Fifth Edition

ADVERTISING & PROMOTION

Supplemental Aspects of
Integrated Marketing
Communications

Terence A. Shimp
University of South Carolina

Special acknowledgement to John H. Lindgren Jr. (Jack), University of Virginia, for the media contribution to this fifth edition. Jack is responsible for blending the visual imagery of the world of advertising and marketing with the magic of electronic media, bringing the thoughts and ideas represented in this book to life in the classroom.

THE DRYDEN PRESS

A DIVISION OF HARCOURT COLLEGE PUBLISHERS

Fort Worth   Philadelphia   San Diego   New York   Orlando   Austin   San Antonio
Toronto   Montreal   London   Sydney   Tokyo

PUBLISHER	Mike Roche
ACQUISITIONS EDITOR	Bill Schoof
MARKET STRATEGIST	Lisé Johnson
DEVELOPMENTAL EDITOR	Tracy Morse
PROJECT EDITOR	Denise Netardus
ART DIRECTOR	Scott Baker
PRODUCTION MANAGER	James McDonald

ISBN: 0-03-021113-1
Library of Congress Catalog card Number: 99-74297

Address for Domestic Orders
Harcourt, Inc., 6277 Sea Harbor Drive, Orlando, FL 32887-6777
1-800-782-4479

Address for International Orders
Harcourt, Inc., 6277 Sea Harbor Drive, Orlando, FL 32887-6777
407-345-3800
(fax) 407-345-4060
(e-mail) hbintl@harcourtbrace.com

Address for Editorial Correspondence
Harcourt College Publishers, 301 Commerce Street, Suite 3700, Fort Worth, TX 76102

Web Site Address
http://www.harcourtcollege.com

Printed in the United States of America
9 0 1 2 3 4 5 6 7 8 048 9 8 7 6 5 4 3 2

The Dryden Press
Harcourt College Publishers

To my wonderful and changing family, and in special tribute to the most recent additions: Henry Franklin (thanks John and Susan for grandson number two!) and Ethan David (thanks Julie and Brad for creating this miraculous fighter!).

The Dryden Press Series in Marketing

Assael
Marketing

Avila, Williams, Ingram, and LaForge
The Professional Selling Skills Workbook

Bateson and Hoffman
Managing Services Marketing: Text and Readings
Fourth Edition

Blackwell, Blackwell, and Talarzyk
Contemporary Cases in Consumer Behavior
Fourth Edition

Boone and Kurtz
Contemporary Marketing WIRED
Ninth Edition

Boone and Kurtz
Contemporary Marketing 1999

Churchill
Basic Marketing Research
Third Edition

Churchill
Marketing Research: Methodological Foundations
Seventh Edition

Czinkota, Dickson, Dunne, Griffin, Hoffman, Hutt,
Lindgren, Lusch, Ronkainen, Rosenbloom, Sheth, Shimp,
Siguaw, Simpson, Speh, and Urbany
Marketing: Best Practices

Czinkota and Ronkainen
Global Marketing

Czinkota and Ronkainen
International Marketing
Fifth Edition

Czinkota and Ronkainen
*International Marketing Strategy: Environmental
Assessment and Entry Strategies*

Dickson
Marketing Management
Second Edition

Dunne and Lusch
Retailing
Third Edition

Engel, Blackwell, and Miniard
Consumer Behavior
Eighth Edition

Ferrell, Hartline, Lucas, Luck
Marketing Strategy

Futrell
*Sales Management: Teamwork, Leadership, and
Technology*
Fifth Edition

Grover
Theory & Simulation of Market-Focused Management

Ghosh
Retail Management
Second Edition

Hoffman/Bateson
Essentials of Services Marketing

Hutt and Speh
*Business Marketing Management: A Strategic View of
Industrial and Organizational Markets*
Sixth Edition

Ingram, LaForge, and Schwepker
Sales Management: Analysis and Decision Making
Fourth Edition

Lindgren and Shimp
Marketing: An Interactive Learning System

Krugman, Reid, Dunn, and Barban
Advertising: Its Role in Modern Marketing
Eighth Edition

Oberhaus, Ratliffe, and Stauble
Professional Selling: A Relationship Process
Second Edition

Parente
Advertising Campaign Strategy: A Guide to Marketing Communication Plans
Second Edition

Reedy
Electronic Marketing

Rosenbloom
Marketing Channels: A Management View
Sixth Edition

Sandburg
Discovering Your Marketing Career CD-ROM

Schaffer
Applying Marketing Principles Software

Schaffer
The Marketing Game

Schellinck and Maddox
Marketing Research: A Computer-Assisted Approach

Schnaars
MICROSIM

Schuster and Copeland
Global Business: Planning for Sales and Negotiations

Sheth, Mittal, and Newman
Customer Behavior: Consumer Behavior and Beyond

Shimp
Advertising, Promotion, and Supplemental Aspects of Integrated Marketing Communications
Fifth Edition

Talarzyk
Cases and Exercises in Marketing

Terpstra and Sarathy
International Marketing
Eighth Edition

Watson
Electronic Commerce

Weitz and Wensley
Readings in Strategic Marketing Analysis, Planning, and Implementation

Zikmund
Exploring Marketing Research
Seventh Edition

Zikmund
Essentials of Marketing Research

Harcourt College Outline Series

Peterson
Principles of Marketing

DRYDEN

soon to become

**Harcourt
College Publishers**

A Harcourt Higher Learning Company

Soon you will find The Dryden Press' distinguished innovation, leadership, and support under a different name . . . a new brand that continues our unsurpassed quality, service, and commitment to education.

We are combining the strengths of our college imprints into one worldwide brand: Harcourt Our mission is to make learning accessible to anyone, anywhere, anytime—reinforcing our commitment to lifelong learning.

We'll soon be Harcourt College Publishers. Ask for us by name.

**One Company
"Where Learning
Comes to Life."**

Preface

Since the inception of this textbook some 18 years ago, the worlds of marketing and marketing communications have changed dramatically. At the same time, marketing and its communications component have become more interwoven. Both small and large firms are seeking varied, more effective ways of communicating effectively and efficiently with their targeted audiences. The competition is more intense than ever, and the marketplace is filled with communications clutter. All firms are challenged to break through this clutter and reach their audiences with interesting and persuasive messages.

Brand managers and marketing communicators in other capacities have dedicated themselves to enhancing the equity of their brands and satisfying the demands for greater accountability. Companies are increasingly embracing a strategy of integrated marketing communications. Whether a student is taking this course simply to learn more about the dynamic nature of this field or to make a career in advertising, promotions, or another aspect of marketing, this textbook continues to provide them with a contemporary view of the role and the importance of marketing communications. I have attempted, in this fifth edition, to expand coverage to satisfy the needs of students in advertising as well as marketing. I emphasize the importance of integrated marketing communications concepts in enhancing the equity of brands and provide a thorough coverage of all aspects of an integrated marketing communications program: advertising, promotions, packaging and branding strategies, point-of-purchase communications, marketing-oriented public relations, event- and cause-oriented sponsorships, and personal selling. These topics are made even more accessible in this edition through expanded use of examples and applications. I continue to cover appropriate academic theories and concepts to provide formal structure to the illustrations and examples.

This textbook is intended for use in undergraduate or graduate courses in marketing communications, advertising, promotion strategy, promotion management, or other courses with similar titles. Professors and their students should find this book substantive but highly readable, imminently current but also appreciative of the evolution of the field, and, above all, a textbook that thoroughly blends marketing communications practice in its varied forms with research and theory.

Organization

The textbook is organized in six parts. Part One introduces the student to the fundamentals of integrated marketing communications. Chapter 1 overviews the topic and discusses the importance of marketing communications in modern marketing. It emphasizes that the various marketing communications elements must be integrated to "speak with a single voice" rather than treated as separate and independent practices. The chapter explains how integrated marketing communications accomplishes the objective of enhancing brand equity through a systematic process of brand-concept management leading to high levels of brand awareness and strong, favorable, and unique brand associations. Enhancing brand equity is a theme woven throughout the text.

Chapter 2 outlines the marketing communications management process within an integrative framework. This framework postulates that marketing communications decisions include a set of general choices (with respect to targets, objectives, and budgets), specific choices (in terms of mixing communications elements and making message, media, and momentum decisions), and measuring the results of communications activities. These decisions are directed toward enhancing a brand's equity.

Chapter 3 examines three interrelated environmental factors that influence decision making involving all aspects of marketing communications: the physical environment, regulation of marketing communications practices, and ethical issues in marketing communications. The first section explores major developments relating to the physical environment and implications that "green marketing" holds for marketing communicators. A second section reviews governmental regulation and industry self-regulations of marketing communication practices. Particular emphasis is placed on the Federal Trade Commission's regulation of deceptive and unfair marketing practices. A final section examines various ethical issues involving matters of targeting communications at vulnerable groups, deceptive advertising, and other cases of potentially unethical marketing communications practices.

Part Two builds a foundation for a better understanding of the nature and function of marketing communications by providing a practical and theoretical overview of its targets. Chapter 4 examines the demographic, psychographic, and geodemographic factors that are used to target marketing communications. Major emphasis is placed on examining important demographic developments such as (1) population statistics, (2) the changing age structure of the population, (3) the growth of the singles market, and (4) ethnic population developments. Psychographic targeting is discussed with emphasis on the VALS 2 classification scheme. The final section describes geodemographic targeting and overviews the Claritas's PRIZM service that is in wide use for this purpose.

Chapter 5 provides further foundation for targeting activities by examining both the process and fundamentals of communication and reviewing fundamentals of buyer behavior. Behavioral foundations of marketing communications are approached from two perspectives: first, the logical thinking person as embodied in the consumer information processing approach, and second, the hedonic-experiential perspective of the pleasure-seeking, feeling person. Particular detail is devoted to describing marketing communications activities that are necessary for promoting consumer attention, comprehension, and learning of marketing messages.

Chapter 6 continues the overview of buyer behavior and the role of targeting communication efforts by discussing the central concepts of attitudes and persuasion. These topics are important because marketing communications and promotion represent organized efforts to influence and persuade customers to make choices that are compatible with the marketing communicator's interests while simultaneously satisfying the customer's needs. A major section examines practical marketing communications efforts to influence the consumer's motivation, opportunity, and ability to process marketing messages.

Part Three consists of two chapters. Chapter 7 looks at the adoption and diffusion processes and examines the role of marketing communications in facilitating these processes and achieving acceptance for new products. Particular attention is devoted to discussions of how marketing communicators facilitate product adoption and diffusion by establishing a new product's relative advantages, showing how the product is compatible with the consumer's past behavior and consumption values, removing perceptions of product complexity, and facilitating product trial. The role of word-of-mouth influence also receives considerable treatment.

Chapter 8 describes the initial elements responsible for a brand's image, namely the brand name, logo, and package. Another major topic treated in this chapter is the ever-growing practice of point-of-purchase communications. The point of purchase is the critical point where the brand name, logo, and package come face to face with the customer. Marketing communicators are increasing their appreciation of the importance of point-of-purchase communications. Expanded investment in this marketing communications component is explained in terms of the valuable functions that P-O-P performs for consumers, manufacturers, and retailers. The chapter devotes considerable attention to the various forms of P-O-P communication tools, presents results from the POPAI Consumer Buying Habits Study, and provides detailed evidence regarding the impact that displays can have in increasing a brand's sales volume during the display period.

Part Four contains seven advertising chapters. Chapter 9 overviews the advertising management process and provides detailed discussions of advertising objective setting and budgeting. Chapter 10 provides a detailed study of the creative-strategy aspect of the advertising management process. Topics include requirements for effective advertising messages, advertising planning, means-end chains and MECCAS models, creative message strategies, and corporate image/issue advertising.

Chapter 11 expands the coverage of advertising message creation by examining advertising endorsers and various message appeals employed in advertisements. Endorser characteristics and selection receive initial discussion. Coverage then turns to specific message appeals, including fear, guilt, humor, sex, subliminal messages, and comparative advertisements.

Chapter 12 provides an analysis of advertising media. It devotes primary attention to evaluating the characteristics and strengths/weaknesses of five major advertising media: out-of-home, newspapers, magazines, radio, and television. The chapter also explores interactive advertising media (including Internet advertising) and alternative advertising media (Yellow Pages, video advertising, and product placements in movies). Chapter 13 focuses exclusively on direct advertising and database marketing. Direct-mail advertising, catalog marketing, telephone marketing, and the role of databases are the topics examined in this chapter.

Chapter 14 provides thorough discussions of the four major activities involved in media strategy: (1) target-audience selection, (2) objective specification, (3) media and vehicle selection, and (4) media-buying activities. In-depth discussion focuses on media-selection considerations such as reach, frequency, gross ratings points, effective rating points, and the efficiency-index procedure. Also explored are advertising timing considerations (pulsed, flighted, and continuous schedules). Receiving prominent attention in this context is a new perspective on media buying termed the shelf-space model, also referred to as the principle of recency planning. The next section covers cost-per-thousand (CPM) computations. A concluding section reviews a computerized media planning (the Adplus program) and presents actual media plans for the introduction of the Saab 9-5 and the rejuvenation of Diet Dr Pepper.

The last chapter in Part Four, Chapter 15, examines the measurement of advertising effectiveness. The chapter describes media- and message-based research methods. Media research methods include audience measurement for magazines (MRI and SMRB), radio (Arbitron), and television (Nielsen). Message-based research methods are discussed under five general categories of measures:

1. recognition and recall (Starch, Bruzzone Tests, and Burke Day-After Recall)
2. emotions (Warmth Monitor, TRACE, and BBDO's Emotional Measurement System)
3. physiological arousal (galvanometer, pupillometer, and voice-pitch analysis)
4. persuasion (ASI theater testing and ARS persuasion testing)
5. sales response (IRI's BehaviorScan and Nielsen's SCANTRACK)

Part Five discusses the burgeoning practice of sales promotion. Chapter 16 offers an overview of promotion by explaining its targets, the reasons underlying its rapid growth, and its capabilities and limitations. The chapter also describes the conditions under which deal-oriented sales promotions are profitable.

Chapter 17 focuses on trade-oriented promotions. The chapter describes the most important and widely used forms of trade promotions: off-invoice allowances, bill-back allowances, slotting allowances, contests and incentives, cooperative advertising and vendor support programs, specialty advertising programs, and trade shows. Considerable discussion is devoted to the practices of forward buying, diverting, and the advent of manufacturer-oriented, everyday low pricing that has been effective in diminishing these practices. Efficient consumer response (ECR), category management, and account-specific marketing also receive prominent treatment.

The subject of Chapter 18 is consumer-oriented sales promotions. Primary emphasis is placed on the objectives that various sales promotions are able to accomplish for manufacturers and the types of rewards they provide to consumers. Detailed discussion is devoted to sampling, couponing, premiums, price-offs, bonus packs, refunds and rebates, contests and sweepstakes, phone cards, and overlay and tie-in promotions. The chapter concludes with a three-step procedure for evaluating sales promotion ideas.

Part Six includes chapters on marketing-oriented public relations (MPR) and personal selling. Chapter 19, on public relations, includes a discussion of the historically entrenched practice of reactive public relations as well as the more recent practice of proactive public relations. A special section is devoted to negative publicity, including suggestions for managing rumors and urban legends. The last major section covers both cause and event marketing, and the two specific aspects of sponsorship marketing.

Chapter 20 introduces students to the job of the salesperson. The chapter describes the salesperson's task and the kinds of activities performed by salespeople. Also discussed are determinants of salesperson performance and characteristics of outstanding salespeople. The chapter emphasizes that all the advertising, sales promotions, point-of-purchase programs, and sponsorships are of little value without effective personal selling. A company's equity and the equity of its individual brands are influenced, in large measure, by the efforts of its sales force.

Changes and Improvements in the Fifth Edition

The fifth edition of *Advertising, Promotion, and Supplemental Aspects of Integrated Marketing Communications* reflects many changes beyond those described so far. To make this book more accessible to a larger range of students, we have revised the look and feel of the book and greatly enhanced the supplemental package that accompanies this text for both the student and the instructor. Major changes include the following:

- The fifth edition includes an updated and improved CD-ROM PowerPoint presentation. The amount of audio and video is expanded from the CD-ROM that accompanied the previous edition. Designed by John H. Lindgren Jr., University of Virginia, this powerful software is easily adaptable for instructors who wish to introduce additional material. The CD-ROM contains over one hour of video, as well as hundreds of still pictures, animations, build slides, and viewers.
- The text retains the same number of chapters (20) as covered in the prior edition, but some of the chapters have been rearranged to reflect a more logical progression. The present Chapter 8, "Brand Names, Logos, Packages, and Point-of-Purchase Materials," was covered in the last part of the text in the prior edition. By moving this material earlier in the text, we are able to highlight the fact that these activities play a critical role in brand-equity enhancement and also set the stage for subsequent chapters on advertising and sales promotions. A small but important change is made in Part Four, where Chapter 13, "Direct Advertising and Database Marketing," is inserted before the media strategy chapter, in contrast to the fourth edition, where it was covered after the media strategy chapter. The primary advantage of this adjustment is that Chapter 14, "Media Strategy," and Chapter 15, "Assessing Advertising Effectiveness," are treated as a related unit rather than being interrupted by the direct advertising material. A final change is that "Personal Selling Fundamentals" (Chapter 8 of the fourth edition) is now the concluding Chapter 20, which locates it at a point that does not interrupt the flow of the other aspects of marketing communications.
- In addition to end-of-chapter questions and exercises, the fifth edition includes a special section on Internet exercises. These are challenging yet enjoyable exercises that nicely supplement the text material.

- A key theme throughout the textbook is that the objective of integrated marketing communications is to enhance a brand's equity. The coverage of brand equity is substantially expanded in Chapter 1 and then tapped into throughout the text.
- The entire textbook has been thoroughly updated. The text provides state-of-the-art coverage of major academic articles and practitioner writings on all aspects of marketing communications. These writings are presented at an accessible level to students and accompanied by copious illustrations, examples, and special inserts.
- The more attractive four-color design will appeal to students and professors alike.

A Premier Instructional Resource Package

The learning package provided with *Advertising, Promotion, and Supplemental Aspects of Integrated Marketing Communications,* Fifth Edition, was specifically designed to meet the needs of instructors facing a variety of teaching conditions and to enhance students' experience with the subject. We have attempted to address both the traditional and the innovative classroom environment by providing an array of high quality and technologically advanced items to bring a contemporary, real-world feel to the study of advertising, promotion, and integrated marketing communications.

Instructor's Manual   This comprehensive and valuable teaching aid, authored by Dave Jones, La Salle University, includes a list of chapter objectives, chapter summaries, detailed chapter outlines, content explanations of transparencies, where to use each transparency, and answers to discussion questions and more. The instructor's manual also serves as a resource to the CD-ROM PowerPoint presentation software.

Testing Resources   This valuable resource provides testing items for instructors' reference and use. The test bank contains over 1,600 multiple choice, true/false, and short answer questions in levels of varying difficulty. The test bank is authored by Martin Meyers, University of Wisconsin—Stephens Point.

The test items are also available in a computerized format, which allows instructors to select problems at random by level of difficulty or type, customize or add test questions, and scramble questions to create up to 99 versions of the same test. The RequestTest phone-in testing service is also available to all adopters. Individual tests can be ordered by question number via fax, mail, phone, or e-mail with a 48-hour turnaround period. Finally, Dryden can provide instructors with software for installing their own on-line testing program, which allows tests to be administered over network or individual terminals. This program allows instructors to grade tests and store results with greater flexibility and convenience.

Four-Color Overhead Transparencies   Available in acetate form are over 100 four-color teaching transparencies that highlight key concepts for presentation in the classroom. In addition to including many important visuals presented in the text, this package contains supplemental ads and exhibits not found in the text. This transparency package provides an easy display format to reinforce important concepts to students. Notes explaining each transparency's content and where to use it are found in the instructor's manual.

CD-ROM PowerPoint Presentation Software   This innovative PowerPoint package (developed by John H. Lindgren Jr., University of Virginia) covers all the material found in the textbook, in addition to numerous other outside supplemental examples and materials found in radio, television, and print media. The CD-ROM contains over one hour of

video; hundreds of still pictures, animations, build slides, and viewers; and allows students to analyze copy in class. An entire course can be developed around this powerful presentation tool. The CD-ROM has been prepared in a PowerPoint format to be easily supplemented by instructors who wish to introduce additional materials.

Video Package   This video package has been prepared to provide a relevant and interesting visual teaching tool for the classroom. Each video segment is relevant to chapter material and gives students the opportunity to apply what they are learning to real-world situations. The video material enables instructors to better illustrate concepts to students. The varied collection of interesting and creative television advertisements complement the company profiles. Another hour of television commercials and video footage is contained on the CD-ROM PowerPoint Presentation Software.

Internet Resources for Integrated Marketing Communications   New to this edition, *Internet Resources for Integrated Marketing Communications,* authored by Gemmy Allen (Mountain View College, Dallas County Community College District) and Georganna Zaba (The Value Exchange, Inc.), gives students hands-on experience while reinforcing the textbook concepts. Students expand their knowledge and learn to use the Internet, the most comprehensive communications tool in the world. Application-oriented questions challenge students to utilize critical-thinking skills as they visit Internet sites and use e-mail, discussion groups, chat, and other Internet resources. Today's employers expect students to know how to use the Internet. With *Internet Resources for Integrated Marketing Communications,* students will build skills that make them more marketable.

A comprehensive **instructor's manual** is available for use with *Internet Resources for Integrated Marketing Communications.* The instructor's manual includes teaching suggestions for group assignments, individual assignments, tips on using the workbook to enhance the course, and much more.

Web Site Internet Support

Visit the Dryden Web site at http://www.harcourtcollege.com for the latest support material for the Dryden series in marketing. The site contains a wealth of Internet resources specific to the topic areas of this textbook. These resources include relevant links to publications, advertising agencies, data and resources, advertising trends, information on careers, national and international business news, Internet exercises, company profiles, time-management aids, and much more.

More Web Support

The Dryden Press has partnered with WebCT to assist adopters with Web-based education materials. Framework includes reading assignments, goals, self-quizzes, Web-based activities, and much more. Your local Dryden sales representative can provide you with more details.

The Dryden Press will provide complimentary supplements or supplement packages to those adopters qualified under our adoption policy. Please contact your sales representative to learn how you may qualify. If as an adopter or potential user you receive supplements you do not need, please return them to your sales representative or send them to:

Attn: Returns Department
Troy Warehouse
465 South Lincoln Drive
Troy, MO 63379

Acknowledgments

My friend and colleague, professor John H. Lindgren Jr. (Jack), of the University of Virginia, deserves special recognition and sincere appreciation for his contributions to this fifth edition. Jack developed the multi-media supplements that serve to create an exciting, dynamic, and enjoyable teaching environment for classroom presentation of the material contained in *Advertising, Promotion, and Supplemental Aspects of Integrated Marketing Communications*, Fifth Edition.

I am grateful to a number of people for their assistance in this project. I sincerely appreciate the thoughtful comments from the following people who provided constructive feedback regarding the fourth edition: Avery Abernethy, Auburn University; Soumava Bandyopadhyay, Lamar University; Ron Bauerly, Western Illinois University; Gordon "Skip" Brunner, Southern Illinois University; Renée Fonetenot, University of New Orleans; Monle Lee, Indiana University–South Bend; Darrel Muehling, Washington State University; and Linda Swayne, University of North Carolina–Charlotte.

Several other individuals deserve special thanks. I am especially grateful to Scott Swain, who developed the Internet exercises for the fifth edition, and Tracy Dunn, who proofed the final copy pages. My appreciation extends to a number of former Ph.D. students who have shared with me their experiences in using the textbook and have provided useful suggestions for change: Avery Abernethy, Auburn University; Craig Andrews, Marquette University; Paula Bone, West Virginia University; Elnora Stuart, Winthrop University; Ken Manning, Colorado State University; and David Sprott, Washington State University. Also, a special thank you to Martin Meyers, University of Wisconsin–Stephens Point, for authoring the test bank, and to Dave Jones, La Salle University, for authoring the instructor's manual.

I am also grateful to the many useful comments from the following reviewers in previous editions of this textbooks: Craig Andrews, Marquette University; Charles S. Areni, Texas Tech University; Guy R. Banville, Creighton University; M. Elizabeth Blair, Ohio University; Barbara M. Brown, San Jose State University; Gordon C. Bruner II, Southern Illinois University; Newell Chiesl, Indiana State University; Robert Dyer, George Washington University; Denise Essman, Drake University; P. Everett Fergenson, Iona College; James Finch, University of Wisconsin–La Crosse; Linda L. Golden, University of Texas at Austin; Stephen Grove, Clemson University; Robert Harmon, Portland State University; Ronald Hill, Villanova University; Clayton Hillyer, University of Conneticut; Stewart W. Husted, Lynchburg College; Patricia F. Kennedy, University of Nebraska; Russell Laczniak, Geoffrey Lantos, Bentley College; Iowa State University; Monle Lee, Indiana University–South Bend; J. Daniel Lindley, Bentley College; Therese A. Maskulka, Lehigh University; John McDonald, Market Opinion Research; John Mowen, Oklahoma State University; Darrel D. Muehling, Washington State University; Kent Nakamoto, Virginia Tech University; Darrel Nasalroad, University of Central Oklahoma; Edward Riordan, Wayne State University; Alan Sawyer, University of Florida; Stanley Scott, Boise State University; Douglas Stayman, Cornell University; Jeffrey Stoltman, Wayne State University; Linda Swayne, University of North Carolina, Charlotte; John A. Taylor, Brigham Young University; Carolyn Tripp, Western Illinois University; and Josh Wiener, Oklahoma State University.

Finally, my great appreciation goes out to Bill Schoof, Lisé Johnson, Tracy Morse, Denise Netardus, Scott Baker, James McDonald, Annette Coolidge, Sam Burkett, and Marcia Masenda at The Dryden Press for their understanding, cooperation, and expertise throughout this project.

Terence A. Shimp
University of South Carolina
April 1999

About the Author

Terence A. Shimp received his doctorate from the University of Maryland in 1974. He is professor of marketing and distinguished foundation fellow in the Darla Moore School of Business, University of South Carolina–Columbia. He is program director of the marketing department at the University of South Carolina. Professor Shimp teaches courses in marketing communications and research philosophy and methods. He has earned a variety of teaching awards, including the Amoco Foundation Award that named him the outstanding teacher at the University of South Carolina in 1990.

He has published widely in the areas of marketing, consumer behavior, and advertising. His work has appeared frequently in respected outlets such as the *Journal of Consumer Research, Journal of Marketing Research, Journal of Marketing, Journal of Advertising, Journal of Advertising Research,* and *Journal of Public Policy and Marketing.* His coauthored article with Brian Till entitled "Endorsers in Advertising: The Case of Negative Celebrity Information," was named the outstanding article published in the *Journal of Advertising* in 1998. "A Critical Appraisal of Demand Artifacts in Consumer Research," published with Eva Hyatt and David Snyder in the *Journal of Consumer Research,* received that journal's award for the top article published during the period 1990–1992.

Professor Shimp is past president of the Association for Consumer Research and current president of the *Journal of Consumer Research* policy board. He is on the editorial policy boards of the *Journal of Consumer Research, Journal of Consumer Psychology, Journal of Marketing, Marketing Letters, Journal of Public Policy and Marketing,* and *Journal of Marketing Communications.* He has represented the Federal Trade Commission and various state agencies as an expert witness in issues concerning advertising regulation.

Brief Contents

Contents

PART

ONE

Part One—The Concept, Practice, and Environment of Integrated Marketing Communications

Part One introduces the student to the fundamentals of integrated marketing communications. Chapter 1 overviews the topic and discusses the importance of marketing communications in modern marketing. The chapter emphasizes the necessity of integrating the various marketing communications elements to "speak with a single voice" rather than treating them as separate and independent practices. Chapter 1 explains how integrated marketing communications accomplishes the objective of enhancing brand equity through a systematic process of brand-concept management that leads to high levels of brand awareness and strong, favorable, and unique brand associations.

Chapter 2 outlines the marketing communications management process within an integrative framework. This framework postulates that marketing communications decisions include a set of general choices (with respect to targets, objectives, and budgets), specific choices (in terms of mixing communications elements and making message, media, and momentum decisions), and measuring the results of communications activities. These decisions are directed toward ultimately enhancing a brand's equity.

Chapter 3 examines three interrelated environmental factors that influence decision making in all aspects of marketing communications: the physical environment, regulation of marketing communications practices, and ethical issues in marketing communications. The first section explores major developments relating to the physical environment and implications that "green marketing" holds for marketing communicators. A second section reviews governmental regulation and industry self-regulations of marketing communications practices. Particular emphasis is placed on the Federal Trade Commission's regulation of deceptive and unfair marketing practices. A final section examines various ethical issues involving matters of targeting communications at vulnerable groups, deceptive advertising, and other cases of potentially unethical marketing communications practices.

Overview of Integrated Marketing Communications

CHAPTER OBJECTIVE

This chapter introduces the topic of marketing communications and suggests why it is such a critical component of modern marketing. We first overview the nature and importance of different elements of marketing communications. Next examined is the concept of brand equity with detailed discussion of why efforts to enhance a brand's equity are crucial to long-term success. Finally, we discuss the features and advantages of integrated marketing communications (IMC). All communication elements (advertising, personal selling, sales promotions, packaging, point-of-purchase materials, and so on) must be tightly interwoven for the successful management of brand equity.

Opening Vignette: Branding Energy

Natural gas and electricity are mere commodities, don't you agree? It doesn't matter who supplies these sources of energy, all electricity and natural gas are identical regardless of the source. Right? Well, this might be how consumers used to look at energy sources back in the days when energy distribution was closely regulated and suppliers were restricted to tight geographic markets. But deregulation of energy distribution, primarily natural gas and electricity, has eliminated geographic monopolies. Deregulation has forced energy companies to compete for customers just as do the long-distance telephone carriers. Where only AT&T used to deliver long-distance telephone service, now there are well-known competitors such as Sprint, MCI, and others. The same is happening with natural gas and electricity.

Branding is the name of the game. Utility companies are developing brand names that will enable them to compete in distant markets. Although natural gas and electricity are invisible products, utility companies intend to create strong brand-name awareness and positive images that will enable them to command more residential and commercial customers. The stakes are high in the utilities industry, which annually generates over $200 billion in revenue. EnergyOne, Enron, Cinergy Inc., and Entergy Corp. are just a few of the branded utilities that have begun using sophisticated marketing communications. For example, Entergy Corp. sponsored a Professional Golfers' Association tournament in 1999. EnergyOne and Enron both hired major advertising agencies to develop exciting advertising campaigns. Enron spent $25 million to advertise on the Super Bowl. Cinergy Inc. paid

Source: Adapted from Kathryn Kranhold, "Power Companies Work Hard to Sell Electricity Like Soap Suds," *The Wall Street Journal Interactive Edition*, March 17, 1998; Daniel Shannon, "Power Play," *Promo*, September 1996, 18. See also Clark W. Gellings, *Effective Power Marketing* (Tulsa, OK: PennWell, 1997).

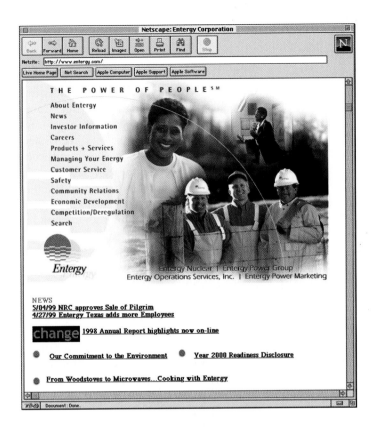

$6 million to put its name on the Cincinnati Reds Riverfront Stadium, which resulted in a dramatic increase in brand awareness.

Through brand naming, advertising, and other forms of marketing communications, utility companies one day may be as well known as the brands of telephone service we use and the gasoline brands (Texaco, BP, Amoco, etc.) that we readily identify and even prefer.

THE NATURE OF MARKETING COMMUNICATIONS

*M*arketing communications is a critical aspect of a company's overall marketing mission and a major determinant of its success. The marketing communications component of the marketing mix has increased in importance dramatically during the past decade. Indeed, it has been claimed that "marketing in the 1990s is communication and communication is marketing. The two are inseparable."[1]

www.redcross.com

All modern organizations—business as well as not-for-profit concerns (museums, symphony orchestras, the Red Cross, and so forth)—use various forms of marketing communications to promote their offerings and achieve financial and non-financial goals. The primary forms of marketing communications include advertisements, salespeople, store signs, point-of-purchase displays, product packages, direct-mail literature, free samples, coupons, publicity releases, and various other communication devices.

Collectively, the preceding activities constitute what traditionally has been termed the **promotion** component of the marketing mix. (As you will recall from an introductory marketing course, the marketing mix for a brand consists of four sets of interrelated decision spheres: *product, price, place (or distribution), and promotion decisions*.) Although this "4P" characterization of marketing has led to widespread use of the term "promotion" for describing communications with prospects and customers, the term "marketing communications" is now preferred by most marketing practitioners as well as many educators.

Elements of Marketing Communications

Marketing communications can be understood best by examining the two constituent elements, communication and marketing. **Communication** is the process whereby thoughts are conveyed and meaning is shared between individuals or between organizations and individuals. **Marketing** is the set of activities whereby businesses and other organizations create transfers of value *(exchanges)* between themselves and their customers. Of course, marketing is more general than marketing communications per se, but much of marketing involves communications activities. Taken together, **marketing communications** represents the collection of all elements in a brand's marketing mix that facilitate exchanges by establishing shared meaning with the brand's customers or clients.

To avoid later confusion, it will be helpful at this point to provide brief definitions of the major types of marketing communications. Before reviewing these definitions, it will be useful to evaluate an actual marketing situation. Consider the line of salted snacks marketed by Frito-Lay under the brand name *Wow!* (The exclamation point is part of the name.) Frito-Lay introduced the *Wow!* brand of potato chips to American consumers in March 1998. These new fat-free chips are fried in a substance called olestra, which is a soybean-based product that was invented by scientists at Procter & Gamble, the world-renowned consumer goods company. Frito-Lay introduced the *Wow!* brand using an aggressive advertising and sales promotion program. Media advertising exceeded $40 million in 1998.[2] Because consumers were expected to be skeptical that a fat-free snack product could really taste good, it was critical that the product be extensively sampled so that consumers could learn for themselves that *Wow!* tastes virtually identical to the fat-laden and higher-calorie snack products that people have long consumed. Bins with trial-size bags priced at three for 99 cents were available in stores and were supported with in-store displays that featured the theme, "*Wow!* All the taste and half the calories." To further generate an opportunity for consumers to try *Wow!*, coupons for a free trial size were distributed nationally as free-standing inserts (FSIs) in Sunday newspapers. Frito-Lay also launched an Internet site as an additional means of communicating *Wow!* and building a positive image for this brand.

www.wowchips.com

Using the *Wow!* brand introduction as our point of departure, let's now briefly examine the major forms of marketing communications.

Personal selling is a form of person-to-person communication whereby salespeople inform, educate, and persuade prospective buyers to purchase the company's products or services. Frito-Lay's sales force called on hundreds of retail buyers in an effort to convince them to add *Wow!* products to their existing lines of salted snacks. These selling efforts were simplified by providing introductory discounts to retailers and assuring them that heavy advertising, sampling, and couponing initiatives would successfully move *Wow!* products out of their stores.

Advertising, such as Frito-Lay's $40 million campaign to introduce *Wow!*, involves either *mass* communication via newspapers, magazines, radio, television, and other media (billboards, the Internet, etc.), or *direct* communication that is pinpointed to each business-to-business customer or ultimate consumer. Both forms of advertising are paid for by an identified sponsor (the advertiser), but are considered to be nonpersonal because the sponsoring firm is simultaneously communicating with multiple receivers, perhaps millions, rather than with a specific person or small group. Direct advertising, also called *database marketing,* has experienced huge growth in recent years due to the effectiveness of targeted communications and the computer technology that has made it possible.

Sales promotion consists of all marketing activities that attempt to stimulate quick buyer action or immediate sales of a product. In comparison, advertising is designed to accomplish other objectives, such as creating brand awareness and influencing customer attitudes. Sales promotions are directed both at the trade (wholesalers and retailers) and consumers. *Trade-oriented sales promotion* includes the use of various types of allowances to encourage wholesaler and retailer response. *Consumer-oriented sales promotions* involve the use of coupons, premiums, free samples, contests/sweepstakes, rebates, and other devices. Frito-Lay used both trade-oriented promotions (off-invoice and display allowances) and consumer-oriented promotions (sampling and couponing) to successfully introduce *Wow!*

Sponsorship marketing is the practice of promoting the interests of a company and its brands by associating the company or one of its brands with a specific *event* (such as a major athletic competition like the World Cup in soccer) or charitable *cause* (such as the United Way). At the time of this writing, Frito-Lay is not known to be using the *Wow!* brand to sponsor any particular event, but it is easy to imagine that it is only a matter of time before a contest celebrating beauty or athletic prowess carries the *Wow!* sponsorship.

Publicity, like advertising, describes nonpersonal communication to a mass audience; but unlike advertising, the sponsoring company does not pay for advertising time or space. Publicity usually assumes the form of news items or editorial comments about a company's products or services. These items or comments receive free print space or broadcast time because media representatives consider the information pertinent and newsworthy for their audiences. It is in this sense that publicity is "not paid for" by the company receiving its benefits. Frito-Lay's public relations department spun out voluminous press releases that provided magazines and other news media with stories about *Wow!* snack foods and the remarkable fat substitute, olestra, that made it possible to develop a low-calorie and no-fat salty snack food.

Point-of-purchase communications encompass displays, posters, signs, and a variety of other materials that are designed to influence buying decisions at the point of purchase. In-store displays played a critically important role in attracting consumers' attention to trial-size samples of *Wow!* products.

In sum, marketing communication managers have a variety of communication tools at their disposal. The relative importance and specific application of these tools depends on the particular circumstances confronting a brand at any point in time. As will be developed throughout the text, each marketing communication tool has its own unique role to play.

www.cocacola.com
www.levis.com
www.motorola.com
www.intel.com
www.kodak.com
www.ibm.com

BRANDS, BRAND EQUITY, AND BRAND EQUITY ENHANCEMENT

Marketing communicators in their various capacities (as advertisers, salespeople, public relations professionals, and so on) develop and deliver messages regarding different types of objects: products, services, stores, events, and even people. Although these terms capture different forms of marketing objects, one term will suffice as a summary means for describing all forms of marketing objects. That term is "brand." *Wow!* salted snacks is a brand. So are EnergyOne and Enron. Coca-Cola, Levi's, Motorola, Intel, Kodak, and IBM are famous brand names. Regardless of brand fame, the point that deserves particular emphasis is that most marketing communications occurs at the brand level.

Discussion throughout this text focuses on *brand-level* marketing communications. It is critical for students to fully appreciate that the term "brand" is a convenient (and appropriate) label for describing any object of concerted marketing efforts. The New York Yankees and Boston Celtics are brands whose reputations must be nurtured and protected. The TV program "60 Minutes" is a brand with a stake in building, or at least maintaining, its substantial equity. A final example to drive home the point is that even *you* can be thought of as a brand. In fact, the well-known marketing consultant and author, Tom Peters (of *In Search of Excellence* fame) has written about marketing the brand called *you*.[3]

www.yankees.com

www.celtics.com

www.CBS.com

www.tpgls.com

A well-known and respected brand is an invaluable asset. Brands perform several roles for the firms that market them.[4] An important economic role is to enable a firm to achieve economies of scale by producing a brand in mass quantities. Another invaluable economic role is that a successful brand can create barriers to entry for competitors who might want to introduce their own brands. Brands also perform a critical strategic role by providing a key means for differentiating one company's offering from competitive brands. A strong brand image enables a manufacturer to gain leverage vis-à-vis retailers and other marketing intermediaries. From the consumer's perspective, respected brands offer an assurance of consistent performance and provide a signal of whatever benefits (such as status or prestige) that consumers seek when purchasing particular products and brands. More than this, a brand is a covenant with the consumer whereby the mere mention of the name triggers expectations about what the brand will deliver in terms of quality, convenience, status, and other critical buying considerations.[5]

Robert Wehling, Senior Vice President responsible for advertising and marketing research for Procter & Gamble, provides keen insight about the role brands perform for consumers when describing several of P&G's venerable brands:

www.pg.com

> *When you [the consumer] have a brand like Tide [detergent], you don't have to think a lot about it. You know that it's going to give you the best performance, the best value and get the job done without question. Great brands bring an element of simplicity to what is a very complex world. I believe as strongly as I possibly could that we're [i.e., P&G] going to be selling Tide and Crest and Pampers and Folgers and Downy 50 years from now, and they're going to be bigger and better than they are today.[6]*

The *Global Focus* insert provides more of Robert Wehling's views on the role of brands.

The Concept of Brand Equity

To appreciate the concept of brand equity requires first that we have a clear understanding of the meaning of the term "brand." The American Marketing Association defines a **brand** as a "name, term, sign, symbol, or design, or a combination of them intended to identify the goods and services of one seller or group of sellers and to differentiate them from those of competition."[7] A brand thus exists when a product, retail outlet, or service receives its own name, term, sign, symbol, design, or any particular combination of these elements. All

GLOBAL FOCUS: GLOBAL BRANDS AND A GLOBAL FIASCO

Many observers consider Procter & Gamble to be the world's leading packaged goods company. P&G operates in more than 70 countries and offers dozens of brands in many product categories. Robert Wehling, Senior VP of advertising and marketing research at P&G, defines a global brand as "[O]ne that has a clear and consistent equity—or identity—with consumers across geographies. It is generally positioned the same from one country to another. It has essentially the same product formulation, delivers the same benefits and uses a consistent advertising concept."

Interestingly, Mr. Wehling believes that only three of P&G's many famous brands truly have achieved global brand stature. These are Pringles (chips), Pantene (shampoo and conditioner), and Always/Whisper (a feminine product that is marketed under two names in different countries). One of the major obstacles to accomplishing global brand status is that Asian consumers are extremely diverse and require unique brands and brand positioning customized to each culture.

On the humorous side, efforts to globalize a brand can meet with unexpected resistance and unanticipated results. A near-disastrous experience occurred with one P&G marketing effort in Japan. American managers in Japan thought that Pampers should be advertised in that country using the same television commercial that was running for that brand in the U.S. That commercial depicted an animated stork delivering Pampers diapers to consumers' homes. The same commercial, when dubbed with Japanese and aired on Japanese television, was a flop. With surprise and dismay, research was undertaken to determine the problem. Interviews with Japanese consumers quickly revealed that they were confused as to why a stork would be delivering diapers. Unlike American custom, which includes the myth that babies are delivered by storks, Japanese folklore presents the story that babies are delivered to deserving parents in giant peaches that float on the river. Needless to say, this commercial was quickly pulled from the Japanese airways and replaced with more culturally appropriate advertising. By reverse logic, imagine how American consumers (or consumers in some other country that presents the stork myth) would respond to a TV commercial for disposable diapers showing a baby floating on a river in a giant peach.

Source: Robert L. Wehling, "Even At P&G, Only 3 Brands Make Truly Global Grade So Far," *Advertising Age*, January 1998, 8.

---

organizations and their products can be considered brands. We live in a world of brands. It just so happens, however, that some brands are better known and more respected than others. For example, the American Marketing Association was mentioned earlier. As someone who is studying marketing, you may belong to a student chapter of that organization or at least have heard of it, but most people probably have never heard of this brand. By way of comparison, consider another organization whose identifying letters also are AMA, the American Medical Association. This latter AMA is undoubtedly better known to a much larger percent of the American population and even throughout the world. In context of the present discussion, it is suggested that the American Medical Association has greater brand equity than does the American Marketing Association. Let us now explore in some detail the meaning of brand equity.

www.ama.org (marketing)

www.ama-assn.org (medical)

Brand equity has been defined in many ways, and numerous approaches have been developed to measure it.[8] This book's approach to describing brand equity is from the perspective of the consumer.[9] From the consumer's perspective, a brand possesses equity to the extent that consumers are familiar with the brand and have stored in their memory warehouses favorable, strong, and unique brand associations.[10] That is, brand equity from the consumer's perspective consists of two forms of brand knowledge: *brand awareness* and *brand image*. For example, the Adidas brand of athletic shoes substantially increased its advertising budget in 1998 by a whopping 25 percent over the previous year's ad budget.

Adidas' director of sales and marketing explained that the purpose of this increase was to: (1) raise consumer awareness of the Adidas name and (2) pound home the message that Adidas is an authentic and high-performance athletic shoe.[11] You will note that he does not refer to brand equity per se, but this is precisely what he's talking about in reference to raising awareness and conveying a desired performance image for the Adidas brand.

www.adidas.com

Figure 1.1 graphically portrays two dimensions of brand knowledge—awareness and image—and the subsequent discussion will describe each dimension in some detail.[12]

Brand Awareness.   Brand awareness is an issue of whether a brand name comes to mind when consumers think about a particular product category and the ease with which the name is evoked. Stop reading for a moment and consider all brands of toothpaste that come immediately to your mind. Probably Crest and Colgate came to mind, because these brands are the market-share leaders among American brands of toothpaste. You, perhaps, also thought of brands such as Aquafresh, Mentadent, and Arm & Hammer insofar as these brands also obtain a large share of toothpaste purchases. But did you think of Close-Up, Pepsodent, or Aim? Maybe so; probably not. These brands are not nearly as widely known or frequently purchased as are their more successful counterparts. As such, they have less brand equity than, say, Colgate and Crest.

www.colgate.com

www.mentadent.com

www.armhammer.com

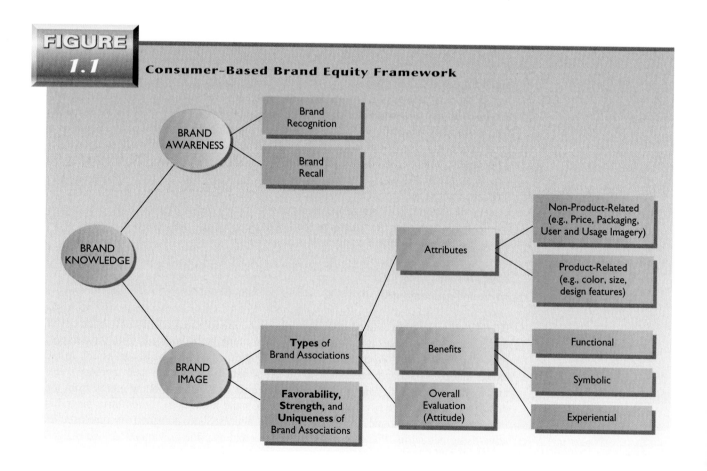

FIGURE 1.1   **Consumer-Based Brand Equity Framework**

Brand awareness is the basic dimension of brand equity. From the vantage point of an individual consumer, a brand has no equity unless the consumer is at least aware of the brand. Achieving brand awareness is the initial challenge for new brands. Maintaining high levels of brand awareness is the task faced by all established brands.

Figure 1.1 shows two levels of awareness: brand recognition and brand recall. *Brand recognition* reflects a relatively superficial level of awareness, whereas *brand recall* reflects a deeper form of awareness. Consumers may be able to identify a brand if it is presented to them on a list or if hints/cues are provided. However, fewer consumers are able to retrieve a brand name from memory without any reminders or cues. It is this deeper level of brand awareness—recall—to which marketers aspire. Through effective and consistent marketing communication efforts, some brands are so well known that virtually every living person of normal intelligence can recall the brand. For example, most people who are conscious of computers would likely mention the name *Windows* if asked to name a software package that has been designed as an operating system.

Brand Image.   The second dimension of consumer-based brand knowledge is a brand's image. Brand image can be thought of in terms of the types of associations that come to the consumer's mind when contemplating a particular brand. An *association* is simply the particular thoughts or images that a consumer has about a brand, much in the same fashion that we have thoughts about other people. For example, what thoughts and images come immediately to mind when you think of your best friend? You undoubtedly associate your friend with certain physical characteristics, features, strengths, and perhaps frailties. Likewise, brands are linked in our memories with specific thoughts, or associations. As shown in Figure 1.1, these associations can be conceptualized in terms of their: (1) type, (2) favorability, (3) strength, and (4) uniqueness.

To illustrate these points, it will be helpful to return to our earlier discussion of Frito-Lay's *Wow!* chips and the associations one consumer, Chuck, has for this brand. Chuck is a life-long lover of potato chips. (It will be instructive to refer back to Figure 1.1 before reading the following description.) He, like so many other consumers, has to be careful about his eating habits both for appearance and health reasons. After trying *Wow!* chips with some skepticism that they would taste as good as regular chips, Chuck learned that *Wow!* chips taste virtually the same as regular chips. He further learned from media reports and his own observations that *Wow!* chips are made by Frito-Lay, cooked in olestra, lower in calories than regular chips, free of saturated fat, available in ridged as well as smooth versions, and perhaps are slightly higher priced than other potato chip brands. All of these thoughts represent *types of associations* in Chuck's memory about *Wow!* All of these thoughts, with the exception of *Wow's!* higher price, represent *favorable brand associations* as far as Chuck is concerned. Insofar as *Wow!* was the pioneer brand of chips to be cooked with olestra, Chuck considers the brand and the product subcategory virtually synonymous, and, as such, his thoughts, or associations, about *Wow!* are held *strongly*. Because olestra represents a new form of fat substitute, *unique thoughts* about *Wow!* are evoked when Chuck thinks of this brand. In other words, in Chuck's mind *Wow!* and olestra are linked inextricably because he associates olestra only with *Wow!* Of course, over time as other brands of salty snack foods made with olestra appear on the market, Chuck's unique association of olestra with *Wow!* will probably weaken. But for the time being, olestra and *Wow!* are virtually synonymous as far as Chuck is concerned.

We can see from this illustration that Chuck associates *Wow!* potato chips with various *attributes* (e.g., made with olestra), *benefits* (less fattening, healthier, good tasting), and that he possesses an overall favorable evaluation, or *attitude*, toward this brand. These associations for Chuck are held strongly and are favorable and somewhat unique. Frito-Lay, the makers of *Wow!*, would love to have millions of Chucks in its market. To the extent that Chuck is prototypical of other consumers, it can be said that *Wow!* has high brand equity.

IMC FOCUS: GARDEN-BURGER AND THE "SEINFELD" FINALE

Gardenburger, Inc.—a small company located in Portland, Oregon, with 1997 sales of approximately $57 million—makes vegetable patties and markets them to supermarkets, restaurants, and other outlets under the Gardenburger® brand name. In 1998 this company made a bold move to increase its brand equity vis-à-vis competitive brands of vegetable patties. The product category of vegetable patties is small but growing. Executives at Gardenburger believed that their brand could be substantially enhanced if more consumers knew about the brand. Toward this end, the decision was made to advertise Gardenburger patties on television, including a placement on the concluding episode of "Seinfeld," which aired in May 1998. A single 30-second ad on the Seinfeld finale cost more than $1.2 million and consumed approximately 10 percent of Gardenburger's annual advertising budget.

Was the investment worth it? According to a company press release, the "Seinfeld" placement along with ads aired on lesser-known television programs and in magazines (for illustration, see Figure 1.2), resulted in huge gains. Sales in the vegetable burger category increased by over 100 percent from the same period a year earlier, and Gardenburger's sales were over 400 percent higher than the comparable period in the previous year. Only time will tell whether Gardenburger can sustain this rapid sales growth, but research conducted by the NPD Group determined that the Gardenburger commercial was the second highest recalled and third most liked of the 28 commercials that ran during the finale episode of "Seinfeld"—a program that reached an audience estimated at 106 million.

Source: "Gardenburger's Ad on Last Episode of Seinfeld Pays Off Big!" *Yahoo Finance PR Newswire* (http://biz.yahoo.com), June 3, 1998.

Gardenburger Ad

FIGURE 1.2

In contrast to *Wow!*, many brands have relatively little equity. This is because consumers are: (1) only faintly aware of these brands or, worse yet, are completely unaware of them or (2) even if aware, do not hold strong, favorable, and unique associations about these brands. The above *IMC Focus* (where IMC is shorthand for Integrated Marketing Communications) describes a relatively unknown brand (see Figure 1.2) that attempted to build its brand equity through advertising.

Enhancing Brand Equity

In general, efforts to enhance a brand's equity are accomplished through the initial choice of positive brand identity (that is, the selection of a good brand name or logo) but mostly through marketing and marketing communication programs that forge favorable, strong, and unique associations in the consumer's mind between a brand and its attributes/benefits. It is impossible to overstate the importance of efforts to enhance a brand's equity. Products that are high in quality and represent a good value potentially possess high brand equity. But effective and consistent marketing communication efforts are needed to build upon and maintain brand equity. A favorable brand image (refer back to Figure 1.1) does not happen automatically. Sustained marketing communications are generally required to create favorable, strong, and perhaps unique associations about the brand. For example, it could be claimed that one of the world's greatest brands, Coca-Cola, is little more than colored sugar water. This brand, nevertheless, possesses immense brand equity because its managers are ever mindful of the need for continuous advertising executions that sustain the Coca-Cola story and build the image around the world. In the United States alone, the Coca-Cola Co. commanded approximately 44 percent of the nearly $55 billion carbonated soft-drink market in 1998.[13] Consumers don't buy this "colored sugar water" merely for its taste; they instead purchase a lifestyle and an image when selecting Coca-Cola over other available brands. It is effective advertising, exciting sales promotions, creative sponsorships, and other forms of marketing communications that are responsible for Coca-Cola's positive image and massive market share.

One major by-product of efforts to increase a brand's equity is that consumer *brand loyalty* toward the brand might also increase. Indeed, long-term growth and profitability are largely dependent on creating and reinforcing brand loyalty. The following quote from two respected marketing practitioners sums up the nature and importance of brand loyalty:

> *While marketers have long viewed brands as assets, the real asset is brand loyalty. A brand is not an asset. Brand loyalty is the asset. Without the loyalty of its customers, a brand is merely a trademark, an ownable, identifiable symbol with little value. With the loyalty of its customers, a brand is more than a trademark. A trademark identifies a product, a service, a corporation. A brand identifies a promise. A strong brand is a trustworthy, relevant, distinctive promise. It is more than a trademark. It is a trustmark of enormous value. Creating and increasing brand loyalty results in a corresponding increase in the value of the trustmark[14]*

Research has shown that when firms communicate unique and positive messages via advertising, personal selling, sales promotion, and other means, they are able to differentiate their brands effectively from competitive offerings and insulate themselves from future price competition.[15] Marketing communications play an essential role in creating positive brand equity and building strong brand loyalty. However, this is not always accomplished with traditional advertising or other conventional forms of marketing communications. For example, Starbucks, the virtual icon for upscale coffee, does very little advertising, yet this brand has a near cult-like following. The average Starbucks consumer visits a Starbucks outlet an estimated 18 times a month, a situation of nearly unparalleled brand loyalty.[16]

www.starbucks.com

www.pepsi.com

Roger Enrico, CEO of PepsiCo, provides us with a fitting conclusion to this section in the following implicit description of the importance of PepsiCo efforts to build brand equity.

> *In my mind the best thing a person can say about a brand is that it's their favorite. That implies something more than simply they like the package, or the taste. It means they like the whole thing—the company, the image, the value, the quality and on and on. So as we think about the measurements of our business, if we're only looking at this year's bottom line and profits, we're missing the picture. We should be looking at market share, but also at where we stand vis-à-vis our competitors in terms of consumer awareness and regard for our brands. You always know where you stand in the P&L because you see it every month. But what you need to know, with almost the same sense of immediacy, is where you stand with consumers and your customers.[17]*

Co-Branding and Ingredient Branding

Products typically carry a single brand, and marketing communications for that brand are designed to enhance solely that brand's equity. However, in recent years there has been a variety of initiatives whereby two or more brands enter into a partnership that potentially serves to enhance both brands' equity and profitability. You need only look at your bank card (e.g., Visa) to see that your card likely carries the name of an organization such as your college or university. The two have entered into an alliance for their mutual benefit. You also regularly see the NutraSweet logo on well-known brands such as Diet Coke and Crystal Light, which in turn benefit from the improved taste that NutraSweet provides.[18] Ocean Spray, the well-known marketer of cranberry products, has entered into branding alliances with a number of other famous branded products, including Post's Cranberry Almond Crunch cereal, Nabisco's Cranberry Newtons (cookies), and Kraft's Stove Top Stuffing with Cranberries.[19] Tyson (of chicken fame) has allied with Pillsbury's Green Giant Create a Meal in which it offers fully cooked chicken and beef items intended specifically for Pillsbury's Create a Meal Starter vegetable and sauce blends.[20] The examples are virtually endless, but the common theme is that brands that enter into an alliance do so on grounds that their images are similar, that they appeal to the same market segment, and that the co-branding initiative is mutually beneficial. The most important requirement for successful co-branding is that there is a "logical fit between the two brands such that the combined brand or marketing activity maximizes the advantages of the individual brands while minimizing the disadvantages."[21]

www.nutrasweet.com

www.oceanspray.com

www.nabisco.com

www.tyson.com

www.pillsbury.com

Ingredient branding is a special type of alliance between branding partners. For example, my Dell computer has a sticker on it that reads "Intel Inside." Intel, the well-known maker of disk drives, microchips, and other computer "ingredients," built incredible brand equity for its brand through the use of clever, aggressive, and continuous advertising. Now computer manufacturers are willing to attach the "Intel Inside" sticker to their "boxes" because the equity of Intel holds potential for enhancing their own brand equity. The NutraSweet example given above is actually better thought of as another case of successful ingredient marketing. Other well-known instances of ingredient branding include various ski-wear brands that make prominent note of the Gore-Tex fabric from which they are made and cookware makers that tout the fact that their skillets and other cookware items are made with DuPont's Teflon nonstick coating.[22] Although ingredient branding is in many instances beneficial for both the ingredient and "host" brands, a potential downside for the host brand is that it runs the risk of being turned into a mere commodity. This would happen if the equity of the ingredient brand is so great that it overshadows the host brand.[23] This situation would arise, for example, if skiers knew that their ski jacket was made of Gore-Tex fabric but they had no awareness of the company that actually manufactured their jacket.

www.goretex.com

www.dupont.com

MANAGING BRAND CONCEPTS

Brands must be strategically managed in a continuous effort to enhance equity and to increase consumer loyalty. This has been termed **brand-concept management,** which can be defined as "the planning, implementation, and control of a brand concept throughout the life of the brand."[24] A brand concept, in other words, is the *specific meaning* that brand managers create and communicate to the target market. Managing a specific brand concept, or meaning, can be accomplished by appealing to any of three categories of basic consumer needs: functional, symbolic, or experiential.[25] Upon a quick review of the consumer-based brand equity framework presented earlier (Figure 1.1), you will see that these three categories are shown as a specific type of association termed *benefits*. The distinction between benefits and needs should not trouble us insofar as it simply involves a matter of perspective. That is to say, consumers have needs and brands have attributes and features that satisfy those needs. Brand benefits are then the need-satisfying features provided by brands. So as you can see, needs and benefits can be thought of, metaphorically speaking, as flip sides of the same coin.

Brand-concept management directed at **functional needs** attempts to provide solutions to consumers' current consumption-related problems or potential problems by communicating that the brand possesses specific benefits capable of solving these problems. The advertisement for Breathe Right (Figure 1.3) is an appeal to the consumer's need (or his or her bedmate's need) to reduce the offensive noise of snoring and to restore "peace and tranquility" (see ad wording). Appeals to functional needs are the most prevalent form of brand-concept management. In industrial selling, for example, salespeople typically appeal to their consumers' functional needs for higher-quality products, faster delivery time, or better service. Consumer goods marketers also regularly appeal to consumers' needs for convenience, safety, good health, cleanliness, and so on, all of which are functional needs that can be satisfied by brand benefits.

FIGURE 1.3

An Appeal to Functional Needs

Whereas many brands are marketed based primarily on their functionality, others are marketed to satisfy *psychological desires.* Appeals to **symbolic needs** include those directed at consumers' desire for self-enhancement, group membership, affiliation, and belongingness. Brand-concept management directed at symbolic needs attempts to associate brand use with a desired group, role, or self-image. Marketers of brands in categories such as personal beauty products, jewelry, alcoholic beverages, and cigarettes frequently appeal to symbolic needs.

www.timex.com

The advertisement for Timex (Figure 1.4) illustrates an appeal to symbolic needs. This ad does not tout the accurate time-keeping ability of Timex watches or describe specific

An Appeal to Symbolic Needs

So much about a family is revealed in its faces.

The New Family *of* Fashion Watches.
TIMEX

product attributes or other functional benefits; rather, it appeals to symbolic needs by directly associating itself with the Austin family, an attractive and apparently successful group of young professionals. Six distinct Timex watches are displayed in juxtaposition against the photo of the six Austin siblings. Minimal advertising copy simply claims that "So much about a family is revealed in its faces." The message is subtle but clear: Owners of Timex watches are stylish, discriminating, yet individualistic.

The Kohler advertisement in Figure 1.5 reflects another brand that is advertised to appeal to symbolic needs. Presumably this ad appeals to consumers who desire the lifestyle conveyed by the stylishly dressed and sophisticated professional shown alongside the advertised sink (which, in keeping with the tone of the ad, is referred to as a "lavatory" and not a "sink").

Consumers' **experiential needs** represent their desires for products that provide sensory pleasure, variety, and cognitive stimulation. Brand-concept management directed at

Another Appeal to
Symbolic Needs

experiential needs promotes brands as being out of the ordinary and high in sensory value (looking elegant, feeling wonderful, tasting or smelling great, sounding divine, being exhilarating, and so on) or rich in the potential for cognitive stimulation (exciting, challenging, mentally entertaining, and so on). Look at the ad in Figure 1.6 for the Cadillac DeVille. Cadillac has historically appealed to an older target audience, although currently the brand has experienced a renaissance of sorts among aging baby boomers. Through its juxtaposition with a child who is learning to ride a bicycle and enjoying the exhilaration of this new experience, the Cadillac DeVille advertisement promises a similar experience for the adult who can remember his bicycle-riding days. The visual "promise" is put in words at the bottom of the ad: "[D]iscover how DeVille Concours makes you want to grip the

An Appeal to
Experiential Needs

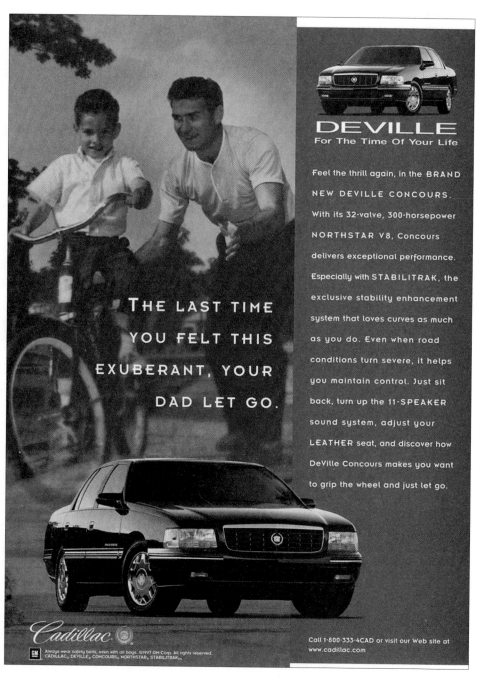

wheel and just let go." This ad, plain and simple, is promising excitement—not an unwise appeal to a target audience of aging baby boomers who are seeking to relive some of the joys of an earlier life when times were perhaps more exciting and less stressful.

www.cadillac.com

It is important to recognize that brands often offer a mixture of functional, symbolic, and experiential benefits. In the case of Timex watches, for example, the brand offers accurate time-keeping (functional benefit), appeals to one's desire to own objects that other successful people possess (symbolic benefit), looks great and is comfortable to wear (experiential benefit). However, the Timex ad (Figure 1.4) does not attempt to communicate all of these but rather appeals only to prospective consumers' symbolic needs. Generally speaking, successful brand-concept management requires a communication strategy that appeals to a *single* type of consumer need (functional, symbolic, or experiential) rather than attempting to be something for everyone—that is, a *generic* brand concept. A brand with multiple, or generic, concepts is difficult to manage because it: (1) competes against more brands (those with purely functional, purely symbolic, purely experiential, and mixed concepts), and (2) may be difficult for consumers to readily understand what it stands for and what its defining characteristics are.[26]

It is the responsibility—and indeed the obligation—of brand managers to supervise brands carefully, to adjust brand meanings when necessary (due to competitive challenges, changes in consumer preferences, and so on) and continuously strive to enhance brand equity.

INTEGRATED MARKETING COMMUNICATIONS

There has been a distinct trend in recent years toward a practice that has come to be termed *integrated marketing communications*, or simply *IMC*. In fact, this trend is one of the most important marketing developments of the 1990s. Companies in the past often treated the communication elements as virtually separate activities, whereas current marketing philosophy holds that integration is absolutely imperative for success, as clearly summarized in the following quotes:

> *The marketer who succeeds in the new environment will be the one who coordinates the communications mix so tightly that you can look from [advertising] medium to medium, from program event to program event, and instantly see that the brand is speaking with one voice.*[27]
>
> *The basic reason for integrated marketing communications is that marketing communication will be the only sustainable competitive advantage of marketing organizations in the 1990s and into the twenty-first century.*[28]

Integrating the various communications elements seems so elementary that the student may be wondering, Why is this such a big deal? Actually, many organizations traditionally have treated advertising, sales promotions, point-of-purchase displays, and other communication tools virtually as separate practices. The reluctance to change is due to managerial parochialism and fears that change might lead to budget cutbacks in their areas of control (such as advertising) and reductions in their authority and power. Corporations' advertising agencies also have resisted change because of their reluctance to broaden their function beyond just advertising. However, many advertising agencies have recently expanded their roles by merging with other companies or creating new departments that specialize in the growth areas of sales promotions, marketing-oriented public relations, event/sponsorship marketing, and direct marketing.[29]

www.fallon.com

The award-winning advertising agency Fallon McElligott of Minneapolis realized that success for it and its clients required more than just a dependence on advertising. The agency's founder and chairman, Patrick Fallon, recognized that the agency needed managers with marketing experience broader than just advertising. The agency hired an integrated marketing manager, and Fallon McElligott was transformed from an agency known mostly by its print advertising to one that could assist its clients in most any form of marketing communications. This integrated approach has enabled Fallon McElligott to attract notable clients such as McDonald's Arch Deluxe, United Airlines, Holiday Inn, the USA Network, and Miller Lite Beer.[30]

www.mcdonalds.com

www.ual.com

www.holiday-inn.com

www.usanetwork.com

Many firms, including suppliers of marketing communication services as well as their clients, have increasingly adopted an integrated approach to their communication activities.[31] This growth is not restricted to North America, but has spread to the United Kingdom, elsewhere in Europe, and also to Latin America.[32] Although IMC received its primary initial acceptance by manufacturers of consumer packaged goods, the practice has also been adopted by numerous retail and service marketers.[33] It now seems certain that IMC is not a passing fad; rather, this philosophy now appears to be a permanent feature of the marketing communications landscape around the world and in many different types of marketing organizations.[34] As Don Schultz, a pioneer of IMC, puts it, "Integration just plain makes sense for those planning to succeed in the 21st-century marketplace. Marketers, communicators, and brand organizations simply have no choice."[35]

Let us now explore in some detail the features of integrated marketing communications.

A Definition of IMC

The following definition captures one widely voiced perspective:

> *IMC is the process of developing and implementing various forms of persuasive communications programs with customers and prospects over time. The goal of IMC is to influence or directly affect the behavior of the selected communications audience. IMC considers all sources of brand or company contacts which a customer or prospect has with the product or service as potential delivery channels for future messages. Further, IMC makes use of all forms of communication which are relevant to the customer and prospects, and to which they might be receptive. In sum, the IMC process starts with the customer or prospect and then works back to determine and define the forms and methods through which persuasive communications programs should be developed.[36]*

Key Features of IMC

This definition suggests five features that undergird the philosophy and practice of integrated marketing communications. These features are listed in Table 1.1 and discussed hereafter.

1. **Affect Behavior.** The goal of IMC is to *affect the behavior* of the communications audience. This means that marketing communications must do more than just influence brand awareness or enhance consumer attitudes toward the brand.

TABLE 1.1	Five Key Features of IMC

1. Affect behavior.
2. Start with the customer or prospect.
3. Use any and all forms of contacts.
4. Achieve synergy.
5. Build relationships.

Instead, successful IMC requires that communication efforts be directed at encouraging some form of behavioral response. The objective, in other words, is to move people to action. We must be careful not to misconstrue this point. An integrated marketing communications program *ultimately* must be judged in terms of whether it influences behavior; but it would be simplistic and unrealistic to expect an action to result from every communication effort. Prior to purchasing a new brand, consumers generally must be made aware of the brand and its benefits and influenced to have a favorable attitude toward it. Communication efforts directed at accomplishing these intermediate, or pre-behavioral, goals are fully justified. Yet eventually—and preferably sooner rather than later—a successful marketing communications program must accomplish more than encouraging consumers to like a brand or, worse yet, merely familiarizing them with its existence. This partially explains why sales promotions and direct-to-consumer advertising are used so extensively—both practices yield quicker results than other forms of marketing communications.

To better understand IMC's objective to affect behavior, consider the situation faced by the U.S. dairy industry. Throughout most of the 1980s and into the 1990s, the industry touted milk as the drink that "does the body good." Research by the dairy industry revealed that most consumers got the message and perceived milk as a nutritious drink. The problem, however, was that average per capita consumption dropped by over 14 percent. Consumers had positive attitudes toward milk, but they simply were not drinking it as much as in the past. Hence, a new communications campaign was initiated with the theme, "Milk. Help Yourself." The advertising was designed to influence behavior—that is, to get people to drink milk more often. The J. Walter Thompson ad agency prepared eight different commercials to present milk with different meals and snacks throughout the day. In a morning commercial, for example, milk was shown being poured into a glass with surrounding shots of a waffle oozing with syrup and a powdered doughnut descending from a bag.[37]

www.jwtworld.com

The predicament faced by producers of natural food products is another instance in which a behavioral-oriented communications program was needed. Research conducted to gauge consumers' feelings about 10 natural products (free-range chickens, organic fruits, and so on) revealed that natural products have a good image, but not many people were buying them. Only 6 percent of the sampled consumers had purchased free-range chickens during the year preceding the survey, yet 43 percent thought that free-range chickens were superior to conventional chickens.[38] This is a classic illustration of buyer behavior not following directly from attitudes. In a case such as this, the goal of marketing communications would be to convert these good feelings toward natural products into product consumption—it does little good to have consumers like your product but not buy it!

2. **Start with the Customer or Prospect.** A second key feature of IMC is that the process *starts with the customer or prospect* and then works back to the brand communicator in determining the most appropriate and effective methods through which persuasive communications programs should be developed. The IMC approach avoids an "inside-out" (from company to customer) approach in identifying contact methods and communication vehicles and instead starts with the customer ("outside-in") to determine those communication methods that will best serve the customers' information needs and motivate them to purchase the brand. The following discussion about the importance of using any form of "contact" that is most appropriate for the target audience is a natural extension of being customer focused.

3. **Use Any and All Forms of Contacts.** IMC uses all forms of communication and *all sources of brand or company contacts* as potential message delivery channels. The term **contact** is used here to mean any message medium that is capable of reaching target customers and presenting the communicator's brand in a favorable light. The key feature of this third element of IMC is that it reflects a willingness to use whatever communication outlets (contacts) are best for reaching the target audience rather than pre-committing to any single medium or subset of media.

Brand message contacts include a virtually endless list of possibilities. For example, the author once observed a sticker for Jell-O pudding affixed to bananas—one product (bananas) was being used as a contact channel for reaching consumers about another (Jell-O). A more dramatic illustration of a unique form of contact involves the introduction of Smirnoff's premium brand of vodka, Smirnoff Black. In introducing this brand, Smirnoff wanted to create excitement as well as to dramatize Smirnoff's Russian connection. Toward this end, Smirnoff officials employed BFG Communications of Hilton Head, South Carolina, to accomplish the job. BFG put together a production in which troupes of three or four actors—who were dressed in 19th-century Russian outfits as czar, czarina, Rasputin, and perhaps a ballerina—went to bars and generated attention and enthusiasm for Smirnoff Black by creating a ruckus and providing entertainment for patrons. In markets such as Philadelphia, Dallas, Atlanta, and Denver, the troupes visited as many trendy bars as possible, and while there provided free samples of Smirnoff Black and explained the distillation intricacies of the brand.[39] The Russian entertainment motif served to attract bar-attendees' attention and also helped build an appropriate association in consumers' minds between the Smirnoff Black brand and its Russian heritage.

www.smirnoff.com

Another illustration of a unique form of contact was a promotion for Mountain Dew. In order to entice teens to purchase multiple packs of Mountain Dew, PepsiCo contacted over 250,000 teenagers once a week for six months through their beepers. Entertaining messages from sports stars and other celebrities were tied into opportunities for the teens to receive desirable items such as Burton snowboards, Killer Loop sunglasses, and other items.[40]

www.burton.com

www.KillerLoop.com

A final example of an unusual form of contact comes from the marketing of rap music. In the summer of 1998 a newcomer on the national rap scene, Master P. Pushed, came out with an album titled "MP Da Last Don." The album sold nearly 500,000 copies in its first week and became the number one album in the country. What accounted for this smashing success? In large part it was due to the use of so-called "street teams" that distributed free tapes at schools, in housing projects, and elsewhere.[41] These teams talked up the "brand" (i.e., the album) and generated a groundswell of enthusiasm among potential rap-music purchasers. For a final illustration of using multiple contact methods, see the *IMC Focus* about Bayer Select.

It should be clear that adherents to IMC are not tied to any single communication method (such as mass media advertising) but instead use whatever media and contacts best enable the communicator to deliver the brand-concept message to the designated audience. Direct-mail advertising, promotions at sporting and entertainment events, advertisements on packages of other brands, slogans on T-shirts, in-store displays, and Internet pages are all potentially important contact methods for reaching present and prospective customers. Thus, the IMC objective is to reach the target audience efficiently and effectively using whatever contact methods are appropriate. Television advertising, for example, may be the best medium for contacting the audience for some brands, while less traditional (and even unconventional) contact methods may best serve other brands' communication and financial needs. The chairman and CEO of Young & Rubicam, a major Madison Avenue ad agency, succinctly yet eloquently captured the essence of the foregoing discussion when stating: "At the end of the day, we [i.e., ad agencies] don't deliver ads, or direct mail pieces, or PR and corporate identity programs. We deliver results."[42]

www.yandr.com

The value of this particular IMC feature, i.e., using whatever form of contact that is most appropriate, is that it challenges an over-dependence on mass-media advertising that characterizes much past marketing practice in the U.S. In contrast to a dependence on advertising, many brand managers in Europe have concluded that traditional mass media advertising often is too costly and ineffective. Many European managers have long relied on contact methods other than advertising to build brand awareness and enhance brand image.[43] For example, the high-end clothier Hugo Boss created its exclusive image primarily through the use of event sponsorships such as tennis, golf, and ski competitions.[44]

www.bayeraspirin.com

4. **Achieve Synergy.** Inherent in the definition of IMC is the need for *synergy.* All of the communication elements (advertising, point-of-purchase, sales promotions, events, and so on) must speak with a *single voice;* coordination is absolutely critical to achieving a strong and unified brand image and moving consumers to action.[45] The failure to closely coordinate all communication elements can result in duplicated efforts or—worse yet—contradictory messages about a brand being conveyed to consumers. A VP of Marketing at Nabisco fully recognized the value of speaking with a single voice when describing her intention to integrate all of the marketing communication contacts for Nabisco's Oreo brand of cookies. This executive captured the essential quality of synergy when stating that under her leadership, "Whenever consumers see Oreo, they'll be seeing the same message."[46]

www.oreo.com

In general, the single-voice, or synergy principle, on which IMC rests involves selecting for a brand a specific *positioning statement.* A **positioning statement** is the key idea that encapsulates what a brand is intended to stand for in its target market's mind. True IMC practitioners, such as Oreo's VP of Marketing, know that it is critical that they continuously convey this message, or positioning statement, on every occasion where the brand comes into contact with the target audience.

IMC Focus: A Big Challenge Requires Creative Marketing Communications

Bayer is a name that is virtually synonymous with aspirin. But after years of challenges from nonaspirin competitors in the pain relief industry (such as acetaminophen-based Tylenol and ibuprofen-based Advil), Sterling Health USA decided to extend the Bayer name to a line of aspirin-free pain relievers, each designed to attack a specific symptom: sinus, menstrual, nighttime, and general pain and headache. They chose the name Bayer Select to suggest the symptom-specific, or select, nature of pain relief provided by this new brand.

Bayer Select's brand concept is clearly an appeal to consumers' functional needs for relief from various forms of pain. Sterling's objective was to reach millions of consumers with the message that Bayer stands for more than just aspirin. Television was a useful medium for conveying this message, but the product manager for Bayer Select recognized that TV alone would not be sufficient because many people do not watch much TV, especially during the times when it is most efficient to advertise.

Strategies were devised for reaching consumers in as many productive ways as possible. Ads were prepared for placement in doctors' waiting rooms and run in various special-interest magazines. One billion coupons were distributed during the course of the first-year campaign (an average of four coupons for every man, woman, and child in the United States). Bayer arranged with Emergency Medical Services (EMS) to contribute financial assistance to volunteers and to distribute telephone procedures for emergencies. This agreement effectively amounted to a free public-service campaign for EMS, and it created a favorable association for Bayer Select by associating its name with a worthy cause. A special advertising campaign also was developed to appeal specifically to Hispanic consumers. All told, Sterling invested $116 million to introduce this new product line, with all messages communicating the concept that Bayer Select "puts the help where it hurts."

Source: Adapted from Patricia Winters, "$116M Intro for Bayer Select Isn't Just Ads," *Advertising Age*, November 23, 1992, 37.

---

5. **Build Relationships.** A fifth characteristic of IMC is the belief that successful marketing communications requires *building a relationship between the brand and the customer.* It can be argued, in fact, that relationship building is the key to modern marketing and that IMC is the key to relationship building.[47] A relationship is an enduring link between a brand and consumers; it entails repeat purchases and perhaps even loyalty. Companies have learned that it is more profitable to build and maintain relationships than it is to continuously search for new customers. This explains the growth in frequent-flyer and many other so-called "frequency," "loyalty," or "ambassador" programs.

The Marketing Support Director for Southwestern Bell Telephone Co. nicely captures the value of relationship building in the following passage:

> *Every customer contact should make us easier to do business with and let our customers know we care. Southwestern Bell employees, from operators to service technicians to sales representatives, make 70 million customer contacts every month. In a competitive arena where customer loyalty can turn on a dime, making the most of those contacts is essential.*[48]

Changes in Marketing Communication Practices

The adoption of an IMC mind-set necessitates some fundamental changes in the way marketing communications have traditionally been practiced. The following interrelated changes are particularly prominent.

Reduced Faith in Mass Media Advertising

www.swbell.com

Many marketing communicators now realize that communication methods other than media advertising often better serve the needs of their brands. As we noted previously, the objective is to contact customers and prospects effectively; media advertising is not always the most effective or financially efficient medium for accomplishing this objective. But of course this does not mean that media advertising is unimportant or in threat of extinction. The point instead is that other communication methods should receive careful consideration before automatically assuming that mass media advertising is the solution.

Increased Reliance on Highly Targeted Communication Methods. Direct mail, specialty interest magazines, cable TV, and alternative media such as the Internet are just some of the contact methods that enable communications that are more pinpointed than mass-media advertising. The use of database marketing is a key aspect of this second feature. Today many business-to-business and consumer-oriented companies maintain large, up-to-date databases of present and prospective customers. These customers and prospects are periodically contacted via direct-mail messages.

Greater Demands Imposed on Marketing Communications Suppliers. Marketing communication suppliers such as advertising agencies, sales promotion firms, and public relations agencies have historically offered a limited range of services. Now it is increasingly important for suppliers to offer multiple services—which is why some major advertising agencies have expanded their offerings beyond just advertising services to include sales promotion assistance, public relations, database marketing, and event marketing support.

Increased Efforts to Assess Communications' Return on Investment. A final key feature of IMC is that it demands that systematic efforts be undertaken to determine whether communication efforts yield a reasonable return on their investment. All managers, and marketing communicators are no exception, must increasingly be held financially accountable for their actions. The investment in marketing communications must be assessed in terms of the profit-to-investment ratio to determine whether changes are needed or whether other forms of investment might be more profitable.[49]

Obstacles to Implementing IMC

Brand managers typically utilize outside suppliers, or specialized services, to assist them in managing various aspects of marketing communications. These include advertising agencies, public relations firms, sales promotion agencies, direct advertising firms, and special event marketers. Herein is a major reason why marketing communication efforts often do not meet the ideals described in this chapter. Integration requires tight coordination among all elements of a communications program. However, this can become complicated when different specialized services operate independently of one another and when the brand marketer's lack of careful organization impedes communication activities.[50]

Perhaps the greatest obstacle to integration is that few providers of marketing communication services have the far-ranging skills to plan and execute programs that cut across all major forms of marketing communications. Advertising agencies, which traditionally have offered a greater breadth of services than other specialists, are well qualified to develop mass media advertising campaigns; most, however, do not also have the ability to conduct direct-to-customer advertising, and even fewer have departments for sales promotions, special events, and publicity campaigns. Although many advertising agencies have expanded their services, integrated marketing communications awaits major changes in the culture of marketing departments and service providers before it becomes a reality on a large scale.[51] It has been suggested that firms might need to create a key organizational position that is responsible for all forms of marketing communication, and that might be headed by an executive with a title such as MarCom director.[52]

Summary

This chapter discusses the importance of brand equity and brand-concept management and introduces the fundamentals of integrated marketing communications. The concept of brand equity is described as the value in a brand resulting from high brand name awareness and strong, favorable, and perhaps unique associations that consumers have in memory about a particular brand. Marketing communications play an important role in enhancing brand equity. This is accomplished through the process of brand-concept management—overseeing a brand throughout its life cycle. Brand concepts are managed by appealing to customers' functional, symbolic, and experiential needs through effective communications.

The chapter overviews the fundamentals of integrated marketing communications (IMC). IMC is an organization's unified, coordinated effort to promote a brand concept through the use of multiple communication tools that "speak with a single voice." One of several key features of IMC is the use of all sources of brand or company contacts as potential message delivery channels. Another key feature is that the IMC process starts with the customer or prospect rather than the brand communicator to determine the most appropriate and effective methods for developing persuasive communications programs. The use of database marketing and highly pinpointed communication methods (such as direct mail and specialty interest magazines) to affect behavioral responses, along with attempts to measure the impact of marketing communications, are significant developments associated with the growing practice of integrated marketing communications.

Discussion Questions

1. Use the framework in Figure 1.1 and describe all personal associations that the following brands hold for you: (1) the new VW Beetle, (2) *Wow!* potato chips, (3) *The Wall Street Journal,* and (4) the New York Yankees (baseball team).

2. Roger Enrico, CEO of PepsiCo, was quoted in the text as saying: "In my mind the best thing a person can say about a brand is that it's their favorite." Identify two brands that you regard as your favorites. Describe the specific associations that each of these brands hold in your mind and that thus make them two of your favorites.

3. Parmalat USA, a division of an Italian-owned company, introduced shelf-stable milk in East Coast U.S. markets in the mid-1990s. Shelf-stable milk, as the name suggests, is liquid milk that does not require refrigeration until the container is opened. Shelf-stable milk is the dominant form of milk in many European and South American countries, but most people in the United States are accustomed to drinking refrigerated milk. Assume you are the advertising agency for Parmalat's brand of shelf-stable milk. Suggest three magazine advertising headlines for this product, one appealing to functional needs, another to symbolic needs, and the last to experiential needs. Explain precisely how your three headlines reflect each type of consumer need.

4. Identify a magazine advertisement that reflects a brand-concept management strategy appealing to consumers' symbolic needs. What specific aspect of this ad led you to conclude that the ad appeals to symbolic needs?

5. Identify another magazine advertisement that reflects a brand-concept management strategy appealing to consumers' experiential needs. Offer a specific explanation as to why you believe this ad appeals to experiential needs.

6. The choice of a brand concept is not an arbitrary decision by some creative advertiser to appeal to functional, symbolic, or experiential needs. To the contrary, there are characteristics of the brand, the competition, and consumers that suggest when a particular brand-concept orientation is most appropriate. Describe some of the factors that likely come into play, using the category of wristwatches to illustrate your discussion.

7. Assume that your college or university is currently undertaking a huge marketing communications campaign targeted to high school students. Explain how your school might use event marketing and sales promotions to increase enrollment.

8. Offer your views on the following statement: "The basic reason for integrated marketing communications is that marketing communication will be the only sustainable competitive advantage of marketing organizations in the 1990s and into the twenty-first century."

9. Given your understanding of IMC and its fundamental characteristics, describe the probable outcome of practicing nonintegrated, rather than integrated, marketing communications.

10. One key feature of IMC is the emphasis on affecting behavior and not just its antecedents (such as brand awareness or favorable attitudes). For each of the following situations, indicate the specific behavior(s) that marketing communications might attempt to affect: (1) your university's advertising efforts; (2) a professional baseball team's promotion for a particular game; (3) a not-for-profit organization's efforts to recruit more volunteers; and (4) Gatorade's sponsorship of a volleyball tournament.

11. IMC also emphasizes utilizing all economically effective contact methods as potential message delivery channels. Assume you are advertising a product that is marketed specifically to high school seniors. Identify seven contact methods (include no more than two forms of mass media advertising) you might use to reach this audience.

Internet Exercises

1. Identify a magazine ad that mentions a Web site dedicated to the advertised brand. First, classify the magazine ad according to its brand-concept management strategy (i.e., whether it appeals predominantly to symbolic, experiential, or functional needs) and explain why this advertisement represents the selected brand-concept strategy. Then, visit the brand's Web site and assess whether the same brand-concept strategy is used as in the magazine ad. If you believe it is, provide specific examples to document the similarity. If not, why do you think the strategies are different and is this a violation of the one-voice, or synergy, principle underlying IMC?

2. Using the framework in Figure 1.1, write down all of the personal associations the Viagra brand holds for you. Visit the Viagra Web site (www.viagra.com/consumer) and identify which of your personal associations are reinforced and provide specific examples of this reinforcement. After leaving the site, write down any new personal associations you have with Viagra.

3. Visit the Coca-Cola Web site (www.coke.com). Using the frame in Figure 1.1, assess the focus of the Web site regarding the development of brand associations (i.e., attributes, benefits, or overall attitude). Provide specific examples to support your assessment and explain why you think the other types of associations were *not* the focus of the Web site.

4. One key characteristic of IMC discussed in this chapter is the belief that marketing communications requires building a relationship between the brand and the customer. Visit the Green Giant Web site (www.greengiant.com) and do the following:
   a. identify the characteristics of the consumers you think Green Giant is targeting for relationships
   b. provide specific examples of attempts to build enduring links to these consumers
   c. describe the *actions* encouraged by the Web site and relate these actions to the sustenance of a relationship with consumers.

Chapter One Endnotes

1. Don E. Schultz, Stanley I. Tannenbaum, and Robert F. Lauterborn, *Integrated Marketing Communications* (Lincolnwood, Ill.: NTC Publishing Group, 1993), 46.

2. This and other facts are based on Stephanie Thompson, "Frito Looks to *Wow!* 'Em with Sample Blitz," *Brandweek,* March 9, 1998, 1, 6.

3. Tom Peters, "The Brand Called You," *Fast Company,* August/September 1997, 83–94.

4. This discussion follows Leslie De Chernatony and Francesca Dall'Olmo Riley, "Expert Practitioners' Views on Roles of Brands: Implications for Marketing Communications," *Journal of Marketing Communications* 4 (June 1998), 87–100.

5. Jacques Chevron, "Of Brand Values and Sausage," *Brandweek,* April 20, 1998, 22.

6. Robert Wehling, cited in *Marketing Science Institute Review* (spring 1998), 7.

7. Cited in Kevin Lane Keller, *Strategic Brand Management: Building, Measuring, and Managing Brand Equity* (Upper Saddle River, NJ: Prentice-Hall, 1998), p. 2.

8. Highly readable and insightful discussions of brand equity are provided in two excellent books written by David A. Aaker: *Managing Brand Equity* (New York: The Free Press, 1991), and *Building Strong Brands* (New York: The Free Press, 1996).

9. The following discussion borrows liberally from the research and writings of Kevin Lane Keller, especially Keller, *Strategic Brand Management* (Chapter 2) and Kevin Lane Keller, "Conceptualizing, Measuring, and Managing Customer-Based Brand Equity," *Journal of Marketing* 57 (January 1993), 1–22. It will be noted that Keller refers to "customer," whereas in this text our reference will be to consumers. The term consumer typically is used to describe end-users, whereas customer more often refers to marketing intermediaries such as wholesalers, agents, and retailers.

10. Keller, "Conceptualizing, Measuring, and Managing Customer-Based Brand Equity," 2.

11. Terry Lefton, "Adidas Goes to Image Pitch with '98 $$ Boost," *Brandweek,* January 26, 1998, 37.

12. This figure is from ibid., 7.

13. "Coke's Market Share Rises to 43.9% as PepsiCo Slips," *The Wall Street Journal Interactive Edition,* February 13, 1998 (http://interactive.wsj.com).

14. Larry Light and Richard Morgan, *The Fourth Wave: Brand Loyalty Marketing* (New York: Coalition for Brand Equity, 1994), 11.

15. William Boulding, Eunkyu Lee, and Richard Staelin, "Mastering the Mix: Do Advertising, Promotion, and Sales Force Activities Lead to Differentiation?" *Journal of Marketing Research* 31 (May 1994), 159–172.

16. Bill McDowell, "Starbucks Is Ground Zero in Today's Coffee Culture," *Advertising Age,* December 9, 1996, 1, 49.

17. "The PepsiCo Empire Strikes Back," *Brandweek,* October 7, 1996, 60.

18. Stephanie Thompson, "Branding Buddies," February 23, 1998, 26.

19. Ibid.

20. Ibid., 28.

21. Keller, *Strategic Brand Management,* 285. For an excellent academic treatment of this issue, see C. Whan Park, Sung Youl Jun, and Allan D. Shocker, "Composite Branding Alliances: An Investigation of Extension and Feedback Effects," *Journal of Marketing Research* 33 (November 1996), 453–466.

22. Sally Goll Beatty, "Intel Wannabes Unleash a Flood of New Ads on TV," *The Wall Street Journal Interactive Edition,* January 14, 1998 (http://interactive.wsj.com).

23. Ibid.

24. C. Whan Park, Bernard J. Jaworski, and Deborah J. MacInnis, "Strategic Brand Concept-Image Management," *Journal of Marketing* 50 (October 1986), 136.

25. Ibid.

26. For further discussion of this point, see ibid.

27. Quoting Spencer Plavoukas, chairman of Lintas (New York), and cited in Laurie Petersen, "Pursuing Results in the Age of Accountability," *Adweek's Marketing Week,* November 19, 1990, 21.

28. Schultz, Tannenbaum, and Lauterborn, *Integrated Marketing Communications,* 47.

29. For further discussion of the resistance to integrate, see Scott Hume, "New Ideas, Old Barriers," *Advertising Age,* July 22, 1991, 6.

30. Richard A. Melcher, "Hot Ship in the Heartland," *Business Week,* January 13, 1997, 51.

31. Fred Beard, "IMC Use and Client-Ad Agency Relationships," *Journal of Marketing Communications* 3 (December 1997), 217–230.

32. Patricia B. Rose, "Practioner Opinions and Interests Regarding Integrated Marketing Communications in Selected Latin American Countries," *Journal of Marketing Communications* 2 (September 1996), 125–140.

33. Glen J. Nowak, Glen T. Cameron, and Denise Delorme, "Beyond the World of Packaged Goods: Assessing the Relevance of Integrated Marketing Communications for Retail and Consumer Service Marketing," *Journal of Marketing Communications* 2 (September 1996), 173–190.

34. Don E. Schultz and Philip J. Kitchen, "Integrated Marketing Communications in U.S. Advertising Agencies: An Exploratory Study," *Journal of Advertising Research* 37 (September/October 1997), 7–18.

35. Don E. Schultz, "Integration Is Critical for Success in 21st Century," *Marketing News,* September 15, 1997, 26.

36. This is the working definition of IMC developed by members of the marketing communications faculty of the Medill School at Northwestern University. The definition was reprinted in Don E. Schultz, "Integrated Marketing Communications: Maybe Definition Is in the Point of View," *Marketing News,* January 18, 1993, 17.

37. Based on Skip Wollenberg, "Dairy Industry Ads Touting Milk As Complement to Favorite Foods," *The State,* October 12, 1994, B12.

38. Leah Rickard, "Natural Products Score Big on Image," *Advertising Age,* August 8, 1994, 26.

39. Elaine Underwood, "Dramatic Entrance," *Brandweek,* December 2, 1996, 26–27.

40. Bruce Orr, "Dew Gets Personal: Brand-Building with Beepers," *Marketing News,* July 6, 1998, 13.

41. Patrick M. Reilly, "Phat Sales: 'Street Teams' Create Rap Stars with Curbside Technique," *The Wall Street Journal Interactive Edition,* June 25, 1998.

42. Peter A. Georgescu, "Looking at the Future of Marketing," *Advertising Age,* April 14, 1997, 30.

43. This argument is made particularly well by Erich Joachimsthaler and David A. Aaker in "Building Brands Without Mass Media," *Harvard Business Review* (January/February 1997), 39–50.

44. Ibid., 44.

45. This "one-voice perspective" is widely shared by various writers on the topic of IMC. See Schultz, Tannenbaum, and Lauterborn, Integrated Marketing Communications; Tom Duncan, "Integrated Marketing? It's Synergy," *Advertising Age,* March 8, 1993, 22; and Glen J. Nowak and Joseph Phelps, "Conceptualizing the Integrated Marketing Communications' Phenomenon: An Examination of Its Impact on Advertising Practices and Its Implications for Advertising Research," *Journal of Current Issues and Research in Advertising* 16 (spring 1994), 49–66.

46. Judann Pollack, "Nabisco's Marketing VP Expects 'Great Things,'" *Advertising Age,* December 2, 1996, 40.

47. See Schultz, Tannenbaum, and Lauterborn, *Integrated Marketing Communications,* 52–53.

48. Pat Long, "Customer Loyalty, One Customer At a Time," *Marketing News,* February 3, 1997, 8.

49. For discussion of how to assess the ROI for marketing communications, see Don E. Schultz, "Trying to Determine ROI for IMC," *Marketing News,* January 3, 1994, 18; and Don E. Schultz, "Spreadsheet Approach to Measuring ROI for IMC," *Marketing News,* February 28, 1994, 12.

50. Kim Cleland, "Few Wed Marketing, Communications," *Advertising Age,* February 27, 1995, 10.

51. Ibid.

52. Schultz, Tannenbaum, and Lauterborn, *Integrated Marketing Communications.*

The Marketing Communications Process

CHAPTER OBJECTIVE

The opening vignette touches on several issues—objective setting, targeting, and budgeting—that are the subject of this chapter. The chapter's general purpose is to build a comprehensive framework that fully integrates the various aspects of managerial decision making related to marketing communications strategy and tactics. This framework will provide a useful model for both thinking about and discussing the role of marketing communications in building brand equity.

Opening Vignette: A Korean Car Company Aims at College Students

You probably are familiar with automobile models manufactured by Hyundai and maybe even Kia, but have you ever heard of Daewoo cars? Daewoo is a huge Korean conglomerate that markets consumer electronics, heavy equipment, and other products. Now it has moved into automobile marketing. Three Daewoo models were introduced to the United States in 1998—the Lanos, Leganza, and Nubira. Big deal, another car company, so what? Well, the interesting thing about Daewoo's automobile introduction in the United States is the manner in which the cars were marketed. The company recruited about 2,000 college students from hundreds of colleges and universities to become Daewoo Campus Advisors (DCAs). Students selected as DCAs received free trips to Korea where they toured Daewoo auto plants and dealerships to gain in-depth product knowledge. Back on campus, DCAs were hired to work about 10 hours per week passing out information about Daewoo cars, giving presentations to student groups, and promoting what were called "ride-and-drive events." The DCAs received commissions up to $400 on referrals and also received the opportunity to purchase Daewoo cars at significant discounts.

Daewoo chose this interesting means of marketing its cars in the U.S. for several reasons. First, it provided a way of building Daewoo's brand equity with young people, who are said to have more brand-preference flexibility when choosing an automobile than older consumers who have already owned multiple cars. Second, it was a less-expensive method for Daewoo to get its cars noticed quickly compared to the mass-media advertising favored by most automobile marketers. Finally, by focusing on college students, Daewoo realized an opportunity to reach budding professionals who, if favorably impressed, would spread the word about Daewoo upon leaving campuses.

Daewoo started its college-oriented marketing efforts in university towns such as Atlanta, Boston, Philadelphia, Orlando, Chicago, and San Diego. Daewoo's campus advisors at colleges and universities in these cities promoted the various Daewoo models and some were given free use of Daewoo vehicles for several months to demonstrate them to friends and acquaintances and to drive prospects to local Daewoo showrooms.

Source: Adapted from Al Urbanski, "The Old College Try," *Promo*, July 1998, 48–50.

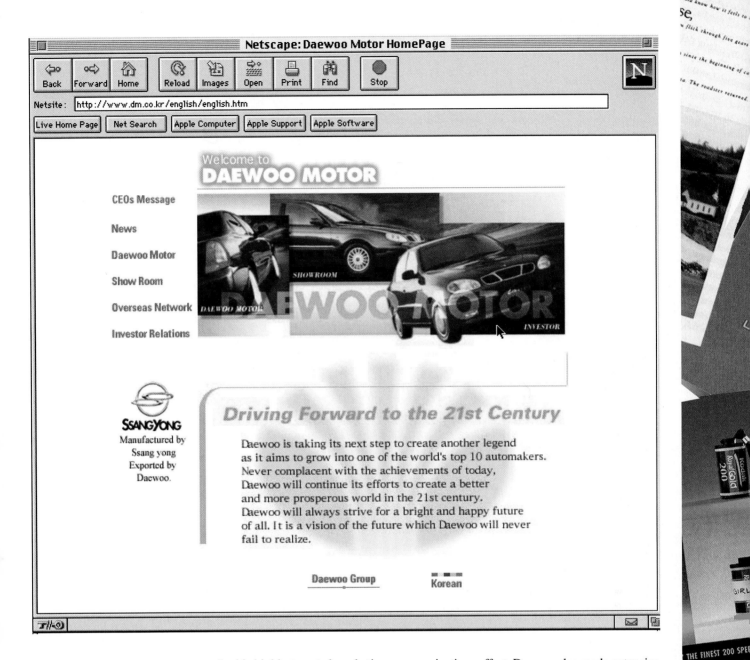

In this highly targeted marketing communications effort, Daewoo also made extensive use of the Internet to promote its cars with banner ads on frequently visited sites that appeal to college-age young adults. The only other media that accompanied the launch of Daewoo were local newspaper and radio ads.

A MODEL OF THE MARKETING COMMUNICATIONS DECISION PROCESS

The elements and relations of the comprehensive framework are illustrated in Figure 2.1. This framework, or model, contains four general components, each of which is designated by a Roman numeral: (I) structuring the organization for marketing communications decisions, (II) monitoring and managing the marketing environment, (III) making brand-level marketing communications decisions, and (IV) enhancing brand equity.

The *brand-level decision process* is the cornerstone of the model and represents the bulk of this chapter's discussion. This process consists of a set of *general choices* (relating to targeting, objective setting, and budgeting), a set of *specific choices* (involving the mixture, or integration, of communications elements and the choice of messages, media, and

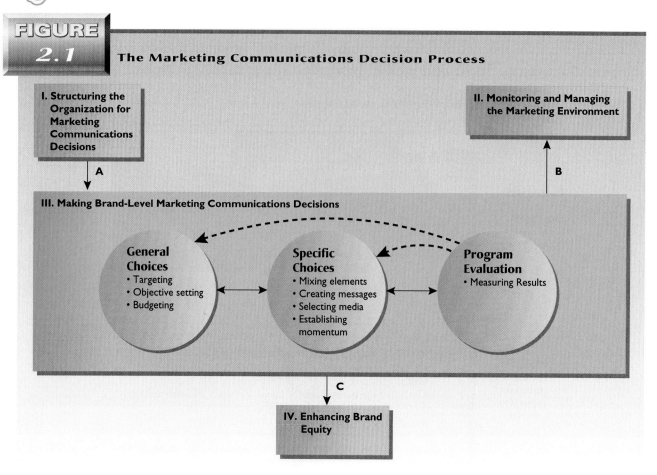

FIGURE 2.1

The Marketing Communications Decision Process

I. Structuring the Organization for Marketing Communications Decisions

II. Monitoring and Managing the Marketing Environment

A

B

III. Making Brand-Level Marketing Communications Decisions

General Choices
- Targeting
- Objective setting
- Budgeting

Specific Choices
- Mixing elements
- Creating messages
- Selecting media
- Establishing momentum

Program Evaluation
- Measuring Results

C

IV. Enhancing Brand Equity

momentum), and *program evaluation* (measuring MarCom results). It is very important at this point that you scan and achieve a basic understanding of the model in Figure 2.1 in preparation for the following discussion, which fleshes out the model's skeleton.

Notice first that the decision process is influenced by the *marketing organizational structure* (relation A in Figure 2.1), which represents the arrangement employed by a firm to perform its marketing and marketing communications functions. An organizational structure has great influence on how a company makes communications decisions and how these decisions are implemented. The model also shows that effective marketing communications decisions require active efforts to *monitor and manage the environment.* (The term **environment** is used in this context to include all forces external to an organization that influence its decision making and opportunities for success. Included are competitive, social-cultural, economic, and regulatory forces.) Relation *B* in Figure 2.1 illustrates that marketing communications decisions are directed toward actively managing, rather than merely reacting to, the environment. The ultimate objective of successful marketing communications, as with all aspects of marketing, is to *enhance brand equity* (relation *C* in Figure 2.1).

Structuring the Organization

A company's marketing organizational structure is instrumental in determining how well it is able to manage its environment, satisfy its customers, and implement effective marketing communications decisions. In recent years many well-known companies (including Procter & Gamble, Campbell Soup, Coca-Cola, Pepsi-Cola, IBM, Ford Motor Co., General Motors, and Mitsubishi Motor Sales of America) have revamped their marketing structures in order to: (1) better serve their immediate customers (wholesalers, brokers, and retailers); (2) do a better job in satisfying their ultimate consumers' needs; and (3) to outperform competitors.

www.campbellsoup.com

www.ford.com

www.gm.com

www.mitsucars.com

Pressures to Reorganize.   All three *C*s (customers, consumers, and competitors) have exerted pressure on companies to reorganize.[1] Having over the years become more sophisticated and economically powerful, retailers expect more service and support from their manufacturer suppliers than received in past years. Greater choices than ever are available to consumers, thereby forcing each company to do a better job in order to win consumers' loyalty and beat competitors.

For example, Pepsi-Cola used to organize its marketing of soft drinks by channel of distribution—retail (such as grocery stores), vending machines, and fountain sales. This structure necessitated three separate organizations to market Pepsi-Cola nationally. Pepsi accordingly reorganized its marketing department into four large regions, with the staff in each region responsible for all customers—retail, vending, and fountain—within the region. The advantage of such a regionalized marketing structure is that it enables the marketing staff to be more responsive to customer needs and competitive actions.[2]

Increasing numbers of firms are reorganizing to better reflect special regional demands. For example, Campbell Soup reorganized its marketing department into more than 20 regional units. Each unit contains a combined marketing and sales force and directs its own promotional budget, media-buying power, and marketing communications strategies. In the past, these decisions were made by Campbell's centralized national office.[3]

www.fritolay.com

Frito-Lay—the well-known marketer of snack foods—carved its market into seven regions. As with other regional marketing efforts, this permitted Frito-Lay to target its programs fully and to accommodate regional differences in consumer taste preferences better.[4] As with other regionalized marketing structures, it is now possible for Frito-Lay to develop marketing communications programs that best serve the special regional needs of retail customers and final consumers while placing the company in a stronger competitive position.

It is not only packaged-good companies that utilize the brand management organizational structure. For example, Ford has 13 brand managers for 16 specific vehicles and also a brand manager for multipurpose vehicles (Explorer, Expedition, and Windstar) and another for trucks.[5] General Motors also has turned to a brand management system. Its brand managers work with manufacturing and engineering personnel to assure that specific customer needs are matched to each car and truck that is designed. In other words, as discussed in Chapter 1, the process at GM starts with the customer and works back to the engineers and the factory.[6]

From Brand Management to Category Management.   The most dramatic marketing restructuring in many years took place at Procter & Gamble (P&G) in 1987. This marketing superstar of packaged goods established a category management structure that alters (but does not abolish) the traditional brand-management system that it innovated in 1931.[7] Under this new system, each of P&G's product categories (detergents, soaps, snacks, cookies, paper products, etc.) has its own manager: a *category manager*. Advertising, sales, manufacturing, research, engineering, and other staffs report directly to the category manager, who has direct profit responsibility.[8]

The reorganization reduced internal bickering for resources among brand managers and curtailed the tendency toward excessive short-term orientation fostered by the brand-management system, as discussed in the following *IMC Focus*. All brand managers (for example, the managers of Tide and Cheer) within a particular product category report directly to a category manager (detergent in this example). The category manager has responsibility for allocating resources among brand managers and seeing that long-term

IMC FOCUS: BRAND MANAGEMENT—THE ART OF RECONCILIATION

The brand management form of marketing organization places individual brand managers in charge of one or several brands. A brand manager literally serves as the brand champion, fighting for budget dollars to support the brand and pushing for more advertising, periodic sales promotions, and point-of-purchase programs to boost the brand's volume and market share. Brand managers typically are recruited from prestigious MBA programs. After serving apprenticeships as assistant brand managers or brand associates for periods as short as two years, the stars among this pool of young MBAs—typically in their late 20s or early 30s—assume positions as brand managers. For example, Procter & Gamble has approximately 80 brand managers.

The brand management system of marketing organization worked well for many companies for years. However, major developments in the 1980s created pressures for significant organizational changes. Three primary forces forced many companies, especially marketers of consumer packaged goods, to reorganize their marketing functions: (1) the realization that consumer preferences often differ considerably across regions of the country; (2) the availability of immediate sales-performance data that made it possible for manufacturers and retailers alike to determine which brands are meeting sales objectives and which marketing programs are effective in achieving manufacturers' and retailers' separate objectives; and (3) the power shift from manufacturers to retailers, which afforded retailers a greater say in how brands are marketed by manufacturers.

The old brand management system was no longer adequate because long-term brand equity often was subordinated to short-term interests. Individual managers faced various conflicts that oftentimes were resolved in ways that were expedient but not compatible with long-term brand-equity development and corporate welfare. Consider the following conflicts faced by a typical brand manager:

◆ Should I (the brand manager) focus on boosting the brand's short-term sales volume, or should I work toward building long-term brand equity?

◆ Should my perspective focus on my individual career (such as increasing the brand's short-term sales and market share) or that of the company as a whole (such as brand longevity and the company's best long-term interests)?

◆ Should my orientation be more national or regional in scope?

◆ Should I spend my time working more on tactical maneuvers (i.e., devising day-to-day programs) or on developing long-range strategic plans?

In most every instance, the opponent on the left side of the conflict won out over the one on the right. That is, brand managers were excessively short-term oriented, too tactical, too national, and perhaps too interested in enhancing self-interests. For these reasons, many companies have reorganized their marketing organizations to reconcile these conflicting interests. The operative word here is *reconcile,* not supplant. Successful brand management necessitates that both sides of the various conflicts receive due accord. However, the emergence of category management systems reflects a growing recognition that long-term corporate welfare requires that brand manager's personal well-being be subordinated to the best interests of the brands and product categories they manage.

objectives and overall corporate welfare are paramount over short-term expediencies and individual brand performance.[9]

www.tide.com

www.cheer.com

Monitoring and Managing the Environment

Every organization operates in a dynamic relation with its environment. As introductory marketing courses emphasize, a variety of external forces constitute the environment for marketing decisions. These include economic, competitive, technological, social-cultural, demographic, and regulatory influences. Marketing communications managers must continuously monitor environmental developments to enable a firm to *manage* rather than merely *react to* environmental forces.

Monitoring the Environment. Developing successful marketing communications necessitates continuous monitoring of competitors, societal events, economic developments, regulatory activity, and even the company's internal situation. **Environmental**

monitoring, or what also is referred to as performing a *situation analysis,* involves two general activities. First, an *internal analysis* must be made of an organization's *strengths* and *weaknesses.* Financial considerations and personnel matters are the primary issues in an internal analysis. A company with strong financial reserves and a talented team of communications specialists has numerous opportunities for developing creative programs that have impact, whereas an impoverished firm is limited in what it can accomplish. Only time will tell, for example, whether Daewoo's modest marketing communication efforts (described in the *Opening Vignette*) will be sufficient for creating high levels of brand awareness and positive brand images for Daewoo's automobile models.

In an *external analysis,* the second component of environmental monitoring, factors that are likely to influence communications effectiveness and product success are thoroughly reviewed. The economic situation, competitive activity, social-cultural developments, the legal climate, and channel of distribution considerations—the *opportunities* and *threats* that confront a brand at a point in time—are typical factors involved in an external situation analysis. The important aspects of environmental monitoring can be remembered with the well-known acronym **SWOT**—the analysis of a brand's strengths, weaknesses, opportunities, and threats.

www.sherwinwilliams.com

To illustrate the nature of an external analysis, consider the Dutch Boy brand of paint that has been marketed for over 80 years. This brand, which historically was directed at a mass audience rather than to any particular segment, was not doing well until it was purchased by the more financially secure Sherwin Williams company. Sherwin Williams's marketing research revealed that nearly 40 percent of all paint purchases were made at the time by younger, fashion-oriented consumers. Dutch Boy was repositioned to appeal to this particular target market by increasing advertising expenditures, and the messages emphasized consumers' lifestyles by showing users painting with Dutch Boy and then enjoying the fruits of their labor—fashionable high-sheen results emulating the European decorating style that had become increasingly popular in the United States.[10]

Managing the Environment. **Environmental management** captures the idea that through its marketing communications efforts and other marketing activities a firm can attempt to modify existing environmental conditions.[11] In other words, managers in specific areas of marketing communications (advertising, sales promotion, and so on) must attempt to influence and alter environmental circumstances so that the organization's interests are best served. While organizations are not able to manage their environments completely, it is nevertheless critical to maintain their monitoring efforts so they are constantly prepared to alter policies, strategies, and tactics to achieve compatibility with environmental circumstances. Successful companies anticipate environmental developments and prepare in advance, rather than simply react to significant changes after they have occurred.

www.nike.com
www.reebok.com

For example, athletic-shoe companies have been remarkably effective in managing their environments. Changes in the cultural and social environment (such as the increased emphasis on health and fitness) have provided opportunities for new types of athletic shoes that are customized to meet the demands of specific sports (for instance, running shoes, aerobic shoes, cross-training shoes, hiking shoes). Nike's initial success was largely attributed to being in the vanguard of the running trend, while Reebok's early success was due in large part to spotting the need for special aerobic shoes. These companies have also effectively withstood the competitive inroads of many domestic and foreign competitors by building prestigious and quality brand images through a combination of effective advertising and good product performance. With increased competition from designer brands of footwear (DKNY, Tommy Hilfiger, etc.), declining consumer loyalty, and criticism over its low pay and alleged abusive treatment of Asian workers (where athletic footwear often is made), it will be interesting to see whether Nike can return itself to the high-flying success that it enjoyed through the mid-1990s.[12]

www.donnakaran.com

www.tommyhilfiger.com

The operative theme in the previous discussion is that organizations must be proactive in dealing with their various environments and not simply reactive. Effective environmental management requires anticipating forthcoming changes and anticipatory action rather than belated reaction after competitors have already responded to the changes. Many declining industries in the United States (such as women's dress shoes, steel manufacturing, and consumer electronics) were notoriously slow in responding to environmental changes.

Enhancing Brand Equity

The touchstone of all marketing communications activities is ultimately the ability to enhance a brand's equity. Enhancing equity depends, of course, on the suitability of all marketing-mix elements. Marketing communications nonetheless play a pivotal role by informing customers about new brands and their relative advantages and by elevating a brand's image. As established in Chapter 1, brand equity is enhanced when consumers become *familiar* with the brand and hold *favorable, strong,* and perhaps *unique* associations in memory about the brand.[13]

A brand has no equity if consumers are unfamiliar with it. Upon consumers being made aware of a brand, the amount of equity depends on how favorably they perceive the brand's features and benefits as compared to competitive brands and how strongly these views are held in memory. Outstanding brands such as Lexus, Motorola, Coca-Cola, Levi's, and Microsoft have gained their equity based on superior product quality supported by effective and consistent marketing communications programs. Rarely can marketing communications alone create brand equity, but inferior or inadequate marketing communications can severely mitigate the equity that a quality brand otherwise might enjoy.

www.lexus.com

www.microsoft.com

Companies that have a true commitment to equity enhancement attempt to build *long-term relationships* with their customers. These companies realize that "you do not manage a company by focusing on R&D (an input), production (an output), or finance (a scoreboard), but rather by a thorough driving orientation toward the market and the customer."[14] Building relations involves listening to the customer and focusing on retaining existing customers.[15] The following *IMC Focus* describes a form of relation-building, called *micromarketing,* that represents one of the major marketing developments of the 1990s.

MAKING BRAND-LEVEL MARKETING COMMUNICATIONS DECISIONS

Having overviewed the general factors that engender, influence, or constrain marketing communications activities in all of their various forms, we now turn attention to the specific elements of the decision process. Since the following discussion refers again to Figure 2.1, it will be helpful to review the model before reading about its specific features.

IMC FOCUS: INCREASING EFFICIENCY VIA MICROMARKETING

The three decades following World War II (1950 through 1970) represented a time when companies could easily achieve sales growth and profits. The population was growing, consumers had increasingly greater disposable incomes, and competition from abroad was weak because many foreign competitors were recovering from the economic devastation of World War II. Needless to say, those unprecedented prosperous days are long past. Marketers now must fight for every percentage point of market share and for every dollar of profit. Competitive pressures demand efficiency with every dollar invested in marketing communications. The world of modern marketing has moved from the *mass marketing* of yesteryear to the *micromarketing* of today.

To fully appreciate the changes that have occurred, it is necessary to examine the nature of mass marketing during its heyday in the 1950s through the 1970s. During this period, marketers directed their advertising and other communications efforts at rather crudely designated target markets and relied on network television to reach general audiences across the United States. Much of the advertising was wasted because many message recipients were not strong prospects for the advertised product. However, for the reasons noted earlier (growing population size, etc.), mass marketing efforts were still profitable in spite of their crudeness and imprecision. Intensified competition and skyrocketing media costs now demand more precise target market specification. The availability of detailed marketing information makes it possible to implement and pinpoint communications efforts.

The practice of **micromarketing** involves focusing marketing communications on targets that provide the greatest opportunity while attempting to minimize messages aimed at the wrong targets.[a] The micromarketer operates by answering three fundamental questions: *Who* exactly are the consumers most likely to become users of a brand? *Where* are they located? *How* can they be reached most efficiently with the tools of marketing communications?[b]

Answering the *who* and *where* questions is facilitated by the ready availability to managers of information about both retail product movement and customers' product-usage patterns. For example, massive computerized databases containing checkout scanner data inform managers of the volume of brand movement from retail shelves. This information, along with rich databases on household characteristics and purchase patterns, reveals the prime targets for marketing communications efforts. Marketers know who (in terms of demographic and socioeconomic characteristics) their best customers are and where they are to be found (in terms of geographic locations and specific retail outlets where they shop).

Answering the *how* question amounts to determining the most efficient ways to reach the target customers. The trend has moved away from national network advertising toward more spot advertising, focused couponing efforts, targeted sampling, greater usage of direct mailings, and more selectively placed in-store promotions. In general, the micromarketer of the 1990s is seeking ways to accomplish greater impact with more selectively placed marketing communications dollars.[c]

---

[a]This definition is based on Danny L. Moore, "What Is Micromarketing?" *Aim* 2, no. 2 (1990), 7. [*Aim* is a publication of the Nielsen research company.]

[b]Ibid. See also Howard Hunt, "How to Become a Micromarketer," *Aim* 2, no. 2 (1990), 13–16.

[c]See Richard Gibson, "Marketers' Mantra: Reap More with Less," *The Wall Street Journal*, March 22, 1991, B1.

The model shows that *general choices* (targeting, objective setting, and budgeting) influence *specific choices* regarding the mixture of communications elements and the determination of messages, media, and momentum. *Program evaluation*—in the form of measuring the results from MarCom efforts—follows from the general choices made and specific plans implemented. The outcome from program evaluation efforts, in turn, feeds back (dashed lines in Figure 2.1) to the general and specific choices. Corrective actions (increased sales-promotion expenditures, new advertising campaigns, and so on) are required when measured results indicate that performance has fallen below expectations.

General Choices

Targeting. As noted in the *IMC Focus* that described the fundamentals of micromarketing, *targeting* allows marketing communicators to deliver more precisely their messages and to prevent wasted coverage to people falling outside the targeted market. Hence, selection of target segments is a critical first step toward effective and efficient marketing communications.

Companies identify potential target markets in terms of various characteristics: demographics, lifestyle characteristics (also called psychographics), product usage patterns, and geographic location. It is crucial to recognize, however, that most profitable segments are not based on a single characteristic (such as gender, age, ethnicity, and so on). Rather, meaningful market segments generally represent consumers who share a *combination of characteristics* and demonstrate similar behavior.

Consider, for example, the segmentation implications of a new brand of premium-priced, nonfat ice cream. The market segment for this new brand is not just women, not just men, not just younger people or older people, and, in general, not any group of people sharing any single characteristic. Rather, a meaningful segment would possess several or more shared characteristics—for example, people who live in urban or suburban areas, earn annual incomes in excess of $50,000, are older than 35, and are health- and weight-conscious.

In general, a meaningful market segment consists of a group of potential consumers who: (1) can be readily *measured and identified* with respect to variables that will be used for segmentation purposes (for example, age, income, and lifestyle preferences), (2) exhibit relatively *homogeneous response tendencies* to a brand's marketing-mix elements, and (3) are *economically accessible* via distribution and media channels. People who respond in a similar way to marketing-mix variables (e.g., prefer nonfat to regular ice cream and are willing to pay a premium price), who shop in similar outlets, and read, listen to, and view similar programs do so because of their similar interests in life, not because they share a single common characteristic. Hence, meaningful and profitable market segmentation efforts typically require that segment members share various demographic, lifestyle, and possibly geographical characteristics. Advertisers and other marketing communicators sometimes pretend to be segmenting markets when they designate an audience in terms such as *women aged 18 to 49*, but such broad groupings are too crude to satisfy the characteristics described above.

Another form of targeting is the strategy of directing marketing communications toward the businesses that handle products purchased by consumers rather than at consumers themselves. This is illustrated in the following *IMC Focus*, which describes a *push-oriented* advertising effort by the National Cattlemen's Beef Association that was designed to increase sales of veal.

Objective Setting. Marketing communications managers' general and specific choices are grounded in underlying goals or **objectives** to be accomplished for a brand. Of course, the content of these objectives varies according to the different capabilities of the marketing communications elements. For example, whereas mass media advertising is ideally suited for creating consumer awareness of a new or improved brand, point-of-purchase communications are perfect for influencing in-store brand selection, and personal selling is unparalleled when it comes to informing business-to-business customers and retailers about product improvements. Nevertheless, as established in Chapter 1, all marketing communications elements must be integrated, "speak with a single voice," and aim to accomplish the same ultimate behavioral objective—that is, to generate action from customers and prospects.

Specific chapters later in the text detail the objectives that each component of the marketing communications mix is designed to accomplish; for present purposes it will suffice merely to list various objectives that marketing communications managers hope to accomplish:

- ◆ Facilitate the successful introduction of new brands.
- ◆ Build sales of existing brands by increasing frequency of use, variety of uses, or the quantity purchased.
- ◆ Inform the trade (wholesalers, agents/brokers, retailers) and consumers about brand improvements.
- ◆ Build a brand's or company's image.

IMC FOCUS: VEAL ADS TARGETED TO CHEFS

Suppose your product is under severe attack and sales are falling like the proverbial lead balloon. Imagine further that your advertising budget is not sufficient to change the negative attitudes that have been engendered toward your product. This is precisely the situation encountered by beef ranchers who in the mid-1990s were faced with rapidly declining sales of veal, which, of course, is the meat harvested from milk-fed calves. Advertising by animal-rights activists had convinced many consumers not to order veal because, according to the activists' claims, calves are raised in cruel circumstances. The activists' argument is not without merit, and many consumers refuse to eat veal.

Nonetheless, cattlemen believe they have a legitimate right to raise calves. Each of us has to decide for ourselves whether it is "right" to eat veal, but our present concern is with the issue of targeting advertising rather than with the controversy that surrounds this product. The trade association needed a way to counter the anti-veal sentiment that had been created by the activist advertising effort. But the association had a budget of only slightly more than $1 million. Surely such a small budget could not reach many consumers nor allow sufficient momentum (as discussed later in the chapter) to have much impact. What to do? The decision was made to best use this small ad budget by targeting advertising efforts at chefs rather than at consumers. Attractive ads were placed in magazines that chefs read, such as *Restaurant Business Magazine* and *Bon Appetit*. What effect did this campaign have? Veal consumption rose by 20 percent, which was due, at least in part, to the advertising that targeted chefs.

Source: Adapted from "Veal Industry Focuses on Chefs in Countering Animal-Rights Ads," *The Wall Street Journal Interactive Edition*, March 18, 1998.

- ◆ Generate sales leads.
- ◆ Persuade the trade to handle the manufacturer's brands.
- ◆ Stimulate point-of-purchase sales.
- ◆ Develop brand awareness, acceptance, and insistence.
- ◆ Increase customer loyalty.
- ◆ Let consumers know where to buy a new brand.
- ◆ Improve corporate relations with special-interest groups.
- ◆ Offset bad publicity about a brand.
- ◆ Generate good publicity.
- ◆ Counter competitors' marketing communications efforts.
- ◆ Provide customers with reasons for buying immediately instead of delaying a purchase choice.

Budgeting. An organization's financial resources are budgeted to specific marketing communications elements to accomplish the objectives established for its various brands. The amount of resources allocated typically results from an involved process in most sophisticated corporations. Companies use different budgeting procedures in allocating funds to marketing communications managers and other organizational units. At one extreme is *top-down budgeting (TD)*, in which senior management decides how much each subunit receives. At the other extreme is *bottom-up budgeting (BU)*, in which managers of subunits (such as at the product-category level) determine how much is needed to achieve their objectives; these amounts are then combined to establish the total marketing budget.

Most budgeting practices involve a combination of top-down and bottom-up budgeting. For example, in the *bottom-up/top-down process (BUTD)*, subunit managers submit budget requests to a chief marketing officer (say, a vice president of marketing), who coordinates the various requests and then submits an overall budget to top management for approval. This is the form of budgeting used at Procter & Gamble: Within each of approximately 40 product categories, brand managers submit budgets to the category manager, who in turn coordinates an overall category budget. The many category budgets are coordinated by a vice president

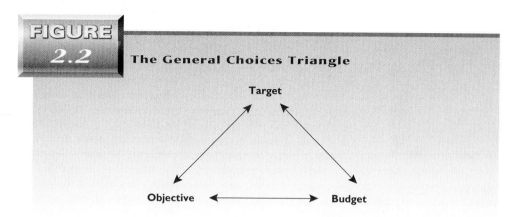

FIGURE 2.2 **The General Choices Triangle**

of marketing and then are submitted to top management for approval. The *top-down/bottom-up process (TDBU)* reverses the flow of influence; top managers first establish the total size of the budget and then divide it among the various subunits.

Research has shown that combination budgeting methods (BUTD and TDBU) are used more often than the extreme methods (TD or BU).[16] The BUTD process is by far the most frequently used, especially in more sophisticated firms where marketing departments have greater influence than finance departments.[17]

A Concluding Mantra. *Mantra* is a Hindu word meaning incantation or recitation (of a song, word, statement, or passage). The following statement serves as a mantra to summarize the preceding discussion of general choices within the brand-level decision process:

> *All marketing communications should be: (1) designed according to a particular* **target market,** *(2) created to achieve a* **specific objective,** *and (3) undertaken to accomplish the target market objective* **within budget constraint.**

Figure 2.2 graphically illustrates this mantra. The target market is shown as the pinnacle of the triangle, with the objective and budget at its base. The double-headed arrow between objective and budget signifies that each influences the other. That is, more lofty objectives require larger budgets, and smaller budgets necessitate less lofty objectives. The double-headed arrows between the target market and both objective and budget again reflect the reciprocal relationship between these elements. For example, vying with competitors for larger, more profitable target markets requires larger budgets.

Specific Choices

Marketing communications managers make a variety of specific decisions in the pursuit of achieving brand-level objectives. Initially they must choose how best to integrate, or mix, the various communications elements to achieve target market objectives within their budgets. Then they must decide what types of messages to use, which media to deliver messages, and the degree of momentum to support the media effort (refer again to Figure 2.1).

Mixing Elements. A fundamental issue confronted by all companies is deciding exactly how to allocate resources among the various marketing communications tools (briefly discussed in Chapter 1): personal selling, advertising, sales promotion, and other communications elements. The mix for industrial-goods manufacturers typically emphasizes personal selling with supplementation from trade advertising, technical literature, and trade shows.[18]

For consumer-goods manufacturers, mixture decisions are, in many respects, more complicated and controversial because greater options are available. Personal selling is important in a consumer-goods company's *push efforts,* but the real difficulty and controversy arises when deciding how best to *pull* a product through the channel.[19] The issue boils down in large part to a decision of how much to allocate to advertising and to sales promotion. Over the past decade or so, the trend has moved toward greater expenditures on sales promotion. Indeed, sales promotion's share of the total promotional budget has grown from less than 60 percent in the late 1970s to approximately 70 percent today.

What is the *optimum mixture* of expenditures between advertising and sales promotion? Unfortunately, no specific answer is possible because the marketing communications-mix decision is what is called an *ill-structured problem.*[20] This means that for a given level of expenditure there is no way of determining the mathematical optimum allocation between advertising and sales promotion in order to maximize sales or profit. At least four factors account for this inability to determine a mathematically optimum mix.[21]

First, advertising and sales promotion are somewhat interchangeable—both tools can accomplish some of the same objectives. Because of this, it is impossible to know exactly which tool or combination of tools is better in every situation.

Second, advertising and sales promotion produce a *synergistic effect*—their combined results are greater than what they would achieve individually. This makes it difficult to determine the exact effects that different combinations of advertising and sales promotion might generate.

Third, advertising and sales promotion not only operate synergistically with each other, they also interact with other elements of the marketing mix. Thus, the effectiveness of these tools is impossible to evaluate without considering the overall marketing mix.

Fourth, the optimum advertising and sales-promotion mix is affected by various market forces—the nature of the buying process, characteristics of the market, the extent of competition, and so on.

Thus, it is impossible to account for all of the preceding factors in determining an optimum mixture of advertising and sales-promotion expenditures. It is more reasonable to develop a workable, *satisfactory mixture* that addresses the following key considerations:[22]

1. A careful *cost-value analysis* of each proposed mix has to be performed to determine whether distribution, sales, and profit objectives can be achieved in view of the intended expenditure.

2. An *evaluation* must be made of how well the proposed levels of advertising and sales promotion fit and complement one another.

3. Strategies must consider the differing purposes of advertising and sales promotion. A key *strategic consideration* is whether short- or long-term schemes are more important given a brand's life-cycle stage. An appropriate mixture for mature brands is likely to be different from the mixture for brands recently introduced. New brands may require a proportionately much larger investment in sales promotions (such as couponing and sampling) to generate trial purchases, whereas mature brands might require proportionately greater advertising investment to maintain or enhance a brand's image.

4. *Brand equity* represents a final consideration in evaluating a satisfactory combination of advertising and sales promotion. Poorly planned or excessive sales promotions can damage a brand's equity by cheapening its image. If a brand is frequently placed on sale or if some form of deal (price-offs, discounts) is regularly offered, consumers will delay purchasing the brand until its price is reduced. This causes the brand to become an object purchased more for its price discount than for its nonprice attributes and benefits.

The matter of properly mixing advertising and sales promotion is aptly summarized in the following quote:

> As one views the opportunities inherent in ascertaining the proper balance between advertising and [sales] promotion, it should be quite clear that both should be used as one would play a pipe organ, pulling out certain stops and pushing others, as situations

and circumstances change. Rigid rules, or continuing application of inflexible advertising-to-promotion percentages, serve no real purpose and can be quite counterproductive in today's dynamic and ever-changing marketing environment. A short-term solution that creates a long-term problem is no solution at all.[23]

The short-term "solution" refers to spending excessive amounts on promotion efforts to create quick sales while failing to invest sufficiently in advertising to build a brand's long-term equity. That is, excessive sales promotion can rob a brand's future. An appropriate mixture involves spending enough on sales promotion to ensure sufficient sales volume in the short term while simultaneously spending enough on advertising to ensure the growth or preservation of a brand's equity position. Many brand managers seem unaware of or disregard the damage caused by short-term thinking. For example, the marketing of Schlitz beer excessively emphasized price discounts and promotions, and the effect in five years was a transition from a profitable brand earning $48 million to one losing $50 million.[24]

Creating Messages. Managers of every marketing communications element must choose how best to present their persuasive arguments to achieve established objectives. Subsequent chapters will address specific message issues relating to each marketing communications tool. The following points merely illustrate the variety of message issues faced by the various marketing communications managers:

- ◆ *Sales managers* decide on the form and content of sales presentations. One important consideration, for example, is whether the presentation should follow a fixed script (a canned presentation) or vary from prospect to prospect.

- ◆ *Public relations directors,* when faced with adverse publicity, choose how best to defend their company's products without appearing excessively contrite or defensive. A public relations representative walks a fine line between being an apologist and a dogmatist. Effective public relations requires sincere but forceful support of any company products under attack.

- ◆ *Advertising creative directors* have numerous message choices. What image to create, how to position the brand, and what specific types of appeals to employ (sex appeal? humor? fear?) are just some of the many alternatives. The following *Global Focus* illustrates advertising efforts in Asia that were designed to enhance the equity of two brands.

- ◆ *Sales promotion managers* must decide what specific information and appeals to include in price-off coupons, premium offers, and sweepstakes and contests.

- ◆ *Sponsorship marketers* have innumerable possibilities in determining how best to present their brands and the events or causes with which the brands are associated.

Selecting Media. All marketing communications messages require an instrument, or medium, for transmission. Though the term *media* is typically applied to advertising media (television, magazines, radio, etc.), the concept of media is relevant to all MarCom tools. For example, personal sales messages can be delivered via face-to-face communications or by telemarketing; these media alternatives have different costs and effectiveness. Point-of-purchase materials are delivered in a variety of ways—via in-store signs, electronically, musically, and otherwise. Each of these represents a different medium. Detailed discussions of media are reserved for specific chapters that follow. Advertising media are discussed in particular detail, and considerable attention also is devoted to the media of consumer promotions.

Establishing Momentum. The word **momentum** refers to an object's force or speed of movement—its *impetus*. A train has momentum as it races down the tracks; a spacecraft has momentum as it is launched into orbit; a hockey player has momentum when he skates past the defensive opposition. Marketing communications programs also

GLOBAL FOCUS: APPEALING TO NATIONAL PRIDE IN CHINA AND PAMPERING PETS IN SOUTH KOREA

Nike's Chinese Advertising Effort

The People's Republic of China (PRC) is a huge country with a massive population. Many firms in Europe, North America, and elsewhere are virtually salivating at the prospects of getting their brands accepted by millions of Chinese consumers. Nike is no exception. This company, famous for its irreverent advertising and the exportation of American pop culture throughout the globe, has adopted a different advertising approach in China. Although Chinese youth are familiar with Michael Jordan and other athletic stars who endorse Nike shoes, Nike executives have decided not to use Jordan or other American stars in new commercials running in China. The approach, instead, is to appeal to Chinese nationalism. One commercial focuses on Chinese basketball star Hu Weidong, who plays for the Nangang Jiangsu Dragons. While showing Hu Weidong and other players taking shots, the ad states: "American cowboys are not the only ones who can make great shots. China also has sharpshooters."

It is easy to understand why Nike decided to appeal to Chinese pride rather than using a "typical" American advertising approach. China is a market with enormous potential, and the government of the PRC desires to boost national pride. Chinese spent only $2 billion on sneakers as of the late 1990s compared to over $17 billion spent on athletic footwear in the U.S. in 1997, but the potential for substantial sales growth is much greater in China than in the U.S. Showing sensitivity to Chinese consumers (as well as to government officials), Nike hired Chinese-speaking art directors and copywriters to customize commercials to Chinese culture rather than imposing American culture on the people of the PRC.[a]

Advertising Pet Food in South Korea

Dogs are pampered, overfed, and treated as integral "family" members in many North American and European households. But in South Korea dogs historically have been regarded as guard animals and fed only table scraps. However, with the relatively recent advent of apartment living in South Korea, dogs now are beginning to receive the same form of spoiled treatment that American dog owners lavish on their pets. In response to this change in the concept of pet food in South Korea, U.S.-based Mars Inc. decided to begin advertising its Pedigree brand on television.

Although pet food advertising had never been banned in South Korea, local pet-food manufacturers avoided advertising for fear that it would be considered inappropriate to encourage people to buy what, for South Koreans, had heretofore been regarded as a frivolous product. Sensitive to the possibility of criticism, Mars avoided any pampering-type claims in its commercials and instead emphasized the health-promoting qualities of Pedigree. Commercials portrayed active, healthy dogs, while an off-camera announcer exclaimed, "Don't they look very healthy? To raise excellent dogs, feed your dogs Pedigree." Some consumers, in reacting to the commercials, said that it had never occurred to them to feed their dogs pet food until they saw advertisements for Pedigree.

The dog food industry in Korea is minuscule by American standards, but by being the first to advertise in South Korea, Pedigree has an opportunity to become a pet-food icon and achieve a dominant market share that later entrants will have difficulty stealing. Gaining advertising momentum will be critical to Pedigree's brand-equity enhancement and long-term success in South Korea. The brand is off to a good start, but continual advertising will be essential to familiarize consumers with the brand and to forge strong, favorable, and unique associations toward Pedigree in consumers' minds.[b]

Source: [a]Adapted from Fara Warner, "Nike Tones Down Bad-Boy Image to Boost Sales in China's Market," *The Wall Street Journal Interactive Edition*, November 10, 1997.

[b]Adapted from Yoo-Lim Lee, "Taboos No Longer Dog South Korea Pet Foods," *Advertising Age*, February 20, 1995, I-13.

have, or lack, momentum. Simply developing an advertising message, personal sales presentation, or publicity release is insufficient. The effectiveness of each of these message forms typically requires both a sufficient amount of effort and continuity of that effort. This is the meaning of momentum as it relates to marketing communications. Insufficient momentum is ineffective at best and a waste of money at worst.

www.hyundai.com

www.mazda.com

www.isuzu.com

As is the case with almost every decision faced by marketing communications managers, momentum is a relative matter: No level of momentum is equally appropriate for all situations. For example, the amount of investment appropriate for one advertiser may be woefully inadequate for another. Hyundai, Mazda, and Isuzu spend a much larger portion of their sales on advertising than their larger competitors, Toyota, Honda, Ford, and General Motors. In general, newer brands must spend more to get established and to create strong, favorable, and perhaps unique brand images. Ford Motor Company spent $110 million to launch its Ford *Contour* and Mercury *Mystique* models. With a first-year goal of selling 250,000 of these vehicles in a highly competitive market, and to recoup the $6 billion investment in developing these models, heavy advertising was essential.[25] Mars Inc., makers of Pedigree brand pet food, faced a similar challenge when advertising Pedigree pet food in South Korea (as discussed in the *Global Focus*).

www.mars.com

Critical to the concept of momentum is the need to *sustain* an effort rather than starting and stopping advertising for a while, then discontinuing it for a longer while, and so on. In other words, some companies never create nor sustain momentum because their marketplace presence is inadequate. "Out of sight, out of mind" is probably more relevant to brands in the marketplace than to people. We generally do not forget our friends and family, but today's brand friend is tomorrow's stranger unless it is kept before our consciousness. Because consumers make hundreds of purchase decisions in many different product categories, they require continuous reminders of brand names and their benefits if these brands are to stand a strong chance of becoming serious purchase candidates.

At one point in 1997 Toyota Motor had only a 16-day supply of the fast-selling Camry. Yet it launched a big advertising campaign that aggressively encouraged consumers to purchase Camrys. Some marketing observers were critical of this campaign, saying that it was unwise to advertise when insufficient product was available to fulfill orders. In response, the vice president of Toyota Sales USA asserted that even when demand is strong it is important "to keep your momentum in the marketplace going."[26] This executive obviously appreciates the value of achieving and maintaining a brand's momentum!

www.toyota.com

Program Evaluation

After marketing communications objectives are set, elements selected and mixed, messages and media chosen, and programs implemented and possibly sustained, the programs must be evaluated. This is accomplished by measuring results of MarCom efforts against the objectives that were established at the outset. For a local advertiser, say, a sporting-goods store that is running an advertised special on athletic shoes for a two-day period in May, the results are the number of Nike, Reebok, Adidas, and other brands sold. If you tried to sell an old automobile through the classified pages, the results would be the number of phone inquiries you receive and whether you ultimately sold the car. For a national manufacturer of a branded product, results typically are not so quick to occur. Rather, a company invests in point-of-purchase communications, sales promotions, and advertising and then waits, often for many weeks, to see whether these programs deliver the desired sales volume.

Regardless of the situation, it is critical to evaluate the results of marketing communications efforts. Throughout the business world there is increasing demand for *accountability*, which requires that research be performed and data acquired to determine whether marketing communications efforts have accomplished the objectives they were expected to achieve. Results can be measured in terms of sales volume or based on *nonsales* accomplishments.

Nonsales outcomes (called communication measures) will be discussed in detail in later chapters (especially in Chapter 15 on measuring advertising effectiveness), but a few comments are in order at this time. A *communication measure* concerns a nonsales target;

brand awareness, message comprehension, attitude toward the brand, and purchase intentions are typical communication measures. All of these are communication (rather than sales) objectives in the sense that an advertiser has attempted to communicate a certain message argument or overall impression. Thus, the goal for an advertiser of a relatively unknown brand may be to increase brand awareness in the target market by 30 percent within six months of starting a new advertising campaign. This objective (a 30 percent increase in awareness) would be based on knowledge of the awareness level prior to the campaign's debut. Post-campaign measurement would then reveal whether the target level was achieved.

It is essential to measure results of all marketing communications programs. Failure to achieve targeted results prompts corrective action (see dashed lines, or feedback loops, in Figure 2.1). Corrective action might call for greater investment, a different combination of communications elements, revised creative strategy, different media allocations, or a host of other possibilities. Only by systematically setting objectives and measuring results is it possible to know whether marketing communications programs are working as well as they should.

Summary

This chapter provides a model of the marketing communications process to serve as a useful integrative device for better structuring and understanding the topics covered throughout the remainder of the text. The model (Figure 2.1) contains four general components: marketing structure, environmental monitoring and management, a brand-level marketing communications decision process, and brand-equity enhancement.

The marketing structure, which involves the organizational arrangement for accomplishing a firm's marketing task, plays an instrumental role in determining the importance of marketing communications in the overall marketing mix and how marketing communications decisions are made and implemented. The communications decision process, which is the guts of the model, is aimed at enhancing brand equity.

The brand-level communications decision process consists of a set of general choices, specific choices, and program evaluation. General choices include choosing target markets, objectives, and budgets. Specific choices involve determining a mixture of marketing communications tools (advertising, sales promotions, etc.) and establishing message, media, and momentum plans. These decisions are evaluated by comparing measured results against brand-level communications objectives.

Discussion Questions

1. Discuss the difference between the brand-management and category-management organizational structures at Procter & Gamble.

2. Explain how changes in the so-called three *C*s of marketing (customers, consumers, and competitors) have imposed pressures on companies to alter their marketing organizational structures.

3. Explain the concept of *environmental management*. Compare this idea with the notion presented in many introductory marketing texts that the environment is uncontrollable.

4. Objectives and budgets are necessarily interdependent. Explain this interdependency and provide an example to support your point.

5. What is the distinction between top-down (TD) and bottom-up (BU) budgeting? Why is BUTD budgeting used in companies that are more marketing-oriented, whereas TDBU budgeting is found more frequently in finance-driven companies?

6. Marketing communications has been described as an ill-structured problem. Explain what this means.

7. Why do you think that marketing communications budgets have been reallocated in recent years to increase sales promotion expenditures and reduce advertising expenditures?

8. Two of the most important considerations in achieving a balance between advertising and sales promotion are strategic and brand equity factors. Explain precisely how these considerations are relevant to the decision about the relative influence placed on advertising and sales promotion. Select a brand of a well-known grocery product as a basis for motivating your discussion.

9. Explain the concept of *momentum*. Using the same brand that you selected for answering the previous question, describe your understanding of how this brand accomplishes a suitable level of momentum.

10. Assume you are in charge of fund-raising for an organization on your campus—say, the student chapter of the American Marketing Association. It is your job to identify a suitable project and to manage the project's marketing communications. For the purpose of this exercise, identify a fund-raising project idea, and apply the model in Figure 2.1 (repeated on page 45) to show how you might go about promoting this project. Be sure to address all aspects of the model, but focus particularly on the elements in the brand-level communications decision process.

FIGURE
2.1   **The Marketing Communications Decision Process**

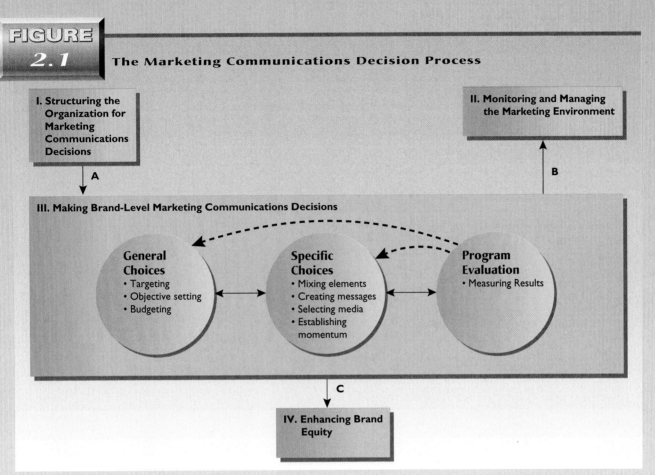

11. Select a well-known brand of your choice. Analyze this brand's marketing communications activities at the general- and specific-choice levels. Describe the specific choices and programs this brand has employed in the past year or so. You cannot be expected to know exactly how the brand is promoted, but your casual observations should provide some idea. Moreover, by reviewing the *Business Periodical Index* in your library or CD-ROM directories, you should be able to identify various recent articles that describe your chosen brand's marketing communications activities.

Internet Exercises

1. Visit the Levi Strauss company Web site (www.levistrauss.com) and access the 6/17/98 press release. What product campaign does this press release announce? Analyze the brand's marketing communication activities at the general- and specific-choice levels based on (a) this press release, (b) information available on the product's own Web site (www.levi.com), and (c) your personal experience with the brand. Use Figure 2.1 and the discussion in the chapter to guide your efforts.

2. Pretend you are the manager for one of your favorite brands (visit the brand's Web site to learn specific details about the brand). You have been asked to investigate the possibility of diverting a portion of your advertising budget to Internet advertising (i.e., advertising beyond just having a Web site). Using a recent study of Internet users and usage (such as those available at www.nielsenmedia.com, www.commerce.net, www.personal.umich.edu/~sgupta/hermes, or www.cyberatlas), discuss the following:

a.   How would Internet advertising reach your brand's target market (e.g., Is your target market on-line? Where is your target market on-line? What are the advertising options on the Internet?).

    b.   How might Internet access, usage, and on-line behavior correlate with actual purchasing behavior (i.e., relate Internet advertising to segmentation goals)?

3.   Using the Internet itself as a resource (e.g., www.cyberatlas, www.commerce.net), identify the issues related to the accountability of Internet advertising. Be sure to (a) list at least three measures currently in use and describe what they actually measure and (b) decide whether these measures can provide useful feedback for advertising objectives.

*C*hapter Two Endnotes

1. Laurie Freeman, "Why Marketers Change," *Advertising Age,* February 22, 1988, 24.

2. "The Marketing Revolution at Procter & Gamble," *Business Week,* July 25, 1988, 72–76.

3. "Marketing's New Look," *Business Week,* January 26, 1987, 64–69.

4. Jennifer Lawrence, "Frito Makes Regional Advances," *Advertising Age,* July 4, 1988, 21.

5. Mary Connelly, "Ford Division Revamps Brand Structure, Adds Managers," *Advertising Age,* July 28, 1997, 2.

6. Jean Halliday, "GM's Brand Management Report Card," *Advertising Age,* March 9, 1998, 1, 26.

7. For fascinating reading on the evolution of the brand management system, see George S. Low and Ronald A. Fullerton, "Brands, Brand Management, and the Brand Manager System: A Critical-Historical Evaluation," *Journal of Marketing Research* 31 (May 1994), 173–190. For an update on Procter & Gamble's brand management system, see Jack Neff, "P&G Redefines the Brand Manager, *Advertising Age,* October 13, 1997, 1, 18, 20.

8. "The Marketing Revolution at Procter & Gamble," 73.

9. An interesting—albeit mathematically sophisticated—treatment of the profitability of a category-management organizational structure is provided in Michael J. Zenor, "The Profit Benefits of Category Management," *Journal of Marketing Research* 31 (May 1994), 202–213.

10. Adapted from Cyndee Miller, "Dutch Boy Repositions Itself to Reach Upscale, Fashion-Oriented Consumers," *Marketing News,* July 4, 1988, 1.

11. Carl P. Zeithaml and Valarie A. Zeithaml, "Environmental Management: Revising the Marketing Perspective," *Journal of Marketing* 48 (spring 1984), 46–53.

12. An interesting discussion of Nike and its leader, Phil Knight, is presented in Jackie Krentzman, "The Force behind the Nike Empire," *Stanford,* January/February 1997, 64–70.

13. Kevin Lane Keller, "Conceptualizing, Measuring, and Managing Customer-Based Brand Equity," *Journal of Marketing* 57 (January 1993), 2.

14. "A New Survival Course for CEO's," *Marketing Communications,* September 1985, 21–26, 94.

15. For further discussion of retention marketing, see Laura A. Liswood, "Once You've Got 'Em, Never Let 'Em Go," *Sales and Marketing Management,* November 1987, 73–77. For a theoretical yet highly readable account of relational marketing, see F. Robert Dwyer, Paul H. Schurr, and Sejo Oh, "Developing Buyer-Seller Relationships," *Journal of Marketing* 51 (April 1987), 11–27.

16. Nigel F. Piercy, "The Marketing Budgeting Process: Marketing Management Implications," *Journal of Marketing* 51 (October 1987), 45–59.

17. Ibid. See 55, fig. 2.

18. Donald W. Jackson, Jr., Janet E. Keith, and Richard K. Burdick, "The Relative Importance of Various Promotional Elements in Different Industrial Purchase Situations," *Journal of Advertising* 16, no. 4 (1987), 25–33.

19. The terms *push and pull* are metaphors that characterize the nature of the promotional thrust through the channel of distribution. *Push* suggests a forward thrust from manufacturer to the trade (wholesalers or retailers) on to the consumer; personal selling to the trade is the primary push technique. *Pull* means that a manufacturer promotes directly to consumers, who it is hoped will pressure retailers to stock the promoted product. In actuality, manufacturers use a combination of pull and push techniques. These techniques complement one another and are not perfectly substitutable.

20. Thomas A. Petit and Martha R. McEnally, "Putting Strategy into Promotion Mix Decisions," *The Journal of Consumer Marketing* 2 (winter 1985), 41–47.

21. This discussion is based on Petit and McEnally, 43.

22. The following key issues are adapted from Joseph W. Ostrow, "The Advertising/Promotion Mix: A Blend or a Tangle," *AAAA Newsletter,* August 1988, 6–7. Note that this article title refers to advertising versus promotion. Mr. Ostrow, like other marketing practitioners, drops the leading word *sales* when referring to sales promotion. Whereas in the academic marketing community we refer to promotion in a general sense to include all forms of promotional tools

(advertising, personal selling, sales promotion, etc.), practitioners use the word *promotion* in reference to sales promotion per se.

23. Ostrow, "The Advertising/Promotion Mix: A Blend or a Tangle," 7.

24. Cited in "The Purest Treasure," *The Econom'st,* September 7, 1991, 67.

25. Raymond Serafin, "Ford Contours Ad Blast," *Advertising Age,* July 18, 1994, 1.

26. Quoted in Sally Goll Beatty, "Auto Makers Bet Campaigns Will Deliver Even If They Can't," *The Wall Street Journal Interactive Edition,* October 13, 1997.

Environmental, Regulatory, and Ethical Issues in Marketing Communications

CHAPTER OBJECTIVES

After studying this chapter, you should be able to:

1. Appreciate the role marketing communications play in "green" marketing.
2. Understand the four general principles that apply to all environmental marketing efforts.
3. Explain the role and importance of governmental efforts to regulate marketing communications.
4. Understand deceptive advertising and the three elements that guide the determination of whether a particular advertisement is potentially deceptive.
5. Explain the regulation of unfair business practices and the three major areas where the unfairness doctrine is applied.
6. Understand the role that states perform in regulating unfair or deceptive marketing communications practices.
7. Understand the process of advertising self-regulation.
8. Appreciate the ethical issues in marketing communications.
9. Explain why the targeting of products and marketing communications is a heatedly debated practice.

Opening Vignette: Trash Bags, Degradability, Ethics, and Regulation

Assume you are the vice president of marketing and sales for the consumer products division of a large chemical company. One of your products, plastic trash bags, is likely to experience lost sales because your competitors are promoting their brands as degradable. To nontechnical consumers, the word degradable implies that these trash bags will literally disintegrate within a relatively short period after they leave the consumer's curbside and are buried in a landfill. Although these bags *are* photodegradable (they will degrade if left out in the sun and rain for an extended period), you know they are *not* biodegradable. That is, they will not disintegrate when placed in landfills; rather, like most everything else that is buried in landfills, these so-called degradable bags will remain intact for decades.

You know your own yet-to-be introduced degradable brand is not biodegradable either. However, your regular brand of nondegradable trash bags may lose shelf space to competitive brands and sales to environmentally concerned consumers who think they are serving the environment by using your competitors' degradable bags. You could introduce a photodegradable bag, but you know that it, like the competitors' bags, is not truly degradable and will not solve the solid waste problem. Hence, if you introduce a new bag labeled

degradable, you can prevent potential lost sales to competitors, but, at the same time, you will be misleading consumers into thinking that they are purchasing a truly degradable bag.

What would you do if you were placed in this position? Would you introduce your own brand of degradable trash bag, or would you be willing to suffer the consequences of lost sales to unethical competitors? Perhaps available to you are alternatives other than the choice between merely introducing or not introducing a degradable bag. Before reading on, think about what you would have done if you had been the key decision maker in this situation. Think about the consequences of your decision for your company, its employees, and for your career. Attempt, as best you can, to balance idealistic and practical considerations. Write down what you would do and fully justify your choice.

OVERVIEW

The situation described in the opening vignette is not hypothetical. Something very similar to this confronted the Mobil Chemical Company in the late 1980s, a time when American consumers were beginning to be concerned with saving the environment. At the same time, many marketers were beginning to respond to consumers' concerns, sometimes in exploitative ways. Mobil's brand of regular Hefty trash bags was, in fact, losing shelf space in supermarkets and experiencing lost sales to brands such as First Brands' degradable Glad bags. Nonetheless, Mobil fully recognized that degradable bags were no panacea. Mobil's general manager of solid-waste-management solutions stated: "Mobil has concluded that biodegradable plastics will *not* [emphasis added] help solve the solid waste problem."[1]

This acknowledgment notwithstanding, Mobil in 1989 introduced its own line of degradable trash bags. No advertising was undertaken; rather, the promotional burden fell entirely on the Hefty package itself. The package was labeled Hefty® Degradable*, with the asterisk qualifying the degradable property as photodegradable ("*Activated by Exposure to the Elements"). The package front included a scene of a pine tree with bright sunlight shining through and an osprey preparing to land on the tree—all presumably chosen as emblematic of the implied claim that Hefty bags are themselves compatible with the environment. The back of the package made additional claims about Hefty bags' degradability.

www.mobil.com

www.firstbrands.com

www.glad.com

Shortly after Mobil introduced Hefty® Degradable, the Federal Trade Commission requested both Mobil and First Brands (Glad bags) to provide substantiation for the degradability claims. By the spring of 1990 Mobil voluntarily decided to discontinue using degradability claims on its trash bag packages. Nonetheless, in the summer of 1990 the attorneys general of seven states (California, Massachusetts, Minnesota, New York, Texas, Washington, and Wisconsin) brought suits against Mobil on grounds that it had engaged in deceptive communications and consumer fraud by falsely claiming that trash bags degrade in landfills. Although refusing to admit wrongdoing, Mobil settled the suits out of court and agreed to pay the states $150,000 to fund environmental educational programs.[2]

This case encapsulates much of the material covered in this chapter. In particular, the chapter addresses three major topics: (1) *environmental matters* and their implications for marketing communications, (2) the *regulation* of marketing communications practices, and (3) *ethical issues* in marketing communications. All three topics are interrelated: Many ethical issues confronting contemporary marketing communicators occur over environmental marketing efforts, and regulation (from federal and state governmental bodies and by industry self-regulators) is needed due in large part to unethical marketing communications practices, many of which now occur in the area of green marketing.[3] It also should be apparent that the topics in this chapter relate to the "environmental monitoring and management" aspect of the marketing communications decision framework that was covered in Chapter 2.

THE PHYSICAL ENVIRONMENT AND GREEN MARKETING COMMUNICATIONS

The United States, as well as much of the industrialized world, is in the throes of a garbage crisis. More than 70 percent of over 200 million tons of trash disposed of each year in the United States is buried in landfills, and the landfills are reaching capacity.[4] Public-opinion surveys reveal that increasing numbers of Americans are showing concern for the physical environment and demanding that companies do something to ensure a cleaner and safer environment.[5] Surveys reveal that many consumers say they are willing to pay more for products that do not harm the environment.[6]

It is easy to understand why so many companies have responded to environmental concerns by introducing environmentally oriented products and undertaking aggressive marketing communications programs to promote these products. These actions are referred to as *green marketing*.[7] Unfortunately, for every truly green product there are probably an equal number of bogus entries. This is why green marketing sometimes is referred to in such unflattering terms as *greenscam, greenwashing,* and *big green lies*.[8] Companies have jumped on the green bandwagon and exploited consumers' sensitivity to products claiming to be recyclable, degradable, safe for the ozone layer, and so on. One source estimates that only 15 percent of all green claims are true, 15 percent are outright false, and the remainder fall into a gray area.[9]

It is not enough for companies merely to claim they are environmentally sensitive; consumers are becoming increasingly skeptical and are turned off by exploitative efforts that do not deliver on environmental-safety promises. As one journalist put it: "Declarations of environmental sensitivity cannot be taken at face value. Everybody wears green on St. Patrick's Day, too—but it doesn't make them Irish."[10]

Responses to Environmental Problems

There have been a number of legitimate responses to environmental problems. Some of these responses have been in the form of *new* or *revised products*. For example, personal computers are now equipped with energy-efficient features and are made with some recycled materials. Furniture manufacturers make environmentally friendly furniture from recycled wood, plastic, and even paper. These items then are finished with water- rather than chemical-based materials that emit potentially harmful gases. Cordless lawn mowers powered by rechargeable batteries are available. In addition to being noiseless and easy to start and maintain, battery-charged lawn mowers reduce pollution significantly. Indeed, it is estimated that a gasoline mower running for only 30 minutes produces as much pollution as driving a car from Philadelphia to the District of Columbia![11] Many companies today have accepted their responsibility not to harm the environment, and products and production processes are becoming cleaner.[12] A strong case has been made that environmental improvements represent an economic and competitive opportunity for companies.[13]

IMC FOCUS: AN ALLIANCE WITH MR. CLEAN TO ENHANCE HONDA'S IMAGE

Managers of Honda Motor decided to develop a corporate campaign that would solidify Honda's reputation as an environmentally friendly car company. They faced the challenge of somehow developing an icon that could be associated with the Honda Accord and thus serve to entrench in consumers' minds a strong, favorable, and somewhat unique image of the Honda Accord as a "clean" automobile. Who of all marketplace icons better represents the quality of cleanliness than Mr. Clean himself? In case you don't know, Mr. Clean is a bald, muscled, and earring-wearing cartoon character that Procter & Gamble has used for decades on its famous old brand of household cleaner named, of course, *Mr. Clean.*

Although realizing that environmental concerns are not a high priority for most consumers, Honda managers nonetheless were eager to bolster the Accord's reputation for fuel efficiency and cleanliness. After undertaking negotiations with P&G officials, both companies agreed that partnering these two brands [recall the discussion of co-branding in Chapter 1] would be mutually advantageous. Honda would benefit by enhancing its environmental image, and P&G's *Mr. Clean* brand would get a lot of free publicity from Honda's advertising. Honda invested approximately $25 million in an ad campaign that presented the Mr. Clean character strutting around Honda Accords in TV commercials as well as displayed in dealer showrooms throughout America, with six-foot-high cutouts of Mr. Clean placed next to four-cylinder LEV (low-emission vehicle) Honda Accords.

Source: Adapted from "Honda to Use Mr. Clean to Add Muscle to Environmental Claims," *The Wall Street Journal Interactive Edition,* September 26, 1997.

Of more relevance here are the marketing communications efforts that appeal to environmental sensitivities. In addition to advertisements that promote green products, the major green communications efforts involve packaging, seal-of-approval programs, cause-oriented communication efforts, and point-of-purchase displays.

Green Advertising. Environmental appeals in advertising were commonplace in American advertising for a short period in the early-to-mid-1990s, but the initial enthusiastic response to the deteriorating physical environment has waned. Nevertheless, there are three types of green advertising appeals when this form of advertising occasionally surfaces: those that: (1) address a relationship between a product/service and the biophysical environment (see Figure 3.1 for Tom's of Maine); (2) promote a green lifestyle without highlighting a product or service; or (3) present a corporate image of environmental responsibility (see Figure 3.2 for Toyota—people drive us and Figure 3.3 for Dow).[14] A content analysis of green TV commercials and magazine revealed that most green ads refer to the environmental implications of the advertised brand or company in very general terms without specifically identifying the advertised product's environmental benefits or the specific environmental actions the company had taken to mitigate the problems.[15]

www.phillips66.com

For a recent exception to the declining use of environmental claims in advertising, see the *IMC Focus.*

www.honda.com

www.hanes.com

Packaging Responses. Consumer concern about the environmental damage from packaging materials has resulted in a number of positive corporate responses, including the following: (1) Soft drinks and other products are packaged in recyclable plastic bottles. (2) McDonald's switched from polystyrene clamshell containers to paperboard packages for its burgers and other sandwiches. (3) Hanes, a leading maker of pantyhose with its L'eggs

Green Advertising Addressing
the Biophysical Environment

brand, changed from the famous plastic egg container to a cardboard container that main-tained the famous silhouette of the plastic egg. This changeover from plastic to cardboard cost millions of dollars in packaging materials and displays.[16] (4) The major detergent makers all introduced concentrated detergents as a way of achieving smaller packages and thus less waste disposal to be placed in already crowded landfills. (5) A company from Maine, the Goodkind Pen Company, manufacturers and markets a pen that is made from birch scraps. Goodkind's Woody brand comes in a plastic package that can be snapped open for easy product removal, and then, at the request of the company, mailed back for another use.[17]

On the negative front, there is evidence that package materials often are wasted. For example, over 40 percent of juice containers, milk cartons, and other dairy products contain a smaller amount of product—from 1 percent to 6 percent less—than what the package labels promise.[18] This short-filling problem is partially due to profit-skimming and also results, more innocently, from poorly calibrated packing machines. Whatever the reason, the fact remains that packaging materials are wasted due to short-filling.[19]

FIGURE 3.2

Green Advertising Promoting an Image of Environmental Responsibility

Seal-of-Approval Programs. About 30 countries around the world have programs that are designed to assist consumers in identifying environmentally friendly products and brands.[20] In Germany, for example, the Blue Angel seal represents a promise to consumers that a product carrying an environmental claim is in fact legitimate. One prominent eco-labeling program in the United States is Green Seal, a Washington, D.C., non-profit organization. Green Seal has developed standards and awarded seals to companies that meet environmental standards, which fewer than 20 percent of all products in the category are able to satisfy. General Electric, for example, received a seal for developing compact fluorescent light bulbs. In addition to Green Seal, there are various product category-specific seal programs such as the "chasing arrows logo" that specifies recycled paperboard content. Programs such as these provide consumers with assurance that the products carrying these seals truly are environmentally friendly.[21]

www.greenseal.com

www.ge.com

Green Advertising Promoting
an Image of Environmental
Responsibility

Cause-Oriented Programs.   Cause-oriented marketing is practiced when companies sponsor or support worthy causes. (See Chapter 19 for further details.) In doing so, the marketing communicator anticipates that associating the company and its brands with a worthy cause will generate goodwill. It is for this reason that companies sponsor various environmental causes. At one time General Motors planted a tree for every Chevrolet Geo car sold. Evian, a company that markets mineral water, had representatives visit college campuses to raise environmental awareness and recruit new members for the World Wildlife Fund. Cause-oriented programs can be effective if they are not overused and if consumers perceive a company's involvement in an environmental cause as sincere and not just naked commercialism. Unfortunately, many companies spend much more on promoting cause-oriented environmental programs than they spend on the programs themselves.[22]

www.evian.com

www.worldwildlife.org

Point-of-Purchase Programs.   In-store displays provide an ideal setting to communicate a brand's environmental merits. A display called Environmental Centers, developed by the makers of Arm & Hammer, illustrates a creative application. These end-of-aisle units merchandised Arm & Hammer products along with select other brands of environmentally safe products. The displays also provided shoppers with free pamphlets from environmental groups. A particularly interesting illustration of environmental marketing at the point of purchase is provided in the *Global Focus*, describing green marketing at Loblaws, an innovative Canadian supermarket chain.

www.loblawsqueensquay.com

In addition to using the point of purchase as a vehicle for promoting a brand's environmental virtues, attention is also focusing on conservation in the construction of these displays. Billions of dollars are invested in plastic, wood, metal, paper, and other materials that are used in constructing point-of-purchase displays.[23] However, many of the displays sent by manufacturers to retailers are never used and simply end up in landfills. Closer consultations with retailers regarding their point-of-purchase needs would lead to fewer unused and summarily discarded displays, and increased use of permanent displays (those engineered to last at least six months) would substantially reduce the number of temporary displays that are quickly discarded.

Guidelines for Green Marketing

The significance of the environmental problem demands that marketing communicators do everything possible to ensure that green claims are credible, realistic, and believable. To assist companies in knowing what environmental claims can and cannot be communicated in advertisements, on packages, and elsewhere, the Federal Trade Commission—the U.S. government's agency responsible for regulating matters such as deceptive and unfair business practices (described subsequently in the chapter)—promulgated guides for environmental marketing claims.[24] These guides outline four general principles that apply to all environmental marketing claims:

1. Qualifications and disclosures should be sufficiently clear and prominent to prevent deception.
2. Claims should make clear whether they apply to the product, the package, or a component of either.
3. Claims should not overstate an environmental attribute or benefit, either expressly or by implication.
4. Comparative claims should be presented in a manner that makes the basis for the comparison sufficiently clear to avoid consumer deception.

The FTC guidelines also address specific categories of environmental claims such as "environmentally friendly," "degradable," and "recyclable." The guides describe the basic elements necessary to substantiate each form of environmental claim, and provide examples of specific claims that do and do not provide adequate support. The FTC's document is must reading for any firm that is considering making a claim about its product's environmental friendliness. A "new and improved" version of the FTC's guidelines was made available in 1996.[25]

In addition to the guidelines established by the FTC, a task force of attorneys general representing 10 states developed a set of recommendations for environmental marketers. These recommendations provide guidelines for labeling, packaging, and advertising products on the basis of environmental attributes.[26] Marketing communicators are offered four general recommendations for making appropriate environmental claims: (1) make the

GLOBAL FOCUS: LOBLAWS' LINE OF GREEN PRODUCTS

Major corporate initiatives typically require bold leadership from an individual who is committed to accomplishing an ideal or grand vision. This certainly was the situation at the Canadian supermarket chain, Loblaws, when it was in the vanguard of the environmental movement in the early 1990s by embarking on a program that merchandised a complete line of private-branded products under the GREEN name. Loblaws' CEO Dave Nichol got the idea from a monograph, *The Green Consumer Guide,* he had picked up on a visit to England. Within months, Loblaws' GREEN line of environmentally friendly products became a reality.

All GREEN products are packaged in bright green packages made from recycled paper. And all provide environmental informa-

tion along with the logo, *SOMETHING CAN BE DONE!* In the first year alone, GREEN products generated nearly $52 million in sales revenue for Loblaws. A high-efficiency light bulb that sold for $20 was one of the most interesting products carried in Loblaws' stores when the GREEN-label program was introduced. Although the price to consumers was nearly 10 times more than conventional bulbs, these high-efficiency bulbs saved shoppers about $32 over their life by reducing energy costs and the costs of bulb replacement—and consumers couldn't get enough of the bulbs. Ideas for adding new GREEN products come from all over the world; indeed, according to Nichol, most of the new ideas come from outside North America.

Source: Based on Carolyn Lesh, "Loblaws," *Advertising Age,* January 29, 1991, 38.

claims specific, (2) have claims reflect current disposal options, (3) make the claims substantive, and (4) make supportable claims.[27]

Make Specific Claims.   This guide is intended to prevent marketing communicators from using meaningless claims such as "environmentally friendly" or "safe for the environment." The use of specific environmental claims enables consumers to make informed choices, reduces the likelihood that claims will be misinterpreted, and minimizes the chances that consumers will think that a product is more environmentally friendly than it actually is. In general, it is recommended that environmental claims be as specific as possible—not general, vague, incomplete, or overly broad.

Reflect Current Disposal Options.   This guide is directed at preventing environmental claims that are technically accurate but practically unrealizable due to local trash-disposal practices. For example, most communities dispose of trash by burying it in public landfills. Because paper and plastic products do not degrade when buried, it is misleading for businesses to make environmental claims that their products are degradable, biodegradable, or photodegradable. As illustrated in the *Opening Vignette,* products such as trash bags may be photodegradable, but once buried in a landfill they do not experience further degradation.

www.aurorafoods.com

Make Substantive Claims.   Some marketing communicators use trivial and irrelevant environmental claims to convey the impression that a promoted brand is environmentally sound. An illustration of a nonsubstantive claim is a company promoting its polystyrene foam cups as "preserving our trees and forests." Another trivial claim is when single-use products such as paper plates are claimed to be "safe for the environment." Clearly, a paper plate is not unsafe to the environment in the same sense that a toxic chemical is unsafe; however, paper plates and other throwaways do not actually benefit the environment but rather exacerbate the landfill problem.

Make Supportable Claims.   This recommendation is straightforward: Environmental claims should be supported by competent and reliable scientific evidence. The purpose of this recommendation is to encourage businesses to make only those environmental claims that can be backed by facts. The injunction to businesses is clear: Don't claim it unless you can support it!

Some companies are indeed showing restraint in making environmental claims. Such restraint not only benefits consumers and society at large, but it also supports the long-run interests of businesses themselves. Misleading consumers with false environmental claims is a short-run tactic that provides a company a Pyrrhic victory at best. Long-term growth achieved from consumer allegiance is obtained only by developing legitimate product offerings and promoting these offers with honest and supportable claims.

What Does the Future Hold for Green Marketing and Who Is the Green Consumer?

About a decade ago, a Harvard Business School professor asserted that green products are to the 1990s what "lite" products were to the 1980s.[28] In retrospect, it would seem that this claim is, at minimum, subject to debate and may even represent a case of excessive enthusiasm. There now is little evidence that many brands are being promoted on the basis of their environmental efficacy. Nonetheless, it is clear that the green movement is here to stay to one degree or another. Indeed, because many countries outside North America and Western Europe have far greater environmental problems, it may be that the opportunity for responsive green marketing is stronger in these countries than in highly advanced economies.

Is there a group of consumers who are especially responsive to environmental claims, and, if so, what are their characteristics? The development of effective, targeted communications requires answers to these questions.[29] A study of over 3,000 consumers has established some discernible characteristics of consumers who are environmentally conscious. In particular, these consumers are interested in new products, are information seekers who talk with others about products, are careful shoppers who are somewhat price sensitive, and are skeptical about advertising in general.[30] It is apparent from these characteristics that green consumers are careful, thoughtful shoppers who must be treated with respect: "Treated fairly, they may be receptive; treated poorly, they may not only switch brands, but also take others with them."[31]

REGULATION OF MARKETING COMMUNICATIONS

Advertisers, sales managers, and other marketing communicators are faced with a variety of regulations and restrictions that influence their decision-making latitude. The history of the past century has shown that regulation is necessary to protect consumers and competitors from fraudulent, deceptive, and unfair practices that some businesses choose to perpetrate. Whatever the rationale, the fact remains that governmental regulation can have a significant impact on business organizations, as perhaps exemplified in the *Global Focus* that describes the recent ban in China on direct sales.

www.amway.com

www.avon.com

www.marykay.com

www.service.mattel.com

When Is Regulation Justified?

Strict adherents to the ideals of free enterprise would argue that government should rarely if ever intervene in the activities of business. However, more moderate observers believe

GLOBAL FOCUS: CHINA'S BAN ON DIRECT SALES

A number of companies that are well known for their direct-sales form of marketing—such as Amway (cleaning products), Avon (cosmetics), and Mary Kay Corp. (cosmetics)—had aggressively expanded their direct selling activity in the People's Republic of China (PRC) throughout the 1990s. This form of selling seemed perfect given the stage of economic development in the PRC and in view of that country's rapid move toward economic liberalization and capitalism. A number of other companies like Mattel Inc. (toys) were teaming up with companies such as Avon and Amway in order to avail themselves of the direct sellers' huge sales forces. Business was good, both for the companies and the sales reps in China who were able to improve their standard of living. By 1997, Amway had approxi-

mately 80,000 sales reps who generated $178 million in sales, and Avon had nearly 50,000 representatives who produced $75 million.

Then in April 1998, the Chinese government banned direct selling. The ban was imposed after some companies (but not any of the respectable companies mentioned heretofore) began setting up so-called pyramid schemes and cheating consumers. While Amway, Avon, and Mary Kay Corp. were never involved in any of these abuses, the Chinese government decided to ban all direct selling efforts. The ban on direct selling has forced companies such as Avon to open its own Avon stores, and thousands of Chinese have lost their direct selling jobs.

Source: Tara Parker-Pope and Lisa Bannon, "Avon's New Calling: Selling Mattel's Barbie Doll in China," *The Wall Street Journal Interactive Edition,* May 1, 1997; Normandy Madden, "China's Direct Sales Ban Stymies Marketers," *Advertising Age,* May 18, 1998, 56; "Avon Faces Shortfall, Job Losses in China Over Direct-Sales Ban," *The Wall Street Journal Interactive Edition,* July 6, 1998.

---

that regulation is justified in certain circumstances. Regulation is perhaps needed most when *consumer decisions are based on false or limited information.*[32] Under such circumstances, consumers are likely to make decisions they would not otherwise make and, as a result, incur economic, physical, or psychological injury. Competitors are also harmed because they lose business they might have otherwise enjoyed.

In theory, regulation is justified if the benefits realized exceed the costs. What are the benefits and costs of regulation?[33] Regulation offers three major benefits: First, *consumer choice* among alternatives is improved when consumers are better informed in the marketplace. For example, consider the Alcoholic Beverage Labeling Act, which requires manufacturers to place the following warning on all containers of alcoholic beverages:

> GOVERNMENT WARNING: (1) According to the Surgeon General, women should not drink alcoholic beverages during pregnancy, due to the risk of birth defects. (2) Consumption of alcoholic beverages impairs your ability to drive a car or operate machinery, and may cause health problems.[34]

This regulation serves to inform consumers that drinking has negative consequences. Pregnant women will benefit themselves and their unborn children in particular if this warning prompts them to refrain from drinking alcoholic beverages.[35] It is unlikely, however, that warning labels alone have a major impact in curbing drinking among pregnant women.[36]

A second benefit of regulation is that when consumers become better informed, *product quality tends to improve* in response to consumers' changing needs and preferences. For example, when consumers began learning about the dangers of fat and cholesterol, manufacturers started marketing healthier food products. When regulators prevented makers of aspirin and analgesic products from making outrageously false and misleading claims, companies introduced new alternatives such as Tylenol, Advil, Motrin, and Aleve as a means of taking market share away from entrenched aspirin brands.[37]

A third regulatory benefit is *reduced prices* resulting from a reduction in a seller's "informational market power." For example, prices of used cars undoubtedly would fall if dealers were required to inform prospective purchasers about a car's defects, since consumers would not be willing to pay as much for automobiles with known problems.

Regulation is not costless. Companies often must incur the *cost of complying* with a regulatory remedy. For example, U.S. cigarette manufacturers are required to rotate over the course of a year four different warning messages for three months each. Obviously, this is more costly than the previously required single warning message. *Enforcement costs* incurred by regulatory agencies and paid for by taxpayers represent a second cost category. The *unintended side effects* that might result from regulations represent a third cost to both buyers and sellers. A regulation may unintentionally harm sellers if buyers switch to other products or reduce their level of consumption after regulation is imposed. The cost to buyers may increase if sellers pass along, in the form of higher prices, the costs of complying with a regulation. In sum, regulation is theoretically justified only if the benefits exceed the costs.

The following sections examine the two forms of regulation that affect many aspects of marketing communications: governmental regulation and industry self regulation.

Regulation of Marketing Communications by Federal Agencies

Governmental regulation takes place at both the federal and state levels. All facets of marketing communications (personal selling, sales promotion, advertising, telemarketing, etc.) are subject to regulation, but advertising is the one area in which regulators have been most active. This is because advertising is the most conspicuous aspect of marketing communications. The discussion that follows examines federal governmental regulation of advertising in the United States. Readers who wish to know more about advertising regulation in European Union countries are directed to the source cited in the following footnote.[38]

www.ftc.gov

The Federal Trade Commission (FTC) is the U.S. government agency that has primary responsibility for regulating advertising at the federal level. The FTC was created in 1914 primarily to prevent anticompetitive practices—that is, it functioned to protect businesses rather than consumers. By 1938, Congress realized that the FTC's mandate should be expanded to offer more assistance to consumers as well as businesses, especially in the area of false and misleading advertising. The Wheeler-Lea Amendment of 1938 accomplished this objective by changing a principal section of the original FTC Act of 1914 from "unfair methods of competition" to "unfair methods of competition and unfair or deceptive acts or practices in commerce." This seemingly minor change enhanced the FTC's regulatory powers appreciably and provided a legal mandate for the FTC to protect consumers against fraudulent business practices. The FTC's regulatory authority cuts across three broad areas that directly affect marketing communicators: deceptive advertising, unfair practices, and information regulation.

Regulation of Deceptive Advertising.   In a general sense, consumers are deceived by an advertising claim or campaign when (1) the impression left by the claim or campaign is false—that is, there is a *claim-fact discrepancy*, and (2) the false claim or campaign is *believed* by consumers. The important point is that a false claim is not necessarily deceptive by itself. Rather, consumers must believe a claim in order to be deceived by it: "A false claim does not harm consumers unless it is believed, and a true claim can generate harm if it generates a false belief."[39]

Although the FTC makes deception rulings case by case, it does employ some general guidelines in deciding whether deceptive advertising has occurred, as illustrated by the environmental guidelines previously discussed. Deception policy at the FTC is not inscribed in granite but rather is subject to shifts, depending on the regulatory philosophy of different FTC chairpersons and the prevailing political climate. Under the Reagan administration, lasting from 1980–1988, the FTC's enforcement policy against deception reflected the conservative political mood and the corresponding opposition to business regulation. However, in recent years the FTC has become more vigorous in opposing advertisers who make false and misleading claims.

The current deception policy declares that the FTC will find a business practice deceptive "if there is a representation, omission or practice that is likely to mislead the consumer acting reasonably in the circumstances, to the consumer's detriment."[40] The three elements that follow provide the essence of this policy.[41]

1. *Misleading.* There must be a representation, omission, or a practice that is likely to mislead the consumer. A *misrepresentation* is defined by the FTC as an express or implied statement contrary to fact, whereas a *misleading omission* is said to occur when qualifying information necessary to prevent a practice, claim, representation, or reasonable expectation or belief from being misleading is not disclosed.

2. *Reasonable Consumer.* The act or practice must be considered from the perspective of the reasonable consumer. The FTC's test of reasonableness is based on the consumer's interpretation or reaction to an advertisement—that is, the commission determines the effect of the advertising practice on a reasonable member of the group to which the advertising is targeted. The following quote indicates that the FTC evaluates advertising claims case by case in view of the target audience's unique position—its education level, intellectual capacity, mental frame of mind, and so on.

   > For instance, if a company markets a cure to the terminally ill, the practice will be evaluated from the perspective of how it affects the ordinary member of that group. Thus, terminally ill consumers might be particularly susceptible to exaggerated cure claims. By the same token, a practice or representation directed to a well-educated group, such as a prescription drug advertisement to doctors, would be judged in light of the knowledge and sophistication of that group.[42]

3. *Material.* The representation, omission, or practice must be material. A *material representation* involves information that is important to consumers and that is likely to influence their *choice* or *conduct* regarding a product. In general, the FTC considers information to be material when it pertains to the central characteristics of a product or service (including performance features, size, price). Hence, if an athletic-shoe company falsely claimed that its brand possesses the best shock-absorption feature on the market, this would be a material misrepresentation to the many runners who make purchase choices based on this factor. On the other hand, for this same company to falsely claim that it has been in business for 25 years—when in fact it has been in business for only 22 years—likely would not be regarded as material, since most consumers would not make a purchase choice based on this claim.

www.kraftfoods.com

An important case involving the issue of materiality was brought by the FTC against Kraft, Inc., and its advertising of Kraft Single American cheese slices.[43] The FTC challenged Kraft on grounds that advertisements for Kraft Singles falsely claimed that each slice contains the same amount of calcium as *five* ounces of milk. In point of fact, each slice of Kraft Singles begins with five ounces of whole milk, but during processing 30 percent, or 1.5 ounces of milk, is lost. In other words, each slice contains only 70 percent of the amount of calcium claimed in Kraft's advertisements.[44] Kraft responded that its $11 million advertising campaign did not influence consumer purchases. Kraft's legal counsel argued that the advertisements: (1) did not convey the misleading representation claimed by the FTC, but (2) even if this representation had been conveyed, it would not have mattered because calcium is a relatively unimportant factor in consumers' decision to purchase Kraft Singles. (Out of nine factors rated by consumers in a copy test, calcium was rated no higher than seventh.)

Whereas the FTC's position was that Kraft's advertising was likely to mislead consumers, Kraft's defense was that its calcium claim, whether false or not, is nondeceptive because the difference between 5 ounces of milk and 3.5 ounces is an immaterial difference to consumers. Or, in other words, Kraft's defense amounted to the following: Yes, we (Kraft) made claims about the calcium benefits of Kraft Singles, but the issue of deceptiveness is moot because the difference in calcium content between what we claimed (a single slice contains the calcium equivalency of 5 ounces of milk) and what is reality (a single slice contains the calcium equivalency of 3.5 ounces of milk) is immaterial to consumers and hence not deceptive.

After hearing detailed testimony on the matter and following an appeal process, the five commissioners of the FTC determined that Kraft's advertising claim *was* material.[45] Accordingly, the FTC ordered Kraft to cease and desist (literally, "stop and go no more," or discontinue) further misrepresentations of Kraft Singles' calcium content. The Kraft case has generated much discussion and controversy. The articles cited in the following endnote are worthwhile reading for this particular case as well as its broader significance for advertising practice and public policy involving deceptive advertising.[46]

Regulation of Unfair Practices.   As noted at the beginning of this section, the Wheeler-Lea Amendment of 1938 gave the Federal Trade Commission authority to regulate unfair, as well as deceptive, acts or practices in commerce. Unfairness is necessarily a somewhat vague concept. For this reason, the unfairness doctrine received limited use by the FTC until 1972, when in a famous judicial decision *(FTC v. Sperry & Hutchinson Co.)* the Supreme Court noted that consumers as well as businesses must be protected from unfair trade practices.[47] Unlike deception, a finding of unfairness to consumers may go beyond questions of fact and relate merely to public values.[48] The criteria used to evaluate whether a business act is unfair involve such considerations as whether the act: (1) offends public policy as it has been established by statutes, (2) is immoral, unethical, oppressive, or unscrupulous, and (3) causes substantial injury to consumers, competitors, or other businesses.[49]

The Federal Trade Commission's right to regulate unfair advertising was a matter of considerable dispute for years, because the precise meaning of "unfair" was not clear.[50] The dispute was ended in 1994 when Congress devised a definition of unfairness that is satisfactory to all parties. Advertising unfairness is defined as "acts or practices that cause or are likely to cause *substantial injury to consumers*, which is *not reasonably avoidable* by consumers themselves and *not outweighed by countervailing benefits to consumers or competition*" (emphasis added).[51] The italicized features of the definition point out the intentions of Congress to balance the interests of advertisers with those of consumers and to prevent capricious applications of the unfairness doctrine by the FTC.

The FTC has applied the unfairness doctrine in three major areas: (1) advertising substantiation, (2) promotional practices directed to children, and (3) trade regulation rules.

1. *Advertising Substantiation.* The ad-substantiation program is based on a simple premise: It is unfair for advertisers to make claims about their products without having a *reasonable basis* for those claims. According to the FTC, unfairness results from imposing on the consumer the unavoidable economic risk that the product may not perform as advertised if neither the consumer nor the manufacturer has a reasonable basis for belief in the product claim. In other words, the ad-substantiation program requires advertisers to have documentation (test results or other data) indicating that they have a reasonable basis for making a claim prior to the dissemination of advertisements.[52]

   www.walgreens.com
   www.advil.com

   The FTC charged Walgreen, a large retail drugstore chain, with making unsubstantiated claims for Advil pain reliever. Walgreen had advertised Advil as a "prescription pain reliever . . ." and "an anti-inflammatory . . . source of comfort for people who experience arthritis pain." The FTC ruled that Walgreen did not have a reasonable basis for this claim. The case was dropped when Walgreen consented not to make unsubstantiated claims for Advil or other analgesic drug products.[53]

2. *Unfairness Involving Children.* Because children are more credulous and less well-equipped than adults to protect themselves, public-policy officials are especially concerned with protecting youngsters. When applied to cases involving children, the unfairness doctrine is especially useful because many advertising claims are not deceptive per se but are nonetheless potentially unethical, unscrupulous, or inherently dangerous to children. For example, the FTC considered one company's use of Spider Man vitamin advertising unfair because such advertising was judged capable of inducing children to take excessive and dangerous amounts of vitamins.[54]

3. *Trade Regulation Rules.* Whereas most Federal Trade Commission actions are taken on a case-by-case basis, the use of trade regulation rules (TRRs) enables the FTC to issue a regulation that restricts an *entire industry* from some unfair and objectionable practice. For example, the FTC issued a TRR to vocational schools that would have required the schools to disclose enrollment and job placement statistics in their promotional materials. The rule was later rejected by a court of appeals on grounds that the FTC had failed to define the unfair practices that the rule was designed to remedy.[55] In recent years the FTC has used industry-wide trade regulation rules sparingly. The new definition of unfairness is likely to impose stringent limits on the FTC's blanket application of the unfairness doctrine.

Information Regulation.   Although the primary purpose of advertising regulation is the prohibition of deceptive and unfair practices, regulation also is needed at times to provide consumers with information they might not otherwise receive.[56] Many believe that the corrective advertising program is the most important of the FTC's information provision programs.[57]

Corrective advertising is based on the premise that a firm that misleads consumers should have to use future advertisements to rectify any deceptive impressions it has created in consumers' minds. In other words, the purpose of corrective advertising is to prevent a firm from continuing to deceive consumers rather than to punish the firm.

www.oral-care.com

www.warner-lambert.com

The most prominent corrective advertising order to date is the case of Warner-Lambert's Listerine mouthwash. According to the FTC, Warner-Lambert had misled consumers for a number of years and required them to run this corrective statement: "Listerine will not help prevent colds or sore throats or lessen their severity." The corrective campaign ran for 16 months at a cost of $10.3 million to Warner-Lambert, most of which was spent on television commercials.

Several studies evaluated the effectiveness of the Listerine corrective advertising order.[58] The FTC's own study revealed only partial success for the Listerine corrective campaign. On the positive side, there was a 40 percent drop in the amount of mouthwash used for the misconceived purpose of preventing colds and sore throats; on the negative side, 57 percent of Listerine users continued to rate cold and sore throat effectiveness as a key attribute in their purchasing decision (only 15 percent of Scope users reported a similar goal), and 39 percent of Listerine users reported continued use of the mouthwash to relieve or prevent a cold or sore throat.

The FTC walks a fine line when issuing a corrective advertising order and specifying the remedial action a deceptive advertiser must take. The objective is to restore the marketplace to its original position prior to the deceptive advertising so that a firm does not continue to reap the rewards of its past deceptive practices. However, there is always the possibility that the corrective advertising effort may go too far and severely damage the firm and perhaps, unintentionally, hurt other companies in the industry. Fortunately, a national study of a corrective advertising order against STP oil additive determined that corrective advertising action in this case worked as intended: False beliefs were corrected without injuring the product category or consumers' overall perceptions of the STP Corporation.[59]

www.fda.gov

Regulation of Product Labeling.   The Food and Drug Administration (FDA) is the federal body responsible for regulating information on the packages of food and drug products. The FDA was inactive until recent years. Under a new director, the FDA in 1991 took action against Procter & Gamble's Citrus Hill brand of concentrated orange juice. Citrus Hill's package falsely represented the brand as being fresh orange juice when in fact the product is concentrated. The FDA made a point of showing its revived regulatory vigilance by literally seizing 2,000 cases of Citrus Hill orange juice from a Minnesota warehouse. Just two days after the FDA action, P&G agreed to remove all references to "fresh" from its packaging.[60] The action against P&G's Citrus Hill had strong symbolic impact and notified other marketers that the FDA was prepared to regulate strongly against deceptive and misleading package labeling.

Regulation of Marketing Communications by State Agencies

Individual states have their own statutes and regulatory agencies to police the marketplace from fraudulent business practices. Most, if not all, states have departments of consumer affairs or consumer protection. During the sweeping deregulation climate in Washington under the Reagan administration, states became more vigorous in their own regulatory activities. The **National Association of Attorneys General (NAAG),** which includes attorneys general from all 50 states, has played a particularly active role. For example, the NAAG issued guidelines directed at advertising practices in the airline and car-rental industries. In another instance, attorneys general from 22 states filed a complaint against Honda of America, alleging that Honda's three-wheel, all-terrain vehicles are "rolling death traps."[61]

www.volvo.com

A particularly interesting case involved a lawsuit filed by the Texas attorney general against Volvo North America. Volvo had produced a television commercial showing Bear Foot, a monster truck with huge wheels, running over a string of automobiles. All of the automobiles collapsed except the Volvo station wagon. An investigation revealed, however, that the Volvo had been reinforced with steel and wood while the other cars had their roof supports severed.[62] This case is reminiscent of similar advertising practices that were chastised two decades ago. For example, Campbell Soup Co. produced a commercial in which marbles were placed at the bottom of the bowl so that the food stock would rise to the top and give the soup a hearty appearance.

Another important case of state regulation of marketing communications practices involves the tobacco industry. As of late 1998, four states had reached settlements with tobacco companies over the marketing of tobacco products. The state of Minnesota, for example, arrived at a settlement with major tobacco companies (Brown & Williamson, Philip Morris, and R. J. Reynolds) that banned: (1) product placement in movies, (2) any marketing of cigarettes to kids, (3) advertising of cigarettes on billboards, transit vehicles, and at arenas and stadiums, and (4) the use of premium objects and specialty advertising items.[63] It is noteworthy that this type of ban is not restricted to the United States. In 1998 the Parliament of the European Union approved virtually a total ban on tobacco advertising, although the ban will not go into effect until 2001 or 2002.[64]

www.bw.com

www.philipmorris.com

www.rjrt.com

There is every indication that states will remain active in their efforts to regulate advertising deception and other business practices.[65] This poses a potentially significant problem for many national advertisers who might find themselves subject to multiple, and perhaps inconsistent, state regulations. It is somewhat ironic that many national companies would prefer to see a stronger Federal Trade Commission. In other words, these firms are better off with a single regulatory agency that: (1) institutes uniform national guidelines and rules, and (2) keeps the marketplace as free as possible from the fly-by-night operators that tarnish the image of all businesses.

Advertising Self-Regulation

Self-regulation, as the name suggests, is undertaken by advertisers themselves rather than by governmental bodies. Thus, self-regulation is in a sense a form of *private government* whereby peers establish and enforce voluntary rules of behavior.[66] Advertising self-regulation has flourished in many countries, particularly in highly developed countries such as Canada, France, and the United Kingdom.[67] In the United States self-regulation has resulted in response to heightened consumer criticism of advertising and stricter government controls.[68] Four major groups sponsor self-regulation programs: (1) advertising associations (e.g., American Association of Advertising Agencies, Association of National Advertisers), (2) special industry groups (e.g., the Council of Better Business Bureaus), (3) media associations, and (4) trade associations.[69]

www.commercepark.com/AAA

www.ana.net

www.bbb.org

The *advertising clearance process* is a form of self-regulation that takes place behind the scenes before a commercial or other advertisement reaches consumers. Prior to its media appearance, a magazine advertisement or television commercial undergoes a variety of clearance steps, including: (1) advertising agency clearance, (2) approval from the advertiser's legal department and perhaps also from an independent law firm, and (3) media approval (such as television networks' guidelines regarding standards of taste).[70] A finished ad that makes it through the clearance process and appears in advertising media is then subject to the possibility of post hoc regulation from the FTC, NAAG, and the National Advertising Review Board.

The National Advertising Review Council.   Self-regulation by the Council of Better Business Bureaus' National Advertising Review Council (NARC) has been the most publicized and perhaps most effective form of self-regulation. NARC consists of three review units: the Children's Advertising Review Unit (CARU), the National Advertising Division (NAD), and the National Advertising Review Board (NARB). CARU monitors children's television programming and commercials, whereas the NAD and NARB were established with the goal of sustaining "high standards of truth and accuracy in national advertising [to adults]."[71] NARB is the umbrella-like term applied to the combined NAD/NARB self-regulatory mechanism; however, by strict definition, NARB is a court consisting of 50 representatives who are formed into five-member panels to hear appeals of NAD cases when one or more of the involved parties is dissatisfied with the initial verdict.[72] NAD is the investigative arm of NARB and is responsible for "receiving or initiating, evaluating, investigating, analyzing and holding initial negotiations with an advertiser on complaints or questions from any source involving truth or accuracy of national advertising."[73]

The number of cases investigated and resolved each year varies, but NAD/NARB often becomes involved in about 100 or so cases. Cases are brought to the NAD by competing advertisers, initiated by the NAD staff itself, or originate from local Better Business Bureaus and consumer groups. Food and beverages and child-directed ads are the categories most frequently involved.[74] For example, Gerber Products challenged three print ads by Beech-Nut, its competitor, which claimed that "the other leading brand also adds sugar to their instant fruit cereals, but Beech-Nut adds only fruit. We wouldn't dream of adding sugar or salt or other things your baby doesn't need." Gerber claimed its products do not contain salt or sugar. Beech-Nut agreed to comply with NAD's recommendation that future ads should be modified to indicate only that Beech-Nut does not add any refined sugar to its cereals.

www.gerber.com

www.beechnut.com

NAD/NARB Complaint Resolution Process.   The preceding cases illustrate some of the fundamentals of the NAD/NARB self-regulatory process. This section details the specific activities that are involved from the time a complaint is initiated until it is resolved.[75]

Step 1: Complaint Screening and Case Selection. The self-regulatory process begins with the NAD screening complaints against allegedly deceptive or misleading advertising. Complaints originate from four major sources: (1) competitors, (2) consumers and consumer groups, (3) Better Business Bureaus, and (4) NAD's own monitoring activities. The NAD pursues those complaints that it regards as having merit.

Step 2: Initial NAD Evaluation. Some cases are administratively closed because they fall outside NAD's jurisdiction, but in most cases NAD contacts the advertiser to open a dialogue. There are three possible outcomes from this dialogue: (1) The disputed advertisement is found acceptable; (2) the advertisement is considered questionable; or (3) the advertisement is deemed unacceptable because NAD feels it violates a precedent or may be misinterpreted by consumers.

Step 3: Advertiser's Initial Response. Advertisers can respond to NAD by providing sufficient substantiation to show that the disputed advertising claim is justified or by discontinuing or modifying the claim (as in the Beech-Nut case).

Step 4: NAD's Final Evaluation. All ads that have been discontinued or modified are publicly reported by NAD in outlets such as *Advertising Age* that reach the advertising community. Ads for which advertisers have provided substantiation are then reviewed by NAD to assess the adequacy of the evidence provided. In most instances NAD rules that the disputed claims have been adequately substantiated. Claims that NAD considers insufficiently substantiated are subject to appeal to NARB. Since its inception in 1971, the NAD has heard about 3,300 cases as of 1996, and only 91 cases had been appealed to the NARB.[76]

Step 5: Advertiser's Final Response. The NAD's ruling may be upheld, reversed, or dismissed by NARB. However, because NAD/NARB is merely a self-regulatory body without legal jurisdiction or power, the ultimate resolution of disputed cases depends on voluntary cooperation between advertisers and NAD/NARB.

In conclusion, self-regulation has a variety of potential benefits to consumers and businesses. It can strengthen effectiveness by "discouraging exaggerated or misleading promises which lower the believability and selling power of advertising."[77] Self-regulation may also reduce the need for government regulation. Furthermore, because advertisers are strongly motivated to point out their competitor's deceptive advertising practices, their efforts to protect themselves help to maintain the general integrity of advertising and, in so doing, to protect consumers. Thus, the evidence seems to indicate that consumers have benefited substantially from NAD/NARB's self-regulatory efforts.[78] Consumers also benefit from the broadcast media's self-regulation of the types of advertisements it is willing to broadcast on radio or television.[79]

ETHICAL ISSUES IN MARKETING COMMUNICATIONS

Advertisers, sales promoters, package designers, sales personnel, telemarketers, public relations representatives, and point-of-purchase designers regularly make decisions that have ethical implications. This section examines many of the ethical issues involved with all elements of marketing communications.

Ethics in our context involves matters of right and wrong, or *moral,* conduct pertaining to any aspect of marketing communications. Hence, for our purposes, ethics and morality will be used interchangeably and considered synonymous with societal notions of *honesty, honor, virtue,* and *integrity* in matters of marketing communications conduct. It is relatively easy to define ethics, but it is difficult to identify what is or is not ethical conduct in marketing communications. Indeed, throughout the field of marketing (as well as elsewhere in society) there is a lack of consensus about what is ethical conduct.[80] Consensus notwithstanding, we nevertheless can identify marketing communications practices that are especially susceptible to ethical challenges. The following sections examine, in order, ethical issues in: (1) the targeting of marketing communications efforts, (2) advertising, (3) public relations, (4) personal selling and telemarketing, (5) packaging communications, and (6) sales promotions.

The Ethics of Targeting

According to widely accepted dictates of the marketing concept and sound marketing strategy (such as described in Chapter 2), firms should direct their offerings at specific segments of customers rather than use a scatter or shotgun approach. Nonetheless, ethical dilemmas are sometimes involved when special products and corresponding marketing communications efforts are directed at particular segments.[81] Especially open to ethical debate is the practice of targeting products and communications efforts at segments that, for various psychosocial and economic reasons, are vulnerable to marketing communications—such as children and minorities.[82]

Targeting to Children. Advertising and in-school marketing programs continuously urge kids to desire various products and brands. Critics often contend that many of the products targeted to children are unnecessary and that the communications are exploitative. Because it would involve debating personal values to discuss what kids do or do not need, the following presentation merely presents the critics' position and allows you to draw your own conclusions.

www.gatorade.com

Consider the advertising of Gatorade to kids. Advertisements claimed that Gatorade is the "healthy alternative for thirsty kids." Nutritionists and other critics charged that Gatorade is unnecessary for kids and no better than water—no harm or benefit arises from its consumption.[83] If indeed Gatorade does not benefit kids, is it ethical to urge them to encourage their gatekeeping parents to purchase this product?

Another criticized aspect of children-directed marketing communications is the practice of using posters, book covers, free magazines, advertising (such as the Channel One school news program), and other so-called learning tools.[84] Disguised as educational materials, these communications oftentimes are little more than attempts to persuade schoolchildren to want the promoted products and brands. Critics contend these methods are unethical because they use children's trust in educational materials as a deceptive means of hawking merchandise.[85]

In addition to classroom tactics, critics also question the ethics of practices such as placing products in movies (for instance, the famous Reese's Pieces in the movie *E.T.*) and supporting the product-movie connection with tie-in merchandise programs. Another criticized practice is the use of magazine *advertorials*—that is, advertisements disguised as editorial opinions. For example, *Seventeen* magazine runs a personal-advice column providing answers to makeup and wardrobe questions. Sometimes, however, the editorial-seeming advice is little more than a product plug.[86]

www.seventeen.com

Marketers also have been criticized for targeting adult products to pre-adults. The Miller Brewing Company, for example, was challenged for using a television commercial for its Molson Ice brand that focuses on a label displaying 5.6 percent alcoholic content at the same time that an off-camera announcer utters that Molson Ice is a "bolder" drink. A spokesperson for the Center for Science in the Public Interest asserted that the Molson Ice commercial appeals to kids because they "drink to get drunk" and higher alcohol content is "what they want in a beer."[87] The beer industry itself would be opposed to this advertising inasmuch as one of the brewing industry's advertising guidelines explicitly states that beer advertising "should neither state nor carry any implication of alcohol strength."[88]

www.rjrt.com

By far the greatest controversy to erupt in many years involving claims of unfair targeting to children was the advertising campaign for Camel cigarettes using the anthropomorphized camel character known as "Old Joe" or "Smooth Joe." An illustrative advertisement is shown in Figure 3.4. This campaign, which was introduced in 1987 by R. J. Reynolds, the makers of Camel cigarettes, was widely criticized as responsible for increased smoking among teenagers. The campaign consistently portrayed Smooth Joe as a swank character in various social settings, aided perhaps by the ubiquitous cigarette hanging in his lips or dangling from his fingertips.

With cigarette smoking among teenagers on the rise, many parties urged a ban be imposed on Joe Camel advertisements. Responsible commentators argued that such a ban would be unfair to advertisers and in violation of their First Amendment rights.[89] Under pressure from anti-smoking activists, the U.S. Congress, and the Federal Trade Commission, R. J. Reynolds discontinued its use of the Old Joe advertising campaign in 1998, although the character will still appear in advertising outside the United States.[90]

Research has been conducted to determine whether the Joe Camel advertising campaign was indeed responsible for more positive smoking attitudes and increased smoking among youth. The research is itself highly controversial and has been both celebrated and pilloried.[91] Has the Joe Camel campaign unethically targeted nonadults? Is it responsible for increased smoking? Is it unethical? These are complicated questions and simple answers are not possible. These are issues that need to be debated both in and outside the classroom. The following *IMC Focus* includes a provocative position on the topic. It is presented here *not* as the final statement on the issue but rather as an intelligent statement that should serve to spark further discussion.

www.anheuser-busch.com
www.aap.org
www.apha.org

Example of Controversial
Advertising

Another celebrated advertising controversy involving children is Anheuser-Busch's use of frogs and lizards in advertising beer. Numerous consumer activists have been joined by the American Academy of Pediatrics and the American Public Health Association in demanding that Anheuser-Busch stop using animated characters—such as the lizards, Frank and Louie—in advertising beer. The concern is that these ads reach young children who, the contention goes, perceive such advertising to be cool and thus may develop the belief at a too-early age that beer drinking is the hip thing to do.[92]

Targeting to Minorities. Makers of alcohol and tobacco products frequently employ billboards and other advertising media to target brands to African-Americans and

IMC Focus: An Adman's Struggle with Joe Camel and Free Speech

Last week, just over the Howard Street Bridge, I crossed a camel's path. Stopped at a traffic light on my way to a business meeting, I glanced up and saw the camel rising above the brick building tops in vibrant, unnatural hues, stretching, it seemed, far into the sky.

I thought he saw me, too; he winked at me with a grin. And there was an understanding between us—camel and man, man and camel.

But his wink and grin were not meant for me alone.

I am a local advertising professional, and the camel is the symbol for Camel cigarettes. He speaks to the city from high atop Howard Street and North Avenue on his billboard perch. As an "adman," I am impressed by the camel. The cartoonish, humanistic depiction of the desert beast in a jazz jam session with his camel buddies is intriguing. It doesn't ask for your attention, it grabs it. And once you are hooked, as it were, on the visual, the message is clear: Camels are cool; they're fun; they make you part of the desirable crowd. All of this, conveyed in just a glance.

More than that, the cartoons speak most persuasively to the "target market" the company wishes to reach. All in all, it is an expert use of the medium and an excellent piece of advertising.

As a man, as a father, I am appalled by the camel. To me, he is perverse, a distortion. Strip away his sleek, tan exterior and what is left? Not a camel, but a purplish, black-plumed raven forlornly whispering to the children of the streets when their parents and teachers are not looking. He beckons the poor, preying upon their weaknesses and panhandling their few coins.

The spectacle leaves me between a rock and a camel's hump—and not only for selfish reasons. Of course, being a glad participant in the free-enterprise system, I am all for the aggressive manufacturing and marketing of any legal product. Beyond that, I believe that free speech, even for ignoble, detestable causes, should be protected without reservation.

But is it free speech to lure children with images they've been taught to trust, cartoon images, to a product the surgeon general has called an addiction that can lead to death? In fact, *The New York Times Magazine* recently reported that "the product kills more than 420,000 Americans a year—surpassing the combined deaths from homicide, suicide, AIDS, automobile accidents, alcohol and drug abuse."

I came to the conclusion that, yes, it is free speech. People are, and should be, allowed to convey whatever message they choose. That is the American way.

But freedom of expression also includes the freedom *not* to express one's self. No one forces an advertising agency to devise strategies and create images for a tobacco company targeting an inappropriate market. No one forces the media outlets to provide them a forum. And finally, no one should overlook them when it comes time to pass out blame.

But it is not enough, either, to merely ignore the camel. Those of us in the marketing business know exactly what he's up to; we should be the first to denounce him. Even in public and professional life, there is a place for personal morality and common decency.

These meager thoughts passed through my head as I sat at that light just over the Howard Street Bridge. When the signal turned green, I waited for a group of school kids to cross the street, then I gently pulled away. A couple of blocks later, I was stopped again at a light. This time, under a billboard for malt liquor.

Source: George DesRoches, "An Adman's Struggle with Joe Camel and Free Speech," *Advertising Age*, September 26, 1994, 23.

Hispanics. Billboards advertising alcohol and tobacco are disproportionately more likely to appear in inner-city areas.[93] Two celebrated cases illustrate the concerns involved.[94] A national uproar ensued when R. J. Reynolds (RJR) was preparing to introduce Uptown, a brand of menthol cigarette aimed at African-Americans and planned for test marketing in Philadelphia where African-Americans make up 40 percent of the population.[95] Because African-Americans have more than a 50 percent higher rate of lung cancer than whites, many critics, including the U.S. government's secretary for Health and Human Services, were incensed by the product launch.[96] In response to the public outcry, RJR canceled test marketing, and the brand died.[97]

Following in the wake of Uptown's demise, critics challenged another firm, the Heileman Brewing Co., for introducing its PowerMaster brand of high-alcohol malt liquor targeted to inner-city residents—a brand containing 5.9 percent alcohol compared to the 4.5 percent content of other malt liquors.[98] Brewing industry supporters claimed that rather than being exploitative, PowerMaster and other malt liquors merely meet the demand among African-Americans and Hispanics, who buy the vast majority of malt liquor.[99] Nonetheless, the U.S. Treasury Department's Bureau of Alcohol, Tobacco, and

Firearms (ATF), which regulates the brewing and liquor industries, would not permit the Heileman Brewing Co. to market malt liquor under the name PowerMaster. The ATF arrived at this decision because it considered the name PowerMaster as promoting the brand's alcoholic content in violation of federal regulations.

www.atf.treas.gov

Other Instances of Targeting. The controversy over targeting is not restricted to children and minorities. The R. J. Reynolds tobacco company was again widely criticized when preparing to introduce its Dakota brand of cigarettes to young, economically downscale women. RJR's plans to test market Dakota in Houston were squashed when critics created an outcry in response to what was considered to be exploitative marketing.[100]

www.discus.health.org

Another area of criticism was the practice of breweries promoting their brands to college students during spring breaks at beaches. Responding to the criticism, beer companies have largely curtailed sponsoring spring break events.[101] More recently, however, the Distilled Spirits Council of the United States voted in 1996 to lift its voluntary ban on advertising "hard" liquor on television and radio. This self-imposed ban had been in effect for nearly a half century, and during this period no liquor ads were aired in the United States. Although there remains only a small amount of liquor advertising on TV and radio, and most of that has been placed on limited market cable programs, critics nonetheless have raised a variety of concerns regarding the resumption of liquor advertising over America's airways. The primary concern is that liquor advertising will encourage young consumers to hold more favorable views toward hard liquor and to increase consumption. Only time will tell whether these concerns are well-founded.[102]

Is Targeting Unethical or Just Good Marketing? The foregoing discussion points out instances where advertising and other forms of marketing communications are criticized because they are directed at specific target markets. Proponents of targeting practices respond to such criticisms by arguing that targeting benefits rather than harms consumers. Targeting, according to the proponents' view, tailors products to consumers and provides them with products best suited to their particular needs and wants. Not to be targeted, according to the advocates' position, is to have to choose a product that better accommodates someone else's needs.[103]

The issue is, of course, more complicated than whether targeting is good or bad. Sophisticated marketing practitioners and students fully accept the strategic justification for target marketing. There is the possibility, however, that some instances of targeting are concerned not with fulfilling consumers' needs and wants but rather with exploiting consumer vulnerabilities—so that the target marketer gains while society loses. Herein rests the ethical issue that cannot be dismissed with a mere claim that targeting is sound marketing. You should discuss the ethical ramifications of targeting in class and benefit from the views of your professor and fellow students.[104]

Ethical Issues in Advertising

The role of advertising in society has been debated for centuries. Advertising is claimed by its practitioners to be largely responsible for the good things in life and is criticized by its opponents as the cause of much of what is bad. Following is a succinct yet elegant account of why advertising is so fiercely criticized:

> *As the voice of technology, [advertising] is associated with many dissatisfactions of the industrial state. As the voice of mass culture it invites intellectuals' attack. And as the most visible form of capitalism it has served as nothing less than a lightning-rod for social criticism.[105]*

A variety of ethical criticisms have been leveled against advertising. Because the issues are complex, it is impossible in this chapter to treat each criticism in great detail. The purpose of this discussion is merely to introduce the basic issues.[106] The following criticisms are illustrative rather than exhaustive.

Advertising Is Untruthful and Deceptive.

The majority (roughly two-thirds) of American consumers think that advertising often is untruthful.[107] As mentioned earlier in the regulatory discussion, deception occurs when an advertisement falsely represents a product and consumers believe the false representation to be true. Is advertising deceptive according to this general definition? Some advertising *is* deceptive—the existence of governmental regulation and industry self-regulation attests to this fact. It would be naive, however, to assume that most advertising is deceptive. The advertising industry is not much different from other institutions in a pluralistic society. Lying, cheating, and outright fraud are universal, occurring at the highest levels of government and in the most basic human relationships (for example, unfaithful husbands and wives). Advertising is not without sin, but neither does it hold a monopoly on it.

Advertising Is Manipulative.

The criticism of manipulation asserts that advertising has the power to influence people to behave atypically, or do things they would not do if they were not exposed to advertising. Taken to the extreme, this suggests that advertising is capable of moving people against their own free wills. What psychological principles would account for such power to manipulate? As will be discussed in detail later in Chapter 11, the evidence certainly does not support subliminal advertising, which has provided advertising critics with the most provocative explanation underlying the claim of manipulation.

In general, the contention that advertising manipulates is without substance. Undeniably, advertising does attempt to persuade consumers to purchase particular products and brands. But persuasion and manipulation are not the same thing. Persuasion is a legitimate form of human interaction that all individuals and institutions perform.

Advertising Is Offensive and in Bad Taste.

Advertising critics contend that many advertisements are insulting to human intelligence, vulgar, and generally offensive to the tastes of many consumers. Several grounds exist for this criticism: (1) inane commercials of the "ring around the collar" genre, (2) sexual explicitness or innuendo in all forms of advertisements, (3) television commercials that advertise unpleasant products (hemorrhoid treatments, diarrhea products, etc.), and (4) repetitive use of the same advertisements ad infinitum, ad nauseam.

Undeniably, much advertising is disgusting and offensive. Yet, the same can be said for all forms of mass media presentations. For example, many network television programs verge on the idiotic, and theater movies are often filled with inordinate amounts of sex and violence. This certainly is not to excuse advertising for its excesses, but a balanced view demands that critical evaluations of advertising be conducted in a broader context of popular culture and other forms of mass media presentations.

Advertising Creates and Perpetuates Stereotypes.

The contention at the root of this criticism is that advertising tends to portray certain groups in very narrow and predictable fashion: African-Americans and other minorities were historically portrayed disproportionately in working-class roles rather than in the full range of positions they actually occupy; women too were stereotyped as homemakers or as sex objects; and senior citizens sometimes were, and still are, characterized as feeble and forgetful people.

Advertising has been guilty of perpetuating stereotypes. However, it would be unfair to blame advertising for creating these stereotypes, which, in fact, are perpetuated by all elements in society. Spreading the blame does not make advertising any better, but it does show that advertising is probably not any worse than the rest of society.

People Buy Things They Do Not Really Need.

A frequently cited criticism suggests that advertising causes people to buy items or services that they do not need. This criticism is a value-laden judgment. Do you need another pair of shoes? Do you need a college education? Who is to say what you or anyone else needs? Advertising most assuredly influences consumer tastes and encourages people to undertake purchases they may not otherwise make, but is this unethical?

Advertising Plays upon People's Fears and Insecurities. Some advertisements appeal to the negative consequences of not buying a product—rejection by members of the opposite sex, bad breath, failure to have provided for the family if one should die without proper insurance coverage, and so on. (For an example of an advertisement appealing to insecurity, see Figure 3.5.) Some advertisers must certainly plead guilty to this charge. However, once again, advertising possesses no monopoly on this transgression.

An Appeal to Insecurity

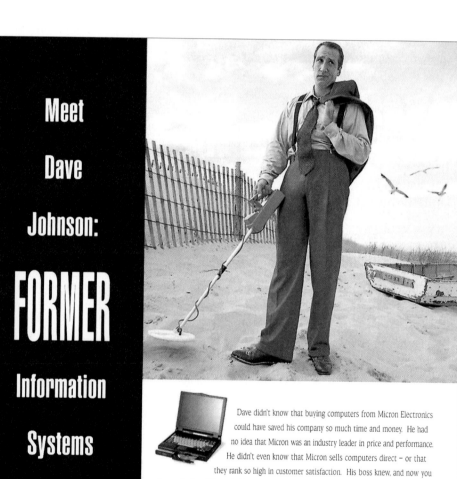

Meet Dave Johnson:

FORMER

Information Systems Manager

Dave didn't know that buying computers from Micron Electronics could have saved his company so much time and money. He had no idea that Micron was an industry leader in price and performance. He didn't even know that Micron sells computers direct – or that they rank so high in customer satisfaction. His boss knew, and now you know. See how Micron desktops, servers and portables can provide your company with a complete network solution. More information on our TransPort XKE high-performance portable computers, now with voice recognition software, is just a call or a click away.

MICRON™ TRANSPORT® XKE
Intel 200MHz or 233MHz Pentium® Processor with MMX™ technology
Dragon Systems' NaturallySpeaking Personal voice recognition software
20X CD-ROM drive with AutoPlay™ technology
13.3" XGA display
Microsoft® Windows® 95
Microsoft Office 97 Small Business Edition
Starting at:
$4,199
Bus lease $133/mo.

888-209-8037
www.micronpc.com

Now You Know.™

In sum, the institution of advertising is certainly not free of criticism. What should be clear, however, is that advertising reflects the rest of society, and any indictment of advertising probably applies to society at large. It is doubtful that advertisers and other marketing practitioners are any less ethical in their practices than are other elements of society.[108] Responsible advertising practitioners, knowing that their practice is particularly susceptible to criticism, have a vested interest in producing legitimate advertisements. The following *IMC Focus* provides illustrations of two company's commitment to ethical advertising and marketing communications.

www.dhc.com

Ethical Issues in Public Relations

Publicity, the one aspect of public relations that relates primarily to marketing communications, involves disseminating positive information about a company and its products and handling negative publicity. Because publicity is like advertising in that both are forms of mass communications, many of the same ethical issues apply and need not be repeated. The one distinct aspect worthy of separate discussion is the matter of *negative publicity*.

There have been a number of celebrated cases in recent years in which companies have been widely criticized for marketing unsafe products. The way firms confront negative publicity has important strategic as well as ethical ramifications. (Discussion of strategic issues is delayed until Chapter 19.) The primary ethical issue concerns whether firms confess to product shortcomings and acknowledge problems or, instead, attempt to cover up the problems.

www.johnsonandjohnson.com

Consider, for example, the case of Tylenol capsules. Seven people in the Chicago area died in 1982 after ingesting cyanide-poisoned capsules. The publicity people at Johnson & Johnson (J&J), the makers of Tylenol, could have claimed that the problem was not of their making but rather was the fault of an isolated lunatic in Chicago. Such a position would have led J&J to continue selling Tylenol in all markets except Chicago. However, because it was unknown at the time whether the capsules had been poisoned at the factory or by a deranged person in retail outlets, the cautionary and ethical response was to remove Tylenol from store shelves throughout the country. This is precisely what J & J chose to do in taking the moral high road. It turned out that the problem was restricted to Chicago, but the ethics of the situation required caution to prevent the possibility of widespread deaths around the country.

Ethical Issues in Personal Selling and Telemarketing

The possibility for unethical behavior is probably greater in personal selling, including telemarketing, than any other aspect of marketing communications. This is because much of personal selling occurs on a one-on-one basis in the privacy of a customer's office or via the telephone. It is easier under such circumstances, compared to the case of mass communications, to make unsubstantiated claims and undeliverable promises. In other words, a salesperson is in a position to say things that are not subjected to public scrutiny.

As an example, imagine that you are at an automobile dealership and have decided to purchase a new car. After committing to your car of choice, the salesperson convinces you to pay for the additional application of a paint sealant and rustproofing to protect your new car—so he argues—against the harsh weather. Believing that the salesperson has your best interests at heart, you spend several hundred dollars for these add-ons. It is only later that you learn that many experts, including engineers at General Motors, caution that these add-ons are both unnecessary and overpriced.[109] Has the salesperson been unethical, or is he just doing his job?

IMC FOCUS: TWO ILLUSTRATIONS OF EXEMPLARY ETHICS STATEMENTS

An Extract from Caterpillar Corp.'s Code of Worldwide Business Conduct

"The company's most valuable asset is a reputation for integrity. If that becomes tarnished, customers, investors, suppliers, employees, and those who sell our products and services will seek affiliation with other, more attractive companies. We intend to hold to a single high standard of integrity everywhere. We will keep our word. We won't promise more than we can reasonably expect to deliver; nor will we make commitments we don't intend to keep. In our advertising and other public communications, we will avoid not only untruths, but also exaggeration and overstatement."

An Extract from Dayton Hudson Corp.'s General Policy on Advertising

"We are an honest-dealing business. No deceptions. No shortcuts. No gray areas. Being honest is not only right, it's good business. The trust of our customers is one of our greatest assets. That trust must be reinforced and preserved by our advertising practices. The basis of our advertising is providing clear and accurate information that our customers need to make their buying decisions."

Source: Patrick E. Murphy, *80 Exemplary Ethics Statements* (Notre Dame, IN: University of Notre Dame Press, 1998), 42, 65.

Each person's moral fiber is the primary determinant of how truthful she or he is behind a customer's closed doors or when delivering a sales pitch by telephone. Companies' penalty and reward structures also have some effect on salespeople's ethical conduct, but it is most often a personal matter.[110]

Ethical Issues in Packaging

Four aspects of packaging involve ethical issues: (1) label information, (2) packaging graphics, (3) packaging safety, and (4) environmental implications of packaging.[111]

Label information on packages can mislead consumers by providing exaggerated information or by unethically suggesting that a product contains more of desired attributes (for instance, nutrition) or less of undesired attributes (such as cholesterol or fat) than is actually the case. Packaging graphics are unethical when the picture on a package is not a true representation of product contents (like when a children's toy is made to appear much bigger on the package than it actually is). Another case of unethical behavior is when a store brand is packaged so that it looks virtually identical to a well-known national brand. *Unsafe packaging* problems are particularly acute with dangerous products that are unsafe for children and the package is not tamper-proof. *Environmental issues* in packaging are typified by the discussion of Hefty trash bags earlier in the chapter. Packaging information is misleading and unethical when it suggests environmental benefits that cannot be delivered.

In a study of packaging ethics, completed questionnaires were received from nearly 600 packaging practitioners representing businesses throughout the United States. Respondents shared their opinions regarding various aspects of packaging ethics.[112] Some of the survey highlights include the following practices that practitioners consider unethical: (1) using the word *light* in reference to a product's texture and not its caloric content; (2) packaging store brands to mimic national-brand packages; (3) being aware of safety hazards with a package's design but doing nothing to remedy the problems; (4) charging more per unit for a large package than a small package; and (5) not attending to environmental problems when packaging materials are available for doing so. The following *IMC Focus* describes a packaging decision by Bristol-Myers Squibb that represents a wonderful illustration of smart marketing and *ethical* packaging.

www.bms.com

IMC FOCUS: EXCEDRIN: TWO PACKAGES, SAME PRODUCT

Excedrin is the fourth-highest selling analgesic brand in the United States. This brand for decades has been used by consumers to fight headaches and muscle pains. In 1998 Excedrin Extra Strength was approved by the Food and Drug Administration (FDA) as the first over-the-counter treatment for mild to moderate migraine relief.

This decision by the FDA posed a wonderful opportunity for Bristol-Myers Squibb, the makers of Excedrin, but it also created a major marketing and packaging challenge. The FDA required Bristol-Myers to develop a new package that would alert migraine sufferers to the distinct warnings about the use of Excedrin, warnings different than those already on the packaging and designed primarily for users suffering regular headaches and muscle pains.

Working with officials at the FDA, the marketing people at Bristol-Myers decided to develop two packages, one for the "regular" Excedrin and the other for the new "Excedrin Migraine." But in point of fact, Excedrin and Excedrin Migraine are the *identical product*. It may have been possible to mislead consumers into thinking that Excedrin Migraine was a dramatic new product formulation, but Bristol-Myers decided to be upfront with consumers and take a responsible course of action. Advertising messages for the "new" Excedrin Migraine were straightforward in stating, "Next to Excedrin, there's a new package—same medicine—called Excedrin Migraine." You might wonder why a company would want two separate packages for the identical product. The reason is straightforward: Having separate packages enables more overall shelf space, and sales revenue is correlated with the amount of retail space that a brand is able to garner.

Source: Adapted from Yumiko Ono, "Upfront Ad for Excedrin Touts Different Packages for Same Item," *The Wall Street Journal Interactive Edition*, April 9, 1998.

Ethical Issues in Sales Promotions

Ethical considerations are involved with all facets of sales promotions, including manufacturer promotions directed at the trade (wholesalers and retailers) and to consumers. As will be detailed later in Chapter 17, retailers have recently gained considerable bargaining power vis-à-vis manufacturers. One outcome of this power shift has been retailers' increased demands for deals by manufacturers. *Slotting allowances* illustrate the power shift. This practice (thoroughly discussed in Chapter 17) requires manufacturers to pay retailers a per-store fee for their willingness to handle a new stock unit from the manufacturer. Critics of slotting allowances contend this practice represents a form of bribery and is therefore unethical.

Consumer-oriented sales promotions (including practices such as coupons, premium offers, rebates, sweepstakes, and contests) are unethical when the sales promoter offers consumers a reward for their behavior that is never delivered—for example, failing to mail a free premium object or to provide a rebate check. Sweepstakes and contests are potentially unethical when consumers think their odds of winning are much greater than they actually are.[113]

As a matter of balance, it is important to note that marketers are not the only ones guilty of unethical behavior in the area of sales promotions. Consumers also engage in untoward activities such as submitting coupons at the point of checkout for items not purchased or submitting phony rebate claims. One woman, who eventually was sentenced to 20 years in prison and $1 million in fines, obtained in excess of $700,000 from manufacturers by submitting thousands of rebate claims using fictitious names and addresses. She paid people to steal proofs-of-purchase from products in stores or from discarded packages in store trash receptacles and then mailed these in for rebates.[114]

Fostering Ethical Marketing Communications

As alluded to throughout the preceding discussion, primary responsibility for ethical behavior resides within each of us when placed in any of the various marketing communicator roles. We can take the easy route and do those things that are most expedient, or we can pursue the moral high road and treat customers in the same honest fashion that we expect to be treated. In large part it is a matter of our own personal integrity. *Integrity* is perhaps the pivotal concept of human nature.[115] Although difficult to precisely define, integrity involves avoiding deceiving others or behaving purely in an expedient fashion.[116] Hence, marketing communications itself is not ethical or unethical—it is the degree of integrity exhibited by communications practitioners that determine whether their behavior is ethical or unethical.

Placing the entire burden on individuals is perhaps unfair, because how we behave as individuals is largely a function of the organizational culture in which we operate. Businesses can foster ethical or unethical cultures by establishing *ethical core values* to guide marketing communications behavior. Two core values that would go a long way toward enhancing ethical behavior are these: (1) treat customers with respect, concern, and honesty—the way you would want to be treated or the way you would want your family treated; and (2) treat the environment as though it were your own property.[117]

Firms can encourage ethical marketing communications behavior in their employees by suggesting that employees apply each of the following tests when faced with an ethical predicament: (1) act in a way that you would want others to act toward you *(the Golden Rule);* (2) take only actions that would be viewed as proper by an objective panel of your professional colleagues *(the professional ethic);* and (3) always ask, "Would I feel comfortable explaining this action on television to the general public?" *(the TV test).*[118]

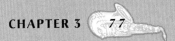

S ummary

This chapter examines a variety of issues related to the physical environment, the regulation of marketing communications, and ethical behavior. In the first section, environmental, or *green*, marketing is described, and implications for marketing communications are discussed. Marketing communicators have responded to society's environmental interests by developing more environmentally friendly packaging and undertaking other communications initiatives. Recommendations provided to marketing communicators for making appropriate environmental claims are to: (1) make the claims specific; (2) have claims reflect current disposal options; (3) make the claims substantive; and (4) make supportable claims.

The second major section looks at the regulation of marketing communications activities. The regulatory environment is described with respect to both government regulation and industry self-regulation. The Federal Trade Commission's role is explained in terms of its regulation of deception, unfair practices, and information regulation. Specific topics covered include the advertising substantiation program, trade regulation rules, and the corrective advertising program. Self-regulation by the Council of Better Business Bureaus' National Advertising Division (NAD) and National Advertising Review Board (NARB) are discussed, emphasizing the process by which the NAD/NARB regulates national advertising.

The final section examines ethical marketing communications behavior. The ethics of each of the following marketing communications activities are discussed: the targeting of marketing communications efforts, advertising, public relations, personal selling and telemarketing, packaging communications, and sales promotions. A concluding discussion examines how firms can facilitate ethical behavior.

D iscussion Questions

1. The opening vignette concluded by asking you to think about the following questions: If you were the manager in this situation, would you introduce your own brand of degradable trash bag, or would you be willing to refrain from introducing a falsely claimed degradable trash bag and, consequently, to suffer lost sales to unethical competitors? Identify marketing alternatives other than *introduce versus don't introduce* that might have been available to the Mobil Chemical Company in the Hefty trash bag situation.

2. Some consumers are more concerned about the physical environment than others. Provide a specific profile of what in your opinion would be the socioeconomic and psychographic (i.e., lifestyle) characteristics of the "environmentally concerned" consumer.

3. The chapter quoted a Harvard Business School professor as claiming that green products would be to the 1990s what *lite* products were to the 1980s. Can you offer any reasons why this assertion may be overstated?

4. Some nutritionists claim that Gatorade is neither helpful nor harmful to children. If indeed Gatorade for children is little more than an inert substance, is it unethical in your opinion for that company to advertise the product actively?

5. What is your opinion regarding the ethics of product placements in movies targeted at children? Identify the arguments on both sides of the issue, and then present your personal position.

6. What is your opinion regarding the ethics of advertorials in magazines targeted to teenagers? Identify the arguments on both sides of the issue, and then present your personal position.

7. Marketers of malt liquor claim they focus on inner cities because African-Americans and Hispanics are the heavy consumers of this product. Is this practice ethical? Identify the arguments on both sides of the issue, and then present your personal position.

8. Advertising is often accused of various ethical violations. The criticisms of advertising mentioned in the chapter include claims that advertising is deceptive, manipulative, offensive, and

plays on people's insecurities and fears. Provide evidence from your own personal experience to support any of these claims.

9. What is the distinction between a deceptive and an unfair business practice?

10. In your opinion, should a firm be required to have substantiating evidence (test results or other data) for an advertising claim prior to making the claim? Why or why not? Give examples of products where it is likely that substantiating evidence probably was not available prior to the advertiser making a claim. (Hint: health and dietary supplements.)

11. Give examples of advertising claims that, if found false, probably would be considered material and those that probably would be evaluated as immaterial.

12. What is your opinion of the defense Kraft used in claiming that calcium is an immaterial product attribute?

13. In theory, corrective advertising represents a potentially valuable device for regulating deceptive advertising. In practice, however, corrective advertising must perform a very delicate balancing act by being strong enough without being too forceful. Explain the nature of this dilemma.

14. In the text discussion on salesperson ethics, the issue was raised about a hypothetical car salesman's efforts to encourage new car buyers to have their automobiles rustproofed. Has the salesperson been unethical, or is he just doing his job?

15. As noted in the text, the Distilled Spirits Council of the United States voted in 1996 to lift its voluntary ban on advertising "hard" liquor on television and radio, a self-imposed ban that had been in effect for nearly a half century. In your opinion, what are the arguments on both sides of the issue regarding the removal of this ban? If you were an executive employed by the Distilled Spirits Council, would you have urged a return to the airways? Is this return to advertising distilled spirits via electronic media unethical or, alternatively, is it a matter of a gutsy business decision by the Distilled Spirits Council that was long overdue?

16. What is your view regarding Anheuser-Busch's use of humorous TV commercials that portray animated characters Frank, Louie, and a remaining cast of lizard and frog characters? Is this form of advertising simply a marvelous creative execution, or is it insidious in its potential to encourage kids to like the concept of drinking beer, and perhaps Budweiser in particular?

Internet Exercises

1. Green Seal is the independent, nonprofit organization dedicated to protecting the environment by promoting the manufacture and sale of environmentally preferable consumer products. Most notably, this organization devises rigorous standards for various product categories and contracts with Underwriter's Laboratories to test products. Products that meet the standards are awarded "Green Seals." Visit Green Seal at http://solstice.crest.org/environment/GreenSeal/index.html and address the following questions:
   a. Using the Green Seal Web site as a source, describe the process manufacturers must undertake in order to get evaluated for a "Green Seal" of approval.
   b. Within product categories, four specific classes of requirements must be met (see http://solstice.crest.org/environment/GreenSeal/standards.html). List and describe these requirements using a particular product class of interest to you.
   c. Looking at the current list of product categories evaluated by Green Seal, select the three that you believe manufacturers are most likely to see a return on their "investment" (annual certification fee plus product modification costs) in a "Green Seal." Justify your selections in terms of consumers' likelihood of awareness, affinity, and action based on the presence or knowledge of a Green Seal.

2. Parents and public policy makers have become increasingly concerned about the solicitation of information from children over the Internet. In particular, many brands which depend on children for revenues have been accused of setting up sites that require children to provide personal information about themselves and/or their families in order to "earn" a promotional gift or gain

access to on-line games. In response, the Better Business Bureau's *Children's Advertising Review Unit (CARU)* included an Internet-specific section in its regulatory guidelines for advertising to children. Access these guidelines at http://www.bbb.org/advertising/caruguid.html#media and respond to the following questions:

a.   Identify a brand which you consider to be a "kids" product and visit its Web site. Name the brand and provide its Web site address. Does the Web site appear to be targeting children? If so, how? If not, why do you think this "kids" brand has a Web site designed for non-kids?

b.   Is the manufacturer of the brand compliant with CARU's guidelines? Provide specific details to support your conclusion.

c.   Do you think self-regulation will work for on-line advertising aimed at children? Why or why not? What are the alternatives to self-regulation?

3.   Imagine two identically sized shampoo bottles. The first one bears the promotional label "25% Free," whereas the second one bears the promotional label "25% More Free." Which bottle contains more free product? Confused? Most people probably are. The answer is that the first bottle has more free product since its percentage is derived from the larger bonus size. The second bottle calculates its percentage from the smaller regular size. With this marketplace phenomenon in mind, pursue the following issues utilizing the Federal Trade Commission's Web site (www.ftc.gov) as a source:

a.   Is the % Free execution covered under current FTC guidelines regarding pricing or labeling? If so, cite the guideline and describe how this execution is in violation.

b.   Do you consider the % Free execution to be deceptive? Why or why not? If so, state the FTC's general guidelines as discussed in the text (or as available on the FTC Web site) and establish deception for this particular case. If you do not consider it to be deceptive, defend your point of view against the charge that it is deceptive.

C hapter Three Endnotes

1.   Quoted at p. 12 in Jennifer Lawrence, "Mobil," *Advertising Age,* January 29, 1991, 12–13. Many of the facts in the following description are based on this article.

2.   Jennifer Lawrence and Christy Fisher, "Mobil, States Settle Degradability Suits," *Advertising Age,* July 1, 1991, 4.

3.   The interrelation between ethical issues and regulation is discussed by George M. Zinkhan, "Advertising Ethics: Emerging Methods and Trends," *Journal of Advertising* 23 (September 1994), 1–4.

4.   William L. Rathje, "Once and Future Landfills," *National Geographic,* May 1991, 117–134.

5.   Jacquelyn Ottman, "Ignore Environmental Issues At Your Own Peril," *Brandweek,* May 9, 1994, 17; and "How to Deal with Tougher Customers," *Fortune,* December 3, 1990, 38–48.

6.   Stefan Bechtel, *Keeping Your Company Green* (Emmaus, Penn.: Rodale Press, 1990), 1.

7.   The concept of green marketing has various dimensions beyond this general explanation. For a review of the nuances, see William E. Kilbourne, "Green Advertising: Salvation or Oxymoron?" *Journal of Advertising* 24 (summer 1995), 7–20.

8.   Alecia Swasy, "Color Us Green," *The Wall Street Journal,* March 22, 1991, B4.

9.   Penelope Wang, "Going for the Green," *Money,* September 1991, 98.

10.   Bob Garfield, "Beware: Green Overkill," *Advertising Age,* January 29, 1991, 26.

11.   James Dulley, "Cordless, Rechargeable Lawn Mowers Cut Grass, Pollution," *The State,* July 24, 1994, Home section, 17.

12.   Stuart L. Hart, "Strategies for a Sustainable World," *Harvard Business Review,* January–February 1997, 66–76.

13.   Michael E. Porter and Claas van der Linde, "Green and Competitive: Ending the Stalemate," *Harvard Business Review,* September–October 1995, 120–134.

14.   This classification is based on Subhabrata Banerjee, Charles S. Gulas, and Easwar Iyer, "Shades of Green: A Multidimensional Analysis of Environmental Advertising," *Journal of Advertising* 24 (summer 1995), 21–32.

15.   *Ibid.* For additional discussion of the types of environmental advertising claims and their frequency of use, see Les Carlson, Stephen J. Grove, and Norman Kangun, "A Content Analysis of Environmental Advertising Claims: A Matrix Method Approach," *Journal of Advertising* 22 (September 1993), 27–39.

16.   "L'eggs to Scrap Plastic 'Egg' Package," *Marketing News,* August 19, 1991, 20.

17.   Jacquelyn Ottman, "Product Take-Back Is a New Marketing Tool," *Marketing News,* January 20, 1997, 8.

18.   Bruce Ingersoll, "Got Milk?" *The Wall Street Journal Interactive Edition,* July 18, 1997.

19.   For review of a report on the short-filling problem, go to the worldwide web at the following URL: http://www.ftc.gov/opa/9707/milk.htm.

20. Jacquelyn Ottman, "Consider Eco-Labels," *Marketing News,* November 18, 1996, 14.

21. Ibid.

22. See Jeffery D. Zbar, "Wildlife Takes Center Stage As Cause-Related Marketing Becomes a $250 Million Show for Companies," *Advertising Age,* June 28, 1993, S1–2.

23. Douglas B. Leeds, "A New Shade of Green," *Promo,* September 1993, 108.

24. Published in the *Federal Register* on August 13, 1992 (57 FR 36,363 (1992)). These guides also available on-line at http://www.ftc.gov/bcp/grnrule/green02.htm. See also, Jason W. Gray-Lee, Debra L. Scammon, and Robert N. Mayer, "Review of Legal Standards for Environmental Marketing Claims," *Journal of Public Policy & Marketing* 13 (spring 1994), 155–159.

25. These updated guidelines are available on-line at http://www.ftc.gov/opa/9610/grnguid2.htm

26. Julie Vergeront (principal author), *The Green Report: Findings and Preliminary Recommendations for Responsible Environmental Advertising* (St. Paul: Minnesota Attorney General's Office, November 1990). The following discussion is a summary of the recommendations in *The Green Report.*

27. The Federal Trade Commission's guidelines are similar in stating that environmental claims should: (1) be substantiated; (2) be clear as to whether any assumed environmental advantage applies to the product, the package, or both; (3) avoid being trivial; and (4) if comparisons are made, make clear the basis for the comparisons.

28. Bechtel, *Keeping Your Company Green.*

29. Pam Scholder Ellen, Joshua Lyle Wiener, and Cathy Cobb-Walgren, "The Role of Perceived Consumer Effectiveness in Motivating Environmentally Conscious Behaviors," *Journal of Public Policy & Marketing* 10 (fall 1991), 102–117.

30. L. J. Shrum, John A. McCarty, and Tina M. Lowrey, "Buyer Characteristics of the Green Consumer and Their Implications for Advertising Strategy," *Journal of Advertising* 24 (summer 1995), 71–82.

31. Ibid.

32. Michael B. Mazis, Richard Staelin, Howard Beales, and Steven Salop, "A Framework for Evaluating Consumer Information Regulation," *Journal of Marketing* 45 (winter 1981), 11–21.

33. The following discussion is adapted from Mazis, et al.

34. *Alcohol Beverage Labeling Act of 1988,* S.R.2047.

35. A thorough review of research pertaining to warning labels is provided by David W. Stewart and Ingrid M. Martin, "Intended and Unintended Consequences of Warning Messages: A Review and Synthesis of Empirical Research," *Journal of Public Policy & Marketing* 13 (spring 1994), 1–19.

36. Janet R. Hankin, James J. Sloan, and Robert J. Sokol, "The Modest Impact of the Alcohol Beverage Warning Label on Drinking During Pregnancy Among a Sample of African-American Women," *Journal of Public Policy & Marketing* 17 (spring 1998), 61–69.

37. For a fascinating history of advertising and regulatory activity in the aspirin/analgesic industry, see Charles C. Mann and Mark L. Plummer, "The Big Headache," *The Atlantic Monthly,* October 1988, 39–57.

38. Ross D. Petty, "Advertising Law in the United States and European Union," *Journal of Public Policy & Marketing* 16 (spring 1997), 2–13.

39. J. Edward Russo, Barbara L. Metcalf, and Debra Stephens, "Identifying Misleading Advertising," *Journal of Consumer Research* 8 (September 1981), 120. For a thorough review of advertising deception, see also David M. Gardner and Nancy H. Leonard, "Research in Deceptive and Corrective Advertising: Progress to Date and Impact on Public Policy," *Current Issues & Research in Advertising* 12 (1990), 275–309.

40. Public copy of letter dated October 14, 1983, from FTC Chairman James C. Miller III to Senator Bob Packwood, Chairman of Senate Committee on Commerce, Science, and Transportation.

41. For a more thorough discussion of these elements and other matters surrounding FTC deception policy, see Gary T. Ford and John E. Calfee, "Recent Developments in FTC Policy on Deception," *Journal of Marketing* 50 (July 1986), 82–103.

42. Chairman Miller's letter to Senator Packwood.

43. The advertising campaign ran in 1984 and 1985, but the FTC did not file a complaint until 1987.

44. These points of fact are offered by Jacob Jacoby and George J. Szybillo, "Consumer Research in FTC Versus Kraft (1991): A Case of Heads We Win, Tails You Lose?" *Journal of Public Policy & Marketing* 14 (spring 1995), 2.

45. Ruling of the Federal Trade Commission, Docket No. 9208, January 30, 1991.

46. Jef I. Richards and Ivan L. Preston, "Proving and Disproving Materiality of Deceptive Advertising Claims," *Journal of Public Policy & Marketing* 11 (fall 1992), 45–56; Jacoby and Szybillo, "Consumer Research in FTC Versus Kraft," 1–14; David W. Stewart, "Deception, Materiality, and Survey Research: Some Lessons from Kraft," *Journal of Public Policy & Marketing* 14 (spring 1995), 15–28; Seymour Sudman "When Experts Disagree: Comments on the Articles by Jacoby and Szybillo and Stewart," *Journal of Public Policy & Marketing* 14 (spring 1995), 29–34.

47. For further discussion, see Dorothy Cohen, "Unfairness in Advertising Revisited," *Journal of Marketing* 46 (winter 1982), 74.

48. Dorothy Cohen, "The Concept of Unfairness as It Relates to Advertising Legislation," *Journal of Marketing* 38 (July 1974), 8.

49. Cohen, "Unfairness in Advertising Revisited," 8.

50. The nature of the dispute is clearly played out in alternative positions presented by the president of the American Advertising Federation and the legal affairs director for the Center for Science in the Public Interest. See alternative positions argued by Wally Snyder (AAF) and Bruce A. Silverglade (CSPI) in "Does FTC Have an

'Unfair' Future?" *Advertising Age,* March 28, 1994, 20.

51. Christy Fisher, "How Congress Broke Unfair Ad Impasse," *Advertising Age,* August 22, 1994, 34.

52. For further discussion, see Dorothy Cohen, "The FTC's Advertising Substantiation Program," *Journal of Marketing* 44 (winter 1980), 26– 35; and Debra L. Scammon and Richard J. Semenik, "The FTC's 'Reasonable Basis' for Substantiation of Advertising: Expanded Standards and Implications," *Journal of Advertising* 12, no. 1 (1983), 4–11.

53. Cited in the "Legal Developments in Marketing" section of the *Journal of Marketing* 52 (January 1988), 131.

54. Cohen, "Unfairness in Advertising Revisited," 74.

55. Ibid., 75.

56. 50.Ivan L. Preston, "A Review of the Literature on Advertising Regulation," in *Current Issues and Research in Advertising 1983,* ed. James H. Leigh and Claude R. Martin, (Ann Arbor: University of Michigan, 1983), 14.

57. The following discussion borrows heavily from the excellent review article by William L. Wilkie, Dennis L. McNeill, and Michael B. Mazis, "Marketing's 'Scarlet Letter': The Theory and Practice of Corrective Advertising," *Journal of Marketing* 48 (spring 1984), 11. See also Gardner and Leonard, "Research in Deceptive and Corrective Advertising."

58. See ibid. for review.

59. Kenneth L. Bernhardt, Thomas C. Kinnear, and Michael B. Mazis, "A Field Study of Corrective Advertising Effectiveness," *Journal of Public Policy & Marketing* 5 (1986), 146–162. This article is "must reading" for anyone interested in learning more about corrective advertising.

60. Steven W. Colford, "FDA Getting Tougher," *Advertising Age,* April 29, 1991, 1, 53; David Kiley, "FDA Seizes Citrus Hill," *Adweek's Marketing Week,* April 29, 1991, 6–7.

61. Paul Harris, "Will the FTC Finally Wake Up?" *Sales and Marketing Management,* January 1988, 57–59.

62. David Kiley, "Candid Camera: Volvo and the Art of Deception," *Adweek's Marketing Week,* November 12, 1990, 4–5; Raymond Serafin and Gary Levin, "Ad Industry Suffers Crushing Blow," *Advertising Age,* November 12, 1990, 1, 76–77; Raymond Serafin and Jennifer Lawrence, "Four More Volvo Ads Scrutinized," *Advertising Age,* November 26, 1990, 4.

63. Betsy Spethmann, "When the Smoke Clears," *Promo,* July 1998, 33–35, 114.

64. Ernest Beck and Julie Wolf, "European Parliament Passes Extensive Ban on Tobacco Ads," *The Wall Street Journal Interactive Edition,* May 14, 1998.

65. See Andrew J. Strenio, Jr., "The FTC in 1988: Phoenix Or Finis?" *Journal of Public Policy & Marketing* 7 (1988), 21–39.

66. Jean J. Boddewyn, "Advertising Self-Regulation: True Purpose and Limits," *Journal of Advertising* 18, no. 2 (1989), 19–27.

67. Jean J. Boddewyn, "Advertising Self-Regulation: Private Government and Agent of Public Policy," *Journal of Public Policy & Marketing* 4 (1985), 129–141.

68. Priscilla A. LaBarbera, "Analyzing and Advancing the State of the Art of Advertising Self-Regulation," *Journal of Advertising* 9, no. 4 (1980), 27.

69. *Ibid.,* 28. See also Martha Rogers, "Advertising Self-Regulation in the 1980s: A Review," *Current Issues & Research in Advertising* 13 (1991), 369–392.

70. For a thorough discussion, see Eric J. Zanot, "Unseen but Effective Advertising Regulation: The Clearance Process," *Journal of Advertising* 14, no. 4 (1985), 44–51, 59.

71. *Statement of Organization and Procedures of the National Advertising Review Board* (Washington, D.C.: National Advertising Review Board, June 19, 1980).

72. Eric J. Zanot, "A Review of Eight Years of NARB Casework: Guidelines and Parameters of Deceptive Advertising," *Journal of Advertising* 9, no. 4 (1980), 20.

73. *Statement of Organization and Procedures.*

74. "NAD Tackles 103 Cases in '88," *Advertising Age,* January 16, 1989, 49.

75. The following discussion borrows heavily from the thorough presentation by Gary M. Armstrong and Julie L. Ozanne, "An Evaluation of NAD/NARB Purpose and Performance," *Journal of Advertising* 12, no. 3 (1983), 19–23.

76. John McDonough, "25 Years of Self-Regulation," *Advertising Age,* December 2, 1996, c1–c2.

77. LaBarbera, "Analyzing and Advancing the State of the Art of Advertising Self-Regulation."

78. Armstrong and Ozanne, "An Evaluation of NAD/NARB Purpose and Performance," 25.

79. See Avery M. Abernethy, "Advertising Clearance Practices of Radio Stations: A Model of Advertising Self-Regulation," *Journal of Advertising* 22 (September 1993), 15–26; Herbert J. Rotfeld, Avery M. Abernethy, and Patrick R. Parsons, "Self-Regulation and Television Advertising," *Journal of Advertising* 19 (December 1990), 18–26.

80. O. C. Ferrell and Larry G. Gresham, "A Contingency Framework for Understanding Ethical Decision Making in Marketing," *Journal of Marketing* 49 (summer 1985), 87–96.

81. For a provocative discussion of the dysfunctional social effects resulting from implementations of the marketing concept, see Steven H. Star, "Marketing and Its Discontents," *Harvard Business Review* 67 (November/December 1989), 148–154.

82. A provocative and informative discourse on the issue of consumer vulnerability is presented in N. Craig Smith and Elizabeth Cooper-Martin, "Ethics and Target Marketing: The Role of Product Harm and Consumer Vulnerability," *Journal of Marketing* 61 (July 1997), 1–20.

83. Laura Bird, "Gatorade for Kids," *Adweek's Marketing Week,* July 15, 1991, 4–5.

84. "Selling to Children," *Consumer Reports* (August 1990), 518–519.

85. Ibid.

86. Ibid.

87. Eben Shapiro, "Molson Ice Ads Raise Hackles of Regulators," *The Wall Steeet Journal,* February 25, 1994, B1, B10.

88. Guideline 8 in the Industry Advertising Code. Published in an undated pamphlet distributed by the Department of Consumer Awareness and Education, Anheuser-Busch, Inc., St. Louis, Mo.

89. Brett Shevack, "Ban Joe Camel Campaign? That's Unfair," *Advertising Age,* September 20, 1993, 28.

90. Yumiko Ono and Bruce Ingersoll, "RJR Banishes Joe Camel, Adds Some Sexy Smokers," *The Wall Street Journal Interactive Edition,* July 11, 1997.

91. For reviews of this research and alternative perspectives, see Jean J. Boddewyn, "Where Should Articles on the Link between Tobacco Advertising and Consumption Be Published?" *Journal of Advertising* 22 (December 1993), 105–107; Lawrence C. Soley, "Smoke-filled Rooms and Research: A Response to Jean J. Boddewyn's Commentary," *Journal of Advertising* 22 (December 1993), 108–109; Richard W. Pollay, "Pertinent Research and Impertinent Opinions: Our Contributions to the Cigarette Advertising Policy Debate," Journal of Advertising 22 (December 1993), 110–117; Claude R. Martin, Jr., "Ethical Advertising Research Standards: Three Case Studies," *Journal of Advertising* 23 (September 1994), 17–29; and Claude R. Martin, Jr., "Pollay's Pertinent and Impertinent Opinions: 'Good' versus 'Bad' Research," *Journal of Advertising* 23 (March 1994), 117–122.

92. Rekha Balu, "Anheuser-Busch Amphibian Ads Called Cold-Blooded by Doctors," *The Wall Street Journal Interactive Edition,* April 10, 1998.

93. "Fighting Ads in the Inner City," *Newsweek,* February 5, 1990, 46.

94. For further reading about these and other controversial cases, see Smith and Cooper-Martin, "Ethics and Target Marketing."

95. Dan Koeppel, "Insensitivity to a Market's Concerns," *Adweek's Marketing Week,* November 5, 1990, 25.

96. "A 'Black' Cigarette Goes Up in Smoke," *Newsweek,* January 29, 1990, 54.

97. "RJR Cancels Test of 'Black' Cigarette," *Marketing News,* February 19, 1990, 10.

98. Laura Bird, "An 'Uptown' Remake Called PowerMaster," *Adweek's Marketing Week,* July 1, 1991, 7.

99. "Fighting Ads in the Inner City."

100. For more discussion of this case, see Smith and Cooper-Martin, "Ethics and Target Marketing."

101. Jeffery D. Zbar, "Spring Break: Inflatable Beer Bottles Gone, but Other Marketers Move In," *Advertising Age,* April 1, 1991, 16.

102. For an interesting article on this issue, see Hae-Kyong Bang, "Analyzing the Impact of the Liquor Industry's Lifting of the Ban on Broadcast Advertising," *Journal of Public Policy & Marketing* 17 (spring 1998), 132–138.

103. See John E. Calfee, "'Targeting' the Problem: It Isn't Exploitation, It's Efficient Marketing," *Advertising Age,* July 22, 1991, 18.

104. For additional insight on the issue, see Smith and Cooper-Martin, "Ethics and Target Marketing."

105. Ronald Berman, "Advertising and Social Change," *Advertising Age,* April 30, 1980, 24.

106. The interested reader is encouraged to review the following three articles for an extremely thorough, insightful, and provocative debate over the social and ethical role of advertising in American society. Richard W. Pollay, "The Distorted Mirror: Reflections on the Unintended Consequences of Advertising," *Journal of Marketing* 50 (April 1986), 18–36; Morris B. Holbrook, "Mirror, Mirror on the Wall, What's Unfair in the Reflections of Advertising?" *Journal of Marketing* 51 (July 1987), 95–103; Richard W. Pollay, "On the Value of Reflections on the Values in 'The Distorted Mirror,'" *Journal of Marketing* (July 1987), 104–109. Professors Pollay and Holbrook present alternative views of whether advertising is a "mirror" that merely reflects societal attitudes and values or a "distorted mirror" that is responsible for unintended and undesirable social consequences.

107. John E. Calfee and Debra Jones Ringold, "The 70% Majority: Enduring Consumer Beliefs about Advertising," *Journal of Public Policy & Marketing* 13 (fall 1994), 228–238.

108. Stephen B. Castleberry, Warren French, and Barbara A. Carlin, "The Ethical Framework of Advertising and Marketing Research Practitioners: A Moral Development Perspective," *Journal of Advertising* 22 (June 1993), 39–46.

109. "The Eight Biggest Rip-Offs in America," *Money,* August 1995, 147.

110. Joseph A. Bellizzi and Robert E. Hite, "Supervising Unethical Salesforce Behavior," *Journal of Marketing* 53 (April 1989), 36–47.

111. These issues were identified by Paula Fitzgerald Bone and Robert J. Corey, "Ethical Dilemmas in Packaging: Beliefs of Packaging Professionals," unpublished working paper, West Virginia University Department of Marketing, 1991. The following discussion is guided by this paper. The authors identified a fifth ethical aspect of packaging (the relationship between a package and a product's price) that is not discussed here.

112. Ibid.

113. For an insightful discussion of sales promotion practices and related consumer psychology that result in exaggerated expectations of winning, see James C. Ward and Ronald Paul Hill, "Designing Effective Promotional Games: Opportunities and Problems," *Journal of Advertising* 20 (September 1991), 69–81.

114. Bob Gatty, "Atlanta Woman Guilty of Rebate Fraud," *Promo,* February 1994, 18.

115. Jeffrey P. Davidson, "The Elusive Nature of Integrity: People Know It When They See It, but Can't Explain It," *Marketing News,* November 7, 1986, 24.

116. Ibid.

117. Donald P. Robin and R. Eric Reidenbach, "Social Responsibility, Ethics, and Marketing Strategy: Closing the Gap between Concept and Application," *Journal of Marketing* 51 (January 1987), 44–58.

118. Based on Gene R. Laczniak and Patrick E. Murphy, "Fostering Ethical Marketing Decisions," *Journal of Business Ethics* 10 (1991), 259–271 (264).

PART

TWO

Part Two—Integrated Marketing Communications from the Customer's Perspective: Targeting, Communicating, and Persuading

Part Two builds a foundation for a better understanding of the nature and function of marketing communications by providing a practical and theoretical overview of its targets. Chapter 4 examines the demographic, geodemographic, and psychographic factors used in targeting marketing communications. Major emphasis is placed on the examination of important demographic developments such as (1) population statistics, (2) the changing age structure of the population, (3) the growth of the singles market, and (4) ethnic population developments. Psychographic targeting is discussed with emphasis on the VALS 2 classification scheme. The final section describes geodemographic targeting and overviews the Claritas PRIZM service that is in wide use for this purpose.

Chapter 5 provides further foundation for targeting activities by examining both the process and fundamentals of communication, and reviewing fundamentals of consumer behavior. Behavioral foundations of marketing communications are approached from two perspectives: first, the logical thinking person as embodied in the consumer information processing approach, and second, the hedonic-experiential perspective of the pleasure-seeking, feeling person. Particular detail is devoted to describing the marketing communication activities necessary to promote consumer attention, comprehension, and learning of marketing messages.

Chapter 6 continues the overview of buyer behavior and the role of targeting communication efforts by discussing the central concepts of attitudes and persuasion. These topics are important because marketing communications represents an organized effort to influence and persuade customers to make choices that are compatible with the communicator's interests while simultaneously satisfying the customer's needs. A major section examines practical marketing communication efforts to influence the consumer's motivation, opportunity, and ability to process marketing messages.

Demographic, Psychographic, and Geodemographic Targets of Marketing Communications

CHAPTER OBJECTIVES

After studying this chapter, you should be able to:

1. Discuss the importance of targeting marketing communications to specific consumer groups.

2. Understand the role of demographics, psychographics, and geodemographics in targeting consumer groups.

3. Appreciate major demographic developments such as changes in age structure of the United States population and ethnic population growth.

4. Describe the nature of psychographic targeting and the VALS 2 system.

5. Explain the meaning of geodemographics and understand the role for this form of targeting.

Opening Vignette: Targeting the Extreme Generation

Downhill biking, mountain boarding, street lugeing, sky surfing, river running, skateboarding, and snowboarding are just some of the "alternative" sports that have a growing following among the extreme generation, or "boarding culture." Appealing mostly to males but attracting females as well, these extreme sports are the fashion for many young people who span the Gen X and Gen Y age groups (described later in the chapter).

Surveys show that in 1998 there were about 6.5 million skateboarders, 4.5 million snowboarders, 2 million wakeboarders (people who do water stunts on boards pulled by powerboats), and 1 million all-terrain boarders (fearless individuals who use 3-1/2-foot-long boards with 6-inch inner-tube-like wheels to ride down off-season ski slopes and other hills). By 2000 it is expected that the number of skateboarders and snowboarders will have doubled over their 1998 levels and that the number of wakeboarders will have increased six-fold. Early in the 21st century there will be millions of Americans who compete in some form of alternative sport.

The business opportunities that arise from this boarding culture are considerable for board manufacturers, shoe marketers, and apparel makers (not to mention hospitals). Marketing communicators have responded to this growing trend by featuring sky surfers, streetboarders, and other alternative-sport risk takers in their advertisements; by sponsoring extreme sporting events; and by establishing endorsement relationships with little-known (to the general public) but highly respected celebrities (among the alternative sports crowd). For example, Vans Inc., a California-based maker of alternative sport shoes, hired

Lee Dancie, who is a star in the sport of street luge. Vans shoes along with brands from its competitors (Airwalk, Etnies, DC, etc.) are known as "shredders," "riders," or "skaters" by the youth who participate in various boarding sports. Whereas sneaker sales in the United States are growing only at the rate of 2 percent per year, footwear geared to boarders is achieving annual gains of 20 to 50 percent.

The major sneaker marketers such as Nike and Reebok entered the alternative footwear business somewhat belatedly, but their massive marketing resources make them a force with whom the smaller companies such as Vans will have to contend. Perhaps the major companies will not be able to steal away consumers from Vans and other smaller companies because their traditional-sports images may be fundamentally incompatible with the risk-seeking, alternative-pursuing, independence-aspiring lifestyle that attracts the boarding culture to the extreme sports in which they participate.

Sources: Adapted primarily from Joseph Pereira, "Going to Extremes: Board-Riding Youths Take Sneaker Maker on Fast Ride Uphill," *The Wall Street Journal Interactive Edition*, April 16, 1998; and Myra Stark, "The Extreme Generation," *Brandweek*, September 1, 1997, 19.

OVERVIEW

*T*he opening vignette portrays one aspect of a changing marketplace, namely, the increasing trend toward alternative and extreme forms of athletic participation. The practice of marketing communications is vastly more complicated than it used to be, due in large part to significant changes in the demographic and lifestyle fabric of American society.

The Importance of Targeting Consumer Groups

This chapter's purpose is to expand the discussion of *targeting* that was introduced in Chapter 2. At that point it was emphasized that the targeting of customers and *micromarketing* efforts allow marketing communicators to deliver more precisely their messages and prevent wasted coverage to people falling outside the targeted market. Meaningful and profitable market segmentation efforts typically require that segment members share demographic and lifestyle characteristics. Hence, selection of target segments is a critical first step toward effective and efficient marketing communications. In this chapter we will focus on three sets of consumer characteristics that singularly or in combination influence what people consume and how they respond to marketing communications: *demographic, psychographic,* and *geodemographic* characteristics.

Demographic variables include characteristics such as age, income, and ethnicity. By monitoring demographic shifts, marketers are better able to: (1) identify and select market segments, (2) forecast product sales, and (3) select media for reaching target customers.[1] Aspects of consumers' lifestyles—their activities, interests, and opinions—represent their **psychographic** characteristics. Purchasing patterns often are influenced more by our lifestyles than our demographic backgrounds. **Geodemographics** include a combination of demographic and lifestyle characteristics of consumers within geographic clusters such as ZIP-code areas and neighborhoods. Knowing that consumers who share similar demographic and psychographic profiles tend to reside in geographic proximity to one another offers marketing communicators, particularly direct mailers, an especially effective and efficient means for reaching consumers who are most receptive to marketing messages. Marketing research firms have developed classification, or clustering, systems that identify relatively distinct geodemographic segments of consumers. (These will be discussed in a concluding section.)

Separate sections are devoted to all three groups of "-graphics" (demographics, psychographics, and geodemographics), but major emphasis in this chapter is devoted to demographic characteristics insofar as the demographic landscape is particularly dynamic. Three major demographic topics are examined: (1) the age structure of the U.S. population (e.g., the baby boom and bust); (2) the changing American household (e.g., the increase in the number of single-person households); and (3) ethnic population developments. It will be helpful to place these topics in context by first examining population growth and geographic distribution of the U.S. population.

POPULATION GROWTH AND GEOGRAPHIC DISPERSION

The total population of human beings on the earth will be slightly over 6 billion people in 2000.[2] The world population is expected to grow to approximately 8 billion people by the year 2025. Correspondingly, the U.S. population will be around 275 million people by 2000 and will reach approximately 335 million by 2025.[3] Perhaps the most interesting aspect of the U.S. population is the shifts that have taken place in its *geographical distribution.* Historically, the population was concentrated in the industrial Northeast and Midwest, but by the year 2000 a solid majority of Americans will live in the South or West. Population increases have been modest in the Northeast and Midwest but explosive in the South and West; in fact, projections indicate that 70 percent of foreseeable U.S. population growth will take place in these two regions.[4]

THE CHANGING AGE STRUCTURE

One of the most dramatic features of the American population is its *relentless aging.* The median age of Americans was 28 in 1970, 30 in 1980, and 33 in 1990; it rose to its present level of nearly 36 in 2000 and is expected to increase to 38 by 2025.[5] Table 4.1 presents

TABLE 4.1	**Population of the United States by Age Group, as of 1998**	
	AGE	POPULATION SIZE
Children and Teens		
	Under 5	18,983,000
	5–9	19,928,000
	10–14	19,268,000
	15–19	19,535,000
		77,714,000
Young Adults		
	20–24	17,768,000
	25–29	18,545,000
	30–34	20,014,000
		56,327,000
Middle Agers		
	35–39	22,602,000
	40–44	21,962,000
	45–49	18,978,000
	50–54	15,907,000
		79,449,000
Olders		
	55–59	12,587,000
	60–64	10,332,000
		22,919,000
Elders		
	65–69	9,530,000
	70–74	8,782,000
		18,312,000
The Very Old		
	75–79	7,227,000
	80–84	4,739,000
	85+	4,045,000
		16,011,000
Total U.S. Population		270,732,000

Source: http//www.census.gov/population/estimates/nation/intfile2-1.txt

1998 population figures distributed by age group. Following sections will examine major age groupings of the U.S. population and the implications these hold for marketing communications efforts. Discussion starts with the so-called baby-boom generation and also includes separate sections devoted to middle-aged and mature consumers, children and teenagers, and the much-touted Generation X and Y groups.

The Baby-Boom Generation

The changing age structure in the United States is attributable in large part to what demographers term the **baby boom**—the birth of 75 million Americans between 1946 and 1964. This population-boom period followed the end of World War II (in 1945) and persisted for nearly two decades. Using the year 2000 as a point of reference, the oldest baby boomer will be 54 years old at the start of the new millennium, whereas the youngest person to be classified in this category will be 36. The effects of the baby boom (and subsequent bust) have been manifested in the following major population developments:

1. The original baby boomers created a *mini baby boom* as they reached childbearing age. As shown in Table 4.1, there were in 1998 nearly 78 million children and teenagers in the United States.

2. Due to a low birthrate from the mid-1960s through the 1970s (prior to the time when most baby boomers were of child-bearing age), relatively few babies were born. There now are fewer young adults (ages 20–34) than was the case in prior generations.

3. The number of middle agers (people aged 35 to 54) has increased dramatically. This maturing of the baby boomers has probably been the most significant demographic development faced by marketers during the decade of the 1990s.

The preceding developments hold considerable promise for many marketers but have caused problems for others. Marketers who appealed to the teenage and young-adult markets during the 1970s and 1980s suffered in the 1990s as the sizes of these markets declined. The blue jeans industry is a case in point. Blue jeans sales reached a peak in 1981, when an estimated 600 million pairs were sold in the United States alone.[6] Since then, sales have declined, due in large part to the baby-boom generation's changing tastes and preferences as they have matured and turned to other types of clothing. This explains why Levi Strauss, for example, introduced Dockers apparel, a line aimed at aging baby boomers. Not many years ago Levi's corporate revenues were obtained primarily through sales of jeans; now Dockers represent a substantial portion of sales and profits.

On the positive side, the baby-boom generation offers tremendous potential for many marketers. Research shows that baby boomers are an attractive market for high-tech products, quality durable goods, and investments such as insurance, real estate, and securities.[7] Figure 4.1 illustrates the types of financial products that are actively marketed to more affluent baby boomers, in this case the Kaufmann Mutual Fund. The appliance maker, Whirlpool, appeals to affluent boomers who want the very best appliance quality with a line of items named Whirlpool Gold.[8]

Moreover, just because baby boomers are aging does not necessarily mean they are getting psychologically old or are significantly altering their consumption patterns from a younger age. Rather, there are indications that baby boomers are retaining many of their more youthful consumption habits and, in a sense, are taking longer to grow up or are unwilling to change.[9] For example, the rather dramatic increase in hair-color product purchases by baby boomers reflects this tendency for boomers to prolong youth and to gravitate toward products that support their youth obsession.[10] Manufacturers of health-care items, exercise machines, and food products (such as Progresso soup; see Figure 4.2) have actively appealed to baby boomers' passion for remaining in youthful shape. Because boomers represent the "epicenter of society," advertisers will march in lockstep with this group and continue to reflect their characteristics and appeal to their purchase interests and needs.[11] For example, in an appeal to baby boomers as well as to younger women, Anheuser-Busch has developed a beer, named Catalina Blonde, that is low in calories (86) and alcohol content (2.5 percent).[12] The athletic footwear maker, New Balance Inc., caters to baby boomers by offering shoes that come in wider widths than just the medium-size width offered by mainstream companies like Nike.

An important point of clarification is needed before concluding this section and moving on to the next age group. In particular, it is tempting to think of baby boomers as a monolithic group of people who think alike, act the same, and purchase identical products. Such an impression would be erroneous. Baby boomers do *not* represent a true market segment. That is, just because millions of Americans share one commonality (all were born between 1946 and 1964), this does not mean they are virtual clones of one another. Within this age cohort, there are distinct differences among people with respect to age, income,

ethnicity, lifestyle choices, and product/brand preferences. Hence, although it is convenient to speak of baby boomers as a single group, it would be mistaken to conclude that they represent an actionable market segment. The advice presented in Chapter 2 is worth repeating: Meaningful and profitable market segmentation efforts typically require that segment members share various demographic, lifestyle, and possibly geographical characteristics; broad groupings such as all baby boomers are much too crude to satisfy the characteristics of a meaningful market segment. In sum, baby boomers are a significant age cohort and, en masse, represent a powerful economic force, but they do not constitute a specific market segment.

Advertising to Health-
Conscious Baby Boomers

Middle-Aged and Mature Consumers

With an aging U.S. population, the 1990s was the decade of marketing to middle-aged baby boomers and mature consumers. Although somewhat arbitrary, we can think of middle age as starting at age *35* and ending at age *54* at which point maturity is reached. Actually, there is some disagreement over the dividing point between middle age and maturity.[13] Sometimes a 65-and-over classification is used, because age 65 normally marks retirement. In this text we will use the U.S. Bureau of the Census's designation, which classifies **mature people** as those who are *55 and older.* As of 1998 there were roughly 79.4 million Americans between the middle ages of 35 and 54 (see Table 4.1). Because most of these individuals constitute the previously described baby boomers born between 1946 and 1964, no further commentary about middle-aged consumers is needed at this point.

Turning to mature consumers, in the year 2000 there will be approximately 59 million U.S. citizens aged 55 or older, representing about 21 percent of the total U.S. population. Historically, many marketers have ignored the mature market or have treated this group in unflattering ways by focusing on "repair kit products" such as dentures, laxatives, and arthritis remedies.[14] Not only are mature consumers numerous, they also are wealthier and more willing to spend than ever before. Mature Americans control nearly 70 percent of the net worth of all U.S. households. People aged 65 and older are particularly well-off and have the highest *discretionary income* (i.e., income unburdened by fixed expenses) and the most assets of any age group.[15] The number of people in this 65+ age category is huge, totaling in excess of 35 million by 2000, which will represent approximately 13 percent of the total population.

A variety of implications accompany marketing communications efforts that are directed at the mature market. In advertising aimed at this group, it is advisable to portray them as active, vital, busy, forward-looking, and concerned with looking attractive and being romantic.[16] The advertisement in Figure 4.3 (for Kellogg's cereal) represents a good application of this advice. Many college students (and certainly this professor) would be happy to emulate the physical condition of the man featured in the Kellogg advertisement. Advertisers now generally appeal to the mature market in a flattering fashion as typified by the use of attractive, middle-aged models to represent clothing, cosmetics, and other products that had been the exclusive advertising domain of youthful models.

A Positive Appeal to Mature Consumers

It again is important to point out that just because mature consumers share a single commonality (i.e., aged 55 or older), they by no means represent a homogeneous market segment. Indeed, the Bureau of the Census divides people aged 55 and older into four distinct age segments: 55 to 64 *(olders);* 65 to 74 *(elders);* 75 to 84 *(the very old);* and 85 and over. On the basis of age alone, consumers in each of these groups differ—sometimes dramatically—in terms of lifestyles, interest in the marketplace, reasons for buying, and spending ability. Moreover, it is important to realize that age alone is not the best indicator of how an individual lives or what role consumption plays in that lifestyle. In fact, research has identified four groups of mature consumers based on a combination of health and self-image characteristics. Based on a national mail survey of over 1,000 people aged 55 and older, respondents were classified into four groups: Healthy Hermits, 38 percent; Ailing Outgoers, 34 percent; Frail Recluses, 15 percent; and Healthy Indulgers, 13 percent.[17] Brief descriptions follow.

Healthy Hermits, though in good health, are psychologically withdrawn from society. They represent a good market for various services such as tax and legal advice, financial services, home entertainment, and do-it-yourself products. Direct mail and print advertising are the best media for reaching this group. *Ailing Outgoers* are diametrically opposite to Healthy Hermits. Though in poor health, they are socially active, health-conscious, and interested in learning to do new things. Home health care, dietary products, planned retirement communities, and entertainment services are some of the products and services most desired by this group. They can be reached via sales promotions and through select mass media tailored to their positive self-image and active, social lifestyle. *Frail Recluses* are withdrawn socially and are in poor health. Various health and medical products and services, home entertainment, and domestic-assistance services (e.g., lawn care) can be successfully marketed to this group via mass-media advertising appeals. *Healthy Indulgers* are in good health, are relatively wealthy, and are socially active. They are independent and want the most out of life. Mature consumers in this group represent a good market for financial services, leisure/travel entertainment, clothes, luxury goods, and high-tech products and services. They are accessible via in-store promotions, direct mail, and specialized print media.

Children and Teenagers

At the other end of the age spectrum are children and teenagers. The group of young Americans aged 19 and younger has fallen dramatically from 40 percent of the population in 1965 (during the baby-boom heyday) to a projected total of approximately 29 percent of the population in 2000. Yet, this is still a substantial group, with 80 million occupants in 2000. (See Table 4.1 for specific breakouts by age group—i.e., under 5, 5 to 9, 10 to 14, and 15 to 19.)

Marketers typically refer to children aged 4 through 12 as "kids" to distinguish this cohort from toddlers and teenagers. It is estimated that children in this broad grouping either directly spend or influence the spending of billions of dollars worth of purchases each year. Aggregate spending by children aged 4–12 or in behalf of this age group roughly doubled every decade in the 1960s, 1970s, and 1980s. Spending in the 1990s tripled. Spending by or for this age group in 1997 alone totaled more than $24 billion.[18]

Children of *preschool age* represent a substantial cohort that has grown substantially in recent years. More babies were born in the United States in 1990 (4.2 million) than at any time since the baby boom peak of 4.3 million babies born in 1957.[19] Products and services appealing to the family and home have increased to cater to this mini baby boom. The appeal to the parents of preschoolers goes beyond these products, however, and includes fashion items as illustrated by the ads for Baby Gap in Figure 4.4 and for Mickey & Co. shown in Figure 4.5.

Elementary-school-age children, aged 6 to 11, directly influence product purchases and indirectly influence what their parents buy.[20] These children are influential in their parents' choice of clothing and toys and even the brand choice of products such as toothpaste.[21]

FIGURE
4.4

An Appeal to Parents
of Preschoolers

FIGURE
4.5

Another Appeal to Parents
of Preschoolers

Advertising and other forms of marketing communications aimed at young children, or their families, have increased substantially in recent years. The advertisement for the Compaq Presario (Figure 4.6) typifies such an appeal. Marketing communicators have encroached on classrooms at all grade levels with promotional messages sometimes disguised as learning tools—often to the chagrin of parents and educators, who have questioned the ethics of these practices.

Teenagers, who total in the United States approximately 27 million 13- to 19-yearolds, have tremendous earning power and considerable influence in making personal and household purchases.[22] This group, which marketing consultants have dubbed *Generation Y* (in contrast to the generation that preceded it, *Generation X*) is an age cohort of substantial buying influence.[23] Indeed, one study estimated that American teenagers spent on average $84 a week and $141 billion total in 1998.[24] Teenagers have purchasing influence

An Appeal to Parents of Elementary-School-Age Children

TABLE 4.2

Teen Shopping Behaviors

BEHAVIOR	TOTAL	MALE	FEMALE
Ask parents before buying	17.4%	14.4%	20.5%
Always looks for manufacturer's name	20.7	19.9	21.5
Careful of how much is spent	33.3	27.9	38.9
Doesn't buy unknown brands	21.2	25.1	17.0
Buys what friends approve of	15.8	18.3	13.2
Reads labels before buying	19.6	13.6	25.9
Shops for specials	33.4	24.3	42.9
Changes brands often	15.9	15.3	16.5
Settles for another brand	21.5	18.5	24.6
Buys on spur of the moment	25.3	23.7	26.9
Believes advertising gives true picture	15.1	14.4	15.7
Keeps up with style changes	24.5	19.9	27.1
First to try new product	13.9	11.6	16.2

Source: Simmons Market Research Bureau, cited in *Advertising Age,* July 18, 1994, 3.

and power far greater than ever before, which, again, accounts for the growth of marketing communications programs that are aimed at this group. Table 4.2 presents an interesting portrait of teenager buying styles and differences between males and females. These results, which are based on a national survey of 2,800 teenagers, reveal that teenage girls are more cautious, careful, and price-conscious shoppers than are boys.

Teenagers are noted for being highly conformist, narcissistic, and fickle consumers.[25] These characteristics pose great opportunities and challenges for marketing communicators. An accepted product can become a huge success when the teenage bandwagon selects a brand as a personal mark of the in-crowd. However, today's accepted product or brand can easily become tomorrow's passé item. The Levi brand of jeans, for example, has lost some of its prior appeal to teenagers, who seem to favor, at least for the time being, brands such as Tommy Hilfiger, Paris Blues, Mudd, and JNCO.[26] The same can be said for the Nike brand, which as of the late 1990s was not nearly the hot commodity it had been throughout the 1980s until the mid-1990s.

Generation X

No age cohort has received more ink and air time in recent years than has *Generation X,* the group that includes most college students. Scholarly treatment of this cohort identifies it as Americans born between 1961 and 1981.[27] However, to avoid overlap with the baby-boomer generation (1946–1964), we will define this age cohort as people born between *1965* and *1981.* Hence, as of 2000, Generation X will constitute over 50 million Americans in the age category 19 to 35. Because Gen Xers were born immediately after the baby boom, which ended in 1964, this group also is referred to as *baby busters* and *twentysomethings*—the latter label reflecting the fact that most people in this cohort are in their 20s. The labels do not end there, however; indeed, Generation X has been subjected to more clichés than any group in history, most of which are deprecatory: slackers, cynics, whiners, grunge kids, and hopeless. As is typically the case when a group is stereotyped, these labels characterize only a subset of Gen Xers and are much too general to begin to capture the complexity of this group and the differences among its occupants.[28] One study has classified Gen Xers into four groups based on their attitudinal profiles: Yup & Comers, Bystanders, Playboys, and Drifters. (See the following *IMC Focus.*)

IMC FOCUS: SUBSEG-MENTS OF GEN XERS

Yup & Comers: This group, which has the highest levels of education and income, accounts for 28 percent of Gen Xers. They tend to focus on intangible rewards rather than material wealth, and are confident about themselves and their futures. This clearly is not a group of people who fit the stereotypical labels attached to Generation X.

Bystanders: Representing 37 percent of Gen Xers, bystanders consist predominantly of female African-Americans and Hispanics. Although their disposable income is relatively low, this subsegment of Gen Xers has a flair for fashion and loves to shop.

Playboys: This predominantly white and male group accounts for 19 percent of the Generation X cohort. Playboys adhere to a "pleasure before duty" lifestyle, and are self-absorbed, fun-loving, and impulsive.

Drifters: This smallest subset, representing 16 percent of Gen Xers, is closest to the Generation X stereotype. They are frustrated with their lives, are among the least educated, seek security and status, and choose brands that offer a sense of belonging and self-esteem.

Source: A survey from Yankelovich Partners, cited in "Don't Mislabel Gen X," *Brandweek,* May 15, 1995, 32, 34.

Contrary to their stereotypical portrayal, Gen Xers are not monolithic. The generalizations are incorrect and generally unfair.[29] As a group they are no more cynical, disenfranchised, or inclined to whine than most people. Marketing communications directed to twentysomethings must use appeals targeted to specific subgroups such as Yup & Comers rather than stereotypes that do not adequately reach any subsegment. Because many Gen Xers have disdain for the stereotypical yuppies of the 1980s, advertising that eschews raw materialism and appeals instead to people who love their work, with or without earning large financial rewards, has a good prospect of striking a responsive chord.[30]

Once again it is important to emphasize that the Gen X age cohort, however it is labeled, is not a unified group in terms of demographics or lifestyle preferences and should not be misconstrued as a single market segment. Indeed, the four groupings described in the *IMC Focus* are themselves somewhat of a simplification but do offer some refinement of the general differences among the over 50 million Americans who have been simplistically collapsed into a single category.

A few comments about the college "market" segment of Generation X will conclude this section. It is estimated that college students possess $30 billion in spending power, which makes you and your peers attractive to many marketers.[31] A recent study of college students reveals that students watch considerably less television than their parents (15 hours versus 35-plus hours per week), are unlikely to read a daily newspaper other than a college paper, and listen to radio more than they view TV (16 hours versus 15 hours).[32] Programs that distribute samples on campus are especially effective in reaching students and encouraging trial and repeat purchase behavior. Needless to say, the Internet is an increasingly important medium for reaching college students with product news and brand messages.

THE EVER-CHANGING AMERICAN HOUSEHOLD

A household represents an independent housing entity, either rental property (e.g., an apartment) or owned property (a condominium or house). As of 2000, there will be approximately *103 million* households in the United States, which means, with a U.S. population of approximately 275 million in 2000, that there are, on average, around 2.67 people per household.[33] The traditional American household—as portrayed stereotypically in baby-boomer television programs such as *Leave It to Beaver* and *Happy Days*—used to consist of the mother, father, and two or three children. Millions of such households still exist in the United States, but the percentage of these types of families is declining as the result of dramatic societal changes.

American households have been altered forever by the combined effects of changes in marriage patterns, increased numbers of working women, and rising divorce rates. Households are growing in number, shrinking in size, and changing in character. The number of new households has grown twice as fast as the population, while household size has declined.

In 1950, *families* (married couples with or without children) constituted 90 percent of all households, whereas in 2000 fewer than 70 percent of all households are family units. *Nonfamily households*—that is, a person living alone or with one or more unrelated persons—are experiencing a huge increase and will constitute nearly one-third of all households in 2000.

The changing composition of the American household has tremendous implications for marketing communicators, especially advertisers. Advertising will have to reflect the widening range of living situations that exist. This is particularly true in the case of households with a single occupant. *Singles* represent a large and ever-growing group. America's more than 30 million households of single men and single women hold in their grasp nearly $500 billion in purchasing power![34] It is little wonder that they are a highly coveted group of consumers.

Many advertisers make special appeals to the buying interests and needs of singles, appealing in food ads, for example, to such needs as ease and speed of preparation, maintenance simplicity, and small serving sizes. Reaching singles requires special media-selection efforts because singles: (1) tend not to be big prime-time television viewers but are skewed instead toward the late-fringe hours (after 11 p.m.); (2) are disproportionately more likely than the rest of the population to view cable television; and (3) are disproportionately heavy magazine readers.

ETHNIC POPULATION DEVELOPMENTS

America has always been a melting pot, but it became even more so in recent decades—especially the 1970s, the "decade of the immigrant." The numbers of immigrants admitted to the United States in the 1970s surpassed any year since 1924.[35] On top of this, nearly 10 million people, mostly Latin Americans and Asians, immigrated to the United States during the 1980s.[36] The largest ethnic groups in the United States are African-Americans and Hispanic-Americans, both of which are experiencing rapid growth. By the early 21st century, ethnic minorities will represent one of three people in the United States. In recognition of the growing role of ethnic groups, the following sections examine population developments and marketing communications implications for African-, Hispanic-, and Asian-Americans.

A few background statistics will be helpful to set the stage for these discussions. First, as of 2000, the population of approximately 275 million Americans will be distributed in roughly the following fashion:[37]

White, not Hispanic	72 percent
Black, not Hispanic	12 percent
Hispanic, of any race	11 percent
Asian and Pacific Islanders	4 percent
American Indians, Eskimos, and Aleut	1 percent

Non-Hispanic whites' share of the U.S. population is projected to decline from 72 percent to 68 percent of the total population by the year 2010.[38] The implication is obvious: Marketers and marketing communicators need to do a better job in developing products, marketing programs, and marketing communications strategies that are designed to meet the unique needs of ethnic groups. Ethnicity plays an important role in directing consumer behavior.[39] As a case in point, Table 4.3 reflects differences in ethnic groups' ownership of electronic products.

	TABLE 4.3	Ethnic Groups' Ownership of Consumer Electronic Products	
PRODUCT	AFRICAN-AMERICANS	HISPANIC-AMERICANS	ASIAN-AMERICANS
VCR	73.5%	73.1%	89.4%
Camera	67.6	58.7	89.4
Microwave	66.8	62.3	79.1
Answering machine	47.2	27.5	50.0
Videogame system	42.3	39.8	41.8
Dishwasher	34.6	26.1	46.9
Compact disc player	31.9	26.7	45.5
Personal computer	19.8	9.6	30.5
Beeper	16.9	14.0	19.5
Camcorder	15.0	17.1	35.6
Cellular phone	10.3	6.7	24.3

Source: Market Segment Research; cited in Christy Fisher, "Poll: Hispanics Stick to Brands," *Advertising Age,* February 15, 1993, 6.

African-Americans

By the year 2000, non-Hispanic African-Americans will total approximately 33.6 million individuals, or 12.2 percent of the U.S. population. African-Americans are characterized more by their common heritage than by skin color. This heritage "is conditioned by an American beginning in slavery, a shared history of discrimination and suffering, confined housing opportunities, and denial of participation in many aspects of the majority culture."[40] Although many black Americans share a common culture in that they have similar values, beliefs, and distinguishable behaviors, African-Americans do *not* represent a single market any more than whites do.

Several factors explain why African-Americans are attractive consumers for many companies. Several notable reasons account for this: (1) The African-American population is growing faster than the rest of the population; (2) the average age of black Americans is considerably younger than that for whites; (3) African-Americans are geographically concentrated—approximately two-thirds of all blacks live in the top 15 U.S. markets; and (4) African-Americans tend to purchase prestige and name-brand products in greater proportion than do whites.

These impressive figures notwithstanding, many companies make no special efforts to communicate with African-Americans. This is foolish, for research indicates that blacks are responsive to advertisements placed in black-oriented media and to advertisements that make personalized appeals by using African-American models and advertising contexts with which blacks can identify, such as the advertisements in Figures 4.7 and 4.8. Major corporations are developing effective programs for communicating with black consumers. For example, Sears, Roebuck & Co. in 1997 launched its first ad campaign that specifically targeted African-Americans.[41] American automobile manufacturers are increasingly targeting messages to African-Americans.[42] To some extent, this is in response to foreign automobile manufacturers that have had particular success with younger African-American purchasers.

Although greater numbers of companies are realizing the importance of directing special marketing communications efforts to black consumers, it is important to emphasize that the black consumer market is *not* homogeneous. African-Americans exhibit different purchasing behaviors according to their lifestyles, values, and demographics. Therefore, companies must use different advertising media, distribution channels, advertising themes, and pricing strategies as they market to the various subsegments of the African-American population.

An Appeal to African-
Americans

Hispanic-Americans

The U.S. Hispanic population grew from only 4 million in 1950 to approximately 31.4 million in 2000 and now represents about 11 percent of the U.S. population. The U.S. Census Bureau predicts that Hispanics will comprise the largest ethnic group, with an estimated population of 41.1 million by 2010. The largest percentage of Hispanics are Mexican Americans, but large numbers of Puerto Rican Americans, Latin Americans from Central and South America, and Cuban Americans also reside in the U.S. Hispanic Americans are concentrated in five states: California, Texas, New York, Florida, and Illinois. It is estimated that by 2025 Hispanics will constitute 43 percent of the California population, 38 percent of Texas, and 24 percent of Florida.[43] Compared to the majority white population, Hispanic-Americans are younger, have larger families, tend to live more in urban clusters, and are becoming increasingly mobile as they begin to fan out from the five states in which they are concentrated.

Another Appeal to African-Americans

Marketing communicators have generally not devoted sufficient attention to Hispanic-Americans. For example, only about one-third of U.S. marketers target Hispanic consumers.[44] The frequency of Hispanics' appearances in television advertising is considerably less than their proportion of the population.[45] Marketing communicators need to be aware of several important points when attempting to reach Hispanic consumers:

1. First, a large percentage of Hispanic-Americans speak only Spanish or just enough English to get by; consequently, many Hispanics can be reached only via Spanish-language media. The following statistics indicate the percentages of Hispanics who speak Spanish and/or English at home[46]:

   - Only Spanish   21 percent
   - Mostly Spanish   28 percent
   - Spanish and English   15 percent
   - Mostly English   23 percent
   - Only English   13 percent

2. Because a large percentage of Hispanics use primarily Spanish media, it is important to target messages to some (but not all) Hispanics using this method.

3. It appears that a key in designing effective advertising for Hispanics is to advertise to them in their *dominant language*.[47] As the above percentages indicate, approximately half of Hispanic-Americans speak only or mostly Spanish at home.

Hence, reaching these consumers requires the use of Spanish. However, for Hispanics who are English-dominant, it makes greater sense to appeal to this group in English with advertising copy that reflects Hispanic values and culture.

4. Advertisers must be very careful in using the Spanish language. A number of snafus have been committed when advertisers translated their English campaigns to Spanish. For example, Frank Perdue, an East Coast marketer of chickens, had his famous slogan ("It takes a strong man to make a tender chicken") translated into Spanish so he could read it to Hispanics. Amusingly (probably to everyone except Frank), the Spanish version erroneously substituted "a sexually excited man" for "a strong man."[48]

The Spanish-speaking market represents a golden opportunity for businesses. Many companies consider Anglo advertising to be sufficient for reaching Hispanic consumers. Research has shown that television commercials fail to portray Hispanics as often as their numbers would suggest, and when they are portrayed in commercials it is typically in crowd scenes.[49] However, marketers such as Coca-Cola, Pepsi, and McDonald's, to name some of the more prominent, are now investing heavily in Hispanic-oriented advertising and sales promotions.

Asian-Americans

Asians in the United States include many nationalities: Chinese, Filipino, Japanese, Asian Indian, Korean, and Vietnamese among others. Asian-Americans have been heralded as the newest "hot ethnic market." The demographics support this optimistic outlook. As of the year 2000, over 10.5 million Asians (and Pacific Islanders, which are grouped with Asians by the Census Bureau) will live in the United States. By 2025 the U.S. Census Bureau has projected that nearly 21 million Asian and Pacific Islanders will reside in the United States. Asian-Americans on average are better educated, have higher incomes, and occupy more prestigious job positions than any other segment of American society—including whites. The median income for all U.S. households in 1997 was slightly over $37,000; in comparison, the median income for Asians and Pacific Islanders exceeded $45,000.[50]

It is important to emphasize that just as there is no single black or Hispanic market, there certainly does not exist a single Asian market. Moreover, unlike other ethnic groups, such as Hispanics, who share a similar language, Asian-Americans speak a variety of uniquely different languages. Between Asian nationalities there are considerable differences in product choices and brand preferences. Even within each nationality there are variations in terms of English-language skills and financial well-being. Indeed, it is estimated that over 50 percent of all Asian-Americans over the age of 5 do not speak English fluently, and many are "linguistically isolated" insofar as they live in homes where no adults speak any English.[51]

Some firms have been successful in marketing to specific Asian groups by customizing marketing programs specifically to their values and lifestyles rather than merely translating Anglo programs. For example, Metropolitan Life, an insurance company, conducted research that determined that Asian parents' top priority was their children's security and education. Metropolitan translated this finding into a successful campaign targeted to Korean and Chinese Americans. An advertisement portrayed a baby in a man's arms with the heading "You protect your baby. Who protects you?" This ad, along with the attraction of Asians to Metropolitan Life's sales force, resulted in a substantial increase in insurance sales to Asians.[52]

Reebok's sales among Asian-Americans increased substantially after that company used tennis star Michael Chang in its advertisements.[53] Mainstream marketers have greater media options than before for reaching Asian-Americans: Asian-language radio stations are now burgeoning in areas where large concentrations of Asians live, and direct marketing via the mail is an outstanding medium for micromarketing to specific groups of Asian-Americans.[54]

PSYCHOGRAPHIC TARGETING

The preceding discussion has described a variety of demographic factors and the implications they hold for marketing communicators. Demographics tell only part of the story, however. It is for this reason that marketing communicators also investigate consumers' attitudes, emotions, and lifestyles, which collectively are referred to as psychographic characteristics. When marketers first began to segment markets, they relied on the various demographic variables described earlier. More sophisticated marketers came to realize that demographics generally provide an insufficient basis for identifying and catering to differences in consumer demand. Starting in the 1970s, marketers turned to psychographic characteristics as a means of obtaining a richer understanding of marketplace dynamics and differences in consumer behavior.[55]

In general, psychographics represents a combination of consumers' *a*ctivities, *i*nterests, and *o*pinions. Marketing researchers customize measures of these **AIO** items to suit the needs of their particular product categories and brands. For example, a maker of a mountain board, snowboard, or other form of equipment intended for "alternative athletes" (see *Opening Vignette*) might design a study to determine the particular activities, interests, and opinions—collectively, lifestyles—that best characterize the users of its brand and the competition. This information would be useful in designing advertising messages and selecting appropriate media vehicles. Table 4.4 lists illustrative AIO components.

Numerous marketing research firms conduct psychographic studies for individual clients. These studies are typically customized to the client's specific product category. In other words, AIO items included in a psychographics study are selected in view of the unique characteristics of the product category. Consider, for example, a study investigating the psychographic characteristics of past purchasers of sports utility vehicles (SUVs). With reference to Table 4.4, such research undoubtedly would include questions that would relate to consumers' work, hobbies, entertainment, and sports activities along with items that would tap into family, recreation, and community activities and social, political, and cultural opinions. It likely would be found that purchasers of the Jeep Grand Cherokee and the Toyota Land Cruiser are similar demographically (i.e., nearly equivalent in terms of age and income) but different psychographically.

In addition to psychographic studies that are customized to a client's particular needs, available also are "off-the-shelf" services that develop psychographic profiles of people that are independent of any particular product or service. Perhaps the best known of these is the

TABLE 4.4

Illustrative AIO Components

ACTIVITIES	INTERESTS	OPINIONS
Work	Family	About Themselves
Hobbies	Home	Social issues
Social events	Job	Politics
Vacation	Community	Business
Entertainment	Recreation	Economics
Club membership	Fashion	Education
Community	Food	Products
Shopping	Media	Future
Sports	Achievement	Culture

Source: Del I. Hawkins, Roger J. Best, and Kenneth A. Coney, *Consumer Behavior: Implications for Marketing Strategy,* 6th ed. (Chicago: Irwin, 1995), 329.

Values and Lifestyles (VALS) classification model developed by the Stanford Research Institute, or SRI. In the most recent model, known as *VALS 2*, eight categories are identified based on a combination of demographic and lifestyle factors such as age, income, education, level of self-confidence, health, and interest in consumer issues. Figure 4.9 portrays the eight VALS 2 categories in a two-dimensional format. The horizontal dimension represents three self-orientations: (1) *principle-oriented* consumers who are guided by their views of how the world should be; (2) *status-oriented* consumers who are guided by the actions and opinions of others; and (3) *action-oriented* consumers who are guided by a desire for social or physical activity, variety, and risk taking. The vertical dimension is based on consumers' resources (income, education, intelligence, health, etc.), and ranges from minimal resources at the bottom to abundant resources at the top. The eight VALS 2 categories can be summarized as follows:[56]

Principle-oriented consumers are guided by their views of how the world should be:

1. *Fulfillers* (11 percent of population; median age 48) are mature, responsible, well-educated professionals who are well-informed about current affairs. They have high incomes but are practical, value-oriented consumers. Their leisure activities center on their homes. Fulfillers are a potential target market for manufacturers of

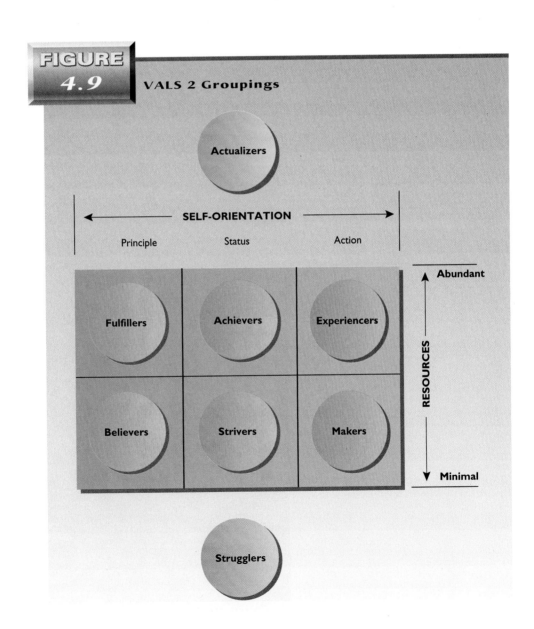

FIGURE 4.9   VALS 2 Groupings

health-conscious products featured as low in cholesterol, salt, sugar, and fat. The advertisement in Figure 4.10 represents an appropriate appeal to Fulfillers.

2. *Believers* (16 percent of population; median age 58) are conservative and predictable consumers who favor established brands and American-made products. They have more modest incomes than fulfillers and their lives are centered around their families, churches, communities, and the nation. They represent a target market for "buy American" manufacturers like Chrysler-Plymouth and Wal-Mart.

Status-oriented consumers are guided by the actions and opinions of others:

3. *Achievers* (13 percent of population; median age 36) are successful, work-oriented people who mainly derive satisfaction from their jobs and families. A politically conservative group who respects authority and the status quo, achievers favor established products and services that reflect their level of success to their peers. Achievers are a target market for high-end automobile manufacturers, high-end clothing manufacturers, and expensive specialty shops.

4. *Strivers* (13 percent of population; median age 34) are similar to achievers but with fewer economic, social, and psychological resources. Style is important to them as they strive to emulate the people they wish they could be. Manufacturers who copy expensive products like designer handbags may find strivers to be a receptive target market.

Action-oriented consumers are guided by a desire for social or physical activity, variety, and risk taking:

5. *Experiencers* (12 percent of population; median age 26) exhibit high energy levels, which they devote to physical exercise and social activities. The youngest of the

An Appeal to Fulfillers

segments, experiencers are adventurous and spend heavily on clothing, fast food, music, and other youthful activities. Experiencers are a promising target market for fast-food restaurants, clothing manufacturers, and health clubs. Perhaps the advertisement for Oscar de La Renta perfume (Figure 4.11) is aimed at Experiencers.

6. *Makers* (13 percent of population; median age 30) are practical, self-sufficient consumers who focus on family, work, and physical recreation. Makers have little interest in the broader world and are only interested in those material possessions that have a practical or functional purpose. Sporting-goods manufacturers and companies offering family-oriented activities and products might find makers to be an attractive target market.

Two other groups of consumers are characterized by resource levels either below or above the other six categories:

7. *Strugglers* (14 percent of population; median age 61) have the lowest incomes and too few resources to be included in any consumer self-orientation. They do tend to be brand-loyal consumers within their limited means. They represent a market for manufacturers of products emphasizing value within the household products and food categories.

8. *Actualizers* (8 percent of population; median age 43) enjoy the highest incomes, strongest self-esteems, and abundant resources. Image is important as they buy the finer things in life. They represent a potential market for manufacturers of high-end products like luxury automobiles, yachts, and Concorde airline travel.

Marketers use the detailed information from the VALS 2 model to position their brands, select media vehicles, and determine the sizes of the various potential market segments

An Appeal to Experiencers

TABLE 4.5

Activities of the Eight VALS 2 Groups

ACTIVITY	ACTUALIZERS	FULFILLERS	BELIEVERS	ACHIEVERS	STRIVERS	EXPERIENCERS	MAKERS	STRUGGLERS
Buy hand tools	148	65	105	63	59	137	170	57
Barbecue outdoors	125	93	82	118	111	109	123	50
Do gardening	155	129	118	109	68	54	104	80
Do gourmet cooking	217	117	96	103	53	133	86	47
Drink coffee daily	120	119	126	88	87	55	91	116
Drink domestic beer	141	88	73	101	87	157	123	50
Drink herbal tea	171	125	89	117	71	115	81	68
Drink imported beer	238	93	41	130	58	216	88	12
Do activities with kids	155	129	57	141	112	89	116	32
Play team sports	114	73	69	104	110	172	135	34
Do cultural activities	293	63	67	96	45	154	63	14
Exercise	145	114	69	123	94	143	102	39
Do home repairs	161	113	85	82	53	88	171	58
Camp or hike	131	88	68	95	84	156	158	33
Do risky sports	190	48	36	52	59	283	171	7
Socialize weekly	109	64	73	90	96	231	94	62

Note: Table entries are index numbers. The number 148 under Actualizers for "Buy hand tools" means that this group is 48 percent more likely to buy this product than are all groups on average.

Source: SRI International.

and their corresponding product needs. Moreover, as shown in Table 4.5, various buyer behaviors are related to VALS 2 lifestyle groupings. With 100 representing the base rate, or average level of consumption, perusal of Table 4.5 reveals distinct differences among the eight groups in terms of their consumption behaviors. In terms of exercise activity, for example, it can be seen that Actualizers (index = 145) and Experiencers (index = 143) are the most likely to exercise, whereas Strugglers (index = 39) and Believers (index = 69) are the least likely to engage in this activity. Actualizers and Experiencers also are disproportionately more likely than all other groups to drink imported beer (indices of 238 and 216, respectively)—perhaps this is why they feel the need to exercise!

Although psychographic variables provide useful marketing information for segmentation purposes, these characteristics, compared to demographic variables, are more difficult to identify and measure. Secondary research of published data will tell a marketer how many male consumers aged 25 to 34 live in a particular market; however, secondary research cannot tell a marketer how many male Achievers aged 25 to 34 live in a particular market. Often, marketers use psychographic variables *along with* other variables when segmenting markets.

GEODEMOGRAPHIC TARGETING

The word **geodemographic** is a conjunction of geography and demography, which beautifully describes this form of targeting. The premise underlying geodemographic targeting is that people who reside in similar areas, such as neighborhoods or postal ZIP-code zones, also share demographic and lifestyle similarities. Hence, knowing where people live also provides some information regarding their general marketplace behaviors. Several companies have developed services that delineate geographical areas into common groups, or clusters, wherein reside people with similar demographic and lifestyle characteristics. These companies (and their services, in parentheses) include CACI (ACORN), Donnelly Marketing (ClusterPlus), National Decision Systems (Vision), and Claritas (PRIZM). The following section describes Claritas's PRIZM system of geodemographic profiling.[57]

PRIZM, which stands for *Potential Rating Index by Zip Markets,* is a classification system that delineates every neighborhood in the United States into 62 clusters, or groups, based on their unique demographic and lifestyle characteristics. These clusters are labeled with colorful and descriptive names such as *blue-blood estates, pools and patios, bohemian mix, towns and gowns, coalburg and corntown, shotguns and pickups, golden ponds, Norma Raeville, tobacco roads, Hispanic mix,* and *hard scrabble.* Bohemian mix, for example, describes those neighborhoods in upscale urban areas (e.g., San Francisco, Manhattan, and Boston) that are occupied by a mixture of white-collar workers, students, actors, writers, artists, aging hippies, and so on. This is the group that Absolut vodka (see Figure 4.12 for illustrative appeal) aimed for with considerable success. Many other wanna-be brands in the liquor category and elsewhere have attempted to emulate Absolut's success. *Golden ponds,* named after the 1980s movie *(On Golden Pond)* starring Henry Fonda, Jane Fonda, and Katharine Hepburn, characterizes those small and rustic communities located at mountain, lake, and beach resorts where senior citizens retire among local neighbors. Such communities offer prime prospects for purveyors of investment products, recreational offerings, and health-care services.

Many major marketers use PRIZM, Donnelly's ClusterPlus, or other geodemographic clustering services to help them with important marketing communication decisions. Selecting geographical locales for spot television advertising and identifying candidates for direct mailing are just two of the decisions that are facilitated by the availability of geodemographic data.

An Appeal to the
Bohemian Mix

Summary

This chapter has emphasized the importance of targeting communication efforts to specific demographic, psychographic, or geodemographic groups. Three major demographic developments are reviewed in this chapter: (1) the age structure of the U.S. population, (2) the changing American household, and (3) ethnic population developments.

The presentation covers a variety of topics relevant for marketing communicators. Some of the major demographic developments discussed include: (1) the continuous shifting of the U.S. population to the South and West; (2) the progressive aging of the U.S. population from an average age of 33 in 1990, to nearly 36 years old in 2000, and to an expected average age of 38 by 2025; (3) the dramatic increase in the percentage of single American adults in the past two decades; and (4) the explosive growth of ethnic minorities—particularly Hispanics—in the United States, so that by early in the next century minorities will represent one of three Americans.

Marketing communicators have in recent decades targeted customers using knowledge about their activities, interests, and opinions (or, collectively, their lifestyles) to better understand what people want and how they respond to advertising, direct mail, and other forms of marketing communications. The term *psychographics* describes this form of targeting effort. Many customized studies are conducted to identify psychographic segments directly applicable to the marketer's product category and brand, but syndicated research systems such as SRI's VALS 2 system also provide useful information for making important marketing communications decisions. The VALS 2 system classifies people into one of eight groups based on a combination of their self-orientation and resources: Actualizers, Fulfillers, Believers, Achievers, Strivers, Experiencers, Makers, and Strugglers.

A final section reviews the role of geodemographic targeting. This form of targeting basically identifies clusters of consumers who share similar demographic and lifestyle characteristics. Donnelly's ClusterPlus and Claritas's PRIZM are two well-known and respected clustering systems that identify meaningful groupings of geographical units such as ZIP-code areas.

Discussion Questions

1. Demographers tell us that households in the United States are growing in number, shrinking in size, and changing in character. Assume that you are the vice president of marketing for a corporation that manufactures refrigerators and other kitchen appliances. What specific implications do these changes hold for your company?

2. As a percentage of the total population, Americans aged 19 and younger represent a much smaller percentage of the total population today (approximately 29 percent) than they did a quarter of a century ago (approximately 40 percent in 1965). In light of this development, what would you do if you were the CEO of a firm that markets exclusively youth-oriented products?

3. References are often made to the children's market, the singles market, the mature market, the African-American market, Hispanic market, Asian market, and so on. Are these truly markets in the rigorous sense of market segmentation? First identify the requirements that a market segmentation basis must satisfy, and then respond to the question. Review appropriate material in Chapter 2 if necessary.

4. African-American, Hispanic-American, and Asian-American consumers do not signify three homogeneous markets; rather, they represent many markets composed of people who merely share a common race and/or language. Explain.

5. Explain the reasons for the relentless aging of the U.S. population, and discuss some implications this will have on marketing and marketing communications into the first decade of the 21st century.

6. If the 1980s was the decade of the baby boomers and yuppies, and the 1990s the decade of mature consumers, to whom will the first decade of the next millennium pay tribute?

7. Due to rather dramatic changes in the population composition of the United States, it is not difficult to argue that advertising in the 1960s and 1970s was a lot easier than it is today. From your reading of the chapter, provide three or four reasons to support this argument.

8. Assume you are brand manager of a food product that is consumed by all Americans—blacks, whites, Hispanics, Asians, and others. You are considering running an extended advertising campaign on prime-time television that uses Hispanic actors and appeals to Hispanic consumers. Aside from cost considerations, what reservations might you have about this type of campaign?

9. When the mature market was discussed, it was noted that advertising aimed at this group should portray them as vital, busy, forward-looking, and attractive/romantic. Interview several mature consumers and coalesce their views on how they perceive advertising directed at them and their peers. Your interview results along with those from fellow students should lead to an interesting class discussion.

10. What are your views on the targeting of special products to children? As context for your essay, review the discussion on the ethics of targeting in Chapter 3.

11. In which of the Generation X groups (yup & comers, bystanders, playboys, and drifters) would you place yourself? Are these categories useful or too crude in your opinion? Relate these four categories to the discussion of psychographics. Are these four categories a form of psychographic categorization?

12. Based on your personal background and using the VALS 2 system, how would you categorize most of the adults with whom you and your family associate?

13. Identify magazine advertisements that reflect appeals to at least five of the eight VALS 2 groups.

14. Describe in as much detail as possible the neighborhood in which you were raised. Come up with a label (similar to the PRIZM cluster names) that metaphorically captures the essence of your neighborhood.

*I*nternet Exercises

1. Select three different products of interest to you. Now visit a popular Web search site (e.g., www.hotbot.com, www.excite.com, www.yahoo.com) and search using the product category or brand name. Carefully observe the various types of ads that appear with each search.
   a. Select the VALS2 category you feel best describes you. Why did you select this category?
   b. Do the three products you selected reflect your VALS2 category?
   c. Do you think the Web ads that appeared for each product were designed to appeal to your VALS2 category? If so, what specific features of the ads seem to fit with the description of your VALS2 category? If not, which VALS2 category does each ad appear to be targeting and what features of the ads led to your conclusion?

2. One often hears the Internet described as a mass of electronically linked "communities." Thus, knowing where people tend to reside in these communities may provide information regarding their general marketplace behaviors (we could call this cyber-geodemographics). For example, knowing that a person has a college e-mail address and that she or he accesses the Internet from a campus domain may be of interest to many marketers. Describe at least two "neighborhoods" on the Internet and come up with a label (similar to the PRIZM cluster names) that metaphorically capture the essence of these neighborhoods.

*C*hapter Four Endnotes

1. Thomas S. Robertson, Joan Zielinski, and Scott Ward, *Consumer Behavior* (Glenview, Ill.: Scott, Foresman and Company, 1984), 340.

2. According to the International Programs Center of the U.S. Bureau of the Census, the world population as of December 22, 1998 was approximately 5.96 billion people. Information about the world population is available at the Bureau of the Census' Web site: http//www.census.gov/cgi-bin/ipc/popclockw.

3. These estimates are available online at http://www.census.gov/population/estimates/nation/intfile2-1.txt.

4. Tom Morganthau, "The Face of the Future," *Newsweek,* January 27, 1997, 58.

5. http://www.census.gov/population/estimates/nation/intfile-2.txt.

6. "Beyond the Blue Horizon," *Time,* August 20, 1984, 106.

7. Robert B. Settle and Pamela L. Alreck, "The Psychology of Expectations," *Marketing Communications,* March 1988, 19–27.

8. Tobi Elkin, "Whirlpool Goes for Boomer Gold," *Brandweek,* November 24, 1997, 9.

9. Ken Dychtwald and Greg Gable, "Portrait of a Changing Consumer," *Business Horizons,* January/February 1990, 62–73.

10. Yumiko Ono, "Some Hair-Color Sales Get Boost As Baby Boomers Battle Aging," *The Wall Street Journal,* February 3, 1994, B7. Also, Joe Schwartz, "Boomer," *Brandweek,* October 1996, 42.

11. The "epicenter of society" expression is attributed to Fred Elkind, an executive with the Ogilvy & Mather advertising agency. Cited in Christy Fisher, "Boomers Scatter in Middle Age," *Advertising Age,* January 11, 1993, 23.

12. Desiree J. Hanford, "Anheuser-Busch Targets Consumers Battling Their Growing Beer Bellies," *The Wall Street Journal Interactive Edition,* April 6, 1998.

13. William Lazer, "Dimensions of the Mature Market," *The Journal of Consumer Marketing* 3 (summer 1986), 24.

14. The expression "repair kit" is from Charles D. Schewe, "Marketing to Our Aging Population: Responding to Physiological Changes," *The Journal of Consumer Marketing* 5 (summer 1988), 61–73. Other discussions of marketers' unflattering treatment of older consumers and recommendations for avoiding such treatment include Randall Rothenberg, "Ad Industry Faulted on Over-50's," *The New York Times,* May 11, 1988, 42; and Melinda Beck, "Going for the Gold," *Newsweek,* April 23, 1990, 74–76.

15. Christy Fisher, "Boomers Bringing Buying Power," *Advertising Age,* November 16, 1992, S2.

16. Rick Adler, "Stereotypes Won't Work with Seniors Anymore," *Advertising Age,* November 11, 1996, 32; "Market Profile: The Graying of America's Consumer," *POPAI News* 7, no. 1 (1983), 5.

17. The research was performed by George P. Moschis and is reported in "Survey: Age Is Not Good Indicator of Consumer Need," *Marketing Communications,* November 21, 1988, 6. See also George P. Moschis and Anil Mathur, "How They're Acting Their Age," *Marketing Management* 2, no. 2 (1993), 40–50.

18. Lisa Bannon, "For Toys and Clothes, the Six-to-12 Set Is Showing Teenage Purchasing Habits," *The Wall Street Journal Interactive Edition,* October 13, 1998.

19. Christy Fisher, "Wooing Boomers' Babies," *Advertising Age,* July 22, 1991, 3, 30.

20. See Horst H. Stipp, "Children As Consumers," *American Demographics,* February 1988, 27–32; Ellen Graham, "As Kids Gain Power of Purse, Marketing Takes Aim at Them," *The Wall Street Journal,* January 19, 1988, 1; John Schwartz, "Portrait of a Generation," *Newsweek Special Issue,* summer 1991, 6–9; and Monte Williams, "'Parental Guidance' Lost on This Crop," *Advertising Age,* July 30, 1990, 1, 28.

21. *Youth Monitor* (winter 1987), Yankelovich, Skelly and White/Clancy, Shulman, Inc.

22. For an academic treatment on the topic, see Sharon E. Beatty and Salil Talpade, "Adolescent Influence in Family Decision Making: A Replication with Extension," *Journal of Consumer Research* 21 (September 1994), 332–341; Kay M. Palan and Robert E. Wilkes, "Adolescent–Parent Interaction in Family Decision Making," *Journal of Consumer Research* 24 (September 1997), 159–169. A provocative treatment on teenagers' work, study, and spending behaviors is available in Steven Waldman and Karen Springen, "Too Old, Too Fast?" *Newsweek,* November 16, 1992, 80–87.

23. T. L. Stanley, "Get Ready for Gen Y," *Brandweek,* May 15, 1995, 36–37.

24. Carol Krol and Alice Z. Cuneo, "Marketers Finding Gen Y a Profitable Playground," *Advertising Age,* October 12, 1998, 57.

25. Graham, "As Kids Gain Power of Purse, Marketing Takes Aim at Them." Also, Selina S. Guber, "The Teenage Mind," *American Demographics,* August 1987, 42–44.

26. Wendy Bounds, "Inside Levi's Race to Restore a Well-Known, Tarnished Brand," *The Wall Street Journal Interactive Edition,* August 4, 1998.

27. William Strauss and Neil Howe, *Generations: The History of America's Future, 1584–2069* (New York: William Morrow and Company, Inc., 1991). For a less technical treatment written by an advertising person, see also Karen Ritchie, *Marketing to Generation X* (New York: Lexington Books, 1995).

28. For an intelligent critique of the stereotypical treatment of the Gen X label, see David Ashley Morrison, "Beyond the Gen X Label," *Brandweek,* March 17, 1997, 23–25.

29. Jeff Giles, "Generalizations X," *Newsweek,* June 6, 1994, 62–72.

30. Judith Langer, "Twentysomethings: They're Angry, Frustrated and They Like Their Parents," *Brandweek,* February 22, 1993, 18–19.

31. Daniel Shannon, "In a Class by Itself," *Promo,* July 1994, 50–56, 76.

32. Ibid., 54.

33. http://www.census.gov/population/projections/nation/hh-fam/tableln.txt.

34. Patricia Braus, "Sex and the Single Spender," *American Demographics,* November 1993, 28–34.

35. "Lands of Our Fathers," *Newsweek,* January 17, 1983, 22.

36. Michael J. McDermott, "Marketers Pay Attention! Ethnics Comprise 25% of the U.S.," *Brandweek,* July 18, 1994, 26.

37. http://www.census.gov/population/projections/nation/nsrh/nprh9600.txt.

38. Ibid.

39. See Douglas M. Stayman and Rohit Deshpande, "Situational Ethnicity and Consumer Behavior," *Journal of Consumer Research* 16 (December 1989), 361–371; and Cynthia Webster, "Effects of Hispanic Ethnic Identification on Marital Roles in the Purchase Decision Process," *Journal of Consumer Research* 16 (September 1994), 319–331.

40. James F. Engel, Roger D. Blackwell, and Paul W. Miniard, *Consumer Behavior,* 8th ed. (Fort Worth: The Dryden Press, 1995), 647.

41. Alice Z. Cuneo, "New Sears Label Woos Black Women," *Advertising Age,* May 5, 1997, 6.

42. Raymond Serafin and Riccardo A. Davis, "Detroit Moves to Woo Blacks," *Advertising Age,* April 11, 1994, 10.

43. Morganthau, "The Face of the Future," 58.

44. Jeffery D. Zbar, "Gallup: Few Targeting Hispanics," *Advertising Age,* November 4, 1996, 55.

45. Thomas H. Stevenson and Patricia E. McIntyre, "A Comparison of the Portrayal and Frequency of Hispanics and Whites in English Language Television Advertising," *Journal of Current Issues and Research in Advertising* 17 (spring 1995), 65–74.

46. Christy Fisher, "Marketing to Hispanics," *Advertising Age,* January 23, 1995, 29, 37.

47. Sigfredo A. Hernandez and Larry M. Newman, "Choice of English vs. Spanish Language in Advertising to Hispanics," *Journal of Current Issues and Research in Advertising* 14 (fall 1992), 35–46.

48. "Snafus Persist in Marketing to Hispanics," *Marketing News,* June 24, 1983, 3.

49. Robert E. Wilkes and Humberto Valencia, "Hispanics and Blacks in Television Commercials," *Journal of Advertising* 18, no. 1 (1989), 19–25.

50. "Money Income in the United States: 1997," U.S. Department of Commerce, Bureau of the Census, Table A.

51. Christy Fisher, "Marketers Straddle Asia-America Curtain," *Advertising Age,* November 7, 1994, S2.

52. John Schwartz, Dorothy Wang, and Nancy Matsumoto, "Tapping into a Blossoming Asian Market," *Newsweek,* September 7, 1987, 47–48.

53. Cyndee Miller, "'Hot' Asian-American Market Not Starting Much of a Fire Yet," *Advertising Age,* January 21, 1991, 12.

54. "Targeting the Asian-American Market in Direct Mail," *Asian Connection* 1, no. 1 (1995), 3.

55. Joseph T. Plummer, "The Concept and Application of Life Styles Segmentation," *Journal of Marketing* 38 (January 1974), 33–37.

56. The following discussion is based on Martha Farnsworth Riche, "Psychographics for the 1990s," *American Demographics,* July 1989, 24–31, 53.

57. Michael J. Weiss, *The Clustering of America* (New York: Harper & Row, 1988).

The Communication Process and Fundamentals of Buyer Behavior

CHAPTER OBJECTIVES

After studying this chapter, you should be able to:

1. Understand the objectives that marketing communications efforts attempt to accomplish.
2. Appreciate the elements of the communications process.
3. Understand the nature of meaning in marketing communications using a perspective known as semiotics.
4. Describe marketing communicators' usage of three forms of figurative language (simile, metaphor, and allegory).
5. Discuss two models of consumer behavior: the consumer processing model (CPM) and the hedonic, experiential model (HEM).
6. Describe the eight stages of consumer information processing.
7. Explain the fundamental features of the hedonic, experiential model.

Opening Vignette: Losing Sales to Bottled Water, the Plight of Diet Soft Drinks

Do you drink diet or regular soft drinks, or perhaps is bottled water your cold beverage of choice? If you are like many consumers in your age group, the chances are reasonably strong that you do not drink diet soft drinks such as Diet Coke or Diet Pepsi. Diet soft drinks commanded 30 percent of the total market in 1990 for carbonated soft drinks, but their share has now plummeted to less than 25 percent of the category. Although a share reduction of five or six points may seem relatively trivial, in a category where carbonated soft drinks generate over $50 billion in annual sales, a 5 percent decline amounts to a huge $2.5 billion revenue reduction.

Why the change in consumption habits in just a decade? Although many people still enjoy diet soft drinks, the majority of consumers prefer bottled water or regular cola. These consumers consider regular colas to have a better taste and are not concerned with the extra calories. They regard bottled water as a healthier and more fashionable beverage— the drink that fits the times. And the sales trend reflects a dramatic shift in consumption patterns. Whereas diet soft drinks are experiencing annual sales growth of less than 2 percent, bottled water has enjoyed growth exceeding 25 percent in recent years.

What would you do if you were the brand manager of Diet Coke or Diet Pepsi in view of your brand's diminishing equity and declining sales and profits? The status quo is an unacceptable option. Your job is to protect your brand's historical stature and restore growth. Now, of course, a better-tasting product might help, but the fact remains that millions of consumers prefer the taste of diet colas over regular colas, so perhaps taste is not the cul-

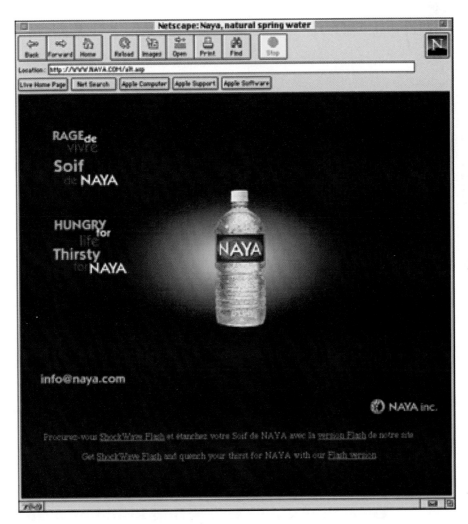

prit. Is it a brand image problem? As discussed in the prior chapter, consumers, especially teenagers, often are fickle in their preferences, and you covet the teens who now consume bottled water and regular colas in preference to diet drinks. What about an advertising overhaul? Would it be possible to change the image of diet soft drinks such that drinking brands like Diet Coke and Diet Pepsi would be as "hip" as drinking bottled water?

Brand managers for Diet Coke and Diet Pepsi apparently think they can change their brand's images and restore some of the lost luster to diet drinks. Diet Coke, for example, introduced a campaign called "You Are What You Drink" reminiscent of Coca-Cola's advertising of Tab in the 1970s. Like the old Tab ads, which delivered the message that "Tab is for beautiful people," the revitalized Diet Coke campaign consisted of different spots all featuring attractive women guzzling the brand from a bottle. From a brand-equity perspective (recall detailed discussion in Chapter 1), the objective of Diet Coke's advertising is to create an association between the brand and user imagery. This is to say that the advertising hopes to build a strong, positive connection between the brand and the type of people who consume Diet Coke. If the advertised models drinking Diet Coke are hip, then the subtle (or not-so-subtle) message conveyed to young consumers is that it also is hip for them to drink this brand.*

*T*he opening vignette captures the essence of much of the content of this chapter, which addresses the communication process, the nature of meaning and meaning transfer, and fundamentals of consumer behavior. All of these topics are essential to an appreciation of marketing communications. The chapter begins with a discussion of communication objectives; turns next to a formal description of the communication process; considers then

*Source: Adapted from Nikhil Deogun and Sally Goll Beatty, "Ads Try to Make Diet Sodas Cool for Today's Teenagers," *The Wall Street Journal Interactive Edition*, May 14, 1997.

the nature of meaning and the semiotics of marketing communications; and finally concludes with a detailed description of how consumers receive, process, and respond to information obtained from marketing communications.

COMMUNICATION OBJECTIVES

All marketing communications efforts are directed at accomplishing one or more of the following objectives[1]:

1. Building product category wants.
2. Creating brand awareness.
3. Enhancing attitudes and influencing intentions.
4. Facilitating purchase.

Objective 1: Building Category Wants

Every marketing organization is interested ultimately in having people select its specific offering rather than choosing a competitive offering, as the discussion in the *Opening Vignette* illustrated in the "wars" between diet soft drinks and bottled water. However, consumers have to want the general product category, say, diet soft drinks, before they buy a specific brand, for example, Diet Coke, in that category. This is what marketers mean by building category wants, also referred to as creating *primary demand*. Every new product introduction brings with it the responsibility for the innovator to build consumer wants aggressively. And marketers in established categories, such as diet soft drinks, must do everything possible to maintain or build their category.

Objectives 2 and 3: Creating Brand Awareness, Enhancing Attitudes, and Influencing Purchase Intentions

Once category wants are created, marketers compete against one another for shares of total customer expenditures, each attempting to establish *secondary demand* for its particular brand. Each marketer must direct its efforts at creating awareness for its brand and favorably influencing attitudes and intentions. Brands in the soft drink and bottled water categories compete for the consumer's interest and use image-oriented advertising campaigns in attempts to sway consumer purchase loyalty.

Awareness involves familiarizing consumers—via advertising, sales promotion, and other marketing communications—about a brand, informing people about its special features and benefits, and showing how it is different and hopefully superior in a functional or symbolic sense to competitive brands. If the communicator is successful in creating consumer awareness, consumers may form favorable *attitudes* toward the company's brand and possibly develop an *intention* to purchase that brand the next time a product want arises.

Objective 4: Facilitating Purchase

Whether consumers ultimately purchase the marketer's brand depends on whether the promotion and marketing communications variables *facilitate purchasing*. That is, advertising may generate consumer awareness and build favorable attitudes, but if a new brand is unavailable at the point of purchase or if consumers evaluate it as, say, overpriced compared to its competitors, then the likelihood of that brand being purchased is reduced. But if a company's marketing communications efforts are really effective, consumers will understand why the brand is higher priced and perhaps will find it more desirable because of its premium price. Effective advertising, attractive in-store displays, and other marketing communications variables serve to facilitate purchasing and possibly overcome impediments created by the nonpromotional marketing mix variables (product, price, and distribution).

Achieving the various communication objectives—from creating brand awareness to facilitating purchase—requires efforts to enhance a brand's equity and to carefully manage a brand concept throughout the brand's life cycle. As previously noted in Chapter 1, efforts to enhance a brand's equity are accomplished through the initial choice of positive brand identity (i.e., the selection of a good brand name or logo) but mostly through marketing and marketing communications programs that forge favorable, strong, and possibly unique associations between the brand and its features and benefits.[2] A favorable brand concept, or brand meaning, must be carefully managed throughout a brand's life cycle. This brand concept is accomplished by promoting a brand as appealing to any of three categories of basic consumer needs (functional, symbolic, or experiential) and remaining consistent in this appeal. A maker of jeans, for example, would not typically introduce a new brand by initially appealing to consumers' functional need for durability only shortly thereafter to reposition the brand as hip or sexy. Such inconsistency would confuse consumers and dilute the brand's concept. Politicians often are chastised for waffling, and brands suffer a similar fate when their consumer constituencies are unsure of a brand's positioning or meaning.

THE COMMUNICATION PROCESS

The word *communication* is derived from the Latin word *communis,* which means "common." Communication then can be thought of as the process of establishing a commonness, or oneness, of thought between a sender and a receiver.[3] The key point in this definition is that there must be a commonness of thought developed between sender and receiver if communication is to occur. Commonness of thought implies that a *sharing* relationship must exist between sender (an advertiser, for instance) and receiver (the consumer).

Consider a situation in which a salesperson is delivering a presentation to a purchasing agent who appears to be listening to what the salesperson is saying but who actually is thinking about a personal problem. Contrary to what an observer might perceive, communication is *not* occurring because thought is not being shared. The reason for the lack of communication in this instance is, of course, the inattentiveness of the intended receiver. Although sound waves are bouncing against his eardrums, he is not actively receiving and thinking about what the salesperson is saying.

An analogy can be drawn between a human receiver and a television set. A television set is continuously bombarded by electromagnetic waves from different stations; yet it will only receive the station to which the channel selector is tuned. Human receivers are also bombarded with stimuli from many sources, and, like the television set, people are selective in what information they choose to process.

Both sender and receiver must be active participants in the same communicative relationship in order for thought to be shared. Communication is something one does *with* another person, not something one does *to* another person. A British advertising researcher conveys the same idea when she reminds us that the question for advertisers is not "What does advertising do to people?" but rather "What do people do with advertising? What do people use advertising for?"[4]

Elements in the Communication Process

All communication activities involve the following eight elements:

1. a source
2. encoding
3. a message
4. a channel
5. a receiver

6. decoding

7. the possibility of noise

8. feedback potential

As shown in the model in Figure 5.1, the **source** (or sender) is a person or group of people (such as a business firm) who has thoughts (ideas, sales points, etc.) to share with some other person or group of people. The source encodes a message to accomplish the four communication objectives described previously. **Encoding** is the process of translating thought into a symbolic form. The source selects specific *signs* from a nearly infinite variety of words, sentence structures, symbols, and nonverbal elements to encode a message that will communicate effectively with the target audience. The **message** itself is a symbolic expression of a sender's thoughts. In marketing communications, the message takes the form of an advertisement, a sales presentation, a package design, point-of-purchase cues, and so on.

The **message channel** is the path through which the message moves from source to receiver. Companies use broadcast and print media and print to channel advertising messages to current and potential customers. Messages also are transmitted to customers directly via salespeople, by telephone, direct-mail brochures, point-of-purchase displays, and indirectly via word of mouth.

The **receiver** is the person or group of people with whom the sender attempts to share ideas. In marketing communications, receivers are the prospective and present customers of an organization's product or service. **Decoding** involves activities undertaken by receivers to interpret—or derive meaning from—marketing messages. (Because the meaning formation process plays such a crucial role in all marketing communications, the following section discusses the nature of meaning in detail.)

A message moving through a channel is subject to the influence of extraneous and distracting stimuli. These stimuli interfere with reception of the message in its pure and original form. Such interference and distortion is called **noise.** Noise may occur at any stage in the communication process (see Figure 5.1). For example, at the point of message encoding, the sender may be unclear about what the message is intended to accomplish. A likely result is a poorly focused and perhaps even contradictory message rather than a message that is

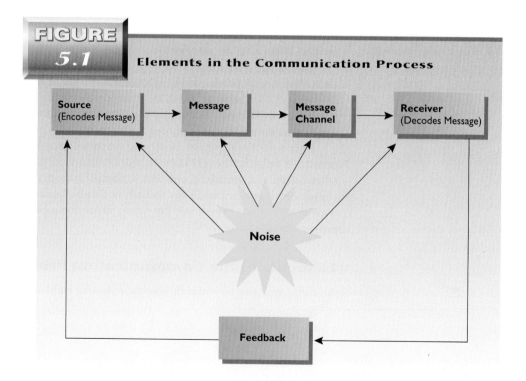

FIGURE 5.1

Elements in the Communication Process

clear-cut and integrated. Noise also occurs in the message channel—a fuzzy television signal, a crowded magazine page on which an advertisement is surrounded by competitive clutter, and a personal sales interaction that is interrupted repeatedly by telephone calls. Noise also can be present at the receiver/decoding stage of the process. An infant might cry during a television commercial and block out critical points in the sales message; passengers in an automobile might talk and not listen to a radio commercial; or the receiver simply may not possess the knowledge base needed to understand fully the promotional message.

The final element, **feedback,** affords the source a way of monitoring how accurately the intended message is being received. Feedback allows the source to determine whether the original message hit the target accurately or whether it needs to be altered to evoke a clearer picture in the receiver's mind. Thus, the feedback mechanism offers the source some measure of control in the communication process. Advertisers frequently discover that their target markets do not interpret campaign themes exactly as intended. Using research-based feedback from their markets, management can reexamine and often correct ineffective or misdirected advertising messages.

MARKETING COMMUNICATIONS AND MEANING

Fundamental to the communication process is the concept of *meaning.* Marketers attempt to convey meaning about their brands while consumers acquire meanings that may or may not be the same as that intended by the marketing communicator. This section discusses the nature of meaning in marketing communications using a perspective known as semiotics. **Semiotics,** broadly speaking, is the study of meaning and the analysis of meaning-producing events.[5] The fundamental concept in semiotics is the sign.

The Nature of Signs

Marketing communications in all of its various forms uses signs to create messages and convey meanings. A **sign** is something physical and perceivable by our senses that represents, or signifies, something (the *referent)* to somebody (the *interpreter)* in some *context.*[6] Consider the pickup truck as a consumption object. The primary and explicit, or *denotative,* meaning of pickup truck is straightforward: a vehicle with a cab compartment for passengers and space in the rear for hauling objects. The secondary and implicit, or *connotative,* meaning of pickup truck is considerably more diverse. A pickup truck connotes good taste and intelligent consumer behavior to some individuals, whereas to others it suggests a crude, indecorous lifestyle.

Thus the same sign, pickup truck, means different things to different people at different times and in different contexts. All meaning is *meaning in context.*[7] The image of the pickup truck has changed dramatically in recent years. Historically, pickups were owned almost exclusively by rural people and laborers and were used primarily for work and secondarily for pleasure. However, in more recent times the pickup truck has taken on meaning as a dual-purpose vehicle, used first for pleasure and only secondarily for work. The director of the University of Michigan's Office for the Study of Automotive Transportation had this to say about the modern meaning of the pickup: "You can take it almost anywhere and it's almost viewed as a status symbol. It isn't a view that people driving these things are clods, but risk takers."[8] It must be recognized, of course, that the positive, status-symbol meaning of the pickup is uniquely American. It is difficult to imagine pickup trucks achieving the level of stature in European or Asian countries that they have achieved in the United States, which further highlights the point that all meaning is meaning in context.

Communication is effective when signs are common to both the sender's and the receiver's fields of experience. A field of experience, also called the *perceptual field,* is the sum total of a person's experiences during his or her lifetime. The larger the overlap, or commonality, in their perceptual fields, the greater the likelihood that signs will be decoded by the receiver in the manner intended by the sender.

Advertisers, salespersons, and other marketing communicators sometimes employ signs that are not part of their target audience's perceptual field. Effective communication is severely compromised when, for example, marketing communicators use words or other signs that customers do not understand. This is especially problematic when developing communication programs for consumers in other cultures. The challenge of advertising and other marketing communications tools is to use signs that contain meaning for consumers and to endow their brands with this meaning.

The Meaning of Meaning

Although we use signs to share meaning with others, the two terms *(signs* and *meanings)* should not be construed as synonymous.[9] Signs are simply stimuli that are used to evoke an intended meaning within another person. But words and nonverbal signs do not have meanings per se; instead, *people have meanings for signs.* Meanings are internal responses people hold for external stimuli. Many times people have different meanings for the same words, as the prior discussion of pickup trucks illustrated.

If signs have no meaning, it follows that meaning cannot be transmitted. "Only messages are transmittable, and meanings are not in the message, they are in the message-users."[10] Good communicators select verbal and nonverbal signs that elicit intended meanings. Marketing communicators must be especially careful to signs that will evoke the intended meaning in prospective buyers. All too often companies communicate their product offerings in terms familiar to themselves but not in terms familiar to their potential customers.

Up to this point we have referred to meaning in the abstract. Now a definition is in order. **Meaning** can be thought of as the *perceptions (thoughts) and affective reactions (feelings)* to stimuli evoked within a person when presented with a sign, such as a brand name, in a particular *context*.[11] It should be clear at this point that meaning is internal, rather than external, to an individual. Meaning, in other words, is *subjective.*

Imagine, for example, two consumers seated in front of a television set watching a commercial for a new brand of cat food. For one consumer, the commercial represents a display of adorable animals consuming a brand that this consumer now will consider buying for her own cat. For the other, who is not a pet lover, the commercial represents a disgusting portrayal of unappealing animals eating an unappetizing product. Clearly the identical message has decidedly different meanings for these two consumers.

Meaning Transfer: From Culture, to Object, to Consumer

The culture and social systems in which marketing communications take place are loaded with meaning. Through socialization, people learn cultural values, form beliefs, and become familiar with the physical manifestations, or artifacts, of these values and beliefs. The artifacts of culture are charged with meaning, which is transferred from generation to generation. For example, the Lincoln monument and Ellis Island are signs of freedom to Americans. To Germans and many other people throughout the world, the now-crumbled Berlin wall signified oppression and hopelessness. Comparatively, yellow ribbons signify crises and hopes for hostage release and the safe return of military personnel. Pink ribbons signal support for breast cancer victims, while red ribbons have grown into an international symbol of solidarity on AIDS.[12] The Black Liberation flag with its red, black, and green stripes—representing blood, achievement, and the fertility of Africa—symbolizes civil rights.

Marketing communicators draw meaning from the *culturally constituted world* (i.e., the everyday world filled with artifacts such as the preceding examples) and transfer that meaning to consumer goods. Advertising is an especially important instrument of meaning transfer. The role of advertising in transferring meaning has been described in this fashion:

> *Advertising works as a potential method of meaning transfer by bringing the consumer good and a representation of the culturally constituted world together within the frame of a particular advertisement. . . . The known properties of the culturally constituted*

world thus come to reside in the unknown properties of the consumer good and the transfer of meaning from world to [consumer] good is accomplished.[13]

When exposed to advertising, the consumer is not merely drawing information from the ad but is actively involved in assigning meaning to the advertised brand.[14] To demonstrate the preceding points, consider the following advertising illustrations. First, a mid-1990s advertisement for the Honda Accord was designed to convey the point that four out of five Accords sold in America are manufactured here. Beyond stating this fact in the ad copy, the two-page advertisement presented large photos of five icons of American culture: a hamburger, cowboy boots, an oversized bicycle (not like the sleek, European racing bikes), a baseball, and a jazz ensemble. By associating itself with these well-known symbols of American consumer culture, Honda pulled meaning from the "culturally constituted world" of the consumers in its target audience who would immediately recognize the five icons as uniquely American. The obvious intent was to persuade consumers that the Accord, embedded as it was among the five icons of American popular culture, is made in America and thus is itself American. Stated verbally, most Americans would counterargue such a claim, fully realizing that the Honda is a Japanese product. But presented at a non-verbal level and merely via association, viewers of this ad may have become somewhat more inclined to accept the Honda Accord as at least quasi-American. This certainly was the advertiser's intent; whether the advertisement achieved this objective is an empirical issue that Honda's advertising research undoubtedly investigated.

Drawing Measuring from the Culturally Constituted World

The advertisement in Figure 5.2 for *Hefty One Zip Slider Bags* hopes to convey to consumers that this brand zips tightly and locks in freshness (see copy at bottom of ad). It is one thing to make the claim, but quite another to convey this meaning to consumers in an attention-gaining and memorable fashion. The ad accomplishes this with the visualization that superimposes a standard door lock on a bag of grapes enclosed in a slider bag. The lock signifies, of course, a device that prevents intruders from entering a protected space. This is precisely the meaning that Hefty desires for its *One Zip Slider Bags*—a "device" for locking in freshness and keeping out contaminating odors. Hefty's advertising agency has pulled meaning from the culturally constituted world—namely, consumers' knowledge that locks are designed to repel intruders—with intentions that this meaning will be transferred to its brand of slider food bags.

Another Illustration of Drawing Meaning from the Culturally Constituted World

The advertisement for the Hermes' Harnais watch in Figure 5.3 embeds this brand in the context of implements from the sport of polo. Polo is a sport that appropriately represents the use of leather and epitomizes high class and luxury, which is just the image Hermes of Paris would hope to attach to its Harnais brand.

The Use of Signs and Symbols in Marketing Communications

As noted earlier, a sign is the basic element in the study of meaning. This section presents a more fine-tuned treatment of signs by distinguishing between *signs* and *symbols*.[15]

Sign Relations.   Signs are used here in a more specific sense than the earlier discussion. Specifically, an object is a **sign** of something if both the object and referent (what the object represents, or signifies) belong to the *same cultural context*. A sign derives its meaning from other items in its context and vice versa. For example, the famous Ralph Lauren Polo logo signifies a sense of high status, financial well-being, and even royalty, because of the sport's association with the British royal family. Ralph Lauren was obviously well aware of this when selecting the word *Polo* to signify his company's products. When purchasing a brand such as Polo, one is buying the whole context of the sign, which brings some degree of truth to the aphorism, "you are what you own."

Figure 5.4 illustrates another sign relation. This magazine advertisement for Bacardi rum apparently attempts to signify that this brand is fashionable. This is accomplished by portraying a professional woman ("Banker by Day") dressed in the accoutrements of late-1990s hip culture—midriff-revealing leather pants with pierced belly button. The intended message is clear: Bacardi rum is the brand for hip professionals.

Illustration of a
Sign Relation

GLOBAL FOCUS: JAPLISH—MEANING TRANSFER IN JAPANESE COMMERCE

The process of meaning transfer is universal; however, the specific signs used to transfer meaning are variable and cultural specific. Take the practice of using foreign language or foreign-sounding language for domestic marketing purposes. In the United States, foreign languages are used sparingly in advertising and other marketing communications. By comparison, much package labeling, brand naming, and advertising in Japan uses English names or combines English and Japanese language in what is referred to as *Japlish*. Products are marketed in Japan with names like *deodoranto* (deodorant), *appuru pai* (apple pie), and *Pocari Sweat* (a sports drink). Japanese automobiles have been marketed with English-sounding names such as *Bongo Wagon* and *Cherry Vanette*.

The use of English names or English transmutations symbolizes the Japanese people's desire to be modern and cosmopolitan. The use of English in Japanese brand names involves consumers with a product by investing that brand with connotations that the native Japanese language is less able to achieve. Since English-sounding words and phrases connote positive notions such as modernity, Japanese marketers hope that such positive connotations will transfer to the consumer goods they advertise.

Japanese marketing communicators' use of English sometimes approaches the bizarre. In beverage packaging, for example, cans are frequently adorned with poetic statements in English. The following example is illustrative:

> *Welcome to heaven*
> *As Time brings*
> *softness*
> *found in this can.*
> *(Mild coffee)*

Try to match the following "Japlished" names with the products they represent. (The answers appear in brackets following the source information.)

Brand Name	Product
1. Clean Life, Please	A. shampoo
2. I've	B. chocolate candy
3. Love-love	C. coffee creamer
4. Volume Up Water	D. cigarettes
5. Hope	E. cleaning gloves
6. Mouth Jazz	F. electric razor
7. Creap	G. mouthwash
8. Meltykiss	H. hairspray
9. Super Winky	I. condoms

Source: Based on John F. Sherry Jr. and Eduardo G. Camargo, "'May Your Life Be Marvelous': English Language Labeling and the Semiotics of Japanese Promotion," *Journal of Consumer Research* 14 (September 1987), 174–188. The quiz is from "Goofy, Twisted English Sells in Japan," an Associated Press release published in *The State*, January 6, 1995, A4. [Answers: 1E, 2A, 3F, 4H, 5D, 6G, 7C, 8B, 9I]

Brands often obtain desired meanings by virtue of their foreign or foreign-sounding names. Consumers in the United States perceive Swiss and German names as conveying artisanship, Italian names as suggesting styling, and French names as communicating avant-garde. Experimental research has shown that the use of French brand names on nail polish and fragrance products resulted in these brands being perceived as more pleasure yielding, or hedonic, than when the identical products were branded with English names.[16] Japanese companies love to use English-like brand names to convey desired meanings to consumers in Japan. As the *Global Focus* points out, Japanese advertising executives routinely concoct slogans in a form of English that Western observers call *Japlish*.

Symbol Relations.   An object is a **symbol** of something else (a referent) when the object and referent have no prior intrinsic relationship but rather are arbitrarily or metaphorically related. Symbol usage is widespread in marketing communications. Prudential Insurance advertises itself as *The Rock* and portrays itself in the context of the Rock of Gibraltar. The rock metaphor symbolizes strength and security, in the desire by Prudential's marketing executives that the company will be perceived as strong and safe. Merrill Lynch features a bull in its advertising, undoubtedly because in financial circles the bull is a symbol of growth and prosperity. Nike has made famous the "swoosh" symbol to identify its brand and impart the notion of speed—a key performance attribute, especially when this brand was introduced in the heyday of the jogging and road-running craze.

When establishing symbolic relations, marketing communicators often utilize *figurative,* or nonliteral, language. Figurative language involves expressing one thing (such as a brand) in terms normally used for denoting another thing (such as an idea or object) with which it may be regarded as analogous.[17] Three forms of figurative language used by marketing communicators are simile, metaphor, and allegory.[18]

Simile uses a comparative term such as like or as to join items from different classes of experience. "Love is like a rose" exemplifies the use of simile.[19] For many years, viewers of the soap opera *Days of Our Lives* have listened to the program open with the intonation of the simile: "Like sands through an hourglass, so are the days of our lives." A tourist advertisement for Jekyll Island, a popular resort on the coast of Georgia, illustrates the use of simile in advertising. The ad proclaimed: "Jekyll Island, Georgia. Like the tide, it draws you back again and again." Of course, the suggestion being made by the ad sponsor is that satisfied tourists return again and again to Jekyll Island, the same way that the drifting tide returns inexorably to the shore.

Metaphor differs from simile in that the comparative term (as, like) is omitted (love is a rose; she has a heart of gold; he has stone hands). Metaphor applies a word or a phrase to a concept or object that it does not literally denote in order to suggest a comparison and to make the abstract more concrete. When used in advertising, metaphors create a picture in consumers' minds and tap into meaning shared both by the advertiser and consumer.[20] For example, Jaguar XJ-S is claimed to be "the stuff of legends"; Wheaties is the "cereal of champions"; Budweiser is the "king of beers"; and Chevrolet is "the heartbeat of America." The advertiser in using metaphor hopes that by repeatedly associating its brand with a well-known and symbolically meaningful referent, the meaning contained in the referent will eventually transfer to the brand.[21] Kids who identify with sports stars eat Wheaties in hopes that they too can become champions.[22] Murphy Wood Floor Cleaner (see advertisement in Figure 5.5) employs metaphor in its headline comparison with Old Faithful. (As known by most Americans and tourists who have visited the American West, Old Faithful is the name of a famous geyser located in Wyoming's Yellowstone National Park that spews hot water and vapor at somewhat regular intervals averaging every 78 minutes.) The ad portrays Murphy Oil Soap erupting in an Old Faithful representation. The Old Faithful metaphor is used in this context to suggest that Murphy Just Squirt & Mop oil soap is a "trusted old friend—to make cleaner wood floors just a squirt away."

Allegory, a word derived from a Greek term meaning *other-speak,* represents a form of *extended metaphor.* Allegorical presentation equates the objects in a particular narrative (such as the advertised brand in a television commercial) with meanings outside the narrative itself.[23] In other words, "allegory conveys meaning in a story-underneath-a-story, where something other than what is literally represented is also occurring."[24] In addition to the use of metaphor, another determining characteristic of allegorical presentation is *personification.*[25]

Through personification, the abstract qualities in a narrative assume human characteristics. Examples of allegorical characters in advertising include:

1. Mr. Clean, who personifies heavy-duty cleaning ability in the brand of cleaner whose package he adorns;
2. Mr. Goodwrench (Chevrolet), who exemplifies professional, efficient car service;
3. The Pillsbury dough boy, who signifies the joy of making (and eating) cookies and fond remembrances (see Figure 5.6).

Allegory is often used in promoting products that are difficult to advertise without upsetting or offending some audience members. Advertisers have found that using personifications (e.g., human-like animals or person-like product characters) makes advertising of these potentially offensive or risqué products more palatable to audiences. For example, the successful, albeit much-criticized, advertising campaign for Camel cigarettes employed the camel personification known as Old Joe or Smooth Joe. Joe was the embodiment of hip. In the many executions of this campaign, Joe was always portrayed as a cool, adventurous, swinging-single-type character. The implications were that smoking Camels was itself the with-it thing to do. Although there are distinct ethical issues associated with this campaign (as previously noted in Chapter 3), there is no questioning its effectiveness. Two years after Old Joe's introduction, Camel shipments rose 11.3 percent and market share increased from

FIGURE 5.5

The Use of Metaphor
in Advertising

Something New From Old Faithful.

Introducing an easy way to take beautiful care of your wood floors. New Murphy®
Just Squirt & Mop. Just one squirt cleans your wood safely and gently, while
preserving your floor's finish and natural glow. Trust an old friend like
Murphy to make cleaner wood floors just a squirt away.

LOVE YOUR WOOD.

3.9 to 4.3 percent.[26] This may seem a pittance, but every share point in the cigarette industry amounts to sales in the hundreds of millions of dollars. The critics of smoking, especially concerning youth, were outraged by RJR's advertising of Camel cigarettes; indeed, Joe Camel in its allegorical splendor became the rallying point around which criticism of tobacco advertising was based and restrictions were eventually imposed.[27]

Budweiser's advertising with frogs and lizards represents another application of allegory in advertising a product category that is subject to criticism, particularly as it relates to drinking by underage consumers. Consider the television commercials that include disaffected lizard character (Louie) and his straight man sidekick (Frank). What is the allegorical representation, or story underneath a story, in these humorous lizard executions? Could it be that Louie and Frank represent competitors envious of Budweiser's success, and could it be that the frogs (who recite Bud–Weis–Er) personify Budweiser itself, the good guy in this

FIGURE
5.6

Allegorical Personification:
The Pillsbury Dough Boy

allegory? An interesting class discussion might debate these questions as well as the ethics of this particular ad campaign, which is said to have great appeal to teens and preteens.

Allegory certainly is not restricted to taboo products. Consider the two advertisements for Chevron gasoline with its Techron additive, one for a green station wagon (Figure 5.7) and the other for a blue pickup truck (Figure 5.8). In both executions the vehicle is made to look human (called "anthropomorphizing" by anthropologists) and in fact serves to personify the lifestyle of the intended market segment. The ad with the green station wagon is aimed at young mothers ("soccer moms") who constantly are on the go, and the blue pickup ad is directed at macho males who want a high-performing pickup truck. On the surface, both ads are just cutesy ways of advertising a boring product (i.e., gasoline). Slightly below the surface, however, both ads are attempting to persuade consumers that

Allegorical Personification:
Chevron Gasoline

the choice of Chevron gasoline reflects good judgment ("She uses her head"; and, for him, "Keep all your horses happy").

Summary of Meaning within Marketing Communications

This section has described the nature of meaning in marketing communications and the elements involved in meaning transfer. Perhaps the most important lesson to learn is that marketers utilize a variety of different signs, nonverbal as well as verbal, in their efforts to accomplish communication objectives. In the final analysis, marketing communicators hope to manage brand concepts by creating desired meanings for their brands. Meaning is the fundamental concept in all of marketing communications. It is the foundation of the brand image component of brand equity that was introduced in Chapter 1 as a core concept throughout the text.

FIGURE 5.8

Allegorical Personification:
Chevron Gasoline

Because meaning resides in the minds of people and not in messages per se, it is important to understand the psychological factors that determine how consumers derive meaning from messages. Accordingly, the following sections elaborate on some of the issues only alluded to so far.

BEHAVIORAL FOUNDATIONS OF MARKETING COMMUNICATIONS: THE CONSUMER PROCESSING MODEL (CPM)

Marketing communicators direct their efforts toward influencing consumers' brand-related *beliefs, attitudes, emotional reactions*, and *choices*. Ultimately, the objective is to encourage consumers to choose the marketer's brand rather than competitive offerings. To accomplish this goal, marketing communicators design advertising messages, promotions, packaging cues, brand names, sales presentations, and other communication activities. Because a fundamental understanding of consumer behavior is essential to appreciate fully the intricacies of marketing communications, the ideas presented in this section lay an important foundation for subsequent topical chapters.

This section examines how consumers process and respond to marketing communications stimuli and make choices among brands. The discussion focuses on the first of two models that describe how consumers process information and go about choosing from among the many alternatives typically available in the marketplace: the *consumer processing model (CPM)* and the *hedonic, experiential model (HEM)*.[28] From a consumer-processing perspective, behavior is seen as rational, highly cognitive, systematic, and reasoned. The hedonic, experiential perspective, on the other hand, views consumer behavior as driven instead by emotions in pursuit of "fun, fantasies, and feelings."[29]

A very important point needs to be emphasized before moving on to discussions of each model. In particular, it must be recognized that consumer behavior is much too complex and diverse to be captured perfectly by two extreme models. Rather, you should think of these models as bipolar perspectives that anchor a continuum of possible consumer behaviors—ranging, metaphorically speaking, from the "icy-blue cold" CPM framework to the "red-hot" HEM perspective (see Figure 5.9). At one end of the continuum is consumer behavior that is based on *pure reason*—cold, logical, and rational; the behavior best described by the CPM perspective. At the other end is consumer behavior that is based on *pure passion*—hot, spontaneous, and perhaps even irrational; the behavior best described by the HEM perspective. In between these extremes rests the bulk of consumer behavior, most of which is not based on pure reason or pure passion, and is neither red hot nor icy-blue cold. Rather, most behavior ranges, again in metaphorical terms, from cool to warm. In the final analysis, we will examine the rather extreme perspectives of consumer behavior but recognize that oftentimes both perspectives are applicable to understanding how and why consumers behave as they do.

The information-processing situation faced by consumers and the corresponding communication imperatives for marketing communicators have been described in the following terms:

The consumer is constantly being bombarded with information which is potentially relevant for making choices. The consumer's reactions to that information, how that information is interpreted, and how it is combined or integrated with other

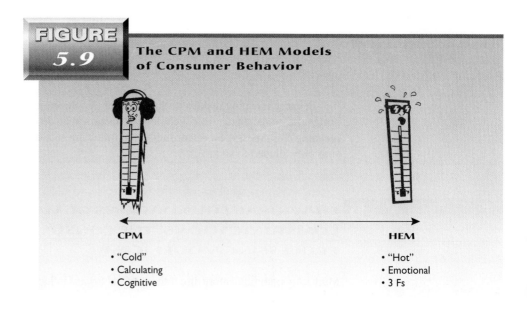

FIGURE 5.9

The CPM and HEM Models of Consumer Behavior

CPM
- "Cold"
- Calculating
- Cognitive

HEM
- "Hot"
- Emotional
- 3 Fs

information may have crucial impacts on choice. Hence, [marketing communicators'] decisions on what information to provide to consumers, how much to provide, and how to provide that information require knowledge of how consumers process, interpret, and integrate that information in making choices.[30]

The following sections discuss consumer information processing in terms of eight interrelated stages:[31]

1. *Exposure* to information.
2. Selective *attention.*
3. *Comprehension* of attended information.
4. *Agreement* with comprehended information.
5. *Retention* in memory of accepted information.
6. *Retrieval* of information from memory.
7. *Decision making* from alternatives.
8. *Action* taken on the basis of the decision.

Exposure to Information

The marketing communicator's fundamental task is to deliver messages to consumers, who, it is expected, will process the messages and be persuaded to undertake the course of action advocated by the marketer. By definition, **exposure** simply means that consumers come in contact with the marketer's message (they see a magazine ad, hear a radio commercial, and so on). Although exposure is an essential preliminary step to subsequent stages of information processing, the mere fact of exposing consumers to the marketing communicator's message does not ensure that the message will have any impact. Gaining exposure is a *necessary* but *insufficient* condition for communication success. In practical terms, exposing consumers to a brand's message is a function of key managerial decisions regarding: (1) the size of the budget, and (2) the choice of media and vehicles in which to present a brand message. In other words, a high percentage of a target audience will be exposed to a brand's message if sufficient funds are allocated and wise choices of media outlets are made; insufficient budget and/or poor media selection invariably result in low levels of exposure.

Selective Attention

Attention means to focus on and consider a message to which one has been exposed. Consumers attend to only a small fraction of marketing communications stimuli because demands placed on attention are great; therefore, attention is highly *selective.* Selectivity is necessary because information-processing capacity is limited, and effective utilization of this capacity requires the consumer to allocate mental energy (processing capacity) to only messages that are relevant and of interest to current goals.[32] For example, once their initial curiosity is satisfied, most people who have no interest in owning a dog would, upon exposure to the ad in Figure 5.10, pay relatively little attention to the detailed comments about Pedigree Puppy food, because the product has little relevance to them. On the other hand, dog owners and lovers could be expected to devote *conscious attention* to the advertisement insofar as it holds a high level of relevance to their interests. Please note that *conscious attention* is highlighted in the previous sentence. This is to distinguish this deliberate, controlled form of attention from an *automatic* form of relatively superficial attention that occurs due to factors such as stimulus novelty (discussed subsequently) even when a message holds little personal relevance to the consumer.[33]

There are three kinds of attention: involuntary, nonvoluntary, and voluntary. **Involuntary attention** requires little or no effort on the part of a receiver. A stimulus intrudes upon a resisting person's consciousness. In this case, attention is gained on the basis of the

Illustration of
Selective Attention

intensity of the stimulus—examples include a loud sound and a bright light. **Nonvoluntary attention,** sometimes called *spontaneous attention,* occurs when a person is attracted to a stimulus and continues to pay attention because it holds his or her interest. A person in this situation neither resists nor willfully attends to the stimulus initially; however, he or she continues to pay attention because the stimulus has some benefit or relevance. Generally, advertisers create messages to gain the nonvoluntary attention of an audience, since in most situations consumers do not willfully search out advertising messages. Therefore, advertisements must attract and maintain attention by being interesting and, often, entertaining. Finally, **voluntary attention** occurs when a person willfully notices a stimulus. A consumer who is considering the purchase of, say, new snow skis will consciously direct his or her attention to ski advertisements. Also, people who have recently made important purchase decisions will voluntarily attend to messages to reassure themselves that their decisions were correct.

As this discussion indicates, attention is highly selective. Attention selectivity is determined both by properties of the marketing stimulus itself and by factors that rest in the consumer's background and psychological makeup. The following discussion reviews three sets of appeals that marketing communicators employ to attract consumers' attention to advertisements or to other marketing messages.[34]

Appeals to Cognitive and Hedonic Needs.   Consumers are most likely to attend to messages that serve their cognitive needs and those that make them feel good and bring pleasure (hedonic needs). Regarding **cognitive needs,** consumers are most likely to attend to those stimuli that are congruent with their informational goals. A student who wants to move out of a dormitory and into an apartment, for example, will be on the lookout for information pertaining to apartments. Classified ads and overheard conversations about apartments will be attended to even when the apartment seeker is not actively looking for information. Similarly, advertisements for food products are especially likely to be noticed when people are hungry. For this reason, many restaurant and fast-food marketers advertise on the radio during the after-work rush hour. Fast-food advertisers also promote their products on late-night television for the same reason.

Hedonic needs are satisfied when consumers attend to messages that make them feel good. People are most likely to attend to those stimuli that have become associated with *rewards* and that relate to those *aspects of life that they value highly.* For example, the use of babies (Figure 5.11), appetizing food items (Figure 5.12), and warm family scenes

Hedonic Appeal to the
Love for Babies

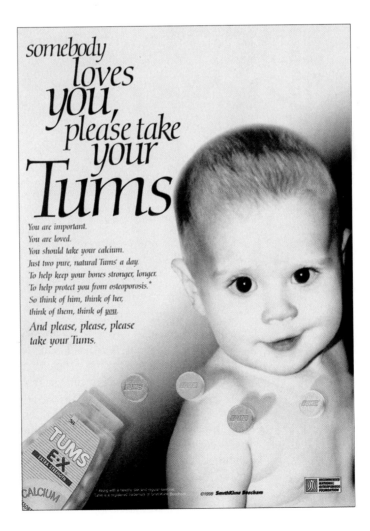

Hedonic Appetitive Appeal

(Figure 5.13) are just some of the commonly used stimuli in advertisements. These appeals are inherently pleasurable to most people because they are firmly associated in our memories with past good times, enjoyment, and those things we value in life.

Use of Novel Stimuli.   There are a wide variety of novel forms of marketing messages. In general, **novel** marketing communications use *unusual, distinctive,* or *unpredictable* devices. Such stimuli tend to produce greater attention than those that are familiar and routine. This can be explained by the behavioral concept of *human adaptation.* People adapt to the conditions around them: As a stimulus becomes more familiar, people become desensitized to it. Psychologists refer to this as *habituation.* For example, if you drive past a billboard on the way to school or work each day, you probably notice it less on each

occasion. If the billboard were removed, you probably would notice it was no longer there. In other words, we notice by exception.

Examples of novelty abound, as illustrated in Figures 5.14 and 5.15. The advertisement for Ziploc's Slide-Loc storage bags (Figure 5.14)—a product category that is not one of high relevance to most consumers—benefits from the attention-getting usage of vegetable pieces formed in the shape of a human ear. The natural eye flow from the top to bottom of the "ear" leads the reader of this ad conveniently to the headline, which provides a rationale for this novel visual when stating "That ought to perk up a few ears." Figure 5.15 for the Mercury Cougar further illustrates a novel device to gain the reader's attention. Notice again that the reader naturally follows the flow of the unique, amusement-park-like road configuration directly to the visual of the automobile and from there to the headline and body copy at the bottom. Both examples represent a key point: The effective use of novelty involves not just attracting attention but also directing that attention to key visual and verbal information.

Use of Intense Stimuli.   **Intense stimuli** (those that are louder, more colorful, bigger, brighter, etc.) increase the probability of attracting attention. This is because it is difficult for consumers to avoid intense stimuli, thus leading to involuntary or nonvoluntary attention. One need only walk through a shopping mall, department store, or supermarket and observe the various packages, displays, sights, sounds, and smells to appreciate the special efforts marketing communicators take to attract consumers' attention.

Advertisements, too, utilize intensity to attract attention. For example, the advertisement for cheese from the America's Dairy Farmers trade association (see Figure 5.16) catches the reader's attention by highlighting a huge wedge of cheese fastened by ropes to a camping-type vehicle. In addition to attracting attention, this caricature is apparently

FIGURE
5.14

The Use of Novelty
to Attract Attention

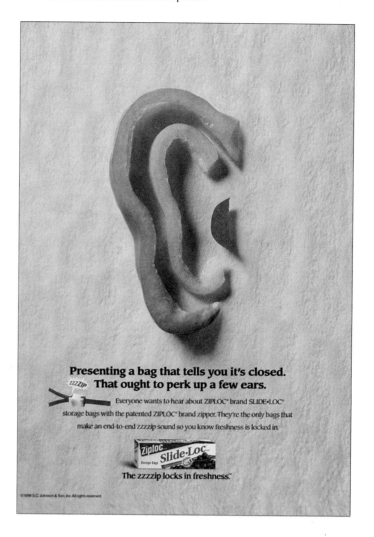

intended to remind consumers not to forget the cheese when packing for a camping trip or other excursion. The use of an intense lightning charge in the Allstate insurance advertisement (Figure 5.17) further illustrates the effective use of this attention-gaining technique. Once again, notice that the ad suitably directs attention from the lone cloud to the house via the lightning charge and then on to the all-important body copy.

Use of Motion. Advertisers sometimes use motion to attract and direct consumer attention. The flipping coin in Figure 5.18 (for Amstel light) captures attention, directs eye flow down the bottle to the brand name and then on to the resolution of the heads and tails alternatives posed at the onset of the coin's free fall. The use of motion in the Dodge Neon advertisement (Figure 5.19) further illustrates the use of this method both to gain the reader's attention and, in this case, direct that attention to the $1,500 cash-back offer, which is the ad's key selling point.

In sum, attention involves allocating limited processing capacity in a selective fashion. Effective marketing communications are designed to activate consumer interests by appealing to those needs that are most relevant to a market segment. This is no easy task; marketing communications environments (stores, advertising media, noisy offices during sales presentations) are inherently cluttered with competitive stimuli and messages that also vie for the prospective customer's attention. Research shows that advertising *clutter,* whether real or perceived, reduces advertising effectiveness.[35] Television commercials appearing later in a stream of multiple commercials and those for low-involvement products are particularly susceptible to clutter effects.[36]

FIGURE 5.15

Another Illustration of Novelty in Advertising

Comprehension of What Is Attended

To comprehend is to understand and create meaning out of stimuli and symbols. Communication is effective when the meaning a marketing communicator intends to convey matches what consumers actually extract from the messages. The term **comprehension** often is used interchangeably with *perception;* both terms refer to *interpretation.* Because people respond to their perceptions of the world and not to the world as it actually is, the topic of comprehension, or perception, is one of the most important subjects in marketing communications.[37]

The perceptual process of interpreting stimuli is called **perceptual encoding.** Two main stages are involved.[38] **Feature analysis** is the initial stage whereby a receiver examines the basic features of a stimulus (such as size, shape, color, and angles) and from this makes a preliminary classification. For example, we are able to distinguish a motorcycle from a bicycle by examining features such as size, presence of an engine, and the number of controls. Lemons and oranges are distinguished by their colors and shapes.

The second stage of perceptual encoding, **active synthesis,** goes beyond merely examining physical features. The *context* or situation in which information is received plays a major role in determining what is perceived and interpreted, or, in other words, what meaning is acquired. Interpretation results from combining, or *synthesizing,* stimulus features with expectations of what should be present in the context in which a stimulus is perceived. For example, a synthetic fur coat placed in the window of a discount clothing store (the context) is likely to be perceived as a cheap imitation; however, the same coat, when attractively merchandised in an expensive boutique (a different context) might now be considered a high-quality, stylish garment.

The Use of Intensity
to Attract Attention

A humorous way to better understand the difference between feature analysis and active synthesis is by examining cartoons. Witty cartoonists often use humor in subtle ways. They insert characters and props in cartoons that require the reader to draw from his or her own past experiences and recollections in order to perceive (comprehend) the humor. Before reading on, consider the cartoon in Figure 5.20 from Gary Larson's now-discontinued "The Far Side." The readily recognized features in this cartoon (feature analysis) are three Neanderthal characters, a mammoth, and a spear that has fallen short of the mammoth. These features are not humorous per se; rather, humor is *comprehended* by active synthesis on the reader's part. Some people immediately pick up on the humor, while others see no humor at all. Understanding the cartoon requires that one generalize to the situation in the cartoon from what happens in a basketball game when a player fires up a shot that completely misses the basket. At that instance fans from the opposing team spontaneously hoot in unison "Airrrr ball . . . airrrr ball." Gary Larson has generalized to the plight of the Neanderthal man who has failed to reach the mammoth with his spear and who then is ridiculed by his chums: "Airrrrr spearrrr . . . airrrrr spearrrr! . . ."

The important point in the preceding discussion is that consumers' comprehension of marketing stimuli is determined by stimulus features and by characteristics of the consumers themselves. Expectations, needs, personality traits, past experiences, and attitudes toward the stimulus object all play important roles in determining consumer perceptions.[39] Due to the subjective nature of the factors that influence our perceptions, comprehension is oftentimes *idiosyncratic,* or peculiar to each individual. Figure 5.21 provides a humorous, albeit revealing, illustration of the idiosyncrasy of perception. "The Investigation" illustrates that each individual's personal characteristics and background influence how he or she perceives someone else.

FIGURE
5.17

Another Illustration of
Intensity in Advertising

An individual's *mood* also can influence his or her perception of stimulus objects. Research has found that when people are in a good mood they are more likely to retrieve positive rather than negative material from their memories; are more likely to perceive the positive side of things; and, in turn, are more likely to respond positively to a variety of stimuli.[40] These findings have important implications for both advertising strategy and personal selling activity. Both forms of marketing communications, especially personal selling, are capable of placing consumers in positive (or negative) moods and may enhance (or mitigate) consumer perceptions and attitudes toward marketers' offerings.

Miscomprehension. People sometimes *misinterpret* or *miscomprehend* messages so as to make them more consistent with their existing beliefs or expectations. This typically is done without conscious awareness; nonetheless, distorted perception and message miscomprehension are common.

The Use of Motion to Attract Attention

A dramatic but tragic case that points out the consequences of misperception occurred in 1988, when the crew of the USS *Vincennes* shot down an Iranian commercial airliner in the Persian Gulf. The stressed-out crew had been alerted that Iranian F-14 warplanes were in the area; therefore, they expected to see an F-14 warplane attacking their ship. They saw what they thought to be a warplane and shot it down. The "warplane" actually was a commercial airliner, and 290 innocent passengers were killed—a tragic case of human error.[41]

An example of selective perception in a marketing context can be seen in a study that examined viewer miscomprehension of three forms of televised communication: programming content, commercials, and public-service announcements (PSAs). Nearly 3,000 people from test sites throughout the United States were exposed to two communication units from a pool of 60 different communications (25 commercials, 13 PSAs, and 22 program excerpts). Respondents answered six true/false questions immediately after viewing the

Another Illustration of Motion in Advertising

Dodge Neon.

Dodge Neon with $1500 cash back.

Now it's even easier to take off in a Dodge Neon. After $1,500 cash back, Neon's just $10,155 for starters, $12,830 nicely equipped* with lots of neat stuff like A/C, automatic, power front windows, power locks and power mirrors. Or get low 1.9% APR financing for up to 60 months.† But you better move quick. They're going pretty fast these days.

Neon 🐏 **The New Dodge**

For more info call 1-800-4-A-DODGE. Or visit our Web site at www.4adodge.com

Always use seat belts. Remember a backseat is the safest place for children.   *Includes destination. MSRPs after cash back exclude tax. Base sedan higher.   †1.9%/60 mos. financing on Neon = $17.48 per month per $1,000 financed for qualified buyers. Or get $1,500 cash back.

communications. Two of the six statements were always true, and the remainder were always false; half related to objective facts, and half were inferences. A high rate of miscomprehension was revealed across all three forms of communications, with an average miscomprehension of nearly 30 percent.[42]

Agreement with What Is Comprehended

A fourth information-processing stage involves the matter of whether the consumer *yields to,* or agrees with, a message argument that he or she has comprehended. It is crucial from a marketing communications perspective that consumers not only comprehend a message but that they also agree with the message (as opposed to countering it or rejecting it outright). Comprehension by itself does not ensure that the message will change consumers' attitudes or influence their behavior.

Agreement depends on whether the message is credible and whether it contains information and appeals that are compatible with the values that are important to the consumer. For example, a consumer who is more interested in the symbolic implications of consuming a particular product than in acquiring functional value is likely to be persuaded more by a message that associates the advertised brand with a desirable group than one that talks about mundane product features.

FIGURE 5.20

Humorous Illustration of Active Synthesis

"Airrrrr spearrrr ... airrrrr spearrrr! ..."

Retention and Search/Retrieval of Stored Information

These two information processing stages, retention and information search and retrieval, are discussed together because both involve *memory* factors related to consumer choice. The subject of memory is a complex topic that has been studied extensively, leading to sophisticated theorizing about its structure and functioning. These technicalities need not concern us here, however, because our interest in the subject is considerably more practical.[43]

From a marketing-communications perspective, memory involves the related issues of what consumers remember (recognize and recall) about marketing stimuli and how they access and retrieve information when making consumption choices. The subject of memory is inseparable from the process of learning, so the following paragraphs first discuss the basics of memory, then examine learning fundamentals, and, finally, emphasize the practical application to marketing communications of memory and learning principles.

Elements of Memory. Memory consists of long-term memory *(LTM);* short-term, or working, memory *(STM);* and a set of sensory stores *(SS)*. Information is received by one or more sensory receptors (sight, smell, touch, and so on) and passed to an appropriate SS, where it is rapidly lost (within fractions of a second) unless attention is allocated to the stimulus. Attended information is then transferred to STM, which serves as the center for current processing activity by integrating information from the sense organs and from LTM. *Limited processing capacity* is the most outstanding characteristic of STM; individuals can process

FIGURE 5.21

Humorous Illustration of Selective Perception

only a finite amount of information at any one time. An excessive amount of information will result in reduced recognition and recall. Furthermore, information in STM that is not thought about or rehearsed will be lost from STM in about 30 seconds or less.[44] (This is what happens when you get a phone number from a telephone directory but then are distracted before you have an opportunity to dial the number. You must refer to the directory a second time and then repeat the number to yourself—rehearse it—so that you will not forget it again.)

Information is transferred from STM to LTM, which cognitive psychologists consider to be a virtual storehouse of unlimited information. Information in LTM is organized into coherent and associated cognitive units, which are variously called *schemata, memory organization packets,* or *knowledge structures.* All three terms reflect the idea that LTM consists of associative links among related information, knowledge, and beliefs.[45] The concept of a knowledge structure is illustrated in Figure 5.22, a representation that captures a baby boomer's schema for the Volkswagen Beetle, a car she first owned during her college years in the 1960s and repurchased in 1998 when the new Beetle was introduced. (Historical note: The VW Beetle had its heyday in the United States in the 1960s and 1970s but then lost its brand equity and market share. But like phoenix ascending from the ashes, the new VW Beetle was reintroduced in 1998 to stunning consumer acceptance.)

The marketing practitioner's job is to provide positively valued information that consumers will store in LTM and that will increase the odds of ultimately choosing the marketer's brand over competitive options. Stated differently, the marketing communicator's

FIGURE 5.22

A Consumer's Knowledge Structure for the VW Beetle

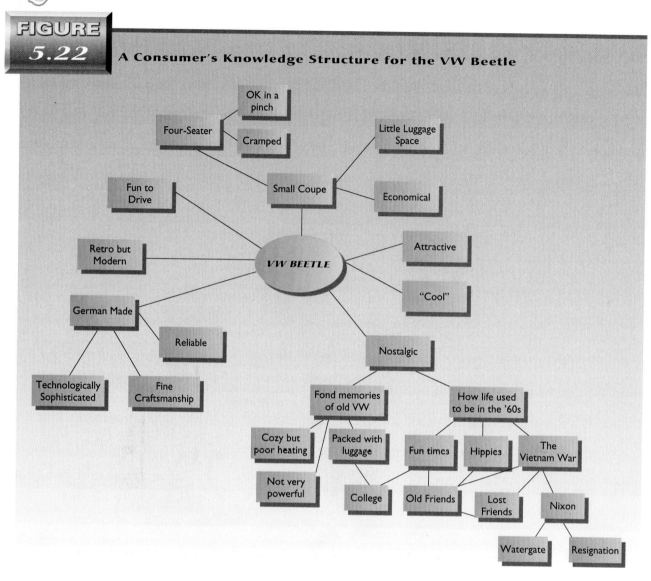

task is to facilitate consumer learning. **Learning** represents changes in the content or organization of information in consumers' long-term memories, that is, changes in their knowledge structures related to a particular brand.[46]

Marketing communicators continuously attempt to alter consumers' long-term memories, or knowledge structures, by facilitating learning of information that is compatible with the marketer's interest. For example, the advertisement for Whirlpool refrigerators (Figure 5.23) is an attention-getting attempt to facilitate consumers' learning that Whirlpool refrigerators have a filtration system that enables better-tasting water and ice to be served conveniently from the door.

Types of Learning. Two primary types of learning are relevant to marketing communications activity.[47] One type is the *strengthening of linkages among specific memory concepts,* such as between the marketer's brand (one memory concept) and some feature or benefit of that brand (another memory concept). In general, linkages are strengthened by *repeating* claims, presenting them in a more *concrete* fashion (a topic given more detail shortly), and being *creative* in conveying a product's features. Metaphorically, the marketing communicator wishes to build mental "ropes" (rather than flimsy strings) between a brand and positive features/benefits of that brand.

Facilitating Consumer's
Learning

With water this pure and good, you might even *want* to drink eight glasses a day.

Downing that daily dose of H_2O has never been easy... until now. With the exclusive Whirlpool® UltraEase™ Filtration System, our new refrigerators serve up fresh, better-tasting water and ice right from the door. And only Whirlpool puts the filter *outside* on the bottom panel – that

saves you the trouble of taking out food. Just a simple turn of a knob lets you replace the filter – no sweat. To soak up even more about our refrigerators, visit **www.whirlpool.com** or call 1-800-253-1301. We think you'll find it all very refreshing.

A Job Well Done.™

Marketing communicators facilitate a second form of learning by *establishing entirely new linkages*. Returning to our discussion of brand equity back in Chapter 1, the present notion of establishing new linkages is equivalent to the previously discussed idea of enhancing brand equity by building a strong, favorable, and perhaps unique association between the brand and a new feature or benefit. Hence, the terms "linkage" and "association" are interchangeable in this context. Both involve a relation between a brand and its features/benefits that are stored in a consumer's memory.

The advertisement for Kingsford Match Light (Figure 5.24) illustrates a rather typical effort to establish new linkages in consumers' minds via advertising—in this case, linking the brand and the promise that this brand of charcoal can be lighted and ready for cooking in about 10 minutes. The clever visual (an anthropomorphized grill), the headline, and

Establishing a New Linkage
Between a Brand and a
Desirable Feature

body copy all combine in this creative effort in hopes of building a strong link in consumers' memories between the Kingsford brand and this highly desirable feature.

Search and Retrieval of Information. Information that is learned and stored in memory only impacts consumer choice behavior when it is searched and retrieved. Precisely how retrieval occurs is beyond the scope of this chapter.[48] Suffice it to say that retrieval is facilitated when a new piece of information is linked, or associated, with another concept that is itself well known and easily accessed. When introducing Luvs diapers, Procter & Gamble used a simple but creative strategy to make it easy for consumers to remember that this brand is available in separate designs for boys and girls. Taking advantage of the widely recognized cue that blue signifies boys and pink girls, P&G gave Luvs diapers two different colors and packaged them in pink and blue boxes, thereby successfully conveying the gender distinctiveness of the Luvs brand.

The Use of Concretizing and Imagery.   Concretizing and imagery are used extensively in marketing communications to facilitate both consumer learning and retrieval of brand information. **Concretizing** is based on the straightforward idea that it is easier for people to remember and retrieve *tangible* rather than abstract information. Claims about a brand are more concrete (versus abstract) when they are made perceptible, palpable, real, evident, and vivid. Examples of concretizing abound. Here are a few illustrations:

1. An advertisement for Johnson's baby powder positioned the brand to be capable of making the user's body feel "as soft as the day you were born." To concretize this claim, a series of age-regression scenes revealed, first, a shot of a woman in her 30s, then a shot as she looked in her 20s, next as an early teenager, and finally as a baby. Accompanying music was played throughout to the lyrics "make me, make me a baby." This beautiful and somewhat touching ad made concrete Johnson's claim that its baby powder will make the user feel "as soft as the day you were born."

2. The makers of Anacin tablets needed a concrete way to present that brand as "strong pain relief for splitting headaches." The idea of a splitting headache was concretized by showing a hard-boiled egg splitting with accompanying sound effects.

3. Aqua-Fresh toothpaste is advertised as a triple-action toothpaste—whitens teeth, fights cavities, and freshens breath. Most toothpaste brands are mono-color, typically white, but in concretizing its triple-action properties, Aqua-Fresh is a three-color striped paste.

4. Tinactin, a treatment for athlete's foot, concretized its relief properties by showing a person's pair of feet literally appearing to be on fire (representing the fiery sensation of athlete's foot), which is "extinguished" by an application of Tinactin.

5. To convey the notion that Purina brand Hi Pro dog food will recharge an active dog and keep it running, a magazine ad portrayed the brand in the form of a battery, which is a widely recognized apparatus for charging electrical objects. In effect, the battery in this symbolic concretization conveyed pictorially the more abstract claim contained in the ad's body copy.

6. To establish in consumers' minds that Tums E-X is "twice as strong as Rolaids," the commercial showed a sledge hammer behind Tums and a regular-sized hammer behind Rolaids. The commercial then showed the sledge hammer driving in a nail twice as quickly as the regular hammer, thus concretizing Tums' claim.

7. A more recent Tums advertisement (see Figure 5.25) claims in its headline that "scientific studies find Tums to be the purest form of calcium available." This claim is concretized with the visual display of a package of Tums inside an empty milk bottle and with the juxtaposed words "calcium" and "Tums" forming the new word Calciums. The chances are good that the two concepts, Tums and calcium, will be firmly linked in the memories of the many consumers exposed to this clever magazine advertisement—an apt illustration of the maxim that "a picture is worth a thousand words."

8. Finally, the ad for Paper Mate rubberized barrel pens (Figure 5.26) beautifully illustrates how a verbal advertising statement ("the uncommonly comfortable Paper Mate") can be concretized. The ad says it all, so no further commentary is required.

The preceding examples highlight the important role of concretizing in advertising. Underlying some of the illustrations is the use of imagery. **Imagery,** by definition, is the

The Use of Concretizing to Facilitate Consumer Learning

representation of sensory experiences in short-term, or working, memory—including visual, auditory, and other sensory experiences.[49] To better understand the notion of imagery, think of the following words: CD-ROM, skateboard, dancing, duck-billed platypus, satisfaction, and standard deviation. The first two, CD-ROM and skateboard, no doubt evoke distinct images in your mind; dancing also probably elicits a visualization, and some of you might even possess a visual concept for the platypus. It is doubtful, however, that you have an image for satisfaction or standard deviation, both of which are inherently abstract concepts.

Mental imagery plays an important role in various aspects of consumer information processing: comprehension, recall, retrieval, attitude formation, and choice. For practical purposes, the issue is this: What can marketing communicators do to elicit imagery? Three strategies are possible: (1) use visual or pictorial stimuli, (2) present concrete verbal stimuli, and (3) provide imagery instructions.[50] Only the first two of these will be discussed, as the third is not used extensively in marketing communications (although advertisers and sales people occasionally instruct listeners or readers to imagine themselves engaged in some behavior).

Pictures and visuals are best remembered (compared with abstract or concrete verbalizations) because pictures are especially able to elicit imagery. A more formal explanation is provided by the **dual-coding theory,** which holds that pictures are represented in memory in verbal as well as visual form, whereas words are less likely to have visual representations.[51] The advertisements for Tums (Figure 5.25) and Paper Mate (Figure 5.26) nicely illustrate advertising efforts to exploit the benefits of visual imagery and dual coding.

FIGURE 5.26

Another Example of the Use of Concretizing to Facilitate Consumer Learning

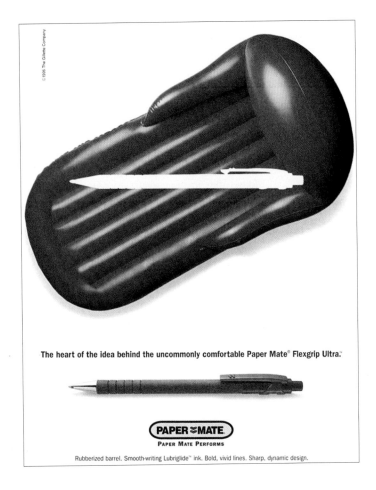

The heart of the idea behind the uncommonly comfortable Paper Mate® Flexgrip Ultra.™

PAPER≋MATE.
PAPER MATE PERFORMS

Rubberized barrel. Smooth-writing Lubriglide™ ink. Bold, vivid lines. Sharp, dynamic design.

Research has shown that information about product attributes is better recalled when the information is accompanied with pictures than when presented only as prose.[52] The value of pictures is especially important when verbal information is itself low in imagery.[53]

Consumer researchers have found that people remember significantly greater numbers of company names when the names are paired with meaningful pictorials. The name "Jack's Camera Shop," for example, is better remembered when the store name is presented along with a jack playing card shown holding a movie camera to its eye.[54] Many marketing communicators use similar pictorials, as can be proven by perusing the yellow pages of any city telephone directory and by surfing the Internet.

Finally, effective visual imagery in advertising can place the audience member in a number of imagined or fantasy-like situations that are conducive to sales of the marketer's product. For example, the advertisement may place the consumer behind the wheel of a powerful sports car cruising down a beautiful country road; in a pair of new basketball shoes leaping high off the floor over an opponent to make an acrobatic, Jordanesque dunk shot; in a dazzling outfit attending an important social event; basking in the sun on an ocean liner cruising toward the Caribbean; rushing toward an important meeting carrying a new leather briefcase; or delivering packages of food and toys to needy people on Christmas Eve.

Imagery and concretizing have numerous potential applications for advertising, point-of-purchase displays, personal selling, and other marketing communications practices.[55] Much of what we feel and visualize internally is based on what we see. Perhaps as much as 70 to 80 percent of what we learn is visual.[56]

It is fitting to conclude this section by noting that although the discussion has focused on visualization, imagery also is elicited by appeals to other senses—auditory, olfactory (smell), and tactile. Marketing communicators appeal to our various senses and evoke images that activate our emotions, influence our cognition, and enhance the memorability of marketing messages. Recall for a moment the sweet smell of a Victoria's Secret lingerie store. Think about the soft, comfortable feel of an old flannel shirt or pair of favorite sweat pants. Just imagine what a movie (or TV commercial) would be like if it contained just scenes and conversations without background music or noises.

The Special Case of Olfactory Stimuli.

Marketing practitioners appeal to the sense of smell, *olfaction,* with a variety of point-of-purchase displays and advertising practices. Store environments are filled with smells, including the use of aromatic discs that emit pleasant and purchase-enhancing odors. Packages and magazine advertisements sometimes are encapsulated with scents that are emitted when scratch-and-sniff patches are rubbed; and sales promotions and point-of-purchase materials embody the scents contained in the products they are designed to promote.

Smells can evoke strong images of products, product usage, and consumption situations. Moreover, olfactory stimuli are able to attract attention, motivate information processing, influence memories, affect store and product evaluations, and activate behavior.[57]

Deciding among Alternatives

The six preceding stages have examined how consumers receive, encode, and store information that is pertinent to making consumption choices. Stored in consumers' memories are numerous information packets for different consumption alternatives. This information is in the form of bits and pieces of *knowledge* (e.g., Adidas is a brand of athletic shoes), specific *beliefs* (e.g., the BMW X5 is an attractive SUV), and *evaluations of purchase consequences* (e.g., manufacturer reputability is more important than price when buying sophisticated electronic equipment).

The issue for present discussion is this: When contemplating a purchase from a particular product category, how does a consumer decide which brand to purchase? The simple answer is that she or he simply chooses the "best" brand. However, it is not always clear what the best brand is, especially when considering that the consumer likely has stored in long-term memory a wide variety of information (facts, beliefs, etc.) about each brand in his or her consideration set. Some of the information is positive, and some of it is negative; occasionally the information is contradictory; oftentimes the information is incomplete.

The following discussion provides some insight into how consumers react in this situation. It will become clear that consumers often resort to simplifying strategies, or *heuristics,* to arrive at decisions that are at least satisfactory if not perfect. Before we describe specific heuristics, it should be instructive to review a decision that all of us have made and that, in many respects, is one of the most important decisions we will ever make: which college or university to attend.

For some of you, there really was no choice—you went to a school you had always planned on attending, or perhaps your parents insisted on a particular institution. Others, especially those of you who work full- or part-time or have family responsibilities, may have selected a school purely as a matter of convenience or affordability; in other words, you really did not seriously consider other institutions. But some of you actively evaluated many colleges and universities before making a final choice. The process was probably done in the following manner: You received information from a variety of schools and formed preliminary impressions of these institutions; you established criteria for evaluating schools (academic reputation, distance from home, cost, curricula, availability of financial assistance, quality of athletic programs, etc.); you formed weights regarding the relative importance of these various criteria; and you eventually integrated this information to arrive at the all-important choice of which college to attend. Now, let's use this example to understand better the different types of heuristics and the terminology that follows.

The simplest of all decision heuristics is **affect referral.**[58] With this strategy the individual simply calls from memory his or her attitude, or affect, toward relevant alternatives and picks that alternative for which the affect is most positive. In the college decision, for example, you may decide that you like a school simply because your friends attend it. There is no need to go through a rigorous decision-making process. In general, this type of choice strategy would be expected for frequently purchased items where risk is minimal. Such items typically are regarded as low-involvement purchases.

Consider, by comparison, the use of a **compensatory heuristic.** To understand how and why compensation operates, it is important to realize that rarely is a particular alternative completely superior or dominant over other consumption alternatives. Although a brand may be preferable with respect to one, two, or several benefits, it is unlikely that it is superior to its alternatives in terms of all attributes or benefits that consumers are seeking. (If you're having trouble appreciating the idea that alternatives are rarely dominant, consider the situation with people. Have you ever known another person who is more intelligent, more honest, more attractive, more athletic, more caring, and who has a better sense of humor than everyone else? If the answer is yes, do your best to marry him or her!)

When making choices under *nondominant* circumstances, consumers must give something up in order to get something else. That is, high-involvement decision making most always requires *trade-offs.* If you want more of a particular benefit, you typically have to pay a higher price; if you want to pay less, you often give something up in terms of performance, dependability, prestige, or durability. Returning to the university choice decision, illustrative trade-offs concern tuition cost versus the quality of education, the size of school versus the quality of athletic programs, or the desirability of the school versus its proximity or distance from home.

In general, when applying principles of compensation, the chosen alternative probably is not the best in terms of all criteria; rather, its superiority on some criteria offsets, or compensates for, its lesser performance on other criteria.[59] In short, the consumer typically cannot have it all unless she or he is willing to pay super-premium prices to obtain *crème de la crème* brands.

In addition to compensatory choice behavior, consumers use a variety of so-called **noncompensatory heuristics.** The only one to be discussed here is the **conjunctive heuristic,** which is derived from the word *conjoin,* meaning to unite or combine.[60] In using this heuristic, the consumer establishes cutoffs, or *minima,* on all pertinent choice criteria. An alternative is retained for further consideration only if it meets or exceeds *all* minima. As seen in the hypothetical university choice, for example, a particular consumer may establish these cutoffs: A viable school must have a respected undergraduate major in advertising, be no farther than approximately 500 miles from home, and cost no more than $8,000 per year. All schools meeting these criteria receive further consideration.

The foregoing discussion should not be misinterpreted as meaning that consumers invariably use only a compensatory or only a noncompensatory choice heuristic. On the contrary, a more likely possibility, especially in high-involvement decisions, is that **phased strategies** are used—that is, a combination of heuristics is applied in sequence (in phase) with one another.[61] For example, after the future university student has exercised a conjunctive strategy to eliminate schools that do not satisfy all of his or her minima, he or she might then apply a compensatory heuristic to arrive at a choice from the remaining options that do satisfy all the minima.

Acting on the Basis of the Decision

It might seem that consumer choice behavior operates in a simple, lockstep fashion. This, however, is not necessarily the case. *People do not always behave in a manner consistent with their preferences.*[62] A major reason is the presence of events, or *situational factors,* that disrupt, inhibit, or otherwise prevent a person from following through on his or her intentions.[63] Situational factors are especially prevalent in the case of low-involvement consumer behavior. Stock-outs, price-offs, in-store promotions, and shopping at a different store are just some of the factors that lead to the purchase of brands that are not necessarily the most preferred and that would not be the predicted choice based on some heuristic, such as affect referral.

What all this means for marketing communicators is that all aspects of marketing (as discussed in Chapter 1) must be coordinated and integrated in order to get consumers to act favorably toward the marketer's offering.

A CPM Wrap-Up

A detailed account of consumer information processing has been presented to this point. As noted in the introduction, the CPM perspective provides an appropriate description of consumer behavior when the behavior is deliberate, thoughtful, or, in short, highly cognitive.

Much consumer behavior and the behavior of business-to-business buyers is of this nature. On the other hand, behavior also is motivated by emotional, hedonic, and experiential considerations. Therefore, we need to consider the HEM perspective and the implications it holds for marketing communicators.

BEHAVIORAL FOUNDATIONS OF MARKETING COMMUNICATIONS: THE HEM PERSPECTIVE

It again is imperative to emphasize that the *rational* consumer processing (CPM) and *hedonic, experiential* (HEM) models of information processing and decision making are *not* mutually exclusive. Indeed, there is impressive evidence that individuals comprehend reality by these rational and experiential processes operating interactively with one another, with their relative influence contingent on the nature of the situation and the amount of emotional involvement—the greater the emotional involvement, the greater the influence of experiential processes.[64] Hence, the HEM model probably better explains how consumers process information and make decisions when they are carefree and happy and confronted with positive outcomes.[65]

Whereas the CPM perspective views consumers as pursuing such objectives as "obtaining the best buy," "getting the most for the money," and "maximizing utility," the HEM perspective recognizes that people often consume products for the sheer fun of it or in the pursuit of amusement, fantasies, or sensory stimulation.[66] Product consumption from the hedonic perspective results from the *anticipation* of having fun, fulfilling fantasies, or having pleasurable feelings. Comparatively, product choice behavior from the CPM perspective is based on the thoughtful evaluation that the chosen alternative will be more functional and provide better results than will other alternatives.

Thus, viewed from an HEM perspective, products are more than mere objective entities (a bottle of perfume, a stereo system, a can of soup) and are, instead, subjective symbols that precipitate *feelings* (love, pride) and promise *fun* and the possible realization of *fantasies*. Products most compatible with the hedonic perspective include the performing arts (opera, modern dance), the so-called plastic arts (photography, crafts), popular forms of entertainment (movies, rock concerts), fashion apparel, sporting events, leisure activities, and recreational pursuits (such as the boarding sports noted in the *Opening Vignette* to Chapter 4).[67] It is important to realize, however, that any product—not just these examples—may have hedonic and experiential elements underlying its choice and consumption. For example, a lot of pleasant feelings and fantasizing are attached to contemplation of purchasing products such as new skis, an automobile, a bicycle, or furniture. Even Procter & Gamble, which is noted for its matter-of-fact advertising style, altered its historical emphasis on performance claims for Tide detergent and focused more on the emotions associated with clean, fresh laundry.[68]

The differences between the HEM and CPM perspectives hold meaningful implications for marketing communications practice. Whereas verbal stimuli designed to affect consumers' product knowledge and beliefs are most appropriate for communicating CPM-relevant products, the communication of HEM-relevant products emphasizes nonverbal content or emotionally provocative words and is intended to generate images, fantasies, and positive emotions and feelings.

A vivid contrast between the CPM and HEM orientations is illustrated in the differences in the advertisements for the Land Rover Discovery (Figure 5.27) and De Beers diamonds (Figure 5.28). The former ad uses verbal content to explain in some detail why the Discovery 4x4 is an all-terrain vehicle perfect for tough and hazardous road conditions. The ad exemplifies the CPM approach in that it attempts to move the consumer through all the CPM stages discussed previously. That is, Land Rover expects the consumer to attend to the message arguments, agree with them, retain them in memory, and to use this information in ultimately choosing the Discovery over other SUV offerings.

Comparatively, the De Beers diamond ad (Figure 5.28) provides no information about product attributes and benefits. Rather, the ad in its striking elegance appeals directly to the emotions of romance and pride.

The prior discussion and examples have emphasized advertising, but it should be apparent that the differences between CPM and HEM perspectives apply as well to other

FIGURE 5.27

An Advertisement Exemplifying the CPM Approach

Don't confuse buying a 4x4 with buying a car.

An Advertisement
Exemplifying the
HEM Approach

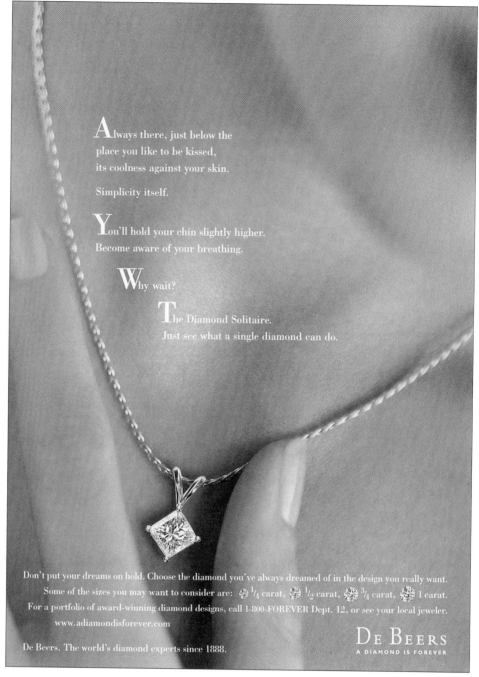

forms of marketing communications, especially personal selling. A salesperson may emphasize product features and tangible benefits in attempting to make a sale, or he or she may also attempt to convey the fun, fantasies, and pleasures that prospective customers can enjoy with product ownership. Successful salespersons employ both approaches and orient the dominant approach to the consumer's specific "hot buttons." That is, successful salespersons know how to adapt their presentations to different customers—it is hoped, of course, doing it honestly and maintaining standards of morality. (Chapter 20 discusses adaptive selling in some detail.)

Finally, no single marketing communications approach, whether aimed at CPM or HEM processing, is effective in all instances. What works best depends on the specific nature of the product category, the competitive situation, and the character and needs of the targeted market segment. Integrating the discussion in Chapter 1, brand concepts managed with appeals to *functional* needs are most congenial with the CPM perspective, whereas the HEM perspective offers a more appropriate approach for appealing to *symbolic* and *experiential* needs.

Summary

Marketing communications efforts attempt to achieve various objectives. These include building product category needs, creating brand awareness, enhancing brand attitudes, influencing purchase intentions, and facilitating purchase. These objectives are realized by managing brands throughout their life cycles. Brand concepts are managed by appealing to customers' functional, symbolic, and experiential needs through effective communication.

Communication is the process of establishing a commonness or oneness of thought between a sender and a receiver. The process consists of the following elements: a source who encodes a message; a channel that transmits the message; a receiver who decodes the message; noise, which interferes with or disrupts effective communication at any of the previous stages; and a feedback mechanism that affords the source a way of monitoring how accurately the intended message is being received.

The concept of signs explains how thought is shared between senders and receivers and how meaning is created. The larger the overlap, or commonality, in their perceptual fields, the greater the likelihood that the sender's signs will be decoded by the receiver in the manner intended.

Signs are used to share meaning, but signs and meaning are not synonymous. Meanings describe people's internal responses toward signs. Meaning is found within an individual's perceptual field. No two people have exactly the same meaning for the same sign; each sign elicits a meaning specific to each individual's field of experience.

Meaning is acquired through a process whereby stimuli (signs in the form of words, symbols, etc.) become associated with physical objects and evoke within individuals responses that are similar to those evoked by the physical objects themselves. Marketing communicators use a variety of techniques to make their brands stand for something, to embellish their value, or, in short, to give them meaning. This is accomplished by relating the brand to a desirable referent in some context (a sign relation), or relating the brand to a symbolic referent that has no prior intrinsic relation to the brand (forging a symbol relation). Simile, metaphor, and allegory are forms of figurative language that perform symbolic roles in marketing communications.

This chapter also describes the fundamentals of consumer choice behavior. Two relatively distinct perspectives on choice behavior are presented: the consumer processing model (CPM) and the hedonic, experiential model (HEM). The CPM approach views the consumer as an analytical, systematic, and logical decision maker. According to this perspective, consumers are motivated to achieve desired goals. The CPM process involves attending to, encoding, retaining, retrieving, and integrating information so that a person can achieve a suitable choice among consumption alternatives.

The HEM perspective views consumer choice behavior as resulting from the mere pursuit of fun, fantasy, and feelings. Thus, some consumer behavior is based predominantly on emotional considerations rather than on objective, functional, and economic factors.

The distinction between the CPM and HEM views of consumer choice is an important one for marketing communicators. The techniques and creative strategies for affecting consumer choice behavior clearly are a function of the prevailing consumer orientation. Specific implications and appropriate strategies are emphasized throughout the chapter.

Discussion Questions

1. Discuss the nature and importance of feedback. In what ways do marketing communicators receive feedback from present and prospective customers?

2. Assume you are a key marketing executive with General Motors Corporation. What forms of feedback would be most important to you as a way of assessing the long-run success potential of a new automobile you introduced to the market six months ago?

3. A reality of communication is that the same sign often means different things to different people. The red ribbon, for example, means different things to different groups. Provide a good example from your own personal experience in which the same sign had different meanings. What are the implications for marketing communications?

4. Some magazine advertisements show a picture of a product, mention the brand name, but have virtually no verbal content except, perhaps, a single statement about the brand. Locate an example of this type, and explain what meaning you think the advertiser is attempting to convey. Ask two friends to offer their interpretations of the same ad, and then compare their responses to determine the differences in meaning that these ads have for you and your friends.

5. How can a marketing communicator (such as an advertiser or salesperson) reduce noise when communicating a product message to a customer?

6. The famous California Raisins commercial humanized raisins by using claymatic characterizations. Raisins dressed in sunglasses and sneakers were shown dancing to "I Heard It through the Grapevine." Explain how this ad illustrates allegorical presentation in advertising.

7. Give two examples each of the use of sign and symbol relations in marketing communications.

8. Provide one example each of the use of simile and metaphor in marketing communications.

9. In the late 1980s Seven-Up introduced a line extension called 7Up Gold, a caffeinated drink with a ginger-ale taste, a cinnamon-apple overtone, and a reddish caramel hue. 7Up Gold was not a cola or a lemon-lime drink; in fact, it fit no established soft-drink category. Seven-Up executives had high hopes that 7Up Gold would capture around a 1 percent share of the annual U.S. soft-drink market. Unfortunately, after Seven-Up invested millions of dollars advertising and promoting 7Up Gold, the brand had gained only one-tenth of 1 percent of the market. 7Up Gold was dumped from the company's product line. Using concepts presented in this chapter, offer your explanation of why 7Up Gold failed.

10. When discussing exposure as the initial stage of information processing, it was claimed that gaining exposure is a necessary but insufficient condition for success. Explain.

11. There are numerous examples of marketing communicators' use of bright colors, loud sounds, and other intense stimuli to attract consumers' attention. Can you think of any drawbacks in using intense stimuli? Be specific.

12. Explain why attention is highly selective and what implication selectivity holds for marketing communicators.

13. All marketing communications environments are cluttered. Explain what this means and provide several examples. Do not restrict your examples just to advertisements.

14. Explain each of the following related concepts: perceptual encoding, feature analysis, and active synthesis. Using a supermarket product of your choice, explain how package designers for that industry implicitly use concepts of feature analysis in designing packages.

15. Linkages between memory concepts (for example, between a brand and a product benefit) are strengthened by frequently repeating a claim, presenting the claim in concrete fashion, or conveying it in a creative manner. Considering only the latter two ways (being concrete or creative), illustrate how you would use these approaches in advertising the following claim: "With Keen's nonalcoholic brew, you don't have to give up taste when you give up alcohol."

16. Distinguish between compensatory and noncompensatory heuristics.

17. In what sense would attending a Saturday afternoon college football game represent an hedonic- or experiential-based behavior?

18. Overpopulation is a major problem for much of the developing world. Complicating government efforts to reduce birth rates is the fact that many men, perhaps especially in Latin cultures, consider fathering children a sign of virility. Thus, efforts to reduce populations by encouraging men to have vasectomies often fall on deaf ears. Using concepts from this chapter, with particular attention to concretizing, what kind of promotional campaign would you develop to encourage Latin American men to consider having a vasectomy?

19. Figure 5.22 presents one consumer's knowledge structure for the VW Beetle. Construct your knowledge structure for this vehicle. Then illustrate your knowledge structure for the one automobile that you most covet owning.

20. When discussing allegory, the text suggested that Budweiser's television commercials with lizards (Frank and Louie) represent an application of allegory. What is your interpretation of the Frank & Louie ads? What story is being told underneath the superficial commercial story?

Internet Exercises

1. Internet advertisements must draw attention away from consumers' primary goals for using the Internet, namely, entertainment and informational pursuits. Expose yourself to some current Web ads and answer the following questions:
   a. Identify and describe at least four specific techniques that Web advertisers use to grab *attention*. What are the strengths and limitations of each technique?
   b. Do Web ads seem capable of capturing all three types of attention (i.e., involuntary, nonvoluntary, and voluntary)? Explain your answer.

2. Locate two examples of Web ads that are predominantly CPM-oriented and two Web ads that take an HEM approach.
   a. Describe the ads in detail and explain why you categorized each as either CPM- or HEM-oriented.
   b. "Click through" on the ads and describe the ensuing marketing communications. Is the CPM or HEM perspective maintained or altered? Explain why you think the ad and subsequent marketing communications were arranged in this way.

Chapter Five Endnotes

1. These objectives were delineated by John R. Rossiter and Larry Percy, *Advertising and Promotion Management* (New York: McGraw-Hill, 1987), 131.

2. Kevin Lane Keller, "Conceptualizing, Measuring, and Managing Customer-Based Brand Equity," *Journal of Marketing* 57 (January 1993), 1–22.

3. Wilbur Schramm, *The Process and Effects of Mass Communications* (Urbana: University of Illinois Press, 1955), 3.

4. Judie Lannon, "New Techniques for Understanding Consumer Reactions to Advertising," *Journal of Advertising Research* 26 (August/September 1986), R6–9.

5. For more in-depth treatments of semiotics in marketing communications and consumer behavior, see David Glen Mick, "Consumer Research and Semiotics: Exploring the Morphology of Signs, Symbols, and Significance," *Journal of Consumer Research* 13 (September 1986), 196–213; Eric Haley, "The Semiotic Perspective: A Tool for Qualitative Inquiry," in *Proceedings of the 1993 Conference of the American Academy of Advertising,* ed. Esther Thorson (Columbia, Mo.: The American Academy of Advertising, 1993), 189–196; and Birgit Wassmuth et al., "Semiotics: Friend or Foe to Advertising?" in *Proceedings of the 1993 Conference of the American Academy of Advertising,* ed., Esther Thorson (Columbia, Mo.: The American Academy of Advertising, 1993), 271–276. For interesting applications of a semiotic analysis, see Morris B. Holbrook and

Mark W. Grayson, "The Semiology of Cinematic Consumption: Symbolic Consumer Behavior in *Out of Africa,*" *Journal of Consumer Research* 13 (December 1986), 374–381; Edward F. McQuarrie and David Glen Mick, "On Resonance: A Critical Pluralistic Inquiry into Advertising Rhetoric," *Journal of Consumer Research* 19 (September 1992), 180–197; Linda M. Scott, "Understanding Jingles and Needledrop: A Rhetorical Approach to Music in Advertising," *Journal of Consumer Research* 17 (September 1990), 223–236; and Teresa J. Domzal and Jerome B. Kernan, "Mirror, Mirror: Some Postmodern Reflections on Global Advertising," *Journal of Advertising* 22 (December 1993), 1–20. For an insightful treatment on "deconstructing" meaning from advertisements and other marketing communications, see Barbara B. Stern, "Textual Analysis in Advertising Research: Construction and Deconstruction of Meanings," *Journal of Advertising* 25 (Fall 1996), 61–73.

6. This description is based on John Fiske, *Introduction to Communication Studies* (New York: Routledge, 1990); and Mick, "Consumer Research and Semiotics," 198.

7. Robert E. Klein III and Jerome B. Kernan, "Contextual Influences on the Meanings Ascribed to Ordinary Consumption Objects," *Journal of Consumer Research* 18 (December 1991), 311–324. See also Mary Jo Bitner, "Servicescapes: The Impact of Physical Surroundings on Customers and Employees," *Journal of Marketing* 56 (April 1992), 57–71.

8. Jean Halliday, "Pickups Gather Momentum As Status Symbols," *Advertising Age,* June 24, 1996, 20.

9. The subsequent discussion is influenced by the insights of David K. Berlo in *The Process of Communication* (San Francisco: Holt, Rinehart & Winston, 1960), 168–216.

10. Berlo, *The Process of Communication,* 175. On this point, see also Stern, "Textual Analysis in Advertising Research: Construction and Deconstruction of Meanings."

11. This interpretation is adapted from Roberto Friedmann and Mary R. Zimmer, "The Role of Psychological Meaning in Advertising," *Journal of Advertising* 17, no. 1 (1988), 31; and Klein and Kernan, "Contextual Influences on the Meanings Ascribed to Ordinary Consumption Objects."

12. Rick Fleury, "The Most Powerful Icon of the '90s?" *Brandweek,* November 30, 1992, 14; and Marc Peyser, "Tyranny of the Red Ribbon," *Newsweek,* June 28, 1993, 61.

13. Grant McCracken, "Culture and Consumption: A Theoretical Account of the Structure and Movement of the Cultural Meaning of Consumer Goods," *Journal of Consumer Research* 13 (June 1986), 74.

14. For further discussion, see Grant McCracken, "Advertising: Meaning or Information," in *Advances in Consumer Research,* vol. 14, ed. Melanie Wallendorf and Paul F. Anderson (Provo, Utah: Association for Consumer Research, 1987), 121–124.

15. These distinctions and the following discussion are based on Jeffrey F. Durgee, "Richer Findings from Qualitative Research," *Journal of Advertising Research* 26 (August/September 1986), 36–44. Durgee also discusses a third form of signs, called *signal relations,* but the present treatment focuses only on signs and symbols.

16. France Leclerc, Bernd H. Schmitt, and Laurette Dube, "Foreign Branding and Its Effects on Product Perceptions and Attitudes," *Journal of Marketing Research* 31 (May 1994), 263–270.

17. Kristine Bremer and Moonkyu Lee, "Metaphors in Marketing: Review and Implications for Marketers," *Advances in Consumer Research* 24 (Provo, UT: Association for Consumer Research, 1997), 419.

18. The following discussion is based on four articles by Barbara B. Stern: "Figurative Language in Services Advertising: The Nature and Uses of Imagery," in *Advances in Consumer Research,* vol. 15, ed. Michael J. Houston (Provo, Utah: Association for Consumer Research, 1987), 185–190; "How Does an Ad Mean? Language in Services Advertising," *Journal of Advertising* 17, no. 2 (1988), 3–14; "Medieval Allegory: Roots of Advertising Strategy for the Mass Market," *Journal of Marketing* 52 (July 1988), 84–94; and "Other-Speak: Classical Allegory and Contemporary Advertising," *Journal of Advertising* 19, no. 3 (1990), 14–26.

19. Stern, "Figurative Language in Services Advertising."

20. Nancy A. Mitchell, Diane M. Badzinski, and Donna R. Pawlowski, "The Use of Metaphors As Vivid Stimuli to Enhance Comprehension and Recall of Print Advertisements," in *Proceedings of the 1994 Conference on the American Academy of Advertising,* ed., Karen Whitehall King (Athens, GA: The American Academy of Advertising, 1994), 198–205.

21. A highly readable treatment of metaphors and their marketing implications is provided by Bremer and Lee, "Metaphors in Marketing: Review and Implications for Marketers," 419–424.

22. There is research that suggests, although does not definitively establish, that the use of metaphors in advertising aimed at elementary school-aged children may retard children's recall of advertising content. See Donna R. Pawlowski, Diane M. Badzinski, and Nancy Mitchell, "Effects of Metaphors on Children's Comprehension and Perception of Print Advertisements," *Journal of Advertising* 27 (Summer 1998), 83–98.

23. Stern, "How Does an Ad Mean? Language in Services Advertising," 186.

24. Stern, "Other-Speak: Classical Allegory and Contemporary Advertising," 15.

25. Stern, "Medieval Allegory: Roots of Advertising Strategy for the Mass Market," 86. (Stern also recognizes moral conflict as an additional characteristic but notes that moral conflict is less relevant to the use of allegory in advertising than in its historical application. See Stern, "Other-Speak: Classical Allegory and Contemporary Advertising.")

26. Laura Bird, "Joe Smooth for President," *Adweek's Marketing Week,* May 20, 1991, 20–22.

27. For discussion of issues related to tobacco advertising effectiveness and subsequent ad restrictions, see Richard W. Pollay et al., "The Last Straw? Cigarette Advertising and Realized Market Shares Among Youths and Adults, 1979–1993," *Journal of Marketing* 60 (April 1996), 1–16; Sandra E. McKay, Mary Jane Dundas, and John W. Yeargain, "The FDA's Proposed Rules Regulating Tobacco and Underage Smoking and the Commercial Speech Doctrine," *Journal of Public Policy & Marketing* 15 (fall 1996), 296–302.

28. What is being called the consumer processing model (CPM) is more conventionally called the consumer information processing (CIP) model. CPM is chosen over CIP for two reasons: (1) It is nominally parallel to the HEM label and thus simplifies memory; and (2) the term "information" is too limiting inasmuch as it implies that only verbal claims (information) are important to consumers and that other forms of communications (e.g., nonverbal statements) are irrelevant. This latter point was emphasized by Esther Thorson, "Consumer Processing of Advertising," *Current Issues & Research in Advertising* 12, ed. J. H. Leigh and C. R. Martin, Jr. (Ann Arbor: University of Michigan, 1990), 198–199.

29. Elizabeth C. Hirschman and Morris B. Holbrook, "Hedonic Consumption: Emerging Concepts, Methods, and Propositions," *Journal of Marketing* 46 (summer 1982), 92–101; Morris B. Holbrook and Elizabeth C. Hirschman, "The Experiential Aspects of Consumption: Consumer Fantasies, Feelings, and Fun," *Journal of Consumer Research* 9 (September 1982), 132–140.

30. James B. Bettman, *An Information Processing Theory of Consumer Choice* (Reading, Mass.: Addison-Wesley, 1979), 1.

31. William J. McGuire, "Some Internal Psychological Factors Influencing Consumer Choice," *Journal of Consumer Research* 4 (March 1976), 302–319.

32. Bettman, *An Information Processing Theory of Consumer Choice,* 77.

33. For an excellent treatment of this distinction as well as a broader perspective on factors determining consumer attention, comprehension, and learning of advertising messages, see Klaus G. Grunert, "Automatic and Strategic Processes in Advertising Effects," *Journal of Marketing* 60 (October 1996), 88–102.

34. This discussion is based broadly on Deborah J. MacInnis, Christine Moorman, and Bernard J. Jaworski, "Enhancing and Measuring Consumers' Motivation, Opportunity, and Ability to Process Brand Information from Advertisements," *Journal of Marketing* 55 (October 1991), 32–53.

35. For example, Paul Surgi Speck and Michael T. Elliott, "The Antecedents and Consequences of Perceived Advertising Clutter," *Journal of Current Issues and Research in Advertising* 19 (fall 1997), 39–54. In addition to being disliked by consumers, advertising clutter has also been shown to have undesirable effects for the advertising community, at least in the case of magazine circulation. See Louisa Ha and Barry R. Litman, "Does Advertising Clutter Have Diminishing and Negative Returns?" *Journal of Advertising* 26 (Spring 1997), 31–42.

36. Peter H. Webb, "Consumer Initial Processing in a Difficult Media Environment," *Journal of Consumer Research* 6 (December 1979), 225–236; Peter H. Webb and Michael L. Ray, "Effects of TV Clutter," *Journal of Advertising Research* 19 (June 1979), 7–12.

37. A thorough discussion of comprehension processes is provided by David Glen Mick, "Levels of Subjective Comprehension in Advertising Processing and Their Relations to Ad Perceptions, Attitudes, and Memory," *Journal of Consumer Research* 18 (March 1992), 411–424.

38. Bettman, *An Information Processing Theory of Consumer Choice,* 79.

39. For discussion of the effects of attitudes on perception, see Russell H. Fazio, David R. Roskos-Ewoldsen, and Martha C. Powell, "Attitudes, Perception, and Attention," in *The Heart's Eye: Emotional Influences in Perception and Attention,* ed., Paula M. Niedenthal and Shinobu Kitayama (San Diego: Academic Press, 1994), 197–216.

40. Alice M. Isen, Margaret Clark, Thomas E. Shalker, and Lynn Karp, "Affect, Accessibility of Material in Memory, and Behavior: A Cognitive Loop," *Journal of Personality and Social Psychology* 36 (January 1978), 1–12; Meryl Paula Gardner, "Mood States and Consumer Behavior: A Critical Review," *Journal of Consumer Research* 12 (December 1985), 281–300.

41. "A Case of Human Error," *Newsweek,* August 15, 1988, 18–19.

42. Jacob Jacoby and Wayne D. Hoyer, "Viewer Miscomprehension of Televised Communication: Selected Findings," *Journal of Marketing* 46 (fall 1982), 12–26. It is relevant to note that the Jacoby and Hoyer research has stimulated considerable controversy. See Gary T. Ford and Richard Yalch, "Viewer Miscomprehension of Televised Communications—A Comment," *Journal of Marketing* 46 (fall 1982), 27–31; Richard W. Mizerski, "Viewer Miscomprehension Findings Are Measurement Bound," *Journal of Marketing* 46 (fall 1982), 32–34; and Jacob Jacoby and Wayne D. Hoyer, "On Miscomprehending Televised Communications—A Rejoinder," *Journal of Marketing* 46 (fall 1982), 35–43.

43. Several valuable sources for technical treatments of memory operations are available in the advertising and marketing literatures. See Bettman, "Memory Functions," *An Information Processing Theory of Consumer Choice,* chap. 6; James B. Bettman, "Memory Factors in Consumer Choice: A Review," *Journal of Marketing* 43 (spring 1979), 37–53; Andrew A. Mitchell, "Cognitive Processes Initiated by Advertising," in *Information Processing Research in Advertising,* ed. R. J. Harris (Hillsdale, N.J.: Lawrence Erlbaum Associates, 1983), 13–42; Jerry C. Olson, "Theories of Information Encoding and Storage: Implications for Consumer Research," in *The Effect of Information on Consumer and Market Behavior,* ed. A. A. Mitchell (Chicago: American Marketing Association, 1978), 49–60; Thomas K. Srull, "The Effects of Subjective Affective States on Memory and Judgment," in *Advances in Consumer Research,* vol. 11, ed. T. C. Kinnear (Provo, Utah: Association for Consumer Research, 1984); and Kevin Lane Keller, "Advertising Retrieval Cues on Brand Evaluations," *Journal of Consumer Research* 14 (December 1989), 316–333.

44. Richard M. Shiffrin and R. C. Atkinson, "Storage and Retrieval Processes in Long-Term Memory," *Psychological Review* 76 (March 23, 1969), 179–193.

45. See Mitchell, "Cognitive Processes Initiated by Advertising."

46. Ibid. See also Grunert, "Automatic and Strategic Processes in Advertising Effects."

47. Mitchell, "Cognitive Processes Initiated by Advertising."

48. A good discussion is provided by Darlene V. Howard, "General Knowledge," *Cognitive Psychology* (New York: Macmillan, 1983), chap. 6.

49. Kathy A. Lutz and Richard J. Lutz, "Imagery-Eliciting Strategies: Review and Implications of Research," in *Advances in Consumer Research,* vol. 5, ed. H. Keith Hunt (Ann Arbor: Association for Consumer Research, 1978), 611–620. For more recent in-depth treatments of imagery, see Deborah J. MacInnis and Linda L. Price, "The Role of Imagery in Information Processing: Review and Extensions," *Journal of Consumer Research* 13 (March 1987), 473–491; Paula Fitzgerald Bone and Pam Scholder Ellen, "The Generation and Consequences of Communication-Evoked Imagery," *Journal of Consumer Research* 19 (June 1992), 93–104; Darryl W. Miller and Lawrence J. Marks, "Mental Imagery and Sound Effects in Radio Commercials," *Journal of Advertising* 21 (December 1992), 83–93; Alvin C. Burns, Abhijit Biswas, and Laurie A. Babin, "The Operation of Visual Imagery as a Mediator of Advertising

Effects," *Journal of Advertising* 21 (June 1993), 71–85; and Richard L. Oliver, Thomas S. Robertson, and Deborah J. Mitchell, "Imaging and Analyzing in Response to New Product Advertising," *Journal of Advertising* 22 (December 1993), 35–50. For an interesting alternative perspective on how imagery can detract from learning, see H. Rao Unnava, Sanjeev Agarwal, and Curtis P. Haugtvedt, "Interactive Effects of Presentation Modality and Message-Generated Imagery on Recall of Advertising Information," *Journal of Consumer Research* 23 (June 1996), 81–88.

50. Lutz and Lutz, "Imagery-Eliciting Strategies," 611–620.

51. Allan Paivio, "Mental Imagery in Associative Learning and Memory," *Psychological Review* 76 (May 1969), 241–263; John R. Rossiter and Larry Percy, "Visual Imaging Ability as a Mediator of Advertising Response," in *Advances in Consumer Research,* vol. 5, ed. H. Keith Hunt (Ann Arbor: Association for Consumer Research, 1978), 621–629.

52. Michael J. Houston, Terry L. Childers, and Susan E. Heckler, "Picture-Word Consistency and the Elaborative Processing of Advertisements," *Journal of Marketing Research* 24 (November 1987), 359–369.

53. H. Rao Unnava and Robert E. Burnkrant, "An Imagery-Processing View of the Role of Pictures in Print Advertisements," *Journal of Marketing Research* 28 (May 1991), 226–231.

54. Kathy A. Lutz and Richard J. Lutz, "The Effects of Interactive Imagery on Learning: Application to Advertising," *Journal of Applied Psychology* 62 (August 1977), 493–498.

55. For an extensive list of visual imagery "principles," see John R. Rossiter, "Visual Imagery: Applications to Advertising," in *Advances in Consumer Research,* vol. 9, ed. A. A. Mitchell (Ann Arbor: The Association for Consumer Research, 1982), 101–106.

56. Roger N. Shepard, "The Mental Image," *American Psychologist* 33 (February 1978), 125–137.

57. Marketing and consumer researchers have generally neglected the study of olfactory stimuli. For exceptions, see Paula Fitzgerald Bone and Swati Jantrania, "Olfaction as a Cue for Product Quality," *Marketing Letters* 3 (July 1992), 289–296; Eric R. Spangenberg, Ayn E. Crowley,

and Pamela W. Henderson, "Improving the Store Environment: Do Olfactory Cues Affect Evaluations and Behaviors?" *Journal of Marketing* 60 (April 1996), 67–80. For the role of olfaction in influencing memory, refer to Frank R. Schab, "Odors and the *Remembrance of Things Past," Journal of Experimental Psychology: Learning, Memory, and Cognition* 16, no. 4 (1990), 648–655; and Frank R. Schab, "Odor Memory: Taking Stock," *Psychological Bulletin* 109, no. 2 (1991), 242–251.

58. Peter L. Wright, "Consumer Choice Strategies: Simplifying vs. Optimizing," *Journal of Marketing Research* 11 (February 1975), 60–67.

59. The best-known illustration of compensation in consumer behavior is Fishbein and Ajzen's theory of reasoned action, which states that one's attitude toward performing an act is the sum of one's beliefs regarding the outcomes of the act weighed by one's evaluations of those outcomes. Further discussion of the attitudinal component of this model will be delayed until the next chapter, which describes attitude formation and change in the context of the general topic of persuasion.

60. For discussion of other noncompensatory heuristics, see Bettman, *An Information Processing Theory of Consumer Choice,* or any standard consumer behavior text.

61. Bettman, *Information Processing Theory,* 184.

62. Martin Fishbein and Icek Ajzen, *Beliefs, Attitude, Intention, and Behavior: An Introduction to Theory and Research* (Reading, Mass.: Addison Wesley, 1975).

63. For further reading on the role of situational variables, see Russell W. Belk, "Situational Variables and Consumer Behavior," *Journal of Consumer Research* 2 (December 1975), 157–164.

64. Veronika Denes-Raj and Seymour Epstein, "Conflict between Intuitive and Rational Processing: When People Behave against Their Better Judgment," *Journal of Personality and Social Psychology* 66, no. 5 (1994), 819–829.

65. Ibid.

66. Hirschman and Holbrook, "Hedonic Consumption."

67. Ibid., 91.

68. Pat Sloan and Judann Pollack, "P&G Preparing for New Tide Approach," *Advertising Age,* January 19, 1998, 3.

Persuasion in Marketing Communications

CHAPTER OBJECTIVES

After studying this chapter, you should be able to:

1. Understand the nature and role of attitudes in marketing communications.
2. Describe three attitudinal components.
3. Appreciate the role of persuasion in marketing communications.
4. Explain six tools of persuasion.
5. Understand the elaboration likelihood model (ELM) and its implications for marketing communications.
6. Explain three basic attitude change strategies.
7. Understand practical marketing communications efforts that enhance consumers' motivation, opportunity, and ability to process messages.

Opening Vignette: Selling Calcium

The National Academy of Sciences' Food and Nutrition Board has since 1941 established Recommended Dietary Allowances (RDAs) for vitamins and minerals, including calcium. For more than 50 years the RDA for calcium remained unchanged at 1200 mg per day for adolescents and 800 mg for adults. In 1994 scientists at the National Institutes of Health (NIH) concluded that calcium intake is important in all stages of life but that most people were not getting enough. The NIH recommended much higher RDAs for daily calcium intake across many age groups. In support of NIH's conclusions, the National Academy of Sciences in 1997 issued new guidelines for calcium intake. The new levels now are called AIs (adequate intakes) rather than RDAs. The new AIs recommend that children and teens, aged 9–18, consume a daily minimum of 1,300 mg of calcium, that people aged 19 through 50 intake at least 1,000 mg, and that individuals aged 51 or older increase consumption to at least 1,200 mg. The message is clear: Most of us need more calcium in our diets to prevent low bone mass and osteoporosis, or brittle bone disease.

Boosted by the new guidelines from the National Academy of Sciences, Tropicana orange juice introduced a new advertising campaign for a calcium-fortified version of its Pure Premium orange juice. The ad campaign had a powerful story to tell, namely, that Tropicana Pure Premium orange juice had been reformulated with a newly patented calcium source called FruitCal—a highly soluble form of calcium that absorbs as well as calcium in milk and better than calcium carbonate, the form used in leading calcium supplements.

Though on the one hand the advertising story was easy to tell in view of the FruitCal argument, Tropicana also faced a challenge in convincing consumers that its Pure Premium juice not only was healthy but also good tasting. When Tropicana initially

162

Inside the browser window:

Location: http://www.colemangroup.com/casestudies/tropicana/trop_single.html

Live Home Page | Net Search | Apple Computer | Apple Support | Apple Software

Challenge
Create a proprietary bottle structure for the 13 ounce single serve offering of Pure Premium juice for the convenience store channel of distribution.

Solution
The new bottle includes an orange shape on the upper portion providing distinction for the brand in an ownable fashion along with an enhanced grip area. While plastic was considered as an option given transportability considerations, clear glass was more consistent with the brand's premium positioning.

introduced calcium-fortified orange juice in 1995, prior to the FruitCal invention, it had a whiter color and mildly chalky texture compared to unfortified orange juice. Many consumers were put off by the color, taste, and texture of the original Pure Premium juice. Now the challenge was to convince people that reformulated Tropicana Pure Premium was both good tasting and good for you.

Apparently the advertising worked, as Tropicana Pure Premium's sales volume increased by 20 percent over the prior year. Figure 6.1 presents a magazine ad from the campaign. In addition to the advertising copy, which focuses on delicious taste as well as the properties of FruitCal, notice the clever headline (Bone Appetit), which of course plays on the well-known French saying, *bon appetit.* Notice also how the ad directs the reader's eye flow from the model's knee to the sliced orange on the top right side of the page and in turn from its flowing juice down to the all-important body copy. The pictorial and body copy work together to tell a very convincing and persuasive story for this reformulated brand of orange juice.

Source: Background information about calcium guidelines and FruitCal is from http://www.non-dairy.org. Other details are adapted from Elizabeth Jensen, "New Juice Ad Touts Calcium Without the Chalky Undertaste," *The Wall Street Journal Interactive Edition,* August 15, 1997.

*T*he opening vignette touches on the two interrelated topics treated in this chapter, *attitudes* and *persuasion.* To understand one topic requires an understanding of the other. Attitude is a mental property of the consumer, whereas persuasion is an effort by a marketing communicator to influence the consumer's attitude and behavior in some manner. This

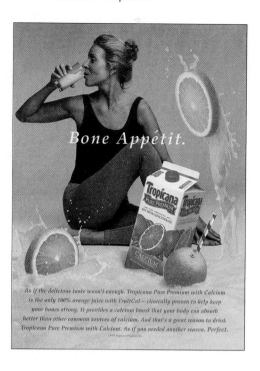

chapter first describes the core attitude concept and then discusses several frameworks that explain how attitudes are formed and changed and how persuasion occurs. In effect, we will be studying marketing communications from the consumer's perspective. The chapter builds upon the fundamentals explained in the previous chapter and provides insight into why marketing communicators' messages sometimes succeed and at other times fail to influence consumers' attitudes and behavior.

THE NATURE AND ROLE OF ATTITUDES

What Is an Attitude?

Attitudes are *hypothetical constructs;* they cannot be seen, touched, heard, or smelled. Because attitudes cannot be observed, a variety of perspectives have developed over the years in attempting to describe them.[1] The term *attitude* will be used here to mean a general and enduring positive or negative feeling toward or evaluative judgment of some person, object, or issue.[2]

Beyond this basic definition are three other notable features of attitudes. They: (1) are *learned,* (2) are *relatively enduring,* and (3) *influence behavior.*[3] Consider the following examples of attitudes that express feelings and evaluations with varying degrees of intensity: "I like Diet Pepsi," "I really like the initiatives undertaken by Mothers Against Drunk Driving (MADD)," "I'm not sure I like Jesse Ventura" (the ex-wrestler who by some incredible twist of fate became governor of Minnesota); "I favor recycling," and "I love Neil Young" (the old rock & roller). All of these attitudes are learned and will likely be retained until there is some strong reason to change them. Moreover, it can be expected that the holders of these attitudes would behave consistently with their evaluations—drinking Diet Pepsi, supporting MADD with a financial contribution, questioning Jesse Ventura's actions as governor, recycling aluminum cans, purchasing a new album by Neil Young, and so on.

The preceding description focuses on feelings and evaluations, or what is commonly referred to as the **affective** component; this is generally what is referred to when people use the word *attitude.* However, attitude theorists recognize two additional components, cognitive and conative.[4] The **cognitive** component refers to a person's *beliefs* (i.e., knowledge and thoughts) about an object or issue ("the euro should greatly simplify currency transactions while traveling throughout Europe"; "WOW! potato chips made with Olestra taste as good as the 'real thing'," i.e., fat-laden chips). The **conative** component represents one's *behavioral tendency,* or *predisposition* to act, toward an object. In consumer-behavior terms, the conative component represents a consumer's intention to purchase a specific item. Generally speaking, attitudes predispose people to respond to an object, such as a brand, in a consistently favorable or unfavorable way.[5]

A clear progression is implied: from initial cognition, to affection, to conation. An individual becomes aware of an object, such as a new brand, then acquires information and forms beliefs about the brand's ability to satisfy consumption needs (*cognitive* component). Beliefs are integrated, and feelings toward and evaluations of the product are developed (*affective* component). On the basis of these feelings and evaluations, an intention is formed to purchase or not to purchase the new product (*conative* component). An attitude, then, is characterized by progressing from thinking (cognitive), to feeling (affective), to behaving (conative).[6]

An illustration will help clarify the notion of attitude progression. Consider the case of Doug, who recently purchased a new sports utility vehicle, a Land Rover Discovery (see Figure 5.27 in Chapter 5 for a view of this brand). When in the process of making a brand-choice decision, Doug knew precisely what he wanted in a new SUV: a lot of passenger and luggage space, the ability to drive off-road during hunting and fishing trips, an attractive but rugged vehicle, unpretentious status, and good resale value. He acquired information about the Discovery and other models from friends and acquaintances, from advertisements, from on-line searching, and from dealer visitations. He formed beliefs about product features and about specific SUV models as a result of this information search-and-processing activity. These beliefs (representing the cognitive-attitude component) led Doug to form specific feelings toward and evaluations of various SUV models (affective component). He also liked the Jeep Cherokee but had heard that this model may be less reliable than some comparably priced SUVs. Overall, his most positive affect was toward the Land Rover Discovery, and his intention to purchase this model (conative component) finally materialized when he drove the new SUV away from the Land Rover dealership.

PERSUASION IN MARKETING COMMUNICATIONS

The foregoing discussion of attitudes provides us with useful concepts as we turn now to the strategic issue of how marketing communicators influence customers' attitudes and behaviors through persuasive efforts. Salespeople attempt to convince customers to purchase one product rather than another. Advertisers appeal to consumers' intellect or to their fantasies and feelings in attempting to create desired images for their brands so that consumers will someday purchase them. Brand managers use coupons, samples, rebates, and other devices to induce consumers to try their products and to purchase them now rather than later.

Persuasion is the essence of marketing communications. Marketing communicators—along with people in other persuasion-oriented roles (e.g., theologians, parents, teachers, politicians)—attempt to guide people toward the acceptance of some belief, attitude, or behavior by using reasoning and emotional appeals.[7] The actual process by which this occurs is examined later in the chapter. First, however, it will be useful to provide some brief discussion on the ethics of persuasion inasmuch as the word *persuasion* may suggest to you something manipulative, exploitative, or unethical.

The Ethics of Persuasion

At times, marketing communicators' persuasion efforts are undeniably unethical. Shrewd operators bamboozle the unsuspecting and credulous into buying products or services that are never delivered. Elderly consumers, for example, are occasionally hustled into making advance payments for household repairs (e.g., roof repairs) that are never performed. Unscrupulous realtors sell swamp land in Florida. Telemarketers sometimes get our attention under the pretense that they are conducting marketing research or representing a charitable cause and then try to sell us something.

Yes, persuasion by *some* marketing communicators is unethical. Of course, so sometimes are persuasive efforts by government officials, the clergy, teachers, your friends, and even you. Persuasion is a part of daily life in all its facets. The practice of persuasion can be noble or deplorable. There is nothing wrong with persuasion per se; it is the practitioners of persuasion who sometimes are at fault. To adapt an old adage: Don't throw the persuasion baby out with the bath water; just make sure the water is clean.

Multiple Forms of Persuasion

It would be erroneous to think that persuasion is a single method, practice, or technique. Rather, there are as many persuasion methods in theory as there are persuasion practitioners. This is a bit of an exaggeration, but it serves to emphasize that persuasion practices are highly diverse.

Another important point is that the topic of persuasion can be viewed from two perspectives. The first involves examining persuasion from the perspective of the *persuader* and studying the persuasive techniques used by practitioners. The other perspective focuses on the *persuadee* by exploring what factors cause a person to be persuaded. The next section looks at persuasion from the persuader's perspective; a later section then takes a persuadee-oriented view.

TOOLS OF INFLUENCE: THE PERSUADER'S PERSPECTIVE

Persuaders in all capacities of life routinely use a variety of tools, which have evolved throughout the millennia to influence people. They are widely understood by many persuaders, if only tacitly. Persuadees, such as consumers, learn these tactics—again, if only tacitly—and form knowledge, or schemas, about persuaders' persuasive tactics. A well-known persuasion researcher coined the catchy phrase *schemer schema* to capture the idea that people form rather strong and stable intuitive theories about marketers' efforts to influence their actions.[8]

A social psychologist, Robert Cialdini, has spent much of his professional career studying the persuasive tactics used by car dealers, insurance salespeople, fund-raisers, waiters, and other persuasion practitioners. His studies, involving both work in the field (as car salesperson, fund-raiser, etc.) and laboratory research, have identified six tools of influence that cut across persuasion practices. These are: (1) reciprocation, (2) commitment and consistency, (3) social proof, (4) liking, (5) authority, and (6) scarcity.[9]

Before discussing these influence tools, it is important to note that these tactics work because much of our behavior occurs in a rather automatic, noncontrolled, and somewhat mindless fashion. In other words, due to limitations on our information processing capacities (as discussed in the previous chapter) and time pressures, we often make judgments and choices without giving a great deal of thought to the matter. Cialdini refers to this as *click, whirr behavior.* He uses this term in reference to patterns of behavior (called *fixed-action patterns*) that appear throughout the animal kingdom. Many animal species (including *Homo sapiens*) will, under special circumstances, engage in patterns of scripted behavior in response to some trigger feature. For example, mother hens will automatically act motherly on hearing the sound *cheep-cheep.*[10] That single sound activates maternal behavior; if a football could emit the sound *cheep-cheep,* a mother turkey would act motherly toward it, taking it under her wing and nurturing it; however, she will not nurture her own offspring if they are unable to make that sound.

Humans sometimes also operate in a click, whirr fashion. Something triggers a response *(click)*, and then an automatic, scripted pattern of behavior follows *(whirr)*. We are not fully aware of this happening (if we were, it would not happen), but, as we will see, persuaders know how to click on, or trigger, our behavior. Out whirrs a response that results in our purchasing a product, making a donation, or doing something else that favors the persuader's interests (but not necessarily the persuadee's).

Reciprocation

As part of the socialization process in all cultures, people acquire a *norm of reciprocity*. As children we learn to return a favor with a favor, to respond to a nicety with another nicety. Knowing this, marketing communicators sometimes give gifts or samples with hopes that customers will reciprocate by purchasing products. We see this with in-store sampling of food items in supermarkets. Anyone who has ever attended a Tupperware party (or other product party of this sort) knows that the hostess often distributes free gifts at the beginning with designs that attendees will reciprocate with big purchases. College students are encouraged to make application for another credit card after being baited by an offer for a free T-shirt emblazoned with their university's logo.

This happens not only with individual consumers, but also in business-to-business marketing interactions. For example, pharmaceutical companies hold *dinner meetings* with physicians. A sales rep invites a small group of physicians to dinner at an expensive restaurant; exposes them to a product presentation before dinner; wines and dines them; then, afterwards, presents them with, say, a $100 "honorarium" for having given their time and attention. Research shows that 80 percent of dinner meetings produce increased sales of the presented brand. Click-whirr: "Something nice was done for me; I should return the favor."[11]

You would be correct if you are thinking that reciprocation tactics do not always work. Sometimes we "see through" the tactic and realize that the nicety is not really a sincere offering but rather a come-on to get us to respond in kind. In saying this, an important theme carries through the entire discussion of influence tactics: No influence tactic is equally effective under all circumstances. Rather, the effectiveness of a tactic is *contingent on the circumstances*: Whether and when a tactic is effective depends on the persuasion circumstances and the characteristics of the persuader and persuadee. As a student of marketing communications, it is critical that you incorporate this "it depends" thinking into your understanding of marketing practices. No influence tactic is universally effective. Rather, the situation or circumstances determine whether and when a tactic might be successful.

With regard to reciprocation, this tactic is most effective when the persuadee perceives the gift giver as honest and sincere. Party plans like the Tupperware parties typify this situation in that the persuader (the host or hostess) is often friends with the persuadees who attend.

Commitment and Consistency

After people make a choice (a commitment), there often is a strong tendency to remain faithful to that choice. Consistency is a valued human characteristic. We admire people who are consistent in their opinions and actions. We sometimes feel ashamed of ourselves when we say one thing and do something different. Hence, the marketing communicator might attempt to click-whirr the consumer by getting him or her to commit to something (commitment is the click, or trigger) and then hope that the consumer will continue to act in a manner consistent with this commitment.

Consider the tactic often used by automobile salespeople. They get the consumer to commit to a price and then say they have to get their sales manager's approval. At this point the consumer has psychologically committed to buying the car. The salesperson, after supposedly taking the offer to the sales manager, returns and declares that the manager would not accept the price. Nevertheless, the consumer, now committed to owning the car, will often increase the offer. In the trade this is referred to as *lowballing* the consumer, a tactic that is widespread because it is effective (albeit not entirely ethical).

When would you expect commitment and consistency to be most effective in marketing communications? (Think first before reading on.) Again, the apparent sincerity of the persuader would play a role. The tactic is unlikely to work when it is obviously deceitful and self-serving. From the persuadee's perspective, it would be expected that consumers are most likely to remain consistent when they are *highly ego-involved* in their choices. In other words, it is hard not to be consistent when a great amount of thought and psychological energy have gone into a choice.

Social Proof

What do I do? How should I behave? The principle of social proof is activated in circumstances where *appropriate behavior is somewhat unclear.* Not knowing exactly what to do, we take leads from the behavior of others; their behavior provides *social proof* of how we should behave. For example, suppose someone asks you for a charitable donation. The appropriate amount to give is unclear, so you might ask the fund-raiser what amount others are giving and then contribute a similar amount. As discussed in the following chapter, new-product developers sometimes encourage widespread adoption by giving new products to opinion leaders and trendsetters, who, it is expected, will provide social proof for others to adopt the same behavior. In general, we are most likely to accept the actions of others as correct "when we are unsure of ourselves, when the situation is unclear or ambiguous, when uncertainty reigns."[12]

Liking

This influence tactic deals with the fact that we are most likely to adopt an attitude or undertake an action when a likable person promotes that action. There are various manifestations of likability. Two of the more prominent in marketing communications are physical attractiveness and similarity. Research (described in detail in Chapter 11) has shown that people respond more favorably to others whom they perceive to be like themselves and physically attractive. This explains why models in advertising, individuals on magazine covers, and celebrity endorsers are typically attractive people to whom consumers can relate and like. The montage presented as Figure 6.2 shows a small sampling of celebrities who have been used in the ongoing "Milk Mustache" advertising campaign undertaken by the National Fluid Milk Processing Promotion Board. These individuals (including the animated characters) represent various demographic categories and appeal to different consumer groups.

Authority

Most people are raised to respect authority figures (parents, teachers, coaches, etc.) and to exhibit a sense of duty toward them. It therefore comes as no surprise that marketing communicators sometimes appeal to authority. Because marketers cannot invoke the same types of sanctions as real authority figures (e.g., parents withholding allowances), appeals to authority in the marketplace typically use surrogates of real authority figures. For example, advertisers sometimes use medical authorities to promote their products' virtues. Broadcasters often air *infomercials* that devote 30-minute programs to weight-loss, skincare, exercise equipment, hair-restoration products, and other items of this sort. Frequently these products are endorsed by medical doctors, entertainers, and athletes, upon whose authority the consumer is promised the product will perform its function.

Scarcity

This influence tactic is based on the principle that things become more desirable when they are in great demand but short supply. Simply put, an item that is rare or becoming rare is more valued. Salespeople and advertisers use this tactic when encouraging people to buy immediately with appeals such as "only a few are left," "we won't have any more in stock by the end of the day," and "they're really selling fast."

The Role of Linking: A Montage from the Milk Mustache Campaign

FIGURE 6.2

The theory of **psychological reactance** helps explain why scarcity works.[13] This theory suggests that people react against any efforts to reduce their freedoms or choices. Removed or threatened freedoms and choices are perceived as even more desirable than previously. Thus, when products are made to seem less available, they become more valuable in the consumer's mind. Of course, appeals to scarcity are not always effective. But if the persuader is credible and legitimate, then an appeal may be effective. (Click-whirr: "Not many of this product remain, so I better buy now and pay whatever it takes to acquire it.") The *Global Focus* insert provides a dramatic use of the scarcity appeal in Singapore.

THE INFLUENCE PROCESS: THE PERSUADEE'S PERSPECTIVE

The persuasive efforts by two advertisers will serve to illustrate the following discussion. In the advertisement for ATROVENT nasal spray (see Figure 6.3), reason after reason, argument upon argument is presented to convince consumers to ask their doctor about this

GLOBAL FOCUS: THE KIASU SYNDROME IN SINGAPORE

In the Hokkien dialect of Chinese, the word *kiasu* means the "fear of losing out." Singaporeans, according to a lecturer in the philosophy department at the National University, will take whatever they can secure, even if they are not sure they really want it. The majority of Singaporeans apparently share a herd mentality—no one wants to be different, and most conform to what others do.

Marketers, needless to say, have exploited this cultural characteristic of Singapore to sell all types of products. McDonald's, for example, popularized a cartoon character, "Mr. Kiasu," whose motto is "Better grab first, later no more"—a rather transparent application of the scarcity appeal. In TV ads using the cartoon character, Mr. Kiasu is shown jumping a queue and ordering 20 burgers to make sure he gets enough.

Performance Motors, a Singaporean automobile dealership, announced that it was moving its location and offered for sale 250 limited-edition BMW 316i models, priced at $78,125 for a manual transmission and $83,125 for automatic. All 250 models were sold within four days, and the dealer was forced to order another 100, which were quickly sold even though delivery was unavailable for months.

The kiasu mentality makes Singaporeans virtually "sitting ducks" for users of the scarcity tactic. In a society where conformity is highly treasured and the fear of losing out reigns supreme, marketers can readily capitalize by promoting the scarcity of their offerings. As always, however, such a tactic is likely to achieve success only in those situations in which there is in fact scarcity. Singaporean consumers otherwise would become skeptical of such transparent attempts to mislead them and reject such blatant attempts to sell products by using deceit.

Source: Adapted from Ian Stewart, "Public Fear Sells in Singapore," *Advertising Age,* October 11, 1993, 18. Singaporeans even make fun of themselves regarding their kiasu behavior. "Mr. Kiasu" is a popular comic book character, and a small cottage industry has sprung up around the character. See http://www.asiapages.com.sg/direct/text/comic.htm.

---

treatment for runny noses. On the other hand, the ad for Godiva chocolates (Figure 6.4) says virtually nothing (at least in words) about the advertised product. Rather, it simply portrays luscious shots of unwrapped chocolate and attractive gift-wrapped boxes—certainly an appetizing and eye-catching appeal to consumers in the emotional throes of the holiday season.

These contrasting persuasive efforts highlight the fact that there are many different ways in which to use persuasion. The following section identifies four factors that are fundamental in the persuasion process. Two factors (message arguments and peripheral cues) deal with persuasion vehicles under the marketing communicator's control. The other two (receiver involvement and initial position) apply to persuadee characteristics.

Message Arguments

The *strength or quality of message arguments* (e.g., the reasons given in Figure 6.3 to encourage consumer interest in ATROVENT nasal spray) is often the major determinant of whether and to what extent persuasion occurs. Consumers are much more likely to be persuaded by convincing and believable messages than by weak arguments. It may seem strange, then, that much advertising fails to present substantive information or compelling arguments. One reason is that the majority of advertising, particularly television commercials, is for product categories (like soft drinks) in which inter-brand differences are modest or virtually nonexistent. Another reason for advertising that promotes images rather than presents facts is that emotion, as discussed in Chapter 5, plays a key role in driving consumer choice.

Peripheral Cues

A second major determinant of persuasion is the presence of cues that are *peripheral to the primary message arguments.* These include such elements as background music, scenery, and graphics. As will be explained in a later section, under certain conditions these cues

An Argument-Based
Persuasive Effort

may play a more important role than message arguments in determining the outcome of a persuasive effort.

Receiver Involvement

The *personal relevance* that a communication has for a receiver is a critical determinant of the extent and form of persuasion. Highly involved consumers (i.e., those for whom an advertisement is most relevant) are motivated to process message arguments when exposed to marketing communications, whereas uninvolved consumers are likely to exert minimal attention to message arguments and perhaps to process only peripheral cues. The upshot is that involved and uninvolved consumers have to be persuaded in

PART 2   Integrated Marketing Communications from the Customer's Perspective

An Emotion-Based
Persuasive Effort

different ways. This will be detailed fully in a following section that presents an integrated model of persuasion.

Receiver's Initial Position

Scholars agree that persuasion results not from external communication per se but from the *self-generated thoughts* that people produce in response to persuasive efforts. Persuasion, in other words, is self-persuasion, or, stated poetically, "thinking makes it so."[14] These self-generated thoughts include both cognitive and emotional responses. These responses are directed at message arguments and executional elements or may involve emotional reactions and images related to using the advertised brand (e.g., "Godiva chocolate is scrumptious"; "Godiva chocolate is ridiculously expensive").[15]

Two primary forms of cognitive responses are supportive arguments and counterarguments.[16] These responses are subvocal rather than vocalized; they are the thoughts elicited spontaneously in response to advertisements and other persuasive efforts. **Supportive arguments** occur when a receiver *agrees* with a message argument. For example, a person reading the ATROVENT nasal spray advertisement may respond favorably to a product that is not a steroid and will not keep you awake or put you to sleep (see highlighted statements in Figure 6.3). **Counterarguments** arise when the receiver *challenges* a message claim. Another person reading the same ATROVENT ad may react that a runny nose can be suitably treated with a tissue and that a prescription drug for such a minor problem is sheer excess.

Whether a persuasive communication accomplishes its objectives depends on the balance of cognitive and emotional responses. If counterarguments outnumber supportive arguments, it is unlikely that many consumers will be convinced to undertake the course of action advocated. Marketing communications, however, may effectively persuade consumers if more supportive than negative arguments are registered or if emotional responses are predominantly positive.

AN INTEGRATED MODEL OF PERSUASION

The various factors overviewed now are combined into a coordinated theory of persuasion. Figure 6.5 presents a model of alternative mechanisms, or routes, by which persuasion occurs.[17] This explanation is based on psychologists Petty and Cacioppo's *elaboration likelihood model* (ELM) and on marketing scholars MacInnis and Jaworski's integrative framework.[18]

FIGURE 6.5

An Integrated Model of Persuasion

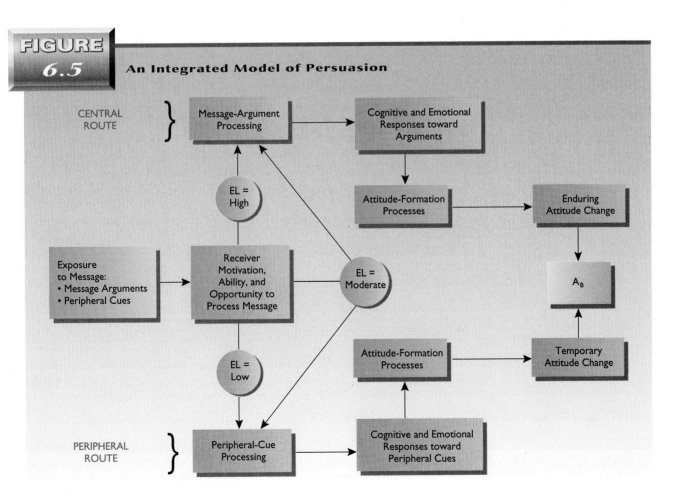

It should be clear by this point in the chapter that there is no single mechanism by which persuasion occurs. Instead, there are a variety of possibilities. Understanding why this is so requires that you understand the concept of elaboration. **Elaboration** deals with mental activity in response to a message such as an advertisement. People elaborate on a message when they think about what the message is saying, evaluate the arguments in the message, and perhaps react emotionally to some of the claims.

Whether and to what extent a person engages in elaboration depends on that person's motivation, ability, and opportunity to process (i.e., to attend to and comprehend) a marketing message's selling claims. **Motivation** is high when a message relates to a person's present goals and needs and is thus relevant to that individual. Generally speaking, consumers are more motivated to process messages the more involved they are in the subject matter of a message. **Opportunity** involves the matter of whether it is physically possible for a person to process a message; opportunity is restricted when a message is presented too quickly, when the sound is too low, or when an individual is distracted. **Ability** concerns whether a person is familiar with message claims and is capable of comprehending them. Consumers, on occasion, are motivated but unable to process message claims.

Together, these three factors (motivation, opportunity, and ability, or **MOA** for short) determine each individual's *elaboration likelihood* for a particular message. **Elaboration likelihood** represents the chance or prospect that a message receiver will elaborate on a message by thinking about and reacting to it and comparing it with his or her preexisting thoughts and beliefs regarding the product category, the advertised brand, and competitive brands. (Note the close similarity between elaboration likelihood and the concept of *active synthesis* that was discussed in the previous chapter.) We can envision an elaboration likelihood continuum ranging from a low likelihood at one end to a high likelihood at the other.

The elaboration likelihood (*EL*) is *low* when the MOA factors are themselves low. This would be the case when a consumer is confronted with an advertisement for a product that she or he is not interested in (hence low motivation). The elaboration likelihood is *high* when the MOA factors are high. Doug, the previously mentioned purchaser of a Land Rover Discovery vehicle, exhibited a high elaboration likelihood for information about SUVs because he was determined to buy a new SUV and, at the outset of the buying process, was uncertain as to which model was best for him. In many marketplace situations, consumers' ELs for messages are at a *moderate* level rather than being low or high. Note in Figure 6.5 that these three EL levels are shown in circles extending from the box labeled *Receiver Motivation, Ability, and Opportunity to Process Message.*

In general, the strength of one's elaboration likelihood will determine the type of process by which attitudes toward the advertised brand will be formed or changed. The model in Figure 6.5 shows two mechanisms—or "routes"—in metaphorical terms—by which persuasion occurs: at the top, a *central route,* and at the bottom, a *peripheral route.* There is also an implicit *dual route* that results from a moderate elaboration likelihood level and combines features of both the central and peripheral routes.

The Central Route

Upon *exposure* to a message consisting of message arguments and peripheral cues (see the *Exposure to Message* box in Figure 6.5), the receiver's level of motivation, ability, and opportunity will determine the elaboration likelihood level. When EL is high, the receiver will focus predominantly on message arguments rather than peripheral cues (see the *Message-Argument Processing* box in Figure 6.5). This situation defines the activation of the so-called central route.

When the central route is activated, the receiver will listen to, watch, or read about a brand's attributes and benefits but will not necessarily accept them at face value. Rather, because the consumer is motivated to acquire information about the product category, she or he will react to the arguments with subvocal cognitive and emotional responses (see the *Cognitive and Emotional Responses toward Arguments* box in Figure 6.5). The consumer may accept some of the arguments but counterargue with others. She or he may also emit emotional reactions to the arguments—"That's a lie!" or "Who do they think they're kidding?"

The nature of the cognitive and emotional processing—whether predominantly favorable (supportive arguments and positive emotional responses) or predominantly unfavorable (counterarguments and negative emotional reactions)—will both determine whether the persuasive communication influences attitudes and the direction of that influence. This takes us to the box labeled *Attitude-Formation Processes* in Figure 6.5, which addresses how attitudes under the central route are formed or changed. There are, in fact, several possibilities, two of which are discussed in the following sections: *emotion-based* persuasion and *message-based* persuasion.[19]

Emotion-Based Persuasion.   When a consumer is highly involved in a marketing communications message, say, a TV commercial, there is a tendency to relate aspects of the message to his or her personal situation. The consumer may vicariously place himself or herself into the commercial, relate to the product and people in the commercial, and *empathically* experience positive emotions (e.g., a sense of pride, romantic feelings, nostalgia) or negative emotions (e.g., anguish, fear). Under these circumstances, attitudes toward the advertised brand (depicted as A_B in Figure 6.5) stand a good chance of being changed in the direction of the experienced emotion—positive emotional reactions leading to positive brand attitudes and negative reactions leading to negative attitudes. Moreover, because the consumer's elaboration likelihood is high, it is to be expected that any attitude change experienced under the central route will be relatively enduring (see *Enduring Attitude Change* box in Figure 6.5).

Consider, for example, an award-winning advertising campaign undertaken by the South Carolina Department of Highways. This ongoing campaign is directed at persuading people (especially teenagers and young adults) not to drink and drive. Commercials graphically depict the aftermath of accidents and the personal tragedy suffered by the driver and the victims of his or her drunken driving. Many viewers of these commercials find themselves emotionally involved with the people and situations depicted. They vicariously experience the anguish that the drama presents. Research indicates that the campaign has successfully influenced many people in the target audience to hold negative attitudes toward driving after drinking or riding with someone who has been drinking.

Message-Based Persuasion.   The second central-route attitude-formation process results from processing message arguments. When consumers are sufficiently motivated and able to process a message's specific arguments or selling points, their cognitive responses may lead to changes in *beliefs* about the advertised brand or changes in *evaluations* of the importance of brand attributes and benefits. In either or both cases, the result is a change in attitudes toward the brand.

The process just described has been fully developed in the well-known theory of reasoned action (TORA). This theory proposes that all forms of planned and reasoned behavior (versus unplanned, spontaneous, impulsive behavior) have two primary determinants: attitudes and normative influences.[20] Many of you have learned about this theory in a psychology or consumer behavior course, so rather than explain the entire theory, the present discussion will just describe the attitudinal component.[21]

Attitude formation according to TORA can best be described in terms of the following equation.

$$A_B = \sum_{i=1}^{n} b_i \bullet e_i$$ **Equation 6.1**

where:

A_B = *attitude* toward a particular brand

b_i = the *belief,* or expectation, that owning that brand will lead to outcome i

e_i = the positive or negative *evaluation* of the ith outcome

A consumer's attitude toward a brand (or, more technically, toward the act of owning and consuming the brand) is determined by his or her beliefs regarding the outcomes, or consequences, of owning the brand weighed by the evaluations of those outcomes. **Outcomes** (expressed in Equation 6.1 as $i = 1$ through n, where n is typically fewer than 7) involve those aspects of product ownership that the consumer either desires to obtain (e.g., good gas mileage with an automobile) or to avoid (e.g., frequent breakdowns). **Beliefs** (the b_i term in Equation 6.1) are the consumer's subjective probability assessments, or expectations, regarding the likelihood that performing a certain act (e.g., buying Brand X automobile) will lead to a certain outcome. In theory, the consumer who is in the market for a product has a separate belief associated with each potential outcome for each brand he or she is considering buying. Doug, the previously mentioned purchaser of a Land Rover Discovery, considered outcomes such as passenger and luggage space, the ability to drive off-road during hunting and fishing trips, an attractive but rugged vehicle, unpretentious status, and good resale value to be the most important factors in choosing an SUV. Doug formed, or already had in memory, specific beliefs about each of these attributes for each SUV model that he seriously considered.

Because all outcomes are not equally important or determinant of consumer choice, we need to introduce a term that recognizes this influence differential. This term is the evaluation component, e_i, in Equation 6.1. **Evaluations** represent the subjective value, or importance, that consumers attach to consumption outcomes. For example, Doug may have considered ruggedness to be the most important consideration in selecting an SUV, followed by resale value, and then passenger and luggage space. The *IMC Focus* elaborates on the role of evaluations in its discussion of product *freshness*.

Hence, Equation 6.1 and the corresponding discussion represent the attitude formation process that results from the integration (see the summation symbol in Equation 6.1) of beliefs regarding individual outcomes of brand ownership weighed by their evaluation. Attitudes toward a brand are more positive when a brand is perceived favorably with respect to valued outcomes and less positive when a brand is perceived unfavorably on these outcomes.

Attitude Change Strategies. With Equation 6.1 in mind, we can identify three strategies that marketing communicators employ in attempting to change consumer attitudes.[22] One strategy is an attempt to influence consumers' brand-related *beliefs* (the b_i term in Equation 6.1). Consider the following efforts to influence consumers' beliefs:

1. Many American consumers consider the BMW to be an automobile that is excessively expensive to maintain. Accordingly, a campaign was introduced to advertise BMW as "the car that tunes itself."[23]

2. When you think of safety, what automobile comes to mind? If you're like most people, the car that occurred to you probably is a Volvo. Knowing this fact, marketers at Swedish-made Saab undertook a major ad campaign to put Saab in a safety class with Volvo. In an effort to enhance consumers' belief regarding Saab's safety, print ads included copylines such as "Safety marries performance. They elope"; "If there were elephants in Sweden, we'd have a safety test for that, too"; "If Saab makes the safest cars in Sweden, and Sweden makes the safest cars in the world . . ."[24]

3. A concrete example of an advertising effort to influence beliefs appears in Figure 6.7. Wilson, the maker of Ultra 500 golf balls, would like golfers to believe that this ball has the same aerodynamic qualities as a rocket. People know that rockets are propelled to great distances and with incredible accuracy, precisely the benefits every golfer seeks in a golf ball.

A second attitude-change strategy is to influence existing *evaluations* (the e_i term in Equation 6.1). This strategy involves getting consumers to reassess a particular outcome associated with brand ownership and to alter their evaluations of the outcome's value. For

IMC FOCUS: CAN A COMPETITIVE ADVANTAGE BE GAINED FROM ADVERTISING "FRESHNESS"?

Back in the 1970s, the marketing people at Procter & Gamble were in search of a new advertising campaign for their Jif brand of peanut butter. They asked a national sample of consumers to rate the importance of a list of attributes in their peanut butter choice. More consumers rated product *freshness* as "highly important" than any other attribute. The brand marketers at P&G and their advertising agency saw this as an exciting opportunity to advertise a product superiority claim for Jif that no other brand had ever advertised. The new advertising campaign was tested in several markets. The result: Consumers couldn't care less! In actuality, consumers almost never experienced a problem with newly opened jars of peanut butter and could not even differentiate among the freshness levels of different brands.

In retrospect, managers at P&G realized that their survey was probably flawed and hence misled the advertising folks into thinking that freshness was a more important purchase consideration than it actually was. Had researchers asked consumers to volunteer the product attributes that were important to their brand choice, rather than giving them a list of attributes to rate for importance, freshness would rarely have been mentioned. The moral is straightforward: Bad research equals bad direction for creative advertising and bad results.

Let's move forward two decades. The product category now is soft drinks rather than peanut butter, and the protagonist is the Pepsi-Cola Company instead of P&G. The situation, however, is similar. Pepsi undertook a $20 million to $30 million advertising campaign to introduce *freshness dating* for Diet Pepsi. (An introductory advertisement is shown in Figure 6.6.) The freshness-dating program involved placing easy-to-read expiration dates on cans. Pepsi's competitors were highly critical of this initiative and asserted that advertising soft-drink freshness simply "opens a can of worms" because, in their opinion, consumers have no concerns about soft drinks losing their freshness.

Only the marketing folks at Pepsi-Cola know with certainty whether the freshness strategy for Diet Pepsi was a success or flop like Jif's campaign. However, because carbonated soft-drink sales in the United States represented nearly $50 *billion* at the time of the freshness dating program (meaning that each gain or loss in share point amounted to revenues of approximately $500 million!), it is easy to understand why Diet Pepsi's brand managers were willing

Diet Pepsi's Freshness Dating Program

FIGURE 6.6

to give the freshness dating program a chance. Quick calculations immediately reveal that a market share increase of, say, just one-tenth of 1 percent would justify the program and the advertising campaign. That is, a 0.1 percent increase in share would increase Diet Pepsi's revenues by $50 million, which would easily compensate for the cost of introducing and advertising freshness dating.

Source: The information about Jif peanut butter is adapted from Brad Morgan, "Spreading a Fresh-ness *[sic]* Lesson Gleaned from Campaign History," *Brandweek,* April 25, 1994, 18. The Pepsi commentary is adapted from Marcy Magiera and Emily DeNitto, "Pepsi Takes Fresh Angle in New Ad Effort," *Advertising Age,* April 4, 1994, 8.

example, Tylenol advertised the fact that it, unlike some competitive brands of pain reliever, contains no caffeine. Tylenol's advertising objective was to get consumers to place a negative value on the presence of caffeine in pain relievers and by doing so to have a more favorable attitude toward Tylenol and less favorable attitudes toward brands that are not caffeine free.

An Effort to Influence
Consumers' Beliefs

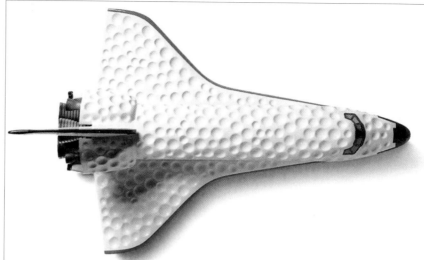

A third strategy used by marketing communicators to change attitudes is to get consumers to *add an entirely new outcome* into how they judge brands in a product category. This outcome, of course, would be one on which the marketer's product fares especially well. The opening vignette described how Tropicana Pure Premium orange juice had been reformulated with a newly patented calcium source called FruitCal—a highly soluble form of calcium. The advertising campaign that trumpeted this product introduction attempted to modify the way consumers evaluate orange juice by focusing on a purchase consideration—calcium—that most consumers had heretofore never considered when making a brand selection from the orange juice category.

An advertisement for Neutrogena No-Stick Sunscreen further illustrates an effort to introduce a new outcome into consumers' set of choice criteria. All brands in this category can claim to block the sun, so Neutrogena's advertising encouraged consumers to evaluate brands in terms of a new consideration—whether sunscreen is nongreasy and eliminates

**FIGURE
6.8**

An Effort to Introduce
a New Outcome

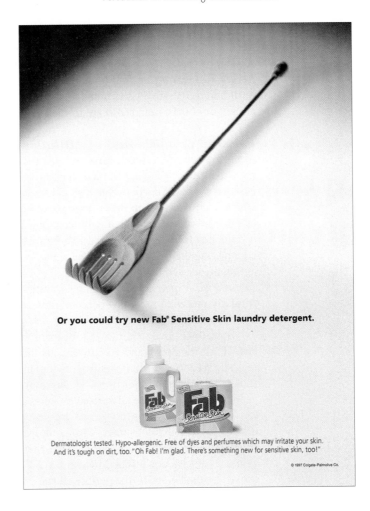

sticking sand. Of course, competitive brands could not, at the time of Neutrogena's introductory advertising campaign, make a comparable claim, and, as such, Neutrogena gained
an advantage in the minds of those consumers bothered by sticking sand.

A final illustration of an effort to introduce a new outcome into consumers' purchase
consideration is provided in Figure 6.8. This advertisement, with its marvelous juxtaposition against the visually prominent back scratcher, encourages consumers to incorporate
protection against sensitive skin as a laundry detergent purchase factor right up there in
importance with being tough on dirt.

The Peripheral Route

When the MOA factors—motivation, opportunity, and ability (see Figure 6.5)—are at *low*
levels, a different form of persuasion is involved. Specifically, when the consumer is *not* motivated to attend to and comprehend message arguments, she or he may nonetheless attend to
a message's *peripheral* features. The peripheral route is shown at the bottom of Figure 6.5,
where attention focuses on processing peripheral cues rather than message arguments.

As previously noted, peripheral cues involve elements of a message that are unrelated
(and hence peripheral) to the primary selling points in the message. For example, a TV
commercial's peripheral cues might include the background music, the scenery, or attractive models. In the case of a sales presentation, peripheral cues would include a salesperson's physical appearance, how he or she is dressed, and his or her accent.

The consumer, having attended to a peripheral cue, may experience thoughts or emotions in response to the cue ("The music is exhilarating"; "What a beautiful dress"; "The scenery is gorgeous"). These responses (labeled *Cognitive and Emotional Responses toward Peripheral Cues* in Figure 6.5) might produce an attitude toward the advertisement itself and/or the advertised brand.[25] Classical conditioning provides one account of how attitudes toward a brand (A_B) are formed via the peripheral route.

Classical Conditioning of Attitudes.   Perhaps you are familiar with the experiments in which the famous Russian scientist, Ivan Pavlov, trained dogs to salivate on hearing a bell ring.[26] Pavlov trained dogs to salivate to a bell by establishing a systematic *contingency relation* between that object and a nonneutral object (i.e., meat powder), which itself *was* able to make dogs salivate. Trial after trial, dogs would hear a bell ring and then would be presented with meat powder. In this situation, meat powder was an *unconditioned stimulus (US),* and salivation was an *unconditioned response (UR).* By repeatedly pairing the bell (a *conditioned stimulus,* or *CS*) with the meat powder, the bell itself eventually caused the dog to salivate. The dog, in other words, had been trained to emit a *conditioned response (CR)* upon hearing the bell ring. The dog had learned that the bell regularly preceded meat powder, and thus the ringing bell caused the dog to predict that something desirable—the meat powder—was forthcoming.

Something analogous to this happens with consumers when processing peripheral cues. For example, brand advertisements that include adorable babies, sexy people, and majestic scenery can elicit positive emotional reactions. (Think of these peripheral cues as analogous to meat powder [the US], the emotional reactions as analogous to the dog's salivation [the UR], and the advertised brand as analogous to the bell in Pavlov's experiments [the CS].) The emotion contained in the cue may become associated with the brand, thereby influencing consumers to like the brand more than they did prior to viewing the commercial. In other words, through their repeated association, the CS (advertised brand) comes to elicit a conditioned response (CR) similar to the unconditioned response (UR) evoked by the US itself (the peripheral cue).[27]

Temporary versus Enduring Attitude Change.   According to the ELM theory on which the foregoing discussion is based, people experience only *temporary* attitude change when persuaded via the peripheral route in comparison to the relatively *enduring* change experienced under the central route. Thus, in circumstances in which receivers think about and process message arguments (i.e., when the elaboration likelihood is high and the central route is invoked), attitudes that are formed will be relatively enduring and somewhat resistant to change. Comparatively, when the elaboration likelihood is low (because the communication topic is not particularly relevant to the message recipient), attitude change may nevertheless occur (by virtue of receivers' processing peripheral cues) but will be only temporary unless consumers are exposed continuously to the peripheral cue. There is some evidence, however, that the use of peripheral cues in advertising can influence attitudes and even shape choice behavior so long as the advertised brand is *not* dominated by a competitive brand that is superior with respect to all pertinent choice criteria.[28]

Dual Routes

The central and peripheral paths represent endpoints on a continuum of persuasion strategies and are not intended to imply that persuasion is an either-or proposition. In other words, in many cases there is a combination of central and peripheral processes operating simultaneously.[29] This is shown in Figure 6.5 when the MOA factors produce a *moderate* elaboration likelihood level. In this instance, which no doubt captures the majority of situations in marketing communications, consumers can be expected to process both message arguments and peripheral cues. As such, attitudes toward the brand result from a combination of central- and peripheral-route attitude-formation processes.

PRACTICAL IMPLICATIONS: ENHANCING CONSUMERS' PROCESSING MOTIVATION, OPPORTUNITY, AND ABILITY

In recognizing alternative paths to attitude formation and thus to persuasion, the ELM points out that the form of persuasion will depend both on the *characteristics* of the market (consumers' motivation, opportunity, and ability to process marketing messages) and the *strengths* of the marketing communicator's relative market position. If consumers are interested in learning about a product, and a company's brand has clear advantages over competitive brands, then the persuasion tactic to be taken is obvious: *Design a message telling people explicitly why your brand is superior.* The result should be equally clear: Consumers will be swayed by your arguments, which will lead to relatively enduring attitude change and a strong chance they will select your brand over its competitors.

However, the marketplace reality is that most brands in a product category are similar, and, because of this, consumers generally are not anxious to devote mental effort toward processing messages that provide little new information. Thus, the marketing communicator, faced with this double whammy (only slightly involved consumers and a me-too brand), has to find ways to enthuse consumers sufficiently such that they will listen to and/or read the communicator's message. Here, peripheral cues become more significant. It matters not only what salespeople say, for example, but also how professionally they appear and whether they have style. It is not just what a television commercial says but how it is said, what props are used, what music is played in the background, how attractive the models are, and so on. In practice, then, persuasive marketing communications efforts include a combination of message arguments and peripheral cues.

The discussion to this point should have made it clear that the marketing communicator is most likely to achieve the best results (in terms of influencing consumers' attitudes and brand-choice behavior) when consumers are motivated, able, and have the opportunity to process messages. Hence, anything a marketing communicator can do to enhance these MOA factors likely will result in increased communication effectiveness. This is because increases in motivation, opportunity, or ability result in greater message elaboration; greater elaboration likelihood, in turn, facilitates central-route processing and the possibility for more enduring attitude change. Figure 6.9 provides a framework for the following discussion of how marketing communicators can enhance each of the MOA factors.[30]

Enhancing Motivation to Attend and Process Messages

As an advertiser or marketing communicator in another capacity, our goal is to increase the likelihood that consumers will be motivated to both *attend* and *process* the information we present in our messages. Among other desirable outcomes, increased processing motivation has been shown to strengthen the impact of brand attitudes on purchase intentions.[31] Figure 6.9 shows that the communicator's objective is to increase the consumer's motivation both to *attend to* the message and *process* brand information. The relationship with the discussion of attention and comprehension in the previous chapter should be apparent.

Marketing communicators attract attention by appealing to hedonic needs with shots of mouth-watering food items or by employing sex appeals. As further shown in Figure 6.9, attention also can be attracted by using novel stimuli, intense or prominent cues, complex pictures, and, in the case of broadcast ads, edits and cuts of the sort one sees with MTV-like videos.

To enhance consumers' motivation to *process* brand information, marketing communicators can use rhetorical questions (see Figure 6.10 for the motion sickness patch), fear appeals, and drama to increase the relevance of the brand to consumers' self-interests.

FIGURE 6.9 Enhancing Consumers' Motivation, Opportunity, and Ability to Process Brand Information

I. Enhance Consumers' MOTIVATION to . . .

   A. *Attend to the message by . . .*

- Appealing to hedonic needs (appetite appeals, sex appeals)
- Using novel stimuli (unusual pictures, different ad formats, large number of scenes)
- Using intense or prominent cues (action, loud music, colorful ads, celebrities, large pictures)
- Heightening ad complexity (complex pictures; edits and cuts)

   B. *Process brand information by . . .*

- Increasing relevance of brand to self (asking rhetorical questions, using fear appeals, using dramatic presentations)
- Increasing curiosity about the brand (opening with suspense or surprise, using humor, presenting little information in the message)

II. Enhance Consumers' OPPORTUNITY to . . .

   A. *Encode information by . . .*

- Repeating brand information
- Repeating key scenes
- Repeating the ad on multiple occasions

   B. *Reduce processing time by . . .*

- Creating Gestalt processing (using pictures and imagery)

III. Enhance Consumers' ABILITY to . . .

   A. *Access knowledge structures by . . .*

- Providing a context (employing verbal framing)

   B. *Create knowledge structures by . . .*

- Facilitating exemplar-based learning (using concretizations, demonstrations, and analogies)

Opening a message with suspense or surprise also enhances motivation to attend a message, as illustrated by the ad for Total cereal in Figure 6.11 with its surprisingly atypical X-ray graphic. The advertisement for Minolta copiers (Figure 6.12) is an outstanding effort to enhance processing motivation by increasing the magazine reader's suspense. The

FIGURE 6.10

The Use of Rhetorical Questioning to Enhance Processing Motivation

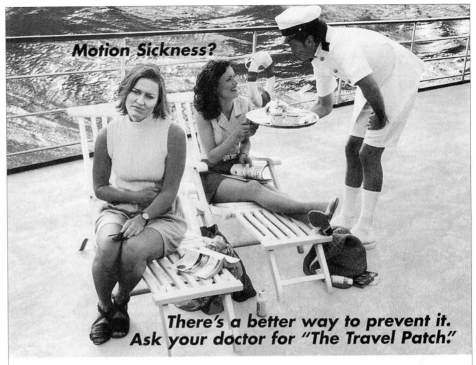

cobra's head virtually demands the reader's attention and provokes curiosity. This ingenious pictorial draws attention to the snake charmer along the exaggerated length of his musical instrument, and then pulls the reader's attention to the headline and body copy via the return path of the instrument's shadow. Readers who have a need for a copier (such as small business owners and office managers) are encouraged to read the advertisement now that their attention has been drawn to the issue of avoiding risk, which is depicted in the pictorial and discussed in the body copy. The previously reviewed ad for ATROVENT nasal spray, Figure 6.3, offers an additional depiction of an unexpected or surprising graphic, namely, a foot chained to a box of tissue, to enhance the consumer's processing motivation.

Additional ways to enhance processing motivation include using humor or presenting little information (and thereby encouraging the consumer to think about the brand). All of

The Use of Surprise to
Enhance Processing
Motivation

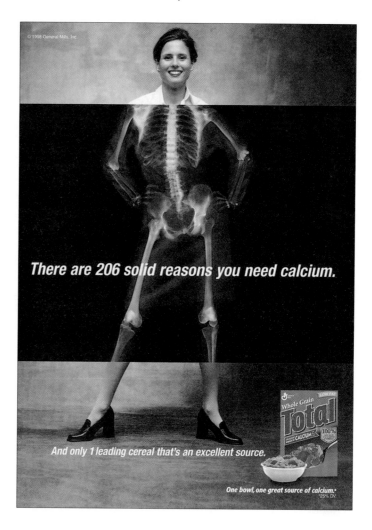

these techniques can serve to heighten consumers' motivation to process brand information and learn about the brand's pertinent attributes, benefits, and need-satisfying potential.

Enhancing Opportunity to Encode Information and Reduce Processing Time

Marketing messages have no chance of effectiveness unless consumers comprehend information about the brand and incorporate it with information related to the product category in their existing memory structure. Hence, the communicator's goal is to get consumers to *encode* information and, toward this end, to make it as simple and quick as possible for them to do so. The secret to facilitating encoding is *repetition*: The marketing communicator should repeat brand information, repeat key scenes, and repeat the advertisement on multiple occasions. Through repetition consumers have increased opportunity to encode the important information the communicator wishes to convey.

Opportunity to process also is enhanced by *reducing the time* it takes to process the information. The use of pictures and imagery create a form of total-message processing (or Gestalt processing) whereby the consumer can readily encode the totality of the message rather than having to process information bit by bit. The magazine ad for Pro Penn tennis balls (Figure 6.13) demands little processing effort or time from the reader in its graphic depiction showing only the tennis ball, but nothing else in the room, withstanding the onslaught of the puppy's unbridled enthusiasm. The previously described ad for

FIGURE 6.12

The Use of Suspense to Enhance Processing Motivation

MAYBE THE BEST WAY TO HANDLE RISK IS TO AVOID IT ALTOGETHER.

That's why Minolta created the No-Risk Guarantee. It takes you out of harm's way by letting you decide whether you're happy with the copier's performance.

Even better. It covers our EP 9760 Pro Series Copier, which was recently voted first overall in productivity in the high-volume class.*

Here's how it works: If you're not completely satisfied with our copier within the first three years of normal operation, we will replace it with an identical or comparably equipped model, free of charge. In other

See an authorized Minolta copier dealer for complete details.

words, it works or it walks. An award-winning copier combined with an iron-clad guarantee? The only risk involved is passing this opportunity up.

For more information, call 1-800-9-MINOLTA.

*Source: Thomas A. Minnella, author *The Copier Productivity Primer*

NO-RISK COPIERS
ONLY FROM THE MIND OF MINOLTA   MINOLTA

Godiva chocolate (Figure 6.4) also uses an attention-attracting pictorial that readily communicates the desired message: This brand is a perfect gift for the "chocoholics" on one's holiday list.

Enhancing Ability to Access and Create Knowledge Structures

In general, people are most able to process new information that relates to something they already know or understand. If one knows a lot about computers, then information presented in computer language is readily comprehended. The marketing communicator's task is to enable consumers either to *access* existing knowledge structures or to *create* new knowledge structures. As described in Chapter 5, a brand-based knowledge structure

FIGURE
6.13

The Use of Pictorials to
Create Gestalt Processing

represents the associative links in the consumer's long-term memory between the brand and information, knowledge, and beliefs about that brand.

To facilitate consumer accessing of knowledge structures, marketing communicators need to *provide a context* for the text or pictures. One way of accomplishing this is with *verbal framing.* This means that pictures in ads are placed in context of, or framed with, appropriate words or phrases. Figure 6.14 for Behr paint uses verbal framing with the gradually fading headline that encourages consumers to draw on their own knowledge structure that exterior house paints, just like the headline, fade over time. Returning again to Figure 6.7, we see another illustration of framing. Immediately following the picture of the dimpled rocket is the headline "Designed by rocket scientists who know what it means to land where you're supposed to." The picture now makes sense and ties in beautifully with the message the advertiser wants consumers to encode, that Ultra 500 golf balls are designed by experts who understand the science of projectile flight. All in all, this ad represents a splendid effort to draw from consumers' positive views about rocket science and to create the impression that the golfer is getting the benefits of this science (distance and precision) when purchasing this brand of golf ball. (The student will see a similarity here with the discussion in the prior chapter on the semiotics of marketing communications. There it was explained that communicators draw from the culturally constituted world—or universe of existing meanings—and transfer these meanings to their promoted brands.)

FIGURE 6.14

Employing Verbal Framing to Enable Knowledge Structure Access

Sometimes marketing communicators need to *create* knowledge structures for information they want consumers to have about their brands. This is accomplished by facilitating *exemplar-based learning*. An *exemplar* is a specimen or model of a particular concept or idea. By using concretizations (as discussed in the previous chapter), demonstrations, or analogies, the marketing communicator can facilitate learning by appealing to exemplars. Consider, for example, the concept of freshness. Assume your task is to activate from consumers' long-term memories exemplars of their efforts to identify freshness when grocery shopping. What grocery products might you use to convey efforts to identify product freshness? Now, return to Figure 6.6 and see what the advertisers of Diet Pepsi did when promoting the introduction of freshness dating. They presented pictures of products that people routinely inspect for freshness (squeeze an orange; pinch a loaf of bread) and, by analogy, communicated the idea that consumers should check arrows on Diet Pepsi cans to assure that the contents are not dated. Figure 6.15 for Sealy mattresses facilitates exemplar-based learning with the spine-ball demonstration. Figure 6.16 uses a vivid demonstration of the dangers of flash fires with the graphic analogy showing how unsealed flammable liquids placed too close to a gas pilot light might ignite spontaneously.

The foregoing discussion has emphasized that advertisers and other marketing communicators benefit from enhancing consumers' motivation, opportunity, and ability to process marketing messages. A variety of communication devices are available to marketing communicators to achieve their goals in the hopes of influencing consumers' brand-related attitudes, purchase intentions, and, ultimately, their behavior. Marketing communications do not just happen; rather, sophisticated communications are planned, orchestrated, and engineered toward the objective of accomplishing specific persuasion goals.

Facilitating Exemplar-Based Learning

Another Illustration of
Facilitating Exemplar-
Based Learning

A flash fire. It happens when invisible fumes creep along your floor and
make contact with a gas pilot light. So please make sure flammable liquids are tightly sealed
and stored far away from gas appliances. For more information on home fire safety,
see an Allstate Agent or call 1-888-ALLSFTY. **Being in good hands is the only place to be."**

Allstate
You're in good hands.

Summary

Marketing communications in its various forms (advertising, personal selling, point-of-purchase displays, and so on) involves efforts to persuade consumers by influencing their attitudes and ultimately their behavior. This chapter describes the role and nature of attitudes and different mechanisms by which they are formed and changed. From the marketing communicators' perspective, attitude formation and change represent the process of persuasion.

The nature of persuasion is discussed with particular emphasis on the elaboration likelihood model (ELM). Two alternative persuasion mechanisms are described: a central route, which explains persuasion under conditions when the receiver is involved in the communication topic, and a peripheral route, which accounts for persuasion when receivers are not highly involved.

Three attitude-formation processes are described in some detail: emotion-based persuasion, message-based persuasion, and classical conditioning. The first two are mechanisms for attitude change under the central route, whereas classical conditioning is a peripheral-route process. Practical efforts to enhance consumers' motivation, opportunity, and ability to process marketing messages are discussed and illustrated.

Discussion Questions

1. Explain the cognitive, affective, and conative components of an attitude. Provide examples of each using your attitude toward the idea of personally pursuing a career in selling and sales management.

2. Distinguish between message arguments and peripheral cues as fundamental determinants of persuasion. Provide several examples of each from actual television commercials or other advertisements.

3. Receiver involvement is the fundamental determinant of whether people may be persuaded through a central or a peripheral route. Explain.

4. There are three general strategies for changing attitudes. Explain each, using a hotel chain as your illustration.

5. Assume that your target audience is composed of people who can afford to purchase a $30,000 electric-powered automobile but who have negative attitudes toward electric-powered vehicles. (Note: The power source for such automobiles is a large battery that is plugged into an electrical outlet for recharging. These automobiles have a range of only several hundred miles before recharging is required, so long-distance travel is virtually precluded.) Using material from the chapter, how would you attempt to change their attitudes if you were the advertising agency responsible for this campaign? Be specific.

6. Have you personally experienced unethical persuasive efforts from marketing communicators? Under what circumstances would you most expect to find unethical marketing communications, and when would unethical communications most likely be effective in marketing? Draw upon the elaboration likelihood model (Figure 6.5) in forming your answer.

7. In the discussion of the influence tactic of reciprocation, you were introduced to the concept of contingency, or it-depends, thinking. Which it-depends factors might explain when the scarcity tactic would and would not be effective?

8. Assume that you are the fund-raiser for a social or professional fraternity or sorority. Explain how in this situation you could use each of the six influence tactics discussed in the text. Be specific.

9. Describe the similarity between active synthesis (discussed in the prior chapter) and the concept of elaboration.

10. Provide detailed explanations as to how the advertisements in Figures 6.15 and 6.16 facilitate exemplar-based learning.

Internet Exercises

1. Pretend you are in charge of advertising for an online retailer (e.g., www.gap.com, www.egghead.com, www.amazon.com, www.cdnow.com). You know that consumers have positive evaluations for the convenience of online shopping but many are distrustful of unknown retailers and of giving out credit card numbers online.
   a. Using material from this chapter, explain how you would attempt to change consumers' attitudes about the risks of online shopping.
   b. Visit several actual online retailers and describe instances where the retailers have addressed consumers' risk perceptions.

2. Visit the Internet sites of approximately five to 10 brands that appeal to you. Based on the framework in Figure 6.9, identify at least one example of each of the following efforts to enhance consumers' MOA factors:
   a. Locate an effort to increase consumers' motivation to process brand information.
   b. Identify an Internet advertisement that attempts to enhance consumers' opportunity to encode information.
   c. Find an advertisement that uses an exemplar to assist consumers in either accessing or creating a new knowledge structure.

Chapter Six Endnotes

1. A number of major theories of attitudes and attitude-change processes have developed over the last half-century. Seven particularly significant theories are reviewed in Richard E. Petty and John T. Cacioppo, *Attitudes and Persuasion: Classic and Contemporary Approaches* (Dubuque, Iowa: Wm. C. Brown Company, 1981). For another review, see Richard E. Petty, Rao H. Unnava, and Alan J. Strathman, "Theories of Attitude Change," in *Handbook of Consumer Behavior,* ed. T. S. Robertson and H. H. Kassarjian (Englewood Cliffs, N.J.: Prentice-Hall, 1991), 241–280.

2. This definition adheres to Petty and Cacioppo, *Attitudes and Persuasion,* 7, and also reflects the concept of attitude popularized by Fazio and his colleagues. See, for example, Russell H. Fazio, Jeaw-Mei Chen, Elizabeth C. McDonel, and Steven J. Sherman, "Attitude Accessibility, Attitude-Behavior Consistency, and the Strength of the Object-Evaluation Association," *Journal of Experimental Social Psychology* 18, 1982, 339–357. On a technical note, the definition makes no distinction between what some authors properly consider to be the distinct constructs of *affect* (or feeling states) and *attitude* (or evaluative judgments). For discussion, see Joel B. Cohen and Charles S. Areni, "Affect and Consumer Behavior," in *Handbook of Consumer Behavior,* ed. T. S. Robertson and H. H. Kassarjian (Englewood Cliffs, N.J.: Prentice-Hall, 1991), 188–240.

3. Daniel J. O'Keefe, *Persuasion: Theory and Research* (Newbury Park, Calif.: Sage Publications, 1990), 18.

4. See, for example, Richard P. Bagozzi, Alice M. Tybout, C. Samuel Craig, and Brian Sternthal, "The Construct Validity of the Tripartite Classification of Attitudes," *Journal of Marketing Research* 16 (February 1979), 88–95; and Richard J. Lutz, "An Experimental Investigation of Causal Relations among Cognitions, Affect, and Behavioral Intention," *Journal of Consumer Research* 3 (March 1977), 197–208.

5. This is the classic viewpoint of attitude popularized by Gordon W. Allport, "Attitudes," in *A Handbook of Social Psychology,* ed. C. A. Murchinson (Worcester, Mass.: Clark University Press, 1935), 798–844.

6. The view that this strict progression applies to every behavior and that cognition must necessarily precede affect is not uncontested. Various alternative "hierarchies of effect" have been postulated. For further discussion, see Thomas E. Barry, "The Development of the Hierarchy of Effects," in *Current Issues and Research in Advertising,* ed. James H. Leigh and Claude R. Martin, Jr. (Ann Arbor: Division of Research, Graduate School of Business, University of Michigan, 1987), 251–296.

7. A similar account is offered by Kathleen Kelley Reardon, *Persuasion in Practice* (Newbury Park, Calif.: Sage Publications, 1990), 2.

8. Peter Wright, "Schemer Schema: Consumers' Intuitive Theories about Marketers' Influence Tactics," in *Advances in Consumer Research* 13, ed. Richard J. Lutz (Provo, Utah: Association for Consumer Research, 1985), 1–3. An elaborate and thorough discussion of consumers' persuasion knowledge is provided

by Marian Friestad and Peter Wright, "The Persuasion Knowledge Model: How People Cope with Persuasion Attempts," *Journal of Consumer Research* 21 (June 1994), 1–31. An empirical demonstration of consumers' persuasion knowledge vis-à-vis that of advertising researchers is available in Marian Friestad and Peter Wright, "Persuasion Knowledge: Lay People's and Researchers' Beliefs about the Psychology of Advertising," *Journal of Consumer Research* 22 (June 1995), 62–74.

9. Cialdini actually discusses seven influence tactics, but the seventh, instant influence, cuts across all the others and need not be discussed separately. Also, he refers to influence tactics as "weapons" of influence. Because the term *weapons* implies that the persuadee is an adversary, I prefer instead the term *tools* insofar as many modern marketing practitioners view their customers as participants in a long-term relation-building process and not as adversaries or victims. The following sections are based on Cialdini's insightful work. See Robert B. Cialdini, *Influence: Science and Practice,* 2d ed. (Glenview, Ill.: Scott, Foresman, 1988).

10. Ibid., 2.

11. "Pushing Drugs to Doctors," *Consumer Reports,* February 1992, 87–94.

12. Cialdini, *Influence: Science and Practice,* 123.

13. Jack W. Brehm, *A Theory of Psychological Reactance* (New York: Academic Press, 1966). See also Mona Clee and Robert Wicklund, "Consumer Behavior and Psychological Reactance," *Journal of Consumer Research* 6 (March 1980), 389–405.

14. Richard M. Perloff and Timothy C. Brock, "'And Thinking Makes It So': Cognitive Responses to Persuasion," in *Persuasion: New Directions in Theory and Research,* ed. M. E. Rioloff and G. R. Miller (Beverly Hills, Calif.: Sage Publications, 1980), 67–99. See also Robert E. Burnkrant and H. Rao Unnava, "Effects of Self-Referencing on Persuasion," *Journal of Consumer Research* 22 (June 1995), 17–26.

15. Deborah J. MacInnis and Bernard J. Jaworski, "Information Processing from Advertisements: Toward an Integrative Framework," *Journal of Marketing* 53 (October 1989), 8.

16. Peter L. Wright, "The Cognitive Processes Mediating the Acceptance of Advertising," *Journal of Marketing Research* 10 (February 1973), 53–62. Also see Amitava Chattopadhyay and Joseph W. Alba, "The Situational Importance of Recall and Inference in Consumer Decision Making," *Journal of Consumer Research* 15 (June 1988), 1–12.

17. Readers familiar with Petty and Cacioppo's ELM model may wonder why it is not presented. Although it is suitable for guiding academic research and graduate study, my own experience in teaching the ELM has revealed that students often have some difficulty in following the model. The reworking of Petty and Cacioppo's model is intended to provide a more

accessible structure for students without doing disservice to their theory.

18. Petty and Cacioppo, *Attitudes and Persuasion;* MacInnis and Jaworski, "Information Processing from Advertisements." For an excellent application of ELM predictions, see Paul W. Miniard, Sunil Bhatla, Kenneth R. Lord, Peter R. Dickson, and H. Rao Unnava, "Picture-Based Persuasion Processes and the Moderating Role of Involvement," *Journal of Consumer Research* 18 (June 1991), 92–107.

19. The discussion of what is termed here emotion-based persuasion is guided by the presentation in MacInnis and Jaworski, "Information Processing from Advertisements."

20. Martin Fishbein and Icek Ajzen, *Belief, Attitude, Intention, and Behavior: An Introduction to Theory and Research* (Reading, Mass.: Addison-Wesley, 1975); Icek Ajzen and Martin Fishbein, *Understanding Attitudes and Predicting Social Behavior* (Englewood Cliffs, N.J.: Prentice-Hall, 1980).

21. The normative component of the theory concerns the influence that important others (also called referent groups) have on our intentions and behavior.

22. Richard J. Lutz, "Changing Brand Attitudes through Modification of Cognitive Structure," *Journal of Consumer Research* 1 (March 1975), 49–59.

23. Fara Warner, "BMW Ads Challenge Maintenance Myth," *Advertising Age,* June 20, 1994, 5.

24. Jim Henry, "Saab Takes on Volvo, BMW in First Campaign Via Martin," *Advertising Age,* August 18, 1997, 4.

25. For a thorough review of research involving the attitude toward the ad construct, see Scott B. MacKenzie and Richard J. Lutz, "An Empirical Examination of the Structural Antecedents of Attitude Toward the Ad in an Advertising Pretesting Context," *Journal of Marketing* 53 (April 1989), 48–65.

26. Pavlov also used a metronome in other experiments and the results were the same as with the bell.

27. For a more detailed account of classical conditioning, see Terence A. Shimp, "Neo-Pavlovian Conditioning and Its Implications for Consumer Theory and Research," in *Handbook of Consumer Behavior,* ed. T. S. Robertson and H. H. Kassarjian (Englewood Cliffs, N.J.: Prentice-Hall, 1991), 162–187.

28. Paul W. Miniard, Deepak Sirdeshmukh, and Daniel E. Innis, "Peripheral Persuasion and Brand Choice," *Journal of Consumer Research* 19 (September 1992), 226–239.

29. Indirect demonstration of this is provided in a series of experiments conducted by Michael Tuan Pham, "Cue Representation and Selection Effects of Arousal on Persuasion," *Journal of Consumer Research* 22 (March 1996), 373–387.

30. The ensuing discussion is based on the work of Deborah J. MacInnis, Christine Moorman, and Bernard J. Jaworski, "Enhancing and Measuring Consumers' Motivation,

Opportunity, and Ability to Process Brand Information from Ads," *Journal of Marketing* 55 (October 1991), 32–53.

31. Scott B. MacKenzie and Richard A. Spreng, "How Does Motivation Moderate the Impact of

Central and Peripheral Processing on Brand Attitudes and Intentions?" *Journal of Consumer Research* 18 (March 1992), 519–529.

PART

THREE

Part Three—New Products, Brand Names, Logos, Packages, and Point-of-Purchase Materials

Chapter 7 looks at the adoption and diffusion processes and examines the role of marketing communications in facilitating these processes and achieving acceptance for new products. Particular attention is devoted to discussions of how marketing communicators facilitate product adoption and diffusion by establishing a new product's relative advantages, showing how the product is compatible with the consumer's past behavior and consumption values, removing perceptions of product complexity, and facilitating product trial. The role of word-of-mouth influence also receives considerable treatment.

Chapter 8 describes the initial elements responsible for a brand's image, namely the brand name, logo, and package. Another major topic covered in this chapter is the ever-growing practice of point-of-purchase (P-O-P) communications. The point-of-purchase is the critical point where the brand name, logo, and package come face to face with the customer. Marketing communicators are increasingly appreciative of the importance of point-of-purchase communications. Expanded investment in this marketing communications component is explained in terms of the valuable functions that P-O-P performs for consumers, manufacturers, and retailers. The chapter devotes considerable attention to the various forms of P-O-P communication tools, presents results from the POPAI Consumer Buying Habits Study, and provides detailed evidence regarding the impact that displays can have in increasing a brand's sales volume during the display period.

Marketing Communications and New Product Adoption

CHAPTER OBJECTIVES

After studying this chapter, you should be able to:

1. Appreciate the role of marketing communications in facilitating the introduction of new products.

2. Explain five innovation-related characteristics that influence consumers' adoption of new products.

3. Describe the diffusion process and the various groups of adopters.

4. Understand efforts employed by marketing communicators to manage the diffusion process.

5. Appreciate the role of word-of-mouth communications in facilitating new product adoption.

Opening Vignette: Steve Jobs Does a Job with the iMac

In Chapter 5 you read about imagery, which, roughly speaking, involves visualization, or mental representation, of an object or event. Imagine for the moment, if you will, the appearance of the very first personal computer you ever used. (Close your eyes and imagine that first computer.) The odds are very high that the computer was a three-piece unit with a "footprint" (the processing unit) and separate monitor and keyboard. The shape probably was "masculine," that is, angular. The color was dull, probably light beige. The machine was functional but not very attractive—exemplary of the dictum that "form follows function."

Now step back in time to 1997 and place yourself in the shoes of Steve Jobs, the founder of Apple Computer, who in 1997 made a return to Apple as quasi-CEO after a hiatus away from the company in pursuit of other interests. The company was moribund prior to his return. Nothing exciting was happening. Market share was declining. The company's future was in doubt. New products, streamlined operations, and a general infusion of enthusiasm were badly needed. Less than two years after his arrival, the iMac computer (Figure 7.1) was launched. (The name iMac, by the way, is a clever conjunction of "i" for Internet and "Mac," an abbreviated version of Macintosh, the name of the famous computer introduced under Jobs' initial reign at Apple Computer Inc. in 1984.)

What's so special about the iMac? For starters, it was virtually an instant success upon introduction in August 1998, selling about a quarter million units in the first six weeks after launch. The iMac was one of the hottest products on the market during the holiday season of 1998. Although a very good PC, the iMac's retail price at $1,299 was, if anything, at a premium level compared to functionally competitive PCs. Indeed, specification-wise the original iMac was nothing exceptional with only 32MB of RAM, a 4GB hard drive, and a 233-MHz processing chip.

However, the iMac's design was special. With five novel colors (for computers), translucent case, one-piece unit, rounded (versus angular) shape, and preinstalled software, the iMac was unlike any personal computer that consumers had seen. Beyond its unique design, the iMac was perhaps the most user-friendly computer to ever hit the market. Essentially all the user had to do was plug it in and turn it on—no setup, no hassle. This perhaps explains why nearly one third of the iMac buyers were first-time computer owners.

A perfect machine? Actually, the iMac has its flaws, the most notable being the absence of a floppy drive and little ability to add any peripherals. Limitations aside, the marketplace response was overwhelming, which suggests that this innovative computer's advantages outweighed its disadvantages in the minds of its thousands of satisfied purchasers. Inspired by iMac's success, other computer companies have introduced their own products encased in translucent covers.

Sources: Adapted from "iMac's Success Spawns Imitators of Translucent Product Casing," *The Wall Street Journal Interactive Edition,* January 4, 1999; also, http://cgi.pathfinder.com/time/digital/yir/1998/apple.html; and http://cnet.com/Content/Reports/Special/Awards98/ss01.html.

FIGURE
7.1

NEW PRODUCTS AND MARKETING COMMUNICATIONS

*I*ntroducing a stream of new products is absolutely essential for most companies' success and long-term growth. Despite the huge investments and concerted efforts to introduce new products and services, many are never successful. It is impossible to pinpoint the percentage of new ideas and products that eventually fail because organizations vary in their definitions of success. However, failure-rate estimates typically range between 35 to 45 percent, and the rate may be increasing.[1] The purpose of this chapter is to explain the role of marketing communications in facilitating successful new product introductions and reducing the product failure rate.

An organization's marketing communications specialists have a number of responsibilities to ensure new-product success. Perhaps this can best be appreciated by conceptualizing the process by which consumers become trial and repeat purchasers of new products.[2] In other words, achieving new product success requires that consumers undertake a trial purchase of a new brand and then become long-term repeat purchasers. (The notions of trial and repeat purchase are particularly apt for inexpensive consumer packaged goods, but even expensive durable goods like automobiles are tried via test drives and then repeat purchased when the consumer is in the market for another new car.) The model in Figure 7.2 indicates with circles the three main stages through which an individual becomes an adopter of a new product. These stages are the awareness, trier, and repeater classes. The blocks surrounding the circles are mostly marketing communications tools that play a role in moving consumers from initial awareness, through product trial, and ultimately to becoming a repeat purchaser.

The first step in facilitating adoption is to make the consumer aware of a new product's existence. Figure 7.2 shows that four variables influence the **awareness class:** free samples, coupons, advertising, and distribution. The first three variables are distinctly marketing communication variables, and the fourth, distribution, is closely allied in that the sales force is responsible for gaining distribution, providing reseller support, and making point-of-purchase materials available to the trade. Successful introduction of new products typically requires an effective advertising campaign, widespread product distribution backed up with point-of-purchase materials, and, in the case of inexpensive package goods, extensive couponing and sampling.

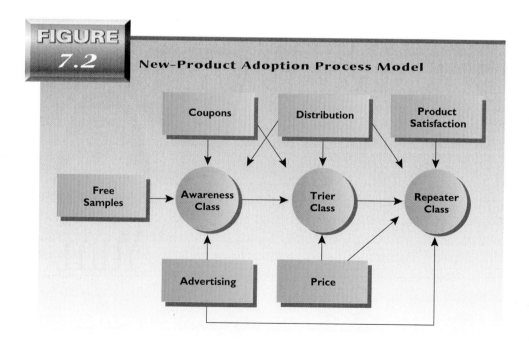

FIGURE 7.2

New-Product Adoption Process Model

Once a consumer becomes aware of a new product or brand, there is an increased probability that he or she will actually try the new offering. Coupons, distribution, and price are the variables that affect the **trier class** (see Figure 7.2). For durable goods, trial may involve test driving a new automobile or visiting a computer store to acquire hands-on experience with a machine such as the iMac. In the case of inexpensive packaged goods, trial more likely involves purchasing a new brand to test its performance characteristics— its taste, cleaning ability, or other pertinent benefit.

Repeat purchasing, demonstrated by the **repeater class,** is a function of four primary forces: advertising, price, distribution, and product satisfaction. That is, consumers are more likely to continue to purchase a particular brand if advertising reminds them about the brand, if the price is considered reasonable, if the brand is accessible in retail outlets, and if product quality is considered satisfactory.

Marketing communications plays a major role in influencing five innovation-related characteristics that undergird consumers' attitudes toward new products and hence their likelihood of adopting innovative products: (1) relative advantages, (2) compatibility, (3) complexity, (4) trialability, and (5) observability.[3]

Relative Advantage

The degree to which a product innovation is perceived as better than existing alternatives is termed *relative advantage*. **Relative advantage** is a function of whether a person *perceives* the new product to be better than competitive offerings, rather than whether the product is actually better by objective standards. Round tea bags are *perceived* as making a better cup of tea, but consumers may not actually be able to discern any difference from tea brewed in square bags in a blind taste test.

Relative advantage is positively correlated with an innovation's adoption rate—that is, the greater an innovation's relative advantages compared to existing offerings, the more rapid the rate of adoption to be expected. In general, relative advantages exist to the extent that a new product offers: (1) better performance compared to other options, (2) increased comfort, (3) savings in time and effort, or (4) immediacy of reward. The iMac (*Opening Vignette*) offered relative advantages in the sense of being considered easy to use (thus saving time and effort) and requiring little start-up hassle (thus providing an immediate reward). Figure 7.3 for Clorox 2 Bleach-Free illustrates a distinct relative advantage in this new product that is capable of removing tough stains without fading clothes. The advertisement for the Olympus Stylus Epic Zoom 80 (Figure 7.4) illustrates another product innovation offering a meaningful relative advantage in the form of being the smallest 35mm zoom camera on the market.

A dramatic case of product success due to relative advantage was achieved by the 3M Company when it introduced its Scotch-Brite Never Rust soap pads to compete against the entrenched S.O.S. and Brillo pads. 3M immediately obtained a substantial share of this product category's total market by offering an alternative to the rusty soap pads with which consumers had contended for decades.[4]

Relative advantages depend on the inherent characteristics of the product itself, but can also be influenced by persuasive communications. For example, overnight package delivery services (such as FedEx) offer the real relative advantage of quicker delivery in comparison to conventional mailing; however, advertising must accentuate this real advantage in order for potential users to appreciate fully the advantages of using overnight delivery. Advertising also serves to negate the relative advantages claimed by marketers of competitive products, as can be seen in the FedEx advertisement (Figure 7.5) that points out the relative *dis*advantages of the United States Postal Service's Priority Mail.

Compatibility

The degree to which an innovation is perceived to fit into a person's way of doing things is termed **compatibility.** A new product is more compatible to the extent that it matches consumers' needs, personal values, beliefs, and past experiences. The greater its compatibility,

An Illustration of
Relative Advantage

the more rapid a new product's rate of adoption. Innovations that are compatible with a person's existing situation are less risky, more meaningful, and require less effort to incorporate into one's consumption lifestyle.

The makers of waterbeds, for example, can claim relative advantages over traditional mattresses (such as better body support), but many consumers shun this form of bedding because waterbeds are surrounded by a hippie-culture image and tales of flooded apartments and seasick users.[5] Most consumers simply consider waterbeds incompatible with their concept of what bedding should be.

Another product innovation that has distinct relative advantages but that suffers from compatibility problems is steel-framed homes. These homes offer unmatched protection from wind, fire, and termites. Most consumers, however, would not consider building a steel home due to perceptions of higher cost (a relative disadvantage) and, more important, because wood framing, rather than steel, better matches their concept of how a house "should be" constructed.

Sometimes the only way to overcome perceptions of incompatibility is through heavy advertising to convince consumers that a new way of doing things truly is superior to an existing solution. Consider the case of ultra-high-temperature milk (UHT), which is a heat-treated product that lasts for up to six months on the shelf and tastes the same as "regular" milk. Shelf-stable milk is standard fare throughout much of Europe and Latin America. For example, market shares of UHT milk are 95 percent in France, 90 percent in Belgium, 80 percent in Spain, 55 percent in Germany, and 55 percent in Italy.[6] In the United States, however, sales of UHT are negligible.

Another Illustration of Relative Advantage

Italy's Parmalat entered the massive U.S. market with intents of changing America's preference to shelf-stable milk. After several years on the market, Parmalat's market share pales in comparison to sales of refrigerated milk. The problem is one of incompatibility. Americans are wedded to refrigerated milk. Parmalat will have to advertise heavily to stand any chance of large numbers of American consumers regularly purchasing UHT instead of conventional refrigerated milk.[7] Of course, because success breeds further success, products that suffer from images of incompatibility often do not have sufficient funds to overcome their status.

An innovator that has the financial resources, though, can launch a successful future and establish itself as the product leader and benefit from corresponding pioneering advantages. The *Global Focus* illustrates this with Microsoft's launch of *Windows 95*. Although *Windows 98* has since been introduced, the initial worldwide launch of *Windows 95* paved the way for subsequent versions of the Windows platform.

Advertising a Competitor's
Relative Disadvantages

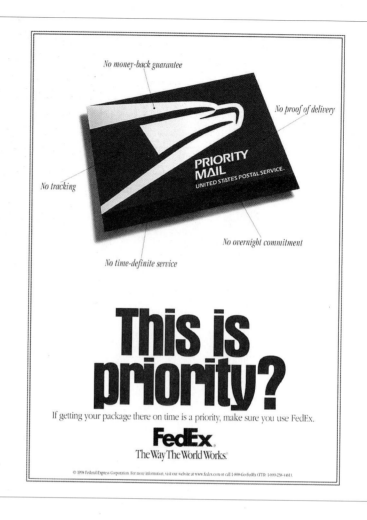

Marketing communicators are largely responsible for ensuring compatibility in the minds of customers by choosing advertising appeals that serve to position a product as compatible with the target market's beliefs, past experiences, and needs. An interesting illustration of this is the marketing of grapefruit by the Florida Department of Citrus, which repositioned this product so that it would fit better into consumers' workday lives. Many people consider the time required preparing a grapefruit to be incompatible with the hectic pace of their lives. Advertisements were developed to convince consumers that slicing a grapefruit in half and scooping out the fruit with a spoon is not the only way to eat grapefruit. Potential buyers were informed, as simple as it may seem, that grapefruit can be quickly peeled and eaten much like an orange. The objective of this campaign was to make the grapefruit more compatible with consumers' fast-paced lifestyles.[8]

Complexity

Complexity refers to an innovation's degree of perceived difficulty. The more difficult an innovation is to understand or use, the slower the rate of adoption. Home computers were adopted slowly because many homeowners perceived them too difficult to understand and use. Advertisers have confronted this by creating subtle (and not-so-subtle) television commercials to convey the idea that anyone can easily learn to use a computer, even little kids. Companies have also redesigned their products and introduced new computers that are easier to use. The success of the iMac attests to the value of making product use simple. As noted in the *Opening Vignette*, approximately one-third of iMac's purchasers upon introduction in 1998 were first-time computer owners. Thousands of people apparently believed that the iMac did not exceed their threshold level for complexity.

GLOBAL FOCUS: THE BIG HOOPLA SURROUNDING THE INTRODUCTION OF *WINDOWS 95*

Months upon months of anticipation, incredible media hype, and the unusual talk-show appearances of the typically ultraprivate Bill Gates preceded the launching of Microsoft Corporation's *Windows 95* on August 24, 1995. Borrowing heavily from new-product introduction techniques used by consumer packaged-goods companies, Microsoft turned the launching of *Windows 95* into a sensational global rollout in 22 countries.

Pundits predicted that this new software product's total introductory marketing expenditures would reach $700 million—including Microsoft's own advertising and publicity stunts along with advertising by retailers and computer hardware companies. The global introduction of *Windows 95* used all imaginable forms of marketing communications, including heavy advertising on TV and in print, massive in-store promotions, and a variety of public relations and publicity activities. These massive expenditures and creative communications were easily justified considering the prediction that 62 million copies of *Windows 95* would be sold in the first year of introduction as installations in new PCs or as upgrades to existing machines.

Microsoft simultaneously launched *Windows 95* around the world using heavy advertising and a variety of alternative media and publicity stunts. For example, 10 days before its Canadian debut, the giant letter *O* appeared on the CN Tower in Toronto, the tallest building in that city. Over the next nine days, other letters were added, until they spelled *Windows 95:* a spectacle 300 feet above the ground that could be seen by the entire city. In England, airline travelers saw the *Windows 95* logo painted on fields. A four-story-high *Windows 95* box on a barge sailed into Sydney on launch day in a carnival-like atmosphere replete with musicians and dancers. In Paris, Microsoft hosted a gathering of 7,000 influential people in the Palais des Congres, while in Vienna a huge group gathered at the famous Stephansdom Cathedral. And in Poland, journalists were taken on a submarine ride to see what a world "without windows" looks like.

Needless to say, these ambitious and clever publicity stunts created incredible levels of product awareness and interest. It is not surprising that Microsoft sold $30 million worth of *Windows 95* on its launch day, an unprecedented success for software introduction. The extraordinary success of *Windows 95* made the subsequent introduction of *Windows 98* a relatively simple undertaking, as likely will be the case when *Windows '01, '04,* and later versions are brought to market.

Source: Adapted from various press reports, including Bradley Johnson, "Windows 95 Opens with Omnimedia Blast," *Advertising Age,* August 28, 1995, 1, 32; and "Heights, and Depths, of Hype," *Advertising Age,* August 28, 1995, 33.

The advertisement in Figure 7.6 for the Mitsubishi is a further effort to overcome concerns about product complexity. On the surface this ad apparently appeals only to people with large fingers who have difficulty with the small buttons on other cellular phones. In this sense, the ad is simply promoting a relative advantage. One might conjecture, however, that the ad is attempting at a slightly deeper level to overcome concerns by some consumers (perhaps senior citizens?) that cell phones are too difficult to use.

Trialability

The extent to which an innovation can be used on a limited basis prior to making a full-blown commitment is referred to as **trialability.** In general, products that lend themselves to trialability are adopted at a more rapid rate. Trialability is tied closely to the concept of *perceived risk.* Test drives of new automobiles, free samples of food products at local supermarkets, and small packages of new detergents all permit the consumer to try a new product on an experimental basis. The trial experience serves to reduce the risk of a consumer's being dissatisfied with a product after having permanently committed to it through an outright purchase. As will be discussed in detail in Chapter 18, sampling is an incomparable promotional method for encouraging trial by reducing the risk that accompanies spending money on a new, untried product.

Facilitating trial is typically more difficult with durable products than with inexpensive packaged goods. Automobile companies allow consumers to take test drives, but what do you do if you are, say, a computer manufacturer or a lawnmower maker? If you are creative, you do what companies like Apple Computer and John Deere did in novel efforts to give people the opportunity to try their products. Apple developed a "Test Drive a Macintosh" promotion that gave interested consumers the opportunity to try the computer in the

Offsetting Perceived
Product Complexity

comfort of their own homes for 24 hours at no cost. John Deere offered prospective mower purchasers a 30-day free test period whereby the consumer could try the mower for this period and then return it, no questions asked, if not fully satisfied.

Observability

Observability is the degree to which the product user or other people can observe the positive effects of new product usage. The more a consumption behavior can be sensed (seen, smelled, etc.), the more *visible* it is said to be. Thus, driving an automobile with a new type of engine is less visible than driving an automobile with a unique body design; wearing a new perfume fragrance is less visible than adopting an *avant-garde* hairstyle. In general, innovations that are high in visibility lend themselves to rapid adoption if they also possess relative advantages, are compatible with consumption lifestyles, and so on.

Consider the situation confronted by a maker of tea bags in the United Kingdom. Tetley was the number two brand of tea in the United Kingdom with little prospect of increasing that position. The company researched ways to physically differentiate its brand but with little success until it developed the idea of a *round* tea bag. Marketing research revealed that consumers perceive the round bag (versus the traditional square bag) to make a better cup of tea. Armed with these results, Tetley introduced round bags in England and quickly earned sales increases of 40 percent and the number one market position. Success with the round tea bag also has been achieved in Canada and the United States. In test marketing in the northeastern United States, Tetley's market share jumped from 15 percent to over 20 percent. Tetley's round tea bags can attribute much of their success to their visible, easily observed, and communicable "advantage."[9]

In general, products whose benefits lack observability are generally slower in adoptability.[10] The steel-framed house, for example, is not visible to all except the owners and immediate neighbors after the house has been completed. This advantage, in other words, may be real but unobserved.

The important role of product observability is further illustrated by Nike's use of Air Pockets in its athletic shoes marketed in the late 1980s. These highly visible inserts in the heel section of Nike shoes clearly conveyed the product benefit of comfort by showing that running and jumping in Nike shoes is like landing on a protective mattress. Nike could have designed its shoes so that the air pocket was concealed from observation; instead, they decided to make the feature conspicuous and in so doing provided themselves with the easily communicable point that Nike shoes are more comfortable than competitive brands. Reebok's Pump shoe marketed in the early 1990s further illustrates product-benefit visibility. In the athletic shoe industry, this is called *exposing the technology*. By any name, this practice simply recognizes the basic fact that consumers are more likely to adopt a new product when its advantages are observable.

Because status from brand ownership is one form of consumption advantage, albeit an advantage high in symbolism rather than functionality, it perhaps is not surprising that many well-known brands of fashion wear (e.g., Tommy Hilfiger, Polo by Ralph Lauren) plaster the outside of clothing with prominent brand names observable to the world. Consumers have become walking billboards for designer brands, a case of observability incarnate.

Breathe Right was a product introduced in the mid-1990s to allow easier breathing during exercise or while sleeping. Sales were slow when first introduced, so the company sent a case of Breathe Right to all National Football League team trainers. While wearing the highly visible Breathe Right, running back Herschel Walker scored two touchdowns during a game when his Philadelphia Eagles played the Washington Redskins. Almost immediately thereafter sales increased dramatically.[11] Another highly observable new product is the Swiffer, a new type of mop from Procter & Gamble (see *IMC Focus*). At the time of this writing the product is undergoing test marketing, so only time will tell whether it ultimately achieves global success.

THE DIFFUSION PROCESS

In comparison to the adoption process, which focuses on the individual consumer (a micro viewpoint), the **diffusion process** is concerned with the broader issue of how an innovation is communicated and adopted *throughout the marketplace* (a macro viewpoint). In simple terms, diffusion is the process of spreading out. In a marketing communications sense, this means that as time passes a new product is adopted by more and more customers. By analogy, consider what happens when gas is released into a small room: The fumes eventually spread throughout the entire room. Similarly, product innovations spread ideally to all parts of a potential market. The word *ideally* is used because, unlike the physical analogy, the communication of an innovation in the marketplace often is impeded by factors such as unsuitable communication channels, competitive maneuverings, and other imperfect conditions.

PART 3   New Products, Brand Names, Logos, Packages, and Point-of-Purchase Materials

IMC Focus: The Globalization of the Swiffer

When companies develop new products, they typically test them in a couple of test markets prior to full-scale commercialization. Provided the testing yields positive results, these products are introduced to the entire domestic market or are rolled out on a market-by-market basis. Where appropriate, successful new products are later introduced in other countries in which the firm has a marketing presence.

P&G, which has been on a new product introduction binge of late, introduced a disposable mop into test marketing in 1998. The light-weight mop consists of a ready-to-assemble handle and disposable cleaning cloths that use static electricity to pick up dust, hair, and other dirt. Convenience and ease of use are prominent relative advantages. Another reason why this product has a good chance of succeeding is due to observability of product performance. The user of this product will be able to readily observe the product picking up hair and other dirt; comparatively, it is difficult with traditional mops to observe whether they have actually accomplished anything beyond merely pushing dirt and dust from one spot to another.

The marketing folks at Procter & Gamble "broke the mold" when test marketing this product. Unlike the typical approach of test marketing products only in the United States, P&G simultane-

ously tested its new mop in two American cities (Cedar Rapids, Iowa, and Pittsfield, Massachusetts) and in Sens, France. With the brand name "Swiffer" used in France as well as the United States, this is the first P&G brand that was global from the outset. P&G officials say the brand name is meant to convey speed and ease of use and to be used as both a noun and a verb, as in "I'm going to 'Swiffer' the hardwood floors." (See Figure 7.7.)

The Swiffer

Source: Adapted from Jack Neff, "P&G Marks First with U.S., Euro Test of Swiffer," *Advertising Age*, August 24, 1998, 32.

This section deals with the *aggregate behavior* of groups of customers who adopt products at different points in time following a product's introduction. Examined are the characteristics that typify each group.[12] It should be noted that the classification scheme discussed hereafter is insightful but also somewhat simplified, which typically is the case when complex human behavior is categorized into a small set of categories.[13]

Adopter Categories

As a product spreads through the marketplace over time, it is adopted by different types of consumers. Five general groups have been identified: (1) innovators, (2) early adopters, (3) early majority, (4) late majority, and (5) laggards. As a matter of convention, these five categories are presumed to follow a normal (bell-shaped) statistical distribution with respect to each group's average (mean) time of adoption following the introduction of an innovation (see Figure 7.8). That is, in accordance with the properties of a normal distribution, 68 percent of all people who ultimately adopt an innovation fall within plus (late majority) or minus (early majority) one standard deviation of the mean time of adoption. The other adopter categories are interpreted in a similar manner. Although the categorization is arbitrary, it has been useful in the study of the diffusion process.

Innovators.   The small group of **innovators,** constituting only 2–3 percent of all adopters, are the first people to accept a new idea or product. Innovators are extremely *venturesome* and are more willing to take risks—a requirement of innovation. That is, the first people to adopt a new product, especially if it is expensive, incur the risk that the product

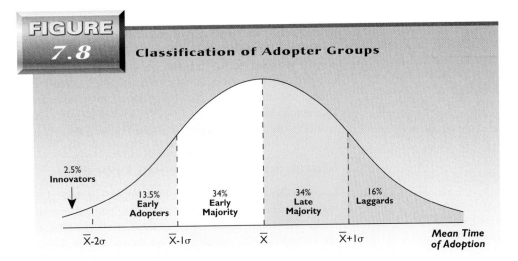

FIGURE 7.8

Classification of Adopter Groups

2.5%
Innovators

13.5%
Early Adopters

34%
Early Majority

34%
Late Majority

16%
Laggards

$\overline{X}-2\sigma$ $\overline{X}-1\sigma$ $\overline{X}$ $\overline{X}+1\sigma$ *Mean Time of Adoption*

will not work as well as expected, that money will be lost, and possibly that they will be embarrassed by a bad decision. Consider, for example, the risk of being among the very first people in a community to own an electric-powered automobile. Not many people are willing to be the first to invest $30,000 or more in a product that may turn out to have little resale value.

Another characteristic of innovators is that they are willing to seek social relationships outside of their local peer group—that is, they are *cosmopolites.* Innovators also tend to be younger, higher in social status, and better educated than later adopter groups. Innovators interact mostly with other innovators and rely heavily on *impersonal* informational sources (e.g., media reports, on-line searches, salespeople) rather than other people, to satisfy their information needs. Innovators generally have been found to display a broader range of interests than noninnovators.[14]

Early Adopters.   **Early adopters** are the second group to adopt an innovation. The size of this group is defined statistically as 13.5 percent of all potential adopters.[15] Early adopters are *localites,* in contrast to innovators, who were described as cosmopolites. The early adopter is well integrated within his or her community and is respected by his or her friends.[16] Because of this respect, the early adopter is often sought for advice and information about new products and services. The respect he or she commands among peers makes the early adopter a very important determinant of the success or failure of an innovation. *Opinion leaders* come primarily from the early adopter group. Their characteristics and role in the diffusion process are discussed later in the chapter.

Early Majority.   Approximately one-third of all potential adopters of an innovation fall into the early majority group. As shown in Figure 7.8, the **early majority** adopt the product prior to the mean time of adoption. Members of this group are deliberate and cautious in their adoption of innovations.[17] They spend more time in the innovation decision process than the two earlier groups. Though the group displays some opinion leadership, it is well below that shown by early adopters. This group is slightly above average in education and social status but below the levels of the early adopter group.

Late Majority.   As shown in Figure 7.8, the **late majority** consists of 34 percent of potential adopters just following the average adoption time. The key word that characterizes the late majority is *skepticism.*[18] By the time they adopt an innovation, the majority of the market has already done so. Peers are the primary source of new ideas for consumers in the late majority, who make little use of mass media. Demographically, they are below average in education, income, and social status.

Laggards. The final group to adopt an innovation is referred to as **laggards;** they represent the bottom 16 percent of potential adopters. These people are bound in tradition.[19] As a group, laggards focus on the past as their frame of reference. Their collective attitude may be summarized as, "If it was good enough for my parents, it's good enough for me." Laggards are tied closely to other laggards and to their local community and have limited contact with the mass media. This group, as might be expected, has the lowest social status and income of all adopter groups. If and when laggards adopt an innovation, it usually occurs after one or more innovations have replaced the earlier innovation.

Managing the Diffusion Process

Consider the following product innovation. The animal-health unit of Switzerland's Novartis introduced an antidepressant drug to the U.S. marketplace in early 1999. You might think, "What's so innovative about that?" Well, the drug, called Clomicalm, was marketed not for individuals' personal use but for their dogs. There apparently are about 7 million dogs in the United States that suffer from a syndrome called "separation anxiety," manifestations of which are destroying furniture, howling, or inappropriate elimination when their owners are away from home. Clomicalm is a meat-flavored pill priced at $1 per day for the minimum treatment length of two to three months.[20] What did Novartis, the maker of this doggie antidepressant pill, do to facilitate successful product diffusion? Read on.

Firms such as Novartis hope to manage the diffusion process so that a new product or service such as Clomicalm accomplishes the following objectives:[21]

1. Secure initial sales as quickly as possible (*a rapid takeoff*).
2. Achieve cumulative sales in a steep curve (*rapid acceleration*).
3. Secure the highest possible sales potential in the targeted market segment (*maximum penetration*).
4. Maintain sales for as long as possible (*a long-run franchise*).

Figure 7.9 displays the *desired* diffusion pattern that satisfies the preceding conditions and compares it with the *typical* diffusion pattern. The typical pattern involves a relatively slow takeoff, a slow rate of sales growth, maximum penetration below the full market potential, and a sales decline sooner than what would be desired.

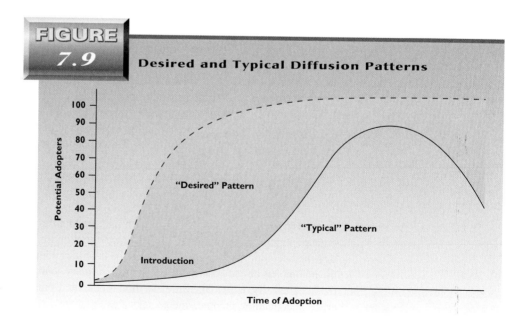

FIGURE 7.9

Desired and Typical Diffusion Patterns

What can marketing communications do to make the typical pattern more like the desired pattern? First, *rapid takeoff* can be facilitated by having a marketing communications budget that is sufficiently large to permit: (1) aggressive sales force efforts that are needed to secure trade support for new products, (2) intensive advertising to create high product-awareness levels among the target market, and (3) sufficient sales promotion activity to generate desired levels of trial-purchase behavior. Novartis embarked on a major marketing campaign to persuade pet owners to take their anxious dogs to see a veterinarian. Millions of dollars were invested in radio and magazine advertising, including ad placements in *Parade*, *Reader's Digest*, and *People*. Advertisements portrayed a sad-looking dog with an emotional appeal in the headline reading "Some dogs just hate to be alone" (see Figure 7.10). In addition to the consumer-oriented advertising, a major promotional campaign was aimed at training vets and encouraging them to prescribe Clomicalm to the owners of separation-anxious dogs. All in all, this was an earnest effort to secure a rapid takeoff.

Second, *rapid acceleration* may be accomplished by: (1) ensuring that product quality is suitable and will promote positive word-of-mouth communication, (2) continuing to advertise heavily to reach later adopter groups, (3) ensuring that the sales force provides reseller support, and (4) using sales promotion creatively so that incentives are provided for repeat-purchase behavior. Following the introduction of Clomicalm, Novartis continued supporting its resellers' (i.e., vets) selling efforts and offered attractive promotional deals to consumers to accelerate the adoption rate.

Advertisement of Clomicalm

Third, *maximum penetration* can be approached by: (1) continuing the same strategies that stimulated rapid acceleration and, where appropriate, (2) revising the product and advertising strategies as necessary to appeal to the needs of later adopters.

Finally, a *long-run franchise* can be maintained by ensuring that: (1) the old product continues to meet the market's needs, (2) distribution is suitable to reach the market, and (3) advertising continues to remind the market about the product. Only time will tell whether Clomicalm achieves a long-run franchise. Its success will assuredly encourage the introduction of new brands from competitors and necessitate continued advertising and promotional effort to offset competitive efforts and position Clomicalm as the best brand for treating Fido's separation anxiety.

STIMULATING WORD-OF-MOUTH INFLUENCE

People in all buying capacities—consumers buying automobiles, industrial purchasing agents buying new equipment, physicians ordering drug products, hospitals ordering supplies, athletic teams purchasing equipment, and so on—rely on two major sources of information to assist them in making decisions: impersonal and personal sources. *Impersonal sources* include information received from television, magazines, the Internet, and other mass-media sources. *Personal sources,* the subject of this section, include word-of-mouth influence from friends, acquaintances, and from business associates in the case of organizational buying decisions.[22] Research has shown that the more favorable information a potential product adopter has received from peers, the more likely that individual is to adopt the new product or service.[23]

Opinion Leaders

An **opinion leader** is a person who frequently influences other individuals' attitudes or overt behavior.[24] Opinion leaders perform several important functions: They inform other people (followers) about new products, they provide advice and reduce the follower's perceived risk in purchasing a new product, and they offer positive feedback to support or confirm decisions that followers have already made. Thus, an opinion leader is an informer, persuader, and confirmer. Consider the phenomenon of movie critiques and the role of the critic. These individuals preview movies before the general public and write reviews, which then are aired on TV or printed in newspapers. The critics' comments serve to influence moviegoers' choice of movies and possibly confirm their own opinions about the movies they have seen.[25]

Opinion leadership influence is typically restricted to one or several consumption topics rather than applying universally across many consumption domains. That is, a person who is an opinion leader with respect to issues and products in one consumption area—such as, movies, computers, skiing, or cooking—is not generally influential in other unrelated areas. It would be very unlikely, for example, for one person to be respected for his or her knowledge and opinions concerning all four of the listed consumption topics. Moreover, opinion leaders are found in every social class. In most instances, opinion leadership influence moves *horizontally* through a social class instead of vertically from one class to another.

Opinion leader profiles are distinctly different from others. In general, opinion leaders: (1) are more *cosmopolitan* and have greater contact with the mass media than do followers; (2) are usually more *gregarious* than the general population and have more social contacts—and thus more opportunity for discussing and conveying information—than followers; (3) tend to have slightly *higher socioeconomic status* than followers; (4) are generally more *innovative* than followers; and (5) are willing to act differently than other people, to withstand criticism and rejection, and, in general, have a *need to be unique.*[26]

What motivates opinion leaders to give information? It seems that opinion leaders are willing to participate in word-of-mouth (WOM) communications with others because they derive satisfaction from sharing their opinions with others and explaining what they know about new products and services. In order to do so, opinion leaders continually strive (and often feel obligated) to keep themselves informed.

GLOBAL FOCUS: JAPANESE TEENAGE GIRLS AND *KUCHIKOMI*

Kuchikomi is a word that refers to the swift network of word-of-mouth advertising that connects teenage girls in Japan. Never was *kuchikomi* more apparent than in the success of the Tamagotchi craze that hit Japan in 1996 and then spread globally. Because there is little space in Japan for people to own pets, the Tamagotchi toy provided a substitute outlet for the desire to own an animal. Meaning "cute little egg," Tamagotchi is a plastic toy with an embedded electronic chip that emits chirps of affection based on the owner's behavior. After an extraterrestrial creature hatches from the toy "egg," the owner presses select buttons on a tiny screen to feed, clean, and care for the virtual pet. Proper care is rewarded with affectionate chirps.

Bandai Co. Ltd., the innovator of this product, estimated initial sales of about 300,000 Tamagotchies at $16 each. However, without any advertising and relying primarily on the word of mouth generated by teenage girls and other owners, sales volume reached 23 million units sold in Japan in slightly over one year. Since then Bandai has exported the Tamagotchi to over 25 other countries.

The Tamagotchi is just one example of the *kuchikomi* power of Japan's teenage girls. Many Japanese consumer product companies do not just wait for Japanese girls to engage in word-of-mouth behavior, but solicit their opinions when in process of developing new products. "Girl guides," as they are called, are recruited by Japanese companies to test proposed new products and provide feedback on preliminary television commercials. They also are paid to "cheerlead" new products. For example, Dentsu Eye Inc., a marketing consultancy, paid schoolgirls a total of $78,000 to talk up a previously unknown product at their schools. Brand awareness quickly grew to 10 percent of high-school students. Dentsu Eye's executives estimated that using television advertising to achieve a comparable level of brand awareness would have cost at least $1.5 million.

Sources: Adapted from Aki Maita, "Tamagotchi," *Ad Age International*, December 1997, 10; Norihiko Shirouzu, "Japan's High-School Girls Excel in the Art of Setting Trends," *The Wall Street Journal Interactive Edition*, April 24, 1998.

Prestige is at the heart of WOM. "We like being the bearers of news. Being able to recommend gives us a feeling of prestige. It makes us instant experts."[27] Being an expert in marketplace matters does bring prestige. Researchers have referred to the marketplace expert as a *maven*.[28] **Market mavens** are "individuals who have information about many kinds of products, places to shop, and other facets of markets, and initiate discussions with consumers and respond to requests from consumers for market information."[29] In other words, the market maven is looked upon as an important source of information and receives prestige and satisfaction from supplying information to friends and others.

The key to generating good WOM is by finding *cheerleaders*—that is, consumers who will "get the talk started."[30] Usually this is a carefully selected target group that is most likely to love a new movie, a new book, or other product or service. (The *Global Focus* insert describes the cheerleading role of Japan's teenage girls.) In the book industry, cheerleading is stimulated by giving free copies of a new book to a select group of opinion leaders. Microsoft accomplished the same thing by providing preproduction versions of *Windows 95* to about 1 million influential computer insiders, analysts, and journalists.[31] Converse successfully introduced its All Star 2000 basketball shoe by going into 10 markets prior to the brand's launch and supplying advance pairs to local hero basketball players, a practice suitably referred to as "seeding" the market.[32]

Positive word-of-mouth communication is a critical element in the success of a new product or service. Unfavorable WOM, on the other hand, can have devastating effects on adoption, because consumers seem to place more weight on negative information in making evaluations than on positive information.[33]

Marketing communicators can do several things to minimize negative word of mouth.[34] At the minimum, companies need to show customers that they are responsive to legitimate complaints. Manufacturers can do this by providing detailed warranty and complaint-procedure information on labels or in package inserts. Retailers can demonstrate their responsiveness to customer complaints through employees with positive attitudes, store signs, and inserts in monthly billings to customers. Companies also can offer toll-free numbers and e-mail addresses to provide customers with an easy way to voice their complaints and provide suggestions. By being responsive to customer complaints, companies can avert negative—and perhaps even create positive—WOM.[35]

Summary

The continual introduction of new products and services is critical to the success of most business organizations. The concepts of adoption and diffusion explain the processes by which new products and services are accepted by more and more customers as time passes. Marketing communications can facilitate the process by communicating a new product's relative advantages, showing how it is compatible with consumers' existing purchase preferences and values, reducing real or perceived complexity, enhancing the product's communicability, and making it easy to try.

The diffusion process is concerned with the broader issue of how an innovation is communicated and adopted throughout the marketplace. Diffusion, in simple terms, is the process of spreading out. Diffusion scholars have identified five relatively distinct groups of adopters. These groups, moving from the first to adopt an innovation to the last, are innovators, early adopters, early majority, late majority, and laggards. Research has shown that these groups differ considerably in terms of such variables as socioeconomic status, risk-taking tendencies, and peer relations.

Opinion leadership and word-of-mouth influence are important elements in facilitating more rapid product adoption and diffusion. Opinion leaders are individuals who are respected for their product knowledge and opinions. Opinion leaders inform other people (followers) about new products and services, provide advice and reduce the follower's perceived risk in purchasing a new product, and confirm decisions that followers have already made. In comparison to followers, opinion leaders are more cosmopolitan, more gregarious, have higher socioeconomic status, and are more innovative. Positive word-of-mouth influence is often critical to new-product success. It appears that people talk about new products and services because they gain a feeling of prestige from being the bearer of news. Marketing communicators can take advantage of this prestige factor by stimulating cheerleaders, who will talk favorably about a new product or service.

Discussion Questions

1. A product for dogs, branded as PureBreath, was introduced in capsule form for purposes of controlling canine halitosis. Priced at around $7 for a month's supply, PureBreath is available in food, drug, and mass merchandise outlets. Using PureBreath for illustration, explain the process by which marketing variables can influence consumers to become part of the awareness, trier, and repeater classes for this brand (refer to Figure 7.2).

2. Based on what you now know about factors that facilitate the adoption process (relative advantages, compatibility, etc.), what is the likelihood that PureBreath will receive widespread consumer acceptance?

3. What determines whether a new product or service has relative advantages over competitive offerings? Identify the relative advantages of each of the following: disposable cameras, disposable contact lenses, fat-free pastries, and electrically powered automobiles. Given that each of the above products also has relative disadvantages compared to its predecessor product, present a general statement (a statement with universal applicability) that would explain why consumers are willing to adopt new products even though they almost invariably have relative disadvantages.

4. What is meant when we say that a potential adopter of a product or service "vicariously tries" the product before adopting it? What can marketing communicators do to promote vicarious trial?

5. Pick a new product or service of your choice, and describe in detail how that product or service satisfies, or fails to satisfy, the following success requirements: relative advantages, compatibility, communicability, trialability, and observability.

6. Suppose you are the manager of a new restaurant located in your college or university community that caters primarily to the campus population. Your fledgling restaurant cannot yet

afford media advertising, so the promotional burden rests upon stimulating positive word-of-mouth communications. Present a specific strategy for how you might go about stimulating positive WOM.

7.   The researchers who conceived the concept of the market maven devised a scale to measure consumers' responses to the following six items:
1.   I like introducing new brands and products to my friends.
2.   I like helping people in providing them with information about many kinds of products.
3.   People ask me for information about products, places to shop, or sales.
4.   If someone asked where to get the best buy on several types of products, I could tell him or her where to shop.
5.   My friends think of me as a good source of information when it comes to new products or sales.
6.   Think about a person who has information about a variety of products and likes to share this information with others. This person knows about new products, sales, stores, and so on, but does not necessarily feel he or she is an expert on one particular product. This description fits me well.

Respondents are asked to rate each item on a seven-point scale, from strongly disagree (= 1) to strongly agree (= 7); thus, total scores range from a low of 6 (strongly disagrees to all items) to 42 (strongly agrees to all items). Administer the scale to two friends whom you regard as market mavens and to two friends who are not market mavens. See if the mavens receive predictably higher scores than the nonmavens. Also, comment on whether you think these six items do a good job of measuring market mavenness. What additions or deletions, if any, would you make?

8.   With reference to the All Star 2000 example that described how Converse's marketing team "seeded" 10 markets with free shoes to local basketball heroes, explain how you would go about seeding a product of your choice in a single market of your choice.

1 nternet Exercises

1.   Innovative brand managers are beginning to explore the potential of the Internet to provide consumers with virtual "test drives" and virtual "free samples." For example, Clairol (www.clairol.com) provides consumers with the opportunity to use a digital photo of themselves to try out new hairdos and new colors right online (Clairol also provides head-shots of models to choose from if you do not have a photo handy.) Revlon (www.revlon.com) provides a similar service with its line of cosmetics. Hewlett-Packard (www.hp.com) offers online demonstrations that simulate an in-store experience for its extensive line of consumer and scientific electronic products.

   a.   Locate another brand that provides an online trial experience for consumers. Describe the brand and the brand experience. If you cannot find such an example, describe how a favorite brand of yours might create a virtual brand experience.

   b.   Which of the five innovation-related characteristics (i.e., relative advantages, compatibility, complexity, trialability, and observability) are most likely influenced by the virtual brand experience described in part (a)? Explain your answer in detail.

   c.   Can you think of any pitfalls in giving consumers convenient and riskless methods of product experience such as online virtual experiences?

2.   Internet access is itself a branded service. Though the Internet is growing rapidly (especially in the U.S.), most people still do *not* have access. In fact, in many countries relatively few people have access to the Internet. Thus, Internet access providers are keenly interested in new product adoption processes. Use Figure 7.2 to explain the process by which marketing variables can influence consumers to become part of the awareness, trier, and repeater classes for Internet access.

Chapter Seven Endnotes

1. William Boulding, Ruskin Morgan, and Richard Staelin, "Pulling the Plug to Stop the New Product Drain," *Journal of Marketing Research* 34 (February 1997), 164.

2. The following discussion is adapted from Chakravarthi Narasimhan and Subrata K. Sen, "New Product Models for Test Market Data," *Journal of Marketing* 47 (winter 1983), 13, 14.

3. Everett M. Rogers, *Diffusion of Innovations,* 4th ed. (New York: The Free Press, 1995). For a fascinating application of these innovation determinates to the issue of smoking cessation, see William H. Redmond, "Product Disadoption: Quitting Smoking as a Diffusion Process," *Journal of Public Policy & Marketing* 15 (spring 1996), 87–97.

4. Eben Shapiro, "Minnesota Mining's Wool Pads Grab Sizable Chunk of Business," *The Wall Street Journal,* January 13, 1994, B6.

5. Gregory A. Patterson, "Waterbed Makers Target Younger, Groovier Snoozers," *The Wall Street Journal,* April 28, 1994, B1, 5.

6. Maureen Kline, "Italy's Parmalat Seeks to Fill U.S. Cups with New Long-Lasting Milk Product," *The Wall Street Journal,* March 11, 1994, B5.

7. Parmalat pursued a $5 million advertising campaign in 1997, but this amount is inadequate in view of the challenge confronting this new (for Americans) form of milk. See Gerry Khermouch, "Parmalat Piggy-backs on 'Got Milk?' " *Brandweek,* December 16, 1996, 4.

8. Elaine Underwood, "A New Way to Think about Grapefruit," *Adweek's Marketing Week,* January 28, 1991, 17.

9. Kevin Doyle, "Tetley," *Incentive,* April 1993, 24–25.

10. For further discussion of the role of visibility, see Robert J. Fisher and Linda L. Price, "An Investigation into the Social Context of Early Adoption Behavior," *Journal of Consumer Research* 19 (December 1992), 477–486.

11. Laurie Freeman, "Breathe Right," *Advertising Age,* June 26, 1995, S4.

12. For further discussion, see Hubert Gatignon and Thomas S. Robertson, "A Propositional Inventory for New Diffusion Research," *Journal of Consumer Research* 11 (March 1985), 849–867.

13. For further discussion of limitations with the traditional diffusion paradigm, see David Glen Mick and Susan Fournier, "Paradoxes of Technology: Consumer Cognizance, Emotions, and Coping Strategies," *Journal of Consumer Research* 25 (September 1998), 123–143, especially at 140.

14. Thomas S. Robertson and James N. Kennedy, "Prediction of Consumer Innovators: Application of Discriminant Analysis," *Journal of Marketing Research* 5 (February 1968), 64–69, citing *America's Tastemakers, Research Reports Nos. 1 and 2* (Princeton, N.J.: Opinion Research Corporation, 1959).

15. That is, the area under the normal curve between one and two standard deviations from the mean.

16. Rogers, *Diffusion of Innovations.*

17. Ibid.

18. Ibid.

19. Ibid.

20. Elyse Tanouye, "When It Looks Like a Dog's Life, Novartis May Help with a Canine Antidepressant," *The Wall Street Journal Interactive Edition,* January 5, 1999.

21. This section is adapted from Thomas S. Robertson, Joan Zielinski, and Scott Ward, *Consumer Behavior* (Glenview, Ill.: Scott, Foresman and Company, 1984), 380–382.

22. R. Bruce Money, Mary C. Gilly, and John L. Graham, "Explorations of National Culture and Word-of-Mouth Referral Behavior in the Purchase of Industrial Services in the United States and Japan," *Journal of Marketing* 62 (October 1998), 76–87.

23. Johan Arndt, "Role of Product-Related Conversation in the Diffusion of a New Product," *Journal of Marketing Research* 4 (August 1967), 291–295; Dorothy Leonard-Barton, "Experts as Negative Opinion Leaders in the Diffusion of a Technological Innovation," *Journal of Consumer Research* 11 (March 1985), 914–926.

24. Rogers, *Diffusion of Innovations.*

25. Jehoshua Eliashberg and Steven M. Shugan, "Film Critics: Influencers or Predictors?" *Journal of Marketing* 61 (April 1997), 68–78.

26. This fifth point is based on research that has detected a new dimension of opinion leadership termed *public individuation.* In a study of college students' wine-consumption attitudes and behavior, the researchers obtained support that opinion leaders in this category are more publicly individuated. See Kenny K. Chan and Shekhar Misra, "Characteristics of the Opinion Leader: A New Dimension," *Journal of Advertising* 19, no. 3 (1990), 53–60.

27. This quote is from the famous motivational researcher Ernest Dichter, in Eileen Prescott, "Word-of-Mouth: Playing on the Prestige Factor," *The Wall Street Journal,* February 7, 1984, 1.

28. A *maven* (or mavin) is considered an expert in everyday matters.

29. Lawrence F. Feick and Linda L. Price, "The Market Maven: A Diffuser of Marketplace Information," *Journal of Marketing* 51 (January 1987), 83–97.

30. Prescott, "Word-of-Mouth."

31. Bradley Johnson, "Microsoft Chase Starting Up Windows 95," *Advertising Age,* August 28, 1995, 4.

32. Steve Gelsi and Matthew Grimm, "Marketing by Seed," *Brandweek,* October 7, 1996, 20.

33. Paul M. Herr, Frank R. Kardes, and John Kim, "Effects of Word-of-Mouth and Product-Attribute Information on Persuasion: An Accessibility-Diagnosticity Perspective," *Journal of Consumer Research* 17 (March 1991), 454–462; Richard J. Lutz, "Changing Brand Attitudes through

Modification of Cognitive Structure," *Journal of Consumer Research* 1 (March 1975), 49–59; and Peter Wright, "The Harassed Decision Maker: Time Pressures, Distractions, and the Use of Evidence," *Journal of Applied Psychology* 59 (October 1974), 555–561.

34. Marsha L. Richins, "Negative Word-of-Mouth by Dissatisfied Consumers: A Pilot Study," *Journal of Marketing* 47 (winter 1983), 76.

35. Ibid.

Brand Names, Logos, Packages, and Point-of-Purchase Materials

CHAPTER OBJECTIVES

After studying this chapter, you should be able to:

1. Understand the role of brand naming and the requirements for developing effective brand names.
2. Explain five steps in the brand-naming process.
3. Appreciate the role of logos.
4. Describe the various elements underlying the creation of effective packages.
5. Explain the VIEW model for evaluating package effectiveness.
6. Describe a five-step package-design process.
7. Appreciate the role of point-of-purchase advertising.
8. Discuss the Consumer Buying Habits Study and its implications for point-of-purchase advertising.
9. Describe the role of displays in influencing brand sales.

Opening Vignette: Transforming Bell Labs into Lucent Technologies

Corporations in the United States are changing their names at an unparalleled rate. Over 1,000 U.S. corporations changed their names between 1989 and 1997. A name change offers a company an opportunity for a new start and a means to effectively reshape itself. Perhaps no name change in recent years has created more interest and commentary than that of Lucent Technologies, which was a spin-off from AT&T that had been known as Bell Labs. Bell Labs dates back to the days of creative genius, Alexander Graham Bell, whose invention of the telephone ultimately gave rise to the telecommunications giant known as AT&T. As the research arm of AT&T, Bell Labs has been the home of many scientists and inventors, including seven Nobel laureates. From the labs of these inventors have originated such products as the dial tone, voice mail, and laser technology. It is from this renowned company that Lucent Technologies came into being.

A San Francisco company called Landor Associates designed a new corporate name. The objective given Landor Associates was to develop a name that would distance the new company from AT&T while at the same time capitalize on the equity accumulated over the years in the Bell Labs tradition. One name considered but rejected was AGB Technologies, with the AGB representing the initials of the famous inventor of the telephone. Landor also considered name variations including "net" and "systems," but quickly determined that these were overused corporate names with over 12,000 companies with the root word "net" and also more than 12,000 with "system" in their names.

FIGURE
8.1

Landor generated in excess of 700 possible names and 50 logo candidates. The objective was to identify a name and logo that would portray an image of creativity and project the qualities of speed and energy. Ultimately Lucent Technologies was selected as the new corporate name. The dictionary meaning of lucent is "shining" or "clear." However, a Lucent spokesman said that Lucent was chosen in part because of its "empty-vessel" quality. The empty-vessel expression implies that the name does not have much meaning associated with it and that subsequent marketing communications would thus be able to create the exact meaning desired without contending with past associations already accumulated in people's memories.

In addition to the name, the now-famous hand-drawn red circle was selected to represent Lucent Technologies (see Figure 8.1). Landor's creative director supported this selection by saying that the circle is a good symbol for knowledge, which is made more humanistic by being hand-drawn. The inflamed circle has been the butt of many jokes, with media critics ridiculing it with expressions such as "the million-dollar coffee stain," "a big red zero," and "a flaming goose egg." Derision aside, executives at Lucent Technologies fully supported the name and logo with an introductory communications campaign estimated at $100 million. In terms of enhancing brand awareness and image, a Lucent spokesperson commented that the company accomplished in one year what many competitors have taken 50 or more years to achieve.

Sources: Adapted from Maricris G. Briones, "When a Rose Is No Longer a Rose," *Marketing News*, April 13, 1998, 1–2; Noreen O'Leary, "Who Loves 'Lucent'?" *Brandweek*, April 7, 1997, 42–43.

INTRODUCTION

*T*his chapter provides a critical linkage between the previous seven chapters and the 12 chapters that follow. To this point in the text, we have discussed integrated marketing communications, developed the importance of brand-equity enhancement, examined the fundamentals of communicating with consumers and the role of persuasion, and described efforts undertaken by marketing communicators to facilitate the adoption of new brands. Subsequent chapters will focus on advertising, promotions, marketing-oriented public relations, sponsorship and event marketing, and personal selling. Brand names, logos, and packages are critical to all of these efforts, and the point-of-purchase is the point where all of the components of an integrated marketing communications program ultimately come together.

The marketing communicator's intermediate goal is enhancing brand equity with the ultimate goal of channeling consumer behavior toward the marketer's brand. That is, our goal, as established in Chapter 1, is to influence customers' behavior. We want people to buy our brand rather than competitors' brands. We want them to purchase sooner rather than later, more rather than less, frequently rather than intermittently, and so on. Having a good brand name, a good logo, an appealing package, and an eye-catching point-of-purchase display enables the brand marketer to achieve the ultimate goal of influencing consumer behavior. We now turn our attention to each of these topics.

BRAND NAMING

A brand is a company's unique designation, or trademark, which distinguishes its offering from other product category entries.[1] Many marketing executives regard brand naming to be one of the most important aspects of marketing management.[2] Product and brand managers consider it critical to choose an appropriate brand name, largely because that choice can influence early trial of a brand and affect sales volume.[3] The brand name identifies a company's offering and differentiates it from others on the market. The brand name and package graphics work together to communicate and position the brand's image. In short, a brand's name is crucially important—indeed, a name "is the cerebral switch that activates an image in the mind of the audience."[4]

A good brand name can evoke a feeling of trust, confidence, security, strength, durability, speed, status, and many other desirable associations. The name chosen for a brand: (1) affects the speed with which consumers become aware of the brand, (2) influences the brand's image, and (3) thus plays a major role in brand-equity formation.[5] Achieving consumer awareness of a brand name is the critical initial aspect of brand-equity enhancement. Brand name awareness has been characterized as the "gateway" to consumers' more complicated learning and retention of associations that constitute a brand's image.[6]

Through brand names, a company can create excitement, elegance, exclusiveness, and influence consumers' perceptions and attitudes.[7] For example, 99 percent of the customers of Polo brand clothing have never seen nor will ever play a match of polo, yet Ralph Lauren through the wise choice of the Polo name was able to endow this brand with a high-status cachet.[8] The name Lucent Technologies (*Opening Vignette*) provides this company with a memorable name unlike most any other name in the telecommunications industry.

www.bmw.com

www.mazda.com

Creating a strong brand name is invaluable for several reasons: First, a strong brand generates consistent sales volume and revenue year after year. Names like McDonald's, Coca-Cola, Sony, BMW, and Levi's are known, respected, and insisted upon around the world. (See the *Global Focus* for lists of outstanding global brands.) Second, a strong brand commands a higher price and larger gross margin. Perhaps the best demonstration of the price-premium value of a strong brand is in the area of so-called "twin automobiles." These are automobiles that are made in the same factory and that are virtually identical in terms of product features but that carry different brand names. Examples include the following "twins": Dodge Colt/Mitsubishi Mirage, Chevrolet Nova/Toyota Corolla, Ford Tempo/Mercury Topaz, Dodge Omni/Plymouth Horizon, and the Mercury Tracer/Mazda 323. Research has shown that consumers do not perceive the twins as identical and that they are willing to pay higher prices for the twins on the right side of the slash marks vis-à-vis those on the left. This is because the twins on the right are perceived as brands from parent companies that have better reputations than those on the left.[9]

Third, a solid brand provides a platform for introducing new brands. Indeed, the dominant brand strategy in recent years has been to extend well-known brands into other product categories (so-called *brand extensions*).[10] In the first five months of one recent year, only 5 percent of the over 6,000 new products introduced to U.S. stores bore new brand names.[11] Fourth, a strong brand provides the manufacturer with leverage when dealing with distributors and retailers. Finally, without a strong brand, the marketer is forced to compete on the basis of price, thus requiring a low-cost product.[12]

What Constitutes a Good Brand Name?

What determines whether a brand name is a good name? This is a complex question that precludes a straightforward answer. Researchers, however, have investigated the determinants of good brand names. Although the accumulated knowledge is nowhere close to the point of specifying scientific principles, there is some consensus regarding the fundamental requirements that guide brand name selection. A good brand name should accomplish the following tasks: (1) distinguish the brand from competitive offerings, (2) describe the brand and its attributes/benefits, (3) achieve compatibility with a brand's desired image and with its product design or packaging, and (4) be memorable and easy to pronounce and spell.[13]

GLOBAL FOCUS: GLOBAL BRANDS HIGH IN STATURE AND VITALITY

A major advertising agency, Young & Rubicam (Y&R), explored consumers' perceptions of hundreds of brand names by conducting interviews with 23,300 consumers in 16 countries: Australia, Brazil, China, France, Germany, Hungary, Italy, Japan, Mexico, the Netherlands, Poland, Russia, South Africa, Thailand, the United Kingdom, and the United States. Consumers rated each brand in terms of: (1) the esteem with which it is held, (2) its familiarity, (3) its personal relevance, and (4) its differentiation from other brands. Y&R combined the first two measures to form an index of brand stature—an indicator of a brand's current performance, and the third and fourth items into an index of brand vitality—an indicator of brand potential. Following are lists of the top 25 brands in terms of stature and vitality; note that Coca-Cola is the top brand in both categories.

STATURE	VITALITY
1. Coca-Cola	1. Coca-Cola
2. Kodak	2. Nike
3. Sony	3. Adidas
4. Mercedes-Benz	4. Sony
5. Pepsi-Cola	5. Ferrari
6. Nestlé	6. Reebok
7. Gillette	7. Disney
8. Colgate	8. Porsche
9. Adidas	9. Pepsi-Cola
10. Volkswagen	10. Mercedes-Benz
11. Nescafé	11. BMW
12. Ford	12. Kodak
13. Panasonic	13. Rolls-Royce
14. Phillips	14. Levi's
15. Levi's	15. Chanel
16. Honda	16. Nestlé
17. BMW	17. Pierre Cardin
18. Toyota	18. Nescafé
19. Rolls-Royce	19. Christian Dior
20. Fanta	20. Harley Davidson
21. Disney	21. Jaguar
22. Palmolive	22. McDonald's
23. Lux	23. Polaroid
24. Nivea	24. Volkswagen
25. McDonald's	25. Benetton

Source: "Upstart Brands Steal Spotlight from Perennials," *Advertising Age International*, September 19, 1994, 1-13, 1-14.

Distinguish the Brand from Competitive Offerings. It is desirable for a brand to have a unique identify, something that clearly differentiates it from competitive brands. Failure to distinguish a brand from competitive offerings creates consumer confusion and increases the chances that consumers will mistakenly select another brand. For example, Sears introduced its own distinctively named brand of jeans to compete against the well-known Levi's, Lee, and other brands. Marketers at Sears chose the evocative name Canyon River Blues to distinguish this brand from the category leaders as well as to evoke a positive, rustic brand image.

www.sears.com

Some marketers attempt to hitchhike on the success of better known brands by using names that are similar to the well-known brands. However, the Federal Trademark Dilution Act of 1995 protects owners of brand names and logos from other companies using the identical or similar names. (In legal terms, brand names and logos are referred to as "trademarks.") The objective of this legislation is to protect trademarks from losing their distinctiveness.[14] Stealing well-known brand names is widely practiced in some newly emerging market economies. Chinese marketers are particularly flagrant in using facsimiles of famous brand names on their own domestically manufactured products. For example, toothpaste is packaged under the Colgate-sounding name, Cologate; and a local brand of sunglasses are named Ran Bans, which is obviously similar to Bausch & Lomb's well-known Ray Ban brand.[15]

www.bausch.com

www.rayban.com

Describe the Brand and Its Attributes/Benefits. It is important to note in this regard that a brand name need not state a specific benefit but may rather simply suggest an abstract promise.[16] Post-It (note pads), I Can't Believe It's Not Butter (margarine), and Healthy Choice (low-fat foods) illustrate brand names that do outstanding jobs in describing their respective products. The name Wow! potato chips (described back in Chapter 1) does not reflect a specific benefit, but it certainly suggests that this brand has extraordinary taste.

www.healthychoice.com

Research has been conducted on the issue of brand name "suggestiveness." Suggestive brand names are those that imply particular attributes or benefits in context of a product category. For example, the name Healthy Choice for food products intimates that this brand is low in fat content and calories. The name Outback for Subaru's sports utility vehicle suggests a product that is durable and rugged—capable of taking on the challenge of the famous Australian outback. Research has demonstrated that suggestive brand names facilitate consumer recall of advertised benefit claims that are consistent in meaning with the brand name. On the other hand, these same suggestive names reduce the recallability of benefit claims after a brand has been repositioned to stand for something different than its original meaning.[17]

Brand names sometimes are created rather than selected from words found in a dictionary. Compaq (a computer brand) is a created name, as are many automobile brand names such as Acura, Altima, Geo, Lexus, Lumina, and Sentra. These names were created from morphemes, which are the semantic kernels of words. For example, Compaq, which combines two morphemes (com and paq), is an excellent name for suggesting the product's benefits of a computer and compactness. The automobile name Acura indicates precision in product design and engineering.

Achieve Compatibility with a Brand's Desired Image and with Its Product Design or Packaging. Again, Healthy Choice is an ideal name for a category of fat-free and low-fat food items that are targeted toward weight- and health-conscious consumers. The name clearly suggests that the consumer has an alternative and that Healthy Choice is the right choice. Another brand name that is perfectly compatible with the brand's desired image is Second Nature, which is the brand name for a line of recycled tablets and legal pads (see Figure 8.2). (Notice that the "o" in Second is formed from three chasing arrows that symbolize environmental consciousness, and that the words Second and Nature are colored in environmentally congruent green against a woodsy-brown background.) Second Nature is an excellent name that suggests that writing pads carrying this name are not made from virgin wood but rather are recycled—hence, the rebirth of nature, or Second Nature. The name also serves as a subtle injunction to the user that using recycled writing materials should be virtually an automatic decision, as implied by the vernacular expression "it's second nature."

www.kfc.com

Because marketplaces are dynamic and consumer preferences and desires change over time, some brand names lose their effectiveness and have to be changed to avoid negative images. A case in point is Kentucky Fried Chicken. This name was compatible with the product for well over two decades, but a name change was needed when health consciousness swept the nation. A change from Kentucky Fried Chicken to simply KFC was undertaken with hopes of preventing the negative implications associated with the word fried.

Be Memorable and Easy to Pronounce. Finally, a good brand name is one that is easy to remember and pronounce. To facilitate memory and pronunciation, many brand names are short, one-word names (e.g., Tide, Bold, Shout, Edge, Bounce, Cheer). Probably few words are as memorable as those learned in early childhood, and among the first

FIGURE 8.2

Second Nature: A Name Compatible with the Brand's Desired Image

words learned are animal names. This likely explains marketers' penchant for using animals as brand names; for example, automobile companies are using or have used names such as Mustang, Thunderbird, Bronco, Cougar, Lynx, Skyhawk, Skylark, Firebird, Jaguar, and Ram.

In addition to their memorability, animal names also conjure up vivid images. This is very important to the marketing communicator because, as discussed in Chapter 5, concrete and vivid images facilitate consumer information processing. Dove soap, for example, suggests softness, grace, gentleness, and purity. Ram (for Dodge trucks) intimates strength, durability, and toughness.

Some Exceptions to the "Rules." The foregoing discussion has identified four guidelines for brand naming. The observant student will note, however, that some successful brand names seem entirely at odds with the above "rules." Why is this the case? First, some brands become successful in spite of their names. (Analogously, some people achieve prominence even though their names may not be the ones they personally would have chosen or that a "namemeister" would have selected as more ideal.) The first brand in a new product category can achieve tremendous success regardless of its name if the brand offers customers distinct advantages over alternative solutions to their problems. Second, in all aspects of life there are exceptions to the rules, and this certainly is the case in brand naming. There simply are many ways to "skin a cat."

A third major exception to the above "rules" is that brand managers and their brand-name consultants sometimes intentionally select names that, at inception, are virtually meaningless. You may recall from Lucent Technologies discussion in the *Opening Vignette* that the name Lucent was selected because for many people this word has relatively little meaning or associations—the empty-vessel philosophy of brand naming. Slates is another brand name selected precisely for this purpose. Slates, by the way, is the brand name for a line of dress pants marketed by Levi Strauss & Co. The name, Slates, was selected to be purposefully vague, perhaps only hinting at slate rock and its thin, durable strength. Levi Strauss hired a California company called Lexicon to assist in selecting a name for dress slacks. This naming consultant said that its key criterion in ultimately recommending this name was that it was "an empty vessel into which its marketers could pour their meaning."[18] In other words, rather than selecting a name already rich in meaning and filled with associations, there are advantages in using a relatively neutral name that a marketing communications campaign can endow with intended meaning.

The Brand Naming Process

Brand naming involves a rather straightforward process as determined by a survey of over 100 product and brand managers who represent both consumer- and industrial-goods products. Figure 8.3 lists these steps, and the following discussion describes each.

Step 1: Specify Objectives for the Brand Name. As with all managerial decisions, the initial step is to identify the objectives to be accomplished. Most managers are concerned with selecting a name that will successfully position the brand in the minds of

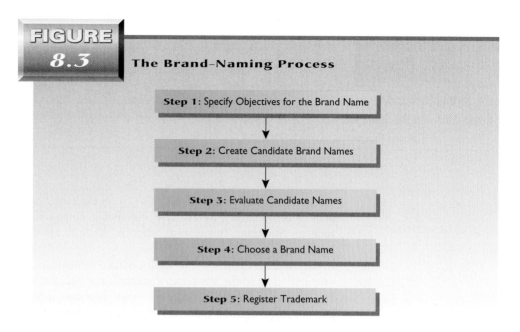

the target audience, provide an appropriate image for the brand, and distinguish it from competitive brands.[19]

Step 2: Create Candidate Brand Names. Brand name candidates often are selected using creative-thinking exercises and brainstorming sessions. Also, with the choice of the Lucent and Slates names, companies frequently use the services of naming consultants to generate candidate names. The survey of product and brand managers noted above determined that on average 46 candidate names were created for each brand-naming assignment.[20]

Step 3: Evaluate Candidate Names. The many names generated are evaluated using criteria such as relevance to the product category, favorability of images suggested by the name, and overall appeal. Product and brand managers consider it key that names be easy to recognize and recall.[21]

Step 4: Choose a Brand Name. The criteria noted in steps 1 and 3 are used by managers to select a final name from the candidate field. In many firms this choice is a matter of subjective judgment rather than the product of rigorous marketing research.[22]

Step 5: Register Trademark. Most companies apply for trademark registration. Some companies submit only a single name for registration, whereas others submit multiple names (on average, five names). One survey found that three names are rejected for every registered name.[23] A naming consultant indicated that the number of rejections is even higher, noting that about 75 percent of the names his firm generates are already taken upon searching federal registrations.[24]

The Role of Logos

Related to the brand name is a graphic design element called a brand logo. To identify their brands, companies use logos with or without brand names.[25] Not all brand names possess a distinct logo, but many do. For example, the Nike swoosh is virtually as famous as the company name. Consumers learn these logos and easily recognize the brands on which the

FIGURE
8.4

Sailor Jack, the Famous
Cracker Jack

logos are emblazoned. (As test of this, take a moment and visualize the logos for each of the following well-known brands: Pepsi, Ralph Lauren's Polo, Tommy Hilfiger clothing, Starbucks coffee, Mercedes-Benz automobiles, Toyota automobiles, Arm & Hammer baking soda, and Cracker Jack popcorn treat.)

Logo designs are incredibly diverse, ranging from highly abstract designs to those that depict nature scenes and from very simple to complex depictions. Generally speaking, good logos are those that are: (1) recognized readily, (2) convey essentially the same meaning to all target members, and (3) evoke positive feelings.[26] The logo for Cracker Jack, the sweetened popcorn snack item, perhaps typifies a readily recognized and feel-good design. What American kid can forget the Sailor Jack logo that has appeared on the Cracker Jack package during most of the 20th century? (Figure 8.4 shows the periodic updates in the Sailor Jack design since its inception in 1910.[27])

Although logos undoubtedly perform a valuable communications role and influence brand equity both via their effect on brand awareness and image, published research on logos is surprisingly absent. However, a major recent study determined that the best strategy for enhancing the likeability of a logo is to choose a design that is moderately elaborate rather than one that is too simple or too complex. Also, natural designs (as opposed to abstract illustrations) were found to produce more favorable consumer responses.[28]

P ACKAGING

Growing numbers of marketing communicators appreciate the crucial role performed by brand packaging. The increasingly important communications role of packaging has given rise to expressions such as "Packaging is the least expensive form of advertising"; "Every package is a five-second commercial"; and "The package is the product."[29] The "advertising" role of packaging is critical inasmuch as research reveals that shoppers spend an incredibly short amount of time—on the order of 10 to 12 seconds—viewing brands prior to moving on or selecting an item and placing it in the shopping cart.[30]

The growth of supermarkets and other self-service retail outlets has necessitated that the package perform marketing functions beyond the traditional role of merely containing and protecting the product. The package also serves to: (1) draw attention to a brand, (2) break through competitive clutter at the point of purchase, (3) justify price/value to the consumer, (4) signify brand features and benefits, and (5) ultimately motivate consumers' brand choices. Packaging is particularly important for differentiating homogenous or unexciting brands from available substitutes. Packaging accomplishes this by working uninterruptedly to say what the brand is, how it is used, and what it can do to benefit the user.[31] In short, packages perform a major brand-equity enhancing role by creating or fortifying brand awareness and, along with other marketing communications tools, building brand images.

Packaging Structure

There is a tendency for consumers to impute characteristics from a package to the brand itself, a tendency termed *sensation transference*.[32] A package communicates meaning about a brand via its various symbolic components: color, design, shape, size, physical materials, and information labeling. These components taken together represent what is referred to as the *packaging structure*.[33] All of these structural elements must interact harmoniously to evoke within buyers the set of meanings intended by the brand marketer. The notion underlying good packaging is *Gestalt*. That is, people react to the whole, not to the individual parts.

The Use of Color in Packaging. Colors have the ability to communicate many things to prospective buyers, including quality, taste, and the product's ability to satisfy various psychological needs. Research studies have documented the important role that color plays in affecting our senses. In one study researchers tested color's cueing role using vanilla pudding as the experimental product. The researchers altered the color of vanilla pudding by adding food colors to create dark brown, medium brown, and light brown "flavors." The pudding, which actually was identical in all three experimental versions (namely vanilla), was perceived as tasting like chocolate. Moreover, the dark brown pudding was considered to have the best chocolate flavor and to be the thickest. The light brown pudding was perceived to be the creamiest, possibly because cream is white in color.[34]

The strategic use of colors in packaging is effective because colors affect people emotionally. For example, the so-called high-wavelength colors of red, orange, and yellow possess strong excitation value and induce elated mood states.[35] *Red* is often described in terms such as active, stimulating, energetic, and vital. Close-Up toothpaste is one well-known brand that effectively uses red in its packaging. *Orange* is an appetizing color that is often associated with food. Popular food brands using orange packaging include Wheaties, Uncle Ben's rice, and Sanka coffee, and Kellogg's Mini-Wheats cereal. *Yellow*, a good attention getter, is a warm color that has a cheerful effect on consumers. Cheerios, Kodak, and Pennzoil are just a few of the many brands that use yellow packages.

www.wheaties.com

www.unclebens.com

www.pennzoil.com

Green connotes abundance, health, calmness, and serenity. Green packaging is sometimes used for beverages (e.g., Heineken beer, Seven-Up), often for vegetables (e.g., Green Giant), and most always in packaging for mentholated products (e.g., Salem cigarettes). Green also has come to stand for environmentally friendly products and as a cue to consumers of reduced-fat, low-fat, and fat-free products.[36] *Blue* suggests coolness and refreshment. Blue is often associated with laundry and cleaning products, including brands such as Windex and Downey fabric softeners. Finally, *white* signifies purity, cleanliness, and mildness. Gold Medal flour, Special K cereal, and Lean Cuisine are a few food brands that feature white packages.

www.leancuisine.com

In addition to the emotional impact that color brings to a package, elegance and prestige can be added to products by the use of polished reflective surfaces and color schemes using white and black or silver and gold.[37] The metallic silver labels on cans of LeSueur peas, for example, contribute to this brand's premium-quality image.

However, it is pertinent to note that the meaning of color varies from culture to culture. The above comments are based on North American culture and are not directly applicable elsewhere. Readers from other cultures should identify exceptions to the above comments and illustrate packages that do not adhere to the color usage described above.

Design and Shape Cues in Packaging. Design refers to the organization of the elements on a package. An effective package design is one that permits good eye flow and provides the consumer with a point of focus. Package designers bring various elements together in a package to help define a brand's image. These elements include—in addition to color—shape, size, and label design. One way of evoking different feelings is through the choice of slope, length, and thickness of lines on a package. *Horizontal lines* suggest restfulness and quiet, evoking feelings of tranquillity. There appears to be a physiological reason for this reaction—it is easier for people to move their eyes horizontally than vertically; vertical movement is less natural and produces greater strain on eye muscles than horizontal movement. *Vertical lines* evoke feelings of strength, confidence, and even pride. *Slanted lines* suggest upward movement to most people in the Western world, who read from left to right and thus view sloped lines as ascending rather than descending.

Shapes, too, arouse certain emotions and have specific connotations. Generally, round, curving lines connote femininity, whereas sharp, angular lines suggest masculinity. A package's shape also affects the apparent volume of the container. In general, if two packages have the same volume but a different shape, the taller of the two will appear to hold a greater volume inasmuch as height is usually associated with volume. Packages also can be shaped so as to convey information about their product contents. The *IMC Focus* describes an interesting package design for the Whipper Snapple brand of fruit drinks.

Packaging Size. Many product categories are available in several product sizes. Soft drinks, for example, come in eight- and 12-ounce bottles, one- and two-liter containers, and in six-, 12-, and 24-unit packs. Manufacturers offer different-sized containers to satisfy the unique needs of various market segments, to represent different usage situations, and also to gain more shelf space in retail outlets. An interesting issue arises from the consumer's perspective with regard to the size of the container. In particular, does the amount of product consumption vary depending on the size of the container? For example, do consumers consume more content from a larger package than a smaller version? Preliminary research on this matter reveals a tendency for consumers to indeed consume more content from larger than smaller packages. The primary reason for this behavior is that consumers perceive they gain lower unit prices from larger than smaller packages.[38] This finding is not universal across all products, however, because consumption for some products (such as laundry bleach or vitamins) is relatively invariant.

Physical Materials in Packaging. Another important consideration is the materials that make up a package. Some marketers are inclined to emphasize cost over all other considerations. The selection of package materials based primarily on cost considerations may be the result of a misguided engineering or accounting decision; the most important consideration should be the marketing-communications implications of the materials chosen. Increased sales and profits often result when upgraded packaging materials are used to design more attractive and effective packages.

Packaging materials can arouse consumer emotions, usually subconsciously. Packages constructed of metal evoke feelings of strength, durability, and coldness; plastics connote lightness, cleanliness, and perhaps cheapness. Materials that are soft, such as velvet, are associated with femininity. Foil has a high-quality image and can evoke feelings of prestige.[39] Wood arouses feelings of masculinity. The men's cologne English Leather, for example, has enjoyed much success using a wooden box and a bottle with a large wooden knob as a cap. English Leather's name and rectangular package present an overall image of masculinity by blending design, shape, brand name, and materials in a consistent fashion.

Product Information on Packages. Product information can come in several forms. In a sense, all of the previous package components (such as color and design) inform consumers (or convey meaning) about what is inside the package. However, when

IMC FOCUS: PACKAGE DESIGN FOR WHIPPER SNAPPLE

Whipper Snapple, from Triarc Beverage, is a packaged "smoothie" product that was successfully launched in 1998. The brand was inspired by the growth of so-called smoothie bars that originated on the West Coast and then spread elsewhere in the United States. (Smoothie bars serve fruit drinks made from fresh fruit blended and thickened with dairy products. Sometimes these drinks also contain herbal ingredients.) The marketing folks at Triarc quickly jumped on the smoothie-bar trend and were confident that a packaged smoothie-type product would represent a grand extension to the Snapple line of iced tea and other beverages.

Marketing executives and brand managers knew that a packaged smoothie product would require an eye-catching and appealing brand name and package. Approximately 1,000 brand names were contemplated, names that were generated by employees, advertising agencies, prospective consumers, and

naming consultants. Eventually the name Whipper Snapple was selected, a name derived from "whippersnapper," a noun referring to a young, presumptuous person. Testing revealed that the name appealed to consumers from all age groups and geographic regions of the United States.

The packaging decision was just as challenging. The objective was to design a package that would signal Whipper Snapple's dairy content in an unmistakable way at the point of purchase. After much deliberation, it was decided to mold an ice-cream-style swirl into the bottle to convey the impression that Whipper Snapple mixes fruit and dairy products in a smoothie-drink fashion. With the creative inputs of a product innovation and design consultant, the Whipper Snapple package came into existence. With a clever brand name, a swirling container suggesting a dairy product, and bright, appetizing fruit shots on the label, Whipper Snapple's packaging structure provided an attractive lure to consumers to give this brand a try.

Source: Adapted from Gerry Khermouch, "Triarc's Smooth Move," *Brandweek*, June 22, 1998, 26–32.

used in the more restricted sense, product information refers to key words on the package, information on the back panel, ingredients, warnings, pictures, and illustrations. An example of the effectiveness of information included on packages comes from a field experiment that measured weekly sales of bread. When a "Made with 100 percent Natural Ingredients: No Artificial Additives" statement was affixed to the package, sales volume increased. When the message was removed, sales returned to their prior level.[40]

The words *new, improved*, and *free* frequently appear on packages. These words stimulate immediate trial purchases or restore a brand purchase pattern for previous consumers who have switched to other brands. Furthermore, these key words presumably offer consumers change, novelty, and excitement.

There is some question whether the key words just cited have been overworked in the marketplace. One study suggests that the new and improved claims on packages do not significantly affect consumer evaluations of certain household and personal-care products.[41] More research is necessary to support or refute this point. Perhaps there is a need for new motivating words. Some examples may be the use of numerals, as in Gleem II (toothpaste) and Clorox 2 (laundry bleach). These names inform consumers that there is a new and improved version of an old brand without directly using such hackneyed words.[42]

In some instances, putting a short, memorable slogan on a package is a good marketing tactic. Slogans on packages are best used when a strong association has been built between the brand and the slogan through extensive and effective advertising. The slogan on the package, a concrete reminder of the brand's advertising, can facilitate the consumer's retrieval of advertising content and thereby enhance the chances of a trial purchase.

Evaluating the Package: The VIEW Model

A number of individual features have been discussed in regard to what a package communicates to buyers, but what exactly constitutes a good package? Although, as always, no single response is equally suitable across all packaging situations, four general features can be used to evaluate a particular package. These are visibility, information, emotional appeal, and workability, which are conveniently remembered with the acronym **VIEW.**[43]

Visibility.   *Visibility* signifies the ability of a package to attract attention at the point of purchase. The objective is to have a package stand out on the shelf yet not be so garish that it detracts from a brand's image. Brightly colored packages are especially effective at gaining the consumer's attention. Novel packaging graphics, sizes, and shapes also enhance a package's visibility.

Many brands in product categories such as soft drinks, cereal, and candy alternate packages throughout the year with special seasonal and holiday packaging as a way of attracting attention.[44] By aligning the brand with the shopping mood fitting the season or holiday, companies provide consumers with an added reason for selecting the specially packaged brand over more humdrum brands that never vary their package design.

Information.   The second consideration, *information*, deals with product usage instructions, claimed benefits, slogans, and supplementary information that are presented on or in a package (such as cooking recipes and sales promotion offers). Package information is useful for: (1) stimulating trial purchases, (2) encouraging repeat purchase behavior, and (3) providing correct product-usage instructions.[45] The objective is to provide the right type and quantity of information without cluttering the package with excessive information that could interfere with the primary information or cheapen the look of the package.

www.gardenburger.com

Figure 8.5 presents an illustration of packaging information for the Gardenburger brand of veggie patties. This illustration includes the front and side panels from the package along with nutrition facts from the back panel. The front panel portrays an appetizing shot of a hamburger-style Gardenburger and prominently notes that this product is fat-free. The side panel presents a photo of the creator of the Gardenburger and also notes that this product promotes healthy eating and a healthy environment. Also indicated is the fact that the company contributes part of its profits to organizations that share its environmental vision. Finally, the section on Nutrition Facts indicates the caloric and fat content of Gardenburgers and other relevant details.

Emotional Appeal.   The third component of the VIEW model component, *emotional appeal*, is concerned with the ability of a package to evoke a desired feeling or mood. Package designers attempt to arouse specific feelings (elegance, prestige, cheerfulness, fun, nostalgia, etc.) through the use of color, shape, packaging materials, and other devices. Packages for some brands contain virtually no emotional content and emphasize instead informational content, while packages of other brands emphasize emotional content and contain very little information.

What determines whether information or emotion is emphasized in a brand's package? The major determinant is the nature of the product category and the underlying consumer behavior involved. Recognizing the distinction drawn in Chapter 5 between the consumer processing model (CPM) and the hedonic, experiential model (HEM), it should be expected that greater informational influence in packaging would go along with CPM-oriented consumer behavior, whereas more emotional influence would be associated with HEM-oriented behavior.

In other words, if consumers make brand-selection decisions based on objectives such as obtaining the best buy or making a prudent choice (CPM-type objectives), then packaging must provide sufficient concrete information to facilitate the consumer's selection. When, however, product and brand selections are made in the pursuit of amusement, fantasies, or sensory stimulation (HEM-type objectives), packaging must contain the requisite emotional content to activate purchase behavior.

Illustration of Packaging Information for Gardenburger Veggie Patties

FIGURE 8.5

This discussion should not be taken as suggesting that all packaging emphasizes information or emotion. Although the packaging of brands in some categories does emphasize one or the other, there are many product categories where it is necessary for packaging to blend informational and emotional content so as to simultaneously appeal to consumers' rational and symbolic needs. Cereal is a case in point. Consumers require nutritional information to intelligently select from among the dozens of available brands, but cereal choice also is driven by emotional factors—wholesomeness, nostalgia, excitement, and so on. General Mills, for example, has used pictures of fictitious Betty Crocker on its boxes for over 50 years. This virtual icon on the supermarket shelves symbolizes middle America, wholesomeness, and family. Over the years, General Mills has periodically changed the photo of Betty Crocker to keep in step with the times. In 1996, General Mills introduced the most recent Betty Crocker—a digitally morphed amalgam of the photos of 75 women in celebration of General Mills's 75th birthday (see Figure 8.6.).

www.generalmills.com

www.wowchips.com

An executive with Apple Designsource Inc., a branding and package design firm, explained the emotional appeal that his firm tried to create in packaging for Wow! potato chips (see Figure 8.7). First, the Wow! package was designed to appeal primarily to

The Changing Faces
of Betty Crocker

female, health-oriented shoppers and at the same time be attractive to male, heavy users. Second, to overcome potential skepticism regarding Wow!'s taste, a taste claim was integrated into the Wow! brandmark (see "All the taste, fat free"). Third, a rich packaging material (mylar foil) and colorful graphics were chosen to convey a premium product-usage experience.[46] This same design firm also created packages for Tostitos corn chip and salsa items. Figure 8.8 is an advertisement from Apple designsource Inc. that was directed at potential clients (not consumers). This ad highlights the various packaging features that were designed to create a desired image for the Tostitos brand.

www.tostitos.com

Workability.   The final component of the VIEW model, *workability*, refers to how a package functions rather than how it communicates. Several workability issues are prominent: (1) Does the package protect the product contents? (2) Does it facilitate easy storage on the part of both retailers and consumers? (3) Does it simplify the consumer's task in accessing and using the product? (4) Does it protect retailers against unintentional breakage from consumer handling and from pilferage? (5) Is the package environmentally friendly?

Numerous packaging innovations in recent years have enhanced workability. These include pourable-spout containers for motor oil and sugar, microwaveable containers for many food items, aseptic cartons, zip-lock packaging, less-mess toothpaste containers, and single-serving bags and boxes. Cereal companies, for example, have introduced one-ounce bags of presweetened cereal products for kids and adults who are on the go and would not otherwise eat cereal during the school or work week. Companies also are developing "smart packages" that include magnetic strips, bar codes, and electronic chips that can communicate with appliances, computers, and consumers. For example, packages of microwaveable foods eventually will be programmed to "tell" microwaves how long the food item should be cooked.[47] Upjohn, maker of the hair-loss product Rogaine, developed packaging to prevent consumer pilferage of the $30 bottles of Rogaine. The new package contains electronic sensors that require deactivation at the store register.[48]

www.upjohn.com

A host of environmentally safe packaging innovations have served to increase what might be called societal workability. Many of the changes have involved moves from plastic to recyclable paper packages; for example, many fast-food chains eliminated the use of foam packaging, and other firms have transformed their packages from plastic to cardboard containers. Another significant environmental initiative has been the increase in spray containers as substitutes for ozone-harming aerosol cans.

Workability is, of course, a relative matter. The objective is to design a package that is as workable as possible yet is economical for the retailer and consumer. For example,

Emotional Appeals in the
Packaging of Wow!

consumers prefer food packages that completely prevent food from getting stale or spoiling, but the manufacturer's ability to provide this degree of workability is limited by cost. At the other extreme, some marketers skimp in their package design and use inexpensive packages that are unsuitable because they are difficult to use and frustrate consumers.

In conclusion, most packages do not perform well on all of the VIEW criteria, but packages need not always be exemplary on all four VIEW components because the relative importance of each criterion varies from one product category to another. Emotional appeal dominates for some products (e.g., perfume), information is most important for others (e.g., staple food items), while visibility and workability are generally important for all products. In the final analysis, the relative importance of packaging requirements depends, as always, on the particular market and the competitive situation.

Designing a Package

Designing a package is not as simple as what it may seem merely by walking through a supermarket and gazing at the thousands of packages located on the shelves. Because package

Rationale for Tostitos' Packaging Graphics

design is so critical to a brand's success, a systematic approach is recommended. Figure 8.9 provides a five-step package-design process. The subsequent discussion describes each of these stages.[49]

Step 1: Specify Brand-Positioning Objectives.   This initial stage of the packaging design process requires the brand-management team to specify how the brand is to be positioned in the consumer's mind and against competitive brands. What identity or image is desired for the brand? For example, it would appear that Tostitos' brand-management team selected a dual positioning strategy for that brand, namely that it is both an authentic nacho chip and a fun brand (see Figure 8.8).

Step 2: Conduct a Product Category Analysis.   Having established what the brand represents (step 1) and thus what the packaging must convey, it is essential to study

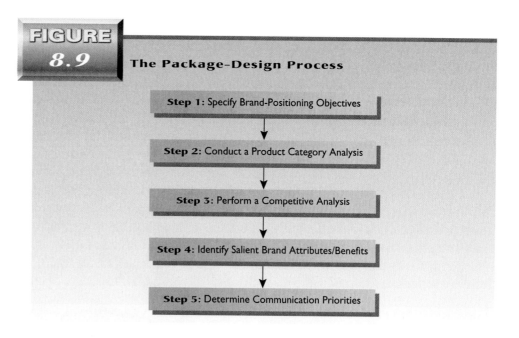

the product category and related categories to determine relevant trends or anticipated events that would influence the packaging decision. The point, in other words, is that to be forewarned is to be forearmed.

Step 3: Perform a Competitive Analysis. Armed with knowledge about competitors' use of packaging colors, shapes, graphical features, and materials, the package designer is thus prepared to create a package that conveys the desired image yet is sufficiently unique and differentiating to capture consumer attention.

Step 4: Identify Salient Brand Attributes/Benefits. As noted earlier, research reveals that shoppers spend an incredibly short amount of time—on the order of 10 to 12 seconds—viewing brands prior to moving on or selecting an item and placing it in the shopping cart.[50] It is imperative, therefore, that the package not be too cluttered with information and that it feature benefits that are most important to consumers. A general rule for identifying packaging benefits is that "the fewer, the better."[51]

Step 5: Determine Communication Priorities. Having identified the most salient brand benefits (step 4), this phase of the process simply forces the package designer to establish verbal and visual priorities for the package. Although perhaps three benefits may have been identified in step 4 as essentially equal in importance, the designer must prioritize which of the three is to capture the greatest visual/verbal attention on the package. This is a very tough decision insofar as it is tempting to devote equal attention to all important brand benefits. It is critical that the package designer acknowledge that the package "advertisement" at the point of purchase occurs in an incredibly cluttered environment for a very short duration. Upon reconciling oneself to this fact, it is much easier to devote package space to the most important brand benefit rather than clutter the package with too many messages.

POINT-OF-PURCHASE ADVERTISING

Brand names and packages, the topics of prior sections in this chapter, confront head on at the point of purchase the ultimate arbiter of their effectiveness, the consumer. The point of purchase, or store environment, provides brand marketers with a final opportunity to affect consumer behavior. The point of purchase is an ideal time to communicate with consumers because this is the time at which many product- and brand-choice decisions are made. It is the time and place at which all elements of the sale (consumer, money, and product) come together.[52] The consumer's in-store behavior has been described in the following terms that highlight the importance of point-of-purchase marketing communications:

> *Shoppers are explorers. They're on safari, hunting for bargains, new products and different items to add excitement to their everyday lives. Three of every four are open to new experiences as they browse the aisles of supermarkets and search for bargains at drugstores and mass merchandisers.*[53]

This translates into an opportunity to make a measurable impact just when shoppers are most receptive to new product ideas and alternative brands. Promotion-savvy marketers realize that the store environment is the last best chance to make a difference. Marketers attempt to influence buying decisions at the point of purchase using a variety of displays, signs, and other communication vehicles.

The Spectrum of P–O–P Materials

Point-of-purchase materials include various types of signs, mobiles, plaques, banners, shelf talkers, mechanical mannequins, lights, mirrors, plastic reproductions of products, checkout units, full-line merchandisers, wall posters, and other items.

Industry officials classify these P-O-P materials into three categories:[54]

◆ *Permanent P-O-P:* **Permanent P-O-P materials** include displays and signs that are intended for use for six months or more. (Note, however, that the six-month dividing line is an arbitrary convention established by POPAI, the Point-of-Purchase Advertising Institute.) Illustrations of three award-winning permanent displays are presented in Figures 8.10 through 8.12.[55]

www.actmedia.com

◆ *Temporary P-O-P:* **Temporary P-O-P materials** include displays and signs that are intended for fewer than six months. Illustrations of three award-winning temporary displays are presented in Figures 8.13 through 8.15.[56]

◆ *In-Store Media:* **In-store media** include advertising and promotion materials such as P-O-P radio, shopping-cart advertising, shelf talkers, and coupon dispensers. A third-party company (i.e., a company other than the brand manufacturer or retailer) executes these in-store media. For example, ActMedia, a company well-known in the P-O-P industry, provides a variety of services to its clients and operates in a capacity similar to that of an advertising agency representing its clients' mass-media advertising needs. ActMedia's in-store services include (1) "POP Radio" (in-store radio programs that carry commercials in over 14,000 stores nationwide); (2) "ActMedia Carts" (shopping carts with signs that are available in 8,000 stores nationwide (see Figure 8.16); and (3) "ShelfTalk"—shelf extensions that promote brands in over 17,000 stores nationwide (see example in Figure 8.17). Brand marketers pay ActMedia advertising rates to secure in-store radio time or shopping-cart and shelf-talker space in specific markets or on a nationwide basis.

What Does P–O–P Accomplish?

Companies are increasingly investing promotional dollars in point-of-purchase materials. Annual expenditures in the United States on in-store promotional materials now exceed $13 billion.[57] This investment in point-of-purchase materials is justified inasmuch as

Permanent Display
for Candy Bars

in-store materials provide useful services for all participants in the marketing process: manufacturers, retailers, and consumers.

Accomplishments for Manufacturers. For *manufacturers,* P-O-P keeps the company's name and the brand name before the consumer and reinforces a brand image that has been previously established through advertising. P-O-P also calls attention to sales promotions and helps stimulate impulse purchasing. Consider, for example, a point-of-purchase effort undertaken by the American Dairy Association (ADA). The ADA, a trade association for producers of cheese and other dairy products, hired the A.C. Nielsen research firm to investigate whether stores that use point-of-purchase materials to promote cheese enjoy higher sales levels than do nonparticipants. A football-related promotion was tested ("Kick Off the Season with Cheese"). A.C. Nielsen employees monitored more than 700 grocery stores over a three-week period in 13 major markets in the United States. The ADA's in-store "Kick Off" promotion used a football motif including small banners, varsity letters, case flags, and helmet mobiles—all drawing shopper attention to cheese. Over half of the 700 monitored stores used these point-of-purchase materials, while the remaining stores used no in-store promotions. Some of the stores that chose to use ADA's promotional materials also created their own displays to further attract consumer attention.

Test results convincingly established the effectiveness of P-O-P materials in this particular application. In the stores that did not participate in the "Kick Off" promotion, cheese sales averaged $4,184. Stores that used the ADA promotional package (banners, mobiles,

FIGURE
8.11

Permanent Display for
Sesame Street Toys

etc.) experienced average sales of $5,392—a 29 percent increase over the nonpromoting stores. Stores that supplemented the promotional package with their own displays enjoyed 38 percent greater sales than the nonpromoting stores, or average sales of $5,790 per store. These results, according to an ADA marketing executive, prove "beyond a shadow of a doubt" that point-of-purchase materials are an effective way to increase sales volume.[58]

Service to Retailers.   P-O-P serves *retailers* by attracting the consumer's attention, increasing his or her interest in shopping, and extending the amount of time spent in the store—all of which lead to increased revenue and profits for retailers. Furthermore, P-O-P helps retailers utilize available space to the best advantage by displaying various products in the same unit, as is done with the candy display illustrated in Figure 8.10. P-O-P displays also enable retailers to better organize shelf and floor space and to improve inventory control, volume, stock turnover, and profitability.

Value to Consumers.   *Consumers* are served by point-of-purchase units that deliver useful information and simplify the shopping process. Permanent and temporary P-O-P units provide this value to consumers by setting particular brands apart from similar items and simplifying the selection process. The Kodak display (Figure 8.12) provides

Permanent Display
for Kodak Film

consumers with a number of film options and enables relatively easy and swift decisions regarding the most appropriate film for one's photographic needs.

In addition to benefiting all participants in the marketing process, point-of-purchase plays another important role: It serves as the capstone for an *integrated marketing communications program*. P-O-P by itself may have limited impact, but when used in conjunction with advertisements and sales promotions, P-O-P can create a synergistic effect. Indeed, research by Information Resources Inc.—the well-known provider of optical scanning data—has shown that when P-O-P reinforces a brand's advertising message, the increase in sales volume averages more than 100 percent compared to advertising alone.[59]

Functions Performed by P–O–P Materials

The functions performed by P-O-P materials are, in general, fourfold: informing, reminding, encouraging, and merchandising.

Informing. *Informing* consumers is P-O-P's most basic communications function. Signs, posters, displays, and other P-O-P materials alert consumers to specific items and provide potentially useful information.

Motion displays are especially effective for this purpose. Motion displays, though typically more expensive than static displays, represent a sound business investment because they attract significantly higher levels of shopper attention. Evidence from three studies shows that motion displays are often worth the extra expense.[60]

Temporary Display
for Alpo Dog Food

Researchers tested the relative effectiveness of motion and static displays for Olympia beer by placing the two types of displays in a test sample of Californian liquor stores and supermarkets. Each of the sampled stores was stocked with either static or motion displays. Another sample of stores, serving as the control group, received no displays. Over 62,000 purchases of Olympia beer were recorded during the four-week test period. Static displays in liquor stores increased Olympia sales by 56 percent over stores with no displays (the control group). In supermarkets, static displays improved Olympia sales by a considerably smaller, though nonetheless substantial, amount (18 percent). More dramatic, however, was the finding that motion displays increased Olympia sales by 107 percent in liquor stores and by 49 percent in supermarkets.

A second test of the effectiveness of motion displays used S. B. Thomas' English muffins as the focal product. Two groups of 40 stores each were matched by store volume and customer demographics. One group was equipped with an S. B. Thomas' English muffin post sign that moved from side to side. The other 40 stores used regular floor displays with no motion. Records of product movement revealed that sales in the stores stocked with motion displays were over 100 percent greater than in stores with static displays.

www.eveready.com

Temporary Display
for Michelob Beer

Researchers conducted a study of motion displays for Eveready batteries in Atlanta and San Diego. Studied in each city were six drugstores, six supermarkets, and six mass-merchandise stores. The stores were divided into two groups, like the English muffin study. Some newspaper advertising appeared during the test period, but special pricing was the primary promotional element. For mass merchandisers, the static displays increased sales during the test period by 2.7 percent over the base period, but, surprisingly, sales in the drug and food outlets utilizing the static displays were slightly less (each 1.6 percent lower) than those not using the static displays. By comparison, the motion displays uniformly increased sales by 3.7 percent, 9.1 percent, and 15.7 percent in the drugstore outlets, supermarkets, and mass merchandisers, respectively.

All three sets of results convincingly demonstrate the effectiveness of motion displays. The consumer information-processing rationale (see Chapter 5) is straightforward: Motion displays attract attention. Attention, once attracted, is directed toward salient product features, including recognition of the displayed brand's name. Brand name information activates consumers' memories pertaining to brand attributes previously processed from media advertising. Information on brand attributes, when recalled, supplies a reason for the consumer to purchase the displayed brand.

Permanent Display for
Goldfish Crackers

Hence, a moving display performs the critical in-store function of bringing a brand's name to active memory. The probability of purchasing the brand increases, perhaps substantially (as in the case of S. B. Thomas' English muffins), if the consumer is favorably disposed toward the brand. The Eveready display was less effective apparently because the selling burden was placed almost exclusively on the display. Without prior stimulation of demand through advertising, the static display was ineffective, and the motion display was not as effective as it might have been.

Reminding.   A second point-of-purchase function is *reminding* consumers of brands they have previously learned about via broadcast, print, or other advertising media. This reminder role serves to complement the job already performed by advertising before the consumer enters a store.

To fully appreciate the reminder role served by point-of-purchase materials, it is important at this point to address a key principle from cognitive psychology: the **encoding specificity principle.** In simple terms, this principle states that information recall is enhanced when the context in which people attempt to *retrieve* information is the same or similar to the context in which they originally *encoded* the information.[61] (Encoding is the placing of information items into memory.)

ActMedia In-Store Advertising Cart

A nonmarketing illustration—one that may bring back some unpleasant memories—will serve to clarify the exact meaning and significance of the encoding specificity principle. Recall a time when you were studying for a crucial exam that required problem-solving skills. You may have been up late at night trying to solve a particularly difficult problem, perhaps in accounting, calculus, or statistics. Eventually the solution came to you, and you felt well prepared for the next morning's exam. Sure enough, the exam had a problem very similar to the one you worked on the night before. However, to your considerable disappointment, your mind went blank, and you were unable to solve the problem. But after the exam, back in your room, the solution hit you like the proverbial ton of bricks.

Encoding specificity is the "culprit." Specifically, the context (your room) in which you originally encoded information and formulated a solution to the problem was different from the context (your classroom) in which you subsequently were asked to solve a similar problem. Hence, contextual retrieval cues were unavailable in the classroom to readily facilitate your recall of how you originally solved the problem.

Returning to the marketplace, consider the situation in which consumers encode television-commercial information about a brand and its unique features and benefits. The advertiser's expectation is that consumers will be able to retrieve this information at the point of purchase and use it to select the advertiser's brand over competitive offerings. It

ActMedia ShelfTalk In-Store Advertising

doesn't always work like this, however. Our memories are fallible, especially since we are exposed to an incredible amount of advertising information. Hence, although we may have encoded advertising information at one time, we may not be able to retrieve it without a reminder cue at the point of purchase.

Consider, for example, the ongoing pink-bunny-pounding-a-drum advertising campaign. Most everyone is aware of this campaign, but many consumers have difficulty remembering the advertised brand. (Think for a moment; which brand is it?) When facing brands of Duracell, Eveready, and Energizer on the shelf, the consumer may not connect the pink-bunny advertising with any specific brand. Here is where point-of-purchase materials can perform a critically important role. Energizer (the pink-bunny brand) can facilitate encoding specificity by using shelf signs or packaging graphics that present the bunny and the Energizer name together (just as they appeared together in advertisements). Accordingly, by providing consumers with encoding-specific retrieval cues, chances are that consumers will recall from earlier advertisements that Energizer is the battery brand that powers the unceasing drum-pounding bunny.

The crucial point is that media advertising and P-O-P communications must be tightly integrated so that in-store reminder cues can capitalize on the background work accomplished by media advertising. Signs, displays, and in-store media provide the culmination for an integrated marketing communications campaign and increase the odds that consumers will select a particular brand over alternatives.

Encouraging.   *Encouraging* consumers to buy a specific item or brand is P-O-P's third function. Effective P-O-P materials influence product and brand choices at the point of purchase and encourage impulse buying. Many parents, and perhaps especially grandparents, would have great difficulty not purchasing a Sesame Street character from the irresistible school-bus display in Figure 8.11.

Merchandising.   The *merchandising* function is served when point-of-purchase displays enable retailers to utilize floor space effectively and boost retail sales by assisting consumers in making product and brand selections.

www.clairol.com

The merchandising role is well illustrated with the information-center displays developed by Clairol to merchandise women's hair-coloring products and to answer consumers' questions concerning these products. Product information appeared on large, colorful header signs above Clairol products that were placed on the display's shelves. The information center made product selection easy: Color-coded labels identified product subcategories and shelf dividers separated the various products. When the information center displays were first introduced to retail accounts, Clairol's sales increased an average of 32 percent, and shelf space devoted to Clairol products averaged 15 percent more linear feet.[62]

Interactive Displays

www.leggs.com

Interactive displays are computerized units with liquid-crystal displays that allow consumers to answer questions pertaining to their product-category needs and help them make well-informed product choices. L'eggs Products, for example, used an interactive unit—called the Pantyhose Advisor—that was available in 2,000 food and drug chains and mass merchandisers. The 14-inch units "asked" shoppers questions about their height, weight, the occasion for which they were buying pantyhose, and the style of shoes they would be wearing. The unit then recommended two styles of pantyhose and the appropriate size from the L'eggs and Just My Size brands of pantyhose. This unit reduced the confusion women face when choosing among a wide variety of styles and shades.[63]

www.kalkan.com

Kal Kan, makers of Expert pet food, introduced the Select-A-Diet interactive unit to assist pet owners in choosing the right nutritional formula of Expert pet food. The unit, attached to supermarket shelves, presented shoppers with a series of questions regarding their pet's age, weight, and activity level. The unit then recommended the best formula of food for the pet.[64]

An interactive unit from Kelly-Springfield presented automobile tire shoppers with questions on car type, driving habits, and tire style performance, and consumers responded via a touch keypad. The unit recommended three tire choices from which the consumer could choose.[65]

An especially clever interactive display was developed to assist shoppers in choosing the "right" bottle of wine. Consumers used a touch-screen monitor to select wines based on quality, price, type, and food pairing. The display provided reviews and ratings for the wines contained in a particular retailer's inventory. Information in the computerized display was periodically updated via modem with inventory and price changes.[66]

A final illustration is a display for Pantene, a Procter & Gamble line of hair-care products. Pantene had experienced weak distribution and poor in-store visibility. Sales were being lost due to these problems and because retail sales personnel were not always well informed about Pantene's advantages. Procter & Gamble and a display-design firm developed an impressive interactive display for Pantene. The display included a video monitor that continuously showed animated graphics to attract customer traffic. After being instructed to touch the screen, customers were guided through a series of multiple-choice questions to find out what products had been designed for their particular hair condition. A printout of Pantene's hair-care prescription was automatically provided. The customer then selected the recommended product directly from the display below the monitor. Tests conducted in two markets revealed sales increases in excess of 400 percent.[67]

One Result of P–O–P: Increased In-Store Decision Making

Studies of consumer shopping behavior have shown that a high proportion of all purchases in supermarkets, drugstores, and other retail outlets are unplanned. In a general sense, this means that many product- and brand-choice decisions are made while the consumer is in the store rather than beforehand. Point-of-purchase materials play a role—perhaps the major role—in influencing unplanned purchasing and in increasing sales. The following section discusses research on unplanned purchasing, and a subsequent section then presents impressive evidence on the role of P-O-P displays in increasing sales volume.

The 1995 POPAI Consumer Buying Habits Study.   This study, conducted by the Point-of-Purchase Advertising Institute (POPAI), is the most recent of a series of studies conducted by this trade association.[68] As with previous undertakings, this study confirms that in-store media, signage, and displays heavily influence consumers' purchase decisions. In conducting this study, researchers interviewed approximately 4,200 consumers who were shopping in the stores of 22 leading supermarket chains and four mass merchandisers—Bradlees, Kmart, Target, and Wal-Mart. Interviews transpired in stores located in 14 major markets throughout the United States.

The 1995 Buying Habits Study was conducted in the following manner.[69] Shoppers aged 16 or older were screened by researchers to determine that they were on a "major shopping trip." Researchers then interviewed qualified shoppers both before they began their shopping (entry interviews) and after they had completed their shopping trips (exit interviews). During the preshopping entry interviews, researchers used an *unaided* questioning format to ask shoppers about their planned purchases on that particular occasion and probed for brand buying intentions. Then, during postshopping exit interviews, researchers gathered supermarket shoppers' register tapes or physically inventoried shoppers' carts at the mass merchandise stores. Interviews were conducted during all times of day and every day of the week.

By comparing shoppers' planned purchases obtained during entry interviews and actual purchases during exit interviews, it was possible to classify every brand purchase into one of four types of purchase behaviors:

1. **Specifically planned:** This category represents purchases of a brand that the consumer had indicated an intention to buy. For example, the purchase of Diet Pepsi would be considered a specifically planned purchase if a consumer mentioned her intention to purchase that brand and in fact bought Diet Pepsi. According to the 1995 Consumer Buying Habits Study (see Table 8.1), 30 percent of supermarket purchases and 26 percent of mass merchandise purchases were specifically planned.

2. **Generally planned:** This classification applies to purchases for which the shopper indicated an intent to buy a particular product (say, a soft drink) but had no specific brand in mind. The purchase of Diet Pepsi in this case would be classified as a generally planned purchase rather than a specifically planned purchase. Generally planned purchases constituted 6 percent of those in supermarkets and 18 percent in mass merchandise stores (see Table 8.1).

TABLE 8.1	Results from the 1995 POPAI Consumer Buying Habits Study	
TYPE OF PURCHASE	SUPERMARKET	MASS MERCHANDISING STORE
1. Specifically planned	30%	26%
2. Generally planned	6	18
3. Substitute	4	3
4. Unplanned	60	53
In-store decision rate (2 + 3 + 4)	70%	74%

Source: *The 1995 POPAI Consumer Buying Habits Study* (Washington, D.C.: The Point-of-Purchase Advertising Institute, 1995), 18.

3. **Substitute purchases:** Purchases where the shopper does not buy the product or brand he or she indicated in the entry interview constitute substitute purchases. For example, if a consumer said she intended to buy Diet Pepsi but actually purchased Tab, her behavior would be classified as a substitute purchase. These represented just 4 percent of supermarket purchases and 3 percent of mass merchandise purchases.

4. **Unplanned purchases:** Under this heading are purchases for which the consumer had no prior purchase intent. If, for example, a shopper buys Diet Pepsi without having informed the interviewer of this intent, the behavior would be recorded as an unplanned purchase. Sixty percent of the purchases in supermarkets and 53 percent of those in mass merchandise stores were classified as unplanned.

Notice in Table 8.1 that the summation of generally planned, substitute, and unplanned purchases constitutes the in-store decision rate. In other words, the three categories representing purchases that are not specifically planned all represent decisions influenced by in-store factors. The in-store decision rates are 70 and 74 percent for supermarkets and mass merchandise stores, respectively. These percentages indicate that approximately seven out of 10 purchase decisions are influenced by in-store factors. It is apparent that P-O-P materials represent a very important determinant of consumers' product- and brand-choice behaviors.

A technical point needs to be addressed at this time. It is important to recognize that not all purchases recorded as unplanned by interviewers are truly unplanned. Rather, some purchases are recorded as unplanned simply because shoppers are unable or unwilling to inform interviewers of their exact purchase plans. This is not to imply that the POPAI research is seriously flawed, but rather that the measurement of unplanned purchases probably is somewhat overstated due to the unavoidable bias just described. Other categories may be biased also. For example, by the same logic, the percentage of specifically planned purchases is probably somewhat understated. In any event, POPAI's findings are important even if they are not precisely correct.

The summary statistics in Table 8.1 represent types of purchases aggregated over literally hundreds of product categories. It should be apparent that in-store decision rates vary greatly across product categories. To emphasize this point, Tables 8.2 and 8.3 present categories with the highest and lowest in-store decision rates for supermarkets (Table 8.2) and mass merchandise stores (Table 8.3).

The data presented in Tables 8.2 and 8.3 make it clear that in-store decision rates vary substantially. Supermarket products that are virtual staples (e.g., produce) and mass merchandise products that are essential and regularly purchased items (e.g., disposable diapers) have the lowest in-store purchase rates because most consumers know they are going to purchase these items when they go to the store. On the other hand, nonnecessities and items that generally do not occupy top-of-the-mind thoughts (e.g., first-aid supplies

TABLE 8.2

Product Categories with the Five Highest and Five Lowest In-Store Decision Rates: Supermarket Purchases

CATEGORY	IN-STORE DECISION RATE
Highest in-store decision rate	
First aid	93%
Toys, sporting goods, crafts	93
Houseware/hardware	90
Stationery	90
Candy/gum	89
Lowest in-store decision rate	
Produce	33
Meat, seafood	47
Eggs	53
Coffee	58
Baby food/formula	58

Source: *The 1995 POPAI Consumer Buying Habits Study* (Washington, D.C.: The Point-of-Purchase Advertising Institute, 1995), 19.

and garbage bags) are especially susceptible to the influence of in-store stimuli. It is clear that for these types of products, brand marketers must have a distinct presence at the point of purchase if they hope to sway purchase decisions toward their brands.

The Brand Lift Index.   POPAI and its research collaborator (the Meyers Research Center) have developed a measure—called the **brand lift index**—to gauge the average increase of in-store decision purchases when P-O-P is present versus when it is not.[70] This index simply indicates how in-store P-O-P materials (signs and displays) affect the

TABLE 8.3

Product Categories with the Five Highest and Five Lowest In-Store Decision Rates: Mass Merchandise Purchases

CATEGORY	IN-STORE DECISION RATE
Highest in-store decision rate	
Apparel accessories	92%
Foils, food wraps	91
Hardware, electric, plumbing	90
Infant/toddler wear	90
Garbage bags	88
Lowest in-store decision rate	
Disposable diapers	35
Baby food	35
Eyedrops and lens care	52
Prerecorded music, videos	54
Coffee, tea, cocoa	55

Source: *The 1995 POPAI Consumer Buying Habits Study* (Washington, D.C.: The Point-of-Purchase Advertising Institute, 1995), 20.

	BRAND LIFT INDEX
Supermarket categories	
Butter/margarine	6.47
Cookies	6.21
Soft drinks	5.37
Beer/ale	4.67
Mixers	4.03
Sour cream/cottage cheese	3.79
Cereal	3.73
Hand and body soaps	3.62
Packaged cheese	3.57
Canned fish	3.55
Salty snacks	3.50
Mass merchandise categories	
Film/photofinishing	47.67
Socks/underwear/pantyhose	29.43
Cookies/crackers	18.14
Small appliances	8.87
Foils, food wraps, and bags	7.53
Adult apparel	7.45
Pet supplies	5.55
Packaged bread	5.01

Source: *The 1995 POPAI Consumer Buying Habits Study* (Washington, D.C.: The Point-of-Purchase Advertising Institute, 1995), 24.

likelihood that customers will buy a product that they had not specifically planned to buy. Table 8.4 shows the brand lift indexes for the products sold in supermarkets and mass merchandise stores that have the highest brand lift indexes from displays. For example, the index of 47.67 for film and photofinishing products in mass merchandise stores indicates that shoppers are over 47 times more likely to make an in-store purchase decision for these products when promoted by displays than if there were no displays. (Students: Note very carefully that the index of 47.67 does not mean that sales of film and other photofinishing items are over 47 times greater when a display is used. Rather, this index merely reveals that consumers are over 47 times more likely to make an in-store decision in the presence versus absence of displays.) And supermarket shoppers are 3.5 times more likely to make in-store decisions to purchase salty snacks when these items are displayed compared to when they are not displayed. Needless to say, displays can have incredible influence on consumer behavior.

The Impact of Displays on Brand Sales

Practitioners are vitally interested in knowing whether the cost of special P-O-P displays is justified. It has only been in recent years, however, that good research evidence has been available to provide answers to this question. Two important studies in particular have examined the impact of displays on a brand's temporary sales.

The POPAI/Kmart/P&G Study. This notable study was conducted by a consortium of a trade association (POPAI), a mass merchandiser (Kmart), and a consumer-goods manufacturer (Procter & Gamble).[71] The study investigated the impact that displays have on sales of P&G brands in six product categories: paper towels, shampoo, toothpaste, deodorant, coffee, and fabric softener. The test lasted for a period of four weeks, and P&G's brands were sold at their regular price throughout this period. Seventy-five Kmart stores in the United States were matched in terms of brand sales, store volume, and shopper demographics and then assigned to three panels of 25 stores each:[72]

> *Control panel.* The 25 stores in this group contained the advertised brands in their normal shelf position with no display or other advertising present.
>
> *Test panel 1.* These 25 stores carried the advertised brands on display.
>
> *Test panel 2.* These stores contained the advertised brands either on a different display or on the same display as in test panel 1 but at a different location in the store.

Specific differences in displays/locations between test panels 1 and 2 are shown in Table 8.5. For example, paper towels were displayed in a mass waterfall display at two different (but undisclosed) store locations; shampoo was displayed in either a special shelf unit display or a floorstand display; and coffee was displayed either on a pallet outside the coffee aisle or a full pallet at the end of the coffee aisle—called an endcap display.

The last column in Table 8.5 compares the percentage sales increase in each set of test stores (with displays) against the control stores where P&G brands were sold in their regular (nondisplay) shelf locations. It can be readily observed that positive sales increases materialized for all products and both test conditions; in some instances the increases were nothing short of huge. P&G's brands of shampoo and deodorant experienced modest increases during the four-week test of only about 18 percent (test 1), whereas paper towels and coffee experienced triple-digit increases in both display conditions—sales increases of 773.5 percent for paper towels (test 2) and 567.4 percent for coffee (test 2).

TABLE 8.5

Display Information for POPAI/Kmart/P&G Study

PRODUCT CATEGORY	TEST PANELS AND DISPLAYS	TEST PANEL SALES VERSUS CONTROL PANEL SALES (PERCENTAGE INCREASE)
Paper towels	Test 1: Mass waterfall (MW) display	447.1%
	Test 2: MW display in a different location	773.5
Shampoo	Test 1: Shelf unit	18.2
	Test 2: Floorstand	56.8
Toothpaste	Test 1: Floorstand in toothpaste aisle	73.1
	Test 2: ¼ pallet outside toothpaste aisle	119.2
Deodorant	Test 1: Powerwing	17.9
	Test 2: Powerwing in a different store location	38.5
Coffee	Test 1: ¼ pallet outside coffee aisle	500.0
	Test 2: Full pallet on endcap of coffee aisle	567.4
Fabric softener	Test 1: Full pallet on endcap of laundry aisle	66.2
	Test 2: ¼ pallet outside laundry aisle	73.8

Source: *POPAI/Kmart/Procter & Gamble Study of P-O-P Effectiveness in Mass Merchandising Stores* (Washington, D.C.: Point-of-Purchase Advertising Institute, 1993).

www.warner-lambert.com

The POPAI/Warner-Lambert Benylin Study. Another important study extends the POPAI/Kmart/P&G findings obtained from mass merchandise stores in the United States to drugstores in Canada.[73] POPAI and Warner-Lambert Canada jointly investigated the effectiveness of P-O-P displays on sales of health items in drugstores. Eighty stores from four major drugstore chains participated (Shoppers Drug Mart, Jean Coutu, Cumberland, and Pharmaprix), and testing was conducted in three major cities: Toronto, Montreal, and Vancouver. Two brands were involved in the testing: Benylin cough syrup and Listerine mouthwash. This section discusses the Benylin study, and the following section describes the Listerine study.

For the Benylin test, stores were divided into four groups: One group offered regularly priced Benylin in its normal shelf position; a second group merchandised Benylin in the normal shelf position but at a feature (i.e., discounted) price; a third group of stores displayed Benylin at a feature price on endcap displays; and the final group employed in-aisle floorstand displays of Benylin at a feature price. Sales data were captured during a two-week period in each store to gauge display effectiveness.

The effectiveness of both feature pricing and displays is determined simply by comparing sales volume during the test period in store groups 2 through 4 with sales in group 1 —the baseline group. These comparisons reveal the following:

- Stores in group 2 (Benylin located at its regular shelf position but feature priced) enjoyed 29 percent greater sales volume of Benylin than the stores in group 1 (Benylin at both its regular price and shelf location). This 29 percent increment reflects simply the effect of feature pricing inasmuch as both store groups sold Benylin from its regular shelf location.

- Stores in group 3 (Benylin on an endcap display and feature priced) enjoyed 98 percent greater sales of Benylin than did stores in group 1. This increment reflects that the endcap display and feature price combination had a substantial impact on the number of units sold. The large percentage increase in comparison to group 2 (i.e., 98 percent versus 29 percent) reflects the incremental impact of the endcap display location over the effect of feature pricing per se.

- Stores in group 4 (Benylin displayed in-aisle and feature priced) realized 139 percent greater sales volume than the baseline stores, which indicates that this location, at least for this product category, is more valuable than is the endcap location.

www.listerine.com

The POPAI/Warner-Lambert Listerine Study. Stores were divided into four groups for this test: One group offered regularly priced Listerine in its normal shelf position; a second group of stores offered Listerine in the normal shelf position but at a feature price; a third group displayed Listerine at a feature price on endcap displays at the *rear* of the store; and the fourth group displayed Listerine at a feature price on endcap displays at the *front* of the store. Sales data were captured during a two-week period in each store to gauge display effectiveness.

Again, the effectiveness of displays can be determined simply by comparing sales volume of groups 2 through 4 with sales in baseline group 1.

- Stores in group 2 (Listerine located at its regular shelf position but feature priced) enjoyed 11 percent greater sales volume of Listerine than the stores in group 1 (where Listerine was regular priced and located in its regular shelf position).

◆ Stores in group 3 (Listerine at a rear endcap display and feature priced) experienced 141 percent greater sales of Listerine than the stores in group 1.

◆ Stores in group 4 (Listerine at a front endcap display and feature priced) enjoyed 162 percent greater sales volume than the baseline stores.

Both sets of results reveal that these two drugstore products, Benylin and Listerine, benefited greatly when feature priced and merchandised from prized locations. The Listerine study results came as a bit of surprise to industry observers, however, who expected the advantage of the front endcap location to be substantially greater in comparison to the rear endcap location. The premium price that manufacturers pay for front endcap placement (versus rear endcap positioning) may not be fully justified in light of these results. Additional research with other product categories is needed before any definitive answer is possible.

The Use and Nonuse of P–O–P Materials

Although P-O-P materials can be very effective for manufacturers and perform several desirable functions for retailers, the fact remains that perhaps as much as 40 to 50 percent of all P-O-P materials supplied by manufacturers are never used by retailers.[74]

Reasons Why P-O-P Materials Go Unused.   Five major reasons explain why retailers choose not to use P-O-P materials. First, there is no incentive for the retailer to use certain P-O-P materials because these materials are inappropriately designed and do not satisfy the retailer's needs. Second, some displays take up too much space for the amount of sales they generate. Third, some materials are too unwieldy, too difficult to set up, too flimsy, or have other construction defects.[75] A fourth reason many signs and displays go unused is because they lack eye appeal. Finally, retailers are concerned that displays and other P-O-P materials simply serve to increase sales of a particular manufacturer's brand during the display period, but that the retailer's sales and profits for the entire product category are not improved. In other words, a retailer has little incentive to erect displays or use signage that merely serves to transfer sales from one brand to another but that does not increase the retailer's overall sales and profits for the product category. (The subsequent discussion of category management in Chapter 17 will emphasize that increased pressures have been imposed by retailers on manufacturers to develop merchandising programs that build category growth and profits rather than merely serving the manufacturer's brand needs.)

Persuading Retailers to Use P-O-P Materials.   Encouraging retailers to use P-O-P materials is a matter of basic marketing. Persuading the retailer to enthusiastically use a display or other P-O-P device means that the manufacturer must view the material from the retailer's perspective. First and foremost, P-O-P materials must satisfy the retailer's needs and the needs of the retailer's customer (the consumer) rather than just those of the manufacturer. This is the essence of marketing, and it applies to encouraging the use of P-O-P materials just as much as promoting the acceptance of their products.

P-O-P materials must be designed so that

1. They are the right size and format;

2. They fit the store decor;

3. They are user friendly—that is, easy for the retailer to attach, erect, or otherwise use;

4. They are sent to stores when they are needed (e.g., at the right selling season);

5. They are properly coordinated with other aspects of the marketing communications program (they should tie in to a current advertising or sales promotion program); and

6. They are attractive, convenient, and useful for consumers.[76]

Summary

The brand name is the single most important element found on a package. The brand name works with package graphics and other product features to communicate and position the brand's image. The brand name identifies the product and differentiates it from others on the market. A good brand name can evoke feelings of trust, confidence, security, strength, durability, speed, status, and many other desirable associations. A good brand name must satisfy several fundamental requirements: It must describe the product's benefits, be compatible with the product's image, and be memorable and easy to pronounce. A major section in this chapter is devoted to a five-step process for selecting a brand name. Another section discusses the nature and role of brand logos.

The second major section of the chapter focuses on packaging. The package is perhaps the most important component of the product as a communications device. It reinforces associations established in advertising, breaks through competitive clutter at the point of purchase, and justifies price/value to the consumer. Package design relies upon the use of symbolism to support a brand's image and to convey desired information to consumers. A number of package cues are used for this purpose, including color, design, shape, brand name, physical materials, and product information labeling. These cues must interact harmoniously to evoke within buyers the set of meanings intended by the marketing communicator. Package designs can be evaluated by applying the VIEW model, which contains the elements of visibility, informativeness, emotionality, and workability. A concluding section describes a five-step process for package design.

The last major section in the chapter is devoted to point-of-purchase advertising. The point of purchase is an ideal time to communicate with consumers. Accordingly, anything that a consumer is exposed to at the point of purchase can perform an important communications function. A variety of P-O-P materials—signs, displays, and various in-store media—are used to attract consumers' attention to particular products and brands, provide information, affect perceptions, and ultimately influence shopping behavior. P-O-P displays, which are distinguished broadly as either temporary or permanent, perform a variety of useful functions for manufacturers, retailers, and consumers.

Research has documented the high incidence of consumers' in-store purchase decision making and the corresponding importance of P-O-P materials in these purchase decisions. The 1995 Point-of-Purchase Advertising Institute (POPAI) Consumer Buying Habits Study classified all consumer purchases into four categories: specifically planned, generally planned, substitutes, and unplanned decisions. The combination of the last three categories represent in-store decisions that are influenced by P-O-P displays and other store cues. In-store decisions represent 70 percent of supermarket purchase decisions and 74 percent of the decisions in mass merchandise stores. Research on the effectiveness of displays—such as the joint undertaking by POPAI, Kmart, and Procter & Gamble—provides evidence that displayed brands sometimes enjoy gigantic, triple-digit increases in sales volume during the display period.

Discussion Questions

1. Assume you operate a company that creates brand names by using a morpheme, or combination of morphemes, that best captures the primary selling feature a client wishes to convey with its new product. Your first client is a company that plans to go into business to compete against Dunkin Donuts. However, the company's unique advantage is that its donuts are made with a fat substitute and hence are fat-free. The client wants a name for its future donut shops to convey that its donuts are fat-free but tasty. Create two names you consider appropriate and justify the logic underlying each.

2. Select a product category of personal interest and analyze the brand names for three competitive brands in that category. Analyze each brand name in terms of the fundamental requirements that

were described in the text. Order the three brands according to which has the best, next best, and worst brand name. Support your ranking with specific reasons.

3. As reported in an issue of *The Wall Street Journal Interactive Edition* (July 8, 1997), two Atlanta entrepreneurs started a retail personal computer business named StupidPC. They arrived at that name during a give-and-take session in which they exchanged possible names for their proposed store. After a period of labeling each other's ideas as "stupid," one of the men suggested that they might as well call their store StupidPC. The name stuck. What are your thoughts on this name? What are its pros and cons? Be specific.

4. According to an article in *The Wall Street Journal Interactive Edition* (June 1, 1998), a Boston diamond wholesaler developed a special way for cutting diamonds that gives diamonds perfect symmetry and extra sparkle. The wholesaler developed a viewing device (called the "proportion scope") that allows consumers to see a diamond with eight perfect hearts and eight arrows when they peer through the scope. The inventor of this specially cut diamond gave his gems the brand name "Hearts on Fire." Evaluate this name by applying concepts from the chapter. Propose an alternative name.

5. Sports utility vehicles (SUVs) have names such as the Ford Explorer, Chevy Blazer, Mercury Mountaineer, Lincoln Navigator, Subaru Outback, Mazda Navajo, Infinity QX-4, Honda Passport, Jeep Wrangler, Dodge Dakota, Olds Bravada, and so on. On January 28, 1999, the Ford Motor Company purchased the Volvo Motor Company of Sweden. Assume that Ford executives decide to add an upscale Volvo SUV to their expanded product line. What would you name this new vehicle? What is your rationale for this name?

6. One job of packaging is to "drive associations established in advertising into the consumer's mind." Discuss specifically what this means, using several marketplace illustrations to support your explanation.

7. What is sensation transference? Provide two specific examples to support your answer.

8. In your opinion, why do so many marketers use the words new and improved on their product packages? Justify why you think this usage is effective or ineffective.

9. Can you identify any brands that avail themselves of the "power" of the encoding specificity principle with their packaging? (Next time you go to the supermarket, cruise the aisles to identify examples of packages that use advertising slogans or symbols on their packages.)

10. Select a packaged-goods product category, and apply the VIEW model to three competitive brands within that category. Define all four components of the model, and explain how each applies to your selected product. Then use the following procedures to weigh each component in the model in terms of your perception of its relative packaging importance in your chosen product category:
    a. Distribute 10 points among the four components, with more points signifying more importance and the sum of the allocated points totaling exactly 10. (This weighting procedure involves what marketing researchers refer to as a constant sum scale.)
    b. Next, evaluate each brand in terms of your perception of its performance on each packaging component by assigning a score from 1 (does not perform well) to 10 (performs extremely well). Thus, you will assign a total of 12 scores: four for each VIEW component for the three different brands.
    c. Combine the scores for each brand by multiplying the brand's performance on each component by the weight of that component (from step a) and then summing the products of these four weighted scores.

       The summed score for each of your three chosen brands will reflect your perception of how good that brand's packaging is in terms of the VIEW model—the higher the score, the better the packaging in your opinion. Summarize the scores for the three brands for an overall assessment of each brand's packaging.

11. What functions can point-of-purchase materials accomplish that mass-media advertising cannot?

12. Explain why the 1995 POPAI Consumer Buying Habits Study probably overestimates the percentage of unplanned purchases and underestimates the percentage of specifically planned and generally planned purchases.

13. Although not presented in the chapter, the 1995 POPAI Consumer Buying Habits Study revealed that the percentage of in-store decisions for coffee was 57.9 percent, whereas the comparable percentage for salsa, picante sauce, and dips was 88.1 percent. What accounts for the 30.2 percent difference in in-store decision making for these two products? Go beyond these two product categories and offer a generalization as to what product categories likely have high and low proportions of in-store decision making.

14. The 1995 POPAI Consumer Buying Habits Study also revealed that the highest average brand lift index from signage (rather than displays) in mass merchandise stores was dishwashing soaps, with an index of 21.65. Provide an exact interpretation of this index value.

15. The discussion of the S. B. Thomas' English muffin study pointed out that in stores using motion displays, sales increased by 473 percent. By comparison, sales of Eveready batteries, when promoted with motion displays, increased anywhere from 3.7 percent to 15.7 percent, depending on the type of store in which the display was placed. Provide an explanation that accounts for the tremendous disparity in sales impact of motion displays for English muffins compared to batteries.

16. Why were motion and static displays considerably more effective at increasing Olympia beer sales in liquor stores than in supermarkets?

Internet Exercise

Consider the following press release:

"Peapod, Inc. (www.peapod.com) is the leading Internet supermarket, providing consumers with broad product choices and local delivery services. The Company currently provides such services in seven metropolitan markets in the United States and serves over 98,000 customers. Peapod also is a leading provider of targeted media and research services to consumer goods companies, offering its unique medium for targeting promotions and advertising at the point of purchase and conducting cost-effective research."

Visit Peapod and select the "Test Drive" option to sample their services. This "Test Drive" will only activate if you provide a zip code from one of the serviced metropolitan markets. You can find an appropriate zip code at www.zipaddress.com. Browse the store for several different products, perhaps including some that you regularly purchase and others that you buy infrequently.

a.   Are the initial product options presented by brand names alone, brand names and logos, or brand names and package images? Compare your response to the initial product options for your frequently versus infrequently purchased items.

b.   Do you think there are differences in the roles of brand name and packaging for consumers shopping at online stores versus regular stores? Explain.

c.   Describe the "Personal Lists" and "Previous Orders" options on the Peapod shopping screens. Discuss the implications of these options for in-store purchase decision making.

d.   Is there any form of POP advertising at the Peapod site? Compare any such advertising to that in a regular store.

Chapter Eight Endnotes

1.   For a thorough discussion of the technical and legal aspects of trademarks, see Dorothy Cohen, "Trademark Strategy Revisited," *Journal of Marketing* 55 (July 1991), 46–59.

2.   Mark Landler and Zachary Schiller, "What's in a Name: Less and Less," *Business Week,* July 8, 1991, 66–67.

3.   Chiranjeev Kohli and Douglas W. LaBahn, "Observations: Creating Effective Brand Names: A Study of the Naming Process," *Journal of Advertising Research* 37 (January/February 1997), 67–75.

4.   Rob Osler, "The Name Game: Tips on How to Get It Right," *Marketing News,* September 14, 1998, 50.

5.   Kevin Lane Keller, "Conceptualizing, Measuring, and Managing Customer-Based Brand Equity," *Journal of Marketing* 57 (January 1993), 9.

6. Joseph W. Alba, J. Wesley Hutchinson, and John G. Lynch, "Memory and Decision Making," in *Handbook of Consumer Behavior*, ed. Thomas S. Robertson and Harold H. Kassarjian (Englewood Cliffs, NJ: Prentice-Hall, 1991), 1–49.

7. France Leclerc, Bernd H. Schmitt, and Laurette Dubé, "Foreign Branding and Its Effects on Product Perceptions and Attitudes," *Journal of Marketing Research* 31 (March 1994), 263–270.

8. Moran, "Packaging Can Lend Prestige," 59.

9. Mary W. Sullivan, "How Brand Names Affect the Demand for Twin Automobiles," *Journal of Marketing Research* 35 (May 1998), 154–165.

10. David A. Aaker, *Managing Brand Equity* (New York: The Free Press, 1991); Kevin Lane Keller and David A. Aaker, "The Effects of Sequential Introduction of Brand Extensions," *Journal of Marketing Research* 29 (February 1992), 35–50.

11. Landler and Schiller, "What's in a Name: Less and Less," 67.

12. Graham Phillips, "The Role of Advertising—Or, the Importance of a Strong Brand Franchise," from a talk in 1986 to senior U.S. marketing executives under the auspices of The Conference Board.

13. These requirements represent a summary of views from a variety of sources, including Kevin Lane Keller, *Strategic Brand Management: Building, Measuring, and Managing Brand Equity* (Upper Saddle River, NJ: Prentice-Hall, 1998), 136–140; Daniel L. Doden, "Selecting a Brand Name That Aids Marketing Objectives," *Advertising Age*, November 5, 1990, 34; and Walter P. Margulies, "Animal Names on Products May Be Corny, but Boost Consumer Appeal," *Advertising Age*, October 23, 1972, 78.

14. For further discussion, see Jeffrey M. Samuels and Linda B. Samuels, "Famous Marks Now Federally Protected Against Dilution," *Journal of Public Policy & Marketing* 15 (fall 1996), 307–310.

15. Marcus W. Brauchli, "Chinese Flagrantly Copy Trademarks of Foreigners," *The Wall Street Journal*, June 20, 1994, B1, B2.

16. Doden, "Selecting a Brand Name That Aids Marketing Objectives."

17. Kevin Lane Keller, Susan E. Heckler, and Michael J. Houston, "The Effects of Brand Name Suggestiveness on Advertising Recall," *Journal of Marketing* 62 (January 1998), 48–57. See also J. Colleen McCracken and M. Carole Macklin, "The Role of Brand Names and Visual Clues in Enhancing Memory for Consumer Packaged Goods," *Marketing Letters* 9 (April 1998), 209–226.

18. Elaine Underwood, "Levi's New Dress Code," *Brandweek*, August 19, 1996, 26.

19. Kohli and LaBahn, "Observations: Creating Effective Brand Names," 69.

20. Ibid.

21. Ibid., 71.

22. Ibid., 72.

23. Ibid., 73.

24. Osler, "The Name Game."

25. Pamela W. Henderson and Joseph A. Cote, "Guidelines for Selecting or Modifying Logos,"

Journal of Marketing 62 (April 1998), 14–30. This article is must reading for anyone interested in learning more about logos.

26. Ibid., 15.

27. Ian P. Murphy, "All-American Icon Gets a New Look," *Marketing News*, August 18, 1997, 6.

28. Ibid.

29. Michael Gershman, "Packaging: Positioning Tool of the 1980s," *Management Review*, August 1987, 33–41.

30. Peter R. Dickson and Alan G. Sawyer, "The Price Knowledge and Search of Supermarket Shoppers," *Journal of Marketing* 54 (July 1990), 42–53; John Le Boutillier, Susanna Shore Le Boutillier, and Scott A. Neslin, "A Replication and Extension of the Dickson and Sawyer Price-Awareness Study," *Marketing Letters* 5 (January 1994), 31–42.

31. John Deighton, "A White Paper on the Packaging Industry," Dennison Technical Papers, December 1983, 5.

32. An interesting article about package meaning is available in Robert L. Underwood and Julie L. Ozanne, "Is Your Package an Effective Communicator? A Normative Framework for Increasing the Communicative Competence of Packaging," *Journal of Marketing Communications* 4 (December 1998), 207–220.

33. Herbert M. Meyers and Murray J. Lubliner, *The Marketer's Guide to Successful Package Design* (Chicago: NTC Business Books, 1998), 2.

34. Gail Tom, Teresa Barnett, William Lew, and Jodean Selmants, "Cueing the Consumer: The Role of Salient Cues in Consumer Perception," *The Journal of Consumer Marketing* 4 (spring 1987), 23–27.

35. This comment and parts of the following discussion are based on statements appearing in Joseph A. Bellizzi, Ayn E. Crowley, and Ronald W. Hasty, "The Effects of Color in Store Design," *Journal of Retailing* 59 (spring 1983), 21–45. Many of the brand name examples in this section were suggested in "Color Is Prime 'Silent Communicator,'" *Marketing News*, April 25, 1986, 15.

36. "Frito Bets 'Reduced' Pitch Is in the Chips," *Brandweek*, January 23, 1995, 18.

37. Dennis J. Moran, "Packaging Can Lend Prestige to Products," *Advertising Age*, January 7, 1980, 59–60.

38. Brian Wansink, "Can Package Size Accelerate Usage Volume?" *Journal of Marketing* 60 (July 1996), 1–14.

39. Kevin Higgins, "Foil's Glitter Attracts Manufacturers Who Want Upscale Buyers," *Marketing News*, February 3, 1984, 1.

40. William H. Motes and Arch G. Woodside, "Field Test of Package Advertising Effects on Brand Choice Behavior," *Journal of Advertising Research* 24 (February/March 1984), 39–45.

41. Edward H. Asam and Louis P. Bucklin, "Nutrition Labeling for Canned Goods: A Study of Consumer Response," *Journal of Marketing* 37 (April 1973), 36–37.

42. "Packaging Plays Starring Role in TV Commercials," *Marketing News*, January 30, 1987, 6.

43. Dik Warren Twedt, "How Much Value Can Be Added through Packaging," *Journal of Marketing* 32 (January 1968), 61–65.

44. Patricia Winters, "Rapt Up in Packages," *Advertising Age,* December 3, 1990, 4.

45. Kerry J. Smith and Daniel Shannon, "Let Your Package Do the Talking," *Promo,* February 1995, 29–32.

46. James Steinberg, "Controversial Products Helped by Packaging," *Brandweek,* January 26, 1998, 20.

47. "Packaging 2000," *Brandweek,* October 16, 1995, 40.

48. Terry Lefton, "Whole New Card Game," *Brandweek,* April 28, 1997, 18.

49. This discussion is adapted from Meyers and Lubliner, *The Marketer's Guide to Successful Package Design,* 55–67.

50. Dickson and Sawyer, "The Price Knowledge and Search of Supermarket Shoppers"; Le Boutillier, Le Boutillier, and Neslin, "A Replication and Extension of the Dickson and Sawyer Price-Awareness Study."

51. Meyers and Lubliner, *The Marketer's Guide to Successful Package Design,* 63.

52. John A. Quelch and Kristina Cannon-Bonventre, "Better Marketing at the Point-of-Purchase," *Harvard Business Review* (November/December 1983), 162–169.

53. "Impact in the Aisles: The Marketer's Last Best Chance," *Promo,* January 1996, 25.

54. POPAI's First Annual P-O-P Buyers Survey (Englewood, N.J.: Point-of-Purchase Advertising Institute, 1993), 1.

55. These examples are drawn from the Point-of-Purchase Design Annual, The 40th Merchandising Awards (New York: Point-of-Purchase Advertising Institute, 1998).

56. Ibid.

57. "P-O-P Gains, But Girds for Tobacco Withdrawal," *Promo* (The 1998 Annual Report of the Promotion Industry), July 1998, S9.

58. "A.C. Nielsen Research Reveals Cheese Sales Skyrocket with In-Store Promotions," *POPAI News,* Marketplace 1990, 19.

59. Doug Leeds, "Accountability Is In-Store for Marketers in '94," *Brandweek,* March 14, 1994, 17.

60. The Effect of Motion Displays on the Sales of Beer; The Effect of Motion Displays on Sales of Baked Goods; The Effect of Motion Displays on Sales of Batteries (Englewood, N.J.: Point-of-Purchase Advertising Institute, undated).

61. Margaret W. Matlin, *Cognition* (New York: Holt, Rinehart & Winston, Inc., 1989), 109.

62. Adapted from "Marketing Textbook: Clairol's Haircoloring Information Center," *POPAI News,* 1983, 3.

63. "The L'eggs Egg Goes Interactive," *POPAI News,* March/April 1990, 28.

64. "Interactive Unit Is Pet Project for Dog and Cat Food Marketer," *POPAI News,* June/July 1991, 9.

65. "Kelly-Springfield Electronic Performance Tire Fitment Center," *POPAI News,* Marketplace 1991, 35.

66. "Interactive Kiosks Dispense Wine Information," *Promo,* October 1993, 84.

67. This description is based on trade literature from Intermark Corporation, the developers of Procter & Gamble's Pantene merchandising center (1985).

68. *Measuring the In-Store Decision Making of Supermarket and Mass Merchandise Store Shoppers* (Englewood, N.J.: Point-of-Purchase Advertising Institute, 1995).

69. This and all following details are according to the 1995 Point-of-Purchase (POPAI) Consumer Buying Habits Study, ibid.

70. Ibid., 23.

71. POPAI/Kmart/Procter & Gamble Study of P-O-P Effectiveness in Mass Merchandising Stores (Englewood, N.J.: Point-of-Purchase Advertising Institute, 1993).

72. This study is in adherence with POPAI's guidelines for appropriate sales-effectiveness research. See POPAI's *Association of In-Store Marketing Guidebook to Research Methodologies for the In-Store Marketing Industry* (Englewood, N.J.: Point-of-Purchase Advertising Institute, 1993), 4.

73. POPAI/Warner-Lambert Canada P-O-P Effectiveness Study (Englewood, N.J.: The Point-of-Purchase Advertising Institute, 1992).

74. John P. Murry, Jr. and Jan B. Heide (1998), "Managing Promotion Program Participation within Manufacturer-Retailer Relationships," *Journal of Marketing* 62 (January 1998), 58. POPAI/Progressive Grocer Supermarket Retailer Attitude Study (Englewood, N.J.: Point-of-Purchase Advertising Institute, 1994), 2.

75. Don E. Schultz and William A. Robinson, *Sales Promotion Management* (Lincolnwood, Ill.: NTC Business Books, 1982), 279.

76. Adapted from Schultz and Robinson, *Sales Promotion Management,* 278–279. For further insights on gaining retailer participation in P-O-P programs, see Murry, Jr. and Heide (1998), "Managing Promotion Program Participation within Manufacturer-Retailer Relationships."

PART
FOUR
Advertising Management •
Packaging and Branding
Demographic, Psychographic, and
Strategy • Supportive Marketing Communications Tools •
Management and Integrated Marke
The Concept

Part Four—Advertising Management

Part Four contains seven advertising chapters. Chapter 9 overviews the advertising management process and provides detailed discussions of advertising objective setting and budgeting.

Chapter 10 provides a detailed study of the creative-strategy aspect of the advertising management process. Topics include requirements for effective advertising messages, advertising planning, means-end chains and MECCAS models, creative message strategies, and corporate image/issue advertising.

Chapter 11 expands the coverage of advertising message creation by examining the advertising endorsers and the various message appeals employed in advertisements. Endorser characteristics and selection receive initial discussion. Coverage then turns to specific message appeals, including fear appeals, humor, sex, subliminal messages, and comparative advertisements.

Chapter 12 provides an analysis of advertising media. The chapter devotes primary attention to evaluating the characteristics and strengths and weaknesses of five major advertising media: out-of-home, newspapers, magazines, radio, and television. Chapter 12 also explores interactive advertising media (including Internet advertising) and alternative advertising media (Yellow Pages, video advertising, and product placements in movies).

Chapter 13 focuses exclusively on direct advertising and database marketing, which represent a growing form of advertising. Direct-mail advertising, catalog marketing, telephone marketing, and the role of databases are the topics examined in this chapter.

Chapter 14 provides thorough discussions of the four major activities involved in media strategy: target audience selection, objective specification, media and vehicle selection, and media-buying activities. In-depth discussion focuses on media selection considerations such as reach, frequency, gross ratings points, effective rating points, and the efficiency-index procedure. Also explored are advertising timing considerations (pulsed, flighted, and continuous schedules), the shelf-space model of media selection, and cost-per-thousand (CPM) computations.

The last chapter in Part Four, Chapter 15, examines the measurement of advertising effectiveness. The chapter describes media- and message-based research methods. Media-based research methods include audience measurement for magazines (MRI and SMRB), radio (Arbitron), and television (Nielsen). Message-based research methods are discussed under five general categories of measures: (1) recognition and recall (Starch, Bruzzone Tests, and Burke Day-After Recall); (2) emotions (Warmth Monitor, TRACE, and BBDO's Emotional Measurement System); (3) physiological arousal (galvanometer, pupillometer, and voice- pitch analysis); (4) persuasion (ASI theater testing and ARS persuasion testing); and (5) sales response (IRI's BehaviorScan and Nielsen's SCANTRACK).

Overview of Advertising Management

CHAPTER OBJECTIVES

After studying this chapter, you should be able to:

1. Explain why advertising is an investment in the brand equity bank.
2. Describe the functions of advertising.
3. Understand the role for advertisement objectives and the requirements for setting good objectives.
4. Describe the hierarchy-of-effects model and its relevance for setting advertising objectives.
5. Explain the distinction between direct and indirect advertising objectives.
6. Understand the role of sales as an advertising objective and the logic of "vaguely right versus precisely wrong" thinking.
7. Understand the nature and importance of advertising budgeting.
8. Explain the relation between a brand's share of market (SOM) and share of voice (SOV).
9. Explain the various rules of thumb, or heuristics, that guide practical advertising budgeting.

Opening Vignette: With Soaring Sales, Why Advertise?

Viagra, the male anti-impotence pill introduced in 1998, was one of the most successful prescription drugs ever. The months following introduction witnessed Viagra as the source of fun and pun on late-night talk shows, in cocktail-party chatter, and in jokes shared among employees at work. Believers in Viagra's effectiveness spoke glowingly of Viagra's wonders. With all this free publicity that Viagra received following its introduction, it might seem that to invest in advertising on Viagra would have been a "waste" of money.

But this is not how executives at Pfizer, the pharmaceutical company that introduced Viagra, looked at the situation. Indeed, in addition to millions of dollars invested in advertising to physicians, more than $60 million was spent on advertising aimed at consumers. A spokesperson for Pfizer commented, in response to the "why advertise" question, that "there is a risk in not advertising." The risk to which he refers is twofold: One form is the risk that consumers will use Viagra along with other drugs that they shouldn't, which could cause death due to a fatal interaction of the drugs. A second form of risk is the competitive challenge from other pharmaceutical companies that will inevitably introduce their own products to compete against Viagra.

Pfizer's decision to advertise Viagra heavily was supported by professionals from medical advertising agencies, who shared the following reactions to Pfizer's advertising decision:

♦ Penny Hawkey, executive creative director at Medicus Communications, said, "You can never do enough to gain top-of-mind [awareness]. You need to get there

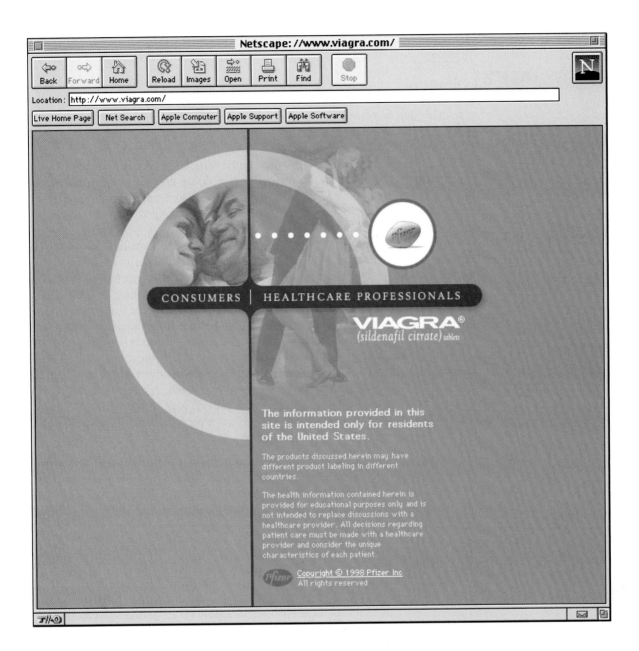

and stay there. You have to claim the hill so whoever is coming in behind you doesn't have a shot. The faster the better."

◆ Ed Rady, president of Medicus Medical Education, commented: "If I were them [Pfizer], I would try to capture as big a share of this market as possible before others come."

◆ Jerry Lee, managing director of HMC Advertising & Marketing, an ad agency that specializes in drug advertising, proffered that a brand has to control its own image. "If you don't create your own brand image, other people will take it and control it for you, and you can't let that happen."

These professionals fully understand and appreciate the value of advertising. They understand the importance of gaining momentum. They know that a successful brand remains successful only by protecting itself from the inroads of competitors. They know that, like Viagra itself, advertising is an "anti-impotence" mechanism—it can be used effectively to build on existing brand strength and to protect against declining strength in the marketplace.

Source: Adapted from Sally Goll Beatty, "Just What Goes in a Viagra Ad? Early Reports Say Dancing Couples," *The Wall Street Journal Interactive Edition,* June 17, 1998.

Overview

*A*dvertising is costly, often its effects are uncertain, and sometimes it takes a while before it has any impact on customers' buying behavior. It is for these reasons that many companies think it appropriate occasionally to reduce expenditures on advertising or to eliminate advertising entirely. Companies find it particularly seductive to pull funds out of advertising during economic downturns—every dollar not spent on advertising is one more dollar added to the bottom line. And companies sometimes consider it unnecessary to advertise when their brands, such as Viagra in the *Opening Vignette*, already are enjoying great success without advertising.

Such behavior implicitly fails to consider the fact that advertising is not just a current expense (as the term is used in accounting parlance) but rather is an *investment*. Although businesspeople fully appreciate the fact that building a new, more efficient production facility or purchasing a new computer system are investments in their companies' futures, many of these same people often think advertising is an expense that can be reduced or even eliminated when financial pressures call for cost-cutting measures.

However, Procter and Gamble—the world's largest advertiser with global advertising spending exceeding $2.5 billion—is one company that fully appreciates advertising's investment role. P&G's ex-CEO, Edwin L. Artzt, considers advertising a long-term investment that shouldn't be intruded upon by short-term needs. Artzt aptly draws an analogy between advertising and exercise in that both provide long-term benefits. Moreover, like exercise, it is easy to stop advertising or postpone it because there is no immediate penalty for the interruption. Here is what Artzt has to say about the value of advertising.

> *If you want your brand to be fit, it's got to exercise regularly. When you get the opportunity to go to the movies or do something else instead of working out, you can do that once in a while—that's [equivalent to] shifting funds into [sales] promotion. But it's not a good thing to do. If you get off the regimen, you will pay for it later.*[1]

www.bah.com

www.kelloggs.com

www.generalmills.com

This viewpoint is captured further in the advice of a vice president at Booz, Allen & Hamilton, a major marketing consultant, when asked what great companies such as Procter & Gamble, Kellogg, General Mills, Coca-Cola, and Pepsi-Cola have in common. All of these companies, in his opinion, are aware that *consistent investment spending* is the key factor underlying successful advertising. "They do not raid their budgets to ratchet earnings up for a few quarters. They know that advertising should not be managed as a discretionary variable cost."[2] This point should remind you of our discussion back in Chapter 2 where we discussed the importance of *momentum*. Advertising momentum is like exercise. Stop exercising, and you will lose conditioning and probably gain weight. Stop advertising, and your brand likely will lose some of its equity and market share as well.

Investment in the Brand Equity Bank

As established in Chapter 1, the objective of marketing communications is to enhance the equity in a firm's brands. You will recall that a brand's equity is enhanced by marketing communications that create brand awareness and forge favorable, strong, and perhaps unique associations in the consumer's memory between the brand and its features and benefits.[3] When advertising and other forms of marketing communications create unique and positive messages, a brand becomes differentiated from competitive offerings and is relatively insulated from future price competition.[4]

One advertising professional has claimed that "strong advertising represents a deposit in the brand equity bank."[5] This clever expression nicely captures the advertising challenge. It also correctly notes that not all advertising represents a deposit in the brand equity bank, only advertising that is *strong*—that is, different, unique, clever, memorable, and the like.

This chapter, the first of seven chapters devoted to advertising, first overviews the general advertising management process and then focuses on two advertising management tasks: establishing advertising objectives and setting advertising budgets. The objective in this and subsequent chapters is to demonstrate how advertising can be effectively managed to enhance brand equity.

The Magnitude of Advertising

Advertising is big business, to say the very least. Ad expenditures in the United States alone totaled approximately $200 billion in 1998.[6] This amounts to over $700 in advertising for each of the nearly 270 million men, women, and children in the United States as of 1998. Advertising spending is also considerable in other major industrialized countries, but not nearly to the same magnitude as in the United States.

www.pathfinder.com

www.sears.com

Some American companies invest over $1 billion a year on domestic advertising. In 1996, for example, Procter & Gamble spent $2.6 billion; General Motors, $2.4 billion; Philip Morris, $2.3 billion; Time Warner, $1.4 billion; and Sears, Roebuck & Co., $1.3 billion.[7] Table 9.1 lists the top 100 brands in U.S. advertising expenditures for 1997. Even the U.S. government advertised to the tune of over $670 million.[8] The government's advertising goes to such efforts as drug control, military recruiting, the Postal Service, Amtrak rail services, and anti-smoking campaigns.[9]

Advertising Functions

These massive investments suggest that many firms have faith in the effectiveness of advertising. In general, advertising is valued because it is recognized as performing a variety of critical communications functions for the business firms and other organizations: (1) informing, (2) persuading, (3) reminding, (4) adding value, and (5) assisting other company efforts.[10]

Informing.   Advertising makes consumers *aware* of new brands, *educates* them about brand features and benefits, and facilitates the creation of positive *brand images*. Because advertising is an efficient form of communication, capable of reaching mass audiences at a relatively low cost per contact, it facilitates the introduction of new brands and increases demand for existing brands, largely by increasing consumers' *top of mind awareness* (*TOMA*) for established brands in mature product categories.[11] Advertising performs another valuable information role—both for the advertised brand and the consumer—by teaching *new uses* for existing brands. This practice, termed *usage expansion advertising,* is typified by the following illustrations:[12]

- Campbell's soup, which is typically eaten for lunch and during other informal eating occasions, was advertised as being suitable for eating during formal family dinners or even at breakfast.
- Gatorade, which originally was used during heavy athletic activity, was advertised for use to replenish liquids during flu attacks.
- Special K, a breakfast cereal, was advertised for afternoon or late-night snacking.

Top 100 Advertisers in 1997

RANK	BRAND	TOTAL MEASURED ADVERTISING (IN MILLIONS)
1	Sears stores	$664.6
2	Chevrolet Cars and Trucks	656.3
3	McDonald's restaurants	580.5
4	Ford cars and trucks	569.9
5	Dodge cars and trucks	551.8
6	AT&T telephone services	475.9
7	Toyota cars and trucks	453.8
8	MCI telephone services	435.0
9	Burger King restaurants	427.0
10	Circuit City stores	400.1
11	Nissan cars and trucks	347.0
12	Kellogg's breakfast foods	340.3
13	Honda cars and trucks	335.6
14	Macy's stores	315.3
15	American Express credit cards	314.6
16	JC Penney stores	311.0
17	Chrysler cars and trucks	301.3
18	Sprint telephone services	288.8
19	General Motors cars, trucks & financial services	279.3
20	General Mills cereals	271.1
21	Tylenol remedies	253.6
22	Buick cars	252.9
23	Jeep vehicles	250.4
24	Cadillac cars	247.6
25	Visa credit cards	242.0
26	Miller beers	236.2
27	Kmart stores	233.5
28	Mazda cars and trucks	232.2
29	Pontiac cars and trucks	229.5
30	Oldsmobile cars and trucks	228.6
31	Saturn cars	215.8
32	Nike shoes	207.2
33	Budweiser beers	207.0
34	IBM computers	202.5
35	Target stores	193.4
36	Microsoft software	193.2
37	Kraft foods	189.5
38	Home Depot stores	188.7
39	Taco Bell restaurants	188.2
40	Bell Atlantic telephone services	185.0
41	Plymouth cars, trucks and vans	177.7
42	Wendy's restaurants	172.2
43	L'Oreal haircare & cosmetics	171.5
44	Best Buy stores	169.2
45	Wal-Mart stores	168.9
46	KFC restaurants	168.5
47	Mercury cars	161.2
48	Coke & Diet Coke beverages	159.8
49	Montgomery Ward stores	155.5
50	Dillard's stores	154.5

Top 100 Advertisers in 1997 *(continued)*

RANK	BRAND	TOTAL MEASURED ADVERTISING (IN MILLIONS)
51	Pizza Hut restaurants	$147.2
52	Radio Shack electronics stores	145.8
54	Mattel toys	140.9
55	Lexus cars and trucks	138.5
56	BellSouth telephone services	135.1
57	Lincoln cars	134.3
58	Pepsi & Diet Pepsi beverages	129.8
59	Mitsubishi cars and trucks	129.3
60	U.S. Postal Service	129.0
61	Prudential financial services	129.0
62	Kodak photo equipment	128.7
63	Coors beers	126.0
64	Clairol haircare products	125.2
65	Wrigley's gums	123.4
66	Domino's Pizza	122.6
67	Phillips Magnavox electronics	122.0
68	Post cereals	121.3
69	Hewlett-Packard computer equipment	117.7
70	Campbell's soups	115.1
71	Marlboro cigarettes	114.5
72	Advil remedies	113.1
73	HBO cable TV	112.1
74	Boston Market restaurants	111.6
75	Blockbuster entertainment	111.2
76	Canon optical & business machines	109.7
77	MasterCard credit cards	109.3
78	Hyundai cars	108.3
79	Volkswagen cars	106.6
80	Compaq computers	106.6
81	U.S. dairy products	106.4
82	Disney entertainment	106.1
83	Infiniti cars and trucks	105.7
84	GTE telephone services	105.4
85	Franklin Mint collectibles	105.3
86	Quaker cereals & foods	102.6
87	Walgreens drug stores	102.3
88	Mercedes-Benz cars and trucks	101.6
89	Southwest Airlines	101.3
90	Crest dental care	101.2
91	Acura cars	100.6
92	Gateway computers	99.6
93	Revlon cosmetics	98.7
94	Ameritech telephone services	96.6
95	Charles Schwab financial services	94.8
96	Hallmark cards	91.7
97	Cover Girl cosmetics	91.4
98	Isuzu cars and trucks	91.3
99	Fidelity financial services	90.2
100	Mervyn's stores	90.2

Source: R. Craig Endicott, "Top 100 Megabrands," *Advertising Age,* July 13, 1998, S1–S13.

www.gillette.com

Persuading. Effective advertising persuades customers to try advertised products and services. Sometimes the persuasion takes the form of influencing *primary demand*—that is, creating demand for an entire product category. More frequently, advertising attempts to build *secondary demand,* the demand for a specific company's brand. Consider Gillette's introduction of the Mach3 razor in 1998. Gillette invested nearly three-quarters of a billion dollars to develop the Mach3, and corporate success (including maintaining a very attractive stock price) demanded huge sales volume in order to garner a good return on the investment in Mach3. Gillette executives knew they would have to advertise heavily to convince consumers that the Mach3 was worth its relatively high price. Accordingly, plans were made to spend $300 million on global advertising.[13] The Mach3 may turn out to be less successful than intended, but the advertising support Gillette executives put behind the brand gave it every opportunity to succeed.

Reminding. Advertising keeps a company's brand fresh in the consumer's memory, as typified in the *Opening Vignette* that described the anti-impotence pill, Viagra. When a need arises that is related to the advertised product, past advertising impact makes it possible for the advertiser's brand to come to the consumer's mind as a purchase candidate. Effective advertising also increases the consumer's interest in a mature brand and thus the likelihood of purchasing a brand that otherwise might not be chosen.[14] Advertising, furthermore, has been demonstrated to influence *brand switching* by reminding consumers who have not recently purchased a brand that the brand is available and that it possesses favorable attributes.[15]

Adding Value. There are three basic ways by which companies can add value to their offerings: innovating, improving quality, or altering consumer perceptions. These three value-added components are completely interdependent.

> *Innovation without quality is mere novelty. Consumer perception without quality and/or innovation is mere puffery. And both innovation and quality, if not translated into consumer perceptions, are like the sound of the proverbial tree falling in the empty forest.*[16]

Advertising adds value to brands by influencing consumers' *perceptions.* Effective advertising causes brands to be viewed as more elegant, more stylish, more prestigious, and perhaps superior to competitive offerings. Effective advertising, then, can lead to increased market share and greater profitability.[17] It is little wonder why the world's largest advertiser, Procter & Gamble, fully appreciates advertising's value-added role and considers it "an investment in the brand-equity bank."

Assisting Other Company Efforts. Advertising is just one member of the marketing communications team. Advertising is at times a scorer that accomplishes goals by itself. At other times advertising's primary role is as an assister that facilitates other company efforts in the marketing communications process. For example, advertising may be used as a vehicle for delivering sales promotions such as coupons and sweepstakes and attracting attention to these sales promotion tools.

Another crucial role of advertising is to assist sales representatives. Advertising presells a company's products and provides salespeople with valuable introductions prior to their personal contact with prospective customers. Sales effort, time, and costs are reduced because less time is required to inform prospects about product features and benefits. Moreover, advertising legitimizes or makes more credible the sales representative's claims.[18]

Advertising also enhances the results of other marketing communications. For example, consumers can identify product packages in the store and recognize the value of a product more easily after seeing it advertised on television or in a magazine. Advertising also can augment the effectiveness of price deals. One study found that customers were more responsive to retailers' price deals when retailers advertised that fact compared to when retailers offered a deal but did not advertise it.[19]

Although the discussion has made it clear that advertising is an extremely important business function, perhaps especially in the United States, it is pertinent to note that advertising's importance varies from country to country. This variance is not just in terms of advertising expenditures, but also in terms of consumer perceptions of advertising. The *Global Focus* presents some interesting information in this regard.

THE ADVERTISING MANAGEMENT PROCESS

www.jwtworld.com

www.dyr.com

A completed advertisement, such as a television commercial or a magazine ad, results from the collective efforts of various participants. Four major groups are involved in the total advertising process: (1) companies and other organizations that advertise—such as Procter & Gamble, McDonald's, the U.S. government, and so on; (2) advertising agencies—such as Ogilvy and Mather, J. Walter Thompson, and Tokyo-based Dentsu—that are responsible for creating and placing ads for their clients; (3) advertising production companies—that is, independent businesses that photograph, film, and otherwise produce advertisements; and (4) advertising media—including newspapers, television, and so on.

Although the advertising industry involves a number of collective efforts, the following discussion is restricted to the first group, the advertisers themselves. The discussion of the advertising-management process is based on the framework in Figure 9.1, which consists of advertising strategy formulation, strategy implementation, and efforts to assess advertising effectiveness.

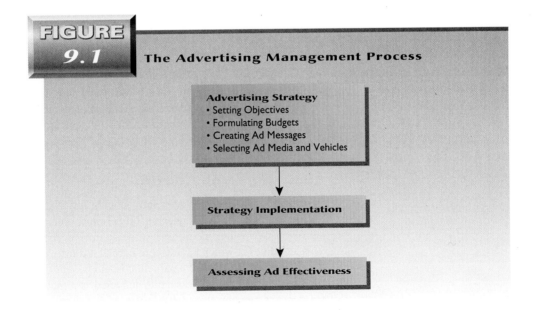

FIGURE 9.1   **The Advertising Management Process**

Advertising Strategy
• Setting Objectives
• Formulating Budgets
• Creating Ad Messages
• Selecting Ad Media and Vehicles

Strategy Implementation

Assessing Ad Effectiveness

GLOBAL FOCUS: THE CASE OF ADVERTISING IN CHINA AND RUSSIA

Lenin, Trotsky, Stalin, and Chairman Mao are probably rolling over in their graves. Businesspeople in the former Soviet Union and in the People's Republic of China are advertising their wares just the way it has been done in the West for generations. This form of product news was unavailable to consumers in these countries for decades, until the recent collapse of the former Soviet Union and the movement in the People's Republic of China toward economic reforms.

To provide a backdrop for the subsequent discussion of Chinese and Russian consumers' attitudes toward advertising, the following list includes responses of people in 20 countries to the statement, "If advertising were banned tomorrow, I would miss it."[a]

COUNTRY	AGREE (PERCENTAGE)	DISAGREE (PERCENTAGE)	COUNTRY	AGREE (PERCENTAGE)	DISAGREE (PERCENTAGE)
Australia	52%	48%	Latvia	36%	51%
Belgium	32	62	Lithuania	43	45
Bulgaria	57	43	Luxembourg	50	49
Denmark	48	50	Netherlands	34	59
Egypt	21	79	New Zealand	51	47
Estonia	49	47	South Africa	68	16
Finland	51	48	Switzerland	41	55
Germany	38	61	Turkey	44	45
Italy	38	59	United Kingdom	43	55
Japan	78	21	Uruguay	71	28

Note: The responses do not always sum to 100 percent due to "I don't know" answers.

Attitudes toward Advertising in China. The amount of advertising in the People's Republic of China has increased dramatically in recent years as economic reforms have swept through that country. Although advertising expenditures in China are trivial by Western standards, the increases are rather dramatic, and Chinese consumers have exhibited great faith in advertising. In fact, it was found to be the preeminent factor consumers in the People's Republic use to identify leading brands. The following table presents ranked responses for six countries, including China, based on reasons that influence consumers' choice of brand leaders.[b]

REASON	CHINA	FRANCE	ITALY	SPAIN	UNITED KINGDOM	UNITED STATES
Advertising	1	6	10	6	7	7
Highest quality	2	3	2	2	3	4
Trust them	3	1	1	1	1	2

(Continued)

Advertising Strategy

Advertising strategy involves four major activities (see Figure 9.1). The first two, objective setting and budgeting, are described later in this chapter. Message strategy is a third aspect that is the subject of Chapters 10 and 11. Media strategy, the topic of Chapters 12, 13, and 14, involves the selection of media categories and specific vehicles to deliver advertising messages.

Strategy Implementation

Strategy implementation deals with the tactical, day-to-day activities that must be performed to carry out an advertising campaign. For example, whereas the decision to emphasize television over other media is a strategic choice, the selection of specific types of programs and times at which to air a commercial is a tactical implementation matter. Likewise, the decision to emphasize a particular brand benefit is a strategic message consideration, but the actual way the message is delivered is a matter of creative implementation. This text focuses more on strategic than tactical issues.

(Continued)

REASON	CHINA	FRANCE	ITALY	SPAIN	UNITED KINGDOM	UNITED STATES
Stand test of time	4	1	3	3	2	1
Best value	5	5	5	4	4	6
Best service	6	4	3	4	6	3
Sells the most	7	7	7	8	8	8
Industry standard	8	8	6	7	4	4
Most innovative	9	9	9	10	9	9
Growing fastest	10	10	8	9	10	10

Note: Reasons with the same number for a particular country indicate tied responses.

Remember that consumers in the People's Republic have had little free choice for decades. Now that increased opportunities are available, consumers in that fledgling economy are somewhat like babies learning to talk—the only way to do it is to copy others. This is precisely what Chinese consumers are doing: They are emulating Western brand preferences and learning about products principally from advertising.[c]

Attitudes toward Advertising in Russia.

www.gallup.com

www.roper.inter.net

A 1994 study by Gallup International found that Russians' attitudes were more positive toward advertising than were the attitudes held by consumers in more economically developed countries.[d] However, just one year later, a 1995 study performed by Roper Starch Worldwide learned that only 9 percent of Russian and Ukrainian respondents believed that advertising provides good information, and only 10 percent of these same respondents thought that it respects consumers' intelligence. These percentages compare with total global results of 38 percent and 30 percent, respectively.[e]

The reasons for the diminished attitudes toward advertising in just one year may simply reflect the state of flux in Russian society, along with consumers' disgruntlement with the economic changes that have yet to deliver the quality-of-life improvements so anticipated. When expectations are not fulfilled, a natural tendency is to lash out at presumed reasons for the failure, and advertising has always been a lightning rod for criticism.[f]

[a]Laurel Wentz, "Major Global Study Finds Consumers Support Ads," *Advertising Age,* October 11, 1993, I1.
[b]Andrew Geddes, "Want to Be a Brand Leader? All You Need Is to Advertise," *Advertising Age,* June 20, 1994, I23.
[c]Ibid.
[d]Steven Gutterman, "Study: Russians Quick to Embrace Ads as Comrades," *Advertising Age,* June 20, 1994, I19.
[e]Leah Rickard, "Ex-Soviet States Lead World in Ad Cynicism," *Advertising Age,* June 5, 1995, 3.
[f]For further reading on consumer responses to advertising in Russia, see J. Craig Andrews, Srinivas Durvasula, and Richard G. Netemeyer, "Testing the Cross-National Applicability of U.S. and Russian Advertising Belief and Attitude Measures," *Journal of Advertising* 23 (March 1994), 71–82; and Ludmilla Gricenko Wells, "Western Concepts, Russian Perspectives: Meanings of Advertising in the Former Soviet Union," *Journal of Advertising* 23 (March 1994), 83–95.

Assessing Advertising Effectiveness

Assessing effectiveness is a critical aspect of advertising management—only by evaluating results is it possible to determine whether objectives are being accomplished. This often requires that baseline measures be taken before an advertising campaign begins (to determine, for example, what percentage of the target audience is aware of the brand name) and then afterward to determine whether the objective was achieved. Because research is fundamental to advertising control, Chapter 15 is devoted exclusively to evaluating advertising effectiveness.

SETTING ADVERTISING OBJECTIVES

Earlier in Chapter 2, which introduced the overall marketing communications process, the relations among target markets, objectives, and budgets were presented with the following mantra:

*All marketing communications should be (1) designed with a particular **target market** in mind, (2) created to achieve a specific **objective**, and (3) undertaken to accomplish the objective toward the target market **within budget constraint.***

We now continue with this theme as it relates specifically to advertising objective setting and budgeting. These activities are the bedrock of all subsequent advertising decisions. Advertising strategy built on a weak foundation is virtually guaranteed to fail. Intelligent objectives and an adequate budget are critical for advertising success.

Advertising objectives are goals that advertising efforts attempt to achieve. Setting good advertising objectives is possibly the most difficult task of advertising management, yet these objectives provide the foundation for all remaining advertising decisions.[20] There are three major reasons why it is essential that advertising objectives be established *prior to* making decisions regarding message selection and media determination, which are the guts of an advertising program:[21]

1. Advertising objectives are an expression of *management consensus.* The process of setting objectives literally forces top marketing and advertising personnel to agree on the course that a brand's advertising will take for the following planning period as well as the tasks it is to accomplish for a specific brand.

2. Objective setting *guides* the budgeting, message, and media aspects of a brand's advertising strategy. Objectives determine how much money should be spent and provide guidelines for the kinds of message strategy and media choice needed to accomplish a brand's marketing communications objectives.

3. Advertising objectives provide *standards* against which results can be measured. As will be detailed later, good objectives set precise, quantitative yardsticks of what advertising hopes to accomplish. Subsequent results can then be compared with these standards to determine whether the advertising accomplished what it was intended to do.

Who, What, Where, When, and How Often?

Several categories of advertising objectives guide advertising strategy. These categories can be framed in terms of the following questions: *who? what? where? when?* and *how often?*[22]

Who? The most basic consideration underlying advertising-strategy formulation is the choice of *target market.* Objectives related to the *who* question specify the target market in terms of its basic needs to which the brand appeals and its defining features—that is, its demographics, psychographics, geodemographics, or other characteristics that influence choice behavior. Two advertisements from the breakfast cereal category illustrate the choice of target market. Consider first the advertisement for Kellogg's Special K cereal (Figure 9.2). This ad obviously is targeted primarily at young women who are concerned with their physical appearance. Consumers in the target group to which Special K appeals are mostly in the age group 16–35, are concerned with their sex appeal and image, and are socially active.[23] By comparison, the advertisement for Quaker Oats (Figure 9.3) is aimed at middle-aged males who are robust yet concerned with their health. The target for Quaker Oats is not all middle-aged men but is limited primarily to those who have an above-average educational level and who are responsive to health appeals.

www.quakeroats.com

What? The *what* question involves two sets of considerations: (1) what emphasis? and (2) what goals? The *emphasis* issue relates to the features and benefits to be emphasized and the emotions to be evoked when advertising a brand. For example, whereas Kellogg's Special K cereal appeals to the desire for a slim and attractive appearance, Quaker Oats appeals to the need for wholesome eating so as to preserve a long, healthy, and active life.

Kellogg's Special K

It's not doing you any good
tucked away in your bottom drawer.

Great Taste Never Looked So Good.

*Great toasted taste. 110 calories. And it's fat free. Maybe
that's just what your diet and exercise plan needs.*

® Kellogg Company, ©1996 Kellogg Company

The *goals* issue deals with the specific communication or sales objectives that need to be accomplished at the present stage in a brand's life cycle. Advertising may be designed to accomplish several goals: (1) to make the target market aware of a new brand, (2) to facilitate consumer understanding of a brand's attributes and its benefits compared to competitive brands, (3) to enhance attitudes and influence purchase intentions, (4) to invite product trial, and (5) to encourage repeat purchase behavior. We will discuss goal objectives in more detail shortly.

Where? When? How Often? Which geographic markets need to be emphasized, what months or seasons are best, and how often should the brand be advertised are additional issues that need to be addressed when setting advertising objectives.

Although advertising practitioners must take all of the preceding categories into consideration when setting objectives, subsequent attention focuses exclusively on defining the goals. This is because other considerations are all situation specific, but the goal issue is relevant to all situations and brands.

FIGURE 9.3

Quaker Oats

A full appreciation of how advertising goals (objectives) are set requires that we first look at advertising from the customer's perspective. That is, advertisers establish objectives that are designed to move customers eventually to purchase the advertiser's brand. A framework called the *hierarchy of effects* is appropriate for accomplishing this understanding.

The Hierarchy of Effects

The **hierarchy-of-effects** metaphor implies that for advertising to be successful it must move consumers from one goal to the next goal, much in the same way that a person climbs a ladder—one step, then another, and another until the top of the ladder is reached.

Although a variety of hierarchy-of-effects models have been formulated, all are predicated on the idea that advertising moves people from an initial state of unawareness about a brand to purchasing that brand eventually.[24] Intermediate stages in the hierarchy represent progressively closer steps to brand purchase. The hierarchy in Figure 9.4 goes a step further by establishing brand loyalty as the top step on the ladder of advertising effects.[25]

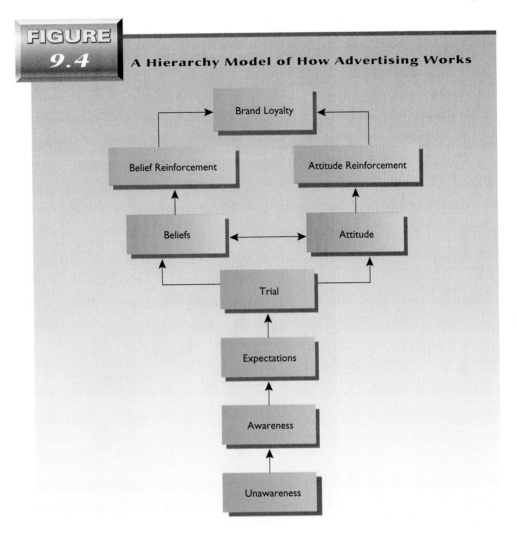

FIGURE 9.4 — A Hierarchy Model of How Advertising Works

The meaning of each of these stages, or hierarchy steps, is best understood by examining an actual advertisement. Each stage is italicized as we progress through the following discussion. Consider the advertisement for the Oil of Olay bath soap in Figure 9.5. When this brand was first introduced to the market, consumers were initially *unaware* of the brand's existence and of its special features (some no doubt remain unaware to this day). The initial advertising imperative, therefore, was to make people *aware* of the Oil of Olay brand name. Creating brand awareness is absolutely essential for success; however, mere brand name awareness generally is not sufficient to get people to buy a brand, particularly when that brand competes in a category with other well-known brands. Advertising has to persuade consumers that the Oil of Olay soap is somehow different and better than competitive brands, that it is especially effective in promoting beautiful, soft skin. The ad, in other words, must influence consumer *expectations* that Oil of Olay will make the user's skin softer and more beautiful. To the extent the consumer develops this expectation, she or he may undertake a *trial* purchase of Oil of Olay the next time there is a need to replenish soap.

Upon using the product, the consumer will form *beliefs* about Oil of Olay's performance benefits and an overall *attitude,* or evaluation, toward the brand. Beliefs and attitude are mutually reinforcing, as illustrated by the double-headed arrow linking these two elements in Figure 9.4. To elaborate, as discussed in Chapter 6, the consumer will form an overall evaluation of Oil of Olay along some implicit good-to-bad spectrum. If Oil of Olay

The Hierarchy of Effects
in an Oil of Olay Ad

lives up to the consumer's expectations about soft and beautiful skin, the attitude most likely will be positive; on the other hand, the attitude can be expected to be somewhat ambivalent or even negative if the brand fails to meet expectations. Once the attitude is formed, the consumer's additional exposures to Oil of Olay advertisements serve to *reinforce* the attitude. In turn, the consumer can be expected to develop a somewhat resolute belief that Oil of Olay does (or does not) soften and beautify the skin. This key belief, which the advertising is directed at influencing, also is subject to reinforcement via additional advertising exposures. In Figure 9.4 these are referred to as *belief reinforcement* and *attitude reinforcement*.

As long as the brand continues to satisfy expectations and a superior brand is not introduced, the consumer may become a *brand loyal* purchaser of Oil of Olay. This indeed is the ultimate advertising objective, because, as has been mentioned in several preceding chapters, it is much cheaper to retain present customers than it is to continuously prospect for new ones.

There are four implicit aspects of the model in Figure 9.4 that require further discussion, each of which is posed as a question: (1) Which comes first, attitude or behavior? (2) Which is more important in influencing the consumer, advertised information about a brand or the consumer's personal experiences in using the brand? (3) Is brand loyalty a guaranteed outcome? (4) What implications does the model hold for setting advertising objectives?

Which Comes First, Attitude or Behavior?

Scholars and practitioners of advertising have assumed for many years that advertising first influences consumers' attitudes toward advertised brands, and then people act on those attitudes by selecting those brands they like most.[26] That is, it has been assumed that consumers first form attitudes toward brands and then behave toward them, either by purchasing or rejecting particular brands. More recent thinking has rejected this assumption.[27] In Figure 9.4, attitudes follow—instead of precede—actual (trial) experience with a brand. Although there *are* instances in which attitudes precede behavior (e.g., a consumer loves a particular piece of jewelry long before purchasing it), especially in the case of expensive product purchases (e.g., the purchase of a new automobile), more often than not consumers have, at most, an *expectation* before they try a particular brand. That is, an attitude preceding behavior is the exception rather than the rule.

The advertising imperative, then, is to influence expectations and encourage trial purchase behavior. The advertised brand then has to be evaluated on it own merits. If the brand is obviously a good one (that is, it performs its function as well as or better than competitive alternatives), consumers will discern this fact and likely include it in at least some of their purchases of this item. If, on the other hand, it is difficult for consumers to objectively judge product performance, then advertising plays another important role. In particular, when the outcome of product quality is difficult to judge objectively—or is *ambiguous*—product-usage experience has been shown to be influenced by prior advertising appeals. For example, if the consumer is unable to ascertain objectively whether a pain reliever truly works faster than competitive pain relievers (that is, the results are ambiguous), prior exposure to credible advertising can influence judgment such that the consumer perceives the advertised brand to be faster-working than its competition.[28]

Which Is More Important, Advertised Information or Personal Experience?

When consumers are passive learners of information (as typically is the case with purchase decisions in most product categories), a true attitude (that is, something more than an expectation) results only after one has acquired direct, or firsthand, experience using a product. A true attitude typically follows rather than precedes product usage experience. In other words, actual usage experience (eating a food product, drinking a beverage, using a camcorder, watching a movie, or bathing with Oil of Olay) is extremely informative and convincing, whereas merely learning from advertising about how a product is supposed to taste or perform is far less revealing. As "proof," answer this question: "Which do you trust more, an advertisement that says a certain brand of food will taste good or your tongue's feedback regarding how good the food tastes?" Personally, my tongue has been a very reliable source of information for many years. I don't recall it ever misleading me. I trust it completely. I don't have this same confidence in advertising. It is *not* that I find most advertisements to mislead or deceive, but, rather, that I simply have more faith in my own sensory experiences than I do in someone else's opinion. In sum, the tongue knows with certainty, whereas advertisers can only conjecture! (Of course, *tongue* is used here in an inclusive sense to capture all sensory receptors that are applicable to gauging the specific product benefits that are relevant to the circumstances of a particular buying situation.)

Is Brand Loyalty a Guaranteed Outcome?

The answer is a resounding *No!* In some instances, strong brand loyalty does develop. Some consumers, for example, always purchase the same brand of cola; others always smoke the same brand of cigarette; and there are those who use the same brand of deodorant, toothpaste, or shampoo. In many other instances, however, the consumer never forms a strong preference for any one brand. Rather, the consumer continuously shifts his or her allegiance from one brand to the next, constantly trying, trying, and trying but never developing a strong commitment to any particular brand. Consumer behavior can be like dating; some people continue to "play the field" but never become committed to anyone.

Brand loyalty is a goal that the advertiser aspires to achieve. Obtaining the consumer's loyalty requires: (1) providing a brand that meets the consumer's needs, and (2) continuously advertising the brand's merits to reinforce the consumer's brand-related beliefs and attitudes (see Figure 9.4 as a graphic reminder of this point). Impressive empirical evidence is available that demonstrates that a brand's advertising has the "good" long-run effect of making consumers less price sensitive and more brand loyal. This same study also determined that sales promotions have the "bad" long-run effect of reducing loyalty by effectively rewarding consumers for being more price-sensitive and less loyal.[29]

Brand marketers and advertisers should do everything economically possible to generate loyal consumers, although most assuredly only a fraction of the target market will become loyalists. Nevertheless, as the nineteenth-century British poet Robert Browning exclaimed, "A man's reach should exceed his grasp, Or what's a heaven for?"

What Are the Implications for Objective Setting?   Advertising objectives must be set in accordance with the circumstances that characterize the advertiser's particular brand and competitive situation. To understand this more fully, let us continue the discussion of advertising goals alluded to previously. As noted, advertising is undertaken to accomplish goals such as: (1) making consumers aware of a new brand, (2) influencing their expectations about a brand's attributes and benefits, and (3) encouraging them to try the brand.

The first goal, awareness, is essential for new or unestablished brands. That is, creating high levels of awareness is an important prerequisite to swaying consumer choice toward the marketer's brand. Unless consumers are aware of a brand, that brand cannot be a member of their *consideration set* of viable purchase alternatives. Getting a brand considered (or, stated another way, moving that brand into consumers' consideration sets) has been demonstrated to influence the odds that it will be chosen—even if it is not more favorably evaluated.[30] Hence, creating awareness toward one's brand is a precondition to accomplishing any subsequent advertising goals.

Advertising must also instill in consumers expectations about brand performance, which, if verified by the outcomes of brand-usage experience, will evolve into specific beliefs. That is, prior to usage one merely *expects* a certain outcome; after usage, one forms a *belief* about the brand's ability to fulfill that expectation. As noted, the Oil of Olay advertisement (Figure 9.5) was designed for consumers to expect that their skin would feel softer and be more beautiful upon using this brand.

All good advertising must inspire some expectation about the brand's capabilities or what consumers will "become" upon using the brand. The collage of advertisements in Figure 9.6 illustrates advertising efforts to create various forms of expectations. The advertisement for General Foods' Viennese Chocolate Café promises the consumer a rich, creamy-tasting coffee with a hint of eventual romance when serving this brand to a special friend. The Rembrandt mouth-rinse ad assures the consumer that this brand, unlike the competitors shown in the background, is alcohol free and hence will not burn: "Gentle on your mouth, tough on bad breath." Kodak's advertisement for Royal Gold 200 vows that this brand of film produces the clearest possible pictures "for the moments that matter most." Finally, the seasonal ad for Wonderbra makes an oblique promise of enhanced sexiness with the claim, "Who needs mistletoe?"[31]

Much advertising is designed to encourage consumers to undertake a trial purchase, oftentimes by encouraging brand switching.[32] The Rembrandt mouth rinse ad (Figure 9.6), for example, contains a free trial offer. To encourage trial usage of this new mouth rinse, the company offers a monetary refund for dissatisfied users and, more generously, a free

A Collage of Expectation-Creating Advertisements

FIGURE 9.6

tube of another brand in Rembrandt's product line (a $4.99 value). Because most advertisements can simply hope to entice, enthuse, and whet one's appetite—or, in general, create expectations—a more compelling mechanism for generating trial purchases is required. And, indeed, this is the role of the *sales promotions* component of marketing communications. An advertisement is merely the vehicle for a sales promotion offer such as that provided by Rembrandt.

Finally, as clearly indicated in Figure 9.4, the purpose of advertising for mature brands is to *reinforce* beliefs about brand benefits. This objective is accomplished when an advertiser sticks with a particular promise and advertises this point repeatedly over time. There is reason to believe that advertising repetition serves to enhance consumer brand awareness and, to a smaller degree, also to enhance brand preference and market share.[33] To prevent the advertising from becoming stale, it is advisable to develop periodically different executions of the same theme.

Requirements for Setting Good Advertising Objectives

An advertising objective is a specific statement about a planned advertising execution in terms of what that particular advertisement is intended to accomplish. That goal is based on the current, or anticipated, competitive situation in the product category and the problems that the brand must confront or the opportunities that are available for it to seek.

The specific content of an advertising objective depends entirely on the brand's idiosyncratic situation. Hence, it is not feasible to discuss objective content without current details (such as market research information) about the advertising context. We can, however, describe the requirements that all good advertising objectives must satisfy. Let us first start by making it clear that not all statements of ad objectives are good. Consider the following examples:

Example A: Brand X's advertising objective this year is to increase sales revenue.

Example B: Brand X's advertising objective this year is to increase overall brand awareness from 60 to 80 percent.

These extreme examples differ in two important respects. First, Example B is obviously more specific. Second, whereas Example A deals with a sales objective, Example B involves a nonsales goal. The sections that follow describe the specific criteria that good advertising objectives must satisfy.[34] Figure 9.7 summarizes these criteria.

Objectives Must Include a Precise Statement of Who, What, and When.

Objectives must be stated in precise terms. At a minimum, objectives should specify the target audience (who), indicate the specific goal—such as awareness level—to be accomplished (what), and indicate the relevant time frame (when) in which to achieve the objective. For example, the advertising campaign for Rembrandt mouth rinse (Figure 9.6) might include objectives such as these: (1) "Within six months from the beginning of the

FIGURE 9.7 **Criteria That Good Advertising Objectives Must Satisfy**

- ◆ Include a precise statement of who, what, and when
- ◆ Be quantitative and measurable
- ◆ Specify the amount of change
- ◆ Be realistic
- ◆ Be internally consistent
- ◆ Be clear and in writing

campaign, research should show that 80 percent of all consumers who use mouth rinse are familiar with the Rembrandt brand." (2) "Within six months from the beginning of the campaign, research should show that at least 50 percent of the target audience know that Rembrandt is an alcohol-free alternative to the established brands." (3) "Within one year from the beginning of the campaign, Rembrandt's market share should be 2 percent higher than at the beginning of the campaign."

Advertising objectives provide valuable agendas for communication between advertising and marketing decision makers and offer benchmarks against which to compare actual performance. These functions can be satisfied, however, only if objectives are stated precisely.

Example B represents the desired degree of specificity and, as such, would give executives something meaningful to direct their efforts toward as well as a clear-cut benchmark for assessing whether the advertising campaign has accomplished its objectives. Example A, by comparison, is much too general. Suppose sales have actually increased by 2 percent during the course of the ad campaign. Does this mean the campaign was successful since sales have in fact increased? If not, how much increase is necessary for the campaign to be regarded as a success?

Objectives Must Be Quantitative and Measurable.   This requirement demands that ad objectives be stated in quantitative terms so as to be measurable, as are the hypothetical objectives given for Rembrandt mouth rinse. A nonmeasurable objective for Rembrandt would be a vague statement such as "Advertising should increase consumers' knowledge of product features." This objective lacks measurability because it fails to specify the product features for which consumers are to possess knowledge.

Objectives Must Specify the Amount of Change.   In addition to being quantitative and measurable, objectives must specify the amount of change they are intended to accomplish. Example A (to increase sales) fails to meet this requirement. Example B (to increase awareness from 60 to 80 percent) is satisfactory because it clearly specifies that anything less than a 20 percent awareness increase would be considered unsuitable performance.

Objectives Must Be Realistic.   Unrealistic objectives are as useless as having no objectives at all. An unrealistic objective is one that cannot be accomplished in the time allotted to the proposed advertising investment. For example, a brand that has achieved only 15 percent consumer awareness during its first year on the market could not realistically expect a small advertising budget to increase the awareness level to, say, 65 percent next year.

Objectives Must Be Internally Consistent.   Advertising objectives must be compatible (internally consistent) with objectives set for other components of the marketing communications mix. It would be incompatible for a manufacturer to proclaim a 25 percent reduction in sales force size while simultaneously stating that advertising's objective is to increase retail distribution by 20 percent. Without adequate sales force effort, it is doubtful that the retail trade would give a brand more shelf space.

Objectives Must Be Clear and in Writing.   For objectives to accomplish their purposes of fostering communication and permitting evaluation, they must be stated clearly and in writing so that they can be disseminated among their users and among those who will be held responsible for seeing that the objectives are accomplished.

Using Direct versus Indirect Advertising Objectives

Direct objectives are those that seek a *behavioral response* from the audience. Behavioral responses from recipients of advertising include such actions as buying an advertised brand, shopping at an advertised store, and sending money to a charity in response to an advertised request for donations. The advertisement for the American Red Cross (Figure 9.8)

Direct Advertising Objective

illustrates a situation for which a direct objective is suitable. In this case, the objective is to generate donations shortly after the advertisement is inserted in various magazines.

Indirect objectives, by comparison, are aimed at accomplishing prebehavioral responses or, in other words, achieving communication outcomes that precede behavior (e.g., increasing brand awareness, enhancing brand image).[35] The advertisement for Hennessy cognac (Figure 9.9) is aimed at accomplishing an indirect goal (creating an expectation of smoothness and enhancing brand image) that might eventuate into brand sales. This ad facilitates exemplar-based learning (as discussed in Chapter 6) by using an analogy between the smooth taste of Hennessy cognac and the incomparably fine and delicate feeling of silk.

Indirect Advertising Objective

When Are Direct Objectives Appropriate?   Direct objectives are appropriate when the purpose of the advertising is to initiate certain behaviors or actions. There are four primary instances of this form of advertising:[36]

1. *Advertising by retailers.* Sometimes retail advertising merely informs prospective customers about a new store or attempts to elevate a store's image. This type of advertising would be regarded as *indirect* in that the purpose is *not* to generate immediate buyer action. On the other hand, much of the advertising undertaken by department stores, mass merchandisers, specialty retailers, and other types of retailer outlets promotes new or sale items and is designed to generate immediate action. This type of advertising has a direct objective: to sell merchandise immediately or in the very near future. With such a short time frame in mind and with knowledge of product sales volume when the merchandise is not on special,

it is reasonable for the retail advertiser to state the ad objective in terms of a direct measure such as sales volume.

www.circuitcity.com

For example, assume that Circuit City, a specialty electronics store, maintains past sales records indicating that on a typical Friday-through-Sunday weekend it sells an average of 15 camcorders in each of its stores. Suppose Circuit City runs a 25 percent-off price special on all camcorders for next weekend only. Newspaper ads announcing the special are placed on Thursday and Friday in all markets where Circuit City has retail outlets. The purpose of the sale is to increase store traffic and double the number of camcorders sold compared to a typical weekend. In this case, the direct advertising objective—to sell an average of 30 camcorders in each store next weekend—represents a precise, quantitative, measurable, and possibly realistic advertising objective.

2. *Direct-response advertising.* Much advertising via the mail or in mass media (such as television or newspapers) is designed to generate immediate action. When an advertiser of inexpensive apparel runs an ad in the *Parade* supplement to the Sunday newspaper announcing the availability of three pairs of slacks for a total price of $39.95, the purpose is plain and simple: to sell tons of slacks. The purpose is not to create brand awareness or to enhance the company's image; rather, the objective is for thousands of consumers to place an order within the next week or so. Under circumstances such as this, it is perfectly appropriate to set a planned volume level as the advertising objective.

www.wvi.com

Similarly, when World Vision, a charitable organization, runs newspaper advertisements throughout the United States informing the public that 28 million people in Bangladesh are homeless following devastating floods, the purpose is to generate donations for the Bangladesh Flood Relief. World Vision's advertising objective is to generate an immediate behavioral response: financial donations.

3. *Sales-promotion advertising.* Sales promotions in the form of coupons, contests, and premium offers are delivered via advertisements in media such as newspapers and magazines. This form of advertising is expected to generate quick buyer action, which is then measured by the number of coupons redeemed or the number of people who enter a contest. In such instances, it is appropriate for the advertiser/sales promoter to establish a direct objective such as "obtain a 3 percent coupon redemption level" or "encourage 100,000 people to enter a contest."

4. *Business-to-business advertising.* Businesses that market their products to other businesses rather than to final consumers often use advertising as a means of generating prospects for their salespeople. Thus, the effectiveness of the advertising can be gauged by the number of telephone or mail inquiries received from prospective customers.

Consider the case of a manufacturer of medical equipment that announces its most recent product innovation in a trade publication read by the manufacturer's primary prospects. The advertisement provides the company's 800 number and an Internet site for interested parties to call or go on-line for further information. The number of expected inquiries represents an appropriate advertising objective, and the number actually received within, say, the next two months indicates the success of the advertisement.

When Are Indirect Objectives Appropriate? Indirect, or communication, objectives are perhaps more appropriate in all advertising situations other than the four just

IMC FOCUS: ADVER-TISING EXPENDITURES INCREASING AT A FASTER RATE THAN SALES REVENUE

www.mcdonalds.com

McDonald's restaurants and the famous golden arch symbolize fast-food service and the American lifestyle around the world. McDonald's stores are located from A (Australia) to Z (Zimbabwe) and in most every country in between. Heavy advertising is crucial to McDonald's expansion throughout the globe and the maintenance of success in its existing outlets.

Fully appreciating the value of advertising, McDonald's increased its advertising expenditures by 27 percent in the two-year period, 1995–96. Unfortunately, sales volume did not maintain

pace; McDonald's worldwide sales increased by only 12.5 percent during this two-year period when ad expenditures were boosted by 27 percent. Total ad spending increased 9 percent in 1997 to nearly $550 million; however, the 9 percent increase in ad expenditures produced only a 5.7 percent increase in sales revenue.

The moral is clear: The mere act of heavy advertising is not tantamount to business success. The reality is that advertising cannot always compensate for a company's fundamental marketing problems or serve to fully offset intense competitive pressure. Thus, rather than looking at McDonald's advertising as having failed, perhaps the more pertinent question is: How bad might things have been without the heavy advertising?

Source: Adapted from Richard Gibson, "McDonald's Sales Fail to Keep Pace with Its Advertisement Expenses," *The Wall Street Journal Interactive Edition,* April 3, 1998.

described. This is especially the case for national advertisers, in contrast to local advertisers such as the neighborhood supermarket, whose reason for advertising typically is indirect rather than direct. For example, the local McDonald's franchise near your campus advertises to generate immediate store traffic, but McDonald's corporate advertising at the national level is typically designed to accomplish indirect objectives such as announcing new menu items, conveying the idea that McDonald's is a good corporate citizen by its practices such as hiring elderly people, or creating the impression that McDonald's is a fun place to take your family. Speaking of McDonald's, the *IMC Focus* notes that this fast-food franchiser's corporate advertising has perhaps not been all that effective in recent years.

Should Sales Represent the Advertising Objective?

An advertising objective such as "Increase Brand X's sales revenue by 10 percent over last year's sales" is a direct advertising objective. Advertising practitioners and educators since the early 1960s have traditionally rejected the use of sales volume by national advertisers in setting their advertising objectives.[37] On the other hand, a relatively recent perspective asserts that sales or market-share gains should *always* represent the objective of any advertising effort. The following discussions present the traditional view (favoring a nonsales objective) and then a heretical position (preferring a sales objective) on this matter.

The Traditional View.   This point of view asserts that using sales or market share as the objective for a branded product's advertising effort is unsuitable for two major reasons. First, a brand's sales volume during any given period is the consequence of a host of factors in addition to advertising. These include the prevailing economic climate, competitive activity, and all of a brand's marketing-mix variables—price level, product quality, distribution efficiencies, personal-selling activity, and so forth. It is virtually impossible, according to the traditional view, to determine precisely the role advertising has had in influencing sales in a given period, because advertising is just one of many possible determinants of sales and profit performance. The following analogy about American football accents this point:

Some argue that evaluating advertising only by its impact on sales is like attributing all the success (or failure) of a football team to the quarterback. The fact is that many other elements can affect the team's record—other players, the competition, and the bounce of the ball. The implication is that the effect of the quarterback's performance should be measured by the things he alone can influence, such as how he throws the ball, how he calls the plays, and how he hands off. If, in a real-world situation, all factors remained constant except for advertising (for example, if competitive activity were static), then it would be feasible to rely exclusively on sales to measure advertising effectiveness. Since such a situation is, in reality, infeasible, we must start dealing with response variables that are associated more directly with the advertising stimulus.[38]

A second reason that sales response is claimed to represent an unsuitable objective for advertising effort is that the effect of advertising on sales is typically delayed, or *lagged.* That is, advertising during any given period does not necessarily influences sales in the current period but may influence sales during later periods. This is particularly the case for durable goods. For example, the advertising of a particular automobile model this year may have limited effect on some consumers' purchasing behavior because these consumers are not presently in the market for a new automobile. On the other hand, this year's advertising can influence consumers to select the advertised model next year when they *are* in the market. Thus, advertising may have a decided influence on consumers' brand awareness, product knowledge, expectations, attitudes, and, ultimately, purchase behavior, but this influence may not be evident during the period when advertising's effect on sales is measured. It therefore is argued by advocates of the traditional view on objective setting that nonsales goals (brand awareness, ad copy comprehension, expectations, and attitude toward the brand) should provide the basis for setting advertising objectives and that using sales as the goal is misguided.

A Heretical View. On the other hand, some advertising specialists contend that advertisers should always state objectives in terms of sales or market-share gains and that failure to do so is a cop-out. The logic of this nontraditional view is that advertising's purpose is not just to create brand awareness, or to convey copy points, or to influence expectations, or to enhance attitudes, but rather to generate sales. Thus, according to this position, it is always possible to measure, if only vaguely and imprecisely, whether advertising has contributed to increased sales. Indirect objectives such as increases in brand awareness are claimed to be "precisely wrong," in contrast to sales measures that are asserted to be "vaguely right."[39]

To better understand the logic of this *vaguely right versus precisely wrong* thinking (which, for short, is labeled VR vs. PW), we need to examine closely the constituent oppositional elements: wrong versus right and precise versus vague. (See Figure 9.10.) First, the issue of *right* versus *wrong* concerns the advertising objective. The heretical, or VR vs. PW, view contends that sales is always the right objective and that any other objective is wrong. Second, the issue of *precise* versus *vague* refers to the determination of whether advertising has accomplished the objective. With a communication objective such as brand awareness, it can be concluded with relative certainty that any registered change in brand awareness

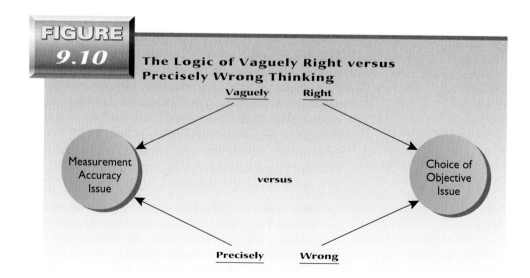

FIGURE 9.10

The Logic of Vaguely Right versus Precisely Wrong Thinking

Vaguely   Right

Measurement Accuracy Issue

versus

Choice of Objective Issue

Precisely   Wrong

that has occurred since onset of an ad campaign, or post-awareness minus pre-awareness, is due to the advertising effort. Hence, the amount of influence advertising has had on brand awareness can be measured *relatively precisely.* However, as described above, because many factors influence a brand's sales level, the effect advertising has had on sales can be measured only somewhat crudely, imprecisely, or, in the language of VR vs. PW, *vaguely.*

Thus, the VR vs. PW perspective makes the very important point that advertisers, and perhaps especially their agencies, might be deceiving themselves into thinking that advertising is effective when it leads to increases in consumer awareness or some other indirect objective. However, Leonard Lodish, the author of the vaguely right versus precisely wrong perspective, argues that advertising is not accomplishing its job unless sales and market share are increasing. If advertising's sole accomplishment is to create higher awareness levels or more positive brand images, but not to increase sales or market share, then such advertising *is* ineffective.

Although there is no simple resolution as to whether the traditional or heretical view is more correct, one thing is certain: To an ever-increasing degree companies and their chief executives and financial officers are demanding greater *accountability* from advertising. Increasing pressure is being placed on advertising agencies to develop campaigns that produce bottom-line results—increases in sales, market share, and return on investment.[40] This accountability from advertising necessitates that efforts be undertaken to determine whether advertising campaigns do indeed increase sales. Although it is difficult to measure the precise effect advertising has on sales, in a world of integrated marketing communications and increased demands for accountability, it is critical that advertisers and their agencies measure, as best they can, advertising's effect on augmenting a brand's sales volume, market share, and profitability.

BUDGETING FOR ADVERTISING

The advertising budget is, in many respects, the most important decision made by advertisers. If too little money is spent on advertising, sales volume will not achieve its potential, and profits will be lost. If too much money is spent, unnecessary expenses will reduce profits. Of course, the dilemma faced by brand managers is determining what spending level is "too little" or how much is "too much." As with most marketing and business decisions, the "devil is in the doing"!

Budgeting is one of the most difficult advertising decisions. This difficulty arises because it is hard to determine precisely how effective advertising has been or might be in the future. To understand this point we need to understand the concept of an advertising-sales-response function. The **advertising-sales-response function** is the amount of sales revenue generated at each level of advertising expenditure—that is, X_1 in advertising yields Y_1 in sales, X_2 in advertising produces Y_2 in sales, X_3 in advertising generates Y_3 in sales, and so on. Because the advertising-sales-response function is influenced by a multitude of factors (such as quality of advertising execution, intensity of competitive advertising efforts, and customer taste at any point in time) and not solely by the amount of advertising investment, it is difficult to know with any certainty what amount of sales a particular level of advertising expenditure will generate.

Another complication is the fact that advertising budgets are largely the result of organizational political processes.[41] Separate organizational units view the advertising budget differently.

> *For the accounting department, it's an expense, usually the largest after rent and payroll. For the marketing team, it's the big push that make the phones ring and it's never big enough. For top management, it's an investment, a speculation formulated to bring in the most revenue for the least amount of cash.*[42]

Research has shown that the size of the advertising budget is positively influenced by the political power of the marketing department.[43]

Advertising Budgeting in Theory

In theory, advertising budgeting is a simple process, provided one accepts the premise that the best (optimal) level of any investment is the level that *maximizes profits*. This assumption leads to a simple rule for establishing advertising budgets: Continue to invest in advertising as long as the marginal revenue from that investment exceeds the marginal cost. Profits are maximized at the point where marginal revenue is equal to marginal cost.

The reader may recall from basic economics that marginal revenue (*MR*) and marginal cost (*MC*) are the change in total revenue and total cost, respectively, that result from producing and selling an additional item. That is,

$MC = $ (Change in total cost)/(Change in quantity) $ = \Delta TC/Q$; and

$MR = $ (Change in total revenue)/(Change in quantity) $ = \Delta TR/Q$.

The symbol, Δ, which is the Greek letter *delta,* stands for "change in." Hence, the profit-maximization rule is then a matter of straightforward economic logic: Profit maximization can occur only at the point where $MR = MC$. At any quantity level below this point (where $MR > MC$), profits are not maximized because at a higher level of output more profit can be earned. Similarly, at any level above this point (where $MC > MR$), there is a marginal loss.[44]

In practical terms, this means that advertisers should continue to increase their advertising investment as long as it is profitable to do so. For example, suppose a company is currently spending $10 million advertising a particular brand and is considering the investment of another $2 million. Should the additional expenditure be made? The answer is simple: only if the additional advertising generates more than $2 million in additional revenue for the brand. Now say the same company is contemplating a further advertising expenditure of $1 million for this brand later in the same advertising period. Again, the company should go ahead with the advertising if it is confident that the $1 million ad expenditure will yield more than $1 million in additional revenue.

It is evident from this simple exercise that setting the advertising budget is a matter of answering a series of *if–then* questions—*if* $X are invested in advertising, *then* what amount of revenue will be generated? Because budgets are set before the fact, this requires that the if–then questions be answered in advance. In order to employ the profit-maximization rule for budget setting, the advertising decision maker must know the advertising-sales-response function for every brand for which a budgeting decision will be made. Because such knowledge is rarely available, theoretical (profit maximization) budget setting is an ideal that is generally nonoperational in the real world of advertising decision making.

Budgeting Considerations in Practice

Advertising decision makers must consider several different factors when establishing advertising budgets: the ad objective, competitive advertising activity, and the amount of funds available for advertising. It should be obvious that these three considerations are not independent of one another. For example, the specific objective for a particular advertising campaign might hinge on competitive advertising activity.

What Is the Ad Objective?   A key consideration underlying ad budget determination is the *objective* that advertising is designed to accomplish. That is, the level of the budget should follow from the specific objective established for advertising; more ambitious objectives require larger advertising budgets. If advertising is intended to increase a brand's market share, then a larger budget is needed than would be required if the task were simply to maintain consumer awareness of the brand name.

How Much Are Competitors Spending?

www.att.com

www.sprint.com

www.mci.com

Competitive advertising activity is another important consideration in setting ad budgets. In highly competitive markets, more must be invested in advertising in order to increase or at least maintain market position. For example, in the telecommunications industry, annual advertising expenditures in a recent year for each of the industry leaders were as follows: AT&T Corp. ($1.06 billion), Sprint Corp. ($481 million), Bell Atlantic Corp. ($479 million), and MCI Communications Corp. ($476 million).[45] The total advertising expenditure for these four telecommunication giants was approximately $2.5 billion. Taking each company's advertising expenditures as a percent of this total yields what is called **share of voice,** or **SOV.** Thus, AT&T's SOV is 42.4 percent, which is followed by Sprint, Bell Atlantic, and MCI all having SOVs of approximately 19 percent each.

www.pizzahut.com

www.dominos.com

www.littlecaesers.com

SOV and share of market (**SOM**) are correlated: Brands having larger SOVs also generally realize larger SOMs. For example, in the $25 billion U.S. pizza market, the top three market share leaders are Pizza Hut (SOM = 23.3 percent, SOV = 54.5 percent), Domino's (SOM = 10.9 percent, SOV = 29 percent), and Little Caesars (SOM = 8.5 percent, SOV = 16.2 percent).[46] The relationship between SOM and SOV is two-way: A brand's SOV is partially responsible for its SOM level. At the same time, brands with larger SOMs can afford to achieve higher SOVs, whereas smaller share brands often are limited to relatively small SOVs in comparison to their better-off competitors.

www.coors.com

www.millerlite.com

To illustrate these points, Table 9.2 presents SOM and SOV data for the top-10 U.S. beer brands as of 1997. It first will be noted that the correspondence between SOM and SOV is far from perfect. The four brands with double-digit SOMs (Budweiser, Bud Light, Miller Lite, and Coors Light) also have double-digit SOVs. However, Budweiser's and Bud Light's

TABLE 9.2   **Top-10 Beer Brands' SOMs and SOVs (1997)**

BRAND	TOTAL SALES ($ BILLIONS)	SOM	MEDIA EXPENDITURES ($ MILLIONS)	SOV
1. Budweiser	$ 35.6	29.2%	$ 98.4	20.4%
2. Bud Light	22.8	18.7	55.7	11.5
3. Miller Lite	16.2	13.3	149.0	30.8
4. Coors Light	13.7	11.2	91.9	19.0
5. Busch	7.9	6.5	2.4	0.5
6. Natural Light	7.1	5.8	0.1	0.0
7. Miller Genuine Draft	5.5	4.5	21.5	4.4
8. Miller High Life	4.7	3.9	61.1	12.6
9. Busch Light	4.5	3.7	0.0	0.0
10. Milwaukee's Best	3.9	3.2	3.1	0.6
TOTAL	$121.9	100%	$483.2	100%

Source: Gerry Khemmouch, "Pockets of Success Tempered by Concern," *Brandweek,* June 15, 1998, S28.

SOVs are disproportionately lower than their SOMs, whereas Miller Lite's and Coors Light's SOVs are proportionately higher. The number three and four brands must spend proportionately more heavily to maintain or grow market share, whereas the leading two brands from Anheuser-Busch (Bud and Bud Light) are able to spend proportionately less, at least for the present time, due to their entrenched positions and high brand equities. Nonetheless, sustained advertising effort at the current levels by Miller Lite and Coors Light would assuredly steal share eventually from Budweiser and Bud Light if these brands continued to spend at the proportionately low levels established in 1997. The bottom six brands in Table 9.2 are all relatively small market, or *niche*, brands that spend relatively little on advertising to maintain their relatively small market shares. Busch, Natural Light, and Busch Light are products of the Anheuser-Busch brewery. Corporate officials apparently think that these brands' market shares can be maintained (but certainly not grown) by virtually renouncing the need for any advertising. It would seem that Anheuser-Busch is willing to retain these brands as niche players while simultaneously committing fully to Bud Light and Budweiser with high ad expenditures and large SOVs. Among the bottom tier of the top-10 beers, only Miller High Life, with a 12.6 SOV, appears poised to steal some market share, perhaps from Budweiser.

The SOM-SOV relationship is a jousting match of sorts between competitors. If large market-share brands reduce their SOVs to too low a level, they are vulnerable to losing market share to aggressive competitors. On the other hand, if market followers (such as Miller Lite and Coors Light in Table 9.2) become too aggressive, then the leading brands are forced into increasing their advertising expenditures to offset the competitive challenge. Figure 9.11 identifies four general situations that compare the advertiser's share of market ("your" share) and the competitor's share of voice.[47] Implications for ad budgeting are now discussed.

www.mgdtaproom.com

1. *Cell A*—In this situation, your SOM is relatively low and your competitor's SOV is relatively high. Miller Genuine Draft in Table 9.2 in comparison to Budweiser exemplifies this situation. The recommendation is to *decrease* ad expenditures and find a niche that can be defended against other competitors.

2. *Cell B*—Your SOM in this situation is relatively high and your competitor has a high SOV. This characterizes Bud Light in Table 9.2 vis-à-vis Miller Lite and

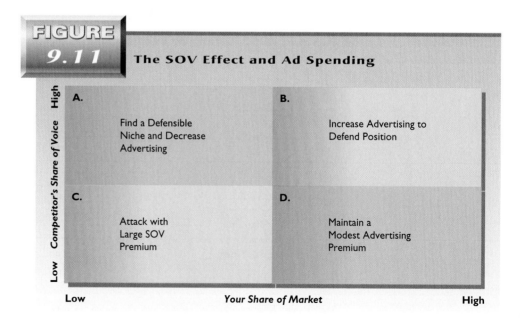

FIGURE 9.11 The SOV Effect and Ad Spending

Competitor's Share of Voice (High / Low)

A. Find a Defensible Niche and Decrease Advertising

B. Increase Advertising to Defend Position

C. Attack with Large SOV Premium

D. Maintain a Modest Advertising Premium

Your Share of Market (Low / High)

Coors Light. Bud Light probably should *increase* its advertising expenditures to defend its present market share position. Failure to do so likely will result in a share loss to these aggressive competitors.

3. *Cell C*—In this situation your SOM is low and your competitor's SOV is itself low. (There is no close parallel to this situation in Table 9.2.) The general recommendation in such a situation is to aggressively attack the competitor whose SOV is low with a *large SOV premium* vis-à-vis that competitor. This is, in other words, a good opportunity to wrest market share from a moribund or complacent competitor.

4. *Cell D*—In this situation you have the attractive position where you hold a high market share but your competitor is nonaggressive and has a relatively low SOV. Hence, it is possible for you to retain your present large share by *maintaining only a modest advertising spending premium* over your competitor.

In sum, these are simply guidelines for determining a brand's advertising budget rather than hard-and-fast rules. The general point to be stressed is that advertising budgets must be set with knowledge of what competitors are doing. This is because the opportunity for growth in market share or the challenge to maintain an existing share position depends in large part on the quality and effectiveness of competitive advertising effort. Moreover, brand marketers should generally set advertising budgets on a market-by-market basis, rather than nationally, because the competitive warfare actually takes place in the individual markets.[48]

How Much Money Is Available?   A third major consideration is the *amount of funds available* for advertising. In the final analysis, advertising budget setting is determined in large part by decision makers' perceptions of how much they can afford to spend on advertising. Because top management often views advertising budgets with suspicion and considers them to be inflated, advertising managers face the challenge of convincing upper management that proposed budgets are indeed affordable. This is no easy task, especially when hard data on advertising effectiveness are unavailable. It is for this reason that advertising budget setters have tended to use simple decision rules for making budgeting decisions.

Budgeting Methods

In view of the difficulty of accurately predicting sales response to advertising, companies ordinarily set budgets by using judgment, applying experience with analogous situations, and using rules of thumb, or *heuristics,* as guides to setting budgets.[49] Although criticized because they do not provide a basis for advertising budget setting that is directly related to the profitability of the advertised brand, these heuristics continue to be widely used.[50] The practical budgeting methods most frequently used by both industrial advertisers and consumer-goods advertisers in the U.S. and Europe are the percentage-of-sales, objective-and-task, competitive parity, and affordability methods.[51]

Percentage-of-Sales Budgeting.   In using the **percentage-of-sales method,** a company sets a brand's advertising budget by simply establishing the budget as a fixed percentage of *past* (e.g., last year's) or *anticipated* (e.g., next year's) sales volume. Assume, for example, that a company allocates 3 percent of anticipated sales to advertising and that the company projects next year's sales for a particular brand to be $100,000,000. Its advertising budget would be set at $3,000,000.

A survey of the top 100 consumer-goods advertisers in the United States found that slightly over 50 percent employ the percentage-of-anticipated-sales method and 20 percent use the percentage-of-past-sales method.[52] This is to be expected, since budget setting should logically correspond to what a company expects to do in the future rather than being based on what it accomplished in the past.

What percentage of sales revenue do most companies devote to advertising? Actually, the percentage is highly variable. For example, based on the 200 industries that spent the largest percentages of sales on advertising in 1998, the highest percentage of sales devoted to advertising for any of the 200 industries was 14.9 percent for dolls and stuffed toys. The only other industries with double-digit advertising-to-sales ratios were watches and clocks (14.4 percent), sugar and confectionery products (14.2 percent), cleaners and polish preparations (13.1 percent), games, toys and children vehicles (12.8 percent), distilled and blended liquor (11.9 percent), books and publishing (11.7 percent), wine and brandy (11.2 percent), cutlery, hand tools, and general hardware (11.2 percent), food products (10.5 percent), and agricultural chemicals (10.3 percent). Most industries average less than 5 percent advertising-to-sales ratios. These, of course, are industry averages, and advertising-to-sales ratios vary considerably across firms within each industry.[53]

The percentage-of-sales method is frequently criticized as being illogical. Criticism is based on the argument that the method reverses the logical relationship between sales and advertising. That is, the true ordering between advertising and sales is that advertising causes sales, or, stated alternatively, sales are a function of advertising:

$$Sales = f(Advertising).$$

Contrary to this logical relation, implementing the percentage-of-sales method amounts to reversing the causal order by setting advertising as a function of sales:

$$Advertising = f(Sales).$$

By this logic and method, when sales are anticipated to increase, the advertising budget also increases; when sales are expected to decline, the budget is reduced.

The illogic of the percentage-of-sales method is demonstrated by the fact that this method could lead to potentially erroneous budgeting decisions such as cutting the advertising budget when a brand's sales are expected to decline. For example, many firms reduce advertising budgets during economic downswings. However, rather than decreasing the amount of advertising, it may be wiser during these times to increase advertising to prevent further sales erosion. When used blindly, the percentage-of-sales method is little more than an arbitrary and simplistic rule of thumb substituted for what needs to be a sound business judgment. Used without justification, this budgeting method is another application of precisely wrong (versus vaguely right) decision making.[54]

In practice, most sophisticated marketers do *not* use percentage of sales as the sole budgeting method. Instead, they employ the method as an initial pass, or first cut, for determining the budget and then alter the budget forecast depending on the objectives and tasks that need to be accomplished.

The Objective-and-Task Method. The **objective-and-task method** is generally regarded as the most sensible and defendable advertising budgeting method. In using this method, advertising decision makers must clearly specify what role they expect advertising to play for a brand and then set the budget accordingly. The role is typically identified in terms of a communication objective (e.g., increase brand awareness by 20 percent) but could be stated in terms of sales-volume or market-share expectations (e.g., increase market share from 15 to 20 percent).

The objective-and-task method is the advertising budget procedure used most frequently by both consumer and industrial companies. Surveys have shown that over 60 percent of consumer-goods companies and 70 percent of industrial-goods companies use this budgeting method.[55] These percentages represent a dramatic increase compared with the 12 percent of respondents in a 1974 survey who said they used the objective-and-task method.[56]

The following steps are involved when applying the objective-and-task method:[57]

www.vw.com

1. The first step is to establish *specific marketing objectives* that need to be accomplished, such as sales volume, market share, and profit contribution.

Consider the marketing and advertising challenge in the United States that faced Volkswagen several years ago. Although this once-vaunted automobile company had achieved huge success in the 1960s and 1970s with its VW "beetle," by the mid-1990s Volkswagen was confronted with what perhaps was its final opportunity to recapture the American consumer, who had turned to other imports and domestic models because VW had not kept up with what Americans wanted.[58] Sales of its two leading brands, the *Golf* and *Jetta,* had each dropped by about 50 percent compared to the prior years. Volkswagen's marketing objective (not to be confused with its specific advertising objective, which is discussed next) was, therefore, to substantially increase sales of the *Golf* and *Jetta* models and its overall share of the U.S. automobile market—from only about 21,000 *Golfs* and *Jettas* sold in 1993 to a goal of selling 250,000 Volkswagen models in the near future.

2. The second step in implementing the objective-and-task method is to assess the *communication functions* that must be performed to accomplish the overall marketing objectives.

   Volkswagen had to accomplish two communication functions to realize its rather audacious marketing objective: First, it had to substantially increase U.S. consumers' awareness of the *Golf* and *Jetta* brand names, and, second, it had to establish an image for Volkswagen as a company that offers "honest, reliable, and affordable cars."[59] In summary terms, Volkswagen had to enhance brand equities for these brands.

3. The third step is to determine *advertising's role in the total communication mix* in performing the functions established in step 2.

   Given the nature of its products and communication objectives, advertising was a crucial component in Volkswagen's mix.

4. The fourth step is to establish specific advertising goals in terms of the levels of *measurable communication response* required to achieve marketing objectives.

   Volkswagen might have established goals such as: (1) increase awareness of the *Jetta* model from the present level of, say, 45 percent of the target market to 75 percent, and (2) expand the percentage of survey respondents who rate Volkswagen products as high quality from, say, 15 percent to 40 percent. Both of these objectives are specific, quantitative, and measurable.

5. The final step is to establish the *budget* based on estimates of expenditures required to accomplish the advertising goals.

   In view of Volkswagen's challenging objectives, the decision was made to invest approximately $100 million in an advertising campaign in hopes of gaining higher brand awareness levels, enhancing the company's image among American consumers, and, ultimately, substantially increasing sales of VW products. The CEO of Volkswagen's advertising agency explained that the advertising challenge was "to come up with hard, clear, product-focused ads that give car buyers the kind of information they need to make an intelligent choice."[60]

www.3m.com

The Competitive Parity Method.   The **competitive parity method** (also called the **match-competitors method**) sets the ad budget by basically following what competitors are doing. A company may learn that its primary competitor is devoting 10 percent of sales to advertising and then decide next year to spend the same percentage advertising its own brand. On the other hand, armed with information on competitors' spending, a company may decide not merely to match but to exceed its expenditures. Consider the case of Minnesota Mining & Manufacturing (3M) when it introduced its new Scotch Brite Never

Rust wool soap pads to compete against the entrenched S.O.S. and Brillo brands. Based on research that revealed that consumers despised rusty soap pads, 3M introduced its Never Rust brand as the first major innovation in the soap-impregnated wool pad category since Brillo entered the market in 1917. Knowing it had a super product, 3M greatly outspent its rival brands during its introductory year by investing an estimated $30 million on advertising in a category that totaled just $120 million in sales potential. The Scotch Brite Never Rust brand quickly acquired a major market share against its competitors, who, according to one critic, were essentially doing nothing.[61]

Affordability Method. In the **affordability method,** only the funds that remain after budgeting for everything else are spent on advertising. Only the most unsophisticated and impoverished firms would be expected to budget in this manner. This method and the competitive parity heuristic are used most frequently by smaller firms that tend to follow industry leaders. However, affordability and competitive considerations influence the budgeting decisions of all companies.

In the final analysis, most advertising budget setters combine two or more methods rather than depending exclusively on any one heuristic. For example, an advertiser may have a fixed percentage-of-sales figure in mind when starting the budgeting process but subsequently adjust this figure in light of anticipated competitive activity, funds availability, and other considerations.

Companies often find it necessary to adjust their budgets during the course of a year in line with sales performance. Many advertisers operate under the belief that they should "shoot when the ducks are flying."[62] In other words, advertisers spend most heavily during periods when products are hot and cut spending when funds are short; however, they should always maintain a decent ad budget even when sales take a downturn.

Ad Budgeting and Competitive Interference

Brands compete in a competitive context, and advertising budgets must be set with an eye to the actions of competitors. This is especially important in view of the fact that a brand's advertising must compete for the consumer's recall with the advertising from competitive brands, a situation of potential competitive interference. If "your" brand were the only one advertising in a particular product category, it probably could get by with a substantially smaller ad budget than what is necessitated when competitors also are aggressively advertising their brands. The mere fact of increasing advertising expenditures is *not* guaranteed to have a substantial impact on augmenting a brand's sales volume.[63]

There are reasons to expect that *familiar brands* are less susceptible to the interference, or *clutter,* from competitive advertising. Unfamiliar brands that compete in a world of advertising clutter are, in effect, at a competitive disadvantage in conveying their points of uniqueness vis-à-vis established brands.[64] Established brands' market shares tend to exceed their advertising shares of voice.[65] New brands need to avoid heavily cluttered media and perhaps turn to alternatives to traditional advertising media—such as by using infomercials (discussed in Chapter 12) or event marketing (discussed in detail in Chapter 20).

Overcoming competitive interference is not just a matter of spending more but rather one of *spending more wisely*. Recent research provides an answer to why this is important. Researchers have offered a psychological theory called the *encoding variability hypothesis,* in which the term *encoding* refers to transferring information into memory, to explain how advertisers can be smarter spenders.[66] The **encoding variability hypothesis,** in its barest details, contends that people's memories for information are enhanced when multiple *pathways,* or connections, are created between the object to be remembered and the information about the object that is to be remembered.

In the case of advertising, the brand represents the object to be remembered, and the brand's attributes and benefits designate the object's information. Advertising can create multiple pathways, and thus enhance memory for the advertised information, by varying (recall the name *encoding variability hypothesis)* at least two aspects of the advertising execution: (1) the advertising *message* itself or (2) the advertising *medium* in which the message is placed. That is, altering how the ad is presented (its message) and where the ad is placed (its medium) should enhance memory for the advertised information and hence mitigate the effects of competitive interference. This results because multiple pathways are created when the same brand is advertised with varied messages or in multiple media. In other words, when Brand X is advertised with a single message in a single medium, just a single pathway is established in memory. When, however, Brand X is advertised in two media, there are two potential pathways established in memory whereby consumers can retrieve information about Brand X. Increasing both the number of message executions and the number of media to convey these messages serves to increase the number of pathway permutations. Thus, increased also is the probability that consumers will be able to retrieve key information about Brand X when they are in the market for the product category in which that brand competes.

Summary

This chapter offers an introduction to advertising, an overview of the advertising-management process, and detailed discussions of advertising objective setting and budgeting. Advertising is shown to perform five major functions: informing, persuading, reminding, adding value, and assisting other company efforts.

Advertising objective setting depends on the pattern of consumer behavior and information that is involved in the particular product category. Toward this end, an introductory section presents a hierarchy-of-effect model of consumers' responses to advertisements and discusses the implications for setting advertising objectives. Requirements for developing effective advertising objectives also are discussed. A final section describes the arguments both promoting and opposing the use of sales volume as the basis for setting advertising objectives.

The chapter concludes with an explanation of the advertising budgeting process. The budgeting decision is one of the most important advertising decisions and also one of the most difficult. The complication arises with the difficulty of determining the sales response to advertising. In theory, budget setting is a simple matter, but the theoretical requirements are generally unattainable in practice. For this reason, advertising practitioners use various rules of thumb (heuristics) to assist them in arriving at satisfactory, if not optimal, budgeting decisions. Percentage-of-sales budgeting and objective-and-task methods are the dominant budgeting heuristics.

Discussion Questions

1. Of the five advertising functions described in the chapter, which is the most important?

2. Provide two examples of usage-expansion advertising other than those illustrated in the chapter.

3. A manufacturer of office furniture has established the following advertising objective for next year: Increase sales by 20 percent. Comment on this objective's suitability. Provide a better objective.

4. Apply Figure 9.4 (A Hierarchy Model of How Advertising Works) to explain the evolution of a relationship between two people, beginning with dating and culminating in a wedding.

5. Now do the same thing as in question 4 using a relatively obscure brand as the basis for your application of Figure 9.4.

6. What reasons can you give for certain industries investing considerably larger proportions of their sales in advertising than other industries?

7. Why is it so difficult to measure precisely the specific impact that advertising has on sales and profits?

8. Compare the difference between precisely wrong and vaguely right advertising objectives. Give an example of each.

9. Some critics contend that the use of the percentage-of-sales budgeting technique is illogical. Explain.

10. How would it be possible for an advertising budget setter to use two or more budgeting heuristics in conjunction with one another? Explain how this could be done.

11. How do local businesses in your college or university community identify their advertising objectives? Interview three or four local businesses, and investigate whether they set formal ad objectives and, if not, whether they have some rather clear-cut, though implicit, objectives in mind.

12. While interviewing the same businesses from the previous question, investigate their advertising budgeting practices. Determine whether they establish formal ad budgets, and identify the specific budgeting methods used.

13. Construct a picture to represent your understanding of how the encoding variability hypothesis applies to an advertising context.

Internet Exercises

1. *Advertising Age* is a trade journal that serves as a source of marketing, advertising and media news, information, and analysis. This journal also provides on-line data. Go to www.adage.com/dataplace/index.html and follow the "100 LEADING NATIONAL ADVERTISERS" link. Here you will find dozens of "top 5," "top 10," and "top 25" lists of brands organized by brand and manufacturer. These lists are based on market share and they provide market share and advertising spending figures.
   a. Select one of the brand category lists (e.g., "Top 10 Coffee Brands") and calculate SOM and SOV figures for each brand.
   b. Locate each brand in the appropriate cell of Figure 9.11.
   c. Recommend an ad spending strategy for each set of brands according to cell position.

2. Internet search engines (e.g., Yahoo!, Infoseek, Excite) are among the most popular sites for brands to advertise. The reason, of course, is that search-engine sites have the highest traffic on the Web. Placing a "banner" on these Web sites is like placing a billboard alongside a busy road or a print ad in a high-circulation magazine. However, banners can be used a little more adaptively. For example, search engines typically select which advertisements to show a particular Internet user based on that user's searching topics or "keywords." Thus, the advertisements are conceptually matched in real time to consumers' information needs. Using the text's description of the encoding variability hypothesis, compare and contrast Internet advertising on search-engine Web sites with magazine advertising and billboard advertising.

3. As discussed in the chapter, one function of advertising is to assist other company efforts. Locate the Web site of a brand that interests you and evaluate its contribution to other brand and company efforts. Specifically, discuss whether or not the Web site (a) delivers or attracts attention to sales promotion tools, (b) assists sales representatives, and (c) enhances the results of other marketing communications (e.g., pictures of packaging, references to other ad medium efforts).

Chapter Nine Endnotes

1. Jennifer Lawrence, "P&G's Artzt on Ads: Crucial Investment," *Advertising Age,* October 28, 1991, 1, 53.

2. Bernard Ryan, Jr., *It Works! How Investment Spending in Advertising Pays Off* (New York: American Association of Advertising Agencies, 1991), 11.

3. David A. Aaker, *Managing Brand Equity* (New York: The Free Press, 1991); Kevin Lane Keller, "Conceptualizing, Measuring, and Managing Customer-Based Brand Equity," *Journal of Marketing* 57 (January 1993), 1–22.

4. Willam Boulding, Eunkyu Lee, and Richard Staelin, "Mastering the Mix: Do Advertising, Promotion, and Sales Force Activities Lead to Differentiation?" *Journal of Marketing Research* 31 (May 1994), 159–172.

5. John Sinisi, "Love: EDLP Equals Ad Investment," *Brandweek,* November 16, 1992, 2.

6. Robert J. Coen, "Ad Revenue Growth Hits 7% in 1997 to Surpass Forecasts," *Advertising Age,* May 18, 1998, 50.

7. "100 Leaders by U.S. Advertising Spending," *Advertising Age,* September 29, 1997, s4.

8. Ibid.

9. "Uncle Sam, the Advertiser," *Advertising Age,* November 17, 1997, 83.

10. These functions are similar to those identified by the noted advertising pioneer James Webb Young. For example, "What Is Advertising, What Does It Do," *Advertising Age,* November 21, 1973, 12.

11. Giles D'Souza and Ram C. Rao, "Can Repeating an Advertisement More Frequently than the Competition Affect Brand Preference in a Mature Market?" *Journal of Marketing* 59 (April 1995), 32–42. See also A. S. C. Ehrenberg, "Repetitive Advertising and the Consumer," *Journal of Advertising Research* (April 1974), 24–34.

12. The term "usage expansion advertising" and the examples are from Brian Wansink and Michael L. Ray, "Advertising Strategies to Increase Usage Frequency," *Journal of Marketing* 60 (January 1996), 31–46.

13. Sharon T. Klahr, "Gillette Puts $300 Mil Behind Its Mach3 Shaver," *Advertising Age,* April 20, 1998, 6.

14. Karen A. Machleit, Chris T. Allen, and Thomas J. Madden, "The Mature Brand and Brand Interest: An Alternative Consequence of

Ad-Evoked Affect," *Journal of Marketing* 57 (October 1993), 72–82.

15. John Deighton, Caroline M. Henderson, and Scott A. Neslin, "The Effects of Advertising on Brand Switching and Repeat Purchasing," *Journal of Marketing Research* 31 (February 1994), 28–43.

16. *The Value Side of Productivity: A Key to Competitive Survival in the 1990s* (New York: American Association of Advertising Agencies, 1989), 12.

17. Ibid., 13–15. See also, Larry Light and Richard Morgan, *The Fourth Wave: Brand Loyalty Marketing* (New York: Coalition for Brand Equity, American Association of Advertising Agencies, 1994), 25.

18. The synergism between advertising and personal selling is not always a one-way flow from advertising to personal selling. In fact, one study has demonstrated a reverse situation, in which personal sales calls sometimes pave the way for advertising. See William R. Swinyard and Michael L. Ray, "Advertising-Selling Interactions: An Attribution Theory Experiment," *Journal of Marketing Research* 14 (November 1977), 509–516.

19. Albert C. Bemmaor and Dominique Mouchoux, "Measuring the Short-Term Effect of In-Store Promotion and Retail Advertising on Brand Sales: A Factorial Experiment," *Journal of Marketing Research* 28 (May 1991), 202–214.

20. Charles H. Patti and Charles F. Frazer, *Advertising: A Decision-Making Approach* (Hinsdale, Ill.: The Dryden Press, 1988), 236.

21. Ibid., 237–239.

22. This formulation has its origins in a broadly similar scheme constructed by John R. Rossiter and Larry Percy, "Advertising Communication Models," working paper, N.S.W. Institute of Technology, Sydney, Australia, September 22, 1983.

23. These statements are not based on any known research that has been conducted by Kellogg's but are purely conjectural.

24. For thorough discussions, see Thomas E. Barry, "The Development of the Hierarchy of Effects: An Historical Perspective," *Current Issues and Research in Advertising,* vol. 10, ed. James H. Leigh and Claude R. Martin, Jr. (Ann Arbor: Division of Research, Graduate School of Business Administration, University of Michigan, 1987), 251–296; Ivan L. Preston, "The Association Model of the Advertising Communication Process," *Journal of Advertising* 11, no. 2 (1982), 3–15; and Ivan L. Preston and Esther Thorson, "Challenges to the Use of Hierarchy Models in Predicting Advertising Effectiveness," in *Proceedings of the 1983 Convention of the American Academy of Advertising,* ed. Donald W. Jugenheimer (Lawrence, Kans.: American Academy of Advertising, 1983).

25. Adapted from Light and Morgan, *The Fourth Wave,* 21.

26. Most traditional hierarchy-of-effect models make this assumption. These include the well-known AIDA (awareness, interest, desire, action) and DAGMAR (awareness, comprehension, conviction, action) models of advertising. DAGMAR is an acronym for the book published under the title *Defining Advertising Goals for Measured Advertising Results* by Russell H. Colley (New York: Association of National Advertisers, 1961).

27. See especially Robert E. Smith and William R. Swinyard, "Information Response Models: An Integrated Approach," *Journal of Marketing* 46 (winter 1982), 81–93; and Robert E. Smith, "Integrating Information from Advertising and Trial: Processes and Effects on Consumer Response to Product Information," *Journal of Marketing Research* 30 (May 1993), 204–219.

28. Relevant research on this topic includes John Deighton, "The Interaction of Advertising and Evidence," *Journal of Consumer Research* 11 (December 1984), 763–770; Stephen J. Hoch and John Deighton, "Managing What Consumers Learn from Experience," *Journal of Marketing* 53 (April 1989), 1–20; Stephen J. Hoch and Young-Won Ha, "Consumer Learning: Advertising and the Ambiguity of Product Experience," *Journal of Consumer Research* 13 (September 1986), 221–233; and Young-Wa Ha and Stephen J. Hoch, "Ambiguity, Processing Strategy, and Advertising-Evidence Interaction," *Journal of Consumer Research* 16 (December 1989), 354–360.

29. Carl F. Mela, Sunil Gupta, and Donald R. Lehmann, "The Long-Term Impact of Promotion and Advertising on Consumer Brand Choice," *Journal of Marketing Research* 34 (May 1997), 248–261.

30. Prakash Nedungadi, "Recall and Consumer Consideration Sets: Influencing Choice without Altering Brand Evaluations," *Journal of Consumer Research* 17 (December 1990), 263–276.

31. In the United States and in other predominantly Christian cultures, mistletoe is hung at Christmastime in some households. Tradition "obligates" a show of affection, such as a kiss, when two people meet under the mistletoe.

32. For further discussion of advertising's role in encouraging brand switching, see Deighton, Henderson, and Neslin, "The Effects of Advertising on Brand Switching and Repeat Purchasing."

33. D'Souza and Rao, "Can Repeating an Advertisement More Frequently than the Competition Affect Brand Preference in a Mature Market?"

34. The following discussion is influenced by the classic work on advertising planning and goal setting by Russell Colley. His writing, which came to be known as the DAGMAR approach, set a standard for advertising objective setting. See Colley, *Defining Advertising Goals for Measured Advertising Results.*

35. Patti and Frazer, *Advertising: A Decision-Making Approach,* 241.

36. Ibid.

37. The traditional view was most compellingly articulated by Russell H. Colley in *Defining Advertising Goals for Measured Advertising Results.*

38. David A. Aaker and John G. Myers, *Advertising Management,* 2d ed. (Englewood Cliffs, N.J.: Prentice-Hall, 1982), 93–94.

39. Leonard M. Lodish, *The Advertising and Promotion Challenge: Vaguely Right or*

Precisely Wrong? (New York: Oxford University Press, 1986), chap. 5.

40. See Kevin J. Clancy, "The Coming Revolution in Advertising: Ten Developments Which Will Separate Winners from Losers," *Journal of Advertising Research* (February/March 1990), 47-52. See also Jon Berry, "Repositioning? Forget It. Sales Are All That Counts," *Brandweek,* August 23, 1993, 13; and Gary Stibel, "Investing in Advertising: The Proof Is in the Profit," *Brandweek,* November 8, 1993, 16.

41. Nigel Piercy, "Advertising Budgeting: Process and Structure as Explanatory Variables," *Journal of Advertising* 16, no. 2 (1987), 34–40.

42. Kathleen Weeks, "How to Plan Your Ad Budget," *Sales and Marketing Management,* September 1987, 113.

43. Piercy, "Advertising Budgeting."

44. For further discussion, review any standard economics text. For example, N. Gregory Mankiw, *Principles of Economics* (Fort Worth, TX: The Dryden Press, Harcourt Brace College Publishers, 1998).

45. "100 Leaders by U.S. Advertising Spending."

46. Karen Benezra, "Caesars' Fall," *Brandweek,* January 26, 1998, 21–25.

47. Adapted from James C. Schroer, "Ad Spending: Growing Market Share," *Harvard Business Review* 68 (January-February 1990), 48. See also John Philip Jones, "Ad Spending: Maintaining Market Share," *Harvard Business Review* 68 (January-February 1990), 38–42.

48. Ibid.

49. Gary L. Lilien, Alvin J. Silk, Jean-Marie Choffray, and Murlidhar Rao, "Industrial Advertising Effects and Budgeting Practices," *Journal of Marketing* 40 (January 1976), 21.

50. Fred S. Zufryden, "How Much Should Be Spent for Advertising a Brand?" *Journal of Advertising Research* (April/May 1989), 24–34.

51. The extensive use of the percentage-of-sales and objective-and-task methods in an industrial context has been documented by Lilien et al., while support in a consumer context is provided by Kent M. Lancaster and Judith A. Stern, "Computer-Based Advertising Budgeting Practices of Leading U.S. Consumer Advertisers," *Journal of Advertising* 12, no. 4 (1983), 6. A thorough review of the history of advertising budgeting research is provided in J. Enrique Bigne, "Advertising Budget Practices: A Review," *Journal of Current Issues and Research in Advertising* 17 (fall 1995), 17–32.

52. Lancaster and Stern, "Computer-Based Advertising."

53. All ratios are based on "1998 Advertising-to-Sales Ratios for the 200 Largest Ad Spending Industries," *Advertising Age,* June 29, 1998, 22.

54. See Lodish, *The Advertising and Promotion Challenge,* chap. 6.

55. Charles H. Patti and Vincent J. Blasko, "Budgeting Practices of Big Advertisers," *Journal of Advertising Research* 21 (December 1981), 23–29; Vincent J. Blasko and Charles H. Patti, "The Advertising Budgeting Practices of Industrial Marketers," *Journal of Marketing* 48 (fall 1984), 104–110. See also C. L. Hung and Douglas C. West, "Advertising Budgeting Methods in Canada, the UK and the USA," *International Journal of Advertising* 10 (no. 3, 1991), 239–250.

56. Andre J. San Augustine and William F. Foley, "How Large Advertisers Set Budgets," *Journal of Advertising Research* 15 (October 1975), 13.

57. Adapted from Lilien et al., "Industrial Advertising and Budgeting," 23.

58. This description is based on Kevin Goldman, "Volkswagen Has a Lot Riding on New Ads," *The Wall Street Journal,* January 31, 1994, B5.

59. Ibid.

60. Ibid.

61. Eben Shapiro, "Minnesota Mining's Wool Pads Grab Sizable Chunk of Business," *The Wall Street Journal,* January 13, 1994, B6.

62. Kathleen Weeks, "How to Plan Your Ad Budget," *Sales and Marketing Management,* September 1987, 114.

63. Leonard M. Lodish, Magid Abraham, Stuart Kalmenson, Jeanne Livelsberger, Beth Lubetkin, Bruce Richardson, and Mary Ellen Stevens, "How T.V. Advertising Works: A Meta-Analysis of 389 Real World Split Cable T.V. Advertising Experiments," *Journal of Marketing Research* 32 (May 1995), 125–139.

64. Robert J. Kent and Chris T. Allen, "Competitive Interference Effects in Consumer Memory for Advertising: The Role of Brand Familiarity," *Journal of Marketing* 58 (July 1994), 97–105; Robert J. Kent, "How Ad Claim Similarity and Target Brand Familiarity Moderate Competitive Interference Effects in Memory for Advertising," *Journal of Marketing Communications* 3 (December 1997), 231–242.

65. Jones, "Ad Spending: Maintaining Market Share."

66. H. Rao Unnava and Deepak Sirdeshmukh, "Reducing Competitive Ad Interference," *Journal of Marketing Research* 31 (August 1994), 403–411.

Creative Advertising Strategy

CHAPTER OBJECTIVES

After studying this chapter, you should be able to:

1. Understand the role of advertising agencies and the relationship between agency and client.
2. Appreciate the factors that promote creative and effective advertising.
3. Describe a five-step program used in formulating advertising strategy.
4. Describe the features of a creative brief.
5. Explain the concept of means-end chains and their role in advertising strategy.
6. Understand the MECCAS model and its role in guiding message formulation.
7. Describe the laddering method that provides the data used in constructing a MECCAS model.
8. Explain alternative creative strategies that play a role in the development of advertising messages.
9. Describe the role of corporate image and issue advertising.

Opening Vignette: Two of the Greatest Ads in the History of Advertising

Miss Clairol: "Does She . . . or Doesn't She?"

Imagine yourself employed as a creative copywriter in a New York advertising agency in the year 1955. You have just been assigned creative responsibility for a product that heretofore (as of 1955) had not been nationally marketed or advertised. The product: hair coloring. The brand: Miss Clairol. Your task: Devise a creative strategy that will convince millions of American women to purchase Miss Clairol hair coloring.

The person actually assigned this task was Shirley Polykoff, a copywriter for the Foote, Cone & Belding agency. Her story of how she came up with the famous line, "Does she . . . or doesn't she?" provides a fascinating illustration of the creative process in advertising. At the time of the Miss Clairol campaign, there was no hair-coloring business. In fact, according to Ms. Polykoff, at-home hair-coloring jobs invariably turned out blotchy. Women were ashamed to color their own hair at home. A product that provided a natural look stood a strong chance of being accepted, but women would have to be convinced that an advertised hair-coloring product would, in fact, give them that highly desired natural look.

Shirley Polykoff explains the background of the famous advertising line that convinced women Miss Clairol would produce a natural look:

> *In 1933, just before I was married, my husband had taken me to meet the woman who would become my mother-in-law. When we got in the car after dinner, I asked him, "How'd I do? Did your mother like me?" and he told me his mother had said, "She paints her hair, doesn't she?" He asked me, "Well, do you?" It became a joke between my husband*

and me; anytime we saw someone who was stunning or attractive we'd say, "Does she, or doesn't she?" Twenty years later [at the time she was working on the Miss Clairol account], I was walking down Park Avenue talking out loud to myself, because I have to hear what I write. The phrase came into my mind again. Suddenly, I realized, "That's it. That's the campaign." I knew that [a competitive advertising agency] couldn't find anything better. I knew that immediately. When you're young, you're very sure about everything.[a]

Macintosh Computer: "1984"

Apple Computer had just developed the world's most user-friendly computer and needed breakthrough advertising to introduce its new Macintosh brand, which was a revolution in computing technology. Steve Jobs, the founder of Apple who was only 29 at the time of the Macintosh introduction, instructed his advertising agency, Chiat/Day, to create an explosive television commercial that would convey the message that the Macintosh is truly a revolutionary machine. The creative people at Chiat/Day had a challenging task before them, especially since Macintosh's main competitor was the powerful and much larger "Big Blue" (IBM). [In 1984, dear student, Compaq, Dell, and Gateway were nonexistent. It was only Apple versus IBM in the personal computer business, and IBM was the well-established leader known for its corporate computers.] However, Chiat/Day produced a commercial in which IBM was obliquely caricatured as the much-despised and feared institution reminiscent of the big-brother theme in George Orwell's book *1984*. The one-minute commercial created in this context, dubbed "1984," was run during the 1984 Super Bowl football game and was never repeated on commercial television. This was not because it was ineffective; to the contrary, its incredible word-of-mouth-producing impact negated the need for repeat showings.

> The commercial . . . opens on a room of zombie-like citizens staring at a huge screen where Big Brother is spewing a relentless cant about "information purification . . . unprincipled dissemination of facts" and "unification of thought."
>   Against this ominous backdrop, a woman in athletic wear [a white jersey top and bright red running shorts, which was the only primary color in the commercial] runs in and hurls a sledgehammer into the screen, causing a cataclysmic explosion that shatters Big Brother. Then the message flashes on the TV screen: "On January 24th, Apple Computer will introduce Macintosh. And you'll see why 1984 won't be like 1984."[b]

This remarkable advertising is considered by some to be the greatest TV commercial ever made.[c] (See key scenes in Figure 10.1.) It grabbed attention; it broke through the clutter of the many commercials aired during the Super Bowl; it was memorable; it was discussed by millions of people; and, ultimately, it played an instrumental role in selling truckloads of Macintosh computers. Figure 10.1 presents some key scenes from this famous commercial.

[a]Based on an interview by Paula Champa in "The Moment of Creation," *Agency,* May/June 1991, 32.
[b]Based on Bradley Johnson, "The Commercial, and the Product, That Changed Advertising," *Advertising Age,* January 10, 1994, 1, 12–14.
[c]Bob Garfield, "Breakthrough Product Gets Greatest TV Spot," *Advertising Age,* January 10, 1994, 14; "The Most Famous One-Shot Commercial Tested Orwell, and Made History for Apple Computer," *Advertising Age,* November 11, 1996, A22.

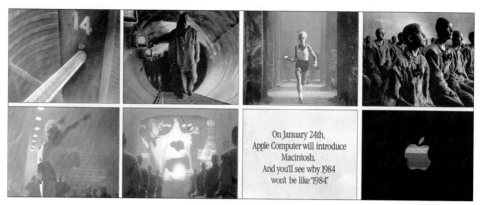

W hat is the process by which advertising messages are created? What makes a good advertising message? What are the different types of creative strategies, and when and why are they used? What is the role of corporate advertising?

The present chapter, which is the first of two to examine the message aspect of advertising, surveys these questions. First addressed is the relationship between advertisers and their advertising agencies. Next considered is the matter of what makes effective advertising and the related subject of creative advertising. A third section covers the process underlying the formulation of advertising strategy. A fourth section introduces the concept of means-end chains as a mechanism to bridge the advertiser's creative process with the values that drive consumers' product and brand choices. A following section describes seven creative strategies often used by advertising practitioners. Finally, the discussion moves away from brand-oriented advertising to corporate image and issue advertising.

THE RELATIONSHIP BETWEEN CLIENT AND ADVERTISING AGENCY

Message strategies and decisions are most often the joint enterprise of the companies that advertise (the clients) and their advertising agencies. This section examines the role of an advertising agency, describes how agencies are organized, and reviews the issue of agency compensation.

The Role of an Advertising Agency

www.mckinsey.com

www.bcg.com

www.atkearney.com

Businesses routinely employ the services of outside specialists: lawyers, financial advisors, management consultants, tax specialists, and advertising agencies. By their very nature, these "outsiders" bring knowledge, expertise, and efficiencies that companies do not possess within their own ranks. A management consulting firm (such as McKinsey and Company, the Boston Consulting Group, or A. T. Kearney) is capable of finding solutions to its clients' complex business problems. By saving clients large sums or recommending attractive earnings opportunities, consulting firms perform extremely valuable functions and fully justify their not-so-meager fees. Similarly, advertising agencies can provide great value to their clients when agencies develop highly effective and profitable advertising campaigns. Some of the world's biggest and best advertising agencies are listed in Table 10.1, which includes the world's top 25 advertising agencies, their headquarters locations, and gross revenues.

AGENCY	HEADQUARTERS	WORLDWIDE GROSS INCOME, 1997 (IN MILLIONS OF U.S. DOLLARS)
1. Dentsu	Tokyo	$1,927.1
2. McCann-Erickson Worldwide	New York	1,451.4
3. J. Walter Thompson Co.	New York	1,120.9
4. BBDO Worldwide	New York	989.6
5. DDB Needham Worldwide	New York	920.2
6. Grey Advertising	New York	918.3
7. Euro RSCG Worldwide	New York	883.2
8. Leo Burnett Co.	Chicago	878.0
9. Hakuhodo	Tokyo	848.0
10. Ogilvy & Mather Worldwide	New York	838.4
11. Young & Rubicam	New York	780.8
12. Publicis Communication	Paris	625.0
13. Ammirati Puris Lintas	New York	621.0
14. D'Arcy Masius Benton & Bowles	New York	606.8
15. Bates Worldwide	New York	520.0
16. Foote, Cone & Belding	New York	511.1
17. Saatchi & Saatchi	London	489.6
18. TBWA International	New York	476.3
19. Bozell Worldwide	New York	404.3
20. Lowe & Partners Worldwide	New York	300.5
21. Carlson Marketing Group	Minneapolis	285.2
22. Wunderman Cato Johnson	New York	280.5
23. TMP Worldwide	New York	263.7
24. Rapp Collins Worldwide	New York	260.5
25. Asatsu	Tokyo	229.8

Source: R. Craig Endicott, "Agency Report," *Advertising Age,* April 27, 1998, S1–S14

Alternative Ways to Perform the Advertising Function.   In general, advertisers have three alternative ways to perform the advertising function. First, a company can maintain its own *in-house advertising operation.* This necessitates employing an advertising staff and absorbing the overhead required to maintain the staff's operations. Such an arrangement is unprofitable unless a company does a large and continuous amount of advertising. Even under these conditions, most businesses choose instead to use the services of advertising agencies.

A second arrangement is to contract for advertising services with a *full-service advertising agency.* Full-service agencies perform research, provide creative services, conduct media planning and buying, and undertake a variety of client services. They also may be involved in the advertiser's total marketing process and, for a fee, may perform other marketing services including sales promotion, publicity, package design, strategic marketing planning, and sales forecasting.

Why would an advertiser want to employ the services of a full-service agency? The advantages include: (1) acquiring the services of specialists with in-depth knowledge of current advertising and other marketing communications insights and skills, (2) obtaining negotiating muscle with the media, and (3) being able to coordinate advertising and marketing efforts. The major disadvantages are that: (1) some control over the advertising function is lost when it is performed by an agency rather than in-house, (2) agencies sometimes cater to larger clients and neglect smaller clients, and (3) agencies occasionally are inefficient in media buying.[1]

A third alternative is to purchase advertising services *a la carte.* That is, rather than depending on a single full-service agency to perform all advertising and related functions, an advertiser may recruit the services of a variety of firms with particular specialties in creative work, media selection, production, advertising research, and so on. This arrangement's advantages include: (1) the ability to contract for services only when they are needed, (2) the availability of high-caliber creative talent, and (3) potential cost efficiencies. The disadvantages include: (1) a tendency for specialists (so-called *boutiques*) to approach client problems in a stereotyped rather than innovative fashion, (2) a lack of cost accountability, and (3) the financial instability of many smaller boutiques.[2]

Many advertisers actually employ a combination of the different advertising options rather than using one of them exclusively. For example, a firm may have its own in-house agency but contract with boutiques for certain needs. Although in-house agencies and boutiques experienced considerable growth in earlier decades, full-service agencies now are preferred, especially by larger advertisers.

Advertising Agency Organization

A full-service advertising agency performs at least four basic functions for the clients it represents: (1) creative services, (2) media services, (3) research services, and (4) account management. In addition to these functions, many advertising agencies have expanded their offerings to include direct marketing, public relations, and even sales promotion services. This expansion is in response to clients' urging for enhanced integration marketing communications services that was detailed in Chapter 1.

Creative Services. Advertising agency copywriters, production people, and creative directors are all responsible for developing advertising copy and campaigns to serve their clients' best interests. As established in the general overview of marketing communications (Chapter 2), the task of an advertising agency's creative services department is to develop for its clients campaigns that are aimed at specific *target markets,* that are designed to achieve specific *objectives,* and that accomplish these objectives within *budget constraint.*

Media Services. This unit of an advertising agency is charged with the task of selecting the best advertising media for reaching the client's target market, achieving ad objectives, and meeting the budget. *Media planners* are responsible for developing overall media strategy (where to advertise, how often, when, etc.), and *media buyers* then procure specific vehicles within particular media that have been selected by media planners and approved by clients. The complexity of media buying requires the use of computer analysis and continuous research of changing media costs and availability.

Research Services. Full-service advertising agencies employ research specialists who study their clients' customers' buying habits, purchase preferences, and responsiveness to advertising concepts and finished ads. Focus groups, mall intercepts, ethnographic studies by trained anthropologists, and acquisition of syndicated research data are just some of the services performed by agencies' research specialists.

Account Management. This facet of an advertising agency provides the mechanism to link the agency with the client. Account managers act as liaisons so that the client does not need to interact directly with several different service departments and specialists. In most major advertising agencies, the account management department includes management supervisors and account executives. *Account executives* are involved in tactical decision making and day-to-day contact with brand managers and other client personnel. Account executives are responsible for seeing that the client's interests, concerns, and preferences have a voice in the advertising agency and that the work is being accomplished on schedule. Account executives report to *management supervisors,* who are more involved in actually getting new business for the agency and working with clients at a more strategic level. Account executives are groomed for positions as management supervisors.

Agency Compensation

Advertising agencies have three sources of compensation.[3]

1. *Commissions from media* (TV, magazines, etc.) for advertisements aired or printed on behalf of the agency's clients provide the primary source of ad agency compensation. Historically, U.S. advertising agencies charged a standard commission of 15 percent of the gross amount of the billing.[4] To illustrate, suppose the Creative Advertising Agency buys $200,000 of space in a certain magazine for its client, ABC Company. When the invoice for this space comes due, Creative would remit payment of $170,000 to the magazine ($200,000 less the 15 percent discount), bill ABC for the full $200,000, and retain the remainder, $30,000, as revenue for services rendered. The $30,000 revenue realized by Creative was, in the past, regarded as a fair amount of compensation to the agency for its creative expertise, media-buying insight, and ancillary functions performed in behalf of its client, ABC Company.

   The 15 percent compensation system has, as one may suppose, been a matter of some controversy between company marketing executives and managers of advertising agencies. The primary area of disagreement is the matter of whether 15 percent compensation is too much (the marketing executives' perspective) or too little (the ad agencies' perspective). The disagreement has spurred the growth of alternative compensation systems. Indeed, a study by the Association of National Advertisers (ANA) revealed that only 9 percent of advertisers still pay a 15 percent commission.[5]

   The most common compensation method today is a *labor-based fee system* by which advertising agencies are compensated much like lawyers, tax consultants, and management consultants. That is, agencies carefully monitor their time and bill clients an hourly fee based on this time commitment. This system, reportedly used by slightly over one half of advertisers in the ANA study, involves price negotiations between advertisers and agencies such that the actual rate of compensation is based on mutual agreement concerning the worth of the services rendered by the advertising agency.[6] Ford Motor Company, for example, has implemented a new compensation system whereby it negotiates a base fee with its agencies to cover the cost of services provided, and additionally offers incentive payments that are tied to brand performance goals such as targeted revenue levels.[7]

   Although there are a growing number of alternatives to the commission system, it probably will not vanish entirely. Rather, a *reduced commission system,* by which the ad agency is compensated with a flat fee that is less than 15 percent, has experienced increased usage.

2. The second form of agency compensation involves *hourly fees for specific services rendered for clients.* For example, a focus group study performed on behalf of the client would be charged on an hourly basis.

3. *Markups on the cost of outside purchases* are a third form of compensation. Outside purchases include an agency's acquisition of photographic and broadcast-production services on behalf of its clients. For example, suppose Creative Advertising Agency had a production company produce a TV commercial for its client, ABC Company, at a cost of $750,000. Creative would typically charge ABC a percentage markup—say, 17.65 percent, which in this case would amount to $132,375.

In many respects, the matter of agency compensation boils down to an issue of what is *fair and workable.* Agencies and clients are not in complete harmony on this issue. In general, agencies have historically preferred standard media commissions with additional fees for extra services rendered, whereas advertisers now prefer labor-based fee systems or media commission systems (but less than 15 percent) with maximum (ceiling) and minimum (floor) percentage adjustments for additional services rendered or excluded.

WHAT MAKES EFFECTIVE ADVERTISING?

How do advertising agency and client working together come up with effective advertisements? No simple answer is possible, but toward this end we first must attempt to understand the meaning of *effective advertising.* It is easy, in one sense, to define effective advertising: Advertising is effective if it accomplishes the advertiser's objectives. This perspective defines effectiveness from the "output" side, or in terms of what it accomplishes. It is much more difficult to define effective advertising from an "input" perspective, or in terms of the composition of the advertisement itself. There are many viewpoints on this issue. Practitioners are broadly split on the matter. For example, a practitioner of direct-mail advertising probably has a different opinion about what constitutes effective advertising than does Shirley Polykoff, the creator of the Miss Clairol campaign, or Steve Hayden, the inspirational source behind the "1984" Macintosh commercial.

Although it is impractical to provide a singular, all-purpose definition of what constitutes effective advertising, it is possible to talk about general characteristics.[8] At a minimum, good (or effective) advertising satisfies the following considerations:

1. *It must extend from sound marketing strategy.* Advertising can be effective only if it is compatible with other elements of an integrated and well-orchestrated marketing communications strategy.

2. *Effective advertising must take the consumer's view.* Consumers buy product benefits, not attributes. Therefore, advertising must be stated in a way that relates to the *consumer's*—rather than the marketer's—needs, wants, and values.

3. *Effective advertising is persuasive.* Persuasion usually occurs when there is a benefit for the consumer in addition to the marketer.

4. *Advertising must find a unique way to break through the clutter.* Advertisers continuously compete with competitors for the consumer's attention. This is no small task considering the massive number of print advertisements, broadcast commercials, and other sources of information available daily to consumers. Indeed, the situation in television advertising has been characterized as "audiovisual wallpaper"—a sarcastic implication that consumers pay just about as much attention to commercials as they do to the detail in their own wallpaper after seeing it for years.[9]

5. *Good advertising should never promise more than it can deliver.* This point speaks for itself, both in terms of ethics (recall the discussion in Chapter 3) and in terms of smart business sense. Consumers learn quickly when they have been deceived and will resent the advertiser.

6. *Good advertising prevents the creative idea from overwhelming the strategy.* The purpose of advertising is to persuade and influence; the purpose is not to be cute for cute's sake or humorous for humor's sake. The ineffective use of humor results in people remembering the humor but forgetting the selling message.

The following quote aptly summarizes the essentials of effective advertising:

> [It] is advertising that is created for a specific customer. It is advertising that understands and thinks about the customer's needs. It is advertising that communicates a specific benefit. It is advertising that pinpoints a specific action that the consumer takes. Good advertising understands that people do not buy products—they buy product benefits. . . . Above all, [effective advertising] gets noticed and remembered, and gets people to act.[10]

Being Creative

Effective advertising is usually *creative.* That is, it differentiates itself from the mass of mediocre advertisements; it is somehow different and out of the ordinary. Advertising that is the same as most other advertising is unable to break through the competitive clutter and fails to grab the consumer's attention.

It is easier to give examples of creative advertising than to exactly define it. Many advertising practitioners would consider the following four examples to be effective, creative advertising:

◆ The pink bunny campaign for Energizer batteries. This is the campaign where a pink drum-beating bunny is shown in a variety of situations, all of which dramatize the bunny's endurance, and, by association, the durability of Energizer batteries. This ongoing campaign has employed a variety of executions of the same underlying theme: Energizer batteries, like the drum-beating bunny that affirms the argument, are still going, and going, and going.

   www.energizer.com

◆ Pepsi-Cola has historically telecast a variety of commercials that poke fun at its competitor, Coca-Cola. None has been more effective than the outstanding commercial in which a security camera captures the antics of a Coke delivery man in a supermarket. While the famous Hank Williams song "Your Cheating Heart" plays in the background, the delivery man approaches a Pepsi cooler that is adjacent to his own Coca-Cola cooler. The security camera catches the delivery man sneaking a look at the Pepsi cooler, opening it, and then removing a can of Pepsi—at which time dozens of Pepsi cans cascade to the floor in a huge noise that catches the attention of shoppers, much to the delivery man's chagrin. This classic advertisement (key scenes of which are shown in Figure 10.2) is an outstanding attention-getter that subtly conveys the message that perhaps Pepsi *is* better than Coke.

◆ A commercial for the Volkswagen Golf automobile represents a third illustration of creative advertising. The commercial's purpose was to convey the point that Golf is a roomy automobile with adequate storage space. Two college-aged men

Key Scenes from Pepsi-Cola's "Security Camera" TV Commercial

"Security Camera": *Pepsi-Cola Co. via BBDO.*

are shown driving around aimlessly on a sunny afternoon and refraining from any conversation (see key scenes in Figure 10.3). The sole sound in the commercial is background music with the minimalist lyrics "Da da da" being repeated. As the passenger fidgets with a plunger-activated miniature puppet, the driver spots an ugly, old easy chair that has been discarded. The men place it in the hatchback area of the car and drive away, only shortly thereafter to return the chair to where they found it after experiencing its foul smell. This simple ad dramatizes the key copy point that the Volkswagen Golf is a roomy car while holding the viewer's attention in an entertaining manner. This commercial was selected as *Advertising Age's* best TV commercial of 1997.[11]

www.adage.com

www.starship.com

◆ Consider, finally, the advertising for Budweiser beer. Through much of the 1990s the name Budweiser was driven to the point of instant recognition by a trio of frogs that in commercial after commercial chanted Bud-weis-er! Then, after the frogs began losing their appeal, Anheuser-Busch's ad agency (Goodby, Silverstein & Partners of San Francisco) extended the campaign by introducing the anthropomorphic lizards "Louie" and "Frank." In these humorous commercials Louie seethes with jealousy that frogs were chosen for the Budweiser gig, while Frank reproves him to "get over it."

Most readers probably vividly remember some or even all of these commercials. They appealed to you because they offered solid reasons for wanting to watch them, and they made their selling points in an entertaining, creative fashion.

But what is creativity? Unfortunately, there are no simple answers to this elusive aspect of advertising.[12] It is beyond the purpose of this text to attempt a thorough explanation of the creative process. Let the following three accounts suffice. First, Jack Smith, vice chairman and creative director of the Leo Burnett advertising agency in Chicago, describes creativity as "a sensitivity to human nature and the ability to communicate it. The best creative [advertising] comes from an understanding of what people are thinking and feeling."[13] John O'Toole, former president of the American Association of Advertising Agencies, describes advertising creativity as "a new combination of familiar elements that forces involvement and memorability."[14] Perhaps jazz musician Charlie Mingus said it best: "Creativity is more than just being different. Anybody can play weird, that's easy. What's hard is to be simple as Bach. Making the simple complicated is commonplace, making the complicated simple, awesomely simple, that's creativity."[15]

In sum, effective, creative advertising must make a relatively lasting impact on consumers. This means getting past the clutter from other advertisements, activating attention, and giving consumers something to remember about the advertised product. In other words,

Key Scenes from Volkswagen Golf's "Da da da" TV Commercial

advertising *must make an impression.* Based on the above perspectives on creativity, this means developing ads that are *empathetic* (i.e., that understand what people are thinking and feeling), that are *involving and memorable,* and that are *"awesomely simple."* The following *IMC Focus* describes a brilliant creative advertising campaign for Absolut Vodka.

ADVERTISING PLANS AND STRATEGY

Advertising messages can be developed in an ad hoc fashion without much forethought, or they can be created systematically. **Advertising plans** provide the framework for the systematic execution of advertising strategies. To appreciate the role of an advertising plan, imagine a soccer team approaching an upcoming game without any idea of how it is going to execute its offense or defense. Without a game plan, the team would have to play in the same spontaneous fashion as do players in a "pick up" game. Under such circumstances there would be numerous missed assignments and overall misexecution. The team very likely would lose unless they played a badly mismatched opponent.

So it is with advertising. Companies compete against opponents who generally are well prepared. This means that a firm must enter the advertising "game" with a clear plan in mind. An advertising plan evaluates a product or brand's advertising history, proposes where the next period's advertising should head, and justifies the proposed strategy for maintaining or improving a brand's competitive situation.

To put an advertising plan into action requires: (1) careful evaluation of customer behavior related to the brand, (2) detailed evaluation of the competition, and (3) a coordinated effort to tie the proposed advertising program to the brand's overall marketing strategy. Because an advertising plan involves a number of steps and details that are beyond the scope of this chapter, attention now turns to the plan's direct result: advertising strategy. **Advertising strategy** is what the advertiser says about the brand being advertised. It is the formulation of an advertising message that communicates the brand's primary benefit or how it can solve the consumer's problem.[16]

A Five-Step Program

Formulating an advertising strategy requires that the advertiser undertake the following formal, five-step program:[17]

1. Specify the key fact
2. State the primary marketing problem
3. State the communications objective
4. Implement the creative message strategy
5. Establish mandatory corporate/divisional requirements

www.ftd.com

Each step can be illustrated by considering an advertising campaign undertaken by Florists' Transworld Delivery Association (FTD). FTD is an association of over 24,000 independent retail florists that are affiliated to enjoy the economic efficiencies of mass marketing and advertising while simultaneously maintaining their ownership and legal independence.[18]

Competition in the retail florist industry has increased rather dramatically in the past decade. Street vendors, supermarkets, and nontraditional retail outlets all compete with conventional retail florists. As a result, the market share of retail florists has fallen from a high of nearly 75 percent of the over $12 billion cut-flower market to around 50 percent, a loss of several billion dollars in sales.

IMC Focus: ABSOLUTELY BRILLIANT!

Imported brands of vodka were virtually nonexistent in the United States until the early 1980s. Three brands (Stolichnaya from Russia, Finlandia from Finland, and Wybrowa from Poland) made up less than 1 percent of the total United States vodka market. In 1980 Carillon Importers, Ltd., began marketing Absolut Vodka from Sweden, a brand that at the time was completely unknown in the United States. In addition to having a great name (suggesting the unequivocally best, or *absolute*, vodka), the brand's most distinguishing feature was a unique bottle—crystal clear with an interesting shape.

With a small advertising budget and the capability of advertising only in print media, Carillon's advertising agency, TBWA, set about the task of rapidly building brand awareness. The agency's brilliant idea was to simply feature a full-page shot of the bottle with a two-word headline. The first word would always be the brand name, Absolut, used as an adjective to modify a second word describing the brand or its consumer. Figure 10.4 presents two advertisements that typify the campaign, Absolut Jersey and Absolut Citron.

www.huntlas.co.2a

Business grew rapidly from the very beginning, facilitated somewhat by American consumers temporarily boycotting the major competitive brand of imported vodka, Stolichnaya, after Russia invaded Afghanistan. Sales growth has never abated. This in large part is due to consistently creative advertising and strong budgetary support given to the brand. The advertising budget grew from only $750,000 in 1981 to now over $20 million.

www.seagram.com

Absolut is the most heavily advertised spirits brand anywhere in the world. Although Absolut is now marketed by Seagrams and not Carillon Importers, Inc., its advertising remains creative and its sales volume high.

Illustrations of Absolut's Classic Advertising Campaign

FIGURE 10.4

Step 1: Specify the Key Fact.   The **key fact** in an advertising strategy is a single-minded statement from the *consumer's point of view* that identifies why consumers are or are not purchasing the product/service/brand or are not giving it proper consideration.

Research performed for FTD undoubtedly revealed that many American consumers have found that they can purchase cut flowers at lower prices from supermarkets and other outlets than traditional retail florists. The key fact that underlies FTD's advertising strategy is that many consumers are price conscious when purchasing cut flowers, which leads them to low-price retailers (such as supermarkets) rather than to FTD retail florists.

Step 2: State the Primary Marketing Problem.   Extending from the key fact, this step states the problem from the *marketer's point of view*. The primary marketing problem may be an image problem, a product perception problem, or a competitive problem.

Retail florists are faced with the reality that many consumers, especially younger people, are either unaware of or disinterested in whether a florist is an FTD member. FTD-affiliated florists are concerned that they will continue to lose younger consumers to low-cost competitors.

Step 3: State the Communications Objective.   This is a straightforward statement about *what effect the advertising is intended to have on the target market and how it should persuade consumers.*

Today's younger consumers represent FTD's consumer of the future, so it is imperative that FTD create name awareness and educate consumers about what FTD members have to offer.

Step 4: Implement the Creative Message Strategy.   The guts of the overall advertising strategy is the creative message strategy, sometimes also called the *creative platform*. The creative platform for a brand is summarized in a single statement called a "positioning statement." A **positioning statement** is the key idea that encapsulates what a brand is intended to stand for in its target market's mind and with consideration of how competitors have attempted to position their brands. Implementing creative message strategy thus requires: (1) defining the target market, (2) identifying the primary competition, (3) choosing the promise, and (4) offering reasons why.

Defining the Target Market.   You will recall from the discussion in Chapter 4 that the target market for a brand's advertising strategy and related marketing program is defined in terms of demographics, geodemographics, psychographics, or product-usage characteristics.

FTD's target market consists of all consumers who occasionally or frequently purchase cut flowers, with special emphasis on younger consumers, who, on the one hand, are the least concerned about their florists being FTD-affiliated and, on the other, are critical to FTD because they represent the core market in the future.

Identifying the Primary Competition.   Who are the primary competitors in the segment the brand is attempting to tap, and what are their advantages and disadvantages? Answering this question enables an advertiser to know exactly how to position a brand against consumers' perceptions of competitive brands' advantages and disadvantages.

FTD's primary competitors are supermarkets and other vendors of low-priced cut flowers. Their advantage is lower price, but they are unable to offer extensive services.

Choosing the Promise.   This aspect of the creative platform amounts to selecting a brand's primary benefit or major selling idea. In most cases, the promise is a consumer benefit or solution to a problem.

The primary benefit to consumers of purchasing from an FTD retail florist is the promise of full services such as mailing, attractive wrapping, and knowledgeable sales assistance—services one cannot obtain from outlets such as supermarkets.

Offering Reasons Why. These are the facts supporting the promise. In some instances advertisers can back up advertising claims with factual information that is relevant, informative, and interesting to consumers. Many times it is impossible physically to prove or support the promise being made, such as when the promise is symbolic or psychological. In these instances, advertisers turn to authority figures, experts, or celebrities to support the implicit advertising promise.

FTD's promise is that its members are caring and knowledgeable merchants—in other words, they know their business, understand the consumer's needs, and are interested in building long-term relations with their customers. The ability to offer quality and professional service sets FTD member florists apart from their low-cost competitors.

Step 5: Establish Mandatory Requirements. The final step in formulating an advertising strategy involves the mandatory requirements that must be included in an ad. This aspect of advertising strategy is relatively technical and uncreative. Basically, it reminds the advertiser to include the corporate slogan or logo (in this case, the Roman god Mercury delivering flowers), a standard tag line ("The professional florists"), any regulatory requirements (as with beer and cigarette advertising), and so on.

In sum, advertising strategy lays out the details for the upcoming advertising campaign. It insists on a disciplined approach to analyzing the product/brand, the consumer, and the competition. A single-minded benefit, or positioning statement, is the outcome. The strategy becomes a blueprint, road map, or guide to subsequent advertising efforts. Every proposed tactical decision is evaluated in terms of whether it is compatible with the strategy.

Constructing a Creative Brief

A systematic approach to creative advertising makes sense in theory, but ultimately the people who write advertising copy—so-called *creatives* or *copywriters*—must summon their full creative talents to develop effective advertising. Creatives often complain that marketing research reports and other such directives excessively constrain their opportunities for full creative expression. On the other hand, one cannot forget that advertising is a business with an obligation to sell products. Even though research has shown that advertising copy is based on copywriters' own implicit theories of how advertising works on consumers, they do not have the luxury to create for the mere sake of engaging in a creative pursuit.[19] Their ultimate purpose is to write advertising copy that affects consumers' expectations, attitudes, and eventually purchase behavior (hopefully, sooner rather than later).

In many advertising agencies, the work of copywriters is directed by a framework known as a **creative brief,** which is a document designed to inspire copywriters by channeling their creative efforts toward a solution that will serve the interests of the client. Ogilvy & Mather, a widely acclaimed worldwide advertising agency, offers the following guidelines for constructing a creative brief to its account executives (that is, personnel who manage the advertising for clients).[20] (It is unnecessary to attempt to memorize the guidelines, but it will be useful to peruse them in order to appreciate the objective they are intended to accomplish.)

1. *What is the background to this job?* The answer to this question requires a brief explanation regarding why the advertising agency is being asked by the client to perform a certain advertising job—such as launching a new brand, gaining back lost sales from a competitor, or introducing a new version of an established product. Part of this explanation would include an analysis of the competitive environment.

2. *What is the strategy?* The response to this question articulates a specific advertising strategy to accomplish the job. This strategy statement gives the creatives an understanding of how their creative work must fit into the overall strategy. For example, the strategy statement may indicate that a new brand is to be launched during September using a football motif. Copywriters are required to work within this context but still have freedom to be creative.

3. *What is our task on this job?* Creatives are told exactly what they are being asked to produce—perhaps a series of TV commercials along with supporting magazine inserts.

4. *What is the corporate and/or brand positioning?* Established brands typically have positionings vis-à-vis competitive brands in the category. Creatives are reminded that their creative work must reflect the brand's positioning statement. If, for example, an automobile brand is positioned as the most fuel-efficient alternative, then the advertising must creatively express this fact.

5. *What are the client's objectives for this job?* This guideline simply reminds everyone what the client wants the advertising to accomplish. Knowing this, creatives can then design appropriate advertisements to achieve that objective.

6. *Whom are we talking to?* This is a precise description of the exemplary target market. With knowledge of the demographic, geodemographic, or psychographic characteristics of the intended customer, creatives have a specific target at which to direct their efforts. This is as essential in advertising as it is in certain athletic events. For example, the late golf sage, Harvey Penick, offered the following advice to pupils trying to improve their golf games: "Once you address the golf ball, hitting it has got to be the most important thing in your life at that moment. Shut out all thoughts other than picking out a target and taking dead aim at it."[21] His point to golfers about taking "dead aim" is also applicable to advertising creatives: You can't hit a target unless you know where to aim!

7. *What do they currently think/feel about our product/service?* The advice here is for creatives to create research-based advertising that speaks to the target customer in terms of his or her perceptions (thoughts and feelings) about the brand rather than relying on the suppositions of the client or advertising agency.

8. *What do we want them to think/feel about our product/service?* Is there a current perception that needs to be changed? For example, if a large number of consumers in the target market consider the brand to be overpriced, how can we change that perception and convince them that the brand actually is a good value due to its superior quality?

9. *What do we want them to do?* This guideline is reminiscent of the integrated marketing communications mind-set presented in Chapter 1, in which creating specific customer action is a key component of the IMC model. In the present context, creatives must focus on a specific consumer action. The advertising might be designed to get prospects to request further information, to order a videotape containing detailed product information, or to purchase the brand within, say, the next 30 days.

10. *What is the single-minded proposition?* This proposition, or positioning statement, directs the creative idea. It should be the most differentiating and motivating message about the brand that can be delivered to the target market. It should focus on brand benefits rather than product features.

11. *Why should our audience believe this proposition?* Because credibility and believability are key to getting the audience to accept the key proposition, this section of the creative brief supports the proposition with evidence about product features that back up the proposition.

12. *How should we be speaking to them?* This guideline calls for a short statement about the crucial feelings or thoughts that the advertisement should evoke in its intended audience. For example, the ad might be intended to move the audience emotionally, to make them feel deserving of a better lifestyle, or to get them to feel anxious about a currently unsafe course of behavior.

In sum, the creative brief is a document prepared by an advertising agency's executive on a particular account and is intended both to inspire advertising copywriters and to channel their creative efforts. A truly valuable creative brief requires that the document be developed with a full understanding of the client's advertising needs. It also necessitates the acquisition of market research data that informs the agency about the competitive environment and about consumers' current perceptions of the to-be-advertised brand and its competition.

MEANS-END CHAINS AND ADVERTISING STRATEGY

The preceding discussion has emphasized that the consumer is, or at least should be, the foremost determinant of advertising messages. The notion of a means-end chain provides a useful framework for understanding the relationship between consumers and advertising messages. Based on sophisticated research that investigates human values and studies what attributes and consequences consumers seek in products, a means-end chain is constructed by linking *attributes* of products (the means), *consequences* of these attributes for the consumer, and the *personal values* (the ends) that the consequences reinforce.[22]

Attributes are features or aspects of advertised brands. For example, automobile attributes include size, storage capacity, engine performance, aesthetic features, and so on. **Consequences** are what consumers hope to receive (benefits) or avoid (detriments) when consuming products. Status, convenience, performance, safety, and resale value are positive consequences (benefits) associated with automobiles, while breakdowns, mishandling, and poor resale value are negative consequences (detriments) that consumers wish to avoid.

Values represent those enduring beliefs people hold regarding what is important in life.[23] They pertain to end states or behaviors that people desire in their lives; they transcend specific situations, and they guide selection or evaluation of behavior.[24] Values are formed during early childhood but undergo some change throughout life. In general, values determine the relative desirability of consequences and serve to organize the meanings for products and brands in consumers' memories.[25] What should be clear is that values represent the starting point, the catalyst, and the source of motivation for all forms of human behavior. Consumer behavior, like other facets of behavior, involves the pursuit of valued states, or outcomes. Product attributes and their consequences (benefits and detriments) are not sought per se, but rather are desired as means to achieving valued end states. Every meaningful act of consumption can be seen as an attempt to achieve valued end states. Hence, from the consumer's perspective, the *ends* (values) drive the *means* (attributes and their consequences). Let's now examine more fully the values that energize human behavior.

The Nature of Values

Psychologists have conducted extensive research on values and constructed numerous value typologies. This chapter takes the view that 10 basic values appear to adequately represent the important human values that are shared by people in a wide variety of culturally diverse countries. Table 10.2 lists these 10 values.[26] The research underlying the identification of these 10 values involved: (1) presenting a large number of potential values to respondents, (2) asking them to rate these candidate items in terms of the importance of each "as a guiding principle in my life," and (3) using appropriate statistical procedures to reduce the list of original value candidates to a more manageable subset. Respondents to the survey were from 20 culturally diverse countries: Australia, Brazil, People's Republic of China, Estonia, Finland, Germany, Greece, Holland, Hong Kong, Israel, Italy, Japan, New Zealand, Poland, Portugal, Spain, Taiwan, United States, Venezuela, and Zimbabwe. The research consistently demonstrated across these 20 countries that all people seem to share the same set of universal values. Each value is now briefly described.[27]

1. *Self-Direction.* Independent thought and action is the defining goal of this value type. It includes the desire for freedom, independence, choosing one's own goals, and creativity.

10 Universal Values

1. Self-Direction
2. Stimulation
3. Hedonism
4. Achievement
5. Power
6. Security
7. Conformity
8. Tradition
9. Benevolence
10. Universalism

Source: Shalom H. Schwartz, "Universals in the Content and Structure of Values: Theoretical Advances and Empirical Tests in 20 Countries," *Advances in Experimental Social Psychology* 25 (1992), 1–65.

2. *Stimulation.* This value derives from the need for variety and achieving an exciting life.

3. *Hedonism.* Enjoying life and receiving pleasure are fundamental to this value type.

4. *Achievement.* Enjoying personal success through demonstrating competence according to social standards is the defining goal of this value type. Being regarded as capable, ambitious, intelligent, and influential is part of the achievement value.

5. *Power.* The power value entails the attainment of social status and prestige along with control or dominance over people and resources (wealth, authority, social power, and recognition).

6. *Security.* The essence of this value type is the longing for safety, harmony, and the stability of society. This value includes concern for personal and family safety and even national security.

7. *Conformity.* Self-discipline, obedience, politeness, and, in general, the restraint of actions and impulses that are likely to upset or harm others and violate social norms are at the root of this value type.

8. *Tradition.* This value encompasses respect, commitment, and acceptance of the customs that one's culture and religion impose.

9. *Benevolence.* The motivational goal of benevolence is the preservation and enhancement of the welfare of one's family and friends. It includes being honest, loyal, helpful, a true friend, and loving in a mature manner.

10. *Universalism.* Universalism represents a life goal whereby individuals are motivated to understand, appreciate, tolerate, and protect the welfare of all people and nature. It incorporates notions of world peace, social justice, equality, unity with nature, environmental protection, and wisdom.

Advertising Applications of Means–End Chains

The creation of effective advertisements demands that the brand marketer possess a clear understanding of what consumers value from the product category. Because consumers differ in what they value from a particular product, it is meaningful to discuss values only at the level of a particular market segment. A brand advertiser, armed with knowledge of segment-level values, is in a position to know what brand attributes and consequences to emphasize to a particular market segment as the means by which that brand can help consumers achieve a valued end state. A formal model, called **MECCAS**—an acronym for *Means-End Conceptualization of Components for Advertising Strategy*—provides a procedure for applying the concept of means-end chains to the creation of advertising messages.[28]

Table 10.3 presents and defines the various levels of the MECCAS model. Note that the components include a *value orientation,* a *leverage point,* an *executional framework, brand consequences,* and *brand attributes.*[29] The *value orientation* represents the consumer value or end level on which the advertising strategy focuses and can be thought of as the *driving force* behind the advertising execution. Every other component is geared toward achieving the end level. Study the definitions carefully in Table 10.3 before moving on to the following applications of the MECCAS approach. It is important to note that these applications are the author's post hoc interpretations. It is unknown whether the advertisers in these cases actually performed formal means-end analyses in developing their ads.

www.jaguar.com

Jaguar XJS Convertible.   A magazine advertisement for the Jaguar *XJS* is shown in Figure 10.5. (Examine it carefully before reading on.) The *value orientation* serving as the driving force in this advertisement is a dual appeal to the target audience's desire for stimulation and self-direction (freedom). The *leverage point* is the verbal copy that expressively mentions these values ("You pulled out of the driveway, gave mom and dad a wave, and experienced an excitement and freedom you'd never known before. The Jaguar XJS 4.0L Convertible has the performance and stunning looks to get that feeling back—in a hurry."). The *executional framework* supports this statement with an action shot of an obviously successful young professional experiencing a sense of excitement and open-road freedom as her new automobile zips down the road. Product performance and appearance are the *consequences* associated with choosing this automobile model, and a variety of brand *attributes* (e.g., Connolly leather, mirror-matched walnut fascia and trim) support the promise of consequences to be obtained from purchasing the Jaguar *XJS.*

TABLE 10.3	**MECCAS: Means-End Conceptualization of Components for Advertising Strategy**
COMPONENT	DEFINITION
Value orientation	The end-level (terminal or instrumental value) to be focused on in the advertising; it serves as the driving force for the advertising execution.
Leverage point	The manner by which the advertising will tap into, reach, or activate the key value, or end level, that serves as the advertisement's driving force.
Executional framework	The overall scenario for the advertisement or action plot. The executional framework provides the mechanism for communicating the value orientation and the overall tone and style for the advertisement.
Brand consequence	The major positive consequences, or benefits of using the brand, that the advertisement verbally or visually communicates to consumers.
Brand attributes	The brand's specific attributes or features that are communicated as a means of supporting the consequences of using the brand.

FIGURE 10.5

MECCAS Illustration for Jaguar XJS

www.scjohnsonwax.com

Shout Gel. A magazine advertisement for Shout Gel laundry stain remover is shown in Figure 10.6. (Examine it carefully before reading on.) The *value orientation* in this ad is an appeal to conformity, that is, a good-parent's desire to take care of their children and to avoid the embarrassment of sending kids into public looking unkempt or dirty. The *leverage point* in this straightforward ad is the copy under the shots of the disheveled boy ("Concentrated Stain Maker") and the brand ("Concentrated Stain Remover"). In this case, it is not so much what the ad says as it is what it implies, and the implication is clear: Shout Gel will get children's clothing clean, which will make parents feel good about doing their job and conforming with society's expectation that this is what good parents do. The *executional framework* is a very clever juxtaposition of a red-headed, spiked-hair kid against an adjoining shot of Shout Gel's package with its built-in red brush. The brand consequences and attributes are clearly stated in the ad's body copy.

MECCAS Illustration
for Shout Gel

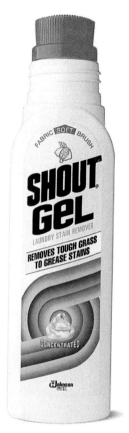

**CONCENTRATED
STAIN MAKER.**

**CONCENTRATED
STAIN REMOVER.**

Remove tough stains - from grass to grease - with Shout® Concentrated Gel.
The power of a gel. The penetration of a brush. Really tough stains have just met their match.

Shout Concentrated Gel. | **Want a tough stain out? Shout it out!®**

www.army.mil

The Army. The illustration in Figure 10.7 (please read before continuing) is a magazine ad for the U.S. Army. Note first that this advertisement is directed more at parents of
prospective recruits than at the recruits themselves. The *value orientation* that is the driving force behind this advertisement is an appeal to benevolence, the welfare of a family
member in this case. The *leverage point* is the scene of proud and loving parents who
appear to be pleased that their son is in the army. The *executional framework* is a warm
family scene in the parents' living room. The advertising creatives could have selected a
variety of other locations in which to place this "family moment." But by portraying an obviously middle-class situation, a statement is being made to other loving and successful
parents, namely that the army also is a wise choice for them and their child. The *consequences* and *attributes* are clearly stated in the body copy, all of which attest to why the

FIGURE
10.7

MECCAS Illustration
for U.S. Army

"The Army helped me give my son
what was best for him."

If you've always dreamed of giving your son a good education, look into the opportunities the Army has to offer. The Army can give your son the opportunity of earning up to $30,000 through the Montgomery GI Bill plus the Army College Fund. In the Army, he'll also gain self-confidence, learn discipline, develop character, and become motivated — the basics he needs to go far in college and in life. The Army can give your son something that money can't buy — an edge on life. For more information, call 1-800-USA-ARMY today. **ARMY. BE ALL YOU CAN BE.**

army is a good opportunity for one's child and thus a wise choice for those parents who support their child's decision to enlist.

www.world.sony.com

Sony Handycam Camcorder. A final illustration is presented in Figure 10.8. (Examine it carefully before reading on.) This magazine advertisement portrays a Little League baseball player at bat. In white lettering against a dark background the ad declares: "The ball charges toward the plate. Your knees buckle. Your body is utterly paralyzed with fear. Ah, the joys of parenthood." The driving force, or *value orientation*, in this clever ad is an appeal to parents' need for security—that is, protection against a technological

FIGURE 10.8

MECCAS Illustration for Sony
Handycam Camcorder

problem that would prevent them from capturing on videotape an important event in their child's life. The *leverage point* is the above-noted verbal copy that portrays the sense of trepidation a technologically challenged parent may experience when wondering whether an electronic product will perform at some critical moment. The *executional framework* is a baseball situation, probably selected because many parents can identify with the fast action of the game and the uncertainty surrounding events in the game: "Will he hit the ball this time at bat?" "Will he catch the ball when it comes in his direction?" Dependable performance is the primary *consequence* associated with choosing the Sony Handycam, and a variety of brand *attributes* (such as five continuous hours on one tape and one battery; steady shot stabilization) support the dependable-performance promise.

In conclusion, the important point to remember about the MECCAS approach is that it provides a systematic procedure for linking the advertiser's perspective (the possession of brand attributes and consequences) with the consumer's perspective (the pursuit of products and brands to achieve desired end states, or values). Effective advertising does not focus on product attributes/consequences per se; rather, it is directed at showing how the advertised brand will benefit the consumer and enable him or her to achieve what he or she most desires in life—self-determination, stimulation, hedonism, and the other values listed in Table 10.2. Products and brands vary in terms of which values they are capable of satisfying; nonetheless, all are capable of fulfilling some value(s), and it is the role of sophisticated advertising to identify and access these values. Advertising and other forms of marketing communications are most relevant to the consumer and thus most effective for the advertised brand when they are based on strong linkages between the right set of attributes, consequences, and values.[30] The next section briefly describes how the "right set" of attributes, consequences, and values is determined.

The Laddering Method

Laddering is a marketing research technique that has been developed to identify linkages between attributes (A), consequences (C), and values (V). The method is termed laddering because it leads to the construction of a hierarchy, or ladder, of relations between a brand's attributes/consequences and consumer values. **Laddering** involves in-depth, one-on-one interviews using primarily a series of directed probes typified by a question such as "Why is that important to you?"[31] With reference to the camcorder product category, imagine that an interviewer asks a father why it might be important to him to use a camcorder that allows for five continuous hours on one tape and one battery. He responds that this would enable him to take the camcorder to outside events (such as baseball games). A follow-up probe by the interviewer ("Why is that important to you?") further prompts our hypothetical father to reply that this would assure him of capturing important moments in his children's lives without constantly worrying whether the camcorder would perform upon demand. In response to a further, why-is-that-important prompt, he comments that being a good parent requires that children are left with visual images (photos, videotapes) of their childhood to enjoy when they are adults looking back on their earlier lives.

We see in this hypothetical description that a product attribute (five continuous hours of tape on one battery) is linked in this consumer's mind with the removal of doubt as to whether the camcorder will perform on demand (a consequence). This consequence is, in turn, linked to the value of security and being a good parent. The advertisement in Figure 10.8 apparently is based on the view that there is a substantial market segment of parents who view the camcorder product in this fashion. Laddering is an invaluable research tool for determining how to link product attributes and their consequences with consumers' desired end states, or values.

ALTERNATIVE CREATIVE STRATEGIES

The use of advertising to access consumer values opens the possibility of a variety of different creative approaches to provide the executional framework and to leverage the value orientation of the advertising strategy. Several relatively distinct creative advertising strategies have evolved over the years. In fact, the bulk of contemporary advertising can be conceptualized in terms of seven creative categories. These are summarized in Table 10.4 and are described in detail in the following sections.[32] It is important to note at the outset that these seven creative strategies are relatively distinct, but, as is the case with most category schemes, these creative strategies sometimes have "fuzzy borders" when applying them to specific advertising executions. Whereas some advertisements are exemplars of a single creative strategy, others can be classified into two or even three categories.

Generic Strategy

An advertiser employs a **generic strategy** when making a claim that could be made by any company that markets a brand in that product category. The advertiser makes *no* attempt to

TABLE 10.4

Summary of Creative Strategy Alternatives

ALTERNATIVE	MOST SUITABLE CONDITIONS	COMPETITIVE IMPLICATIONS
Generic Straight product or benefit claim with no assertion of superiority.	Monopoly or extreme dominance of product category.	Serves to make advertiser's brand synonymous with product category; may be combated through higher-order strategies.
Preemptive Generic claim with assertion of superiority.	Most useful in growing or awakening market where competitive advertising is generic or nonexistent.	May be successful in convincing consumer of superiority of advertiser's product; limited response options for competitors.
Unique Selling Proposition Superiority claims based on unique physical feature or benefit.	Most useful when point of difference cannot be readily matched by competitors.	Advertiser obtains strong persuasive advantage; may force competitors to imitate or choose more aggressive strategy (e.g., *positioning*).
Brand Image Claims based on psychological differentiation, usually symbolic association.	Best suited to homogeneous goods where physical differences are difficult to develop or may be quickly matched; requires sufficient understanding of consumers to develop meaningful symbols/associations.	Most often involves prestige claims that rarely challenge competitors directly.
Positioning Attempts to build or occupy mental niche in relation to identified competitor.	Best strategy for attacking a market leader; requires relatively long-term commitment to aggressive advertising efforts and understanding consumers.	Direct comparison severely limits options for named competitor; counterattacks seem to offer little chance of success.
Resonance Attempts to evoke stored experiences of prospects to endow product with relevant meaning or significance.	Best suited to socially visible goods; requires considerable consumer understanding to design message patterns.	Few direct limitations on competitor's options; most likely competitive response is imitation.
Emotional Attempts to provoke involvement or emotion through ambiguity, humor, or the like, without strong selling emphasis.	Best suited to discretionary items; effective use depends upon conventional approach by competitors to maximize difference; greatest commitment is to aesthetics or intuition rather than research.	Competitors may imitate to undermine strategy of difference or pursue other alternatives.

Source: Charles F. Frazer, "Creative Strategy: A Management Perspective," *Journal of Advertising* 12, no. 4 (1983), 40.

differentiate its brand from competitive offerings or to claim superiority. This strategy is most appropriate for a company that *dominates a product category*. In such instances, the firm making a generic claim will enjoy a large share of any primary demand stimulated by advertising.

For example, Campbell's dominates the prepared-soup market in the United States, selling nearly two-thirds of all soup. Any advertising that increases overall soup sales naturally benefits Campbell's. This explains the "Soup is good food" campaign used by Campbell's in the early 1990s. This advertising extolled the virtues of eating soup without arguing why people should buy Campbell's soup. Campbell's subsequently followed this campaign with another one that simply declared, "Never underestimate the power of soup." Along similar lines, AT&T's "Reach out and touch someone" campaign, which encouraged more long-distance calling, was a wise strategy in light of this company's grasp on the long-distance phone market.

Preemptive Strategy

www.chase.com

Preemptive strategy is employed when an advertiser makes a generic-type claim but does so with an *assertion of superiority*. This strategy is used most often by advertisers in product or service categories where there are few, if any, functional differences among competitive brands. Preemptive advertising is a clever strategy when a meaningful superiority claim is made because it effectively precludes competitors from saying the same thing. Any branch of the military service could claim that they enable recruits to "be all you can be" (see the use of this claim in Figure 10.7), but no other branch could possibly make such a claim after the army adopted this as its unique statement. The huge Chase Bank, which resulted from the merger of Chase Manhattan and Chemical banks, undertook a $45 million advertising campaign shortly after the merger that referred to Chase as "the Relationship Company." In a clear recognition of the value of preemption, the chief marketing officer for Chase justified the campaign by stating "The idea is to stamp that word [relationship] on our brand enough to preempt the use of it by anyone else in the category."[33]

www.visine.com

www.nissan-usa.com

The maker of Visine eyedrops advertised that this brand "gets the red out." All eyedrops are designed to get the red out, but, by making this claim first, Visine made a dramatic statement that the consumer will associate only with Visine. No other company would make this claim now for fear of being labeled a mimic. An advertisement for Hanes' Smooth Illusions pantyhose used a brilliant preemptive claim in comparing that brand to "Liposuction without surgery." Another clever preemptive campaign was introduced by Nissan Motor Corporation several years ago with its advertising of the *Maxima*. Preceding the campaign, the *Maxima* competed against models such as the Ford *Taurus* and the Toyota *Cressida* in the upper-middle segment of the industry, a segment which at the time had experienced a 25 percent sales decline over a two-year period. To avoid stiff price competition and price rebates, Nissan wanted a more upscale and high-performance image for the *Maxima*. Based on extensive research, *Maxima's* advertising agency devised a brilliant preemptive line which touted the *Maxima* as the "four-door sports car." Of course, other sedans have four doors, but *Maxima* preempted sports-car status for itself with this one clever claim. Its sales immediately increased by 43 percent over the previous year despite a price increase, and *Maxima* began appealing to more upscale consumers.[34]

www.patek.com

A final illustration of the preemptive strategy is the advertising for the luxury Swiss brand of watches named Patek Philippe. Magazine advertisements for this brand portrayed happy scenes of a parent enjoying the company of his or her same-sex child. Corresponding advertising copy simply asserted "You never actually own a Patek Philippe. You merely take care of it for the next generation." Such a claim could be made by any maker of luxury watches, but in appropriating this claim with its implicit assertion of superiority Patek Philippe has preempted competitors from using the heritage tact in advertising their own brands.

Unique Selling-Proposition Strategy

With the **unique selling-proposition (USP)** strategy, an advertiser makes a superiority claim based on a unique product attribute that represents a *meaningful, distinctive consumer benefit*. The main feature of USP advertising is identifying an important difference that makes a brand unique and then developing an advertising claim that competitors either cannot make or have chosen not to make. The translation of the unique product feature into a relevant consumer benefit provides the unique selling proposition. The USP strategy is best suited for a company with a brand that possesses a relatively lasting competitive advantage, such as a maker of a technically complex item or a provider of a sophisticated service.

The Gillette Sensor razor used a USP when claiming that it is "the only razor that senses and adjusts to the individual needs of your face." The Dodge *Caravan* had a unique selling proposition, if only temporarily, when it was able to claim that it was "the first and the only minivan with a driver's air bag." Nicoderm CQ's USP is contained in the claim that this product is the only nicotine-substitute patch "you can wear for 24 hours" (see Figure 10.9).

In many respects the unique selling-proposition strategy is the optimum creative technique. This is because it gives the consumer a clearly differentiated reason for selecting the advertiser's brand over competitive offerings. The only reason USP advertising is not used more often is because brands in most product categories are pretty much homogeneous. They have no unique physical advantages to advertise and therefore are forced to use strategies favoring the more symbolic, psychological end of the strategy continuum.[35]

FIGURE 10.9

Illustration of a USP Creative Strategy

One stop-smoking patch is better at calming the cravings that can tempt you to reach for that first cigarette:

NICODERM® CQ™ IS BETTER THAN THE OTHER PATCH AT CALMING MORNING CRAVINGS.*

CQ is the only patch you can wear for 24 hours. And it's the only patch that gives you 3 strengths* so you can step down your dose gradually.† (Gradual is the method doctors and pharmacists prefer.)

The power to **Calm.**
The power to **Comfort.**
The power to help you **Quit** successfully.™

Partners in Helping You Quit

AMERICAN CANCER SOCIETY®

SB *SmithKline Beecham* NicoDerm CQ helps reduce withdrawal symptoms, including nicotine craving and irritability, associated with quitting smoking. *Refers only to non-prescription patches. †Light smokers start at Step 2. Helps you to stop smoking when used as directed in enclosed user's guide. Nicotrol is a registered trademark of Pharmacia A.B. ©1997 SmithKline Beecham Consumer Healthcare L.P.

Brand-Image Strategy

Whereas the USP strategy is based on promoting physical and functional differences between the advertiser's product and competitive offerings, the **brand-image strategy** involves *psychological,* rather than physical, differentiation. Advertising attempts to develop an image or identity for a brand by associating the product with symbols. In imbuing a brand with an image, advertisers draw meaning from the culturally constituted world (that is, the world of artifacts and symbols) and transfer that meaning to their brands. In effect, the properties of the culturally constituted world that are well known to consumers come to reside in the unknown properties of the advertised brand.[36]

Developing an image through advertising amounts to giving a brand a *distinct identity* or *personality.* This is especially important for brands that compete in product categories where there is relatively little physical differentiation and all brands are relatively homogeneous (beer, soft drinks, cigarettes, bluejeans, etc.). Thus Pepsi at one time was referred to as the soft drink for the "new generation." Mountain Dew has consistently presented itself as a hip, outrageous brand for teens who drink the beverage in outdoor settings.[37]

Brand image advertising might also be described as *transformational.* **Transformational advertising** associates the experience of using an advertised brand with a unique set of psychological characteristics that would *not* typically be associated with the brand experience to the same degree without exposure to the advertisement. Such advertising is transforming (versus informing) by virtue of endowing brand usage with a particular experience that is different from using any similar brand. By virtue of repeated advertising, the brand becomes associated with its advertisements and the people, scenes, or events in these advertisements.[38] Transformational advertisements contain two notable characteristics:[39]

1. They make the experience of using the brand richer, warmer, more exciting, or more enjoyable than what would be the case based solely on an objective description of the brand.

2. They connect the experience of using the brand so tightly with the experience of the advertisement that consumers cannot remember the brand without recalling the advertising experience. Marlboro cigarettes and cowboys, for example, are inextricably woven together in many consumers' memories.

The following *Global Focus* describes a very successful transformational advertisement for a brand of television marketed in India under the name Private.

Positioning Strategy

Successful advertising must, according to **positioning strategy,** implant in the customer's mind *a clear meaning of what the product is and how it compares to competitive offerings.* Effective positioning requires that a company be fully aware of its competition and exploit competitive weaknesses. A brand is positioned in the consumer's mind relative to competition. The originators of the positioning concept, Jack Trout and Al Ries, contend that successful companies must be "competitors' oriented," must look for weak points in their competitors' positions, and then launch marketing attacks against those weak points.[40]

These same management consultants claim that many marketing people and advertisers are in error when operating under the assumption that marketing is a battle of products. Their contrary position is this:

> There are no best products. All that exists in the world of marketing are perceptions in the minds of the customer or prospect. The perception is the reality. Everything else is an illusion.[41]

This perhaps is a bit overstated, but the important point is that how good (or how prestigious, dependable, sexy, etc.) a brand is depends more on what people think than on objective reality. And what people think is largely a function of effective advertising that builds strong brand images.

GLOBAL FOCUS: NOT NECESSARILY A BETTER TV, BUT A BETTER TV COMMERCIAL

Videocon, a local India-based electronics company, faced stiff competition in its own country from the likes of such global giants as Sanyo and Sony. But on the merits of a clever TV commercial, Videocon's brand of 14-inch TV sets became the dominant brand in India.

The 14-inch set has traditionally been the Indian family's second TV set. With a 20 percent market share and a product with technological advantages over competitive brands, Videocon needed a creative way to differentiate its brand. When Videocon's advertising agency analyzed the market, it became clear that most 14-inch sets were positioned as solutions to family conflicts over channel choices—apparently a universal problem in all families. Privacy *is* the key benefit provided by ownership of a second, 14-inch set, but marketers of all brands can make the same claim, which hardly provides any form of uniqueness. Indeed, advertising of 14-inch TV sets had been rather dull and unimaginative in India until Videocon's advertising agency went to work.

The agency first gave Videocon's 14-inch set a great brand name, Private. Then it went about the task of creating advertising that would truly transform the experience of owning this brand. One television spot, for example, showed a mother telling her teenage daughter to go to bed. In her room, the girl proceeded to turn on her Private set and began dancing when Elvis Presley's "Jailhouse Rock" appeared on the set. The mother, hearing the noise of the daughter's dancing, peered through the keyhole, recognized the song, and broke into a dance herself. Meanwhile, the daughter, hearing a noise outside her room, peeked through the keyhole and shrieked upon seeing her mother dancing.

The response to this commercial was immediate. In a matter of only months, Private's market share jumped from 20 to 39 percent! This massive gain was accomplished with an advertising investment of only $310,000.

Source: Adapted from Mir Maqbool Alam Khan, "India's 'Private' Positioning Is a Hit with Public," *Advertising Age,* January 16, 1995, I4.

www.pontiac.com

Numerous examples are available to illustrate positioning strategies. The automobile industry relies heavily on positioning. For example, Pontiac's positioning theme at one time was "We build excitement." Volvo positioned itself as "a car you can believe in," and supported the claim by showing in advertising how sturdy the product is. Chevrolet used a patriotic theme in promoting itself as "the heartbeat of America." Toyota positioned itself as a maker of quality automobiles. ("Who could ask for anything more?")

It is important to realize that positioning strategy is *not* mutually exclusive of other strategies. Advertising positions brands in consumers' minds in comparison to competitive brands. This positioning can be implemented using USP, brand-image, or other creative approaches.

Resonance Strategy

When used in the advertising-strategy sense, the term *resonance* is analogous to the physical notion of resonance, which refers to noise resounding off an object. In similar fashion, an advertisement resonates *(patterns)* the audience's life experiences. Resonant advertising strategy extends from psychographic research and structures an advertising campaign to pattern the prevailing lifestyle orientation of the intended market segment.

Resonant advertising does not focus on product claims or brand images but rather seeks to present circumstances or situations that find counterparts in the real or imagined experiences of the target audience. Advertising based on this strategy attempts to match "patterns" in an advertisement with the target audience's stored experiences.

www.buick.com

The two advertisements in Figure 10.10 for the Buick LeSabre illustrate use of resonance strategy. The ad on the left portrays a young family enjoying time together on their porch, while the ad on the right side portrays a successful young couple relaxing in the comfort of their living room. Both ads refer to the safety of home and then suggest that the LeSabre's safety features make driving that automobile as safe as being at home.

Illustration of Resonant Creative Strategy

FIGURE
10.10

*The 1997 LeSabre.
The family's safely home...*

Out there, you rely on things like the safety
of LeSabre's dual air bags.* You rely on the
performance of its anti-lock brakes. And your family
relies on you. For more reasons why you and your
family can rely on LeSabre, visit our Web site at
http://www.buick.com or call 1-800-4A-BUICK.

©1996 GM Corp. All rights reserved. LeSabre is a registered trademark of GM Corp. Buckle up. America! **BUICK**
*Always wear safety belts, even with air bags.

*LeSabre.
The comfort and safety of home...
on the road.*

Its comfort will put you at ease. Its arsenal of safety
features will give you a sense of inner peace. Make you feel
almost invulnerable. That's why those who want to
feel at home on the road drive the Buick LeSabre. For
your peace of mind, drive LeSabre. For more details, visit our
Web site at www.lesabre.buick.com or call 1-800-4A-BUICK.

©1997 GM Corp. All rights reserved. LeSabre is a registered trademark of GM Corp. Buckle up, America!

Emotional Strategy

Much contemporary advertising aims to reach the consumer at a visceral level through the use of emotional strategy.[42] Many advertising practitioners and scholars recognize that products are often bought on the basis of emotional factors and that appeals to emotion can be very successful if used appropriately and with the right products. The use of emotion in advertising runs the gamut of positive and negative appeals, including appeals to romance, nostalgia, compassion, excitement, joy, fear, guilt, disgust, and regret.[43]

Though the emotional strategy can be used when advertising virtually any product, emotional advertising seems to work especially well for products that naturally are associated with emotions (e.g., foods, jewelry, cosmetics, fashion apparel, soft drinks, and long-distance telephoning). The magazine advertisement in Figure 10.11, which says virtually nothing about product characteristics, typifies the use of an emotional appeal for Lever 2000 Bodywash.

Illustration of Emotional
Creative Strategy

In Sum

Seven general forms of creative strategy have been discussed. These strategic alternatives provide a useful aid to understanding the different approaches available to advertisers and the factors influencing the choice of creative strategy.

It would be incorrect to think of these strategies as pure and mutually exclusive. Because there is some unavoidable overlap, it is possible that an advertiser may consciously or unconsciously use two or more strategies simultaneously. For example, a positioning strategy can be used in conjunction with any of the other strategies. An advertiser can position a brand against competitors' brands using emotional strategy, image strategy, a unique selling proposition, or other possibilities.

It is also worth noting that some advertising experts contend that advertising is most effective when it reflects both ends of the creative advertising continuum—that is, by addressing both rational product benefits and symbolic/psychological benefits. A New York advertising agency, Lowe Marschalk, provided evidence in partial support of the superiority of combined benefits over only rational appeals. The agency tested 168 television commercials, 47 of which contained both rational and psychological appeals and 121 of which contained rational appeals only. Using recall and persuasion measures, the agency found that the ads containing both rational and psychological appeals outperformed the rational-only ads by a substantial margin.[44]

CORPORATE IMAGE AND ISSUE ADVERTISING

The type of advertising discussed to this point is commonly referred to as product- or brand-oriented advertising. Such advertising focuses on a product or, more typically, a specific brand and attempts ultimately to persuade consumers to purchase the advertiser's product/brand.

Another form of advertising, termed **corporate advertising,** focuses not on specific products or brands but on a corporation's overall image or on economic/social issues relevant to the corporation's interests. This form of advertising is widespread and increasing.[45] Consistent spending on corporate advertising can serve to boost a corporation's equity, much in the same fashion that product-oriented advertising is an investment in the brand-equity bank.[46]

Two somewhat distinct forms of corporate advertising are discussed in the following sections: (1) image advertising and (2) issue, or advocacy, advertising.[47]

Corporate Image Advertising

This type of corporate advertising has been defined as follows:

> *Corporate image advertising is aimed at creating an image of a specific corporate personality in the minds of the general public and seeking maximum favorable images amongst selected audiences (e.g., stockholders, employees, consumers, suppliers, and potential investors). In essence, this type of advertising treats the company as a product, carefully positioning and clearly differentiating it from other similar companies and basically "selling" this product to selected audiences. Corporate image advertising is not concerned with a social problem unless it has a preferred solution. It asks no action on the part of the audience beyond a favorable attitude and passive approval conducive to successful operation in the marketplace.*[48]

Corporate image advertising attempts to increase a firm's name recognition, establish goodwill for the company and its products, or identify itself with some meaningful and socially acceptable activity. For example, the two "Think different" ads in Figure 10.12 for Apple Computer associate this company with two famous personages (Amelia Earhart, an American pilot who presumably died—her body was never recovered—while attempting to cross the Pacific in 1937, and Alfred Hitchcock, the producer of suspenseful TV programs) attempt to convey the impression that Apple Computer, Inc. is a daring company. Like other corporate image advertisements, these ads attempt to accomplish two overriding objectives: increase consumer recognition of the Apple name and enhance the company's image. In general, research has found that executives regard name identity and image building to be the two most important functions of corporate advertising.[49]

Corporate image advertising is directed at more than merely trying to make consumers feel good about a company. Companies are increasingly using the image of their firms to enhance sales and financial performance.[50] Corporate advertising that does not contribute to increased sales and profits is difficult to justify in today's climate of accountability.[51]

Corporate Issue (Advocacy) Advertising

The other form of corporate advertising is **issue,** or **advocacy, advertising.** When using issue advertising a company takes a position on a controversial social issue of public importance "in hopes of swaying public opinion."[52] It does so in a manner that supports the

Illustration of Corporate Image Advertising

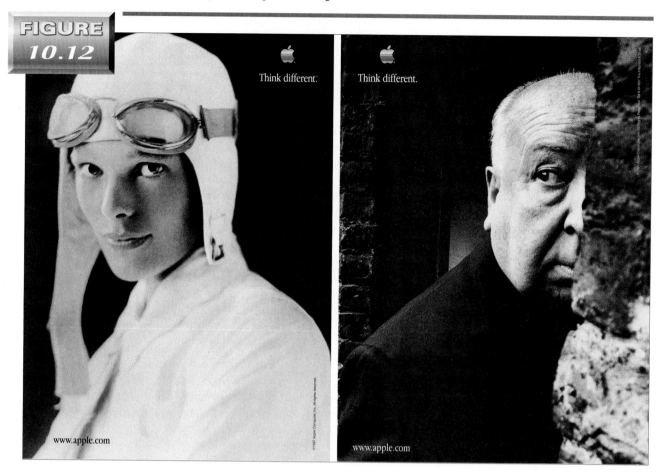

company's position and best interests while expressly or implicitly challenging the opponent's position and denying the accuracy of their facts.[53]

An example of issue (advocacy) advertising is presented in Figure 10.13. The advertisement is just one of several ads undertaken by Philip Morris in a campaign that describes smokers' rights and efforts to accommodate differences between smokers and nonsmokers.

Issue advertising is a topic of considerable controversy.[54] Business executives are divided on whether this form of advertising represents an effective allocation of corporate resources. What, for example, does the Philip Morris ad hope to accomplish? Will it ultimately increase product sales and profits? How?

Critics question the legitimacy of issue advertising and challenge its status as a tax-deductible expenditure. Since further discussion of these points is beyond the scope of this chapter, the interested reader is encouraged to review the sources contained in the last endnote.[55]

FIGURE 10.13

Illustration of Corporate Issue Advertising

Our position, word by word.

Accommodation

Accommodation is the reasonable way for smokers and nonsmokers to work out their differences.

That is our position at Philip Morris. And it turns out that most Americans share this view.

In a recent USA TODAY/CNN poll among both smokers and nonsmokers, nearly 7 out of 10 respondents said they think that rather than banning smoking in public places, smokers should be allowed to smoke in separate, designated areas.

Philip Morris has a program that helps owners of businesses, such as restaurants, bars and hotels, to accommodate the choices of both smoking and nonsmoking customers by setting up designated smoking and non-smoking areas.

The program works because it respects the rights and wishes of both groups. So both get what they want.

That's accommodation.

You could also call it a win-win situation.

For a free copy of our booklet, *Smoking Issues,* which contains more information about The Accommodation Program, as well as information on other issues relating to smoking, please call us at 1-800-852-3445, Ext. 221.

PHILIP MORRIS U.S.A.

We want you to know where we stand.

| Facts Matter | Businesses where smoking has been banned have reported, in some cases, up to a 30% loss in sales. Some restaurants have been forced to fire employees and others have even had to close down. |

© 1994 Philip Morris Inc.

Summary

The chapter examines creative advertising, advertising-strategy formulation, means-end models, creative strategies, and corporate image and issue advertising. An important initial question asks, What are the general characteristics of effective advertising? Discussion points out that effective advertising must: (1) extend from sound marketing strategy, (2) take the consumer's view, (3) be persuasive, (4) break through the competitive clutter, (5) never promise more than can be delivered, and (6) prevent the creative idea from overwhelming the strategy.

Creative advertising formulation involves a multistep process. The strategy is initiated by specifying the key fact advertising should convey to the target market. This key fact is translated, in step 2, into the primary marketing problem. Extending from this problem statement is the selection of specific communications objectives. The guts of advertising strategy consists, in step 4, of designing the creative message strategy. This involves selecting the target market, identifying the primary competition, and choosing the primary benefit to emphasize. The last step in the process involves ensuring that the advertisement meets all corporate/divisional requirements.

The next major subject covered in this chapter is the concept of means-end chains and the advertising framework extending from the MECCAS (means-end conceptualization of components for advertising strategy) model. Means-end chains and MECCAS models provide bridges between product attributes (the means), the consequences to the consumer of realizing product attributes, and the ability of these consequences to satisfy consumption-related values (the end). MECCAS models provide an organizing framework for developing creative ads that simultaneously consider attributes, consequences, and values.

The use of advertising to tap consumer values leaves open the possibility of a variety of different creative strategies. Seven specific strategies—generic, preemptive, unique selling proposition, brand image, positioning, resonance, and emotional—are described and illustrated with examples.

The final subject discussed is corporate advertising. A distinction is made between conventional product- and brand-oriented strategy and advertising that focuses on facilitating corporate goodwill, enhancing its image, and advocating matters of economic or social significance to a corporation. Two forms of corporate advertising, image and issue (advocacy) advertising, are also described.

Discussion Questions

1. One requirement for effective advertising is the ability to break through competitive clutter. Explain what this means, and provide several examples of advertising methods that successfully accomplish this.

2. Explain the meaning of the MECCAS model, and describe an advertising campaign of your choice in terms of this model—that is, discuss specifically the value orientation, leverage point, and so on.

3. Explain the differences between unique selling-proposition and brand-image strategies, and indicate the specific conditions under which each is more likely to be used.

4. Positioning strategy is not mutually exclusive of other creative advertising strategies. Explain what this means, and discuss how positioning can be achieved using different types of creative strategies. Provide examples of actual advertisements to buttress your points.

5. What is a resonant advertising strategy? Explain the similarity between resonant advertising and what some advertising practitioners call slice-of-life advertising.

6. A television commercial for Miller Genuine Draft beer started out by showing scenes of people experiencing a stifling summer day while fantasizing about a cold beer. In a subsequent scene,

Miller Genuine Draft came into the picture, and, as people opened cans of beer, the urban setting miraculously changed from a hot summer day to snow-covered streets. Describe how this television commercial represents a form of preemptive strategy.

7. Explain the preceding commercial in terms of means-end chain components (attributes, consequences, and values).

8. Some critics contend that advocacy, or issue, advertising should not be treated as a legitimate tax-deduction expenditure. Present and justify your opinion on this matter.

9. Select two advertising campaigns that have been on television for some time, and describe in detail what you think their creative message strategies are.

10. Review magazine advertisements, and locate specific examples of the seven creative strategies that were discussed in the chapter. Be sure to justify why each ad is a good illustration of the strategy with which you identify it.

11. Along the lines of the FTD case described in the chapter, select an advertising campaign, and reconstruct in detail your interpretation of all the steps in the campaign's advertising strategy.

*I*nternet Exercises

Currently, Internet advertising is dominated by "banners" (rectangular strips of space on a Web page allotted to advertisers). Banners are typically small in comparison to the visual field of a computer monitor so that they do not obscure Web page content or take too long to download. Early banners simply begged consumers to "click through" (i.e., click on the banner) to visit a company or brand Web site. However, sponsors soon realized that most people do not click through but are still exposed to the banner. Recognizing this lost opportunity to communicate, sponsors have begun to require banners to not only encourage click through but also to serve as a stand-alone brand communication effort. Given the small size of banners, these requirements present a formidable challenge for banner designers. To investigate this issue, visit several sites where banner advertising is prevalent (e.g., any search engine, online newspapers). Based on your observations and the material covered in the chapter, discuss the following:

1. Are banner ads effective from the standpoint of the MECCAS model? Be sure to discuss each component of the model and provide examples to support your argument.

2. Is there evidence for each of the seven creative strategies discussed in the chapter in the banners you observed? Provide specific examples for those strategies you find to be represented and describe how these examples typify the strategy. If a strategy is not represented, explain why you think it is absent (other than inadequate sampling on your part).

*C*hapter Ten Endnotes

1. George Donahue, "Evaluating Advertising Services: Part II," *Marketing Communications,* April 1982, 61.

2. Ibid., 64.

3. Wes Perrin, *Advertising Realities: A Practical Guide to Agency Management* (Mountain View, Calif.: Mayfield Publishing, 1992), 74–75.

4. The discount paid to advertising agencies for outdoor advertising is typically 16.67 percent.

5. Judann Pollack, "ANA Survey: Under 50% Pay Agency Commissions," *Advertising Age,* June 15, 1998, 18.

6. Ibid.

7. Gregory White, "Ford's Better Idea for Agencies: Incentives Instead of Commissions,"

The Wall Street Journal Interactive Edition, September 10, 1998.

8. The following points are a mixture of the author's views and perspectives presented by A. Jerome Jewler, *Creative Strategy in Advertising* (Belmont, Calif.: Wadsworth, 1985), 7–8; and Don E. Schultz and Stanley I. Tannenbaum, *Essentials of Advertising Strategy* (Lincolnwood, Ill.: NTC Business Books, 1988), 9–10.

9. Stan Freberg, "Irtnog Revisited," *Advertising Age,* August 1, 1988, 32.

10. Schultz and Tannenbaum, *Essentials of Advertising Strategy,* 75. This quote actually describes what these authors term "creative advertising," but they use *creative* in the same

sense as the present use of *good,* or *effective,* advertising.

11. Bob Garfield, "The Best TV: VW," *Advertising Age,* May 18, 1998, s1.

12. For an interesting discussion on creativity and the creative process in advertising, see Vincent J. Blasko and Michael P. Mokwa, "Paradox, Advertising and the Creative Process," in *Current Issues and Research in Advertising,* ed. J. H. Leigh and C. R. Martin, Jr. (Ann Arbor: Graduate School of Business Administration, University of Michigan, 1989), 351–366.

13. Terence Poltrack, "Stalking the Big Idea," *Agency,* June 1991, 26.

14. Ibid.

15. Lou Centlivre, "A Peek at the Creative of the '90s," *Advertising Age,* January 18, 1988, 62.

16. Schultz and Tannenbaum, *Essentials of Advertising Strategy,* 4.

17. The following discussion is an adaptation from Don E. Schultz, Dennis Martin, and William P. Brown, *Strategic Advertising Campaigns* (Lincolnwood, Ill.: NTC Business Books, 1987), 240–245.

18. This discussion is broadly based on Leah Rickard, "FTD Fights Back in $16M Image Ads," *Advertising Age,* September 27, 1993, 12.

19. Arthur J. Kover, "Copywriters' Implicit Theories of Communication: An Exploration," *Journal of Consumer Research* 21 (March 1995), 596–611.

20. These guidelines are based on an undated document ("How to Write a Creative Brief") from the Ogilvy & Mather Worldwide.

21. Harvey Penick with Bud Shrake, *Harvey Penick's Little Red Book* (New York: Simon & Schuster, 1992), 45.

22. This discussion is based on various writings by Professors Gutman and Reynolds, who, along with several colleagues, have popularized means-end theory in advertising. For example, see Jonathan Gutman, "A Means-End Chain Model Based on Consumer Categorization Processes," *Journal of Marketing* 46 (spring 1982), 60–72; Thomas J. Reynolds and Jonathan Gutman, "Advertising Is Image Management," *Journal of Advertising Research* 24 (February/March 1984), 27–36; Thomas J. Reynolds and Jonathan Gutman, "Laddering Theory, Method, Analysis, and Interpretation," *Journal of Advertising Research* 28 (February/March 1988), 11–31; and Thomas J. Reynolds and Alyce Byrd Craddock, "The Application of MECCAS Model to the Development and Assessment of Advertising Strategy: A Case Study," *Journal of Advertising Research* 28 (April/May 1988), 43–59.

23. For further discussion of cultural values, see Lynn R. Kahle, Basil Poulos, and Ajay Sukhdial, "Changes in Social Values in the United States during the Past Decade," *Journal of Advertising Research* 28 (February/March 1988), 35–41; Sharon E. Beatty, Lynn R. Kahle, Pamela Homer, and Shekhar Misra, "Alternative Measurement Approaches to Consumer Values: The List of Values and the Rokeach Value Survey," *Psychology and Marketing* 2, no. 3 (1985), 181–200; Wagner A. Kamakura and Jose Afonso Mazzon, "Value Segmentation: A Model for the Measurement of Values and Value Systems," *Journal of Consumer Research* 18 (September 1991), 208–218; and Wagner A. Kamakura and Thomas P. Novak, "Value-System Segmentation: Exploring the Meaning of LOV," *Journal of Consumer Research* 19 (June 1992), 119–132.

24. Shalom H. Schwartz, "Universals in the Content and Structure of Values: Theoretical Advances and Empirical Tests in 20 Countries," *Advances in Experimental Social Psychology* 25 (1992), 4.

25. J. Paul Peter and Jerry C. Olson, *Consumer Behavior: Marketing Strategy Perspectives* (Homewood, Ill.: Irwin, 1990).

26. Schwartz, "Universals in the Content and Structure of Values."

27. These descriptions are based on ibid., pp. 5–12.

28. Jerry Olson and Thomas J. Reynolds, "Understanding Consumers' Cognitive Structures: Implications for Advertising Strategy," in *Advertising and Consumer Psychology,* ed. L. Percy and A. Woodside (Lexington, Mass.: Lexington Books, 1983), 77–90.

29. The language used in Table 10.3 is adapted from that employed in the various writings of Gutman and Reynolds, such as those cited in note 22. It is the author's experience that students are confused with the terminology originally used. The present terminology is more user friendly without doing a disservice to the original MECCAS conceptualization.

30. Thomas J. Reynolds and David B. Whitlark, "Applying Laddering Data to Communications Strategy and Advertising Practice," *Journal of Advertising Research* 35 (July/August 1995), 9.

31. Reynolds and Gutman "Laddering Theory, Method, Analysis, and Interpretation," 12.

32. The following discussion is based on Charles F. Frazer, "Creative Strategy: A Management Perspective," *Journal of Advertising* 12, no. 4 (1983), 36–41. For another perspective on creative strategies, see Henry A. Laskey, Ellen Day, and Melvin R. Crask, "Typology of Main Message Strategies for Television Commercials," *Journal of Advertising* 18, no. 1 (1989), 36–41.

33. Terry Lefton, "Cutting to the Chase," *Brandweek,* April 7, 1997, 47.

34. This description is based on "Four-Door Sports Car," *1990 Winners of the Effie Gold Awards: Case Studies in Advertising Effectiveness* (New York: American Marketing Association of New York and the American Association of Advertising Agencies, 1991), 124–131.

35. An interesting debate on the issue of whether a USP strategy is appropriate even for parity products is available in the offsetting views of Dennis Chase and Bob Garfield, "Can Unique Selling Proposition Find Happiness in Parity World?" *Advertising Age,* September 21, 1992, 58.

36. Grant McCracken, "Culture and Consumption: A Theoretical Account of the Structure and Movement of the Cultural Meaning of Consumer Goods," *Journal of Consumer Research* 13 (June 1986), 74.

37. "Mountain Dew Stays True to Its Positioning," *Advertising Age,* May 18, 1998, 26.

38. Christopher P. Puto and William D. Wells, "Informational and Transformational Advertising: The Differential Effects of Time," in *Advances in Consumer Research,* vol. 11, ed. Thomas C. Kinnear (Provo, Utah: Association for Consumer Research, 1984), 638–643. See also David A. Aaker and Douglas M. Stayman, "Implementing the Concept of Transformational Advertising," *Psychology & Marketing* 9 (May/June 1992), 237–253.

39. Ibid., 638.

40. Jack Trout and Al Ries, "The Positioning Era: A View Ten Years Later," *Advertising Age,* July 16, 1979, 39–42.

41. Al Ries and Jack Trout, *The 22 Immutable Laws of Marketing* (New York: Harper Business, 1993), 19.

42. Frazer "(Creative Strategy")" refers to this as "affective strategy," but "emotional strategy" is more descriptive and less subject to alternative interpretations.

43. For a variety of perspectives on the use of emotion in advertising, see Stuart J. Agres, Julie A. Edell, and Tony M. Dubitsky, *Emotion in Advertising: Theoretical and Practical Explorations* (New York: Quorum Books, 1990).

44. Kim Foltz, "Psychological Appeal in TV Ads Found Effective," *Adweek,* August 31, 1987, 38.

45. David W. Schumann, Jan M. Hathcote, and Susan West, "Corporate Advertising in America: A Review of Published Studies on Use, Measurement, and Effectiveness," *Journal of Advertising* 20 (September 1991), 35–56. This article provides a thorough review of corporate advertising and is must reading for anyone interested in the topic. For evidence of the increase in corporate advertising, see Mercedes M. Cardona, "Corporate-Ad Budgets At Record High: ANA Survey," *Advertising Age,* April 27, 1998, 36.

46. Mercedes M. Cardona, "Study Establishes Link of Corp. Ads, Branding," *Advertising Age,* August 24, 1998, 32.

47. This distinction is based on a classification by S. Prakash Sethi, "Institutional/Image Advertising and Idea/Issue Advertising As Marketing Tools: Some Public Policy Issues," *Journal of Marketing* 43 (January 1979), 68–78. Sethi

actually labels the two subsets of corporate advertising as "institutional/image" and "idea/issue." For reading ease they are shortened here to image versus issue advertising.

48. Ibid.

49. See Charles H. Patti and John P. McDonald, "Corporate Advertising: Process, Practices, and Perspectives (1970–1989)," *Journal of Advertising* 14, no. 1 (1985), 42–49.

50. Lewis C. Winters, "Does It Pay to Advertise to Hostile Audiences with Corporate Advertising?" *Journal of Advertising Research* 28 (June/July 1988), 11–18.

51. Lori Kesler, "Merger Craze Colors Image," *Advertising Age,* October 5, 1987, S1–4.

52. Bob D. Cutler and Darrel D. Muehling, "Advocacy Advertising and the Boundaries of Commercial Speech," *Journal of Advertising* 18, no. 3 (1989), 40.

53. Sethi, "Institutional/Image Advertising," 70.

54. For discussion of the First Amendment issues surrounding the use of advocacy advertising, see Cutler and Muehling, "Advocacy Advertising and the Boundaries of Commercial Speech"; and Kent R. Middleton, "Advocacy Advertising, The First Amendment and Competitive Advantage: A Comment on Cutler & Muehling," *Journal of Advertising* 20 (June 1991), 77–81.

55. Louis Banks, "Taking on the Hostile Media," *Harvard Business Review* (March/April 1978), 123–130; Barbara J. Coe, "The Effectiveness Challenge in Issue Advertising Campaigns," *Journal of Advertising* 12, no. 4 (1983), 27–35; David Kelley, "Critical Issues for Issue Ads," *Harvard Business Review* (July/August 1982), 80–87; Ward Welty, "Is Issue Advertising Working?" *Public Relations Journal* (November 1981), 29. For an especially thorough and insightful treatment of issue advertising, particularly with regard to the measurement of effectiveness, see Karen F. A. Fox, "The Measurement of Issue/Advocacy Advertising," in *Current Issues and Research in Advertising,* vol. 9, ed. James H. Leigh and Claude R. Martin, Jr. (Ann Arbor: Division of Research, Graduate School of Business Administration, University of Michigan, 1986), 61–92.

Message Appeals and Endorsers in Advertising

CHAPTER OBJECTIVES

After studying this chapter, you should be able to:

1. Describe the role of endorsers in advertising.
2. Explain the requirements for an effective endorser.
3. Discuss the role of Q-ratings in selecting celebrity endorsers.
4. Describe the role of humor in advertising.
5. Explain the logic underlying the use of fear appeals in advertising.
6. Understand the nature of guilt appeals in advertising.
7. Discuss the role of sex appeals in advertising, including the downside of such usage.
8. Explain the meaning of subliminal messages and symbolic embeds.
9. Appreciate the role of music in advertising.
10. Understand the role of comparative advertising and the considerations that influence the use of this form of advertising.

Opening Vignette: Dead Is Alive . . . in Celebrity Endorsements

Celebrities—chosen primarily from the entertainment business or the athletic field—are mainstays of North American advertising. This is understandable in as much consumers readily identify with these stars, often regarding them as heroes and heroines for their accomplishments, personalities, and physical appeal.

Advertisers have fondly used celebrities in advertising because their famous attributes—including beauty, courage, talent, athleticism, grace, power, and sex appeal—often represent the attractions desired for the brands they endorse. The repeated association of a brand with a celebrity may ultimately lead consumers to think the brand possesses the attractive qualities that are similar to the celebrity's. More generally, consumers may like a brand merely because they like the celebrity who endorses it. Regardless of the specific mechanism by which celebrities enhance the value of brands, the undeniable fact is that they are often worth the millions of dollars advertisers pay for their services.

There is, nevertheless, a distinct *downside* to using celebrity endorsers. Suppose a celebrity is convicted of a crime or has his or her image blemished in some way during the course of an advertising campaign. What are the potential negative implications for the endorsed brand? Frankly, there are no simple answers to this provocative question, and researchers are just beginning to explore the issue in a sophisticated fashion.

FIGURE
11.1

Illustration Using
a Dead Celebrity

Bogart wore khakis.

GAP
KHAKIS

In the meantime, many advertisers and advertising agencies are reluctant to use celebrity endorsers. Their concern is not without justification. Consider some of the celebrity-related incidents making news during the past decade:

◆ Boxer Mike Tyson—an active endorser before a series of mishaps—was convicted on a rape charge and served a prison sentence.

◆ Actress Cybill Shepherd had a lucrative endorsement deal with the beef industry but embarrassed the industry by revealing to the press that she avoided eating beef.

◆ Entertainer Michael Jackson was arraigned on child-molestation charges.

◆ Tennis player Jennifer Capriati's promising career was sidetracked with emotional problems and allegations of drug abuse.

◆ Ex-football player and actor O. J. Simpson was indicted for, but not convicted of, murder.

Because of the risks of such incidents after the consummation of a million-dollar celebrity-endorsement contract, there has been increased scrutiny in selecting celebrity endorsers.

No selection procedure is fail-safe, however, and it is for this reason that some advertisers and their agencies avoid celebrity endorsements altogether. An alternative is to use the "endorsements" of celebrities who are no longer living: Babe Ruth, Marilyn Monroe, James Dean, and Natalie Wood have all been used in advertisements, for instance. Famous actor Humphrey Bogart (best known for his performances in *Casablanca* and *The Maltese Falcon*) died decades ago (in 1957) but was used recently as part of the Gap's khakis advertising campaign (see Figure 11.1). As illustrated in the previous chapter (Figure 10.12), Apple Computer used two dead celebrities (Amelia Earhart and Alfred Hitchcock) in its "Think different" ad campaign.

Dead celebrities are well known and respected by consumers in the target audiences to whom they appeal, and, best of all, their use in advertising is virtually risk free inasmuch as they cannot engage in behaviors that will sully their reputations and resonate adversely to the brands they posthumously endorse.

Sources: Brian D. Till and Terence A. Shimp, "Endorsers in Advertising: The Case of Negative Celebrity Information, *Journal of Advertising* 27 (Spring 1998), 67–82; Kevin Goldman, "Dead Celebrities Are Resurrected as Pitchmen," *The Wall Street Journal,* January 7, 1994, B1–2; Cyndee Miller, "Some Celebs Just Now Reaching Their Potential, and They're Dead," *Marketing News,* March 29, 1993, 2, 22.

*T*his chapter's objective is to overview some of the common approaches to advertising creation. First examined is the use of endorsers in advertising. Discussion turns then to five types of messages that are widespread in advertising: (1) humor, (2), fear appeals, (3) guilt appeals, (4) sex appeals, and (5) subliminal messages. The chapter concludes with reviews of the music's role in advertising and the use of comparative advertisements.

Where possible, an attempt is made to identify *generalizations* about the creation of effective advertising messages. It is important to realize, however, that generalizations are not the same as scientific laws or principles. These higher forms of scientific truth (such as Einstein's general theory of relativity and Newton's law of gravity) have not been established in the realm of advertising, for several reasons: First, the buyer behavior that advertising is designed to influence is complex, dynamic, and variable across situations, which consequently makes it difficult to arrive at straightforward explanations of how communication elements operate in all situations and across all types of market segments. Second, advertisements are themselves highly varied entities that differ in numerous respects rather than just in terms of their use of humor, or sex, or fear, or any other single dimension. This complexity makes it difficult to draw specific research conclusions about any particular feature of advertising. Third, because the scientific knowledge of advertising is based on research that necessarily has been conducted under somewhat unnatural conditions (such as laboratory experiments with college students), it is impossible to draw clear-cut inferences to applied marketing settings.

Thus, the findings presented and the conclusions drawn should be considered tentative rather than definitive. We should heed the philosopher's advice: "Seek simplicity and distrust it."[1] In other words, it would be naïve and misleading to suggest that any particular advertising technique will be universally successful under all circumstances. Rather, the effectiveness of any message format depends on circumstances such as the nature of the competition, the advertising environment, and the extent of consumer involvement. Throughout the text we have emphasized the importance of this "it-depends" mind-set, and it is important that you bring such an orientation to your reading of the following sections.

THE ROLE OF ENDORSERS IN ADVERTISING

The products in many advertisements receive explicit endorsements from a variety of popular public figures. In addition to celebrity endorsements, products also receive the explicit or tacit support of noncelebrities. This latter form of *typical-person endorsement* will be discussed in a following section.

Celebrity Endorsers

Television stars, movie actors, famous athletes, and dead personalities *(Opening Vignette)* are widely used in magazine ads, radio spots, and television commercials to endorse products. By definition, a celebrity is a personality (actor, entertainer, or athlete) who is known to the public for his or her accomplishments in areas other than the product class endorsed.[2] Celebrities are in great demand as product spokespersons. Perhaps as many as one-fourth of all commercials employ celebrity endorsements.[3]

Advertisers and their agencies are willing to pay huge salaries to those celebrities who are liked and respected by target audiences and who will, it is hoped, favorably influence consumers' attitudes and behavior toward the endorsed products. For the most part, such investments are justified. For example, consumers' attitudes and perceptions of quality are enhanced when celebrities endorse products.[4] Moreover, stock prices have been shown to increase when companies announce celebrity-endorsement contracts.[5] Of course, it should not be assumed that celebrity endorsers are effective for all brands and in every situation. In fact, from our discussion (in Chapter 6) of the elaboration likelihood model and alternative persuasion routes (central and peripheral) that are part of this model, it should be apparent that celebrity endorsers would be especially effective when consumers' motivation to process message arguments is relatively *low*.[6] That is, celebrity endorsers and the peripheral route go hand in hand.

www.jordan.sportsline.com

www.tigerwoods.com

www.stl.cardinals.com

www.samsosa.com

www.rogermaris.com

www.2131.com

Top celebrities receive enormous payments for their endorsement services. Top celebrity fees average $2 to $3 million a year for the endorsement of a single product.[7] Michael Jordan, the famous ex-basketball player who retired in 1999, is estimated to earn in excess of $30 million yearly from endorsement deals with a broad range of local and national advertisers.[8] To put this amount in perspective, a person earning a not-so-paltry annual income of $100,000 would have to work 300 years at that salary to earn as much as Michael Jordan receives in a single year from his endorsement activities! Tiger Woods (golfer) also obtains huge sums for his endorsements. Baseball sluggers Mark McGwire (St. Louis Cardinals) and Sammy Sosa (Chicago Cubs) surpassed Roger Maris's (late of the New York Yankees) 37-year-old record of 61 home runs in a single season. McGwire smashed 70 home runs and Sosa finished with 66 four-baggers. And Cal Ripken (Baltimore Orioles) ended his streak of playing in 2,632 baseball games without missing a single game—an amazing streak extending over 16 years. One can only imagine the lucrative endorsements that await these three men, who are wonderful athletes and apparently good human beings.

The Importance of Matchup.   What makes a celebrity an effective endorser for a particular product? Basically, there has to be a *meaningful relationship,* or *matchup,* between the celebrity, the audience, and the product.[9] Bill Cosby (see Figure 11.2) is an ideal endorser for Jell-O Pudding. Cosby's television and movie persona as a lovable and somewhat mischievous character represents a perfect match with the rather amusing nature of pudding and the fun-enhancing mood that parents wish for their children when serving this brand. Martina Hingis (Figure 11.3) is an appropriate endorser for Clairol's Daily Defense shampoos. She is known as an outstanding tennis player who is outdoors on a daily basis. Her attractiveness and profession tie in well to this product's protective ingredients and its promise to protect users' hair from the harshness of outdoor activities.

Can you think of endorsements where the fit between celebrity and brand is inappropriate? Why, in your opinion, is the matchup poor?

Illustration of Celebrity
and Brand Matchup

How Are Celebrities Selected?

How Are Celebrities Selected? Needless to say, the selection of high-priced celebrity endorsers is typically undertaken with considerable thought on the part of brand managers and their advertising agencies. Their selection process is facilitated with *Performer Q-Ratings* that are commercially available from a New York-based firm called Marketing Evaluations. As will shortly become apparent, the *Q* in a Q-Rating signifies *quotient.*

In determining Q-Ratings for entertainers, athletes, and other famous personages, Marketing Evaluations evaluates approximately 1,500 public figures by mailing questionnaires to a representative national panel of individuals. Panel representatives are asked two straightforward questions for each person: (1) Have you heard of this person? (a measure of *familiarity*); and (2) if so, do you rate him or her poor, fair, good, very good, or one of your favorites? (a measure of *popularity*). The calculation of each performer's Q-Rating, or quotient, is accomplished by determining the percentage of panel members who respond that a particular performer is "one of my favorites" and then dividing that number by the percentage who indicate that they have heard of that person. In other words, the popularity percentage is divided by the familiarity percentage, and the quotient is that person's

Another Illustration of Celebrity and Brand Matchup

Q-Rating. This rating simply reveals the proportion of a group familiar with a person and who regard that person as one of their favorites.

For example, results from a survey by Marketing Evaluations revealed that Bill Cosby was known by 95 percent of people surveyed and considered a favorite by 45 percent. Hence, his Q-Rating (which is expressed without decimal points) was approximately 47 (i.e., 45 divided by 95 = 47). Comparatively, in this same survey, Roseanne Barr had a Q-Rating of only 16, which was obtained by dividing the 15 percent of respondents who considered her one of their favorites by the 93 percent who were familiar with her.[10] It comes as little surprise that advertisers have not flocked to Roseanne to sign her up to endorse their products.

Sears turned to Q-Ratings when attempting to change its stodgy image. Sears became the official sponsor of singer Phil Collins' U.S. tour after perusing Performer Q-Ratings and learning the following: Whereas the average Q-Rating for a male musician is 19, Collins' rating among adults ages 18 and older was 34. Among Sears' most desirable target audience of women aged 18 to 34, his rating was an exceptional 48.[11]

Performer Q-Ratings provide valuable information to brand managers and advertising agencies, but there is more to selecting a celebrity to endorse a brand than simply scouring through the pages of Q-Ratings. A survey of advertising executives illuminates the factors these executives consider when making their celebrity-selection decisions.[12] The major considerations, in order of decreasing importance, are: (1) celebrity credibility, (2) celebrity and audience matchup, (3) celebrity and brand matchup, (4) celebrity attractiveness, and (5) miscellaneous considerations.

Celebrity Credibility. A celebrity's trustworthiness and expertise (jointly referred to as *credibility*) is the primary reason for selecting a celebrity endorser. People who are trustworthy and perceived as knowledgeable on a particular issue, such as a brand's effectiveness, are best able to convince others to undertake a course of action. It is little wonder that Michael Jordan was selected to endorse Gatorade insofar as his public persona is one of trustworthiness, and as a give-it-all-you-have athlete he should know something about the merits of a sports drink. Larry King probably also performs this role when participating in the ongoing milk-mustache advertising campaign (Figure 11.4).

www.shaq.com

www.granthill.com

www.whymilk.com

Celebrity/Audience Matchup. Shaquille O'Neal, Grant Hill, and other NBA superstars who endorse basketball shoes match up well with the predominantly teenage audience who aspire to slam dunk the basketball, block shots, intercept passes, and sink 24-foot jump shots. Also, the milk-mustachioed celebrities (see collage in Figure 11.5) match up well with a variety of demographic audiences whom the National Fluid Milk Processor Promotion Board desired to reach with its advertising campaign.

Celebrity/Brand Matchup. Advertising executives require that the celebrity's image, values, and decorum be compatible with the image desired for the advertised brand. Bill Cosby matches up well with Jell-O pudding, as previously noted, because his image fits well with that brand. Grant Hill is an ideal endorser for Italian-headquartered Fila athletic shoes due to his reputation for being a marvelous basketball player who has a solid educational background (Duke University) and is not sullied with a "bad-boy" image. Cal Ripken, who played in 2,632 consecutive baseball games, would match extremely well with any brand that promotes itself as durable, long-lasting, dependable, consistent, and the like.

Celebrity Attractiveness. In selecting celebrity spokespeople, advertising executives evaluate different aspects that can be lumped together under the general label *attractiveness*. These include friendliness, likability, physique, and occupation as some of the more important dimensions of the attractiveness concept. The milk-mustachioed celebrities (Figure 11.5) are attractive in a variety of ways that appeal to different target audiences. But, of course, attractiveness alone is subordinate in importance to credibility and matchup with the audience and brand.

Miscellaneous Considerations. Finally, ad executives in selecting celebrities consider additional factors, such as: (1) how much it will cost to acquire a celebrity's services, (2) the likelihood that the celebrity will get into trouble after an endorsement is established, (3) how difficult or easy he or she is to work with, and (4) how many other brands the celebrity is endorsing. If a celebrity is overexposed—that is, endorsing too many products—his or her perceived credibility and likability may suffer.[13] Golfer Tiger Woods, for example, may be somewhat overexposed. At least one advertiser (Reebok) found it difficult to work with basketball player Shaquille O'Neal, which may have diminished this superstar's endorsement value.[14]

Illustration of a Credible Celebrity

Typical-Person Endorsers

A frequent advertising approach is to show regular people—that is, noncelebrities—using or endorsing products. The young family in Figure 11.6 illustrates the use of a typical-person endorsement in the implication that "affordable safety" is crucial to them in protecting their treasured child.

Many advertisements that portray typical-person users often include *multiple people* rather than a single individual. Is there any reason why multiple sources should be more effective than a single source? Yes, there is: The act of portraying more than one person increases the likelihood an advertisement will generate higher levels of message involvement and correspondingly greater message elaboration (recall the discussion on involvement and elaboration

Collage of Milk-Mustache Ads

in the context of the Elaboration Likelihood Model in Chapter 6). In turn, greater elaboration increases the odds that strong message arguments will favorably influence attitudes.

This line of reasoning was tested in an experiment that manipulated: (1) one versus four person-in-the-street endorsers for a new pizza chain advertisement and (2) strong versus weak arguments favoring eating this chain's pizza. As theorized, the four-person advertisement was found to be more effective (as measured by cognitive responses and attitude measures) than the single source when message arguments were strong. On the other hand, the single source was superior when weak arguments were offered. The practical implication for advertisers is that increasing the number of endorsers will not necessarily increase persuasive impact; the message arguments themselves must also be influential.[15]

Illustration of a Typical Person Endorsement

Endorser Attributes

Now that a distinction has been made between the two general types of advertising endorsers, it is important to explain more formally endorser attributes and the role they play in facilitating communications effectiveness. Extensive research has demonstrated that two basic attributes contribute to an endorser's effectiveness: attractiveness and credibility. Each involves a different mechanism by which the endorser affects consumer attitudes and behavior.[16] Some of these points have already been mentioned, but a formal treatment will now ensure that these key concepts are fully understood.

Attractiveness: The Process of Identification. **Attractiveness** does *not* mean simply physical attractiveness—although that can be a very important attribute—but includes any number of virtuous characteristics that receivers may perceive in an endorser: intellectual skills, personality properties, lifestyle characteristics, athletic prowess, and so on. The general concept of attractiveness consists of three related ideas: *similarity, familiarity,* and *liking.*[17] That is, an endorser is considered attractive to receivers if they share a sense of similarity or familiarity with him or her or if they simply like the endorser regardless of whether the two are similar in any respect. Martina Hingis (refer back to Figure 11.3), would seem to epitomize the use of attractiveness and capture all dimensions of that concept. That is, Hingis, in addition to her physical beauty, is attractive to tennis fans who are similar to her (in the sense that they also play or enjoy tennis), are familiar with her (via watching her play on TV and reading about her), and like her (due to her generally pleasant demeanor and fiery competitive spirit). The *Global Focus* section describes an extremely successful Japanese endorser who represents a variety of attractive attributes.

One study has demonstrated that a matchup between spokesperson and audience similarity is especially important when the product or service in question is one where audience members are *heterogeneous* in terms of their taste and attribute preferences. For example, because people differ greatly in terms of what they like in restaurants, plays, and movies, a spokesperson perceived to be similar to the audience is expected to have the greatest effect in influencing their attitudes and choices. On the other hand, when preferences among audience members are relatively *homogeneous* (such as might be expected with services such as plumbing, dry cleaning, and auto repair), the matchup between spokesperson and audience similarity is not that important. Rather, it is the spokesperson's *experience or expertise* with the product/service that appears to have the greatest influence in shaping the audience's attitudes and subsequent behavior.[18]

When receivers find something in an endorser that they consider attractive, persuasion occurs through an **identification process.** That is, when receivers perceive a source to be attractive, they *identify with* the endorser and are very likely to adopt the attitudes, behaviors, interests, or preferences of the source.

Advertising researchers have not studied attractiveness extensively, and what little research has been conducted has focused primarily on the physical-attractiveness dimension.[19] Research has supported the rather intuitive expectation that physically attractive endorsers produce more favorable evaluations of ads and advertised products than do less attractive communicators.[20] However, empirical evidence suggests that attractive endorsers are more effective only when the endorser's image is *compatible with the nature of the endorsed product.*

In other words, an attractive endorser does not necessarily benefit a product if there is a poor *matchup* between the endorser and the product. An experiment tested this possibility by comparing the effectiveness of two actors, one who was handsome (Tom Selleck) and the other who was not (Telly Savalas). Two products were examined, one an attractiveness-related product (a luxury automobile) and the other an attractiveness-unrelated product (a home computer). As predicted by the *matchup hypothesis,* when handsome Tom Selleck endorsed the luxury automobile, subjects' attitudes toward the advertisement were significantly more favorable than when unhandsome Telly Savalas endorsed the same car. However, no significant difference between these two endorsers was detected for the attractiveness-unrelated home computer product.[21]

Credibility: The Process of Internalization. In its most basic sense, credibility refers to the tendency to believe or trust someone. When an information source, such as an endorser, is perceived as credible, audience attitudes are changed through a psychological process called internalization. **Internalization** occurs when the receiver accepts the endorser's position on an issue as his or her own. An internalized attitude tends to be maintained even if the source of the message is forgotten or if the source switches to a different position.[22]

GLOBAL FOCUS: JAPAN'S MOST POPU-LAR CELEBRITY, GEORGE TOKORO

George Tokoro is Japan's most popular celebrity according to a survey conducted by Dentsu Inc., Japan's largest advertising agency. Mr. Tokoro is famous in Japan for his broad smile, contorted facial expressions, and slapstick sense of humor. These features have endeared him to the Japanese, possibly because he is a virtual antithesis of the no-nonsense, ultra-serious Japanese workingman. Tokoro is big fan of American products and has enjoyed much success endorsing brands such as Chevy Cavaliers and Coca-Cola. Chevy Cavaliers weren't doing very well in Japan until George Tokoro was hired to endorse this brand. Through Mr. Tokoro's offbeat personality and goofy antics, the Cavalier became a "hot" product virtually overnight. He also was largely responsible for reversing a big sales slump that Coca-Cola had experienced in Japan. For his considerable talents, Tokoro grosses nearly $700,000 per commercial. His attractiveness to Japanese consumers fully justifies this handsome level of remuneration and benefits the brands he endorses.

Source: Norihiko Shirouzu, *The Wall Street Journal Interactive Edition*, July 28, 1997.

Two important properties of endorser credibility are expertise and trustworthiness. **Expertise** refers to the knowledge, experience, or skills possessed by an endorser as they relate to the communications topic. Hence, athletes are considered to be experts when it comes to the endorsement of sports-related products. Expertise is a perceived rather than an absolute phenomenon. Whether an endorser is indeed an expert is unimportant; all that matters is how the target audience perceives the endorser. An endorser who is perceived as an expert on a given subject is more persuasive in changing audience opinions pertaining to his or her area of expertise than an endorser who is not perceived as possessing the same characteristic. This no doubt explains the extensive use of athletes to endorse sports-related products.

Trustworthiness refers to the honesty, integrity, and believability of a source. While expertise and trustworthiness are not mutually exclusive, often a particular endorser is perceived as highly trustworthy but not particularly expert. An endorser's trustworthiness depends primarily on the audience's perception of his or her endorsement motivations. If the audience believes that an endorser is motivated purely by self-interest, he or she will be less persuasive than someone the audience perceives as having nothing to gain by endorsing the product or as being completely objective. Interestingly, research with ethnic minorities reveals that when a spokesperson matches the audience's ethnicity, spokesperson trustworthiness is enhanced, which, in turn, promotes more favorable attitudes toward the advertised brand.[23]

Advertisers capitalize on the value of trustworthiness by selecting endorsers who are widely regarded as being honest, believable, and dependable people. This probably explains why celebrities such as Bill Cosby and Michael Jordan are successful endorsers. They simply appear to be individuals who can be trusted.

Advertisers also use the *overheard conversation technique* to enhance trustworthiness. A television advertisement might show a middle-aged person overhearing one man explain to another why his brand of arthritis pain-relief medicine is the best on the market. In this case, the commercial attempts to have audience members place themselves in the position of the person overhearing the conversation. An experiment tested whether a hidden-camera endorser (one who is presumably extolling the virtues of a product without being aware of it) is more persuasive than a typical-person endorser (one who is aware of his or her spokesperson role). The researchers hypothesized that the hidden-camera endorser should be considered more trustworthy because he or she makes favorable product claims but does not come across as having ulterior motives. The hidden-camera spokesperson was, in fact, shown to be more trustworthy.[24]

In general, endorsers must establish that they are not attempting to manipulate the audience and that they are objective in their presentations. By doing so, they establish themselves as trustworthy and, therefore, credible.

THE ROLE OF HUMOR IN ADVERTISING

Politicians, actors and actresses, public speakers, professors, and indeed all of us at one time or another use humor to create a desired reaction. Advertisers also turn to humor in the hopes of achieving various communication objectives—to gain attention, guide consumer comprehension of product claims, influence attitudes, enhance recallability of advertised claims, and, ultimately, create customer action. The use of humor in advertising is extensive, representing approximately 25 percent of all television advertising in the United States and over 35 percent in the United Kingdom.[25] A study based on a sampling of television advertisements from four countries (Germany, Korea, Thailand, and the United States) determined that humorous advertisements in all of these countries generally involve the use of *incongruity resolution*. For example, in a Bud Light beer commercial one character arrives with a flashlight in hand, while the other character exclaims, "I said Bud Light." A study of magazine advertising in the United States determined that the vast majority of ads using humor employ incongruity-based humor.[26] This form of advertising has been characterized as Huh? Aha! Ha-Ha! humor. That is, an initial discrepancy reaction (Huh?) provokes an effort to resolve the meaning of the ad (Aha!) and then, when the humor is detected, a Ha-Ha! response is promoted.[27]

Whether humor is effective and what kinds of humor are most successful are matters of some debate among advertising practitioners and scholars.[28] A survey determined that advertising agency executives consider the use of humor to be especially effective for getting people to attend to advertisements and creating brand awareness.[29] A thorough review of research on the effects of humor leads to the following tentative conclusions:[30]

◆ Humor is an effective method for *attracting attention* to advertisements.

◆ Humor enhances *liking* of both the advertisement and the advertised brand.

◆ Humor does *not* necessarily harm *comprehension*.

◆ Humor does *not* offer an advantage over nonhumor at *increasing persuasion*.

◆ Humor does *not* enhance *source credibility*.

◆ The nature of the product affects the appropriateness of using humor. Specifically, humor is more successfully used with established rather than new products. Humor also is more appropriate for products that are more feeling-oriented, or experiential, and those that are not very involving (such as inexpensive consumer packaged goods).

www.motel6.com

When used correctly and in the right circumstances, humor can be an extremely effective advertising technique. The subtle humor of Tom Bodett in radio ads for Motel 6 has undoubtedly had an impressive impact on that hotel chain's revenue. Although humor is used relatively infrequently in magazine advertising (compared to TV and radio), the ad in Figure 11.7 vividly demonstrates how humor, albeit of a morbid type in this case, can serve to effectively attract attention and convey the key message argument: that Eastpak backpacks are "Guaranteed for life. Maybe longer."[31]

A complication of using humor in advertising is that humorous appeals are not equally effective for all. Using data on magazine readership patterns from the *Starch* magazine readership database (see Chapter 15 for details about *Starch* data), researchers determined that men had higher attention scores than women for humorous ads and that magazines with predominantly white audiences had higher attention scores for humorous ads than did those with predominantly African-American readers.[32] This finding obviously should not be interpreted as meaning that blacks and women lack a sense of humor; rather, what it likely reflects is a bias in advertising that caters more to the special interests of white males over females or minority audiences.

The Use of Humor in
Magazine Advertising

In addition to demographic differences in responsiveness to humor, research evidence also shows that humorous ads are more effective than nonhumorous ads *only when consumers' evaluations of the advertised brand are already positive.* When prior evaluations are negative toward the advertised brand, humorous ads have been shown to be less effective than nonhumorous ads.[33] This finding has a counterpart in interpersonal relations: When you like someone, you are more likely to consider his or her attempt at humor to be funny than if you do not like that person.

In sum, humor in advertising can be an extremely effective device for accomplishing a variety of marketing communications objectives. Nonetheless, advertisers should *proceed cautiously* when contemplating the use of humor. First, the effects of humor can differ due to differences in audience characteristics—what strikes some people as humorous is not at all funny to others.[34] Second, the definition of what is funny in one country or region of a country is not necessarily the same in another place. Finally, a humorous message may be so distracting to an audience that receivers ignore the message content. Thus, advertisers should carefully research their intended market segments before venturing into humorous advertising.

THE USE OF FEAR APPEALS

Earlier in Chapter 6 it was noted that marketing communicators employ a variety of techniques to enhance consumers' information-processing motivation, opportunity, or ability. The use of fear is expected to be especially effective as a means of enhancing motivation. The unfortunate fact is that consumers in the late-twentieth century live in a world where crime and health-related problems abound. Advertisers, in attempting to motivate customers to process information and to take action, invoke fear appeals by identifying either: (1) the negative consequences of *not using the advertised product* or (2) the negative consequences of *engaging in unsafe behavior* (such as drinking and driving, smoking).

Fear–Appeal Logic

The underlying logic when using fear appeals is that fear will stimulate audience involvement with a message and thereby promote acceptance of message arguments.[35] The appeals may take the form of *social disapproval* or *physical danger*. For example, mouthwashes, deodorants, toothpastes, and other products use fear appeals when emphasizing the social disapproval we may suffer if our breath is not fresh, our underarms are not dry, or our teeth are not cavity-free. Smoke detectors, automobile tires, unsafe sex, portable phones, driving under the influence of alcohol and other drugs, and being uninsured (see Figure 11.8) are a sampling of products and themes that advertisers use to induce fear of physical danger or impending problems. Health-care ads (such as for Havrix Hepatitis A vaccine in Figure 11.9) are frequent users of fear appeals, and advertising agencies justify the use of such appeals with logic such as, "Sometimes you have to scare people to save their lives."[36]

Appropriate Intensity

Aside from the basic ethical issue of whether fear should be used at all, the fundamental issue for advertisers is determining *how intense* the fear presentation should be. Should the advertiser employ a slight amount of threat merely to get the consumer's attention, or should a heavy dose of fear appeal be used so the consumer cannot possibly miss the point the advertiser wishes to make? Numerous fear-appeal studies have been performed by psychologists and marketing researchers, but the fact remains that there still is no consensus on the optimum level of fear. Some studies have reported that a low level of fear is most effective,[37] whereas other researchers contend that a moderate fear level is more effective than levels of fear that are either too low or too high.[38]

In an attempt to reconcile these apparently contradictory findings, two marketing researchers arrived at the conclusion that differences in research findings are probably attributable to the different definitions of high, moderate, and low fear appeals employed in different studies. These researchers summarized the early fear-appeal literature by concluding

Neither extremely strong nor very weak fear appeals are maximally effective. It seems that appeals at a somewhat moderate level of fear are best. A simple explanation for this might be that if an appeal is too weak, it just does not attract enough attention. If it is too strong, on the other hand, it may lead people to avoid the message or ignore

FIGURE
11.8

An Insurance Company's
Appeal to Fear

A flood isn't the worst thing that can happen to you.

Not being insured for one is.

A flood moves with frightening speed. In minutes, a flood can wash away everything you and your family have spent a lifetime building.

But often the worst isn't the flood. It's finding out, too late, that you're not covered for flood damage.

You're probably not covered.

The truth is, 90% of all natural disasters in this country involve floods. Yet, as many find out too late, most homeowner's insurance policies don't cover flood damage.

Everyone runs the risk of being a flood victim. In fact, between 25%

and 30% of flood insurance claims come from "low risk" areas. It could happen to you.

Give yourself peace of mind.

Fortunately, now you can protect your home and property with flood insurance from the National Flood Insurance Program.

Return the coupon or call your insurance company, agent or this toll-free number: 1-888-CALL FLOOD, extension 159. Act now, since it takes 30 days before your coverage begins. Because with floods, you can never say never.

1-888-CALL FLOOD ext. 159
Please send me information about NFIP.
MAIL TO: FEMA/MSC, PO BOX 1038,
JESSUP, MD 20797-9408
Do you have an insurance agent or company? Yes ☐ No ☐
If yes, who is your insurance agent and/or company?
_____
Mag. Issue Date_____
Your Name_____
Address_____
City_____
State_____ Zip_____ Tel.(___)_____

NFIP
National Flood Insurance Program
Administered by FEMA

 We can't replace your memories, but we can help you build new ones.

NFIP, 500 C Street SW, Washington, D.C. 20472 ⬥ TDD #1-800-427-5593 ⬥ http://www.fema.gov/fema/nfip96-43.shm   FEMA

the message's recommendations as being inadequate to the task of eliminating the feared event.[39]

This conclusion, which has been termed the *inverted-U explanation* (from the form of functional relation—literally an inverted U—between the level of fear intensity and the degree of persuasive effectiveness), has not stood up under scrutiny.[40] An alternative *degree-of-relevance explanation* holds that the optimum level of fear depends on how much relevance a topic has for an audience—the greater the relevance, the lower the optimal level of fear. In other words, people who are highly involved in a topic can be motivated by

A Drug Company's
Use of a Fear Appeal

a relatively *small* amount of fear, whereas a more intense level of fear is required to motivate uninvolved people.[41]

www.michelin.com

To illustrate the relation between fear intensity and issue relevance, let us compare a low-fear campaign for Michelin tires with the much more intense fear-appeal campaigns to discourage drinking and driving. As you may recall, the long-standing Michelin campaign contains a series of television commercials that show adorable babies sitting on or surrounded by tires. These commercials are subtle reminders (low levels of fear) for parents to consider buying Michelin tires to ensure their children's safety. A low-level of fear is all that is needed in this situation, because safety for their children is perhaps the most relevant concern for most parents.

Consider, by comparison, the level of fear needed to reach high school students and other young people who are the targets of public service announcements (PSAs) to discourage drinking and driving. The last thing many young people want to hear is what they should or should not be doing. Hence, although safety is relevant to most everyone, it is less relevant to young people who consider themselves invulnerable. Consequently, very intense fear-appeal PSAs are needed to impress upon high schoolers the risk in which they place themselves and their friends when drinking and driving.[42]

THE USE OF GUILT APPEALS

Like fear, guilt is an appeal to a negative emotion. People feel guilty when they have broken rules, violated their own standards or beliefs, or have behaved irresponsibly.[43] Appeals to guilt are powerful because they motivate emotionally mature individuals to undertake

An Illustrative Guilt Appeal

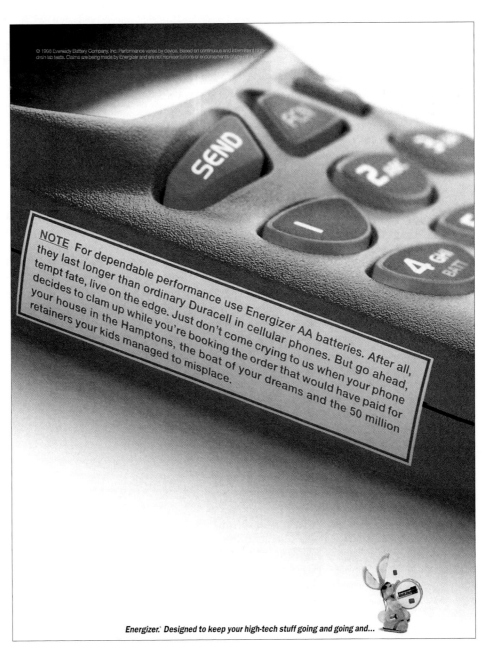

GLOBAL FOCUS: IS THE USE OF SEX APPEAL GREATER IN FRENCH OR AMERICAN ADVERTISING?

Americans often stereotype France as a glamorous society with avant-garde fashions, sexy models, high-stepping and scantily clad chorus-line dancers, and greater openness in sexual expression with fewer sexual hang-ups. If these stereotypes have any truth, then it might be expected that French advertisers would use sex appeals in advertising even more than their usage by American advertisers. Researchers tested this hypothesis by comparing the advertising content in a sample of French and American magazines. One news (*L'Express* and *Time*) and one women's (*Madame Figaro* and *McCall's*) magazine from each country was selected. Six issues were randomly selected from each magazine, and all full-page or larger ads were subjected to content analysis. The final sample consisted of 279 American and 259 French advertisements.

www.lexpress-net.com

www.mccalls.com

The analysis revealed that 24 percent of the French advertisements used sexual appeal compared to only 8.6 percent of the American ads, which represents a statistically significant difference. With respect to the types of models appearing in the sexually oriented ads, 9.3 percent of the French advertisements contained only males, 83.3 percent only females, and 7.4 percent both males and females. Comparatively, in the American advertisements using sexually suggestive models, 4.5 percent had only male models, 81.8 percent had only female models, and 13.6 percent used both male and female models.

Hence, it appears that French advertisers are somewhat more inclined to use sexual appeals, but both French and American advertisers are far more likely to use female than male models when using sex in advertising. On balance, these results would seem to suggest that French consumers are more receptive to sexual appeals than Americans. A variety of cultural factors no doubt are implicated in the explanation for this difference, which should make for interesting class discussion.

Source: Abhijit Biswas, Janeen E. Olsen, and Valerie Carlet, "A Comparison of Print Advertisements from the United States and France," *Journal of Advertising* 21 (December 1992), 73–81. For further reading about French advertising, see Ronald E. Taylor, Mariea Grubbs Hoy, and Eric Haley "How French Advertising Professionals Develop Creative Strategy," *Journal of Advertising* 25 (spring 1996), 1–14.

responsible action leading to a reduction in the level of guilt. Advertisers and other marketing communicators appeal to guilt and attempt to persuade prospective customers by asserting or implying that feelings of guilt can be relieved by using the promoted product.[44] Consider, for example, the advertisement for Energizer batteries in Figure 11.10. This ad subtly suggests that it would be irresponsible to install poor-quality batteries in one's cellular phone, that doing so may have negative consequences (such as losing an important order), and that using Energizer batteries will remove the guilt associated with failing to behave responsibly.

In general, guilt appeals focus on one's past or future transgressions or failure to care for others.[45] The advertisement for Havrix vaccine (Figure 11.9) previously illustrated the use of fear in advertising. It also represents an appeal to anticipatory guilt. That is, the ad induces a sense of guilt in the reader by suggesting blame for failing to have family members vaccinated prior to traveling to a high-risk area where a loved one could contract hepatitis A. An in-depth analysis of a broad spectrum of magazines revealed that about one out of 20 ads contains an appeal to guilt.[46]

THE USE OF SEX IN ADVERTISING

Sex appeals in advertising are used frequently and with increasing explicitness. Whereas the use of such explicit sex was unthinkable not many years ago, it now represents part of the advertising landscape.[47] The trend is not restricted to the United States; indeed, sexual explicitness is more prevalent and more overt elsewhere—for example, in Brazil and certain European countries. See the *Global Focus* for a discussion of different uses of sex appeals in American and French magazine advertising.

Whether and under what conditions such advertising is effective remain largely unexplored issues.[48] Complicating the matter is the fact that sex in advertising actually takes two forms: *nudity* and *suggestiveness*. It is uncertain which form is more effective.[49] An example of suggestiveness is the Right Guard ad featuring basketball player Charles Barkley portrayed in a garish fox-hunting outfit (Figure 11.11). Of course, the outfit and surrounding scene are merely convenient props for the sexually suggestive claim in the upper left-hand corner of the ad: "One cannot smell like a hound and expect to catch any foxes." The suggestion is clear: Men should use Right Guard deodorant if they want to attract or appeal to women.

What Role Does Sex Play in Advertising?

www.guess.com

Actually, it has several potential roles. First, sexual material in advertising acts as an initial *attentional lure* while also retaining that attention for a longer period—often by featuring

The Use of Sexual Suggestiveness in Advertising

attractive models in provocative poses.[50] This is called the *stopping-power role* of sex.[51] There is little doubt that the magazine ad for Guess Jeans (Figure 11.12) is a strong attention-getter.

   A second potential role is to *enhance recall* of message points. Research suggests, however, that sexual content or symbolism will enhance recall only if it is appropriate to the product category and the creative advertising execution.[52] Sexual appeals produce significantly better recall when the advertising execution has an appropriate relationship with the advertised product.[53] The advertisements for Right Guard deodorant and Guess Jeans

Illustration of the Stopping-Power Role of Sex

might be considered instances of appropriate usage of sex inasmuch as sexual appeal is a key attribute of both of these products.

A third role performed by sexual content in advertising is to *evoke emotional responses* such as feelings of arousal or even lust.[54] These reactions can increase an ad's persuasive impact, with the opposite occurring if the ad elicits negative feelings such as disgust, embarrassment, or uneasiness.[55] The appeal to lust is typified by a Diet Coke television commercial in which a group of women was shown watching with palpable pleasure a sexy construction worker at a nearby site take his shirt off and open a Diet Coke as part of his lunch break.

Whether sexual content elicits a positive or a negative reaction depends on the *appropriateness or relevance* of the sexual content to the advertised subject matter. An interesting marketing experiment tested this by varying magazine ads for two products, a ratchet wrench set (a product for which sexual appeal is irrelevant) and a body oil (a relevant sex-appeal product). The study also manipulated three versions of dress for the female model who appeared in the ads: In the *demure* model version, she was shown fully clothed in a blouse and slacks; in the *seductive* model version, she wore the same clothing as in the demure version, but the blouse was completely unbuttoned and knotted at the bottom, exposing some midriff and cleavage; and in the *nude* model version, she was completely undressed. Study findings revealed that the seductive model/body oil combination was perceived most favorably by all respondents, whereas the nude model/body oil combination was perceived as the least appealing advertisement. Females regarded the nude model/ratchet set as least appealing.[56] This study was conducted over two decades ago, and it is uncertain whether the same finding would be obtained in the sexually more explicit society in which we now live.

Sexual content stands little chance of being effective unless it is directly relevant to an advertisement's primary selling point. When used appropriately, however, sexual content is capable of eliciting attention, enhancing recall, and creating a favorable association with the advertised product.

The Downside of Sex Appeals in Advertising

The presentation to this point has indicated that when used appropriately, sex appeals in advertising can be effective. The discussion would be incomplete, however, without mentioning the potential hazards of using sex appeals. There is evidence to suggest that the use of explicit sexual illustrations in advertisements may interfere with consumers' processing of message arguments and reduce message comprehension.[57] Moreover, many people are offended by advertisements that portray women (and men) as brainless sex objects.[58] For example, an outcry ensued in response to an advertisement for Old Milwaukee beer featuring the so-called "Swedish Bikini Team"—a boat full of beautiful Scandinavian-looking women wearing blue bikinis who appeared out of nowhere in front of a group of fishermen. Female employees of Stroh's Brewery Co., the makers of Old Milwaukee, sued their employer, claiming that the advertisement created an atmosphere conducive to sexual harassment in the workplace.[59] Regardless of the merits of this particular case, the general point is that sex in advertising can be demeaning to females (and males) and, for this reason, should be used cautiously.

An advertising campaign for Calvin Klein jeans featuring teenagers in provocative poses created a public outcry, and Calvin Klein discontinued the campaign after critics dubbed it kiddie porn.[60] The use of sex in advertising is a matter of concern to people and regulatory bodies throughout the world.[61] For further discussion, see the *Global Focus*.

S UBLIMINAL MESSAGES AND SYMBOLIC EMBEDS

The word *subliminal* refers to the presentation of stimuli at a rate or level that is below the conscious threshold of awareness. One example is self-help audiotapes (such as tapes to help one quit smoking) that play messages at a decibel level indecipherable to the naked

GLOBAL FOCUS: WORLDWIDE CONCERN ABOUT SEX AND DECENCY IN ADVERTISING

Many people throughout the world are troubled by advertising they consider to be indecent. But, of course, what is considered indecent in one country may not necessarily be seen the same way in another. The International Chamber of Commerce (ICC) Code of Advertising Practice states that "advertising should be decent"; that is, "prepared with a due sense of social responsibility . . . [and] not be such as to impair public confidence in advertising."

Three categories of advertising indecency that are matters of concern around the world include advertisements that are sexist or sexy or that sexually objectify their models. Sexist ads are those that demean one sex in comparison with the other, particularly through sex-role stereotyping; sexy ads use sexual imagery or suggestiveness; and sexual objectification occurs when ads use women (or men) as decorative or attention-getting objects with little or no relevance to the product category. (Does the Guess Jeans ad in Figure 11.12 sexually objectify women?)

The nature and extent of government regulation of indecent sex-oriented advertising varies considerably, from a relatively laissez-faire attitude in the United States and western Europe to stringent controls in various Muslim countries. Following are some examples of government regulations of advertising in different countries:

- In Malaysia, the Ministry of Information's Advertising Code states that women should not be the principal objects of an advertisement or intended to attract sales unless the advertised product is relevant to women.
- The Ministry of Information in Saudi Arabia prevents any advertising depicting veiled or unveiled women.
- Indian law forbids the depiction of a woman's figure or any female body part if the depiction is derogatory to women or immoral.
- Portuguese law prohibits sex discrimination or the subordination or objectification of women in advertising.
- Norway requires that advertising not portray men or women in an offensive manner or imply any derogatory judgment of either sex.

The regulation of advertising (on grounds of decency or otherwise) is complex and controversial, because regulation curtails the rights of advertisers to communicate with their public and impinges on the rights of people to receive information and images in any form they consider nonobjectionable. Regulators in all countries are placed in a tricky position when attempting to balance the rights and interests of advertisers, consumers, and society at large.

Source: Jean J. Boddewyn, "Controlling Sex and Decency in Advertising around the World," *Journal of Advertising* 20 (December 1991), 25–36.

ear. Stimuli that cannot be perceived by the conscious senses may nonetheless be perceived *subconsciously*. This possibility has generated considerable concern from advertising critics and has fostered much speculation from researchers. The reason for the concern is clear: A large percentage of American people believe that subliminal methods are used by advertisers.[62] Representatives of the advertising community, however, disavow the widespread use of subliminal advertising.[63]

Original outcry occurred in response to research by James Vicary in 1957, who claimed to have increased sales of Coca-Cola and popcorn in a New Jersey movie theater by using subliminal messages. At five-second intervals during the movie *Picnic*, subliminal messages saying "Drink Coca-Cola" and "Eat Popcorn" appeared on the screen for a mere 1-3,000th of a second. Although the naked eye could not possibly have seen these messages, Vicary claimed that sales of Coca-Cola and popcorn increased 58 and 18 percent respectively.[64] Though Vicary's research is scientifically meaningless because he failed to use proper experimental procedures, the study nonetheless raised public concerns about subliminal advertising and led to congressional hearings.[65] Federal legislation was never enacted, but since then subliminal advertising has been the subject of criticism by advertising critics, a matter of embarrassment for advertising practitioners, and an issue of theoretical curiosity to advertising scholars.[66]

The fires of controversy were fueled again in the 1970s with the publication of three provocatively titled books: *Subliminal Seduction, Media Sexploitation,* and *The*

Clam Plate Orgy.[67] The author of these books, Wilson Key, claimed subliminal advertising techniques are used extensively and have the power to influence consumers' choice behaviors.

A Challenge

Many advertising practitioners and marketing communications scholars discount Key's arguments and vehemently disagree with his conclusions. Part of the difficulty in arriving at clear answers as to who's right and who's wrong stems from the fact that commentators differ in what they mean by subliminal advertising. In fact, there are three distinct forms of subliminal stimulation. A first form presents *visual stimuli* at a very rapid rate by means of a device called a tachistoscope (say, at 1-3,000th of a second such as in Vicary's research). A second form uses *accelerated speech* in auditory messages. The third form involves the *embedding of hidden symbols* (such as sexual images or words) in print advertisements.[68]

This last form, *embedding,* is what Key has written about and is the form that advertising researchers have studied. However, it is important to remember that embeds (for example, the word *SEX* airbrushed into an advertisement) are not truly subliminal since they are visible to the naked eye. Nonetheless, the remaining discussion of subliminal messages is restricted to the practice of embedding.

To better appreciate embedding, consider an advertisement for Edge shaving cream that ran in magazines in the 1980s. This ad featured a picture of a lathered-up man with a look of near ecstasy on his face and a prominent shot of the Edge Gel can grasped in his fingertips. Below his lips were scenes of a nude woman on her back with knees raised, a facial portrayal of an attractive blond woman, and a scene of a sexy male on a surfboard surfing through a water tunnel. Aside from the Freudian symbolism associated with the water tunnel and the look of ecstasy on the man's face, the ad also included three vague nude figures airbrushed into the shaving lather above the man's lip.

Are embedded symbols in advertisements effective? To answer this we first need to examine the process that would have to operate in order for embedding to influence consumer choice behavior. The Edge shaving gel advertisement provides a useful vehicle for motivating this discussion. The first step in the process requires that the consumer consciously or subconsciously process the embedded symbol (the nude figures in the Edge magazine ad). Second, as the result of processing the cue, the consumer would have to develop a greater desire for Edge shaving gel than he had before seeing the ad. Third, because advertising is done at the brand level and because advertisers are interested in selling their brands and not just any brand in the product category, effective symbolic embedding would require that consumers develop a desire for the specific brand, Edge in this case, rather than just any brand in the category. Finally, the consumer would need to transfer the desire for the advertised brand into actual purchase behavior.

Is there evidence to support this chain of events? Despite a few limited studies on the issue, there are a variety of practical problems that *probably prevent embedding from being effective in a realistic marketing context.*[69] Perhaps the major reason why embedding in advertising has little effect is because the images have to be concealed to preclude detection by consumers. Many consumers would resent such tricky advertising efforts if they knew they existed. Thus, precluding detection from consumers means that embedding is a relatively weak technique in comparison to more vivid advertising representations. Because the majority of consumers devote relatively little time and effort in processing advertisements, a weak stimulus means that most consumers could not possibly be influenced.[70]

Even if consumers did attend to and encode sexual embeds under natural advertising conditions, there remains serious doubt that this information would have sufficient impact to affect product or brand choice behavior. Standard (supraliminal) advertising information itself has a difficult time influencing consumers. There is no theoretical reason to expect that subliminal information is any more effective. For example, do you really think that men would run out to buy Edge shaving gel just because they consciously or subconsciously spot a nude woman in the advertisement for that product?

In sum, the topic of subliminal advertising (particularly the Wilson Key variety of symbolic embeds) makes for interesting speculation and discussion, but scientific evidence in support of its practical effectiveness is virtually nonexistent. The following quotation appropriately sums up the issue:

> *A century of psychological research substantiates the general principle that more intense stimuli have a greater influence on people's behavior than weaker ones. While subliminal perception is a bona fide phenomenon, the effects obtained are subtle and obtaining them typically requires a carefully structured context. Subliminal stimuli are usually so weak that the recipient is not just unaware of the stimulus but is also oblivious to the fact that he/she is being stimulated. As a result, the potential effects of subliminal stimuli are easily nullified by other ongoing stimulation in the same sensory channel or by attention being focused on another modality. These factors pose serious difficulties for any possible marketing application.*[71]

THE FUNCTIONS OF MUSIC IN ADVERTISING

Music has been an important component of the advertising landscape virtually since the beginning of recorded sound. Jingles, background music, popular tunes, and classical arrangements are used to attract attention, convey selling points, set an emotional tone for an advertisement, and to influence listeners' moods. Well-known entertainers, nonvocal musical accompaniment, and unknown vocalists are used extensively in promoting everything from fabric softeners to automobiles.

Many advertising practitioners and scholars think that music performs a variety of useful communication functions. These include *attracting attention,* putting consumers in a *positive mood,* making them *more receptive to message arguments,* and even *communicating meanings* about advertised products.[72]

Although music's role in marketing has until recently been an incredibly understudied subject, brief commentary on a few studies will convey a sense of the type of research that is being conducted.[73] In one study using classical conditioning procedures, music represented the unconditioned stimulus in an effort to influence experimental subjects' preference for a ballpoint pen, which represented the conditioned stimulus.[74] An *unconditioned stimulus* (US) is one that evokes pleasant feelings or thoughts in people. A *conditioned stimulus* (CS) is one that is emotionally or cognitively neutral prior to the onset of a conditioning experiment. In simple terms, classical conditioning is achieved when the pairing of US and CS results in a transfer of feeling from the US (music in the present case) to the CS (the ballpoint pen).

Experimental subjects in this study were informed that an advertising agency was trying to select music for use in a commercial for a ballpoint pen. Subjects then listened to music while they viewed slides of the pen. The positive US for half the subjects was music from the movie *Grease,* and the negative US for the remaining subjects was classical Asian Indian music. The simple association between music and the pen influenced product preference—nearly 80 percent of the subjects exposed to the *Grease* music chose the advertised pen, whereas only 30 percent of the subjects exposed to the Indian music chose the advertised pen.[75]

Music's Role at the Point of Purchase

Although falling outside of an advertising context, two additional studies of music are noteworthy in that they provide dramatic evidence regarding the potential impact music can have on consumers' buying behavior at retail venues. A first experiment examined the effects of *background music* in a supermarket setting. A supermarket chain was studied over a nine-week period by comparing sales volume during days when slow-tempo background music was played (72 beats per minute or slower) versus days when fast-tempo music was in the background (94 beats per minute or more). The researcher found that daily sales volume averaged approximately $16,740 on days when slow-tempo music was played but only about $12,113 when fast-tempo music was played—an average increase of $4,627, or *38.2 percent* per day! The slow-tempo music apparently *slowed the pace* at which customers moved through the store and increased their total expenditures because they had a longer opportunity to purchase more.[76]

In a second field experiment, the same researcher examined the effects of background music on restaurant customers' purchase behavior. A restaurant alternated playing slow- and fast-tempo music on Friday and Saturday nights over a one-month period. Slow music increased the amount of time customers remained seated at their tables—an average of 56 minutes per customer group during slow-music nights compared to an average of 45 minutes during fast-music nights. Also, customers during slow-music nights spent significantly larger amounts on alcoholic beverages (an average of $30.47 per customer group) compared to fast-music nights ($21.62 per customer group).[77]

In the final analysis, music appears to be effective in creating customer moods and stimulating buying preferences and choices. Of course, considerably more research is needed to understand fully the scientific role of music in accomplishing different marketing communications functions. Marketplace wisdom, as manifested by marketing communicators' nearly universal use of music in advertisements and in retail settings, clearly suggests that music is an effective form of nonverbal communication. However, the type of music used in advertising and the specific role music performs undoubtedly varies considerably across cultures inasmuch as music does not mean the same thing to all people around the world.[78]

THE ROLE OF COMPARATIVE ADVERTISING

The practice in which advertisers *directly* or *indirectly* compare their products against competitive offerings, typically claiming that the promoted item is superior in one or several important purchase considerations, is called comparative advertising. Comparative ads vary both with regard to the explicitness of the comparisons and with respect to whether the target of the comparison is named or referred to in general terms.[79] Salespeople have always used comparative messages in arguing the advantages of their products over those of their competitors. Likewise, print advertisers (newspapers, magazines) have used comparative claims for decades. It was not until the early 1970s, however, that television commercials in the United States began making direct-comparison claims. Since then all media have experienced notable increases in the use of comparative advertising.

To better appreciate comparative advertising, it will be useful to examine a couple of examples. Figure 11.13 represents an indirect-comparison ad whereby Zest compares itself with "regular soap" without mentioning any specific brand. The ad in Figure 11.14 for Extra Strength Tylenol compares itself directly, albeit visually, against competitor Excedrin. This clever ad conveys the point that Tylenol, unlike Excedrin, is caffeine-free. The questions posed below ask whether and under what conditions comparative advertising is most effective.

Is Comparative Advertising More Effective?

In deciding whether to use a comparative advertisement rather than a more conventional noncomparative format, an advertiser must confront questions such as the following:

◆ How do comparative and noncomparative advertisements compare in terms of differential impact on brand awareness, consumer believability and comprehension of advertising claims, and source credibility?

Illustration of an Indirect
Comparative Ad

**HARD WATER & SOAP
LEAVE A DRYING FILM BEHIND.**

If your soap won't lather well and your skin feels dry, these are signs that you might have hard water (and up to 70% of the U.S. does). You see, regular soap combined with the minerals in hard water can leave a drying film you can feel on your skin. But not Zest.

**HARD WATER & ZEST
RINSE CLEAN AWAY.**

Zest is specially formulated to work in hard water. It lathers up and rinses clean away. With no drying soap film left behind. Just cleaner, smoother skin. In Body Wash and Bar.

ZEST MAKES HARD WATER EASY ON YOUR SKIN.

♦ Do comparative and noncomparative ads differ with regard to effects on brand preferences, buying intentions, and purchase behavior?

♦ What are the effects of copy claim variation and substantiation on the performance of competitive advertisements?

♦ How do factors such as consumer brand preference and the advertiser's competitive position influence the effectiveness of comparative advertising?

♦ Under what specific circumstances should an advertiser use comparative advertising?[80]

Illustration of a Direct Comparative Ad

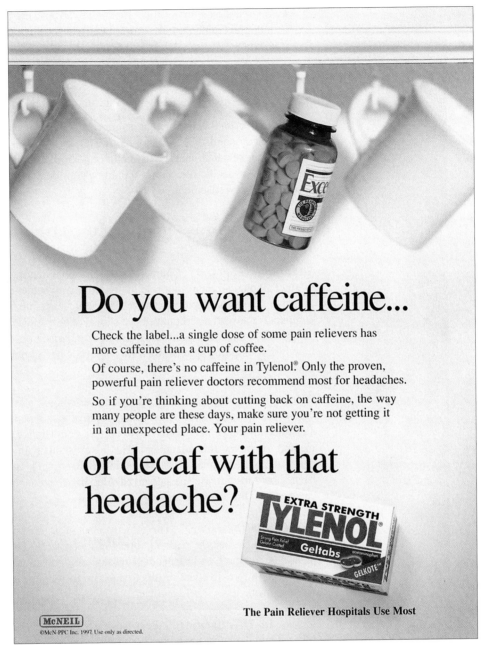

Researchers have performed a number of comparative-advertising studies since the mid-1970s.[81] Findings are at times inconclusive and even contradictory. Lack of definitive results is to be expected, however, because advertising is a complex phenomenon that varies from situation to situation in terms of executional elements, audience characteristics, media characteristics, and other factors. However, a major analysis of research that has tested comparative versus noncomparative advertising suggests the following conclusions:[82]

♦ Comparative advertising is better (than non-comparative ads) in enhancing brand awareness (i.e., brand name recall).

♦ Comparative advertising promotes better recall of message points.

♦ However, comparative advertising is perceived as somewhat less believable than noncomparative advertising.

♦ Comparative (versus noncomparative) advertising is responsible for generating more favorable attitudes toward the sponsoring brand, especially when the brand is a new (versus established) brand.

♦ Comparative advertising generates stronger intentions to purchase the sponsored brand.

♦ Comparative advertising generates more purchases than noncomparative ads.

It is obvious from this listing that a variety of advantages accrue to the use of comparative versus noncomparative advertising. However, as always is the case, one form of advertising is not universally superior to another under all circumstances. The following sections identify some specific issues that should be considered when considering whether to use a comparative advertisement.

Considerations Dictating the Use of Comparative Advertising

Situational Factors. Characteristics of the audience, media, message, company, and product all play an important role in determining whether comparative advertising is more effective than noncomparative advertising. For example, product superiority claims in a comparative advertisement have been shown to be evaluated significantly less favorably by people who had a prior preference for the comparison brand (the brand that the advertised brand was compared against) than for subjects who did not have a prior preference for that brand.[83]

Distinct Advantages. Comparative advertising is particularly effective for promoting *brands that possess distinct advantages* relative to competitive brands.[84] When a brand has a distinct advantage over competitive brands, comparative advertising provides a powerful method to convey this advantage. The advertisement for Tylenol (Figure 11.14) typifies this situation. Relative to noncomparative advertising, comparative advertising has also been shown to increase the perceived similarity between a challenger brand in a product category and the category leader.[85]

The Credibility Issue. The effectiveness of comparative advertising increases when comparative claims are made to appear *more credible.* There are various ways to accomplish this: (1) have an independent research organization support the superiority claims, (2) present impressive test results to back up the claims, and (3) use a trusted endorser as spokesperson.

Assessing Effectiveness. Because comparative advertisements make claims for an advertised brand relative to another brand and because consumers encode this comparative information in a relative fashion, *measurement techniques* in assessing the effectiveness of comparative advertising are most sensitive when questions are worded in a relative fashion. This is to say that for maximal sensitivity, the question context, or wording, should match the consumer's encoding mind-set. For example, with reference to the Zest advertisement (Figure 11.13), there are two alternative questions that could be framed to ascertain whether consumers perceive Zest as an effective brand in lathering up and rinsing away soap film: (1) How likely is it that Zest is effective when bathing in hard water? *(nonrelative* framing) or (2) How likely is it that Zest is more effective than regular soaps when bathing in hard water? *(relative* framing). Research has shown that relative framing does a better job of assessing consumers' beliefs after being exposed to comparative advertisements.[86]

S ummary

This chapter discusses both the role of celebrity endorsers and the nature and effectiveness of specific advertising techniques such as humor and fear appeals. Discussion of celebrity and typical-person endorsers indicates that endorsers have influence on consumers via the attributes of attractiveness and credibility. Attractiveness operates through an identification mechanism, whereas credibility functions via the process of internalization.

Widely used advertising techniques discussed in this chapter include humor, fear appeals, guilt, sex appeals, subliminal messages, the use of music, and comparative advertisements. Discussion covers empirical research and indicates when each of these advertising techniques is most effective.

D iscussion Questions

1. Using the concepts of attractiveness, expertise, and trustworthiness, explain what makes Michael Jordan an effective endorser.

2. Identify two product categories where Michael Jordan would not make an effective endorser. Justify your reasoning, and do not use products that would be ridiculous for Jordan or any other man to endorse.

3. Suppose you are the brand manager for Jell-O and are looking for a celebrity to replace Bill Cosby as the endorser for that brand. What person would you select to replace Mr. Cosby if you were in charge of this account? Fully justify the rationale behind your choice.

4. Magic Johnson announced to the world in November 1991 that he had just tested positive for HIV, a precursor to AIDS, and would be retiring from professional basketball. Try to place yourself in the position of Converse's vice president of marketing in November 1991. Would you have allowed Magic to continue endorsing Converse (his contract was written through 1995), or would you have amicably terminated the contract and sought another endorser?

5. A relatively new form of advertising is referred to as the long commercial (30 to 60 minutes in length), or *infomercial*. These commercials typically are aired during fringe times and frequently promote products such as diet aids, balding cures, and exercise products. Invariably these infomercials turn to physicians and other health professionals to buttress claims about the promoted brand's efficacy. Using concepts from this chapter, explain why health professionals are used in this form of advertising.

6. You have probably seen a number of public service announcements along the lines described in the fear-appeals section to discourage drinking and driving. In your opinion, is this form of advertising effective in altering the behavior of people your age? Be specific in justifying your answer.

7. The fear of getting AIDS should be relevant to many college students. Accordingly, would you agree that a relatively weak fear appeal should suffice in influencing students to either abstain from sexual relations or practice safe sex? If you disagree, then how can you reconcile your disagreement with the degree-of-relevance explanation?

8. Develop a list of products for which you feel fear appeals might be a viable approach to persuading consumer acceptance of a brand. What kinds of products do not lend themselves to fear appeals? Explain why you feel these products would be inappropriate.

9. Consumers occasionally find television commercials to be humorous and enjoyable. Some advertising pundits claim that such commercials may capture attention but are frequently ineffective in selling products. What is your stance on this issue? Justify your position.

10. The advertising agency for an automobile-tire manufacturer is considering using a fear-appeal message to promote its client's tires. What would you suggest to the advertising agency in terms of fear-appeal strength?

11. Explain why an advertiser would prefer to change consumer attitudes through an internalization process rather than through compliance or identification.

12. Distinguish between an attractive and a credible source. Provide two or three examples of well-known product spokespersons who, in your opinion, are high in both attractiveness and credibility. Justify why you consider these individuals to possess both attributes.

13. Provide two or three examples of music in advertisements that you think are particularly effective. For each example, explain precisely why you consider the music to be effective.

14. Photo copy several examples of comparative advertisements from magazines. Analyze each ad in terms of why you think the advertiser used a comparative-advertising format and whether you think the advertisement is effective. Justify your position.

15. Collect advertisements from magazines, and locate two or three illustrations of each of the following: credible sources, attractive sources, and trustworthy sources. Explain why you chose each example to illustrate a particular source characteristic.

16. In an article titled "Understanding Jingles and Needledrop: A Rhetorical Approach to Music in Advertising" (see endnote 72), it has been suggested that music in commercials is able to communicate specific meanings to listeners and viewers. In other words, music can talk (communicate) to people by conveying a sense of speed, excitement, sadness, nostalgia, and so on. Identify two commercials where the music is communicating a specific emotion or other state or action to consumers, and identify this emotion or state/action.

17. Too much sex is used in advertising. Comment.

*I*nternet Exercises

1. Q-ratings (a.k.a. Q-scores) represent one source of valuable information to brand managers and advertising agencies. To get a better idea of how Q-ratings are developed, visit www.qscores.com. While visiting this site, answer the following questions:
   a. Describe the studies that produce Q-scores. What is the purchase price for these studies?
   b. Using the free example provided on the Web site, name the performer and provide the total sample data. Additionally, verify the calculation of the Q-score.
   c. Starting in November 1997 a new type of Q-score has become available, namely, "Performers of the Past." Why do you think this new Q-score was introduced? What are the advantages and disadvantages of using past performers?
   d. Access the actual questionnaire for the past performer Q-scores on the Web site and pick "one of your favorites" from the list. Identify one or more product categories where you think this past performer would make an effective endorser. Explain your choices in terms of the endorser attributes described in the chapter.
   e. Q-scores are also given for cartoon characters since they are used heavily in endorsements and licensing. Since cartoons are fictional, is it appropriate to assess their endorser "attributes"? That is, can cartoons be attractive, credible, trustworthy, or possess expertise in the perceptions of consumers?

2. The Better Business Bureau has a special advertising review board called the *Children's Advertising Review Unit (CARU)*. CARU has published its self-regulation guidelines at <u>www.bbb.org/advertising/caruguide.html</u>. Using these guidelines, address the following issues:

a. CARU provides extensive guidelines on the use of cartoon characters. Do these guidelines indicate whether it is the attributes of cartoon character endorsers, children, or both that put children at risk?

b. What are the guidelines concerning comparative advertising? Why should adults be less susceptible to comparative advertising than children?

Chapter Eleven Endnotes

1. Abraham Kaplan, *The Conduct of Inquiry: Methodology for Behavioral Science* (New York: Intext Educational Publishers/Chandler, 1964).

2. Hershey Friedman and Linda Friedman, "Endorser Effectiveness by Product Type," *Journal of Advertising Research* 19 (October/November 1979), 63–71.

3. This estimate is a rough extrapolation of a 33 percent estimate by Spielman and a 20 percent estimate by Miciak and Shanklin. See H. M. Spielman, "Pick Product Presenter Prudently," *Marketing News,* September 8, 1987, 5; and Alan R. Miciak and William L. Shanklin, "Choosing Celebrity Endorsers," *Marketing Management* 3 (winter 1994), 51–59.

4. See, for example, R. B. Fireworker and H. H. Friedman, "The Effects of Endorsements on Product Evaluation," *Decision Sciences* 8 (July 1977), 576–583; and H. H. Friedman, Salvatore Termini, and R. Washington, "The Effectiveness of Advertisements Utilizing Four Types of Endorsers," *Journal of Advertising* 5 (summer 1976), 22–24.

5. Jagdish Agrawal and Wagner A. Kamakura, "The Economic Worth of Celebrity Endorsers: An Event Study Analysis," *Journal of Marketing* 59 (July 1995), 56–62.

6. S. Ratneshwar and Shelly Chaiken, "Comprehension's Role in Persuasion: The Case of Its Moderating Effect on the Persuasive Impact of Source Cues," *Journal of Consumer Research* 18 (June 1991), 52–62.

7. "Star Turns That Can Turn Star-Crossed," *U.S. News & World Report,* December 7, 1987, 57.

8. Jeff Jensen, "Jordan Still King of Ad Presenter Game," *Advertising Age,* April 25, 1994, 3; Randall Lane, "The Forbes All-Stars," *Forbes,* December 19, 1994, 266–278.

9. Michael A. Kamins, "An Investigation into the 'Match-Up' Hypothesis in Celebrity Advertising: When Beauty May Be Only Skin Deep," *Journal of Advertising* 19, no. 1 (1990), 4–13.

10. David Finkle, "Q-Ratings: The Popularity Contest of the Stars," *The Wall Street Journal,* June 7, 1992, in special section ("Themes of the Times"), 1.

11. Kevin Goldman, "Sears, Seeking to Change Image, Plans to Sponsor Phil Collins Tour," *The Wall Street Journal,* January 4, 1994, B8.

12. This survey and the following discussion are based on Miciak and Shanklin, "Choosing Celebrity Endorsers."

13. Carolyn Tripp, Thomas D. Jensen, and Les Carlson, "The Effects of Multiple Product Endorsements by Celebrities on Consumers' Attitudes and Intentions," *Journal of Consumer Research* 20 (March 1994), 535–547.

14. Jeff Jensen, "Team Reebok-Shaq: Is Big Trouble Afoot?" *Advertising Age,* February 21, 1994, 1, 36.

15. David J. Moore and Richard Reardon, "Source Magnification: The Role of Multiple Sources in the Processing of Advertising Appeals," *Journal of Marketing Research* 24 (November 1987), 412–417.

16. It is important to note that although the present discussion is framed in terms of endorser characteristics, more general treatment of the topic refers to source characteristics. For a classic treatment of the subject, see Herbert C. Kelman, "Processes of Opinion Change," *Public Opinion Quarterly* 25 (spring 1961), 57–78. For a more current treatment, see Daniel J. O'Keefe, *Persuasion Theory and Research* (Newbury Park, Calif.: Sage, 1990), chap. 8.

17. H. C. Triandis, *Attitudes and Attitude Change* (New York: John Wiley & Sons, 1971).

18. Lawrence Feick and Robin A. Higie, "The Effects of Preference Heterogeneity and Source Characteristics on Ad Processing and Judgements about Endorsers," *Journal of Advertising* 21 (June 1992), 9–24.

19. For information about how to measure attractiveness, see Roobina Ohanian, "Construction and Validation of a Scale to Measure Celebrity Endorsers' Perceived Expertise, Trustworthiness, and Attractiveness," *Journal of Advertising* 19, no. 3 (1990), 39–52.

20. W. Benoy Joseph, "The Credibility of Physically Attractive Communicators: A Review," *Journal of Advertising* 11, no. 3 (1982), 15–24; Lynn R. Kahle and Pamela M. Homer, "Physical Attractiveness of the Celebrity Endorser: A Social Adaptation Perspective," *Journal of Consumer Research* 11 (March 1985), 954–961.

21. Kamins, "An Investigation into the 'Match-Up' Hypothesis."

22. Richard E. Petty, Thomas M. Ostrom, and Timothy C. Brock, eds., *Cognitive Responses in Persuasion* (Hillsdale, N.J.: Lawrence Erlbaum Associates, 1981), 143.

23. Rohit Deshpande and Douglas Stayman, "A Tale of Two Cities: Distinctiveness Theory and Advertising Effectiveness," *Journal of Marketing Research* 31 (February 1994), 57–64.

24. James M. Hunt, Theresa J. Domzal, and Jerome B. Kernan, "Causal Attributions and Persuasion: The Case of Disconfirmed Expectancies," in *Advances in Consumer Research,* vol. 9, ed. Andrew Mitchell (Ann Arbor, Mich.: Association for Consumer Research, 1982), 287–292.

25. Marc Weinberger and Harlan Spotts, "Humor in U.S. Versus U.K. TV Advertising," *Journal of Advertising* 18, no. 2 (1989), 39–44. For further discussion of differences between American and British advertising, see Terence Nevett, "Differences between American and British Television Advertising: Explanations and Implications," *Journal of Advertising* 21 (December 1992), 61–71.

26. Harlan E. Spotts, Marc G. Weinberger, and Amy L. Parsons, "Assessing the Use and Impact of Humor on Advertising Effectiveness: A Contingency Approach," *Journal of Advertising* 26 (fall 1997), 17–32.

27. H. Shanker Krishnan and Dipankar Chakravarti, "Processes Underlying the Effects of Humorous Ad Executions on Brand Claims Memory," Indiana University Working Paper, 1998.

28. A thorough review of the issues is provided in two valuable reviews: Paul Surgi Speck, "The Humorous Message Taxonomy: A Framework for the Study of Humorous Ads," *Current Issues and Research in Advertising,* vol. 3, ed. J. H. Leigh and C. R. Martin, Jr. (Ann Arbor: Graduate School of Business Administration, University of Michigan, 1991), 1–44; Marc G. Weinberger and Charles S. Gulas, "The Impact of Humor in Advertising: A Review," *Journal of Advertising* 21 (December 1992), 35–59.

29. Thomas J. Madden and Marc G. Weinberger, "Humor in Advertising: A Practitioner View," *Journal of Advertising Research* 24, no. 4 (1984), 23–29.

30. Based on Weinberger and Gulas, "The Impact of Humor in Advertising: A Review," 56–57.

31. Differences in the use of humor across advertising media are demonstrated in Marc G. Weinberger, Harlan Spotts, Leland Campbell, and Amy L. Parsons, "The Use and Effect of Humor in Different Advertising Media," *Journal of Advertising Research* 35 (May/June 1995), 44–56.

32. Thomas J. Madden and Marc G. Weinberger, "The Effects of Humor on Attention in Magazine Advertising," *Journal of Advertising* 11, no. 3 (1982), 4–14.

33. Amitava Chattopadhyay and Kunal Basu, "Humor in Advertising: The Moderating Role of Prior Brand Evaluation," *Journal of Consumer Research* 27 (November 1990), 466–476.

34. See Yong Zhang, "Responses to Humorous Advertising: The Moderating Effect of Need for Cognition," *Journal of Advertising* 25 (spring 1996), 15–32.

35. On a technical note, advertisers make threats that appeal to audience fears. Fear is the emotional response to a threat. Thus, it would be technically more correct to talk about "threat appeals" than fear appeals. This distinction notwithstanding, the conventional approach has been to talk about fear appeals rather than threat appeals. For in-depth treatment of this issue, see

Michael S. LaTour and Herbert J. Rotfeld, "There Are Threats and (Maybe) Fear-Caused Arousal: Theory and Confusions of Appeals to Fear and Fear Arousal Itself," *Journal of Advertising* 26 (fall 1997), 45–60.

36. This is a quote from the Jerry Della Femina, a well-known advertising agency executive and former copywriter. Cited in Emily DeNitto, "Healthcare Ads Employ Scare Tactics," *Advertising Age,* November 7, 1994, 12.

37. The classic demonstration is a study on dental hygiene practices. See I. Janis and S. Feshbach, "Effects of Fear-Arousing Communications," *Journal of Abnormal and Social Psychology* 48 (January 1953), 78–92.

38. Michael L. Ray and William L. Wilkie, "Fear: The Potential of an Appeal Neglected by Marketing," *Journal of Marketing* 34 (January 1970), 54–62.

39. Ibid., 55.

40. For further discussion, see Herbert J. Rotfeld, "Fear Appeals and Persuasion: Assumptions and Errors in Advertising Research," *Current Issues and Research in Advertising,* vol. 11, ed. J. H. Leigh and C. R. Martin, Jr. (Ann Arbor: Graduate School of Business Administration, University of Michigan, 1988), 21–39.

41. Peter Wright, "Concrete Action Plans in TV Messages to Increase Reading of Drug Warnings," *Journal of Consumer Research* 6 (December 1979), 256–269. For an explanation of the psychological mechanism by which fear-intensity operates, see Punam Anand Keller and Lauren Goldberg Block, "Increasing the Persuasiveness of Fear Appeals: The Effect of Arousal and Elaboration," *Journal of Consumer Research* 22 (March 1996), 448–459.

42. For further reading on the use of fear appeals in antidrinking-and-driving campaigns, see Karen Whitehill King and Leonard N. Reid, "Fear Arousing Anti-Drinking and Driving PSAs: Do Physical Injury Threats Influence Young Adults?" *Current Issues and Research in Advertising,* vol. 12, ed. J. H. Leigh and C. R. Martin, Jr. (Ann Arbor: Graduate School of Business Administration, University of Michigan, 1990), 155–175. Other relevant articles on fear appeals include John F. Tanner, James B. Hunt, and David R. Eppright, "The Protection Motivation Model: Normative Model of Fear Appeals," *Journal of Marketing* 55 (July 1991), 36–45; Tony L. Henthorne, Michael S. LaTour, and Rajan Natarajan, "Fear Appeals in Print Advertising: An Analysis of Arousal and Ad Response," *Journal of Advertising* 22 (June 1993), 59–70; and James T. Strong and Khalid M. Dubas, "The Optimal Level of Fear-Arousal in Advertising: An Empirical Study," *Journal of Current Issues and Research in Advertising* 15 (fall 1993), 93–99

43. Carroll E. Izard (1977), *Human Emotions,* New York: Plenum.

44. Robin Higie Coulter and Mary Beth Pinto, "Guilt Appeals in Advertising: What Are Their Effects?" *Journal of Applied Psychology,* 80 (December 1995), 697–705; Bruce A. Huhmann and Timothy P. Brotherton, "A Content Analysis of Guilt Appeals in Popular Magazine Advertisements," *Journal of Advertising* 26 (summer 1997), 35–46.

45. Huhmann and Brotherton, "A Content Analysis of Guilt Appeals in Popular Magazine Advertisements," 36.

46. Ibid.

47. A content analysis of magazine advertising indicates that the percentage of ads with sexual content had not changed over a two-decade period. What changed, however, was that sexual illustrations had become more overt. Female models were more likely than male models to be portrayed in nude, partially nude, or suggestive poses. See Lawrence Soley and Gary Kurzbard, "Sex in Advertising: A Comparison of 1964 and 1984 Magazine Advertisements," *Journal of Advertising* 15, no. 3 (1986), 46–54.

48. For a review of the scientific issues involved in studying sex in advertising, see Robert S. Baron, "Sexual Content and Advertising Effectiveness: Comments on Belch et al. (1981) and Caccavale et al. (1981)," in *Advances in Consumer Research,* vol. 9, ed. Andrew Mitchell (Ann Arbor, Mich.: Association for Consumer Research, 1982), 428–430.

49. Michael A. Belch, Barbro E. Holgerson, George E. Belch, and Jerry Koppman, "Psychophysiological and Cognitive Responses to Sex in Advertising," in *Advances in Consumer Research,* vol. 9, ed. Andrew Mitchell (Ann Arbor, Mich.: Association for Consumer Research, 1982), 424–427.

50. Baron, "Sexual Content and Advertising Effectiveness," 428.

51. B. G. Yovovich, "Sex in Advertising—The Power and the Perils," *Advertising Age,* May 2, 1983, M4.

52. Larry Percy, "A Review of the Effect of Specific Advertising Elements upon Overall Communication Response," in *Current Issues and Research in Advertising,* vol. 2, ed. J. H. Leigh and C. R. Martin, Jr. (Ann Arbor: Graduate School of Business Administration, University of Michigan, 1983), 95.

53. David Richmond and Timothy P. Hartman, "Sex Appeal in Advertising," *Journal of Advertising Research* 22 (October/November 1982), 53–61.

54. Michael S. LaTour, Robert E. Pitts, and David C. Snook-Luther, "Female Nudity, Arousal, and Ad Response: An Experimental Investigation," *Journal of Advertising* 19, no. 4 (1990), 51–62.

55. Baron, "Sexual Content and Advertising Effectiveness," 428.

56. Robert A. Peterson and Roger A. Kerin, "The Female Role in Advertisements: Some Experimental Evidence," *Journal of Marketing* 41 (October 1977), 59–63.

57. Jessica Severn, George E. Belch, and Michael A. Belch, "The Effects of Sexual and Non-sexual Advertising Appeals and Information Level on Cognitive Processing and Communication Effectiveness," *Journal of Advertising* 19, no. 1 (1990), 14–22.

58. "Sex Still Sells—But So Does Sensitivity," *Business Week,* March 18, 1991, 100; Michele Ingrassia, "Going One Step Ogle the Line?" *Newsweek,* March 14, 1994.

59. Ira Teinowitz and Bob Geiger, "Suits Try to Link Sex Harassment Ads," *Advertising Age,* November 18, 1991, 48.

60. Cyndee Miller, "Sexy Sizzle Backfires," *Marketing News,* September 25, 1995, 1, 2.

61. A study of consumers in Denmark, Greece, New Zealand, and the U.S. revealed consistent criticism of sexist role portrayals. See Richard W. Pollay and Steven Lysonski, "In the Eye of the Beholder: International Differences in Ad Sexism Perceptions and Reactions," *Journal of International Consumer Marketing* 6 (volume 2, 1993), 25–43.

62. Three surveys have demonstrated this fact. For the most recent review of these surveys, see Martha Rogers and Kirk H. Smith, "Public Perceptions of Subliminal Advertising: Why Practitioners Shouldn't Ignore This Issue," *Journal of Advertising Research* 33 (March/April 1993), 10–18.

63. Martha Rogers and Christine A. Seiler, "The Answer Is No: A National Survey of Advertising Industry Practitioners and Their Clients about Whether They Use Subliminal Advertising," *Journal of Advertising Research* 34 (March/April 1994), 36–45.

64. This description is adapted from Martin P. Block and Bruce G. Vanden Bergh, "Can You Sell Subliminal Messages to Consumers?" *Journal of Advertising* 14, no. 3 (1985), 59.

65. Vicary himself acknowledged that the study that initiated the original furor over subliminal advertising was based on too small an amount of data to be meaningful. See Fred Danzig, "Subliminal Advertising—Today It's Just Historic Flashback for Researcher Vicary," *Advertising Age,* September 17, 1962, 42, 74.

66. For example, see Sharon E. Beatty and Del I. Hawkins, "Subliminal Stimulation: Some New Data and Interpretation," *Journal of Advertising* 18, no. 3 (1989), 4–8.

67. Wilson B. Key, *Subliminal Seduction: Ad Media's Manipulation of a Not So Innocent America* (New York: Signet, 1972); *Media Sexploitation* (New York: Signet, 1976); *The Clam Plate Orgy: And Other Subliminal Techniques for Manipulating Your Behavior* (New York: Signet, 1980). Key has since written *The Age of Manipulation: The Con in Confidence, the Sin in Sincere* (New York: Holt, 1989).

68. For a sophisticated treatment of visual imagery and symbolism in advertising (though not dealing with subliminal advertising per se), see Linda M. Scott, "Images in Advertising: The Need for a Theory of Visual Rhetoric," *Journal of Consumer Research* 21 (September 1994), 252–273.

69. Ronnie Cuperfain and T. K. Clarke, "A New Perspective of Subliminal Perception," *Journal of Advertising* 14, no. 1 (1985), 36–41; Myron Gable, Henry T. Wilkens, Lynn Harris, and Richard Feinberg, "An Evaluation of Subliminally Embedded Sexual Stimuli in Graphics," *Journal of Advertising* 16, no. 1 (1987), 26–31; William E. Kilbourne, Scott Painton, and Danny Ridley, "The Effect of Sexual Embedding on Responses to Magazine Advertisements," *Journal of Advertising* 14, no. 2 (1985), 48–56.

70. For discussion of the practical difficulties with implementing subliminal advertising and the

questionable effectiveness of this advertising technique, see Timothy E. Moore, "Subliminal Advertising: What You See Is What You Get," *Journal of Marketing* 46 (spring 1982), 41; and Joel Saegert, "Why Marketing Should Quit Giving Subliminal Advertising the Benefit of the Doubt," *Psychology & Marketing* 4 (summer 1987), 107–120.

71. Moore, "Subliminal Advertising: What You See Is What You Get," 46.

72. Very good reviews of music's various advertising functions are available in Gordon C. Bruner II, "Music, Mood, and Marketing," *Journal of Marketing* 54 (October 1990), 94–104; Linda M. Scott, "Understanding Jingles and Needledrop: A Rhetorical Approach to Music in Advertising," *Journal of Consumer Research* 17 (September 1990), 223–236; and James J. Kellaris, Anthony D. Cox, and Dena Cox, "The Effect of Background Music on Ad Processing: A Contingency Explanation," *Journal of Marketing* 57 (October 1993), 114–125.

73. In addition to those reviewed here, the following studies are recommended reading: Deborah J. MacInnis and C. Whan Park, "The Differential Role of Characteristics of Music on High- and Low-Involvement Consumers' Processing of Ads," *Journal of Consumer Research* 18 (September 1991), 161–173; James J. Kellaris and Robert J. Kent, "The Influence of Music on Consumers' Temporal Perceptions: Does Time Fly When You're Having Fun?" *Journal of Consumer Psychology* 1, no. 4 (1992), 365–376; James J. Kellaris and Robert J. Kent, "An Exploratory Investigation of Responses Elicited by Music Varying in Tempo, Tonality, and Texture," *Journal of Consumer Psychology* 2, no. 4 (1993), 381–402.

74. Gerald J. Gorn, "The Effects of Music in Advertising on Choice Behavior: A Classical Conditioning Approach," *Journal of Marketing* 46 (winter 1982), 94–101.

75. A replication of this study failed to obtain supporting evidence, thereby calling into question the ability to generalize from Gorn's prior research. See James J. Kellaris and Anthony D. Cox, "The Effects of Background Music in Advertising," *Journal of Consumer Research* 16 (June 1989), 113–118.

76. Ronald E. Milliman, "Using Background Music to Affect the Behavior of Supermarket Shoppers," *Journal of Marketing* 46 (summer 1982), 86–91. For additional insights on the role of music in altering individual's perception of time, see Kellaris and Kent, "An Exploratory Investigation of Responses Elicited by Music Varying in Tempo, Tonality, and Texture."

77. Ronald E. Milliman, "The Influence of Background Music on the Behavior of Restaurant Patrons," *Journal of Consumer Research* 13 (September 1986), 286–289.

78. For a fascinating discussion of cross-cultural differences, see Noel M. Murray and Sandra B. Murray, "Music and Lyrics in Commercials: A Cross-Cultural Comparison Between Commercials Run in the Dominican Republic and in the United States," *Journal of Advertising* 25 (summer 1996), 51–64.

79. See Darrell D. Muehling, Donald E. Stem, Jr., and Peter Raven, "Comparative Advertising: Views from Advertisers, Agencies, Media, and Policy Makers," *Journal of Advertising Research* 29 (October/November 1989), 38–48.

80. These questions are adapted from Stephen B. Ash and Chow-Hou Wee, "Comparative Advertising: A Review with Implications for Further Research," in *Advances in Consumer Research*, vol. 10, ed. R. P. Bagozzi and A. M. Tybout (Ann Arbor, Mich.: Association for Consumer Research, 1983), 374.

81. A sampling of significant comparative advertising research includes the following: Cornelia Droge and Rene Y. Darmon, "Associative Positioning Strategies through Comparative Advertising: Attribute versus Overall Similarity Approaches," *Journal of Marketing Research* 24 (November 1987), 377–388; Cornelia Pechmann and David W. Stewart, "The Effects of Comparative Advertising on Attention, Memory, and Purchase Intentions," *Journal of Consumer Research* 17 (September 1990), 180–191; Cornelia Pechmann and S. Ratneshwar, "The Use of Comparative Advertising for Brand Positioning: Association versus Differentiation," *Journal of Consumer Research* 18 (September 1991), 145–160; Cornelia Pechmann and Gabriel Esteban, "Persuasion Processes Associated with Direct Comparative and Noncomparative Advertising and Implications for Advertising Effectiveness," *Journal of Consumer Psychology* 2, no. 4 (1993), 403–432; Randall L. Rose, Paul W. Miniard, Michael J. Barone, Kenneth C. Manning, and Brian D. Till, "When Persuasion Goes Undetected: The Case of Comparative Advertising," *Journal of Marketing Research* 30 (August 1993), 315–330.

82. Dhruv Grewal, Sukuman Kavanoor, Edward F. Fern, Carolyn Costley, and James Barnes, "Comparative Versus Noncomparative Advertising: A Meta-Analysis," *Journal of Marketing* 61 (October 1997), 1–15.

83. V. Kanti Prasad, "Communications Effectiveness of Comparative Advertising: A Laboratory Analysis," *Journal of Marketing Research* 13 (May 1976), 128–137.

84. Terence A. Shimp and David C. Dyer, "The Effects of Comparative Advertising Mediated by Market Position of Sponsoring Brand," *Journal of Advertising* 7, no. 3 (1978), 13–19.

85. Gerald J. Gorn and Charles B. Weinberg, "The Impact of Comparative Advertising on Perception and Attitude: Some Positive

Findings," *Journal of Consumer Research* 11 (September 1984), 719–727.

86. Rose, Miniard, Barone, Manning, and Till, "When Persuasion Goes Undetected: The Case of Comparative Advertising"; Paul W. Miniard, Randall L. Rose, Michael J. Barone, and Kenneth C. Manning, "On the Need for Relative Measures When Assessing Comparative Advertising Effects," *Journal of Advertising* 22 (September 1993), 41–57.

Analysis of Advertising Media

CHAPTER OBJECTIVES

After studying this chapter, you should be able to:

1. Describe the five major advertising media.
2. Discuss out-of-home advertising and its strengths and limitations.
3. Discuss newspaper advertising and its strengths and limitations.
4. Discuss magazine advertising and its strengths and limitations.
5. Discuss radio advertising and its strengths and limitations.
6. Discuss television advertising and its strengths and limitations.
7. Describe the various forms of TV advertising (such as network and cable).
8. Discuss the features of Internet advertising.
9. Discuss the so-called alternative advertising media (such as product placements in movies and virtual signage).

Opening Vignette: Revamping Miller Lite's Image Required a Media Overhaul

As discussed in Chapter 9, Miller Lite in 1997–1998 dramatically increased its advertising expenditures and share of voice (SOV) in an effort to build the brand's market share. Most people are familiar with the quirky "Dick" campaign that was designed to create a hip image for Miller Lite and to position it as the beer of choice for young adults aged 21 to 28, which is regarded as a crucial demographic in the beer category. Miller Lite's ad agency, Fallon McElligott of Minneapolis, knew that the choice of advertising media would be critical to the successful redefinition of the brand.

Miller Lite and its agency were decisive in their belief that that national TV was the best medium for redefining the brand. Prime-time programming was considered especially important for reaching the greatest number of prospective 21- to 28-year-old beer drinkers. Miller Lite had previously avoided prime-time TV advertising on national networks due to higher prices, but the importance of quickly changing the brand's image necessitated purchasing the more expensive, yet more efficient TV medium that would be capable of best reaching the target audience. The "Dick" campaign also was extended to cable TV in view of the fact that this medium is drawing larger audiences.

www.millerlite.com/html/home-frame2

In total, network TV spending on Miller Lite advertising increased by over 60 percent to approximately $110 million during 1997, and cable spending rose by 78 percent to over $12 million. At the same time, Miller cut back on more traditional media that were considered ineffective for boosting the desired new image for Miller Lite. Outdoor and radio advertising were virtually eliminated. However, Miller's magazine advertising soared to over $7 million

with placements in hip young male magazines including *Maxim, Bikini,* and *POV.* This contrasts with Miller Lite's traditional magazine advertising that has featured mainstream magazines such as *Sports Illustrated.*

Post Mortem: The advertising campaign and revamped media schedule represented bold efforts to reposition Miller Lite in hopes of reversing what had become a very unattractive sales trend. It was anticipated that a hip, new image for the brand along with a revamped media schedule would drive meaningful increases in sales, market share, and profits. Although early results (as of 1997) indicated a volume increase of nearly 2 percent, this increase may have been fueled more by price promotions than by the advertising effort. In early 1999, the "Dick" campaign was considered ineffective and, thus, replaced with more traditional advertising aimed at a broader market.

Source: Adapted from James B. Arndorfer, "Media Strategy Crucial to Revamp of Miller's Image," *Advertising Age,* August 3, 1998, s12.

The previous two chapters have examined the message component of advertising strategy. Though effective messages are essential for successful advertising, these messages are of little use unless advertising media effectively reach the intended target audience. This and the following two chapters are devoted to media considerations. The present chapter examines the mass media (e.g., magazines, television, out-of-home advertising, and the Internet); Chapter 13 focuses on the use of direct advertising that is targeted to individual households and other "addressable" customers; and Chapter 14 explores the various factors and analytic methods that are used in making media-selection decisions.

The Miller Lite "story" in the *Opening Vignette* makes it abundantly clear that ad message and media considerations are inextricably related. Media and message represent a hand-in-glove relationship, where each must be compatible with and fit the other. It has been said that advertising creatives "can't move until they deal with a media strategist."[1] This is to say that creatives and media specialists must team up to design advertisements that effectively and efficiently deliver the right brand concept to the intended target audience, which in Miller Lite's case (*Opening Vignette*) is predominantly young males aged 21 to 28. Surveys of advertising practitioners reveal that the most important consideration in selecting advertising media is the ability to reach a specific audience effectively.[2]

OVERVIEW OF MAJOR MEDIA

Media versus Vehicles

Advertising industry terminology conventionally distinguishes between advertising media and vehicles. **Media** are the general communication methods that carry advertising messages, that is, television, magazines, newspapers, and so on. **Vehicles** are the specific broadcast programs or print choices in which advertisements are placed. Hence, for example, television is a specific medium, and *Friends, NBC Evening News,* and *Monday Night Football* are vehicles for carrying television advertisements. Magazines are another medium, and *Time, Business Week, Ebony,* and *Cosmopolitan* are vehicles in which magazine ads are placed.

www.nbc.com

www.cgi.pathfinder.com/time

www.businessweek.com

www.ebony.com

www.cosmopolitan.com

Characteristics of Traditional Major Advertising Media

Virtually any environment in which messages can be printed, sung, blared, or announced in any other fashion is a potential advertising medium. Ads on blimps; on the walls of restrooms; on T-shirts; on buses and bus stops; on shopping carts in stores; on store floors; on race cars and boats; on the apparel of golfers, tennis players, and other athletes; and on signs that trail behind small airplanes and products appearing in movies and television programs are just some of the spots where advertising is placed. These "special purpose" media are, of course, minor in relation to the traditional advertising media: television, radio, newspaper, magazines, and out-of-home advertising on billboards.

These five media are known as the *major* advertising media, within which the majority of advertising expenditures are placed. Table 12.1 classifies the advertising expenditures and their percentage of total advertising in each of these five major media for 1997. Approximately $73 billion in advertising expenditures were placed in these major media by national advertisers, with television advertising in its various forms (network, spot, cable, and syndicated) representing the dominant medium. It should be noted that total advertising in newspapers has been estimated at over $36.6 billion, a figure over twice as large as the $17.4 billion amount shown in Table 12.1. The difference in estimates is that the larger figure includes local newspaper advertising, whereas the smaller amount is advertising in newspapers by national advertisers.[3]

Each medium and each vehicle has a set of unique characteristics and virtues (see Figure 12.1). Advertisers attempt to select those media and vehicles whose characteristics are most compatible with the advertised brand in reaching its target audience and conveying its intended message. As Figure 12.1 indicates, if the objective is to demonstrate product

TABLE 12.1

U.S. Major Media Expenditures, 1997

MEDIUM	EXPENDITURES (IN MILLIONS OF DOLLARS)	PERCENTAGE OF TOTAL
Television		
Network TV	$15,225.1 (40.0% of TV)	
Spot TV	14,534.6 (38.2% of TV)	
Cable TV	5,781.9 (15.2% of TV)	
Syndicated TV	2,515.0 (06.6% of TV)	
Total Television	$38,056.6	51.98%
Newspapers	17,427.5	23.80
Magazines	13,717.7	18.74
Radio	2,549.8	3.48
Out-of-Home	1,462.7	2.00
TOTAL	$73,214.3	100.00%

FIGURE 12.1 Which Media Do It Best?

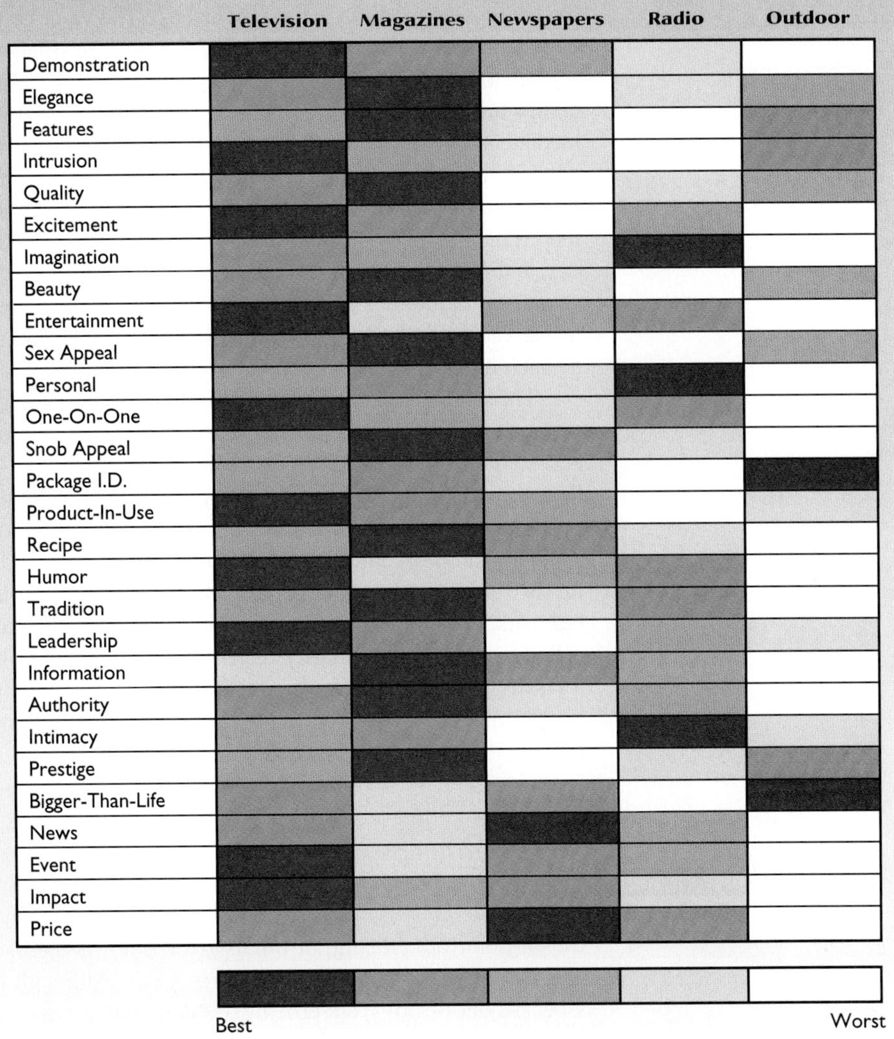

	Television	Magazines	Newspapers	Radio	Outdoor
Demonstration					
Elegance					
Features					
Intrusion					
Quality					
Excitement					
Imagination					
Beauty					
Entertainment					
Sex Appeal					
Personal					
One-On-One					
Snob Appeal					
Package I.D.					
Product-In-Use					
Recipe					
Humor					
Tradition					
Leadership					
Information					
Authority					
Intimacy					
Prestige					
Bigger-Than-Life					
News					
Event					
Impact					
Price					

Best   Worst

features, *television* is the best medium, followed by magazines, newspapers, radio, and out-of-home advertising. Television is also particularly powerful in terms of its entertainment and excitement value and its ability to have an impact on the viewer. *Magazines* are strong in terms of elegance, beauty, prestige, and tradition. *Newspapers* offer newsworthiness and low prices. *Radio,* which is especially personal, allows for the listener's imagination to play a part, while *out-of-home,* or outdoor, advertising is especially appropriate for package identification.

A Forewarning

The following sections will be devoted to each of the five major advertising media, placing considerable emphasis on each medium's strengths and limitations. Because it would be easy to misinterpret these discussions and the conclusions to be drawn, a few words of caution are in order. In particular, it might be tempting to play a count-'em game when examining each medium's strengths and limitations. That is, the reader might erroneously conclude that one medium is superior to another simply because more advantages and fewer limitations are listed. But this assuredly is not the intent of the following discussions.

The overall value or worth of an advertising medium depends on the advertiser's specific needs in a particular situation and the overall budget available for advertising a brand. No advertising medium is always the best. The value or worth of a medium depends on the circumstances confronting a brand at a particular time: its advertising objective, the target market toward whom this objective is aimed, and the available budget. An analogy will clarify this point. Suppose someone asked you: "What type of restaurant is best?" An immediate single answer is difficult to offer, because you undoubtedly would recognize that what is best in a restaurant depends on a person's particular needs on a specific dining occasion. In some circumstances price and speed of service are of essence, and restaurants like McDonald's would win out by this criterion. On other occasions, ambiance rules the day, and a classy French restaurant might be considered ideal. In yet another situation, the consumer is looking for a balance between dining elegance and reasonable price, and hence a middle-of-the-road eating establishment would serve the purpose. In sum, there is no such thing as a universally "best" restaurant.

The same is true of advertising media. What medium is "best" depends entirely on the advertiser's objectives, the creative needs, the competitive challenge, and budget availability. The best medium, or combination of media, is determined not by counting advantages and limitations but by conducting a careful examination of the advertised brand's needs and resources.

The presentation of ad media progresses in the following order: First discussed is the smallest and most unusual ad medium, out-of-home advertising. Coverage turns next to the two print media, newspapers and magazines, and then to the two electronic media, radio and television. In addition to these major media, later sections are devoted to the so-called *new media*—primarily Internet advertising. Finally, a brief discussion is devoted to a variety of unique advertising media (such as product placements in movies) that are relatively small in comparison to the major media but that nonetheless play an important role for advertisers in select situations.

OUT–OF–HOME ADVERTISING

Out-of-home advertising, or *outdoor* for short, is the oldest form of advertising with origins dating back literally thousands of years. Although billboard advertising is the major aspect of out-of-home advertising, outdoor encompasses a variety of other delivery modes: advertising on bus shelters, giant inflatables (e.g., the Goodyear blimp; see the *IMC Focus),* various forms of transit advertising (including ads painted on buses and trucks), shopping-mall displays, skywriting, T-shirts emblazoned with brand logos, and so on. The one commonality among these is that they are seen by consumers outside of their homes (hence the name) in contrast to television, magazines, newspapers, and radio, which are received in the home (or in other indoor locations).

Outdoor advertising is regarded as a supplementary, rather than primary, advertising medium. As shown in Table 12.1, out-of-home advertising expenditures in 1997 amounted to approximately $1.46 billion, which represents 2 percent of total advertising expenditures in the five major media. Product categories that historically have spent the most on outdoor advertising include tobacco products and alcohol. However, these two categories, which increasingly have come under fire for excessive outdoor advertising in inner-city areas, have dramatically reduced outdoor advertising. Municipal bans on billboard advertising of cigarette and liquor ads have been upheld by the U.S. Supreme Court.

Billboard Advertising

Although there are a variety of out-of-home advertising vehicles, billboard advertising is the major outdoor medium. Advertising on billboards is designed with name recognition

IMC FOCUS: BLIMPS AS AN ADVERTISING MEDIUM

Most people enjoy blimps. There is something very special about seeing such a large object meandering in the sky with no apparent goal in mind or haste to get anywhere. Unlike airplanes, which rush inexorably to their destinations, blimps just seem to be there—floating without worries, unconstrained by time, there only for the enjoyment of the observer.

It is perhaps this warm and fuzzy feeling that people get when spotting a blimp that makes them such an attractive advertising medium. When flying above population centers, attention is virtually guaranteed. Who can resist looking at a blimp? And if one cannot resist, the advertiser is assured that consumers will be exposed to the brand name festooned on the blimp. Unlike other advertising media, such as television and magazines, in which the advertiser competes in a cluttered environment for the prospective customer's attention, blimp advertisers have the luxury of an uncluttered clear blue sky.

Growing numbers of advertisers are turning to the blimp as an alternative medium. In addition to its other advantages, blimp advertising also has a relatively low cost. The per-month charge for a full-size blimp (approximately $300,000–$400,000) costs an advertiser approximately the same as only one or two 30-second network television commercials or two full-page ads in a single magazine. In addition to the venerable Goodyear blimp, other blimp advertisers include Met Life, Blockbuster, Fuji, Gulf Oil, and Budweiser.

www.goodyear.com
www.metlife.com

www.blockbuster.com
www.fujifilm.co.jp
www.gulf.ca
www.anheuser-busch.com

Fuji Photo Film Co. took great delight in being selected as the sole blimp to carry network television cameras in telecasting the World Cup soccer championship that was contested in the United States in 1994. Fuji's marketing executives decided to spend millions of dollars in hopes of reaching over a billion worldwide television viewers who were expected to watch the games. For the worldwide *blimp pops*—the brief time when a television network shows a blimp floating above a sports arena and gives it a quick plug—Fuji was willing to pay an estimated $20 million to reach millions of people on multiple occasions. Indeed, Fuji anticipated achieving 30 billion total exposures, which at a price of $20 million would yield a cost per thousand (discussed in detail in Chapter 13) of approximately only 67 cents. By comparison, a $250,000 television commercial that reaches 15 million households has a cost per thousand of $12.50. It is little wonder that Fuji and other advertisers see considerable value in blimp advertising. Of course, blimp advertising is unable to accomplish the same image-oriented goals as television, but it is a superb medium for yielding high levels of brand awareness.

Sources: Wendy Bounds, "Fuji's Spirits Soar as Its Blimp Is Winner of a World Cup Contest," *The Wall Street Journal*, June 21, 1994, B1, B5; and William Spain, "Blimps No Longer Just Flights of Fancy," *Advertising Age*, August 1, 1994, 27–28.

as the primary objective. The major forms of billboard advertising are poster panels and painted bulletins.

Poster Panels. These billboards are what we regularly see alongside highways and in other heavily traveled locales. Posters are silk-screened or lithographed and then brought and pasted in sheets to the billboard. Companies typically sell billboard space on a monthly basis. Posters can be either 8-sheet or 30-sheet, literally designating the number of sheets of paper required to fill the allotted billboard space. An *8-sheet poster* is 6 feet, 2 inches high by 12 feet, 2 inches wide, although the actual viewing area is a slightly smaller 5 feet by 11 feet (or, in other words, 55 square feet of viewing space). The much larger *30-sheet poster* is 12 feet, 3 inches high by 24 feet, 6 inches wide, with a 9 feet, 7 inches by 21 feet, 7 inch viewing area (or approximately 207 square feet of viewing space). Figure 12.2 presents an example of a poster panel.

Painted Bulletins. Painted bulletins are hand painted directly on the billboard by artists hired by the billboard owner. Standard bulletins measure 14 feet high by 48 feet wide and represent a total viewing space of 672 square feet. These bulletins are generally repainted every several months to provide a fresh look. Advertisers typically purchase these large bulletins for a one- to three-year period with the objective of achieving a consistent and relatively permanent presence in heavily traveled locations. An example of a painted bulletin is shown in Figure 12.3.

Example of a Poster Panel

Buying Out-of-Home Advertising

www.gannett.com

www.gateway.com

www.3m.com

Outdoor advertising is purchased through companies that own billboards, called *plants.* Plants are located in all major markets throughout the nation. Companies like Gannett, Gateway, and 3M are some of the larger plants that have operations in multiple metropolitan areas throughout the United States. To simplify the national advertiser's task of buying outdoor space in multiple markets, buying organizations, or agents, facilitate the purchasing of outdoor space at locations throughout the country.

Plants have historically sold poster-advertising space in terms of so-called *showings.* A showing is the percent of the population that is theoretically exposed to an advertiser's billboard message. Showings are quoted in increments of 25 and are designated as #25, #50, #75, and #100. The designation #50, for example, means that 50 percent of the population in a particular market is expected on any given workday to pass the billboards on which an advertiser's message is posted.

In recent years plants have converted to gross rating points (GRPs) as the metric for quoting poster prices. As discussed thoroughly in the following chapter, GRPs represent the percentage and frequency of an audience being reached by an advertising vehicle. Specifically, one outdoor GRP means reaching 1 percent of the population in a particular market a single time. Outdoor GRPs are based on the daily duplicated audience (meaning that some people may be exposed on multiple occasions each day) as a percentage of the total potential market. For example, if four billboards in a community of 200,000 people achieve a daily exposure to 80,000 persons, the result is 40 gross rating points. As with traditional showings, GRPs are sold in blocks of 25, with 100 and 50 being the two most-purchased levels.[4]

FIGURE 12.3

Example of a Painted Bulletin

Outdoor Advertising Strengths and Limitations

Outdoor advertising in the form of posters and bulletins presents the advertiser with several unique strengths and problems, which are summarized in Table 12.2.

Outdoor Advertising's Strengths.   A major strength of outdoor advertising is its *broad reach and high frequency levels.* Outdoor advertising is effective in reaching virtually all segments of the population. The number of exposures is especially high when signs are strategically located in heavy-traffic areas.

Another advantage is *geographic flexibility.* Outdoor advertising can be strategically positioned to supplement other advertising efforts in select geographic areas where advertising support is most needed.

Low cost per thousand is a third advantage. Outdoor advertising is the least expensive advertising medium on a cost-per-thousand basis.

Because outdoor advertising is literally bigger than life, *product identification is substantial.* The ability to use large representations offers marketers excellent opportunities for brand and package identification.

Outdoor advertising also provides an excellent opportunity to reach consumers as a *last reminder before purchasing.* This explains why frequently purchased products and services (like soft drinks, beer, and restaurants) are the heaviest users of outdoor advertising. Advertisers in these categories hope to have their brands seen just prior to the consumer's brand choice.

Outdoor Advertising's Limitations.   A significant problem with outdoor advertising is *nonselectivity.* Outdoor advertising can be geared to general groups of consumers (such as inner-city residents) but cannot pinpoint specific market segments (say, professional African-American men between the ages of 25 and 39). Advertisers must turn to other advertising media (such as radio and magazines) to pinpoint audience selection.

	Outdoor Advertising Strengths and Limitations	
STRENGTHS		**LIMITATIONS**
Broad reach and high frequency levels		Nonselectivity
Geographic flexibility		Short exposure time
Low cost per thousand		Difficult to measure audience size
Prominent brand identification		Environmental problems
Opportune purchase reminder		

Short exposure time is another drawback. "Now you see it, now you don't" appropriately characterizes the fashion in which outdoor advertising engages the consumer's attention. For this reason, outdoor messages that have to be read are less effective than predominantly visual ones.

It also is *difficult to measure outdoor advertising's audience.* The lack of verified audience measurement is regarded by some as a significant impediment that must be overcome if outdoor advertising is to become a more widely used advertising medium.[5]

A final outdoor advertising problem involves *environmental concerns.* Billboards, the so-called "litter on a stick," have been banned in some manner by several U.S. states and more than 1,000 local governments.[6] Although some would argue that attractive billboards *can* enliven and even beautify neighborhoods and highways with attractive messages, others consider this advertising medium to be ugly and intrusive. This largely is a matter of personal taste. The articles cited in the following footnote explore the issue in some depth, including a discussion of the value and potential hazards attendant to the growing use of *changeable message signs*, that is, billboards that vary the advertising message on a schedule of every 4 to 10 seconds.[7]

NEWSPAPERS

Newspapers in the United States reach approximately 57 million households during the week and nearly 61 million on Sundays.[8] Newspapers have historically been the leading advertising medium, but recently television surpassed newspapers as the medium that receives the greatest amount of advertising expenditures. This is partially attributable to the fact that newspaper readership has been on a constant cycle of decline for a number of years.

Local advertising is clearly the mainspring of newspapers. However, newspapers have become more active in their efforts to increase national advertising. These efforts have been facilitated by the Newspaper Advertising Bureau (NAB), a nonprofit sales and research organization. The NAB offers a variety of services that assist both newspapers and national advertisers by simplifying the task of buying newspaper space and by offering discounts that make newspapers a more attractive medium. Moreover, the trend toward regional marketing has led to greater use of newspaper advertising by major consumer packaged-goods companies.

Buying Newspaper Space

In the past, a major problem in buying newspaper space, especially for regional or national advertisers that purchased space from newspapers in many cities, was that newspaper page size and column space varied, thereby preventing an advertiser from preparing a single advertisement to fit every newspaper. Analogously, imagine what it would be like to advertise on television if, rather than having fixed 15-, 30-, or 60-second commercials for all networks and local stations, some local stations ran only 28-second commercials, while others preferred 23-second, 16-second, or 11-second commercials. Buying time on television would be nightmarish for advertisers. So it was in buying newspaper space until the 1980s, when the advertising industry adopted a standardized system known as the **Standardized Advertising Unit (SAU) system.** The implementation of the SAU system made it possible for advertisers to purchase any one of 56 standard ad sizes to fit the advertising publishing parameters of all newspapers in the United States.

Under this system, advertisers prepare advertisements and purchase space in terms of column widths and depth in inches. There are six column widths:

1 column: 2¹/₁₆ inches

2 columns: 4¼ inches

3 columns: 6⁷/₁₆ inches

4 columns: 8⅝ inches

5 columns: 10¹³/₁₆ inches

6 columns: 13 inches

www.chicagotribune.com

www.suntimes.com

Space depth varies in size from 1 inch to 21 inches. Thus, an advertiser can purchase an ad as small as 1 inch by 2¹/₁₆ inches or as large as 13 inches by 21 inches with numerous in-between combinations of column widths and depths in inches. A chosen size for a particular advertisement can then be run in newspapers throughout the country. Space rates can be compared from newspaper to newspaper and adjusted for circulation differences. For example, assume that the daily SAU column-inch rate for the *Chicago Tribune* (circulation: 665,000) is $476, whereas the same rate in the competitive *Chicago Sun Times* (circulation: 491,000) is $406.[9] On the surface, the *Sun Times* is cheaper than the *Tribune,* but when adjusted to a per-thousand-readers basis, the cost per thousand of procuring a column inch in the *Tribune* is approximately $0.72 (i.e., $476 ÷ 665) compared to a cost of about $0.83 (i.e., $406 ÷ 491) to advertise in the *Sun Times*. Hence, it is actually cheaper to advertise in the *Tribune*. Of course, the advertiser must observe audience characteristics, newspaper image, and other factors when making an advertising decision rather than considering only cost.

The choice of an advertisement's position must also be considered when buying newspaper space. Space rates apply only to advertisements placed *ROP* (run of press), which means that the ad appears in any location, on any page, at the discretion of the newspaper. Premium charges may be assessed if an advertiser has a preferred space positioning, such as at the top of the page in the financial section. Whether premium charges are actually assessed is a matter of negotiation between the advertiser and the newspaper.

Newspaper Advertising Strengths and Limitations

As with all advertising media, newspaper advertising has various strengths and limitations (see Table 12.3).

Newspaper Advertising's Strengths. Because people read newspapers for news, they are in the *right mental frame to process advertisements* that present news of store openings, new products, sales, and so forth.

Mass audience coverage is a second strength of newspaper advertising. Over 58 percent of adults read a daily paper, and on Sundays readership increases to about 67 percent.[10] Coverage is not restricted to specific socioeconomic or demographic groups but rather extends across all strata. However, newspaper readers on average are considerably more economically upscale than television viewers. College graduates are over 60 percent more likely to read a newspaper than the population at large.[11] Because economically

STRENGTHS	LIMITATIONS
Audience in appropriate mental frame to process messages	Clutter
	Not a highly selective medium
Mass audience coverage	Higher rates for occasional advertisers
Flexibility	Mediocre reproduction quality
Ability to use detailed copy	Complicated buying for national advertiser
Timeliness	Changing composition of readers

TABLE 12.3 Newspaper Advertising Strengths and Limitations

upscale consumers are relative light TV viewers, newspaper advertising provides a relative inexpensive medium for reaching these consumers. Special-interest newspapers also reach large numbers of potential consumers. For example, the vast majority of college students read a campus newspaper.

Flexibility is perhaps the greatest strength of newspapers. National advertisers can adjust copy to match the specific buying preferences and peculiarities of localized markets. Local advertisers can vary copy through in-paper inserts targeted to specific ZIP Codes. In addition, advertising copy can be placed in a newspaper section that is compatible with the advertised product. Retailers of wedding accessories advertise in the bridal section, providers of financial services advertise in the business section, sporting-goods stores advertise in the sports section, and so forth.

The *ability to use detailed copy* is another strength of newspaper advertising. Detailed product information and extensive editorial passages are used in newspaper advertising to an extent unparalleled by any other medium.

Timeliness is a final significant strength of newspaper advertising. Short lead times (the time between placing an ad and running it) permit advertisers to tie in advertising copy with local market developments or newsworthy events. Advertisers can develop copy or make copy changes quickly and thereby take advantage of dynamic marketplace developments.

Newspaper Advertising's Limitations. *Clutter* is a problem in newspapers, as it is in all of the other major media. A reader perusing a newspaper is confronted with large numbers of ads, all of which compete for the reader's limited time and only a subset of which receive the reader's attention. It is noteworthy, however, that a national survey of consumers revealed that they perceived newspapers as being significantly less cluttered with advertisements than television, radio, and magazines.[12]

A second limitation of newspaper advertising is that newspapers are *not a highly selective medium*. Newspapers are able to reach broad cross sections of people but, with few exceptions (such as campus newspapers), are unable to reach specific groups of consumers effectively. A large survey of advertising agencies found that most agency personnel consider newspapers to fare poorly in comparison to network television in efficiently reaching specific audiences.[13]

Occasional users of newspaper space (such as national advertisers who infrequently advertise in newspapers) *pay higher rates* than do heavy users (such as local advertisers) and have difficulty in securing preferred, non-ROP positions. In fact, newspapers' price lists (called rate cards) charge higher rates for national than local advertisers. This partially explains the role of cooperative advertising, which is described in detail in Chapter 17.

Newspapers generally offer a *mediocre reproduction quality*. For this and other reasons, newspapers are not generally known to enhance a product's perceived quality, elegance, or snob appeal, as do magazines and television (see Figure 12.1).

Buying difficulty is a particularly acute problem in the case of the national advertiser who wishes to secure newspaper space in a variety of different markets. Each newspaper must be contacted individually, and, on top of this, the rates charged to national advertisers are typically higher than those charged to local advertisers. Fortunately, as mentioned previously, the Newspaper Advertising Bureau (NAB) is making great strides toward facilitating the purchase of newspaper space by national advertisers. One NAB program is known by the acronym CAN DO, which stands for Computer Analyzed Newspaper Data On-Line System. This program provides national advertisers with pertinent information about newspapers in terms of cost per thousand (abbreviated **CPM,** with the *M* being the Roman numeral for 1,000) and demographic information on age, household income, and household size.[14]

A final significant problem with newspaper advertising involves the *changing composition of newspaper readers.* While most everyone used to read a daily newspaper, readership has declined progressively over the past two decades. The most faithful newspaper readers are individuals aged 45 and older, but the large and attractive group of consumers aged 30 to 44 are reading daily newspapers less frequently than ever.[15] Daily newspaper readership in this age group has fallen dramatically in the last quarter century.

MAGAZINES

Although considered a mass medium, there are literally hundreds of special-interest magazines, each appealing to audiences that manifest specific interests and lifestyles. In fact, Standard Rates and Data Services, the technical information source for the magazine industry, identifies well over 1,000 consumer magazines in dozens of specific categories, such as automotive (e.g., *Motor Trend*); general editorial (e.g., the *New Yorker*); sports (e.g., *Sports Illustrated*); women's fashions, beauty, and grooming (e.g., *Glamour*); and many others. In addition to consumer magazines, there are hundreds of other publications classified as farm magazines or business publications. Advertisers obviously have numerous options when selecting magazines to promote their products.

Buying Magazine Space

A number of factors influence the choice of magazine vehicles in which to advertise. Most important is selecting magazines that reach the type of people who constitute the advertiser's target market. However, because the advertiser typically can choose from several alternative vehicles to satisfy the target-market objective, cost considerations also play an extremely important role.

Advertisers who are interested in using the magazine medium can acquire a wealth of data about the composition of a magazine's readership (in terms of demographic and lifestyle profiles). This information is provided in each magazine's *media kit* that is made available to ad agencies and prospective advertisers. For example, Figure 12.4 presents *Rolling Stone's* adult demographic profile. The first column contains audience size expressed in thousands (000); column two then presents percentage breakdowns for each demographic subgroup; and the last column indexes each percent against that group's proportionate population representation. Men, for example, are substantially more likely to read *Rolling Stone* than are women (63.4 percent vs. 36.6 percent). Also, the readership of this magazine is disproportionately drawn from young adults, especially those in the 18–24 (41.3 percent) and 25–35 (29.7 percent) age groups. Obviously, this magazine, with its more than 8.7 million readers, is a very appropriate vehicle for reaching college students and graduates. Another demographic profile (of *Cosmopolitan* readers) is provided in Figure 12.5.

Media kits also provide prospective advertisers with pertinent cost information in the form of a *rate card.* A rate card for *Rolling Stone* magazine is presented in Figure 12.6. This card includes advertising rates for different page sizes (e.g., full page, ¾ page) and black and white (B&W), four-color (4/C), and two-color (2/C) ads. For example, an advertiser would pay $84,445 to place a full-page, four-color ad in *Rolling Stone* on a one-time

Rolling Stone Adult
Demographic Profile

ADULT DEMOGRAPHIC PROFILE

	AUD(000)	% COMP	INDEX
TOTAL ADULTS	8,757	100.0	100
MEN	5,553	63.4	132
WOMEN	3,204	36.6	70
AGE			
18-24	3,612	41.3	324
25-34	2,604	29.7	142
25-44	4,364	49.8	115
35-44	1,760	20.1	90
45+	781	8.9	20
18-34	6,216	71.0	211
18-39	7,146	82.2	180
Median Age	27.5 years		
EDUCATION			
Att/Graduated College+	5,343	61.0	127
Attending College	1,815	20.7	296
HOUSEHOLD INCOME			
HHI $75,000+	1,810	20.7	105
HHI $60,000+	2,911	33.2	109
HHI $50,000+	3,912	44.7	112
HHI $40,000+	4,918	56.2	109
HHI $30,000+	6,243	71.3	111
Median HHI	$45,213		
EMPLOYMENT STATUS			
Total Employed	7,035	80.3	123
White Collar	3,502	40.0	104
MARITAL STATUS			
Single	5,161	58.9	255
LOCALITY TYPE/COUNTY SIZE			
MSA Central City/Suburban	7,720	88.2	110
A/B County	6,793	77.6	109

Source: 1998 Spring MRI

("open") rate basis. However, by contracting to advertise 25 times (25x) in a single year, the per-page rate for the advertiser would drop to $74,315. As is typical in magazines' price policies, cumulative discounts are available based on the number of pages advertised in *Rolling Stone* during 12 consecutive months. Cumulative quantity discounts offered by magazines provide clear incentives for advertisers to maintain continuity with a particular magazine.

Although every magazine has its own media kit, advertisers and their agencies do not have to contact each magazine to obtain them. Standard Rate and Data Services, or SRDS, compiles media kits and then makes these available (of course, for a fee) to advertisers and their agencies. Most recently SRDS has developed a CD-ROM version of its print directory, named the Electronic Media Kit Library. Media buyers use the Electronic Media Kit Library to expedite and simplify the search for business or consumer publications. To

FIGURE 12.5

Cosmopolitan
Demographic Profile

COSMOPOLITAN
Demographic Profile

	Audience	%Comp.	Index
Readers per Copy	5.82		
Age			
Total Women	13,970	84.8	163
18-24	4,298	30.8	252
25-34	4,011	28.7	142
18-34	8,309	59.5	183
35-49	3,824	27.4	88
Median	31.3		
HHI			
$30,000+	9,544	68.3	113
$40,000+	7,463	53.4	112
Median	$42,678		
Education			
Attended/Graduated College+	8,241	59.0	125
Employment			
Total Employed	9,682	69.3	120
Full-Time	7,577	54.2	121
Marital Status			
Single	5,601	40.1	202
Married	5,648	40.4	73
Div/Wid/Sep	2,720	19.5	79
Other			
Women w/children	6,497	46.5	106
Working Women w/children	4,506	32.3	112
County			
A/B	10,838	77.6	110
C/D	3,132	22.4	77

Source: 1998 Spring MRI; Women

search for a class of magazines, such as those targeted to people interested in a vegetarian lifestyle, all the media buyer need do is input a key word—in this case, *vegetarian*—and all magazines that have this word or a variant in their title will be called up. Information for each magazine (or *book* as they are referred to by the advertising industry) includes editorial features, rates, readership profiles, circulation, competitive data, editorial calendars, contact persons at the magazine, and additional information. Needless to say, SRDS's print directory and the Electronic Library provide media buyers with invaluable information and greatly simplify their work.

FIGURE 12.6

Rolling Stone 1998 General Rate Card

Rolling Stone
1998 GENERAL RATE CARD

4/C	OPEN	7x	13x	25x	39x	50x	75x	100x
FULL PAGE	$84,445	$81,915	$78,535	$74,315	$72,625	$69,245	$66,715	$64,180
3/4 PAGE	$76,000	$73,720	$70,680	$66,880	$65,360	$62,320	$60,040	$57,760
1/2 PAGE	$50,670	$49,150	$47,125	$44,590	$43,580	$41,550	$40,030	$38,510
1/4 PAGE	$25,335	$24,575	$23,565	$22,295	$21,790	$20,775	$20,015	$19,255

2/C	OPEN	7x	13x	25x	39x	50x	75x	100x
FULL PAGE	$80,225	$77,820	$74,610	$70,600	$68,995	$65,785	$63,380	$60,975
3/4 PAGE	$72,200	$70,035	$67,150	$63,540	$62,095	$59,205	$57,040	$54,875
1/2 PAGE	$48,135	$46,695	$44,770	$42,360	$41,400	$39,475	$38,030	$36,585
1/4 PAGE	$24,070	$23,350	$22,390	$21,185	$20,705	$19,740	$19,020	$18,295

B&W	OPEN	7x	13x	25x	39x	50x	75x	100x
FULL PAGE	$76,000	$73,720	$70,680	$66,880	$65,360	$62,320	$60,040	$57,760
3/4 PAGE	$68,400	$66,350	$63,615	$60,195	$58,825	$56,090	$54,040	$51,985
1/2 PAGE	$45,600	$44,235	$42,410	$40,130	$39,220	$37,395	$36,025	$34,660
1/4 PAGE	$22,800	$22,120	$21,205	$20,065	$19,610	$18,700	$18,015	$17,330
1/8 PAGE	$11,400	$11,060	$10,605	$10,035	$9,805	$9,350	$9,010	$8,665

SPREADS	OPEN	7x	13x	25x	39x	50x	75x	100x
PAGE 4/C	$168,890	$163,830	$157,070	$148,630	$145,250	$138,490	$133,430	$128,360
PAGE 2/C	$160,450	$155,640	$149,220	$141,200	$137,990	$131,570	$126,760	$121,950
PAGE B&W	$152,000	$147,440	$141,360	$133,760	$130,720	$124,640	$120,080	$115,520
1/2 4/C	$101,340	$98,300	$94,250	$89,180	$87,160	$83,100	$80,060	$77,020
1/2 B&W	$91,200	$88,470	$84,820	$80,260	$78,440	$74,790	$72,050	$69,320

4TH COVER	OPEN
	$105,560

RATEBASE: 1,250,000
RATECARD #42
EFFECTIVE ISSUE #778 (COVER DATE: 1/22/98)

www.mediamark.com

The CPM (cost-per-thousand) measure introduced earlier is used by advertisers to compare different magazine buys. Cost-per-thousand information for each magazine is available from two syndicated magazine services: Mediamark Research, Inc. (MRI) and Simmons Market Research Bureau (SMRB). These services provide CPM figures for general reader categories (e.g., "total men") and also break out CPMs for subgroups (e.g., "men aged 18 to 49," "male homeowners"). These more specific subgroupings enable the advertiser to compare different magazine vehicles in terms of cost per thousand for reaching the target audience (or *CPM-TM)* rather than only in terms of gross CPMs. Cost-per-thousand data are useful in making magazine-vehicle selection decisions, but many other factors must be taken into account.

Magazine Advertising Strengths and Limitations

Magazine advertising too has both strengths and limitations, depending on the advertisers' needs and resources (see Table 12.4).

www.tvgen.com

www.nationalgeographic.com

www.cnnsi.com

Magazine Advertising Strengths.   Some magazines reach *very large audiences.* For example, magazines like *TV Guide, Modern Maturity, Reader's Digest, National Geographic*, and *Sports Illustrated* have total audiences (as measured by MRI and SMRB) that exceed 20 million readers.

However, the ability to pinpoint specific audiences (termed *selectivity*) is the feature that most distinguishes magazine advertising from other media. If a potential market exists for a product, there most likely is at least one periodical that reaches that market. Selectivity enables an advertiser to achieve effective, rather than wasted, exposure. This translates into more efficient advertising and lower costs per thousand target customers.

Magazines are also noted for their *long life.* Unlike other media, magazines are often used for reference and kept around the home (and barber shops, beauty salons, and dentists' and doctors' offices) for weeks. Magazine subscribers often pass along their copies to other readers, further extending a magazine's life.

In terms of qualitative considerations (refer again to Figure 12.1), magazines as an advertising medium are exceptional with regard to elegance, quality, beauty, prestige, and snob appeal. These features result from the *high level of reproduction quality* and from the surrounding editorial content that often transfers to the advertised product. For example, food items advertised in *Bon Appetit* always look elegant; furniture items in *Better Homes and Gardens* look tasteful; and clothing items in *Cosmopolitan,* and *Gentlemen's Quarterly (GQ)* appear especially fashionable.

www.epicurious.com

www.betterhomesandgardens.com

www.gq.com

Magazines are also a particularly good source for providing *detailed product information* and for conveying this information with a *sense of authority.* That is, because the editorial

TABLE 12.4	Magazine Advertising Strengths and Limitations	
STRENGTHS	LIMITATIONS	
Some magazines reach large audiences	Not intrusive	
Selectivity	Long lead times	
Long life	Clutter	
High reproduction quality	Somewhat limited geographic options	
Ability to present detailed information	Variability of circulation patterns by market	
Authoritative conveying of information		
High involvement potential		

content of magazines often contains articles that themselves represent a sense of insight, expertise, and credibility, the advertisements carried in these magazines convey a similar sense of authority, or correctness.

A final and especially notable feature of magazine advertising is its creative ability to get consumers *involved in ads* or, in a sense, to attract readers' interest and to encourage them to think about the advertised brands. This ability is due to the self-selection and reader-controlled nature of magazines in comparison to more intrusive media such as radio and television. A cute, albeit unintentional, portrayal of this ability appeared in the *Family Circus* comic strip, which typically presents the thoughts of preschool-age children as they contemplate the world around them. This particular strip opens with Billy saying to his sister, Dolly: "I'll tell you the difference between TV, radio, and books. . . . TV puts stuff into your mind with pictures and sound. You don't even hafta think." In the next box he states: "Radio puts stuff into your mind with just sounds and words. You make up your own pictures." And in the final section, Billy proclaims: "Books are quiet friends! They let you make up your own pictures and sounds. They make you *think*."[16] Substitute the word "magazines" for "books," and you have a pretty good characterization of the power of magazine advertising.

www.revlon.com

www.rolls-royce.com

www.canadianmist.com

www.transamerica.com

www.toyota.com

www.cgi.pathfinder.com/people

In addition to the standard magazine advertising practices that are appealing and attention gaining, magazine advertisers sometimes go to dramatic lengths to enhance reader involvement. For example, Revlon and Estee Lauder have offered eye-shadow and blusher samples on the pages of fashion magazines. Rolls-Royce included a scent strip in one of its ads that imitated the smell of the leather interior of its cars. Two liquor brands, Canadian Mist whiskey and Absolut vodka, used ads with microchips to play songs when the page opened. (A New York woman reported a case of "Absolut chaos" when she walked into her apartment building to a chorus of noisy mailboxes full of magazine ads gone haywire.[17]) TransAmerica included a pop-up ad in *Time* magazine that featured the insurance company's distinctive pyramidal-shaped building set against the San Francisco skyline. An especially creative magazine advertising effort to enhance reader involvement was Toyota's use of three-dimensional viewfinders in 14 million copies of *Time, People,* and *Cosmopolitan* magazines. The ads were designed to show off the new look of the redesigned *Corolla.* Readers looked into the viewfinder and saw a very realistic three-dimensional portrayal of the car. The ad received exceptionally high recall scores. Recall levels were 83 percent among males and 76 percent among females as compared with average recall rates for a four-page auto ad of 39 percent for males and 31 percent for females.[18]

Magazine Advertising Limitations. Several limitations are associated with magazine advertising. First, unlike TV and radio, which by their very nature infringe on the attention of the viewer/listener, magazine advertising is *not intrusive;* readers control whether to be exposed to a magazine ad.

A second limitation is *long lead times.* In newspapers and the broadcast media, it is relatively easy to change ad copy on fairly short notice and in specific markets. Magazines, by comparison, have long closing dates that require advertising materials to be on hand for a full month or longer.

As with other advertising media, *clutter* is a problem with magazine advertising. In certain respects clutter is a worse problem with magazines than, say, television, because readers can become engrossed in editorial content and skip over advertisements so as not to have their reading disrupted.

Magazine advertising also provides fewer *geographic options* than do other media. For example, *Cosmopolitan* offers advertisers the opportunity to place ads just in any of seven regions or any particular state. An advertiser that is interested only in select markets—say, Dallas/Fort Worth and Houston, Texas—would probably refrain from advertising in *Cosmopolitan* (or in other magazine vehicles) because much of the magazine circulation would be wasted on readers outside these two metropolitan areas. It is important to note, however, that greater selectivity is provided by some magazines. *Sports Illustrated*, for example, offers advertising rates for five key regions, all 50 states, and 50 metropolitan areas. An advertiser could choose to advertise in *Sports Illustrated* only in the Dallas/Fort Worth area, and in so doing pay $8,796 for a full-page, 4/C ad.[19] As can be seen by these two illustrations, there is variance in magazine selectivity.

A final limitation of magazine advertising is *variability in circulation patterns* from market to market. *Rolling Stone,* for example, is more read in metropolitan than rural areas. Hence, advertisers who are interested, say, in reaching young males would not be very successful in reaching nonmetropolitan readers. This would necessitate placing ads in one or more additional magazines than *Rolling Stone,* which would up the total cost of the media buy. Radio, TV, or both might better serve the advertiser's needs and provide more uniform market coverage.

R ADIO

Radio is a nearly ubiquitous medium: Nearly 100 percent of all homes in the United States have radios; most homes have several radios; virtually all cars have a radio; and more than 50 million radios are purchased in the United States each year.[20] These impressive figures indicate radio's strong potential as an advertising medium. Although radio has always been a favorite of local advertisers, it is only in recent years that regional and national advertisers have begun to appreciate radio's advantages as an advertising medium. This trend is largely due to the fact that Americans are listening more now than anytime in recent decades. One study found that Americans aged 12 and older average 24 hours a week listening to the radio.[21]

Buying Radio Time

Radio advertisers are interested in reaching target customers at a reasonable expense while ensuring that the station format is compatible with the advertised brand's image and its creative message strategy. Several considerations influence the choice of station. *Station format* (classical, progressive, country, top 40, talk, and so forth) is a major consideration. Certain formats are obviously most appropriate for particular products and brands.

A second consideration is the *choice of geographic areas to cover.* National advertisers buy time from stations whose audience coverage matches the advertiser's geographic areas of interest. This typically means locating stations in preferred metropolitan statistical areas (MSAs) or in so-called *areas of dominant influence* (ADIs), which number approximately 200 in the United States and correspond to the major television markets.

A third consideration in buying radio time is the *choice of day part.* Most stations offer anywhere from two- to five-day parts. Table 12.5 lists a typical radio time schedule, with different day parts designated by letter combinations and descriptions (in parentheses).

Rate structures vary depending on the attractiveness of the day part; for example, AAAA is priced higher than AAA, which is priced higher than AA, and so on. Information about rates and station formats is available in *Spot Radio Rates and Data,* a source published by the Standard Rate and Data Services.

TABLE 12.5	Typical Radio Time Schedule	

DAY PART	TIME
AAAA *(A.M. Drive)*	AAAA *(AM Drive)*—Monday through Saturday, 6:00 to 10:00 A.M.
AAA *(P.M. Drive)*	AAA *(PM Drive)*—Monday through Saturday, 3:00 to 7:00 P.M.
AA *(Midday)*	Monday through Friday, 10:00 A.M. to 3:00 P.M.; Saturday and Sunday, 6:00 A.M. to 8:00 P.M.
A *(Evening)*	Monday through Sunday, 7:00 P.M. to midnight.
B *(Overnight)*	B *(Overnight)*—Tuesday through Sunday, midnight to 6:00 A.M.

Radio Advertising Strengths and Limitations

This section examines the advantages and also explores some of the problems with radio advertising (see the summary in Table 12.6).

Radio Advertising Strengths.   The first major strength of radio is that it is second only to magazines in its *ability to reach segmented audiences.* An extensive variety of radio programming enables advertisers to pick specific formats and stations to be optimally compatible with both the composition of their target audience and their creative message strategies. Radio can be used to pinpoint advertisements to specific groups of consumers: teens, Hispanics, sports fanatics, news enthusiasts, conservatives, liberals, and so on. One media director explains radio's *narrowcasting* versatility this way:

> *There's classical music to reach the same kind of educated, high income adults [who] read* Smithsonian *or* Travel and Leisure, *only at less cost. You've got a yen to reach working women? Try an all news station in a.m. drive time. Blacks? Stations like WBLS in New York reach them more efficiently than TV's* Soul Train *or black magazines such as* Ebony *and* Essence. *You've got teen stations, old lady stations, stations which reach sports nuts, young adults and middle-of-the-roaders. So don't think of radio as a mass medium unless sheer tonnage at the lowest CPM is your game. The radio networks are made up of hundred of stations with different formats, audiences, signal strengths, coverage, etc.*[22]

A second major advantage of radio advertising is its *ability to reach prospective customers on a personal and intimate level.* Local store merchants and radio announcers sometimes are extremely personable and convincing. Their messages come across as if they were personally speaking to each audience member.

www.jwtworld.com

A former CEO of J. Walter Thompson USA, one of the largest advertising agencies in the United States, metaphorically described radio as a "universe of private worlds" and a "communication between two friends."[23] In other words, people select radio stations in much the same way that they select personal friends. People listen to those radio stations with which they closely identify. Because of this, radio advertising is likely to be received when the customer's mental frame is most conducive to persuasive influence. Radio advertising, then, is a personal and intimate form of "friendly persuasion."[24]

Economy is a third advantage of radio advertising. In terms of target audience CPM, radio advertising is considerably cheaper than other mass media. Over the past quarter century, radio's cost per thousand has increased less than any other advertising medium.[25]

Radio Advertising Strengths and Limitations	
STRENGTHS	LIMITATIONS
Ability to reach segmented audiences	Clutter
Intimacy	No visuals
Economy	Audience fractionalization
Short lead times	Buying difficulties
Transfer of imagery from TV	
Use of local personalities	

www.vtbear.com

Short lead times are another relative advantage of radio advertising. Because radio production costs are typically inexpensive and scheduling deadlines are short, copy changes can be made quickly to take advantage of important developments and changes in the marketplace. For example, a sudden weather change may suggest an opportunity to advertise weather-related products. A radio spot can be prepared quickly to accommodate the needs of the situation. A spokesperson for the Vermont Teddy Bear Company, which is a regular advertiser on radio, describes it this way: "We can react very quickly [when advertising on radio]. We can change the copy according to what we have in stock, or to a specific occasion or holiday."[26]

A very important advantage of radio advertising is its ability to *transfer images from television advertising.* A memorable television advertising campaign that has been aired frequently effects in consumers a mental association between the sight and sound elements in the commercial. This mental image can then be transferred to a radio commercial that uses the TV sound or some adaptation of it.[27] The radio commercial thus evokes in listeners a mental picture of the TV ad—much in the fashion that Billy described in childlike terms in the *Family Circus* cartoon mentioned earlier. The advertiser effectively gains the advantage of TV advertising at the lower cost of radio.[28]

www.snapple.com

A final strength of radio advertising is its ability to avail itself of the reputations and the sometimes bigger-than-life persona of *local personalities.* Snapple Natural Beverages, for example, gained much of its early success when it started advertising on a New York radio show hosted by the highly controversial Howard Stern. More recently, Snapple signed up conservative talk-show host Rush Limbaugh to promote its Snapple Diet Iced Tea. As explained by a spokesperson for Snapple's ad agency, "this brand [Snapple] is one of those brands that does best when it's passed by word-of-mouth—when someone you know tells you Snapple is a great drink."[29]

Radio Advertising Limitations. Radio's foremost limitation, one it shares with other ad media, is that it is *cluttered* with competitive commercials and other forms of noise, chatter, and interference. Radio listeners frequently switch stations, especially on their car radios, to avoid commercials.[30]

A second limitation is that radio is the only major medium that is *unable to employ visualizations.* However, radio advertisers attempt to overcome the medium's visual limitation by using sound effects and choosing concrete words to conjure up mental images in the listener. It is important to note that many advertising campaigns use radio as a supplement to other media rather than as a stand-alone medium. This reduces radio's task from one of creating visual images to one of *reactivating images* that already have been created via television or magazines.

A third problem with radio advertising results from a high degree of *audience fractionalization*. On the one hand, selectivity is a major advantage of radio advertising, but at the same time the advertiser is unable to reach a diverse audience because each radio station and program has its own unique set of audience demographics and interests.

A final limitation is the *difficulty of buying radio time*. This problem is particularly acute in the case of the national advertiser who wishes to place spots in different markets throughout the country. With nearly 10,000 commercial radio stations operating in the United States, buying time is complicated by unstandardized rate structures that include a number of combinations of fixed and discount rates.

TELEVISION

Television is practically ubiquitous in the United States and throughout the rest of the industrialized world. Television sets are present in over 98 percent of all American households, which, as of 1998, number approximately 98 million.[31] As an advertising medium, television is uniquely personal and demonstrative, yet it is also expensive and subject to considerable competitive clutter. Consumers consider television the most cluttered of all ad media.[32]

Before we elaborate upon television's specific strengths and weaknesses, it first will be instructive to examine two specific aspects of television advertising: (1) the different programming segments, or so-called day parts, and (2) the alternative outlets for television commercials (network, spot, syndicated, cable, and local).

Television Programming Segments

Advertising costs, audience characteristics, and programming appropriateness vary greatly at different times of the day and during different days of the week. Like radio, these times of day are referred to as day parts. The three major day parts are prime time, daytime, and fringe time, each of which has its own strengths and weaknesses.[33]

Prime Time.   The period between 8 P.M. and 11 P.M. (or between 7 P.M. and 10 P.M. in some parts of the country) is known as *prime time*. The best and most expensive programs are scheduled during this period. Audiences are largest during prime time, and the networks naturally charge the highest rates for prime-time advertising. Popular prime-time programs sometimes reach as many as 20 to 25 million households. Advertisers must pay dearly to reach the huge numbers of households that popular prime-time programs deliver. The popular hit comedy *Seinfeld* (NBC) charged $575,000 for each 30-second commercial aired on that program during 1997–98 in its final year of original (pre-syndication) programming.[34]

Daytime.   The period that begins with the early morning news shows and extends to 4:30 P.M. is known as *daytime*. Early daytime appeals first to adults with news programs and then to children with special programs designed for this group. Afternoon programming, with its special emphasis on soap operas, talk shows, and financial news appeals primarily to people working at home, retirees, and, according to rumor, college students in dormitories.

Fringe Time.   The period preceding and following prime time is known as *fringe time*. Early fringe starts with afternoon reruns and is devoted primarily to children but becomes more adult oriented as prime time approaches. Late fringe appeals primarily to young adults.

Network, Spot, Syndicated, Cable, and Local Advertising

Television messages are transmitted by local stations, which are either locally owned cable television systems or are affiliated with the four major commercial networks (ABC, CBS,

NBC, and Fox) or with an independent cable network (such as TBS, the Turner Broadcasting System). This arrangement of local stations and networks allows for different ways of buying advertising time on television.

Network Television Advertising.   Companies that market products nationally often use network television to reach potential customers throughout the country. The advertiser, typically working through an advertising agency, purchases desired time slots from one or more of the major networks (ABC, CBS, Fox, and NBC) and advertises at these times on all local stations that are affiliated with the network. The cost of such advertising depends on the time of day when an ad is aired, the popularity of the television program in which the ad is placed, and the time of year—advertising rates are higher in the first (January through March) and fourth quarters (October through December) when more people are inside watching television and ratings are at their peak. The average cost for all 30-second prime-time television commercials during the fourth quarter of 1998 was $189,000, with some of the most popular programs commanding well over $250,000 for 30 seconds of commercial time.[35] Table 12.7 presents the 10 most expensive prime-time advertising buys for the 1998–99 season.

Network television advertising, although expensive in terms of per-unit cost, can be a cost-efficient means to reach mass audiences. Consider a 30-second commercial that costs $300,000 and reaches 20 percent of the 98 million American households, or 19.6 million households. Although $300,000 is a lot to pay for 30 seconds of commercial time, reaching 19.6 million households means that the advertiser would have paid approximately only $15.31 to reach every 1,000 households.

Network advertising is inefficient, and in fact unfeasible, if the national advertiser chooses to concentrate efforts only on select markets. For example, some brands, though marketed nationally, are directed primarily at consumers in certain geographic locales. In this case, it would be wasteful to invest in network advertising, which would reach many areas where target audiences are not located.

Spot Television Advertising.   The national advertiser's alternative to network television advertising is *spot advertising*. As the preceding discussion intimated and as the name suggests, this type of advertising is placed (spotted) only in selected markets.

Spot advertising is particularly desirable when a company rolls out a new brand market by market before it achieves national distribution; when a marketer needs to concentrate on particular markets due to poor performance in these markets or aggressive

TABLE 12.7

The Ten Most Expensive Prime-Time TV Ad Buys, 1998–99

SHOW	COST PER 30 SECONDS
ER (NBC)	$565,000
Frasier (NBC)	475,000
Friends (NBC)	425,000
Drew Carey Show (ABC)	375,000
Monday Night Football (ABC)	375,000
Veronica's Closet (NBC)	345,000
X-Files (Fox)	330,000
Jessie (NBC)	325,000
Touched by an Angel (CBS)	275,000
Ally McBeal (Fox)	265,000

Source: *Advertising Age,* September 21, 1998, 1.

competitive efforts; or when a company's product distribution is limited to one or a few geographical regions. Also, spot advertising is useful even for those advertisers who use network advertising but need to supplement the national coverage with greater amounts of advertising in select markets that have particularly high brand potential. Greater use of spot television advertising is harmonious with the growing practices of regional-oriented marketing and geodemographic segmentation of consumer markets.

www.disney.com

www.spe.sony.com/tv

Syndicated Advertising.   Syndicated programming occurs when an independent company—such as Buena Vista Television Advertising Sales (an affiliate of the Walt Disney Company) or Columbia TriStar Television Distribution—markets a TV show to as many network-affiliated or cable television stations as possible. Because an independent firm markets syndicated programs to individual television stations, the same syndicated program will appear on, say, NBC stations in some markets and on ABC or CBS stations in other markets.

Syndicated programs are either original productions or shows that first appeared on network television. During the 1997–1998 television season, the most costly *original* syndicated programs (and their costs per 30-second commercial) were *Entertainment Tonight* ($72,000), *Wheel of Fortune* ($65,000), *Jeopardy!* ($57,000), *The Oprah Winfrey Show* ($52,000), *Xena* ($40,000), and the *Rosie O'Donnell Show* ($37,000). In the same season, the most expensive *off-network* syndicated programs were *Home Improvement* ($105,000), *X-Files* ($92,000), *Seinfeld* ($81,000), *The Simpsons* ($65,000), *Frasier* ($62,000), and *Mad About You* ($58,000).[36]

Cable Advertising.   Unlike network television, which is free to all owners of television sets, cable television requires users to subscribe (pay a fee) to a cable service and have their sets specially wired to receive signals via satellite or other means. Though cable television has been available since the 1940s, only recently have advertisers turned to cable as a valuable advertising medium. Growing numbers of major national companies now advertise on cable TV. Cable television's household penetration increased from less than 25 percent of all households in 1980 to a level now nearly 70 percent of the 98 million U.S. households with television sets.[37] Advertising spending on cable TV is climbing steadily. As of 1998, total ad spending on cable TV amounted to nearly 70 percent ($9 billion) of that invested in commercial time on the four major networks ($13 billion).[38] Table 12.8 provides advertising expenditures for the top four broadcast networks and the top 25 cable networks.

Viewership of cable TV has increased dramatically over the past 15 years, to the point where combined ratings for the dozens of cable-TV networks increased from less than 4 percent in 1985 to over 20 percent by the late 1990s. Comparatively, combined prime-time ratings for the four major networks dropped from approximately 45 percent to 34 percent during this same period.[39]

Cable advertising is attractive to national advertisers for several reasons. First, because cable networks focus on narrow areas of viewing interest (so-called "narrowcasting"), advertisers are able to reach more *finely targeted audiences* (in terms of demographics and psychographics) than when using network, syndicated, or spot advertising. Indeed, cable stations are available to reach almost any imaginable viewing interest. A brand marketer can select cable stations that appeal to a variety of specific viewing interests such as cooking and eating (such as the Food Network), golfing (The Golf Channel), sports in general (ESPN and ESPN2), music entertainment (e.g., MTV, M2, MuchMusic, The Nashville Network, and VH1), health and fitness (e.g., America's Health Network, Fit TV, and Kaleidoscope Television), nature, science, and animal life (e.g., Animal Planet, Discovery Channel, and Outdoor Life Network), and general education (e.g., The History Channel, Knowledge TV, and the Travel Channel).

TABLE 12.8   **Total Ad Spending on Top Four Broadcast Networks and Top 25 Cable Networks, 1997**

BROADCAST NETWORK	AD SPENDING ($ BILLION)
NBC	$ 5.230
ABC	4.109
CBS	3.099
Fox	2.368
TOTAL	$14.806

CABLE NETWORK	AD SPENDING ($ BILLION)
ESPN	$0.696
Nickelodeon	0.494
TBS	0.470
USA	0.454
TNT	0.409
Lifetime	0.373
MTV	0.371
The Nashville Network	0.344
Discovery Channel	0.278
A&E	0.267
Cable News Network	0.266
The Family Channel	0.199
CNBC	0.141
FX	0.117
Headline News	0.117
The Weather Channel	0.104
VH1	0.102
Comedy Central	0.100
The Learning Channel	0.091
Black Entertainment TV	0.084
E! Entertainment TV	0.080
The Sci-Fi Channel	0.078
Cartoon Network	0.069
ESPN2	0.057
Country Music TV	0.024
TOTAL	$5.785

Source: "Total Ad Spending on Network Vs. Cable, 1997," *Adweek,* May 18, 1998, 13.

A second reason why cable advertising appeals to national advertisers is that high network advertising prices and declining audiences have compelled advertisers to *experiment with media alternatives* such as cable. A third reason for cable advertising's growth is the *demographic composition of cable audiences.* Cable subscribers are more economically upscale and younger than the population as a whole. By comparison, the heaviest viewers of network television tend to be more economically downscale. It is little wonder that the upscale characteristics of cable viewers have great appeal to many national advertisers.

Local Television Advertising.   Television advertising historically has been dominated by national advertisers, but local advertisers are turning to television in ever greater numbers. Local advertisers often find that the CPM advantages of television, plus the advantage of product demonstration, justify the choice of this advertising medium. Local television advertising is particularly inexpensive during the fringe times preceding and following prime-time programming.

Television Advertising Strengths and Limitations

Like the other forms of media, advertising on television has a number of both strengths and limitations (see the summary in Table 12.9).

Television's Strengths. Beyond any other consideration, television possesses the unique capability to *demonstrate a product in use.* No other medium can reach consumers simultaneously through both auditory and visual senses. Viewers can see and hear a product being used, identify with the product's users, and imagine themselves using the product.

Television also has *intrusion value* unparalleled by other media. That is, television advertisements engage one's senses and attract attention even when one would prefer not to be exposed to an advertisement. In comparison, it is much easier to avoid a magazine or newspaper ad by merely flipping the page, or to avoid a radio ad by changing channels. But it is often easier to sit through a television commercial rather than attempting to avoid it either physically or mentally. Of course, as will be discussed shortly, remote devices have made it easier for viewers to avoid television commercials via zipping and zapping.

A third relative advantage of television advertising is its combined *ability to provide entertainment* and *generate excitement.* Advertised products can be brought to life or made to appear even bigger than life. Products advertised on television can be presented dramatically and made to appear more exciting and less mundane than perhaps they actually are.

Television also has the unique ability to *reach consumers one on one,* as is the case when a spokesperson or endorser espouses the merits of a particular product. Like a personal sales presentation, the interaction between spokesperson and consumer takes place on a personal level.

More than any other medium, television is *able to use humor* as an effective advertising strategy. As discussed in the previous chapter, many of the most memorable commercials are those using a humorous format.

In addition to its effectiveness in reaching ultimate consumers, television advertising also is *effective with a company's sales force and the trade.* Salespeople find it easier to sell new or established brands to the trade when a major advertising campaign is planned. The trade has added incentive to increase merchandise support (e.g., through advertising features and special display space) for a brand that is advertised on television.

In the final analysis, the greatest relative advantage of television advertising is its *ability to achieve impact.* Impact is that quality of an advertising medium that activates the consumer's awareness and "enlivens his [or her] mind to receive a sales message."[40]

Television Advertising Limitations. As an advertising medium, television suffers from several distinct problems. First, and perhaps most serious, is the *rapidly escalating advertising cost.* The cost of network television advertising has more than tripled over

STRENGTHS	LIMITATIONS
Demonstration ability	Rapidly escalating cost
Intrusion value	Erosion of viewing audiences
Ability to generate excitement	Audience fractionalization
One-on-one reach	Zipping and zapping
Ability to use humor	Clutter
Effective with sales force and trade	
Ability to achieve impact	

TABLE 12.9 — **Television Advertising Strengths and Limitations**

the past two decades. A dramatic illustration of this is the increasing cost of buying advertising time during the Super Bowl. In 1975, a 30-second commercial cost $110,000. By 1999, Anheuser-Busch paid $2 million per 30-second commercial, or $20 million in total, for exclusive rights in the beer category for placing 20 ads on Super Bowl XXXIII.[41] Table 12.7 earlier revealed how expensive it is for advertisers to buy prime time on the 10 top-rated programs. In addition to the cost of buying air time, it is very costly to produce television commercials. The average cost of making a national 30-second commercial exceeds $300,000![42]

A second problem is the *erosion of television viewing audiences.* Videocassette recorders, syndicated programs, cable television, the Internet, and other leisure and recreational alternatives have diminished the number of people viewing network television. The four major networks' share of television audiences during prime time fell from 91 percent in 1979 to around 60 percent today. Program *ratings*—that is, the percentage of households tuned in to a particular program—have consistently fallen over the past 40 years. Whereas the top-rated programs used to have ratings in the 50s (meaning that over 50 percent of all television households were tuned in to these programs), the top-rated programs now rarely exceed a 20 rating. For example, *Gunsmoke* was the top-rated program from 1957 to 1961 with ratings consistently around 40, and, from 1972 to 1976, *All in the Family* was the leading program with ratings above 30. However, only about 10 programs had a 20 share or greater in 1998.[43]

There also has been substantial *audience fractionalization.* Advertisers cannot expect to attract large homogeneous audiences when advertising on any particular program due to the great amount of program selection now available to television viewers.

Fourth, even when people are viewing cable as well as network television, much of their time is spent switching from station to station, zapping or zipping commercials. *Zapping* occurs when viewers switch to another channel when commercials are aired, prompting one observer to comment (only partially with tongue in cheek) that the remote control "zapper" is the greatest threat to capitalism since Karl Marx.[44] Research reveals that perhaps as high as one-third of a potential audience for TV commercials may be lost to zapping.[45] Although zapping is extensive, one intriguing study presented evidence suggesting that commercials that are zapped are actively processed prior to being zapped and may have a greater positive effect on brand-purchase behavior than commercials that are not zapped.[46]

In addition to zapping, television viewers also engage in zipping. *Zipping* takes place when ads that have been recorded with a VCR along with program material are fast-forwarded (zipped through) when the viewer watches the prerecorded material. Research has shown that zipping is extensive.[47]

Clutter is a fifth serious problem with television advertising. Clutter refers to the growing amount of nonprogram material: commercials, public service messages, and promotional announcements for stations and programs. As noted earlier, consumers perceive television to be the most cluttered of all major advertising media.[48] Clutter has been created by the network's increased use of promotional announcements to stimulate audience viewing of heavily promoted programs and by advertisers' increased use of shorter commercials. Whereas 60-second commercials once were prevalent, the duration of the vast majority of commercials today is only 30, 20, or 15 seconds.[49] The effectiveness of television advertising has suffered from the clutter problem, which creates a negative impression among consumers about advertising in general, turns viewers away from the television set, and perhaps reduces brand name recall.[50]

Infomercials

Discussion of television advertising would not be complete without at least a brief mention of the *infomercial.* Introduced to television in the early 1980s, the long commercial, or **infomercial,** is an innovative alternative to the conventional, short-form of television commercial. By comparison, infomercials are full-length commercial segments run on cable

IMC Focus: Kodak's Infomercial

www.kodak.com

Kodak in 1997 introduced a 30-minute infomercial to promote its new DC210 Digital Zoom Camera. Up to this time Eastman Kodak had little sales and profit to show for the $500 million it had invested in digital imaging. The infomercial, which cost nearly $400,000 to produce, included a toll-free number that invited viewers to request a $175 coupon that was good toward the purchase of the camera and other Kodak products at retail locations. Follow-up research indicated that approximately one out of 12 callers who received the discount coupon ordered the camera at a retail outlet, an impressive statistic in view of the fact that the DC210's retail price was $899 at the time of the promotion.

Retail sales in cities where the DC210 infomercials were aired exceeded by 80 percent sales of these digital cameras in cities without infomercials. Moreover, retail selling time was substantially reduced insofar as consumers already were pre-sold by the infomercial. Kodak officials concluded that the infomercial was a cost-effective way to introduce consumers to the advantages of digital imaging.

Source: Adapted from "Digital Profits: A Case Study of Kodak's Infomercial," *Infomercial and Direct Response Television Sourcebook '98*, a supplement to *Adweek Magazines*, 20–21.

(and sometimes network) television that typically last 28 to 30 minutes and combine product news and entertainment. Infomercials account for nearly one-fourth of the programming time for most cable stations.[51] Sales of products generated by infomercial programs exceed $1 billion.[52] Total Gym, the top-grossing infomercial product in 1997, alone yielded revenues just below $100 million.[53]

It is claimed that a successful infomercial uniquely blends both entertainment and selling. Here, according to an industry spokesperson, is what an infomercial must do to be successful:

> *With an infomercial you're asking people to find you by accident. Once they find you, they must find the show so compelling, so entertaining, that they watch 'till the very end. By that time they've got to be so excited that they pick up the telephone and give the producers money.[54]*

In the early years, infomercials were restricted primarily to unknown companies selling skin care, balding treatment, exercise equipment, and various feel-good products. However, the growing respectability of this form of advertising has encouraged a number of well-known consumer-goods companies to promote their brands via infomercials. Some of the better known brands that have turned to infomercials include Avon, Braun, Clairol, Chrysler, Estee Lauder, Hoover, Pioneer, Procter & Gamble, and Sears.[55] Manufacturers of consumer durables are increasingly using infomercials. For example, Kodak used a 30-minute infomercial to promote its DC210 Digital Zoom Camera (see *IMC Focus*), as did Phillips Consumer Electronics in marketing its digital videodisc player. General Motors' Chevrolet division featured famous baseball star Cal Ripken Jr. in an infomercial touting its new Silverado pickup truck.

The cost of producing an infomercial starts at around $150,000 and can reach as high as $850,000.[56] National cable rates typically cost the advertiser $3,000 to $20,000 per 30-minute show.[57] Cable programming obviously does not deliver the numbers of consumers that network programming generates, but numerous advertisers have found the infomercial to be an extremely effective promotional tool for moving merchandise. This long-form commercial is apparently here to stay. Although consumers have complaints with infomercials (e.g., that some make false claims and are deceptive),[58] this form of long commercial appears to be especially effective for consumers who are brand- and price-conscious, who are innovative and impulsive, and who place high importance on shopping convenience.[59]

NTERACTIVE ADVERTISING MEDIA

Conventional advertising media have served advertisers' needs for many years, but recently there have been increased efforts on the part of advertisers and their agencies to locate new advertising media that are less costly, less cluttered, and potentially more effective than the established media. Some observers have gone so far as to claim that traditional advertising is on its deathbed.[60] The contention is that new, interactive media are superior to the traditional media due to their ability to provide consumers with virtually full control over the commercial information they choose to receive or avoid.

The Concept of Interactive Media

Traditional advertising media (magazines, TV, etc.) vary in the degree to which they are able to generate mental activity from consumers. Nonetheless, all of these media engage the consumer in a relatively passive fashion: The consumer listens to and/or sees information about the advertised brand, but he or she has limited control over the amount or rate of information receipt. What you see (or hear) is what you get. There is action, but there is no interaction. Whereas action involves a flow in one direction, *interaction* entails reciprocal behavior. This idea of *reciprocity* generally defines the nature of the new, interactive media.

It is easy to define the term *interaction* but it is difficult to precisely identify the specific media that should be included within the bounds of *interactive media*. One observer claims that defining interactive media is as difficult as lassoing Jell-O.[61] Another spokesperson says, "Anyone who claims definitive knowledge about interactive technology and its potential effects on advertising or on anything else in life should be given wide berth these days. It's just too soon to tell."[62] The point of both statements is that this is a fledgling industry that is just beginning to develop, and as such it will be some time before the specific form and character of the industry takes clear shape.

Complexities aside, interactive advertising is defined here as encompassing all media that enable the *user* (who no longer is a "receiver" in the traditional, passive model of communication) to *control the amount or rate of information* that she or he wishes to acquire from a commercial message. The user can choose to devote one second or 15 minutes to a message. He or she is, for all intents and purposes, involved in a "conversation" with the commercial message at a subvocal level. A request for additional information occurs with the push of a button, the touch of a screen, or the click of a mouse. In all instances, the user and source of commercial information are engaged in a give-and-take exchange of information—intercourse rather than mere transmission and reception. By analogy, an American football quarterback and receivers are somewhat equivalent to the traditional media: The quarterback throws the ball, and the receivers attempt to catch it. Comparatively, in rugby, players toss the ball back and forth as they advance the ball downfield—each passes and each receives; their relation is analogous to the give-and-take reciprocity that defines interactive media.

So defined, interactive commercial media at this time include the following:[63]

- ◆ CD-ROM
- ◆ Virtual reality
- ◆ The Internet
- ◆ Interactive 800 numbers

The following discussion will focus on the first three forms of interactive media, while the following chapter discusses interactive 800 numbers.

The CD–ROM and Virtual Reality

CD-ROM. Advertisers have not as yet utilized CD-ROM software as a significant advertising medium, but the only thing holding back greater utilization is the relative paucity of owners of multimedia computers—that is, computers capable of providing both video and audio presentations via CD-ROM drives. As greater numbers of households and businesses purchase or upgrade to multimedia computers, advertisers will use this medium to present consumers with detailed product information. The marketing of tourism is a particularly appropriate category for CD-ROM communication. Imagine a tourist location responding to prospective tourists' requests for information by mailing a CD that they could play in their home computers. This CD would contain the sights (video as well as still pictures) and sounds (music, wildlife sounds, the sound of the beach, etc.) of the area and would present this information in a newsworthy and entertaining fashion. CD-ROM software also has considerable potential in the area of business-to-business marketing. Audio/video CD presentations of new products can be mailed to prospective customers, with prospects encouraged to call for additional information or to invite a personal sales visitation.

Virtual Reality. Artificial reality arcades are appearing across the country in which participants pay as much as $6 for a four-minute game. Wearing a virtual reality helmet or goggles and wearing a specially designed glove, the participant interacts with animated objects and enjoys lifelike sensations when moving his or her head or touching something with the glove. It was only a matter of time before marketers began using this medium for commercial purposes. One of the initial users was Bubble Yum, a brand of gum for children, which fielded a 16-market tour by taking a virtual reality machine to malls around the United States. More than 18,000 people, mostly youngsters, "traveled" to Planet Bubble Yum; the objective of their trip was to compete against others to see who could catch the most chunks of three-dimensional animated Bubble Yum flying through the air.[64] Future ingenious applications of virtual reality in commercial contexts will undoubtedly be seen, though the potential applications may be restricted to marketing to the teens and pre-teens who seem to be most intrigued by this technology.

The Internet

The Internet is a huge worldwide network of interconnected computers that permits the electronic transfer of information.[65] A major research organization has claimed that the "Internet revolution is sweeping the globe with such swiftness that companies are desperately trying to understand what is occurring, what it all means, where it is going, and how to leverage this new opportunity."[66] Millions of people throughout the world have access to the Internet and to the World Wide Web (the Web, or WWW). Following are some key aspects of Internet users:[67]

♦ Approximately 35 million U.S. households were on-line (i.e., had Internet access) as of 1999, and the number of on-line households is expected to rise to 57 million by 2002.

♦ Approximately 24 million non-U.S. households were on-line in 1999.

♦ The average age of Web users in the United States is about 35.

♦ Women represent about 42 percent of the on-line population.

♦ Internet users are economically upscale in comparison to the general population. Specifically, more than 65 percent of Internet users have incomes of $50,000 or more (compared with 35 percent of the total U.S. population), and more than 75 percent have attended or graduated college.

Internet Advertising. Thousands of marketers have turned to the Internet as a prospective medium for promoting their brands and transacting sales. Although research suggests that consumers find Internet advertising only "somewhat valuable" in comparison to traditional ad media,[68] on-line advertising revenue climbed to approximately $2 billion in 1998 and is projected to reach $4 billion by 2000.[69] Microsoft alone spent over $30 million on

Internet advertising in 1997.[70] However, as of 1998, the average Internet advertiser invested only about $700,000 in this ad medium.[71]

Internet advertisers use two general forms of advertising: banner ads and sponsorships. *Banner ads* are the more common form of Internet advertising. These are typically small, static ads that are placed in context of frequently visited Web sites. Banner ads cost approximately $25 to $35 per 1,000 visits.[72] A recent survey determined that larger and more-complicated Internet ads (e.g., those with pop-up boxes or scroll-down mechanisms aimed at distracting) are more eye-catching and memorable than are standard (i.e., static) banner ads.[73] The other form of Internet advertising is *sponsorship advertising,* whereby an advertiser is a partial or exclusive sponsor of a Web site and benefits from the many visitations to that site. For example, IBM paid $1 million to be sole sponsor of the National Football League's Superbowl.com Web site. The site generated more than 8 million hits.[74]

Though dating back only to 1994, the Internet has potential to become an incredibly huge and invaluable advertising medium. It is only fair to say, however, that leading advertisers do not yet fully understand how to use the Internet effectively as an advertising medium. Perhaps the best way to appreciate the Internet's potential as an advertising medium is by comparing it with more conventional media. Two metaphors help clarify the capabilities of Internet communications. For instance, Internet Web sites have been described as an "electronic yellow pages" in comparison to the standard Yellow Pages supplement to telephone directories, which provides information about products, stores, and services. This information is ordered alphabetically by the business type, and the consumer who is interested in locating a particular product or service scans the Yellow Pages in search of prospective suppliers of the product or service. Upon encountering prospective suppliers, the Yellow Pages user acquires information about the supplier's services, location, and telephone number. In similar fashion, the user, or surfer, of the Net goes to Web sites in search of specific information or merely in the pursuit of news or entertainment value. Whereas the real Yellow Pages are limited to only the printed information, electronic yellow pages allow the user, using links, to dig deeper and deeper for additional information or entertainment. Like the Yellow Pages, Web sites are effective only to the extent that they are able to both attract and hold the surfer's attention.

However, unlike the Yellow Pages, the Internet user can place an immediate order for the advertised brand. It is for this reason that the Internet can also be described as a "cyberspace 800 number." Of course, 800 (that is, toll-free) numbers enable telephone callers to both acquire additional information about products and services and to place orders. The great promise of the Internet is that it will serve as an electronic shopping mall whereby shoppers locate suppliers, place orders, have charges placed against their credit cards, and receive shipments of products by expedited mail service. Consumer confidence and the potential for misuse of credit-card numbers are the only impediments to the Internet serving as a major forum for transacting commercial exchanges.

Both metaphors convey the Internet and its World Wide Web shell as media for the consumer both to interact with the marketer and to transact commercial exchanges. Because the present profile of Internet and WWW users is that of a young, economically upscale, and computer-knowledgeable person, advertising via the Net must satisfy the nonpromotional standards that have been informally established.[75] In other words, surfers will choose to devote their attention to those Web sites that offer informational or entertainment value. They will look to buy, but they do not want to be sold aggressively. Marketers face a challenge in making their messages acceptable and enjoyable while simultaneously conveying information about brand virtues without being perceived as hucksters.

Measuring Internet Effectiveness. A major concern for commercial users of the Internet is one of *measuring* the effectiveness of their advertising. In the early years, no research services measured Internet usage in a fashion similar to the service provided by the A.C. Nielsen Company in its measurement of television viewership. But research services eventually evolved to measure the frequency with which Web sites are visited, the length of the visitations, and the path by which surfers arrive at particular sites. This information is invaluable to marketers in gauging the effectiveness of their Internet advertising and in determining how to improve their efforts.[76]

Interactive advertising on the Internet will not supplant the traditional advertising media, but advertisers and their agencies now have a revolutionary new medium for reaching present users of their brands and prospective customers. Just as advertising was altered forever with the introduction of television in the late 1940s, another seismic shift has occurred with the opportunity to advertise on the Net. In the spirit of the Interactive Marketing Communications mind-set that pervades this text, Internet advertising should provide brand marketers with an additional medium that complements more traditional media. The Internet enables the brand marketer to extend and deepen relationships with consumers that have been initially established via traditional media.[77]

ALTERNATIVE ADVERTISING MEDIA

In this final section, several alternative or unconventional media options available to advertisers are identified. As noted at the beginning of the chapter, virtually any space is a potential medium for a marketer's advertisement. In this section brief discussion is devoted to the Yellow Pages, videos for VCRs, product placements in movies, virtual signage, and a potpourri of additional alternatives.

Yellow Pages Advertising

Over 6,000 localized Yellow Pages directories are distributed annually to hundreds of millions of consumers.[78] There currently are more than 4,000 headings for different product and service listings. Local businesses place the majority of Yellow Pages ads, but national advertisers also are frequent users of the Yellow Pages. For example, both General Motors and U-Haul have invested more than $20 million in Yellow Pages advertising.[79]

www.gm.com

www.uhaul.com

Research shows that users of Yellow Pages tend to be younger (aged 25 to 49); are employed in professional, technical, clerical, or sales positions; have relatively high household incomes ($60,000 or more); and are better educated than the population at large.[80] Reasons for using Yellow Pages include: (1) saving time spent shopping around for information; (2) saving energy and money; (3) finding information quickly; and (4) learning about products and services.[81] In a typical week, it is estimated that 60 percent of all American adults use the Yellow Pages at least once. This clearly is a valuable advertising medium.

Video Advertising

This form of advertising involves capturing key visual and audio information about a brand and distributing this information to business customers or final consumers. Because over 90 percent of American households own at least one VCR, the video advertising medium is capable of reaching most everyone. One company, Technicolor Video Services, promotes itself as being able to deliver videotapes via the mail at a total cost of less than $1.50 per tape. Although there is limited research to verify the effectiveness of video advertising, firms in this industry maintain (albeit not without self-interest) that video advertising is both more effective and less expensive than comparable print advertising in the form of brochures. It is claimed that business customers and consumers are less likely to throw away an unsolicited video compared to a brochure and that videos are more persuasive.[82] Although unverified in a scientific sense, it stands to reason that video advertising is potentially more entertaining than comparable print advertising and thus more effective in gaining attention and influencing memorability of an advertising message.

Product Placements in Movies

Product placements in movies date back to the 1940s, yet the frequency of occurrence is greater now than ever. The typical price for a product placement ranges between $25,000 to $225,000 or even higher if the sponsoring brand demands a highly prominent placement.[83] Does it work? Public evidence of whether such "advertising" is effective is essentially nonexistent, though there is some evidence that brand awareness increases significantly with more prominent placements.[84] Beyond building brand name awareness, it can be expected that product placements serve further to enhance brand attitudes in a fashion akin to the *peripheral route* of persuasion that was discussed in Chapter 6. It would seem that advertisers have little to lose and more to gain when using this form of relatively inexpensive advertising.[85]

Virtual Signage

Unbeknownst to television viewers, the brand logos sometimes seen on sports fields, tennis courts, and other sporting venues actually are not there. That is, computer technology is used to "paint" an advertiser's logo at sporting venues. Attendees at the sporting event cannot see the signs, because they are not there, but television viewers have no idea that what they are viewing is merely a computer-generated image rather than a "real" sign. Virtual signs have been used in boxing, football, tennis, baseball, and basketball coverage. These signs enable advertisers to use state-of-the-art graphics to attract and hold viewer attention during the actual playing of a sporting event. Companies such as Imagine Video Systems and Princeton Video Image charge about $20,000 for a half-inning of national baseball coverage.[86] Advertisers in the United States have enthusiastically embraced virtual signage as a potentially promising advertising medium, but in Europe regulators such as the European Broadcasting Union have categorically banned virtual advertising from events in which it holds broadcasting rights.[87]

Potpourri of Alternative Media

Creative advertisers have unlimited sources to convey their messages. For example, some companies sell advertising space in restrooms. An enterprising firm called The Fruit Label Co. has used apples and other fruit and vegetable items to carry mini-ads for movies such as *Liar, Liar* and *Jurassic Park*.[88] Another firm sells advertising space on gas nozzles (see advertisement for the Sales Pumper in Figure 12.7). Levi's advertised 501 jeans on the back cover of *Marvel Comics* and *DC Comics*. This was an excellent medium insofar as these two comic book companies sell more than 10 million combined copies of their comic books every month! The comics provided Levi's with an outlet for reaching the notoriously difficult-to-reach segment of boys aged 12 to 17. The *Global Focus* section describes several interesting alternative advertising media that are in use around the world.

    This brief discussion of alternative media has been intended merely to demonstrate that the imagination (and perhaps good taste) are the only limits to the choice of advertising media. Creative advertisers find many ways to reach customers using alternative media that either substitute for or complement more conventional advertising media. We must be mindful, however, of the advice about integrated marketing communications that was presented in Chapter 1: Effective communications require that all points of contact with customers speak with a single voice. Multiple media are to little avail if their messages are inconsistent or possibly even in conflict.

400 PART 4 Advertising Management

An Alternative Advertising
Medium, the "Sales Pumper"

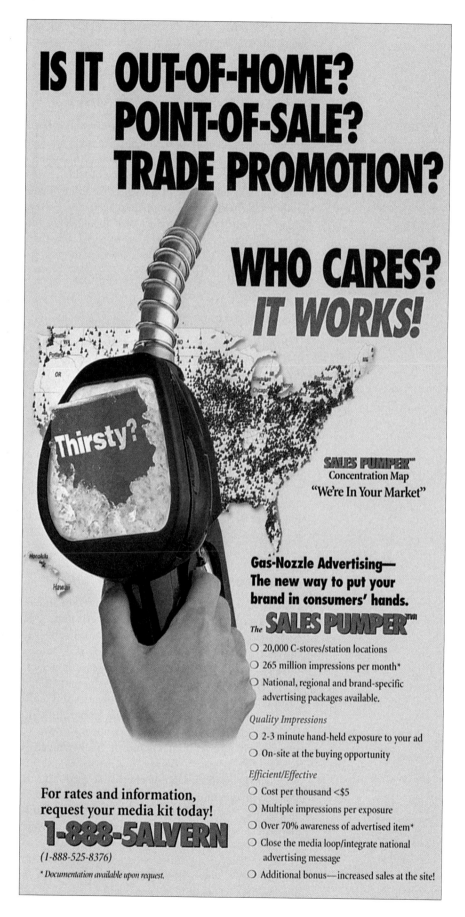

GLOBAL FOCUS: ALTERNATIVE ADVERTISING MEDIA AROUND THE WORLD

Car Advertising in Spain

Americans over the age of 30 might remember advertisers' using Volkswagen Beetles back in the late 1960s and early 1970s as advertising vehicles (in the most literal sense of the term) for their brands. Now a company called Logocar is doing the same thing in the Spanish capital of Madrid. Logocar has recruited car owners who are willing to have their vehicles covered in a vinyl skin that bears an advertising message. Figure 12.8 shows an ad for Pall Mall cigarettes. Car owners receive $230 per month for allowing their cars to serve as roving billboards. Advertisers are charged a basic cost of $29,000 per month for a 25-car advertising fleet.[a]

Sailboat Advertising in Egypt

An advertising axiom says advertise where the customers are. An advertiser in Egypt can find no better place to reach potential consumers than on the Nile River, where millions of Egyptians reside nearby. The ancient sailboats that travel the Nile are called *feluccas*. These boats have huge white sails that represent an ideal location for advertising messages. Coca-Cola signed a two-year contract to have its logo displayed on the sails of boats owned by one of Cairo's popular felucca operators. The cost to Coke was around $8,000. Some Egyptians have criticized the commercialization of the Nile, while others fear excessive clutter from too many feluccas carrying advertising messages. Their concern echoes critics of outdoor advertising in the United States., who refer to billboards as "litter on a stick." In Egypt, the potential counterpart to this criticism is "litter on a sail."[b]

Free Telephone Service in Sweden ... But at a Cost

An enterprising company in Sweden, Gratistelefon Svenska AB, came up with the creative idea of giving away local and long-distance telephone service to residential customers. To receive this free service, customers must be willing to listen to 10-second advertising spots every three minutes during a phone conversation. In addition, customers must provide Gratistelefon with detailed personal information (family size, hobbies, tastes, and demographics) when signing on for free service. Advertisements can then be customized to customers based on their market segmentation profiles. The potential beauty of this advertising medium is that advertisers have the caller's undivided attention during the 10 seconds when an ad is transmitted. Gratistelefon has patented its process in dozens of other countries, and now this form of "gratis telephone" also is available in countries such as Australia and the Philippines.[c]

Sources:

[a] "Drivers Paid to Carry Ads," *Ad Age International*, April 1997, i18.

[b] Amy Dockser Marcus, "Latest Ad Trend in Cairo: Company Logos on Sailboats," *The Wall Street Journal Interactive Edition*, July 18, 1997.

[c] Gautam Naik, "For Free Calls, Users Must Listen to Marketing Pitches," *The Wall Street Journal Interactive Edition*, September 29, 1997.

The Logo Car in Madrid, Spain

Summary

Five major media are available to advertising media planners: television, radio, magazines, newspapers, and outdoor advertising. Each medium has unique qualities with both strengths and weaknesses. The chapter provides a detailed analysis of each medium. In addition to these traditional media, advertisers are beginning to take advantage of new interactive media, including especially the Internet.

Discussion Questions

1. What are the advantages and disadvantages of cable television advertising? Why are more national advertisers turning to cable television as a viable advertising medium?

2. Assume you are brand manager for a product line of thermos containers. Your products range from thermos bottles to small ice chests. You have $3 million to invest in a four-week magazine advertising campaign. What magazines would you choose for this campaign? Justify your choices.

3. Cigarettes and liquor products were responsible for a very large percentage of all billboard advertising. Why did these two product categories dominate the billboard medium?

4. Changeable message signs are billboards that vary the advertising message on a schedule of every 4 to 10 seconds. What, in your opinion, is the value of this technology to the advertiser and what are the potential hazards to society?

5. Assume you are a manufacturer of various jewelry items. Graduation rings for high school and college students are one of the most important items in your product line. You are in the process of developing a media strategy aimed specifically at high school students. With an annual budget of $5 million, what media and specific vehicles would you use? How would you schedule the advertising over time?

6. Examine a copy of the most recent Spot Radio Rates and Data available in your library and compare the advertising rates for three or four of the radio stations in your hometown or university community.

7. Identify five magazines that are of interest to you. Using the criteria in Figure 12.1 that are especially relevant to magazines (such as elegance), construct a rank ordering of the magazines. Your ordering should range from the magazine that best meets the criteria to the magazine that, in your opinion, is worst with respect to the criteria.

8. Pick your favorite clothing store in your university community (or hometown), and justify the choice of one radio station that the clothing store should select for its radio advertising. Do not feel constrained by what the clothing store may be doing already; focus instead on what you think is most important. Be certain to make explicit all criteria used in making your choice and all radio stations considered.

9. Identify three home pages on the Web that you consider particularly effective. What, in your opinion, contributes to their effectiveness?

10. Magazine A is read by 20,450,000 people and costs $80,000 for a full-page, four-color advertisement. Magazine B reaches 15,700,000 readers and costs $65,000 for a full-page, four-color advertisement. Holding all other factors constant, in which magazine would you choose to advertise?

11. Radio is the only major medium that is nonvisual. Is this a major disadvantage? Thoroughly justify your response.

12. One advertiser declared: "Infomercials are junk. I wouldn't waste my money advertising on this medium." What is your response to this assertion?

13. How responsive do you think most North American consumers would be to a service for gratis telephone service such as described in the *Global Focus* insert?

Internet Exercises

1. Companies are increasingly willing to pay for market research related to the Web. Demographics, attitudes, and behaviors are monitored by countless surveys in an effort to understand and predict the future of Internet commerce (see http://www.nua.ie for weekly, monthly, and annual compilations of Internet surveys and articles about Internet surveys). Interestingly, with so much focus on what Web users are doing and why they are doing it, few seem to be asking "when are they doing it?" Imagine being an advertiser and finding that the only information about television and radio usage was the total number of users, their demographic profiles, and which channels they watched (but not when they watched the channels). Use the chapter material related to media characteristics and practices to discuss the following issues:

   a. Is banner advertising more similar to outdoor or magazine advertising? Support your answer with specific comparisons of the advertising implications associated with each medium.

   b. Banner ads are often "affiliated" with certain search engine keywords. In what sense does this give the ads a "timeliness" characteristic?

   c. Describe how the following aspects of Web sites could allow for "premium" banner ad pricing: (a) Web site sponsorship (b) Special Web "events" such as online concerts, interviews, or broadcasts, and (c) Time of day (considering time zones as well).

2. While everyone acknowledges the commerce potential of the Internet, few are as hopeful about its brand-building capacity. Part of the skepticism is based on the less-than-encouraging results from banner ads and "interstitials" (pop-up ad pages). These ads generate very few brand Web site visits. For those consumers who do visit a brand Web site, many are disappointed to find no extra brand benefits. Instead, they find traditional advertising-style information about the brand or the company. In reality, the only profitable, accountable Web sites are those that are themselves branded. In this regard, the principles of integrated marketing communications suggest a somewhat simple solution for many brands—make the Web site part of the brand. More specifically, Web sites can offer new brand benefits or enhance existing benefits. Select a product or service that you think this idea would apply to and discuss the following questions:

   a. How could new or enhanced brand benefits be offered for your brand by using a Web site?

   b. Apply this idea by developing a media strategy that accommodates the Internet as a part of the brand's offer. What media and specific vehicles would you use? How will advertising be scheduled over time?

Chapter Twelve Endnotes

1. Thom Forbes, "Consumer Central: The Media Focus Is Changing—And So Is the Process," *Agency,* winter 1998, 38.

2. Karen Whitehill King and Leonard N. Reid, "Selecting Media for National Accounts: Factors of Importance to Agency Media Specialists," *Journal of Current Issues and Research in Advertising* 19 (fall 1997), 55–64.

3. All values are based on "Leading National Advertisers," *Advertising Age,* September 28, 1998, s50. The larger estimate for newspaper advertising is based on figures from Robert J. Coen (McCann-Erickson Worldwide), whereas the smaller newspaper figure is *Advertising Age's* estimate.

4. Anthony F. McGann and J. Thomas Russell, *Advertising Media: A Managerial Approach* (Homewood, Ill.: Irwin, 1988), 272.

5. Adam Snyder, "Outdoor, Forecast: Sunny, Some Clouds," *Adweek's Marketing Week,* July 8, 1991, 18–19.

6. Ibid.

7. Myron Laible, "Changeable Message Signs: A Technology Whose Time Has Come," *Journal of Public Policy & Marketing* 16 (spring 1997), 173–176; Frank Vespe, "High-Tech Billboards: The Same Old Litter on a Stick," *Journal of Public Policy & Marketing* 16 (spring 1997), 176–179; and Charles R. Taylor, "A Technology Whose Time Has Come or the Same Old Litter on a Stick? An Analysis of Changeable Message Boards," *Journal of Public Policy & Marketing* 16 (spring 1997), 179–186.

8. *Marketer's Guide to Media* 1998–99, vol. 21 (New York: BPI Communications), 190.

9. These figures are based on ibid., 192.

10. Ibid., 190.

11. Ibid.

12. Michael T. Elliott and Paul Surgi Speck, "Consumer Perceptions of Advertising Clutter and Its Impact across Various Media," *Journal of Advertising Research* 38 (January–February 1998), 29–41.

13. Karen Whitehill King, Leonard N. Reid, and Margaret Morrison, "Large-Agency Media Specialists' Opinions on Newspaper Advertising for National Accounts," *Journal of Advertising* 26 (Summer 1997), 1–18. This same article indicates that ad agencies consider the newspaper as an advertising medium to be less effective in most all respects compared to network television.

14. "Shedding the Local Image," *Marketing Communications,* September 1982, 43.

15. Joe Schwartz and Thomas Exter, "The News from Here," *American Demographics,* June 1991, 50–53.

16. Bill Keane, "The Family Circus," ©1992, Bill Keane, Inc., August, 9, 1992.

17. "The Escalating Ads Race," *Newsweek,* December 7, 1987, 65.

18. "3-D Glasses Double Ad's Impact," *Marketing Communications,* January 1988, 10.

19. Based on *Sports Illustrated's* rate card #56, January 12, 1998, 5.

20. Marc Beauchamp, "Radio Days," *Forbes,* November 30, 1987, 200, 204.

21. Riccardo A. Davis, "It's Not a New Medium, but Radio Still a Hot One," *Advertising Age,* May 9, 1994, 49.

22. Cyril C. Penn, "Marketing Tool Underused," *Advertising Age,* September 25, 1978, 122.

23. Burt Manning, "Friendly Persuasion," *Advertising Age,* September 13, 1982, M8.

24. Ibid.

25. Kerry J. Smith, "Cranking Up the Volume," *Promo,* October 1994, 106.

26. "Radio Lets Vermont Teddy Bear Constantly Fine-Tune Its Ads," *Advertising Age* (special advertising section), October 18, 1993, R4.

27. Rhody Bosley, "Radio Study Tells Imagery Potential," *Advertising Age* (advertising supplement), September 6, 1993, R3.

28. For further reading on the nature and value of imagery in advertising, see Paula Fitzgerald Bone and Pam Scholder Ellen, "The Generation and Consequences of Communication-Evoked Imagery," *Journal of Consumer Research* 19 (June 1992), 93–104; and Darryl W. Miller and Lawrence J. Marks, "Mental Imagery and Sound Effects in Radio Commercials," *Journal of Advertising* 21 (December 1992), 83–93.

29. "Radio's Personalities Help Find Snapple's Sales Targets," *Advertising Age* (special advertising section), October 18, 1993, R3.

30. A thorough study of this behavior was conducted by Avery M. Abernethy, "The Accuracy of Diary Measures of Car Radio Audiences: An Initial Assessment," *Journal of Advertising* 18 (no. 3, 1989), 33–49.

31. *Marketer's Guide to Media* 1998–99, 20.

32. Elliott and Speck, "Consumer Perceptions of Advertising Clutter and Its Impact across Various Media."

33. The following discussion is adapted from Anthony F. McGann and J. Thomas Russell, *Advertising Media: A Managerial Approach* (Homewood, Ill.: Irwin, 1988), 141–143.

34. Joe Mandese, "'Seinfeld' Nears Price Ceiling As Sophomore Shows Soar," *Advertising Age,* September 15, 1997, 1.

35. *Marketer's Guide to Media* 1998–99, 25.

36. Joe Mandese, "'X-Files' Usurps 'Seinfeld' for No. 2 Barter Price Slot," *Advertising Age,* January 19, 1998, s2.

37. *Marketer's Guide to Media* 1998–99, 51.

38. Kyle Pope and Leslie Cauley, "In the Battle for TV Ads, Cable Is Now the Enemy," *The Wall Street Journal Interactive Edition,* May 6, 1998.

39. Leslie Cauley, "Ad Buyers Are Warming to Cable As Network-Rating Gap Narrows," *The Wall Street Journal Interactive Edition,* October 5, 1998.

40. Based on famous advertising practitioner Raymond Rubicam as quoted in Richard C. Anderson, "Eight Ways to Make More Impact," *Advertising Age,* May 17, 1982, M23.

41. James B. Arndorfer and Chuck Ross, "A-B Shells Out Record Price for '99 Super Bowl," *Advertising Age,* April 13, 1998, 1.

42. Sally Beatty, "Cost of Making a TV Commercial Leaped 11% in 1997, Survey Shows," *The Wall Street Journal Interactive Edition,* August 19, 1998.

43. Verne Gray, "Share and Share Alike?" *Adweek,* June 1, 1998, 54–55.

44. "The Toughest Job in TV," *Newsweek,* October 3, 1988, 72; Dennis Kneale, "'Zapping' of TV Ads Appears Pervasive," *The Wall Street Journal,* April 25, 1988, 21.

45. John J. Cronin, "In-Home Observations of Commercial Zapping Behavior," *Journal of Current Issues and Research in Advertising* 17 (fall 1995), 69–76.

46. Fred S. Zufryden, James H. Pedrick, and Avu Sankaralingam, "Zapping and Its Impact on Brand Purchase Behavior," *Journal of Advertising Research* 33 (January/February 1993), 58–66.

47. John J. Cronin and Nancy E. Menelly, "Discrimination vs. 'Zipping' of Television Commercials," *Journal of Advertising* 21 (June 1992), 1–7.

48. Elliott and Speck, "Consumer Perceptions of Advertising Clutter and Its Impact across Various Media."

49. For an interesting article that compares the effectiveness of 15- and 30-second commercials, see Surendra N. Singh and Catherine A. Cole, "The Effects of Length, Content, and Repetition on Television Commercial Effectiveness," *Journal of Marketing Research* 30 (February 1993), 91–104.

50. Whether advertising clutter has adverse effects on brand name recall and message memorability is a matter of some dispute. For somewhat different accounts, see Tom J. Brown and Michael L. Rothschild, "Reassessing the Impact of Television Advertising Clutter," *Journal of Consumer Research* 20 (June 1993), 138–146; Robert J. Kent and Chris T. Allen, "Does Competitive Clutter in Television Advertising 'Interfere' with the Recall and Recognition of Brand Names and Ad Claims?" *Marketing Letters* 4, no. 2 (1993), 175–184; Robert J. Kent

and Chris T. Allen, "Competitive Interference in Consumer Memory for Advertising: The Role of Brand Familiarity," *Journal of Marketing* 58 (July 1994), 97–105; and Robert J. Kent, "Competitive Clutter in Network Television Advertising: Current Levels and Advertiser Response," *Journal of Advertising Research* 35 (January/February 1995), 49–57.

51. Julie Steenhuysen, "Adland's New Billion-Dollar Baby," *Advertising Age,* April 11, 1994, S8.

52. Elaine Underwood, "Timex Links into Infomercial Market," *Brandweek,* April 3, 1995, 3.

53. "The Top Ten Grossing Infomercials in 1997," *Infomercial and Direct Response Television Sourcebook '98,* a supplement to *Adweek Magazines,* 18.

54. Steve Dworman, "The Infomercial," special sourcebook issue to *Brandweek,* 1994, 5.

55. Underwood, "Timex Links into Infomercial Market." Kevin Goldman, "P&G Experiments with an Infomercial," *The Wall Street Journal,* July 8, 1994, B9.

56. Steenhuysen, "Adland's New Billion-Dollar Baby," S14.

57. Ibid.

58. Paul Surgi Speck, Michael T. Elliott, and Frank H. Alpert, "The Relationship of Beliefs and Exposure to General Perceptions of Infomercials," *Journal of Current Issues and Research in Advertising* 14 (spring 1997), 51–66.

59. Naveen Donthu and David Gilliland, "Observations: The Infomercial Shopper," *Journal of Advertising Research* 36 (March–April 1996), 69–76.

60. Rolan T. Rust and Richard W. Oliver, "Notes and Comments: The Death of Advertising," *Journal of Advertising* 23 (December 1994), 71–77. See also Roland T. Rust and Sajeev Varki, "Rising from the Ashes of Advertising," *Journal of Business Research* 37 (November 1996), 173–181.

61. Debra Aho Williamson, "Building a New Industry," *Advertising Age,* March 13, 1995, S3.

62. Harry King, "Interactive Future: Is It Sunrise or Sunset for the Ad Business," *Agency,* spring 1994, 44.

63. For a slightly different treatment, see Williamson, "Building a New Industry."

64. This description is based on Debra Aho, "Bubble Yum Steps into Virtual Reality," *Advertising Age,* October 4, 1993, 30.

65. For discussion of some of the technical and economic issues involved with the Internet, see "The Internet: The Accidental Superhighway," *The Economist,* July 1, 1995, 3–18.

66. "The CommerceNet/Nielsen Internet Demographics Survey," October 1995. URL: http://www.commerce.net/information/surveys/execsum/exec_sum .html.

67. "Why Internet Advertising," Report by the Internet Advertising Bureau published as a supplement to *Brandweek,* spring 1997.

68. Robert H. Ducoffe, "Advertising Value and Advertising on the Web," *Journal of Advertising Research* 36 (September/October 1996), 21–35.

69. Kate Maddox, "Internet Ad Sales Approach $1 Billion," *Advertising Age,* April 6, 1998, 32.

70. Kate Maddox, "On-line Advertising Reaches $544.8 Mil, New Report Says," *Advertising Age,* August 3, 1998, 28.

71. Kate Maddox, "ANA Study Finds Marketers Triple 'Net Ad Budgets," *Advertising Age,* May 11, 1998, 63.

72. Vanessa O'Connell, "Soap and Diaper Makers Pitch to Masses of Internet Women," *The Wall Street Journal Interactive Edition,* July 20, 1998.

73. Sally Beatty, "Companies Push for Much Bigger, More-Complicated On-Line Ads," *The Wall Street Journal Interactive Edition,* August 20, 1998.

74. Terry Lefton, "IBM's $1M Super Buy Is Web-Topper; Phoenix Close on $9M NCAA Pact," *Brandweek,* November 24, 1997, 8.

75. Daniel Shannon, "Promoting on the Internet," *Promo,* March 1995, 50.

76. See Debra Aho Williamson, "Digital Planet's Plan to Track Eyeballs," *Advertising Age,* April 24, 1995, 14; and Michael Krantz, "The Medium Is the Measure," *IQ,* September 25, 1995, 20–24.

77. Joseph C. Philport and Jerry Arbittier, "Advertising: Brand Communications Styles in Established Media and the Internet," *Journal of Advertising Research* 37 (March/April 1997), 68–76.

78. This statistic and the remainder of the information in this section are based on Joel J. Davis, *Understanding Yellow Pages* (Troy, Mich.: Yellow Pages Publishers Association, 1995).

79. Ibid., 10.

80. Ibid., 18.

81. Ibid., 19.

82. Based on promotional literature received from Technicolor Video Services. Interested readers can contact this firm at (800) 732-4555.

83. Pola B. Gupta and Kenneth R. Lord, "Product Placement in Movies: The Effect of Prominence and Mode on Audience Recall," *Journal of Current Issues and Research in Advertising* 20 (spring 1998), 47–60.

84. Ibid.

85. For readings on this topic, see *Proceedings of the 1994 Conference of the American Academy of Advertising,* ed. Karen Whitehall King (Athens, Ga.: The American Academy of Advertising, 1994); Barry Sapolsky and Lance Kinney, "You Oughta Be in Pictures: Product Placements in the Top-Grossing Films of 1991," 89; James A. Karrh, "Effects of Brand Placements in Motion Pictures," 90–96; and Stacy Vollmers and Richard Mizerski, "A Review and Investigation into the Effectiveness of Product Placements in Films, 97–102.

86. Terry Lefton, "The New Signage," Brandweek, January 27, 1997, 35; William Porter, "The Virtual Ad: On TV You See It, But at Baseball Games You Don't," *The Wall Street Journal Interactive Edition,* July 30, 1998.

87. Kimberley A. Strassel, "Virtual Ads Vie for Field Position, But Regulators Move to Stop Them," *The Wall Street Journal Interactive Edition,* October 17, 1997.

88. Lisa Bannon, "Jim Carrey Is Coming Soon to a Fruit Bin Near You," *The Wall Street Journal Interactive Edition,* August 21, 1997.

Direct Advertising and Database Marketing

CHAPTER OBJECTIVES

After studying this chapter, you should be able to:

1. Explain direct marketing and the reasons underlying its growth.
2. Describe the characteristics of direct-response advertising.
3. Discuss the distinctive features of direct mail advertising.
4. Explain the role of databases.
5. Perform lifetime value analyses of database entries.
6. Discuss the features and advantages of outbound and inbound telemarketing.

Opening Vignette: An Effective Direct–Mail and Tele–marketing Campaign for the Saab 9–5

In April 1998, Saab, the Swedish automobile maker, introduced a new luxury sedan named the Saab 9-5 (see Figure 13.1). This model represented Saab's first entry in the luxury category and was designed to compete against well-known high-equity brands including Mercedes, BMW, Volvo, Lexus, and Infiniti. A total of 200,000 consumers, including 65,000 current Saab owners and 135,000 prospects, were targeted with the objective of encouraging them to test drive the 9-5. The Martin Agency of Richmond, VA, developed an integrated marketing communications strategy, prominent among which was a direct marketing campaign that consisted of multiple mailings and outbound telemarketing. The effort was designed to engage prospects in a dialogue about the new 9-5 and to learn more about their automobile purchase interests. Mailings provided prospects with brand details, made an appealing offer for them to test drive the 9-5, and fed names of the most qualified prospects to dealers for follow-up.

The Martin Agency designed four mailings: (1) a countdown mailing in December 1997 announced the new Saab 9-5, provided a "teaser" photo of the car, and requested recipients to complete a survey of their automobile purchase interests and needs; (2) a qualification mailing in January 1998 provided respondents to the "countdown" mailing with product information addressing their specific purchase interests (performance, safety, versatility, etc.) and offered a test-drive kit as an incentive for returning an additional survey; (3) a road & track mailing in March 1998 included a special issue from *Road & Track* magazine that was devoted to the Saab 9-5's product-development process; and (4) a test-drive kit mailing in June 1998 extended an offer to test drive the 9-5 for three hours and also provided an opportunity for prospects to win an all-expenses-paid European driving adventure (through Germany, Italy, and Sweden) as incentive for test driving the 9-5.

An outbound telemarketing campaign was conducted between March to July 1998 as a follow-up to the direct mailings. Telephone calls were made to all people who responded

FIGURE 13.1

Saab Global Homepage
(www.saab.com)

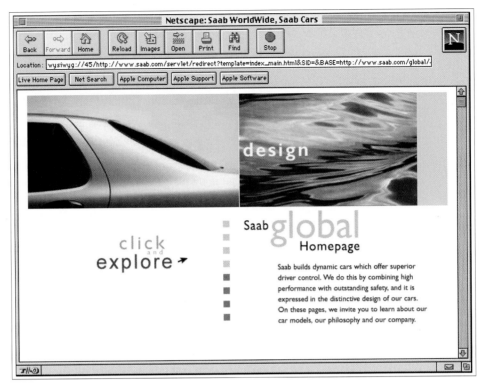

to the "countdown" and "qualification" mailings as well as to all prospects who had automobile leases or loans that were expiring prior to mailing of the test-drive kit. These callings reinforced the European test-drive offer and set up times for local dealers to call back to schedule a test drive.

The direct marketing effort for the 9-5 was fabulously successful. Of the 200,000 initial prospects who were contacted by the introductory mailing, 16,000 indicated interest in test driving the 9-5 (an 8 percent response rate), and more than 2,200 test drives had already been scheduled at the time of this writing.

Source: Information provided by The Martin Agency, Richmond, VA, 1998.

*T*he prior chapter emphasized the major advertising media: television, magazines, newspapers, radio, and outdoor advertising. Historically, these conventional media have been used to reach *mass audiences* and have been judged in terms of cost efficiencies. Advertising in mass media creates brand awareness, conveys product information, and builds or reinforces a brand's image. Marketers such as Saab and The Martin Agency (*Opening Vignette*) now are turning increasingly to direct advertising and database marketing to fine-tune their customer selection, better serve customer needs, and fulfill their own needs by achieving advertising results that can be measured by actual sales response. Mass-media advertising and direct marketing efforts are components of well-designed integrated marketing communication efforts.

This chapter covers the related topics of database marketing and direct marketing, which collectively include direct-response advertising, telemarketing, and direct selling. An overview of direct marketing is provided before turning to each specific topic.

DIRECT MARKETING

Direct marketing was traditionally considered a specialty form of marketing and advertising appropriate only for products and services offered by book publishers, record clubs, correspondence schools, and marketers of inexpensive gadgets and cheap clothing. Today, however, most *Fortune 500* firms as well as medium-sized and small companies now are enthusiastic users of databases and direct-marketing initiatives. Indeed, direct marketing is one of the growth areas in business.

Precisely what is direct marketing? The Direct Marketing Association, a trade group whose members practice various forms of direct marketing, offers the following definition:

> Direct marketing is an *interactive system* of marketing which uses *one or more advertising media* to effect a *measurable response* and/or transaction *at any location.*[1]

Note the italicized features of this definition. First, direct marketing involves *interactive marketing* in that it entails personalized communications between marketer and prospect. Second, direct marketing is not restricted to just direct mail but rather involves *one or more media* (for instance, direct mail with telephone follow-up marketing). Third, marketing via media such as direct mail allows for relatively greater *measurability of response* in comparison to indirect media such as television advertising. It is easier to measure because purchase responses to direct marketing: (1) typically are more immediate than responses to mass-media advertising and (2) can be tracked to specific customers in response to specific marketing efforts. Finally, direct marketing takes place at a *variety of locations*—by phone, at a kiosk, by mail, or by personal visits.

You now have a general understanding of direct marketing; however, the terminology of direct marketing can be confusing because the word *direct* is used in several different ways: direct marketing, direct-response advertising, direct mail, and direct selling. Figure 13.2 provides a framework to help clarify the distinctions among these various *D* words. As shown by the figure, the total marketing process consists of indirect and direct marketing, and Figure 13.2 delineates the latter into its various forms.

Indirect marketing includes the use of intermediaries in the channel of distribution; examples include distributors or dealers in industrial-goods marketing and retailers in consumer-goods marketing. Indirect marketing is what typically comes to mind when one thinks of marketing. However, there has been substantial growth in various forms of interactive home shopping whereby consumers make catalog purchases, engage in electronic shopping, or order from home-shopping television networks. Many manufacturers now bypass retailers and sell directly to consumers, a trend referred to as *disintermediation*.[2] Dell Computer, for example, became the leading marketer of desktop computers by exclusively selling its products directly to consumers without retailer intervention.

www.dell.com

The marketer's purpose with *direct marketing* is to establish a relationship with a customer in order to initiate immediate and measurable responses. Direct marketing is accomplished using direct-response advertising, direct mail (including catalogs), telemarketing, and direct selling.

Direct-response advertising involves the use of any of several media to transmit messages that encourage buyers to purchase directly from the advertiser. *Direct mail* is the most important direct-advertising medium, but it is certainly not the only one. Direct-response advertising also uses television, magazines, and other media with the intent of creating immediate action from customers. *Telemarketing,* the dominant form of direct marketing, includes making outbound calls from telephone salespersons and handling inbound orders, inquiries, and complaints from present or prospective customers. *Direct selling* is the use of salespeople (for example, Avon or Tupperware representatives) to sell directly to the final consumer. Direct selling will not be further discussed in this chapter in that this practice entails all aspects of marketing and is not a marketing communications method per se.

Finally, we need to introduce the practice of database marketing. Database marketing (DBM), which is used both by indirect and direct marketers, involves collecting and electronically storing (in a database) information about present, past, and prospective customers. Typical databases include customers' past purchase details ("buyographic" data) and other types of relevant information (demographic, geographic, and psychographic data). The information is used to profile customers and to develop effective and efficient marketing programs by communicating with individual customers and by establishing long-term communication relationships.[3]

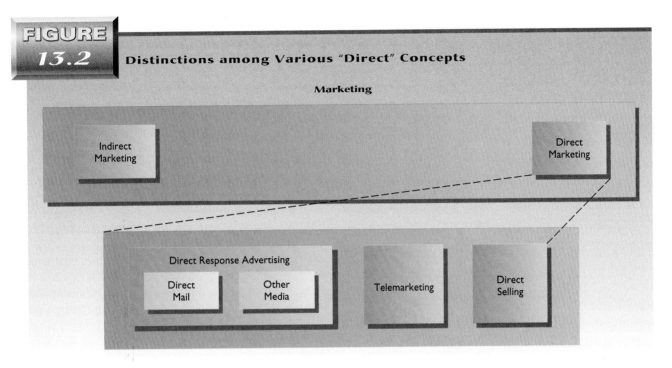

FIGURE 13.2 **Distinctions among Various "Direct" Concepts**

Although database marketing and direct marketing are *not* equivalent, the increased sophistication of database marketing has been largely responsible for the growing use and effectiveness of direct marketing. Moreover, indirect marketers also have increased their use of database marketing.

Direct Marketing's Phenomenal Growth

Historically, direct marketing represented a relatively small part of most companies' marketing efforts. However, direct marketing now is a huge enterprise as reflected in the following statistics:[4]

- U.S. sales revenues attributable to direct marketing reached more than $1.2 trillion in 1997.

- Business-to-business (B-to-B) marketers in 1997 produced sales of $238.6 billion from telephone marketing. Direct marketing expenditures for B-to-B marketers in 1997 totaled $76.6 billion, or about 50 percent of all direct marketing expenditures.

- Consumer direct mail sales amounted to $244.3 billion in 1997 based on expenditures of $76.4 billion.

Lester Wunderman, the famous direct marketing practitioner who coined the expression "direct marketing," recently had this to say: "Direct marketing, today, is scientific, accountable, versatile, multi-dimensional and growing faster than any other form of advertising."[5]

A variety of factors help to explain direct marketing's growth. Fundamental *societal changes* (intensified time pressures, increased use of credit cards, and more discretionary income) have created a need and opportunity for the convenience of direct-marketed products and services. Direct marketing provides shoppers with an easy, convenient, and relatively hassle-free way to buy.

www.blockbuster.com

www.kraft.com

Major advances in *computer technology and database management* have made it possible for companies to maintain huge databases containing millions of prospects and customers. For example, Blockbuster, the movie-rental business, has a database of over 40 million households, and Kraft General Foods has a list of more than 30 million users of its products.

By targeting promotional efforts to a company's best prospects—who can be identified by their past product-category purchasing behavior (buyographics) or in terms of specific geographic, demographic, or psychographic characteristics—direct marketing enables pin-pointed communications, or what is also referred to as *niche marketing.* Increasingly, more powerful and faster computers have enabled "marketers to zero in on ever-smaller niches of the population, ultimately aiming for the smallest consumer segment of all: the individual."[6]

In addition to the growth of consumer-oriented direct marketing, applications of direct marketing by business-to-business marketers also have experienced tremendous expansion. B-to-B expenditures on direct marketing (predominantly telephone sales and direct mail) grew by 8.6 percent from 1992–1997 and are forecast to grow at an annual rate of 8.2 percent from 1997–2002, for total expenditures of $113.4 billion in 2002.[7]

A major reason for this trend is the rising cost of personal sales calls, which on average exceed $250 per call. As a result, telemarketing and direct mail have actually replaced the sales force in some companies, whereas in others direct marketing is used to supplement the sales force's efforts by building goodwill, generating leads, and opening doors for salespeople.

Mail-order selling, telemarketing, and other forms of direct marketing provide attractive options for firms who either prefer to avoid the huge expense of a traveling sales force or desire to supplement sales-force effort with supportive marketing communications. Business-to-business direct marketing can reduce marketing costs substantially and provide firms with larger potential markets. Consider the case of General Binding Corporation (GBC), a marketer of printing-related machines and other printing products. GBC's sales force originally consisted of more than 300 salespersons who sold to tens of thousands of small, medium, and large businesses throughout the country. Escalating sales costs forced the company to find alternatives to in-person sales contact to do business with its many smaller customers. GBC found that mail order proved an efficient distribution method for serving the many customers that make small purchases individually but who collectively represent huge sales potential.[8]

DIRECT-RESPONSE ADVERTISING

As shown in Figure 13.2, direct-response advertising includes direct mail and other media. Direct mail is by far the dominant direct advertising medium, but some of the advertising placed in conventional mass media (newspapers, magazines, and television) is of the direct-response variety. In general, three distinct features characterize direct-response advertising: (1) It makes a *definite offer,* (2) it contains *all the information necessary for the prospect to make a decision,* and (3) it includes a *response device* (coupon, phone number, or both) to facilitate immediate action.[9]

www.nordictrack.com

An illustration of direct-response advertising is the advertisement in Figure 13.3 for the Leg Shaper Plus by NordicTrack. This ad satisfies the requirements of a direct-response advertisement in its appeal to women who read any of the various magazines in which the ad was placed. The ad provides prospective customers with interesting background information and solid reasons to consider purchasing this product. The ad also offers readers a convenient mechanism to actualize their purchase desires in the form of a toll-free 800 number. In addition, a no-risk in-home trial offer allows the purchaser to try the Leg Shaper and return it within 30 days if not fully satisfied. It seems the consumer has little to lose when responding to this offer, which is essential for successful direct marketing.

Illustration of Direct-
Response Advertising

In general, the direct advertiser's objective is to select a medium (or multiple media) that provides maximum ability to segment the market at a reasonable cost. Effective direct-response media selection demands that the marketer clearly define a target market. Consider, for example, the direct-response ad for the Polycom teleconferencing speaker-phone (Figure 13.4). The target market for the Polycom probably consists of managers from small to medium-sized businesses that do not have major teleconferencing facilities but have a need for high-quality and reliable teleconferencing equipment. Advertisements for this product are placed in consumer magazines that reach businesspeople (such as *Business Week, Newsweek, Time, Fortune*) and in business periodicals that cater to particular business specialties.

Direct Mail

Although direct-response advertisers use various media (such as the magazine ads just described), direct mail is the most important direct-response medium. **Direct-mail advertising** refers to any advertising matter sent directly to the person whom the marketer wishes

Another Illustration of
Direct-Response Advertising

to influence; these advertisements can take the form of letters, postcards, programs, calendars, folders, catalogs, videocassettes, blotters, order blanks, price lists, menus, and so on. The direct-mail campaign by The Martin Agency for the Saab 9-5 (*Opening Vignette*) typifies effective direct mailing. In general, direct mail's distinctive features include targetability, measurability, accountability, flexibility, and efficiency.[10]

1. *Targetability*. Direct mail is capable of targeting a precisely defined group of people. For example, The Martin Agency selected just 200,000 consumers to receive mailings for the Saab 9-5. These included 65,000 current Saab owners and 135,000 prospects who were identified based on a statistical model of financial and demographic variables that was created specifically for Saab.

2. *Measurability*. With direct mail it is possible to determine exactly how effective the effort was because the marketer knows precisely how many mailings were sent out and how many people responded. This enables ready calculations of cost-per-inquiry and cost-per-order. As noted in the *Opening Vignette,* over 2,200 consumers signed up for test drives of the Saab 9-5. Dealer sales data will reveal how many of the initial 200,000 mailings resulted in purchases.

3. *Accountability*. Every business decision must be held accountable for results. Marketing communicators increasingly are being required to justify the results of their communication efforts. Direct mailing simplifies this task. Because results can be readily demonstrated (as in the case of the Saab 9-5), brand managers can justify budgets allocated to direct mail.

4. *Flexibility*. Because effective direct mail can be produced relatively quickly (say, in comparison to producing a TV commercial), it is possible for a company to launch a direct-mail campaign that meets changing circumstances. For example, if inventory levels are excessive, a quick postcard or letter may serve to reduce it. Direct mail also offers the advantage of permitting the marketer to test communication ideas on a small-scale basis quickly and out of the view of competitors. Comparatively, a mass-media effort cannot avoid the competition's eyes. Direct mail also is flexible in the sense that it has no constraints in terms of form, color, or size (other than those imposed by cost and practical considerations). It also is relatively simple and inexpensive to change direct-mail ads. Compare this with the cost of changing a television commercial. (Recall from the prior chapter that the average cost of producing a 30-second TV commercial exceeds $300,000.)

5. *Efficiency*. Direct mail makes it possible to direct communication efforts only to a highly targeted group, such as the 200,000 consumers who received mailings for the Saab 9-5. The cost efficiency resulting from such targeting is considerable in comparison to mass-marketing efforts.

An alleged disadvantage of direct mail is its *expense.* On a cost-per-thousand (CPM) basis, direct mail *is* more expensive than other media. For example, the CPM for a particular direct mailing may be as high as $200–$300, whereas a magazine's CPM might be as low as $4. However, compared with other media, direct mail is much less wasteful and will usually produce the highest percentage of responses. Thus, on a *cost-per-order basis,* direct mail is often *less expensive* and a better bargain.

Perhaps the major problem with direct mail is that many people consider it excessively *intrusive and invasive of privacy.* Americans are accustomed to receiving massive quantities of direct mail (on average, American households receive 12.5 pieces of direct mail each week, a third of which is trashed without being read[11]) and so have been "trained" to accept the voluminous amount of direct mail we receive. It is not the amount of direct mail that concerns most people, but rather the fact that virtually any business or other organization that has a product, service, or idea to promote can readily obtain their names and addresses.

Who Uses Direct-Mail Advertising?   As noted earlier, direct mail used to be restricted to fairly specialized businesses—book publishers, record clubs, and so on. But now all types of marketers use direct mail as a strategically important advertising medium. Seventy-seven percent of U.S. companies reported using direct mail in a survey conducted by the Gallup Organization.[12] *Business Week* magazine claims (albeit with some hyperbole) that marketers of all types of consumer goods "are turning from the TV box to the mailbox."[13] Some automobile manufacturers, for example, budget as much as 10 percent of their advertising expenditures to direct mail.[14]

www.pg.com

Both business-to-business companies and marketers of consumer packaged goods have turned increasingly to database marketing and direct mailing as an advertising option.

Packaged-goods companies such as Philip Morris, RJR Nabisco, Ralston Purina, Adolph Coors, Kraft, Gerber Products, Sara Lee, Quaker Oats, Sandoz Consumer, and Procter & Gamble are some of the primary users of database marketing and direct mailings.[15] Product categories that most frequently use databases and direct mailings include beverages, cigarettes, liquor, pet products, lotions/creams, fresh/canned meats and poultry, diet products, fragrances, and vitamins. Direct mailing by these firms is especially valuable when introducing new brands. For example, P&G sometimes uses the mail to distribute samples of new brands. A typical mailing includes: (1) a product sample, (2) attractive coupons to encourage consumers to make a brand purchase following their sample usage, and (3) detailed consumer surveys that provide P&G with names and addresses for its database along with valuable information regarding respondents' purchases of other product categories and brands marketed by P&G.

Why the Trend toward Direct Mailing? At least four factors account for the widespread use of direct mail by all types of marketers. First, the *rising expense of television advertising* along with increased audience fragmentation have led many advertisers to reduce investments in television advertising. Second, as noted earlier, direct mailing enables *unparalleled targeting* of messages to desired prospects. Why? Because, according to one expert, it is "a lot better to talk to 20,000 prospects than 2 million suspects."[16] Third, increased emphasis on *measurable advertising results* has encouraged advertisers to use the medium—namely, direct mail—that most clearly identifies how many prospects purchased the advertised product. Fourth, *consumers are responsive*—surveys indicate that Americans like mail advertisements. For example, Louis Harris & Associates learned that 40 percent of consumers would be "very or somewhat upset" if they could not get mail offers or catalogs.[17]

www.nestle.com

www.heinz.com

In addition to the above reasons for direct mail's surge, this medium also provides marketers with a valuable means for *offsetting competitors' marketing efforts.* For example, the USA Carnation division of Nestlé was faced with a competitive challenge from Heinz, which was introducing its brand of Reward dog food and spending $10 million in introductory advertising and promotions. To blunt this brand introduction, which assuredly would have stolen share from Carnation's own brand, Mighty Dog, Carnation delivered coupons via direct mail for Mighty Dog to user households two weeks prior to Reward's launch. The coupons were of high value and also included a proof-of-purchase premium offer to create purchase continuity. The coupons were mailed to more than 525,000 households. The coupon-redemption rate was an extremely high 6.7 percent, and the premium offer obtained a 13 percent redemption rate, both of which are far above typical redemption rates. The result was that Mighty Dog's share loss to Reward was minimal. Carnation was able to blunt Heinz's brand introduction for a total expenditure of only $400,000.[18]

The Role of Databases

Successful direct mailing necessitates the availability of huge computer databases and the *addressability* inherent in these databases.[19] That is, databases enable contacts with present or prospective customers who can be accessed, or addressed, by companies whose databases contain mailing addresses or telephone numbers. In general, an *address* is "[a]nything that locates the customer uniquely in time and space in a database, so that responses, marketing actions, and respondents can be matched."[20] Database advertising, in comparison to broadcast advertising, does not deal with customers as a mass but rather creates individual relationships with each customer or prospective customer. The following analogy aptly pits addressable media, such as direct mail, against broadcast media:

Broadcast media send communications; addressable media send and receive. Broadcasting targets its audience much as a battleship shells a distant island into submission; addressable media initiate conversations.[21]

Database Assets.   An up-to-date database provides firms with a number of assets, including the ability to:

1. Direct marketing and advertising efforts to those people who represent the best prospects for the offering;
2. Offer varied messages to different groups of customers;
3. Create long-term relationships with customers;
4. Enhance marketing communications productivity; and
5. Calculate the lifetime value of a customer or prospect.[22]

Because of the importance of customer lifetime value, the following section will focus exclusively on this last database asset.

Lifetime Value Analysis.   A key feature of database marketing is the need to consider each address contained in a database from a lifetime-value perspective. That is, each present or prospective customer is viewed as not just an address but rather as a *long-term asset.* **Customer lifetime value** is the *net present value (NPV)* of the profit that a company stands to realize on the average new customer during a given number of years.[23] This concept is best illustrated using the data in Table 13.1.[24]

Assume that a small retailer has a database of 1,000 customers (the intersection of row *A* and the Year 1 column in Table 13.1). The analysis examines the net present value of each customer over a five-year period. Row *B*, the *retention rate,* indicates the likelihood that people will remain customers of this particular retailer during a five-year period. Hence, 40 percent of 1,000 customers in Year 1 will continue to be customers in Year 2, or, in other words, there will be 400 of the initial 1,000 customers remaining in Year 2 (see intersection of row *A* and the Year 2 column). Forty-five percent of these 400 customers, or 180 customers, will remain into Year 3, and so on.

TABLE 13.1

Customer Lifetime Value

	YEAR 1	YEAR 2	YEAR 3	YEAR 4	YEAR 5
Revenue					
A Customers	1,000	400	180	90	50
B Retention rate	40%	45%	50%	55%	60%
C Average yearly sales	$150	$150	$150	$150	$150
D Total revenue	$150,000	$60,000	$27,000	$13,500	$7,500
Costs					
E Cost %	50%	50%	50%	50%	50%
F Total costs	$75,000	$30,000	$13,500	$6,750	$3,750
Profits					
G Gross profit	$75,000	$30,000	$13,500	$6,750	$3,750
H Discount rate	1	1.2	1.44	1.73	2.07
I NPV profit	$75,000	$25,000	$9,375	$3,902	$1,812
J Cumulative NPV profit	$75,000	$100,000	$109,375	$113,277	$115,088
K Lifetime value (NPV) per customer	$75.00	$100.00	$109.38	$113.28	$115.09

Row *C* indicates that the *average yearly sales* in Years 1 through 5 are constant at $150. That is, customers on average spend $150 at this particular retail establishment. Thus, the *total revenue,* row *D,* in each of the five years is simply the product of rows *A* and *C.* For example, the 1,000 customers in Year 1 who spend on average $150 produce $150,000 of total revenue.

Row *E* reflects the *cost* of selling merchandise to the store's customers. For simplification it is assumed that the cost is 50 percent of revenue. *Total costs* in each year, row *F,* are thus calculated by simply multiplying the values in rows *D* and *E.*

Gross profit, row *G,* is calculated by subtracting total costs (row *F*) from total revenues (row *D*). The *discount rate,* row *H,* is a critical component of net present value analysis and requires some discussion. This rate reflects the idea that money received in future years is not equivalent in value to money received today. This is because money received today, say $100, can be immediately invested and begin earning interest. Over time, the $100 grows more valuable as interest accumulates and compounds. Delaying the receipt of money thus means that one gives up the opportunity to earn profit. This being the case, $100 received in the future, say in three years, is worth less than the same amount received today. Some adjustment is needed to equate the value of money received at different times. This adjustment is called a *discount rate* and can be expressed as follows:

$$D = (1 + i)^n$$

where *D* equals the discount rate; *i* equals the interest rate; and *n* equals the number of years before the money will be received. The discount rate given in row *H* of Table 13.1 assumes an interest rate of 20 percent. Thus, the discount rate in Year 3 is 1.44, because the retailer will have to wait two years (from Year 1) to receive the profit that will be earned in Year 3. That is,

$$(1 + .2)^2 = 1.44$$

The *net present value (NPV) profit,* row *I,* is determined by simply taking the reciprocal of the discount rate (i.e., 1 ÷ D) and multiplying the gross profit, row *G,* by that reciprocal. For example, in Year 3, the reciprocal of 1.44 is 0.694, which implies that the present value of $1 received two years later is only about $0.69. Thus, the NPV of the $13,500 gross profit to be earned in Year 3 is $9,375. (You should perform the calculation for Years 4 and 5 to assure that you understand the derivation of NPV.)

The *cumulative NPV profit,* row *J,* simply sums the NPV profits across the years. This summation reveals that the cumulative NPV profit to our hypothetical retailer, who had 1,000 customers in Year 1, of whom 50 remain after five years, is $115,088. Finally, row *K,* the *lifetime value (NPV) per customer,* shows the average worth of each of the 1,000 people who were customers of our hypothetical retailer in Year 1. The average lifetime value of each of these customers expressed as NPV over a five-year period is thus $115.09.

Now that you have an understanding of the concept of lifetime value analysis, we can turn to more strategic concerns. The key issue is this: What can a database marketer do to enhance the average customer's lifetime value? There are five ways to augment lifetime value:[25]

1. *Retention rate.* The greater the number of customers and the longer they are retained, the greater will be the lifetime value. It therefore behooves marketers and advertisers to focus on retention rather than just acquisition. Database marketing is ideally suited for this purpose, because it enables regular communication with customers (through newsletters, frequency programs, and so on) and relationship building.

2. *Referral rate.* Positive relations created with existing customers can influence others to become customers through the positive word of mouth expressed by satisfied customers.

3. *Sales volume.* Existing customers can be encouraged to purchase more, and the more loyal customers are, the more they will buy.

4. *Direct costs.* By altering the channel of distribution via direct marketing efforts, a firm may be able to cut costs and hence increase profit margins.

5. *Marketing communication costs.* Effective DBM can lead to meaningful reductions in marketing communication expenses because direct advertising often is more productive than broadcast advertising.

Two General Types of Mailing Lists.   Success with direct mail depends on the quality of mailing lists contained in a company's database. Mailing lists of past or prospective customers enable direct marketers to pinpoint the best candidates for future purchases. One observer has aptly dubbed mailing lists "windows to our pocketbooks."[26] There are two broad categories of lists: internal (house lists) and external (public lists).

House lists are based on a company's own internal list of present or prospective customers. For example, Blockbuster has a list of over 40 million customers in its database. Because house lists contain the names of customers who previously responded to a company's offering, they are generally more valuable than external lists.

There are various means by which companies acquire names and addresses for their databases. For retailers (such as Blockbuster) and direct marketers, it is simply a matter of saving the names of past customers. The situation is more complicated, however, for manufacturers who market their products through retail outlets. With creativity, they too can generate databases. Following are some methods used to obtain database information:[27]

www.blackanddecker.com

- *In-pack promotions.* When companies include promotional offers in packages, customers must identify their names and addresses in order to receive the promotions. These names are entered into the marketer's database for future contact. Black & Decker built an impressive database by offering free vacuum cleaner bags to its Dust Buster purchasers. Lea & Perrin built a list of their sauce buyers by offering free recipe books.[28]
- *Warranty cards.* When a customer mails a completed warranty card for, say, a new television, the manufacturer has another address for its database.

www.levis.com

- *Registration programs.* Hardware manufacturers often have consumers complete a registration card that reveals the date of product purchase and also provides classification information about the purchaser. Levi Strauss & Co. borrowed this practice by placing registration cards in every pair of Levi's jeans sold in the United States.[29]
- *Rebate programs.* To receive rebates, customers supply information that the database builder enters for future contact.
- *Telemarketing.* Names and addresses can be requested from toll-free callers and entered into the database.

Many companies, especially those in the catalog business, segregate their house lists by the *recency (R)* of a customer's purchase, the *frequency (F)* of purchases, the *monetary value (M)* of each purchase, and the type of products purchased. Companies typically assign point values to accounts based on these classifications. Each company has its own customized procedure for point assignment (i.e., its own R-F-M formula), but in every case more points are assigned to more recent, more frequent, and more expensive purchases. The R-F-M system offers tremendous opportunities for database manipulation and direct-mail targeting. For example, a company might choose to send out free catalogs only to those accounts whose point totals exceed a certain amount. In addition to R-F-M information, house lists often categorize customers by buyographic, geographic, demographic, and perhaps psychographic characteristics.

The other type of mailing list is the **external list,** which comes in two forms. The first, *house lists of other companies,* is bought by a firm to promote its own products. These lists are effective because they comprise the names of people who have responded to another company's direct-response offer. The greater the similarity of the products offered by both the buyer and the seller of the list, the greater the likelihood that the purchased list will be effective.

For example, imagine a company that markets coverings that protect automobile exteriors from exposure to the elements. New automobile purchasers who do not have a garage are the best market for this company's products. The coverings marketer could purchase and merge mailing lists from automobile manufacturers and rental companies and specify names of only those buyers who have purchased an automobile within, say, the past six months and who rent an apartment rather than own their own home. Additionally, this marketer, using geodemographic segmentation (as discussed in Chapter 4), could identify certain geographic areas that are known to consist of smaller homes without garages and send blanket mailings to all households in these areas.

Compiled lists, the second type of external list, include lists compiled by a company for its own purposes or lists purchased from another company that specializes in list compilation. The first type of compiled list is illustrated by a direct-marketing effort at Kimberly-Clark, makers of Huggies disposable diapers. Each year, Kimberly-Clark's database developers identify by name 75 percent of the approximately 3 to 4 million new mothers in the United States. (The names are obtained from hospitals and doctors.) Kimberly-Clark sends the new mothers personalized letters, educational literature about caring for a new baby, and cents-off coupons for Huggies.[30] Huggies' database program has been extremely effective, resulting in market share growth and an accompanying decrease in media expenses.[31]

The other type of compiled list comes from businesses that specialize in compiling lists and selling them to other companies. List compilers are typically involved in businesses that give them access to millions of consumer names and vital statistics. For example, the Lifestyle Selector, a service of National Demographics and Lifestyles, Inc., is a data-list service provided by a company that originally handled processing of warranty cards for dozens of manufacturers. For each of the millions of names on file, the database contains 10 demographic characteristics (age, sex, education, etc.) and 50 lifestyle characteristics (sports participation, travel activities, etc.).

The Lifestyle Selector enables a direct-mail marketer to order a list containing names and addresses that have been identified based on any combination of lifestyle and demographic characteristics. A manufacturer of men's sporting goods, for example, would be able to request a list matching its desired target market—for example, people between the ages of 35 and 54 who play golf and enjoy fashion clothing; who are business executives, professionals, or technicians earning $50,000 or more annually; and who possess an American Express credit card.

Another example is the Lists-on-Disc database of millions of businesses available on a single CD-ROM disc. The list is compiled by a company called American Business Information, which records company names and addresses from nearly 5,000 telephone directories from every town and city in the United States. Users can tap into all businesses contained on the CD or selectively choose companies based on geographic, business type, or other pertinent determinations.

Compiled lists play an important role for marketers of packaged-good products that are less able than business-to-business marketers to maintain customer lists. Compiled lists are not as desirable as house lists, however, because they do not contain information about the willingness of a person to purchase by mail. The characteristics of the members of compiled lists may also be too diversified to serve the purposes of the direct mailer. However, some compiled lists are put together with considerable care and may serve the direct mailer's specific needs.

C ATALOG MARKETING

Catalog marketing, though a form of direct mail, deserves a separate discussion due to its distinctiveness. For clarity, it should be noted that there are four types of catalogs: (1) *retail catalogs* designed by retailers to increase store traffic; (2) *full-line merchandise catalogs* (e.g., JC Penney's catalog); (3) *consumer specialty catalogs* (e.g., the L.L. Bean sporting goods and ready-to-wear catalog); and (4) *industrial specialty catalogs,* which are used by business-to-business marketers to reach smaller customers while freeing up the sales force's time for larger, more promising accounts.

The greatest growth in cataloging has been consumer specialty catalogs. Name a product, and at least one company is probably marketing that item via catalog—food items (cheese, candy, pastry, steaks), clothing, furniture—the list goes on and on. New catalogs are regularly introduced. Levi Strauss & Co. recently introduced a catalog aimed primarily at teenagers.[32] Limited Too, a division of giant retailer Limited Inc., introduced a clothing catalog targeted to preteen girls.[33]

www.limited.com

The growth rate for catalog sales in the United States has exceeded that enjoyed by fixed-site retailers. Various factors account for this. From the *marketer's perspective,* catalog selling provides an efficient and effective way to reach prime prospects. From the *consumer's perspective:* (1) catalogs save time because people do not have to find parking spaces and deal with in-store crowds; (2) catalog buying appeals to consumers who are fearful of shopping due to concerns about crime; (3) catalogs allow people the convenience of making purchase decisions at their leisure and away from the pressure of a retail store; (4) the availability of toll-free 800 numbers, credit-card purchasing, and liberal return policies make it easy for people to order from catalogs; (5) consumers are confident in purchasing from catalogs because merchandise quality and prices are often comparable to what is available in stores; and (6) guarantees are attractive.

Illustrative of this last point, consider the policy of L.L. Bean, the famous retailer from Maine:

> *All of our products are guaranteed to give 100 percent satisfaction in every way. Return anything purchased from us at any time if it proves otherwise. We will replace it, refund your purchase price or credit your credit card, as you wish. We do not want you to have anything from L.L. Bean that is not completely satisfactory.*

Although catalog marketing is pervasive, signs indicate it has reached the mature life-cycle stage: First, industry observers note that the novelty of catalog scanning has worn off for many consumers. Second, as is typically the case when a product or service reaches the maturity stage, the costs of catalog marketing have increased dramatically. A primary reason is that firms have incurred the expenses of developing more attractive catalogs and compiling better mailing lists in an effort to outperform their competitors. Costs have been further strained by third-class postal rate increases in recent years and sharp increases in paper prices.

Some catalog companies have responded to the slowdown by sending out even more catalogs than they mailed in the past. Other companies have scaled back their efforts. Many marginal companies have dropped out, which invariably is the case when an industry reaches maturity. Many catalog companies have found it unprofitable to remain in the catalog business, but the best companies continue to flourish. In their efforts to achieve steady growth, some U.S. catalogers have expanded to markets overseas, and European catalogers have made inroads into the U.S. market (see the *Global Focus* on international catalog expansion).

GLOBAL FOCUS: INTERNATIONAL EXPANSION BY CATALOGERS

www.llbean.com

www.jcrew.com

www.landsend.com

www.eddiebauer.com

International expansion is a major initiative on the part of many U.S. catalogers, including L.L. Bean, J. Crew, Lands' End, Eddie Bauer Inc., Patagonia Inc., and Spiegel. For example, Lands' End has opened a distribution center in Japan and mass mails catalogs to consumers in that country. Lands' End also is actively pursuing German consumers, which is understandable in view of the fact that mail order accounts for nearly 6 percent of overall retail sales in Germany compared with 3 percent in the United States. L.L. Bean mails catalogs to over 100 countries, although nearly 70 percent of its international sales comes from Japan alone. Achieving success in international markets requires that U.S. catalog companies undertake aggressive marketing communications backed up with high-quality offerings, provide reliable and dependable deliv-ery, and achieve high customer-service levels. Catalog companies, just like marketers in every other endeavor, are challenged by the need to enhance brand equity by creating name awareness in countries where they are just beginning to establish an identity and building strong and favorable brand associations among con-sumers in these countries.

European catalogers have also intensified their marketing efforts in the attractive U.S. market. The strongest European cata-logers are huge concerns that offer a vast array of merchandise—everything from clothing and furniture to consumer electronics and appliances. U.S. catalogers, by comparison, tend to concentrate on specialty lines of merchandise. European catalogs are massive, ranging in size from 700 to 1,300 pages. Most European catalog companies are experienced international marketers. For instance, the French cataloger La Redoute earns about one-third of its sales in 12 other countries. Otton Versand, a German cataloger, earns al-most one-half of its sales outside Germany.

Source: Gregory A. Patterson, "U.S. Catalogers Test International Waters," *The Wall Street Journal,* April 19, 1994, B1; Cacilie Rohwedder, "U.S. Cata-log Firms Target Avid Consumers Overseas," *The Wall Street Journal Inter-active Edition,* January 6, 1998.

OUTBOUND AND INCOMING TELEMARKETING

Telephone marketing is *the* dominant form of direct marketing. **Telemarketing** entails both *outbound* telephone usage to sell products over the phone or perform other marketing functions (e.g., arranging test drives for the Saab 9-5) and incoming telephone marketing efforts that are directed at taking orders and servicing customers.

Outbound Telemarketing

As noted earlier, many companies use the telephone to support or even replace their con-ventional sales forces. Telemarketing uses *outbound calls* from telephone salespersons for purposes of: (1) opening new accounts, (2) qualifying advertising leads, and (3) servicing existing business, including reorders and customer service. Outbound telemarketing is used in conjunction with advertising, direct mail, catalog sales, and face-to-face selling.

Outbound telemarketing's versatility applies to both consumer-oriented products and business-to-business marketing. In the consumer arena, outbound telemarketing played a crucial role in the marketing efforts for the Saab 9-5 (*Opening Vignette*). IBM is an effec-tive B-to-B user of telemarketing to cover its small to medium-sized accounts, generate in-cremental sales, enhance the productivity of traditional sales representatives via the leads and information that it provides, and ensure customer satisfaction and buying convenience. IBM has a fully integrated system of mail, catalog, and inbound and outbound telephone activity for its hardware, software, supplies, and services. The strategy is to transform a prospect or a dormant account into an active account and then to service the account with as little in-person sales contact as possible.[34]

www.ibm.com

Who Should Use Outbound Telemarketing?

Who Should Use Outbound Telemarketing?   Telemarketing is not appropriate for all sales organizations. The following eight factors should be considered when evaluating the suitability of introducing a telephone sales force.[35]

1. An initial consideration is an evaluation of *the importance of face-to-face contact;* the more essential it is, the less appropriate is outbound telemarketing.

2. A second consideration is *geographical concentration.* Telephone selling may represent an attractive alternative to in-person selling if customers are highly dispersed; if, however, customers are heavily concentrated (such as apparel makers in Manhattan or automobile manufacturers in Detroit), minimal travel time is required and personal selling is probably preferable.

3. *Economic considerations* involving average order size and total potential should be estimated to determine the cost effectiveness of in-person sales. In cases of small and marginal accounts—such as in the previously noted case of IBM—customers may be served more economically by telephone.

4. A fourth area for evaluation is *customer decision criteria.* Telephone sales may be sufficient if price, delivery, and other quantitative criteria are paramount, but in-person sales may be essential in instances where product quality, dealer reputation, and service are uppermost in importance.

5. A fifth factor is the number of *decision makers* typically involved in purchasing a company's product. Face-to-face contact is typically necessary when several decision makers are involved—for example, when an industrial engineer, a purchasing agent, and a financial representative all contribute to a purchase decision.

6. Another consideration is the *nature of the purchase.* Routine purchases (such as office supplies) can be handled easily by phone, whereas purchases of more complex products will likely require face-to-face interactions.

7. The *status of the major decision maker* is a seventh consideration. The telephone is acceptable for buyers, purchase agents, and engineers but probably not for owners, presidents, and vice presidents.

8. A final consideration is an *evaluation of the specific selling tasks* that telemarketing is or is not capable of performing. For example, telephone representatives may be particularly effective for prospecting and postsale follow-ups, whereas in-person sales effort is needed for the intervening sales task—preapproach, approach, presentation, objection handling, and closing.

These eight factors make it apparent that telephone selling is only appropriate and effective in certain situations. Systematic application of this eight-step process should enable a company to determine whether and to what extent telemarketing is appropriate for serving its customers.

Incoming Telemarketing

Incoming telephone marketing includes both the toll-free (800) number option and the Dial-It (900) number service, which is not a free call for the user.

Toll-Free (800 Numbers).   Toll-free numbers (more commonly called "800 numbers") are virtually everywhere. Every time you open a magazine, turn on the television, or pick up a newspaper, you read or hear, "Call 1-800-XXX-XXXX." An 800-number telecommunication program uses an incoming WATS (wide area telecommunication service) telephone system to encourage potential customers to phone a publicized number (a number with an 800 or 888 prefix) in response to media advertising or other marketing communications. This 800 number, correctly inserted in advertisements, can be used by motivated, self-qualified consumers to request product or service information, place direct orders, express complaints or grievances, request coupons or other sales-promotion materials, and inquire about the nearest dealers or outlets. For example, the consumer receives a direct mailing from Butch Long's Steaks of Nebraska and, attracted by the enticing offer, places an order via the 800 number that is prominently displayed (see Figure 13.5).

Customer-service representatives who receive 800 calls can provide immediate responses to requests for merchandise and product information and can handle complaints. Additionally, representatives can record callers' names and addresses to initiate immediate follow-ups by sending promotional materials. Also, the effectiveness of an advertising campaign can be measured quickly. The advent of sophisticated *call-center technology* (called ACDs for automatic call distributor) has substantially facilitated and improved

Prominent Display
of 800 Number

16 quarter-pound
Butch's Best
Beef Burgers
FREE!
One bite and you'll know why
they're the best!

Reusable
thermal
picnic chest
FREE!
Perfect for family outings,
car trips and more!

4 pairs of
quality stainless
steel scissors
FREE!
The perfect scissors for
every job. Always at hand!

Get this
full-featured
desk-top
calculator FREE!
• Larger keys. Quality feel.
• Easy-to-read display face.
**Yours when you
beat the deadline!**

incoming telephone service. Call centers involve hardware and software technology that efficiently receives and routes calls to telephone representatives. Call-center technology also tracks statistics such as how many calls come into the office at any time, customers' average time on hold, the amount of time sales reps are idle, and so on. This is invaluable information for determining how many representatives to have available at any particular time and results in better customer service and higher sales performance.[36] It is estimated that U.S. companies spent about $1.4 billion on call-center technology in 1997, and that investments in call centers are growing dramatically to the point where total investment by 2002 is expected to be nearly $9 billion.[37]

Toll-free numbers are widely used because they are valuable adjuncts to marketing communications programs. Along with their distinct benefits, 800 numbers also present potential problems. One notable problem arises from improperly trained or unskilled 800 service communicators. A second potential problem is that there may be an insufficient number of lines to handle incoming calls. Third, failure to integrate the 800 number carefully into a company's marketing program can be extremely wasteful. Advertising, sales promotions, and 800 numbers need to be coordinated carefully to achieve their maximum, synergistic effects.

To implement a successful incoming telemarketing program, companies must assure that prospective customers' information needs are fulfilled. Following are eight tips to which any direct marketer should adhere when fulfilling prospects' requests for information:

1. Make sure the person answering the phone is knowledgeable about your company and products.

2. Get the information out fast. That is, if the prospect requests additional information in the form of a brochure or videocassette, the requested item should be mailed within a day or two.

3. The fulfillment envelope must say "Requested Information Enclosed" or the equivalent. There is a good chance the mailing will be trashed if such a *red flag* is not provided.

4. Sequence the contents of the mailing in a logical order, simplifying the reader's task rather than making him or her work for the information that is needed.

5. Personalize the letter.

6. Reinforce the original offer or make a new one.

7. Include a *bounceback* (typically a postage-paid card or envelope) for additional dialogue and database building.

8. Do telemarketing follow-up.[38]

www.att.com

Dial-It (900 Numbers).   The Dial-It, or 900 number, service was introduced by AT&T to permit callers, who pay a fee, to phone a central number and register an opinion on a particular issue. The 900 service is the only national communication medium that can accept simultaneous calls by large numbers of people at a flat rate. The first major use of the Dial-It service was during the Carter–Reagan presidential debate in 1980, when over 700,000 people spent 50 cents each to call a 900 number and register their opinions about who won the debate. Since then, the use of 900-number telemedia activity has increased substantially.

Sleazy sex operations, contest scams, and other unscrupulous efforts have dominated 900-number usage; nonetheless, there are legitimate uses for 900-number technology.[39] One use is to update customers about services that are subject to frequent changes. For example, the American Bankers Association sponsored a 900-number service to inform callers of the most recent interest rates on various financial instruments. Dial-It numbers also are used as sources of sports information, weather updates, and travel information.

Some companies have used 900 numbers in concert with sweepstakes offers. For example, Revlon ran a sweepstakes as part of a freestanding insert (FSI) carried in newspapers. Recipients of the FSI were instructed to call a 900 number and recite a four-digit code to learn if they were instant winners.

Telephone Marketing under Attack

The dramatic increase in the use of telephone marketing has inevitably included some untoward practices. Consumers are besieged by calls from telemarketers at undesirable times, particularly during the dinner hour. More extreme are telemarketing scams that deceive credulous individuals into thinking they are dealing with legitimate businesspeople. Vitamin-pill rip-offs, travel scams, fake AIDS cures, misleading stock "tips," and phony art reproductions are just some of the fraudulent telemarketing practices in recent years. It is estimated that American consumers lose more than $40 billion annually to telephone scam artists, mostly through phony investment schemes and contests.[40]

Many consumers are disgusted with all forms of telephone marketing except 800 numbers. Likewise, in response to consumer complaints, government regulators have taken action to try to prevent further abuses. Telephone marketers will eventually have to clean up their acts or suffer reprisals from irate customers and regulators. The Federal Trade Commission in 1995 introduced the Telemarketing Sales Rule (TSR) to regulate against untoward telemarketing practices. The key provisions of the rule are listed in Table 13.2.[41] In addition to government regulation of telemarketing practices, it is pertinent to note that it has become progressively more difficult for telemarketers to reach prospective customers because norms for answering the telephone have changed in recent years. The *IMC Focus* elaborates on this point.

TABLE 13.2   **Key Provisions of the Telemarketing Sales Rule**

Telemarketers must:
- Initially identify themselves, their business, and the goods or services they are selling to the customer.
- Tell customers the odds of winning any prizes while explaining that no purchase or payment is necessary to win them.
- Clearly and completely explain their offerings and their price(s), payment terms, and the customer's financial commitment by placing a telephone order.
- Obtain and tape record customer's express oral authorization for a sale before checking account debiting.
- Maintain complete employment records; all advertising, marketing, and promotional materials (including telemarketing scripts); and for contests, lists of the names and addresses of all prize winners and descriptions of those prizes valued at $25 or more.
- Identify, maintain lists of, and comply with rules regarding customers who request that they not be contacted again by telemarketers.

Telemarketers must not:
- Assist or facilitate deceptive or abusive telemarketing acts.
- Launder credit cards (i.e., illegally use credit information obtained from one sale toward another unauthorized transaction).
- Use threats, intimidation, or profane or obscene language toward customers.
- Call customers before 8 A.M. or after 9 P.M. (local time zones).

IMC Focus: The Phone Rings but Nobody Answers

Throughout much of the history of the telephone, people welcomed the ringing of their phones. In virtually a Pavlovian-conditioning sense, the sound of a ringing phone signaled a call from a good friend or loved one and a welcome intrusion into lives less hectic than those now experienced by most people at the turn of the century. Social norms about telephone calling and answering developed whereby people refrained from calling at inopportune times (e.g., during the dinner hour) and the receiver felt obligated to answer the phone as quickly as possible. Now in a world of frequent interruptions from unwelcome callers who phone at inappropriate times, impose themselves on the receiver, and who don't understand the word "No," the norms of telephone receivership have changed. Many people no longer are "slaves" to the telephone. With answering machines, voice mail, and Caller ID units, people are screening calls to an unprecedented degree.

According to the marketing-research firm Roper Starch Worldwide, two-thirds of U.S. households have answering machines and fully half use them to screen calls. Other people simply refuse to answer their phones or take them off the hook during certain hours. Needless to say, such behavior complicates the life of the telemarketer by requiring more calls to reach fewer people. Yet, telemarketers often have been their own worst enemies. Their intrusions have effectively trained people to refuse answering their phones. The future of telemarketing is clearly in doubt as growing numbers of consumers find ways to escape unwanted calls.

Source: Adapted from Christina Duff, "Why Answer the Phone? Odds Are, The Call Wasn't Worth the Bother," *The Wall Street Journal Interactive Edition*, January 14, 1998.

Summary

Direct marketing is the most rapidly growing aspect of marketing activity in the United States. Successful direct mailing necessitates the availability of huge computer databases and their inherent addressability. Direct mail is the dominant direct-marketing advertising medium. Its outstanding advantages are that marketers can target messages to specific market segments and determine success (or failure) virtually immediately. Direct mail also permits greater personalization than mass media advertising and is not subject to the clutter of competing ads such as those that appear in other print and broadcast media. On a cost-per-order basis, direct mail is often less expensive and more efficient than alternative media.

Magazines, newspapers, and television are additional media used by direct marketers. Catalog marketing is a form of direct marketing that has enjoyed spectacular success. Factors that account for this growth (which is now abating) include consumer time savings, buying freedom, greater disposable income, and increased confidence in mail-order buying.

Two forms of telephone marketing—in which the telephone is the major direct-marketing medium—are practiced. One, outbound telemarketing, involves calls from telephone salespersons to customers and prospects; the other, incoming telemarketing involves handling inbound calls for orders, inquiries, and complaints. The growth of outbound telemarketing is attributable in large part to the enormous expense of in-person sales contacts, which exceed $250 on average. Telemarketing can be used to support or even replace a conventional sales force.

Incoming telemarketing activities include the well-known toll-free 800-number programs and the lesser-known Dial-It, or 900-number, service. Toll-free programs have experienced tremendous growth, recently aided by the sophisticated call-center technology that efficiently distributes calls to telephone sales reps and tracks a variety of valuable call statistics. Dial-It (900 numbers) was introduced initially by AT&T to permit callers to pay a fee for a phone call to register an opinion on a particular issue. Many unscrupulous operators began using 900 numbers shortly thereafter. Nonetheless, there are potential uses of 900 numbers by legitimate telephone marketers.

Discussion Questions

1. Explain the differences among direct marketing, direct-response advertising, and direct mail.

2. Why has direct marketing enjoyed such rapid growth in recent years?

3. Your company, Computer Supplies, Inc., sells computer paper, ribbons, diskettes, and other items to thousands of business and nonbusiness organizations. Because most orders are relatively small, selling costs are extremely high relative to revenues. The vice president of sales is evaluating the implementation of an outbound telemarketing program directed at all accounts whose annual purchases amount to less than $10,000. What factors should the VP consider? Be specific.

4. Refer to the ad for the Polycom SoundStation teleconferencing system (Figure 13.4). Assume the manufacturer of this product chose to use direct mail to market the product in addition to advertising it in magazines. Explain how you, as vice president of marketing for this company, would acquire a mailing list. What characteristics of businesses would you select in generating the list? Be specific.

5. John Deere, a major company in the lawn-tractor business, includes an 800 number at the bottom of its advertisement. A relatively unknown competitor, Kubota, includes this statement at the bottom of its ads: "To learn more about our tractors and other power products, please write Kubota Tractor Corporation" and supplies its address. How responsive do you think consumers would be in writing for more information? How could a company like Kubota justify not installing an 800-number service?

6. What should government regulators do to prevent telemarketing abuses? What kind of prohibitions, if any, should be placed on telemarketing?

7. Assume you are a direct marketer for a line of merchandise imprinted with major-university logos. These items are targeted to the fans and supporters of university athletic programs. Detail how you would compile a mailing list. Use your college or university for illustration.

8. Conduct five to 10 interviews with nonstudent adults regarding their personal experiences with and evaluations of telemarketing. Are they hassled often? Do they mind having telephone salespeople call them? What specific complaints do they have?

9. Go through a recent consumer magazine and list every advertiser that employs a toll-free 800 number. Describe the specific function that the 800 number is apparently intended to serve for each advertiser.

10. Following is a lifetime value analysis framework similar to that presented in the chapter. Perform the calculations necessary to complete row K.

REVENUE	YEAR 1	YEAR 2	YEAR 3	YEAR 4	YEAR 5
A Customers	2,000	____	____	____	____
B Retention rate	30 percent	40 percent	55 percent	65 percent	70 percent
C Average yearly sales	$250	$250	$250	$250	$250
D Total revenue	____	____	____	____	____
Costs					
E Cost percentage	50 percent	50 percent	50 percent	50 percent	50 percent
F Total costs	____	____	____	____	____
Profits					
G Gross profit	____	____	____	____	____
H Discount rate	1	1.15	____	____	____
I NPV profit	____	____	____	____	____
J Cumulative NPV profit	____	____	____	____	____
K Lifetime value (NPV)	____	____	____	____	____

*I*nternet Exercises

1. You may have noticed that Web sites seem to "know" more and more about you each time you visit. For instance, you may bookmark a popular site such as www.cdnow.com or http://home.microsoft.com and find that the computer on the other end knows not only that you've been there before, but exactly when you last visited, what you were looking at the last time you visited, and so forth. Most Web sites accomplish this with HTTP cookies. A cookie is a small piece of information that's sent to your browser along with an HTML page when you access a particular site. When a cookie arrives, your browser generally saves this information to your hard drive; when you return to that site, some of the stored information will be sent back to the Web server, along with your new request. The Web site www.cookiecentral.com is dedicated to explaining exactly what cookies are and what they can do. Visit this site and present a discussion on how cookies can be, and are being, used to compile direct marketing lists. Additionally, comment on the ethical debate surrounding the use of cookies.

2. Well-known retailers such as L.L. Bean, Gap, and Eddie Bauer are helping to legitimize on-line shopping in the minds of consumers by taking their popular catalogs to the Internet. Strictly speaking, an on-line catalog would not constitute direct marketing since it is not addressed to any particular target. However, some retailers have turned on-line catalogs into direct marketing ventures by tying on-line purchasing to particular targets. For example, during the 1997 holiday season, J. Crew offered a 20% discount to AOL subscribers making an on-line purchase. What are some other ways an on-line retailer could engage in direct marketing?

3. What is your overall evaluation of Saab 9-5's Web site? What do you like and dislike about the site? What additions or deletions would you make if you were the master of this site?

Chapter Thirteen Endnotes

1. *Fact Book on Direct Response Marketing* (New York: Direct Marketing Association, Inc., 1982), xxiii. Italics added.

2. For an insightful and thorough discussion of interactive home shopping (IHS), see Joseph Alba, John Lynch, Barton Weitz, Chris Janiszewski, Richard Lutz, Alan Sawyer, and Stacy Wood, "Interactive Home Shopping: Consumer, Retailer, and Manufacturer Incentives to Participate in Electronic Marketplaces," *Journal of Marketing* 61 (July 1997), 38–53.

3. This description is adapted from Don E. Schultz, "The Direct/DataBase Marketing Challenge to Fixed-Location Retailing," in *The Future of U.S. Retailing: An Agenda for the 21st Century,* ed. Robert A. Peterson (New York: Quorum Books, 1992), 165–184.

4. "The DMA Releases 1997 Forecast on DM's Economic Impact," *Direct Connection* (a newsletter of the Direct Marketing Educational Foundation), winter 1997–98, 4.

5. Lester Wunderman, "Excerpts from New Frontiers in Direct Marketing IV," *Direct Connection* (Newsletter of the Direct Marketing Educational Foundation, winter 1993–1994), 6.

6. Jonathan Berry, John Verity, Kathleen Kerwin, and Gail DeGeorge, "A Potent New Tool for Selling: Database Marketing," *Business Week,* September 5, 1994, 56–57.

7. "The DMA Releases 1997 Forecast on DM's Economic Impact."

8. Jack Miller, "Several Factors Converge to Spawn Mail Order's Business-to-Business Sales Growth," *Marketing News,* July 8, 1983, 8.

9. Bob Stone, "For Effective Direct Results," *Advertising Age,* March 28, 1983, M32.

10. These features and the following descriptions are adapted from a brochure prepared by the United States Postal Service. The brochure is undated, but the brochure was sent to me by Greg Whiteman of the USPS in May 1997.

11. George E. Bardenheier, Jr., "More to Database Brand Building than Filling Up a Lot of Mail Boxes," *Brandweek,* May 2, 1994, 20.

12. "P-B Survey: Direct Mail Is First Among Marketers," *Promo,* June 1996, 106.

13. "What Happened to Advertising," *Business Week,* September 23, 1991, 69.

14. Rebecca Fannin, "Detroit's Direct Route," *Marketing and Media Decisions,* February 1989, 41–44.

15. Laura Loro, "Package Goods Expands Database," *Advertising Age,* August 14, 1995, 29.

16. Don Schultz as quoted in Gary Levin, "Going Direct Route," *Advertising Age,* November 18, 1991, 37.

17. Annetta Miller, "My Postman Has a Hernia!" *Newsweek,* June 10, 1991, 41.

18. Glenn Heitsmith, "Database Promotions: Marketers Move Carefully, but Some Are Still Faking It," *Promo,* October 1994, 39, 46.

19. An excellent review of the history of database marketing is provided in Lisa A. Petrison,

20. Robert C. Blattberg, and Paul Wang, "Database Marketing: Past, Present, and Future," *Journal of Direct Marketing* 7 (summer 1993), 27–43.

20. Robert C. Blattberg and John Deighton, "Interactive Marketing: Exploiting the Age of Addressability," *Sloan Management Review* (fall 1991), 5.

21. Ibid.

22. The list of database assets is adapted from the following sources: Blattberg and Deighton, 14; Rob Jackson and Paul Wang, *Strategic Database Marketing* (Lincolnwood, Ill.: NTC Business Books, 1994), 14–15; Stan Rapp and Thomas L. Collins, *MaxiMarketing,* 216–231; Terry G. Vavra, *Aftermarketing* (Homewood, Ill.: Business One Irwin, 1992).

23. Arthur M. Hughes, *Strategic Database Marketing* (Chicago: Probus, 1994), 17.

24. This table and the following discussion are based on Hughes, *Strategic Database Marketing,* 47–50. There are more sophisticated approaches to lifetime value analysis, but this example contains all of the essential elements needed to understand the fundamentals of the approach.

25. Ibid., 17.

26. Robert J. Samuelson, "Computer Communities," *Newsweek,* December 15, 1986, 66.

27. Edward L. Nash, *Database Marketing: The Ultimate Marketing Tool* (New York: McGraw-Hill, 1993), 15–20.

28. Ibid., 18.

29. Jane Hodges and Alic Z. Cuneo, "Levi's Registration Program Will Seek to Build Database," *Advertising Age,* February 24, 1997, 86.

30. Rapp and Collins, *MaxiMarketing,* 50.

31. Lynn G. Coleman, "Data-Base Masters Become King of the Marketplace," *Marketing News,* February 18, 1991, 13.

32. Carol Krol, "Levi Strauss Moves into Mail-Order Marketing," *Advertising Age,* September 14, 1998, 18.

33. Yumiko Ono, "Limited Too Will Blitz Preteens with Catalogs of Their Very Own," *The Wall Street Journal Interactive Edition,* August 25, 1998.

34. This description is an adaptation of remarks from Peter DiSalvo in "Three Telemarketers Tell How to Hire, Train, Organize for This Profitable Direct Medium," *Marketing News,* July 8, 1983, 4.

35. Hubert D. Hennessey, "Matters to Consider before Plunging into Telemarketing," *Marketing News,* July 8, 1983, 2.

36. Alessandra Bianchi, "Lines of Fire: Automated Call Centers Allow for Sophisticated Competition," *The Wall Street Journal Interactive Edition,* June 24, 1998.

37. Ibid. There is a trade association for call centers called the Incoming Calls Management Institute (ICMI). For more information about call centers, contact ICMI at 800-672-6177.

38. Source: James Rosenfield, "Don't Leave Customers Unfulfilled," *Sales & Marketing Management,* August 1995, 78–79.

39. Cyndee Miller, "It's Not Just for Sleaze Anymore: Serious Marketers Want Consumers to Dial 1-900," *Marketing News,* October 15, 1990, 1-2; Scott Hume, "900 Numbers: The Struggle for Respect," *Advertising Age,* February 18, 1991, S1.

40. Chad Rubel, "Stiffer Rules for Telemarketers as U.S. Cracks Down on Fraud," *Marketing News,* February 26, 1996, 1.

41. "New Telemarketing Rules: What You Need to Know," *Promo,* January 1996, 31.

FOURTEEN

Media Strategy

CHAPTER OBJECTIVES

After studying this chapter, you should be able to:

1. Describe the major factors used in segmenting target audiences for media strategy purposes.
2. Explain the meaning of reach, frequency, gross rating points, effective rating points, and other media concepts.
3. Discuss the logic of the three-exposure hypothesis and its role in media and vehicle selection.
4. Describe the use of the efficiency-index procedure for media selection.
5. Distinguish the differences among three forms of advertising allocation: continuous, pulsed, and flighted schedules.
6. Explain the shelf-space model and its implications for allocating advertising expenditures over time.
7. Describe the STAS measure of advertising effectiveness.
8. Perform cost-per-thousand calculations.
9. Interpret the output from a computerized media model.

Opening Vignette: The Introductory Media Campaign for the Saab 9–5

Despite being a unique automobile, Saab had done relatively little to enhance its brand image in the United States. Saab suffered both from a low level of consumer awareness and a poorly defined brand image. Particularly troubling for Saab was the fact that its product mix had historically attracted younger consumers, but achieving success for its new luxury sedan, the Saab 9-5, would require that the 9-5 appeal to upscale families and relatively affluent older consumers. The objectives of the introductory advertising campaign were to: (1) generate excitement for the new 9-5 model line, (2) increase overall awareness for the Saab name, (3) encourage consumers to visit dealers and test drive the 9-5, and (4) retail 11,000 units of the 9-5 between April and December of 1998.

Marketing research had shown that Saab's strength resided in the fact that consumers perceived Saab products to deliver a unique combination of performance and safety. The Saab 9-5, priced at $29,995, was positioned as a luxury automobile capable of delivering an ideal synthesis of performance and safety. Creative advertising executions were designed to portray Saab as a premium European luxury manufacturer, and for the advertising to have a hint of mystery and wit (see example advertisement in Figure 14.1).

In addition to the direct mail campaign, which was described in Chapter 13, an intensive media campaign was executed. Television commercials for the Saab 9-5 were run throughout the month of May on network TV and network cable, generating a total of 620

FIGURE
14.1

Example Advertisement
for the Saab 9–5

gross rating points. A national newspaper campaign began even earlier, in early March, and ran regular advertisements throughout the remainder of the year in *USA Today* and the *Wall Street Journal*. An aggressive magazine campaign also ran throughout the year with placements in automobile magazines (*Car & Driver*, *Road & Track*, etc.), sports publications (e.g., *Ski* and *Tennis*), home magazines (*Martha Stewart Living*, *Southern Living*, *Architectural Digest*), business and personal finance publications (*Money*, *Forbes*, *Fortune*, *Working Women*, etc.), and general interest magazines (*Time*, *New York Magazine*, and *Vanity Fair*). The ad campaign also included Internet banner ads throughout the year.

This integrated advertising campaign was designed to generate high levels of reach and frequency (concepts introduced later in this chapter) among the target group of older and financially well-off consumers and ultimately to sell at retail 11,000 Saab 9-5 vehicles. The extensive mass-media advertising campaign in conjunction with the intensive direct mailing effort (Chapter 13) provided every opportunity for the Saab 9-5 to achieve its ambitious sales goals for 1998 and enjoy success in future years.

Source: Information provided by The Martin Agency, Richmond, VA, 1998.

*T*he previous two chapters overviewed the major *mass media* (Chapter 12) that advertisers employ in their efforts to reach customers with advertising messages and explored the role of *direct media* (Chapter 13) in further accomplishing this goal. The present chapter builds upon this foundation by exploring the process by which advertisers and media planners select media categories and media vehicles from the vast array of available alternatives. Advertisers are placing more emphasis than ever on media planning, and media planners have achieved a level of unparalleled stature.[1]

THE MEDIA-PLANNING PROCESS

Media categories and vehicles are chosen with the goal of building brands' long-term equity.[2] The choice of media and vehicles is, in many respects, the most complicated of all marketing communications decisions due to the variety of decisions that must be made. In addition to determining which general media categories to use (e.g., television, radio, magazines), the media planner must also pick specific vehicles within each medium and decide how to allocate the available budget among the various media and vehicle alternatives. Additional decisions involve determining when to advertise, choosing specific geographical locations, and deciding how to distribute the budget over time. The complexity of media selection is made clear in the following commentary:

> An advertiser considering a simple monthly magazine schedule, out of a pool of 30 feasible publications meeting editorial environment and targeting requirements, must essentially consider over one billion schedules when narrowing the possibilities down to the few feasible alternatives that maximize campaign goals within budget constraints. Why over one billion possible schedules? There are two outcomes for each monthly schedule, either to use a particular publication or not to do so. Therefore, the total number of possible schedules equals two raised to the 30th power (i.e., 2^{30} = 1,073,741,800). If 10 weekly magazines are involved in a monthly schedule, the choices for each are not to run any advertisement or to run up to 4.3, the average number of weeks in a month. Technically, this presents the planner with nearly 12 million possible schedules from which to choose—that is, $(4.3 + 1^{10}) = 11.9$ million. Now imagine how the options explode when one is also considering 60 prime time and 25 daytime broadcast television network programs, 12 cable television networks, 16 radio networks, 4 national newspapers, and 3 newspaper supplements, with each vehicle having between 4.3 and perhaps as many as 30 or more possible insertions per month.[3]

Media planning involves the process of designing a scheduling plan that shows how advertising time and space will contribute to the achievement of marketing objectives.[4] As shown in Figure 14.2, media planning involves coordination of three levels of strategy formulations: marketing strategy, advertising strategy, and media strategy. The overall *marketing strategy* (consisting of target-market identification and marketing-mix selection) provides the impetus and direction for the choice of both advertising and media strategies. The *advertising strategy*—involving advertising objectives, budget, and message and media strategies—thus extends naturally from the overall marketing strategy.

www.dodge.com

For example, consider a hypothetical new sports utility vehicle (SUV) named the Dodge *Rambler*.[5] Assume that this name was selected as an extension of the *Ram* name that Dodge carries on its truck line and also because the name *Rambler* appropriately connotes a rather carefree and leisurely lifestyle. Assume further that outdoor-oriented men represent the *Rambler's* primary target market and that prospective owners desire practicality along with a carefree, adventuresome image in a sports utility vehicle. The media strategy for the *Rambler* naturally must extend from Dodge's 1999 strategy to sell approximately 20,000 *Ramblers* at retail.

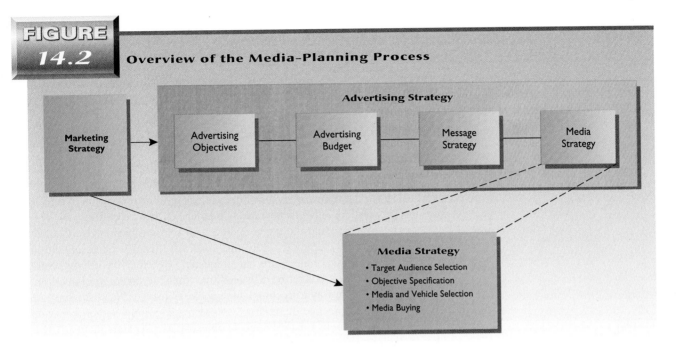

FIGURE 14.2   **Overview of the Media-Planning Process**

Media strategy necessarily evolves from the more general advertising strategy. Let us assume that the Dodge *Rambler* had a $20 million advertising budget in 1999. Assume further that Dodge's objective was to create brand awareness for the *Rambler* among targeted consumers and convey the desired image. Advertising strategy decisions simultaneously impose constraints on media strategy ($20 million is the maximum amount that could be spent on the 1999 *Rambler* campaign) and provide direction for media selection.

The media strategy itself consists of four sets of interrelated activities (see Figure 14.2):

1. Selecting the target audience;
2. Specifying media objectives;
3. Selecting media categories and vehicles; and
4. Buying media.

The following sections discuss the first three activities in detail. No discussion is devoted to media buying because of its specialized nature.

SELECTING THE TARGET AUDIENCE

Successful media strategy requires first that the target audience be pinpointed. Failure to precisely define the audience results in wasted exposures; that is, some nonpurchase candidates are exposed to advertisements while some prime candidates are missed. Saab, for example, selected families and older "empty nesters" (i.e., couples without children living at home) as its primary target for the 9-5's advertising and direct mailing efforts.

Four major factors are used in segmenting target audiences for media strategy purposes: (1) geographic, (2) demographic, (3) product usage (e.g., heavy, medium, and light product users), and (4) lifestyle/psychographics. Product-usage information, when available, generally provides the most meaningful basis for segmenting target audiences.[6]

Geographic, demographic, and psychographic considerations are typically combined for purposes of target-audience definition. Dodge, for example, would define the target audience for the *Rambler* in terms such as the following: men between the ages of 18 and 49 (a demographic variable), who have incomes exceeding $40,000 (also demographic), and who enjoy the outdoors and are carefree and adventurous (psychographic). A target audience defined in such specific terms has obvious implications for both message and media strategy. For example, magazines that appeal to the interests of outdoor enthusiasts would reach prospective customers.

SPECIFYING MEDIA OBJECTIVES

A second aspect of media strategy is establishing specific objectives. Five objectives are fundamental to media planning: reach, frequency, weight, continuity, and cost. Media planners seek answers to the following types of questions: (1) What proportion of the target audience must see, read, or hear our advertising message during a specified period? (a *reach* issue); (2) How often should the target audience be exposed to the advertisement during this period? (a *frequency* issue); (3) How much total advertising is necessary during a particular period to accomplish the reach and frequency objectives (a *weight* issue); (4) How should the advertising budget be allocated over time? (a *continuity* issue); and (5) What is the least expensive way to accomplish the other objectives? (a *cost* issue). Although in actual advertising practice these issues are addressed jointly (rather than independently), the following sections treat each media objective as a separate matter. A later section addresses their interdependence.

Reach

The *percentage of a target audience* that is exposed *at least once* to the advertiser's message during an established time frame (usually *four weeks*) represents **reach.** In other words, reach represents the number of target customers who receive the advertiser's message one or more times during a four-week time period. Other terms used by media planners for describing reach are *1+* (read "one-plus"), *net coverage, unduplicated audience,* and *cumulative audience* (or *"cume"*). Later it will become clear why these terms are interchangeable with reach.

A number of factors determine the reach of an advertising campaign. Generally speaking, more people are reached when a media schedule uses *multiple media* rather than a single medium. For example, if the Saab 9-5 were advertised only on network television, its advertisements would reach fewer people than if it were also advertised on cable TV, in magazines, and in national newspapers. In general, the more media used, the greater the chances that an advertising message will come into contact with people whose media habits differ. A second factor influencing reach is the *number and diversity of media vehicles used.* For example, if Saab's media planners had chosen to advertise the 9-5 regularly in just a couple of magazines rather than the wide variety of magazines listed in the *Opening Vignette,* far fewer consumers would have been reached by the magazine advertising effort. Third, reach can be increased by *diversifying the day parts* used to advertise a brand. For example, network television advertising during prime time and cable television advertising during fringe times would reach more potential automobile purchasers than advertising exclusively during prime time.

Reach by itself is an inadequate objective for media planning because it tells nothing about *how often* target customers are exposed to the advertiser's message. Therefore, frequency of advertising exposures must also be considered.

Frequency

The number of times, on average, within a four-week period that members of the target audience are exposed to (see, read, or hear) media vehicles that are included in a particular media schedule is referred to as *average frequency* (or, for short, **frequency**). To better understand the concept of frequency and how it relates to reach, consider the simplified example in Table 14.1. This example provides information about 10 hypothetical members of the target audience for the Dodge *Rambler* and their exposure to *Rambler* advertisements placed in *Rolling Stone* magazine over four consecutive weeks. Member A, for example, is exposed to *Rambler* ads twice, on weeks two and three; C is never exposed to a *Rambler* ad in *Rolling Stone;* F is exposed only once, on week four; and so on. Notice also in Table 14.1 that for each week, only five of 10 households (50 percent) are exposed to the *Rambler* advertisement in *Rolling Stone.* This reflects that: (1) a single vehicle *(*in this case, *Rolling Stone*) rarely reaches the full target audience, and (2) exposure to an advertising vehicle does not guarantee that consumers will see a particular advertisement.

The frequency distribution and summary reach and frequency statistics are also presented in Table 14.1. The frequency distribution represents the percentage of audience members (i.e., percentage *f*) exposed *f* times (where *f* = 0, 1, 2, 3, or 4) to the *Rambler* advertisement. The cumulative frequency column (i.e., percentage *f+*) indicates the percentage of the 10-member audience exposed at or greater than a certain level of exposures. For example, 70 percent were exposed two or more times to the *Rambler* magazine advertisement.

With this background, we now are in a position to illustrate how reach and frequency are calculated. It can be seen in Table 14.1 that 90 percent of the hypothetical audience for the *Rambler* advertisement have been exposed to one or more ads (i.e., with *f* = 1, %1+ = 90 percent). This figure, 90 percent, represents the reach for this advertising effort. Ninety percent of the target audience have been exposed to the ad one or more times during the four-week advertising period. When discussing reach statistics, advertising practitioners drop the percentage and simply refer to the number. In this case, reach is expressed simply as 90.

Frequency is the average of the frequency distribution. In this situation, frequency equals 2.2. That is, 90 percent of the target audience is reached one or more times, 20 percent are reached one time, 40 percent are reached two times, 20 percent are reached three times, and 10 percent four times. Or, arithmetically,

$$\frac{(1 \times 20) + (2 \times 40) + (3 \times 20) + (4 \times 10)}{90} = \frac{200}{90} = 2.2$$

TABLE 14.1 **Hypothetical Frequency Distribution for Dodge *Rambler* Advertised in *Rolling Stone* Magazine**

					TARGET-AUDIENCE MEMBER						
WEEK	A	B	C	D	E	F	G	H	I	J	TOTAL EXPOSURES
1		x		x	x		x		x		5
2	x	x			x		x		x		5
3	x	x		x				x		x	5
4		x		x		x	x			x	5
Total exposure	2	4	0	3	2	1	3	1	2	2	

SUMMARY STATISTICS

FREQUENCY DISTRIBUTION (*f*)	PERCENTAGE *f*	PERCENTAGE *f+*	AUDIENCE MEMBERS
0	10%	100%	C
1	20	90	F, H
2	40	70	A, E, I, J
3	20	30	D, G
4	10	10	B

Reach (1+ exposures) = 90
Frequency = 2.2
GRPs = 200

Hence, this hypothetical situation indicates 90 percent of Dodge *Rambler's* target audience are reached by the advertising schedule and that they are exposed an average of 2.2 times during the four-week advertising schedule in *Rolling Stone.* This value, 2.2, represents this simplified media schedule's frequency. (The exact frequency actually is 2.22; however, media practitioners round frequency figures to a single decimal place.)

Weight

A third objective involved in formulating media plans is determining how much advertising weight is required to accomplish advertising objectives. Notice at the bottom of Table 14.1 that this hypothetical schedule yields 200 GRPs. **Gross rating points, or GRPs,** are an indicator of the amount of gross weight, or simply **weight,** that a particular advertising schedule is capable of delivering. The term *gross* is the key. The number of GRPs indicates the *gross coverage* or *duplicated audience* that is exposed to a particular advertising schedule. (Compare these terms with the alternative terms given earlier for reach—that is, *net coverage* or *unduplicated audience.*)

Returning to our hypothetical example, the reach (net coverage, unduplicated audience) is 90. The gross rating points (gross coverage, duplicated audience) amount to 200, because audience members are exposed multiple times (2.2 times on average) to the vehicles that carry the *Rambler* advertisement during the four-week ad schedule.

It should be apparent from this discussion that GRPs represent the arithmetic product of reach times frequency.

$$\text{GRPs} = \text{Reach (R)} \times \text{Frequency (F)}$$
$$= 90 \times 2.22$$
$$= 200$$

By simple algebraic manipulation the following additional relations are obtained:

$$R = \text{GRPs} \div F$$
$$F = \text{GRPs} \div R$$

Determining GRPs in Practice. In advertising practice, media planners make media purchases by deciding how many GRPs are needed to accomplish established objectives. However, because the frequency distribution and reach and frequency statistics are unknown before the fact (i.e., at the time when the media schedule is determined), media planners need some other way to determine how many GRPs will result from a particular schedule.

There is, in fact, a simple way to make this determination. GRPs are ascertained by simply summing the ratings obtained from the individual vehicles included in a prospective media schedule. Remember: Gross rating points are nothing more than *the sum of all vehicle ratings in a media schedule.*

But what exactly is meant by ratings? A **rating** is simply the proportion of the target audience presumed to be exposed to a single occurrence of an advertising vehicle in which the advertiser's brand is advertised. For example, considering the hypothetical target audience specifications for the Dodge *Rambler* given earlier, let us assume there are approximately 25 million consumers who satisfy the age and income specifications that define this product's target audience. Assume further that approximately 1.8 million members of this predominantly male audience read *Rolling Stone (RS).* The rating for this target audience in *RS* would therefore be equal to $1.8 \div 25 = .072$. Moving the decimal point over two places (because practitioners express ratings as whole numbers) yields a rating of 7.2. Finally, assume that one full-page ad for the Dodge *Rambler* is to be placed in each of the following magazines during a single week. Although GRPs are typically determined for a full four-week period, this simplified one-week schedule would yield 75.9 GRPs:

MAGAZINE	HYPOTHETICAL RATING
Sports Illustrated	26.3
National Geographic	15.6
Time	14.1
Newsweek	12.7
Rolling Stone	7.2
Total	75.9

The *Global Focus* box presents an interesting example of how GRPs have a different meaning in Mexico compared to the United States.

The Concept of Effective Rating Points (ERPs).

Alternative media schedules are usually compared in terms of the number of GRPs each generates. It is important to realize, however, that a greater number of GRPs does not necessarily indicate superiority. Consider, for example, two alternative media plans, X and Z, both of which require the same budget. Plan X generates 90 percent reach and an average frequency of 2, thereby yielding 180 GRPs. (Note again that reach is defined as the proportion of the audience exposed one or more times—that is, 1+—to an advertising vehicle during the course of a four-week campaign.) Plan Z provides for 166 GRPs from a reach of 52 percent and a frequency of 3.2. Which plan is better? Plan X is clearly superior in terms of total GRPs and reach, but Plan Z has a higher frequency level. If the brand in question requires a greater number of exposures for the advertising to achieve effectiveness, then Plan Z may be superior even though it yields fewer GRPs.

It is for the reason suggested in the preceding comparison that many advertisers and media planners have become critical of the GRP concept, contending that "it rests on the very dubious assumption that every exposure is of equal value, that the 50th exposure is the same as the tenth or the first."[7] Although the GRP concept remains very much a part of media planning, the advertising industry has turned away from the exclusive use of "raw" advertising weight (i.e., GRPs) toward a concept of media *effectiveness*.[8] The determination of media effectiveness takes into consideration *how often* members of the target audience have an opportunity to be exposed to advertising messages for the focal brand. The terms *effective reach* and *effective frequency* often are used interchangeably by media practitioners to capture the idea that an effective media schedule delivers a sufficient, but not excessive, number of ads to the target audience. Because the term "effective reach" creates less confusion when discussing the meaning and calculation of effective rating points (ERPs), that term is preferred in this text over effective frequency.

Effective reach is based on the idea that an advertising schedule is effective only if it does not reach members of the target audience too few or too many times. In other words, there is a theoretical optimum range of exposures to an advertisement with minimum and maximum limits. But what constitutes too few or too many exposures? This, unfortunately, is one of the most complicated issues in all of advertising. The only statement that can be made with certainty is, "It depends!"

It depends, in particular, on considerations such as the advertised brand's awareness level, its competitive position, the audience's degree of loyalty to the brand, message creativity and novelty, and the objectives that advertising is intended to accomplish for the brand. In fact, high levels of weekly exposure to a brand's advertising may be unproductive for loyal consumers because of a leveling off of ad effectiveness.[9] Specifically, brands with higher market shares and greater customer loyalty typically require fewer advertising exposures to achieve minimal levels of effectiveness. Likewise, it would be expected that distinctive advertising requires fewer exposures. The higher up the hierarchy of effects the advertising is attempting to move the consumer, the greater the number of exposures needed to achieve minimal effectiveness. For example, more exposures probably are needed to convince consumers that the Dodge *Rambler* provides the dual advantages of practicality and excitement than merely to make them aware that there is a brand named *Rambler.*

GLOBAL FOCUS: GRPs IN THE UNITED STATES AND MEXICO

Listed below are the top 10 U.S. TV programs based on cost of buying a 30-second ad on each for the 1998–1999 television season. Because viewership changes from week to week and from quarter to quarter, the ratings and share data presented below are rough approximations of the average ratings/shares for each program during the 1998–99 season. For example, the most expensive program, *ER*, is assumed to have had the highest rating at 21.5, followed by *Frasier* and *Friends* at 20.2 and 18.8, respectively. Ratings decreased to 10.5 for the 10th-highest-rated program, *Ally McBeal*. Shares for the top three programs are shown at 41, 35, and 31.

PROGRAM	RATING	SHARE
1. *ER*	21.5	41
2. *Frasier*	20.2	35
3. *Friends*	18.8	31
4. *Drew Cary Show*	17.4	29
5. *NFL Monday Night Football*	15.0	28
6. *Veronica's Closet*	14.3	26
7. *X-Files*	12.9	25
8. *Jessie*	12.4	27
9. *Touched by an Angel*	11.2	22
10. *Ally McBeal*	10.5	24

Calculations of ratings and shares both use the same value in the numerator (which is the number of people exposed to the program) but have different values in the denominator. Specifically, when *ratings* are calculated, the denominator is the total number of TV households in the United States as of the date of the calculation, which as of 1998 was approximately 98 million households. By comparison, when TV *shares* are calculated, the calculation is based *not* on the total number of households, but rather on the total number of sets that are turned on at program air time. Hence, a rating of 21.5 for *ER* means that 21,070,000 households had their sets tuned to that program at air time (i.e., .215 × 98,000,000 = 21,070,000). This percentage when multiplied by 100 is *ER*'s rating, 21.5.

As the name suggests, the concept of *share* represents a particular program's share of market at the time that program is aired or, in other words, its proportion of viewers compared to other programs aired at the same time. Because not all 98 million TV sets are turned on at the time of any program, share values are higher than their corresponding ratings because, of course, the base when calculating share is smaller. In the case of *ER*, its share was 41 compared to a rating of 21.5. Because we know that 21,070,000 viewed that program, we also know that approximately 51.39 million of the 98 million U.S. households were tuned in to any television program at *ER* air time (i.e., 21,070,000 ÷ 0.41 = 51,390,243). Thus, *ER*'s 41 share means that 41 percent of the viewing audience were tuned in to this program. Comparatively, its rating of 21.5 means that 21.5 percent of the 98 million television households viewed this program. It now should be obvious why ratings are always lower than shares.

Interestingly, GRPs do not mean the exact same thing in all countries. Consider the difference between the United States and Mexico. In the United States, GRPs are defined as the percentage of households with televisions that are viewing the program at air time. In Mexico, GRPs mean the percentage of households with their televisions turned *on* that are viewing the program at air time. In other words, GRPs in the United States are based on the accumulation of *ratings,* whereas in Mexico GRPs are based on the accumulation of *shares* and, by American convention, should be thought of as gross share points and not gross rating points. So, for example, if an advertiser placed one ad on each of the first four programs listed, that advertiser would have accumulated 77.9 U.S. GRPs (i.e., 21.5 + 20.2 + 18.8 + 17.4). By Mexican calculations, this same advertiser would have accumulated 136 GRPs (41 + 35 + 31 + 29).

The lesson is clear: The same terms are at times used to mean different things in different countries. For those involved in global marketing and advertising, this application becomes very important. Mexican GRPs are inflated by American standards. U.S. GRPs are deflated by Mexican standards. Neither is right or wrong: Practitioners in each country simply adhere to different conventions.

Sources: The top-10 programs are from Joe Mandese, "'ER' Is Prime-Time Price King in Post-'Seinfeld' Marketplace," *Advertising Age*, September 21, 1998, 1. The information concerning the differences in U.S. and Mexican use of GRPs is from "Mexican Wearout Studied," *rsc Newsletter* 1, no. 3 (1994), 1–2. (This is a publication of the Research Systems Corporation, Evansville, IN.)

How Many Exposures Are Needed? It follows from the foregoing discussion that the minimum and maximum numbers of effective exposures can be determined only by conducting sophisticated research. Because research of this nature is time consuming and expensive, advertisers and media planners generally have used rules of thumb in place of research in determining exposure effectiveness. Advertising industry thinking on this matter has been heavily influenced by the so-called **three-exposure hypothesis,** which addresses the *minimum* number of exposures needed for advertising to be effective. Its originator, an advertising practitioner named Herbert Krugman, argued that a consumer's initial exposure to a brand's advertising initiates a response of "What is it?" The second exposure triggers a response of "What of it?" And the third exposure and those thereafter are merely reminders of the information that the consumer already has learned from the first two exposures.[10] This hypothesis, which was based on little empirical data and a lot of intuition, has virtually become gospel in the advertising industry. Many advertising practitioners have interpreted the three-exposure hypothesis to mean that media schedules are ineffective when they deliver average frequencies of fewer than three exposures to the vehicle in which a brand's advertisement is placed.

Although there is some intuitive appeal to the notion that average frequencies of fewer than three are insufficient, this interpretation of the three-exposure hypothesis both is too literal and also fails to recognize that Krugman's hypothesis had in mind three exposures to an advertising *message* and not three exposures to an advertising *vehicle*.[11] The difference is that vehicle exposure, or what also is referred to as *opportunity to see an ad (OTS)*, is not tantamount to advertising exposure. A reader of a magazine issue certainly will be exposed to some advertisements in that issue, but the odds are that he or she will not be exposed to all, or even most, of them. Likewise, a viewer of a TV program will likely miss some of the commercials placed during a 30- or 60-minute program. Hence, the number of consumers who are actually exposed to any particular advertising message carried in a vehicle—what Krugman had in mind—is less than the number of people who are exposed to the vehicle that carries the message.[12]

Aside from this general misunderstanding of the three-exposure hypothesis, it must also be recognized that no specific number of minimum exposures—whether 3+, 5+, or *x*+—is absolutely correct for all advertising situations. It cannot be overemphasized that what is effective (or ineffective) for one product/brand may not necessarily be so for another. "There is no magic number, no comfortable '3+' level of advertising exposures that works, even if we refer to advertising exposure rather than OTS."[13]

An Alternative Approach: The Efficiency-Index Procedure.   Advertising scholars have proposed an alternative approach to the three-exposure doctrine.[14] The objective of the *efficiency-index procedure* (as it will be referred to here) is to select that media schedule (from a set of alternative schedules) that generates the most exposure value per GRP—or, stated differently, provides a "bigger bang for the buck." This approach entails the following straightforward steps:

1. Estimate the *exposure value* for each level of vehicle exposure, or OTS, that a schedule would produce. Table 14.2 provides a list of OTSs (from 0 to 10+) and a corresponding set of illustrative exposure values. (Please note that these exposure values are not invariant across all situations but instead have to be determined uniquely for each product-market situation.) It can be seen that 0 vehicle

TABLE 14.2	**Exposure Values for Different OTS Levels**
OTS	EXPOSURE VALUE
0	0.00
1	0.50
2	0.63
3	0.72
4	0.79
5	0.85
6	0.90
7	0.94
8	0.97
9	0.99
10+	1.00

exposures has, of course, an exposure value of 0. One exposure adds the greatest amount of value, assumed here to be 0.50 units; a second OTS contributes 0.13 additional units of value (for an overall value of 0.63); a third exposure contributes 0.09 more units to the second exposure (for an overall value of 0.72 units); and so on. One can readily see that this value function reflects decreasing marginal utility with each additional OTS. At an OTS of 10, the maximum value of 1.00 is achieved. Hence, this illustration proposes that OTSs in excess of 10 offer no additional value. By graphing the values in Table 14.2, one can readily see that the function is nonlinear and concave to the origin. In other words, each additional exposure contributes decreasing value.

2. Next estimate the *exposure distribution* of the various media schedules that are under consideration. Computer programs, such as the ADplus program discussed later, are available for this purpose. Table 14.3 illustrates the distributions for two alternative schedules. It can be seen that Schedule 1 will reach 85 percent of the target. That is, if 15 percent of the target are exposed zero times (i.e., OTS = 0 = 15 percent), then the remaining 85 percent are exposed one or more times (1+). Reading down the first two columns in Table 14.3, it can be seen that 11.1 percent of the target audience is estimated to be exposed exactly one time; 12.5 percent of the audience exposed exactly two times; 13.2 percent three times; and so on. The third column shows that the exposure value is obtained by simply multiplying the exposure value of a particular number of exposures from Table 14.2 with the corresponding percentage of target at that number of exposures from Table 14.3. Hence, at an OTS of one exposure, the exposure value is $0.5 \times 11.1 = 5.55$; at an OTS of two exposures, the exposure value is $0.63 \times 12.5 = 7.875$; and so on.

3. After the exposure value at each OTS level is determined, the *total exposure value* is obtained by simply summing the individual exposure values ($5.55 + 7.875 + 9.504 + \ldots + 10.5 = 66.481$ for Schedule 1). The total value for Schedule 2 is similar: 66.482.

TABLE 14.3 — Frequency Distributions and Evaluations of Two Alternative Schedules

	SCHEDULE 1		SCHEDULE 2	
OTS	PERCENTAGE OF TARGET	VALUE	PERCENTAGE OF TARGET	VALUE
0	15.0%	0.000	8.0%	0.000
1	11.1	5.550	21.0	10.500
2	12.5	7.875	17.6	11.088
3	13.2	9.504	13.6	9.792
4	11.0	8.690	10.9	8.611
5	8.4	7.140	8.6	7.310
6	6.3	5.670	6.6	5.940
7	5.0	4.700	5.2	4.888
8	3.9	3.783	3.9	3.783
9	3.1	3.069	3.0	2.970
10+	10.5	10.500	1.6	1.600
Total value:		66.481		66.482
GRPs:		398.600		333.800
Value/GRP:		0.167		0.199
3+ Reach:		61.4%		53.4%

4. Finally, develop an *index of exposure efficiency*. This is accomplished by dividing the total exposure value for each schedule by the number of GRPs produced by that schedule. Total GRPs are determined from the data in Table 14.3 exactly in the same fashion identified earlier when discussing Table 14.1. Specifically, Schedule 1's total of 398.6 GRPs (see bottom of Table 14.3) is calculated as follows: $(1 \times 11.1) + (2 \times 12.5) + (3 \times 13.2) + \ldots + (10 \times 10.5)$. The index of exposure efficiency for Schedule 1 is 0.167 (i.e., $66.481 \div 398.6$), whereas the index value for Schedule 2 is 0.199 (i.e., $66.482 \div 333.8$).

With higher index values representing greater exposure efficiency, it should be clear that the second media schedule in Table 14.3 is more efficient. That is, Schedule 2 has a higher efficiency index than Schedule 1 because Schedule 2 accomplishes an equivalent exposure value (66.482 versus 66.481) but with fewer GRPs and hence less expense. Moreover, whereas Schedule 1 reaches a high percentage of the target audience 10 or more times (i.e., OTS = 10+ = 10.5 percent), Schedule 2 focuses more on reaching the audience at least one time (OTS = 1 = 21 percent) rather than wasting expenditures on reaching the audience 10 or more times.

In concluding this section, it should be further noted from the bottom of Table 14.3 that Schedule 1 is superior to Schedule 2 in terms of its 3+ reach (61.4 percent versus 53.4 percent). However, when using the systematic and logical procedure described here, Schedule 2 is superior to Schedule 1 when applying the criterion of efficiency. In other words, Schedule 2 reaches proportionately fewer audience members three or more times, but it produces an exposure value comparable to that produced by Schedule 1 at a lower expense and with fewer GRPs.

Although this index of exposure efficiency is theoretically more sound than the three-exposure heuristic, the latter is embedded in advertising practice whereas the former has just recently been introduced. We therefore return to standard advertising practice and discuss the heuristics used by advertising practitioners in determining the effective number of exposures. The implication is not that this new procedure should be dismissed out of hand; the point, instead, is that advertising practice has not as yet had time to widely adopt this approach.

Effective Reach in Advertising Practice.   Although effective reach planning is widely practiced by large consumer-product advertisers, media planners remain divided on the matter of what constitutes effective reach.[15] Nevertheless, the mostly widely accepted view is that *fewer than three exposures* during a four-week media schedule is generally considered ineffective, while *more than 10 exposures* during this period is considered excessive. The range of effective reach, then, can be thought of as *three to 10 exposures* during a designated media-planning period, which typically is four weeks.

The use of effective reach rather than gross rating points as the basis for media planning can have a major effect on overall media strategies. In particular, effective reach planning generally leads to using *multiple media* rather than depending exclusively on television, which is often the strategy when using the gross-rating-point criterion. Prime-time television is especially effective in terms of generating high levels of reach (1+ exposures) but may be deficient in terms of achieving effective reach (i.e., 3+ exposures). Thus, the use of effective reach as the decision criterion often involves giving up some of prime-time television's reach to obtain greater frequency (at the same cost) from other media.

This is illustrated in Table 14.4, which compares four alternative media plans involving different combinations of media expenditures from an annual advertising budget of $12 million.[16] Plan A allocates 100 percent of the budget to network television advertising; Plan B allocates 67 percent to television and 33 percent to network radio; Plan C splits the budget between network television and magazines; and Plan D allocates 67 percent to television and 33 percent to outdoor advertising.

Notice first that Plan A (the use of network television only) leads to the lowest levels of reach, effective reach, frequency, and GRPs. An even split of network television and

TABLE 14.4	Alternative Media Plans (Based on a $12 Million Annual Budget and Four–Week Media Analysis)			
	PLAN A: TV (100%)	PLAN B: TV (67%), RADIO (33%)	PLAN C: TV (50%), MAGAZINES (50%)	PLAN D: TV (67%), OUTDOOR (33%)
Reach (1+ exposures)	69%	79%	91%	87%
Effective reach (3+ exposures)	29%	48%	53%	61%
Frequency	2.8	5.5	3.2	6.7
GRPs	193	435	291	583
ERPs	81	264	170	409
Cost per GRP	$62,176	$27,586	$41,237	$20,583
Cost per ERP	$148,148	$45,455	$70,588	$29,340

magazines (Plan C) generates an especially high level of reach (91 percent), while combinations of network television with network radio (Plan B) and network television with outdoor advertising (Plan D) are especially impressive in terms of frequency, GRPs, and the percentage of consumers exposed three or more times.

More to the point, notice that the network-television-only plan in comparison to the remaining plans yields far fewer GRPs and considerably fewer ERPs. (Please note in Table 14.4 that ERPs equal the product of effective reach, or 3+ exposures, times frequency; Plan A, for example, yields 81 ERPs, i.e., 29 × 2.8 = 81.) Plan D, which combines 67 percent network television and 33 percent outdoor advertising, is especially outstanding in terms of the numbers of GRPs and ERPs generated. This is because outdoor advertising is seen frequently as people travel to and from work.

Should we conclude from this discussion that Plan D is the best and Plan A is the worst? Not necessarily! Clearly, the impact from seeing one billboard advertisement is probably far less than being exposed to a captivating television commercial. This points out a fundamental aspect of media planning: *Subjective factors* also must be considered when allocating advertising dollars. Superficially, the numbers do favor Plan D. However, judgment and past experience may favor Plan A on the grounds that the only way to effectively advertise this particular product is by presenting dynamic action shots of people consuming and enjoying the product. Only television could satisfy this requirement.

It is useful to return again to a point established in Chapter 9: *It is better to be vaguely right than precisely wrong.*[17] Reach, frequency, effective reach, GRPs, and ERPs are precise in their appearance but, in application, if used blindly, may be precisely wrong. Discerning decision makers never rely on numbers to make decisions for them. Rather, the numbers should be used solely as additional inputs into a decision that ultimately involves insight, wisdom, and judgment. For further discussion of the role of subjectivity in media buying, see the *IMC Focus.*

www.nielsenmedia.com

Continuity

A fourth general objective the media planner deals with is the timing of advertising. **Continuity** involves the matter of how advertising is allocated during the course of an advertising campaign. The fundamental issue is this: Should the media budget be distributed uniformly throughout the period of the advertising campaign; should it be spent in a concentrated period to achieve the most impact; or should some other schedule between these two extremes be used? As always, the determination of what is best depends on the specific product-market situation. In general, however, a uniform advertising schedule suffers from too little advertising weight at any one time. A heavily concentrated schedule, on the

IMC Focus: Is Super Bowl Advertising Worth the Expense?

Nielsen Media Research determined that the 1998 National Football League Super Bowl between the Denver Broncos and the Green Bay Packers had a 44.5 rating and a 67 share. Advertisers paid $1.3 million for placing a 30-second commercial on this program. Just three years earlier, in 1995, the cost of a 30-second advertisement during the Super Bowl was $1,007,000. Media planners at a company called Media Edge questioned whether the Super Bowl represents a prudent media buy and proposed another way to spend $1,007,000. They developed an alternative media plan that consisted of: (1) buying advertising time on all network programs aired at the same time on Tuesday night (e.g., the *CBS Tuesday Night Movie* and the *Fox Tuesday Night Movie)*; (2) securing advertising time on all network programs aired at the same time on Sunday night (the three major networks' Sunday night movies plus *Married with Children* on Fox); and (3) purchasing a final single spot on Saturday night (Fox's *Cops*). (The Tuesday and Sunday night buys are called *roadblocks,* because advertising purchased on all network programs aired simultaneously acts as a "roadblock" to ensure that all consumers viewing TV at this time will be exposed to the brand's advertising.) This alternative media plan was able to secure 13 prime-time advertising spots, or a total time of 6.5 minutes, compared to purchasing a single 30-second ad on the Super Bowl. Comparative GRPs for the Super Bowl media buy and the alternative plan are as follows:

Group	Super Bowl GRPs	Alternative, 13-Spot GRPs	13-Spot Advantage Over Super Bowl (in %)
Adults 18–49	40	65	+62
Adults 25–54	42	78	+86
Men 18–49	46	63	+37
Men 25–54	48	68	+42

Whereas a single 30-second ad on the 1995 Super Bowl provided 40 GRPs based on the 18–49 age group, 42 GRPs based on the 25–54 group, and so on, the equivalently priced 13 spots yielded considerably more GRPs. For example, for all adults aged 25 to 54, the 78 GRPs from the 13 prime-time spots were 86 percent greater than the 42 GRPs generated by the Super Bowl advertisement.

Hence one can conclude that advertisers should not have advertised on the Super Bowl but rather would have been better served by investing their advertising money elsewhere. Correct? Not necessarily, especially considering advertising *impact*. People react with a relatively unenthusiastic response to advertisements placed on the programs contained in the alternative media buy. Comparatively, advertisements placed on the Super Bowl are, like the program itself, a special event. Consumers look forward to new, dramatic advertisements and often talk about the advertisements well after the Super Bowl is completed. Journalists write about these advertisements in magazines, newspapers and on the Internet, so that advertisers receive a secondary form of brand contact. In short, all advertising does not have equivalent impact. When planners are buying advertising media, considerations, often subjective, other than mere comparisons of cost and rating points have to be factored into the decision.

Source: The 1998 ratings and cost data are from Kyle Pope, "NBC Scores Big With the Super Bowl; Game Is Among Most-Watched Ever," *The Wall Street Journal Interactive Edition*, January 27, 1998. The information about the 1995 Super Bowl is from Rob Frydlewicz, "Missed Super Bowl? Put Your Bucks Here," *Advertising Age,* January 30, 1995, 18.

other hand, suffers from excessive exposures during the advertising period and a complete absence of advertising at all other times.

Advertisers have three general alternatives related to allocating the budget over the course of the campaign: continuous, pulsing, and flighting schedules. To understand the differences among these three scheduling options, consider the advertising decision faced by a regional manufacturer of processed meat products (hot dogs, luncheon meats, etc.). Figure 14.3 shows how advertising allocations might differ from month to month depending on the use of continuous, pulsing, or flighting schedules. Assume the annual advertising budget for a hypothetical brand of hot dogs is $3 million.

Continuous Schedule. In a **continuous** advertising schedule, an equal or relatively equal amount of ad dollars is invested throughout the campaign. The illustration in panel A of Figure 14.3 shows an extreme case of continuous advertising in which the hypothetical hot dog advertiser allocates the $3 million advertising budget in equal amounts of exactly $250,000 each month.

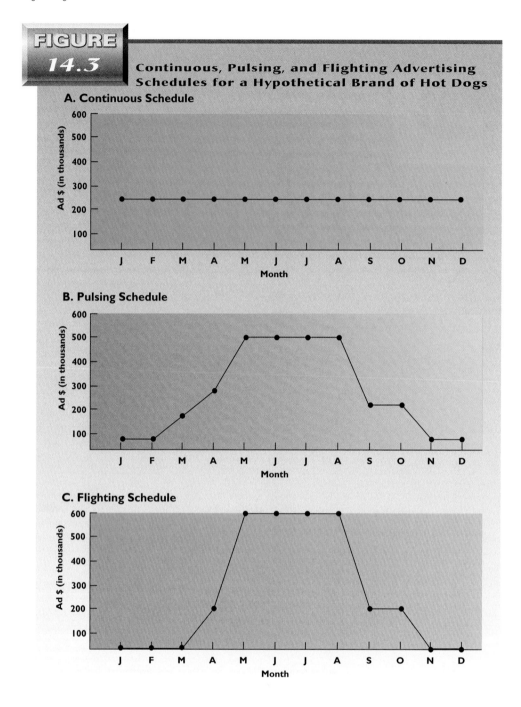

FIGURE 14.3 Continuous, Pulsing, and Flighting Advertising Schedules for a Hypothetical Brand of Hot Dogs

A. Continuous Schedule

B. Pulsing Schedule

C. Flighting Schedule

Such an advertising allocation would make sense only if hot dogs were consumed in essentially equal quantities throughout the year. Although hot dogs are consumed year-round, consumption is particularly high during May, June, July, and August. This calls for a discontinuous allocation of advertising dollars throughout the year.

Pulsing. In a pulsing advertising schedule, some advertising is used during every period of the campaign, but the amount of advertising varies considerably from period to period. In panel B of Figure 14.3, a pulsing schedule for our hypothetical hot dog manufacturer shows the company advertising especially heavy during the high-consumption months of May through August (spending $500,000 each month) but continuing to advertise in every month throughout the year. The minimum advertising expenditure is $50,000 even in the slow months of January, February, November, and December.

Flighting.   In a flighting schedule, the advertiser varies expenditures throughout the campaign and allocates zero expenditures in some months. As demonstrated in panel C of Figure 14.3, the hot dog advertiser allocates $600,000 to each of the four high-consumption months (May through August), $200,000 each to moderate-consumption months (April, September, and October), but zero dollars to five low-consumption months (January, February, March, November, and December).

Thus, pulsing and flighting are similar in that they both involve *differential levels of advertising expenditures* throughout the year, but differ in that some advertising takes place during every period with pulsing but not with flighting. The following analogies may help to eliminate any confusion between pulsing and flighting. Pulsing in advertising is similar to an individual's heartbeat, or *pulse.* One's pulse changes continuously between some lower and upper bounds but is always present in a living person. Comparatively, a flighting schedule is like an airplane, which at times is at ground zero but in flight varies from lower to higher altitudes. Thus, a pulsed advertising schedule is always beating (some advertising is placed in every ad period), whereas a flighted schedule soars at times to very high levels (high levels of advertising) but is nonexistent on other occasions (no advertising during some periods).

The Shelf-Space Model of Advertising.   Some advertising practitioners argue that flighted and pulsed advertising schedules are necessitated by the tremendous increases in media costs, especially the cost of network television advertising. Few advertisers, according to this argument, can afford to advertise consistently heavily throughout the year. According to this argument, advertisers are forced to advertise only at select times, namely during those periods when there is the greatest chance of accomplishing communication and sales objectives. This argument holds further that during those periods when advertising is undertaken there should be sufficient frequency to justify the advertising effort. In other words, the argument favoring flighting goes hand in hand with the goal of achieving effective reach (3+) during any advertising period such as the standard four-week planning schedule.

The wisdom of this argument has been challenged by various advertisers and media specialists, most forcefully perhaps by Erwin Ephron, a New York media specialist. Ephron and his supporters assert that the advertising industry has failed to prove the value of the effective reach (3+) criterion for allocating advertising budgets and that this dubious criterion leads inappropriately to flighted allocations. Ephron has formulated an argument favoring consistent advertising that he terms the **shelf-space model.**[18] This model—also termed the *principle of recency* or the *theory of effective weekly planning*—is built on two interrelated ideas: (1) that consumers' first exposure to an advertisement for a brand is the most powerful, and (2) that achieving a high level of weekly reach for a brand should be emphasized over acquiring heavy frequency.

Because flighting is an on-and-off proposition, let us consider by analogy what would happen to sales of a particular brand if a retailer's shelves were empty sometimes when consumers shopped the store. There obviously would be zero sales during those periods of stockouts where the shelves are empty. Sales would be obtained only when the shelves held some amount of the product. This, in a sense, is the way it is with flighted advertising schedules: The "shelves" are empty during certain periods (when no advertising is being run) and full during others.

Empirical evidence (albeit tentative) has demonstrated that the first exposure to advertising has a greater effect on sales than do additional exposures.[19] (The *IMC Focus* box provides additional discussion on this matter.) Accordingly, Ephron argues that media planners should devise schedules that are geared toward providing a continuous (or near continuous) presence for a brand with the objective of optimizing *weekly reach* rather than effective reach as embodied in the three-exposure hypothesis. Ephron's argument can be summarized as follows:

1. Contrary to the three-exposure hypothesis, which has been interpreted to mean that advertising must *teach* consumers about brands (therefore requiring multiple

exposures), the shelf-space model, or principle of recency, assumes that the role of advertising is <u>not</u> to teach but to influence consumers' *brand selection.* "Unless it's a new brand, a new benefit, or a new use, there is not much learning involved."[20] Hence, the purpose of most advertising is to remind, reinforce, or evoke earlier messages rather than to teach consumers about product benefits or uses.

2. With the objective of influencing brand selection, advertising must therefore reach consumers when they are ready to buy a brand. The purpose of advertising, in other words, is to "rent the shelf" so as to assure a brand presence close to the time when consumers make purchase decisions. *Out of sight, out of mind* is the first principle of advertising according to Ephron.

3. Advertising messages are most effective when they are *close to the time of purchase,* and a single advertising exposure is effective if it reaches consumers close to the time when they are making brand-selection decisions.

4. The cost effectiveness of a single exposure is approximately *three times greater* than the value of subsequent exposures.[21]

5. Hence, rather than concentrating the advertising budget to purchase multiple exposures only at select times throughout the year, planners should allocate the budget to *reach more consumers more often.*

6. In a world without budget constraints, the ideal advertising approach would be to achieve a weekly reach of 100 (i.e., to reach 100 percent of the target audience at least one time) and to sustain this level of reach for all 52 weeks of the year. Such a schedule would yield 5200 weekly reach points. Because most advertisers cannot afford to sustain such a constant level of advertising, the next best approach is to *reach as high a percentage of the target audience as possible for as many weeks as possible.* This goal can be accomplished by using: (1) 15-second TV commercials as well as more expensive 30-second spots; (2) spreading the budget among cheaper media rather than spending exclusively on television advertising; and (3) buying cheaper TV programs (cable, syndicated) rather than exclusively prime-time network programs. All of these strategies free up advertising dollars and permit an advertising schedule that will reach a high percentage of the target audience continuously rather than sporadically.

The concept of scheduling media so as to achieve a continuous rather than sporadic presence has considerable appeal. However, it must be recognized that no single approach is equally effective for all brands. Ephron has recognized as much when suggesting (in the first point above) that for new brands, benefits, or uses, the advertising objective may indeed be to teach rather than merely to remind. Another advertising executive summarizes the issue nicely:

> *We've always believed that the first exposure is the most powerful, yet we don't want to have hard and fast rules. Every brand is a different situation. The leader in a category has different frequency needs than a competitor with less market share. It's not fair to say every brand has the same need for frequency.*[22]

Toward Reconciliation. As a student it may be somewhat disconcerting to receive "mixed signals" such as these. Assuredly, it would be easier if there were hard-and-fast rules or straightforward principles that said, "Here is how you should do it." Marketing communications, unfortunately, is not as simple as this. We repeat a theme that has been emphasized at different points throughout the text: What works best depends on the specific circumstances facing a brand. If the brand is mature and well established, then effective weekly reach (the shelf-space model) is probably an appropriate way to allocate the advertising budget. On the other hand, if the brand is new, or if new benefits or uses for the brand have been developed, or if the advertising message is complex, then the budget should be allocated in a manner that achieves the frequency necessary to teach consumers about brand benefits and uses.

IMC Focus: The STAS Measure of Advertising Effectiveness

Based on in-depth analysis of so-called single-source data, which is covered in the following chapter, a prominent advertising researcher, John Philip Jones, produced provocative findings regarding advertising effectiveness. Jones's research was based on a study of 142 brands that were advertised in the early 1990s representing the following 12 product categories: packaged detergents, liquid detergents, bar soaps, shampoos, toilet tissue, ice cream, mayonnaise, peanut butter, ground coffee, diet carbonated soft drinks, breakfast cereals, and analgesics.

Jones evaluated advertising's short-term sales effect using a measure called STAS, an acronym standing for *short-term advertising strength*. This measure simply registers the difference score between *baseline STAS* (a brand's share of purchases in households that have *not* been exposed to advertising for that brand during the seven days before purchase) and *stimulated STAS* (a brand's share of purchases in the households that have had an opportunity to see at least one TV advertisement for that brand in the seven days before purchase). Thus, Jones's measure of the short-term effects of advertising (STAS) is calculated simply by subtracting *baseline STAS* from *stimulated STAS* and dividing this difference by baseline STAS to yield a ratio. That is, for *each seven-day period* a weekly STAS score is calculated as follows: STAS = (Baseline STAS − Stimulated STAS) ÷ Baseline STAS. Thus, a STAS of 100 for any given week indicates no change in sales when comparing the baseline period of sevens days without advertising exposure to the seven days in which households had an opportunity to see a message for the advertised brand. Any value in excess 100 indicates that advertising has influenced short-term sales, whereas values below 100 indicate a negative effect of advertising exposure. The arithmetic mean of weekly STAS scores is then calculated to yield a yearly average of the weekly ratios. This yearly average STAS, and not the weekly scores, is the value of interest.

Jones's research demonstrated that 70 percent of the ad campaigns he examined yielded positive STAS values (i.e., advertising increased sales immediately), although in many cases the increase was small and temporary. Moreover, 46 percent of the brands he studied achieved *long-term effects* from advertising. Jones's data further reveal that the first exposure generates the highest proportion of sales and that additional exposures add very little to the first. This clearly supports Ephron's similar conclusion based on his shelf-space model of advertising.

Despite these findings, which have had considerable impact on the advertising community, there is some counterevidence suggesting that STAS differentials are not solely the result of advertising exposure but in fact are correlated with sales promotion activity. In other words, what may appear to be the exclusive impact of successful advertising may actually be due at least in part to a brand's sales promotion activity (such as couponing or cent-off dealing) that takes place at the same time that advertising for the brand is running on television. Until research evidence is more definitive on this matter, a reasonable conclusion is that Jones's STAS measure of advertising effectiveness is interesting but perhaps simplistic in the absence of proper experimental or statistical controls for sales promotions, price changes, and other potential determinants of a brand's sales volume.

Source: John Philip Jones, "Single-Source Research Begins to Fulfill Its Promise," *Journal of Advertising Research* 35 (May/June 1995), 9–16. The counterperspective extends from research by Gary Schroeder, Bruce C. Richardson, and Avu Sankaralingam, "Validating STAS Using Behav-iorScan," *Journal of Advertising Research* 37 (July/August 1997, 33–43. For another challenge to the STAS measure, see Gerard J. Tellis and Doyle L. Weiss, "Does TV Advertising Really Affect Sales? The Role of Measures, Models, and Data Aggregation," *Journal of Advertising* 24 (fall 1995), 1–12.

These opposing viewpoints about how advertising works can be distinguished as the "strong" and "weak" models of advertising.[23] The *strong model* takes the position that advertising is important because it teaches consumers about brands and encourages trial purchases leading to the prospect of repeat buying. The *weak model* contends that most advertising messages are not important to consumers and that consumers do not learn much from advertising. This is because advertising usually is for brands that consumers already know about. In this case, advertising merely serves to remind consumers about brands they already know.

A reconciliation between these opposing viewpoints is obtained upon appreciating the fact that advertising at any point in time *does* have influence on a relatively small percentage of consumers, and these are the consumers who happen to be in the market for the product at the time of the advertising. For example, a newspaper advertisement announcing a retailer's special sale for a particular brand of televisions may encourage store traffic and purchases from the relatively small subset of consumers who, at this point in time, need a new television set. Most consumers, however, do not need a new television set at this particular time. It thus may be said that advertising achieves its effectiveness "through a chance encounter with a ready consumer."[24] The advertisement for *Parade* magazine

(Figure 14.4), which is directed at the advertising community and not consumers, nicely illustrates this "chance encounter" idea and the importance of reaching consumers at a time when they are prepared to make a buying decision.

Should it be concluded from this discussion that a single advertising exposure is all that is necessary and that advertising time and space should be scheduled so that recency is optimized and frequency is neglected? Absolutely not. Rather, what you should understand is that the specific advertising situation dictates whether emphasis on reach or frequency is more important. Brands familiar to consumers require less frequency, whereas new or relatively unfamiliar brands require higher levels of frequency. Brands that employ complex messages (e.g., containing technical details or subtle claims) also generally require more frequency.[25]

Illustration of Advertising's "Chance Encounter" and the Value of Achieving Reach

When you're putting together a media plan, shouldn't this be the moment you plan for?

It's the moment of truth. The moment when someone is ready to buy. The challenge is to reach

as many people as possible at that moment, increasing the chances that the product they buy will be yours.

Parade does that better than any magazine in America. 82 million readers. In just 24 hours. Every week.

Call Jennifer Gallo at 212-450-7093.

NOTHING MOVES AMERICA LIKE

Cost Considerations

Media planners attempt to allocate the advertising budget in a cost-efficient manner subject to satisfying other objectives. One of the most important and universally used indicators of media efficiency is the cost-per-thousand criterion. Cost per thousand (abbreviated **CPM,** with the *M* representing the Roman numeral for 1,000) is the cost of reaching 1,000 people. The measure can be refined to mean the cost of reaching 1,000 members of the target audience, excluding those people who fall outside the target market. This refined measure is designated **CPM-TM.**[26]

CPM and CPM-TM are calculated by dividing the cost of an advertisement by a medium's circulation within the total market (CPM) or target market (CPM-TM):

CPM = Cost of Ad ÷ Number of Total Contacts (expressed in thousands)

CPM-TM = Cost of Ad ÷ Number of TM Contacts (expressed in thousands)

The term *contacts* is used here in a general sense to include any type of advertising audience (television viewers, magazine readers, radio listeners, etc.).

To illustrate how CPM and CPM-TM are calculated, consider the following unconventional advertising situation. During every Saturday football game at a major university, a local airplane advertising service flies messages on a trailing device that extends behind the plane. The cost is $300 per message. The football stadium holds 80,000 fans and is filled to capacity every Saturday. Hence, the CPM in this situation is $3.75, which is the cost per message ($300) divided by the number of thousands of people (80) who potentially are exposed to an advertising message trailing from the plane. Now assume that a new restaurant geared toward students uses the airplane advertising service to announce its opening to the 20,000 students who are in attendance at the game. Because the target market in this instance is only a fraction of the total audience, CPM-TM is a more appropriate cost-per-thousand statistic. CPM-TM in this instance is $15 ($300 ÷ 20)—which of course is four times higher than the CPM statistic because the target audience is only one-fourth as large as the total audience.

To further illustrate how CPM and CPM-TM are calculated, consider a more conventional advertising situation on television. Suppose an advertiser promoted its brand on the hospital drama *ER* and that on Thursday evening in the last week of October 1998 this program had a rating of 21.5. This means that 21.5 percent of the approximately 98 million U.S. households—or approximately 21,070,000 households—were tuned in to *ER* on this particular evening. At a cost of $565,000 for a 30-second commercial on this program during the 1998–1999 season, the CPM is as follows:

Total Viewership = 21,070,000 Households

Cost of 30-Second Commercial = $565,000

Thus,

CPM = $565,000 ÷ 21,070

= $26.82

Remember: The denominator in a CPM or CPM-TM calculation is expressed in thousands. In this situation, there are 21,070 thousands of viewers.

If we assume that the target market consists only of women between the ages of 18 and 49 and that this submarket represents 63 percent of the total audience—or 13,274,100 women—then the CPM-TM is

CPM-TM = $565,000 ÷ 13,274.1

= $42.56

The CPM and CPM-TM statistics are useful for comparing different advertising schedules. They must be used cautiously, however, for several reasons. First, these are measures of *cost efficiency*—not of effectiveness. A media schedule may be extremely efficient but totally ineffective because it: (1) reaches the wrong audience (if CPM is used rather than CPM-TM) or (2) is inappropriate for the product category advertised. For instance, compare CPM to using miles-per-gallon calculations for different automobiles. A Hyundai *Excel* may be more efficient than a BMW but less effective for one's purposes.[27]

A second limitation of CPM and CPM-TM measures is their lack of comparability across media. As emphasized in Chapter 12, the various media perform unique roles and are therefore priced differently. A lower CPM for radio does not mean that buying radio is better than buying a more expensive (CPM-wise) television schedule.

Finally, CPM statistics can be misused unless vehicles within a particular medium are compared on the same basis. For example, the CPM for an advertising schedule on daytime television is lower than that for a prime-time schedule, but this represents a case of comparing apples with oranges. The proper comparison would be between two daytime schedules or between two prime-time schedules. Similarly, it would be inappropriate to compare the CPM for a black-and-white magazine ad against a four-color magazine ad unless these two ads are considered equal in terms of their ability to present the brand effectively.

TRADEOFFS, TRADEOFFS, TRADEOFFS

The various media-planning objectives (reach, frequency, weight, continuity, and cost) have now been discussed in some detail. Each was introduced without direct reference to the other objectives. It is important to recognize, however, that these objectives are actually somewhat at odds with one another. That is, given a fixed advertising budget (e.g., $20 million for the Dodge *Rambler*), the media planner cannot simultaneously optimize reach, frequency, and continuity objectives. Tradeoffs must be made because media planners operate under the constraint of fixed advertising budgets. Hence, optimizing one objective (e.g., minimizing CPM or maximizing GRPs) requires the sacrifice of other objectives. This simply is due to the mathematics of constrained optimization: Multiple objectives cannot simultaneously be optimized when constraints (like limited budgets) exist.

For example, with a fixed advertising budget, the media planner can choose to maximize reach or frequency, but not both. With increases in reach, frequency is sacrificed and vice versa—if you want to reach more people, you cannot reach them as often with a fixed advertising budget; if you want to reach them more often, you cannot reach as many. Similarly, with a fixed advertising budget, an advertiser cannot simultaneously increase advertising continuity and also increase reach or frequency. This discussion may remind you of the lesson in basic statistics about the tradeoff between committing Type I and Type II errors while holding sample size constant. That is, with a fixed sample size, decisions to decrease a Type I error (say, from alpha = .05 to .01) must inevitably result in an increase in the Type II, or beta, error, and vice versa. You can't have your cake and eat it too. The advertiser faced with a budget constraint must decide whether frequency is more important (the three-exposure hypothesis) or reach is more important (the shelf-space model).

Thus, each media planner must decide what is best given the particular circumstances surrounding the advertising decision facing his or her brand. As previously discussed, achieving *effective reach* (3+ exposures) is particularly important when brands are new or when established brands have new benefits or uses. In these circumstances, the task of advertising is to teach consumers, and part of teaching is repetition. The more complex the message, the greater the need for repetition to convey the message effectively. However, for established brands that already are well known by consumers, the advertising task is more one of reminding consumers about the brand. The ad budget in this situation is best allocated to achieve the maximum level of *reach*.

Media Planning Software

The media planner is faced with the difficult task of making intelligent tradeoffs among sometimes opposing objectives (reach, frequency, etc.). On top of this, there are literally thousands of possible advertising schedules that could be selected depending on how the various media and media vehicles are combined. Fortunately, this daunting task is facilitated with the availability of computerized models to assist media planners in making media-selection decisions. These models essentially attempt to optimize some goal, or objective function (e.g., selecting a schedule that yields the greatest level of reach), subject to satisfying constraints such as not exceeding the upper limit on the advertising budget. A computer program then searches through the possible solutions and selects a particular media schedule that optimizes the objective function and satisfies all specified constraints.

The functioning of computerized media models will be illustrated with the ADplus software. ADplus is a comprehensive personal computer program that allows the user to evaluate all major advertising media categories and subcategories and to find optimum schedules based on selecting multiple vehicles from within a single advertising medium.

Using for illustration purposes a hypothetical magazine campaign for the Dodge *Rambler* during its introductory month of September 1999, the following steps are involved in using ADplus to develop a media schedule:

1. First, the user must develop a *media database.* This strategic aspect of media planning involves selecting prospective advertising vehicles and specifying their ratings and cost. Table 14.5 illustrates the essential information contained in a media database for the *Rambler.*

2. Next, the user selects the *criterion for schedule optimization.* The available optimization alternatives include maximizing reach (1+), effective reach (3+), frequency, and GRPs. In the illustration to follow, maximize reach (1+) has been selected as the optimizing criterion for *Rambler*'s September campaign.

TABLE 14.5   Media Scheduling Database for the Dodge *Rambler*

MAGAZINE	RATING	COST	MAXIMUM INSERTIONS
Sports Illustrated	37.00	$170,000	4
Field & Stream	19.80	84,630	1
Popular Mechanics	16.00	82,225	1
Playboy	14.50	96,210	1
Hot Rod	11.60	48,080	1
Guns & Ammo	10.30	31,785	1
Golf Digest	10.40	106,610	1
Rolling Stone	10.10	84,445	2
Muscle & Fitness	9.90	27,325	1
Outdoor Life	9.80	58,640	1
Inside Sports	9.40	39,990	1
Ebony	9.30	49,975	1
Road & Track	9.30	64,995	1
Men's Health	9.10	82,955	1
GQ	8.90	51,523	1
Sport	8.30	37,260	1
American Riflemen	7.20	33,057	1
Golf Magazine	7.20	83,085	1
Sporting News	5.60	25,770	4
Sports Afield	5.50	29,700	1

3. Then the user *specifies constraints.* These include: (1) a *budget constraint* and (2) *the minimum and maximum number of ad placements, or insertions, for each vehicle.* The magazine budget constraint for September 1999 is $1 million. Magazine insertion constraints are identified in Table 14.5.

4. Once the user has provided the information required in steps 1 through 3, the ADplus algorithm seeks out the optimum media schedule according to the specified objective function and subject to satisfying the budget and number-of-insertion constraints. The following illustration reveals how this is accomplished.

Hypothetical Illustration

Let us assume that a media planner for the Dodge *Rambler* is in the process of choosing an optimum, four-week schedule—during the September 1999 introduction of the *Rambler*—from among 20 magazines considered appropriate for reaching outdoor-oriented males, aged 18–49, who have incomes of $40,000 or greater. Let us assume further that as of 1999 there were approximately 62 million American males aged 18–49, and that only 44 percent of this group satisfy the *Rambler*'s income target of $40,000 or greater. Thus, the target market is reduced to 27.3 million customers. All subsequent planning is based on this estimate.

The Dodge Rambler Database. The media planner has prepared a database consisting of 20 magazines considered suitable for reaching the target audience (see Table 14.5). In constructing the database, the first determination was the choice of magazines considered appropriate for reaching the Dodge *Rambler*'s target audience. Candidate magazines are listed in the first column of Table 14.5. The second key input was magazine ratings. Ratings (see the second column in Table 14.5) were determined by dividing each magazine's audience size by the size of *Rambler*'s target market, which was estimated as 27.3 million potential customers.[28] Third, costs (the third column) were designated according to the price charged by each magazine for a one-time placement of a full-page, four-color advertisement.[29] Finally, maximum insertions (the last column) were based on each magazine's publication cycle. Seventeen of the 20 magazines are published once per month, whereas *Rolling Stone* is published bimonthly and *Sporting News* and *Sports Illustrated* are published weekly. Hence, only one ad each can be placed during the four-week period in 17 of the magazines, whereas it is possible to place up to two ads in *Rolling Stone* and up to four ads each in *Sporting News* and *Sports Illustrated.*

The Objective Function and Constraints. The information in Table 14.5 was input into the ADplus program by including each magazine's name, cost, rating, and maximum insertions.[30] With this information, the ADplus program was instructed to maximize reach (1+) without exceeding a budget of $1 million for this four-week introductory campaign. Earlier it was indicated that the first-year advertising budget for the *Rambler* totaled $20 million. The media planner has decided to invest $1 million in magazine advertising in the introductory month and another $4 million on TV advertising during this month. The remainder of the budget, $15 million, will be allocated during the end of 1999 and into 2000. (To simplify the discussion, only the magazine component of the media schedule is described here.)

The Optimal Schedule. Given the maximum number of insertions designated for the 20 magazines in Table 14.5, a total of 27 ads could be inserted in these magazines at a total cost of $1,960,015. It will be recalled, however, that a $1 million budget constraint was imposed for magazine advertising in September 1999. It thus is necessary to make a selection from these magazines such that the budget constraint is met and reach is maximized. This is precisely what a media algorithm accomplishes. Given 20 magazines with different numbers of maximum insertions in each, there are numerous combinations of magazines that could be selected. However, in a matter of seconds, the ADplus algorithm identified the single combination of magazines that would maximize reach for an expenditure of $1 million or less. The solution is displayed in Table 14.6.

TABLE 14.6 — ADplus™ Optimum Schedule for the Dodge *Rambler* Magazine Campaign, September 1999

Dodge *Rambler*
September 1999

Target: 27,300,000
Males 18–49, $40,000+

Message/vehicle = 52.5%

FREQUENCY (F) DISTRIBUTIONS

f	VEHICLE % f	VEHICLE % f+	MESSAGE % f	MESSAGE % f+
0	29.9	100.0	57.0	100.0
1	10.7	70.1	5.6	43.0
2	16.5	59.4	9.7	37.4
3	17.7	43.0	11.0	27.7
4	13.2	25.3	8.6	16.7
5	7.3	12.0	4.9	8.1
6	3.2	4.8	2.2	3.3
7	1.1	1.6	0.8	1.1
8	0.4	0.5	0.3	0.3
9	0.1	0.1	0.1	0.1
10+	0.0	0.0	0.0	0.0

SUMMARY EVALUATION

	VEHICLE	MESSAGE
Reach (1+)	70.1%	43.0%
Effective reach (3+)	43.0%	27.7%
Gross rating points (GRPs)	216.8	137.9
Average frequency (f)	3.1	3.2
Gross impressions (000s)	59,186.4	37,634.5
Cost-per-thousand (CPM)	$16.75	$26.35
Cost-per-rating point (CPP)	$4,573	$7,192

VEHICLE LIST	RATING	AD COST	CPM-MSG	ADS	TOTAL COST	MIX
Muscle & Fitness	9.90	$27,325	$19.26	1	$27,325	2.8%
Guns & Ammo	10.30	31,785	21.53	1	31,785	3.2
Hot Rod	11.60	48,080	28.92	1	48,080	4.8
Inside Sports	9.40	39,990	29.68	1	39,990	4.0
Field & Stream	19.80	84,630	29.82	1	84,630	8.5
Sport	8.30	37,260	31.32	1	37,260	3.8
American Riflemen	7.20	33,057	32.03	1	33,057	3.3
Sports Illus.	37.00	170,000	32.06	2	340,000	34.3
Sporting News	5.60	25,770	32.11	3	77,310	7.8
Popular Mechanics	16.00	82,225	35.86	1	82,225	8.3
Ebony	9.30	49,975	37.49	1	49,975	5.0
Sports Afield	5.50	29,700	37.68	1	29,700	3.0
GQ	8.90	51,523	40.39	1	51,523	5.2
Outdoor Life	9.80	58,640	41.75	1	58,640	5.9
Totals:			$26.35	17	$991,500	100.0%

Table 14.6 shows that the optimum schedule consists of three ads in *Sporting News,* two ads in *Sports Illustrated,* and one ad each in *Muscle & Fitness, Guns & Ammo, Hot Rod, Inside Sports, Field & Stream, Sport, American Riflemen, Popular Mechanics, Ebony, Sports Afield, GQ,* and *Outdoor Life.* (Six magazines, including *Golf Digest* and *Golf Magazine* were not included in the final solution. Perusal of Table 14.5 will reveal that these magazines are relatively expensive in view of the ratings delivered.) The total cost is $991,500, which is just under the specified upper limit of $1 million. (Note that the inclusion of any single additional advertisement would have exceeded the imposed budget limit.)

Interpretation of the Solution. Let us carefully examine the data in Table 14.6. Notice first that the boxed section in the upper left-hand corner provides pertinent details about the schedule. The only new piece of information here states that the message/vehicle equals 52.5 percent. This value, 52.5 percent, is a ratio representing the likelihood that consumers who are exposed to the magazine vehicle also will be exposed to the advertising message within it. This ratio, although a rough estimate, was obtained from a survey of media directors who were asked to identify the message/vehicle ratios they employ for different media categories.[31] The corresponding ratios for television, radio, and newspapers have been estimated at 32 percent, 16 percent, and 16 percent, respectively.[32] These ratios mean that roughly one of three TV viewers and one of six radio listeners and newspaper readers are predicted to be exposed to any particular advertisement contained in each medium. These ratios are, of course, imperfect estimates that are not applicable to every advertising situation. For example, people watching the NFL Super Bowl are probably much more likely to view advertisements than normally is the case.

The next pertinent information to observe in Table 14.6 is the *vehicle* and *message frequency distributions.* Conceptually these are identical, but the percentages in the message distribution are lower for the reasons described in the previous paragraph. To interpret the vehicle distribution, recall the earlier discussion of the 10-household market for the Dodge *Rambler* advertised in *Rolling Stone* magazine. It will be helpful to review the concepts of: (1) exposure level (f); (2) frequency distribution, or percent of audience exposed at each level of f (percentage f), and (3) cumulative frequency distribution (percentage $f+$). When f equals zero, the percentage f and percentage $f+$ values in Table 14.6 are 29.9 and 100, respectively. This is to say that the 29.9 of the 27.3 million audience members will not be exposed to any of the 14 magazines that made it into the optimum solution and that are listed at the bottom of Table 14.6. The cumulative frequency when f equals zero is of course 100—that is, 100 percent of the audience members will be exposed zero or more times to magazine vehicles in *Rambler*'s four-week advertising schedule. Note further that percentage f and percentage $f+$ are 10.7 and 70.1 when f equals 1. That is, the media algorithm estimates that 10.7 percent of the target audience will be exposed to exactly one of the 14 magazines, and 70.1 percent of the audience will be exposed to one or more of the magazines during this four-week period in September 1999. Note carefully under the summary evaluation in the middle of Table 14.6 that vehicle reach equals 70.1 percent. With reach defined as the percentage of the target audience exposed one or more times (i.e., 1+), the level of reach is determined merely by identifying the corresponding value in the percentage $f+$ column, which, when f equals 1, is 70.1 percent. It should also be clear that because 29.9 percent of the audience is exposed zero times, the complement of this value (100 percent − 29.9 percent = 70.1 percent) is the percentage of the audience exposed one or more times—that is, the percentage of the audience reached.

Hence, this optimum schedule yields a *vehicle reach* of 70.1, which is the maximum level of reach that any combination of the selected magazines could achieve within a budget constraint of $1 million. This optimum vehicle schedule reaches the audience an average of 3.1 times (see average frequency under the summary evaluation in Table 14.6) and produces approximately 217 GRPs. These GRPs, by the way, are calculated simply by multiplying the ratings for each magazine by the number of ads placed in that magazine [(*Muscle & Fitness* = 9.9 × 1) + (*Guns & Ammo* = 10.3 × 1) + . . . + (*Outdoor Life* = 9.8 × 1) = 216.8 GRPs]. Effective vehicle reach (i.e., 3+) is 43 percent. That is, only 43 percent of the total audience are exposed to three or more vehicles. This value is obtained, of course, by reading across from $f = 3$ to the corresponding *percentage f+* column. The cost per thousand (CPM) is $16.75. [This value is calculated as follows: (1) Audience size is 27,300,000; (2) 70.1 percent, or 19,137,300, of the people are reached by the schedule of magazines shown in Table 14.6; (3) each person reached is done so on average approximately 3.1 times (see Table 14.6); (4) the number of gross impressions, which is the number of people reached multiplied by the average number of times they are reached, is thus 59,186,400 (slightly off due to rounding error); (5) the total cost of this media schedule is

$991,500 (see bottom of "total cost" column in Table 14.6); and (6) hence the CPM is $991,500 ÷ 59,186.4 = $16.75.] Finally, the cost per rating point (CPP) is $4,573 ($991,500 ÷ 216.8 GRPs).

Does Table 14.6 present a good media schedule? In terms of reach, the schedule is the best of all possible schedules that could have been produced from the various combinations of 20 magazines that were input into the ADplus algorithm. No other combination from among these 20 magazines could have exceeded this schedule's vehicle reach of 70.1 percent. Note carefully, however, that this *opportunity to see* (OTS) the advertisement for Dodge *Rambler* is not tantamount to having actually seen the advertisement. Indeed, it can be seen under the message frequency distribution column that the advertising message for Dodge *Rambler* is estimated to reach only 43 percent of the audience one or more times. (By contrast, the vehicle reach is 70.1 percent.) Such an achievement would be inadequate were it not for the fact, as earlier noted, that television advertising is to be run simultaneously with the magazine schedule. The combination of these media can be expected to produce much more impressive numbers and to achieve *Rambler*'s introductory advertising objectives.

It is critical to emphasize that media models such as ADplus do not make the ultimate scheduling decision. All they can do is efficiently perform the calculations needed to determine which single media schedule will optimize some objective function such as maximizing reach or GRPs. Armed with the answer, it is up to the media planner to determine whether the media schedule satisfies other, nonquantitative objectives such as those described in Chapter 12.

THE SAAB 9–5 MEDIA CAMPAIGN

Now that fundamental issues in media scheduling have been identified, it will be useful to consider two actual media campaigns. First discussed is the 1998 campaign for the Saab 9-5 luxury automobile, which was previously discussed in Chapter 13 and also was the subject of this chapter's *Opening Vignette*. Next presented is an award-winning campaign for Diet Dr Pepper.

As described in Chapter 13, Saab, the Swedish automobile maker, introduced a new luxury sedan named the Saab 9-5 in April 1998. This model represented Saab's first entry in the luxury category and was designed to compete against well-known high-equity brands including Mercedes, BMW, Volvo, Lexus, and Infiniti. In addition to innovative and aggressive direct mailing and outbound telemarketing campaigns (the subject of Chapter 13), the Martin Agency representing Saab also developed a thoroughly integrative media schedule. The media schedule is presented in Table 14.7.

It first will be noted from Table 14.7 that TV advertising started in January, which was prior to the 9-5's introduction in April. Network and cable TV advertising ran in late January and into February and then again throughout May following the 9-5's introduction. Note that the initial network TV campaign accumulated 74 GRPs for each of three weeks (the weeks beginning January 19, January 26, and February 2) and that accompanying advertising on cable TV amassed 40 GRPs for each of these same three weeks. Following the 9-5's introduction, the May television schedule accumulated 95 and 60 GRPs, respectively, on network and cable TV. Or, in other words, a total of 620 television GRPs [(95 × 4) + (60 × 4)] were purchased in May.

Table 14.7 further reveals that magazine advertising for the Saab 9-5 started in late January and continued for the remainder of the year without interruption. A wide variety of magazines were used to reach Saab's designated market for the 9-5. These included such outlets as automotive magazines (e.g., *Car & Driver, Road & Track*), sports publications (e.g., *Ski, Tennis*), home magazines (e.g., *Martha Stewart Living, Architectural Digest*), business magazines (e.g., *Money, Forbes, Working Women*), and general interest publications (e.g., *Time, New York Magazine*). National newspaper advertising in *USA Today* and the *Wall Street Journal* also was run throughout the year. And finally, Internet banner advertising was run continuously throughout 1998 on the *Wall Street Journal's Interactive Edition*.

TABLE 14.7

Media Plan for the Saab 9–5

Medium	29	5	12	19	26	2	9	16	23	2	9	16	23	30	6	13	20	27	4	11	18	25	1	8	15	22
(JAN)	JAN				*(FEB)* FEB					*(MAR)* MAR				*(APR)* APR				*(MAY)* MAY					*(JUN)* JUN			
Network TV					74 wk														95 wk							
Network Cable					40 wk														60 wk							
Magazines						■ solid bar ── ■																				
Newspapers																										
USA Today																										
3 PBW (2X)														1X		1X										
SPBW (1X)															1X											
PBW (12X)																										
T Page (58X)	1X			1X	1X	1X		1X		2X	2X	2X	2X	2X	2X	2X	2X	2X	1X	1X		1X		1X		1X
1/4 PBW (8X)											4X	2X	2X													
Wall Street Jrnl																										
3 PBW (2X)														1X		1X										
SPBW (1X)															1X											
PBW (12X)																										
4 col x 14" (63X)	1X	1X		1X	1X	1X		1X	2X	2X	2X	2X	2X	2X	2X	2X	2X	2X	1X	1X	1X	1X	1X	1X	1X	1X
4 col x 8" (8X)											2X	4X	2X													
Interactive		■ solid bar ─── ■																								

Legend:

1X, 2X, etc. = Number of insertions per week placed in *USA Today* or *WSJ* (1X = one insertion, 2X = two insertions, etc.)
3 PBW = 3 pages black & white magazine ad
SPBW = Spread page B&W (ad runs across 2 pages like a centerfold)
PBW = 1-page black & white
T Page = An odd shaped add placement
¼ PBW = ¼ page B&W
Interactive = Internet banner ad placed on *The Wall Street Journal Interactive Edition*

THE DIET DR PEPPER CAMPAIGN

www.drpepper.com
www.yandr.com
www.clioawards.com

An award-winning advertising campaign for Diet Dr Pepper developed by the Young & Rubicam advertising agency provides an exemplary application of media scheduling and

Table 14.7 Continued

	JUL				AUG					SEP				OCT				NOV					DEC			
	29	6	13	20	27	3	10	17	24	31	7	14	21	28	5	12	19	26	2	9	16	23	30	7	14	21
Network TV																										
Network Cable																										
Magazines																										
Newspapers																										
USA Today																										
3 PBW (2X)																										
SPBW (1X)																										
PBW (12X)														1X	3X	2X					3X	1X	2X			
T Page (58X)		1X	1X	1X	1X	1X	1X	1X	1X	1X	1X	1X	2X	1X		1X	2X	2X	2X	2X		1X	1X	2X	2X	1X
1/4 PBW (8X)																										
Wall Street Jrnl																										
3 PBW (2X)																										
SPBW (1X)																										
PBW (12X)														1X	2X	2X	1X			2X	1X	2X	1X			
4 col x 14" (63X)	1X	2X	1X	1X	1X	1X	1X	1X	1X	1X		1X	2X	1X	1X	1X	1X	2X	2X	2X	1X	1X	1X	1X	2X	1X
4 col x 8" (8X)																										
Interactive																										

the advertising creative process around which scheduling takes place. This campaign received a Gold Effie Award from the advertising community in tribute to its accomplishment.[33]

Marketing Situation and Campaign Objectives

Diet Dr Pepper competes in a dynamic and constantly changing category that makes it difficult to increase market share and sustain long-term brand growth. Major factors that challenge the brand's growth include the following:

- ◆ *Sluggish category growth.* The diet, carbonated-soft drink category was growing at an average annual rate of only 1.4 percent.
- ◆ *Growth of new-age beverages.* The new-age segment—consisting of sparkling juices, natural sodas, flavored sodas, and other items—was growing at a rapid rate (10 percent annual growth), posing a strong challenge to Diet Dr Pepper and other diet soft drinks.

♦ *Price sensitivity of soft-drink category.* Price is a major brand-choice determinant in this category, but Diet Dr Pepper is at a competitive disadvantage inasmuch as it is priced higher on a cents-per-ounce basis than Coca-Cola and Pepsi-Cola brands.

♦ *Lack of bottler attention and focus.* Approximately three-fourths of Diet Dr Pepper's volume is distributed via the Coke and Pepsi bottler distribution network, which in many instances causes Diet Dr Pepper to be a low-priority item with insufficient retailer support.

♦ *Inadequate distribution.* Relative to its larger competitors, Diet Dr Pepper's distribution is insufficient in trial-inducing outlets such as fountain/food service and vending machines.

♦ *Greater spending by major competitors.* Diet Dr Pepper's share of voice (SOV) at the onset of the advertising campaign was only 4.8 percent in this highly competitive and advertising-sensitive category.

Campaign Target and Objectives. The target audience for Diet Dr Pepper consists primarily of adults aged 18–49 who are present or prospective diet soft-drink consumers. In view of the above marketing challenges, the objectives for the Diet Dr Pepper advertising campaign (titled "The Taste You've Been Looking For") were as follows:

1. To increase Diet Dr Pepper sales by 4 percent and improve its growth rate to at least 1.5 times that of the diet soft-drink category.

2. To heighten consumers' evaluations of the key product benefit and image factors that influence brand choice in this category: It is refreshing, tastes as good as regular Dr Pepper, is a good product to drink at any time, and is a fun brand to drink.

3. To enhance those key brand-personality dimensions that differentiate Diet Dr Pepper from other diet drinks—particularly that Diet Dr Pepper is a unique, clever, fun, entertaining, and interesting brand to drink.

Creative Strategy and Supportive Promotions

www.cocacola.com

www.pepsi.com

The creative strategy for Diet Dr Pepper positioned the brand as "tasting more like regular Dr Pepper." This was a key claim based on research revealing that nearly 60 percent of initial trial users of Diet Dr Pepper were motivated by the desire to have a diet soft drink that tasted like regular Dr Pepper. The cornerstone of the campaign entailed the heavy use of 15-second commercials, which historically had not been used by Coca-Cola and Pepsi-Cola, which instead preferred the entertainment value of longer commercials. The aggressive use of 15-second commercials enabled Diet Dr Pepper to simply convey its key taste claim ("tastes more like regular Dr Pepper") and differentiate the brand from competitive diet drinks. Moreover, by employing cheaper 15-second commercials, it was possible to buy many more commercial spots and hence to achieve greater reach, frequency, and GRPs for the same advertising budget. Diet Dr Pepper's advertising expenditures totaled $20.27 million.[34]

In addition to the advertising campaign, the brand marketers for Diet Dr Pepper implemented several sales promotion programs to achieve their lofty goals. From January through April, a trade promotion called "The Pepper Advantage" provided bottlers with $30 gift certificates (for use at apparel retailer Eddie Bauer) that they could distribute to retailers to encourage greater display space for Diet Dr Pepper. In addition, attractive coupons were placed on 2- and 3-liter bottles of Diet Dr Pepper to encourage repeat purchasing by consumers.

From April to September, during baseball season, the "Pepper Pastime" promotion was run to enhance sales of Diet Dr Pepper to consumers in convenience stores. Promotions included free bottles of Diet Dr Pepper and premium objects, including autographed baseballs and baseball jerseys emblazoned with the Diet Dr Pepper brand name. During May through August, a promotional tie-in with the Foot Locker chain of athletic stores was undertaken. Purchasers of 12- and 24-packs of Diet Dr Pepper received Foot Locker gift certificates if their pack contained a winning game card inside. Collectively, these sales promotion programs were designed to complement the advertising campaign and substantially boost immediate sales of Diet Dr Pepper products.

Media Strategy

The advertising schedule for Diet Dr Pepper generated a total of 1,858 GRPs, with a cumulative annual reach of 95 and frequency of 19.6. These media-weight values were accomplished with the national media plan summarized as a flowchart in Table 14.8.

The 12 months and the week-beginning dates (Mondays) throughout the year are listed across the top of the flowchart. Table entries reflect the target rating points achieved by each advertised event for each weekly period. The first entry, a 41 for the *NFL Championship Games,* indicates that 41 gross rating points were produced by placing advertisements for Diet Dr Pepper during these televised football games.

It can be seen that the Diet Dr Pepper media plan consisted of: (1) placing advertisements during professional and college football games (the SEC stands for Southeastern Conference); (2) sponsoring various special events (e.g., the *Country Music Awards,* the *Garth Brooks Special,* and golfing events); and (3) continuously advertising during prime time, on late-night television (e.g., *David Letterman*), on syndicated programs, and on cable stations.

At the bottom of Table 14.8 is a summary of GRPs broken down by week (e.g., 86 GRPs during the week beginning January 10), month (e.g., 227 GRPs during January), and quarter (e.g., 632 GRPs produced during the first quarter, January through March). It can be seen that the media schedule was *flighted* insofar as advertisements were placed during approximately two-thirds of the 52 weeks with no advertising during the remaining weeks. In sum, the media schedule was designed to highlight Diet Dr Pepper during a variety of special events and to maintain continuity throughout the year with prime-time network advertising and less expensive support on syndicated and cable programming.

Results

The advertising campaign for Diet Dr Pepper was extremely successful, even surpassing the ambitious goals established for the brand. Sales of Diet Dr Pepper increased by 6.6 percent compared to the increase of only 1.4 percent for other diet soft-drink brands during the same year.[35] Research also revealed that consumer brand ratings of Diet Dr Pepper improved over the previous year and surpassed ratings achieved by Diet Coke and Diet Pepsi on several important dimensions: refreshing, tastes as good as regular, good anytime, fun to drink, and unique.

All in all, "The Taste You've Been Looking For" campaign was extremely successful and served well to enhance Diet Dr Pepper's image and sales volume. The bold and innovative use of 15-second commercials allowed the brand to advertise aggressively, to maintain an almost continuous presence on television, and to differentiate Diet Dr Pepper successfully from competitive diet soft drinks. This is what good advertising is all about. Creative advertising and proper media selection can yield dramatic increases in sales volume and enhance a brand's equity. Diet Dr Pepper certainly is a more valuable brand as a result of these advertising efforts.

TABLE 14.8   Media Plan for Diet Dr Pepper

ADULTS 18–49 GRPs

Category	J27	J3	J10	J17	J24	F31	F7	F14	F21	F28	M7	M14	M21	M28	A4	A11	A18	A25	My2	My9	My16	My23	My30	Jn6	Jn13	Jn20
SPORTS																										
NFL Championship Games				41																						
Road to the Superbowl					10																					
FOX "Game of the Month"																										
NBC "Game of the Month"																										
NBC Thanksgiving Game																										
ABC Monday Night Football																										
4Q Sports Total				41	10																					
SEC Championship Game																										
SEC-CFA Regular Game																										
SEC Thanksgiving Game																										
SEC Local/Conference Fee																										
SEC Sponsorship Total																										
TOTAL SPORTS				41	10																					
EVENTS																										
McDonald's Golf Classic																		1								
Daytime Emmy Awards																					23					
Country Music Awards																		32								
Garth Brooks Special																		12								
Michael Bolton Sponsorship																										
May Event Print																			17	18						
JC Penney LPGA Golf																										
Harvey Penick Special																								1		
Diners Club Golf																										
TOTAL EVENTS																			61	18	17	41	1			
CONTINUITY																										
Prime		53					53				53		54		34	35		35				35				35
May Event Prime Scatter																			29	28						
Late Night		6	5								5				3				3		4					
Syndication		14					14				13				8			8			8					8
Cable		13					14				14				11			11			11					
TOTAL CONTINUITY		86	126	15	86	81			85	68					56	57		54	86	28		86	58			43
Integration-to-date																										
Total Diet Plan		86	126	15	86	81			85	68					56	57		54	147	46	103	127	59			43
A18-49 GRPs/Week																										
Amount Over Budget																										

A18-49 GRPs/Month

JAN	FEB	MAR	APR	MAY	JUN
227	167	238	167	477	102

A18-49 GRPs/Quarter

632	746

Table 14.8 Continued

ADULTS 18–49 GRPs	JUL 27	4	11	18	25	AUG 1	8	15	22	SEP 29	5	12	19	OCT 26	3	10	17	24	NOV 31	7	14	21	28	DEC 5	12	19
SPORTS																										
NFL Championship Games																										
Road to the Superbowl																										
FOX "Game of the Month"														28							24			25		
NBC "Game of the Month"																13				22				20		
NBC Thanksgiving Game																							22			
ABC Monday Night Football																22			20	10		24				25
4Q Sports Total														28		35			20	10	46	24	22	45		25
SEC Championship Game																								33		
SEC-CFA Regular Game															8											
SEC Thanksgiving Game																							6			
SEC Local/Conference Fee																										
SEC Sponsorship Total															8								6	33		
TOTAL SPORTS														28	8	35			20	10	46	24	28	78		25
EVENTS																										
McDonald's Golf Classic																										
Daytime Emmy Awards																										
Country Music Awards																										
Garth Brooks Special																										
Michael Bolton Sponsorship																										
May Event Print																										
JC Penney LPGA Golf																										
Harvey Penick Special																										
Diners Club Golf																										
TOTAL EVENTS																										
CONTINUITY																										
Prime	25					25				26																
May Event Prime Scatter																										
Late Night																										
Syndication																										
Cable																										
TOTAL CONTINUITY	25					25				26																
Integration-to-date																										
Total Diet Plan	25					25				26				28	8	35			20	10	46	24	28	78		15
A18-49 GRPs/Week																										
Amount Over Budget																										

A18-49 GRPs/Month: JUL 75 | AUG 51 | SEP 52 | OCT 91 | NOV 108 | DEC 103

A18-49 GRPs/Quarter: 178 (JUL–SEP) | 302 (OCT–DEC)

Summary

Selection of advertising media and vehicles is one of the most important and complicated of all marketing communications decisions. Media planning must be coordinated with marketing strategy and with other aspects of advertising strategy. The strategic aspects of media planning involve four steps: (1) selecting the target audience toward which all subsequent efforts will be directed; (2) specifying media objectives, which typically are stated in terms of reach, frequency, gross rating points (GRPs), or effective rating points (ERPs); (3) selecting general media categories and specific vehicles within each medium; and (4) buying media.

Media and vehicle selection are influenced by a variety of factors; most important are target audience, cost, and creative considerations. Media planners select media vehicles by identifying those that will reach the designated target audience, satisfy budgetary constraints, and be compatible with and enhance the advertiser's creative message. There are numerous ways to schedule media insertions over time, but media planners have typically used some form of pulsed or flighted schedule whereby advertising is on at times, off at others, but never continuous. The shelf-space model of advertising, which also is known as the principle of recency, challenges the use of flighted advertising schedules and purports that weekly efficient reach should be the decision criterion of choice because this approach ensures that advertising will be run at the time when consumers are making brand-selection decisions.

The chapter has provided detailed explanations of the various considerations used by media planners in making advertising media decisions. These include the concepts of reach, frequency, gross rating points (GRPs), effective rating points (ERPs), and cost and continuity considerations. Media vehicles within the same medium are compared in terms of cost using the cost-per-thousand criterion.

The chapter includes a detailed discussion of a computerized media-selection model called ADplus. This model requires information about vehicle cost, ratings, maximum number of insertions, and a budget constraint and then maximizes an objective function subject to that budget. Optimization criteria include maximizing reach (1+), effective reach (3+), frequency, or GRPs.

The chapter concludes with descriptions of media plans for the Saab 9-5 and Diet Dr Pepper.

Discussion Questions

1. Why is target-audience selection the critical first step in formulating a media strategy?
2. Explain the problems associated with using GRPs as a media-selection criterion. In what sense is the concept of ERPs superior?
3. Why is reach also called *net coverage* or *unduplicated audience?*
4. Referring to the ADplus output for the hypothetical media schedule for the Dodge *Rambler* (Table 14.6), show how the following values were obtained:
   a. Vehicle reach = 70.1 percent; Message reach = 43.0 percent.
   b. Vehicle frequency = 3.1; Message frequency = 3.2.
   c. CPM (Message) = $26.35.
   d. CPM-MSG (*Ebony*) = $37.49. (Hint: You will have to consider *Ebony's* rating from Table 14.5 and the message/vehicle ration of 52.5 percent in order to determine how many of the members of *Rambler's* 27,300,000 target audience would have been exposed to an advertisement for *Rambler* printed in *Ebony*.)
   e. CPP (Vehicle) = $4,573
   f. GRPs (Vehicle) = 216.8
5. *Golf Digest* and *Golf Magazine* were two of six advertising vehicles not included in the optimum media schedule for the Dodge *Rambler*. Why do you think that they were excluded?

6. The chapter endnotes refer to a publication called the *"$ Ad Summary"* that also is generally known as *Leading National Advertisers*. Go to your library and find the most recent version of *LNA*. Identify the advertising expenditures and the media used in advertising the following brands: Diet Coke, Tide detergent, and the Jeep *Cherokee*.

7. With reference to the three-exposure hypothesis, explain the difference between three exposures to an advertising message versus three exposures to an advertising vehicle.

8. When an advertiser uses the latter, what implicit assumption is that advertiser making?

9. Describe in your own words the fundamental logic underlying the shelf-space model of advertising. Is this model always the best model to apply in setting media allocations over time?

10. A TV program has a rating of 17.6. With approximately 99 million television households in the United States as of 2000, what is that program's CPM if a 30-second commercial costs $550,000? Now assume that an advertiser's target audience consists only of people aged 25–54, which constitutes 62 percent of the program's total audience. What is the CPM-TM in this case?

11. Which is more important for an advertiser: maximizing reach or maximizing frequency? Explain in detail.

12. In the ADplus output in Table 14.6, the message/vehicle ratio equals 52.5 percent. Explain in your own words precisely what this means. Why is the ratio for TV lower than this?

13. Reach will be lower for an advertised brand if the entire advertising budget during a four-week period is devoted to advertising exclusively on a single program than if the same budget is allocated among a variety of TV programs. Why is this so?

14. Following are the ratings and number of ad placements on five cable TV programs designated as C1 through C5: C1 (rating=7; placements=6); C2 (rating =4; placements=12); C3 (rating=3; placements=20); C4 (rating=5; placements=10); C5 (rating=6; placements=15). How many GRPs would be obtained from this cable TV advertising schedule?

15. Assume that in Canada there are 21 million TV households. A particular TV prime-time program aired at 9:00 P.M. and had a rating of 18.5 and a 32 share. At the 9:00 air time, how many TV sets were tuned into this or another program? (Hint: Read the introduction of the *IMC Focus* titled "GRPs in the U.S. and Mexico" in order to understand the distinction between ratings and share.)

*I*nternet Exercises

1. Approximately 40% of Internet advertising is sold on a CPM basis while the other 60% is sold by combining CPM with other Internet "traffic" measures (e.g., "click-throughs" and "impressions"). Recently, prominent Internet analysts have concluded that online CPMs are too high, particularly compared to magazines and television. However, as discussed in the text, such comparisons are not valid. Address the following questions to demonstrate your understanding of this point:

   a. Locate a recent Internet survey or report (such as those at www.nua.ie/surveys, www.cc.gatech.edu/gvu, or www.usadata.com). Identify a target market where a premium (on CPM-TM) for Internet advertising (relative to magazines or television) is justified. Be sure to include specific reasons for your choice.

   b. Banner ads typically occupy 480×60 pixels. Most browsers are set by default to a screen size of 640×480 pixels. Thus, the ad-to-edit ratio for one banner ad is $480 \times 60/640 \times 480 = 9.4\%$. Magazines are typically in the 50% range (i.e., 50% ads and 50% copy) while television weighs in at 40% (i.e., 40% commercials and 60% programming). What are the implications of these facts for CPM-TM comparisons?

   c. Consumers on the Internet are arguably more "involved" (since reading, clicking, and typing are required) than consumers in front of a television or consumers listening to a radio. How might this consideration impact comparisons of CPM-TM across the media?

2. Visit www.netratings.com/sample.html and follow the "Top Ten Weekly Properties" link.
   a. How does the information on this Web page relate to the chapter's discussion of "reach"?
   b. Could you develop a reasonable measure of "frequency" using the information on the Web page?

3. Visit www.adage.com/dataplace/index.html. Follow the "Top 200 Brands" link. Now follow the "Top 200 brands: Jan-June 1997" link. Identify the advertising expenditures and media used (all 11 categories) by the #22 and #26 brands (Miller Beer and Budweiser Beer).

*C*hapter Fourteen Endnotes

1. Ave Butensky, "Hitting the Spot," *Agency,* winter 1998, 26.

2. Kate Lynch (VP-director of media research, Leo Burnett, USA) as cited in Laurie Freeman, "Added Theories Drive Need for Client Solutions," *Advertising Age,* August 4, 1997, s18.

3. Kent M. Lancaster, "Optimizing Advertising Media Plans Using ADOPT on the Microcomputer," working paper, University of Illinois, December 1987, 2–3.

4. Arnold M. Barban, Steven M. Cristol, and Frank J. Kopec, *Essentials of Media Planning: A Marketing Viewpoint* (Lincolnwood, IL: NTC Business Books, 1987), 1.

5. This illustration is hypothetical and has no basis in any fact known to the author. American Motors, which later was purchased by the Chrysler Corporation, marketed an automobile under the *Rambler* name in the mid- to late-1960s.

6. Henry Assael and Hugh Cannon, "Do Demographics Help in Media Selection?" *Journal of Advertising Research* 19 (December 1979), 7–11; Hugh M. Cannon and G. Russell Merz, "A New Role for Psychographics in Media Selection," *Journal of Advertising* 9, no. 2 (1980), 33–36, 44.

7. A quote from advertising consultant Alvin Achenbaum cited in B. G. Yovovich, "Media's New Exposures," *Advertising Age,* April 13, 1981, S7.

8. One study found that over 80 percent of advertising agencies use effective reach as a criterion in media planning. See Peggy J. Kreshel, Kent M. Lancaster, and Margaret A. Toomey, "How Leading Advertising Agencies Perceive Effective Reach and Frequency," *Journal of Advertising* 14, no. 3 (1985), 32–38.

9. Gerard J. Tellis, "Advertising Exposure, Loyalty, and Brand Purchase: A Two-Stage Model of Choice," *Journal of Marketing Research* 25 (May 1988), 134–144.

10. Herbert E. Krugman, "Why Three Exposures May Be Enough," *Journal of Advertising Research* 12, no. 6 (1972), 11–14.

11. This point is made especially forcefully by Hugh M. Cannon and Edward A. Riordan, "Effective Reach and Frequency: Does It Really Make Sense? *Journal of Advertising Research* 34 (March/April 1994), 19–28.

12. Ibid., 21.

13. Ibid., 24.

14. Ibid., 25–26. The following illustration is also taken from this source.

15. Peter B. Turk, "Effective Frequency Report: Its Use and Evaluation by Major Agency Media Department Executives," *Journal of Advertising Research* 28 (April/May 1988), 55–59.

16. Adapted from "The Muscle in Multiple Media," *Marketing Communications,* December 1983, 25.

17. Leonard M. Lodish, *The Advertising and Promotion Challenge: Vaguely Right or Precisely Wrong?* (New York: Oxford University Press, 1986).

18. Erwin Ephron, "More Weeks, Less Weight: The Shelf-Space Model of Advertising," *Journal of Advertising Research* 35 (May/June 1995), 18–23.

19. Ibid., 5–18. See also John Philip Jones, "Single-Source Research Begins to Fulfill Its Promise," *Journal of Advertising Research* 35 (May/June 1995), 9–16; Lawrence D. Gibson, "What Can One TV Exposure Do?" *Journal of Advertising Research* 36 (March-April 1996), 9–18; and Kenneth A. Longman, "If Not Effective Frequency, Then What?" *Journal of Advertising Research* 37 (July–August 1997), 44–50.

20. Ephron, "More Weeks, Less Weight: The Shelf-Space Model of Advertising," 19.

21. Ibid., 20.

22. A quote from Joanne Burke, senior VP worldwide media research director, TN Media, New York, in Freeman, "'Effective Weekly Planning' Gets a Boost," S8, S9.

23. Erwin Ephron, "Recency Planning," *Journal of Advertising Research* 37 (July/August 1997), 61–65.

24. Ibid., 61.

25. For elaboration on these points, see Gerard J. Tellis, "Effective Frequency: One Exposure or Three Factors?" *Journal of Advertising Research* 37 (July/August 1997), 75–80.

26. Charles H. Patti and Charles F. Frazer, *Advertising: A Decision-Making Approach* (Hinsdale, IL: The Dryden Press, 1988), 369.

27. This analogy is adapted from Patti and Frazer, *Advertising: A Decision-Making Approach.*

28. For constructing Table 14.5, magazine audience sizes were based on the larger of the estimated audience sizes provided by Simmons Marketing Research Bureau and Mediamark Research, Inc. Figures were obtained from *Marketer's Guide to Media: 1998–99,* vol. 21 (New York: BPI Communications, 1998), 171–177. Because

many of the readers of these magazines do not satisfy the income requirement of $40,000+ or are not within the 18–49 age category targeted for the *Rambler,* each magazine's total audience size was arbitrarily reduced by 50 percent prior to being divided by the target audience size of 27.3 million.

29. This information was obtained from *Marketer's Guide to Media: 1998–99,* 155–159. In actuality, a large advertiser such as Dodge would receive quantity discounts and, thus, would pay only about 60 to 70 percent as much per full-page ad as the costs listed in Table 14.5.

30. A users' manual and operating diskettes for the ADplus program are available in a *Windows* version. This package sells commercially for $449 but is available to educators at a substantially reduced rate. The program was developed by Kent Lancaster and is distributed by Telmar Information Services Corp., 148 Madison Ave., New York, NY 10016 (phone: 212-725-3000), under the title *ADplus for Multi-Media Advertising Planning.*

31. Kent M. Lancaster, Peggy J. Kreshel, and Joya R. Harris, "Estimating the Impact of Advertising Media Plans: Media Executives Describe Weighting and Timing Factors," *Journal of Advertising* 15 (September 1986), 21–29, 45.

32. Lancaster, *ADplus for Multi-Media Advertising Planning,* 17.

33. The following descriptions are based on a summary of Diet Dr Pepper's 1994 advertising campaign prepared by Young & Rubicam. Appreciation for these materials is extended to Chris Wright-Isak and John T. O'Brien.

34. "Ad $ Summary January-December 1994," *Competitive Media: LNA/Media Watch Multi-Media Service* (New York: Competitive Media Reporting, 1995), 208. (It is important to note that this publication, which often is referred to as *Leading National Advertisers [LNA],* is an invaluable source for learning how much particular brands spend on advertising and the specific advertising media they use.)

35. These statistics are based on retail product movement as revealed by Nielsen's ScanTrak service, which is discussed in the following chapter. Based on the Bottler Case Sales Report, Diet Dr Pepper's sales volume increased 7.2 percent compared to a 1.6 percent growth by other diet soft drinks.

Assessing Advertising Effectiveness

CHAPTER OBJECTIVES

After studying this chapter, you should be able to:

1. Explain the rationale and importance of advertising research.
2. Describe the various research methods used in measuring audiences for magazines, radio, and television.
3. Describe the various research techniques used to measure consumers' recognition and recall of advertising messages.
4. Discuss the various measures of emotional response to advertisements.
5. Describe measures of physiological arousal to advertisements.
6. Explain the role of pre/post preference testing and the various research methods involved in this form of advertising research.
7. Explain the meaning and operation of single-source measures of advertising effectiveness.
8. Discuss the measurement of Internet advertising effectiveness.

Opening Vignette: Two Illustrations of Potentially Risky Ad Campaigns

As established throughout the preceding chapters, advertising performs a vital role in enhancing brand equity. However, extensive advertising clutter makes it imperative that ads gain and hold the audience's attention and convey key copy points. This sometimes requires taking risks. Following are two illustrations of risky, albeit potentially effective, advertising campaigns.

Intel and Homer Simpson   In an advertising campaign introduced to the airwaves in late 1998, Intel had a simple objective: Convince prospective PC purchasers that Intel chips make PCs smarter. The objective was straightforward enough, but the challenge was in designing an advertising campaign that would attract and hold attention, convey the desired copy point in a memorable fashion, and ultimately persuade consumers to purchase only those PC brands featuring the famous "Intel Inside" message. Enter Homer Simpson, the simpleton cartoon-character from Fox TV's *The Simpsons* program. Creative artists at Intel's ad agency designed an initial spot that portrayed Homer having his challenged brain replaced with a Pentium chip. The result: Homer-the-simpleton Simpson is transformed into a brainy college professor.

For this spot to achieve its objective, viewers not only needed to grasp the intended humor but they also had to comprehend and remember the key selling point that Intel chips make computers smarter. The commercial unquestionably was humorous, but whether it influenced consumers' beliefs about Intel chips, their ability to recall this information, and their attitudes toward Intel chips remains to be determined by appropriate advertising research.

Dunkin' Donuts Takes on Starbucks   The restaurant coffee business in the United States is estimated to generate $55 billion in annual sales. The market has been dominated by the Seattle-based Starbucks Coffee Co., which, starting in the 1980s, introduced many American consumers to the pleasures of drinking a really good cup of coffee. In an effort to capture a bigger chunk of the restaurant coffee business and steal sales from Starbucks, the 3,400-unit Dunkin' Donuts chain introduced a darker coffee called Cafe Blend to compete against Starbucks' own dark-roast coffees. Creative and effective advertising was needed to start the task of taking market share from Starbucks.

Dunkin' Donuts' ad agency created a 30-second television commercial and designed a $5 million media campaign on spot TV. In an apparent suggestion that the atmosphere at Starbucks is pretentious, the commercial for Dunkin' Donuts featured an obnoxious Starbucks clerk as he routinely insults customers. He corrects one customer's pronunciation from Sumaytra to Sumatra. He informs another that "Your order bores me." The *coup de grâce* in this biting comparative advertisement is a subsequent scene in which insulted customers wait for the obnoxious clerk to leave the store at which time they proudly hold up cups of Dunkin' Donuts' Cafe Blend coffee and inform him that "We're through with you." The obvious implication is that coffee drinkers need not subject themselves to the alleged pretense of Starbucks and can in fact get an equally good-tasting coffee at a less-ostentatious Dunkin' Donuts outlet.

Will this ad encourage Starbucks' customers to try coffee from Dunkin' Donuts? Will Dunkin' Donuts' present customers, who are predominantly working class, form an impression that Dunkin' Donuts is being uppity in its seeming effort to emulate the more upscale Starbucks? Will Starbucks' customers take serious the implied claim that a retail chain well-known for its donuts, but not its coffee, could possibly offer a blend of coffee as good as that sold at Starbucks outlets? In general, will this ad persuade more consumers, whether customers of Starbucks or otherwise, to consider purchasing coffee from a Dunkin' Donuts store? Appropriate advertising research is much needed in order to address these pertinent inquiries.

Sources: The Intel description is adapted from T. L. Stanley, "If Homer Simpson Only Had a Brain! It Happens, in New Intel Campaign," *Brandweek*, October 26, 1998, 3. The Dunkin' Donut description is adapted from Louise Kramer, "Dunkin' Donuts Jabs Rival Starbucks in Humorous TV Ads," *Advertising Age*, November 2, 1998, 10.

*H*undreds of billions of dollars are spent annually worldwide to advertise products and services. Sound business practice requires that efforts be made to determine whether these expenditures are justified. Accordingly, a significant amount of time and money are spent on testing advertising effectiveness. This chapter will describe many of the research techniques used in the advertising-research business.

OVERVIEW OF ADVERTISING RESEARCH

Measuring advertising effectiveness is a difficult and expensive task. Nonetheless, the value gained from undertaking the effort typically outweighs these drawbacks. In the absence of formal research, most advertisers would not know whether proposed ad messages are going to be effective or whether ongoing advertising is doing a good job, nor could they know what should be changed to improve future advertising efforts. Advertising research enables management to increase advertising's contribution toward achieving marketing and corporate goals. To be *accountable* for their actions, advertising executives are virtually obligated to conduct research that determines, as best as possible, whether an advertising campaign is accomplishing its intended goals.

What Does Advertising Research Involve?

Advertising research encompasses a variety of purposes, methods, measures, and techniques. Effectiveness is measured in terms of achieving awareness, conveying copy points, influencing attitudes, creating emotional responses, and affecting purchase choices. Due to growing calls for advertising accountability, advertising research in its various forms is more prevalent and essential than ever.[1]

Sometimes research is done under natural advertising conditions and other times in simulated or laboratory situations. Measures of effectiveness range from paper-and-pencil instruments (such as attitude scales) to physiological devices (e.g., pupillometers that measure eye movement). It should be clear that there is no single encompassing form of advertising research. Rather, the measurement of advertising effectiveness is exceptionally diverse because of the wide variety of questions that advertisers and their agencies are interested in having answered.

Although, as will be seen shortly, a variety of research methods are employed in assessing advertising effectiveness, two general forms of advertising research are practiced. First, **message research** is undertaken to test the effectiveness of creative messages. (Message research is also called copy research, or copytesting, but these terms are too limiting inasmuch as message research involves testing all aspects of advertisements, not just the copy material.) Message research involves both *pretesting* messages during developmental stages (prior to actual placement in advertising media) and *posttesting* messages for effectiveness after they have been aired or printed. Pretesting is performed to eliminate ineffective ads before they are ever run, while posttesting is conducted to determine whether messages achieve their established objectives.

Media research is the second general category of advertising research. Whereas message research asks questions about the message per se, media research attempts to ascertain both the characteristics of an advertising vehicle's audience as well as the size of that audience so that ratings can be determined. For example, people-meter research is performed to estimate television program ratings.

Idealism Meets Reality in Advertising Research

The role, importance, and difficulty of assessing advertising effectiveness perhaps can best be appreciated by examining what an ideal system of advertising measurement would entail and then comparing this against the reality of advertising research.

First, an ideal measure would provide an *early warning signal*—that is, a measure of ad effectiveness at the earliest possible stage in the advertisement development process. The sooner an advertisement is found to be ineffective, the less time, effort, and financial resources will be wasted. Early detection of effective advertisements, on the other hand, enables marketers to hasten the developmental process so that the ads can generate return on investment as quickly as possible.

Second, an ideal measurement system would evaluate advertising effectiveness in terms of the *sales volume generated by advertising,* which is, according to the logic of vaguely-right-versus-precisely-wrong objective setting (see Chapter 9), the only bona fide advertising objective.[2] A measure of advertising effectiveness becomes less valuable the further removed it is from an advertisement's potential for generating sales volume. Hence, an attitude measure is more valuable than a measure of awareness, which is less concerned with the act of purchasing the advertised product.

Third, an ideal measurement system would satisfy the standard research requirements of *reliability and validity.* Advertising measures are reliable when repeated trials yield the same results. Measures are valid when they predict actual marketplace performance.

Finally, an ideal system would permit *quick and inexpensive measurement.* The longer it takes to assess advertising effectiveness and the more it costs, the less valuable is the measuring system.

The ideal conditions just discussed are rarely satisfied. In fact, several are inconsistent. For example, a measurement system capable of predicting sales potential is likely to be expensive. Similarly, one that provides an early warning signal is less likely to be reliable and valid. Advertising research must necessarily deviate from the ideal circumstances described previously. However, the gap between idealism and reality in advertising research is narrowing with advances in technology and greater ingenuity in developing testing procedures.

Advertising Research Methods

Literally dozens of methods for measuring advertising effectiveness have appeared over the years. The following sections discuss some of the more popular methods in use by national advertisers. The media research methods are categorized according to magazine, radio, and television audience size measurement. Message research methods, which are described in a subsequent section, are classified into measures of: (1) recognition and recall, (2) emotions, (3) physiological arousal, (4) persuasion, and (5) sales response.

MEDIA RESEARCH METHODS

The initial task an advertiser faces is to ensure that sufficient numbers of potential customers are actually exposed to, or have an *opportunity to see* (OTS), its advertisements and that audience members match the target audience's desired characteristics. This requires that: (1) media vehicles (television programs, magazine issues, and so on) be distributed, (2) customers be exposed to these vehicles (e.g., by watching the television program, reading a specific magazine issue), and (3) customers be exposed to the advertiser's specific advertisements carried in these vehicles.

A variety of resource materials are available to advertisers for determining potential audience sizes for specific media vehicles. These source materials will be discussed shortly, but an important general resource is the *Competitive Media Report's Ad $ Summary,* which is available in many university and public libraries. This publication provides detailed information pertaining to leading national advertisers (LNAs) and specific expenditure data for literally thousands of national brands. For example, the 1997 volume shows that the two brands covered in the *Opening Vignette,* Dunkin' Donuts and Intel, had media expenditures of approximately $30.5 million and $65.8 million, respectively.[3] Dunkin'

Donuts expenditures were allocated among newspapers, outdoor, spot TV, cable TV, and national spot radio. Intel used a slightly wider array of media consisting of magazines, newspapers, network, cable, syndicated, and spot TV, and national spot radio. Needless to say, this information is valuable to brand managers when studying competitive activity. (It also is useful information for students who want to learn about advertising activity undertaken in specific product categories and for particular brands.)

Magazine Audience Measurement

It may seem that determining the size of a particular magazine's readership would be an easy task. All one needs to do is tally the number of people who subscribe to a magazine, right? Unfortunately, it is not this simple; several complicating factors make subscription counting an inadequate way of determining a magazine's readership. First, magazine subscriptions are collected through a variety of intermediaries, making it difficult to obtain accurate lists of who subscribes to what magazines. Second, magazines often are purchased from newsstands, supermarkets, and other retail outlets rather than through subscriptions, thus completely eliminating knowledge of who purchases what magazines. Third, magazine issues distributed at public locations (doctors' offices, barber shops, beauty salons, and so on) are read by numerous people other than just the subscriber. Finally, individual magazine subscribers often share issues with other people.

www.mediamark.com

For all of these reasons, the number of subscriptions to a magazine and the number of people who actually read the magazine are nonequivalent. Fortunately, there are two services—Simmons Market Research Bureau (SMRB) and Mediamark Research, Inc. (MRI)—that specialize in measuring magazine readership and determining audience size. As will be seen in the following descriptions, these two companies offer very similar, yet competitive, services. It should be noted in advance that magazine audience measurement is replete with difficulties and problems, such as the following: (1) respondents to readership surveys are asked to rate numerous magazines, which can lead to fatigue and hasty or faulty responses; (2) sample sizes often are small, especially for small-circulation magazines, which leads to high margins of sampling error; and (3) sample composition often is unrepresentative of audience readership.[4] Despite these problems, media planners must make the most of the audience estimates and readership profiles generated by Simmons Market Research Bureau and Mediamark Research, Inc.

Simmons Market Research Bureau (SMRB). This research firm assesses magazine vehicle exposure for about 230 consumer magazines. A national probability sample of approximately 20,000 individuals are queried about their magazine-reading habits. Until 1995, SMRB's research staff employed the *through-the-book-technique* to measure magazine readership. Respondents were asked to identify those magazines (by their logos) they may have read or looked through during the past six months; then they were directed to look through stripped-down versions of a recent issue for each magazine. Through a series of questions, SMRB's interviewers attempted to determine whether respondents truly had been exposed to the particular magazine issue.

Starting in 1995, however, Simmons switched to the *recent-reading method* that merely requires respondents to examine a particular magazine issue and to say whether they have read it. This change in methodology cut Simmons's interview length per respondent from its previous two hours to approximately 25 minutes. This change enabled Simmons to increase its assessment of magazine readership from 130 to over 230 magazines.[5]

For each magazine examined, SMRB determines how many of the sampled respondents read that magazine. The statisticians at SMRB then employ statistical inference procedures to generalize vehicle exposure from the sample results to the total population and to demographic subgroups. SMRB also acquires information pertaining to respondents' product and brand usage, television viewing, and radio listening. These sample results are generalized to the total population of the United States. Advertisers and media planners use the readership information along with detailed demographic and product-usage data to evaluate the absolute and relative value of different magazines.

Mediamark Research, Inc. (MRI). MRI provides advertisers and agencies with an alternative magazine-readership measurement. Like SMRB, MRI's research procedure involves interviewing approximately 20,000 adults per year, and MRI obtains readership statistics for over 200 magazines along with product/brand usage and demographic information. However, MRI's measurement technique differs from SMRB's approach: MRI gives each participant a deck of magazine logo cards. The participant then sorts the logo cards into three piles based on whether she or he has read the magazine, has not read it, or is not sure.

Because these two readership services use different research methods, their results are often discrepant. Consider, for example, differences between SMRB's and MRI's estimates for the following four magazines: *Black Enterprise* (2.49 million vs. 3.14 million), *Bon Appetit* (5.73 million vs. 4.96 million), *Golf Digest* (7.47 million vs. 6.56 million), and *Motor Trend* (6.91 million vs. 6.03 million).[6] In percentage terms and using the smaller estimate as the base, these differences are 26.1, 15.5, 13.9, and 14.6 percent, respectively. Media planners are thus faced with the task of determining which service is right or whether both are wrong in their estimates of magazine audience size.[7]

Both SMRB and MRI produce annual multi-volume reports of product and brand-usage data and detailed media information. Using pretzels as an illustration, Table 15.1 provides a pared-down report that will be useful for explaining the construction and interpretation of SMRB and MRI reports.[8]

MRI and SMRB reports are structurally equivalent to the data contained in Table 15.1. Each of the detailed tables in these reports present cross-tabulations of demographic segments or media by product or brand usage. Table 15.1 presents usage of pretzels delineated by age, geographic region, and media vehicles. The table is to be interpreted as follows:[9]

TABLE 15.1

Illustration of a Skeleton MRI Report for Pretzels

BASE: FEMALE HOMEMAKERS	TOTAL U.S. '000	A '000	B % DOWN	C % ACROSS	D INDEX
All Female Homemakers	88052	34928	100.0	39.7	100
18–24	8171	2595	7.4	31.8	80
25–34	19304	7997	22.9	41.4	104
35–44	19465	9460	27.1	48.6	123
45–54	14163	6527	18.7	46.1	116
55–64	10409	4124	11.8	39.6	100
65 or over	16539	4225	12.1	25.5	64
Northeast	18424	9265	26.5	50.3	127
North Central	21134	9469	27.6	45.7	115
South	30862	9359	26.8	30.3	76
West	17632	6655	19.1	37.7	95
TV Guide	20304	8453	24.2	41.6	105
U.S. News & World Report	3790	1827	5.2	48.2	122
USA Today	986	581	1.7	58.9	148

Source: *Mediamark Research Baked Goods, Snacks, and Desserts Report,* P-16 (Mediamark Research Inc., Spring 1996), 353–361.

1. The first row (labeled "All Female Homemakers") shows the occurrence of pretzel purchases in the total U.S. female homemaker population. Thus, of the 88,052,000 female homemakers, 34,928,000, or 39.7 percent (see column C, percentage across), purchased pretzels at least once in the past six months.

2. Each set of detailed entries shows the estimate in four different ways (denoted as columns *A, B, C,* and *D*) for the product category (pretzels in this case), and the specified population grouping.

   a. Column *A,* which is expressed in thousands ('000), presents the survey estimate of total product users in thousands. In the Northeast, for example, there are 9,265,000 female homemakers who reported having purchased pretzels.

   b. Column *B (percentage down)* represents the *composition of buyers* in each demographic group. For example, the 9,265,000 purchasers of pretzels in the Northeast constitutes 26.5 percent of the total (34,928,000) female-homemaker pretzel purchasers; that is, 9,265,000 ÷ 34,928,000 = 26.5 percent.

   c. Column *C (percentage across)* reflects each demographic group's *coverage* with respect to the particular product category. For example, the same number of pretzel purchasers in the Northeast (9,265,000) represents 50.3 percent of all female homemakers in the Northeast.

   d. Column *D (index)* is a measure of the particular demographic group as compared to the total population. For example, 50.3 percent of northeastern homemakers are pretzel purchasers as compared to 39.7 percent of all female homemakers. The index is a calculation of this relationship: (50.3 ÷ 39.7) × 100 = 127. This index indicates that northeasterners are 27 percent more likely than the general population to purchase pretzels. The data in Table 15.1 make it apparent that consumers in the Northeastern and North Central United States are disproportionately more likely to consume pretzels than are residents of the South and West.

The age and magazine-readership data can be interpreted in an analogous fashion. Regarding age, it can be seen that proportionately the greatest consumption is by consumers in the 35–44 and 45–54 age categories. Comparatively, consumers at the extremes (those aged 18–24 and 65 and older) are the least likely to purchase pretzels. Does this mean that pretzel marketers should cater only to the middle-aged groups and neglect the others? Probably not. For example, although people aged 65 or over (index of 64) are proportionately less likely than the population at large to consume pretzels, there are, nonetheless, a total of over 4.2 million people in this age group who *do* consume pretzels. It thus would make little sense to disregard such a large number of consumers simply because the index number is less than 100. Although prudent pretzel marketers would not neglect these older consumers, the index numbers in Table 15.1 suggest that less media weight should be directed at older consumers in comparison to the amount of emphasis, or weight, targeted at the middle-aged consumers.

www.tvgen.com

www.usnews.com

www.usatoday.com

Turning to the media data in Table 15.1, it can be seen that *TV Guide* has the lowest index number (105), with *U.S. News & World Report* (122) and *USA Today* (148) having considerably higher indices. How might an advertiser use these data? Looking just at index numbers, *USA Today* is the best choice, but the index number conveys only part of the story. Note carefully that a pretzel advertisement placed in *USA Today* would potentially reach only 581,000 pretzel purchasers. There would be relatively little wasted coverage with this vehicle, but not many pretzel purchasers would be reached. Comparatively, an advertisement placed in *TV Guide* would have a chance of reaching nearly 8,453,000 potential pretzel consumers. A smaller percentage of *TV Guide's* total audience consumes pretzels, but because this vehicle is read by over 20 million readers, it would reach millions of potential pretzel purchasers.

In using media data supplied in MRI and SMRB reports, the advertiser must weigh various pieces of information in order to make intelligent media-selection decisions. This includes: (1) the size of the potential audience that a vehicle might reach; (2) the attractiveness of its coverage as revealed by the total product purchasers exposed to that vehicle (column *A*) and in comparison to other media (column *D*); (3) its cost compared to other vehicles; and (4) its appropriateness for the advertised brand. It thus should be apparent that selecting advertising vehicles cannot be simplified by merely resorting to a comparison of index numbers or any other single numerical value. These numbers are merely input into a judgment that a careful decision maker must make after considering all of the available information.

Radio Audience Measurement

Radio audiences are measured both nationally and locally. Statistical Research, Inc. (SRI) is the sole provider of national radio network ratings. This company provides a service that goes by the acronym RADAR, which stands for Radio All Dimensions Audience Research. SRI annually recruits about 12,000 individuals, who, during a one-week period, are asked to report on their radio listening. Individuals (over the age of 12) are called daily for one week and asked to recall their listening behavior for the previous 24 hours. RADAR's research provides ratings estimates for network radio programming and audience demographic characteristics. Advertisers use this information to select network programming that matches their intended target audiences.[10]

At the local level, there used to be two major research services that measured radio audience sizes: Arbitron Ratings Co. and Birch Scarborough Research. However, in 1991 Birch discontinued operations, leaving Arbitron as the sole supplier of local radio ratings data. Arbitron measures listening patterns in over 250 markets located throughout the United States. Arbitron researchers obtain data in each market from 250 to 13,000 randomly selected individuals aged 12 or older. Respondents are compensated for maintaining *diaries* of their listening behavior for a *seven-day period.* Subscribers to the Arbitron service (more than 5,000 radio stations, advertisers, and agencies) receive reports that detail people's listening patterns, their station preferences, and demographic breakdowns. This information is invaluable to advertisers and their agencies for purposes of selecting radio stations whose listener composition matches the advertiser's target market.

Television Audience Measurement

As noted in Chapter 12, a 30-second commercial on prime-time television can cost over $500,000 or as little as $150,000. The reason for the disparity is *ratings*! Generally speaking, higher-rated programs command higher prices. Because prices and ratings go hand in hand, the accurate measurement of program audience size, or ratings, is a critically important, multimillion-dollar industry. Advertising researchers continuously seek ways to measure more accurately the size of program audiences. Two measurement systems are Nielsen's People Meter method and SRI's SMART technology.

Nielsen's People Meter. The *People Meter,* by Nielsen Media Research Inc., represents perhaps the most important research innovation since the advent of television audience measurement.[11] Considerable controversy has surrounded its implementation, however, as demonstrated in the following brief review of television audience measurement.

Prior to the introduction of the People Meter system, Nielsen measured television program ratings by combining two data-collection methods. One involved attaching electronic meters to the television sets of a national sample of households (the electronic-meter panel). These electronic meters—called *black boxes*—determined the number of households attuned to particular programs. Statistical inference techniques were used to estimate program ratings on a national basis. A separate national panel of households—the diary panel—maintained diaries of their ongoing viewing habits and supplied pertinent demographic information on household size, income, education, race, and so on. When combined, the data from the two panels indicated the program ratings and demographic characteristics of each program's audience. This information was used by networks to set advertising rates and by advertisers to select programs on which to advertise their products.

This method worked well during a simpler time when fewer program options were available to television viewers. It became less suitable as independent stations, cable networks, and VCRs increased the number of choices available to viewers. Diary data diminished in accuracy because people became less willing or able to maintain precise accounts of their viewing behavior. In response, the People Meter was developed by a British research firm, Audits Great Britain (AGB Television Research). This firm introduced people meters to the United States in 1984, but withdrew from the business several years later. Nielsen followed with its own People Meter system shortly after AGB entered the U.S. market.

What is a People Meter? The **People Meter** is a handheld device slightly larger than a typical television channel selector that has eight buttons for family members and two additional buttons for visitors. A family member (or visitor) must push his or her designated numerical button each time he or she selects a particular program. The meter automatically records what programs are being watched, how many households are watching, and which family members are in attendance. Information from each household's people meter is fed daily into a central computer via telephone lines. This viewing information is then combined with each household's pertinent demographic profile to provide a single source of data about audience size and composition.

The People Meter controversy ensued from the substantial decline—almost 10 percent—in network ratings as a result of the transition from diary panels to people meters. The big three networks (ABC, CBS, and NBC) lost millions of dollars in advertising revenues because smaller-rated programs were unable to command higher prices. The networks have placed much of the blame on people meters, claiming that the meters have fundamental faults responsible for erroneous ratings data.

The problem is not restricted to the United States. Research by Foote, Cone & Belding Communications (FCB) investigated the effect on TV ratings of converting from an existing ratings method (such as diaries) to People Meters. In 15 of the 26 countries examined, People Meter ratings were lower than ratings generated by prior methodology. Table 15.2 provides a sampling of ratings changes from FCB's research.

TABLE 15.2	Illustrative International Rating Changes Following Shift to People Meters
COUNTRY	RATINGS CHANGE
Argentina	Down 20–25%
Australia	Up 10–25%
Brazil	Down 25%
Greece	Down 20–40%
Mexico	Down 30%
Philippines	Down 25%
Puerto Rico	Down 4%
Spain	Down 15%
United Kingdom	Up 15–20%
United States	Down 5–10%

Source: Joe Mandese, "People Meters Shake Up Global TV Ratings," *Advertising Age International,* July 18, 1994, I16.

People Meters likely are here to stay in one form or another, and probably so is the controversy surrounding their use. However, advertisers and their agencies may soon have an alternative to Nielsen's People Meter, which now is the sole service for estimating national TV audiences. The four major networks, which pay Nielsen more than $10 million annually for its data, are growing increasingly critical of Nielsen's data. They claim that Nielsen undercounts major segments of the population, especially young people and viewers watching TV outside the home.[12]

SRI's SMART System.   SRI, the company that provides the RADAR national radio service, has been developing its own TV measurement system called SMART, standing for Systems for Measuring And Reporting Television.[13] The SMART system consists of meters that are attached with Velcro strips to television sets. The attached meters have sensors that enable signals to be picked up from the air. Television viewers log in and out before and after watching TV using a remote-control device. The user-friendly devices contain a dozen icons (telephone, flower, smiley face, apple, heart symbol, etc.) that are selected by family members as their unique log-in symbol. At the time of this writing (late 1998), the SMART system was under pilot testing in Philadelphia. SRI intends to roll out the SMART system throughout the United States by 2001, but the company must obtain nearly $100 million to finance the national effort.[14]

It is interesting to note that Arbitron, of radio-audience measurement fame, introduced a service in 1991 called ScanAmerica to compete with Nielsen's rating system. However, within two years Arbitron discontinued the service due to lack of industry support.[15] It remains to be seen whether SRI's SMART system will provide viable competition for Nielsen's People Meters.

M ESSAGE RESEARCH METHODS

Contemporary message research traces its roots to the 19th century, when measures of recall and memory were obtained as indicators of print-advertising effectiveness.[16] Today, most national advertisers would not even consider airing a television commercial or placing a magazine advertisement before having first tested it. A survey of the largest advertisers and advertising agencies in the United States determined that more than 80 percent of the respondents from each group pretest television commercials before airing them on a national basis.[17] Interestingly, these commercials typically are tested in a preliminary form rather than as finished versions. Following are the major forms of pre-finished commercials:[18]

- *Storyboards.* This pre-finished version presents a series of visual frames and corresponding script of key audio that will be included in a proposed commercial.
- *Animatics.* This is a film or videotape of a sequence of drawings with simultaneous playing of audio to represent a proposed commercial.
- *Photomatics.* A sequence of photographs is filmed or videotaped and accompanied with audio to represent a proposed commercial.
- *Ripamatics.* Footage is taken from existing commercials and spliced together to represent the proposed commercial.
- *Liveamatics.* This pre-finished version entails filming or videotaping live talent to represent the proposed commercial. This version is the closest to a finished commercial, but it does not fully represent the actual settings or talent who will be used in the actual commercial.

Industry Standards for Advertising Research

Message-based research, or copy testing, is in wide use throughout North America, Europe, and elsewhere. Yet, it may be a bit sobering to note that much message-based research is not of the highest caliber. Sometimes it is unclear exactly what the research is attempting to measure; measures often fail to satisfy basic reliability and validity requirements; and results have little to say about whether copytested ads stand a good chance of being effective.

Members of the advertising-research community have been mindful of these problems and have sought a higher standard of performance from advertising researchers. A major document, called **Positioning Advertising Copytesting (PACT),** was formulated by leading U.S. advertising agencies to remedy the problem of mediocre or flawed advertising research. The document is directed primarily at television advertising but is relevant to the testing of advertising in all media.

The PACT document consists of nine copytesting principles.[19] These principles are more than mere pronouncements and instead represent useful guides to how copytesting research should be conducted. It is unnecessary that you attempt to commit these principles to memory; rather, your objective in reading the following principles should be simply appreciating what constitutes good copytesting practice.

Principle 1. A good copytesting system needs to provide measurements that are *relevant to the advertising objectives.* The specific objective(s) that an advertising campaign is intended to accomplish (such as creating brand awareness, influencing brand image, creating warmth) should be the first consideration in determining the methods to assess advertising effectiveness. For example, if the objective for a particular campaign is to evoke strong emotional reactions, a measure of recall would be patently inappropriate.

Principle 2. A good copytesting system is one that requires *agreement about how the results will be used in advance of each specific test.* Specifying the use of research results before data collection ensures that all parties involved (advertiser, agency, and research firm) agree on the research goals and reduces the chance of conflicting interpretations of test results. This principle's intent is to encourage the use of decision rules or action standards that, before actual testing, establish the test results that must be achieved for the test advertisement to receive full media distribution. For example, Commercial X must receive at least a 10 percent increase in persuasion or the commercial will not be run.

Principle 3. A good copytesting system provides *multiple measurements* because single measurements are generally inadequate to assess the performance of an advertisement. Because the process by which advertisements influence customers is complex, multiple measures are more likely to capture the various advertising effects and are therefore preferred over single measures.

Principle 4. A good copytesting system is based on *a model of human response to communications*—the reception of a stimulus, the comprehension of the stimulus, and the response to the stimulus. Because advertisements vary in the impact they are intended to achieve, a good copytesting system is capable of answering questions that are patterned to the underlying model of behavior. For example, if consumers purchase a particular product for primarily emotional reasons, then message research should use a suitable measure of emotional response rather than simply measuring recall of copy points.

Principle 5. A good copytesting system allows for consideration of *whether the advertising stimulus should be exposed more than once.* This principle addresses the issue of whether a single test exposure (showing an ad or commercial to consumers only once) provides a sufficient test of potential impact. Because multiple exposure is often required for advertisements to accomplish their full effect, message research should expose a test ad to respondents on two or more occasions when the communication situation calls for such a procedure.[20] For example, a single-exposure test is probably insufficient to determine whether an advertisement successfully conveys a complex benefit. On the other hand, a single exposure may be adequate if an advertisement is designed solely to create name awareness for a new brand.

Principle 6. A good copytesting system recognizes that a more finished piece of copy can be evaluated more soundly; therefore, a good system requires, at minimum, that *alternative executions be tested in the same degree of finish.* Test results typically vary depending on the degree of finish, as, for example, when testing a photomatic or ripamatic version of a television commercial. Sometimes the amount of information lost from testing a less-than-finished ad may be inconsequential; sometimes it may be critical.

Principle 7. A good copytesting system *provides controls to avoid the bias normally found in the exposure context.* The context in which an advertisement is contained (e.g., the clutter or lack of clutter in a magazine) will have a substantial impact on how the ad is received, processed, and accepted. For this reason, copytesting procedures should attempt to duplicate the eventual actual context of an advertisement or commercial.

Principle 8. A good copytesting system is one that takes into account *basic considerations of sample definition.* This typically requires that the sample be representative of the target audience to which test results are to be generalized and that the sample size be sufficiently large to permit reliable statistical conclusions.

Principle 9. A good copytesting system is one that can *demonstrate reliability and validity.* Reliability and validity are basic requirements of any research endeavor. As applied to message research, a reliable test is one that yields consistent results each time an advertisement is tested, and a valid test is one that is predictive of marketplace performance.

The foregoing principles establish a high set of standards for the advertising-research community. Yet, they should not be regarded in the same sense as the earlier discussion of research ideals. Rather, these principles should be viewed as mandatory if advertising effectiveness is to be tested in a meaningful way.

Assessing Advertising Effectiveness

Enormous efforts have been made by members of the advertising community to ascertain which measures of advertising best predict advertising effectiveness. Particularly notable is a major study, called the Copy Research Validity Project (CRVP), that was funded by the Advertising Research Foundation to assess which of 35 different measures best predict the sales effectiveness of television commercials.[21] Although representing a heroic effort, results from the CRVP are both inconclusive and controversial.[22] Probably the only definitive conclusion that can be made is that no one measure is always most appropriate or universally best. Each brand-advertising situation requires a careful assessment of the objectives that advertising is intended to accomplish. The following sections elaborate on a representative sampling of research procedures that are available for measuring advertising effectiveness. It should be noted that these methods, which are summarized in Table 15.3, examine five different forms of response to advertisements: (1) recognition and recall, (2) emotional reactions, (3) physiological arousal, (4) persuasive impact, and (5) sales response.

Measures of Recognition and Recall

After exposure to an advertisement, consumers may experience varying degrees of awareness, the most basic of which is simply noticing an ad without processing specific executional elements. Advertisers intend, however, for consumers to heed specific parts, elements, or features of an ad and associate those with the advertised brand.[23] Recognition and recall both represent elements of consumers' memories for advertising information, but recognition measures, which can be equated with multiple-choice test questions, tap a more superficial level of memory compared to recall measures, which are similar to essay questions.[24]

TABLE 15.3	Illustrative Message Research Methods

Measures of recognition and recall
- Starch Readership Service (magazines)
- Bruzzone tests (TV)
- Burke day-after recall (TV)

Measures of emotion
- The warmth monitor
- Market Fact's TRACE
- BBDO's Emotional Measurement System

Measures of physiological arousal
- Psychogalvanometer
- Pupillometer
- Voice-pitch analysis (VOPAN)

Measures of persuasion
- ASI theater testing
- ARS laboratory testing

Measures of sales response (single-source systems)
- IRI's BehaviorScan
- Nielsen's SCANTRACK

Several commercial research firms provide advertisers with information on how well their ads perform in terms of generating awareness, which typically is assessed with recognition or recall measures. Three services are described in the following sections: Starch Readership Service (magazine recognition); Bruzzone tests (television recognition); and Burke day-after recall rests (television recall).[25]

Starch Readership Service.   Starch Readership Service measures the primary objective of a magazine ad, namely to be seen and read. Starch examines reader awareness of advertisements in consumer magazines and business publications. Over 75,000 advertisements are studied annually based on interviews with more than 100,000 people involving over 140 publications. Sample sizes range from 100 to 150 individuals per issue, with most interviews conducted in respondents' homes or, in the case of business publications, in offices or places of business. Interviews are conducted during the early life of a publication. Following a suitable waiting period after the appearance of a publication to give readers an opportunity to read or look through their issue, interviewing commences and continues a full week (for a weekly publication), two weeks (for a biweekly), and three weeks (for a monthly publication).

Starch interviewers locate eligible readers of each magazine issue studied. An eligible reader is one who has glanced through or read some part of the issue prior to the interviewer's visit and who meets the age, sex, and occupation requirements set for the particular magazine. Once eligibility is established, interviewers turn the pages of the magazine, inquiring about each advertisement being studied. Respondents are first asked, "Did you see or read any part of this advertisement?" If a respondent answers "Yes," a prescribed questioning procedure is followed to determine the respondent's awareness of various parts of the ad (illustrations, headline, etc.). Respondents are then classified as noted, associated, read-some, or read-most readers according to these specific definitions:[26]

- *Noted* is the percentage of people interviewed who remembered having previously seen the advertisement in the issue being studied.

◆ *Associated* is the percentage of people interviewed who not only *noted* the ad but also saw or read some part of it that clearly indicated the name of the brand or advertiser.

◆ *Read Some* is the percentage of people interviewed who read any part of the ad's copy.

◆ *Read Most* is the percentage of people interviewed who read half or more of the written material in the ad.

For each magazine advertisement that has undergone a Starch analysis, indices are developed for that ad's noted, associated, read-some, and read-most scores. Two sets of indices are established: One index compares an advertisement's scores against the average scores for *all ads* in the magazine issue, and the second (called the ADNORM index) compares an advertisement's scores against other ads in the *same product category* as well as the same size (e.g., full page) and color classifications (e.g., four-color ads). Hence, an advertisement that achieves an average value receives an index of 100. By comparison, a score of 130, for example, would mean that a particular ad scored 30 percent above comparable ads, whereas a score of 70 would indicate it scored 30 percent below comparable ads.

Starch-Rated Advertisement for Vanessa Williams and Milk-Mustache Campaign

Starch-Rated Advertisement
for the Toyota Sienna

Figures 15.1 and 15.2 illustrate two Starch-rated advertisements from the August 31, 1998 issue of *Time* magazine. The first example (Figure 15.1) features actress and singer Vanessa Williams from the ongoing series of milk-mustache advertisements. As can be seen, 73 percent of the respondents remembered having previously seen (or *noted)* the ad, 68 percent *associated* it, and 32 percent *read most* of it. The second illustration (Figure 15.2) is a "crash test" advertisement for the Toyota Sienna. This ad's noted, associated, and read most scores are substantially lower at 49, 46, and 23 percent, respectively.

A basic assumption of the Starch procedure is that respondents in fact do remember whether they saw a particular ad in a specific magazine issue. The Starch technique has sometimes been criticized because in so-called *bogus ad studies* that use prepublication or altered issues, respondents report having seen ads that actually never ran. The Starch organization does not consider such studies valid because of the failure of researchers to follow proper procedures for qualifying issue readers and questioning respondents. Research by the Starch organization demonstrates that when properly interviewed, most respondents are able to identify the ads they have seen or read in a specific issue with a high degree of accuracy; according to this research, false reporting of ad noting is minimal.[27]

Due to inherent frailties of people's memories, it is almost certain that Starch scores do *not* provide exact percentages but rather are biased to some degree by people reporting they have seen or read an ad when in fact they have not. Nonetheless, it is not exact scores that are critical but rather comparisons between scores for the same ad placed in different magazines or comparative scores among different ads placed in the same magazine issue. For example, the milk ad with Vanessa Williams in Figure 15.1 obtained readership index scores of 155 (noted), 162 (associated), and 188 (read most). These indices mean that the milk ad performed 55 percent better than the average noted score for all 31 one-half-page or larger ads tested in this particular issue of *Time,* 62 percent better than the median associated score, and 88 percent better than the median read-most score. ADNORM indices for the Toyota Sienna (Figure 15.2) are 102 (noted), 107 (associated), and 177 (read most). Compared to the other automobile and light truck advertisements in this particular issue of *Time,* the Toyota Sienna performed slightly above average in terms of noted and associated scores, but dramatically above average with respect to its read-most score. Because Starch has been performing these studies since the 1920s and has compiled a wealth of baseline data, or norms, advertisers and media planners can make informed decisions concerning the relative merits of different magazines and informed judgments regarding the effectiveness of particular advertisements.

Bruzzone Tests. The Bruzzone Research Company (BRC) provides advertisers with a test of consumer recognition of television commercials. BRC tests consumer recognition of television commercials by mailing a set of photoboard commercials to a random sample of households and encourages responses by providing a nominal monetary incentive. This token of appreciation along with individuals' inherent interest in the task typically yields a high response rate.[28] A Bruzzone test for a commercial is shown in Figure 15.3.[29] This is a photoboard version of an American Express commercial (titled "Seinfeld/Superman") that first aired in 1998 and was tested shortly thereafter. Note in the upper left corner of Figure 15.3 that respondents are directed to "look over these pictures and words from a TV commercial and answer the questions on the right." At the top of the right side, the recognition question is asked immediately: "Do you remember seeing this commercial on TV?" Toward the bottom of the right side, respondents are then asked to identify the name of the advertised brand (which is not included in the photoboard). Intervening questions ask respondents to indicate their reactions to and liking of the tested commercial. Respondents also describe their feelings toward the commercial by checking any of 27 adjectives that describe the commercial. (See items starting with "Amusing" in the middle of the page on the right side of Figure 15.3.)

Because BRC has performed hundreds of such tests, it has established norms for particular product categories against which a newly tested commercial can be compared. Moreover, BRC has developed an Advertising Response Model (ARM) that links responses to the 27 descriptive adjectives to consumers' attitudes toward both the advertisement and the advertised brand, and ultimately to interest in purchasing the brand. Figure 15.4 presents the ARM analysis for American Express' "Seinfeld/Superman" commercial. Note first in the upper right corner the color coding for this analysis. Specifically, adjectives coded in yellow indicate that the commercial performed better than average (compared to BRC norms); words coded in blue reveal average performance; and those adjectives coded in red indicate below average performance. A review of Figure 15.4 shows that the American Express commercial scored above average on indicators of humor, uniqueness, energy, and appeal, all of which generated an above average "attitude toward the ad" for this commercial. At the same time, the "Seinfeld/Superman" execution performed below average in terms of perceived credibility and relevance. Along with just an average performance on persuasiveness and clarity, the net result was only an average "attitude toward the product" and, in turn, only an average "purchasing interest." Thus, this

Bruzzone-Tested Commercial for American Express ("Seinfeld/Superman")

FIGURE 15.3

Please look over these pictures and words from a TV commercial and answer the questions on the right.

(Superman talking to Seinfeld) It's not like I asked to be famous.

(Seinfeld) Yeah, well, it's the price you pay.

(Superman) You sign a lot of autographs?

(Seinfeld) Oh yeah. You?

(Superman) Some. They ask me to bend stuff a lot.

(Seinfeld) I could see that. What?

(Superman) It's Lois. She's in trouble.

(Seinfeld) Did you look through that building?

(Superman) Well, kind of. It's glass.

(Lois) Superman I've forgotten my wallet.

(Superman) I can't carry any money in this. I'm powerless.

(Seinfeld) I'm not.

(Seinfeld spins around and produces the Name Brand * card.)

(Lois) My hero.

(Announcer) It's a huge comet hurdling toward earth. We're doomed.

(Seinfeld to Superman) I think you better get this one.
(Announcer) You can do more with the Name Brand * card.

Do you remember seeing this commercial on TV? **BRC**

05-1 ☐ Yes   -2 ☐ No   -3 ☐ Not sure-I may have

(If no, skip the rest of these questions and go to the next page.)

How interested are you in what this commercial is trying to tell you or show you about the product?

06-1 ☐ Very interested   -2 ☐ Somewhat interested   -3 ☐ Not interested

How does it make you _feel_ about the product?

07-1 ☐ Good   -2 ☐ OK   -3 ☐ Bad   -4 ☐ Not sure

Please check any of the following if you feel they describe this commercial.

08-1 ☐ Amusing	09-1 ☐ Familiar	10-1 ☐ Pointless
-2 ☐ Appealing	-2 ☐ Fast moving	-2 ☐ Seen a lot
-3 ☐ Believable	-3 ☐ Gentle	-3 ☐ Sensitive
-4 ☐ Clever	-4 ☐ Imaginative	-4 ☐ Silly
-5 ☐ Confusing	-5 ☐ Informative	-5 ☐ True to life
-6 ☐ Convincing	-6 ☐ Irritating	-6 ☐ Warm
-7 ☐ Dull	-7 ☐ Lively	-7 ☐ Well done
-8 ☐ Easy to forget	-8 ☐ Original	-8 ☐ Worn out
-9 ☐ Effective	-9 ☐ Phony	-9 ☐ Worth remembering

Thinking about the commercial as a whole would you say you:

11-1 ☐ Liked it a lot   -4 ☐ Disliked it somewhat
-2 ☐ Liked it somewhat   -5 ☐ Disliked it a lot
-3 ☐ Felt neutral

* We have blocked out the name.
Do you remember which credit card was being advertised?

12-1 ☐ MasterCard   -3 ☐ American Express
-2 ☐ Visa   -4 ☐ Don't know

Does anyone in your household use this type of product?

13-1 ☐ Regularly   -2 ☐ Occasionally   -3 ☐ Seldom or never

2-20

American Express commercial was effective in terms of its entertainment and stimulation value, but it seems to have lacked the requisite persuasiveness, credibility, and relevance to create anything other than just an average interest in the American Express card.

Bruzzone testing provides a valid prediction of actual marketplace performance along with being relative inexpensive compared to other copytesting methods. Because a Bruzzone test cannot be implemented until after a finished TV commercial has actually been aired, it does not provide a before-the-fact indication of whether a commercial should be aired in the first place. Nevertheless, these tests offer important information for evaluating a commercial's effectiveness and whether it should continue to run.

Burke Day-After Recall Testing. Various companies test advertisements to determine whether viewers have been sufficiently influenced to recall having seen the advertisement in a magazine or on television. Gallup & Robinson and Mapes & Ross provide recall testing of ads placed in print media, while ASI and Burke tests consumer recall of television commercials. The Burke and ASI methods are similar, so the following discussion will focus on Burke's procedure.

Burke's day-after recall (DAR) procedure tests commercials that have been aired as part of normal television programming. The day following the first airing of a new commercial, Burke's telephone staff conducts interviews with a sample of 150 consumers. The sample includes individuals who watched the program in which the test commercial was

Bruzzone's Advertising Response Model (ARM) for "Seinfeld/Superman" Commercial

FIGURE 15.4

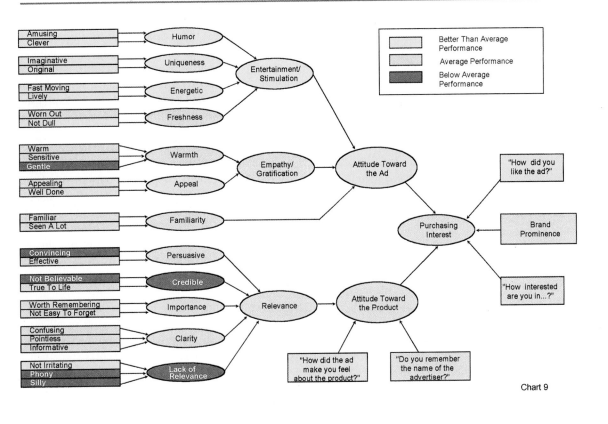

AMERICAN EXPRESS "SEINFELD/SUPERMAN" TV
Advertising Response Model - Among All Who Recognize the Commercials

placed and who were physically present at the time the commercial was aired. These individuals receive a product or brand cue, are asked whether they saw the test commercial in question, and then are asked to recall all they can about it.

For each tested commercial, Burke reports findings as: (1) *claimed-recall scores,* which indicate the percentage of respondents who recall seeing the ad, and (2) *related-recall scores,* which indicate the percentage of respondents who accurately describe specific advertising elements.

Advertisers and agencies use this information, along with verbatim statements from respondents, to assess the effectiveness of test commercials and to identify a commercial's strengths and weaknesses. On the basis of this information, a decision is made to advertise the commercial nationally, to revise it first, or possibly even to drop it.

The Recall Controversy.   Considerable controversy has surrounded the use of DAR testing.[30] For example, Coca-Cola executives reject recall as a valid measure of advertising effectiveness because, in their opinion, recall simply measures whether an ad is received but not whether the message is accepted.[31] It also is known that measures of recall are biased in favor of younger consumers. This is to say that recall scores deteriorate with age progression.[32] Third, there is mounting evidence that the recall scores generated by advertisements are not predictive of sales performance; i.e., regardless of which measure of recall is used, the evidence suggests that sales levels do not increase with increasing levels of recallability.[33] Finally, it has been established that day-after recall testing is biased against certain types of advertising content, as next explained.

Foote, Cone & Belding (FCB), a major advertising agency, claims that DAR tests significantly *understate the memorability* of commercials that employ *emotional or feeling-oriented themes* and are biased in favor of rational or thought-oriented commercials.[34] To test the assertion that DAR testing is biased against emotionally oriented commercials, FCB conducted a study that compared three thinking and three feeling commercials. The six commercials were tested with two methods: the standard DAR measurement described previously and a *masked-recognition test.* The latter test involves showing a commercial to respondents on one day, telephoning them the next, requesting that they turn on their television sets to a given station where the commercial is shown once again (but this time *masked,* i.e., without any brand identification), and then asking them to identify the brand. FCB defines correct brand-name identification by this masked-recognition procedure as *proven recognition* or *true remembering.*[35]

The results from FCB's research, shown in Table 15.4, demonstrate clearly the bias in day-after recall procedures against emotional, feeling commercials. It can be seen that the thinking commercials (coded *A, D,* and *E* in Table 15.4) perform only slightly better under masked-recognition measurement than under the standard DAR test. For example, commercial *A* obtained a DAR score of 49 percent and a masked-recognition score of 56 percent, thereby yielding a ratio of 114 (i.e., 56 ÷ 49). In fact, as shown in Table 15.4, the average ratio for the three thinking commercials is 119. This indicates that an average of only 19 percent more people recognized the advertised brand when prompted again by seeing the product advertised with the brand masked compared to recalling the brand entirely from memory.

Comparatively, Table 15.4 shows that the feeling commercials *(B, C,* and *F)* performed considerably better under masked-recognition than day-after recall procedures. Overall, the masked-recognition method reveals that proven recognition for the three feeling commercials is 68 percent higher than the day-after recall scores (i.e., their average ratio of masked recognition to recall is 168).

TABLE 15.4 Day-After Recall versus Masked-Recognition Research Findings

	DAY-AFTER RECALL	MASKED RECOGNITION	RATIO OF MASKED RECOGNITION TO RECALL
Thinking Commercials			
A	49%	56%	114
D	24	32	133
E	21	24	114
Average	31	37	119
Feeling Commercials			
B	21%	37%	176
C	25	36	144
F	10	23	230
Average	19	32	168

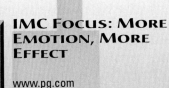

IMC Focus: More Emotion, More Effect

www.pg.com

Procter & Gamble, the huge consumer goods company, spends over $3 billion annually to advertise its many brands. However, P&G officials recently came to the conclusion that the company's internal advertising process probably was too rigid, too time-consuming, and perhaps even too risk-adverse, and that the probable result was suboptimal creative advertising from P&G's ad agencies. Part of the problem was that P&G's rigid rules regarding how advertising should be done imposed limitations on the creative product flowing out of its advertising agencies and perhaps even encouraged formulaic advertisements rather than creative ads attuned to the specific needs of P&G's brands. Moreover, too many P&G personnel were involved in the process, which led to divided accountability and delays in creating new ad campaigns.

Propelled by a passionate desire to improve the advertising process and the quality of creative advertising for its brands, top P&G officials in concert with high-level ad agency representatives proposed several major changes in the advertising process: (1) involve fewer P&G people in the process, (2) have just a single P&G representative work with an ad agency on any particular brand advertising assignment (called "single point accountability"), and (3) allow ad agencies more discretion in developing advertising concepts.

A result of this "paradigm shift" at P&G has been the production of more creative, dramatic, and emotional advertisements. The first illustration of this was an ad for Bounty paper towels. Advertising for this brand historically had involved new executions of the same old theme: Mom arriving just in time to mop up her child's spilled juice with Bounty paper towels followed by a side-by-side product demonstration. Under the new system, a new creative execution for Bounty required only about one-quarter of the time that past ad development required. The ad incorporated an emotional scene in which a father knocks over his own glass of juice to make his pre-school son feel better about his own juice disaster. Commenting on this emotional advertising execution, an official for Bounty's ad agency commented that consumers don't need to be shown how paper towels work, implying that an emotional execution would do a better job in holding viewer attention and enhancing Bounty's equity.

Source: Adapted from Sally Beatty, "P&G Says to Its Ad Agencies: Please Rewrite Our Old Formulas," *The Wall Street Journal Interactive Edition*, November 5, 1998.

These results clearly suggest that day-after recall tests may be biased against emotional, or feeling, commercials. A different research method, such as masked recognition, is needed when testing whether this type of commercial accomplishes suitable levels of awareness.[36]

Measures of Emotions

Advertising researchers have increasingly recognized that advertisements that positively influence receivers' feelings and emotions can be extremely successful for certain products and situations. Research has shown that ads that are better liked—often because they elicit positive emotions—are more likely to be remembered and to persuade.[37] (See the *IMC Focus* for one major company's shift to more emotional advertising.) Along with the trend toward more advertising directed at emotions, there has been a corresponding increase in efforts to measure consumers' emotional reactions to advertisements.[38] As shown in Table 15.3, three such measures are the warmth monitor, the TRACE method, and BBDO's Emotional Measurement System.

The Warmth Monitor. Warmth is one of various emotional responses that advertisements are capable of engendering in consumers. Warmth is considered to occur when a commercial viewer experiences a positive emotional reaction, albeit one that is mild and short-lived. This emotion is precipitated by experiencing a sense of love, family, or friendship.[39] Research has shown that warmth in advertising increases physiological arousal in response to an advertisement, encourages consumers to like the ad, and is correlated with the likelihood of purchasing the advertised product.[40] It is important to note, however, that although warmth and liking are related concepts, they are not equivalent. That is, consumers can like an ad without having a warm response to it.[41]

The warmth monitor is one of several techniques that have been developed to measure emotional reactions to both print ads and television commercials. The **warmth monitor** measures warmth in one of two ways: (1) by having consumers manipulate a computer joystick in response to a commercial, or (2) by having them track their reactions to a commercial on a sheet of paper containing four vertical lines running from top to bottom.[42] From left to right these lines are labeled *absence of warmth, neutral, warmhearted/tender,* and *emotional (moist eyes).* While viewing a test commercial, respondents advance a pencil down the paper, moving it to the left and right to continuously reflect their feelings about the commercial. Respondents are instructed to chart how warm they feel and how warm or good they consider the commercial to be. They are directed to maintain a constant rate of speed in moving their pencils down the page while keeping their eyes fixed on the commercial rather than the page. Most respondents do not need to look down at all and others do so only rarely.[43]

Market Fact's TRACE Method. A technologically more sophisticated measure of consumers' feelings toward advertisements is a technique called TRACE from the research firm Market Facts, Inc. **TRACE** enables consumers to reveal their feelings toward what they are seeing in a television commercial by pressing a series of buttons on a handheld microcomputer. Responses are synchronized with commercial content, and the microcomputer then plays back the consumer's feelings, expressed as a *TRACEline* across the television screen. The TRACEline moves up when the consumer feels good about what is shown and down when he or she feels bad about it. At points of critical movement in the TRACE-line, consumers are asked to discuss why their feelings changed.[44]

BBDO's Emotional Measurement System. Another approach to measuring consumers' emotional reactions to advertisements is the use of photos to reflect different emotions. This nonverbal procedure was devised by the BBDO Worldwide advertising agency to measure reactions to TV commercials because they had found that many people find it difficult to articulate their feelings. Words may not be readily available to describe how we feel, or we may be reluctant to share our feelings using words that may make us seem excessively sentimental. BBDO's Emotional Measurement System was designed to overcome this articulation problem.

BBDO spent three years testing hundreds of photos and refining its nonverbal procedure. This research culminated in a final collection of 53 photos that represent 26 universal emotional reactions: shame, fear, happiness, disgust, and so on. (See Figure 15.5 for two examples.) The Emotional Measurement System is simple to use. After consumers have been exposed to a test commercial, they are given the deck of 53 photos and asked to set aside any or all of the photos that reflect how they felt after viewing the commercial. The frequency with which a particular photo is chosen by the 150 to 600 respondents is then recorded, and a perceptual map is constructed. The perceptual map provides a vivid graphical representation of the emotions that characterize a set of tested commercials and provides a convenient way to show how different commercials compare against one another according to the emotions they evoke.[45]

Measures of Physiological Arousal

Advertising researchers also have turned to a variety of physiological testing devices to measure consumers' affective reactions to advertisements. These include such techniques as the galvanometer (which measures minute levels of perspiration in response to emotional arousal), pupillometric tests (pupil dilation), and voice-pitch analysis. Psychologists have concluded that these physiological functions are indeed sensitive to psychological processes of concern in advertising.[46] All of these physiological functions cited are controlled by the *autonomic nervous system.* (The autonomic nervous system consists of the nerves and ganglia that furnish blood vessels, the heart, smooth muscles, and glands.) Because individuals have little voluntary control over the autonomic nervous system,

FIGURE 15.5

BBDO Emotional Measurement System Photos Reflecting Disgust and Happiness

advertising researchers use changes in physiological functions to indicate the actual, unbiased amount of arousal resulting from advertisements.

In order to appreciate the potential value of such physiological measurement, consider the case of an advertisement that promotes the advertised brand by associating it with a scantily clad model, such as illustrated in the Nike ad (Figure 15.6) showing tennis player Mary Pierce. In pretesting this ad, some men, when asked what they think of it, may indicate that they dislike the ad because they consider it sexist and insulting to women. Others may respond that they really like it and find it appealing. Still others may feign disgust or aggravation in order to make a favorable impression on the interviewer. That is, this latter group of men may actually enjoy the ad but say otherwise in response to an interviewer's query, thereby disguising their true evaluation. Here is where measures of physiological arousal have a potential role to play in advertising research, namely to prevent self-monitoring of feelings and biased responses.

The Galvanometer.   The **galvanometer** (also referred to as a psychogalvanometer) is a device for measuring *galvanic skin response*, or *GSR*. (*Galvanic* refers to electricity produced by a chemical reaction.) When the consumer's autonomic nervous system is activated by some element in an advertisement, a physical response occurs in the sweat glands located in the palms and fingers. These glands open in varying degrees depending on the intensity of the arousal, and skin resistance drops when the sweat glands open. By sending a very fine electric current through one finger, out the other, and completing the circuit through an instrument called a *galvanometer,* testers may measure both the degree and frequency with which an advertisement activates emotional responses.[47] Simply, the galvanometer indirectly assesses the degree of emotional response to an advertisement by measuring minute amounts of perspiration.

There is evidence to indicate that galvanic skin response is a valid indicator of the amount of warmth generated by an advertisement.[48] Many companies have found the galvanometer to be a useful tool for assessing the potential effectiveness of advertisements, direct-mail messages, package copy, and other marketing communications messages. Advertising research practitioners who use the galvanometer claim that it is a *valid* predictor (see PACT principle 9) of an advertisement's ability to *motivate* consumer purchase behavior.[49] Indeed, in recognition of the galvanometer's ability to reveal an advertisement's motivational properties, practitioners refer to GSR research as the Motivational Response Method, or MRM.[50]

Pupillometer.   Pupillometric tests in advertising are conducted by measuring respondents' pupil dilation as they view a television commercial or focus on a printed advertisement. Respondents' heads are in a fixed position to permit continuous electronic

Illustration of Potential
Role for Physiological
Measurement

measurement of changes in pupillary responses. Responses to specific elements in an advertisement are used to indicate positive reaction (in the case of greater dilation) or negative reaction (smaller relative dilation). Although not unchallenged, there has been scientific evidence since the late 1960s to suggest that pupillary responses are correlated with people's arousal to stimuli and perhaps even with their likes and dislikes.[51]

Voice-Pitch Analysis (VOPAN). A complaint leveled against the galvanometer, pupillometric tests, and other physiological measurement devices is that they are capable of indicating the amount of emotional arousal but *not the direction of arousal.* One advertising commentator stated it this way:

> *The problem . . . is that once you have the data, you don't know what to do with it. All you have is a reading of physiological changes in a person. You have to get from there to whether that is good or bad.*[52]

Voice-pitch analysis (VOPAN) is a physiological measurement device that purportedly overcomes the preceding criticism.[53] A specially programmed computer analyzes a person's voice pitch in response to a question about a test commercial and determines how much the pitch differs in relation to the individual's normal, or baseline, pitch level. When an individual has emotional commitment, the vocal chord, which is regulated by the autonomic nervous system, becomes abnormally taut, and the pitch is higher than normal.

Thus, the voice-pitch reading indicates the amount of emotional involvement. Moreover, unlike other psychophysiological measures, the direction of an individual's emotional response can be determined by simply recording whether the individual responds affirmatively or negatively to a question of whether she or he liked the test commercial. *Truthfulness* of response is established by comparing changes in voice pitch over the respondent's pre-interview levels. Changes greater than a certain range indicate conscious or unconscious lies or confused responses.[54]

Voice-pitch analysis is potentially a valuable research technique; unfortunately, research purporting its virtues and validity lacks scientific merit. It is unknown whether VOPAN is a valuable addition to the advertising researcher's repertoire or a case of commercial hype.[55]

Measures of Persuasion (Pre/Post Preference Testing)

Measures of persuasion are used when an advertiser's objective is to influence consumers' attitudes toward and preference for the advertised brand. Advertising effectiveness can be assessed using the persuasiveness criterion by measuring attitudes or preferences both before and after an advertisement is run and determining whether attitudes have become more favorable or preference has shifted toward the advertised brand.

These procedures generally involve: (1) recruiting a sample of representative consumers and having them meet at a central location (a movie theater, a room in a shopping mall, a conference room), (2) initially measuring their attitudes or preferences for a brand that is the focus of the research (the *target* brand), (3) possibly measuring attitudes or preferences toward one or more competitive brands, (4) exposing consumers to a new television commercial for the target brand in context of a television pilot program or some other realistic viewing context, and (5) again measuring attitudes or preferences toward the target and competitive brands following the program and advertising exposure.

Commercial effectiveness is assessed by determining the amount of attitude change for the target brand or preference shift toward that brand. Firms that perform this type of research include, among others, ASI Market Research, Inc. and **rsc** THE QUALITY MEASUREMENT SYSTEM.[56]

ASI Theater Testing.   ASI performs theater testing of new television commercials. A sample of 250 consumers are recruited and invited to attend a preview of new television programs. Once in the ASI theater, they are told that prizes from various product categories will be awarded in a drawing. They then are asked to identify, for each product, the specific brand they would prefer receiving if their name should happen to be drawn (a preference measure). Next they are exposed to a pilot television program followed by test commercials for each of the product categories mentioned in the drawing. After being exposed to a second pilot television program, the participants are led to believe that one product was inadvertently omitted from the list of products for which the drawing will be held and that they will have to complete a new brand-preference sheet that includes the omitted product as well as the others.

Commercial effectiveness is determined by comparing the two sets of brand-preference measures. A commercial is considered effective to the extent that more consumers indicate a higher preference for the test product on the second preference sheet (i.e., after they have been exposed to a commercial for the brand) than on the first sheet (before they were exposed to the test commercial). Based on numerous past studies, ASI has developed norms indicating the actual magnitude of brand-preference shift that advertisers in particular product categories should expect.

In addition to the brand-preference measurement, ASI theaters are equipped with electronic recording dials that permit respondents to register continuously their likes and dislikes regarding the pilot programs and the test commercials.[57] These specific reactions to commercial elements are used to explain the brand-preference shifts.

The ARS Method. A company called **rsc** THE QUALITY MEASUREMENT SYSTEM (or **rsc** for short) is one of the most active of all message-testing research suppliers. This company tests individual video selling propositions as well as entire television commercials. Commercials are tested at varying stages of completion ranging from rough cut (e.g., animatics or photomatics) to finished form. **rsc**'s testing procedure is called the *ARS Persuasion*® method, where ARS stands for Advertising Research System. The ARS testing procedure is as follows:

> *Commercials are exposed in regular ARS test sessions to approximately 1,000 men and women drawn randomly from eight metropolitan areas and invited to preview typical television material. Each test commercial and other unrelated commercials are inserted into the television programs. While at the central location, a measurement of ARS Persuasion*® *is made by obtaining brand preferences before and after exposure to the programs. The ARS Persuasion*® *measure is the percent of respondents choosing the test product over competition after exposure to the TV material minus the percent choosing the test product before exposure.*[58]

In other words, the *ARS Persuasion*® method first has respondents indicate what brands they would prefer to receive among various product categories if their name were selected in a drawing to win a "basket" of free items (the pre measure). Among the list of products and brands is a "target brand" for which, unbeknownst to respondents, they subsequently will be exposed to a commercial that is being tested. After exposure to a television program, within which is embedded the test commercial, respondents again indicate what brands they would prefer to receive if their name were selected in a drawing (the post measure). The *ARS Persuasion*® score is calculated simply as the percentage of respondents selecting the target brand in preference to competitive brands at the post measure minus the percent selecting the brand at the pre measure. A positive score indicates that the test commercial has shifted preference toward the target brand.

The average *ARS Persuasion*® score in testing commercials in the United States is 5.8, which means that on average 5.8 percent more people exposed to test commercials prefer the brand after exposure to its advertising than before exposure.[59] This average score provides a benchmark against which ARS-tested commercials can be evaluated—the higher the score, the greater a commercial's potential persuasive power. **rsc** has tested over 30,000 commercials in its 25-year history, and from these tests it has been able to establish—albeit not without challenge[60]—that its *ARS Persuasion*® scores predict actual sales performance when commercials are aired. That is, higher-scoring commercials generate greater sales volume and larger market share gains. **rsc** principals recently published results based on 155 tested commercials from six countries: Belgium, Canada, Germany, Mexico, UK, and the U.S. The interesting results—and some new concepts—are described in the *Global Focus* box.

The principals at **rsc** have published various articles regarding TV commercial performance. This company, of course, has a vested interest in reporting that its testing system provides accurate predictions of marketplace performance; nonetheless, the fact that articles authored by **rsc** principals have been published in peer-reviewed journals (e.g., the *Journal of Advertising Research*) makes them worthy of further discussion. **rsc**'s *ARS Persuasion*® technique has received a positive independent endorsement from well-known advertising researcher John Philip Jones.[61] Three of the major conclusions that have been drawn by **rsc** about the functioning and effectiveness of advertising are these: (1) ad copy must be distinctive; (2) ad weight without persuasiveness is insufficient; and (3) the selling power of advertising wears out over time.[62]

GLOBAL FOCUS: RELATION BETWEEN *ARS PERSUASION*® SCORES AND MARKET-SHARE GAINS IN SIX COUNTRIES

Based on results of 155 tested commercials from Belgium, Canada, Germany, Mexico, the UK, and the U.S., principals at **rsc** have demonstrated how *ARS Persuasion*® scores relate to market-share changes. A total of 84 brands (some with multiple commercials tested) representing 54 product categories were involved in the analysis. All 155 commercials were tested under the procedures described above, and then market-share levels under in-market circumstances were compared during a period after advertising commenced for the brands versus a period prior to any advertising. Hence, the key issue is whether *ARS Persuasion*® scores accurately predict the magnitude of market-share gain following advertising. In other words, are the scores that **rsc** generates from its laboratory testing predictive of actual marketplace performance? This obviously is a validity issue as described previously under PACT principle 9. Results from these 155 tests are presented in Table 15.5.

To understand what these results reveal, let us carefully examine the first row in Table 15.5. This row includes all commercials that received really low (<2.0) *ARS Persuasion*® scores. **rsc** defines scores of 2.0 or lower as "inelastic," implying that commercials scoring this poorly are probably incapable of driving market-share gains. Now looking at the four columns of positive share-point differences, it will be observed that for those commercials yielding inelastic persuasion scores, only 27 percent generated positive share

gains; in other words, 73 percent of these poorly performing commercials failed to generate in-market share gains. Eighteen percent of these commercials yielded gains of less than ½-share point, and 9 percent generated gains of greater than ½-share point but less than a full share point. None of the inelastic commercials generated gains exceeding a full share point. At the other extreme, 100 percent of the "highly elastic" commercials (persuasion scores of 12+) yielded positive share gains. Indeed, all 100 percent of these outstanding performing commercials produced gains of ½-share point or better, with 92 percent yielding gains of at least 1 share point and 80 percent providing gains of 2+ share points. Cell entries for the "low elastic," "moderately elastic," and "elastic" categories are to be interpreted in similar fashion.

It is apparent from these 155 test cases that *ARS Persuasion*® scores are valid predictors of in-market performance. In sum, the higher the score (or, stated alternatively, the more elastic the score), the greater the likelihood that a tested commercial will produce positive sales gains when the focal brand is advertised under real-world, in-market conditions. This global study thus informs advertisers that they should not place advertising weight behind commercials that have tested poorly. Table 15.5 reveals, in fact, that commercials scoring a 2.0 or lower *ARS Persuasion*® score most likely will not produce a positive share gain, and that a large percentage (i.e., 40 percent) of those scoring in the "low elastic" range (2.0–3.9) also will not generate positive gains. It is only when commercials test in the "moderately elastic" (4.0–6.9) or higher ranges that meaningful share gains can be anticipated.

Source: Adapted from Margaret Henderson Blair and Michael J. Rabuck, "Advertising Wearin and Wearout: Ten Years Later," Table 4, p. 7 (Evansville, IN: **rsc** THE QUALITY MEASUREMENT COMPANY, 1998).

TABLE 15.5 — rsc's 1998 Global Validation Study *ARS Persuasion*® Scores and In-Market Results

ARS PERSUASION® SCORE RANGE	POSITIVE SHARE-POINT DIFFERENCE OF AT LEAST:			
	0.0+	0.5+	1.0+	2.0+
<2.0 ("Inelastic")	18%	9%	0%	0%
2.0–3.9 ("Low elastic")	60%	26%	11%	0%
4.0–6.9 ("Moderately elastic")	80%	55%	43%	20%
7.0–11.9 ("Elastic")	100%	97%	69%	43%
12.0+ ("Highly elastic")	100%	100%	92%	80%

Ad Copy Must Be Distinctive.   What is distinctive ad copy? Research by **rsc** has shown that commercials having *strong selling propositions* are distinctive and thereby tend to achieve higher *ARS Persuasion*® scores.[63] What determines whether a commercial has a strong selling proposition? Research indicates that any differentiating information concerning a new brand or new feature of an existing brand gives a selling proposition a significantly higher chance of a superior score.[64] Although commercials for new brands and those with new features are more persuasive on average, advertising for established brands also can be very persuasive via *brand differentiation*—that is, by distinguishing the advertised brand from competitive offerings and providing consumers with a distinctive reason to buy it.[65]

The foregoing discussion has illustrated a key advertising principle: Effective advertising must be persuasive and distinctive; it must possess a strong selling proposition. Appreciation of this point necessitates rigorous testing of proposed advertisements prior to committing any media dollars to their airing or printing. Reminiscent of the classic parental admonition to young children ("Look before you cross the street"), a similar exhortation can be made to advertisers when formulating advertising messages: "Test before you air or print!" To put it bluntly, it is foolhardy to invest money in a media campaign without first having assured that the advertising message is fully capable of "moving the dial," that is, shifting brand preference toward the advertised brand.

Weight Is Not Enough. A second important finding from **rsc** is that the amount of advertising weight invested in a brand (as indicated by the number of gross rating points during a specified advertising period) does *not* by itself provide a good predictor of sales volume and market share. In other words, merely increasing GRPs does not directly translate into better performance for a brand. Advertising copy *must also be distinctive and persuasive* (as established above) for advertising to have a positive impact on a brand's sales and market share. An advertising practitioner perhaps said it best when stating that "Airing ineffective advertising is like being off-air; it just costs more."[66] It cannot be overemphasized that unpersuasive, nondistinctive advertising is not worth airing or printing.

rsc's test results receive impressive support from a landmark study that analyzed numerous tests based on BehaviorScan single-source data (a methodology that will be thoroughly described in the next section). Leonard Lodish and colleagues concluded from their research that when advertisements are unpersuasive there is no more likelihood of achieving sales volume increases even with doubling and tripling TV advertising weight.[67]

The virtual independence between advertising weight and sales is clearly demonstrated in Table 15.6. The study results presented in this table are based on single-source data and *split-cable tests* for various brands of consumer packaged goods. As will be discussed more fully in a later section about BehaviorScan single-source data, split-cable testing involves either "weight" or "copy" tests. The data in Table 15.6 involve only weight tests whereby two panels of households have an opportunity to see the identical commercial for a particular brand, but the amount of spending, or weight, is varied between the two panels. These households' subsequent purchases of the advertised brand are later compared based on purchase data acquired via optical scanning devices in grocery stores. Split-cable tests generally run for a full year. (The following section on single-source data describes this methodology in greater detail.)

Table 15.6 presents data from 20 split-cable tests, each involving an actual marketplace examination of advertising's influence on the sales of a branded grocery product. In each test, there are two key features of the advertising effort: First is the number of GRPs, or weight, used to advertise the brand; in Table 15.6 this is expressed as the *weight difference* between the two panels of households. A difference of zero would mean that an identical amount of advertising (in terms of GRPs) was aired during the test period to both groups of households. The second key advertising feature is the *ARS Persuasion*® score that the test commercial obtained. Recall that the average *ARS Persuasion*® score is 5.8, so scores in Table 15.6 lower than 5.8 indicate a below-average commercial in terms of persuasiveness, whereas scores above 5.8 indicate above-average performers. Finally, for each test reported in Table 15.6, there is an indication in the last column of whether a statistically significant sales difference occurred between the two panels.

Thus, test 8, for example, shows a weight difference of 1,000 GRPs between the two panels. However, the tested commercial in this case received a below-average *ARS Persuasion*® score of 3.6. Given this combination of a heavy weight difference between the two panels but a relatively unpersuasive commercial, the result was no significant difference

TABLE 15.6	Relations among Advertising Weight, Persuasion Scores, and Sales		
TEST NUMBER	WEIGHT DIFFERENCE	ARS PERSUASION SCORE	SALES DIFFERENCE
1.	334 GRPs	−1.3	NSD*
2.	4,200	0.6	NSD
3.	406	1.8	NSD
4.	1,400	2.6	NSD
5.	695	2.7	NSD
6.	800	2.8	NSD
7.	2,231	3.5	NSD
8.	1,000	3.6	NSD
9.	900	3.7	NSD
10.	1,800	4.0	NSD
11.	947	4.2	NSD
12.	820	4.3	NSD
13.	1,364	4.4	NSD
14.	1,198	4.4	NSD
15.	583	5.9	SD†
16.	1,949	6.7	SD
17.	580	7.0	SD
18.	778	7.7	SD
19.	1,400	9.0	SD
20.	860	9.3	SD

*NSD: Purchases of the advertised brand were *not* significantly different between the two split-cable panels at a 90 percent confidence level.

†SD: Purchases of the advertised brand *were* significantly different between the two split-cable panels at a 90 percent confidence level.

Source: Margaret Henderson Blair, "An Empirical Investigation of Advertising Wearin and Wearout," *Journal of Advertising Research* 27 (December 1987/January 1988), 45–50.

(NSD) in sales. Heavy advertising weight was unable to compensate for an unpersuasive commercial.

Now let us examine test 15, in which the weight difference between the two panels of households amounts to only 583 GRPs. However, the new commercial in this test received an above-average *ARS Persuasion*® score of 5.9. The result: A significant difference (SD) in sales *was* recorded when the tested brand was advertised with a persuasive commercial.

Table 15.6 also demonstrates that no significant sales differences are obtained even in instances of huge weight differences such as in tests 2 (a 4,200 GRP difference) and 7 (a 2,231 GRP difference). These two tests correspond (at the time of the research) with annual ad expenditures of $21 million and $11 million, yet no differential sales response materialized after a full year. Comparatively, note in tests 15 through 20 that significant sales differences are observed even when the weight differences are relatively small in comparison with the weight differences in tests 2 and 7. Also, the *ARS Persuasion*® score is above average in every instance for tests 15 through 20. Hence, it can be concluded that the primary determinant of sales differences in these split-cable tests was the *persuasiveness* of the tested commercials. Whenever the *ARS Persuasion*® score was above the average ARS score (i.e., above 5.8), significant sales differences were detected; in all instances in which the *ARS Persuasion*® score was below average, no significant sales differences were obtained.

Provided these results generalize beyond the tested commercials, the implication is that a commercial's persuasiveness is absolutely critical: Persuasiveness, and not mere advertising weight, is the prime determinant of whether an advertising campaign will translate into improved sales performance. Indeed, investing advertising in nonpersuasive commercials is akin to throwing money away. Advertising weight is important, but only if a commercial presents a persuasive story.[68]

Research conducted by **rsc** for the Campbell's Soup Company provides additional evidence regarding the importance of commercial persuasiveness.[69] Figure 15.7 presents the results of **rsc**'s testing of various commercials for an undisclosed Campbell Soup Company brand, which we will assume to be V8 vegetable juice. Note that the horizontal axis is broken into 18 four-week periods, whereas the vertical axis of the graph depicts market shares for this brand. It can be seen that V8's market share during the first four-week period was 19.6. Notice next that a new commercial (titled "Tastes Great 30," with the 30 signifying a 30-second commercial) was aired during the second four-week period. This commercial, when tested by **rsc,** received an *ARS Persuasion*® score of 5.8. Shortly after airing this new commercial, V8's market shared jumped from 19.6 to 21.4—an increase of nearly 2 share points. Thereafter, V8's market share varied from a low of 20.4 (period 5) to a high of 21.5 (period 4). Then in period 7, when a new commercial started airing ("Beauty Shot Revised 15"), V8's market share jumped by an incredible 4.5 share points. Notice how this result correlates to the strength of the new commercial, which obtained an *ARS Persuasion*® score of 10. Over the next several months, the market share for V8 fell to 22 (period 14). At this point (period 15), another new commercial began airing ("Beauty Shot Poolout 2 15"). This commercial, which obtained an *ARS Persuasion*® score of 10.9, immediately increased V8's sales to a 25.9 market share. By period 18 the share had declined

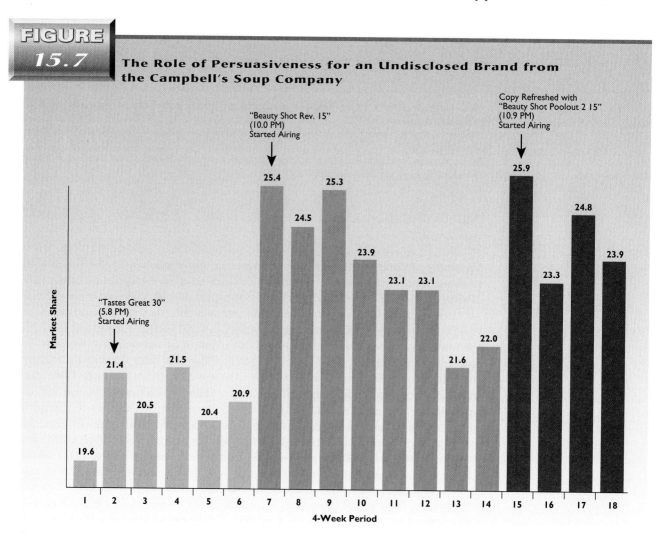

FIGURE 15.7

The Role of Persuasiveness for an Undisclosed Brand from the Campbell's Soup Company

Source: Anthony J. Adams and Margaret Henderson Blair, "Persuasive Advertising and Sales Accountability: Past Experience and Forward Validation," *Journal of Advertising Research* 32 (March/April 1992), 23.

to a 23.9, but in comparison to the initial share of 19.6 in period 1, this still represented a gain of 4.3 share points in slightly more than a year—a substantial market-share gain in an established product category by any standard. These results indicate that persuasive commercials can have a rather dramatic effect in increasing market share.

Advertising Eventually Wears Out.   Another important lesson from the Campbell V8 case presentation is that advertising ultimately *wears out* and hence must be periodically refreshed in order to maintain or increase a brand's sales effectiveness.[70] Research in the academic community as well as by practitioners has convincingly demonstrated that with the accumulation of GRPs for a brand, the persuasive power of that brand's advertising declines over time.[71] This is referred to as **wear out,** the result of which is diminished effectiveness of advertising as GRPs accumulate over time. The implication is that it is important to periodically re-test commercials (using, for example, *ARS Persuasion*® measurement) to determine how much persuasive power remains in a commercial. When the persuasive power falls into the low elastic or inelastic range (see Table 15.5), it probably is time to replace the commercial with a new or revised execution.

Measures of Sales Response (Single-Source Systems)

Determining the sales impact of advertising is, as explained in Chapter 9, a most difficult task. However, substantial efforts have been made in recent years toward developing research procedures that are able to assess the sales-generating ability of advertising.

So-called **single-source systems (SSSs)** have evolved in advertising research to measure the effects of advertising on sales. SSSs became possible with the advent of three technological developments: (1) *electronic television meters,* (2) *optical laser scanning* of universal product codes (UPC symbols) at retail checkout, and (3) *split-cable* technology. Single-source systems gather purchase data from panels of households using optical scanning equipment and merge it with household demographic characteristics and, most important, with information about causal marketing variables that influence household purchases (i.e., television commercials, coupons, in-store displays, trade promotions, etc.). The following sections describe two single-source systems: IRI's BehaviorScan (which was alluded to when discussing Table 15.6) and Nielsen's SCANTRACK.

IRI's BehaviorScan.   Information Resources, Inc.'s (IRI) pioneered single-source data collection when introducing its BehaviorScan service in 1979. IRI now operates BehaviorScan panel households in seven markets around the United States: Pittsfield, Massachusetts; Marion, Indiana; Eau Claire, Wisconsin; Cedar Rapids, Iowa; Grand Junction, Colorado; Midland, Texas; and Visalia, California. These small cities were chosen because they are located far enough from television stations that residents must depend on *cable TV* to receive good reception. Moreover, grocery and drug stores in these cities are equipped with optical scanning devices that read UPC symbols from packages and thereby record exactly what product categories and brands panel households purchase.

In each market, approximately 3,000 households are recruited to participate in a BehaviorScan panel, and about one-third of these households are equipped with electronic meters attached to TV sets. Panel members are eligible for prize drawings as remuneration for their participation. Because each BehaviorScan household has an *identification card* that is presented at the grocery store checkout on every shopping occasion, IRI knows precisely what items each household purchases by merely linking up optically scanned purchases with ID numbers. Panel members also provide IRI with detailed demographic information, including family size, income level, number of televisions owned, the types of newspapers and magazines read, and who in the household does most of the shopping. IRI then combines all of these data into a *single source* and thereby determines which households purchase what products/brands and how responsive they are to advertising and other purchase-causing variables. Thus, **single source data** consists of: (1) household demographic information, (2) household purchase behavior, and (3) household exposure to (or, more technically, the opportunity to see, OTS) new television commercials that are tested under real world, or *in-market,* test conditions.

The availability of cable TV enables IRI (with the cooperation of cable companies and advertisers) to intercept a cable signal before it reaches households, *split the signal,* and send different advertisements to two panels of households (test versus control). Hence, the split-cable feature and optically scanned purchase data enable IRI to know which commercial each household had an opportunity to see and how much of the advertised brand the household purchases.

IRI's BehaviorScan allows for the testing of television commercials. Two types of tests are offered: (1) weight tests and (2) copy tests. In both types of tests, a test commercial is aired in, say, two BehaviorScan markets for up to a full year. With *weight tests,* panel households are divided into test and control groups. The identical commercial is transmitted to both groups, but the number of GRPs, or weight, is varied between the groups during the course of the test period. Any difference between the groups' aggregate purchase behavior for the tested brand is obviously attributable to the advertising weight differential between the two groups—such as described above in context of **rsc**'s weight test results (Table 15.6). The second form of testing, *copy tests,* holds the amount of weight constant but varies commercial content. That is, a test group is exposed during the course of the testing period to a new commercial, whereas a control group has an opportunity to see public service announcements (PSAs) that are inserted in lieu of the new commercial. Regardless of the type of test, upon aggregating purchase data across all households in each of the two groups, it is simple to determine whether differences in advertising copy or weight generate differences in purchase behavior.

To better understand how BehaviorScan's single-source data can be used to show the relationship between advertising and sales activity, consider a situation in which a manufacturer of a new snack food is interested in *copy testing* the effectiveness of a television commercial promoting this product. BehaviorScan would do the following: (1) select two or three cities in which to conduct the test; (2) stock the manufacturer's brand in all grocery stores and perhaps drug stores located in these cities; (3) selectively broadcast a new commercial for the brand using special split-cable television so approximately one-half of the panel members in each market are exposed either to the new commercial or PSAs; (4) record electronically (via optical scanners) grocery purchases made by all panel members; and (5) compare the purchase behavior of the two groups of panel members who were potentially exposed to the new commercial versus PSAs.

If the advertising is effective, a greater proportion of the panel members exposed to the test commercial should buy the promoted item than those only exposed to the public service announcements. The percentage of panel members who undertake a trial purchase behavior would thereby indicate the effectiveness of the new television commercial, and the percentage who make a repeat purchase would indicate how much the brand is liked. The use of split-cable testing (also called split-panel testing) at Frito-Lay, a large U.S.-based maker of various salted snack foods, is described in the *IMC Focus.*

Nielsen's SCANTRACK. The A. C. Nielsen company entered into a joint venture with another research firm, the NPD Group, in 1989 to form the SCANTRACK single-source system. SCANTRACK differs from BehaviorScan in a couple of interesting respects. First, and most important, whereas BehaviorScan collects purchase data via optical scanners located only in supermarkets, SCANTRACK collects purchase data by having its 15,000 panel households use *handheld scanners.* These scanners are located in panel members' homes, usually mounted to a kitchen or pantry wall. Hence, with SCANTRACK panelists record purchases of *every bar-coded product purchased* regardless of the store where purchased—a major grocery chain, independent supermarket, mass merchandiser, or wholesale club.[72]

A second distinguishing characteristic of SCANTRACK is that panel members also use their handheld scanners to enter any coupons used and to record all store deals and in-store features that influenced their purchasing decisions. Panel members transmit purchases

IMC FOCUS: SPLIT-PANEL TESTING AT FRITO-LAY

To test the effectiveness of television advertising for its various brands, marketing researchers and brand managers at Frito-Lay, Inc. commissioned IRI, Inc. to perform 23 split-panel experiments in BehaviorScan markets during a four-year period in the 1990s. All 23 experiments were copy (versus weight) tests that involved comparing one group of households who were exposed to advertising for a Frito-Lay brand (advertising households) against another group who had no opportunity to see the advertising (control households). Each of the 23 tests was conducted in at least two BehaviorScan markets and lasted a full year. In addition to the advertising versus no-advertising condition, Frito-Lay's BehaviorScan tests also were classified in terms of: (1) whether the tested brand was a new brand (e.g., SunChips) or an established brand (e.g., Ruffles), and (2) whether sales for the brand were relatively large (e.g., Doritos) or small (e.g., Rold Gold).

The objective in conducting these tests was to determine whether sales volume would be greater in households exposed to advertisements for Frito-Lay brands versus those households which had no opportunity to be exposed to commercials for these brands. Results from the 23 Frito-Lay BehaviorScan tests are summarized in Table 15.7.

The first notable observation from Table 15.7 is that advertising for 57 percent of the 23 tested brands generated significant increases in sales volume during the one-year test duration. (Though not shown in Table 15.7, the average gain in sales volume between the advertising versus no-advertising household panels was 15

percent across the 12 advertisements that yielded significant sales increases.) A second key finding from Table 15.7 is that advertising for the small sales-volume brands was much more effective in driving sales gains than was advertising for the large brands. In fact, of the 12 small brands tested, 83 percent, or 10 brands, experienced significant increases in sales as a result of their one-year advertising efforts. A third important finding is that advertising for 88 percent of the new brands generated significant sales gains, whereas only 40 percent of the established brands resulted in sales gains from advertising. A fourth notable finding, though not apparent in Table 15.7, is that in all 12 (of 23) cases where advertisements for Frito-Lay brands drove significant sales increases, the effects occurred within the first six months and in 11 of the 12 tests within the first three months. In other words, when advertising works, it works relatively quickly or not at all.

These 23 BehaviorScan tests of Frito-Lay brands reveal that advertising is not always effective; indeed, it was effective in slightly over one-half of the tests. Moreover, as demonstrated earlier when discussing **rsc**'s *ARS Persuasion*® method, this research supports the finding that advertising generally is effective only when it provides distinctive, newsworthy information, such as when introducing new brands or line extensions. Finally advertising works relatively quickly if at all.

Source: Based on Dwight R. Riskey, "How T.V. Advertising Works: An Industry Response," *Journal of Marketing Research* 34 (May 1997), 292–293. For more complete reporting on effectiveness of TV advertising, see Leonard M. Lodish et al., "How T.V. Advertising Works: A Meta-Analysis of 389 Real World Split Cable T.V. Advertising Experiments," *Journal of Marketing Research* 32 (May 1995), 125–139; and Leonard M. Lodish et al., "A Summary of Fifty-Five In-Market Experimental Estimates of the Long-Term Effect of TV Advertising," *Marketing Science* 14 (No. 3 1995), G133–G140.

TABLE 15.7   BehaviorScan Tests of Advertising Effectiveness for 23 Frito-Lay Brands

	ESTABLISHED BRANDS	NEW BRANDS	TOTAL
Large Brands	13% (n=8)*	67% (n=3)	27% (n=11)
Small Brands	71% (n=7)	100% (n=5)	83% (n=12)
Total	40% (n=15)	88% (n=8)	57% (n=23)

*Table entries are to be interpreted as follows: A total of eight (out of 23) tests involved large, established brands. Of the eight tests conducted with this particular combination of brands, only one test, or 13 percent, detected a statistically significant increase in sales volume in those households exposed to advertising compared to the no-advertising control households.

and other data to Nielsen every week by calling a toll-free number and holding up their scanner to the phone, which records the data via a series of electronic beeps. Nielsen's SCANTRACK has provided advertisers and their agencies with invaluable information about the short- and long-term effects of advertising. For example, John Philip Jones' STAS method, as described in Chapter 14, is based on analysis of SCANTRACK data.

MEASURING WEB ADS

As discussed in Chapter 12, online advertising revenue is projected to reach approximately $4 billion by 2000.[73] Though this amount is relatively trivial in comparison to major ad media (TV, newspaper, etc.), major future increases in Internet advertising are probable. As with traditional advertising media, the development of accurate measurement systems is a key determinant of whether Internet advertising will continue to grow at an explosive rate. This is to say that advertisers and their agencies will not continue to invest heavily in this particular medium if the effectiveness of Internet advertisements cannot be assessed reliably and validly. Advertisers initially invested in Internet advertising largely on blind faith, but this will not continue. Indeed, the Advertising Research Foundation concluded that Internet advertising will ultimately succeed as an ad medium only if it becomes possible to gauge effectiveness in such indicators as awareness, recall, and persuasion.[74] Respondents to a survey by the Association of National Advertisers indicated that the two top barriers to increased Internet advertising are the difficulty of tracking return on investment (noted by 68 percent) and the lack of reliable and valid measurement information (cited by 56 percent).[75]

Many research suppliers are scrambling to develop measurement systems comparable to Simmons Market Research Bureau (of magazine rating fame) and **rsc** (of television persuasion notoriety). It frankly is too early to know the exact Internet research suppliers that will rise to the top and whose results will be trusted and respected by the advertising industry. Accurately measuring Internet ratings, audience composition, and advertising effectiveness on the Web are major challenges for the research community. By the next edition of this text, we will have a much clearer idea of which research services have earned the respect of the advertising community. At the present time, all that can be said with assurance is that advertising on the Internet will remain relatively "small potatoes" (compared to TV advertising) until advertisers believe they can determine whether they are receiving a decent return on investment when choosing the Internet over alternative media buys.

Summary

Though difficult and often expensive, measuring advertising effectiveness is essential for advertisers to better understand how well their ads are performing and what changes need to be made to improve performance.

Broadly speaking, advertising research consists of media and message research. Media research measures audience composition and size for media vehicles as a basis for determining ratings. The text discusses two magazine audience measurement services (Simmons Market Research Bureau and Mediamark Research, Inc.), one local radio audience service (Arbitron) and one national service (RADAR), and two television audience measurement systems (Nielsen's people meters and SRI's SMART method).

Message-based research evaluates the effectiveness of advertising messages. Dozens of techniques for measuring advertising effectiveness have evolved over the years. The reason for this diversity is that advertisements perform a variety of functions and multiple methods are needed to test different indicators of advertising effectiveness.

Starch Readership, Bruzzone tests, and Burke day-after recall tests are techniques for measuring recognition and recall. Consumers' emotional reactions to advertisements are measured using techniques such as the warmth monitor, TRACE, and the photograph-based Emotional Measurement System. Various physiological measures (such as galvanic skin response, pupil dilation, and voice pitch) are used to assess physiological arousal activated by advertisements. ASI theater and *ARS Persuasion*® testing are used to measure preference shifts to advertising. The impact of advertising on actual purchase behavior is assessed with single-source data collection systems (IRI's BehaviorScan and Nielsen's SCANTRACK) that obtain optical-scanned purchase data from household panels and then integrate this with television viewing behavior and other marketing variables.

No single advertising-effectiveness measurement technique is ideal, nor is any particular technique appropriate for all occasions. The choice of technique should depend on the specific objective an advertising campaign is intended to accomplish. Moreover, multiple measurement methods are usually preferable to single techniques in order to answer the diversity of questions that are typically involved in attempts to assess advertising effectiveness.

Discussion Questions

1. It is desirable that the measurement of advertising effectiveness focus on sales response rather than on some precursor to sales, yet measuring sales response to advertising is typically difficult. What complicates the measurement of sales response to advertising?

2. PACT principle 2 states that a good copytesting system should establish how results will be used in advance of each copytest. Explain the specific meaning and importance of this copytesting principle. Construct illustrations of an anticipated result lacking a sufficient action standard and one with a suitable standard.

3. In reference to PACT principle 9, explain in your own words what valid measurement means. Suppose a research firm offers television advertisers an inexpensive method of testing commercials in which consumers merely evaluate photographed pictures of key commercial scenes. Comment about the probable validity of this approach.

4. Advertising research often measures vehicle exposure to indicate advertising exposure. What is the difference between these two types of exposure, and why do researchers measure the former when advertising decision makers are really interested in the latter?

5. If you were an account executive in an advertising agency, what would you tell clients to convince them to use (or not to use) the Starch Readership Service?

6. An advertising agency is in the process of arranging research services to assess advertising effectiveness for two clients: One advertising campaign for a unique financial service uses a

number of specific selling points; the other campaign involves a very touching family scene to advertise another client's food product. The agency proposes that day-after recall tests be conducted for both clients. Comment.

7. As advertising manager for a brand of toothpaste, you are considering using a physiological measurement technique to assess consumers' evaluative reactions to your new advertisements. Present an argument in favor of using VOPAN rather than pupil dilation testing or galvanic skin-response measurement.

8. A test of television advertising effectiveness performed by BehaviorScan will cost you, as brand manager of a new brand of cereal, approximately $250,000. Why might this be a prudent investment in comparison to spending $50,000 to perform an awareness study?

9. Assume that several years from now you are purchasing your own home. One day you open your mail to a letter from Information Resources, Inc., (IRI) that requests you to become a BehaviorScan panel member. Would you have any reservations about agreeing to do this? Assume instead that the letter is from Nielsen, instead of IRI, requesting your participation in SCAN-TRACK. What would be your reservations, if any, in this case?

10. Representatives of the major TV networks (ABC, CBS, Fox, and NBC) often claim that people meters are flawed. What are some of the reasons why people meters may not yield precise information about the number of households tuned into a specific television program?

11. Select three national television commercials, identify the objective(s) each appears to be attempting to accomplish, and then propose a procedure for how you would go about testing the effectiveness of each commercial. Be specific.

12. Locate a recent SMRB or MRI publication in your library, and select a product used by large numbers of consumers (soft drinks, cereal, candy bars, etc.). Pick out the index numbers for the 18 to 24, 25 to 34, 35 to 44, 45 to 54, 55 to 64, and 65 and older age categories based on *All Users* columns. Show how the index numbers in column *D* were calculated. Also, identify some magazines that would be especially suitable for advertising to the *Heavy Users* of your selected product category.

13. With the following data, fill in the empty blanks.

BASE: ALL ADULTS	TOTAL U.S. '000	A '000	B % DOWN	C % ACROSS	D INDEX
All Adults	169557	49639	100.0	29.3	100
18–24	14859	6285	"B1" = ___	"C1" = ___	"D1" = ___
25–34	38494	10509	"B2" = ___	"C2" = ___	"D2" = ___

14. Based exclusively on the data in question 13, if you were an advertiser in process of deciding whether to advertise your brand just to people aged 18 to 24, just to the 25 to 34 age group, or to both age groups, what would be your decision? Provide a detailed rationale for your decision.

15. Television commercials are tested in various stages of completion, including storyboards, animatics, photomatics, ripamatics, liveamatics, and finished commercials. What reservations might you have concerning the ability to project results from testing pre-finished commercials to actual marketplace results with real commercials? Be specific and refer to the PACT principles where appropriate.

16. Turn to Table 15.5 and inspect the row in that table having an *ARS Persuasion*® score range of 4.0–6.9 ("Moderately elastic"). With that particular row in mind, interpret the cell entries under each of the four columns of share-point differences. For example, what is the specific interpretation of 55 percent under the column headed 0.5+?

17. In your own words, specifically explain the meaning of the statement that "ad weight without persuasiveness is insufficient." Illustrate your discussion with the Dunkin' Donuts commercial in the *Opening Vignette*.

18. In context of the discussion of single-source data, explain the difference between "weight" and "copy" tests. Illustrate your understanding of the difference between these two types of test with the Intel commercial in the *Opening Vignette*.

19. With reference to Frito-Lay's "copy" tests in Table 15.7, the results reveal that of the 23 commercials tested, only 57 percent of the tests generated significant differences in sales between the commercially exposed and control groups of households. Let us assume that Frito-Lay's results are applicable to television advertising in general. What is your general conclusion from this key finding?

20, Assume that as a brand manager you are considering investing a substantial sum of your advertising funds into Internet advertising. Before making this investment, what specific research questions would you have regarding this particular medium? What questions would you want answered regarding your proposed ad message? (Make whatever assumptions you consider necessary in order to address these questions.)

*I*nternet Exercise

1. As mentioned in the chapter, assessing advertising effectiveness on the Internet presents major challenges for the research community. As more and more consumers view the Internet as a necessity rather than a luxury, so too will advertisers. Large advertisers are still willing to experiment but most complain about the limited video and audio capabilities of the Internet. However, even when Internet technology improves, advertising will only expand if it offers measurable and substantial advantages in effectiveness relative to existing media. To gain a more detailed understanding of the research challenges, discuss the following:

    a. What is the current status of Internet audience measurement and how does it compare to other media? Cite online and offline resources to support your answer.

    b. Devise a copytesting system for Internet ads. Organize your conceptualization and presentation of this system by discussing how it addresses the 9 principles of good copytesting practice. Try to avoid simply regurgitating the 9 principles. Use specific details from the system you have devised.

*C*hapter Fifteen Endnotes

1. William A. Cook and Theodore F. Dunn, " The Changing Face of Advertising Research in the Information Age: An ARF Copy Research Council Survey," *Journal of Advertising Research* 36 (January–February 1996), 55–71.

2. Leonard M. Lodish, *The Advertising and Promotion Challenge: Vaguely Right or Precisely Wrong?* (New York: Oxford University Press, 1986).

3. *LNA/MediaWatch Multi-Media Service Ad $ Summary January–December 1997* (New York: Competitive Media Reporting and Publishers Information Bureau, Inc., 1997).

4. Stephen M. Blacker, "Magazines Need Better Research," *Advertising Age,* June 10, 1996, 23; Erwin Ephron, "Magazines Stall At Research Crossroads," *Advertising Age,* October 19, 1998, 38.

5. Keith J. Kelly, "Simmons Shift Opens Door to Research Peace," *Advertising Age,* October 24, 1994, S20.

6. These data are from *Marketer's Guide to Media 1998–99,* 21 (New York: BPI Communications, 1998), 164–171.

7. For additional information on magazine audience measurement, see Thomas C. Kinnear, David A. Horne, and Theresa A. Zingery, "Valid Magazine Audience Measurement: Issues and Perspectives," in *Current Issues and Research in*

Advertising, ed. James H. Leigh and Claude R. Martin, Jr. (Ann Arbor: Division of Research, Graduate School of Business, University of Michigan, 1986), 251–270.

8. The following information is from *Mediamark Research Baked Goods, Snacks & Desserts Report, P-16* (Mediamark Research Inc., spring 1996, 353–361).

9. The format for this discussion is based on an illustration provided in ibid., iii.

10. This description is adapted from Joel J. Davis, *Advertising Research: Theory and Practice* (Upper Saddle River, NJ: Prentice-Hall, 1997), 611.

11. A sampling of the many articles written about people meters and the surrounding controversy includes Verne Gay, "Vindication?" *Advertising Age,* May 30, 1988, 66; Ira Teinowitz, "People Meters Miss Kids: JWT," *Advertising Age,* July 18, 1988, 35; and Joe Mandese, "Groups Propose TV Rating Changes," *Advertising Age,* September 9, 1991, 33. For a technical analysis, see Roland Soong, "The Statistical Reliability of People Meter Ratings," *Journal of Advertising Research* 28 (February/March 1988), 50–56.

12. Kyle Pope, "TV Networks Decide to Launch a Rival to Nielsen Media Research," *The Wall Street Journal Interactive Edition,* August 3, 1998.

13. Michelle Wirth Fellman, "A SMART Move," *Marketing News,* September 14, 1998, 1, 7, 43.

14. Chuck Ross, "Broadcast Net Declines to Fund SRI's Nielsen Rival," *Advertising Age,* November 9, 1998, 2.

15. Joe Mandese, "Nielsen Marketing May Bring Back TV Viewing Diaries," *Advertising Age,* October 19, 1992, 6.

16. Karen Whitehill King, John D. Pehrson, and Leonard N. Reid, "Pretesting TV Commercials: Methods, Measures, and Changing Agency Roles," *Journal of Advertising* 22 (September 1993), 85–97.

17. Ibid.

18. Descriptions are based on ibid., table 3, 91.

19. Material for this section is extracted from the PACT document, which is published in its entirety in the *Journal of Advertising* 11, no. 4 (1982), 4–29.

20. Herbert E. Krugman, "Why Three Exposures May Be Enough," *Journal of Advertising Research* 12 (December 1972), 11–14.

21. Russell I. Haley and Allan L. Baldinger, "The ARF Copy Research Validity Project," *Journal of Advertising Research* 31 (March/April 1991), 11–32.

22. John R. Rossiter and Geoff Eagleson, "Conclusions from the ARF's Copy Research Validity Project," *Journal of Advertising Research* 34 (May/June 1994), 19–32.

23. Ivan L. Preston, "The Association Model of the Advertising Communication Process," *Journal of Advertising* 11, no. 2 (1982), 3–15.

24. For an in-depth discussion of differences between recognition and recall measures, see Erik du Plessis, "Recognition versus Recall," *Journal of Advertising Research* 34 (May/June 1994), 75–91.

25. For further details on other services, see David W. Stewart, David H. Furse, and Randall P. Kozak, "A Guide to Commercial Copytesting Services," in *Current Issues and Research in Advertising,* ed. James H. Leigh and Claude R. Martin, Jr. (Ann Arbor: Division of Research, Graduate School of Business, University of Michigan, 1983), 1–44; and Surendra N. Singh and Catherine A. Cole, "Advertising Copy Testing in Print Media," in *Current Issues and Research in Advertising,* ed. James H. Leigh and Claude R. Martin, Jr. (Ann Arbor: Division of Research, Graduate School of Business, University of Michigan, 1988), 215–284.

26. These definitions are derived from Roper Starch Worldwide Inc. as available in any Starch Readership Report prepared by this research firm.

27. D. M. Neu, "Measuring Advertising Recognition," *Journal of Advertising Research* 1 (1961), 17–22. For an alternative view, see George M. Zinkhan and Betsy D. Gelb, "What Starch Scores Predict," *Journal of Advertising Research* 26 (August/September 1986), 45–50.

28. David A. Aaker and Donald E. Bruzzone, "Causes of Irritation in Advertising," *Journal of Marketing* 49 (spring 1985), 47.

29. Appreciation for this illustration is extended to Mr. R. Paul Shellenberg, Director of Sales, and Mr. Donald E. Bruzzone, president of Bruzzone Research Company, Alameda, Calif.

30. The value of commercial-recall testing, and Burke's DAR in particular, have been questioned by Joel S. Dubow, "Point of View: Recall Revisited: Recall Redux," *Journal of Advertising Research* 34 (May/June 1994), 92–106.

31. "Recall Not Communication: Coke," *Advertising Age,* December 26, 1983, 6.

32. Joel S. Dubow, "Advertising Recognition And Recall by Age—Including Teens," *Journal of Advertising Research* 35 (September/October 1995), 55–60.

33. Leonard M. Lodish et al., "How T.V. Advertising Works: A Meta-Analysis of 389 Real World Split Cable T.V. Advertising Experiments," *Journal of Marketing Research* 32 (May 1995), 135. See also John Philip Jones and Margaret H. Blair, "Examining 'Conventional Wisdoms' about Advertising Effects with Evidence from Independent Sources," *Journal of Advertising Research* 36 (November/December 1996), 42.

34. Jack Honomichl, "FCB: Day-After-Recall Cheats Emotion," *Advertising Age,* May 11, 1981, 2; and David Berger, "A Retrospective: FCB Recall Study," *Advertising Age,* October 26, 1981, S36, S38.

35. Honomichl, "FCB," 82.

36. Ibid.

37. Steven P. Brown and Douglas M. Stayman, "Antecedents and Consequences of Attitude toward the Ad: A Meta-Analysis," *Journal of Consumer Research* 19 (June 1992), 34–51; Haley and Baldinger, "The ARF Copy Research Validity Project"; David Walker and Tony M. Dubitsky, "Why Liking Matters," *Journal of Advertising Research* 34 (May/June 1994), 9–18.

38. Judie Lannon, "New Techniques for Understanding Consumer Reactions to Advertising," *Journal of Advertising Research* 26 (August/September 1986), RC6–9; Judith A. Wiles and T. Bettina Cornwell, "A Review of Methods Utilized in Measuring Affect, Feelings, and Emotion in Advertising," in *Current Issues and Research in Advertising,* ed. James H. Leigh and Claude R. Martin, Jr. (Ann Arbor: Division of Research, Graduate School of Business, University of Michigan, 1991), 241–275.

39. David A. Aaker, Douglas M. Stayman, and Michael R. Hagerty, "Warmth in Advertising: Measurement, Impact, and Sequence Effects," *Journal of Consumer Research* 12 (March 1986), 366.

40. Ibid. See studies 2 and 3, 371–377.

41. Douglas M. Stayman and David A. Aaker, "Continuous Measurement of Self-Report of Emotional Response," *Psychology & Marketing* 10 (May/June 1993), 199–214.

42. The joystick method is described in Stayman and Aaker, "Continuous Measurement of Self-Report of Emotional Response," whereas the paper-and-pencil approach is detailed in Aaker, Stayman, and Hagerty, "Warmth in Advertising: Measurement, Impact, and Sequence Effects."

43. This description is based on Aaker, Stayman, and Hagerty, "Warmth in Advertising: Measurement, Impact, and Sequence Effects," 368.

44. "New Technology 'TRACES' Reaction to TV Ads," *Marketing News,* May 25, 1984, 3.

45. Sources: "Ad-testing Technique Measures Emotions," Marketing News, April 16, 1990, 9; and Gary Levin, "Emotion Guides BBDO's Ad Tests," *Advertising Age,* January 29, 1990, 12.

46. Paul J. Watson and Robert J. Gatchel, "Autonomic Measures of Advertising," *Journal of Advertising Research* 19 (June 1979), 15–26.

47. "Psychogalvanometer Testing 'Most Predictive,'" *Marketing News,* June 17, 1978, 11.

48. Aaker, Stayman, and Hagerty, "Warmth in Advertising: Measurement, Impact, and Sequence Effects." For an especially thorough and insightful report on the galvanometer, see Priscilla A. LaBarbera and Joel D. Tucciarone, "GSR Reconsidered: A Behavior-Based Approach to Evaluating and Improving the Sales Potency of Advertising," *Journal of Advertising Research* 35 (September/October 1995), 33–53.

49. See LaBarbera and Tucciarone, ibid.

50. Ibid., 40.

51. For detailed discussion of pupil dilation and other physiological measures, see Joanne M. Klebba, "Physiological Measures of Research: A Review of Brain Activity, Electrodermal Response, Pupil Dilation, and Voice Analysis Methods and Studies," in *Current Issues and Research in Advertising,* ed. James H. Leigh and Claude R. Martin, Jr. (Ann Arbor: Division of Research, Graduate School of Business, University of Michigan, 1985), 53–76. See also John T. Cacioppo and Richard E. Petty, *Social Psychophysiology* (New York: The Guilford Press, 1983).

52. Comment by William Wells as quoted in Mark Liff, "Cataloging Some Tools," *Advertising Age,* October 31, 1983, M54.

53. The following discussion is based on material from several sources: Glen A. Brickman, "Voice Analysis," *Journal of Advertising Research* 16 (June 1976), 43–48; Ronald G. Nelson and David Schwartz, "Voice Pitch Gives Marketer Access to Consumer's Unaware Body Responses," *Marketing News,* January 28, 1977, 21; Ronald G. Nelson and David Schwartz, "Voice-Pitch Analysis," *Journal of Advertising Research* 19 (October 1979), 55–59.

54. Nelson and Schwartz, "Voice-Pitch Analysis," 55.

55. For further discussion, see Klebba, "Physiological Measures of Research," 70–73.

56. For details, see Stewart, Furse, and Kozak, "A Guide to Commercial Copytesting Services."

57. Research has demonstrated that the dial-turning method is a reliable and valid means for measuring consumers' feelings and evaluative responses to advertisements. See Michel Tuan Pham, G. David Hughes, and Joel B. Cohen, "Validating a Dial-Turning Instrument for Real-Time Measurement of Affective and Evaluative Responses to Advertising," Report Number 93–116 (Cambridge, Mass.: Marketing Science Institute, September 1993); see also David G. Hughes, "Realtime Response Measures Redefine Advertising Wearout," *Journal of Advertising Research* 32 (May/June 1992), 61–77.

58. Anthony J. Adams and Margaret Henderson Blair, "Persuasive Advertising and Sales Accountability: Past Experience and Forward Validation," *Journal of Advertising Research* 32 (March/April 1992), 25. Note: This quotation actually indicated that respondents are drawn from four metropolitan areas. However, personal correspondence with **rsc** executives indicated

that as of November 24, 1998 there were eight metropolitan areas represented.

59. This average *ARS Persuasion*® score of 5.8 is an increase from **rsc**'s previously published average of 5.7. This change was brought to the author's attention by correspondence dated November 24, 1998 with **rsc**'s Karen M. Harvey, Senior Manager, Marketing Communications Team.

60. Leonard M. Lodish, "J. P. Jones and M. H. Blair on Measuring Advertising Effects—Another Point of View," *Journal of Advertising Research* 37 (September/October 1997), 75–79.

61. John Philip Jones, "Quantitative Pretesting for Television Advertising," in John Philip Jones, ed., *How Advertising Works: The Role of Research* (Newbury Park, CA: Sage Publications, Inc., 1998), 160–169.

62. These conclusions are based on Margaret Henderson Blair and Karl E. Rosenberg, "Convergent Findings Increase Our Understanding of How Advertising Works," *Journal of Advertising Research* 34 (May/June 1994), 35–45.

63. Scott Hume, "Selling Proposition Proves Power Again," *Advertising Age,* March 8, 1993, 31; Lee Byers and Mark Gleason, "Using Measurement for More Effective Advertising," *Admap,* May 1993, 31–35.

64. Hume, "Selling Proposition Proves Power Again."

65. Byers and Gleason, "Using Measurement for More Effective Advertising," 34.

66. The quote is from Jim Donius as cited in Don Bruzzone, "The Top 10 Insights about Measuring the Effect of Advertising," Bruzzone Research Company Newsletter, October 28, 1998, principle 8.

67. Lodish et al., "How T.V. Advertising Works: A Meta-Analysis of 389 Real World Split-Cable T.V. Advertising Experiments," 128.

68. In comparison with the results presented in Table 15.6, research by Lodish et al. does not demonstrate a strong relationship between commercial persuasiveness and sales. See table 11 in "How T.V. Advertising Works," 137.

69. Adams and Blair, "Persuasive Advertising and Sales Accountability: Past Experience and Forward Validation."

70. Lodish et al.'s findings also support this conclusion. See "How T.V. Advertising Works."

71. Margaret Henderson Blair and Michael J. Rabuck, "Advertising Wearin and Wearout: Ten Years Later," Table 4, p. 7 (Evansville, IN: **rsc** THE QUALITY MEASUREMENT COMPANY, 1998).

72. Information from this description is from Schwartz, "Back to the Source," and from Andrew M. Tarshis, "The Single Source Household: Delivering on the Dream," *AIM* (a Nielsen publication) 1, no. 1 (1989).

73. Kate Maddox, "Internet Ad Sales Approach $1 Billion," *Advertising Age,* April 6, 1998, 32.

74. Debra Aho Williamson, "ARF to Spearhead Study on Measuring Web Ads," *Advertising Age,* February 10, 1997, 8.

75. Kate Maddox, "ANA Study Finds Marketers Triple 'Net Ad Budgets," *Advertising Age,* May 11, 1998, 63.

PART

FIVE

Sales Communication · Advertising Management · Packaging and Branding · Demographic, Psychographic

· Sales Promotion · The Concept · Supportive Marketing Communications · Demographic, Psychographic Appeals and Ever

· Strategy · Promotion Management and Integrated Marketing · Communications Tools · The

· Promotion Management · The Concept · Branding · Message Appeals and

Part Five—Sales Promotion Management

Part Five discusses the ever-growing practice of sales promotion. Chapter 16 offers an overview of promotion by explaining its targets, the reasons underlying its rapid growth, and its capabilities and limitations. The chapter also describes the conditions under which deal-oriented sales promotions are profitable.

Chapter 17 focuses on trade-oriented promotions. The chapter describes the most important and widely used forms of trade promotions: off-invoice allowances, bill-back allowances, slotting allowances, contests and incentives, cooperative advertising and vendor support programs, specialty advertising programs, and trade shows. Considerable discussion is devoted to the practices of forward buying, diverting, and the advent of manufacturer-oriented, everyday low pricing that has been effective in diminishing these practices. Efficient consumer response (ECR), category management, and account-specific marketing also receive prominent treatment.

Consumer-oriented sales promotions are the subject of Chapter 18. Primary emphasis is placed on the objectives that various sales promotions are able to accomplish for manufacturers and the types of rewards they provide to consumers. Detailed discussions are devoted to sampling, couponing, premiums, price-offs, bonus packs, refunds and rebates, contests and sweepstakes, phone cards, and overlay and tie-in promotions. The chapter concludes with a three-step procedure for evaluating sales promotion ideas.

Overview of Sales Promotion Management

CHAPTER OBJECTIVES

After studying this chapter, you should be able to:

1. Describe the nature and purposes of sales promotions.
2. Explain the factors that account for the increased investment in sales promotion.
3. Explain the tasks that promotions can and cannot accomplish.
4. Understand nine empirical generalizations about promotions.
5. Discuss the circumstances that determine when sales promotions are profitable.

Opening Vignette: Three Exemplary Cases of Using Promotions Effectively

This vignette overviews recent promotional practices of three brands that fully appreciate the strategically sound use of sales promotions.

McDonald's. This fast-food heavyweight generated global sales in 1997 exceeding $16 billion and invested over $200 million in promotional spending. Some of McDonald's favorite promotions are continuity games, phone cards, and, especially, tie-ins with movies from the Disney studios. Movie tie-ins in 1998 included *Mulan* and *A Bug's Life*. McDonald's promoted its Happy Meals for kids by distributing free toy characters from these movies. McDonald's and Disney entered into a 10-year deal in 1997 whereby McDonald's has exclusive rights (among fast-food chains) to distribute toy characters from the child-oriented movies that regularly flow from Disney's studios. As promotional devices, these Disney-inspired products bring millions of children and parents to McDonald's in the pursuit of a double prize, Happy Meals and Disney toys. What more could a kid want?

Coca-Cola. This colossus of the soft-drink industry had worldwide sales of nearly $19 billion in 1997 and invested approximately $200 million in promotional spending. Coca-Cola regularly uses in-pack and under-the-cap offers including ATM cards. To encourage continuity of purchasing, Coke's MasterCard ATM card giveaway placed cards in a sampling of Coca-Cola case packs that varied in value from $20 to $200. In a separate appeal to teenagers, Coca-Cola implemented a $75 million Coke Card campaign in 1998 whereby loyalty cards were distributed to teenagers for redemption at local restaurants, theaters, and other attractive retail locations. Coca-Cola also is testing a loyalty program using

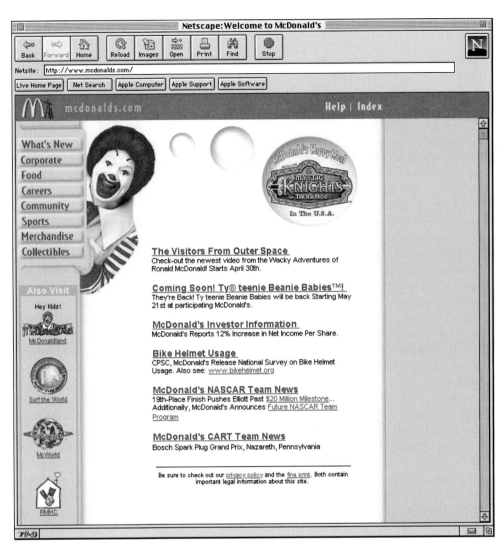

school lunch cards. Students earn points for buying Coke in the cafeteria. The points are redeemable for special offers at local retailers.

Levi's Jeans. With 1997 international sales of nearly $7 billion, Levi Strauss & Co. invested between $50–$64 million in a variety of promotions. Levi's sponsored the Lilith Fair series of music concerts featuring Sarah McLachlan and other female musicians. In Israel Levi's sponsored a 24-hour dance party in the Negev desert. A massive outdoor amphitheater was constructed for performances from some of the world's top bands. Consumers who bought a pair of Levi's during the promotional period received a one-half price reduction from their concert ticket and could obtain a free concert T-shirt with the purchase of a second pair of Levi's. MTV aired live clips from the Israeli concert throughout Europe. The result: a sales jump of 25 percent!

In a promotion for its Slates brand (of dress pants), Levi Strauss appealed to American businessmen by offering a free style guide for trying on a pair of Slates slacks. A mail-in form in the guide entered shoppers into a sweepstakes to win a trip to one of 10 featured cities (New York, San Francisco, Los Angeles, etc.). Buyers of Slates pants received a gift certificate worth $25 for redemption at any of the restaurants featured in the style guide. All in all, this was a creative and successful promotion to attract attention and encourage purchasing of Levi Strauss' new line of dress slacks.

Source: Adapted from Betsy Spethmann, "The Nation's Top-Promoted Brands," *Promo*, December 1998, 40–50.

INTRODUCTION TO SALES PROMOTION

*T*he *Opening Vignette* illustrates effective use of sales promotions by three major companies. The vignette also introduces some terminology you have not previously been exposed to in this textbook. The objective of this chapter and the two chapters that follow is to provide a thorough introduction to sales promotion's role in complementing advertising while performing its own unique functions. Sales promotion's role in influencing the trade—wholesalers, brokers, and retailers—on the one hand, and its part in influencing consumer behavior, on the other, are covered in detail in the two chapters that follow.

What Exactly Is Sales Promotion?

It first will be useful to clarify some terminology. Whereas marketing academics typically refer to the term "sales promotions," practitioners truncate the expression to simply "promotions." This contrast between academia and practice probably originated because one of the 4P elements of the marketing mix (product, place, price, and *promotion*) is applied by academics in reference to *all* forms of marketing communications (advertising, sales promotions, public relations, personal selling, etc.) and not to sales promotions per se. Thus, in the pursuit of terminological precision, academics separate the specific practice of sales promotions from the more inclusive notion of promotion en toto. Practitioners need not concern themselves with this distinction and thus use the more efficient term "promotions" in reference to what professors call "sales promotion." Distinction noted, the author of this text uses the term "marketing communications" to refer to the "whole ball of communications wax" and, like the practitioner, uses the term "promotion" in lieu of or interchangeably with "sales promotion."

Promotion refers to any *incentive* used by a manufacturer to induce the trade (wholesalers and retailers) and/or *consumers* to buy a brand and to encourage the *sales force* to aggressively sell it. Retailers also use promotional incentives to encourage desired behaviors from consumers—come to my store rather than a competitor's; buy one brand rather than another; purchase larger quantities; and so on. The incentive is *additional to the basic benefits* provided by the brand and *temporarily changes its perceived price or value.*[1]

The italicized features require comment. First, by definition, promotions involve incentives (i.e., bonuses or rewards) that are designed to encourage end-user consumers or trade customers to purchase a particular brand sooner, more frequently, in larger quantities, or to engage in some other behavior that will benefit the manufacturer or retailer that offers the promotion. Second, these incentives (sweepstakes, coupons, premiums, display allowances, and so on) are additions to—not substitutes for—the basic benefits a purchaser typically acquires when buying a particular product or service. For example, getting $1 off the price of a new brand of shampoo would be little consolation if the shampoo failed to do an effective job. Third, the target of the incentive is the trade, consumers, the sales force, or all three parties. Finally, the incentive changes a brand's perceived price or value, but only temporarily. This is to say that a sales-promotion incentive for a particular brand applies to a single purchase or perhaps several purchases during a period, but not to every purchase a consumer would make over an extended period.

In contrast to advertising, which typically, though not always, is relatively long-term in orientation and best suited to enhance buyer attitudes and augment brand equity, promotion is more *short-term oriented* and capable of *influencing behavior* (rather than just attitudes or intentions). Indeed, the academically oriented term "sales promotion" precisely captures this short-term, behavioral orientation insofar as *promotions* are designed to promote *sales*. Promotion has the character of urgency in its injunction to act NOW because tomorrow is too late.[2] Promotion has the power to influence behavior because it offers the buyer superior value in the short term.[3] For example, with reference to the *Opening Vignette,* parents and their children got a better value from a McDonald's Happy Meal purchase when they received a free Disney-character bug toy. And Israeli shoppers had a better value by obtaining discounted concert tickets along with their purchase of Levi jeans.

It also is important to note at this point that although consumer packaged-goods companies are the biggest users of promotions, all types of companies utilize promotional incentives on occasion. For example, automobile companies regularly offer rebates and cheap financing to attract purchasers. Retailers woo consumers with special offers, discounts, and incentives to attract immediate purchasing. A Nordstrom store in California, for example, offered shoppers the opportunity to have their name drawn from a raffle and win a $500 shopping spree.[4] Following a strike by its pilots in 1997, American Airlines offered attractive discounts and double frequent-flier miles to lure back customers who boarded other airlines during the strike.

Promotion Targets

To appreciate more fully the role of promotion, consider the following promotion from Schering-Plough, a leader in the foot-care category. Schering-Plough markets two well-known foot-care brands: Lotrimin AF and Tinactin. To gain greater trade support for these brands and to generate excitement and enthusiasm among its own sales force of 152 people, Schering-Plough introduced the "Howwe Gosell" promotion. (This promotional label plays on the name of the famous sportscaster, the late Howard Cosell, who gained celebrity for his outspoken personality and quirky mannerisms while announcing major sporting events, especially boxing matches featuring Muhammad Ali, and football games on *Monday Night Football*.) The promotion appealed to Schering-Plough's sales force to be part of the "team" coached by Howwe Gosell, who encouraged his "players" (the sales force) on to a victory ending in higher sales of Lotrimin AF and Tinactin. In keeping with the football motif, salespeople received "playbooks" and had a chance to score points that would earn them NFL merchandise or expense-paid trips to the Super Bowl. The result: Tinactin and Lotrimin AF gained 19 percent and 14 percent, respectively, in sales volume during the promotional period. Howwe Gosell was a topic of much discussion among the sales force, and the trade devoted more display space to these brands than they had ever previously enjoyed.[5]

For Schering-Plough's foot-care brands to achieve their marketing objectives (sales volume, market share), several things had to happen (see Figure 16.1): First, Schering-Plough's *sales force* had to enthusiastically and aggressively sell these brands to the trade. Second, *retailers* had to be encouraged to allocate sufficient store space to the brands and provide merchandising support to enable them to stand out, if only temporarily, from competitive brands. Third, consumers needed reasons for selecting Lotrimin AF and Tinactin over competitive foot-care brands.

All three groups—the sales force, retailers, and consumers—are targets of sales-promotional efforts (Figure 16.1). Allowances, discounts, contests, and advertising-support programs encourage retailers to stock and promote particular brands. Coupons, samples, premiums, cents-off deals, sweepstakes, and other incentives encourage consumers to purchase a brand on a trial or repeat basis. Trade- and consumer-oriented sales promotions also provide salespeople with the necessary tools for aggressively and

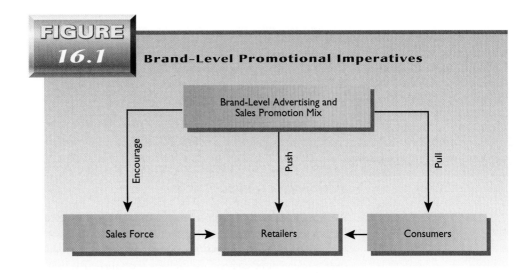

FIGURE 16.1   **Brand-Level Promotional Imperatives**

IMC Focus: Gaining Better Effort from a Manufacturer's Sales Force and from Retail Salespeople

Increasing Dr Pepper's Sales Volume, a Family Affair

The goal at Dr Pepper was to get its top bottlers to increase sales volume for 18 continuous months. The challenge: How? The answer: Make it a family affair. To achieve its ambitious goal, brand management of Dr Pepper designed a clever program that enlisted bottlers' wives. The program gave bottlers an opportunity to receive a fully paid trip with their wives to luxurious sites in Europe. However, rather than presupposing that they knew the best locations for the vacation, marketing people at Dr Pepper recruited a team of bottlers' wives to plan side trips for the vacation. The team was flown to Venice to choose between three deluxe hotels and to Paris to decide whether to rent the Orient Express. Having selected appealing travel options, the program was promoted to bottlers as well as to their wives. Needless to say, wives occasionally pressured their husbands to accomplish program goals and thus become eligible for the exciting vacation opportunity. In the end, 100 bottlers and their spouses received paid vacations. During this period, Dr Pepper sales increased an average 20 percent, which was substantially better than the 12 percent increase that was projected.

Encouraging Retail Salespeople to Sell Packard Bell Computers More Aggressively

Packard Bell at one time was the top brand in home PC sales, only to lose its commanding presence to Compaq, Dell, Gateway, and Hewlett-Packard. In an effort to regain some of its lost market share, Packard Bell designed an innovative program to influence

the retail salespeople who play a major role in directing PC purchases in electronic and computer stores. In conjunction with its promotion agency, Packard Bell developed a "Home Delivery" program that was designed to enhance Packard Bell's equity in the minds of retail salespeople, who are predominantly young males. Upon acquiring a mailing list of names and home addresses, Packard Bell mailed retail salespeople a series of three interactive CD-ROMs that were packaged as take-out food items (a pizza box, Chinese food container, and a chicken bucket). These food items were appropriately themed to the take-out eating habits of the targeted group of youthful male salespeople. Each CD-ROM contained information about the latest features of Packard Bell computers along with interesting supplemental segments including movie trailers, classic TV advertising spots, and music videos. The "Home Delivery" program was a major success. Follow-up research determined that 95 percent of the targeted salespeople wanted to receive more CD-ROMs; 64 percent reported having viewed the CD-ROMs on multiple occasions; and, of greatest significance, 70 percent of the salespeople acknowledged that their perceptions of Packard Bell had improved after viewing the CD-ROMs and that they recommended Packard Bell PCs more often than before.

Sources: The Dr Pepper case is adapted from Betsy Spethmann and Daniel Shannon, "Motivating the Team," *Promo*, October 1996, 41–48. The Packard Bell case is adapted from Tobi Elkin, "Packard Bell Delivers," *Brandweek*, March 2, 1998, R3–R6.

enthusiastically selling to wholesale and retail buyers and for encouraging retail salespeople to devote more effort to selling the manufacturer's brand. Please read the *IMC Focus* that accompanies this section. It examines two cases: (1) a clever effort by Dr Pepper to generate more effort from its own sales force and (2) a brilliant effort from Packard Bell to get retail salespeople to better understand and more aggressively sell its computer products.

www.drpepper.com

www.packardbell.com

INCREASED BUDGETARY ALLOCATIONS TO PROMOTIONS

Advertising spending as a percentage of total marketing communications expenditures has declined in recent years, while promotion spending has steadily increased. Media advertising expenditures as a proportion of total marketing communications expenditures averaged over 40 percent of companies' budgets until the early 1980s, but only a decade later media advertising's portion of the total budget had fallen to around just one quarter.[6]

**TABLE
16.1**

	Marketing Communications Expenditures among Media Advertising, Trade Promotions, and Consumer Promotions, 1987–1997										
	1987	1988	1989	1990	1991	1992	1993	1994	1995	1996	1997
Media Advertising	33%	32%	31%	28%	25%	25%	24%	25%	24%	24%	26%
Trade Promotions	41	42	44	47	48	48	49	49	51	50	50
Consumer Promotions	26	25	26	25	27	27	27	26	25	26	24

Source: Annual Surveys of Promotional Practices for 1987–1997, Chart 25 in *Cox Direct 20ᵗʰ Annual Survey of Promotional Practices* (Largo, FL: Cox Direct, 1998), 40.

Table 16.1 shows how marketers of consumer packaged goods in recent years have allocated expenditures among media advertising, trade promotions, and consumer promotions. Looking at the anchor years, 1987 and 1997, media advertising constituted 33 percent of total expenditures in 1987 but only 26 percent by 1997. On the other hand, trade promotions represented 41 percent of total expenditures in 1987 but 50 percent by 1997. Consumer promotions remained relatively constant throughout this 11-year period, ranging from 24 to 27 percent. The trend, in short, is that advertising expenditures have declined at the expense of greater trade promotions. We now will examine the major reasons underlying this shift.

Factors Accounting for the Shift

A variety of factors account for the shift in budgetary allocations away from advertising and toward trade promotion. However, before we describe the reasons for this shift, it first will be beneficial to briefly review the concepts of push and pull marketing strategies.

Push and pull are physical metaphors characterizing the promotional activities manufacturers undertake to encourage channel members (the trade) to handle products. **Push** implies a forward thrust of effort whereby a manufacturer directs personal selling, trade advertising, and trade-oriented sales promotion to wholesalers and retailers. **Pull** suggests a backward tug from consumers to retailers. This tug, or pull, is the result of a manufacturer's successful advertising and promotion efforts directed at the consumer.

Table 16.2 illustrates the differences between push- and pull-oriented promotional strategies based on two companies' allocations of $20 million among different promotional activities. Company A emphasizes a *push strategy* by allocating most of its promotional budget to personal selling and trade promotions aimed at retail customers. Company

**TABLE
16.2**

Push versus Pull Promotion Strategies		
	COMPANY A (PUSH)	COMPANY B (PULL)
Advertising to Consumers	$ 1,200,000	$13,700,000
Advertising to Retailers	1,600,000	200,000
Personal Selling to Retailers	9,000,000	4,000,000
Sales Promotion to Consumers	200,000	2,000,000
Sales Promotion to Retailers	8,000,000	100,000
TOTAL	$20,000,000	$20,000,000

Source: Arnold M. Barban, Steven M. Cristol, and Frank J. Kopec. *Essentials of Media Planing: A Marketing viewpoint* (Lincolnwood, Ill.: NTC Business Books, 1987). 15.

B, on the other hand, utilizes a *pull strategy* by investing the vast majority of its budget in consumer advertising.

It should be clear that pushing and pulling are *not* mutually exclusive. Both efforts occur simultaneously. Manufacturers promote to consumers (creating pull) and to trade members (accomplishing push). *The issue is not which strategy to use but rather which to emphasize.* Effective marketing involves a *combination of forces*: exerting push to the trade and creating pull from consumers.

Historically, at least through the mid-1970s, the emphasis in consumer packaged-goods marketing was on promotional pull (such as company B's budget in Table 16.2). Manufacturers advertised heavily, especially on network television, and literally forced retailers to handle their brands by creating consumer demand for those heavily advertised items. However, over the past two decades, pull-oriented marketing has become less effective due in large part to the splintering of the mass media and audience fractionalization as discussed in Chapter 12. Along with this reduced effectiveness has come an increase in the use of push-oriented sales promotion practices (such as company A's budget in Table 16.2).[7]

Increased investment in sales promotion, especially trade-oriented sales promotions, has gone hand in hand with the growth in push marketing. Major developments that have given rise to sales promotion are summarized in Table 16.3 and discussed hereafter.[8] It is important to emphasize at this point that these developments are interdependent rather than separate and distinct. Hence, there is no particular order of importance implied by the listing in Table 16.3.

Balance-of-Power Shift. Until roughly around 1980, national manufacturers of consumer packaged goods generally were more powerful and influential than the supermarkets, drugstores, and mass merchandisers that carried the manufacturers' brands. The reason was twofold. First, manufacturers were able to create consumer *pull* by virtue of heavy network-television advertising, thus effectively requiring retailers to handle their brands whether retailers wanted to or not. Second, retailers did little research of their own and, accordingly, were dependent on manufacturers for information such as whether a new product would be successful. A manufacturer's sales representative could convince a buyer to carry a new product using test-market results suggesting a successful product introduction.

The balance of power began shifting when network television dipped in effectiveness as an advertising medium and, especially, with the advent of optical scanning equipment. Armed with a steady flow of data from optical scanners, retailers now know virtually on a real-time basis what products are selling and which advertising and promotion programs are working. Retailers no longer need to depend on manufacturers for facts. Instead, retailers use the facts they now possess to demand terms of sale rather than merely accepting manufacturers' terms. The consequence for manufacturers is that for every promotional dollar used to support retailers' advertising or merchandising programs, one less dollar is available for the manufacturer's own advertising.

TABLE 16.3 **Developments Underlying the Growth of Sales Promotion**

- ◆ Shift in manufacturer versus retailer balance of power
- ◆ Increased brand parity and price sensitivity
- ◆ Reduced brand loyalty
- ◆ Splintered mass market and reduced media effectiveness
- ◆ Emphasis on short-term results in corporate-reward structures
- ◆ Responsive consumers

Increased Brand Parity and Price Sensitivity. In earlier years when truly new products were being offered to the marketplace, manufacturers could effectively advertise unique advantages over competitive offerings. As product categories have matured, however, most new offerings represent only slight changes from existing products, thus resulting, more often than not, in greater similarities between competitive brands. With fewer distinct product differences, consumers have grown more reliant on price and price incentives (coupons, cents-off deals, refunds, etc.) as ways of differentiating parity brands.[9] Because concrete advantages are often difficult to obtain, firms have turned increasingly to promotion as a means of achieving temporary advantages over competitors.

Reduced Brand Loyalty. Consumers probably are less brand loyal than they once were. This is partly due to the fact that brands have grown increasingly similar, thereby making it easier for consumers to switch among brands. Also, marketers have effectively trained consumers to expect that at least one brand in a product category will always be on deal with a coupon, cents-off offer, or refund; hence, many consumers rarely purchase brands other than those on deal. (The term deal refers to any form of sales promotion that delivers a *price reduction* to consumers; coupons and cents-off offers are the most frequent forms of deals.)

One team of researchers investigated the impact that deal promotions have on consumers' price sensitivity using 8¼ years of scanner panel data for a nonfood packaged-good product. These researchers determined that price promotions make consumers more price sensitive in the long run. Moreover, increased usage of price promotions serves, for all intents and purposes, to "train" consumers to search for deals. Nonloyal consumers are especially likely to be trained by marketers' usage of price deals.[10] Another study using scanner panel data discovered that the use of coupons by brands in the liquid detergent category (i.e., brands such as Wisk, Era, and Bold) resulted in increased consumer price sensitivity and reduced brand loyalty.[11]

The upshot of all of this dealing activity is that marketers have created a "monster" in the form of the consumer's insatiable desire for deals. The extensive use of sales promotion has reduced brand loyalty and increased switching behavior, thereby requiring ever-more dealing activity to feed the monster's desire for more deals. If deals resulted in increased brand loyalty and greater long-term sales, their use would be fully justified; however, a major international study of sales promotion activities in Germany, Japan, the United Kingdom, and the United States suggests anything but this result. The study investigated the effects of price-related promotions (such as cents-off deals and coupons) on a brand's sales *after* a promotional period is over. The dramatic finding from this international research, which examined dozens of brands in 25 consumer-goods categories, is that these promotions have virtually *no impact* on a brand's long-term sales or on consumers' repeat-buying loyalty. No strong aftereffects occurred because extra sales for the promoted brands came almost exclusively from a brand's long-term customer base. In other words, the people who normally buy a brand are the ones who are most responsive to the brand's price promotion. Hence, price promotions effectively serve to simply induce consumers to buy on deal what they would have bought at regular prices anyway. In sum, although price-related promotions typically result in immediate and huge sales spikes, these short-term gains do not positively influence long-term brand growth.[12]

Splintering of the Mass Market and Reduced Media Effectiveness. Advertising *efficiency* is directly related to the degree of homogeneity in consumers' consumption needs and media habits. The greater their homogeneity, the less costly it is for mass advertising to reach target audiences. However, as consumer lifestyles have diversified and advertising media have narrowed in their appeal, mass-media advertising's efficiency has weakened. On top of this, advertising effectiveness has declined with simultaneous increases in ad clutter and escalating media costs. These combined forces have influenced many brand managers to devote proportionately larger budgets to sales promotion.

Short-Term Orientation and Corporate Reward Structures. Sales promotions go hand in hand with the brand-management system, which is the dominant organizational structure in packaged-goods firms. The reward structure in firms organized along brand-manager lines emphasizes *short-term sales response* rather than slow, long-term growth. And sales promotion is incomparable when it comes to generating quick sales response. In fact, the majority of packaged-good brand sales are associated with some kind of promotional deal.[13]

Consumer Responsiveness. A final force that explains the shift toward sales promotion at the expense of advertising is that consumers respond favorably to money-saving opportunities and other value-adding sales promotions. A national survey revealed that over 90 percent of the more than 7,500 consumers interviewed had taken advantage of some form of promotion in the past month.[14] Coupons in particular have nearly universal acceptance, with over 80 percent of consumers using coupons.[15]

SALES PROMOTION CAPABILITIES AND LIMITATIONS

Every promotion-mix element is capable of accomplishing certain objectives and not others. As summarized in Table 16.4, sales promotion is well suited for accomplishing certain tasks but is incapable of achieving others.[16]

What Promotions Can Accomplish

Promotions cannot work wonders but are well-suited to accomplishing the following tasks:

Stimulate Sales Force Enthusiasm for a New, Improved, or Mature Product. There are many exciting and challenging aspects of personal selling; there also are times when the job can become dull, monotonous, and unrewarding. For example, imagine what it would be like to repeatedly call on a customer if you never had anything new or different to say about your brands or the marketing efforts that support them. Maintaining enthusiasm would be difficult, to say the least. Exciting sales promotions give salespeople persuasive ammunition when interacting with buyers; they revive enthusiasm and make the salesperson's job easier and more enjoyable. A case in point is the previously described Howwe Gosell promotion for Schering-Plough's two foot-care brands, Lotrimin AF and Tinactin.

www.quakeroatmeal.com

Invigorate Sales of a Mature Brand. As mentioned earlier, sales promotions cannot reverse the sales decline for an undesirable product or brand. However, promotions can invigorate sales of a mature product that requires a shot in the arm. A case in point is the Quaker Oats Cap'n Crunch efforts. After nearly one-quarter of a century on the market, Cap'n Crunch dropped from a 3.2 percent market share to a 2.8 percent share in less than two years. This may appear to be a minuscule drop but in actuality amounted to a $16 million loss in annual sales in the huge ready-to-eat-cereal business where annual sales in the United States exceed $4 billion.

A major promotional effort was needed to invigorate Cap'n Crunch sales. Accordingly, promotional planners at Quaker Oats developed the "Find the Cap'n" sales promotion game to increase brand interest among children between the ages of 6 and 12 and to encourage repeat purchasing. Cap'n Horatio Crunch's picture was temporarily dropped from the cereal package; in his place appeared the question "Where's the Cap'n?" Package directions informed children that they could share in a $1 million reward for finding the Cap'n. Consumers had to buy three boxes of Cap'n Crunch to get clues to Horatio Crunch's whereabouts. At the game's end, 10,000 children's names were drawn from the pool of thousands of correct answers, and each child received $100.

The "Find the Cap'n" promotion involved heavy television and magazine advertising along with the promotion effort. In addition to the cash giveaway, coupons and cents-off deals were used to stimulate consumer purchasing. An incredible 50 percent increase in

TABLE 16.4	Tasks That Sales Promotions Can and Cannot Accomplish

Sales Promotions *Can*

◆ Stimulate sales force enthusiasm for a new, improved, or mature product

◆ Invigorate sales of a mature brand

◆ Facilitate the introduction of new products to the trade

◆ Increase on- and off-shelf merchandising space

◆ Neutralize competitive advertising and sales promotions

◆ Obtain trial purchases from consumers

◆ Hold current users by encouraging repeat purchases

◆ Increase product usage by loading consumers

◆ Preempt competition by loading consumers

◆ Reinforce advertising

Sales Promotions *Cannot*

◆ Compensate for a poorly trained sales force or for a lack of advertising

◆ Give the trade or consumers any compelling long-term reason to continue purchasing a brand

◆ Permanently stop an established brand's declining sales trend or change the basic nonacceptance of an undesired product

sales resulted during the promotion.[17] The *Global Focus* insert presents a similarly successful promotion for Bazooka bubble gum in Argentina.

Facilitate the Introduction to the Trade of New Products and Brands. To achieve sales and profit objectives, marketers continuously introduce new products and add new brands to existing categories. Sales promotions to wholesalers and retailers are typically necessary to encourage the trade to handle new products and brands. In fact, many retailers refuse to carry new items unless they receive extra compensation in the form of off-invoice allowances, display allowances, and slotting allowances. (The following chapter discusses each of these various forms of allowances.)

Increase On- and Off-Shelf Merchandising Space. Trade-oriented sales promotions enable a manufacturer to obtain extra shelf space for a temporary period. This space may be in the form of extra facings on the shelf or off-shelf space in a gondola or end-of-aisle display.[18]

www.topps.com/gum

Neutralize Competitive Advertising and Sales Promotions. Sales promotions can be used to offset competitors' advertising and sales-promotion efforts. For example, one company's 50 cents-off coupon loses much of its appeal when a competitor simultaneously comes out with a $1-off coupon. Bazooka bubble gum's promotion in Argentina, Paraguay, and Uruguay (see *Global Focus*) offset competitors' promotions and won back lost market share.

Obtain Trial Purchases from Consumers. Marketers depend on free samples, coupons, and other sales promotions to encourage trial purchases of new brands. Many consumers would never try new products or previously untried brands without these promotional inducements.

GLOBAL FOCUS: OFF-SETTING THE COMPE-TITION AND REVIVING SALES OF BAZOOKA BUBBLE GUM IN AR-GENTINA

In Latin America as in the United States, Bazooka bubble gum comes wrapped with a Bazooka Kid comic strip, known as *El Pibe Bazooka* to kids in Argentina, Paraguay, and Uruguay. Bazooka commanded over 40 percent of the gum market in these countries, but its share had fallen by over 10 points due to an onslaught of competitors. The maker of Bazooka gum, Cadbury, turned to its promotion agency for ideas to offset competitive inroads. The agency devised a promotion that led to temporarily replacing *El Pibe Bazooka* with Secret Clues that, when placed under a decoder screen, would reveal keys to "Bazooka Super Treasure." Over 150 million Secret Clues hit the market, and 3 million decoder screens were made available to kids through magazine and newspaper inserts and at candy stands and schools. Upon buying Bazooka and placing a Secret Clue under a decoder screen, kids learned immediately whether they would receive instant-win prizes such as T-shirts, soccer balls, and school bags. Kids could also enter a super treasure sweepstakes by mailing in 10 proofs of purchase. Top prizes included multimedia computers for winners and their schools along with stereo systems, TVs, bicycles, and other attractive items.

Consumer response was so overwhelming that Bazooka experienced distribution problems within several weeks of initiating the promotion. Bazooka sales increased by 28 percent and gained back about 7 share points. This successful promotion demonstrates the power of sales incentives that catch the imagination of a receptive target market. Kids were encouraged to buy Bazooka gum to win instant prizes and to purchase the brand on repeated occasions so as to become eligible for very attractive sweepstake awards.

Source: Adapted from Amie Smith and Al Urbanski, "Excellence x 16," *Promo*, December 1998, 136.

Hold Current Users by Encouraging Repeat Purchases. Brand switching is a fact of life faced by all brand managers. The strategic use of certain forms of sales promotion can encourage at least short-run repetitive purchasing. Premium programs, refunds, sweepstakes, and various continuity programs (discussed in Chapter 18) are useful promotions for encouraging repeat purchasing.

www.butterfinger.com

A promotion for the Butterfinger brand of candy nicely illustrates a promotional event that encouraged repeat purchasing. Butterfinger, a popular brand of candy bar with annual sales exceeding $30 million, is a favorite of predominantly male consumers in the 12-to-24 age range. Nestlé, the marketer of Butterfinger, wanted to introduce a promotional event that would reinforce the brand's fun personality and increase purchase frequency. Toward this end, a tie-in arrangement with Bart Simpson and *The Simpsons* television show was established. A mystery program was created featuring Bart on 65 million Butterfinger bars. Consumers participated by collecting "alibis" from candy wrappers in order to identify the mystery culprit. The grand prize for identifying the culprit was a $50,000 cash award. Ten thousand additional winners received "Most Wanted" T-shirts emblazoned with Bart Simpson in his detective outfit. The result was increased purchase frequency and a 51 percent sales gain during the promotion period.[19]

Increase Product Usage by Loading Consumers. The effect of many deal-oriented promotions is to encourage consumer *stockpiling*, that is, to influence consumers to purchase more of a particular brand than they normally would so as to take advantage of the deal. Research has found that when readily stockpiled items are promoted with a deal (e.g., canned goods, paper products, and soap), purchase quantity increases by a substantial magnitude.[20] This practice prompts a critical question: Do these short-term increases resulting from consumer stockpiling actually lead to long-term consumption increases of the promoted product category or do they merely represent borrowed future sales? One study has found that price promotions do not increase category profitability but rather simply serve to shift short-term sales revenue from one brand to another. That is, sales gains in the short term induced by consumer stockpiling are offset by reduced demand in the long term.[21] This finding thus suggests that price-oriented promotions may encourage consumers to load up in the short term, but that this short-term loading simply steals purchases that otherwise would have been made during subsequent periods.

Please note that the foregoing finding is based on research involving a single product, namely, a nonfood item (probably a brand from the household cleaning category) that could not be disclosed by the researchers due to the manufacturer's proprietary concerns. Is this finding generalizable or is the result idiosyncratic to this particular product category? No simple answer is possible, and, as usual, it depends on the specific circumstances surrounding a particular brand and promotional event. Other researchers, however, have provided tentative evidence that establishes when the practice of loading might have positive long-term effects. These researchers have determined that loading does increase consumers' product usage especially when usage-related thoughts about a product are vivid in the consumer's memory. For example, people will not necessarily consume more soup just because they have stockpiled above-average quantities. However, if soup is on their minds (due to the presence of an advertising campaign touting soup's versatility), then consumption is likely to increase. Also, products that are regularly visible (such as perishable items placed in the front of the refrigerator) are likely to receive greater usage when consumers have stockpiled quantities of such products.[22]

This finding receives more recent support from research that has examined the impact of consumer inventory levels on the amount of usage for two product categories, ketchup and yogurt. Researchers predicted that consumption of yogurt would be more sensitive to inventory level insofar as yogurt, unlike ketchup, can be consumed at different times of day and under a variety of usage circumstances (with meals, as a snack, etc.). Their results supported this expectation as the amount of yogurt consumption, but not ketchup, was influenced by the quantity of yogurt available in consumer refrigerators—more yogurt, more (than normal) consumption; more ketchup, no more (than normal) consumption.[23]

Although no simple conclusion is available at this stage of research, the empirical evidence suggests that marketer's price-oriented deals that encourage stockpiling promote increased long-term consumption for some product categories but not others. For example, when consumers stockpile products like yogurt, orange juice, and perhaps salty snacks—all of which are physically visible to consumers as well as perishable—the effect may be to encourage increased short-term consumption without stealing sales from future periods. On the other hand, the use of price deals that lead consumers to stockpile products like ketchup and household cleaning products may simply serve to increase product purchasing in the short term without decreasing long-term consumption. Consumers, in effect, stockpile these items when they go on deal but do not increase their normal amount of product usage. Thus, we would tentatively conclude that price dealing is a useful offensive weapon (that is, for purposes of increasing total consumption) only for items such as yogurt, whereas products such as ketchup should be price promoted only for defensive reasons such as offsetting competitive efforts that attempt to steal market share.

Preempt Competition by Loading Consumers.   When consumers are loaded with one company's brand, they are temporarily out of the marketplace for competitive brands. Hence, one brand's sales promotion serves to preempt sales of competitive brands.

www.crayola.com

Reinforce Advertising.   A final can-do capability of sales promotion is to reinforce advertising. An advertising campaign can be strengthened greatly by a well-coordinated sales promotion effort. A case in point was a combined advertising and promotional effort by Binney & Smith, the manufacturer of Crayola crayons. Crayola crayons has in recent years found itself facing stiff competition—not especially from other crayon makers but from video game marketers and other purveyors of "fun" products that compete for kids' leisure time. Binney & Smith designed an advertising campaign and an accompanying promotion event to generate high levels of awareness among parents of children aged 2 to 12 and increase purchasing of "Big Box" crayons.

To create excitement, and hence awareness and purchasing, Binney & Smith invited consumers via advertising to name a new Crayola color. An accompanying promotion offered prospective winners the opportunity to have their color's name along with their own name printed on a crayon label. In addition, each winner was to receive cash and an all-expenses-paid trip for four to Crayola's 90th anniversary celebration in Hollywood, California. This promotion, which was aimed at consumers, was supported by another promotion that awarded prizes to participating retailers who set up special displays announcing the competition. The result: Over 100,000 entries were received, and phenomenal publicity was obtained—approximately 1,000 print articles and 700 TV news stories devoted space or time to describing this clever promotion. The names of the 16 new colors? Purple mountain's majesty, macaroni & cheese, granny smith apple, pacific blue, tropical rain forest, timber wolf, tumbleweed, tickle me pink, robin's egg blue, cerise, asparagus, denim, shamrock, razzmatazz, wisteria, and mauvelous.[24]

What Promotions Cannot Accomplish

As with other marketing communications elements, there are limits to what sales promotions are incapable of accomplishing. Particularly notable are the following three limitations.

Inability to Compensate for a Poorly Trained Sales Force or for a Lack of Advertising. When suffering from poor sales performance or inadequate growth, some companies consider promotion to be the solution. However, promotions will provide at best a temporary fix if the underlying problem is due to a poor sales force, a lack of brand awareness, a weak brand image, or other maladies that only proper sales management and advertising efforts can overcome.

Unable to Provide the Trade or Consumers with Any Compelling Long-Term Reason to Continue Purchasing a Brand. The trade's decision to continue stocking a brand and consumers' repeat purchasing are based on continued satisfaction with the brand. Satisfaction results from the brand's meeting profit objectives (for the trade) and providing benefits (for consumers). Promotions cannot compensate for a fundamentally flawed or mediocre brand unless the promotions offset the flaws by offering superior value to the trade and consumers.

Incapable of Permanently Stopping an Established Brand's Declining Sales Trend or Changing the Basic Nonacceptance of an Undesired Item. Declining sales over an extended period indicate poor product performance or the availability of a superior alternative. Sales promotions cannot reverse the basic nonacceptance of an undesired brand. A declining sales trend can be reversed only through product improvements or perhaps an advertising campaign that breathes new life into an aging brand. Promotions used in combination with advertising effort or product improvements may reverse the trend, but sales promotion by itself would be a waste of time and money when a brand is in a state of permanent decline.

What Generalizations Can Be Made About Promotions?

The foregoing discussion has referred to research evidence regarding how promotions work and the objectives accomplished. Researchers have vigorously studied the functioning and effectiveness of sales promotions during the past two decades. Their empirical efforts have enabled academics to draw some tentative conclusions. These conclusions, more formally termed empirical generalizations, represent consistent empirical evidence regarding different facets of promotion performance. Nine empirical generalizations are noteworthy (see Table 16.5).[25]

TABLE 16.5   Nine Generalizations about Sales Promotions

1. Temporary retail price reductions substantially increase sales.
2. The greater the frequency of deals, the lower the height of the deal spike.
3. The frequency of deals changes the consumer's reference price.
4. Retailers pass through less than 100% of trade deals.
5. Higher market share brands are less deal elastic.
6. Advertised promotions can result in increased store traffic.
7. Feature advertising and displays operate synergistically to influence sales of discounted brands.
8. Promotions in one product category affect sales of brands in complementary and competitive categories.
9. The effects of promoting higher- and lower-quality brands are asymmetric.

Adapted from Robert C. Blattberg, Richard Briesch, and Edward J. Fox, "How Promotions Work," *Marketing Science* 14 (No. 3, 1995), G122–G132.

Generalization #1: Temporary retail price reductions substantially increase sales.
The evidence is clear that temporary retail price reductions generally result in substantial increases in short-term sales. These short-term sales increases are termed sales spikes.

Generalization #2: The greater the frequency of deals, the lower the height of the deal spike. When manufacturers (and thus retailers) offer frequent deals, consumers learn to anticipate the likelihood of future deals and thus their responsiveness to any particular deal is diminished. In short, infrequent deals generate greater spikes, whereas frequent deals generate less-dramatic sales increases. The psychology of deal responsiveness also entails an issue of *reference prices*. When deals are frequently offered, the consumer's internal reference price (i.e., the price the consumer expects to pay for a particular brand) is lowered, thus making any particular deal price less attractive and generating less responsiveness than would be the case if the deal were offered less frequently.

Generalization #3: The frequency of deals changes the consumer's reference price. A corollary to the above generalization is that frequent deals on a brand tend to reduce consumers' price expectation, or reference price, for that brand. This lowering of a brand's reference price has the undesirable consequence of lowering the brand's equity and thus the seller's ability to charge premium prices. Taken together, generalizations #2 and #3 indicate that excessive dealing has the undesirable effects of both reducing a brand's reference price and diminishing consumer responsiveness to any particular deal.

Generalization #4: Retailers pass through less than 100 percent of trade deals. The simple reality is that manufacturers' trade deals, which typically are offered to retailers in the form of off-invoice discounts, are not always passed on to consumers. Though a manufacturer offers, say, a 15 percent off-invoice allowance, perhaps only 60 percent of retailers will extend this allowance to consumers as lower retail prices. There is no legal obligation for retailer's to pass through trade discounts. Retailers choose to pass along discounts only if their profit calculus leads them to the conclusion that greater profits can be earned from passing discounts to consumers rather than directly "pocketing" the discounts.

Generalization #5: Higher market share brands are less deal elastic. Suppose that a certain brand's price is reduced at retail by 20 percent and that sales volume increases by 30 percent. This would represent an elasticity coefficient of 1.5 ($30 \div 20$), a value indicating that the increase in demand is proportionately one and one-half times greater than the reduction in price. Generalization #5 suggests that for brands holding larger market shares, the deal-elasticity coefficient generally is smaller than is the case for smaller-share brands. The reason is straightforward: Smaller-share brands have proportionately more customers to gain when they are placed on deal, whereas larger-share brands have fewer remaining customers. In short, a larger-share brand when placed on deal gains "less bang for the promotional buck" compared to a smaller-share brand.

Generalization #6: Advertised promotions can result in increased store traffic. On balance the research suggests that store traffic benefits from brand-dealing activity. Upon exposure to a retailer's advertising that features brands on deal, some consumers will switch stores, if only temporarily, so as to take advantage of attractive deals from stores other than those in which they most regularly shop. Retailers refer to this temporary store-switching behavior as consumer "cherry picking," an apt metaphor.

Generalization #7: Feature advertising and displays operate synergistically to influence sales of discounted brands. When brands are placed on price deal, sales generally increase (see generalization #1). When brands are placed on price deal and are advertised in the retailers' advertised features, sales increase even more (see generalization #6). When brands are placed on price deal, are feature advertised, and receive special display attention, sales increase by substantially more. In other words, the combined effects of advertising and display positively interact to boost a dealt brand's retail sales. (This point was made previously in Chapter 8 in its discussion of point-of-purchase advertising.)

Generalization #8: Promotions in one product category affect sales of brands in complementary and competitive categories. An interesting thing often happens when a brand in a particular product category is promoted, namely, sales also increase for brands in complementary and even competitive categories. For example, when Tostitos nacho chips are promoted, sales of complementary salsa brands likely increase as well as might sales of brands in the competitive potato chip category.

Generalization #9: The effects of promoting higher- and lower-quality brands are asymmetric. When a higher-quality brand is promoted, say, via a substantial price reduction, there is a tendency for that brand to attract switchers and thus steal sales from lower-quality brands. However, a lower-quality brand on promotion is proportionately less likely to attract switchers from higher-quality brands. In other words, switching behavior is asymmetric—the proportion of switchers drifting from low- to high-quality brands, when the latter is on deal, is higher than the proportion moving in the other direction when a low-quality brand is on deal.

PROMOTION DEALING IS NOT ALWAYS PROFITABLE

A brand's sales volume is increased almost always during the period of a coupon offering or price-off deal. Consumers are highly responsive to deals, especially when they are advertised.[26] However, increases in sales volume do *not* necessarily lead to increased profits. Indeed, many sales promotion deals spur sales but not profits.

As we will see, whether or not a promotion is profitable *depends on consumers' deal responsiveness within a particular product category.* For example, if consumers are relatively insensitive to deals, sales promotions are necessarily *unprofitable.* This is because per-unit profit margin is reduced during a sales promotion and the additional sales volume is insufficient to offset the reduction in profit margin. Essential to this process is the basic accounting concept of contribution margin. **Contribution margin,** or simply *margin,* is a brand's selling price minus its per-unit variable cost. When a brand is on deal, its variable cost increases due to the expense of offering, say, a coupon worth 50 cents. This results in a reduced margin. When a brand's margin is reduced, profit will increase only if the incremental sales volume is proportionately greater than the percentage reduction in margin.

Consumer Responsiveness to Promotional Deals

The market for any product category is made up of consumers who differ in their responsiveness to deals. Some consumers are loyal to a single brand in a category and buy only that brand. Other consumers have absolutely no brand loyalty and will purchase only those brands that are on deal.[27] Most consumers fall somewhere between these extremes. Figure 16.2 presents a framework showing various segments of consumers in terms of their deal proneness.[28]

As shown in Figure 16.2, a market can be segmented into eight groups based on the pattern of consumers' deal responsiveness. There are two critical points about these groupings and the purchase patterns on which they are based: First, the patterns are obtained from optically scanned purchase data obtained from consumers who are members of household panels such as IRI's BehaviorScan or Nielsen's SCANTRACK (as described in the previous chapter). Second, the eight segments are based on consumers' purchase patterns within a *single product category*. The segmentation of consumers into deal-responsiveness segments is meaningful only on a product-by-product basis inasmuch as consumers exhibit different deal-responsiveness patterns across product categories.

Returning to the eight segments in Figure 16.2, the most general distinction is between consumers who purchase *only when a brand is on deal* (segment 8) and all remaining consumers who do not restrict their purchasing to such times. These *on- and off-deal consumers* fall into two general categories, loyalists and switchers. The distinction between loyalists and switchers is based on purchase behavior when *no brands in a product category are on deal.*

Loyalists are consumers whose purchase patterns reflect that they buy the same brand over and over when no brands are on deal (when the category is off deal). Looking again at Figure 16.2, you can see that some loyalists are deal prone and some are not. **Switchers,**

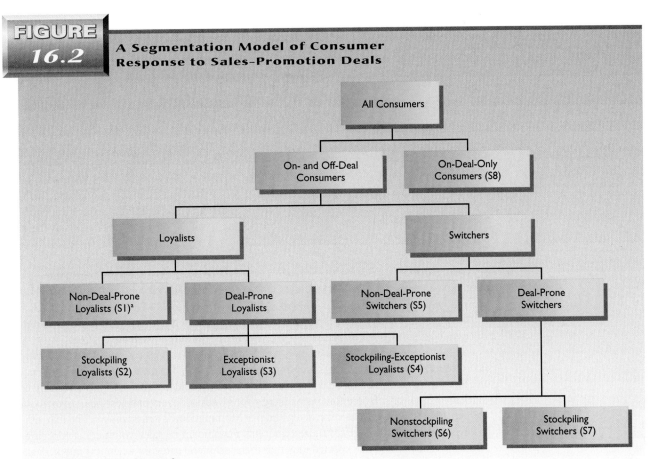

FIGURE 16.2

A Segmentation Model of Consumer Response to Sales-Promotion Deals

[a]S1–S8=Segment 1–Segment 8.

Source: Adapted from Leigh McAlister, "Continued Research into Sales Promotion: Product Line Management Issues" (research report and proposal prepared for the Marketing Science Institute and other sponsors, circa 1986). Adapted with permission.

on the other hand, are consumers who, even when all brands in a category are off deal, nonetheless switch among different brands. Like loyalists, switchers may or may not be deal prone. Now let's track the various types of loyalist and switcher consumers.

Non-deal-prone loyalists (segment 1) are consumers who invariably buy a single brand in a product category and are not influenced by that brand's deals or the deals from competitive brands. Segment 1 represents consumers who are truly brand loyal. Most brands today have relatively few consumers who are non-deal-prone loyalists. **Non-deal-prone switchers** (segment 5) are like their loyalist counterparts insofar as they are not responsive to deals. They switch among brands, but this is due to a need for novelty rather than to avail themselves of deals.

Deal-prone loyalists come in three varieties: (1) **Stockpiling loyalists** (segment 2) purchase only the single brand to which they are loyal but take advantage of savings by stockpiling when that brand is on deal (e.g., buying three instead of the customary one box of their favored cereal when a 75 cents-off deal is offered); (2) **exceptionist loyalists** (segment 3), though loyal to a single brand when all brands in the category are off deal, will make an exception and purchase another, nonpreferred brand when it, but not their preferred brand, is on deal; (3) **stockpiling-exceptionist loyalists** (segment 4) not only make exceptions by choosing nonpreferred brands but also stockpile quantities of other brands when they are on deal.

Deal-prone switchers break into two groups: **Nonstockpiling switchers** (segment 6) are responsive to deals but do not purchase extra quantities when any of their acceptable brands are on deal; **stockpiling switchers** (segment 7) exploit deal opportunities by purchasing multiple units when any acceptable brand is on deal.

Because several of the loyalist and switcher segments are conceptually overlapping, we can eliminate any further need to distinguish between segments 1 and 5, segments 3 and 6, and segments 4 and 7. All subsequent discussion is based on the following five categories of purchase patterns:

1. Promotion insensitives (segments 1 and 5)
2. Stockpiling loyalists (segment 2)
3. Nonstockpiling promotion sensitives (segments 3 and 6)
4. Stockpiling promotion sensitives (segments 4 and 7)
5. On-deal-only consumers (segment 8)

Profit Implications for Each Sales Promotion Consumer Category

The profit implications of dealing in each category will be based on a hypothetical shampoo brand called "MorningGlow."[29] (For the moment, return to Figure 16.2 and identify which segment of the shampoo market you belong to on the basis of your responsiveness, or lack of responsiveness, to shampoo deals.)

Promotion Insensitives (Segments 1 and 5). Assume that the market for shampoo consists entirely of consumers who are *insensitive* to promotional deals. Would it be profitable in such a situation to place MorningGlow on deal? Your answer should be a resounding NO! The reason is depicted in Figure 16.3, which portrays the sales pattern that would result from a market made up entirely of promotion insensitives.

Note first in Figure 16.3 the labels for the horizontal and vertical axes. The horizontal axis is a *time* dimension, which indicates that MorningGlow, like most real brands, is off deal for a period of time, then on deal, then off, and so on. (In actuality, most brands of consumer packaged goods are on deal for approximately four weeks of every business quarter, or about 30 percent of the time.) The vertical axis graphs MorningGlow's *sales volume*. The line indicating MorningGlow's *market share* represents the amount of sales volume that Morning-Glow normally would be expected to garner in the shampoo category when it is not on deal.

The reason it would be unprofitable to place MorningGlow on deal is because promotion insensitives will *not*, by definition, alter their purchase behavior in response to

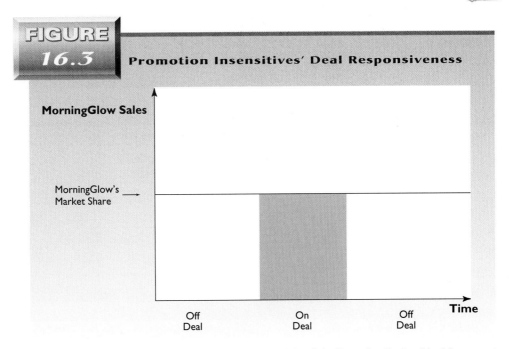

Source: Adapted from Leigh McAlister, "Continued Research into Sales Promotion: Product Line Management Issues" (research report and proposal prepared for the Marketing Science Institute and other sponsors, circa 1986). Adapted with permission.

MorningGlow's dealing activity. Hence, when MorningGlow is placed on deal, the same number of units will be sold that would have been sold without the promotion—except now these units are being sold *at a lower margin*. The total amount of loss from the sales promotion would thus equal the number of units sold when MorningGlow is on deal times the cost per unit of running the deal.

Stockpiling Loyalists (Segment 2).   These shampoo purchasers are loyal to MorningGlow and will stockpile quantities of that brand when it is on deal. Should MorningGlow be placed on deal if all consumers are stockpiling loyalists? The answer again is NO. It would be *unprofitable* for MorningGlow to deal this brand if the shampoo market consists entirely or predominantly of stockpiling loyalists.

The reason is shown in Figure 16.4. Note first from the vertical axis that a *sales depression* would result due to MorningGlow's own sales promotions when the brand is off deal. In other words, sales during off-deal periods are below MorningGlow's regular sales volume because consumers who stockpiled in response to past promotions have no need to now purchase MorningGlow at its regular, non-deal price. When MorningGlow is on deal, sales bump up considerably because stockpiling loyalists take advantage of the deal (see the massive sales increase in Figure 16.4 when MorningGlow is on deal). However, this sales increase when MorningGlow is on deal is simply *borrowed from future sales* that would have occurred if MorningGlow had not been placed on deal. Hence, the deal results in an increase in short-term sales volume, but it is unprofitable because: (1) sales when MorningGlow is on deal are made at a lower margin, and (2) when MorningGlow is off deal, fewer sales are made at the full margin.

Nonstockpiling Promotion Sensitives (Segments 3 and 6).   Nonstockpiling promotion sensitives consists of loyalists (segment 3) and switchers (segment 6) who *take advantage of promotional deals but do not stockpile*. In terms of shampoo purchasing, these consumers will *switch* among several brands of acceptable shampoos depending on which brand is on deal on any particular shopping occasion. They do not choose to stockpile, however. This segment represents a large percentage of consumers in many product categories. For example, one study determined that increases in coffee sales

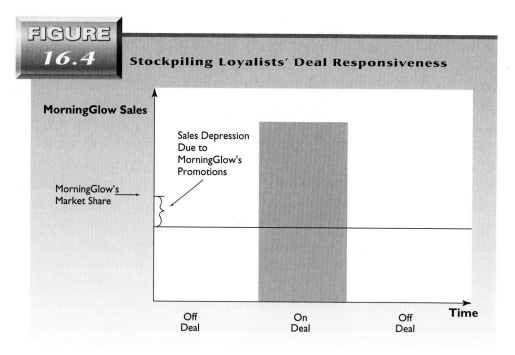

FIGURE 16.4 **Stockpiling Loyalists' Deal Responsiveness**

from promotions were due almost entirely to brand switching (84 percent) rather than from accelerated purchasing (14 percent) or stockpiling (2 percent).[30]

How profitable would a promotional offering by MorningGlow be if the market for shampoo consisted entirely, or predominantly, of consumers who switch among shampoo brands but do not stockpile? Figure 16.5 displays this situation. As in the case of stockpiling loyalists, a *sales depression* exists between MorningGlow's market share and its non-deal, or theoretical baseline, sales level. However, in the present case the depression is due entirely to *competitive promotions*: Specifically, when MorningGlow is off deal, its sales level is below its theoretical market share level (see the depression in Figure 16.5) because consumers who might normally purchase this brand have switched to competitive brands that are on deal. (Of course, when MorningGlow *is* on deal, its sales are bumped up measurably over the baseline level due to capturing purchases from consumers who have switched from competitive shampoo brands that now are off deal.)

MorningGlow's sales during the promotional period are made at a margin, M_D, which stands for the per-unit margin, M, during the period when MorningGlow is on deal, D. If MorningGlow did not deal, its sales volume would remain at a level equal to the blue-colored portion in Figure 16.5 (labeled S_N, or the sales volume when MorningGlow is *not* on deal). These sales would have been made at a margin, M_N. (MorningGlow's profit margin is, of course, greater when it is not on deal compared to when it is; i.e., $M_N > M_D$.) Total sales due to the deal are shown in Figure 16.5 by S_D, which includes incremental sales from the promotion (green-colored area) plus regular nonpromotional sales, S_N.

Let us define R as the ratio of sales volume when MorningGlow is on deal to when it is not on deal (i.e., R equals the ratio of S_D to S_N). We conclude that it will be *profitable* to put MorningGlow on deal only if $R \times M_D > M_N$.

An example will clarify the point. Assume that MorningGlow's sales volume, S_N, is 2,000,000 units when it is *off deal* with a margin, M_N, of 25 cents, and that *on deal* its sales volume, S_D, increases to 4,200,000 units but its margin, M_D, falls, due to the deal, to 15 cents. Hence, in this case R equals 2.1 (4,200,000 ÷ 2,000,000). It thus would be profitable to promote MorningGlow because R times M_D is greater than M_N (that is, $2.1 \times 15 = 31.5 > 25$).

Stockpiling Promotion Sensitives (Segments 4 and 7). This segment switches among brands, depending on which is on deal, and stockpiles extra quantities when an attractive deal is located. In this case, MorningGlow's baseline sales are depressed both by its own dealing activity *and* by competitive dealing. If MorningGlow's

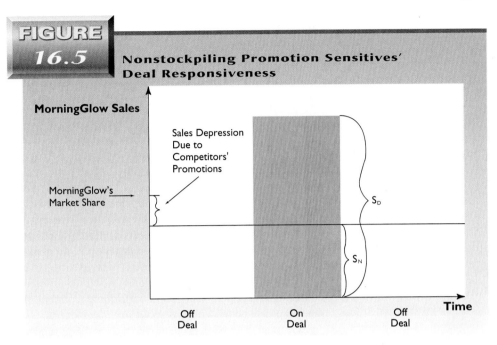

FIGURE 16.5 **Nonstockpiling Promotion Sensitives' Deal Responsiveness**

Source: Adapted from Leigh McAlister, "Continued Research into Sales Promotion: Product Line Management Issues" (research report and proposal prepared for the Marketing Science Institute and other sponsors, circa 1986), 7. Adapted with permission.

dealing activity is profitable when consumers do *not* stockpile (the situation in the previous case), then stockpiling behavior will lead to even greater profitability. This is because MorningGlow will profit both by taking consumers away from competitors during the period MorningGlow is on deal and by preempting competitors' sales in subsequent off-deal periods when consumers are "working off" their stockpiles of MorningGlow.

On-Deal-Only Consumers (Segment 8).   Because, by definition, MorningGlow makes no sales to these consumers *unless it is on deal*, it follows that promotions to a market made up exclusively of on-deal-only consumers will be *profitable*. The total amount of profit would equal the number of units sold, Q, times the profit margin when the brand is on deal, M_D.

In Conclusion

The discussion to this point has provided several guidelines regarding the profitability of dealing:

1. Putting a brand on deal is *unprofitable* if the market is composed of either promotion-insensitive consumers or stockpiling loyalists.
2. Putting a brand on deal is *profitable* if the market contains on-deal-only consumers.
3. Putting a brand on deal may or may not be profitable if the market consists of nonstockpiling or stockpiling promotion-sensitive consumers.

The preceding statements are based on the assumption that a brand's market consists exclusively of one or another type of consumer—for example, promotion insensitives or stockpiling loyalists. This obviously is a simplifying assumption. The market for any product (such as our illustrative shampoo brand, MorningGlow) contains consumers from all segments. The matter of whether promotion is profitable thus depends on the relative composition of customer types.

Fortunately, the availability of scanner data makes it possible for marketing researchers to identify the percentage of consumers who fall into each of these dealing categories. Armed with this information, brand managers can determine whether dealing activity is profitable or whether it merely results in a revenue-increasing but profit-losing endeavor.

Summary

Sales promotion is introduced in this first of three chapters devoted to the topic. The precise nature of sales promotion is described, and specific forms of trade- and consumer-oriented sales promotion are discussed. Sales promotion is explained as having three targets: the trade (wholesalers and retailers), consumers, and a company's own sales force.

The chapter proceeds to discuss the reasons for a significant trend in marketing communications toward greater sales promotion in comparison with advertising. This shift is part of the movement from pull- to push-oriented marketing, particularly in the case of consumer packaged goods. Underlying factors include a balance-of-power transfer from manufacturers to retailers, increased brand parity and growing price sensitivity, reduced brand loyalty, splintering of the mass market and reduced media effectiveness, a growing short-term orientation, and favorable consumer responsiveness to sales promotions.

The chapter also details the specific tasks that sales promotion can and cannot accomplish. For example, sales promotion cannot give the trade or consumers compelling long-term reasons to purchase. However, it is ideally suited for generating trial-purchase behavior, facilitating the introduction of new products, gaining shelf space for a brand, encouraging repeat purchasing, and performing a variety of other tasks. Also discussed are nine empirical generalizations about sales promotions.

Detailed discussion is devoted to the conditions under which the use of price-deal promotions are profitable. Various segments of consumers based on their responsiveness to promotional deals are described. It is concluded that sales promotion is unprofitable if a brand's market is composed of promotion-insensitive or brand-loyal stockpilers; sales promotion is always profitable if the market contains consumers who buy only on deal; and sales promotion may be profitable if the market consists primarily of consumers who switch from brand to brand depending on which brand is on deal.

The following chapter continues with a detailed treatment of sales promotion's role in influencing trade behavior, while Chapter 18 examines its role in influencing the behavior of ultimate consumers.

Discussion Questions

1. The term *promotional inducement* has been suggested as an alternative to sales promotion. Explain why this term is more descriptive than the established one.

2. Describe the factors that have accounted for sales promotion's rapid growth. Do you expect a continued increased in the use of promotion throughout the following decade?

3. Explain in your own words the meaning of push- versus pull-oriented promotional strategies. Using for illustration a well-known supermarket brand of your choice, explain which elements of this brand's marketing communications mix embody push and which embody pull.

4. Assume you are the vice president of marketing for a large, well-known manufacturer of consumer packaged goods (e.g., Procter & Gamble, Lever Brothers, Johnson & Johnson). What steps might you take to restore a balance of power favoring your company in its relations with retailers?

5. Are promotions able to reverse a brand's temporary sales decline and/or a permanent sales decline? Be specific.

6. The allocation of marketing communications dollars to advertising and promotions is influenced by a variety of factors, including life-cycle stage, the degree of brand differentiation, and the degree of brand dominance. Explain how these factors influence the allocation decision.

7. How can promotion techniques generate enthusiasm and stimulate improved performance from the sales force?

8. Offer a specific explanation of why you think the "Find the Cap'n" promotional campaign for Cap'n Crunch cereal was so successful.

9. If a market for a brand were composed entirely of brand-loyal stockpilers, why would promotional deals for this brand necessarily be unprofitable? Why are promotional deals profitable when a market consists of on-deal-only consumers?

10. Why is it critical that objectives be clearly specified when formulating a sales-promotion program?

    Assume you are brand manager of MountainState Bottled Water. This new brand competes in a product category with several well-known brands. Your marketing communications objective is to generate trial purchases among predominantly younger and better-educated consumers. Propose a sales promotion that would accomplish this objective. Assume that your promotion is purely experimental and that it will be undertaken in a small city of only 250,000 people. Also assume that: (1) you cannot afford product sampling, (2) you will not advertise the promotion, and (3) your budget for this experimental promotion is $5,000. What would you do?

12. Generalization #5 in the chapter claimed that higher market share brands are less deal elastic. Construct a realistic example to illustrate your understanding of this empirical generalization.

13. Generalization #8 asserted that promotions in one product category affect sales of brands in complementary and competitive categories. Tostitos tortilla chips was used as an example of this generalization. Provide examples of two additional brands and the complementary and competitive product categories that likely would be affected by promotions for your two illustrative brands.

I nternet Exercises

1. A San Francisco-based company called planet U, inc. (www.planetu.com) is one of the first to bring promotions to the Internet by offering Internet-based coupons. Currently, you can visit planet U or one of its client's Web sites (e.g., www.kroger.com for Kroger's grocery chain of 1400 stores) to select coupons you want to receive in the mail. However, soon (perhaps by the time this textbook goes to press) you will simply select the coupons you want and planet U will upload the information to the point of sale (e.g., Kroger's checkout network). At the point of sale, a card (e.g., a Kroger shopping card) will be used for identification and the coupons will be instantly redeemed. Thus, the coupons will never physically exist but the outcome is the same. Manufacturers and retailers are also quite interested in this new technology since it promises unprecedented promotions accountability. Specific promotions can be linked to particular consumers and their specific transactions. Visit the planet U Web site and respond to the following questions:
   a. List planet U's major clients.
   b. Visit the Web site of one of the clients you listed in part (a). Describe the process of acquiring Internet coupons. Were the coupons available for all types of products or just a subset? Why do you think coupon availability was structured this way?
   c. Describe the two types of reports available to retailers and manufacturers. How could these types of reports change the nature of trade promotions?

2. Most people know that Publisher's Clearing House runs frequent (and sometimes very large) consumer sweepstakes. However, many people do not know that you can enter just as many sweepstakes on the Internet. Publisher's has its own sweepstakes at www.pch.com, but if you are willing to do some Web surfing, you probably will find other sweepstakes via a banner ad or by checking popular brand sites.
   a. Locate a sweepstakes run by a particular brand (recent sweepstakes have been run by M&M's, Coke, L'eggs, and Starwave Software). Describe the process required to enter the sweepstakes.
   b. Internet sweepstakes can be constructed to require consumers to explore a brand's Web site. With which characteristic of integrated marketing communications (see Chapter 1) does this requirement seem to be consistent?
   c. Do you think Internet sweepstakes should award large prizes infrequently or small prizes frequently? Justify your answer in terms of the text's discussion of what promotions can and cannot be expected to accomplish.

Chapter Sixteen Endnotes

1. This definition combines the author's thoughts with those from two sources: Roger A. Strang, "Sales Promotion Research: Contributions and Issues" (unpublished paper presented at the AMA/MSI/PMAA Sales Promotion Workshop, Babson College, May 1983); and James H. Naber, James Webb Young address (University of Illinois, Urbana-Champaign, October 21, 1986).

2. Jacques Chevron, "Branding and Promotion: Uneasy Cohabitation," *Brandweek,* September 14, 1998, 24.

3. Don E. Schultz, William A. Robinson, and Lisa A. Petrison, *Sales Promotion Essentials: The 10 Basic Sales Promotion Techniques ... and How to Use Them* (3rd. ed.). Chicago: NTC Business Books, 1998, 6.

4. "Wave of Early Promotions Draws Out Early Shoppers," *The Wall Street Journal Interactive Edition,* December 1, 1997.

5. Kellie Krumplitsch, "Promotion Explosion: The Reggie Awards," *Brandweek,* April 4, 1994, 29, 32.

6. These figures are based on annual surveys conducted by Donnelly Marketing and now Cox Direct that since 1979 have queried executives from packaged goods, health and beauty aids, and household products companies about their marketing communications expenditures. Trend data are from Cox Direct 20th Annual Survey of Promotional Practices (Largo, FL: Cox Direct, 1998), Chart 63, 74.

7. Alvin A. Achenbaum and F. Kent Mitchel, "Pulling Away from Push Marketing," *Harvard Business Review* 65 (May/June 1987), 38–40; Robert J. Kopp and Stephen A. Greyser, "Packaged Goods Marketing 'Pull' Companies Look to Improved 'Push,'" *The Journal of Consumer Marketing* 4 (spring 1987), 13–22; F. Kent Mitchel, "Strategic Use of A&P," *Marketing Communications,* April 1986, 34–36.

8. For an excellent review of sales promotion trends in the UK, see Ken Peattie and Sue Peattie, "Sales Promotion—Playing to Win?" *Journal of Marketing Management* 9 (1993), 255–269.

9. Bud Frankel and J. W. Phillips, "Escaping the Parity Trap," *Marketing Communications,* November 1986, 93–100.

10. Carl F. Mela, Sunil Gupta, and Donald R. Lehmann, "The Long-Term Impact of Promotion and Advertising on Consumer Brand Choice," *Journal of Marketing Research* 34 (May 1997), 248–261.

11. Purushottam Papatla and Lakshman Krishnamurthi, "Measuring the Dynamic Effects of Promotions on Brand Choice," *Journal of Marketing Research* 33 (February 1996), 20–35.

12. A. S. C. Ehrenberg, Kathy Hammond, and G. J. Goodhardt, "The After-Effects of Price-Related Consumer Promotions," *Journal of Advertising Research* 34 (July/August 1994), 11–21.

13. Robert C. Blattberg and Scott A. Neslin, "Sales Promotion: The Long and the Short of It," *Marketing Letters* 1, no. 1 (1989), 81–97.

14. Scott Hume, "Coupons Score with Consumers," *Advertising Age,* February 15, 1988, 40.

15. *Cox Direct 20th Annual Survey of Promotional Practices* (Largo, FL: Cox Direct, 1998), 22.

16. This discussion is guided by Charles Fredericks, Jr., "What Ogilvy & Mather Has Learned about Sales Promotion," The Tools of Promotion (New York: Association of National Advertisers, 1975); and Don E. Schultz and William A. Robinson, *Sales Promotion Management* (Lincolnwood, Ill.: NTC Business Books, 1986), chap. 3.

17. "Quaker Oats Finds Cap'n Crunch Loot with Hide-and-Seek," *Advertising Age,* May 26, 1986, 53.

18. A facing is a row of shelf space. Brands typically are allocated facings proportionate to their profit potential to the retailer. Manufacturers must pay for extra facings by offering display allowances or providing other inducements that increase the retailer's profit.

19. Krumplitsch, "Promotion Explosion: The Reggie Awards."

20. Chakravarthi Narasimhan, Scott A. Neslin, and Subrata K. Sen, "Promotional Elasticities and Category Characteristics," *Journal of Marketing* 60 (April 1996), 17–30.

21. Carl F. Mela, Kamel Jedidi, and Douglas Bowman, "The Long-Term Impact of Promotions on Consumer Stockpiling Behavior," *Journal of Marketing Research* 35 (May 1998), 250–262.

22. Brian Wansink and Rohit Deshpande, "'Out of Sight, Out of Mind': Pantry Stockpiling and Brand-Usage Frequency," *Marketing Letters* 5, no. 1 (1994), 91–100.

23. Kusum L. Ailawadi and Scott A. Neslin, "The Effect of Promotion on Consumption: Buying More and Consuming It Faster," *Journal of Marketing Research* 35 (August 1998), 390–398.

24. Krumplitsch, "Promotion Explosion: The Reggie Awards."

25. The following discussion is based on the outstanding synthesis of the literature provided by Robert C. Blattberg, Richard Briesch, and Edward J. Fox, "How Promotions Work," *Marketing Science* 14 (No. 3, 1995), G122–G132. The order of generalizations presented here is adapted from Blattberg et al.'s presentation. Please refer to this article for coverage of the specific studies on which the generalizations are based.

26. Albert C. Bemmaor and Dominique Mouchoux, "Measuring the Short-Term Effect of In-Store Promotion and Retail Advertising on Brand Sales: A Factorial Experiment," *Journal of Marketing Research* 28 (May 1991), 202–214.

27. Research has shown that consumers possess a good understanding of when deals are offered by manufacturers as well as how much savings they can enjoy by purchasing on deal. See Aradhna Krishna, Imran S. Currim, and Robert W. Shoemaker, "Consumer Perceptions of Promotional Activity," *Journal of Marketing* 55 (April 1991), 4–16; and Aradhna Krishna, "The Effect of Deal Knowledge on Consumer

Purchase Behavior," *Journal of Marketing Research* 31 (February 1994), 76–91.

28. The following discussion is based on the work of Leigh McAlister, "Continued Research into Sales Promotion: Product Line Management Issues" (research report and proposal prepared for the Marketing Science Institute and other sponsors, circa 1986); also, Leigh McAlister, "A Model of Consumer Behavior," *Marketing Communications,* April 1987, 27–30.

29. Shampoo is an appropriate product category because it is characterized by both switching and loyal purchase patterns. For a fascinating set of experiments using shampoo as the experimental product, see Barbara E. Kahn and Therese A. Louie, "Effects of Retraction of Price Promotions on Brand Choice Behavior for Variety-Seeking and Last-Purchase-Loyal Consumers," *Journal of Marketing Research* 27 (August 1990), 279–289.

30. Sunil Gupta, "Impact of Sales Promotion on When, What, and How Much to Buy," *Journal of Marketing Research* 25 (November 1988), 342–355.

SEVENTEEN

Trade-Oriented Sales Promotion

CHAPTER OBJECTIVES

After studying this chapter, you should be able to:

1. Discuss the objectives of trade-oriented promotions and the factors critical to building a successful trade promotion program.

2. Explain the various forms of trade allowances and the reasons for their usage.

3. Understand forward buying and diverting and how they are created by manufacturers' use of off-invoice allowances.

4. Explain the role of everyday low pricing (EDLP) and pay-for-performance programs in overcoming forward buying and diverting.

5. Describe the concept and practice known as efficient consumer response (ECR).

6. Understand the practice of category management.

7. Describe the role of cooperative advertising and vendor support programs.

8. Discuss the nature and role of specialty advertising.

9. Discuss the nature and role of trade shows.

Opening Vignette: Now You See It, Now You Don't—The Old "Switcharoo" in the Modern Retail Establishment

Do you recall ever going to a certain location in a retail outlet to find a particular brand that had always been there but now the brand was nowhere in sight? Perhaps in its place was another brand, one that you had never previously seen. Where's your preferred brand? Well, it could be that your preferred brand was not selling well and the store's management simply decided to replace it with a brand having better sales prospects. Another possibility is that your preferred brand was the victim of a practice called "stocklifting." Here is how stocklifting works.

Consider the case of Lowe's Home Improvement stores, a large retail chain that merchandises all kinds of home products and competes against Home Depot and other similar retailers. Lowe's stores carried a brand of work and gardening gloves from a company called Wells Lamont, which is the largest garden-glove company in the United States. The shelves at Lowe's were at one time (and perhaps again at some future time) filled with the Wells Lamont brand. But early in 1998, Lowe's shelves were restocked with a brand of gloves from Midwest Quality Gloves Inc., Wells Lamont's archrival. Midwest, in cooperation with Lowe's, cleared the shelves of over 200,000 pairs of Wells Lamont's gloves and replaced them with its own brand. Midwest accomplished this by paying Lowe's a negotiated wholesale price (i.e., a price below the retail price charged to consumers) for the 200,000 pairs of Wells Lamont's gloves.

Why would Midwest Quality Gloves Inc. purchase a competitors' brand, and what would it do with all these gloves? The answer to the first question is straightforward: Midwest

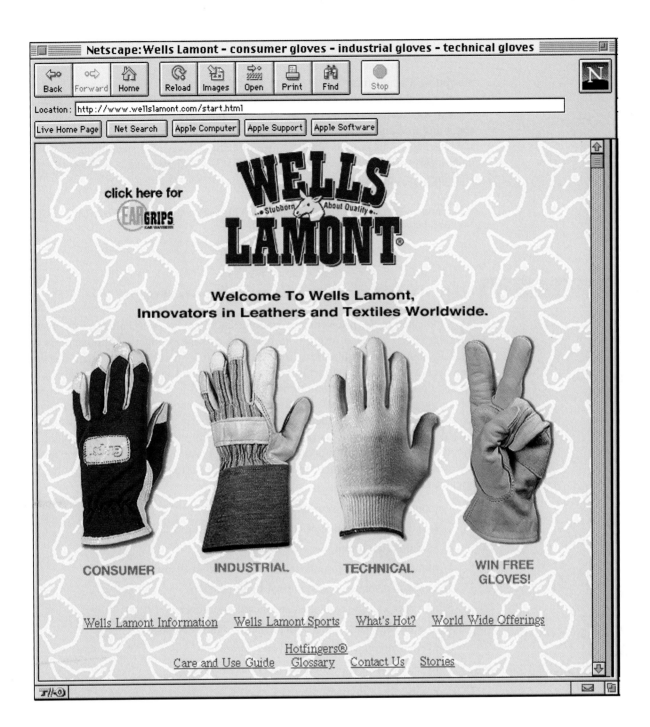

Back Forward Home Reload Images Open Print Find Stop

Location: http://www.wellslamont.com/start.html

Live Home Page Net Search Apple Computer Apple Support Apple Software

click here for
EARGRIPS

WELLS LAMONT
..Stubborn About Quality..

**Welcome To Wells Lamont,
Innovators in Leathers and Textiles Worldwide.**

CONSUMER   INDUSTRIAL   TECHNICAL   WIN FREE
GLOVES!

Wells Lamont Information   Wells Lamont Sports   What's Hot?   World Wide Offerings

Hotfingers®
Care and Use Guide   Glossary   Contact Us   Stories

wanted to gain access to Lowe's shelf space, but could not get its brand accepted as long as Wells Lamont's gloves were the brand of choice in Lowe's stores. The solution: Buy the entire stock of Wells Lamont's gloves and then resell them to so-called liquidators that specialize in reselling stocklifted merchandise. For example, Genco Distribution System is a Pittsburgh-based company that has warehouses throughout the United States in which it inventories stocklifted products and then sells these items to domestic and foreign purchasers at discounted prices. Among other possible outlets for its stocklifted products, Genco could sell garden and work gloves to industrial customers for use by factory workers—a situation where the brand name is not a key buying consideration.

Stocklifting certainly is not restricted to gloves. Pet toys, humidifiers, flashlights, and light bulbs are just a few of the many stocklifted items. The practice of stocklifting is increasing in view of manufacturers' desire to gain prime retail shelf space at whatever expense is required. Stocklifting is not illegal per se, but a manufacturer could be found in violation of federal antitrust legislation if its stocklifting has the effect of effectively precluding a competitor from a market and thus constituting a form of monopoly. Is the practice unethical? Rather than taking a position on this issue, it would seem worthwhile to present your own views and to hear what your professor and fellow students have to say about this growing practice. Consider, however, what a Wells Lamont vice president had to say when asked his opinion about Midwest Quality Glove Inc.'s stocklifting of Wells Lamont's gloves in Lowe's retail outlets. He said: "We sold the product to the customer. It's their inventory, not ours."

Source: Adapted from Yumiko Ono, "Some Vendors Pay Big Sums to Get Competing Goods Off Store Shelves," *The Wall Street Journal Interactive Edition*, May 15, 1998.

INTRODUCTION TO TRADE PROMOTION

*A*s indicated in the prior chapter, trade promotions represent half of every manufacturer dollar invested to promote new and existing products. Manufacturers direct trade promotions at wholesalers, retailers, and other marketing intermediaries (rather than at consumers). A manufacturer's consumer-oriented advertising and promotions are likely to fail unless trade promotions have succeeded in persuading wholesalers to distribute the product and retailers to stock adequate quantities. The special incentives offered by manufacturers to their distribution channel members are then expected to be passed through to consumers in the form of price discounts offered by retailers, often stimulated by advertising support and special displays.[1] As we will see later, however, this does not always occur. Manufacturers have various objectives for using trade-oriented sales promotions:[2]

1. to introduce new or revised products,
2. to increase distribution of new packages or sizes,
3. to build retail inventories,
4. to maintain or increase the manufacturer's share of shelf space,
5. to obtain displays outside normal shelf locations,
6. to reduce excess inventories and increase turnover,
7. to achieve product features in retailers' advertisements,
8. to counter competitive activity, and, ultimately,
9. to sell as much as possible to final consumers.

To accomplish these myriad objectives, several ingredients are critical to building a successful trade-promotion program.[3]

Financial Incentive.   A manufacturer's trade promotion must offer wholesalers and retailers increased profit margins and/or increased sales volume.

Correct Timing.   Trade promotions are appropriately timed when they are: (1) tied in with a seasonal event during a time of growing sales (such as candy sales during Valentine's Day, Halloween, and Christmas), (2) paired with a consumer-oriented sales promotion, or (3) used strategically to offset competitive promotional activity.

Minimize the Retailer's Effort and Cost.   The more effort and expense required, the less likely it is that retailers will cooperate in a program they see as benefiting the manufacturer but not themselves.

Quick Results.   The most effective trade promotions are those that generate immediate sales or increases in store traffic.

Improve Retailer Performance. Promotions are effective when they help the retailer do a better selling job or improve merchandising methods as, for example, by providing retailers with improved displays.[4]

Types of Trade Promotions

Manufacturers in dealing with their channel intermediaries utilize a variety of practices that are intended to encourage certain behaviors on the part of wholesale and retail customers and ultimately to boost the sales and profitability of the manufacturer's brands. These practices can be lumped under the general label "trade promotions," although, as will become apparent, these practices vary greatly in terms of their objectives, implementation, and effectiveness. Common to all, however, is the general objective to induce channel intermediaries (the "trade") to devote greater attention to products of the manufacturer that is offering the promotion rather than to competitive offerings. Following sections discuss five forms of trade promotions:

- ◆ Trade allowances
- ◆ Cooperative advertising and vendor support programs
- ◆ Trade contests and incentives
- ◆ Specialty advertising
- ◆ Trade shows

T RADE ALLOWANCES

Trade allowances are used by manufacturers to reward wholesalers and retailers for performing activities in support of the manufacturer's brand.[5] These allowances, also called trade deals, encourage retailers to stock the manufacturer's brand, discount the brand's price to consumers, feature it in advertising, or provide special display or other point-of-purchase support.[6]

By using trade allowances, manufacturers hope to accomplish two interrelated objectives: (1) increase wholesalers and retailers purchases of the manufacturer's brand and (2) increase consumers' purchases of the manufacturer's brand from retailers. This latter objective is based on the expectation that consumers are receptive to price reductions, and that retailers will in fact pass along to consumers the discounts they receive from manufacturers.

This does not always happen. Retailers often take advantage of allowances without performing the services for which they receive credit. In fact, a study of trade promotion spending revealed that over 80 percent of manufacturers do not feel they get good value for their trade dollars. Moreover, the vast majority of retailers think that trade promotions should serve to increase sales and profits of entire product categories without concern for whether a manufacturer's specific brand benefits from the trade promotion.[7] There is, in short, a substantial rift between manufacturers and retailers over the matter of which party trade promotions are intended to benefit. Manufacturers use trade promotions, of course, to advance their brands' sales and profit performance. Retailers, on the other hand, tend to look upon trade dollars as an opportunity for increasing their profit margins and thus boosting their bottom lines. This schism is not difficult to understand insofar as parties to economic transactions often have conflicting objectives, while at the same time depending upon each other for success.

Major Forms of Trade Allowances

Three major forms of trade allowances are: (1) slotting allowances, (2) bill-back allowances, and (3) off-invoice allowances.

Slotting Allowances. This form of trade allowance applies specifically to the situation where a manufacturer attempts to get one of its brands—typically a new brand—accepted by retailers. Also called a *stocking allowance* or *street money*, a slotting allowance is not something manufactures of branded products choose to offer retailers; to the contrary, retailers impose slotting allowances on manufacturers. Retailers demand this fee of manufacturers supposedly to compensate them for added costs incurred when taking a new brand into distribution and placing it on the shelf. Definitionally, **slotting allowances** are the fees manufacturers pay retailers for access to the slot, or location, that the retailer must make available in its distribution center to accommodate the manufacturer's new brand.

When slotting allowances first appeared in the 1960s, they were used to compensate retailers for the real costs of taking on a new stockkeeping unit, or SKU.[8] The cost at that time averaged $50 per SKU per *account*. However, by the mid-1990s slotting allowances had increased to an average charge of $42 per SKU per *store*, or a total cost to the manufacturer of approximately $1.2 million to introduce one SKU nationally.[9] You probably are thinking, "This sounds like bribery." You also may be wondering, "Why do manufacturers tolerate slotting allowances?" Let's examine each issue.[10]

First, slotting allowances are indeed a form of bribery. The retailer that demands slotting allowances denies the manufacturer shelf space unless the manufacturer is willing to pay the up-front fee—the slotting allowance—to acquire that space for its new brand. Second, manufacturers tolerate slotting allowances because they are confronted with a classic dilemma: Either they pay the fee and eventually recoup the cost through increased sales volume, or they refuse to pay the fee and in so doing accept a fate of not being able to successfully introduce new brands.

The expression "between a rock and a hard place" appropriate describes the reality of slotting allowances from the manufacturer's perspective. Consider, for example, Eastman Kodak's introduction of Supralife alkaline batteries to compete against the likes of Duracell, Eveready, and Ray-O-Vac. After being on the market for only a few years, Supralife's performance was so weak that Kodak decided to discontinue all advertising and, in effect, to accept its destiny as a minor player in the alkaline battery business. Analysts estimate Kodak's battery-business losses at somewhere between $100 million and $200 million. Among other reasons for Supralife's losses is the fact that Kodak in the first year had to pay millions of dollars in slotting allowances.[11]

In certain respects, slotting allowances are a legitimate cost of doing business. When, for example, a large, multi-store supermarket chain takes on a new brand, it does incur several added expenses. These expenses arise because the chain must make space for that new brand in its distribution center, create a new entry in its computerized inventory system, possibly redesign store shelves, and notify individual stores about the new SKU. In addition to these expenses, the chain takes the risk that the new brand will fail. This is a likely result in the grocery industry, where at least half of all new brands are failures. Hence, the slotting allowance provides the retailer with what effectively amounts to an insurance policy against the prospects that a brand will fail.

It is questionable, however, whether the actual expenses incurred by retailers are anywhere near the slotting allowances they charge. Actual charges are highly variable. Some supermarkets charge as little as $5 per store to stock a new item, while others charge as much as $100 per store. Large companies can afford to pay slotting allowances, because their volume is sufficient to recoup the expense. However, brands with small consumer franchises are frequently unable to afford these fees.

How, you might be wondering, are retailers able to impose expensive slotting fees on manufacturers? The reason is straightforward: As noted in the previous chapter, the balance of power has shifted away from manufacturers and toward retailers. Power means being able to call the shots, and increasing numbers of retailers are doing this. Also, manufacturers have hurt their own cause by introducing thousands of new brands each year, most of which are trivial variants of existing products rather than distinct new offerings with meaningful profit opportunities for the retailer. As such, every manufacturer competes against every other manufacturer for limited shelf space, and slotting allowances are simply a mechanism used by retailers to exploit the competition among manufacturers. Furthermore, many grocery retailers find it easy to rationalize slotting allowances on the grounds that their net profit margins in selling groceries are minuscule (typically 1 to 1.5 percent) and that slotting allowances enable them to earn returns comparable to those earned by manufacturers.

Further understanding of the rationale and dynamics underlying slotting allowances is possible by comparing them to apartment prices in any college community. When units are abundant, different apartment complexes compete aggressively with one another and force prices down. On the other hand, when apartments are scarce (which typically is the case on most college campuses), prices are often inflated. The result: You may be forced to pay an arm and a leg to live in a miserable, albeit conveniently located, apartment.

This is also the case in today's marketing environment. Each year retailers are confronted with requests to stock thousands of new brands (potential tenants). The amount of shelf space (the number of apartments) is limited because relatively few new stores are being built. Hence, retailers are able to command slotting allowances (higher rent), and manufacturers are willing to pay the higher rent to "live" in desirable locations.

What can a manufacturer do to avoid paying slotting allowances? Sometimes nothing. But powerful manufacturers such as Procter & Gamble and Kraft, for example, are less likely to pay slotting fees than are weaker national and particularly regional manufacturers. Retailers know that P&G's and Kraft's new brands probably will be successful. This is because P&G and Kraft invest heavily in research in order to develop meaningful new products; they spend heavily on advertising to create consumer demand for these products; and they use extensive sales promotions (e.g., couponing) that serve to create strong consumer pull for their brands.

Another way to avoid paying slotting allowances is simply to refuse to pay them and, if need be, to accept the consequence of being refused shelf space by some, if not most, retail chains. For example, Jays, a well-known brand of potato chips in the Chicago area, refuses to pay slotting allowances. Jays's chief executive explains his decision this way: "Somewhere you have to draw the line. I make my money off potato chips, not soft drinks or beer, and I have no other place to pull money."[12] (The comment about soft drinks and beer is in reference to PepsiCo's Frito-Lay brand and the failed Anheuser-Busch's Eagle brand, both of which were more able than Jays to pay slotting allowances.)

Whereas slotting allowances represent a form of entry fee for getting a new brand entered in a grocery chain's distribution center, some retail chains charge manufacturers with fee to remove unsuccessful brands from their distribution centers. These **exit fees** could just as well be called *deslotting allowances*. Here is how they operate: When introducing a new brand to a supermarket chain, the manufacturer and chain enter into a contractual arrangement. This arrangement stipulates the average volume of weekly product movement during a specified period, say six months, that must be achieved for the manufacturer's brand to be permitted to remain in the chain's distribution center. Then, if the six months have elapsed and the brand has not met the stipulated average weekly movement, the chain will issue a deslotting charge. This charge, or exit fee, is intended to cover the handling costs for the chain to remove the item from its distribution center. One chain has a deslotting charge of $1,200.

This practice may seem to be a marketplace application of the old saying about having salt rubbed into a wound. However, it really represents the fact that retailers, especially in the supermarket industry, no longer are willing to pay for manufacturers' new-product mistakes. There clearly is some economic logic to deslotting charges. Indeed, these charges are another form of insurance policy to protect grocery chains from slow-moving and unprofitable brands. To continue the apartment-rental analogy, a deslotting charge operates in much the same fashion as the stipulation between apartment owner and tenant regarding property damage. If as a tenant you damage an apartment, the apartment owner is fully justified in forfeiting all or part of your rental deposit. As such, your deposit provides the apartment owner with an insurance policy against your potential negligence. This is precisely how an exit fee, or deslotting charge, operates.

Bill-Back Allowances. Another form of trade allowance is the so-called bill-back allowance. Retailers receive allowances for featuring the manufacturer's brand in advertisements (**bill-back *ad* allowances**) or for providing special displays (**bill-back *display* allowances**). As the expression indicates, the bill-back allowance is not deducted directly from the invoice by virtue of ordering products (as is the case with the subsequently discussed off-invoice allowances) but rather is earned by the retailer for performing designated advertising or display services in behalf of the manufacturer's brand. The retailer effectively bills (i.e., charges) the manufacturer for the services rendered, and the manufacturer pays an allowance to the retailer for the services received.

To illustrate, assume that the sales force for the Campbell Soup Company informs its many retailers that during the month of October they will receive a 5 percent discount on all cases of V8 Juice purchased during this period provided that they run newspaper advertisements in which V8 Juice is prominently featured. With proof of having run feature ads in newspapers, retailers then would bill Campbell Soup for a 5 percent advertising allowance. Similarly, Campbell Soup's sales force could offer a 2 percent display allowance whereby retailers could receive a 2 percent discount on all purchases of V8 Juice during the deal period for displaying V8 Juice in a prime display location, such as at the front of the aisle.

Off-Invoice Allowances. The most frequently used form of trade allowance is an off-invoice allowance, which represents a manufacturer's *temporary price reduction* to the trade on a particular brand. **Off-invoice allowances** are, as the name suggests, deals offered periodically to the trade that literally permit wholesalers and retailers to deduct a fixed amount from the invoice. (A slight variant is a deal that provides the trade with free goods for orders meeting or exceeding required quantities.) In offering an off-invoice allowance, the manufacturer's sales force informs retail buyers that a discount of, say, 15 percent can be deducted from the invoice amount for all quantities purchased during the specified deal period. Many manufacturers of consumer packaged goods provide off-invoice allowances at regularly scheduled intervals, which for many brands is for one four-week period during every 13-week business quarter. This means that many brands are on off-invoice deals approximately 30 percent of the year. (The implications of this dealing frequency will be discussed later when describing the retailer practices of forward buying and diverting.)

By using off-invoice allowances, manufacturers hope to increase retailers' purchasing of the manufacturer's brand and increase consumers' purchasing from retailers that are expected to pass the deals on to shoppers in the form of reduced prices. However, as previously stated, retailers do not always comply with these expectations. Rather, retailers receive an off-invoice allowance (of, say, 15 percent) when purchasing the manufacturer's brand but then do not discount their selling prices to consumers or reduce prices by substantially less than the full 15 percent.

Forward Buying and Diverting

Manufacturers' trade allowances make considerable sense in theory, but in practice many retailers do not perform the services necessary to earn the allowances they receive from manufacturers. Large retail chains are particularly likely to take advantage of manufacturers' off-invoice allowances without passing the savings along to consumers. A major reason is that large chains, unlike smaller chains, are able to promote and sell their own *private brands*. Because private brands can be sold at lower prices than manufacturers' comparable brands, large chains are able to use private brands to satisfy the needs of price-sensitive consumers while selling manufacturers' brands at their normal prices and pocketing the trade allowance as extra profit.

A second major problem with manufacturers' off-invoice allowances is that they often induce retailers to *stockpile* products in order to take advantage of the temporary price reductions. Forward buying and diverting are two interrelated practices used by retailers, especially those in the grocery trade, to capitalize on manufacturers' trade allowances. Table 17.1 illustrates these practices.[13]

TABLE 17.1 **Illustration of Forward Buying and Diverting**

1. In preparation for a huge promotional event surrounding the Cinco de Mayo celebration of Mexican independence on May 5, 1999, the hypothetical Beauty Products, Inc.—a manufacturer of personal care products—extends a one-week offer to Texas-based grocery retailers for a 15% *off-invoice allowance* on all orders placed for MorningGlow shampoo during the week beginning April 9, 1999.

2. FB&D Supermarkets of San Antonio, Texas, orders 15,000 cases of MorningGlow shampoo. Beauty Products, Inc., has offered the 15 percent off-invoice allowance to FB&D Supermarkets with the expectation that FB&D will reduce MorningGlow's retail price by 15 percent to consumers during the promotional events associated with the Cinco de Mayo festivities.

3. FB&D sells at the discounted price only 3,000 of the 15,000 cases purchased. (The remaining cases include some that are forward bought and some that will be diverted.)

4. FB&D resells 5,000 cases of MorningGlow at a small profit margin to Opportunistic Food Brokers, Inc.—a company that services grocery retailers throughout the Southwest. (This is the practice of *diverting*.)

5. FB&D later sells the remaining 7,000 cases of MorningGlow to shoppers in its own stores, but at the regular, full price. (These 7,000 cases represent *forward buys*.)

Forward Buying.   As earlier noted, manufacturers' trade allowances are typically available every four weeks of each business quarter (which translates to about 30 percent of the year). During these deal periods, retailers buy larger quantities than needed for normal inventory and warehouse the excess volume, thereby avoiding purchasing the brand at its full price during the remaining 70 percent of the time when a deal is not offered. Retailers often purchase enough products on one deal to carry them over until the manufacturer's next regularly scheduled deal. This is the practice of **forward buying**, which, for obvious reasons, is also called *bridge buying*. Approximately 75 percent of all leading grocer retailers practice forward buying.[14]

When a manufacturer marks down a product's price by, say, 15 percent, retail chains commonly stock up with a 10- to 12-week supply.[15] A number of manufacturers sell 80 to 90 percent of their volume on deal. It is estimated that forward buying costs manufacturers between 0.5 to 1.1 percent of retail prices, which translates into hundreds of millions of dollars annually.[16]

The practice of forward buying has given rise to computer models that enable retail buyers to estimate the profit potential from a forward buy and the optimum weeks of inventory to purchase. The models take into consideration the amount of savings from a deal and then incorporate into their calculations the various added costs from forward buying. These added costs include warehouse storage expenses, shipping costs, and the cost of tying up money in inventory when that money could be used to earn a better return in some other manner.

It may appear that forward buying benefits all parties to the marketing process, but this is not the case. First, retailers' *savings from forward buying often are not passed on to consumers*; indeed, it has been claimed that only 30 percent of trade promotion money that manufacturers provide to wholesalers and retailers actually reaches the consumer.[17]

Second, forward buying leads to *increased distribution costs* because wholesalers and retailers pay greater carrying charges in holding in inventory large quantities of forward-bought items. In fact, the average grocery product takes up to *12 weeks* from the time it is shipped by a manufacturer until it reaches retail store shelves. This delay obviously is not due to transit time but rather reflects storage time in wholesalers' and retailers' warehouses from stockpiling surplus quantities of forward-bought items.[18] Third, manufacturers experience *reduced margins* due to the price discounts that they offer as well as the increased costs that are incurred.

www.campbellsoup.com

A notable case in point is the situation that confronted the Campbell Soup Company with massive forward buying of its chicken noodle soup when that product was placed on trade deal. As much as 40 percent of its annual chicken noodle soup production was sold to wholesalers and retailers in just six weeks when this product was on deal. Because wholesalers and retailers forward-bought chicken noodle soup in large quantities, Campbell had to schedule extra work shifts and pay overtime to keep up with the accelerated production and shipping schedules. After years of falling prey to forward buying, Campbell implemented a *bill and hold program* whereby it invoices (bills) the retailer as soon as the retailer places a forward-bought order but delays shipping (holds) the order until desired quantities are requested by the retailer. This program has smoothed out Campbell's production and shipping schedules by allowing retailers to purchase large amounts at deal prices while delaying shipments until inventory is needed. The bill and hold program has not eliminated forward buying, but the negative consequences for the Campbell Soup Company have been reduced.

Diverting.   **Diverting** occurs when a manufacturer *restricts a deal to a limited geographical area* rather than making it available nationally. In Table 17.1, MorningGlow shampoo is available only in Texas as part of Beauty Products, Inc.'s participation in the Cinco de Mayo festivities. The manufacturer intends for only wholesalers and retailers in that area to benefit from the deal. However, what happens with diverting is that wholesalers and retailers buy abnormally large quantities at the deal price and then use food brokers to resell the excess quantities in other geographical areas. It is estimated that 5 to 10 percent of grocery products sold on trade allowance is diverted.[19] Over 50 percent of retailers acknowledge engaging in the practice of diverting.[20]

Many retailers blame manufacturers for offering irresistible deals and argue that they must take advantage of the deals in any way legally possible in order to remain competitive with other retailers. Manufacturers could avoid the diverting problem by placing brands on national deal only. This solution is more ideal than practical, however, since regional marketing efforts are expanding, and local deals and regional marketing go hand in hand. Further complicating the problem is that products intended for foreign markets sometimes are diverted back into a domestic market. The *Global Focus* describes one instance of this practice.

There are other negative consequences of diverting. First, product quality potentially suffers due to delays in getting products from manufacturers to retail shelves. For example, Tropicana requires its chilled juices to be stored at between 32 and 36 degrees. If unrefrigerated for a few hours, due to careless diverting practices, the product can go bad, and consumers may form negative impressions of this brand.[21] A second and potentially more serious problem could result from product tampering—such as the infamous Tylenol incident in the early 1980s, when seven Chicago residents died from this brand being laced with cyanide by a lunatic.[22] In the event of product tampering, it would be difficult, if not impossible, to identify exactly where a diverted brand may have been shipped.

www.tylenol.com

The prior discussion has perhaps made it seem that retailers are villains when engaging in the practice of forward buying and diverting. This would be an unfair representation inasmuch as retail buyers are simply taking advantage of an opportunity that is provided them by manufacturers that offer attractive trade deals. One retail executive explains his company's forward buying and diverting actions in this fashion: "We are very aggressive when it comes to buying at the best price. We have to be. If we don't, somebody else will."[23]

GLOBAL FOCUS: DIVERTING CIGARETTES

Cigarette prices in the United States increased by as much as 50 percent during the late 1990s. With price increases such as these, it was only a matter of time before enterprising businesses found a way to beat the system. Diverting was the answer. Here is how it works. Large cigarette manufacturers such as Philip Morris and RJR ship their brands to foreign markets at prices below those charged in the United States. Diverters in foreign markets then resell these cigarettes to retailers back in the United States. Until 1999 it was perfectly legal to re-import cigarettes to the United States, but a federal statute went into effect in 2000 that made it illegal to divert tobacco products. Nonetheless, enforcement of this statute will be extremely difficult and costly.

Cigarette diverting has taken a heavy toll on established tobacco distributors and retailers that refuse to divert and thus lose business to their competitors that buy and sell diverted cigarettes. There is skepticism as to whether tobacco manufacturers are actually committed to stopping diverting. Indeed, the skeptics contend that diverting enables manufacturers to maintain the brand loyalty of price-sensitive consumers that otherwise would switch to cheaper brands if their preferred brands were not available at cheaper, diverted prices. Manufacturers deny that they encourage diverting and contend that the practice threatens the equity of their brands.

Source: Adapted from Suein L. Hwang, "'Diverted' Cigarettes Are for Sale, Sparking Inquiries and a Backlash," *The Wall Street Journal Interactive Edition*, January 28, 1999.

E FFORTS TO RECTIFY TRADE PROMOTION PROBLEMS

Because trade promotions spawn inefficiencies, create billions of added dollars in distribution costs, are economically unprofitable for manufacturers, and perhaps inflate prices to consumers, a variety of efforts have been undertaken to fundamentally alter the way business is conducted, especially in the grocery industry.[24] Following sections are devoted to five notable developments that hold important implications for trade promotions. Two of these represent major changes in the interrelations between manufacturers and retailers (namely, the efficient consumer response and category management movements), whereas the final three reflect more specific practices on the part of manufacturers (everyday low pricing, pay-for-performance programs, and account-specific marketing).

Efficient Consumer Response (ECR)

Efficient consumer response (ECR) is a broad-based concept of business management that is oriented toward enhancing efficiencies and reducing costs in the grocery industry. Kurt Salmon Associates, Inc., a consulting firm, issued a report in the early 1990s that estimated that some $30 billion, or 10 percent of total grocery sales, is wasted. This waste, according to the Salmon report, is due to inefficient ordering procedures, maintenance of excessive inventories, and inefficient promotional practices. The report argued that billions of dollars could be saved if ECR were fully implemented throughout the distribution chain. The objective of ECR is to improve efficiencies in the grocery industry between all parties (manufacturers, wholesalers, brokers, and retailers) and reduce costs for everyone, especially the final consumer. ECR also includes the objective of reducing the huge expenditures on trade promotion. Although many of the ECR initiatives go beyond the scope of this chapter, several features are noteworthy:

1. *Improved product-replenishment practices.* The objective is to move products
   more efficiently from manufacturers' production facilities to retailers' shelves.
   Electronic data interchange (EDI) between manufacturers and retailers is a major
   means of reducing the time and cost of order fulfillment. EDI essentially entails
   constant electronic exchanges between trading partners: Retailers are able to
   maintain minimal inventory levels because manufacturers ship required product
   quantities just in time to replenish depleting inventories. For example, the fully

coordinated EDI system between Procter & Gamble and Wal-Mart allows Wal-Mart to carry minimal levels of P&G brands with the assurance that additional quantities of brands like Tide detergent, Pringles chips, and Luvs diapers will be replenished as needed.

2. *Reduced trade promotions.* The objective is to minimize inventory costs in the system, and this necessitates reducing drastically the practices of forward buying and diverting. EDLP pricing and pay-for-performance programs, as discussed below, represent major steps in this direction.

3. *Improved product introductions.* The objective is to respond to consumers' needs for new products rather than simply introducing me-too products and the associated wasteful practices of slotting allowances and failure fees.

In sum, the ultimate objective of ECR is to reduce wasteful practices that lead to excessive grocery prices for consumers and diminished profits for manufacturers, wholesalers, and retailers. As with all revolutions, it will be a matter of years before the benefits of ECR are anywhere close to being fully realized.[25]

Category Management

Manufacturers produce different product lines of which the individual brands in each line constitute a group, or category. Likewise, retailers merchandise multiple brands that compete in each of many categories. A grocery store, for example, has categories of detergents, breakfast cereals, and pain relievers; an appliance dealer has kitchen appliances, video devices, computer equipment, and audio equipment. Although manufacturers and retailers both work with categories, their interests are not necessarily equivalent. Whereas manufacturers are concerned with the profitability of their individual brands, retailers are more interested in the overall profitability of a product category. With growing retailer power, as discussed in the previous chapter, manufacturers have been forced to market their brands with greater concern for the retailer's broader, category interests rather than focusing exclusively on their own profits.

Category management describes the working relationship between manufacturers and retailers that attempts to find ways whereby both parties can be more profitable. The implementation of category management means that retailers and manufacturers must work together, share market intelligence, and develop strategies that are mutually beneficial.[26] Thus, category managers from both the manufacturer and retailer sides of business jointly plan and execute merchandising programs, sales promotion deals, and advertising executions that are agreeable to both parties and improve the category performance for both.

Figure 17.1 presents five interrelated stages involved in the actual process of implementing category management. Although both manufacturers and retailers must individually conduct these same five activities, the following discussion presents the manufacturer's perspective.[27]

1. *Category Review.* A manufacturer would initiate a category management program by conducting a thorough study of the product category. After carefully defining the category (e.g., soft drinks) and its subcategories (colas, noncolas, regular, diet), the manufacturer must gather information pertaining to category sales volume and growth rate, sales by type of retail outlet, household purchasing patterns, and comparisons of the performances of the manufacturer's brands versus its competitors'. The acquisition of these data enables the manufacturer to identify growth opportunities and to develop new or modified marketing strategies that capitalize on the opportunities.

2. *Target Consumers.* This stage requires the manufacturer to acquire an in-depth understanding of the typical consumer in the product category. The consumer is profiled with respect to relevant demographic characteristics (income level, age) and examined with respect to their product-purchase and usage patterns (Where

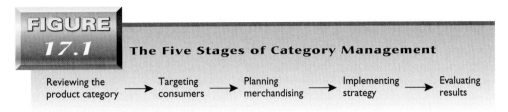

do they shop? How much do they typically purchase?), lifestyles (What activities do they participate in?), and media preferences. Armed with this information, a manufacturer is prepared to know a brand's potential in specific stores and to make intelligent decisions about the choice of advertising media, sales promotions, and product offerings.

3. *Merchandise Planning.* This stage entails developing a detailed strategy for the best mix of brands for each retail account within a particular category. The manufacturer recommends to the retailer an optimum mix of brands, prices, and shelf-space allocation that will enable the retailer to achieve desired volume and profit goals within the category. Sophisticated software applications enable manufacturers to assist retailers in developing product-stocking programs, called *planograms,* that identify the specific products that the store should stock to best appeal to the consumers in its trade area. "By assisting in the development of category-wide shelf-space management strategies, the manufacturer can help the retailer ensure that the right products are in the right stores in the right quantity at the right time."[28]

4. *Strategy Implementation.* Results from the first three stages provide the content for an ongoing interaction between the manufacturer's sales team and a retail chain's category buyer. Merchandising plans are the foundation for the sales team's recommendations to the retailer concerning appropriate product mix, pricing, promotions, and shelf-space allocations for the category. The sales team also explains how the manufacturer's advertising program will target the retailer's consumers and thus generate business for the retailer.

5. *Results Evaluation.* Effective implementation of category management programs requires that manufacturers answer this key question: Did the strategies proposed for the retail account achieve their objectives? If the program has not achieved these objectives, answering this question will direct manufacturers and retailers to alter their strategies; if objectives have been achieved, the prudence of continuing with the previously proposed strategy will be reinforced.

In sum, manufacturers are able to undertake category management programs that are mutually beneficial to themselves and their retail accounts. Sophisticated software applications backed by careful study of consumer behavior, competitor actions, and market developments enable manufacturers and retailers to formulate merchandising programs that suit the needs of all parties: retailers, manufacturers, and consumers.

Everyday Low Pricing (EDLP)

Manufacturers lose billions of dollars every year to inefficient and ineffective trade deals stemming from the trade's practice of forward buying and diverting. It is for this reason that the powerful Procter & Gamble Corporation, under the leadership of then CEO Edwin Artzt, undertook a bold move in the early 1990s to bust the practice of forward buying and diverting. P&G introduced a new form of pricing called everyday low pricing, or EDLP, which the company also refers to as *value pricing*—signifying its desire to compete on the basis of providing product values and not mere price savings. Because some retailers also practice everyday low prices, we will distinguish between "backdoor" EDLP as used by manufacturers from the "frontdoor" variety practiced by retailers.[29] Our interest is with the backdoor variety of EDLP, which for clarity's sake we label EDLP(M) to stand for manufacturers' use of EDLP.

EDLP(M) is a form of pricing whereby a manufacturer charges the same price for a particular brand day in and day out. In other words, rather than charging *high-low prices—* that is, regular, or "high," prices for a period followed by off-invoice, or "low," prices for a shorter period—EDLP(M) involves charging the same price over an extended period. Because no trade allowances are offered the trade, wholesalers and retailers have no reason to engage in forward buying or diverting. Hence, their profit is made from selling merchandise rather than from buying it.

Many retailers and wholesalers initially resisted the move toward EDLP(M), but P&G persisted, and other manufacturers followed suit. Today over 80 percent of P&G's brands are sold via EDLP(M) pricing, and the amount of forward buying and diverting has declined. Nonetheless, manufacturers less powerful than Procter & Gamble have found it difficult to convert to a pure system of everyday low pricing. Even P&G has experienced resistance and has deviated from a pure EDLP pricing with some brands.[30]

Three major reasons account for why some retailers resist manufacturers' EDLP pricing initiatives: First, many retailers have established distribution infrastructures to avail themselves of high-low prices—they developed storage capabilities to take advantage of manufacturers' deals by forward buying. Research has established that the more committed a retailer is to forward buying, the greater the resistance to EDLP(M) pricing.[31] Second, there is some evidence that EDLP(M) pricing benefits the manufacturers that price their products in this fashion more than it does the retailers that pay EDLP(M) rather than high-low prices.[32] Finally, it also has been argued that EDLP(M) pricing takes some of the excitement out of retailing. With EDLP(M) pricing, the retailer charges the same price to consumers day after day. Comparatively, with high-low pricing, there are periods when retailers are able to advertise attractive price savings, which breaks the monotony of never varying the retail price. Although in the long term the consumer realizes no savings from high-low pricing, in the short term it may be exciting to receive an appealing discount.

Although pricing practices by manufacturers—especially those in the grocery industry— remain somewhat in a state of flux, it appears that a pure EDLP(M) pricing system will not dominate. Some combination of EDLP(M) pricing along with periodic promotional funds provided to the trade by manufacturers is the pricing system most likely to endure. One thing is certain, however: Forward buying and diverting are decreasing, and inventories are shrinking.

Pay-for-Performance Programs

As noted earlier, many trade promotions, especially in the grocery industry, are unprofitable for manufacturers because they merely shift future buying to the present when the trade engages in forward buying and diverting. Manufacturers, accordingly, have a strong incentive to devise an alternative system to the traditional off-invoice allowance. One such system is the pay-for-performance program. As the name suggests, **pay-for-performance** is a form of trade allowance that rewards retailers for performing the primary function that justifies a manufacturer's offering a trade allowance—namely, *selling increased quantities of the manufacturer's brands to grocery shoppers.* In other words, pay-for-performance programs are designed to reward retailers for *selling* the brands supported with trade allowances rather than for merely buying these brands. By comparison, off-invoice allowances reward retailers for *merely buying* trade-supported brands.

Pay-for-performance programs also are called *scanner-verified trade promotions* or *scan-downs* because the retail sales volume for a trade-supported brand is recorded via optical scanning devices. Scan-downs essentially entail three facets:[33]

1. A manufacturer establishes with a retailer an agreed-on period during which the retailer receives an allowance for all quantities of a promoted brand that are sold

to consumers at the designated deal price (e.g., an item that regularly sells at $1.99 per unit is to be reduced to $1.79);

2. The retailer's own scanning data verify the exact amount of the promoted brand that has been sold during this period at the deal price (e.g., 5,680 units @ $1.79); and

3. After determining the scanned-down quantity (from step 2), the manufacturer pays the retailer quickly, say within five days, at the designated allowance for the quantity sold. The manufacturer would reimburse the retailer for the reduced margin in selling a certain number of units (e.g., 5,680 units @ a reduced margin of $0.20, or $1,136) and compensate the retailer for the amount of the trade allowance (e.g., 5,680 units @ $0.05, or $284; thus, the manufacturer would mail a check to the retailer totaling $1,420).

In sum, scanner-verified, or pay-for-performance, programs provide incentive to the retailer only for the items that are sold to consumers during the agreed-upon time period. As such and unlike off-invoice allowances, a manufacturer using scan-downs does not pay for allowances where no benefit is received. Rather, retailers get compensated only for items sold to consumers. Hence, this form of pay-for-performance program benefits all parties: consumers, retailers, and manufacturers. Consumers receive reduced prices; retailers obtain allowances for moving increased quantities of manufacturers' promoted brands; and manufacturers increase sales of their brands, if only temporarily, by reducing prices to consumers. By comparison, when using off-invoice allowances, manufacturers have no assurance that the off-invoice allowances given to retailers will be passed on to consumers.

    Pay-for-performance programs are a natural correlate for the efficient consumer response (ECR) initiative that was previously discussed. Only time will tell whether these programs become widely implemented. However, the technological infrastructure is available in the United States to support this new form of trade promotion. Moreover, well-known companies such as A.C. Nielsen and Information Resources Inc. have moved into this emerging business in the role of scanning agents. These scanning agents profit from performing the following functions: (1) collecting scanner data from retailers, (2) verifying the amount of product movement that meets the manufacturer's promotional requirements and warrants compensation, (3) paying the retailer, and (4) collecting funds from the manufacturer along with a commission for services rendered.

Account-Specific Marketing

Account-specific marketing, also called *co-marketing*, is a descriptive term that characterizes promotional and advertising activity that a manufacturer customizes to specific retail accounts. To appreciate this practice fully, it is necessary to place it in context of the earlier-described off-invoice allowance promotion, which is a temporary price reduction that is offered to *all* accounts. With off-invoice programs, a manufacturer's promotion dollars are anything but customized to the needs of specific retail accounts. On the other hand, account-specific marketing, or co-marketing, directs promotion dollars to specific retail customers and develops in concert with the retailer an advertising or promotion program that simultaneously serves the manufacturer's brand, the retailer's volume and profit requirements, and the consumer's needs. Local radio tie-in advertising and loyalty programs using retailers' shopper databases are especially popular account-specific practices.[34]

    When introducing its expensive PhotoSmart photography system—a photo-scanning and printing system for home computers—Hewlett-Packard (HP) developed co-marketing arrangements with a small number of retailers. HP selected prime consumer prospects in each retailers' trade area and mailed invitations that were customized so as to appear that the invitations were from the retailer and not HP. Prospective purchasers were invited to see an in-store demonstration and receive a chance to win a free PhotoSmart system.

    Account-specific marketing is a relatively recent innovation. First introduced by marketers in the packaged goods field, the practice has spread to companies that manufacture

IMC FOCUS: A COMBINED CONSUMER AND TRADE PROMOTION FOR SPAM

Hormel makes a canned meat product, called Spam, that for years has been the source of parody for comedians. Kidding aside, Spam is a pretty good product that has a following among many consumers, as evidenced by the fact that its annual sales exceed $70 million. To boost sales and to lure new consumers to the brand, Hormel introduced the "Spam Stuff" continuity program in 1998. Following in the footsteps of Marlboro, Kool-Aid, and Pepsi, all of which had previously launched "Stuff" programs, Hormel offered consumers points toward the acquisition of free items (such as bean bag characters, boxer shorts, mouse pads, mugs, and T-shirts) with each purchase of Spam products. In addition to offering "freebies" to encourage consumers to try Spam products, Hormel developed some account-specific programs to draw the trade's attention to the brand.

Retailers were provided with Spam advertising materials (called ad slicks) for their advertising "flyers." They also received local advertising support for promoting Spam on radio and in newspapers. To further excite retailer participation, Hormel offered one supermarket per region with a "Spam Day" promotion for the best in-store display. Winning stores received Spam-wear for employees and customers, free Spam burgers grilled in the store's parking lot, and a personal appearance by Spam Cans characters.

Beyond lampooning Spam as a funny product, it would also be understandable if the student were to consider this promotional program somewhat goofy. This surely is a lighthearted attempt on the part of Hormel to increase interest in Spam both from consumers and retailers. Silly as it may seem, programs like this often represent effective ways to encourage retailers to devote greater attention to a brand (e.g., providing increased display space) and to entice consumers to purchase the brand more regularly.

Source: Adapted from Stephanie Thompson, "Hormel Seeks Frequent Spam-sters," *Brandweek*, May 18, 1998, 6.

and market soft goods (e.g., apparel items) and durable items such as the HP PhotoSmart system. Because account-specific marketing requires a lot of effort both in development and implementation and is costly, the future of this practice is uncertain at the time of this writing. It appears that interest among packaged goods companies has peaked already.[35] The future will depend on results. As always, the proof is in the pudding. Account-specific marketing will increase in those industries and for those companies where programs yield increased results but decrease where the returns fail to justify the efforts. The *IMC Focus* describes another application of account-specific marketing.

COOPERATIVE ADVERTISING AND VENDOR SUPPORT PROGRAMS

Another form of trade promotion occurs when manufacturers of branded merchandise pay for part of the expense that retailers incur when advertising manufacturers' brands. Both cooperative advertising and vendor support programs deal with the *advertising relation between manufacturers and resellers*. A fundamental distinction between the two is that cooperative advertising programs are *initiated by the manufacturer*, whereas vendor support programs are *retailer initiated*. The significance of this distinction will become clear in the following discussion.

Cooperative Advertising

Cooperative (co-op) advertising is an arrangement between a manufacturer and reseller (either a retailer or an industrial distributor) whereby the manufacturer pays for all or some of the advertising costs undertaken by the reseller in behalf of the manufacturer's products.[36] Co-op programs permit resellers to place ads promoting the manufacturers' products and their availability. The cost of a co-op ad placement is divided between the manufacturer and reseller according to the terms specified in the cooperative contract.

Though cooperative advertising programs vary, five elements are common to all. These elements are illustrated with the co-op advertising program from Action Industries' Lane Furniture, a well-known manufacturer of reclining chairs, sofas, and other furniture items.

www.actionlane.com

1. *Specified time period:* Co-op funds typically apply to a specified time period. Lane's program applies to funds accrued between January 1 and December 31. These funds can be applied only to advertising that is run during the same period.

2. *Accrual*: The retailer receives from the manufacturer an advertising fund, called an *accrual account*, against which advertising costs are charged. The accrual typically is based either on a fixed amount or a percentage of a retailer's net purchases from the manufacturer during the term of the co-op contract. In the case of Lane, which applies a *fixed accrual*, the retailer accrues $4 on each Lane chair and $8 on each Lane sofa.

   To illustrate a *percentage accrual*, suppose a certain appliance retailer purchases $200,000 in products from a manufacturer in one year. Suppose further that the manufacturer's cooperative program allows 5 percent of purchases to accrue to the retailer's cooperative advertising account. Thus, the retailer would have accrued $10,000 worth of cooperative advertising dollars.[37]

3. *Payment share:* The payment share, also called the *participation rate,* is the amount the manufacturer reimburses the retailer for advertising. Manufacturers generally agree to pay a set percentage ranging from 25 to 100 percent of the cost for each advertisement placed by the retailer. Lane pays 50 percent of each advertisement.[38]

   For example, suppose that a retailer places a $1,000 newspaper ad featuring Lane recliners and sofas. Action Industries, Inc. would pay $500; and the retailer would pay the remaining $500.

4. *Performance guidelines:* These are the manufacturer's requirements that the retailer must satisfy in order to qualify for advertising reimbursement. Guidelines typically deal with suitable media, size and type of logos, the use of trademarks, copy and art directions, and product content.

5. *Billing for reimbursement:* This prescribes how the retailer is to be reimbursed. To receive reimbursement from Action Industries, the retailer must present a copy of the invoice from the newspaper or other medium where the ad was placed, along with evidence of the actual advertising copy in the form of so-called tearsheets.

Why Is Cooperative Advertising Used?   There are several reasons for the use of co-op advertising.[39] First, consumers of infrequently purchased goods (appliances, apparel, and furniture) are responsive to retailer advertisements, especially preceding a major buying decision. In the absence of co-op dollars, however, most retailers would not emphasize a specific manufacturer's products/brands in their advertisements but would rather simply mention the variety of products/brands that the retailer handles. Hence, co-op advertising enables manufacturers to achieve advertising support on a local-market basis and provides them with a way to *associate their products in the consumer's mind with specific retail outlets.*

   Second, manufacturers have found that cooperative advertising *stimulates greater retailer buying and merchandising support.* Retailers, knowing they have accrued co-op dollars, are more likely to aggressively promote and merchandise a specific manufacturer's products. From the manufacturer's perspective, this amounts to greater stocking and more display space for its brands as well as more retail advertising support.

   A third advantage of co-op advertising is that it *enables manufacturers to have access to local media at an advertising rate lower than would be paid if the manufacturer advertised directly rather than through retailers.* This cost savings reflects the fact that local media, particularly newspapers, charge lower advertising rates to local advertisers than to national advertisers. For example, average national rates for advertising in major U.S. newspapers were found to be over 66 percent higher than the average local rates.[40] By using cooperative advertising, a manufacturer thus gets exposure in local markets at a reduced rate.

From the retailer's perspective, cooperative advertising is a relatively inexpensive form of advertising. The advertising is not truly free, however, because the manufacturer's cooperative advertising costs are built into the price of the merchandise. Failure to take advantage of accrued co-op dollars means that the retailer is effectively paying more for the same merchandise than retailers that do utilize co-op funds.

Yet much cooperative advertising accruals are never spent by retailers. Over $11 billion is available annually in co-op funds, and fully one-third of that amount goes unspent each year.[41] Research by the Newspaper Advertising Bureau shows that only about 40 percent of all retailers take advantage of co-op accruals.[42]

Some manufacturers have implemented cooperative advertising programs that make it easier and more lucrative for retailers to utilize co-op funds. The objective is to make the program instructions simpler to read and easier to implement. Advertising media are also offering new programs to attract more co-op dollars. For example, the Newspaper Advertising Bureau has developed a program whereby salespeople of newspaper space are able to identify all the products in a retailer's store that carry co-op advertising, determine how much the retailer has accrued for each product, and then run an ad for the retailer that will use the accrued co-op funds.[43]

Open-Ended Co-op Advertising. The cooperative advertising programs discussed to this point relate the amount of co-op funds to the amount of products purchased by a retailer from a particular manufacturer. The more products purchased, the more co-op funds accrue to the retailer. **Open-ended co-op advertising** involves paying for part of the retailer's advertising cost without relating the reimbursement to the amount of products purchased from the manufacturer.[44]

Open-ended programs make considerable sense when the manufacturer: (1) wants to encourage the use of co-op funds by smaller retailers or (2) when the manufacturer sells through intermediaries and does not have access to retailers' purchase figures. Major advantages of open-ended programs involve simplifying the record-keeping task and, more important, making it possible to use advertising for generating sales rather than relying on sales to generate advertising.

Vendor Support Programs

In contrast to cooperative advertising, **vendor support programs (VSPs)** are *initiated by retailers*. A retailer, such as a supermarket chain, develops an advertising program in consultation with local advertising media and then invites its vendors (i.e., manufacturers) to pay for a specific percentage of the media cost for the proposed campaign. In other words, the retailer creates advertising dollars by exerting its power over a manufacturer, or vendor, which depends on the retailer for its marketplace success.

To illustrate, consider a hypothetical 250-store grocery chain called BuyRight. BuyRight's advertising agency recommends that the chain undertake a major advertising campaign in April. The campaign will cost BuyRight $300,000. Where is the money to come from? Solution: Get 10 vendors (manufacturers) to contribute $30,000 each to BuyRight's April campaign. In return for their participation, manufacturers will receive *feature time and space* in BuyRight's advertisements as well as *extra shelf space*. Extra sales volume, BuyRight assures the manufacturers, will more than compensate for their advertising support funds.

VSPs have clear advantages for the retailer. Indeed, these programs seem to benefit everyone (retailers, ad agencies, media), except perhaps the manufacturers that provide the financial support.[45] Often a manufacturer pays a large sum to support a retailer's advertising efforts but receives very little actual promotion of its own brands to end users. The manufacturer's products may be lost amid the clutter of the other brands featured in, say, a supermarket chain's newspaper advertisement.

Why Do Manufacturers Participate in VSPs?   Vendor support programs are most likely used when the retailer's channel power is greater than that of manufacturers that compete against one another for the retailer's limited shelf space. This is particularly true in the case of smaller, regional manufacturers that have not created strong consumer franchises for their brands. These weaker manufacturers cannot afford to invest in consumer-pull programs, because their promotion funds are almost fully consumed by retailers' vendor support programs. As such, it becomes an irrevocable cycle: The less powerful a manufacturer, the more susceptible it is to retailers' demands for advertising support funds. In turn, the more the manufacturer invests in the retailers' advertising programs, the less funds it has available to build demand for its own brands.

TRADE CONTESTS AND INCENTIVES

Contests and incentive programs are developed by manufacturers to encourage better performance from retail managers and their salespeople. A trade contest typically is directed at store-level or department managers and generally is based on managers *meeting a sales goal* established by the manufacturer. For example, Almay, a division of Revlon, Inc., is a maker of hypoallergenic cosmetics that until the 1990s appealed mostly to middle-aged and medically minded consumers. One of Almay's products, waterproof mascara, reached a point where sales volume leveled off, thereby forcing the marketing staff to consider ways to invigorate the product. Almay's marketers made the resourceful move to introduce a new mascara brand, named Wetproof, to teens and women in their early 20s, consumers with whom Almay had not had much previous success. Some substantial marketing changes were needed to attract this market. Because mass-merchandise cosmetics are typically purchased on impulse, Almay came up with a bold color combination, neon yellow and black, to use in both product packages and merchandise displays. This combination appealed to the youthful market and also differentiated Wetproof from competitive mascaras.

To encourage retailers to handle Wetproof and to support the brand's sales performance, a free gift of a floating air mattress—a product that tied into Wetproof's waterproof feature—was offered to the head buyer on all accounts. To further encourage retail support, a trade contest offered store managers the opportunity to win 35-millimeter cameras, cordless telephones, and other attractive items based on meeting specified sales goals. In a matter of months Wetproof found its way into 16,000 retail outlets, and sales to consumers were vigorous.[46]

Whereas contests are typically related to meeting sales goals, **trade incentives** are given to retail managers and salespeople for performing certain tasks. For example, when running sweepstakes or contests directed to final consumers (discussed fully in the following chapter), manufacturers often encourage retailers to display the object of merchandise that is being offered to consumers. As an incentive to encourage retailer participation, the manufacturer then gives the item to the store or departmental manager when the sales promotion is completed. Bigger prizes in the form of vacations and other high-ticket items are used sometimes as incentives.

Manufacturers employ another form of incentive when they provide financial incentives to retail salespeople to aggressively sell to consumers a select item in the manufacturer's product line. This practice is called **push money**. For example, a manufacturer may pay retail salespeople $25 for every unit of a particular compact disc player that they sell. Of course, the purpose of the push money is to encourage salespeople to favor the manufacturer's model over competitors' offerings and thus to literally "push" the product on consumers.

When structured properly, trade contests and incentives can serve the manufacturer's interests very well. These programs may not serve the retailer's or the consumer's interests, however. For example, push money can cause retail salespeople to be overly aggressive in attempting to persuade consumers to purchase a particular brand. For this reason, many stores have policies that prevent their managers and salespeople from accepting any form of incentive from manufacturers.

S PECIALTY ADVERTISING

Many companies promote their brands to prospective customers by offering free items that carry the brand's name. These gifts include wearable items (especially T-shirts and ballcaps), writing instruments, calendars, desk and office accessories, glasswear and ceramic objects, and a host of other items. This is the practice of specialty advertising. Specialty advertising represents a hybrid form of marketing communications. It is very much like direct-mail advertising in that both pinpoint their communication efforts toward specifically defined audiences. Specialty advertising also resembles public relations in that both engender goodwill. In another respect, specialty advertising is analogous to sales promotion in that both involve the use of incentives given to recipients to encourage certain forms of behavior.

Specialty advertising can be defined as an advertising and promotions medium that utilizes useful or decorative articles to transmit to a target audience an organization's identification and promotional message.[47] Expenditures on ad specialties are small in comparison with other forms of advertising and trade promotions, yet in 1997 the annual expenditures in the United States on specialty merchandise amounted to $9.5 billion.[48] Healthcare and financial services companies are the top users of advertising specialties.[49]

This hybrid form of advertising and promotion can help companies achieve a variety of marketing communications objectives, including: (1) promoting new store openings, (2) introducing new brands, (3) motivating salespeople, (4) establishing new accounts, (5) developing traffic for trade shows, (6) improving customer relations, and (7) activating inactive accounts.[50]

Specialty advertising generally takes two forms. One is the *distribution of items to prospects and customers as a type of reminder advertising.* Typical specialty items in this category include matchbooks, calendars, ballpoint pens, and T-shirts—all of which are inscribed with a company or brand name and perhaps a brief advertising message. A second form of specialty advertising is the *structured promotion,* which calls for planning and analyzing promotion objectives, identifying target audiences, creating promotional themes, budgeting, and developing systems for distributing specialty items.[51] It is this latter, more sophisticated use of specialty advertising that is pertinent to the present discussion. It can be considered a form of trade promotion when the target audience is a company's wholesaler, distributor, retailer, or other intermediate customer. The following cases illustrate how specialty advertising works as a form of structured trade promotion.

www.xerox.com

Xerox undertook a specialty-advertising program to generate sales leads for its printing systems to a designated target audience of 3,800 information-services and data-processing managers. Based on research showing this audience to be composed largely of upscale individuals with sophisticated tastes, the creative appeal centered around a music theme. A promotion was assembled showing how Xerox could orchestrate a system to meet corporate requirements. The first of five music-theme mailings consisted of a record-album package with an imprinted pencil housed in blueprint graphics with copy stating, "For a perfect arrangement, Xerox presents products that work in perfect harmony with your system." A second mailing depicted an orchestra conductor and included a conductor's baton and a response card promising a free gift to those who replied (a recording of Vivaldi's "The Four

Seasons"). Later mailings tied the music theme to the idea that Xerox could orchestrate a system meeting the buyer's needs. The promotion generated a very high response rate: Over one-third of all recipients responded to the specialty advertising. Salespeople found the promotion to be a helpful "door opener" in acquiring appointments.[52]

The Anderson Trucking Service, Inc., of St. Cloud, Minnesota, structured a specialty promotion to increase its name awareness among 2,500 business accounts using competing trucking services. In the first month of this seven-month promotion, a toy horn was mailed to prospective accounts in a box with the copy "In the next six months we are going to be making a lot of noise." The second-month mailing included a letter opener with a folder reading, "Transportation problems are closing in on you . . . let ATS open them up." Following monthly mailings included similar copy with creative giveaway items. For example, "for problems that have you biting your nails," the mailer included a fingernail file, and for those that "have you in a sweat," an encapsulated truck-shaped sponge was included with the copy "Let ATS dry them up." The promotion reportedly resulted in increased revenue of approximately $1 million.[53]

TRADE SHOWS

A trade show is a temporary forum (typically lasting several days) for sellers of a product category (such as small appliances, toys, clothing, furniture, industrial tools, food products, or sporting goods) to exhibit and demonstrate their wares to present and prospective buyers.[54] It is estimated that approximately 4,800 trade shows will be conducted in the United States and Canada by 2000, and that these shows will attract 140 million attendees to the booths of the 1.3 million companies that will exhibit their products at these shows.[55] Trade-show activity is even greater in Europe, representing approximately one-fourth of the total marketing communications budgets for European business-to-business firms (compared to the one-fifth representation among North American companies).[56] Approximately 13 percent of the marketing communications budgets for business-to-business firms are allocated to trade shows.[57]

Trade-show attendees include most of an industry's important manufacturers and major customers. This encapsulated marketplace enables the trade-show exhibitor to accomplish both selling and nonselling functions. Specific functions include: (1) servicing present customers, (2) identifying prospects, (3) introducing new or modified products, (4) gathering information about competitors' new products, (5) taking product orders, and (6) enhancing the company's image.[58]

Trade shows are an excellent forum for introducing new products. Products can be demonstrated and customer inquiries can be addressed at a time when customers are actively soliciting information. This allows companies to gather useful feedback. Positive information can be used in subsequent sales presentations and advertising efforts, while negative information can guide product improvements or changes in the marketing program. Trade shows also provide an ideal occasion to recruit dealers, distributors, and sales personnel. Although there is virtually no published research on the topic, one recent study provided evidence, albeit limited, that trade shows can enhance a company's sales and profits.[59]

Summary

This chapter presents the topic of trade-oriented sales promotions and describes its various widely used forms. As of 1997, trade-oriented sales promotions represented 50 percent of consumer packaged-good companies' promotional budgets. These programs perform a variety of objectives.

Trade allowances, or trade deals, are offered to retailers for performing activities that support the manufacturer's brand. Manufacturers find allowance promotions attractive for several reasons: They are easy to implement, can successfully stimulate initial distribution, are well accepted by the trade, and can increase trade purchases during the allowance period. However, two major disadvantages of buying allowances are that they: (1) often are not passed along by retailers to consumers and (2) may induce the trade to stockpile a product in order to take advantage of the temporary price reduction. This merely shifts business from the future to the present. Two prevalent practices in current business are forward buying and diverting. Another form of trade deal, called a slotting allowance, applies to new-product introductions. Manufacturers of grocery products typically are required to pay retailers a slotting fee for the right to have their product carried by the retailer. Exit fees, or deslotting charges, are assessed to manufacturers whose products do not achieve prearranged levels of sales volume.

To reduce forward buying and diverting, some manufacturers have revised their method of pricing products. Procter & Gamble is most notable in this regard for introducing what it calls value pricing, or what others refer to as everyday low pricing by a manufacturer, or EDLP(M). This method of pricing eliminates the historical practice of periodically offering attractive trade deals and instead charges the same low price at all times. Another major development in the grocery industry that is aimed at curtailing forward buying and diverting is the implementation of pay-for-performance programs, which also are called scanner-verified systems, or scan-downs. With this method of trade allowance, retailers are compensated for the amount of a manufacturer's brand that they sell to consumers, rather than according to how much they purchase from the manufacturer (as is the case with off-invoice allowances). Pay-for-performance programs and everyday low pricing are both part of the paradigm shift in the grocery industry known as efficient consumer response (ECR). Category management is another development that is designed to create better working relations between manufacturers and retailers and to increase efficiency in their relations.

Cooperative advertising and vendor support programs are trade promotions in which manufacturers and retailers jointly pay for the retailer's advertising that features the manufacturer's product. Co-op advertising is initiated by the manufacturer, whereas vendor support programs are initiated by retailers.

Trade contests and incentives encourage retailer performance by offering gifts for meeting sales goals or for performing certain tasks deemed important for the success of the sponsoring manufacturer's products. Push money is one form of trade incentive used to encourage special selling efforts from retail salespeople.

Specialty advertising is a hybrid form of marketing communications that uses articles of merchandise to carry a company's message to its target audience. Specialty advertising is a form of trade-oriented sales promotion when the audience consists of the manufacturer's distributors or other intermediate customers.

Trade shows are a final type of trade-oriented sales promotion. Thousands of companies in North America and Europe participate in trade shows each year. Specific functions of trade shows include: (1) servicing present customers, (2) identifying prospects, (3) introducing new or modified products, (4) gathering information about competitors' new products, (5) taking product orders, and (6) enhancing the company's image.

Discussion Questions

1. A number of retailers have explicit policies that prevent their managers or salespeople from receiving any form of incentives from manufacturers. Are these policies wise? Under what conditions

might manufacturer-sponsored incentives benefit the retail firm above and beyond their obvious material benefits for individual managers or salespeople?

2. Assume you are the marketing manager of a company that manufactures a line of paper products (tissues, napkins, etc.). Your current market share is 7 percent, and you are considering offering retailers an attractive bill-back allowance for giving your brand special display space. Comment on this promotion's chances for success.

3. Identify concepts in Chapter 12 ("Message Appeals and Endorsers in Advertising") that would be relevant to a furniture company's efforts to develop an effective exhibition at a trade show attended by major furniture retailers from around the country.

4. In your own words, explain the practices of forward buying and diverting. Also, describe the advantages and disadvantages of bill and hold programs.

5. Assume you are a buyer for a large supermarket chain and that you have been asked to speak to a group of marketing students at a nearby university. During the question-and-answer session following your comments, one student remarks: "My father works for a grocery-product manufacturer, and he says that slotting allowances are nothing more than a form of larceny!" How would you defend your company's practice to this student?

6. Explain why selling private brands often enables large retail chains to pocket trade deals instead of passing their reduced costs along to consumers in the form of lower product prices.

7. In your own words, explain why EDLP(M) pricing diminishes forward buying and diverting.

8. In your own words, discuss how pay-for-performance programs, or scan-downs, would, if widely implemented, virtually eliminate forward buying and diverting.

9. It is estimated that at least one-third of the billions of co-op advertising dollars offered by manufacturers go unspent. Why? What could a manufacturer do to encourage greater numbers of retailers to spend co-op dollars? Do you think some manufacturers may not want their retail customers to spend co-op funds?

10. In discussing open-ended co-op programs, the text stated that this type of cooperative advertising makes it possible to use advertising for generating sales rather than relying on sales to generate advertising. Explain precisely what this means.

11. You are the Midwest sales manager for a product line marketed by a large, highly respected national manufacturer. Most of your products hold market shares of 30 percent or higher. The promotion manager for a big midwestern grocery chain approaches you about a vendor support program his company is in the process of putting together. It will cost you $50,000 to participate. What would be the reasons for and against your participation? On balance, would it be in your company's long-term interest to participate in this or other VSPs?

12. Assume that you are the marketing director for a hospital located in your hometown or college/university community. Your birthing center is operating far below capacity, so your objective is to gain visibility for the center and greater usage. Design a specialty advertising program to accomplish this objective.

13. In your view, is stocklifting an unethical practice? Fully justify your response and be certain to explicitly detail the specific criteria you have applied in arriving at the determination that stocklifting is or isn't an unethical practice.

*I*nternet Exercise

Many businesses have attempted to establish a presence on the Internet "just in case" something revolutionary happens with e-commerce. Some retailers, on the other hand, have found that their revolution is now. Clothes, computer products, gourmet food, and books are just some of the products that are regularly turning profits. Some of these online retailers are simply a distribution system behind a virtual storefront (such as Dell computers, Amazon bookstores), whereas others also have physical stores (such as Gap and Barnes and Noble). Retailers with physical stores almost certainly have experience with trade promotions but it is not clear how trade promotions are evolving in virtual retailing, especially since many trade promotions are tied to physical shelving, displays, and activities.

Visit a favorite retailer on the Internet. Pretend that you are a manufacturer of a product that could be sold by this retailer. Fully describe how you could implement the following forms of trade allowances in the virtual retailing arena:

1. Bill-back allowances

2. Off-invoice allowances

3. Cooperative advertising

*C*hapter Seventeen Endnotes

1. Robert C. Blattberg and Alan Levin, "Modeling the Effectiveness and Profitablilty of Trade Promotions," *Marketing Science* 6 (spring 1987), 125.

2. These objectives are adapted from a consumer-promotion seminar conducted by Ennis Associates, Inc., and sponsored by the Association of National Advertisers, Inc. (New York, undated). See also Chakravarthi Narasimhan, "Managerial Perspectives on Trade and Consumer Promotions," *Marketing Letters* 1, no. 3 (1989), 239–251.

3. Don E. Schultz and William A. Robinson, *Sales Promotion Management* (Lincolnwood, Ill.: NTC Business Books, 1986), 265–266.

4. For further reading, see Kenneth G. Hardy, "Key Success Factors for Manufacturers' Sales Promotions in Package Goods," *Journal of Marketing* 50 (July 1986), 13–23.

5. Rajiv Lal, "Manufacturer Trade Deals and Retail Price Promotions," *Journal of Marketing Research* 27 (November 1990), 428–444.

6. Ronald C. Curhan and Robert J. Kopp, "Obtaining Retailer Support for Trade Deals: Key Success Factors," *Journal of Advertising Research* 27 (December 1987/January 1988), 51–60.

7. This study is by Cannondale Associates as reported in Christopher W. Hoyt, "You Cheated, You Lied," *Promo,* July 1997, 64.

8. Retailers designate each size and form of manufacturers' brands with specific SKU codes. For example, six packs of 12-ounce Coca-Cola cans and single one-liter Coke bottles represent two different SKUs.

9. Christopher W. Hoyt, "The Slotting Weevil," *Promo,* February 1997, 68.

10. For discussion of the legal issues surrounding the use of slotting allowances, see Joseph P. Cannon and Paul N. Bloom, "Are Slotting Allowances Legal under the Antitrust Laws?" *Journal of Public Policy and Marketing* 10, no. 1 (1991).

11. Julie Liesse, "Kodak Brand Calls Retreat in the Battery War," *Advertising Age,* October 15, 1990, 3, 69.

12. Karen Benezra, "Not Playing the Slots," *Brandweek,* March 27, 1995, 36.

13. This illustration is adapted from Zachary Schiller, "Not Everyone Loves a Supermarket Special," *Business Week,* February 17, 1992, 64.

14. Christopher W. Hoyt, "Retailers and Suppliers Are Still Miles Apart," *Promo,* February 1996, 49.

15. Ronald Alsop, "Retailers Buy Far in Advance to Exploit Trade Promotions," *The Wall Street Journal,* October 9, 1986, 37.

16. Robert D. Buzzell, John A. Quelch, and Walter J. Salmon, "The Costly Bargain of Trade Promotion," *Harvard Business Review* 68 (March/April 1990), 145.

17. Schiller, "Not Everyone Loves a Supermarket Special," 64.

18. Patricia Sellers, "The Dumbest Marketing Ploy," *Fortune,* October 5, 1992, 88.

19. Jon Berry, "Diverting," *Adweek's Marketing Week,* May 18, 1992, 20.

20. Hoyt, "Retailers and Suppliers Are Still Miles Apart."

21. Berry, "Diverting," 22.

22. Ibid.

23. Ibid.

24. An insightful demonstration of why trade promotions are unprofitable is provided in Magid M. Abraham and Leonard M. Lodish, "Getting the Most out of Advertising and Promotion," *Harvard Business Review* 68 (May/June 1990), 50–60.

25. For a fuller account of the ECR "movement," see Chapter 6 in Barbara E. Kahn and Leigh McAlister, *Grocery Revolution: The New Focus on the Consumer* (Reading, MA: Addison-Wesley, 1997).

26. *Category Management* (Northbrook, IL: Nielsen Marketing Research, 1992), 10.

27. The discussion is adapted from ibid., especially 112–121.

28. Ibid., 119.

29. For discussion of everyday low pricing by retailers, see Stephen J. Hoch, Xavier Dreze, and Mary E. Purk, "EDLP, Hi-Lo, and Margin Arithmetic," *Journal of Marketing* 58 (October 1994), 16–27.

30. Jack Neff, "Diaper Battle Puts EDLP on Injured List," *Advertising Age,* August 14, 1995, 3, 33.

31. Kenneth Craig Manning, "Development of a Theory of Retailer Response to Manufacturers' Everyday Low Cost Programs" (Ph.D. dissertation, University of South Carolina, 1994).

32. Christopher W. Hoyt, "More Cracks in the EDLP-ECR Marble," *Promo,* December 1993,

57. See also Hoch, Dreze, and Purk, "EDLP, Hi-Lo, and Margin Arithmetic."

33. Kerry E. Smith, "Scan Down, Pay Fast," *Promo,* January 1994, 58–59; "The Proof Is in the Scanning," *Promo,* February 1995, 15.

34. *Cox Direct 20th Annual Survey of Promotional Practices* (Largo, FL: Cox Direct, 1998), 50, 65.

35. Betsy Spethmann, "Wake Up and Smell the Co-Marketing," *Promo,* August 1998, 43–47.

36. Shantanu Dutta, Mark Bergen, George John, and Akshay Rao, "Variations in the Contractual Terms of Cooperative Advertising Contracts: An Empirical Investigation," *Marketing Letters* 6 (January 1995), 15.

37. The most frequently used rates of accrual are 2, 3, and 5 percent, with consumer-goods companies offering slightly higher accrual rates than industrial-goods companies. See ibid., 16–17.

38. The average payment share, or participation rate, is approximately 74 percent for consumer-goods companies and 69 percent for industrial-goods companies according to Dutta et al., "Variations in the Contractual Terms of Cooperative Advertising Contracts . . ."

39. Stephen A. Greyser and Robert F. Young, "Follow 11 Guidelines to Strategically Manage Co-op Advertising Program," *Marketing News,* September 16, 1983, 5.

40. *Newspaper Rate Differentials 1987* (New York: American Association of Advertising Agencies, 1988).

41. Martin Everett, "Co-op Advertising and Computers," *Sales and Marketing Management,* May 1987, 56.

42. Renee Blakkan, "Savory Deals Tempt Hungry Retailers," *Advertising Age,* March 7, 1983, M11.

43. Ibid.

44. Ed Crimmins, "Why Open-Ended Co-op Is on the Rise," *Sales and Marketing Management,* December 1986, 64, 67.

45. Ed Crimmins, "Dispelling the Hype of 'Vendor Support,'" *Sales and Marketing Management,* December 9, 1985, 54–57.

46. "Almay Catches the Wave with Wetproof Mascara," *Adweek's Marketing Week,* March 25, 1991, 26, 28.

47. Success Stories: 30 Award-Winning Specialty Advertising Promotions from the 34th Annual Golden Pyramid Competition (Irving, Texas: Specialty Advertising Association International, 1992), inside front cover.

48. "Where Merchandise Carries the Message," *Promo's 5th Annual Sourcebook,* 1998, 15.

49. Ibid.

50. "The Case for Specialty Advertising," Specialty Advertising Association International, Irving, Texas, undated. See also Dan S. Bagley III, Understanding Specialty Advertising (Irving, Texas: Specialty Advertising Association International, 1990).

51. Richard G. Ebel, "Specialties: Gifts of Motivation," *Marketing Communications,* April 1986, 75–80.

52. Success Stories: 25 Award-Winning Specialty Advertising Promotions (Irving, TX: Specialty Advertising Association International, 1988), 15.

53. Success Stories: 30 Award-Winning Specialty Advertising Promotions from the 34th Annual Golden Pyramid Competition, 6.

54. The trade show is not strictly a form of sales promotion. It, nonetheless, is appropriate to discuss trade shows in context of sales promotions inasmuch as trade shows, like certain forms of sales promotions, provide an extremely effective mechanism for assisting customers in learning about and trying new products.

55. These estimates are from the Center for Exhibition Industry Research as published in Dale D. Buss, "Cashing in on Trade Shows," *Nation's Business,* November 1996, 21.

56. Srinath Gopalakrishna, Gary L. Lilien, Jerome D. Williams, and Ian K. Sequeira, "Do Trade Shows Pay Off?" *Journal of Marketing* 59 (July 1995), 75. For discussion of trade shows in the U.K., see Jim Blythe, "Does Size Matter?—Objectives and Measures at UK Trade Exhibitions," *Journal of Marketing Communications* 3 (March 1997), 51–59. For comparison between trade shows in the U.K. and U.S., see Marnik G. Dekimpe, Pierre Francois, Srinath Gopalakrishna, Gary L. Lilien, and Christophe Van den Bulte, "Generalizing About Trade Show Effectiveness: A Cross-National Comparison," *Journal of Marketing* 61 (October 1997), 65–73.

57. Cyndee Miller, "Marketing Industry Report: Who's Spending What on Biz-to-Biz Marketing," *Marketing News,* January 1, 1996, 1.

58. Roger A. Kerin and William L. Cron, "Assessing Trade Show Functions and Performance," *Journal of Marketing* 51 (July 1987), 88.

59. Gopalakrishna et al., "Do Trade Shows Pay Off?" 75–83.

Consumer-Oriented Promotions

CHAPTER OBJECTIVES

After studying this chapter, you should be able to:

1. Describe the objectives of consumer-oriented sales promotions.
2. Recognize that many forms of promotions perform different objectives for marketers.
3. Explain the role of sampling, the various types of sampling, and the trends in sampling practice.
4. Explain the role of couponing, the various types of coupons, and the developments in couponing practice.
5. Understand the coupon redemption process and misredemption.
6. Explain the role of premiums, the various types of premiums, and the developments in premium practice.
7. Describe the role of price-off promotions and bonus packages.
8. Discuss the role of rebates and refund offers.
9. Explain the differences between contests and sweepstakes, and the reasons for using each form of promotion.
10. Understand the role of continuity programs.
11. Appreciate the growth of Internet promotions.
12. Evaluate the potential effectiveness of sales promotion ideas.

Opening Vignette: Promotional Disasters

Consumer-oriented promotions are sometimes incredibly successful and generate huge increases in short-term sales. However, achieving success requires careful planning and tight coordination with other aspects of a marketing program. Inadequate forethought leads occasionally to promotional disasters, as typified by the following illustrations.

Hoover Vacuum Cleaners in Britain and Ireland. Maytag Corp., the maker of Hoover vacuum cleaners, developed a promotion to increase vacuum cleaner sales to British and Irish consumers. The promotion offered consumers a pair of round-trip tickets to destinations in Europe or the United States, with the only requirement being that one must purchase a new Hoover cleaner selling in the price range $150 to $375. Guess what most consumers did? You got it; they purchased bottom-of-the line models of Hoover vacuum cleaners. The cost of the free tickets barely offset the revenue generated. Maytag intended to finance the cost of the promotion by earning commissions when consumers booked car rentals and hotel reservations with their flights. However, there was a bigger-than-expected response rate to the promotion, which created major fulfillment problems, and a smaller-than-expected booking of car rentals and hotel reservations. In the final

analysis, the Maytag Corp. suffered from deep consumer discontent and lost, according to one estimate, $49 million from this promotion!

Pepsi-Cola in the Philippines. A Pepsi bottler in the Philippines offered a one million peso grand prize (which, at the time, was approximately equivalent to $36,000) to holders of bottle caps with the number 349 printed on them. To the bottler's (and Pepsi-Co's) great chagrin, a computer error (by the printer that produced the game numbers) created 500,000 bottle caps with the winning number 349 imprinted—making PepsiCo liable for approximately $18 billion! The botched promotion created mayhem for PepsiCo, including attacks on Pepsi trucks and bottling plants and anti-Pepsi rallies. Pepsi's sales plummeted in the Philippines, and market share fell by nine points. To resolve the problem, PepsiCo paid consumers with winning caps $19 apiece. More than 500,000 Filipinos collected about $10 million. The Filipino justice department excused PepsiCo from criminal liability and dismissed thousands of lawsuits. PepsiCo has since implemented procedures for preventing future disasters such as this.

Sloggies Pantyhose in Australia. The makers of Sloggies pantyhose ran a promotion that offered women a free night at a Best Western hotel with submission of a proof of purchase from Sloggies packages. The purchase of pantyhose and corresponding requests for free rooms were overwhelming. Women immediately called to book their free night at Best Western hotels in Australia. But because only 30 Best Western hotels existed at the time in all of Australia, thousands of consumers were told that their free night would not be available for months or even years. Consumer dissatisfaction was rampant and brand equity suffered serious damage.

Sources: The Hoover and Sloggies cases are adapted from Annie Smith, "Learning from the Mistakes of Others," Special report from *Promo* magazine, August 1998, S8–S9. The Pepsi debacle is adapted from Glenn Heitsmith, "Botched Pepsi Promotion Prompts Terrorist Attacks," *Promo,* September 1993, 10.

INTRODUCTION

*T*his chapter discusses the many consumer-oriented sales promotions that are part of the brand manager's arsenal when attempting to influence desired behaviors from present and prospective customers. Building on the base developed in Chapter 16, this chapter focuses exclusively on consumer-oriented promotions. It describes the unique character of each promotion technique and explains the specific objectives each is intended to accomplish.

Before proceeding, it is appropriate to reiterate some advice that was provided in Chapter 2 and repeated in Chapter 9. That guidance involved the relations among target, objectives, and budgets and was summarized in the form of the following mantra:

> *All marketing communications should be (1) designed with a particular **target market** in mind, (2) created to achieve a specific **objective**, and (3) undertaken to accomplish the objective toward the target market **within budget constraint.***

This counsel when considered in context of strategy formulation and decision making about consumer promotions simply advises that the target market is the starting point for all decisions. With a clear target in mind, the brand manager is in a position then to specify intelligently the objective a particular promotion program is supposed to accomplish. The manager also must work diligently to assure that promotion spending does not exceed the budget constraint. This is the challenge that brand managers face when using consumer-oriented promotions to achieve strategic objectives.

Marketer Objectives and Consumer Rewards

What objectives do marketers hope to accomplish by using consumer-oriented promotions? Why do consumers respond to coupons, contests, sweepstakes, and other promotional efforts? Answers to these interrelated questions constitute the core of this chapter.

Marketer Objectives. As discussed in Chapter 16, marketers use promotions to accomplish various objectives. Three general categories of objectives include: (1) generating trial purchases, (2) encouraging repeat purchases, and (3) reinforcing brand images.

Some sales promotions (such as samples and coupons) are used primarily for *trial impact.* A manufacturer employs these promotional tools to prompt nonusers to try a brand for the first time or to encourage retrial for prior users who have not purchased the brand for perhaps an extended period. At other times, manufacturers use promotions to hold onto their current customer base by rewarding them for continuing to purchase the promoted brand or loading them with a stockpile of the manufacturer's brand so they have no need, at least in the short run, to switch to another brand. This is sales promotions' *repeat-purchase objective.* Sales promotions also can be used for *image reinforcement* purposes. For example, the careful selection of the right premium object or appropriate sweepstakes prize can serve to bolster a brand's image.

Consumer Rewards. Consumers would not be responsive to sales promotions unless there was something in it for them—and, in fact, there is. All promotion techniques provide consumers with *rewards* (incentives or inducements) that encourage certain forms of behavior desired by marketers. Rewards are typically in the form of cash savings or free gifts. Sometimes rewards are immediate, while at other times they are delayed.

An *immediate reward* is one that delivers the savings or gift as soon as the consumer performs a marketer-specified behavior. For example, you receive cash savings at the time you redeem a coupon; pleasure is obtained immediately when you try a free food item or beverage. *Delayed rewards* are those that follow the behavior by a period of days, weeks, or even longer. For example, you may have to wait weeks before a free-in-the-mail premium item can be enjoyed. Generally speaking, consumers are more responsive to immediate than delayed rewards. Of course, this is in line with the natural human preference for immediate gratification.

Classification of Sales Promotion Methods

It is insightful to consider each consumer-oriented sales promotion technique in terms of its marketing objective simultaneously with its consumer reward. Table 18.1 presents a six-cell typology that was constructed by cross-classifying the two forms of consumer rewards with the three objectives for using promotions.

Cell 1 includes three sales promotion techniques—samples, instant coupons, and shelf-delivered coupons—that encourage trial purchase behavior by providing consumers with an immediate reward. The reward is either monetary savings, in the case of instant coupons, or a free product, in the case of samples. Media- and mail-delivered coupons, free-in-the-mail premiums, and scanner-delivered coupons—all found in cell 2—are techniques that generate consumer trial yet delay the reward.

Cells 3 and 4 contain promotional tools that are intended to encourage repeat purchasing from consumers. Marketing communicators design these techniques to reward a brand's existing customers and to keep them from switching to competitive brands—or, in other words, to encourage repeat purchasing. Immediate reward tools, in cell 3, include price-offs, bonus packs, and in-, on-, and near-pack premiums. Delayed reward techniques, in cell 4, involve in- and on-pack coupons, refund and rebate offers, phone cards, and continuity programs.

Building a brand's image is primarily the task of advertising; however, sales promotion tools may support advertising efforts by reinforcing a brand's image. By nature, these techniques are incapable of providing consumers with an immediate reward; therefore, cell 5 is empty. Cell 6 contains self-liquidating premiums and two promotional tools, contests and sweepstakes, that can (if designed appropriately) reinforce or even strengthen a brand's image in addition to performing other tasks.

Points of Qualification. Before proceeding, it is important to emphasize that the classification of promotional tools in Table 18.1 is necessarily simplified. First, Table 18.1 classifies each technique with respect to the *primary* objective it is designed to accomplish. It is important to recognize, however, that promotions are capable of accomplishing more than a single objective. For example, bonus packs (cell 3) are classified as encouraging repeat purchasing, but first-time triers also occasionally purchase brands that offer extra

TABLE 18.1 — **Major Consumer-Oriented Forms of Sales Promotions**

CONSUMER REWARD	MARKETER'S OBJECTIVE		
	Generating Trial Purchases	**Encouraging Repeat Purchases**	**Reinforcing Brand Image**
Immediate	**(1)** ◆ Sampling ◆ Instant coupons ◆ Shelf-delivered coupons	**(3)** ◆ Price-offs ◆ Bonus packs ◆ In-, on-, and near-pack premiums	**(5)**
Delayed	**(2)** ◆ Media- and mail-delivered coupons ◆ Free-in-the-mail premiums ◆ Scanner-delivered coupons	**(4)** ◆ In- and on-pack coupons ◆ Rebates/Refunds ◆ Phone cards ◆ Continuity Programs	**(6)** ◆ Self-liquidating premiums ◆ Contests and sweepstakes

volume. The various forms of coupons located in cells 1 and 2 are designed primarily to encourage triers and to attract switchers from other brands, but in actuality these coupons often are redeemed by current purchasers. In other words, though intended to encourage trial purchasing and switching, coupons also invite repeat purchasing.

Second, the tools in Table 18.1 are categorized under the primary objective each is designed to accomplish *toward consumers*. It is important to recognize, however, that manufacturers use consumer-oriented sales promotions also to *leverage trade support*. For example, when a manufacturer informs retailers that a certain brand will be sampled during a designated period, the manufacturer is virtually assured that retailers will purchase extra quantities of that brand and possibly provide extra display space. In other words, consumer-oriented promotions can influence trade behavior as well as consumer action.

Finally, note that two techniques, coupons and premiums, are found in more than one cell. This is because these techniques achieve different objectives depending on the specific form of delivery vehicle. Coupons delivered through the media (newspapers and magazines) or in the mail offer a form of delayed reward, whereas instant coupons that are peeled from a package at the point of purchase offer an immediate reward. Similarly, premium objects that are delivered in, on, or near a product's package provide an immediate reward, while those requiring mail delivery yield a reward only after some delay.

SAMPLING

www.heinz.com

The baby-food division of Heinz foods developed a rather revolutionary product idea: a powdered, instant baby food. Although Heinz's management was optimistic about instant baby food, they knew consumers would resist trying the product because of a natural inertia regarding dramatic product shifts and the fear of treating their babies as guinea pigs for a new product. A further complication was the difficulty of communicating the product's benefits by advertising alone. Heinz needed a way to persuade mothers to try instant baby food. The solution was to employ the services of a company that specializes in delivering samples to mothers of newborn infants. This form of sampling avoided waste distribution and gave mothers firsthand experience with preparing and feeding their babies instant food. Many samplers became loyal users.[1]

This case illustrates the power of sampling as a promotional technique. Most practitioners agree that sampling is the *premier sales-promotion device for generating trial usage*. In fact, some observers believe that sample distribution is almost a necessity when introducing *truly* new products.

By definition, **sampling** includes any method used to deliver an actual- or trial-sized product to consumers. Over 80 percent of manufacturers use sampling as part of their consumer promotion mix for purposes of generating trial or retrial and to leverage trade support.[2] Marketers in the United States invest over $1 billion annually on product sampling.[3]

Marketers deliver samples either alone (*solo* sampling) or in cooperation with other brands (*co-op* sampling). A variety of sample-distribution methods are available:

♦ *Direct mail.* Samples are mailed directly to households targeted by demographic characteristics or in terms of geodemographics (as discussed in Chapter 4). Figure 18.1 is an advertisement for a company (Larry Tucker Targeted Co-op Mailings) that specializes in this form of sample distribution. The figure describes the merits of targeting samples via direct mail. Figure 18.2 (for Crest Multi-Care toothpaste) illustrates how direct mail was used effectively by Procter & Gamble to introduce consumers to this brand. The two foil packets allow separate consumers in the same household to try the new mint-flavored toothpaste.

FIGURE 18.1

Direct Mail Sampling

Street Smart Sampling

Not this house. **Not this house.** **This house.**

Demographically Targeted
With Larry Tucker demographically targeted sampling, you zero in on just the households you want.

That's right! Specific households. Not entire neighborhoods or costly carrier routes. But individual families with a common demographic profile and a high interest in your product category.

Direct Mail Delivered
In fact, we deliver more people in certain demographic segments

than any other medium available. Like adults 50 to 64 (17.5 million households). Or families with young kids (7.5 million households). Or 65 to 75 year olds (7.5 million households).

Which means you reach more people who count. Without paying for the people who don't.

Solo Impact at Co-op Rates
Best of all, your sample will be the only one in the mailing. So you get the impact of solo

sampling at a fraction of the cost of solo mail.

We deliver over 2.5 billion samples, coupons and other offers every year. We can do this because we have our own mailing facility. Don't be fooled. Some co-op mailers don't. And it's a must in the world of sampling.

Find out how affordable street smart sampling is. Call 201-307-8888. Or fax us at 201-307-1200.

Larry Tucker Targeted Co-op Mailings
America's largest targeted co-op program

FIGURE 18.2

Illustration of a Sample Distributed via Direct Mail

♦ *Newspapers and magazines.* Samples often are included in magazines and newspapers. The Sunday newspaper is an increasingly attractive medium for broad-scale sampling, especially when considering that over 60 million American households get a Sunday newspaper. Figure 18.3 is an advertisement from a company (Valassis Communications, Inc.) that offers various formats (including plastic pouches as shown in the figure) for delivering samples via the newspaper.

♦ *Door to door by special distribution crews.* Figure 18.4 provides some information about a company (Impact Media) that offers nationwide delivery of door-to-door samples. Inspection of Figure 18.4 reveals that this form of sampling allows considerable targeting and possesses advantages such as lower cost than in-store or direct-mail sampling and short lead times (between the time a sampling

Newspaper Sampling

FIGURE 18.4

Door-to-Door Sampling

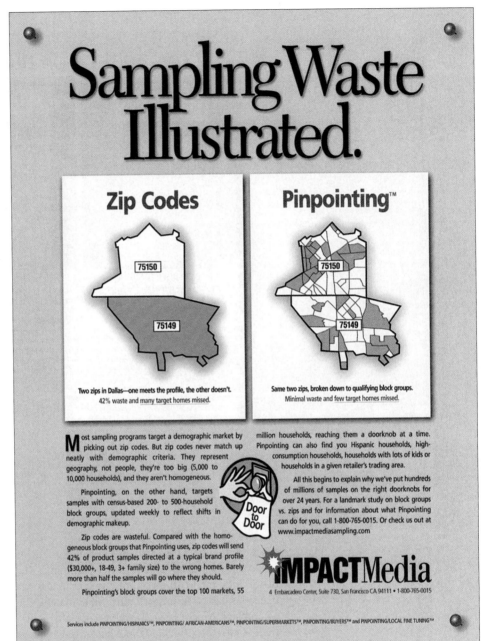

request is made and performed). Companies like Impact Media that specialize in door-to-door sampling target household selection to fit the client's needs. For example, samples can be distributed just in Hispanic neighborhoods if that is the client's desire.

www.impactmedia.com

♦ *On- or in-pack sampling.* This method uses the package of another product to serve as the sample carrier. Figure 18.5 is an advertisement from a company called Co-op Promotions that specializes in this form of promotion. The ad indicates, for example, that Nuprin pain reliever was sampled in Ace bandages.

♦ *High-traffic locations.* Shopping centers, movie theaters, airports, or special events offer forums for sample distribution. More will be said about this form of sampling when later discussing creative forms of sampling.

On- or In-Pack Sampling

◆ *In-store sampling.* Demonstrators provide product samples in grocery stores and other retail outlets for trial while consumers are shopping. It is understandable that in-store is the most frequent form of sampling when considering that this distribution mode offers samples to consumers where and when their purchase decisions can be influenced most immediately.[4] Figure 18.6 is an advertisement by a company (MarketSource) whose specialty is in-store sampling. Note in the figure that a store such as Blockbuster is a venue for sampling to all family members, that Toys 'R' Us is an appropriate outlet for reaching moms and kids, the Medicine Shoppe is a suitable outlet for distributing samples to mature consumers, and so forth.

Sampling Trends

Three major trends have evolved in conjunction with the renewed use of sampling: increased targeting, innovative distribution methods, and efforts to measure sampling's return on investment.

Increased Targeting. Sampling services that specialize in precision distribution (targeting) have emerged in recent years. The distribution of Heinz baby food to mothers of newborns is one example. Another form of targeting is delivering samples to consumers who are either product nonusers or users of competitive brands. The Gillette Company mailed 400,000 Sensor razors to men who use competitive wet razors.

In-Store Sampling

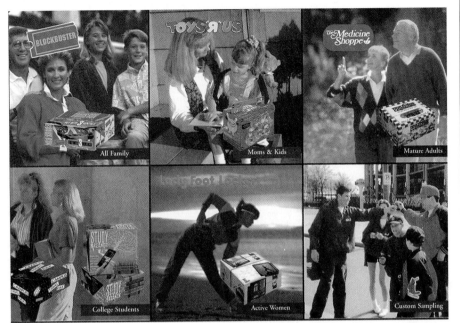

All Family | Moms & Kids | Mature Adults

College Students | Active Women | Custom Sampling

SAMPLING THAT CAN'T BE MISSED

MarketSource Sampling Programs				
Program	**Target**	**Distribution**	**Reach**	**Timing**
• Early Return Bonus	All Family	Blockbuster Video	12MM	Winter/Spring, Summer/Fall
• Bonus Pack	Youth Aged 15-35	Blockbuster Music	700M	May, September
• Body & Soul	Active Women	Lady Foot Locker	750M	May, October
• PrimeTime®	Mature Adults	The Medicine Shoppe	1MM	October
• Diabetes Lifestyle	Consumers w/Diabetes	The Medicine Shoppe	300M	November
• 'R' Treat®	Moms & Kids	Toys 'R' Us	2MM	October
• Baby Registry Bundle	Expectant Mothers	Babies 'R' Us	500M	September-December
• Campus Trial Pak®	College Students	College Stores	2.5MM	August-September
• Study Breaker®	College Students	College Dorms	1.2MM	October
• WhatNext™	High School Students	High Schools	2MM	October
• In-market Sampling	Any Audience	Any Venue	TBD	TBD

MarketSource helps brand managers reach nearly 50 million consumers each year with award-winning sampling programs. Our cooperative programs include integrated promotions to reach targeted consumers through America's leading retailers. We also provide fully customized programs to reach any target audience at any venue. And in all cases, we provide turnkey programs with strict distribution controls – including our own packing and shipping facility. Call Debbi Cheezum at 1-800-888-8108 (609-655-8990 in New Jersey) for more information.

MarketSource
10 Abeel Rd., Cranbury, NJ 08512
Phone: 609-655-8990   Fax: 609-395-0737

How would you reach high-school males? This is one of the most inaccessible markets because they are not particularly heavy television viewers or magazine readers. MarketSource developed a program that reached teenage males by distributing gift packages of product samples (such as shaving cream, razors, mouthwash, and candy) at tuxedo-rental shops. Recipients picked up their sample pack when they arranged to rent a prom tuxedo.[5]

Suppose you wanted to reach young children with free samples. Where would you gain access to this group? Distributors hand out sample packs at stores such as Toys 'R' Us.[6] One sampling executive describes the advantage of this form of targeting sampling in these terms:

When you're giving your product to customers in Toys 'R' Us, you can bet with 99 percent accuracy you're reaching families with children under 12 or grandparents with grandchildren that age. You don't have that kind of certainty of reach with other [forms of marketing communications].[7]

Targeting inner-city residents with samples is problematic due to the fact that around 30 percent of inner-city mailboxes are broken at any particular time, according to Lafayette Jones, president of a company that specializes in delivering samples to African-Americans and Hispanics.[8] What is Mr. Jones' solution? His company has established a network of approximately 7,000 African-American and Hispanic churches through which samples are distributed. Ministers in these churches often present sample bags to members of the congregation.

www.benadryl.com

A final illustration of targeted sampling involves the distribution of an anti-itch cream named Benadryl. Warner-Lambert, makers of Benadryl, wanted to develop a sampling program that would reach victims of itching caused by mosquito bites, heat rash, poison ivy, and so on. The objective was to contact prospective consumers at "point-of-itch" locations where they would be most receptive to learning about the virtues of Benadryl. The company considered sampling outside retailers' lawn and garden departments, but eliminated that prospect as not quite satisfying its point-of-itch objective. It eventually came up with the clever idea of sampling at KOA Kampsites—locations where people camp, enjoy the outdoors, and . . . itch. Twenty-five million people visit KOA sites every year. During a two-summer period in the late 1990s, Warner-Lambert distributed 6 million Benadryl samples to 550 campsites, thereby achieving effective and cost-efficient sample distribution.[9]

Creative Distribution Methods. Companies are applying numerous creative ways to get sample merchandise into the hands of targeted consumers. United Artists Entertainment, the largest theater chain in the United States with about 2,500 screens in over 500 locations, has an in-theater sampling program that distributes over 9 million samples during a four-week cycle.[10] One company distributed samples of Chunky candy bars to consumers stuck in rush-hour traffic.[11]

Progresso Soup, marketed by the Pillsbury Co., employed a fleet of "Soupermen" to deliver cups of hot soup from backpack dispensers to consumers in cold-weather cities such as Cleveland, Chicago, Detroit, and Pittsburgh (see Figure 18.7). From October through March, sampling teams visited consumers in these cities at sporting events, races, outdoor shows, and other locales—all of which represented ideal locations for getting consumers to try cups of hot Progresso soup.[12]

www.progressosoup.com

FIGURE 18.7

Progresso Soup Sampling

Guinness Trailer Sampling

Guinness Import Co. sampled its unique beer using tractor trailers each equipped with dozens of taps (see Figure 18.8). These trailers travel to Irish musical festivals in cities such as New York, Chicago, and San Francisco. According to a company spokesman, Guinness invested in the trailers because it regards hands-on sampling at special events as a good opportunity to create a unique brand-usage experience and to avoid the clutter of mass-media advertising.[13]

The *IMC Focus* describes a final example of creative sampling.

Estimating Return on Investment. As previously noted when discussing advertising, marketing communicators are increasingly being held accountable for their decisions. Financial officers, senior marketing executives, and chief executives are demanding evidence that investments in advertising and promotions can be justified by the profits they return. Return on investment (ROI) is a tool that can be used to assess whether an investment in a sampling program is cost justified. Table 18.2 lays out the straightforward steps in applying an ROI analysis to a sampling investment.[14]

How Effective Is Sampling?

www.npd.com

How effective is sampling in influencing trial purchase behavior? What influence does it have on stimulating repeat purchase behavior? NPD Research, Inc., a firm that collects data from a panel of over 30,000 households that maintain continuous diaries of packaged-goods purchases, has shed light on these questions. Their composite results for eight brands show that of the households who did not receive free samples (the control group), an average of about 11 percent made trial purchases of the eight brands. By comparison, 16 percent of the recipients of free samples made trial purchases. Moreover, nearly 36 percent of the families who made purchases after receiving a sample repurchased the brand,

IMC FOCUS: SAMPLING MARIE CALLENDER FROZEN FOODS

West of the Rocky Mountains in the United States, Marie Callender is a name well known for homestyle restaurants. The positive brand equity of the Marie Callender name encouraged ConAgra Frozen Foods, a major food producer, to acquire rights to use the Marie Callender name for branding a line of frozen meals, entrees, and pot pies. The line of frozen foods under the Marie Callender name performed well in Western markets, but in the Midwest and Eastern markets sales were sluggish, because the Marie Callender name in these markets had no pre-established brand equity like it had in the West. ConAgra decided it would have to aggressively sample Marie Callender frozen foods to establish the name and generate trade and consumer enthusiasm.

ConAgra developed a clever way to sample its line of Marie Callender frozen foods. Old Airstream trailers were purchased and converted into retro Marie Callender's Mobile Diners. The trailers were sent to six markets: Chicago, Detroit, Grand Rapids, Milwaukee, Pittsburgh, and New England. Samples of meatloaf and gravy with mashed potatoes and fettucine with chicken and broccoli were distributed to over 100,000 consumers in these markets. Live radio broadcasts and in-store point-of-purchase banners announced the Diner visits. As a result of the sampling program, key retail accounts in the six-market area ordered ConAgra's Marie Callender frozen foods and consumers demonstrated their receptiveness to this new brand through their trial and repeat purchases.

Source: Adapted from Stephanie Thompson, "Mobile Marie," *Brandweek*, March 2, 1998, R11.

whereas only 32 percent of the control-group triers repurchased.[15] These results are particularly interesting because they run somewhat contrary to experimental research, which has detected a tendency for sampling to diminish repeat purchasing.[16] Research involving Frito-Lay's sampling of its Sunchips brand determined, however, that there was no difference in the repeat purchase rate for people who were given the brand compared to those who bought it without a prior sample.[17]

TABLE 18.2 Calculating the ROI for a Sampling Investment

◆ **Step 1:** The first determination is the *total cost* of sampling, which includes the cost of the sample goods plus the costs of distribution—mailing, door-to-door distribution, and so on. Assume, for example, that the cost of distributing a trial-sized unit is $0.60 and that 15,000,000 units are distributed; hence, the total cost is $9 million.

◆ **Step 2:** The next step is to calculate the *profit per unit*. This is accomplished by determining the average number of annual uses of the product and multiplying this by the per-unit profit. Assume, for example, that on average six units of the sampled product are purchased per year and that the profit per unit is $1. Thus, each user promises the company a profit potential of $6 when they become users of the sampled brand.

◆ **Step 3:** The next step is to calculate the *number of converters* that are needed for the sampling program to break even. (Converters are individuals who after sampling a brand become users.) Given the cost of the sampling program ($9 million) and the profit potential per user ($6), the number of conversions needed in this case to break even is 1,500,000 (i.e., $9 million divided by $6). This number represents a 10 percent conversion rate just to break even (i.e., 1,500,000 divided by 15,000,000).

◆ **Step 4:** For a sampling to be successful, the conversion rate must exceed the break-even rate with gains in the 10 to 16 percent range. In this case, this would mean a minimum of 1,650,000 people must become users after trying the sampled brand (i.e., 1,500,000 times 1.1) to justify the sampling cost and yield a reasonable profit from the sampling investment.

In sum, there absolutely is no doubt that sampling is an effective stimulant to trial purchasing. However, no single answer is possible regarding the matter of whether sampling increases or decreases repeat purchase behavior. As always, the answer depends on the specific circumstances of the situation. All that can be said is that the impact of sampling on repeat purchase behavior probably is moderated by the quality of the sampled product. In other words, if consumers sample a new product and learn that it is demonstrably superior to alternatives on the market, it stands to reason that the sample-use experience will facilitate further purchasing. If, on the other hand, the product is found wanting in quality or has no relative advantage, sampling is likely to have no effect on subsequent purchasing or, in the worst case, may retard repeat purchasing.

When Should Sampling Be Used?

Promotion managers use sampling to induce consumers to try either a brand that is new or one that is moving into a different market. While it is important to encourage trial usage for new brands, sampling is not appropriate for all new or improved products. Ideal circumstances include the following:[18]

1. Sampling should be used when a new or improved brand is either *demonstrably superior* to other brands or when it has *distinct relative advantages* over brands that it is intended to replace. If a brand does not possess superiority or distinct advantages, it probably is not economically justifiable to give it away. Marketing executives at Procter & Gamble thought their new Jif Smooth Sensations line— which consists of three varieties of peanut butter blended with chocolate, apple cinnamon, and berry—had distinct advantages that would appeal to children and their parents once they tasted the new product. Sampling was ideal for this purpose.[19]

   www.pg.com

2. Sampling should be used when the product concept is so innovative that it is *difficult to communicate by advertising alone.* The earlier example of Heinz instant baby food illustrates this point. In general, sampling enables consumers to learn about product advantages that marketers would have difficulty convincing them of via advertising alone. Procter & Gamble sampled its new line of olestra-made FatFree Pringles to lunchtime crowds in 20 major cities. The brand management team knew that consumers had to taste for themselves that this fat-free version of Pringles tasted virtually the same as regular Pringles chips.[20]

3. Sampling should be used when promotional budgets *can afford to generate consumer trial quickly.* If generating quick trial is not essential, then cheaper trial-impacting promotional tools should be considered.

Sampling Problems

There are several problems with the use of sampling. First, sampling is expensive. Second, mass mailings of samples can be mishandled by the postal service or other distributors. Third, samples distributed door to door or in high-traffic locations may suffer from wasted distribution and not reach the hands of the best potential customers. Fourth, in- or on-package sampling excludes consumers who do not buy the carrying brand. Fifth, in-store sampling often fails to reach sufficient numbers of consumers to justify its expense.

A sixth problem with samples is that they may be misused by consumers. Consider the case of Sun Light dishwashing liquid, a product of Lever Brothers. This product, which smells like lemons and contains 10 percent lemon juice, was extensively sampled some years ago to more than 50 million households. Nearly 80 adults and children became ill after consuming the product, having mistaken the dishwashing liquid for lemon juice!

According to a Lever Brothers' marketing research director, there is always a potential problem of misuse when a product is sent to homes rather than purchased with prior product knowledge at a supermarket.[21]

A final sampling problem, pilferage, can result when samples are distributed in the mail. A case in point occurred in Poland shortly after the Iron Curtain separating eastern from western Europe was literally and symbolically demolished with the fall of communist hegemony in the east. Procter & Gamble mailed 580,000 samples of Vidal Sassoon Wash & Go shampoo to consumers in Poland, the first ever mass mailing of free samples in that country. The mailing was a big hit—so big, in fact, that about 2,000 mailboxes were broken into. The shampoo samples, although labeled "Not for sale," turned up on open markets and were in high demand at a price of 60 cents each. P&G paid nearly $40,000 to the Polish Post, Poland's mail service, to deliver the samples. In addition to the cost of distribution, P&G paid thousands more to have mailboxes repaired.[22]

Due to its expense and because of waste and other problems, the use of sampling fell out of favor for a period of time as many marketers turned to less-expensive promotions, especially couponing. However, with the development of creative solutions and innovations, promotion managers have again become enthusiastic about sampling. Sampling has become more efficient in reaching specific target groups, its results are readily measurable, and the rising costs of media advertising have increased its relative attractiveness.

C OUPONING

A **coupon** is a promotional device that provides cents-off savings to consumers upon its redemption. Coupons are delivered through newspapers, magazines, free-standing inserts, direct mail, in or on packages, and, increasingly, at the point of purchase by package-, shelf-, and electronic-delivery devices. It is important to appreciate the fact that not all delivery methods have the same objective. Instant coupons (that is, those that can be peeled from packages at the point of purchase) provide immediate rewards to consumers and encourage trial purchases as well as repeat buying from loyal consumers. Mail- and media-delivered coupons delay the reward, although they also generate trial purchase behavior. Before discussing these specific coupon delivery modes in detail, it first will be instructive to examine pertinent developments in coupon usage.

Couponing Developments

Background. In 1970, marketers in the United States distributed fewer than 17 billion coupons.[23] The number had increased to nearly 143 billion coupons by 1983.[24] Roughly a decade later, couponing in the United States reached its peak with 327 billion coupons distributed in 1994.[25] Since that time there has been a reduction in the use of coupons. Nonetheless, approximately 276 billion coupons were distributed in 1997.[26] The decrease in couponing has resulted not from diminished marketer interest in this promotional tool but rather is attributable to the fact that marketers have become more adept at targeting coupons to specific consumer groups.

www.gm.com

Virtually all packaged-goods marketers issue coupons. The use of coupons is not, however, restricted to packaged goods. For example, General Motors Corp. mailed coupons valued at $500 or $1,000 to its past customers in hopes of encouraging them to purchase new cars. The Ford Motor Company quickly retaliated by offering to honor GM coupons.[27] Figure 18.9 represents a $400 offer from General Motors to recent college graduates toward the purchase or lease of select GM vehicles. Although referred to as a "certificate," this offer is

FIGURE 18.9

Coupon Offer from
General Motors

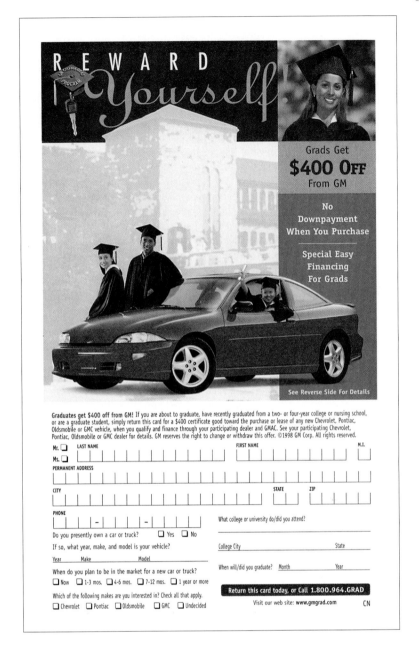

no different than the 75-cent coupon used by a consumer packaged-good company to encourage purchasing of an inexpensive brand.

Surveys indicate that virtually all American consumers (99 percent) use coupons at least on occasion, and that almost all (93 percent) say that they like coupons "somewhat" or "very much."[28] However, research has established that consumers vary greatly in terms of their psychological inclination to use coupons, and that this coupon proneness is predictive of actual coupon redemption behavior.[29]

The appeal of coupons is not limited to American consumers. A major international study found that consumers in every country included in the survey valued coupons. Although vastly more coupons are distributed in the United States than elsewhere, redemption rates (the percentage of all distributed coupons that are taken to stores for price discounts) are higher in most other countries.[30] However, couponing in some countries is virtually nonexistent or in the fledgling stage. For example, in Germany the government

GLOBAL FOCUS: THE USE OF COUPONS BY THE JAPANESE GOVERNMENT

The Japanese economy has been stagnant for several years after recession struck that economy around 1997. The lack of vitality in the Japanese economy is due in part to the Japanese people's pessimism about the economy as well as their penchant for saving a higher percentage of their incomes in comparison to consumers in the United States and other high-powered economies. In hopes of increasing consumer spending, the government initiated massive tax cuts, but the effect was minimal. Trillions of yen were invested in public works projects, but, again, this policy maneuver had little impact on consumer spending. In a sign of perhaps desperation, the Japanese government in 1999 gave away money in the form of coupons. During a two-month period in early 1999, the government distributed shopping vouchers (coupons) totaling around $6 billion.

About 35 million Japanese, including elderly people and families with children up to age 15, were eligible for $170 worth of coupons. The program allowed coupon recipients to spend the coupons within six months of receipt on virtually any item offered by local retailers or services. The only provisions were that consumers could not exchange them for cash or receive any change upon redemption.

It is too early to know whether the coupon program will propel greater spending among Japanese consumers. However, some Japanese were opposed to their government's "gift" program on grounds that coupon recipients would simply spend the vouchers in lieu of their own money. Their concern, in other words, is that no new money would enter the Japanese economy and that taxpayer money would be wasted.

Source: Adapted from Ginny Parker, Associated Press, "Japan Tries Coupons in Bid to Revive Consumer Spending," *Charlotte Observer,* January 30, 1999, 12A.

limits the face value of coupons to 1 percent of a product's value, which effectively eliminates this form of promotion in that country. Only a small amount of couponing occurs in France because the few chains that control the retail grocery market generally oppose couponing.[31] Couponing activity in Japan is in the early stages following the lifting of government restrictions. Speaking of Japan, the *Global Focus* describes a unique use of couponing in that country.

Changes in Coupon Distribution.   There have been significant developments in the distribution of coupons. Changes have been made primarily because of the need to avoid competitive clutter, to increase targeting, and to reduce distribution costs—in step with the trend toward efficient consumer response (ECR), as discussed in the previous chapter. Coupons must stand out so that they will be clipped and ultimately redeemed by consumers. Accordingly, the preferred mode for delivering coupons is the *freestanding insert (FSI),* which, as of 1997, accounted for 80 percent of all coupons distributed in the United States.[32] This is a dramatic change from 20 years ago, when only 15 percent of coupons were distributed by FSI and nearly 75 percent were distributed via newspapers and magazines as run-of-paper coupons (ROPs).[33] The reason for these changes should be obvious: Freestanding inserts capture the consumer's attention more readily and therefore are superior in overcoming competitive clutter.

Another major trend in coupon distribution has been the establishment of *cooperative coupon programs.* These are programs in which a service distributes coupons for a single company's multiple brands or brands from multiple companies. Two such service companies—Valassis Inserts and News America Marketing—are responsible for distributing the billions of FSI coupons. Val-Pak Direct Marketing Systems is a cooperative program for distributing coupons via direct mail.

Economic Impact.   The extensive use of couponing has not occurred without criticism. Some critics contend that coupons are wasteful and may actually increase prices of consumer goods. Whether coupons are wasteful and inefficient remains problematic. However, it is undeniable that coupons are an expensive proposition. For a better understanding of coupon costs, consider the case of the coupon for Brummel & Brown spread (Figure 18.10) that has a face value of 75 cents. The coupon's actual cost to Brummel & Brown, as

FIGURE 18.10

Coupon for Brummel & Brown Spread

shown in Table 18.3, is actually substantially more at $1.34. As can be seen from the table, the major cost element is the face value of 75 cents that is deducted from the purchase price of Brummel & Brown spread upon redemption of the coupon. But the makers of this brand also incur: (1) a hefty distribution and postage cost (40¢), (2) a handling charge that is paid to retailers for their troubles (8¢), (3) a misredemption charge resulting from fraudulent redemptions (7¢), (4) internal preparation and processing cost (2¢), and (5) a redemption cost (2¢).

TABLE 18.3

Full Coupon Cost	
1. Face Value	75¢
2. Distribution and postage cost	40¢
3. Handling charge	8¢
4. Consumer misredemption cost	7¢
5. Internal preparation and processing cost	2¢
6. Redemption cost	2¢
TOTAL COST	$1.34

Source: Adapted from an analysis performed by the McKinsey & Co. consulting firm as reported in Daniel Shannon, "Still a Mighty Marketing Mechanism," *Promo,* April 1996, 85.

The actual cost of $1.34 per redeemed coupon, is nearly 80 percent greater than the face value of 75 cents. Assume that Brummel & Brown distributed 40 million of these FSI coupons and that 2 percent, or 800,000, were redeemed. The total cost to Brummel & Brown of this coupon "drop" would thus amount to $1.072 million. It should be apparent that coupon activity requires substantial investment to accomplish desired objectives.

Obviously, programs that aid in reducing costs, such as cooperative delivery programs, are eagerly sought. Creative and innovative couponing programs are constantly being developed. Coupons are indeed costly, some are clearly wasteful, and other promotional devices may be better. However, the extensive use of coupons either suggests that there are a large number of incompetent marketing executives or that better promotional tools are not available or are economically infeasible. The latter explanation is the more reasonable when considering how the marketplace operates. If a business practice is uneconomical, it will not continue to be used for long. When a better business practice is available, it will replace the previous solution. Conclusion: It appears that coupons are used extensively because marketers have been unable to devise more effective and economical methods for accomplishing the objectives achieved with couponing.

Is Couponing Profitable? Recall the discussion in Chapter 16 that examined when promotional dealing is and is not profitable. Among other conclusions, it was determined that putting a brand on deal is unprofitable if the market is composed entirely of promotion-insensitive consumers or entirely of stockpiling loyalists. On the other hand, dealing a brand is profitable if the market consists exclusively of on-deal-only consumers.

Of course, markets never consist entirely of just one type of consumer. However, there is evidence showing that those households most likely to redeem coupons are also the most likely to buy the brand in the first place. It has been estimated that as much as 70 to 80 percent of coupons are redeemed by a brand's current users.[34] Moreover, most consumers revert to their pre-coupon brand choice immediately after redeeming a competitive brand's coupon.[35]

Hence, when those consumers who redeem would have bought the brand anyway, the effect of couponing, at least on the surface, is merely to increase costs and reduce the per-unit profit margin. However, the issue is more involved than this. Although it is undeniable that most coupons are redeemed by current brand users, competitive dynamics force companies to continue offering coupons to prevent losing consumers to other brands that do offer coupons.

Couponing is a fact of life that will continue to remain an important part of marketing in North America and elsewhere. The real challenge for promotion managers is to continuously seek ways to increase couponing profitability and to target coupons to those consumers who may not otherwise purchase their brands.

The following sections describe the major forms of couponing activity, the objectives each is intended to accomplish, and the innovations designed to increase couponing profitability. The presentation of couponing delivery methods follows the framework presented earlier in Table 18.1.

Point-of-Purchase Couponing

A major trend in couponing distribution is to increase the delivery of coupons at the point of purchase. As was established in Chapter 8, approximately 70 percent of purchase decisions are made in the store. It thus makes sense to deliver coupons at the point where decisions are made. Point-of-purchase coupons come in three forms: instant, shelf delivered, and electronically delivered by optical scanner.

Instantly Redeemable Coupons. Most coupon-distribution methods have delayed impact on consumers because the coupon is received in the consumer's home and held for a period of time before it is redeemed. Instantly redeemable coupons, which are peelable from the package at the point of purchase, represent an immediate reward that can spur the consumer to undertake a trial purchase of the promoted brand. A Wheaties cereal campaign illustrates the use of instant couponing. General Mills, the maker of Wheaties, wanted a promotional program that would provide a significant price reduction and an immediate point-of-purchase incentive for consumers. Rather than use a price-off deal, which often creates problems for retailers, General Mills offered a peel-off coupon attached to the front of the Wheaties package. The coupons were designed to be removed by the consumer and redeemed at checkout. The program gained strong retailer acceptance and high redemption.[36]

www.generalmills.com

Although the instant coupon is a minor form of couponing, it has emerged in recent years as an alternative to price-off deals (in which case every package must be reduced in price). The redemption level for instant coupons is considerably higher than the level for other couponing techniques. Whereas the dominant couponing method (that is, FSIs) generates an average redemption level below 2 percent, the average redemption rate for instant coupons is about 30 percent.[37] One would think that most all purchasers would remove instant coupons at the time of making a purchase so as to receive the savings immediately, but obviously the majority do not take advantage of these instant coupons.

A recent study compared the effectiveness of instant redeemable coupons (IRCs) against freestanding inserts (FSIs) in generating sales for a brand of body wash.[38] The FSI and IRC coupons had face values of either 50 cents or $1. Each coupon type and value combination (that is, 50-cent FSI, $1 FSI, 50-cent IRC, $1 IRC) was placed on the body wash brand in each of two markets for a two-month period. Recorded sales data revealed that the IRCs out-performed FSIs of equal value. Moreover, the 50-cent IRC increased sales volume by 23 percent more than the $1 FSI! This obviously is a counterintuitive finding that requires some explanation.

A spokesperson for the company that conducted this research said that his company had no idea why the 50-cent IRC out-performed the $1 FSI. However, research from the academic front offers an answer. One study found that a 75-cent coupon was not considered any more attractive than a 40-cent coupon.[39] A more directly relevant study determined that higher-value coupons *signal* higher brand prices to consumers.[40] This is true especially when consumers are unfamiliar with a brand. In this situation, high coupon values may "scare them off" by suggesting, or signaling, that these brands are high priced. Perhaps the $1 FSI for the body wash implied to prospective customers that the brand must be high priced or otherwise it could not justify offering such an attractive coupon offer. This being the case, they would not have removed the FSI coupon for later redemption. Comparatively, the 50-cent IRC was available to consumers at the point of purchase where the brand's actual price was available to them. They had no reason to expect a high price; they rather saw an opportunity to receive an attractive discount by simply peeling the coupon and presenting it to the clerk when checking out. Ironically, higher-valued coupons may attract primarily current brand users who know the brand's actual price and realize the deal offered by the attractive coupon, whereas potential switchers from other brands may be discouraged by a higher-valued coupon if to them it signals a high price. This, of course, is particularly problematic in the use of FSIs, a form of coupon received away from the point of purchase and that, as a matter of practicality, include only the coupon value but not the brand's regular price. Such is not the case, however, with IRCs.

It would be unwise to draw sweeping generalizations from this single study based on only one product category (body wash), but the intriguing finding suggests that IRCs are capable of outperforming FSIs. Only with additional research will we know whether this finding holds up for other products.

Shelf-Delivered Coupons.   Shelf-delivered coupon machines, which until recently were called Instant Coupon Machines (see Figure 18.11) but now carry the name Smart-Source™, represent an innovative means of reaching consumers with coupons at the point

FIGURE
18.11

Instant Coupon Machine
(now called SmartSource)

of making a brand-selection decision. Approximately 500,000 SmartSource™ couponing machines are available in over 27,000 supermarket and drugstores nationwide. The machines are attached to the shelf alongside coupon-sponsoring brands. Sponsoring brands pay for a four-week cycle. The cost per store/per cycle is between $40–$55.[41]

The average redemption rate for shelf-delivered coupons is approximately 11 percent.[42] Given the infancy of this coupon-delivery mode, only time will tell whether shelf delivery remains appealing to consumers and profitable for marketers.

www.catalinamktg.com

Scanner-Delivered Coupons. Several electronic systems for dispensing coupons at the point of purchase have been introduced in recent years. Although many of these systems have failed, one system that appears to be a success is from Catalina Marketing Corp., which is available in thousands of stores nationwide. Catalina offers two programs, one called Checkout Coupon and the other Checkout Direct. The Checkout Coupon program delivers coupons based on the particular brands a shopper has purchased. Once the optical scanner records that the shopper has purchased a *competitor's brand,* a coupon from the participating manufacturer is dispensed. For example, Figure 18.12 shows a 50-cent coupon for Lean Cuisine Hearty Portions, a frozen entrée product. This coupon was automatically dispensed to a consumer who purchased a competitive brand, Healthy Choice. By targeting competitors' customers, Catalina's Checkout Coupon program ensures that the manufacturer will reach people who buy the product category but are not currently purchasing the manufacturer's brand. The redemption rate is approximately 9 percent.[43]

The other couponing program from Catalina, called Checkout Direct, enables marketers to deliver coupons only to those consumers who satisfy the coupon-sponsoring manufacturer's specific targeting requirements. The Checkout Direct program allows the coupon user to target consumers in various ways: (1) in terms of a purchase-relevant demographic variable (e.g., distribute coupons only to families with incomes greater than $25,000), (2) with respect to their purchase pattern for a particular product (e.g., direct coupons only to consumers who purchase toothpaste every six weeks), and (3) based on the amount of product usage (e.g., deliver coupons only to heavy users of the product). Once the couponing requirements are established, Catalina's computer operators can identify coupon-target households by analyzing two databases: (1) optical-scanned purchase data and (2) household demographic variables acquired by supermarkets when requiring shoppers to complete a form to receive check-cashing privileges. When shoppers who satisfy the coupon-sponsoring manufacturer's requirement make a purchase (as indicated by their check-cashing ID number), a coupon for the sponsoring manufacturer's brand is automatically dispensed for use on the shopper's next purchase occasion.

Frito-Lay used the Checkout Direct system to increase trial purchases of its new (in 1995) Baked Lays brand. Marketers at Frito-Lay targeted super-heavy users of healthier snack foods such as its own Baked Tostitos. Based on optical scanner data that records and stores consumers' past purchase data, the Checkout Direct system was programmed to issue coupons for Baked Lays only to those consumers who purchased "better-for-you" snacks at least eight times during the past 12 months. When these consumers checked out, the scanner triggered a coupon for Baked Lays. In excess of 40 percent of the coupons were redeemed, and the repeat purchase rate was a very impressive 25 percent.[44]

Checkout Coupon for Lean Cuisine Hearty Portions

FIGURE 18.12

Both Catalina programs are used to encourage trial purchasing. However, because coupons are distributed to consumers when they are checking out of a store and cannot be used until their next visit, the reward is *delayed*—unlike the instant or shelf-delivered coupons. Nevertheless, these scanner-delivered couponing methods are potentially very effective and cost-efficient because they provide a way to carefully target coupon distribution. Targeting, in the case of Checkout Coupon, is directed at competitive-brand users and, in the case of Checkout Direct, is directed at users who satisfy a manufacturer's prescribed demographic or product-usage requirements.

Mail– and Media–Delivered Coupons

These coupon delivery modes initiate trial purchase behavior by offering consumers *delayed* rewards. Mail-delivered coupons represent less than 5 percent of all manufacturer-distributed coupons. Mass-media modes (newspapers and magazines) are clearly dominant, carrying well over 80 percent of all coupons (the bulk of which is in the form of freestanding inserts).

Mail-Delivered Coupons. Marketers typically use mail-delivered coupons to introduce new or improved products. Mailings can be directed either at a broad cross-section of the market or targeted to specific demographic segments. Mailed coupons achieve the *highest household penetration*. Coupon distribution via magazines and newspapers reaches fewer than 70 percent of all homes, whereas mail can reach as high as 95 percent. Moreover, direct mail achieves the *highest redemption rate* (5.7 percent) of all mass-delivered coupon techniques.[45] There also is empirical evidence to suggest that direct-mail coupons *increase the amount of product purchases,* particularly when coupons with higher face values are used by households that own their homes, have larger families, and are more educated.[46]

The major disadvantage of direct-mailed coupons is that they are *relatively expensive* compared with other coupon-distribution methods. Another disadvantage is that direct mailing is especially inefficient and expensive for brands enjoying a high market share. This is because a large proportion of the coupon recipients may already be regular users of the coupon brand, thereby defeating the primary purpose of generating trial purchasing. Mass-mailing inefficiencies account for the rapid growth of efforts to target coupons to narrowly defined audiences such as users of competitive brands.

Media-Delivered Coupons. As earlier noted, approximately 80 percent of all coupons distributed in the United States are via Sunday newspaper freestanding inserts. The major advantage of media coupons is their broad exposure; they are limited only by media circulation. While magazines and newspapers both permit geographical selectivity, magazines also permit demographic and psychographic pinpointing.

Moreover, the cost per thousand for freestanding inserts is only about 50 to 60 percent of that for direct-mail coupons, which largely explains why FSIs are the dominant coupon-delivery mode. Another advantage of FSIs is that they perform an extremely important reminder function for the consumer who peruses the Sunday inserts, clips coupons for brands she or he intends to buy in the coming weeks, and then redeems these at a later date.[47] Finally, there is some evidence that FSIs also perform an advertising function. That is, when perusing the Sunday inserts, consumers are exposed to FSI "advertisements" and are somewhat more likely to purchase promoted brands even without redeeming a coupon.[48] This comes as no great surprise since FSI coupons often are extremely attractive, eye-catching promotional pieces, illustrated by the collage of FSIs in Figure 18.13. Note especially the FSI for Oreo O's cereal. Do you see anything strange, different about this FSI? In comparison to the other five FSIs in Figure 18.13, the Oreo O's FSI contains no coupon. It is an FSI advertisement in the truest sense of the word!

Research has shown that attractive pictures in FSIs function as peripheral cues (as discussed in Chapter 6) and are particularly effective when viewers of the FSI are loyal to a

A Collage of FSI "Advertisements"

FIGURE 18.13

brand other than the one featured in the FSI. In this situation, consumers, loyal as they are to another brand, are not motivated to process arguments about a non-preferred brand featured in the FSI. Hence, the use of attractive pictures (versus message arguments) is necessary to enhance consumer attitudes, if only temporarily, and increase the odds that consumers will clip the FSI coupon.[49]

There are several problems with media-delivered coupons. First, the redemption rate is very low. Magazine on-page and newspaper ROP redemption rates are less than 1 percent, while FSI redemption rates are below 2 percent.[50] Table 18.4 lists several reasons for the drop in FSI redemption. A second problem with media-delivered coupons is that they do not, with the slight exception of FSIs, generate much trade interest. Finally, coupons delivered via magazines and the newspaper are particularly susceptible to misredemption. The latter issue is so significant to all parties involved in couponing that it deserves a separate discussion later.

TABLE 18.4

Reasons for the Drop in FSI Redemption

♦ **Shortened expiration periods:** In 1988 the average expiration period for coupons was 7.6 months, but by 1994 the average had dropped to 3.7 months. Expiration dates have been cut by brand managers as a way of limiting their financial liability and controlling their promotional budgets.*

♦ **Increased Clutter:** In order to decrease costs, more manufacturers have opted to place more than one coupon per FSI page.

♦ **Face-value stagnation:** Face values have increased but, when adjusted for inflation, amount to only about 2 percent.

♦ **Advent of EDLP:** The trend toward EDLP by manufacturers—EDLP(M)—has resulted in a decrease in coupon promotions by major companies such as Procter & Gamble, Kraft, Kellogg, and General Mills.

♦ **Increased targeting:** In an effort to reduce inefficiencies, many brand managers have reduced the use of FSIs and increased the use of electronic checkout coupons and other methods that allow greater targeting.

*For further reading regarding coupon expiration dates, see J. Jeffrey Inman and Leigh McAlister, "Do Coupon Expiration Dates Affect Consumer Behavior?" *Journal of Marketing Research* 34 (August 1994), 423–428.
Source: Adapted from Daniel Shannon, "Couponing into the Millennium," *Promo,* April 1995, 76–77.

In- and On-Pack Coupons

In- and on-pack coupons are included either inside a product's package or as a part of a package's exterior. This form of couponing should not be confused with the previously discussed instant, or peelable, coupon. Whereas IRCs are removable at the point of purchase and redeemable for that particular item while the shopper is in the store, an in- or on-pack coupon cannot be removed until it is in the shopper's home to be redeemed on a subsequent purchase occasion.

Frequently, a coupon for one brand is promoted by another brand. For example, General Mills promoted its brand of granola bars by placing cents-off coupons in cereal boxes. Practitioners call this practice *crossruffing,* a term borrowed from bridge and bridge-type card games where partners alternate trumping one another when they are unable to follow suit.

Though marketers use crossruffing to create trial purchases or to stimulate purchase of products such as granola bars that are not staple items, in- and on-pack coupons carried by the same brand are generally intended to stimulate repeat purchasing. That is, once consumers have exhausted the contents of a particular package, they are more likely to repurchase that brand if an attractive inducement, such as a cents-off coupon, is available immediately. A package coupon has *bounce-back value.* An initial purchase, the bounce, may stimulate another purchase, the bounce back, when a hard-to-avoid inducement such as an in-package coupon is made available.[51]

A major advantage of in- and on-pack coupons is that there are virtually no distribution costs. Moreover, redemption rates are much higher because most of the package-delivered coupons are received by brand users. The average redemption rate for in-pack coupons is around 6 percent, whereas that for on-pack coupons is slightly less than 5 percent.[52] The major limitations of these coupons are that they offer delayed value to consumers, they do not reach nonusers of the carrying brand, and trade interest is relatively low due to the delayed nature of the offer.

The Coupon Redemption Process and Misredemption

As alluded to earlier, misredemption is a problem, especially in the use of media-delivered coupons. The best way to understand how misredemption occurs is to examine the redemption process. A graphic of the process is provided in Figure 18.14.

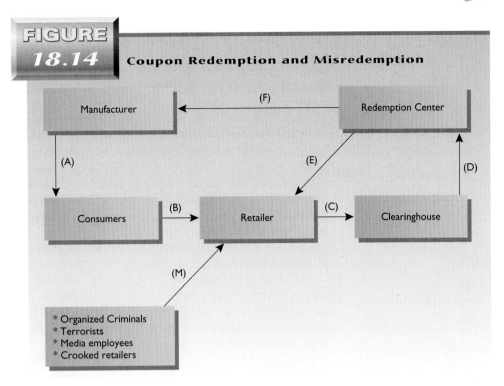

FIGURE 18.14 Coupon Redemption and Misredemption

The process begins with a manufacturer distributing coupons to consumers via FSIs, direct mail, or any of the other distribution modes previously described (see path A in Figure 18.14). Consumers collect coupons, take them to the store, and present them to a checkout clerk, who subtracts each coupon's face value from the shopper's total purchase cost (path B). For the shopper to be entitled to the coupon discount, certain conditions and restrictions must be met: (1) she or he must buy the merchandise specified on the coupon in the size, brand, and quantity directed; (2) only one coupon can be redeemed per item; (3) cash may not be given for the coupon; and (4) the coupon must be redeemed before the expiration date. (Some coupon misredemption occurs because consumers present coupons that do not meet these requirements.)

Retailers, in turn, redeem the coupons they have received in order to obtain reimbursement from the manufacturers that sponsored the coupons. Retailers typically hire another company, called a *clearinghouse,* to sort and redeem the coupons in return for a fee (path C). Clearinghouses, acting on behalf of a number of retail clients, consolidate coupons before forwarding them. Clearinghouses maintain controls by ensuring that their clients sold products legitimately in the amounts they submitted for redemption.

Clearinghouses forward the coupons to *redemption centers* (path D), which serve as agents of the coupon-issuing manufacturers. The redemption center pays off on all properly redeemed coupons (path E) and then is compensated for its services by the manufacturer (path F). If a center questions the validity of certain coupons, it may go to its client, a manufacturer, for approval on redeeming suspected coupons.[53]

The system is not quite as clear-cut as it may appear from this description. Some large retailers act as their own clearinghouses, some manufacturers serve as their own redemption centers, and some independent firms, such as the A.C. Nielsen Co., offer both clearinghouse and redemption-center services.

www.acnielsen.com

However, regardless of the specific mechanism by which a coupon is ultimately redeemed (or misredeemed), the retailer is reimbursed for the amount of the face value paid to the consumer and for payment of a handling charge, which currently is 8 cents per coupon. Herein rests the potential for misredemption: An unscrupulous person could thus make an 83-cent profit from a coupon with a face value of 75 cents. One thousand such misredeemed coupons are worth $830! Exacerbating the potential for misredemption is the fact that many coupons now have face values worth as much as $1 or more. (Note that the coupon for Colgate Total in Figure 18.13 has a $1.50 face value.)

Now with an understanding of the redemption process, how does misredemption occur and who participates in it? Estimates of the misredemption rate have ranged from a low of 15 percent to a high of 40 percent. Many brand managers have assumed a 20 to 25 percent rate of misredemption when budgeting for coupon events. However, a recent study found that past estimates of coupon misredemption have been inflated. It now appears that fraudulent coupon redemption is, on average, closer to 3 or 4 percent rather than the 20–25 percent assumed previously.[54] Although the magnitude of misredemption has been reduced by imposing tighter controls on coupon redemption at all stages of the redemption process, a 3–4 percent misredemption level nevertheless represents millions of dollars lost by manufacturers.

Misredemption occurs at every level of the redemption process. Sometimes *consumers* present coupons that have expired, coupons for items not purchased, or coupons for a smaller-sized product than that specified by the coupon. Some *clerks* take coupons to the store and exchange them for cash without making a purchase. At the *store management* level, retailers may boost profits by submitting extra coupons in addition to those redeemed legitimately. A dishonest retailer can buy coupons on the black market, age them in a clothes dryer, mix them with legitimate coupons, and then mail in the batch for redemption. Shady *clearinghouses* engage in misredemption by combining illegally purchased coupons with real ones and certifying the batch as legitimate.

The major source of coupon misredemption is large-scale *professional misredeemers* (see path M, standing for Misredemption, in Figure 18.14). These professional misredeemers either (1) recruit the services of actual retailers to serve as conduits through which coupons are misredeemed or (2) operate phony businesses that exist solely for the purpose of redeeming huge quantities of illegal coupons. Illegal coupons typically are obtained by removing FSIs from Sunday newspapers.

The following examples represent some recent cases of organized misredemption efforts. The proprietor of Wadsworth Thriftway store in Philadelphia illegally submitted in excess of 1.5 million coupons valued at over $800,000.[55] The top three executives of the Sloans Supermarket in New York were indicted for their role in a 20-year operation that led to $3.5 million in coupon misredemption.[56] Another Philadelphian acted as a middleman between charities, from which he purchased coupons in bulk, and a supermarket employee, who submitted them for repayment by manufacturers or their redemption centers. The middleman earned $200,000 from the couponing scam before he was arrested.[57] Five operators of Shop n' Bag supermarkets in Philadelphia (is there a pattern here?) bought nearly 12 million coupons for only 20–30 percent of their face value and then redeemed them prior to being arrested.[58] And finally, according to *The New York Post,* Mideast terrorists misredeemed perhaps up to $100 million by funneling illegally redeemed coupons through Arab mini-marts and Hispanic bodegas.[59]

PREMIUMS

Many marketers, including business-to-business firms as well as consumer-oriented companies, use premiums. Total expenditures on premiums in the United States amounted to $24 billion in one recent year.[60] Broadly defined, **premiums** are articles of merchandise or services (e.g., travel) offered by manufacturers to induce action on the part of the sales force, trade representatives, or consumers. The *IMC Focus* illustrates some successful premium promotions.

IMC FOCUS: SUCCESSFUL PREMIUM PROMOTIONS

Mountain Dew's Pager Promotion

The marketers at Mountain Dew developed a promotion to appeal to Gen Xers. Based on research indicating that 20 percent of teens in the United States carry pagers, this product was identified as an outstanding promotional item. Advertisements encouraged Mountain Dew consumers to send in 10 proofs of purchase along with $29.99 for receipt of a Motorola Renegade pager and six free months of pager service. The offer didn't stop here. Customers who responded to the offer received weekly messages via their pagers that provided numbers to call for special deals from companies such as Sony, Pizza Hut, K2, Timex, and Taco Bell.

Springs Industries Premium Offer

Spring Industries is a South Carolina-based textile manufacturer that specializes in linen products. In an effort to generate enthusiasm for its Wamsutta brand among key retailers (such as Bloomingdales, Bed, Bath & Beyond, and Linens 'N Things), Springs developed an appealing premium promotion. For every Wamsutta purchase of $25 or more, consumers were given a Herbath gift pack that contained a mixture of aromatic herbs in an attractive bag. Sales of Wamsutta linens increased by 22 percent during the promotion period.

Procter & Gamble's Train Offer

With the objective of increasing sales both to the trade and consumers of six of its brands—Folger's coffee, Jif peanut butter, Sunny Delight juice, Puritan oil, Crisco shortening, and Duncan Hines cake mix—P&G promotion managers developed an innovative premium offer. An O-Gauge model train set from K-line Electric Trains was offered to consumers with three proofs of purchase from any of the six brands plus $79.95 and $4 postage and handling. P&G also offered 15,000 retailers larger O-Gauge train sets with a total purchase of 180 cases of the six brands. This promotion received a positive response from consumers, and retailer orders averaged 20 percent more cases than required to receive the train sets.

Coca-Cola's CD Offer

This soft-drink giant offered free in-pack compact discs to consumers who purchased 12-packs of Coke, Diet Coke, or Sprite. CDs from four different up-and-coming artists were available, which encouraged consumers to make multiple purchases to collect the full set. More than 6 million CDs were given away, which translated into a major sales increase during the promotional period.

Pizza Hut's Basketball Giveaway

Painted basketballs with bold graphics were prepared for this special promotion. These balls, unpainted, sold for $17 in retail stores, but Pizza Hut offered consumers basketballs for only $4.99 with purchases of pizza. Participating retailers received a free basketball plus an opportunity to win NCAA apparel and NCAA tournament tickets. A total of 3.8 million basketballs were self-liquidated (defined later) in less than six weeks.

Sources: The Mountain Dew example is adapted from Dan Hanover, "On the Money," *Promo*, May 1997, P10; the Springs Industries illustration is adapted from Nicole Crawford, "Shining Examples," A *Promo* Magazine Special Report, October 1997, R24; the other examples are adapted from Blair R. Fischer, "The Top 10 Premium Promotions of the Past Ten Years," *Promo*, May 1995, P17.

In general, premiums are a versatile promotional tool, possessing the ability to generate trial, introduce new brands, increase display exposure, and enhance brand equity.[61] Several forms of premium offers are used to motivate consumers: free-in-the-mail premiums; in-, on-, and near-pack premiums; and self-liquidating premiums. All three forms serve fundamentally different purposes. Free-in-the-mail premiums are useful primarily for generating initial brand trial or retrial; in-, on-, and near-pack premiums serve customer-holding purposes; and self-liquidators perform image-reinforcement functions (see Table 18.1). Phone cards represent a unique form of premium offering and are discussed in a separate section.

Free-in-the-Mail Premiums

By definition, a **free-in-the-mail premium** is a promotion in which consumers receive a premium item from the sponsoring manufacturer in return for submitting a required number of proofs of purchase. For example, Procter & Gamble offered a free toy racing car with two proofs of purchase for its Tide or Downy brands (see Figure 18.15). Although children and their parents are the targets of numerous free-in-the-mail premium offers, this promotional tool certainly is not limited to children.

FIGURE
18.15

Free-in-the Mail Premium

In addition to stimulating consumer trial, free-in-the-mail premiums can achieve other objectives. When directed at adult audiences, these premiums can accomplish customer-holding objectives by rewarding consumers' brand loyalties and encouraging repeat-purchase behavior. For example, Figure 18.16 (for a sleeve of Titleist golf balls carrying Tiger Woods' signature) illustrates an offer where consumers must collect two UPCs to be eligible for this attractive premium item.

Perhaps as few as 2–4 percent of consumers who are exposed to free mail-in offers actually take advantage of these opportunities. However, free-in-the-mail premiums can be extremely effective if the premium item is appealing to the target market, as probably was the case with the golf ball offer just noted.

FIGURE 18.16

Another Free-in-
the-Mail Premium

In-, On-, and Near-Pack Premiums

In- and on-pack premiums offer a premium item inside or attached to a package or make the package itself the premium item. For example, in a delightful promotional program for Cap'n Crunch cereal, the box was labeled "Christmas Crunch," and Captain Horatio (the cartoon-character brand icon) was shown on the package dressed like Santa Claus. The package advertised a free Christmas tree ornament inside the box—a premium offer with much appeal to small children during the holiday season. In general, in- and on-package premiums offer consumers immediate value and thereby encourage increased product consumption.

However, this form of premium is not restricted to children. For example, Ralston Purina offered tiny sports-car models in about 11 million boxes of six cereal brands. Ten of these boxes contained scale-model red Corvettes. Lucky consumers turned in the models for real Corvettes.[62]

Near-pack premiums provide the retail trade with specially displayed premium pieces that retailers then give to consumers who purchase the promoted product. Near-pack premiums are less expensive, because additional packaging is not required. Furthermore, near-pack premiums can build sales volume in stores that put up displays and participate fully.

Self-Liquidating Premiums

The **self-liquidating premium** gets its name from the fact that the consumer mails in a stipulated number of proofs of purchase along with sufficient money to cover the manufacturer's purchasing, handling, and mailing costs of the premium item. In other words, the actual cost of the premium is paid for by consumers; from the manufacturer's perspective the item is cost-free, or, in other words, self-liquidating.

The Star Kist Charlie® soccer ball (Figure 18.17) illustrates a self-liquidating premium. Consumers receive with three proofs of purchase and $9.99 a product that at retail likely would sell for around $20.

However, very few consumers ever send for a premium. Companies expect only 0.1 percent of self-liquidators to be redeemed.[63] A circulation of 20,000,000, for example, would be expected to produce only about 20,000 redemptions.

Industry specialists generally concur that the most important consideration in developing a self-liquidator program is that the premium be appealing to the target audience and represent a value. Most sources agree that consumers look for a savings of at least 50 percent of the suggested retail price.[64] Pizza Hut's basketball promotion described earlier in the *IMC Focus* was an attractive self-liquidator inasmuch as consumers could spend only $4.99 for a basketball that sold in retail stores at $17.

Phone Cards

Phone cards, also called phone debit cards, represent a rather unique type of premium offer. Introduced in 1991, this form of promotion incentive is classified in Table 18.1 as performing a customer-holding objective and providing consumers with a delayed reward. This is a bit of a simplification insofar as phone cards also are capable of generating trial purchase behavior or even reinforcing brand image. Because this form of promotion is in its infancy, it is unclear how promotion managers will use phone cards as this form of incentive matures. Although a variety of phone cards are available, the most common type offers a preset amount of long-distance calling time. These cards operate as follows:

> Using a Touch-Tone phone, the caller dials the toll-free number on the back of the card. The call is routed to a computer switch or network containing memory that stores all information related to the card. The cardholder hears a personalized greeting from the marketer, then is prompted to enter an access number imprinted on the card. The system identifies the number, tabulates the amount of time remaining on the card and informs the user of how long he or she can talk. Whether the call is placed across the country or to the house next door, the card entitles the holder to the same amount of time on the phone.[65]

Some interesting phone-card promotions include the following:[66]

- Ryder offered phone cards with 20 minutes of long-distance calling to renters of its moving vans. Ryder dealers distributed 300,000 cards during a six-week promotion, and double-digit sales growth was enjoyed.

- L'eggs pantyhose promoted its Silken Mist line of hosiery with a phone card worth 10 minutes of long-distance calling time. Customers received the calling cards by mailing a proof of purchase.

- Lexus offered a Lexus-logoed phone card good for an hour and a half of long-distance calling time to 150,000 preselected customers. All who took a test drive in the ES 300 Lexus sedan received a free card.

FIGURE
18.17

Self-Liquidating Premium

◆ Gillette included 4,000,000 phone cards worth 5 minutes of free long-distance service in its 10-pack Daisy and Good News brands of disposable razors.

P RICE-OFFS

Price-off promotions (also called cents-off or price packs) entail a reduction (typically ranging from 10 to 25 percent) in a brand's regular price. A price-off is clearly labeled as such on the package. This type of promotion is effective when the marketer's objective is any of the following: (1) to reward present brand users; (2) to get consumers to purchase larger quantities of a brand than they normally would (i.e., to load them), thereby effectively preempting the competition; (3) to establish a repeat purchase pattern after an initial trial; (4) to ensure that promotional dollars do, in fact, reach consumers (no such assurance is possible with trade allowances); (5) to obtain off-shelf display space when such allowances are offered to retailers; and (6) to provide the sales force with an incentive to obtain retailer support.[67]

Price-offs cannot reverse a downward sales trend, produce a significant number of new users, or attract as many trial users as sampling, coupons, or premium packs. Furthermore, *retailers often dislike price-offs* because they create inventory and pricing problems, particularly when a store has a brand in inventory at both the price-off and regular prices. Yet despite trade problems, price-offs have strong consumer appeal.

FTC Price–Off Regulations

Manufacturers cannot indiscriminately promote their brands with continuous or near-continuous price-off labeling. To do so would deceive consumers into thinking the brand is on sale when in fact the announced sale price is actually the regular price.

www.ftc.gov

The Federal Trade Commission controls price-off labeling with the following regulations:

1. Price-off labels may only be used on brands already in distribution with established retail prices;
2. There is a limit of three price-off label promotions per year per brand size;
3. There must be a hiatus period of at least 30 days between price-off label promotions on any given brand size;
4. No more than 50 percent of a brand's volume over a 12-month period may be generated from price-off label promotions;
5. The manufacturer must provide display materials to announce the price-off label offer; and
6. The dealer is required to show the regular shelf price in addition to the new price reflecting the price-off label savings.[68]

BONUS PACKS

Bonus packs are extra quantities of a product that a company gives to consumers at the regular price. For example, Carnation offered consumers 25 percent more hot cocoa mix at the regular price; golf ball manufacturers on occasion reward consumers with an extra pack of three balls when they purchase a dozen. Bonus packs are sometimes used as an *alternative to price-off deals* when the latter are either overused or resisted by the trade. The extra value offered to the consumer is readily apparent and for that reason can be effective in loading current users and thereby removing them from the market—a defensive tactic that is used against aggressive competitors.

A potential drawback of bonus packs is that a large proportion of the bonus-packed merchandise will be purchased by regular customers who would have purchased the brand anyway. Of course, this is not a drawback if the explicit purpose of the bonus-pack offer is to reward a brand's present customers.

REBATES/REFUNDS

A **rebate** (also called a refund) refers to the practice in which manufacturers give cash discounts or reimbursements to consumers who submit proofs of purchase. Unlike coupons, which the consumer redeems at retail checkouts, rebates/refunds are mailed with proofs of purchase to manufacturers. Figure 18.18 illustrates a rebate offer for Suave shampoo and styling aid. Rebates certainly are not restricted to packaged goods. Automobile companies are among the major users of rebate programs. In 1998, for example, General Motors Corp. offered rebates worth as much as $3,000 per vehicle.

Rebates offer consumers delayed rather than immediate value, since the consumer has to wait to receive the reimbursement. In using these programs, manufacturers achieve customer-holding objectives by encouraging consumers to make multiple purchases or by rewarding previous users with a cash discount for again purchasing the manufacturer's brand.

Rebate Offer

Phantom Discounts

Marketers are fond of rebates because they provide an alternative to the use of coupons and stimulate consumer purchase behavior.[69] Rebate offers reinforce brand loyalty, provide the sales force with something to talk about, and enable the manufacturer to flag the package with a potentially attractive deal. Perhaps the major reason manufacturers are using rebates more now than ever is that many consumers never bother to redeem them. Thus, when using rebates manufacturers get the best of both worlds—they stimulate consumer purchases of rebated items without having to pay out the rebated amount because most consumers do not undertake the effort to mail in rebate forms. Hence, rebates can be thought of as a form of *phantom discount.*[70] Needless to say, consumer advocates condemn manufacturers' use of rebates.

One may wonder why consumers purchase rebated items but then fail to take the time to submit forms to receive the rebate amount. Recent research offers an explanation. It appears that at the time of brand choice consumers tend to overweigh the benefit to be obtained from a rebate relative to the future effort required to redeem a rebate offer.[71] In other words, it seems that many consumers engage in a form of self-deception when purchasing rebated merchandise. They find a rebate offer attractive and on that basis decide to purchase a particular brand. Yet, later on at home they are unwilling to commit the time and effort to send in the rebate form. When manufacturers offer rebates, are they exploiting consumers, or are consumers to be blamed for their own inaction? This should make for interesting class discussion.

Rebate Fraud

Consumers engage in their own form of rebate-related fraud. There is, in fact, a huge amount of fraud associated with bogus claims paid out to "professional" rebaters. At one time manufacturers paid out in excess of $500 million annually to these crooks.[72] Fraud occurs when professionals acquire their own cash registers, generate phony cash-register receipts, and send them on to manufacturers to collect refund checks without making required product purchases. Other professionals use computers to design phony UPC codes, which they mail to manufacturers as evidence of purchases they actually have not made. Of course, these professionals do not send in just single refund requests; rather, they submit requests under multiple names and then have refund checks mailed to different P.O. boxes.

Two promotions illustrate this fraudulent practice.[73] One manufacturer ran a $3 refund offer requiring submission of a UPC to be eligible for the refund. Three out of four refund requests had the same misprinted UPC number on them. Investigators determined that *Moneytalk,* a refunding magazine, had misprinted the product's UPC number in one of its issues. In a second case, a manufacturer's rebate forms were available in stores before its product reached store shelves. Nonetheless, this did not deter 2,200 rebate requests from flowing in immediately—all accompanied by bogus cash-register receipts and UPC numbers.

Postal authorities and marketers are taking aggressive efforts to curtail refunding fraud.[74] Many marketers are beginning to state on their refund/rebate forms that they will not send checks to P.O. boxes—as illustrated in the rebate offer for Suave shampoo (Figure 18.18). Others are stating that checks will be mailed only to the return address listed on the envelope. Because organized refund redeemers use computers to generate mailings and return address labels, manufacturers are further deterring fraud by stipulating on their refund/rebate forms that printed mailing labels are prohibited.

CONTESTS AND SWEEPSTAKES

Contests and sweepstakes offer consumers the opportunity to win cash, merchandise, or travel prizes. As noted in Table 18.1, these forms of promotions are used primarily to enhance a brand's image. This is accomplished by associating the brand with an attractive gift that is logically related to the brand. In a **sweepstakes,** winners are determined purely *on the basis of chance.* Accordingly, proofs of purchase cannot be required as a condition for entry. In a **contest,** the consumer must solve the specified contest problem and may be required to submit proofs of purchase.[75] For example, Polaner All Fruit brand of breakfast jam offered consumers a chance to win the historic MacAuley House in Vermont as winner of the "Win your Own Bed & Breakfast" contest. Entrants were required to submit two proofs of purchase and write a short essay in response to the phrase "Breakfast with Polaner All Fruit is better because. . . ."[76] Perhaps the best-known contest of this sort is Guinness Import's annual giveaway of an Irish pub. Figure 18.19 illustrates a contest by Dickies, a manufacturer of work clothes. This contest simply requires entrants to complete in 75 words or less the following statement: "I think my nominee deserves special recognition as Dickies 1998 American Worker of the Year because. . . ." Contests may even encourage repeat purchasing, which is an added benefit of a carefully structured event. The *IMC Focus* shows how repeat purchasing might be encouraged with a clever contest.

Because they require less effort from consumers and generate greater response, sweepstakes are much preferred to contests. The sweepstakes offer for Uncle Ben's rice (Figure 18.20) is a standard sweepstakes offer. Consumers simply complete an entry form to become eligible to win a cruise for two on the famous Windjammer cruise ship.

Dickies American Worker of the Year Contest

IMC FOCUS: A REPEAT–PURCHASE BUILDING CONTEST OF GLEN ELLEN WINE

Glen Ellen wine, based in Sonoma, California, devised a contest with the aid of its promotions agency that served both to enhance the brand's equity and to encourage repeat purchasing. Corks from bottles of Glen Ellen wine were imprinted with symbols of four products—a corkscrew, hat, shirt, or Adirondack chair. The consumer won the product symbolized on the cork and claimed the prize by returning the cork to the company. In addition to the corks imprinted with product symbols, other corks were imprinted with letters. Anyone collecting four corks spelling G-L-E-N was eligible for an annuity worth $1 million.

In addition to encouraging repeat purchasing and getting consumers more involved with the brand, the contest generated considerable excitement among Glen Ellen's salespeople and created a favorable response from retailers, many of whom took on added inventories of the Glen Ellen brand. The contest was publicized with FSI coupons and extensive point-of-purchase displays.

Source: Adapted from "A Simple Twist of Fate," *Promo,* June 1998, 19.

Another reason marketers favor sweepstakes over contests is because the latter form of promotion sometimes goes awry. The Pepsi contest in Philippines (*Opening Vignette*) is an extreme example of a failed contest. The Beatrice Company's Monday Night Football contest illustrates another failed contest. Contestants scratched silver-coated footballs off cards to reveal numbers, hoping to win the prize offered if the numbers on the cards matched the number of touchdowns and field goals scored in the weekly Monday night NFL game. Contest planners intended the chances of getting a match to be infinitesimal. However, to Beatrice's great surprise, a salesman for rival Procter & Gamble put in a claim for a great deal more money than they had planned on paying out.

A computer buff, the salesman cracked the contest code and determined that 320 patterns showed up repeatedly in the cards. By scratching off just one line, he could determine which numbers were underneath the rest. With knowledge of the actual numbers of TDs and field goals scored on a particular Monday night, he would start scratching cards until winning numbers were located. He enlisted friends to assist in collecting and scratching the cards. Thousands of cards were collected, mostly from Beatrice salespeople. The P&G salesman and friends identified 4,000 winning cards worth $21 million in prize money! Beatrice discontinued the game and refused to pay up.[77]

PepsiCo blew it again in a contest conducted in the United States. Contestants participated in a spell-your-surname contest with letters printed on bottle caps. Because very few caps bore vowels, PepsiCo assumed that only a small number of people would win the contest. What the contest planners failed to realize, however, was that many Asian names contain only consonants (such as Ng).[78]

These and other problems lead many companies to shy away from contests. Sweepstakes, on the other hand, have experienced a tremendous increase in popularity. Indeed, approximately three quarters of packaged-goods marketers use sweepstakes.[79] Compared with many other sales-promotion techniques, sweepstakes are relatively inexpensive, simple to execute, and are able to accomplish a variety of marketing objectives. In addition to reinforcing a brand's image and attracting attention to advertisements, well-designed sweepstakes can promote distribution and retailer stocking, increase sales-force enthusiasm, and reach specific groups, such as ethnic markets, through a prize structure that is particularly appealing to consumers in the group.

The effectiveness and appeal of a sweepstakes is generally limited if the sweepstakes is used alone. However, when tied in with advertising, point-of-purchase displays, and other promotional tools, sweepstakes can work effectively to produce significant results.

FIGURE 18.20

Sweepstakes Offer

CONTINUITY PROMOTIONS

Promotions sometimes reward consumers' repeat purchasing of a particular brand by awarding points leading to reduced prices or free merchandise. It is obvious from this description why continuity promotions also are referred to as "loyalty programs" or "point programs." Frequent-flyer programs by airlines and frequent-guest programs by hotels represent one form of loyalty program. Fliers and hotel guests accumulate points that can be redeemed eventually for free flights and lodging. These programs encourage consumers to stick with a particular airline or hotel in order to accumulate requisite numbers of points as quickly as possible.

Many readers will recall the "Pepsi Stuff" promotion that awarded consumers points for each purchase of Pepsi brands, with more points being awarded for purchases of larger-quantity containers. Consumers could redeem points for merchandise items such as T-shirts, caps, sunglasses, sweatshirts, and beach chairs. This summer-long promotion encouraged repeat purchasing of Pepsi products and also bolstered Pepsi's image by associating the brand with a fun promotion. Hormel borrowed the "Pepsi Stuff" idea in developing its own points program for Spam, the processed meat product that is the butt of frequent jokes (see Figure 18.21).

In general, continuity programs reward consumers for purchasing a particular brand repeatedly. Those consumers who are loyal already to the point-program brand are rewarded for what they would have done anyway, namely, buying a preferred brand on a regular basis. In such a case, a point program does not encourage repeat purchasing; it does, however, serve to cement a relation with the consumer that is strong already. On the other hand, point programs can encourage consumers whose loyalty is divided among several brands to purchase more frequently the brand that awards promotion points. This is perhaps where continuity programs have the greatest value.

INTERNET PROMOTIONS

The Internet is becoming a major medium for consumer-oriented promotions. Continuity programs, online couponing, Internet sweepstakes and contests, and Web-based sample

The Spam Stuff
Points Program

offers are now pervasive. Online couponing, for example, is a cheaper and more targeted couponing medium than FSIs or direct mail. Companies such as Catalina Marketing Corp. (www.valupage.com) offer consumers the opportunity to receive upwards of $40 of national-brand coupons by providing information about themselves, such as their ZIP code and preferred supermarket. By answering additional specific questions on the screen, consumers get coupons that are finely targeted to their demographic and lifestyle profiles.[80] A downside to online couponing is that it is susceptible to fraud given the ease of duplicating coupons that are offered in electronic form and thus printable and duplicable in mass quantities.[81]

In addition to providing a medium for distributing promotions to consumers, the Internet also provides an ideal forum for connecting brand marketers who are in process of creating a promotional program with suppliers that specialize in developing such programs. For example, the publishers of *Promo* magazine, a monthly periodical that focuses on the promotion industry, recently introduced a Web site (www.promoxchange.com) that is designed to assist brand managers who are in the planning stage for a promotional program.[82] Brand marketers using PromoXchange answer a series of menu-directed questions regarding their specific promotion needs. Potential suppliers read the answers to these queries and then evaluate whether their companies possess the expertise and resources to fulfill the brand manager's promotional needs. A potential cyberspace relation between client and supplier is thereby formed.

For example, suppose a brand manager is interested in developing a sampling program to generate trial purchasing for a new brand. The manager would enter the PromoXchange Web site, select "sampling" from a menu of offerings, and then answer a series of menu-directed questions. For example, What is the proposed timing of the sampling program? What is the target audience? What type of sampling is preferred?[83] Companies that specialize in sampling programs would then enter into a cyberspace exchange with the brand manager, who would query each prospective supplier with questions such as "Describe similar programs you've conducted with other clients," or "What is your area of expertise?" PromoXchange essentially allows a brand marketer to post a proposed promotion program on the Internet and then receive responses from interested suppliers of the prospective promotion. The initial cyberspace exchange between marketer and prospective suppliers may lead ultimately to other forms of exchange (telephone, face to face) and the possibility of a business relation that meets the needs of both parties.

OVERLAY AND TIE-IN PROMOTIONS

Discussion to this point has concentrated on individual sales promotions. In practice, sales-promotion techniques often are used in combination to accomplish a number of objectives that could not be achieved by using a single promotional tool. Furthermore, these techniques, individually or in conjunction with one another, are used oftentimes to promote simultaneously two or more brands either from the same company or from different firms.

The use of *two or more sales promotion techniques in combination* with one another is called an **overlay,** or **combination, program.** The *simultaneous promotion of multiple brands in a single promotional effort* is called a **tie-in,** or **joint, promotion.** In other words, overlay refers to the use of multiple sales promotion tools, whereas tie-in refers to the promotion of multiple brands from the same or different companies. Overlay and tie-ins often are used together, as the following sections illustrate.

Overlay Programs

Media clutter, as noted repeatedly in past chapters, is an ever-growing problem facing marketers. When used individually, promotion tools (particularly coupons) may never be noticed by consumers. A combination of tools—such as the use of a coupon offer with another promotional device increases the likelihood that consumers will attend a promotional message and process the promotion offer. In addition, the joint use of several techniques in a well-coordinated promotional program equips the sales force with a strong sales program and provides the trade with an attractive incentive to purchase in larger quantities (in anticipation of enhanced consumer response) and to increase display activity. For example, Figure 18.15 (a tie-in between Tide and Downy) overlays a mail-in premium offer on coupons for each of the two participating brands. Figure 18.17 (a tie-in for Star Kist tuna and Kraft Mayo) overlays a self-liquidating premium offer (for Star Kist) on top of a coupon offer for Kraft Mayo. Finally, Figure 18.18, a tie-in offer for various Suave brands, combines rebates with coupons.

Tie-In Promotions

Growing numbers of companies are using tie-ins (group promotions) to generate increased sales, to stimulate trade and consumer interest, and to gain optimal use of their promotional budgets. Tie-in promotions are cost-effective because the cost, say, of distributing coupons is shared among multiple brands. For example, two P&G brands—Tide and Downy—share the expense of the FSI coupon offer and the free-in-the-mail promotion shown in Figure 18.15. The P&G promotion is an intracompany tie-in, but intercompany tie-ins also are used as illustrated by the joint promotion in Figure 18.22 between Green Giant's Create a Meal brand and Tyson's chicken strips.

An Intercompany Tie-In

Implementation Problems.   Tie-in promotions are capable of accomplishing useful objectives, but not without potential problems.[84] Promotion lead time is lengthened because two or more entities have to coordinate their separate promotional schedules. Creative conflicts and convoluted messages may result from each partner trying to receive primary attention for its product/service.

To reduce problems as much as possible and to accomplish objectives, it is important that (1) the profiles of each partner's customers be similar with regard to pertinent demographic or other consumption-influencing characteristics; (2) the partners' images should reinforce each other (e.g., Green Giant and Tyson both are well-known brands with images of consistently high quality); and (3) partners must be willing to cooperate rather than imposing their own interests to the detriment of the other partner's welfare.[85]

RETAILER PROMOTIONS

Discussion to this point has focused on manufacturer promotions that are directed at consumers. Retailers also design promotions for their present and prospective customers. These retailer-inspired promotions are created for purposes of increasing store traffic and offering shoppers attractive price discounts or other deals. Couponing is a favorite promotion among many retailers in the grocery, drug, and mass merchandise areas of business. Some grocery retailers hold special "Coupon Days" when they redeem manufacturer coupons at double or even triple their face value. For example, a grocery store on a "triple-coupon day" would deduct $1.20 from the consumer's bill when she or he submits a manufacturer's coupon with a face value of 40 cents. Retailers typically limit their double- or triple-discount offers to manufacturer coupons having face values of 50 cents or less.

Another form of retailer coupon is illustrated by the example in Figure 18.23. In this instance, Eckerd (a drugstore chain) is offering rolls of Bounty towels for 79 cents, which represents a savings of 60 cents from the regular price of $1.39 per roll. This coupon, by the way, is just one of many from a thick booklet of Eckerd coupons totaling over $700 in potential savings. Note that although these coupons carry the retailer's name (Eckerd in this case), manufacturers support the coupon discounts through so-called account-specific funds provided to retailers (as described in Chapter 17).

FIGURE 18.23

A Store Coupon

A number of retailers offer their customers plastic, frequent-shopper cards that entitle shoppers to discounts on select items purchased on any particular shopping occasion. For example, in a Wednesday advertising flyer, one grocery retailer offered its cardholders savings such as $2.99 on the purchase of two Mrs. Paul's fish filets, $1.25 when buying two cans of Minute Maid juice, and $1.70 discount with the purchase of Freschetta pizza. Customers receive these savings upon submitting their frequent-shopper cards to clerks at checkout, who scan the card number and deduct savings from the shopper's bill when discounted items are scanned. These frequent-shopper cards encourage repeat purchasing from a particular retail chain. Because they are designated with labels such as VIC ("Very Important Customer"), they also serve to elevate the shopper's sense of importance to a store. Finally, frequent-shopper card programs provide retailers with valuable databases containing information on shopper demographics and purchase habits.

Sampling is another form of retailer-based sales promotion that is in wide use. Although many instances of store sampling represent joint programs between stores and manufacturers, retailers are sampling their own store/private label products increasingly.[86]

EVALUATING SALES PROMOTION IDEAS

It should be apparent by this point that numerous alternatives are available to manufacturers and retailers when planning sales promotions. There also are a variety of objectives that effective promotion programs are able to achieve. The combination of numerous alternatives and diverse objectives leads to a staggering array of possibilities. The following straightforward, three-step procedure directs a brand marketer in determining which promotion ideas and approaches have the best chance of succeeding.[87]

Step 1: Identify the Objectives

The most basic yet important step toward successful consumer-oriented promotions is the clear identification of the specific objective(s) that is (are) to be accomplished. Objectives should be specified as they relate both to the trade and to ultimate consumers; for example, an objective may be to generate trial, to load consumers, to preempt competition, to increase display space, and so on.

In this first step, the promotional planner must commit the objectives to writing and state them specifically and in measurable terms. For example, "to increase sales" is too general. In comparison, the objective "to increase display space by 25 percent over the comparable period last year" is specific and measurable.

Step 2: Achieve Agreement

Everyone involved in the marketing of a brand must agree with the objectives developed. Failure to achieve agreement on objectives results in various decision makers (such as the advertising, sales, and brand managers) pushing for different programs because they have different objectives in mind. Also, a specific sales promotion program can more easily be evaluated in terms of a specific objective than a vague generalization.

Step 3: Evaluation System

With specific objectives established and agreement achieved, the following five-point evaluation system should be used to rate any sales promotion program or idea:

1. **How good is the general idea?** Every idea should be evaluated against the promotion's objectives. For example, if the objective is to increase product trial, a sample or a coupon would be rated favorably, while a sweepstakes would flunk this initial evaluation.

2. **Will the sales promotion idea appeal to the target market?** A contest, for example, might have great appeal to children, but for certain adult groups it would have disastrous results. In general, remember that the target market represents the bedrock against which all proposals should be judged.

3. **Is the idea unique, or is the competition doing something similar?** The prospects of receiving both trade and consumer attention depend on developing promotions that are not ordinary. Creativity is every bit as important to the success of sales promotions as it is with advertising.

4. **Is the promotion presented clearly so that the intended market will notice, comprehend, and respond to the deal?** Sales promotion planners should start with one fundamental premise: Most consumers are not willing to spend much time and effort figuring out how a promotion works. It is critical to a promotion's success that instructions be user friendly. Let consumers know quickly and clearly what the offer is and how to respond to it.

5. **How cost-effective is the proposed idea?** This requires an evaluation of whether or not the proposed promotion will achieve the intended objectives at an affordable cost. Sophisticated promotion planners cost out alternative programs and know in advance the likely bottom-line payoff from a promotion.

In sum and as emphasized throughout the text as well as earlier in the chapter, the brand manager must think continually in terms of target, objectives, and budget. In this case, she or he must evaluate every promotion concept in terms of the intended target market, the objectives that are to be achieved, and the budget constraint that is imposed.

S ummary

This chapter focuses on consumer-oriented promotions. The various sales promotion tools available to marketers are classified in terms of whether the reward offered consumers is immediate or delayed and whether the manufacturer's objective is to achieve trial impact, customer holding/loading, or image reinforcement. Specific sales promotion techniques fall into one of five general categories: immediate reward/trial impact, delayed reward/ trial impact, immediate reward/customer holding, delayed reward/customer holding, and delayed reward/image reinforcement.

Specific topics addressed in the chapter include sampling effectiveness; conditions when sampling should be used; coupon usage and growth; couponing costs; coupon misre- demption; reasons for using in- and on-pack premiums and self-liquidators; FTC price-off regulations; differences between refunds and rebates and when each is used; the role of contests and sweepstakes; the innovation of phone cards as promotional incentives; Inter- net promotions; the nature of overlay and tie-in promotions; retailer promotions; and vari- ous other topics.

The first and most critical requirement for a successful sales promotion is that it be based on clearly defined objectives. Second, the program must be designed with a specific target market in mind. It should also be realized that many consumers, perhaps most, de- sire to maximize the rewards gained from participating in a promotion while minimizing the amount of time and effort invested. Consequently, an effective sales promotion, from a consumer-response perspective, must make it relatively easy for consumers to obtain their reward, and the size of the reward must be sufficient to justify the consumers' efforts. A third essential ingredient for effective sales promotions is that programs must be developed with the interests of retailers in mind—not just those of the manufacturer.

D iscussion Questions

1. Why are immediate rewards more effective in inducing consumer behaviors desired by a brand marketer? Use a specific, concrete illustration from your own experience to support your answer.

2. In view of the promotional disasters described in the *Opening Vignette,* what specific moral would you suggest should be taken from these examples? Be specific.

3. One of the major trends in product sampling is selective sampling of targeted groups. Assume you work for a company that has just developed a substitute candy bar that tastes almost as good as a regular candy bar but has far fewer calories. Marketing research has identified the tar- get market as economically upscale consumers, aged 21 to 54, who reside in suburban and urban areas. Explain specifically how you might selectively sample your new product to ap- proximately 5 million such consumers.

4. Compare and contrast sampling and media-delivered coupons in terms of objectives, consumer impact, and overall roles in marketing communication strategies.

5. A packaged-goods company plans to introduce a new bath soap that differs from competitive soaps by virtue of a distinct new fragrance. Should sampling be used to introduce the product?

6. Present your personal views concerning the number of coupons distributed annually in the United States. Is widespread couponing in the best interest of consumers? Could marketers use other promotional methods more effectively and economically to achieve the objectives accom- plished with coupons?

7. Present a position on the following statement (voiced by a student who read a previous edition of this textbook): "I can't understand why in Table 18.1 free-in-the-mail premiums are positioned as accomplishing just a trial-impact function. It would seem that this form of promotion also accomplishes customer holding objectives."

8. Using Table 18.3 as a guide, calculate the full cost per redeemed coupon given the following facts: (1) face value = 75 cents; (2) 20 million coupons distributed at $7 per thousand; (3) redemption rate = 3 percent; (4) handling cost = 8 cents; and (5) misredemption rate = 7 percent.

TABLE 18.3

Full Coupon Cost

1. Face Value	75¢
2. Distribution and postage cost	40¢
3. Handling charge	8¢
4. Consumer misredemption cost	7¢
5. Internal preparation and processing cost	2¢
6. Redemption cost	2¢
TOTAL COST	$1.34

Source: Adapted from an analysis performed by the McKinsey & Co. consulting firm as reported in Daniel Shannon, "Still a Mighty Marketing Mechanism," *Promo*, April 1996, 85.

9. Your company markets hot dogs, bologna, and other processed meats. You wish to offer a self-liquidating premium that would cost consumers approximately $25, would require five proofs of purchase, and would be appropriately themed to your product category during the summer months. Your primary market segment consists of families with school-age children crossing all socioeconomic strata. Suggest two premium items and justify your choice.

10. What is the purpose of the FTC price-off regulations?

11. Compare bonus packs and price-off deals in terms of consumer impact.

12. What is sales promotion crossruffing, and why is it used?

13. How can sales promotion reinforce a brand's image? Is this a major objective of sales promotion?

14. Compare contests and sweepstakes in terms of how they function and their relative effectiveness.

15. Your company markets antifreeze. Sales to consumers take place in a very short period, primarily September through December. You want to tie in a promotion between your product and the product of another company that would bring more visibility to your brand and encourage retailers to provide more shelf space. Recommend a partner for this tie-in promotion and justify the choice.

16. Go through a Sunday newspaper and select five FSIs. Analyze each in terms of what you think are the marketer's objectives in using this particular promotion.

17. What are your thoughts regarding the future of Internet promotions?

18. What retailer-based promotions are you familiar with that are different from the ones described toward the end of the chapter?

Internet Exercises

1. Internet advertising faces a tough challenge. It must grab users' attention away from primary Web-surfing goals such as entertainment, communication, and research. Other media take control of the situation by halting their content and transmitting only the advertisement so that the receiver's choices are to listen/see or to "withdraw" by, for example, channel surfing (that is, zapping) during commercials. Internet Web sites mimicking this approach have found that consumers are much less tolerant of having their own active goals blocked than they are of having mass-media content interrupted. A few innovative companies are seeking to directly address this problem with consumer-based incentives. For example, www.cybergold.com's online "Earn & Spend™" community has nearly 1.5 million registered consumers who earn cash online by clicking on banners, visiting sponsor Web sites, and filling out surveys. The cash can then be spent online back at Cybergold's site that offers a wide variety of products including many from the advertisers. The site also has substantive content such as news, stock quotes, weather, e-mail, chat, and games so that many members also use Cybergold as their portal to the Internet. Visit Cybergold's site and respond to the following questions:
    a. In what ways is Cybergold's promotional concept innovative? In what ways is it an extension of the old Greenbax stamps and stores?
    b. Do you think that seeing an advertiser willing to pay you to view an ad would enhance or detract from the perceived value of the advertised product?
    c. How could Cybergold's advertising clients employ an overlay program?

2. Visit www.mypoints.com. MyPoints runs a program that allows consumers to earn "points" by clicking on banners, buying products online, following links, and so on. These points can be accumulated and then redeemed for other goods such as gift certificates to Target, Sprint long distance credit, books, videos, boat cruises, and frequent-flyer miles. MyPoints claims to have 2 million people signed up and 6000 joining each day. Consumers are asked to provide a "profile" in order to participate in the program. This profile can then be linked to a person's point gathering as well as redemption activity.
    a. How could this "points" program be structured into a continuity program for a specific brand? Illustrate with an example or two.
    b. When do you think offering points versus cash will be more effective for:
        i)   Getting consumers to perform the specific earning activities (banner clicking, site visits, site learning, etc.), and
        ii) Accomplishing the three general categories of promotion objectives (generating trial purchases, encouraging repeat purchases, and reinforcing brand images)?

3. Visit www.prizes.com and answer the following questions:
    a. Describe the "scratch and win" product.
    b. Select a favorite brand. Assume you have been asked to investigate the prospect of running an Internet sweepstakes for this brand. Describe your design and discuss how it facilitates attaining your promotional objectives.

Chapter Eighteen Endnotes

1. "Products on Trial," *Marketing Communications,* October 1987, 73–74.

2. *The 20th Annual Survey of Promotional Practices* (Largo, FL: Cox Direct, 1998), 47.

3. The last available statistic of sampling expenditures was for 1997, at which time total sampling expenditures were approximately $925 million. (Source: *Promo's* 6th Annual Sourcebook '99, 30.) With an annual growth rate almost in the double digits, by 2000 sampling expenditures in the United States undoubtedly exceed $1 billion.

4. *The 20th Annual Survey of Promotional Practices,* 48.

5. Scott Hume, "Prom Night: Free Samples with Tux," *Advertising Age,* March 13, 1989, 53.

6. Russ Bowman, "Freebie Follow-Through," *Marketing and Media Decisions,* February 1989, 102.

7. "Sampling Wins Over More Marketers," *Advertising Age,* July 27, 1992, 12.

8. Terry Lefton, "Try It, You'll Like It," *Brandweek,* May 24, 1993, 32.

9. David Vaczek, "Points of Switch," *Promo,* September 1998, 39–40.

10. Marcy Magiera, "A Real Movie Treat," *Advertising Age,* December 10, 1990, 6.

11. Kate Fitzgerald, "Targeted Sampling Fits in Integrated Mix," *Advertising Age,* July 5, 1993, 22.

12. "Street Walkers," *Promo,* February 1997, 6; Stephanie Thompson, "Progresso Warriors," *Brandweek,* June 23, 1997, 20, 22.

13. Kate Fitzgerald, "Sampling & Singing," *Advertising Age,* June 8, 1998, 32.

14. Adapted from Glenn Heitsmith, "Gaining Trial," *Promo,* September 1994, 108; and "Spend a Little, Get a Lot," Trial and Conversion III: Harnessing the Power of Sampling Special Advertising Supplement (New York: Promotional Marketing Association, Inc., 1996–97), 18.

15. *Insights: Issues 1–13, 1979–1982* (New York: NPD Research, 1983), 6–7.

16. Carol Scott, "Effects of Trial and Incentives on Repeat Purchase Behavior," *Journal of Marketing Research* 13 (August 1976), 263–269. See also Joe A. Dodson, Alice M. Tybout, and Brian Sternthal, "Impact of Deals and Deal Retraction on Brand Switching," *Journal of Marketing Research* 15 (February 1978), 72–81. This research has attribution theory as its foundation. For more discussion of applications of attribution theory in marketing and consumer behavior, see Richard W. Mizerski, Linda L. Golden, and Jerome B. Kernan, "The Attribution Process in Consumer Decision Making," *Journal of Consumer Research* 6 (September 1979), 123–140; and Valerie S. Folkes, "Recent Attribution Research in Consumer Behavior: A Review and New Directions, *Journal of Consumer Research* 14 (March 1988), 548–565.

17. "Sampling Wins Over More Marketers."

18. Charles Fredericks, Jr., "What Ogilvy & Mather Has Learned about Sales Promotion," *The Tools of Promotion* (New York: Association of National Advertisers, 1975).

19. Judann Pollack, "Jif Samples Flavored Peanut Butter," *Advertising Age,* September 28, 1998, 12.

20. Tara Parker-Pope, "P&G Puts Lots of Chips on Plan to Give Away Fat-Free Pringles," *The Wall Street Journal Interactive Edition,* June 23, 1998.

21. Lynn G. Reiling, "Consumers Misuse Mass Sampling for Sun Light Dishwashing Liquid," *Marketing News,* September 3, 1982, 1, 2.

22. Maciek Gajewski, "Samples: A Steal in Poland," *Advertising Age,* November 4, 1991, 54.

23. Roger A. Strang, "The Economic Impact of Cents-Off Coupons," *Marketing Communications,* March 1981, 35–44.

24. Nathaniel Frey, "Sales Promotion Analysis," *Marketing Communications,* August 1988, 14–20.

25. Daniel Shannon, "Couponing into the Millennium," *Promo,* April 1995, 75.

26. *Promo's* 6th Annual Sourcebook '99, 18.

27. Emily R. Sendler and Fara Warner, "Ford Matches Coupon Mailing by GM, And Offers to Honor Rival's Discounts," *The Wall Street Journal Interactive Edition,* April 24, 1998.

28. Kerry J. Smith, "Shoppers Get Promotion Active," *Promo,* July 1995, 70.

29. Donald R. Lichtenstein, Richard G. Netemeyer, and Scot Burton, "Distinguishing Coupon Proneness from Value Consciousness: An Acquisition-Transaction Utility Theory Perspective," *Journal of Marketing* 54 (July 1990), 54–67. For a detailed treatment of factors that influence consumers' coupon redemption behavior, see also Banwari Mittal, "An Integrated Framework for Relating Diverse Consumer Characteristics to Supermarket Coupon Redemption," *Journal of Marketing Research* 31 (November 1994), 533–544.

30. Betsy Spethmann, "Countries Crave Coupons," *Advertising Age,* July 15, 1991, 26.

31. "Global Couponing Gets Mixed Reviews," *Promo,* August 1994, 107.

32. *Promo's* 6th Annual Sourcebook '99, 18. This estimate is from NCH NuWorld Marketing, an Illinois-based coupon clearinghouse company.

33. "Couponing Distribution Trends and Patterns," *PMAA Promotion Update '82* (New York: Promotion Management Association of America, Inc., 1983). Run of paper, or run of press, means that an advertisement carrying a coupon is part of the regular newspaper/magazine pages rather than a separate section or insert.

34. Nathaniel Frey, "Targeted Couponing: New Wrinkles Cut Waste," *Marketing Communications,* January 1988, 40.

35. Kapil Bawa and Robert W. Shoemaker, "The Effects of a Direct Mail Coupon on Brand Choice Behavior," *Journal of Marketing Research* 24 (November 1987), 370–376.

36. Richard H. Aycrigg, *Promotion Update '82* (New York: Promotion Marketing Association of America, Inc., 1982).

37. Daneil Shannon, "Still a Mighty Marketing Mechanism," *Promo,* April 1996, 86.

38. "Checkout: Instant Results," *Promo,* October 1998, 75.

39. Kapil Bawa, Srini S. Srinivasan, and Rajendra K. Srivastava, "Coupon Attractiveness and Coupon Proneness: A Framework for Modeling Coupon Redemption," *Journal of Marketing Research* 34 (November 1997), 517–525.

40. Priya Raghubir, "Coupon Value: A Signal for Price?" *Journal of Marketing Research* 35 (August 1998), 316–324.

41. *Marketer's Guide to Media,* 1998–99, Vol. 21 (New York: BPI Communications, 1998), 129.

42. Shannon, "Still a Mighty Marketing Mechanism," 86.

43. Ibid.

44. "When the Chips Are Down," *Promo* Magazine Special Report, April 1998, S7.

45. Shannon, "Still a Mighty Marketing Mechanism," 86.

46. Kapil Bawa and Robert W. Shoemaker, "Analyzing Incremental Sales from a Direct Mail Coupon Promotion," *Journal of Marketing Research* 53 (July 1989), 66–78.

47. Erwin Ephron, "More Weeks, Less Weight: The Shelf-Space Model of Advertising," *Journal of Advertising Research* 35 (May/June 1995), 18–23.

48. Srini S. Srinivasan, Robert P. Leone, and Francis J. Mulhern, "The Advertising Exposure Effect of Free Standing Inserts," *Journal of Advertising* 24 (spring 1995), 29–40.

49. France Leclerc and John D. C. Little, "Can Advertising Copy Make FSI Coupons More Effective?" *Journal of Marketing Research* 34 (November 1997), 473–484.

50. Shannon, "Still a Mighty Marketing Mechanism," 86.

51. For a technical analysis of the role of crossruffing, see Sanjay K. Dhar and Jagmohan S. Raju, "The Effects of Cross-Ruff Coupons on Sales and Profits," *Marketing Science* 44 (November 1998), 1501–1516.

52. Shannon, "Still a Mighty Marketing Mechanism," 86.

53. "The Route to Redemption," *Advertising Age,* May 30, 1983, 57.

54. "A Drop in the Crime Rate," *Promo,* December 1997, 12.

55. Cecelia Blalock, "Another Retailer Nabbed in Coupon Misredemption Plot," *Promo,* December 1993, 38.

56. Ibid.

57. Cecelia Blalock, "Tough Sentence for Coupon Middle Man," *Promo,* June 1993, 87.

58. "Clipped, Supermarket Owners Charged with Coupon Fraud," *Promo,* May 1997, 14.

59. "Report: Coupon Scams Are Funding Terrorism," *Promo,* August 1996, 50.

60. *Promo's* 6th Annual Sourcebook '99, 12.

61. Glenn Heitsmith, "Value-Added Versatility," *Promo,* May 1994, 26.

62. "Ralston-Purina Offers Adult Incentive in Kids' Cereal Boxes," *Marketing News,* April 25, 1988, 1.

63. Francine Schore, "Inflation Hurts Cheaper Items," *Advertising Age,* October 6, 1980, S19, S20.

64. Ibid.

65. Carolyn Shea, "Calling All Cards: Prepaid Phone Cards Are Ringing Up Sales," *Promo,* March 1995, 42.

66. Ibid., 37–46.

67. Fredericks, "What Ogilvy & Mather Has Learned about Sales Promotion."

68. *Consumer Promotion Seminar Fact Book* (New York: Association of National Advertisers, undated), 7.

69. Ronnie Telzer, "Rebates Challenge Coupons' Redeeming Values," *Advertising Age,* March 23, 1987, S18.

70. William M. Bulkeley, "Rebates' Appeal to Manufacturers: Few Consumers Redeem Them," *The Wall Street Journal Interactive Edition,* February 10, 1998.

71. Dilip Soman, "The Illusion of Delayed Incentives: Evaluating Future Effort-Money Transactions," *Journal of Marketing Research* 35 (November 1998), 427–437.

72. Kerry J. Smith, "Postal Inspectors Target Rebate Fraud," *Promo,* April 1994, 13; Kerry J. Smith, "Marketers Huddle on Rebate Fraud," *Promo,* June 1994, 39.

73. Smith, "Postal Inspectors Target Rebate Fraud."

74. The following examples are from Kerry J. Smith, "The Promotion Gravy Train," *Promo,* August 1995, 51.

75. Daniel Shannon, "Playing to Win," *Promo,* August 1994, 50.

76. Stephanie Thompson, "Polaner Joins Dwelling Giveaway Rush," *Brandweek,* February 2, 1998, 8.

77. Laurie Baum, "How Beatrice Lost at Its Own Game," *Business Week,* March 2, 1987, 66.

78. Ibid.

79. *The 20th Annual Survey of Promotional Practices,* 42.

80. Paulette Thomas, "Shoppers May Be Willing to Trade Privacy for Savings," *The Wall Street Journal Interactive Edition,* June 18, 1998.

81. Robert Storace, "Bringing Online in Line," *Promo,* April 1998, 54–56, 154–156.

82. "PromoXchange Debuts: A Cyberspace Tool for Marketers," *Promo,* October 1998, 11.

83. Ibid.

84. Melvin Scales, "What Tie-in Promotions Can Do for You," *Outlook* (a publication of the Promotion Marketing Association of America) 12 (fall 1988), 10–11.

85. "Creating Synergy through Tie-in Promotions," *Marketing Communications,* April 1988, 45.

86. *The 20th Annual Survey of Promotional Practices,* 63.

87. Don E. Schultz and William A. Robinson, *Sales Promotion Management* (Lincolnwood, Ill.: NTC Business Books, 1986), 436–445.

PART

SIX

Part Six—Public Relations, Sponsorship Marketing, and Personal Selling

Part Six includes chapters on marketing-oriented public relations, or MPR, and personal selling. Chapter 19, on public relations, includes a discussion of the historically entrenched practice of reactive public relations as well as the more recent practice of proactive public relations. A special section is devoted to negative publicity, including the issue of rumors and how to handle them. The last major section covers both cause and event marketing—the two specific aspects of sponsorship marketing.

Chapter 20 introduces students to the job of the salesperson. The chapter describes the salesperson's job and the kinds of activities performed. Also discussed are determinants of salesperson performance and determinants of outstanding salespeople. The chapter emphasizes that advertising, sales promotions, point-of-purchase programs, and sponsorships are of little value without effective personal selling. A company's equity and the equity of its individual brands are influenced in large measure by the efforts of its sales force.

Marketing Public Relations and Sponsorship Marketing

CHAPTER OBJECTIVES

After studying this chapter, you should be able to:

1. Explain the nature and role of marketing public relations (MPR).
2. Distinguish between proactive and reactive MPR.
3. Understand the types of commercial rumors and how to control them.
4. Explain event sponsorships and how to select appropriate events.
5. Explain the nature and use of cause-oriented marketing.

Opening Vignette: Good to the Last Drop—And Good for the Economically Disadvantaged

Kraft Foods' Maxwell House® is a coffee brand that has been available to American consumers since 1892. The slogan "Good to the Last Drop"™ has graced the cans and packages of Maxwell House for most of this time. Although Maxwell House has been a very successful brand throughout the years, competition has intensified and maintaining market share demands continuous effort on the part of Maxwell House to demonstrate that its brand remains relevant to consumers. An integrated marketing communications initiative is essential toward meeting this challenge. One program in the late 1990s illustrates how brand managers for Maxwell House met the challenge.

A philanthropic-like marketing effort was a key component of the IMC initiative that allowed Maxwell House to make a personal connection with consumers and further establish the brand's role as a part of Americana. In particular, Maxwell House aligned the brand with Habitat for Humanity and created the "Build a Home America"™ program. With an objective of building 100 homes in partnership with hard working American families in need in 100 weeks, Maxwell House donated $2 million to Habitat for Humanity and challenged others to match the contribution. A major advertising campaign reinforced Maxwell House's "Good-to-the-last-drop" image and also emphasized the brand's sponsorship of "Build a Home America." Television advertising made a connection between the brand and the worthy sponsorship program via a voiceover that stated: "After more than a century in American homes, Maxwell House is proud to help Habitat for Humanity build 100 homes."

Freestanding inserts and special packaging graphics were additional elements of the integrated marketing program that touted Maxwell House's sponsorship of the home-building program. Further, the Maxwell House Cafe traveled to all 37 markets around the United States where Maxwell House-sponsored homes were built. The Airstream diner, painted in Maxwell House's signature blue and white colors, housed an exhibit on the meaning of home in America. The exhibit traveled to building sites and grocery store loca-

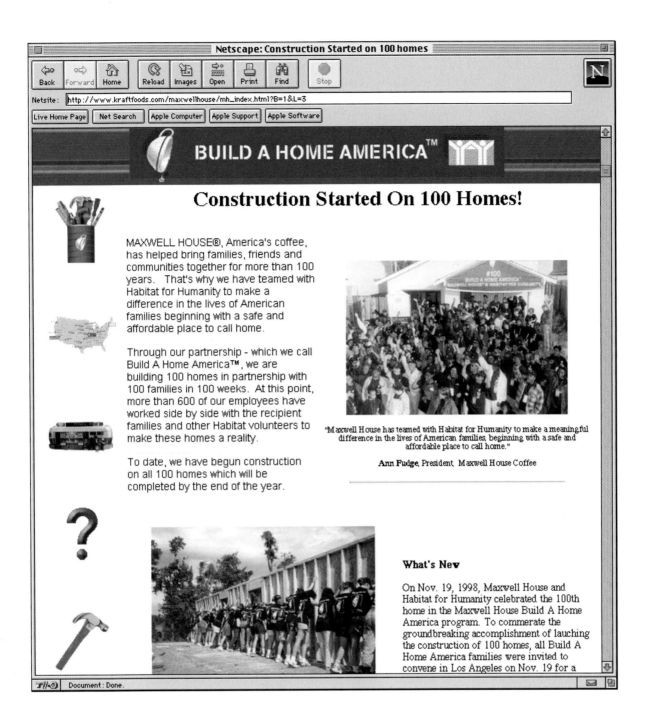

Back Forward Home Reload Images Open Print Find Stop

Netsite: http://www.kraftfoods.com/maxwellhouse/mh_index.html?B=1&L=3

Live Home Page   Net Search   Apple Computer   Apple Support   Apple Software

BUILD A HOME AMERICA™

Construction Started On 100 Homes!

MAXWELL HOUSE®, America's coffee, has helped bring families, friends and communities together for more than 100 years. That's why we have teamed with Habitat for Humanity to make a difference in the lives of American families beginning with a safe and affordable place to call home.

Through our partnership - which we call Build A Home America™, we are building 100 homes in partnership with 100 families in 100 weeks. At this point, more than 600 of our employees have worked side by side with the recipient families and other Habitat volunteers to make these homes a reality.

To date, we have begun construction on all 100 homes which will be completed by the end of the year.

"Maxwell House has teamed with Habitat for Humanity to make a meaningful difference in the lives of American families, beginning with a safe and affordable place to call home."

Ann Fudge, President, Maxwell House Coffee

What's New

On Nov. 19, 1998, Maxwell House and Habitat for Humanity celebrated the 100th home in the Maxwell House Build A Home America program. To commerate the groundbreaking accomplishment of lauching the construction of 100 homes, all Build A Home America families were invited to convene in Los Angeles on Nov. 19 for a

Document: Done.

---

tions, distributing complimentary samples of Maxwell House coffee and coupons. There also was a public relations program whereby house-building volunteers shared their experiences in building homes and encouraged others to participate in Habitat for Humanity efforts.

As should be apparent, Maxwell House's brand managers and their advertising and PR agencies designed an ambitious integrated marketing communications program that involved more than merely contributing money to a worthy cause. Although difficult to attribute success to any single program, Maxwell House's brand managers believe that this program prevented sales erosion at a time when coffee prices were skyrocketing and competition was intensifying. In sum, this program combined some hard-nosed strategic marketing with an element of corporate philanthropy to serve both the requirements of the Maxwell House brand and the housing needs of economically disadvantaged Americans.

Source: Adapted from Stephanie Thompson, "Maxwell Housing," *Brandweek,* May 4, 1998, 24.

*T*his chapter explores the multiple roles performed by the public relations aspect of an integrated marketing communications program. The chapter also treats the related topics of event and cause marketing as part of the more general practice known as sponsorship marketing. These growing aspects of IMC are conceptually aligned with public relations and in some organizations are administratively part of the public relations department.

MARKETING PUBLIC RELATIONS

Public relations, or PR, is an organizational activity involved with fostering *goodwill* between a company and its various publics. PR efforts are aimed at various corporate constituencies, including employees, suppliers, stockholders, governments, the public, labor groups, citizen action groups, and consumers. As just described, PR involves relations with *all* of an organization's relevant publics. In other words, most PR activities do not involve marketing per se but rather deal with general management concerns. This more encompassing aspect of public relations can be called *general PR*. Interactions with employees, stockholders, labor groups, citizen action groups, and suppliers are typically part of a company's general, nonmarketing public relations.

Our concern in this chapter is only with the narrow aspect of public relations involving an organization's interactions with *consumers*. The marketing-oriented aspect of public relations is called *marketing public relations,* or *MPR* for short.[1]

MPR can be further delineated as involving either proactive or reactive public relations.[2] **Proactive MPR** is dictated by a company's marketing objectives. It is offensively rather than defensively oriented and opportunity seeking rather than problem solving. Proactive MPR, as illustrated by the Maxwell House case in the *Opening Vignette,* is a tool for communicating a brand's merits and is used typically in conjunction with advertising, promotions, and personal selling.

Reactive MPR, by comparison, describes the conduct of public relations in response to outside influences. It is undertaken as a result of external pressures and challenges brought by competitive actions, shifts in consumer attitudes, changes in government policy, or other external influences. Reactive MPR deals typically with changes that have *negative consequences* for an organization. Reactive MPR attempts to repair a company's reputation, prevent market erosion, and regain lost sales.

Proactive MPR

The major role of proactive MPR is in the area of product introductions or product revisions. Proactive MPR is integrated with other IMC tools to give a product additional exposure, newsworthiness, and credibility. This last factor, *credibility,* largely accounts for the effectiveness of proactive MPR. Whereas advertising and personal-selling claims are sometimes suspect—because we question salespeople's and advertisers' motives, knowing they have a personal stake in persuading us—product announcements by a newspaper editor or television broadcaster are notably more believable. Consumers are less likely to question the motivation underlying an editorial-type endorsement.

Publicity is the major tool of proactive MPR. Like advertising and personal selling, the fundamental purposes of marketing-oriented publicity are to enhance a brand's equity in a twofold manner: (1) by facilitating brand awareness and (2) by augmenting brand image via forging strong and favorable associations with the brand in the minds of consumers. For example, managers of Maxwell House intended for that brand to be perceived as wholesome and compassionate by virtue of its alliance with Habitat for Humanity and the "Build a Home" program.

www.kraftfoods.com

Companies obtain publicity using various forms of news releases, press conferences, and other types of information dissemination. News releases concerning new products, modifications in old products, and other newsworthy topics are delivered to editors of newspapers, magazines, and other media. Press conferences announce major news events of interest to the public. Photographs, tapes, and films are useful for illustrating product improvements, new products, advanced production techniques, and so forth. Of course, all forms of publicity are subject to the control and whims of the media. However, by disseminating a large volume of publicity materials and by preparing materials that fit the media's needs, a company increases its chances of obtaining beneficial publicity.[3]

Three widely used forms of publicity in marketing-oriented PR are product releases, executive-statement releases, and feature articles.

Product releases announce new products, provide relevant information about product features and benefits, and inform interested listeners/readers how additional information can be obtained. A product release is typically aired on television networks or published in a product section of trade magazines and business publications (such as *Business Week, Forbes, Fortune,* and *The Wall Street Journal*) or in a business or consumer-news section of consumer magazines (such as *Time* or *Newsweek*).

www.newsweek.com

www.time.com

Audiovisual product releases (called video news releases, or VNRs) have gained wide usage in recent years. For example, Hershey introduced its new Hershey Kisses with almonds by showing a 6-foot, 500-pound replica of a Hershey Kiss covered in gold sequins and foil being dropped from a Times Square building (much like the neon apple dropped on New Year's Eve). Hershey's PR agency videotaped the event, distributed tapes to New York networks, and the same evening the event was seen on TV by millions of Americans. For less than $100,000, Hershey's new product received tremendous exposure.

www.hersheys.com

Executive-statement releases are news releases quoting CEOs and other corporate executives. Unlike a product release, which is restricted to describing a new or modified product, an executive-statement release may address a wide variety of issues relevant to a corporation's publics, such as the following:

- ◆ Statements about industry developments and trends;
- ◆ Forecasts of future sales;
- ◆ Views on the economy;
- ◆ Comments on R&D developments or market research findings;
- ◆ Announcements of new marketing programs launched by the company;
- ◆ Views on foreign competition or global developments; and
- ◆ Comments on environmental issues.

Whereas product releases are typically published in the business or product section of a publication, executive-statement releases are published in the *news section*. This location carries with it a significant degree of credibility. Note that any product release can be converted into an executive-statement release by changing the way it is written.

Feature articles are detailed descriptions of products or other newsworthy programs that are written by a PR firm for immediate publication or airing by print or broadcast media or distribution via appropriate Internet sites. Materials such as this are inexpensive to prepare, yet they can provide companies with tremendous access to many potential customers as well as prospective investors.

Reactive MPR

Unanticipated marketplace developments can place an organization in a vulnerable position that demands reactive marketing PR. Nike, for example, has been the focus of intense negative publicity on grounds that this company underpays Asian workers who manufacturer its swoosh-plastered casual shoes and apparel.[4] Product defects and failures are the most dramatic factors underlying the need for reactive MPR. Following are some illustrations of negative-publicity cases that have received widespread media attention.

Product Tamperings: Tylenol and Sudafed. In 1982, seven people in the Chicago area died from cyanide poisoning after ingesting Tylenol capsules. Many analysts predicted that Tylenol would never regain its previously sizable market share. Some observers even questioned whether Johnson & Johnson ever would be able to market anything under the Tylenol name.

Johnson & Johnson's handling of the Tylenol tragedy was nearly brilliant. Rather than denying a problem existed, J&J acted swiftly by removing Tylenol from retail shelves. Spokespersons appeared on television and cautioned consumers not to ingest Tylenol capsules. A tamper-proof package was designed, setting a standard for other companies. As a final good-faith gesture, J&J offered consumers free replacements for products they had disposed of in the aftermath of the Chicago tragedy. Tylenol regained its market share shortly after this campaign began.

In a tragic replay of the Tylenol case, two people in Washington state died in 1991 after ingesting cyanide-laced Sudafed capsules. Following Tylenol's lead, Burroughs Wellcome Co., Sudafed's maker, immediately withdrew the product from store shelves, suspended advertising, established an 800-number phone line for consumer inquiries, and offered a $100,000 reward for information leading to the arrest of the product tamperer. Burrough's quick and effective response resulted in only a brief sales slump for Sudafed.[5]

The Perrier Case. Perrier was the leading brand of bottled water in the United States until 1990 when Source Perrier, the manufacturer, announced that traces of a toxic chemical, benzene, had been found in some of its products. Perrier recalled 72 million bottles from U.S. supermarkets and restaurants and subsequently withdrew the product from distribution elsewhere in the world. The total cost of the global recall was about $166 million. Perrier's sales in the United States declined by 40 percent, and Evian replaced it as the leading imported bottled water.[6] Perrier's business has never fully recovered.

The Pepsi Hoax. Pepsi-Cola was the target of a product tampering hoax when a New Orleans man contacted the Cable News Network and alleged that he had found a syringe in a can of Diet Pepsi. This was only the first of several reported contaminations from different geographical areas. Pepsi officials were confident that the reports were false and that the Pepsi bottling process was completely safe. They reacted to the negative publicity by using the media. A video showing the bottling process of Pepsi products was released shortly after the initial news broke and was seen by an estimated 187 million viewers. It demonstrated the remote possibility that a foreign object, especially something as large as a syringe, could be inserted in cans in the less than one second they are open for filling and capping. That same day, Pepsi-Cola's president and CEO appeared on ABC's *Nightline* along with the Commissioner of the Food and Drug Administration, Dr. David Kessler. Pepsi's CEO insisted that the Diet Pepsi can was 99.9 percent safe, and the FDA Commissioner warned consumers of the penalties for making false claims.

Two days later, Dr. Kessler noted at a news conference that "It is simply not logical to conclude that a nationwide tampering has occurred" and that the FDA was "unable to confirm even one case of tampering." These statements were later broadcast over national TV along with a video news release showing a consumer inserting a syringe into a Diet Pepsi can. She had been caught by the store's surveillance camera. With this exposure, the crisis was essentially over.

To close the issue, Pepsi ran nationwide newspaper advertisements to assuage any residual consumer fears. The headlines to these full-page ads read: "Pepsi is pleased to announce . . . nothing." The ads proceeded to inform readers that "those stories about Diet Pepsi were simply a hoax. Plain and simple, not true." Although volume case sales dropped 2 percent during the period following the hoax, sales returned to normal in a matter of weeks.[7]

Negative publicity can hit a company at any time. The lesson to be learned is that quick and positive responses to negative publicity are imperative. Negative publicity is something to be dealt with head-on, not denied. When done effectively, reactive MPR can virtually save a brand or a company. A corporate response immediately following negative publicity can lessen the inevitable loss in sales.

The Special Case of Rumors and Urban Legends

You have heard them and probably helped spread them since you were a small child in elementary school. They are often vicious and malicious. Sometimes they are just comical. Most always they are false. We are talking about rumors and urban legends. As a technical aside, urban legends and rumors capture slightly different phenomena. Whereas urban legends are a form of rumor, they go beyond rumor by transmitting a story involving the use of *irony;* that is, urban legends convey subtle messages that are in contradiction of what is literally expressed in the story context.[8] As a case in point, consider the following "Gucci Kangaroo" legend:

> *Have you heard about the American tourists who were driving in the outback of Australia? They had been drinking, and it seems that their car hit a kangaroo. Thinking the kangaroo to be dead, the tourists decided to take a gag photograph. They hastily propped the kangaroo up against a fence and dressed it in the driver's Gucci jacket. They proceeded to take photographs of the well-dressed marsupial. Well, it seems that the kangaroo had merely been stunned rather than dead. All of a sudden he revived and jumped away wearing the man's jacket, which also contained the driver's license, money, and airline ticket.*[9]

Technical distinction noted, we need not get hung up in differentiating between the more general case of rumors and the specific instance of urban legends. Hereafter we will refer simply to rumors in an inclusive sense to include urban legends. It further is noteworthy that our interest involves only those rumors that involve products, brands, stores, or other objects of marketing practice. A variety of Internet Web sites focus on rumors and urban legends, and many of these refer to products, technological developments, and even specific brands.[10]

Commercial rumors are widely circulated but unverified propositions about a product, brand, company, store, or other commercial target.[11] Rumors are probably the most difficult problem faced by public relations personnel. What makes rumors so troublesome is that they spread like wildfire and most always state or imply something very undesirable, and possibly repulsive, about the target of the rumor.[12]

Consider the case of the persistent rumor/urban legend that surrounded the Procter & Gamble Company for years. The rumor involved P&G's famous man-in-the-moon logo, which was claimed to be a symbol of the devil. The logo on the left side of Figure 19.1 is the old P&G logo. According to the rumormongers, when the stars in the old logo are connected (as has been done in the figure), the number 666 (a symbol of the Antichrist) is formed. Also, the curls in the man-in-the-moon's beard, which have been circled, also supposedly form 666 when held up to a mirror.

Although nonsensical, this rumor spread for years throughout the Midwest and South. P&G eventually decided to drop the old logo and change to the new logo on the right side of Figure 19.1. The new logo retains the 13 stars, which represent the original United States colonies, but eliminates the curly hairs in the beard that appeared to form the number 666.

Old and New Procter & Gamble Logos

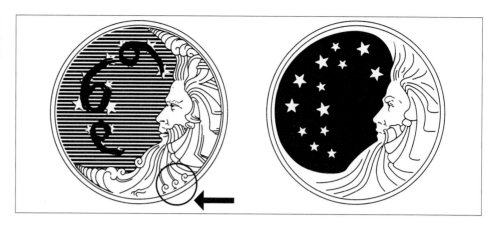

Following are some other rumors/urban legends you may have heard at one time or another. (Some of these are pretty old, so you might want to ask someone else about them.) None are true, but all have been widely circulated.

- The McDonald's Corporation makes sizable donations to the Church of Satan.
- Wendy's hamburgers contain something other than beef, namely red worms. (Other versions of this rumor have substituted McDonald's or Burger King as the target.)
- Pop Rocks (a carbonated, candy-type product made by General Foods) explode in your stomach when mixed with soda.
- Bubble Yum chewing gum contains spider eggs.
- A woman while shopping in a Kmart store was bitten by a poisonous snake when trying on a coat imported from Taiwan.
- A boy and his date stopped at a Kentucky Fried Chicken restaurant on their way to a movie. Later the girl became violently ill, and the boy rushed her to the hospital. The examining physician said the girl appeared to have been poisoned. The boy went to the car and retrieved an oddly shaped half-eaten piece from the KFC bucket. The physician recognized it to be the remains of a rat. It was determined that the girl died from consuming a fatal amount of strychnine from the rat's body.[13]
- In what is referred to as the "Gerber Myth," thousands of consumers sent letters to a post-office box in Minneapolis following a rumor circulating on the Internet (as well as in church bulletins and day-care centers) that Gerber, a baby-food company, was giving away $500 savings bonds as part of a lawsuit settlement. Complying with the rumor's advice, parents mailed copies of their child's birth certificate and Social Security card to the Minneapolis address. For a period of time, the post-office box received daily between 10,000 to 12,000 pieces of Gerber-Myth mail.[14]

The preceding examples illustrate two basic types of commercial rumors: conspiracy and contamination.[15] **Conspiracy rumors** involve supposed company policies or practices that are threatening or ideologically undesirable to consumers. For example, a conspiracy rumor circulated in New Orleans in 1990 claiming that the founder of the Popeyes restaurant chain, Al Copeland, supported a reprehensible politician known to have Ku Klux Klan and Nazi connections. Copeland immediately called a press conference, vehemently denied any connections with the politician, and offered a $25,000 reward for information leading to the source of the rumor. This swift response squashed the rumor before it gained momentum.[16] (For another example of a conspiracy rumor, see the *IMC Focus.*)

IMC FOCUS: A BIZARRE CONSPIRACY RUMOR

The Brooklyn Bottling Corp. introduced an inexpensive line of soft drinks under the name Tropical Fantasy. Priced at 49 cents for a 20-ounce bottle, Tropical Fantasy quickly gained sales momentum and was heading toward becoming the top-selling brand in small grocery stores in many northeastern markets. But then rumor peddlers went to work. Leaflets started appearing in low-income neighborhoods warning consumers away from Tropical Fantasy and claiming that the brand was manufactured by the Ku Klux Klan and "contain[s] stimulants to sterilize the black man." Angry Tropical Fantasy drinkers threatened distributors with baseball bats and threw bottles at delivery trucks. Some stores stopped accepting shipments. Sales of Tropical Fantasy immediately plummeted.

Source: Adapted from "A Storm over Tropical Fantasy," *Newsweek*, April 22, 1991, 34.

Contamination rumors deal with undesirable or harmful product or store features. For example, a rumor started in Reno, Nevada, that the Mexican-imported beer Corona was contaminated with urine. A beer distributor in Reno who handled Heineken, a competitive brand, actually had initiated the rumor. Corona sales fell by 80 percent in some markets. The rumor was hushed when an out-of-court settlement against the Reno distributor required a public statement declaring that Corona is not contaminated.

What Is the Best Way to Handle a Rumor?   When confronted with a rumor, some companies believe that doing nothing is the best way to handle it. This cautious approach is apparently based on the fear that an anti-rumor campaign will call attention to the rumor itself.[17]

An expert on rumors claims that rumors are like fires, and, like fires, time is the worst enemy. His advice is to not merely hope that a rumor will simmer down but rather to combat it swiftly and decisively to PUT IT OUT![18] Table 19.1 recommends steps for rumor control. It will be well worth your time to review these recommendations.

S PONSORSHIP MARKETING

Sponsorships represent a rapidly growing aspect of marketing communications. Sponsorships involve investments in *events* or *causes* for the purpose of achieving various corporate objectives, especially ones involving increased brand awareness, enhanced brand image, and heightened sales volume.[19] The following definition captures nicely the practice of sponsorship marketing:

> [S]ponsorship involves two main activities: (1) an exchange between a sponsor [such as a brand] and a sponsee [such as a sporting event] whereby the latter receives a fee and the former obtains the right to associate itself with the activity sponsored and (2) the marketing of the association by the sponsor. Both activities are necessary if the sponsorship fee is to be a meaningful investment.[20]

Event sponsorships range from supporting athletic events (such as golf and tennis tournaments, college football bowl games, and the Olympics) to underwriting rock concerts and supporting festivals and fairs. *Cause-oriented sponsorships* typically involve supporting causes deemed to be of interest to some facet of society, such as environmental protection, wildlife preservation, and raising funds for charities.

Table 19.2 delineates annual sponsorship spending in North America for one recent year. It can be seen that total sponsorship spending in 1998 amounted to an estimated $6.76 billion. Two thirds of this amount ($4.55 billion) went to various sporting events such as motorsports (e.g., NASCAR), golf and tennis, professional sports leagues and teams, and the Olympics.

TABLE 19.1 Recommended Steps for Rumor Control

A. Alert Procedure

1. On first hearing a rumor, note the location and wording of the allegation and target.
2. Keep alert for any other rumors to see if the original report was spurious.
3. If rumors increase to ten or more, send requests to distributors, franchise managers, and whoever else meets the public to find out who told the rumor to the person reporting it. It is important to specify the regional boundaries of the problem and the characteristics of the participating population. Distribute forms that can be filled out for the above information, as well as fact sheets rebutting the rumor.
4. Check with competitors to see if they share the problem. Try to find out if the target has moved from your company to them or from them to yours, or if it has spread throughout the industry.

B. Evaluation

1. Check for a drop in sales or a slowdown in sales increase.
2. Monitor person-hours required to answer phone calls and mail.
3. Keep tabs on the morale of the company personnel meeting people in the corporation. Do they feel harassed? Do they feel that management is doing enough to help them?
4. Design a marketing survey to find out what percentage of the public believes any part of the rumor.
5. Make an assessment of the threat or potential threat the rumor poses to profits. Is the corporation in danger of appearing to be an inept, impotent, and passive victim of the rumor problem? How much is management's image affected by the way things are going? The next move is a judgment call. If it seems that something more should be done, then it is time to move to the next phase.

C. Launch a Media Campaign

1. Assemble all facts about the extent of the problem to present to co-workers and superiors. Be prepared for resistance from people who support the myth that "pussyfooting is the best policy."
2. Based on information gathered in the previous phases, decide on the geographical regions for implementing the campaign. If it is a local rumor, treat it locally; if it is a national rumor, treat it nationally.
3. Based on information gathered in the previous phases, decide on the demographic features of the carrying population.
4. Select appropriate media outlets and construct appropriate messages.
5. Decide on what points to refute. (Don'd deny *more* than is in the allegation.) If the allegation is of the contamination variety, be careful not to bring up any offensive association or to trigger potential "residuals" in the refutation.
6. Two important points to make in any campaign are that the allegations are *untrue* and *unjust.* It should be implied that the company's business is not suffering, but that "what's right is right" and that people who pass on the rumor are "going against the American sense of fair play!"
7. Line up spokespeople such as scientists, civic and/or religious leaders, rumor experts—whomever you think appropriate—to make statements on the company's behalf.

If all of the above is done properly, the problem is well on the way to being solved.

Source: From Fredrick Koenig, *Rumor in the Marketplace: The Social Psychology of Commercial Hearsay* (Dover, Mass.: Auburn House, 1985), 171–173. Reprinted with permission.

At least four factors account for the growth in sponsorships.[21] First, by attaching their names to special events and causes, companies are able to avoid the clutter inherent in advertising media. For example, Visa USA sponsors the Triple Crown of horse racing consisting of the Kentucky Derby, the Preakness, and the Belmont Stakes. Visa's VP of marketing justified this choice on grounds that horse racing is an uncluttered area thus allowing Visa to receive primary attention from consumers.[22] Second, sponsorships help companies respond to consumers' changing media habits. For example, with the decline in network television viewing, sponsorships offer a potentially effective and cost-efficient way to reach customers. Third, sponsorships help companies gain the approval of various constituencies, including stockholders, employees, and society at large. Finally, the sponsorship of special events and causes enables marketers to target their communication and promotional efforts to specific geographic regions and/or to lifestyle groups. For example, Kodak has been an annual sponsor of the Kodak Albuquerque International Balloon Fiesta. This event attracts thousands of amateur and professional photographers and is thus an ideal venue for creating a strong, positive linkage with the Kodak name.[23]

Now that we have overviewed the general features of sponsorship marketing, following sections detail the practice of event and cause-oriented sponsorships, respectively.

Event Sponsorships

Though relatively small compared to the two major components of the marketing communications mix—advertising and promotions—expenditures on event sponsorship are increasing. As noted in Table 19.2, North American marketers in 1998 invested over $6 billion in various events (another $544 million went to causes). Two-thirds of these expenditures went to sports events with the remainder spent on sponsoring entertainment events and tours, festivals and fairs, and the arts. Event sponsorship is practiced worldwide, with total expenditures easily doubling North American spending.[24]

Thousands of companies invest in some form of event sponsorship. Defined, **event sponsorship** is a form of brand promotion that ties a brand to a meaningful athletic, entertainment, cultural, social, or other type of high-interest public activity. Event marketing is distinct from advertising, promotion, point-of-purchase merchandising, or public relations, but it generally incorporates elements from all of these communication tools. Event sponsorships have a considerable opportunity to achieve success because events reach people when they are receptive to marketing messages and capture people in a relaxed and happy mood.[25]

As with every other marketing communications decision, the starting point for effective event sponsorship is to designate the target market and specify clearly the *objectives* that an event is designed to accomplish. Event marketing has no value unless it accomplishes these objectives. Consider the following example. Procter & Gamble sponsored the Mexican Festival weekend of Cinco de Mayo, the May 5th anniversary of Mexico's victory in its war against France. The objective was to strengthen P&G's relations with Hispanic retailers and consumers in the Los Angeles and Santa Ana areas of California. Over 100 festivals in supermarket parking lots were conducted during and after the official Cinco de Mayo celebration. The result: More than 4 million Hispanic consumers were reached through various Spanish-language media, and nearly 85 percent of the retailers

TABLE 19.2 Estimated Sponsorship Spending in North America for 1998

SPONSORED EVENT/CAUSE	AMOUNT
Sports	$4.55 billion
Entertainment, tours, and attractions	$675 million
Festivals, fairs, and annual events	$578 million
Causes	$544 million
Arts	$413 million
TOTAL	$6.76 billion

Source: "Sponsorships Grow Without the Olympics," *Promo*, July 1998, S16.

participated in the promotion. By supporting an important community event, P&G was able to increase its standing with Hispanic consumers and community leaders.[26]

www.visa.com

Selecting Sponsorship Events.

Marketers use sponsorships of events to develop relationships with consumers, to enhance brand equity, and to strengthen ties with the trade. Successful event sponsorships require meaningful fit among the brand, the event, and the target market. Budget Rent A Car, for example, oriented much of its marketing communications efforts toward women inasmuch as women are the key decision makers on business car rentals, both as business and leisure travelers and as coordinators of company travel. Accordingly, Budget became a major sponsor of women's sporting events—the Ladies Professional Golf Association, the Women's Tennis Association, and the Women's Sports Foundation.[27]

What specific factors should a company consider when selecting an event? The following questions represent a good starting point when evaluating whether an event represents a suitable association for a brand:[28]

1. *Is the event consistent with the brand image, and will it benefit the image?* Unionbay, the jeans and sportswear brand, along with soft drink brand Mountain Dew and snowboard maker Burton all sponsored the 1999 U.S. Open Snowboarding Championships.[29] It would seem that this event matches perfectly the images of all three brands.

2. *Does the event offer a strong likelihood of reaching the desired target audience?* The Old Navy chain of retail clothing stores began in 1999 its sponsorship of Major League Soccer.[30] The demographics of Old Navy's typical customer matches well the demographics of consumers who both participate in soccer and view it live or on television.

3. *Is the event geographically suited?* Procter & Gamble's sponsorship of the Cinco de Mayo Mexican Festival in California typifies an appropriate application of geographic suitability.

4. *Is this event one that the competition has previously sponsored, and is there a risk in sponsoring the event of being perceived as "me-tooistic" and confusing the target audience as to the sponsor's identity?* Sponsor misidentification is not a trivial issue. For example, Coca-Cola paid $250 million to be the official soft drink of the National Football League (NFL) for a five-year period. After sponsoring the NFL for several years, a general survey (not about Coca-Cola per se) asked football fans to name brands that sponsor the NFL. Thirty-five percent of the respondents named Coke as an NFL sponsor. Unfortunately (for Coca-Cola), another 34 percent falsely identified Pepsi Cola as a sponsor![31]

5. *Is the event cluttered?* NASCAR, for example, attracts a large number of sponsors due to the extraordinary growth rate in fan interest. However, recognizing the problem with sponsorship clutter, one observer noted that a brand "can get lost on the bumper" unless it is a prime NASCAR sponsor.[32]

6. *Does the event complement existing sponsorships and fit with other marketing communications programs for the brand?* Many brands sponsor multiple events. In the spirit of integrated marketing communications, it is important that these events "speak with a single voice." (If the notion of speaking with a single voice is unclear, please refer back to the IMC discussion in Chapter 1.)

7. *Is the event economically viable?* This last point raises the all-important issue about budget constraints. Companies that sponsor events must support the sponsorships with adequate advertising, P-O-P, and publicity support. One professional in the sponsorship arena uses the rule of thumb that two to three

Marketing Public Relations and Sponsorship Marketing **CHAPTER 19** 617

times the cost of a sponsorship must be spent in properly supporting it and offers the following advice:

A sponsorship is an opportunity to spend money. But like a car without gasoline, sponsorship without sufficient funds to maximize it goes nowhere. Therein lies the biggest secret to successfully leveraging sponsorship: It's not worth spending money for rights fees unless you are prepared to properly support it.[33]

Creating Customized Events. Firms are increasingly developing their own events rather than sponsoring existing events. For example, managers of the Kibbles and Bits brand of dog food developed the "Do Your Bit for Kibbles and Bits" tour that covered 33 United States cities during a three-month period. The event involved having consumers in each of these cities enter their dogs into a competition to determine which dog would be picked for the brand's next TV commercial based on the quality of tricks the dog would perform to receive Kibbles and Bits food. Over 11,000 people attended the event and 2,500 dogs were entered into the competition. The Kibbles and Bits brand gained anywhere from one to four share points in key markets during this event.[34] In a similar event, Kraft conducted a Talent Search for its Oscar Mayer brand of hot dogs. During a 12-week period in the summer, Oscar Mayer "Wienermobiles" (see Figure 19.2) traveled to 90 markets, and at each location children sang the Oscar Mayer jingle and auditioned to appear in a commercial.[35]

In general, brands are increasingly customizing their own events for at least two major reasons. First, having a customized event provides a brand total control over the event. This eliminates externally imposed timing demands or other constraints and also removes the problem with clutter from too many other sponsors. Also, the customized event is developed to match perfectly the brand's target audience and to maximize the opportunity to enhance the brand's image and sales. A second reason for the customization trend is that there is a good chance that a specially designed event is more effective but less costly than a preexisting event. For example, in 1996 Olympic sponsorships cost $40 million. Many brand managers simply refuse to pay such staggering fees.

It would be simplistic to conclude that a brand manager or higher-level marketing executive should eschew sponsoring well-known and prestigious events. Sponsoring the Olympics or another major sporting or entertainment event can greatly enhance a brand's image and boost sales volume. Indeed, successfully achieving a strong linkage with an event that is valued positively means that the event's prestige and perhaps fun atmosphere may transfer to the sponsoring brand. However, achieving such an outcome requires that a strong, durable, and positive linkage be established between the sponsoring brand or company and the event.[36] All too often individual brands are swamped by larger and

FIGURE 19.2

The Oscar Mayer Wienermobile

better-known sponsoring brands and no solid or durable linkage is formed. This being the case, it is doubtful that the sponsorship represents a good return on investment.

Ambushing Events.   In addition to increased customization, a number of companies engage in what is called ambush marketing, or simply ambushing. **Ambushing** takes place when companies that are not official sponsors of an event undertake marketing efforts to convey the impression that they are.[37] For example, research following the 1996 Summer Olympics in Atlanta determined that 72 percent of respondents to a survey identified Visa as an official sponsor of the Summer Games and that 54 percent named American Express as a sponsor. As a matter of fact, Visa paid $40 million to sponsor the Olympics, whereas American Express simply advertised heavily during the telecast of the Olympic Games.[38] One may question whether it is ethical to ambush a competitor's sponsorship of an event, but a counterargument can be made readily that ambushing is simply a financially prudent way of offsetting a competitor's effort to obtain an advantage over your company or brand. (Your class might consider discussing the ethical aspects of ambushing.)

Measuring Success.   Whether participating as an official sponsor of an event, customizing your own event, or ambushing a competitor's sponsorship, the results from all of these efforts must be measured to determine effectiveness. As always, this requires that the brand marketer first establish specific objectives that the sponsorship is intended to accomplish and then obtain before-and-after measures to ascertain whether the sponsorship has augmented the brand's image or increased sales volume.

As always, accountability is the key. Sponsorships cannot be justified unless there is proof that brand equity and financial objectives are being achieved. It has been asserted that many sponsorship arrangements involve little more than managerial ego trips—that is, key executives sponsor high-profile events as a means of meeting famous athletes or entertainers and gaining great tickets and luxurious accommodations.[39] Whether this cynical perspective is correct is beyond this text to determine, but the point to be emphasized is that a brand's welfare cannot be compromised by executive caprice. One study provides evidence that challenges whether Olympic sponsorships represent a good return on investment. This study demonstrated that stock values actually decline following announcements of Olympic sponsorships, which suggests that analysts and bankers on Wall Street do not regard this form of marketing to be a wise financial investment.[40]

Cause–Related Marketing

A relatively minor aspect of overall sponsorships (representing about 8 percent of total sponsorships; see Table 19.2), **cause-related marketing (CRM)** involves an amalgam of public relations, sales promotion, and corporate philanthropy. The distinguishing feature of CRM is that a company's contribution to a designated cause is *linked to customers' engaging in revenue-producing exchanges with the firm.*[41] Cause-related marketing is based, in other words, on the idea that a company will contribute to a cause every time the customer undertakes some action. The contribution is contingent on the customer performing a behavior (such as buying a product or redeeming a coupon) that benefits the firm.

The following examples illustrate how cause-related marketing operates.

♦ For each Heinz baby-food label mailed in by consumers, H. J. Heinz Company contributed 6 cents to a hospital near the consumer's home.

♦ Nabisco Brands donated $1 to the Juvenile Diabetes Foundation for each certificate that was redeemed with a Ritz brand proof of purchase. Hershey donated 25 cents to local children hospitals for each Hershey coupon redeemed.

◆ Reynolds Metals Company, a maker of aluminum foil and other products, contributed 5 cents to local Meals on Wheels programs every time any of three Reynolds brands was purchased.

◆ Domino's Pizza teamed with Easter Seals in an ambitious CRM effort. Twenty-eight million Domino's Pizza box tops offered customers a coupon worth up to $10 toward the purchase of the electronic game called *SimCity 3000*. When redeeming coupons, consumers were required to send in $5 donations to Easter Seals.[42]

◆ Campbell's Soup donated a can of soup to food banks for every FSI coupon redeemed when purchasing Campbell's products (see Figure 19.3). Notice how this contribution is contingent on a specifically identified consumer behavior and thus exemplifies the workings of cause-oriented marketing.

◆ General Mills issued a check to schools for each box top from one of its various brands shown in Figure 19.4. Notice that the ad encourages parents to send box tops to school with their children. (Children, no doubt, implore their parents to purchase General Mills brands so they can take box tops to school and gain approval from their teachers, who have appealed to them to bring box tops. This is how such programs serve the sponsor's business needs.)

Cause-Related Marketing Illustration

FIGURE 19.3

Another Cause-Related
Marketing Illustration

The *Global Focus* describes a fascinating use of cause-related marketing in Canada.

The Benefits of CRM. Cause-related marketing is corporate philanthropy based on profit-motivated giving.[43] In addition to helping worthy causes, corporations satisfy their own tactical and strategic objectives when undertaking cause-related efforts. By supporting a deserving cause, a company can (1) enhance its corporate or brand image, (2) thwart negative publicity, (3) generate incremental sales, (4) increase brand awareness, (5) broaden its customer base, (6) reach new market segments, and (7) increase a brand's retail merchandising activity.[44]

Research reveals that consumers have favorable attitudes toward cause-related marketing efforts. According to the 1999 Cone/Roper Cause-Related Marketing Report,

GLOBAL FOCUS: A CEREAL WITH A CAUSE

Kellogg Canada introduced a new brand of cereal to Canadian grocery stores without investing any money in advertising. Such an introduction is virtually unheard of in this era of intense competition and spectacular marketing, and yet over 1 million boxes of Kellogg's Nutrific, the new brand, were shipped to stores without the benefit of advertising or even product testing. The brand was launched solely on the strength of a sponsorship relation between Kellogg Canada and the Canadian Breast Cancer Foundation.

Kellogg promised to donate 50 cents for each box of Nutrific it sold with a goal of raising $500,000 for breast-cancer research. Not only did this benefit an extremely important cause and in so doing enhance Kellogg's image, but also this form of product innovation was able to achieve product trial inexpensively among the targeted audience of women. Also, because grocers were supportive of Kellogg's cause-oriented efforts, the marketers of Nutrific were able to gain shelf space without having to pay listing allowances (the name in Canada for slotting allowances).

Source: Adapted from Fara Warner, "Kellogg Launches a Cereal for Charity," *Adweek's Marketing Week*, November 11, 1991, 6.

83 percent of Americans feel more positive about a company that supports a cause they care about. Moreover, 77 percent of consumers want companies to commit to a cause for a long time rather than conducting short-term promotions with several causes.[45] On the downside, about one-half of the sample in another study expressed negative attitudes toward CRM, this negativity is due in large part to consumers' cynicism about the sponsoring firm's self-serving motive.[46]

It's a Matter of Fit.   How should a company decide what cause to support? Although there are many worthy causes, a subset only are relevant to the interests of any brand and its target audience. Selecting an appropriate cause is a matter of fitting the brand to a cause that is naturally related to the brand's attributes, benefits, or image and also relates closely to the target market's interests.[47] For example, Avon and breast cancer offer a natural nexus that fit well with Avon's almost exclusively female market. Likewise, Reynolds' sponsorship of the Meals on Wheels program represents an appropriate fit in that both the company and the cause are involved with food; moreover, the market for Reynolds' products includes many economically fortunate consumers who undoubtedly receive fulfillment from seeing their purchases support a worthy cause.

Accountability.   In the final analysis, brand marketers are obligated to show that their CRM efforts yield sufficient return on investment or achieve other important, nonfinancial objectives. Corporate philanthropy is wonderful, but cause-related marketing is not needed for this purpose—companies can contribute to worthy causes without tying the contribution to consumers' buying a particular brand. However, when employing a cause-related marketing effort, a company intends to accomplish marketing goals (such as improved sales or enhanced image) rather than merely exercising its philanthropic aspirations. Hence, a CRM effort should be founded on specific objectives—just the same as any advertising campaign. Research—such as a pre- and post-test as described for event sponsorships—is absolutely essential to determine whether a CRM effort has achieved its objective and is thereby strategically and financially accountable.

Colgate-Palmolive applies a profit-and-loss formula in measuring the effectiveness of its sponsorship of the Starlight Foundation that grants wishes to seriously ill children. This cause program is based on consumers redeeming freestanding inserts. Using scanner data, Colgate compares product sales in the three weeks following a coupon drop with the average sales for the preceding six months. The difference between these two sales figures is multiplied by the brand's net profit margin, and the event's cost on a per-unit basis is subtracted to determine the incremental profit.[48]

*S*ummary

This chapter covers two major topics: marketing public relations and sponsorship marketing. Public relations (PR) entails a variety of functions and activities that are directed at fostering harmonious interactions with an organization's publics (customers, employees, stockholders, governments, and so forth). An important distinction is made between general public relations (general PR), which deals with overall managerial issues and problems (such as relations with stockholders and employees), and marketing-oriented public relations (MPR). The chapter focuses on MPR.

Marketing PR consists of proactive MPR and reactive MPR. Proactive MPR is another tool, in addition to advertising, personal selling, and sales promotion, for promoting a company's products and brands. Proactive MPR is dictated by a company's marketing objectives. It seeks opportunities rather than solves problems. Reactive MPR responds to external pressures and typically deals with changes that have negative consequences for an organization. Handling negative publicity and rumors are two areas in which reactive PR is most needed.

The other major topic covered in this chapter is sponsorship marketing. Sponsorships involve investments in events or causes in order to achieve various corporate objectives. Event marketing is a rapidly growing facet of marketing communications. Though small in comparison to advertising and other major promotional elements, expenditures on event promotions exceeded $6 billion in 1998. Event marketing is a form of brand promotion that ties a brand to a meaningful athletic, entertainment, cultural, social, or other type of high-interest public activity. Event marketing is growing because it provides companies with alternatives to the cluttered mass media, an ability to segment on a local or regional basis, and opportunities for reaching narrow lifestyle groups whose consumption behavior can be tied to the local event.

Cause-related marketing (CRM) is a relatively minor aspect of overall sponsorship. The distinctive feature of CRM is that a company's contribution to a designated cause is linked to customers engaging in revenue-producing exchanges with the firm. Cause-related marketing serves corporate interests while helping worthy causes.

*D*iscussion Questions

1. Assume you are marketing VP for Nike and that you are considering a cause-related marketing effort. What role might CRM perform for your company? Provide two examples of causes that might be appropriate allies with Nike.

2. Explain how a local business in your area (such as a bank) might use event marketing to its advantage. Be specific in describing the objectives that event marketing would satisfy for a bank and the type of event that would be compatible with these objectives.

3. Assume you are the owner of a restaurant in your college/university community. A rumor about your business has circulated claiming that your head chef has AIDS. Your business is falling off. Explain precisely how you would combat this rumor.

4. Explain the similarities and differences between general public relations, marketing PR, and publicity.

5. What are the advantages of publicity in comparison to advertising? What are some of the objectives that both of these marketing communications techniques satisfy?

6. Some marketing practitioners consider publicity to be too difficult to control and measure. Evaluate these criticisms.

7. As the brand manager of Wow! potato chips (the no-fat, low-calorie brand from Frito-Lay), how might you use proactive MPR to create some inexpensive brand exposure and incremental sales?

8. Assume you are the athletic director of your college or university's athletic department. A major story hits the news claiming that many of your athletes receive inappropriate assistance in writing term papers. How would you handle this negative publicity?

9. Faced with the rumor about Corona beer being contaminated with urine, what course of action would you have taken if the Heineken distributor in Reno had not been identified as starting the rumor? In other words, if the source of the rumor were unknown, what steps would you have taken?

10. Classify the various rumors presented in the text (e.g., P&G's logo, McDonald's Church of Satan connection) as either conspiracy or contamination rumors.

11. Describe two or three commercial rumors, or urban legends, other than those mentioned in the chapter. Identify each as either a conspiracy or a contamination rumor. Describe how you think these rumors started and why people apparently consider them newsworthy enough to pass along. (You might want to locate an urban legend Internet site for ideas.)

12. Is ambushing unethical or just smart, hard-nosed marketing?

13. In 1999, the year after Mark McGwire had slugged a record-smashing 70 home runs while playing for the St. Louis Cardinals, the coffee chain Starbucks contributed $5,000 to child-literacy causes for each home run McGwire hit. Explain why this offer is not a true application of CRM.

*I*nternet Exercises

1. As mentioned in the chapter, there are a surprising number of Web sites dedicated to urban rumors, legends, and hoaxes. Unfortunately for marketing communicators, significant portions of these rumor repositories are dedicated to products, brands, companies, and technological developments pertaining to new products. Equally troubling is the speed and ease with which rumors can now travel on the Internet. To sample the types of rumors currently on the Web, visit http://urbanlegends.miningco.com and www.urbanlegends.com.
   a. Based on your knowledge and experience with rumors and the Internet, are marketing communicators following the advice in the chapter about how to handle a rumor? If so, how? If not, do you think this is by design or are they missing an opportunity to deal with rumors in a better way?
   b. Select at least two of your "favorite" commercial rumors from the Web sites listed above. Are these conspiracy or contamination rumors? Explain.
   c. Assume that you have been tasked with using the Internet to deal with the rumors selected previously. Describe how you would handle the assignment. Be as specific as possible.

2. Events designed specifically for the Internet are beginning to appear as this technology improves and more people gain Web access. For example, popular musical artists are exploiting the Internet by performing "live" online concerts, conducting interviews, and chatting with fans. Other examples include celebrities online, live talk shows, and Internet TV. Find an Internet event and discuss the following (use an event locator such as http://att.yack.com):
   a. Identify the event sponsors.
   b. Evaluate the suitability of the event for the sponsoring brands using the seven criteria discussed in the chapter.

*C*hapter Nineteen Endnotes

1. The dividing line between marketing PR and general PR is not perfectly clear. For further discussion, see Philip J. Kitchen and Danny Moss, "Marketing and Public Relations: The Relationship Revisited," *Journal of Marketing Communications* 1 (June 1995), 105–118.

2. Jordan Goldman, *Public Relations in the Marketing Mix* (Lincolnwood, Ill.: NTC Business Books, 1984).

3. Mark Ivey, "Pitching the Press," *Hemispheres*, August 1994, 23–25.

4. William McCall, "Nike Battles Backlash from Overseas Sweatshops," *Marketing News*, November 9, 1998, 14.

5. Judann Dagnoli, "Brief Slump Expected for Sudafed," *Advertising Age*, March 18, 1991, 53.

6. The facts in this description are from Annetta Miller, Fiona Gleizes, and Elizabeth Bradburn, "Perrier Loses Its Fizz," *Newsweek*, February 27, 1990, 53; Laura Bird, "Perrier Imports New Image from France," *Adweek's Marketing Week*, June 10, 1991, 9; and "Perrier: Heavy Users Came Back," *Advertising Age*, October 21, 1991, 36.

7. Gerry Khermouch, "Pepsi Flack Attack Nips Hoax in the Bud," *Brandweek*, June 21, 1993, 5; Marcy Magiera, "The Pepsi Crisis: What Went Right," *Advertising Age*, June 19, 1993, 14–15; Marcy Magiera, "Pepsi Weathers Tampering Hoaxes," *Advertising Age*, June 21, 1993, 1, 46.

8. For an insightful discussion of urban legends and an interesting experiment testing factors influencing the likelihood that legends will be transmitted, see D. Todd Donavan, John C. Mowen, and Goutam Chakraborty, "Urban Legends: The Word-of-Mouth Communication of Morality Through Negative Story Content," *Marketing Letters* 10 (February 1999), 23–34.

9. Ibid., 23–24.

10. Donavan et al.'s content analysis of 100 urban legends revealed that 45 percent included product references, 12 percent involved warnings about innovations and technology, and 10 percent identified specific brands.

11. This definition is adapted from Fredrick Koenig, *Rumor in the Marketplace: The Social Psychology of Commercial Hearsay* (Dover, Mass.: Auburn House, 1985), 2.

12. For a review of the academic literature related to rumors as well as inspection of three interesting studies, see Michael A. Kamins, Valerie S. Folkes, and Lars Perner, "Consumer Responses to Rumors: Good News, Bad News," *Journal of Consumer Psychology* 6(2), 165–187.

13. These rumors, all of which are false, have been in circulation at one time or another since the 1970s. All are thoroughly documented and analyzed in Koenig's fascinating book *Rumor in the Marketplace*.

14. "Internet-Based 'Gerber Myth' Blamed for Flood of Bogus Mail," *The Wall Street Journal Interactive Edition*, October 23, 1997.

15. Koenig, *Rumor in the Marketplace*, 19.

16. Amy E. Gross, "How Popeyes and Reebok Confronted Product Rumors," *Adweek's Marketing Week*, October 22, 1990, 27.

17. Koenig, *Rumor in the Marketplace*, 163.

18. Ibid., 167.

19. Meryl Paula Gardner and Phillip Joel Shuman, "Sponsorship: An Important Component of the Promotions Mix," *Journal of Advertising* 16, no. 1 (1987), 11–17.

20. T. Bettina Cornwell and Isabelle Maignan, "An International Review of Sponsorship Research," *Journal of Advertising* 27 (spring 1998), 11.

21. The first three factors are adapted from Gardner and Shuman, "Sponsorship: An Important Component of the Promotions Mix," 12.

22. Kate Fitzgerald, "Visa Wins At Races," *Advertising Age*, May 25, 1998, 30.

23. David Vaczek, "Finding America at the Fair," *Promo*, March 1998, 43.

24. Cornwell and Maignan, "An International Review of Sponsorship Research," 1.

25. Glenn Heitsmith, "Event Promotions: Get Them by Their Hearts and Minds," *Promo*, March 1994, 32.

26. Adapted from William A. Robinson, "Adweek's First Annual Achievements in Event Marketing," Promotion section of *Adweek*, November 16, 1987, 12.

27. David J. Sparks, "Why Budget Rent A Car Sponsors Women's Sports," *Brandweek*, August 23, 1993, 29.

28. Adapted from Mava Heffler, "Making Sure Sponsorships Meet All the Parameters," *Brandweek*, May 16, 1994, 16.

29. Becky Ebenkamp, "Unionbay Back to Backing Boards," *Brandweek*, November 30, 1998, 9.

30. Terry Lefton, "Old Navy Kicks in $2M for Soccer," *Brandweek*, February 22, 1999, 4.

31. James Crimmins and Martin Horn, "Sponsorship: From Management Ego Trip to Marketing Success," *Journal of Advertising Research* 36 (July-August 1996), 11–21.

32. Sam Walker, "NASCAR Gets Coup as Anheuser Is Set to Raise Sponsorship Role," *The Wall Street Journal Interactive Edition*, November 13, 1998.

33. Heffler, "Making Sure Sponsorships Meet All the Parameters."

34. Wayne D'Orio, "The Main Event," *Promo*, May 1997, 19.

35. Ibid., 23.

36. For further discussion along these lines, see Crimmins and Horn, "Sponsorship: From Management Ego Trip to Marketing Success," especially Figure 1 and related discussion.

37. Dennis M. Sandler and David Shani, "Olympic Sponsorship Vs. 'Ambush' Marketing: Who Gets the Gold?" *Journal of Advertising Research* 29 (August-September 1989), 9–14.

38. David Shani and Dennis Sandler, "Counter Attack: Heading Off Ambush Marketers," *Marketing News*, January 18, 1999, 10.

39. Crimmins and Horn, "Sponsorship: From Management Ego Trip to Marketing Success," 11.

40. Kathleen Anne Farrell and W. Scott Frame, "The Value of Olympic Sponsorships: Who Is Capturing the Gold?" *Journal of Market Focused Management* 2 (1997), 171–182.

41. P. Rajan Varadarajan and Anil Menon, "Cause-Related Marketing: A Coalignment of Marketing Strategy and Corporate Philanthropy," *Journal of Marketing* 52 (July 1988), 58–74.

42. Theresa Howard, "Domino's Links Easter Seals to CD-ROM," *Brandweek*, January 11, 1999, 10.

43. "Avon Pinning Down an Issue," *Sales & Marketing Management*, September 1994, 58.

44. Varadarajan and Menon, "Cause-Related Marketing."

45. Betsy Spethmann, "Charitable Contributions," *Promo*, February 1999, 31.

46. Deborah J. Webb and Lois a Mohr, "A Typology of Consumer Responses to Cause-Related Marketing: From Skeptics to Socially Concerned," *Journal of Public Policy & Marketing* 17 (Fall 1998), 239–256.

47. Howard Scholssberg, "For a Good Cause," *Promo,* February 1994, 41.

48. Gary Levin, "Sponsors Put Pressure On for Accountability," *Advertising Age,* June 21, 1993, S1.

Personal Selling Fundamentals

CHAPTER OBJECTIVES

After studying this chapter, you should be able to:

1. Explain personal selling's role in the marketing communications mix.
2. Describe the positive features of a job in personal selling.
3. Discuss the principles underlying modern selling philosophy.
4. Describe the type of personal selling jobs and the activities performed.
5. Explain the determinants of salesperson performance.
6. Discuss the characteristics of high-performing salespeople.
7. Describe the role of sales management.

Opening Vignette: What Qualities Are Liked and Disliked in a Salesperson?

A national sample of purchasing agents was surveyed to determine the qualities that they value most in a salesperson. The five most-valued salesperson behaviors and the percentage of 200 responding purchasing agents who agreed that they value these particular behaviors are as follows:

- ◆ Reliability/credibility: 98.6%
- ◆ Professionalism/integrity: 93.7
- ◆ Product knowledge: 90.7
- ◆ Innovation in problem solving: 80.5
- ◆ Presentation/preparation: 69.7

Another survey asked more than 300 business customers in various industries to disclose which aspects of salesperson behavior they found most bothersome. In decreasing order of importance, the customers complained about the salesperson who

- ◆ Is difficult to communicate with;
- ◆ Lacks knowledge of the customer's company;
- ◆ Is overly aggressive; and
- ◆ Makes promises that his or her company cannot deliver.

In purchasing agents' own words, the table on page 627 lists are some of the specific qualities and behaviors in salespeople that are most liked, disliked, and despised—the good, the bad, and the ugly.

The Good	The Bad	The Ugly
1. Honesty	1. No follow-up	1. Wise-ass attitude
2. Loses a sale graciously	2. Walks in without an appointment	2. Calls me "dear" or "sweetheart"
3. Admits mistakes	3. Begins call by talking sports	3. Gets personal
4. Problem-solving capabilities	4. Puts down competitor's products	4. Doesn't give purchasing people credit for any brains
5. Friendly but professional	5. Poor listening skills	5. Whiners
6. Dependable	6. Too many phone calls	6. "BSers"
7. Adaptability	7. Lousy presentation	7. Wines and dines me
8. Knows my business	8. Fails to ask about my needs	8. Plays one company against another
9. Well prepared	9. Lacks product knowledge	9. Pushy
10. Patience	10. Wastes my time	10. Smokes in my office

Source: "PAs [Purchasing Agents] Examine the People Who Sell to Them," *Sales and Marketing Management,* November 11, 1985, 38–41; Richard Whiteley, "How to Push Customers," *Sales and Marketing Management,* February 1994, 29–30.

A good sales force that embodies the positive qualities identified in the *Opening Vignette* is essential for corporate success. Effective personal selling is critical. Indeed, popular business wisdom holds that everything starts with selling. Personal selling provides the push (as in *push strategy*) needed to get customers to carry new products, increase their amount of purchasing, and devote more effort in merchandising a company's brand. At the retail level, personal selling can determine whether a purchase is made and how often consumers shop at a particular store.

This chapter's objective is to present the reader with a broad array of ideas about the nature of personal selling, encouraging a greater appreciation of the opportunities and challenges for career success in this field. Toward this end, the chapter explores several dimensions of personal selling. First examined is personal selling's role in the marketing-communications mix, its advantages and disadvantages, and the attractive characteristics of personal selling and opportunities in this field. A second section explores selling activities, duties, and types of selling jobs. Determinants of salesperson performance and effectiveness are covered in the third section. Finally, the characteristics of excellence in selling are examined.

In concluding this introductory section, it is important to note that many readers of this text will initiate business careers in personal selling positions and move later on into sales management posts. Some will embark on a selling career working with a consumer packaged-goods firm; others will obtain sales employment with a business-to-business organization. Still others will pursue careers in fields such as advertising, public relations, financial services, or other service-oriented organizations. Some may not consider these jobs to be personal selling, but account managers in these fields are heavily involved in selling their companies' services to prospective clients. Selling is part and parcel of many jobs in business, so it is best to maintain an open attitude toward this pursuit and learn as much as possible about it.

OVERVIEW

Personal selling is a form of person-to-person communication in which a salesperson works with prospective buyers and attempts to influence their purchase needs in the direction of his or her company's products or services. The most important feature of this definition is the idea that personal selling involves personal interaction. This contrasts with other forms of marketing communications in which the audience typically consists of many people, sometimes millions (as in the case of mass-media advertising).

Personal Selling's Role in the Marketing Communications Mix

Integrated Marketing Communications and Personal Selling. As explained at various points throughout the text, all elements of marketing communications must work together to achieve overall organizational objectives. From an *integrated marketing communications* perspective, personal selling is inextricably related to all other marketing communications elements. For example, advertising to retailers and to consumers is of little value unless the sales force is able to gain product distribution for new brands and maintain distribution for established brands. Likewise, the creation of clever point-of-purchase displays is of small benefit unless the sales force secures retailer cooperation in using these displays. The sales force also is critical in assuring that trade-oriented promotions work in the manner they are intended and that sufficient products are available to support promotions aimed at consumers.

Personal Selling's Unique Role. Each marketing communications element has its own unique characteristics, purposes, and advantages. The personal selling activity is crucial to enhancing a company's equity and the equity in individual brands. Personal selling's primary purposes include educating customers, providing product usage and marketing assistance, and providing after-sale service and support to buyers. Personal selling, compared to other communications elements, is uniquely capable of performing these functions as a result of the person-to-person interaction mode that characterizes this form of marketing communications. Consequently, various advantages accrue to personal selling compared to other forms of marketing communications.

1. Personal selling contributes to a relatively high level of customer attention, since in face-to-face situations it is difficult for a potential buyer to avoid a salesperson's message.

2. It enables the salesperson to customize the message to the customer's specific interests and needs.

3. The two-way communication characteristic of personal selling yields immediate feedback, so that an alert salesperson can know whether or not his or her sales presentation is working.

4. Personal selling enables a salesperson to communicate a larger amount of technical and complex information than other promotional methods.

5. In personal selling there is a greater ability to demonstrate a product's functioning and performance characteristics.

6. Frequent interactions with a customer permit the opportunity for developing long-term relations and effectively merging selling and buying organizations into a coordinated unit to serve both sets of interests.[1]

The primary disadvantage of personal selling is that it is more costly than other forms of marketing communications because sales representatives typically interact with only one customer at a time. Hence, when considering only the outcomes or results accomplished with the personal-selling effort (an effectiveness consideration), personal selling is generally more *effective* than other elements. However, when considering the ratio of inputs to outputs (cost to results), personal selling is typically less *efficient* than other marketing communications tools. In practice, allocating resources to personal selling and the other elements of marketing communications amounts to an effort at balancing effectiveness and efficiency.

Attractive Features of Personal Selling

Numerous challenging and exciting job opportunities are available in this field. The attractive features of a sales job include freedom of action, variety and challenge, opportunities for career development and advancement, and desirable financial and nonfinancial rewards.[2]

Job Freedom.   In field-sales positions (those outside of retail settings), the individual is primarily responsible for most of his or her day-to-day activities. Many sales positions involve little direct supervision. Salespeople may go days or even weeks without seeing their supervisors. Of course, with freedom comes responsibility. The unsupervised salesperson is expected to conduct his or her business professionally and to achieve sales objectives.

Variety and Challenge.   Managing one's own time presents a challenge that many professional salespeople enjoy. Much like the person who operates his or her own business, a salesperson can invest as much time and energy into the job as desired and can generate the number of rewards for which he or she is willing to work.

Opportunities for Career Development and Advancement.   More and more companies expect their middle- and upper-level managers to have sales experience, because they believe it helps an individual understand a business from the ground-level up. Many top-level corporate executives come from the sales ranks; sales experience provided them with a knowledge of customers, the trade, the competition, and their own company.

Attractive Compensation and Nonfinancial Rewards.   Personal selling is potentially both lucrative and rewarding. Nonfinancial rewards include feelings of self-worth for a job well done and the satisfaction that comes from providing a customer with a solution to a problem or with a product or service that best meets his or her needs.

M ODERN SELLING PHILOSOPHY

Before *modern* selling philosophy, there must have been an earlier variety. Let us label this earlier version *antiquated* and place the two in stark contrast, realizing of course that any such comparison is necessarily simplified.

In a word, antiquated selling is *seller-oriented*. Selling practices in this older view are undertaken with the seller's interests paramount. Manifestations of this approach include high-pressure selling tactics, little effort to understand the customer's business, and little post-sale follow-through or attention to customer satisfaction.

Are these practices truly antiquated in the sense that they no longer are practiced? Certainly not. Some firms and their salespeople remain antiquated, and their selling practices lag behind contemporary forces that have imposed a higher standard on sales performance. These forces include intense competition, sophisticated buying practices, and expectations of reliable and dependable service.

In most prospering firms, modern selling philosophy has supplanted this seller-oriented approach. A *partner-oriented* selling mind-set exists in most successful firms. These firms realize that their own prosperity rests with their customers' successes. Hence, modern partner-oriented wisdom makes customer satisfaction its highest priority. Modern selling practice is based on the following principles.[3]

1. The sales process must be built on a *foundation of trust and mutual agreement.* Selling should not be viewed as something someone does to another; rather, it should be looked upon as something two parties agree to do for their mutual benefit. In fact, it is easy to argue that modern salespeople do not sell but rather facilitate buying. This difference is not merely semantics—it is at the root of the transformation from the antiquated to modern selling philosophies.

2. A *customer-driven atmosphere* is essential to long-term growth. This is a corollary point to the preceding principle. Modern selling requires that the customer's welfare, interests, and needs be treated as equal to the seller's in the partnership between seller and buyer. A customer-oriented approach means avoiding high-pressure tactics and focusing on customer satisfaction. Salespeople have to be trained to know the customer and to speak in a language that the customer understands. Perhaps the preceding points are best summed up in these terms: "Be product centered, and you will make a few sales; be prospect centered, and you will gain many customers."[4]

3. Sales representatives should *act as if they were on the customer's payroll.* The ultimate compliment a salesperson can receive is a comment from a customer to the sales supervisor along these lines: "I'm not sure whether your sales rep works for me or for you."[5] The closer salespeople are to the customer, the better they will be at providing solutions to the customer's problems. However, successful salespeople never forget that their ultimate responsibility resides with their employer. Solving customers' problems and building relations are means to ends; the end itself is performing those behaviors that will maximize the long-term interests of the salesperson's employer.

4. Getting the order is only the first step; *after-sales service is what counts.* No customer problem should be too small to address. Modern selling philosophy calls for doing whatever is necessary to please the customer in order to ensure a satisfying long-term relationship. The *Global Focus* describes how Japanese salespeople achieve success in contrast with their Western counterparts.

5. In selling, as in medicine, *prescription before diagnosis is malpractice.* This principle holds that no one solution is appropriate for all customers any more than any single diagnosis is appropriate for all patients. Customers' problems have to be analyzed by the modern salesperson and solutions customized to each problem. The days of "one solution fits all" are gone. Moreover, because most people like to make their own decisions or at least be involved in making them, a salesperson should treat the customer as a partner in the solution.

6. Salesperson *professionalism and integrity are essential.* Customers expect high standards of conduct from their salespeople and dislike unprofessional, untrustworthy, and dishonest behavior. (As evidence of this, reexamine "The Good, the Bad, and the Ugly" in the *Opening Vignette.*)

GLOBAL FOCUS: SELLING JAPANESE STYLE

Modern selling philosophy and modern selling practice are not the same thing. That is, what *ought* to be and what actually occurs may be worlds apart. The nonequivalence of philosophy and practice is perhaps particularly acute in the United States, where organizational structures and personalities make it difficult for many Americans to behave according to the six principles underlying modern selling practice. For example, the individualistic style and competitive spirit that are part of the American psyche make it difficult for some salespeople to consider their customers' needs as important as their own.

Japanese salespeople's personalities are perhaps better suited to implementing modern selling philosophy. *Respect* is the foundation of Japanese selling. Being respectful (deferential to their customers and dedicated to their needs) is easy for Japanese businesspeople insofar as the feudal roots of Japan placed businesspeople at the bottom of the societal hierarchy. As one writer observes, "Today's Japanese sales reps, if they're good, still behave as if they're at the bottom of the social ladder, respecting and trying to satisfy their customers."

The Japanese selling style is sometimes referred to as "wet"—implying that it is flexible, accommodating, caring, and human. The American style is more likely to be "dry"—or more inflexible, logical, and cut and dried. A notable distinction in how the wet and dry styles are manifested concerns customer service. Upon being informed of a customer problem, an American sales representative might just pass the problem along to the technical support staff with hopes that the problem will be resolved. Japanese sales reps, on the other hand, will personally become involved in solving the problem, work with the support staff, and submit a report to the customer explaining why the product failed and what has been done to prevent that failure from happening again.

Sales & Marketing Management magazine conducted a nonscientific survey of American sales managers who work for Japanese companies to learn whether Japanese marketing and sales personnel are different from, and perhaps better than, their American counterparts. Some of the key findings are these:

- Because individuality and independence are not as highly valued in Japan as America, Japanese marketers and salespeople are less inclined to take credit for successes or blame others for failures.

- Japanese companies, even those located in the United States, rarely use nonfinancial incentives to recognize, praise, or reward salespeople for successful performance. Good performance is simply expected, and special praise is deemed unnecessary.

- Because loyalty to one's employer is a fundamental characteristic of Japanese society, commissions are generally an unnecessary component of compensation packages. Salespeople consider it their duty to create business for their companies; it is the honorable thing to do, and no special compensation is required for doing what duty demands.

- Because Japanese typically stay with one company for their entire professional lives, there is a greater tendency than in the United States to focus on long-term results. American businesspeople, by comparison, frequently switch jobs; hence, compensation and incentive packages are tied to short-term results.

- Japanese businesspeople are more dedicated to their companies than are Americans. Accordingly, Japanese tend to work longer hours, oftentimes working (at least entertaining) until midnight.

Source: Adapted from Bill Kelley, "Culture Clash: West Meets East," *Sales & Marketing Management,* July 1991, 28–34; and George Leslie, "U.S. Reps Should Learn to Sell 'Japanese Style,'" *Marketing News,* October 29, 1990, 6. For an interesting discussion of cultural differences between Japan and the United States, see R. Bruce Money, Mary C. Gilly, and John L. Graham, "Effects of Trait Competitiveness and Perceived Intraorganizational Competition on Salesperson Goal Setting and Performance," *Journal of Marketing* 62 (October 1998), 76–87.

SELLING ACTIVITIES AND TYPES OF PERSONAL-SELLING JOBS

Personal selling has been treated rather generally to this point in the chapter, as if all selling jobs are identical. This section describes the various kinds of activities that salespeople perform and then identifies a variety of selling jobs.

Selling Activities

What exactly does a salesperson do? The specific activities and their range of performance vary greatly across sales positions. Nonetheless, the following ten activities are common to nearly all jobs in personal sales.[6]

Selling Function. This is the typical activity envisioned when thinking of personal selling. Selling functions include planning the sales presentation, making the presentation, overcoming objections, trying to close the sale, and so on.

Working with Orders. Much of a salesperson's time is spent writing up orders, working with lost orders, handling shipment problems, expediting orders, and handling back orders.

Servicing the Product. Servicing activities, which are performed primarily by people who sell technical products such as industrial machinery, include testing a newly sold product to ensure that it is working properly, training customers to use the product, and teaching safety procedures.

www.palmpilot.com

Managing Information. These activities involve receiving feedback from customers and then relaying the information to management. Much of this is done in the course of day-to-day selling. This activity has been greatly facilitated in recent years with advances in computer technology that simplify the salesperson's information-entry task.[7] New handheld computers, called *personal digital assistants*, or PDAs, accept handwritten input via ballpoint pen and then digitize the handwriting. Various brands are on the market, but 3Com's Palm Pilot is perhaps the best-known brand available currently (see Figure 20.1). Gillette, the company that is best known for razors and blades but that also markets

The Palm Pilot from 3Com

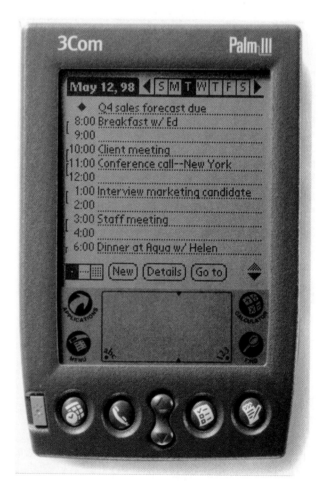

such health- and beauty-aid brands as Noxzema, Cover Girl, and Noxell, has equipped its sales representatives with pen-based computers for gathering important market data. Immediately on entering a retail account, Gillette's sales reps are instructed to gather information on matters such as competitive prices, the presence of in-store promotions, whether new brands or sizes are in the store, and so on. Information gathered on the salesperson's pen-based computer is transmitted to a central database nightly via modem. These data are analyzed, and statistical profiles of product trends and store activity are transferred at a later date back to the salespeople for use in influencing retail accounts to purchase more Gillette products.[8]

www.gillette.com

Servicing the Account.   Account servicing includes activities such as inventory control, stocking shelves, handling local advertising, and setting up and working with point-of-purchase displays. Such activities are performed primarily by salespeople who call on supermarkets, drugstores, mass-merchandise accounts, and other retail outlets.

Attending Conferences and Meetings.   Attending conferences and sales meetings and working at trade shows are activities in which nearly all salespeople participate to some extent. These conferences often are held at attractive locations where recreational activities are available during periods when formal meetings are not being conducted.

Training and Recruiting.   Salespeople who are in more advanced stages of their careers become involved in training new salespeople, traveling with trainees, and similar duties.[9]

Entertaining.   Some sales positions involve entertaining customers through activities such as dining and playing golf. While the antiquated view of selling would hold that you can buy customers by wining and dining them, modern selling philosophy includes a role for customer entertainment but recognizes that customers are earned (through loyal, efficient, dependable service) rather than bought.

Traveling.   Although sales jobs involve some traveling, the amount of time spent out of town is highly variable, ranging from virtually no travel to journeying thousands of miles each month. The increasing availability of e-mail, videoconferencing, and other electronic means of exchange has enabled doing the sales job with less travel.[10]

Types of Sales Jobs

Specific sales jobs are as variable as the companies in which personal selling occurs. However, six major categories encompass the major types of sales jobs: trade selling, missionary selling, technical selling, new-business selling, retail selling, and telephone selling, or telemarketing.[11]

Trade Selling.   A sales representative for a food manufacturer who sells to the grocery and drug industries typifies trade selling. The primary task of trade salespeople is to build sales volume by providing customers with promotional assistance in the form of advertising and sales promotion. Trade selling requires limited prospecting and places greater emphasis on *servicing accounts*. Trade salespeople work for companies such as Gillette, Beecham Products, Johnson & Johnson, Campbell's Soup, Procter & Gamble, and many other consumer packaged-goods organizations.

Missionary Selling.   Like trade salespeople, missionary salespeople typically are employees of manufacturers. However, the difference is that trade salespeople sell *through* their direct customers, whereas a missionary sales force sells *for* its direct customers.[12]

The pharmaceutical industry typifies missionary selling. Nearly two-thirds of all pharmaceutical sales to retailers are through wholesalers. In other words, manufacturers of pharmaceuticals typically market their products to wholesalers who in turn market to pharmacies and other retailers. Thus, the wholesaler is the pharmaceutical manufacturer's direct customer. Sales representatives for pharmaceutical manufacturers (called detail reps or detailers) nonetheless call on physicians and pharmacies to detail (explain) the advantages of the manufacturer's brands compared to competitive offerings. Detail reps are not selling directly to physicians (i.e., selling in the sense that a physician will place an order with the salesperson's company); rather, they are trying to get physicians to prescribe their brands. In so doing, they benefit both the manufacturer (via increased sales volume) and their direct customers (wholesalers).

www.dupont.com

Technical Selling. Technical salespeople are present in industries such as chemicals, machinery, mainframe computers, and sophisticated services (e.g., complicated insurance and other financial programs). They are typically trained in technical fields such as chemistry, engineering, computer science, and accounting. For example, in the chemical division of Du Pont, 95 percent of the company's salespeople start out in a technical field and then are recruited into sales.[13] Later, many sales technicians attain advanced training in business administration. Good technical salespeople must be especially knowledgeable about their company's product lines and must be able to communicate complicated features to prospective customers.

New-Business Selling. This type of selling is prevalent with products such as office copiers, data-processing equipment, personal computers, business forms, and personal insurance. Practitioners use terms such as bird-dogging, cold calling, and canvassing to characterize this type of selling. These terms capture the idea that new-business salespeople must continuously call on new accounts. Salespeople involved in any of the previous categories of sales jobs do some prospecting for new customers, but most of their time is spent working with and servicing existing accounts. New-business salespeople continually work to open new accounts, because sales to most customers are infrequent.

Retail Selling. The distinguishing characteristic of retail selling is that the customer comes to the salesperson. Many retail sales jobs require limited training and sophistication, but others demand salespeople who have considerable product knowledge, strong interpersonal skills, and an ability to work with a diversity of customers.

Telemarketing. Telephone salespeople perform essentially the same types of selling activities as do salespeople who meet customers face to face. Many companies use the telephone to support or even replace their conventional sales forces. Telemarketing uses *outbound calls* from telephone salespersons for purposes of: (1) opening new accounts, (2) qualifying advertising leads, and (3) servicing existing business, including reorders and customer service. Telemarketing is used in conjunction with advertising, direct mail, catalog sales, and face-to-face selling.

Telemarketing's versatility applies to both consumer-oriented products and business-to-business marketing. IBM, for example, uses telemarketing to cover its small- to medium-sized accounts, generate incremental sales, enhance the productivity of traditional sales representatives through the leads and information that it provides, and ensure customer satisfaction and buying convenience. (Other computer companies such as Dell and Gateway rely almost exclusively on *inbound telephone* sales for the bulk of their substantial business, but this form of selling is reactive in comparison to IBM's proactive outbound selling efforts.)

Telemarketing is not appropriate for all sales organizations. The eight factors highlighted in Table 20.1 should be considered when evaluating the suitability of introducing a

Factors in Evaluating the Use of a Telephone Sales Force

1. *How essential is face-to-face contact?* The more essential it is, the less appropriate is telemarketing.

2. *Are customers geographically concentrated or dispersed?* Telephone selling may represent an attractive alternative to in-person selling if customers are *highly dispersed;* if, however, customers are concentrated (such as apparel makers in Manhattan or automobile manufacturers in Detroit), minimal travel time is required, and personal selling is probably preferable.

3. *How large are typical order sizes?* Economic considerations involving average order size and total potential should be estimated to determine whether in-person sales are cost-effective. In cases of small and marginal accounts, customers may be served more economically by telephone.

4. *What decision criteria are important to customers?* Telephone sales may be sufficient if price, delivery, and other quantitative criteria are paramount, but in-person sales may be essential in instances where product quality, dealer reputation, and service are most important.

5. *How many decision makers are typically involved in purchasing a company's product?* Face-to-face contacft is typically necessary when several decision makers are involved—for example, when an industrial engineer, a purchasing agent, and a financial representative all must contribute to a purchase decision.

6. *What is the nature of the purchase?* Routine purchases (such as office supplies) can be handled easily by phone, whereas more complex purchasers will likely require face-to-face interactions.

7. *What is the status of the major decision maker?* The telephone is acceptable for buyers, purchase agents, and engineers but probably not for owners, presidents, and vice presidents.

8. *What specific selling tasks have to be performed?* Telephone representatives may be particularly effective for prospecting and postsale follow-ups, whereas in-person sales effort is needed for the intervening sales task—preapproach, approach, presentation, objection handling, and closing.

telephone sales force.[14] It should be apparent that telephone selling is appropriate and effective in certain situations but not in others. Systematic application of this eight-step process should enable a company to determine whether and to what extent outbound telephone selling is appropriate for serving its customers.

Team Selling

The discussion to this point has suggested that the personal selling process entails selling activity by a single salesperson. This typically is how it has been done in the past—one salesperson calling on customers or prospects and attempting to gain an initial sale or repeat business. However, there has been a trend in recent years toward the formation of selling teams that combine representatives from marketing, logistics, finance, sales, and other corporate units. Procter & Gamble has established customer account teams that are assigned to specific retailers and wholesalers. One of P&G's first teams was assigned to Wal-Mart Stores.[15] P&G salespeople are located virtually on the premises of Wal-Mart's corporate headquarters in Fayettville, Arkansas. Kraft Foods also has an integrated sales team for calling on key retailers.[16] The purpose in both instances is to best represent the customer's interests by capitalizing on the strengths and expertise of various personnel who, in one way or another, play important roles in determining how well the organization fulfills the needs of important customers.

Team selling also is prevalent in business-to-business selling situations. The key aspect of team selling here, as with consumer-goods sales situations, is to include experts drawn from throughout the organization—engineers, product developers, customer service representatives, finance experts, and so on. Usually an account executive coordinates the team's efforts, which are used to produce creative solutions to a customer's purchasing needs.[17]

SALESPERSON PERFORMANCE

Regardless of the type of sales job, certain aptitudes and skills are needed to perform effectively. Indeed, people in all facets of life are ultimately judged in terms of their performance. Typically these evaluations are based on *quantitative assessments:* number of arrests made by a police officer, number of convictions by a prosecuting attorney, number of hits by a baseball player, number of units produced by a factory worker, number of articles published by a professor, and so on. Likewise, salespeople are judged in terms such as the number of units sold, dollar volume, and number of new accounts opened.

Researchers have long been intrigued with explaining and predicting salesperson performance. The fundamental issue is one of identifying the specific factors that determine salesperson effectiveness—the ingredients that distinguish the outstanding salesperson from those who are merely good, or, worse yet, are mediocre or below par. (Stop reading for a few moments, and think about your own ideas on this issue. Jot down what you think are the most important determinants of salesperson success, and later compare your thoughts with the ideas presented.)

Two general points require careful attention prior to discussing the specific determinants of salesperson performance and effectiveness. First, no single factor is able to explain salesperson performance adequately. In a very thorough and insightful analysis of sales research conducted over a 40-year span, researchers examined more than 100 separate studies that related salesperson performance with a wide variety of potential predictors. Results revealed that, on average, no single predictor explained more than *4 percent* of the variability in salesperson performance![18] The conclusion to be drawn is clear: Sales performance is based on various considerations, and no single factor (or even several factors) is capable of adequately explaining something as complex as salesperson performance.

A second general conclusion is that salesperson performance and effectiveness are contingent on a host of factors; indeed, selling performance and effectiveness depend on the total situation in which sales transactions take place. Specifically, salesperson performance depends on: (1) the salesperson's own resources (product knowledge, analytical skills, etc.), (2) the nature of the customer's buying task (e.g., whether it is a first-time or repeat decision), (3) the customer-salesperson relationship (relative power, level of conflict, etc.), and interactions among all three of these general sets of factors.[19]

Detailing all of the various factors upon which salesperson performance and effectiveness are contingent would take us beyond the scope of this overview. We will examine in greater detail six characteristics that have been hypothesized to determine salesperson performance: (1) aptitude, (2) skill level, (3) motivational level, (4) role perceptions, (5) personal characteristics, and (6) adaptability.[20]

Aptitude

An individual's ability to perform certain tasks depends greatly on his or her aptitude, which includes interests, intelligence, and personality characteristics. Because different salespeople have different tasks and activities to perform, some people are better suited to one type of sales job than another. Technical sales positions require individuals with a strong analytical aptitude and technical knowledge in order to explain complex product features to customers. Trade selling requires individuals who have good interpersonal skills and are highly adaptive, because they meet with many different types of customers.

Regardless of the specific type of sales position, all professional salespeople must be *customer oriented* and *empathetic.* They must be able to view the world from the outside in and not just in terms of their own limited perspectives. Salespeople who work for companies that have a general customer, or market, orientation are found to experience reduced role conflict and experience greater job satisfaction.[21]

In terms of the personality aspect of salesperson aptitude, research has shown that salespeople who are *competitive* set higher performance goals for themselves. They in turn, by virtue of setting higher goals, perform at a higher level.[22] Interestingly, salespeople who are intrinsically competitive set high goals for themselves only when they perceive that the organizational climate is itself competitive. Individuals who are not very competitive set low goals for themselves, regardless of whether the organizational climate is or is not perceived to be competitive.[23]

Skill Level

Whereas aptitude is a matter of native ability, skill level refers to an individual's *learned proficiency* at performing necessary selling tasks. These include selling skills (such as knowing how to make a sales presentation), interpersonal skills (such as how to cope with and resolve conflict), and technical skills (such as knowledge about a product's features, performance, and benefits). These skills are partially brought to a sales position as a function of an individual's educational preparation, but also are learned and fostered on the job.

Companies with effective sales programs instill in their sales force the skills needed for success. In fact, many sales organizations prefer to recruit salespeople directly out of college rather than from other sales positions so that they do not have to retrain sales candidates to overcome any bad habits and conflicting skills learned elsewhere.

For example, Armstrong World Industries, a maker of carpeting and other products, is legendary for hiring salespeople directly from college and sending them through the same basic training program that all Armstrong salespeople have undergone for over 60 years. In explaining the company's attitude toward sales training, Armstrong's director of human resources explains: "We prefer to hire people without any biases, conflicting opinions, or bad traits—and then we train them ourselves. We've had great success doing things our way, and if we're doing it that way and other companies aren't, well, then they're doing it wrong."[24] This may sound arrogant, but it merely represents the belief that it is often easier to train than it is to retrain.

One of the most important skills a salesperson can acquire is the ability to *close a sale.*[25] Closing a sale effectively amounts to identifying the appropriate time to ask the customer for an order. A 15-year survey conducted by a national sales training company revealed that 80 percent of salespeople refuse to close when the buyer is ready.[26] This is because too many salespeople use preprogrammed, or *canned,* sales presentations and do not listen carefully to the customer's needs; instead, they feel compelled to complete the presentation before asking for the order.

Another personal selling skill is the ability to get along with one's immediate superior. Indeed, there is evidence showing that being close psychologically and socially to one's supervisor is beneficial to the salesperson.[27] That is, when salesperson and sales manager think in similar fashion and perhaps socialize in the same circles, there is a tendency for the sales manager to attribute inadequate performance on the salesperson's part to factors beyond the salesperson's control rather than to his or her limitations. Does this mean that "sucking up" to the boss pays off? Well, yes and no. The incompetent salesperson will eventually lose out regardless of his or her closeness to the sales manager, but for the competent salesperson, there is a greater chance of being looked upon favorably when he or she is more like his or her superior.

Motivational Level

Motivational level refers to the *amount of time and energy* a person is willing to expend performing tasks and activities associated with a job. Intrinsic motivation is one of the key determinants of successful salespeople.[28] An interesting thing about motivation is that it is *reciprocally related* to performance. That is, motivation is a determinant of performance but also is determined by performance—we often become even more motivated after we have enjoyed some success. Research shows that increased salesperson effort leads to greater job performance and satisfaction.[29]

Another important characteristic of salesperson motivation is the distinction between *working hard* and *working smart.* Motivation is not simply the amount of effort but also how the effort is directed. Salespeople who work smart are typically more effective than those who just work hard.[30] Of course, a truly dynamite combination for a salesperson is to work both smart and hard.

A final pertinent point about salesperson motivation is that people are driven in different ways to accomplish objectives that best suit their unique personalities. Research over a 22-year period by the Gallup Management Consulting Group identified four general personality types in salespeople that represent different manifestations of intrinsic motivation.[31] First, *competitors* have a deep-seated desire to win and to beat specific rivals, such as competitors' salespeople or top performers in their own sales organization. Competitors will work hard to win new accounts to prove that they are better than other salespeople. The *ego-driven* are a second type. These people want to experience the glories of winning. They desire to be the best, to win awards, and to be recognized. Their objective is not necessarily to beat someone; rather, they are motivated to succeed to feed their healthy egos. The next personality type are the *achievers.* These salespeople routinely set higher goals than what is expected of them and are never satisfied with their own performance. These people like accomplishment. They usually make the best sales managers. Finally, *service-oriented* salespeople demonstrate their strength is in building and cultivating relationships with customers. They are generous, caring, and empathetic.

Of course, most salespeople are not pure representations of any one of these types of personalities; instead, they typically represent an amalgam of different typings with particular orientations toward one or two. People are motivated in different ways, but regardless of how they are motivated, success in sales (as with most of life's pursuits) requires a high level of intrinsic motivation.

Role Perceptions

In order to perform their jobs well, salespeople must know what is expected of them and have accurate perceptions of their roles. Their jobs are defined by people both within and outside the organization, including family, sales managers, company executives, and customers. Thus, how well people perform in sales jobs depends on the accuracy of their perceptions of management's stated goals, demands, policies, procedures, and organizational lines of authority and responsibilities. Accurate role perception is a very important determinant of job satisfaction.

Very often salespeople face *role conflicts* that diminish their sales performance. For example, a customer may want special price or advertising concessions that violate the policies of the salesperson's company. Salespeople have been trained to meet customers' needs; however, they have also learned to follow company policies. They play the role of customer satisfier but also of company satisfier. What should sales representatives do? If a salesperson can negotiate differences between the two parties, he or she may be able to resolve the conflict and make the sale.

In general, accurate role perceptions are a very important determinant of sales performance, effectiveness, satisfaction, and organizational commitment.[32] Role ambiguity in the early stage of employment decreases salesperson commitment to their companies and increases turnover.[33] Accurate perceptions are instilled during initial sales training and over time during sales meetings and through periodic interactions with sales supervisors.

Organizational citizenship behaviors, or OCBs, represent a very important aspect of salesperson role perceptions and managerial evaluation of salesperson performance. **Organizational citizenship behaviors** are "discretionary behaviors on the part of a salesperson that directly promote the effective functioning of an organization, without necessarily influencing a salesperson's objective sales productivity."[34] OCBs include helping fellow salespeople or other personnel with important tasks (*altruism*), tolerating less-than-ideal working circumstances without complaining (*sportsmanship*), participating in and being concerned with organizational welfare (*civic virtue*), and going beyond the minimum role requirements of the job—such as working extra hours, never bending the rules, and spending corporate money only when it is in the best interest of the company (*conscientiousness*). Research across a variety of sales situations has determined that these organizational citizenship behaviors have a greater impact than does actual sales success in determining sales managers' overall evaluations of salesperson performance.[35] Salespeople who are more satisfied with their jobs tend to display organizational citizenship behaviors.[36]

Personal Characteristics

Another determinant of salesperson effectiveness is an individual's personal characteristics: Age, physical size, appearance, race, and gender are some of the personal characteristics expected to affect sales performance. Research has shown that these personal factors may be even more important than the other factors in determining sales performance.[37]

It would be erroneous, however, to conclude that one's personal characteristics ensure sales success or failure. To the contrary, personal characteristics merely may make it more or less difficult to succeed in sales. Performance by any individual depends ultimately on his or her ability, skill, motivation level, and disciplined work habits.[38] One can either misuse personal advantages or overcome disadvantages. For example, women and African-Americans were at one time perceived to be less qualified for sales positions than white males. However, the number of sales opportunities for women and minorities have increased significantly in recent years—partly because both groups have overcome what used to be perceived as sales-related disadvantages.[39]

Speaking of gender, the proportion of women employed in nonretail selling positions has increased substantially. The idea that women might even make better salespersons than men has also increased in popularity. Yet, the question of who is better—men or women—is a fruitless one when it is framed in universal terms. One study found no significant differences between male and female salespeople in terms of job commitment, satisfaction, or performance.[40]

No doubt, some women are better salespersons than their male colleagues and vice versa. Whether women or men perform better in the salesperson role no doubt depends on the type of sales job. For example, there is some evidence to suggest that women may outperform men in selling jobs involving relationship building and consultative interaction between salesperson and customer.[41] Women seem to have somewhat better nurturing skills, which thus enables building long-term relations with customers.

In the final analysis, the real determinant of sales success does not depend on one's gender per se but rather the ability to *adapt* oneself to situational circumstances and to call upon a repertoire of what stereotypically are both male and female traits. This ability is called **androgyny,** defined as "the degree to which individuals feel that they are characterized by traits associated with both men and women."[42] Salespeople are generally considered to exhibit a variety of traits, some of which might be thought of as stereotypically male (M) or female (F) traits. These include being empathetic (F), competitive (M), sensitive (F), ambitious (M), and so on. Because adaptability is critical for success in selling and because androgynous people are more adaptable, it follows that successful salespeople are likely to be androgynous—that is, possess both male and female traits. Modest research on this topic has revealed that the highest percentage of salespeople are in fact androgynous (41 percent) and that saleswomen are more androgynous than salesmen.[43]

Adaptability

A final determinant of salesperson effectiveness is one's ability to adapt to situational circumstances. This ability is due in part to personal aptitude but also includes learned skills.

Researchers have built a compelling case that adaptability is an absolutely essential characteristic for success in selling.[44]

Formally, **adaptive selling** is "the altering of sales behaviors during a customer interaction or across customer interactions based on perceived information about the nature of the selling situation."[45] A low level of adaptability occurs when a salesperson uses the same presentation approach and methods during a single sales encounter or across encounters—such as the canned approach noted earlier when discussing the failure of some salespeople to close sales effectively. Effective salespeople adapt their presentation to fit the situation; they are able to pick up signals and "read" the customer's needs. For example, a brief, matter-of-fact presentation may be called for when meeting with a time-pressured and impatient customer, whereas a longer, more-detailed presentation is appropriate when interacting with a customer who wants all the details before making a decision.

Hence, adaptive selling involves: (1) recognizing that different selling approaches are needed in different sales situations; (2) having confidence in one's ability to use a variety of sales approaches across selling encounters as called for by a specific situation; (3) having confidence in one's ability to alter the sales approach during a sales encounter; and (4) actually using different approaches in different situations.[46]

To accentuate the prior discussion on salesperson adaptability, let us make an analogy between salesperson behavior and the action of a baseball pitcher. Imagine what would happen if a pitcher never varied the speed, location, or type of pitches thrown to batters. Batters would quickly learn to expect a certain pitch and would undoubtedly make contact with the ball and perhaps even hit a home run. But, of course, good pitchers know they have to vary their pitches so as to keep batters in suspense and thus complicate their ability to hit the ball. Good pitchers adapt their pitches to any particular batter and also throw different pitches to different batters. Adaptability is a key factor in selling, just as it is in pitching.

EXCELLENCE IN SELLING

What does it take to be a truly outstanding salesperson—to be a high performer and to excel in sales? As is always the case, there are no simple answers. Moreover, achieving excellence in one type of sales endeavor, such as selling personal insurance, undoubtedly requires somewhat different aptitude and skills than achieving excellence when selling sophisticated information systems to corporate buyers. However, although there are differences across sales jobs, there also are similarities.

Specific Characteristics of High Performers

Excellence in selling is associated with a variety of specific characteristics that are reflected in the salesperson's personal features and job behavior. These include the first impression made by a salesperson, his or her depth and breadth of knowledge, adaptability, sensitivity, enthusiasm, self-esteem, extended focus, sense of humor, creativity, risk taking, and sense of honesty and ethics.[47]

The First Impression. The outcome of a sales call is greatly influenced by the customer's first impression of the salesperson. The likelihood that a salesperson's ideas will be accepted depends largely on the *initial encounter.* Determinants of the first impression include personal appearance, dress, body language, eye contact, handshake, punctuality, and courtesy. Table 20.2 lists ten blunders a salesperson should avoid when trying to make a good first impression.

Depth of Knowledge. A salesperson's depth of knowledge reflects how well he or she understands the business, products, company, competitors, and general economic

TABLE 20.2	Ten Blunders to Avoid When Trying to Make a Good First Impression

1. Treating the receptionist and secretary with less respect than you would give the prospect; instead, make a friend of these people if you want to build a relationship with the prospect.
2. Not doing your homework on the company and their needs and problems.
3. Arriving at a sales call ill-prepared—that is, not having all necessary papers, samples, brochures, and so on.
4. Talking too much, which implies that you are not doing enough listening.
5. Giving recommendations without asking your prospect's needs.
6. Making yourself at home in the prospect's office before being asked.
7. Being late.
8. Using sloppy or inappropriate language.
9. Being poorly groomed.
10. Having a negative attitude.

Source: Adapted from "10 Ways to Sabotage a First Impression," *Sales and Marketing Management,* July 1994, 49.

climate related to the sales job. Depth of knowledge is obtained in part through an individual's self-study efforts. Knowledgeable salespeople stay alert to what is going on by listening carefully to customers, keeping abreast of current developments in the industry, and getting the most out of company sales meetings, training programs, and conferences.

Breadth of Knowledge.   Salespeople who have a wide breadth of knowledge are conversant on a broad spectrum of subjects and, therefore, are able to interact effectively with a variety of customers. Salespeople who possess a broad scope of knowledge make customers feel relaxed and are able to share common interests (through comments or discussions concerning world events, athletics, cultural affairs, or whatever the customer's interests may be). One acquires this facet of excellence through expansive reading, taking a variety of courses while in college, continuous studying, and good listening skills. In general, breadth of knowledge is a matter of being alert, attentive, and interested in different people and events. At a minimum, any college graduate who expects to be conversant and effective in a selling position should read a daily newspaper and a weekly magazine such as *Newsweek, Time, Business Week,* and so forth.

Adaptability.   As already discussed, this fourth characteristic of excellence refers to the willingness and ability to adjust one's interactional style toward the customer. Because salespeople interact with a wide variety of customers, those who are more adaptable tend to be more effective. Adaptability in this sense should not be misinterpreted as suggesting that a salesperson should alter his or her presentation to accommodate what each prospect might want to hear, regardless of the truth. Rather, people differ in terms of how open, sociable, and communicative they are, and a salesperson must adjust his or her interactional style to make the customer comfortable.

Sensitivity.   The essence of this fifth feature of excellence is *empathy,* or the ability to place oneself in the other person's position. That is, the successful sales representative shows a genuine interest in the prospect's needs, problems, and concerns. Also, the salesperson demonstrates respect for customers and does not patronize them. Most people are quick to notice a sales representative's positive attitude toward them, to which they react favorably.

Good listening skills are another facet of sensitivity. Based on ratings of factors leading to salesperson *failure,* one study determined that poor listening skills are at the top of the list.[48] Listening enables the salesperson to understand the needs of the customer and to adjust the sales message accordingly.[49] Listening is a rare skill. But why? One reason is that people are usually absorbed in their own lives and activities, and listening to someone else becomes boring for them. Most of us enjoy a conversation only when the other person is finished talking so that we can start talking ourselves. The fact that so many people look upon listening as something irksome reflects the scarcity of good listeners.

Enthusiasm.   Enthusiasm, the sixth quality of excellence, reflects a salesperson's deep-seated commitment to his or her company's products and to customers' needs. Enthusiastic salespeople tend to be more motivated than less enthusiastic people, and customers are responsive to the salesperson's enthusiastic efforts.

Self-Esteem.   This involves feelings of self-worth and personal confidence. A salesperson is more successful if he or she has a positive self-concept, likes his or her product and company, and looks forward to meeting prospects. A salesperson who does not have self-confidence will seldom be successful in selling. Furthermore, a salesperson must have a positive attitude toward the product, company, and sales message. A person who does not fully believe in what he or she sells will be seen as insincere. After all, if the salesperson does not believe in the product, how can the customer?

Extended Focus.   Excellent people in any endeavor have specific goals and purposes— that is, a sense of focus. Said another way, "Most people aim at nothing in life and hit it with amazing accuracy."[50] The term *extended focus* means the ability to focus simultaneously on the specific while considering the big picture. This eighth property of excellence is based on the idea that salespeople must focus their efforts into achieving specific goals; they must not permit themselves to be distracted.

Sense of Humor.   This ninth characteristic of excellence stresses the ability to laugh with others as well as to laugh at oneself. Humor helps customers relax. It also helps customers remember you. There is a difference, however, between having a good sense of humor and being a clown or buffoon.

Creativity.   Salespeople who exhibit this tenth feature have an ability to connect seemingly unrelated ideas and to arrive at unique solutions to problems. This ability is critical in many selling positions, such as trade and technical selling, where the salesperson is often selling a total system rather than a single product. Often competing companies' basic products and nonproduct offerings (e.g., promotional programs) are very similar; hence, what distinguishes one company from the next are the creative solutions that salespeople devise for addressing customers' needs or solving problems. Creativity does not stop with merely coming up with an idea; rather, "it is the quality of the action that puts the idea into being."[51]

Taking Risks.   Closely related to creativity is the eleventh characteristic of excellence, the willingness to take risks. To be creative you must be willing to take risks, recommend solutions that might backfire, and seek change rather than sameness. Excellent salespeople are always looking for new ideas, methods, and solutions that will benefit their customers, themselves, and their companies.

Sense of Honesty and Ethics.   This twelfth quality of excellence is last but certainly not least. Contrary to widespread myths about personal selling, excellence in personal selling requires as high a degree of honesty and ethical behavior as any of life's lasting relationships. The key word is *relationship*. There are some sales jobs where a single transaction between buyer and seller takes place; however, most personal-selling interactions involve building long-term relationships with customers. This is not accomplished with deceit, misrepresentation, or undependable behavior. Truly excellent salespeople are considered by their customers as trustworthy and dependable individuals. We expect these qualities in our friends, and the same expectations carry over on a professional level to the marketplace. You may recall from the *Opening Vignette* those salesperson qualities most valued by purchasing agents. The two most valued qualities are reliability/credibility and professionalism/integrity.

F ROM SELLING TO SALES MANAGEMENT

A natural step in the career life cycles of many successful salespeople is an eventual move from a personal selling position to sales management. In general, sales management involves acquiring, directing, and stimulating competent salespeople to perform tasks that move the organization toward accomplishment of its objectives and mission. Sales management provides a significant link between an organization's corporate and marketing strategies and the salespeople who actuate the marketing transaction. A sales manager has been described as

> *the tactician who translates plans into action. He or she implements the various programs for market analysis, direction of sales effort, training, performance appraisal and compensation . . . [and] also has a longer-term responsibility for planning market development and account coverage in his/her area. He or she provides management with information on the organization's effectiveness and conditions in the marketplace as inputs to management's analysis, planning, and control activities.*[52]

It is interesting to note that many successful salespeople move into sales management only to be dissatisfied or unsuccessful. The reasons are manifold, but some people simply are not cut out for managerial responsibilities. The best managers are team players who obtain satisfaction from overseeing the success of their organizations. Moreover, some salespeople simply prefer to be involved in selling rather than managing others. Outstanding salespeople often receive greater compensation than do sales managers.[53]

Summary

This chapter presents a broad array of ideas about the nature of personal selling. Personal selling's role in the marketing communications mix includes educating customers, encouraging product usage and marketing assistance, and providing after-sale service and support to the buyer. As a career, personal selling includes the attractive features of freedom of action, variety and challenge, opportunities for advancement, and desirable financial and nonfinancial rewards.

A partner-oriented selling mind-set pervades most successful firms today. These firms realize that their success rests upon the successes of their customers. Hence, modern partner-oriented philosophy makes customer satisfaction its highest priority. Modern selling practice is based on the following principles: Trust and mutual agreement must exist between buyer and seller; getting the order is only the first step—after-sales service is what counts; and professionalism and integrity are essential in a salesperson.

Personal selling is a broad field consisting of a variety of different types of sales jobs. Sales activities include making sales presentations, working with orders, servicing the product and the account, managing information, participating in conferences and meetings, training, entertaining, traveling, and working with distributors. Sales jobs include trade selling, missionary selling, technical selling, new-business selling, retail selling, and telemarketing.

Specific determinants of salesperson performance include: (1) aptitude, (2) skill level, (3) motivational level, (4) role perceptions, (5) personal characteristics, and (6) adaptability. Each is discussed in some detail.

A final section examines excellence in selling. Twelve basic characteristics of excellence include the first impression a salesperson makes, his or her depth of knowledge, breadth of knowledge, adaptability, sensitivity, enthusiasm, self-esteem, extended focus, sense of humor, creativity, risk taking, and sense of honesty and ethics.

Discussion Questions

1. Personal selling is more effective but less efficient than advertising. Explain.

2. Many people hold personal selling in low esteem. Many students rebel at the idea of taking a sales job out of college. Why do you think these attitudes persist?

3. Please respond to the following task:[54]

   List all of the *thoughts* that come to your mind when you hear the words *personal selling*. Simply write the first thought that comes to your mind about *personal selling*, the second idea that comes to your mind about *personal selling*, the third thought, and so on. Please number each thought and put only a single thought next to each number. Your *thoughts about personal selling* may be favorable, unfavorable, or neutral.

4. Comment on the following statement: Salespeople must lie and be deceitful in order to succeed.

5. Contrast antiquated and modern selling practices. In rethinking your response to question 2, what additional insight can you offer by taking into consideration the antiquated/modern distinction?

6. One form of sales presentation is called a canned presentation, which means that a salesperson uses the identical presentation time after time. How would you evaluate the canned sales presentation? What are the advantages and disadvantages of this form of presentation?

7. "Sales representatives should act as if they were on the customer's payroll." Evaluate this statement by explaining in your own words what it means and by describing the advantages and disadvantages that may result when a salesperson acts in this manner.

8. In view of the different types of sales jobs described in the chapter (such as trade selling and technical selling), identify the job types you would or would not be willing to take as a first job out of college. Provide your rationale for each decision.

9. No single factor is able to explain salesperson performance adequately. Comment.

10. Distinguish among aptitude, skill, and personal characteristics as unique determinants of salesperson performance. Considering only aptitude and personal characteristics, provide an assessment of whether you possess the aptitude and personal features for a successful career in: (1) computer sales for a company like IBM and (2) trade sales for a company such as Procter & Gamble. Offer reasons why you think you would (or would not) succeed.

11. Distinguish between working hard and working smart. As a student, which behavior better characterizes your own performance? What behaviors would a salesperson manifest in demonstrating an ability to work smart rather than simply hard? Be specific.

12. Based on the 12 characteristics of personal excellence described in the text, which of these do you think most salespeople with whom you have come in contact lack? Do you possess the potential for excellence in selling? Why or why not?

13. Interview three sales representatives, and describe the differences in their philosophies and approaches to personal selling. Compare your findings with the ideas presented in the text.

14. Select five students who are not members of your class and ask them to rate each of the following statements on a five-point scale, with the five places on the scale labeled *strongly agree, agree, neither agree nor disagree, disagree,* and *strongly disagree. I associate a job in personal selling with . . .*
    a. Insincerity and deceit.
    b. Low status and prestige.
    c. Much traveling.
    d. Salespeople being money hungry.
    e. The use of high-pressure tactics.
    f. Low job security.
    g. Just a job, not a career.
    h. Too little monetary reward.
    i. Having an ingratiating personality.
    j. In sum, I prefer a nonsales position much more than sales.
    Summarize the results from your small survey, and draw implications based on the assumption that the five students you queried hold views that are representative of the general student body.[55]

15. Write a two- to three-page essay on why you would or would not be a good salesperson.

1 nternet Exercise

1. Today there are more than 600 software and database productivity tools on the global market designed specifically for sales forces. These tools can give a sales force an advantage relative to competitors. However, many salespersons must travel extensively and have no way to access the software or databases without returning to the home office. To address this problem, some companies equip salespersons with portable computers. Unfortunately, each computer must be individually updated so salespersons end up spending valuable time "calling in" to make or receive updates via telecommunications. An emerging alternative is an Internet-based sales force support system. Such a system has advantages analogous to those of Internet-based e-mail in that it does not require a person to gain access from a particular location. Instead, any point of access will work. Further, with wireless Internet access on the horizon, a salesperson will truly have real time information before, during, and after every sale. Considering these possibilities, answer the following questions:
    a. Which of the selling activities listed in the chapter would be most affected by online sales force support? Justify your choices with specific details.
    b. How would online sales force support affect the implementation of adaptive selling? Be sure to distinguish between personal aptitudes and learned skills.

*C*hapter Twenty Endnotes

1. Gilbert A. Churchill, Jr., Neil M. Ford, and Orville C. Walker, Jr., *Sales Force Management: Planning, Implementation, and Control* 2nd ed. (Homewood, Ill.: Richard D. Irwin, 1985), 67.

2. Gilbert A. Churchill, Jr., Neil M. Ford, and Orville C. Walker, Jr., *Sales Force Management* 5th ed. (Chicago: Richard D. Irwin, 1997), 36–42. Also, Charles Futrell, *Personal Selling: How to Succeed in Sales* (Homewood, Ill.: Business One Irwin, 1992).

3. These points are adapted from two excellent practitioner-oriented books: Anthony Alessandra, James Cathcart, and Phillip Wexler, *Selling by Objectives* (Englewood Cliffs, N.J.: Prentice-Hall, 1988); and Paul Hersey, *Selling: A Behavioral Science Approach* (Englewood Cliffs, N.J.: Prentice-Hall, 1988).

4. C. Conrad Elnes, *Inside Secrets of Outstanding Salespeople* (Englewood Cliffs, N.J.: Prentice-Hall, 1988), 6.

5. Hersey, *Selling: A Behavioral Science Approach,* xi.

6. William C. Moncrief III, "Selling Activity and Sales Position Taxonomies for Industrial Selling," *Journal of Marketing Research* 23 (August 1986), 261–270.

7. Thayer C. Taylor, "A Handy Invention," *Sales and Marketing Management,* January 1994, 77–81.

8. Tony Seideman, "On the Cutting Edge," *Sales and Marketing Management,* June 1994, 18–23.

9. For a discussion of different stages of sales careers, see William L. Cron, Alan J. Dubinsky, and Ronald E. Michaels, "The Influence of Career Stages on Components of Salesperson Motivation," *Journal of Marketing* 52 (January 1988), 78–92.

10. Churchill, Ford, and Walker, *Sales Force Management* 5th ed, 40.

11. Ronald B. Marks, *Personal Selling: An Interactive Approach* (Boston: Allyn and Bacon, 1988), 39.

12. Ibid., 45.

13. "Du Pont Turns Scientists into Salespeople," *Sales and Marketing Management,* June 1987, 57.

14. Hubert D. Hennessey, "Matters to Consider Before Plunging into Telemarketing," *Marketing News,* July 8, 1983, 2.

15. Jennifer Lawrence, "P&G Redirects Sales Force," *Advertising Age,* June 28, 1993, 52.

16. Julie Liesse, "Kraft Retires General in Reorganization," *Advertising Age,* January 9, 1995, 4.

17. Frank V. Cespedes, "Industrial Marketing: Managing New Requirements," *Sloan Management Review* 35 (spring 1994), 45–60.

18. Gilbert A. Churchill, Jr., Neil M. Ford, Steven W. Hartley, and Orville C. Walker, Jr., "The Determinants of Salesperson Performance: A Meta-Analysis," *Journal of Marketing Research* 22 (May 1985), 103–118.

19. Barton A. Weitz, "Effectiveness in Sales Interactions: A Contingency Framework," *Journal of Marketing* 45 (winter 1981), 85–103.

20. The following discussion of the first five factors is based on Churchill, Ford, and Walker, *Sales Force Management* 5th ed., Chapter 9.

21. Judy A. Siguaw, Gene Brown, and Robert E. Widing II, "The Influence of the Market Orientation of the Firm on Sales Force Behavior and Attitudes," *Journal of Marketing Research* 31 (February 1994), 106–116.

22. Steven P. Brown, William L. Cron, and John W. Slocum, Jr., "Effects of Trait Competitiveness and Perceived Intraorganizational Competition on Salesperson Goal Setting and Performance," *Journal of Marketing* 62 (October 1998), 88–98.

23. Ibid.

24. "Armstrong Salespeople Are to the Manor Born," *Sales and Marketing Management,* June 1987, 46.

25. Geoffrey Brewer, "Mind Reading: What Drives Top Salespeople to Greatness?" *Sales and Marketing Management,* May 1994, 82–92.

26. Geoffrey Brewer, "Survey: Sellers Giving Away the Store," *Sales and Marketing Management,* July 1994, 34.

27. Thomas E. DeCarlo and Thomas W. Leigh, "Impact of Salesperson Attraction on Sales Managers' Attributions and Feedback," *Journal of Marketing* 60 (April 1996), 47–66.

28. Brewer, "Mind Reading," 85.

29. Steven P. Brown and Robert A. Peterson, "The Effect of Effort on Sales Performance and Job Satisfaction," *Journal of Marketing* 58 (April 1994), 70–80.

30. Harish Sujan, "Smarter versus Harder: An Exploratory Attributional Analysis of Salespeople's Motivation," *Journal of Marketing Research* 23 (February 1986), 41–50.

31. Brewer, "Mind Reading," 85.

32. Steven P. Brown and Robert A. Peterson, "Antecedents and Consequences of Salesperson Job Satisfaction: Meta-Analysis and Assessment of Causal Effects," *Journal of Marketing Research* 30 (February 1993), 63–77. Also, Scott B. MacKenzie, Phillip M. Podsakoff, and Michael Ahearne, "Some Possible Antecedents and Consequences of In-Role and Extra-Role Salesperson Performance," *Journal of Marketing* 62 (July 1998), 87–98.

33. Mark W. Johnston, A. Parasuraman, Charles M. Futrell, and William C. Black, "A Longitudinal Assessment of the Impact of Selected Organizational Influences on Salespeople's Organizational Commitment during Early Employment," *Journal of Marketing Research* 27 (August 1990), 333–344.

34. Scott B. MacKenzie, Philip M. Podsakoff, and Richard Fetter, "The Impact of Organizational Citizenship Behavior on Evaluations of Salesperson Performance," *Journal of Marketing* 57 (January 1993), 71.

35. Ibid.

36. Richard G. Netemeyer, James S. Boles, Daryl O. McKee, and Robert McMurrian, "An Investigation into the Antecedents of Organizational Citizenship

Behaviors in a Personal Selling Context," *Journal of Marketing* 61 (July 1997), 95–94.

37. Churchill, Ford, Hartley, and Walker, "The Determinants of Salesperson Performance: A Meta-Analysis."

38. This last factor, disciplined work habits, was identified in the extensive research conducted by the Gallup Management Consulting Group. See Brewer, "Mind Reading," 87.

39. See, for example, Michelle Block Morse, "Rich Rewards: For Ambitious Blacks, Selling Can Mean Pride, Power, and High Pay," *Success* 35 (March 1988), 50–61.

40. Patrick L. Schul and Brent M. Wren, "The Emerging Role of Women in Industrial Selling: A Decade of Change," *Journal of Marketing* 56 (July 1992), 38–54.

41. Jane Z. Sojka and Patriya Tansuhaj, "Exploring Communication Differences between Women and Men Sales Representatives in a Relationship Selling Context," *Journal of Marketing Communications* 3 (December 1997), 197–216; Nancy Arnott, "It's a Woman's World," *Sales & Marketing Management,* March 1995, 54–59; and Michele Marchetti, "Women's Movement," *Sales & Marketing Management,* November 1996, 76–82.

42. Rosemary R. Lagace and Jacquelyn L. Twible, "The Androgyny of Salespeople: Gooses and Ganders, or All Geese?" *Journal of Social Behavior and Personality* 5, no. 6 (1990), 641–650.

43. Ibid.

44. See Siew Meng Leong, Paul S. Busch, and Deborah Roedder John, "Knowledge Bases and Salesperson Effectiveness: A Script-Theoretic Analysis," *Journal of Marketing Research* 26 (May 1989), 164–178; Rosann L. Spiro and Barton A. Weitz, "Adaptive Selling: Conceptualization, Measurement, and Nomological Validity," *Journal of Marketing Research* 27 (February 1990), 61–69; Weitz, "Effectiveness in Sales Interactions: A Contingency Framework"; and Barton A. Weitz, Harish Sujan, and Mita Sujan, "Knowledge, Motivation, and Adaptive Behavior: A Framework for Improving Selling Effectiveness," *Journal of Marketing* 50 (October 1986), 174–191.

45. Weitz, Sujan, and Sujan, "Knowledge, Motivation, and Adaptive Behavior," 175.

46. Adapted from Spiro and Weitz, "Adaptive Selling."

47. These characteristics and the following discussion are based on Alessandra, Cathcart, and Wexler, *Selling by Objectives,* 59–76. A related perspective is provided by Lawrence W. Lamont and William J. Lundstrom, "Identifying Successful Industrial Salesmen by Personality and Personal Characteristics," *Journal of Marketing Research* 14 (November 1977), 517–529.

48. Thomas N. Ingram, Charles H. Schwepker, Jr., and Don Hutson. "Why Salespeople Fail," *Industrial Marketing Management,* 21 (1992), 225–230.

49. See Rosemary P. Ramsey and Ravipreet S. Sohi, "Listening to Your Customers: The Impact of Perceived Salesperson Listening Behavior on Relationship Outcomes." *Journal of the Academy of Marketing Science,* 25 (No. 2, 1997), 127–137.

50. Alessandra, Cathcart, and Wexler, *Selling by Objectives,* 73.

51. Ibid., 75.

52. John P. Steinbrink, "Field Sales Management," in *Marketing Manager's Handbook,* ed. Stuart Henderson Britt and Norman F. Guess (Chicago: Dartnell Corporation, 1983), 984.

53. Nancy Arnott, "I'd Rather Be Selling," *Sales and Marketing Management,* July 1995, 77–83.

54. This task is slightly adapted from Steven Lysonski and Srinivas Durvasula, "A Cross-National Investigation of Student Attitudes toward Personal Selling: Implications for Marketing Education," *Journal of Marketing Education,* 20 (May 1998), 164.

55. The statements used in question 14 are adapted from Rosemary R. Lagace and Timothy A. Longfellow, "The Impact of Classroom Style on Student Attitudes toward Sales Careers: A Comparative Approach," *Journal of Marketing Education* (fall 1989), 74.

Glossary

Ability   With reference to marketing, a person's familiarity with message claims and capability of comprehending them.

Account-specific marketing   A descriptive term that characterizes promotional and advertising activity that a manufacturer customizes to specific retail accounts; also called *co-marketing*.

Active synthesis   The second stage of perceptual encoding, active synthesis involves a more refined perception of a stimulus than simply an examination of its basic features. The context of the situation in which information is received plays a major role in determining what is perceived and interpreted.

Adaptive selling   The altering of sales behaviors during a customer interaction or across customer interactions based on perceived information about the nature of the selling situation.

Advertising   A form of either mass communication or direct-to-consumer communication that is nonpersonal and is paid for by various business firms, nonprofit organizations, and individuals who are in some way identified in the advertising message and who hope to inform or persuade members of a particular audience.

Advertising objective   Motive or goal that advertising efforts attempt to achieve. Examples include increasing sales volume, consumer awareness, and favorability of attitudes.

Advertising-sales-response function   The amount of sales revenue generated at each level of advertising expenditure.

Advertising strategy   A plan of action guided by corporate and marketing strategies which determine the following: how much can be invested in advertising; at what markets advertising efforts need to be directed; how advertising must be coordinated with other marketing elements; and, to some degree, how advertising is to be executed.

Advocacy advertising   See **Issue advertising**.

Affective component   The emotional component of an attitude.

Affect referral   The simplest decision heuristic strategy in which the individual calls from memory his or her attitude, or affect, toward relevant alternatives and picks that alternative for which the affect is most positive.

Affordability method   An advertising budgeting method that sets the budget by spending on advertising those funds that remain after budgeting for everything else.

AIO   An acronym for *a*ctivities, *i*nterests, and *o*pinions, a combination representing psychographics.

Allegory   A form of figurative language that equates the objects in a particular narrative (such as an advertised brand in a television commercial) with meanings lying outside the narrative itself.

Ambushing   An activity that takes place when companies that are not official sponsors of an event undertake marketing efforts to convey the impression that they are.

Androgyny   The condition of adapting oneself to situational circumstances and to call upon a repertoire of both male and female traits.

Attractiveness   An attribute that includes any number of virtuous characteristics that receivers may perceive in an endorser. The general concept of attractiveness consists of three related ideas: *similarity, familiarity,* and *liking.*

Attributes   In the means-end conceptualization of advertising strategy, attributes are features or aspects of the advertised product or brand.

Awareness class   The first step in product adoption. Four marketing-mix variables influence the awareness class: samples, coupons, advertising, and product distribution.

Baby boom   The birth of 75 million Americans between 1946 and 1964.

Beliefs   Subjective probability assessments regarding the likelihood that performing a certain act will lead to a certain outcome.

Bill-back allowances   A form of trade allowance in which retailers receive allowances for featuring the manufacturer's brand in advertisements (bill-back ad allowances) or for providing special displays (bill-back display allowances).

Brand-concept management   The planning, implementation, and control of a brand concept throughout the life of the brand.

Brand equity   The goodwill (equity) that an established brand has built up over the period of its existence.

Brand-image strategy   A creative advertising strategy that involves psychological rather than physical differentiation. The advertiser attempts to develop an image for a brand by associating it with symbols.

Category management   A system established by Procter & Gamble whereby a category manager who has direct profit responsibility manages each product category within a company.

Cause-related marketing (CRM)   A relatively narrow aspect of overall sponsorship which involves an amalgam of public relations, sales promotion, and corporate philanthropy. The distinctive feature of CRM is that a company's contribution to a designated cause is linked to customers' engaging in revenue-producing exchanges with the firm.

Cognitive component   The intellectual component of attitude. In marketing, it is the consumer's knowledge, thoughts, and beliefs about an object or issue.

Cognitive needs   Cognitive needs are congruent with consumers' informational goals as opposed to their hedonistic (feelings of good and pleasure) needs. Cognitive needs are met by sources such as print and television advertising.

Commercial rumor   A widely circulated but unverified proposition about a product, brand, company, store, or other commercial target.

Communication   Process whereby individuals share meaning and establish a commonness of thought.

Compensatory heuristic   A choice strategy in which the customer ranks each of the criteria he or she would like a product to meet, decides how well each brand alternative will satisfy these criteria, and integrates this information to arrive at a "score" for each alternative. Theoretically the consumer selects the alternative with the highest overall score. This procedure is likely to be used in risky (high-involvement) circumstances; that is, when a decision involves considerable financial, performance, or psychological risk.

Competitive parity method A budgeting method that sets the advertising budget by basically following what competitors are doing.

Complexity The degree of perceived difficulty of an innovation. The more difficult an innovation is to understand or use, the slower the rate of adoption.

Comprehension The ability to understand and create meaning out of stimuli and symbols.

Conative component The action component of an attitude; a person's behavioral tendency toward an object. In marketing, it is the consumer's intention to purchase a specific item. Also called *behavioral component.*

Concretizing A marketing approach based on the idea that it is easier for people to remember and retrieve *tangible* rather than *abstract* information.

Conjunctive heuristic One of three noncompensatory choice strategies in which the consumer establishes cutoffs, or minima, on all pertinent criteria; an alternative is retained for further consideration only if it meets or exceeds all minima.

Consequences In the means-end conceptualization of advertising strategy, consequences represent the desirable or undesirable results from consuming a particular product or brand.

Conspiracy rumors Unconfirmed statements that involve supposed company policies or practices that are threatening or ideologically undesirable to consumers.

Contact Potential message delivery channels capable of reaching target customers and presenting the communicator's brand in a favorable light.

Contamination rumors Unconfirmed statements dealing with undesirable or harmful product or store features.

Contest A form of consumer-oriented sales promotion in which consumers have an opportunity to win cash, merchandise, or travel prizes. Winners become eligible by solving the specified contest problem.

Continuity A media planning consideration that involves the matter of how advertising should be allocated during the course of an advertising campaign.

Continuous advertising schedule In a continuous schedule, a relatively equal number of ad dollars are invested in advertising throughout the campaign.

Contribution margin The selling price of a brand minus its per-unit variable cost. When a brand is on deal, its variable cost increases due to the expense of offering, for example, a coupon worth 50 cents. This results in a reduced margin.

Cooperative advertising An arrangement between a manufacturer and reseller (either a retailer or an industrial distributor) whereby the manufacturer pays for all or some of the advertising costs undertaken by the reseller in behalf of the manufacturer's products.

Corporate advertising Advertising that focuses on specific products or brands in a corporation's overall image or on economic/social issues relevant to the corporation's interests.

Corporate image advertising A specific form of corporate advertising that attempts to gain name recognition for a company, establish goodwill for it and its products, or identify itself with some meaningful and socially acceptable activity.

Corrective advertising Advertising based on the premise that a firm that misleads consumers should have to use future advertisements to rectify any deceptive impressions it has created in consumers' minds. Its purpose is to prevent a firm from continuing to deceive consumers rather than to punish the firm.

Counterarguments A form of cognitive response that occurs when the receiver challenges message claims.

Coupon A promotional device that provides cents-off savings to consumers upon redeeming the coupons.

CPM An abbreviation for cost per thousand, in which the *M* represents the Roman numeral for 1,000. CPM is the cost of reaching 1,000 people.

CPM-TM A refinement of CPM that measures the cost of reaching 1,000 members of the target market, excluding those people who fall outside of the target market.

Creative brief The work of copywriters is directed by this framework, which is a document designed to inspire copywriters by channeling their creative efforts toward a solution that will serve the interests of the client.

Customer lifetime value The net present value (NPV) of the profit that a company stands to realize on the average new customer during a given number of years.

Decoding The mental process of transforming message symbols into thought; consumers' interpretations of marketing messages. See also **Encoding.**

Demographics These are variables that are measurable population characteristics, including the age distribution, household living patterns, income distribution, ethnic population patterns, and regional population statistics.

Diffusion process In a marketing communications sense, diffusion means that a product or idea is adopted by more and more customers as time passes. In other words, a product "spreads out" through the marketplace.

Direct-mail advertising A form of advertising matter sent directly to the person whom the marketer wishes to influence; these advertisements can take the form of letters, postcards, programs, calendars, folders, catalogs, videocassettes, blotters, order blanks, price lists, menus, and so on.

Direct marketing Activities by which products and services are offered to market segments in one or more media for informational purposes or to solicit responses from present or prospective customers or contributors by mail, telephone, or other access.

Direct objectives With reference to advertising, those objectives that seek a *behavioral response* from the audience.

Dual-coding theory The idea that pictures are represented in memory in verbal as well as visual form, whereas words are less likely to have visual representations.

Early adopters The second group of people to adopt an innovation. The size of this group is defined statistically as 13.5 percent of all potential adopters. Early adopters are localites, in contrast to innovators, who are described as cosmopolites. Early adopters are well integrated within their communities and are respected by their friends.

EDLP(M) pricing This is a form of pricing whereby a manufacturer charges the same price for a particular brand day in and day out. Rather than charging high-low prices (regular, or "high," prices for a period followed by off-invoice, or "low," prices for a shorter period), EDLP(M) involves charging the same price over an extended period.

Effective reach   Based on the idea that an advertising schedule is effective only if it does not reach members of the target audience too few or too many times. What exactly is too few or too many depends on the specific advertising situation, but many media planners consider fewer than three exposures as too few and more than ten as too many.

Efficient consumer response (ECR)   A broad-based concept of business management oriented toward altering industry practices to enhance efficiencies and reduce costs.

Elaboration   The mental activity associated with a consumer's response to a persuasive message. Elaboration involves thinking about what the message is saying, evaluating the arguments in the message, agreeing with some, disagreeing with others, and so on.

Elaboration likelihood model (ELM)   A theory of persuasion and attitude change that predicts two forms of message processing and attitude change: central and peripheral routes. The former occurs under high involvement and leads to a more permanent attitude change than does the latter.

Encoding   The process of putting thoughts into symbolic form. See also **Decoding.**

Encoding specificity principle   A principle of cognitive psychology which states that information recall is enhanced when the context in which people attempt to retrieve information is the same or similar to the context in which they originally encoded the information.

Encoding variability hypothesis   A hypothesis contending that people's memories for information are enhanced when multiple pathways, or connections, are created between the object to be remembered and the information about the object that is to be remembered.

Environmental management   The idea that through its promotional efforts and other marketing activities, a firm can attempt to modify existing environmental conditions.

Environmental monitoring   An action involving two general activities: an *internal analysis* of an organization's strengths and weaknesses and an *external analysis* or review of factors that are likely to influence communications effectiveness and product success.

Ethics   In the context of marketing communications involves matters of right and wrong, or *moral*, conduct.

Evaluations   The subjective value or importance that consumers attach to consumption outcomes.

Event sponsorship   A form of brand promotion that ties a brand to a meaningful cultural, social, athletic, or other type of high-interest public activity.

Exceptionist loyalists   Consumers who, though loyal to a single brand when all brands in the category are off deal, will make an exception and purchase another, nonpreferred brand when it, but not their preferred brand, is on deal.

Executive-statement release   A news release quoting CEOs and other corporate executives.

Exit fee   A *deslotting charge* to cover the handling costs for a chain to remove an item from its distribution center.

Experiential needs   Needs representing desires for products that provide sensory pleasure, variety, and stimulation.

Expertise   The knowledge, experience, or skills possessed by an endorser as they relate to the communications topic.

Exposure   In marketing terms, signifies that consumers come in contact with the marketer's message.

External lists   Mailing lists bought from other companies rather than being based on a company's own internal list of customers.

Feature analysis   The initial stage of perceptual encoding whereby a receiver examines the basic features of a stimulus (brightness, depth, angles, etc.) and from this makes a preliminary classification.

Feature article   A detailed description of a product or other newsworthy programs that are written by a PR firm for immediate publication or airing by print or broadcast media or distribution via appropriate Internet sites

Feedback   Data that afford the source of marketing communications with a way of monitoring how accurately the intended message is being received and offer some measure of control in the communications process.

Forward buying   The practice whereby retailers take advantage of manufacturers' trade deals by buying larger quantities than needed for normal inventory. Retailers often buy enough product on one deal to carry them over until the manufacturer's next scheduled deal; hence, forward buying also is called *bridge buying*.

Free-in-the-mail premium   A promotion in which consumers receive a premium item from the sponsoring manufacturer in return for submitting a required number of proofs of purchase.

Frequency   The number of times, on average, within a four-week period that members of the target audience are exposed to the advertiser's message. Also called *average frequency*.

Functional needs   Those needs involving current consumption-related problems, potential problems, or conflicts.

Galvanometer   A device (also referred to as a psychogalvanometer) for measuring *galvanic skin response* or *GSR*. The galvanometer indirectly assesses the degree of emotional response to an advertisement by measuring minute amounts of perspiration.

Generic strategy   A creative advertising strategy in which the advertiser makes a claim about its brand that could be made by any company that markets the product.

Geodemographics   A combination of demographic and lifestyle characteristics of consumers within geographic clusters such as ZIP-code areas and neighborhoods.

Gross rating points (GRPs)   A statistic that represents the mathematical product of reach multiplied by frequency. The number of GRPs indicates the total weight of advertising during a time frame, such as a four-week period. The number of GRPs indicates the gross coverage or duplicated audience that is exposed to a particular advertising schedule.

Hedonic needs   Needs such as pleasure satisfied by messages that make people feel good. People are most likely to attend those stimuli that have become associated with rewards and that relate to those aspects of life that they value highly.

Hierarchy of effects   A model predicated on the idea that advertising moves people from an initial stage of unawareness about a product/brand to a final stage of purchasing that product/brand.

House lists   Names of customers that are generated from a company's own internal records. Customers' names are often grouped into active, recently active, long-since-active customers, or inquiry categories. A list may be subdivided by the recency of a customer's purchase, the monetary value of each purchase, or the type of products purchased. Customers may be categorized by geographic, demographic, or psychographic characteristics.

Identification process   The source attribute of attractiveness influences message receivers via a process of identification, that is, receivers perceive a source to be attractive and therefore identify with the source and adopt the attitudes, behaviors, interests, or preferences of the source.

Imagery   A mental event involving visualization of a concept or relationship.

In- and on-pack premiums Programs that offer a premium item inside a package, attached to a package, or the package itself is reusable.

Indirect objectives   With reference to advertising, those objectives aimed at eliciting prebehavioral responses, that is, achieving communication outcomes that precede behavior.

Infomercial   A form of television advertising that serves as an innovative alternative to the conventional form of short television commercial. Infomercials are full-length commercial segments run on cable (and sometimes network) television that typically last 30 minutes and combine product news and entertainment.

Innovators   The first group of people to accept a new idea or product. Innovators are extremely venturesome and more willing to take risks.

Intense stimuli   Stimuli that are louder, more colorful, bigger, brighter, and so on, and which are more likely than less intense stimuli to attract attention.

Internalization   The source attribute of credibility influences message receivers via a process of internalization; that is, receivers perceive a source to be credible and therefore accept the source's position or attitude as their own. Internalized attitudes tend to be maintained even when the source of the message is forgotten and even when the source switches to a new position.

Involuntary attention   One of the forms of attention that requires little or no effort on the part of the message receiver; the stimulus intrudes upon a person's consciousness even though he or she does not want it to. See also **Nonvoluntary attention** and **Voluntary attention.**

Issue advertising   A form of corporate advertising that takes a position on a controversial social issue of public importance. It does so in a manner that supports the company's position and best interests. Also called *advocacy advertising.* See also **Corporate image advertising.**

Key fact   In an advertising strategy, a single-minded statement from the *consumer's point of view* that identifies why consumers are or are not purchasing the product/service brand or are not giving it proper consideration.

Laddering   A marketing research technique that has been developed to identify linkages between attributes, consequences, and values. It involves in-depth, one-on-one interviews using primarily a series of directed probes.

Laggards   The final group to adopt an innovation; they represent the bottom 16 percent of potential adopters. These people are bound in tradition and, as a group, focus on the past as their frame of reference.

Late majority   Adopters representing 34 percent of potential adopters just following the average adoption time. The key word that characterizes this group is *skepticism.*

Loyalists   Consumers whose purchase patterns reflect that they buy the same brand over and over when no brands are on deal. Loyalists may or may not be deal prone.

Marketing   Process whereby businesses and other organizations facilitate exchanges, or transfers of value, between themselves and their customers and clients.

Marketing communications   The collection of all elements in an organization's marketing mix that facilitates exchanges by establishing shared meaning with the organization's customers or clients.

Market mavens   Individuals who have information about many kinds of products, places to shop, and other facets of markets, and who initiate discussions with consumers and respond to requests from consumers for market information.

Mature people   According to the U.S. Bureau of the Census, those who are 55 and older.

Meaning   The set of internal responses and resulting predispositions evoked within a person when presented with a sign or stimulus object.

MECCAS   An acronym for *Means-End Conceptualization of Components for Advertising Strategy,* a model for applying the concept of means-end chains to the creation of advertising messages.

Media   The general communication methods that carry advertising messages, that is, television, magazines, newspapers, and so on.

Media planning   An approach that involves the process of designing a scheduling plan that shows how advertising time and space will contribute to the achievement of marketing objectives.

Media research   Advertising research undertaken to test the effectiveness of creative media.

Message   A symbolic expression of a sender's thoughts; the instrument (e.g., advertisement) used to share thought with a receiver. More practically, the term *message* refers to the verbal and nonverbal persuasive techniques used in all forms of marketing communications.

Message channel   The path through which the message moves from source to receiver; for example, from a marketer via a magazine to consumers.

Message research   Also known as *copytesting,* message research is a technique that tests the effectiveness of creative messages. Copytesting involves both pretesting a message during its development stages and posttesting the message for effectiveness after it has been aired or printed.

Metaphor   A form of figurative language that applies a word or a phrase to a concept or an object, such as a brand, that it does not literally denote in order to suggest a comparison with the brand (e.g., Budweiser is "the king of beers").

Micromarketing   The customizing of products and communications to small segments of consumers.

MOA   *M*otivation, *o*pportunity, and *a*bility, the factors that determine each individual's elaboration likelihood for a particular message.

Motivation   One of the factors that determines each individual's elaboration likelihood for a particular message.

National Association of Attorneys General (NAAG)
Includes attorneys general from all 50 states. In recent years this group has played an increasingly active role in regulating advertising deception and other business practices.

Noise Extraneous and distracting stimuli that interfere with reception of a message in its pure and original form. Noise occurs at all stages of the communications process.

Noncompensatory heuristics Choice behavior based on strategies such as conjunctive, disjunctive, or lexicographic heuristics. Contrasts with the compensatory heuristic to choice.

Non-deal-prone loyalists Consumers who invariably buy a single brand in a product category and are not influenced by that brand's deals or the deals from competitive brands.

Non-deal-prone switchers A consumer segment that is not responsive to deals and which switches among brands. This is due to a need for novelty rather than to avail themselves of deals.

Nonvoluntary attention One of three forms of attention that occurs when a person is attracted to a stimulus and continues to pay attention because it holds interest for him or her. A person in this situation neither resists the stimulus nor willingly attends to it initially; however, once his or her attention is attracted, the individual continues to give attention because the stimulus has some benefit or relevance. Also called *spontaneous attention.* See also **Involuntary attention** and **Voluntary attention.**

Objective Marketing managers' goals to be accomplished for a brand.

Objective-and-task method A budgeting method that establishes the advertising budget by determining the communication tasks that need to be established. See also **Percentage-of-sales method.**

Observability The degree to which other people can observe one's ownership and use of a new product. The more a consumption behavior can be sensed by other people, the more observable it is and typically the more rapid is its rate of adoption.

Off-invoice allowance A deal offered periodically to the trade that literally permits wholesalers and retailers to deduct a fixed amount from the invoice.

Open-ended co-op advertising A cooperative advertising program that involves paying for the portion of the retailer's advertising cost without relating the reimbursement to the amount of product purchased from the manufacturer.

Opportunity A term referring to whether it is physically possible for a person to process a message.

Outcomes The aspects of brand ownership that the consumer either desires to obtain or to avoid.

Overlay program The use of two or more sales promotion techniques in combination with one another; also called *combination program.*

Pay-for-performance programs A form of trade allowance that rewards retailers for performing the primary function that justifies a manufacturer's offering a trade allowance—namely, selling increased quantities of the manufacturer's brands to grocery shoppers.

People Meter A handheld device that automatically records what programs are being watched, how many households are watching, and which family members are in attendance.

Percentage-of-sales method A budgeting method that involves setting the budget as a fixed percentage of past or

anticipated (typically the latter) sales volume. See also **Objective-and-task method.**

Perceptual encoding The process of interpreting stimuli, which includes two stages: feature analysis and active-synthesis.

Personal selling A form of person-to-person communication in which the seller attempts to persuade prospective buyers to purchase his or her company's (organization's) product or service.

Phased strategies Procedure in which consumers use a combination of choice heuristics in sequence or in phase with one another to make decisions.

Point-of-purchase (P-O-P) communications Promotional elements, including displays, posters, signs, and a variety of other in-store materials, that are designed to influence the customer's choice at the time of purchase.

Positioning Advertising Copytesting (PACT) A set of nine copytesting principles developed by leading U.S. advertising agencies.

Positioning statement The key idea that encapsulates what a brand is intended to stand for in its target market's mind.

Positioning strategy A creative advertising strategy in which an advertiser implants in the consumer's mind a clear understanding of what the brand is and how it compares to competitive offerings.

Preemptive strategy A creative advertising strategy in which the advertiser that makes a particular claim effectively prevents competitors from making the same claim for fear of being labeled a copycat.

Premiums Articles of merchandise or services offered by manufacturers to induce action on the part of the sales force, trade representatives, or consumers.

Proactive MPR A form of marketing PR that is offensively rather than defensively oriented and opportunity-seeking rather than problem solving. See also **Reactive MPR.**

Product release A publicity tool that announces new product, provides relevant information about product features and benefits, and informs interested listeners/readers how additional information can be obtained.

Promotion The aspect of general marketing that promotion management deals with explicitly. Promotion includes the practices of advertising, personal selling, sales promotion, publicity, and point-of-purchase communications.

Psychogalvanometer A device for measuring galvanic skin response that is used as an indicator of advertising effectiveness, specifically by determining whether the consumer's autonomic nervous system is activated by some element in an advertisement.

Psychographic characteristics Aspects of consumers' lifestyles such as activities, interests, and opinions.

Psychological reactance A theory that suggests that people react against any efforts to reduce their freedoms or choices. When products are made to seem less available, they become more valuable in the consumer's mind.

Publicity Nonpersonal communication to a mass audience that is not paid for by an organization. Examples include news items or editorial comments about an organization's products or services.

Pull strategy Marketing efforts directed to ultimate consumers with the intent of influencing their acceptance of the manufacturer's brand. Manufacturers hope that the consumers will then encourage retailers to handle the brand. Typically used in conjunction with *push strategy*.

Push money   Cash provided to salespeople by the manufacturer to encourage them to push certain products in the manufacturer's line. Also called *spiffs*.

Push strategy   A manufacturer's selling and other promotional efforts directed at gaining trade support from wholesalers and retailers for the manufacturer's product.

Rating   The proportion of the target audience presumed to be exposed to a single occurrence of an advertising vehicle in which the advertiser's brand is advertised.

Reach   The percentage of an advertiser's target audience that is exposed to at least one advertisement over an established time frame (a four-week period represents the typical time frame for most advertisers). Reach represents the number of target customers who see or hear the advertiser's message one or more times during the time period. Also called *net coverage, unduplicated audience*, or *cumulative audience (cume)*.

Reactive MPR   Marketing undertaken as a result of external pressures and challenges brought by competitive actions, changes in consumer attitudes, or other external influences. It typically deals with changes that have negative consequences for the organization. See also **Proactive MPR**.

Receiver   The person or group of people with whom the sender of a communication shares thoughts. In marketing, the receivers are the prospective and present customers of an organization's product or service.

Relative advantage   The degree to which an innovation is perceived as better than an existing idea or object in terms of increasing comfort, saving time or effort, and increasing the immediacy of reward.

Repeater class   This third stage in the adoption process is influenced by four marketing-mix variables: advertising, price, distribution, and product satisfaction.

Sales promotion   Marketing activities intended to stimulate quick buyer action by offering extra benefits to customers. Examples include coupons, premiums, free samples, and sweepstakes. Also called *promotional inducements*.

Sampling   The use of various distribution methods to deliver actual- or trial-size products to consumers. The purpose is to initiate trial-usage behavior.

Semiotics   The study of meaning and the analysis of meaning-producing events.

Shelf-space model of advertising   Also termed the theory of *effective weekly planning*, a model built on the idea that the first exposure to an advertisement for a brand is the most powerful.

Sign   (1) Something physical and perceivable by our senses that represents or signifies something (the referent) to somebody (the interpreter) in some context. (2) Specifically, when both a product/brand and referent belong to the same cultural context.

Simile   A form of figurative language that uses a comparative term such as *like* or *as* to join items from different classes of experience (e.g., "love is like a rose").

Single-source data   consist of household demographic information, household purchase behavior, and household exposure to new television commercials that are tested under real world, or in-market, test conditions.

Single-source systems (SSSs)   Systems which gather purchase data from panels of households using optical scanning equipment

and merge it with household demographic characteristics and, most important, with information about causal marketing variables that influence household purchases.

Slotting allowance   The fee a manufacturer pays a supermarket or other retailer to get that retailer to handle the manufacturer's new product. The allowance is called slotting in reference to the slot, or location, that the retailer must make available in its warehouse to accommodate the manufacturer's product.

Source   In marketing communications, a source is a person, group, organization, or label that delivers a message. Marketing communications sources influence receivers by possessing one or more of three basic attributes: power, attractiveness, and credibility.

Specialty advertising   A hybrid form of marketing communications that combines elements of advertising and, at times, trade-oriented sales promotion. Specialty advertisers imprint merchandise with an advertiser's message and distribute the merchandise without obligation to designated recipients. Specialty advertising complements other forms of advertising by providing another way to keep a company's name before customers and prospects.

Sponsorship marketing   A form of marketing whereby a company invests in special events or causes for the purpose of achieving various promotional and corporate objectives.

Standardized Advertising Unit (SAU) system   A system adopted in the 1980s, making it possible for advertisers to purchase any one of 56 standard ad sizes to fit the advertising publishing parameters of all newspapers in the United States.

Stockpiling-exceptionist loyalists   A consumer segment that not only makes exceptions by choosing nonpreferred brands, but which also stockpiles quantities of other brands when they are on deal.

Stockpiling loyalists   A consumer segment that purchases only the single brand to which it is loyal but which takes advantage of savings by stockpiling when that brand is on deal.

Stockpiling switchers   A consumer segment that exploits deal opportunities by purchasing multiple units when any acceptable brand is on deal.

Supportive arguments   A form of cognitive response that occurs when a receiver agrees with a message's arguments. See also **Counterarguments** and **Source derogations**.

Sweepstakes   A form of consumer-oriented sales promotion in which winners receive cash, merchandise, or travel prizes. Winners are determined purely on the basis of chance.

Switchers   Consumers who, even when all brands in a category are off deal, nonetheless switch among different brands.

SWOT   Acronym for the analysis of a brand's *s*trengths, *w*eaknesses, *o*pportunities, and *t*hreats.

Symbol   A product and referent put together arbitrarily or metaphorically with no prior intrinsic relationship.

Symbolic needs   Internal consumer needs such as the desire for self-enhancement, role position, or group membership.

Telemarketing   The dominant form of direct marketing, entails both outbound telephone usage to sell products over the phone or perform other marketing functions and incoming telephone marketing efforts that are directed at taking orders and servicing customers.

Three-exposure hypothesis   This addresses the *minimum* number of exposures needed for advertising to be effective.

Tie-in   The simultaneous promotion of multiple brands in a single sales-promotion effort; also called *joint promotion*.

TRACE   A measurement technique that enables consumers to reveal their feelings toward what they are seeing in a television commercial by pressing a series of buttons on a handheld microcomputer.

Trade incentives   In contrast to trade contests, trade incentives are given to retail managers and salespeople for performing tasks such as displaying merchandise or selling certain lines of merchandise.

Transformational advertising   Brand image advertising that associates the experience of using an advertised brand with the unique set of psychological characteristics that would not typically be associated with the brand experience to the same degree without exposure to the advertisement.

Trialability   The extent to which an innovation can be used on a limited basis. Trialability is tied closely to the concept of perceived risk. In general, products that lend themselves to trialability are adopted at a more rapid rate.

Trier class   The group of consumers who actually try a new product; the second step in which an individual becomes a new brand consumer. Coupons, distribution, and price are the variables that influence consumers to become triers.

Trustworthiness   The honesty, integrity, and reliability of a source.

Unique selling-proposition (USP) strategy   A creative advertising strategy that promotes a product attribute that represents a meaningful, distinctive consumer benefit.

Values   In the means-end conceptualization of advertising strategy, values represent important beliefs that people hold about themselves and that determine the relative desirability of consequences.

Vehicles   The specific broadcast programs or print choices in which advertisements are placed.

Vendor support programs (VSPs)   A form of cooperative advertising program initiated by retailers whereby the retailer features one or several manufacturers' products in local advertising media and has the manufacturer(s) pay for the advertising.

Voluntary attention   One of three forms of attention that occurs when a person willfully notices a stimulus. See also **Involuntary attention** and **Nonvoluntary attention.**

Warmth monitor   A technique that measures emotional warmth in television commercials.

Wear out   Refers to the ultimately diminished effectiveness of advertising over time.

Credits

by permission of The Point-of-Purchase Advertising Institute. Chapter 9 vignette: Adapted from Sally Goll Beatty, "Just What Goes in a Viagra Ad? Early Reports Say Dancing Couples," *The Wall Street Journal Interactive Edition,* June 17, 1998. Republished by permission of Dow Jones, Inc. via Copyright Clearance Center, Inc. © 1998 *The Wall Street Journal,* Dow Jones & Company, Inc. All Rights Reserved Worldwide. Table 9.1: R. Craig Endicott, "Top 100 Magabrands," *Advertising Age,* July 13, 1998, pp. S1–S13. © 1998 by Crain Communications, Inc. Reprinted by permission. Box on page 281: Richard Gibson, "McDonald's Sales fail to Keep Pace with Its Advertisement Expenses," *The Wall Street Journal Interactive Edition,* April 3, 1998. Republished by permission of Dow Jones, Inc. via Copyright Clearance Center, Inc. ©1998 *The Wall Street Journal,* Dow Jones & Company, Inc. All Rights Reserved Worldwide. Table 9.2: Gerry Khemmouch, "Pockets of Success Tempered by Concern, " Brandweek, June 15, 1998, S28. © 1998 ASM Communications. Figure 9.11: Reprinted by permission of *Harvard Business Review* from, "Ad Spending: Growing Market Share," by James C. Schoer, (January–February 1990), p. 48. © 1990 by the President and Fellows of Harvard College; all rights reserved. Box on page 322: Adapted from Mir Maqbool Alam Khan, "India's Private' Positioning Is a Hit with Public," Advertising Age, January 16, 1995, pp. 14. © 1995 by Crain Communications, Inc. Reprinted by permission. Table 10.1: R. Craig Endicott, "Agency Report," *Advertising Age,* April 27, 1998, pp. S1–S14. © 1998 by Crain Communication, Inc. Reprinted by permission. Table 10.2: Shalom H. Schwartz, "Universals in the Content and Structure of Values: Theoretical Advances and Empirical Tests in 20 Countries," *Advances in Experimental Social Psychology* 25 (1992), 1–65 Table 10.4: Charles F. Frazer, "Creative Strategy: A Managerial Perspective," *Journal of Advertising* 12, no. 4 (1983), p. 40. Reprinted by permission. Box on page 343: Norihiko Shirouzu, *The Wall Street Journal Interactive Edition,* July 28, 1997. Republished by permission of Dow Jones, Inc. via Copyright Clearance Center, Inc. ©1997 *The Wall Street Journal,* Dow Jones & Company, Inc. All Rights Reserved Worldwide. Box on page 354: Jean J. Boddewyn, "Controlling Sex and Decency in Advertising around the World," *Journal of Advertising* 20 (December 1991), pp. 25–36. Reprinted by permission. Chapter 12 vignette: James B. Arndorfer, "Media Strategy Crucial to Revamp of Miller's Image," *Advertising Age,* August 3, 1998, p. S12. © 1998 by Crain Communications, Inc. Reprinted by permission. Figure 12.4: 1998 Spring MRI. Figure 12.5: 1998 Spring MRI. Figure 12.6: 1998 Spring MRI. Table 12.7: "The Ten Most Expensive Prime-Time TV Ad Buys, 1998-99," *Advertising Age,* September 21, 1998, p.1. © 1998 by Crain Communications, Inc. Reprinted by permission. Table 12.8: "Total Ad Spending on Network vs. Cable, 1997," *Adweek,* May 18, 1998, p.13. © 1998 ASM Communications Inc. Box on page 425: Adapted from Christina Duff, "Why Answer the phone? Odds Are. The Call Wasn't Worth the Bother," *The Wall Street Journal Interactive Edition,* January 14, 1998. Republished by permission of Dow Jones, Inc. via Copyright Clearance Center, Inc. ©1998 *The Wall Street Journal,* Dow Jones & Company, Inc. All Rights Reserved Worldwide. Table 14.3. Hugh M. Cannon and Edward A. Riordan, "Effective Reach and Frequency: Does It Really Make Sense?" *Journal of Advertising Research,* 34 (March/April 1994), p. 25. Reprinted by permission. Table 14.4: Adapted from, "The Muscle in Multiple Media," *Marketing Communications,* December 1983, p. 25. Reprinted by permission. Chapter 15 vignette art: THE SIMPSONS ™ & © 1998 Twentieth Century Fox Film Corporation. All rights reserved. Table 15.2: Joe Mandese, "People Meters Shake Up Global TV Ratings," *Advertising Age International,* July 18, 1994, p. 116. © 1994 by Crain Communications, Inc. Reprinted by permission. Figure 15.7: Anthony J. Adams and Margaret Henderson Blair, "Persuasive Advertising and Sales Accountability: Past Experience and Forward Validation," *Journal of Advertising Research* 32 (March/April 1992), p. 23. Reprinted by permission. Box on page 516: Global Focus Box: "Offsetting the Competition and Reviving Sales of Bazooka Bubble Gum in Argentina," adapted from Amie Smith and Al Urbanski, "Excellence x 16," *Promo,* December 1998, p. 136. Used with permission from PROMO. Figure 16.2: Adapted from Leigh McAlister, "Continued Research into Sales Promotion: Product Line Management Issues" (research report and proposal prepared for the Marketing Science Institute and other sponsors, circa 1986). Adapted with permission. Figure 16.3: Adapted from Leigh McAlister, "Continued Research into Sales Promotion: Product Line Management Issues" (research report and proposal prepared for the Marketing Science Institute and other sponsors, circa 1986). Adapted with permission. Box on page 539: Adapted from Suein L. Hwang, "'Diverted' Cigarettes are for Sale, Sparking Inquiries and a Backlash," *The Wall Street Journal Interactive Edition,* January 28, 1999. Republished by permission of Dow Jones, Inc. via Copyright Clearance Center, Inc. ©1999 Dow Jones and Company, Inc. All Rights Reserved. Box on page 544: Adapted from Stephanie Thompson, "Hormel Seeks Frequent Spam-sters," *Brandweek,* May 18, 1998, p. 6. © 1998 ASM Communications, Inc. Chapter 18 vignette: The Hoover and Sloggies cases are adapted from Amie Smith, "Learning from the Mistakes of others," Special report from *Promo* magazine, August 1998, pp. S8–S9. The Pepsi debacle is adapted from Glenn Heitsmith, "Botched Pepsi Promotion Prompts Terrorist Attacks," *Promo,* September 1993, p. 10. Used with permission from PROMO. Chapter 18 vignette photo: © Photopia Box on page 566: Adapted from Stephanie Thompson, "Mobile Marie," *Brandweek,* March 2, 1998, p. R11. ©1998 ASM Communications Inc. Box on page 570: Adapted From Ginny Parker, Associated Press, "Japan Tries Coupons in Bid to Revive Consumer Spending," *Charlotte Observer,* January 30, 1999, p.12A. Reprinted by permission of Associated Press. box 18: Adapted from, "A Simple Twist of Fate," *Promo,* June 1998, p.19. Used with permission from PROMO. Figure 18.7: Reprinted with permission from The Pillsbury Co. Figure 18.11: © Photopia   Table 18.3: "Full Coupon Cost" adapted from an analysis performed by the McKinsey & Co. consulting firm reported in Daniel Shannon, "Still a Mighty Marketing Mechanism," *Promo,* April 1996, p. 85. Used with permission from PROMO. Chapter 19 vignette: Adapted from Stephanie Thompson, "Maxwell Housing," *Brandweek,* May 4, 1998, p. 24. © 1998 ASM Communications Inc. Chapter 19 vignette art: Used with permission. Maxwell House is a registered trademark of Kraft Foods, Inc. Box on page 613: "A Bizarre Conspiracy Rumor" adapted from "A Storm over Tropical Fantasy," *Newsweek,* April 22, 1991, p. 34. © Newsweek, Inc. All Rights Reserved. Reprinted with permission. Table 19.01: From Fredrick Koenig, "Rumor in the Marketplace: The Social Psychology of Commercial Hearsay" (Dover, Mass.: Auburn House, 1985) pp. 171–173. Copyright © 1985 by Auburn House. Reproduced with permission of GREENWOOD PUBLISHING GROUP, INC., Westpoint, CT. Table 19.02: "Sponsorships Grow Without the Olympics," *Promo,* July 1998, p. S16. Used with permission from PROMO. Figure 19.02: David Young Wolff/PhotoEdit. Box on page 621: Adapted from Fara Warner, "Kellog Launches a Cereal for Charity," *Adweek's Marketing Week,* November 11, 1991, p. 6. © 1998 ASM

Name Index

Subject Index

About the Cover

Of Music, Technology, and Integrated Marketing Communications

Individual musical instruments, such as the saxophone, trumpet, or piano played alone can be beautiful, yet the effect can be sublime when multiple instruments are skillfully meshed into an ensemble. Beautiful as they are, musical instruments are limited in their range of sound production. However, advances in computer technology now make sound production virtually unlimited. Computer synthesisers combined with conventional instruments and skilled performers offer unparalleled results for conductors who are knowledgeable and courageous enough to utilize all of the tools available to them.

So it is with integrated marketing communications. The individual elements of the communication mix (such as advertising and sales promotion) may work moderately well by themselves, but the effects are much stronger when managers orchestrate multiple communication tools into coordinated programs. Technology cannot replace the insight and knowledge possessed by marketing communication practitioners, but when the artistic skills of seasoned practitioners are combined with scientific and technological advances, the results can be truly magnificent.